Eric Hobsbawm was born in Alexandria in 1917 and educated in Vienna, Berlin, London and Cambridge. A Fellow of the British Academy and the American Academy of Arts and Sciences, with honorary degrees from universities in several countries, he taught until retirement at Birkbeck College, University of London, and since then at the New School for Social Research in New York. In addition to *The Age of Revolution*, *The Age of Capital* and *The Age of Empire* (all available in Abacus), his books include *Primitive Rebels*, *Labouring Men and Worlds of Labour*, *Industry and Empire*, *Bandits*, *On History*, *Uncommon People*, *Revolutionaries*, *The New Century*, his memoir, *Interesting Times*, and most recently, *Globalisation, Democracy and Terrorism*. All have been translated into several languages.

Also by Eric Hobsbawm in Abacus

THE AGE OF EXTREMES

THE SHORT TWENTIETH CENTURY
1914–1991

Eric Hobsbawm

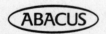

ABACUS

First published in Great Britain by Michael Joseph in 1994
This edition published by Abacus in 1995
Reprinted 1995, 1996 (three times), 1997, 1998, 1999, 2000, 2001,
2002, 2003, 2004, 2006, 2007, 2008

A CIP catalogue record for this book is available from the British Library.

ISBN 978-0-349-10671-7

Printed and bound in Great Britain by Clays Ltd, St Ives plc

Papers used by Abacus are natural, renewable and recyclable
products made from wood grown in sustainable forests and certified
in accordance with the rules of the Forest Stewardship Council.

Mixed Sources
Product group from well-managed
forests and other controlled sources
www.fsc.org Cert no. SGS-COC-004081
© 1996 Forest Stewardship Council

Abacus
An imprint of
Little, Brown Book Group
100 Victoria Embankment
London EC4Y 0DY

An Hachette Livre UK Company
www.hachettelivre.co.uk

www.littlebrown.co.uk

Contents

PART THREE: THE LANDSLIDE

Illustrations

(*Copyright holders are indicated in italics*)

Preface and Acknowledgements

Nobody can write the history of the twentieth century like that of any other era, if only because nobody can write about his or her lifetime as one can (and must) write about a period known only from outside, at second or third-hand, from sources of the period or the works of later historians. My own lifetime coincides with most of the period with which this book deals, and for most of it, from early teen-age to the present, I have been conscious of public affairs, that is to say I have accumulated views and prejudices about it as a contemporary rather than as a scholar. This is one reason why under my professional hat as a historian I avoided working on the era since 1914 for most of my career, though not refraining from writing about it in other capacities. 'My period', as they say in the trade, is the nineteenth century. I think it is now possible to see the Short Twentieth Century from 1914 to the end of the Soviet era in some historical perspective, but I come to it without the knowledge of the scholarly literature, let alone of all but a tiny sprinkle of archive sources, which historians of the twentieth century, of whom there is an enormous number, have accumulated.

It is, of course, utterly impossible for any single person to know the historiography of the present century, even that in any single major language, as, let us say, the historian of classical antiquity or of the Byzantine Empire knows what has been written in and about those long periods. Nevertheless, my own knowledge is casual and patchy even by the standards of historical erudition in the field of contemporary history. The most I have been able to do is to dip into the literature of particularly thorny and controverted questions – say, the history of the Cold War or that of the 1930s – far enough to satisfy myself that the views expressed in this book are tenable in the light of specialist research. Of course, I cannot have succeeded. There must be any number of questions on which I display ignorance as well as controversial views.

This book, therefore, rests on curiously uneven foundations. In addition to the wide and miscellaneous reading of a good many years, supplemented by what reading was necessary to give lecture courses on twentieth-century history to the graduate students of the New School for Social Research, I have drawn on the accumulated knowledge, memories and opinions of someone who has lived through the Short Twentieth Century, as what the social anthropologists call a 'participant observer', or simply as an open-eyed traveller, or what my ancestors would have called a *kibbitzer*, in quite a lot of countries. The historical value of such experiences does not depend on being present on great historic occasions, or having known or even met prominent history-makers or statesmen. As a matter of fact, my experience as an occasional journalist enquiring into this or that country, chiefly in Latin America, has been that interviews with presidents or other decision-makers are usually unrewarding, for the obvious reason that most of what such people say is for the public record. The people from whom illumination comes are those who can, or want to, speak freely, preferably if they have no responsibility for great affairs. Nevertheless, though necessarily partial and misleading, to have known people and places has helped me enormously. It may be no more than the sight of the same city at an interval of thirty years – Valencia or Palermo – which alone brings home the speed and scale of social transformation in the third quarter of the present century. It may be simply a memory of something said in conversations long ago and stored away, sometimes for no clear reason, for future use. If the historian can make some sense of this century it is in large part because of watching and listening. I hope I have communicated to readers something of what I have learned through doing so.

The book also, and necessarily, rests on the information drawn from colleagues, students, and anyone else whom I buttonholed while I was working on it. In some cases the debt is systematic. The chapter on the sciences was submitted to my friends Alan Mackay FRS, who is not only a crystallographer but an encyclopedist, and John Maddox. Some of what I have written about economic development was read by my colleague at the New School, Lance Taylor, formerly of MIT, and much more was based on reading the papers, listening to the discussions and generally keeping my ears open during the conferences organized on various macro-economic problems at the World Institute for Development Economic Research of the UN University (UNU/WIDER) in Helsinki when it was transformed into a major international centre of research and discussion under the direction of Dr Lal Jayawardena. In general, the summers I was able to spend at that admirable institution as a McDonnell Douglas visiting scholar were invaluable to me, not least through its proximity to, and intellectual concern with, the USSR in its last years. I have not always accepted the advice of those I consulted, and, even when I have, the errors are strictly my own. I have derived much benefit from the conferences and colloquia at which academics spend much of their time meeting their colleagues largely for the purpose of picking each others' brains. I cannot possibly acknowledge all the colleagues from whom I have derived benefit or correction on formal or informal occasions, nor even all the information I have incidentally acquired from being lucky enough to teach a particularly international group of students at the New School. However, I think I must specifically acknowledge what I learned about the Turkish revolution and about the nature of Third World migration and social mobility from term papers produced by Ferdan Ergut and Alex Julca. I am also indebted to the doctoral dissertation of my pupil Margarita Giesecke on APRA and the Trujillo Rising of 1932.

As the historian of the twentieth century draws closer to the present he or she becomes increasingly dependent on two types of sources: the daily or periodical press and the periodic reports, economic and other surveys, statistical compilations and other publications by national governments and international institutions. My debt to such papers as the London *Guardian*, the *Financial Times* and the *New York Times* should be obvious. My debt to the invaluable publications of the United Nations and its various agencies, and the World Bank, is recorded in the bibliography. Nor should their predecessor, the League of Nations, be forgotten. Though an almost total failure in practice, its admirable economic enquiries and analyses, culminating in the pioneering *Industrialisation and World Trade* of 1945 deserve our gratitude. No history of economic social and cultural changes in this century could be written without such sources.

Most of what I have written in this book, except obvious personal judgments of the author, readers will have to take on trust. There is no point in overloading a book such as this with a vast apparatus of references or other signs of erudition. I have tried to confine my references to the source of actual quotations, to the source of statistics and other quantitative data – different sources sometimes give different figures – and to the occasional support for statements which readers may find unusual, unfamiliar or unexpected, and some points where the author's controversial view might require some backing. These references are in brackets in the text. The full title of the source is to be found at the end of the volume. This bibliography is no more than a full list of all the sources actually cited or referred to in the text. It is *not* a systematic guide to further reading. A brief pointer to further reading is printed separately. The apparatus of references, such as it is, is also quite separate from the footnotes, which merely amplify or qualify the text.

Nevertheless, it is only fair to point to some works on which I have relied quite a lot or to which I am particularly indebted. I would not want their authors to feel unappreciated. In general I owe much to the work of two friends: the economic historian and indefatigable compiler of quantitative data, Paul Bairoch, and Ivan Berend, formerly President of the Hungarian Academy of Sciences, to whom I owe the concept of the Short Twentieth Century. For the general political history of the world since the Second World War, P. Calvocoressi (*World Politics Since 1945*) has been a sound, and sometimes – understandably – tart guide. For the Second World War I owe much to Alan Milward's superb *War, Economy and Society 1939–45*, and for the post-1945 economy I have found Herman Van der Wee's *Prosperity and Upheaval: The World Economy 1945–1980* and also *Capitalism Since 1945* by Philip Armstrong, Andrew Glyn and John Harrison most useful. Martin Walker's *The Cold War* deserves far more appreciation than most of the lukewarm reviewers have given it. For the history of the Left since the Second World War I am greatly indebted to Dr Donald Sassoon of Queen Mary and Westfield College, University of London, who has kindly let me read his so far uncompleted vast and perceptive study on this subject. For the history of the USSR I am particularly indebted to the writings of Moshe Lewin, Alec Nove, R.W. Davies and Sheila Fitzpatrick; for China to those of Benjamin Schwartz and Stuart Schram; for the Islamic world to Ira Lapidus and Nikki Keddie. My views on the arts owe much to John Willett's works on Weimar culture (and to his conversation), and to Francis Haskell. In chapter 6 my debt to Lynn Garafola's *Diaghilev* should be obvious.

My special thanks go to those who have actually helped me to prepare this book. They are, first, my research assistants Joanna Bedford in London and Lise Grande in New York. I would particularly like to stress my debt to the exceptional Ms Grande, without whom I could not possibly have filled the enormous gaps in my knowledge, and verified half-remembered facts and references. I am greatly indebted to Ruth Syers, who typed my drafts, and to Marlene Hobsbawm, who read the chapters from the point of view of the non-academic reader with a general interest in the modern world, to whom this book is addressed.

I have already indicated my debt to the students of the New School, who listened to the lectures in which I tried to formulate my ideas and interpretations. To them this book is dedicated.

Eric Hobsbawm
London–New York, 1993–94

The Century: A Bird's Eye View

Isaiah Berlin (philosopher, Britain): 'I have lived through most of the twentieth century without, I must add, suffering personal hardship. I remember it only as the most terrible century in Western history.'

Julio Caro Baroja (anthropologist, Spain): 'There's a patent contradiction between one's own life experience – childhood, youth and old age passed quietly and without major adventures – and the facts of the twentieth century . . . the terrible events which humanity has lived through.'

Primo Levi (writer, Italy): 'We who survived the Camps are not true witnesses. This is an uncomfortable notion which I have gradually come to accept by reading what other survivors have written, including myself, when I re-read my writings after a lapse of years. We, the survivors, are not only a tiny but also an anomalous minority. We are those who, through prevarication, skill or luck, never touched bottom. Those who have, and who have seen the face of the Gorgon, did not return, or returned wordless.'

René Dumont (agronomist, ecologist, France): 'I see it only as a century of massacres and wars.'

Rita Levi Montalcini (Nobel Laureate, science, Italy): 'In spite of everything there have been revolutions for the better in this century . . . the rise of the fourth estate, and the emergence of women after centuries of repression.'

William Golding (Nobel Laureate, writer, Britain): 'I can't help thinking that this has been the most violent century in human history.'

Ernst Gombrich (art historian, Britain): 'The chief characteristic of the twentieth century is the terrible multiplication of the world's population. It is a catastrophe, a disaster. We don't know what to do about it.'

Yehudi Menuhin (musician, Britain): 'If I had to sum up the twentieth century, I would say that it raised the greatest hopes ever conceived by humanity, and destroyed all illusions and ideals.'

Severo Ochoa (Nobel Laureate, science, Spain): 'The most fundamental thing is the progress of science, which has been truly extraordinary . . . This is what characterizes our century.'

Raymond Firth (anthropologist, Britain): 'Technologically, I single out the development of electronics among the most significant developments of the twentieth century; in terms of ideas, the change from a relatively rational and scientific view of things to a non-rational and less scientific one.'

Leo Valiani (historian, Italy): 'Our century demonstrates that the victory of the ideals of justice and equality is always ephemeral, but also that, if we manage to preserve liberty, we can always start all over again . . . There is no need to despair, even in the most desperate situations.'

Franco Venturi (historian, Italy): 'Historians can't answer this question. For me the twentieth century is only the ever-renewed effort to understand it.'

(Agosti and Borgese, 1992, pp. 42, 210, 154, 76, 4, 8, 204, 2, 62, 80, 140, 160.)

I

On the 28 June 1992 President Mitterrand of France made a sudden, unannounced and unexpected appearance in Sarajevo, already the centre of a Balkan war that was to cost many thousands of lives during the remainder of the year. His object was to remind world opinion of the seriousness of the Bosnian crisis. Indeed, the presence of a distinguished, elderly and visibly frail statesman under small-arms and artillery fire was much remarked on and admired. However, one aspect of M. Mitterrand's visit passed virtually without comment, even though it was plainly central to it: the date. Why had the President of France chosen to go to Sarajevo on that particular day? Because the 28 June was the anniversary of the assassination, in Sarajevo, in 1914, of the Archduke Franz Ferdinand of Austria-Hungary, which led, within a matter of weeks, to the outbreak of the First World War. For any educated European of Mitterrand's age, the connection between date, place and the reminder of a historic catastrophe precipitated by political error and miscalculation leaped to the eye. How better to dramatize the potential implications of the Bosnian crisis than by choosing so symbolic a date? But hardly anyone caught the allusion except a few professional historians and very senior citizens. The historical memory was no longer alive.

The destruction of the past, or rather of the social mechanisms that link one's contemporary experience to that of earlier generations, is one of the most characteristic and eerie phenomena of the late twentieth century. Most young men and women at the century's end grow up in a sort of permanent present lacking any organic relation to the public past of the times they live in. This makes historians, whose business it is to remember what others forget, more essential at the end of the second millennium than ever before. But for that very reason they must be more than simply chroniclers, remembrancers and compilers, though this is also the historians' necessary function. In 1989 all governments, and especially all Foreign Ministries, in the world would have benefited from a seminar on the peace settlements after the two world wars, which most of them had apparently forgotten.

However, it is not the purpose of this book to tell the story of the period which is its subject, the Short Twentieth Century from 1914 to 1991, although no one who has been asked by an intelligent American student whether the phrase 'Second World War' meant that there had been a 'First World War' is unaware that knowledge of even the basic facts of the century cannot be taken for granted. My object is to understand and explain *why* things turned out the way they did, and how they hang together. For anyone of my age-group who has lived through all or most of the Short Twentieth Century this is inevitably also an autobiographical endeavour. We are talking about, amplifying (and correcting) our own memories. And we are talking as men and women of a particular time and place, involved, in various ways, in its history as actors in its dramas – however insignificant our parts – as observers of our times and, not least, as people whose views of the century have been formed by what we have come to see as its crucial events. We are part of this century. It is part of us. Readers who belong to another era, for instance the student entering university at the time this is written, for whom even the Vietnam War is prehistory, should not forget this.

For historians of my generation and background, the past is indestructible, not only because we belong to the generation when streets and public places were still called after public men and events (the Wilson station in pre-war Prague, the Metro Stalingrad in Paris), when peace treaties were still signed and therefore had to be identified (Treaty of Versailles) and war memorials recalled yesterdays, but because public events are part of the texture of our lives. They are not merely markers in our private lives, but what has formed our lives, private and public. For this author the 30 January 1933 is not simply an otherwise arbitrary date when Hitler became Chancellor of Germany, but a winter afternoon in Berlin when a fifteen-year-old and his younger sister were on the way home from their neighbouring schools in Wilmersdorf to Halensee and, somewhere on the way, saw the headline. I can see it still, as in a dream.

But not only one old historian has the past as part of his permanent present. Over huge stretches of the globe everybody over a certain age, irrespective of their personal background and life-story, has passed through the same central experiences. These have marked us all, to some extent in the same ways. The world that went to pieces at the end of the 1980s was the world shaped by the impact of the Russian Revolution of 1917. We have all been marked by it, for instance, inasmuch as we got used to thinking of the modern industrial economy in terms of binary opposites, 'capitalism' and 'socialism' as alternatives mutually excluding one another, the one being identified with economies organized on the model of the USSR, the other with all the rest. It should now be becoming clear that this was an arbitrary and to some extent artificial construction, which can only be understood as part of a particular historical context. And yet, even as I write, it is not easy to envisage, even in retrospect, other principles of classification which might have been more realistic than that which placed the USA, Japan, Sweden, Brazil, the German Federal Republic and South Korea in a single pigeon-hole, and the state economies and systems of the Soviet region which collapsed after the 1980s in the same compartment as those in East and Southeast Asia which demonstrably did not collapse.

Again, even the world which has survived the end of the October Revolution is one whose institutions and assumptions were shaped by those who were on the winning side of the Second World War. Those who were on the losing side or associated with it were not only silent and silenced, but virtually written out of history and intellectual life except in the role of 'the enemy' in the moral world drama of Good versus Evil. (This may now also be happening to the losers in the Cold War of the second half of the century, though probably not to quite the same extent or for so long.) This is one of the penalties of living through a century of religious wars. Intolerance is their chief characteristic. Even those who advertised the pluralism of their own non-ideologies did not think the world was big enough for permanent coexistence with rival secular religions. Religious or ideological confrontations, such as those which have filled this century, build barricades in the way of the historian, whose major task is not to judge but to understand even what we can least comprehend. Yet what stands in the way of understanding is not only our passionate convictions, but the historical experience that has formed them. The first is easier to overcome, for there is no truth in the familiar but mistaken French phrase *tout comprendre c'st tout pardonner* (to understand all is to forgive all). To understand the Nazi era in German history and to fit it into its historical context is not to forgive the genocide. In any case, no one who has lived through this extraordinary century is likely to abstain from judgement. It is understanding that comes hard.

II

How are we to make sense of the Short Twentieth Century, that is to say of the years from the outbreak of the First World War to the collapse of the USSR which, as we can now see in retrospect, forms a coherent historical period that has now ended? We do not know what will come next, and what the third millennium will be like, even though we can be certain that the Short Twentieth Century will have shaped it. However, there can be no serious doubt that in the late 1980s and early 1990s an era in world history ended and a new one began. That is the essential information for historians of the century, for though they can speculate about the future in the light of their understanding of the past, their business is not that of the racing tipster. The only horse-races they can claim to report and analyse are those already won or lost. In any case, the record of forecasters in the past thirty or forty years, whatever their professional qualification as prophets, has been so spectacularly bad that only governments and economic research institutes still have, or pretend to have, much confidence in it. It is even possible that it has got worse since the Second World War.

In this book the structure of the Short Twentieth Century appears like a sort of triptych or historical sandwich. An Age of Catastrophe from 1914 to the aftermath of the Second World War was followed by some twenty-five or thirty years of extraordinary economic growth and social transformation, which probably changed human society more profoundly than any other period of comparable brevity. In retrospect it can be seen as a sort of Golden Age, and was so seen almost immediately it had come to an end in the early 1970s. The last part of the century was a new era of decomposition, uncertainty and crisis – and indeed, for large parts of the world such as Africa, the former USSR and the formerly socialist parts of Europe, of catastrophe. As the 1980s gave way to the 1990s, the mood of those who reflected on the century's past and future was a growing *fin-de-siècle* gloom. From the vantage-point of the 1990s, the Short Twentieth Century passed through a brief Golden Age, on the way from one era of crisis to another, into an unknown and problematic but not necessarily apocalyptic future. However, as historians may wish to remind metaphysical speculators about 'The End of History', there will be a future. The only completely certain generalization about history is that, so long as there is a human race, it will go on.

The argument of this book is organized accordingly. It begins with the First World War, which marked the breakdown of the (western) civilization of the nineteenth century. This civilization was capitalist in its economy; liberal in its legal and constitutional structure; bourgeois in the image of its characteristic hegemonic class; glorying in the advance of science, knowledge and education, material and moral progress; and profoundly convinced of the centrality of Europe, birthplace of the revolutions of the sciences, arts, politics and industry, whose economy had penetrated, and whose soldiers had conquered and subjugated most of the world; whose populations had grown until (including the vast and growing outflow of European emigrants and their descendants) they had risen to form a third of the human race; and whose major states constituted the system of world politics.*

The decades from the outbreak of the First World War to the

---

* I have tried to describe and explain the rise of this civilization in a three-volume history of the 'long nineteenth century' (from the 1780s to 1914) and tried to analyse the reasons for its breakdown. The present text will refer back to these volumes, *The Age of Revolution, 1789–1848, The Age of Capital, 1848–1875* and *The Age of Empire 1875–1914*, from time to time, where this seems useful.

aftermath of the Second, was an Age of Catastrophe for this society. For forty years it stumbled from one calamity to another. There were times when even intelligent conservatives would not take bets on its survival. It was shaken by two world wars, followed by two waves of global rebellion and revolution, which brought to power a system that claimed to be the historically predestined alternative to bourgeois and capitalist society, first over one sixth of the world's land surface, and after the Second World War over one third of the globe's population. The huge colonial empires, built up before and during the Age of Empire, were shaken and crumbled into dust. The entire history of modern imperialism, so firm and self-confident when Queen Victoria of Great Britain died, had lasted no longer than a single lifetime – say, that of Winston Churchill (1874–1965).

More than this: a world economic crisis of unprecedented depth brought even the strongest capitalist economies to their knees and seemed to reverse the creation of a single universal world economy, which had been so remarkable an achievement of nineteenth-century liberal capitalism. Even the USA, safe from war and revolution, seemed close to collapse. While the economy tottered, the institutions of liberal democracy virtually disappeared between 1917 and 1942 from all but a fringe of Europe and parts of North America and Australasia, as fascism and its satellite authoritarian movements and regimes advanced.

Only the temporary and bizzare alliance of liberal capitalism and communism in self-defence against this challenger saved democracy, for the victory over Hitler's Germany was essentially won, and could only have been won, by the Red Army. In many ways this period of capitalist–communist alliance against fascism – essentially the 1930s and 1940s – forms the hinge of twentieth-century history and its decisive moment. In many ways it is a moment of historical paradox in the relations of capitalism and communism, placed, for most of the century – except for the brief period of antifascism – in a posture of irreconcilable antagonism. The victory of the Soviet Union over Hitler was the achievement of the regime installed there by the October Revolution, as a comparison of the performance of the Russian Tsarist economy in the First World War and the Soviet economy in the Second World War demonstrates (Gatrell/Harrison, 1993). Without it the Western world today would probably consist (outside the USA) of a set of variations on authoritarian and fascist themes rather than a set of variations on liberal parliamentary ones. It is one of the ironies of this strange century that the most lasting results of the October revolution, whose object was the global overthrow of capitalism, was to save its antagonist, both in war and in peace – that is to say, by providing it with the incentive, fear, to reform itself after the Second World War, and, by establishing the popularity of economic planning, furnishing it with some of the procedures for its reform.

Still, even when liberal capitalism had – and only just – survived the triple challenge of slump, fascism and war, it still seemed to face the global advance of revolution, which could now rally round the USSR, which had emerged from the Second World War as a superpower.

And yet, as we can now see in retrospect, the strength of the global socialist challenge to capitalism was that of the weakness of its opponent. Without the breakdown of nineteenth-century bourgeois society in the Age of Catastrophe, there would have been no October revolution and no USSR. The economic system improvised in the ruined rural Eurasian hulk of the former Tsarist Empire under the name of socialism would not have considered itself, nor been considered elsewhere, as a realistic global alternative to the capitalist economy. It was the Great Slump of the 1930s that made it look as though it was so, as it was the challenge of fascism which made the USSR into the indispensable instrument of Hitler's defeat, and therefore into one of the two superpowers whose confrontations dominated and terrified the second half of the Short Twentieth Century, while – as we can also now see – in many respects stabilizing its political structure. The USSR would not have found itself, for a decade-and-a-half in the middle of the century, at the head of a 'socialist camp' comprising a third of the human race, and an economy that briefly looked as though it might out-race capitalist economic growth.

Just how and why capitalism after the Second World War found itself, to everyone's surprise including its own, surging forward into the unprecedented and possibly anomalous Golden Age of 1947–73, is perhaps the major question which faces historians of the twentieth century. There is as yet no agreement on an answer, nor can I claim to provide a persuasive one. Probably a more convincing analysis will have to wait until the entire 'long wave' of the second half of the twentieth century can be seen in perspective, but, although we can now look back on the Golden Age as a whole, the Crisis Decades through which the world has lived since then are not yet complete at the time this is written. However, what can already be assessed with great confidence is the extraordinary scale and impact of the consequent economic, social and cultural transformation, the greatest, most rapid and most fundamental in recorded history. Various aspects of it are discussed in the second part of this book. Historians of the twentieth century in the third millennium will probably see the century's major impact on history as the one made by and in this astonishing period. For the changes in human life it brought about all over the globe were as profound as they were irreversible. Moreover, they are still continuing. The journalists and philosophical essayists who detected 'the end of history' in the fall of the Soviet Empire were wrong. A better case can be made for saying that the third quarter of the century marked the end of the seven or eight millennia of human history that began with the invention of agriculture in the stone age, if only because it ended the long era when the overwhelming majority of the human race lived by growing food and herding animals.

Compared to this, the history of the confrontation between 'capitalism' and 'socialism', with or without the intervention of states and governments such as the USA and the USSR claiming to represent one or the other, will probably seem of more limited historical interest – comparable, in the long run, to the sixteenth and seventeenth-century wars of religion or the Crusades. For those who lived through any part of the Short Twentieth Century they naturally bulked large, and so they do in this book, since it is written by a twentieth-century writer for late-twentieth-century readers. Social revolutions, the Cold War, the nature, limits and fatal flaws of 'really existing socialism' and its breakdown, are discussed at length. Nevertheless, it is important to remember that the major and lasting impact of the regimes inspired by the October revolution was as a powerful accelerator of the modernization of backward agrarian countries. As it happened, its major achievements in this respect coincided with the capitalist Golden Age. How effective, or even how consciously held, the rival strategies for burying the world of our forefathers were, need not be considered here. As we shall see, until the early 1960s, they seemed at least evenly matched, a view which seems preposterous in the light of the collapse of Soviet socialism, though a British prime minister, conversing with an American president, could then still see the USSR as a state whose 'buoyant economy . . . will soon outmatch capitalist society in the race for material wealth' (Horne, 1989, p. 303). However, the point to note is simply that, in the 1980s, socialist Bulgaria and non-socialist Ecuador had more in common than either had with the Bulgaria or Ecuador of 1939.

Although the collapse of Soviet socialism and its enormous and still not fully calculable, but mainly negative, consequences were the most dramatic incident in the Crisis Decades which followed the Golden Age, these were to be decades of *universal* or global crisis. The crisis affected the various parts of the world in different ways and degrees, but it affected all, irrespective of their political, social and economic configurations, because the Golden Age had, for the first time in history, created a single, increasingly integrated and universal world economy largely operating across state frontiers ('transnationally'), and therefore also increasingly across the frontiers of state ideology. Consequently the accepted ideas of institutions of all regimes and systems were undermined. Initially the troubles of the 1970s were seen only as a hopefully, temporary pause in the Great Leap Forward of the world economy, and countries of all economic and political types and patterns looked for temporary solutions. Increasingly it became clear that this was an era of long-term difficulties, for which capitalist countries sought radical solutions, often by following secular theologians of the unrestricted free market who rejected the policies that had served the world economy so well in the Golden Age, but now seemed to be failing. The ultras of *laissez-faire* were no more successful than anyone else. In the 1980s and early 1990s the capitalist world found itself once again staggering under the burdens of the inter-war years, which the Golden Age appeared to have removed: mass unemployment, severe cyclical slumps, the ever-more spectacular confrontation of home-less beggars and luxurious plenty, between limited state revenues and limitless state expenditures. Socialist countries, with their now flagging and vulnerable economies, were driven towards equally or even more radical breaks with their past, and, as we know, towards breakdown. That breakdown can stand as the marker for the end of the Short Twentieth Century, as the First World War can stand as the marker for its beginning. At this point my history concludes.

It concludes – as any book completed in the early 1990s must – with a view into obscurity. The collapse of one part of the world revealed the malaise of the rest. As the 1980s passed into the 1990s it became evident that the world crisis was not only general in an economic sense, but equally general in politics. The collapse of the communist regimes between Istria and Vladivostok not only produced an enormous zone of political uncertainty, instability, chaos and civil war, but also destroyed the international system that had stabilized international relations for some forty years. It also revealed the precariousness of the domestic political systems that had essentially rested on that stability. The tensions of troubled economies undermined the political systems of liberal democracy, parliamentary or presidential, which had functioned so well in the developed capitalist countries since the Second World War. They also undermined whatever political systems operated in the Third World. The basic units of politics themselves, the territorial, sovereign and independent 'nation-states', including the oldest and stablest, found themselves pulled apart by the forces of a supranational or transnational economy, and by the infranational forces of secessionist regions and ethnic groups. Some of these – such is the irony of history – demanded the outdated and unreal status of miniature sovereign 'nation-states' for themselves. The future of politics was obscure, but its crisis at the end of the Short Twentieth Century was patent.

Even more obvious than the uncertainties of world economics and world politics was the social and moral crisis, reflecting the post-1950 upheavals in human life, which also found widespread if confused expression in these Crisis Decades. It was a crisis of the beliefs and assumptions on which modern society had been founded since the Moderns won their famous battle against the Ancients in the early eighteenth century – of the rationalist and humanist assumptions, shared by liberal capitalism and communism, and which made possible their brief but decisive alliance against fascism, which rejected them. A conservative German observer, Michael Stürmer, rightly observed in 1993 that the beliefs of both East and West were at issue:

> There is a strange parallelism between East and West. In the East state doctrine insisted that humanity was the master of its destiny. However, even we believed in a less official and less extreme version of the same slogan: mankind was on the way to becoming master of its destinies. The claim to omnipotence has disappeared absolutely in the East, only relatively *chez nous* – but both sides have suffered shipwreck. (From Bergedorf, 98, p. 95)

Paradoxically, an era whose only claim to have benefited humanity rested on the enormous triumphs of a material progress based on science and technology ended in a rejection of these by substantial bodies of public opinion and people claiming to be thinkers in the West.

However, the moral crisis was not only one of the assumptions of modern civilization, but also one of the historic structures of human relations which modern society inherited from a pre-industrial and pre-capitalist past, and which, as we can now see, had enabled it to function. It was not a crisis of one form of organizing societies, but of all forms. The strange calls for an otherwise unidentified 'civil society', for 'community' were the voice of lost and drifting generations. They were heard in an age when such words, having lost their traditional meanings, became vapid phrases. There was no other way left to define group identity, except by defining the outsiders who were not in it.

For the poet T.S. Eliot 'this is the way the world ends – not with a bang but a whimper.' The Short Twentieth century ended with both.

III

How did the world of the 1990s compare with the world of 1914? It contained five or six billion human beings, perhaps three times as many people as at the outbreak of the First World War, and this in spite of the fact that during the Short Century more human beings had been killed or allowed to die by human decision than ever before in history. A recent estimate of the century's 'megadeaths' is 187 millions (Brzezinski, 1993), which is the equivalent of more than one in ten of the total world population in 1900. Most people in the 1990s were taller and heavier than their parents, better fed, and far longer-lived, though the catastrophes of the 1980s and 1990s in Africa, Latin America and the ex-USSR may make this difficult to believe. The world was incomparably richer than ever before in its capacity to produce goods and services and in their endless variety. It could not have managed otherwise to maintain a global population several times larger than ever before in the world's history. Most people until the 1980s lived better than their parents, and, in the advanced economies, better than they had ever expected to live or even imagined it possible to live. For some decades in the middle of the century it even looked as though ways had been found of distributing at least some of this enormous wealth with a degree of fairness to the working people of the richer countries, but at the end of the century inequality had once again the upper hand. It had also made a massive entry into the former 'socialist' countries where a certain equality of poverty had previously reigned. Humanity was far better educated than in 1914. Indeed, probably for the first time in history most human beings could be described as literate, at least in official statistics, though the significance of this achievement was far less clear at the end of the century than it would have been in 1914, given the enormous and probably growing gap between the minimum of competence officially accepted as literacy, often shading into 'functional illiteracy', and the command of reading and writing still expected at elite levels.

The world was filled with a revolutionary and constantly advancing technology, based on triumphs of natural science which could be anticipated in 1914, but had then barely begun to be pioneered. Perhaps the most dramatic practical consequence of these was a revolution in transport and communications which virtually annihilated time and distance. It was a world which could bring more information and entertainment than had been available to emperors in 1914, daily, hourly, into every household. It let people speak to one another across oceans and continents at the touch of a few buttons, and, for most practical purposes, abolished the cultural advantages of city over countryside.

Why, then, did the century end, not with a celebration of this unparalleled and marvellous progress, but in a mood of uneasiness? Why, as the epigraphs to this chapter show, did so many reflective minds look back upon it without satisfaction, and certainly without confidence in the future? Not only because it was without doubt the most murderous century of which we have record, both by the scale, frequency and length of the warfare which filled it, barely ceasing for a moment in the 1920s, but also by the unparalleled scale of the human catastrophes it produced, from the greatest famines in history to systematic genocide. Unlike the 'long nineteenth century', which seemed, and actually was, a period of almost unbroken material, intellectual *and moral* progress, that is to say of improvement in the conditions of civilized life, there has, since 1914, been a marked regression from the standards then regarded as normal in the developed countries and in the milieus of the middle classes and which were confidently believed to be spreading to the more backward regions and the less enlightened strata of the population.

Since this century has taught us, and continues to teach us, that human beings can learn to live under the most brutalized and theoretically intolerable conditions, it is not easy to grasp the extent of the, unfortunately accelerating, return to what our nineteenth-century ancestors would have called the standards of barbarism. We forget that the old revolutionary Frederick Engels was horrified at the explosion of an Irish Republican bomb in Westminster Hall, because, as an old soldier, he held that war was waged against combatants and not non-combatants. We forget that the pogroms in Tsarist Russia which (justifiably) outraged world opinion and drove Russian Jews across the Atlantic in their millions between 1881 and 1914, were small, almost negligible, by the standards of modern massacre: the dead were counted in dozens, not hundreds, let alone millions. We forget that an international Convention once provided that hostilities in war 'must not commence without previous and explicit warning in the form of a reasoned declaration of war or of an ultimatum with conditional declaration of war', for when was the last war that began with such an explicit or implicit declaration? Or one that ended with a formal treaty of peace negotiated between the belligerent states? In the course of the twentieth century, wars have been increasingly waged against the economy and infrastructure of states and against their civilian populations. Since the First World War the number of civilian casualties in war has been far greater than that of military casualties in all belligerent countries except the USA. How many of us recall that it was taken for granted in 1914 that:

Civilized warfare, the textbooks tell us, is confined, as far as possible, to disablement of the armed forces of the enemy; otherwise war would continue till one of the parties was exterminated. 'It is with good reason . . . that this practice has grown into a custom with the nations of Europe'. (*Encyclopedia Britannica*, XI ed., 1911, art: War.)

We do not quite overlook the revival of torture or even murder as a normal part of the operations of public security in modern states, but we probably fail to appreciate quite how dramatic a reversal this constitutes of the long era of legal development, from the first formal abolition of torture in a Western country in the 1780s to 1914.

And yet, the world at the end of the Short Twentieth Century cannot be compared with the world at its beginning in the terms of the historical accountancy of 'more' and 'less'. It was a qualitatively different world in at least three respects.

First, it was no longer Eurocentric. It had brought the decline and fall of Europe, still the unquestioned centre of power, wealth, intellect and 'Western civilization' when the century began. Europeans and their descendants were now reduced from perhaps a third of humanity to at most one sixth, a diminishing minority living in countries which barely, if at all, reproduced their populations, surrounded by, and in most cases – with some shining exceptions such as the USA (until the 1990s) – barricading themselves against the pressure of immigration from the regions of the poor. The industries Europe had pioneered were migrating elsewhere. The countries which had once looked across the oceans to Europe looked elsewhere. Australia, New Zealand, even the bi-oceanic USA, saw the future in the Pacific, whatever exactly this meant.

The 'great powers' of 1914, all of them European, had disappeared, like the USSR, inheritor of Tsarist Russia, or were reduced to regional or provincial status, with the possible exception of Germany. The very effort to create a single supranational 'European Community' and to invent a sense of European identity to correspond to it, replacing the old loyalties to historic nations and states, demonstrated the depth of this decline.

Was this a change of major significance, except for political historians? Perhaps not, since it reflected only minor changes in the economic, intellectual and cultural configuration of the world. Even in 1914 the USA had been the major industrial economy, and the major pioneer, model and propulsive force of the mass production and mass culture which conquered the globe during the Short Twentieth Century, and the USA, in spite of its many peculiarities, was the overseas extension of

Europe, and bracketed itself with the old continent under the heading 'western civilization'. Whatever its future prospects, the USA looked back from the 1990s on 'The American Century', an age of its rise and triumph. The ensemble of the countries of nineteenth-century industrialization remained, collectively, by far the greatest concentration of wealth, economic and scientific-technological power on the globe, as well as the one whose peoples enjoyed by far the highest standard of living. At the end of the century this still more than compensated for de-industrialization and the shift of production to other continents. To this extent the impression of an old Eurocentric or 'Western' world in full decline was superficial.

The second transformation was more significant. Between 1914 and the early 1990s the globe has become far more of a single operational unit, as it was not, and could not have been in 1914. In fact, for many purposes, notably in economic affairs, the globe is now the primary operational unit and older units such as the 'national economies', defined by the politics of territorial states, are reduced to complications of transnational activities. The stage reached by the 1990s in the construction of the 'global village' – the phrase was coined in the 1960s (Macluhan, 1962) – will not seem very advanced to observers in the mid-twenty-first century, but it had already transformed not only certain economic and technical activities, and the operations of science, but important aspects of private life, mainly by the unimaginable acceleration of communication and transport. Perhaps the most striking characteristic of the end of the twentieth century is the tension between this accelerating process of globalization and the inability of both public institutions and the collective behaviour of human beings to come to terms with it. Curiously enough, private human behaviour has had less trouble in adjusting to the world of satellite television, E-mail, holidays in the Seychelles and trans-oceanic commuting.

The third transformation, and in some ways the most disturbing, is the disintegration of the old patterns of human social relationships, and with it, incidentally, the snapping of the links between generations, that is to say, between past and present. This has been particularly evident in the most developed countries of the western version of capitalism, in which the values of an absolute a-social individualism have been dominant, both in official and unofficial ideologies, though those who hold them often deplore their social consequences. Nevertheless, the tendencies were to be found elsewhere, reinforced by the erosion of traditional societies and religions, as well as by the destruction, or autodestruction, of the societies of 'real socialism'.

Such a society consisting of an otherwise unconnected assemblage of self-centred individuals pursuing only their own gratification (whether this is called profit, pleasure or by some other name) was always implicit in the theory of the capitalist economy. Ever since the Age of Revolution, observers of all ideological colours predicted the consequent disintegration of the old social bonds in practice and monitored its progress. The Communist Manifesto's eloquent tribute to the revolutionary role of capitalism is familiar ('The bourgeoisie . . . has pitilessly torn asunder the motley feudal ties that bound man to his 'natural superiors' and has left remaining no other nexus between man and man than naked self-interest'). But that is not quite how the new and revolutionary capitalist society had worked in practice.

In practice, the new society operated not by the wholesale destruction of all that it had inherited from the old society, but by selectively adapting the heritage of the past for its own use. There is no 'sociological puzzle' about the readiness of bourgeois society to introduce 'a radical individualism in economics and . . . to tear up all traditional social relations in the process' (i.e. where they got in its way), while fearing 'radical experimental individualism' in culture (or in the field of behaviour and morality) (Daniel Bell, 1976, p. 18). The most effective way to build an industrial economy based on private enterprise was to combine it with motivations which had nothing to do with the logic of the free market – for instance with the Protestant ethic; with the abstention from immediate gratification; with the ethic of hard work; with family duty and trust; but certainly not with the antinomian rebellion of individuals.

Yet Marx and the other prophets of the disintegration of old values and social relationships were right. Capitalism was a permanent and continuous revolutionizing force. Logically, it would end by disintegrating even those parts of the pre-capitalist past which it had found convenient, nay perhaps essential, for its own development. It would end by sawing off at least one of the branches on which it sat. Since the middle of the century this has been happening. Under the impact of the extraordinary economic explosion of the Golden Age and after, with its consequent social and cultural changes, the most profound revolution in society since the stone age, the branch began to crack and break. At the end of this century it has for the first time become possible to see what a world may be like in which the past, including the past in the present, has lost its role, in which the old maps and charts which guided human beings, singly and collectively, through life no longer represent the landscape through which we move, the sea on which we sail. In which we do not know where our journey is taking us, or even ought to take us.

This is the situation with which a part of humanity must already come to terms at the end of the century, and more will have to in the new millennium. However, by then it may have become clearer where humanity is going than it is today. We can look backward over the road that brought us here, and this is what I have tried to do in this book. We do not know what will shape the future, although I have not resisted the temptation to reflect on some of its problems, insofar as they arise from the debris of the period that has just come to an end. Let us hope it will be a better, juster and more viable world. The old century has not ended well.

PART ONE

THE AGE OF CATASTROPHE

CHAPTER ONE
The Age of Total War

Lines of grey muttering faces, masked with fear,
They leave their trenches, going over the top,
While time ticks blank and busy on their wrists,
And hope, with furtive eyes and grappling fists,
Flounders in mud. O Jesus, make it stop!

– Siegfried Sassoon (1947, p. 71)

It may be thought better, in view of the allegations of 'barbarity' of air attacks, to preserve appearances by formulating milder rules and by still nominally confining bombardment to targets which are strictly military in character . . . to avoid emphasizing the truth that air warfare has made such restrictions obsolete and impossible. It may be some time until another war occurs and meanwhile the public may become educated as to the meaning of air power.

– *Rules as to Bombardment by Aircraft*, 1921 (Townshend, 1986, p. 161)

(Sarajevo, 1946.) Here as in Belgrade, I see in the streets a considerable number of young women whose hair is greying, or completely grey. Their faces are tormented, but still young, while the form of their bodies betrays their youth even more clearly. It seems to me that I see how the hand of this last war has passed over the heads of these frail beings . . .

This sight cannot be preserved for the future; these heads will soon become even greyer and disappear. That is a pity. Nothing could speak more clearly to future generations about our times than these youthful grey heads, from which the nonchalance of youth has been stolen.

Let them at least have a memorial in this little note.

– *Signs by the Roadside* (Andrić, 1992, p. 50)

I

'The lamps are going out all over Europe,' said Edward Grey, Foreign Secretary of Great Britain, as he watched the lights of Whitehall on the night when Britain and Germany went to war in 1914. 'We shall not see them lit again in our lifetime.' In Vienna the great satirist Karl Kraus prepared to document and denounce that war in an extraordinary reportage-drama of 792 pages to which he gave the title *The Last Days of Humanity*. Both saw the world war as the end of a world, and they were not alone. It was not the end of humanity, although there were moments, in the course of the thirty-one years of world conflict between the Austrian declaration of war on Serbia on 28 July 1914 and the uncondi-tional surrender of Japan on 14 August 1945 – four days after the explosion of the first nuclear bomb – when the end of a considerable proportion of the human race did not look far off. There were surely times when the god or gods, whom pious humans believed to have created the world and all in it, might have been expected to regret having done so.

Mankind survived. Nevertheless, the great edifice of nineteenth-century civilization crumpled in the flames of world war, as its pillars collapsed. There is no understanding the Short Twentieth Century without it. It was marked by war. It lived and thought in terms of world war, even when the guns were silent and the bombs were not exploding. Its history and, more specifically, the history of its initial age of break-down and catastrophe, must begin with that of the thirty-one years' world war.

For those who had grown up before 1914 the contrast was so dramatic that many of them – including the generation of this historian's parents, or, at any rate, its central European members, refused to see any continuity with the past. 'Peace' meant 'before 1914': after that came something that no longer deserved the name. This was understandable. In 1914 there had been no major war for a century, that is to say, a war in which all, or even a majority of, major powers had been involved, the major players in the international game at that time being the six European 'great powers' (Britain, France, Russia, Austria-Hungary, Prus-sia – after 1871 enlarged into Germany – and, after it was unified, Italy), the USA and Japan. There had been only one brief war in which more than two of the major powers had been in battle, the Crimean War (1854–56) between Russian on one side, Britain and France on the other. Moreover, most wars involving major powers at all had been compara-tively quick. Much the longest of them was not an international conflict but a civil war within the USA (1861–65). The length of war was measured in months or even (like the 1866 war between Prussia and Austria) in weeks. Between 1871 and 1914 there had been no wars in Europe at all in which the armies of major powers crossed any hostile frontier, although in the Far East Japan fought, and beat, Russia in 1904–5, thus hastening the Russian revolution.

There had been no *world* wars at all. In the eighteenth century France and Britain had contended in a series of wars whose battlefields ranged from India through Europe to North America, and across the world's oceans. Between 1815 and 1914 no major power fought another outside its immediate region, although aggressive expeditions of imperial or would-be imperial powers against weaker overseas enemies were, of course, common. Most of these were spectacularly one-sided fights, such as the US wars against Mexico (1846–48) and Spain (1898) and the various campaigns to extend the British and French colonial empires, although the worm turned once or twice, as when the French had to withdraw from Mexico in the 1860s, the Italians from Ethiopia in 1896. Even the most formidable opponents of modern states, their arsenals increasingly filled with an overwhelmingly superior technology of death, could only hope, at best, to postpone the inevitable retreat. Such exotic conflicts were the stuff of adventure literature or the reports of that mid-nineteenth-century innovation the war correspondent, rather than matters of direct relevance to most inhabitants of the states which waged and won them.

All this changed in 1914. The First World War involved *all* major powers and indeed all European states except Spain, the Netherlands, the three Scandinavian countries and Switzerland. What is more, troops from the world overseas were, often for the first time, sent to fight and work outside their own regions. Canadians fought in France, Australians and New Zealanders forged their national consciousness on a peninsula in the Aegean – 'Gallipoli' became their national myth – and, more significantly, the United States rejected George Washington's warning against 'European entanglements' and sent its men to fight there, thus determining the shape of twentieth-century history. Indians were sent to Europe and the Middle East, Chinese labour battalions came to the West, Africans fought in the French army. Though military action outside Europe was not very significant, except in the Middle East, the naval war was once again global: its first battle was fought in 1914 off the Falkland Islands, its decisive campaigns, by German submarines and Allied convoys, on and under the seas of the North and mid-Atlantic.

That the Second World War was literally global hardly needs to be demonstrated. Virtually all independent states of the world were involved, willingly or unwillingly, although the republics of Latin America participated only in the most nominal manner. The colonies of imperial powers had no choice in the matter. Except for the future Irish Republic, Sweden, Switzerland, Portugal, Turkey and Spain in Europe, and possibly Afghanistan outside Europe, virtually the whole globe was belligerent or occupied or both. As for the battlefields, the names of Melanesian islands and of settlements in the North African deserts, in Burma and the Philippines became as familiar to newspaper readers and radio listeners – and this was quintessentially the war of the radio news bulletins – as the names of Arctic and Caucasian battles, of Normandy, Stalingrad and Kursk. The Second World War was a lesson in world geography.

Local, regional or global, the wars of the twentieth century were to be on an altogether vaster scale than anything previously experienced. Among seventy-four international wars between 1816 and 1965, which American specialists, who like to do that kind of thing, have ranked by the number of people they killed, the top four occurred in the twentieth century: the two world wars, the Japanese war against China in 1937–39, and the Korean war. They killed upwards of one million persons in battle. The largest documented international war of the post-Napoleonic nineteenth century, that between Prussia/Germany and France in 1870–71, killed perhaps 150,000, an order of magnitude roughly comparable to the deaths in the Chaco war of 1932–35 between Bolivia (pop. *c.* 3 million) and Paraguay (pop. *c.* 1.4 million). In short, 1914 opens the age of massacre (Singer, 1972, pp. 66, 131).

There is not space in this book to discuss the origins of the First World War, which the present author has tried to sketch in *The Age of Empire*. It began as an essentially European war between the triple alliance of France, Britain and Russia on one side, the so-called 'central powers' of Germany and Austria-Hungary on the other, Serbia and Belgium being immediately drawn in by the Austrian attack on one (which actually set off the war) and the German attack on the other (which was part of the German strategic war plan). Turkey and Bulgaria soon joined the central powers, while on the other side the Triple Alliance gradually built up into a very large coalition. Italy was bribed in; Greece, Rumania and (much more nominally) Portugal were also involved. More to the point, Japan joined in almost immediately in order to take over German positions in the Far East and Western Pacific, but took no interest in anything outside its own region, and – more significantly – the USA entered in 1917. In fact, its intervention was to be decisive.

The Germans, then as in the Second World War, were faced with a possible war on two fronts, quite apart from the Balkans into which they were drawn by their alliance with Austria-Hungary. (However, since three of the four Central Powers were in that region – Turkey and Bulgaria as well as Austria – the strategic problem there was not so urgent.) The German plan was to knock out France quickly in the West and then move with equal rapidity to knock out Russia in the East, before the Tsar's empire could bring the full weight of its enormous military manpower into effective action. Then, as later, Germany planned for a lightning campaign (what would in the Second World War be called a *blitzkrieg*) because it had to. The plan almost succeeded, but not quite. The German army advanced into France, among other places through neutral Belgium, and was only halted a few dozen miles east of Paris on the river Marne five to six weeks after war had been declared. (In 1940 the plan was to succeed.) They then withdraw a little, and both sides – the French now supplemented by what remained of the Belgians and by a British land force which was soon to grow enormously – improvised parallel lines of defensive trenches and fortifications which soon stretched without a break from the Channel coast in Flanders to the Swiss frontier, leaving a good deal of eastern France and Belgium in German occupation. They did not shift significantly for the next three-and-a-half years.

This was the 'Western Front', which became a machine for massacre such as had probably never before been seen in the history of warfare. Millions of men faced each other across the sandbagged parapets of the trenches under which they lived like, and with, rats and lice. From time to time their generals would seek to break out of the deadlock. Days, even weeks of unceasing artillery bombardment – what a German writer later called 'hurricanes of steel' (Ernst Jünger, 1921) – were to 'soften up' the enemy and drive him underground, until at the right moment waves of men climbed over the parapet, usually protected by coils and webs of barbed wire, into 'no-man's land', a chaos of waterlogged shell-craters, ruined tree-stumps, mud and abandoned corpses, to advance into the machine-guns that mowed them down. As they knew they would. The attempt of the Germans to break through at Verdun in 1916 (February–July) was a battle of two millions, with one million casualties. It failed. The British offensive on the Somme, designed to force the Germans to break off the Verdun offensive cost Britain 420,000 dead – 60,000 casualties on the first day of the attack. It is not surprising that in the memory of the British and the French, who fought most of the First World War on the western front, it remained the 'Great War', more terrible and traumatic in memory than the Second World War. The French lost almost 20 per cent of their men of military age, and if we include the prisoners of war, the wounded and the permanently disabled and disfigured – those *'gueules cassés'* ('smashed faces') which became so vivid a part of the after-image of the war – not much more than one in three French soliders came through the war without harm. The chances of the five million or so British soldiers surviving the war unharmed were just about evens. The British lost a generation – half a million men under the age of thirty (Winter, 1986 p. 83) – notably among their upper classes, whose young men, destined as gentlemen to be officers who set an example, marched into battle at the head of their men and were consequently mown down first. One quarter of the Oxford and Cambridge students under the age of twenty-five who served in the British army in 1914 were killed (Winter, 1986, p. 98). The Germans, though the number of their dead was even greater than the French, lost only a smaller proportion of their much larger military age-groups – 13 per cent. Even the apparently modest losses of the USA (116,000, against the 1.6 millions of French, the almost 800,000 of British, the 1.8 millions of Germans) actually demonstrate the murderous nature of the Western front, the only one where they fought. For while the USA lost between 2.5 and 3 times as many in the Second World War as in the First, the American forces in 1917–18 were in action for barely a year-and-a-half, compared to the three-and-a-half years of the Second World War, and on only a single narrow sector and not world-wide.

The horrors of warfare on the Western Front were to have even darker consequences. The experience itself naturally helped to brutalize both warfare and politics: if one could be conducted without counting the human or any other costs, why not the other? Most men who served in the First World War –. overwhelmingly as conscripts – came out of it as convinced haters of war. However, those ex-soldiers who had passed through this kind of war without being turned against it sometimes drew from the shared experience of living with death and courage a sense of incommunicable and savage superiority, not least to women and those who had not fought, which was to fill the early ranks of the post-war ultra-right. Adolf Hitler was only one of such men for whom having been a *frontsoldat* was the formative experience of their lives. However, the opposite reaction had equally negative consequences. After the war it became quite evident to politicians, at least in democratic countries, that bloodbaths like 1914–18 would no longer be tolerated by the voters. The post-1918 strategy of Britain and France, like the post-Vietnam strategy of the USA, was based on this assumption. In the short run this helped the Germans to win the Second World War in the West in 1940 against a France committed to crouch behind its incomplete fortifications and, once these had been breached, simply unwilling to fight on; and a Britain desperate to avoid committing itself to the sort of massive land war that had decimated its people in 1914–18. In the longer run democratic governments failed to resist the temptation of saving their own citizens' lives by treating those of enemy countries as totally expendable. The dropping of the atom bomb on Hiroshima and Nagasaki in 1945 was not justified as indispensable for victory, which was by then absolutely certain, but as a means of saving American soldiers' lives. But perhaps the thought that it would prevent America's ally the USSR from establishing a claim to a major part in Japan's defeat was not absent from the minds of the US government either.

While the Western Front settled into bloody stalemate, the Eastern Front remained in movement. The Germans pulverised a clumsy Russian invasion force at the battle of Tannenberg in the first month of war and thereafter, with the intermittently effective help of the Austrians, pushed Russia out of Poland. In spite of occasional Russian counter-offensives, it was clear that the Central Powers had the upper hand, and Russia was fighting a defensive rearguard action against the German advance. In the Balkans the Central powers were in control, in spite of an uneven military performance by the rocky Habsburg empire. The local belligerents, Serbia and Rumania, incidentally, suffered by far the greatest proportional military losses. The Allies, in spite of occupying Greece, made no headway until the collapse of the Central Powers after the summer of 1918. The plan by Italy to open another front against Austria-Hungary in the Alps failed, mainly because many Italian soldiers saw no reason to fight for the government of a state they did not consider theirs, and whose language few of them could speak. After a major military debacle at Caporetto in 1917, which left a literary memory in Ernest Hemingway's novel *A Farewell to Arms*, the Italians had even to be stiffened by transfers from other Allied armies. Meanwhile France, Britain and Germany bled each other to death on the Western Front, Russia was increasingly destabilized by the war she was patently losing, and the Austro-Hungarian empire increasingly tottered towards its break-up, which its local nationalist movements longed for, and to which the Allied foreign ministries resigned themselves without enthusiasm, rightly foreseeing an unstable Europe.

How to break the stalemate on the Western Front was the crucial problem for both sides, for without victory in the West neither could win the war, all the more so since the naval war was also deadlocked. Except for some isolated raiders, the Allies controlled the oceans, but the British and German battle-fleets faced and immobilized each other on the North Sea. Their only attempt to engage in battle (1916) ended indecisively, but since it confined the German fleet to its bases, on balance it was to the Allies' advantage.

Both sides tried to do it by technology. The Germans – always strong in chemistry – brought poison gas onto the battlefield, where it proved both barbarous and ineffective, leaving behind the only genuine case of government humanitarian revulsion against a means of conducting warfare, the Geneva Convention of 1925, by which the world pledged itself not to use chemical warfare. And indeed, though all governments continued to prepare for it and expected the enemy to use it, it was not used by either side in the Second World War though humanitarian feelings did not prevent the Italians from gassing colonial people. (The steep decline in the values of civilization after the Second World War eventually brought poison gas back. During the Iran–Iraq war of the 1980s Iraq, then enthusiastically supported by the Western states, used it freely against both soldiers and civilians.) The British pioneered the caterpillared armoured vehicle, still known by its then code-name of *tank*, but their far from impressive generals had not yet discovered how to use it. Both sides used the new and still frail airplanes, as well as (by Germany) the curious cigar-shaped hydrogen-filled airships, experimenting with aerial bombardment, fortunately not to much effect. Air warfare also came into its own, notably as a means of terrorizing civilians, in the Second World War.

The only technological weapon which had a major effect on warfare in 1914–18 was the submarine, for both sides, unable to defeat each other's soldiers, resorted to starving the other's civilians. Since all Britain's supplies were seaborne, it seemed feasible to strangle the British Isles by increasingly ruthless submarine warfare against shipping. The campaign came close to success in 1917, before effective ways to counter it were found, but it did more than anything else to draw the USA into the war. The British, in turn, did their best to blockade supplies to Germany, i.e. to starve both the German war economy and the German population. They were more effective than they ought to have been, since, as we shall see, the German war economy was not run with the efficiency and rationality on which the Germans prided themselves. Unlike the German military machine, which, in the First as in the Second World War, was strikingly superior to any other. This sheer superiority of the German army as a military force might just have proved decisive, had the Allies not been able to call on the practically unlimited resources of the USA from 1917. As it was, Germany, even hobbled by the alliance with

Austria, secured total victory in the East, driving Russia out of the war, into revolution and out of a large part of her European territories in 1917–18. Shortly after imposing the penal peace of Brest-Litowsk (March 1918) the German army, now free to concentrate in the West, actually broke through the Western Front and advanced on Paris again. Thanks to the flood of American reinforcements and equipment, the Allies recovered, but for a while it looked a close thing. However, it was the last throw of an exhausted Germany, which knew itself to be close to defeat. Once the Allies began to advance in the summer of 1918, the end was only a few weeks away. The Central Powers not only admitted defeat but collapsed. Revolution swept across central and south-eastern Europe in the autumn of 1918, as it had swept across Russia in 1917 (see next chapter). No old government was left standing between the borders of France and the Sea of Japan. Even the belligerents on the victorious side were shaken, although it is difficult to believe that Britain and France would not have survived even defeat as stable political entities; but not Italy. Certainly none of the defeated countries escaped revolution.

If one of the great ministers or diplomats of the past – the ones on whom aspiring members of their countries' foreign services were still told to model themselves, a Talleyrand or a Bismarck – had risen from their graves to observe the First World War, they would certainly have wondered why sensible statemen had not decided to settle the war by some compromise before it destroyed the world of 1914. We must also wonder. Most non-revolutionary and non-ideological wars of the past had not been waged as struggles to death or total exhaustion. In 1914 ideology was certainly not what divided the belligerents, except insofar as the war had to be fought on both sides by mobilizing public opinion, i.e. by claiming some profound challenge to accepted national values, such as Russian barbarism against German culture, French and British democracy against German absolutism, or the like. Moreover there were statesmen who recommended some kind of compromise settlement even outside Russia and Austria-Hungary which lobbied their Allies in this sense with increasing desperation as defeat drew near. Why, then, was the First World War waged by the leading powers on both sides as a zero-sum game, i.e. as a war which could only be totally won or totally lost?

The reason was that this war, unlike earlier wars, which were typically waged for limited and specifiable objects, was waged for unlimited ends. In the Age of Empire, politics and economics had fused. International political rivalry was modelled on economic growth and competition, but the characteristic feature of this was precisely that it had no limit. 'The "natural frontiers" of Standard Oil, the Deutsche Bank or the De Beers Diamond Corporation were at the end of the universe, or rather at the limits of their capacity to expand.' (Hobsbawm, 1987, p. 318.) More concretely, for the two main contestants, Germany and Britain, the sky had to be the limit, since Germany wanted a global political and maritime position like that now occupied by Britain, and which therefore would automatically relegate an already declining Britain to inferior status. It was either/or. For France, then as later, the stakes were less global but equally urgent: to compensate for its increasing, and apparently inevitable, demographic and economic inferiority to Germany. Here also the issue was the future of France as a great power. In both cases compromise would merely have meant postponement. Germany itself, one might have supposed, could wait until its growing size and superiority established the position German governments felt to be their country's due, which would happen sooner or later. Indeed, the dominant position of a twice defeated Germany with no claims to independent military power in Europe was more unchallenged in the early 1990s than the claims of militarist Germany ever were before 1945. Yet that is because Britain and France, as we shall see, were forced after the Second World War, however reluctantly, to accept their relegation to second-rank status, just as Federal Germany, with all its economic strength, recognized that in the post-1945 world supremacy as a single state was, and would have to remain, beyond its power. In the 1900s, at the peak of the imperial and imperialist era, both the German claim to unique global status ('The German spirit will regenerate the world', as the phrase went) and the resistance of Britain and France, still undeniable 'great powers' in a Euro-centred world, were as yet intact. On paper no doubt compromise was possible on this or that point of the almost megalomaniac 'war aims' which both sides formulated as soon as war had broken out, but in practice the only war aim that counted was total victory: what in the Second World War came to be called 'unconditional surrender'.

It was an absurd and self-defeating aim which ruined both victors and vanquished. It drove the defeated into revolution, and the victors into bankruptcy and physical exhaustion. In 1940 France was overrun by inferior German forces with ridiculous ease and speed, and accepted subordination to Hitler without hesitation, because the country had almost bled to death in 1914–18. Britain was never the same again after 1918 because the country had ruined its economy by waging a war substantially beyond its resources. Moreover, total victory, ratified by a penal, dictated peace, ruined what little chances there were of restoring something even faintly like a stable, liberal, bourgeois Europe, as the economist John Maynard Keynes immediately recognized. If Germany was not reintegrated into the European economy, i.e. if the country's economic weight within that economy was not recognized and accepted, there could be no stability. But this was the last consideration in the minds of those who had fought to eliminate Germany.

The peace-settlement, imposed by the major surviving victorious powers (USA, Britain, France, Italy) and usually, if inaccurately, known as the Treaty of Versailles,* was dominated by five considerations. The most immediate was the breakdown of so many regimes in Europe, and the emergence in Russia of an alternative revolutionary Bolshevik regime dedicated to universal subversion, and a magnet for revolutionary forces everywhere else (see chapter 2). Second, there was the need to control Germany which had, after all, almost defeated the entire Allied coalition singlehanded. For obvious reasons this was, and has ever since remained, the major concern of France. Third, the map of Europe had to be re-divided and re-drawn, both to weaken Germany and to fill the large empty spaces left in Europe and the Middle East by the simultaneous defeat and collapse of the Russian, Habsburg and Ottoman empires. The main claimants to the succession, at least in Europe, were various nationalist movements which the victors tended to encourage insofar as they were adequately anti-Bolshevik. In fact, in Europe the basic principle of re-ordering the map was to create ethnic-linguistic nation states, according to the belief that nations had the 'right to self-determination'. President Wilson of the USA, whose opinions were seen as expressing those of the power without whom the war would have been lost, was passionately committed to this belief, which was (and is) more easily held by those far from the ethnic and linguistic realities of the regions which were to be divided into neat nation-states. The attempt was a disaster, as can still be seen in the Europe of the 1990s. The national conflicts tearing the continent apart in the 1990s were the old chickens of Versailles once again coming home to roost.† The remapping of the Middle East was

---

* Technically the Treaty of Versailles only made peace with Germany. Various parks and royal chateaux in the neighbourhood of Paris gave their names to the other treaties: Saint Germain, with Austria; Trianon with Hungary; Sèvres with Turkey; Neuilly with Bulgaria.

† The Yugoslav civil war, the secessionist agitation in Slovakia, the secession of the Baltic states from the former USSR, the conflicts between Hungarians and Rumanians over Transylvania, the separatism of Moldova (Moldavia, formerly Bessarabia), and for that matter Transcaucasian nationalism, are among the explosive problems which either did not exist or could not have existed before 1914.

along conventional imperialist lines – division between Britain and France – except for Palestine, where the British government, anxious for international Jewish support during the war, had incautiously and ambiguously promised to establish 'a national home' for the Jews. This was to be another problematic and unforgotten relic of the First World War.

The fourth set of considerations were those of domestic politics within the victor countries – which meant, in practice, Britain, France and the USA – and frictions between them. The most important consequence of such internal politicking was that the US Congress refused to ratify a peace settlement largely written by or for its President, and the USA consequently withdrew from it, with far-reaching results.

Finally, the victor powers desperately searched for the kind of peace settlement which would make impossible another war like the one that had just devastated the world, and whose after-effects were all around them. They failed in the most spectacular manner. Within twenty years the world was once again at war.

Making the world safe from Bolshevism and re-mapping Europe overlapped, since the most immediate way to deal with revolutionary Russia, if by any chance it survived – this was by no means certain in 1919 – was to isolate it behind a 'quarantine belt' (*cordon sanitaire*, in the contemporary language of diplomacy) of anti-communist states. Since the territory of these was largely or wholly carved out of the formerly Russian lands, their hostility to Moscow could be guaranteed. Going from north to south, these were: Finland, an autonomous region that had been allowed to secede by Lenin; three new little Baltic republics (Estonia, Latvia, Lithuania), for which there was no historical precedent; Poland, restored to independent statehood after 120 years, and an enormously enlarged Rumania, its size doubled by accessions from the Hungarian and Austrian parts of the Habsburg empire and ex-Russian Bessarabia. Most of these territories had actually been detached from Russia by Germany and, but for the Bolshevik Revolution, would certainly have been returned to that state. The attempt to continue this isolation belt into the Caucasus, failed, essentially because revolutionary Russia came to terms with non-communist but revolutionary Turkey, which had no fondness for the British and French imperialists. Hence the briefly independent Armenian and Georgian states, set up after Brest Litowsk, and attempts under the British to detach oil-rich Azerbaijan, did not survive the victory of the Bolsheviks in the Civil War of 1918–20 and the Soviet–Turkish treaty of 1921. In short, in the East the Allies accepted the frontiers imposed by Germany on revolutionary Russia, insofar as these were not made inoperative by forces beyond their control.

This still left large parts, mainly of formerly Austro-Hungarian Europe, to be re-mapped. Austria and Hungary were reduced to German and Magyar rumps, Serbia was expanded into a large new Yugoslavia by a merger with the (formerly Austrian) Slovenia and the (formerly Hungarian) Croatia, as well as with the formerly independent small tribal kingdom of herdsmen and raiders, Montenegro, a bleak mass of mountains whose inhabitants reacted to the unprecedented loss of independence by converting en masse to communism, which, they felt, appreciated the heroic virtue. It was also associated with orthodox Russia, whose faith the unconquered men of the Black Mountain had defended against the Turkish unbelievers for so many centuries. A new Czechoslovakia was also formed by joining the former industrial core of the Habsburg empire, the Czech lands, to the areas of Slovak and Ruthenian country people once belonging to Hungary. Rumania was enlarged into a multi-national conglomerate, while Poland and Italy also benefited. There was absolutely no historical precedent for or logic in the Yugoslav and Czechoslovak combinations, which were constructs of a nationalist ideology which believed in both the force of common ethnicity and the undesirability of excessively small nation-states. All the southern slavs (= Yugoslavs) belonged to one state, as did the western slavs of the Czech and Slovak lands. As might have been expected, these shotgun political marriages did not prove very firm. Incidentally, except for rump Austria and rump Hungary, shorn of most – but in practice not entirely of all – their minorities, the new succession states, whether carved out of Russia or the Habsburg Empire, were no less multinational than their predecessors.

A penal peace, justified by the argument that the state was uniquely responsible for the war and all its consequences (the 'war guilt' clause) was imposed on Germany to keep her permanently enfeebled. This was achieved not so much by territorial losses, though Alsace-Lorraine went back to France, a substantial region in the east to a restored Poland (the 'Polish Corridor' which separated East Prussia from the rest of Germany), and some lesser adjustments to the German borders; rather it was to be ensured by depriving Germany of an effective navy and any air force; limiting its army to 100,000 men; imposing theoretically indefinite 'reparations' (payments for the costs of the war incurred by the victors); by the military occupation of part of western Germany; and, not least, by depriving Germany of all her former overseas colonies. (These were redistributed among the British and their dominions, the French and, to a lesser extent, the Japanese, but, in deference to the growing unpopularity of imperialism, they were no longer called 'colonies' but 'mandates' to ensure the progress of backward peoples, handed over by humanity to imperial powers who would not dream of exploiting them for any other purpose.) Except for the territorial clauses, nothing was left of the Treaty of Versailles by the middle 1930s.

As for the mechanism for preventing another world war, it was evident that the consortium of European 'great powers' which had been supposed to secure this before 1914 had utterly broken down. The alternative, urged on hard-nosed European politicos by President Wilson with all the liberal fervour of a Princeton political scientist, was to set up an all-embracing 'League of Nations' (i.e. independent states) which would settle problems peacefully and democratically before they had got out of hand, preferably by public negotiation ('open covenants openly arrived at'), for the war had also made the habitual and sensible processes of international negotiation suspect as 'secret diplomacy'. This was largely a reaction against the secret treaties arranged among the Allies during the war, in which they carved up post-war Europe and the Middle East with a startling lack of concern for the wishes, or even the interests, of the inhabitants of these regions. The Bolsheviks, discovering these sensitive documents in the Tsarist archives, had promptly published them for the world to read, and an exercise of damage limitation was therefore called for. The League of Nations was indeed set up as part of the peace settlement, and proved an almost total failure, except as an institution for collecting statistics. It did, however, in its early days, settle one or two minor disputes which did not put world peace at much risk, such as that between Finland and Sweden over the Åland Islands.* The refusal of the USA to join the League of Nations deprived it of any real meaning.

It is not necessary to go into the details of interwar history to see that the Versailles settlement could not possibly be the basis of a stable peace. It was doomed from the start, and another war was therefore practically certain. As we have already noted, the USA almost immediately contracted out, and in a world no longer Euro-centred and Euro-determined,

---

* The Åland Islands, situated between Finland and Sweden, and part of Finland, were and are inhabited exclusively by a Swedish-speaking population, whereas the newly independent Finland was aggressively commited to the dominance of the Finnish language. As an alternative to secession to nearby Sweden, the League devised a scheme which guaranteed the exclusive use of Swedish on the islands, and safeguarded them against unwanted immigration from the Finnish mainland.

no settlement not underwritten by what was now a major world power could hold. As we shall see, this was true of the world's economic affairs as well as of its politics. Two major European, and indeed world, powers, were temporarily not only eliminated from the international game, but assumed not to exist as independent players – Germany and Soviet Russia. As soon as either or both these re-entered the scene, a peace settlement based on Britain and France alone – for Italy also remained dissatisfied – could not last. And, sooner or later Germany, or Russia, or both, would inevitably reappear as major players.

What little chance the peace had, was torpedoed by the refusal of the victor powers to reintegrate the losers. It is true that the total repression of Germany and the total outlawing of Soviet Russia soon proved impossible, but adjustment to reality was slow and reluctant. The French, in particular, only abandoned the hope of keeping Germany feeble and impotent unwillingly. (The British were not haunted by the memory of defeat and invasion.) As for the USSR, the victor states would have preferred it not to exist, and, having backed the armies of counter-revolution in the Russian Civil War, and sent military forces to support them, showed no enthusiasm about recognizing its survival. Their businessmen even dismissed the offers of the most far-reaching concessions to foreign investors made by Lenin, desperate for any way to re-start an economy almost destroyed by war, revolution and civil war. Soviet Russia was forced into developing in isolation, even though for political purposes the two outlaw states of Europe, Soviet Russia and Germany, drew together in the early 1920s.

Perhaps the next war might have been avoided, or at least postponed, if the pre-war economy had been restored again as a global system of prosperous growth and expansion. However, after a few years in the middle 1920s when it seemed to have put the war and post-war disruptions behind it, the world economy plunged into the greatest and most dramatic crisis it had known since the industrial revolution (see chapter 3). And this then brought to power, both in Germany and in Japan, the political forces of militarism and the extreme right committed to a deliberate break with the status quo by confrontation, if necessary military, rather than by gradually negotiated change. From then on a new world war was not only predictable, but routinely predicted. Those who became adults in the 1930s expected it. The image of fleets of airplanes dropping bombs on cities and of nightmare figures in gasmasks tapping their way like blind people through the fog of poison gas, haunted my generation: prophetically in one case, mistakenly in the other.

II

The origins of the Second World War have produced an incomparably smaller historical literature than the causes of the First, and for an obvious reason. With the rarest exceptions, no serious historian has ever doubted that Germany, Japan and (more hesitantly) Italy were the aggressors. The states drawn into the war against these three, whether capitalist or socialist, did not want a war, and most of them did what they could to avoid one. In the simplest terms the question who or what caused the Second World War can be answered in two words: Adolf Hitler.

Answers to historical questions are not, of course, so simple. As we have seen, the world situation created by the First World War was inherently unstable, especially in Europe, but also in the Far East, and peace was therefore not expected to last. Dissatisfaction with the status quo was not confined to the defeated states, although these, and notably Germany, felt they had plenty of cause for resentment, as indeed was the case. Every party in Germany, from the Communists on the extreme left to Hitler's National Socialists on the extreme right, concurred in condemning the Versailles Treaty as unjust and unacceptable. Paradoxically, a genuine German revolution might have produced an internationally less explosive Germany. The two defeated countries which were really revolutionized, Russia and Turkey, were too concerned with their own affairs, including the defence of their frontiers, to destabilize the international situation. They were forces for stability in the 1930s, and indeed Turkey remained neutral in the Second World War. However, both Japan and Italy, though on the winning side in the war, also felt dissatisfied, the Japanese with somewhat greater realism than the Italians, whose imperial appetites greatly exceeded their state's independent power to satisfy them. In any case, Italy had come out of the war with considerable territorial gains in the Alps, on the Adriatic and even in the Aegean Sea, even if not quite with all the booty promised to the state by the Allies in return for joining their side in 1915. However, the triumph of fascism, a counter-revolutionary and therefore ultra-nationalist and imperialist movement, underlined Italian dissatisfaction (see chapter 5). As for Japan, its very considerable military and naval force made it into much the most formidable power in the Far East, especially since Russia was out of the picture, and this was to some extent recognized internationally by the Washington Naval Agreement of 1922, which finally ended British naval supremacy by establishing a formula of 5:5:3 for the strength of the US, British and Japanese navies respectively. Yet Japan, whose industrialization was advancing at express speed – even though in absolute size the economy was still quite modest – 2.5 per cent of world industrial production in the late 1920s – undoubtedly felt that it deserved a rather larger slice of the Far Eastern cake than the white imperial powers granted it. Moreover, Japan was acutely conscious of the vulnerability of a country that lacked virtually all natural resources needed for a modern industrial economy, whose imports were at the mercy of disruption by foreign navies, and whose exports were at the mercy of the US market. Military pressure for the creation of a nearby land empire in China, it was argued, would shorten the Japanese lines of communication and thus make them less vulnerable.

Nevertheless, whatever the instability of the post-1918 peace and the probability of its breakdown, it is quite undeniable that what caused the Second World War concretely was aggression by the three malcontent powers, bound together by various treaties from the middle 1930s. The milestones on the road to war were the Japanese invasion of Manchuria in 1931; the Italian invasion of Ethiopia in 1935; the German and Italian intervention in the Spanish Civil War of 1936–39; the German invasion of Austria in early 1938; the German crippling of Czechoslovakia later in the same year; the German occupation of what remained of Czechoslovakia in March 1939 (followed by the Italian occupation of Albania); and the German demands on Poland which actually led to the outbreak of war. Alternatively, we can count these milestones negatively: the failure of the League to act against Japan; the failure to take effective measures against Italy in 1935; the failure of Britain and France to respond to the unilateral German denunciation of the Treaty of Versailles, and notably its military reoccupation of the Rhineland in 1936; their refusal to intervene in the Spanish Civil War ('non-intervention'); their failure to respond to the occupation of Austria; their retreat before German blackmail over Czechoslovakia (the 'Munich Ageement' of 1938); and the refusal of the USSR to continue opposing Hitler in 1939 (the Hitler–Stalin pact of August 1939).

And yet, if one side clearly did not want war and did everything possible to avoid it, and the other side glorified it and, in the case of Hitler, certainly actively desired it, none of the aggressors wanted the war they got, at the time they got it, and against at least some of the enemies they found themselves fighting. Japan, in spite of the military influence on its politics, would certainly have preferred to achieve its objectives – essentially the creation of an East Asian empire – without a *general* war, into which they only became involved because the USA was involved in one. What kind of war Germany wanted, when and against whom, are still matters of argument, since Hitler was not a man who documented his decisions, but two things are clear. A war against Poland (backed by Britain and France) in 1939 was not in his game plan, and the war in which he finally found himself, against both the USSR and the USA, was every German general's and diplomat's nightmare.

Germany (and later Japan) needed a rapid offensive war for the same reasons that had made it necessary in 1914. The joint resources of the potential enemies of each, once united and co-ordinated, were overwhelmingly greater than their own. Neither even planned effectively for a lengthy war, nor relied on armaments that had a long gestation period. (By contrast the British, accepting inferiority on land, put their money from the start into the most expensive and technologically sophisticated forms of armament and planned for a long war in which they and their allies would outproduce the other side.) The Japanese were more successful than the Germans in avoiding the coalition of their enemies, since they kept out of both Germany's war against Britain and France in 1939–40 and the war against Russia after 1941. Unlike all the other powers, they had actually been up against the Red army in an unofficial but substantial war on the Siberian–Chinese border in 1939 and had been badly mauled. Japan only entered the war against Britain and the USA, but not the USSR, in December 1941. Unfortunately for Japan, the only power it had to fight, the USA, was so vastly superior in its resources to Japan, that it was virtually bound to win.

Germany seemed luckier for a while. In the 1930s, as war drew nearer, Britain and France failed to join with Soviet Russia, and eventually Soviet Russia preferred to come to terms with Hitler, while local politics prevented President Roosevelt from giving more than paper backing to the side he passionately supported. The war therefore began in 1939 as a purely European war, and indeed, after Germany marched into Poland, which was defeated and partitioned with the now neutral USSR in three weeks, a purely west European war of Germany against Britain and France. In the spring of 1940, Germany overran Norway, Denmark, the Netherlands, Belgium and France with ridiculous ease, occupying the first four countries, and dividing France into a zone directly occupied and administered by the victorious Germans and a satellite French 'state' (its rulers, drawn from the various branches of French reaction, no longer liked to call it a republic) with its capital in a provincial health resort, Vichy. Only Britain was left at war with Germany, under a coalition of all national forces, headed by Winston Churchill, based on a total refusal to come to any kind of terms with Hitler. It was at this moment that fascist Italy mistakenly chose to slide off the fence of neutrality, on which its government had cautiously been sitting, on to the German side.

For practical purposes, the war in Europe was over. Even if Germany could not invade Britain because of the dual obstacle of the sea and the Royal Air Force, there was no foreseeable war in which Britain could return to the Continent, let alone defeat Germany. The months of 1940–41, when Britain stood alone, are a marvellous moment in the history of the British people, or at any rate those who were lucky enough to live through it, but the country's chances were slim. The USA's 'Hemispheric Defense' re-armament programme of June 1940 virtually assumed that further arms for Britain would be useless and, even after Britain's survival was accepted, the United Kingdom was still seen chiefly as an outlying defence base for America. Meanwhile the map of Europe was re-drawn. The USSR, by agreement, occupied those European parts of the Tsarist empire lost in 1918 (except for the parts of Poland taken over by Germany) and Finland, against which Stalin had fought a clumsy winter war in 1939–40, which pushed the Russian frontiers a little further away from Leningrad. Hitler presided over a revision of the Versailles settlement in the former Habsburg territories that proved shortlived. British attempts to extend the war in the Balkans led to the expected conquest of the entire peninsula by Germany, including the Greek islands.

Indeed, Germany actually crossed the Mediterranean into Africa when its ally Italy, even more disappointing as a military power in the Second World War than Austria-Hungary had been in the First World War, looked like being thrown entirely out of its African empire by the British, fighting from their main base in Egypt. The German Afrika Korps, under one of the most talented generals, Erwin Rommel, threatened the entire British position in the Middle East.

The war was revived by Hitler's invasion of the USSR on 22 June 1941, the decisive date in the Second World War; an invasion so senseless – for it committed Germany to a war on two fronts – that Stalin simply would not believe that Hitler could contemplate it. But for Hitler the conquest of a vast eastern land-empire, rich in resources and slave labour, was the logical next step, and, like all other military experts except the Japanese, he spectacularly underestimated the Soviet capacity to resist. Not, however, without some plausibility, given the disorganization of the Red Army by the purges of the 1930s (see chapter 13), the apparent state of the country, the general effects of the terror, and Stalin's own extraordinarily inept interventions into military strategy. In fact, the initial advances of the German armies were as swift and seemed as decisive as the campaigns in the West. By early October they were on the outskirts of Moscow, and there is evidence that, for a few days, Stalin himself was demoralized and contemplated making peace. But the moment passed, and the sheer size of the reserves of space, manpower, Russian physical toughness and patriotism, and a ruthless war effort, defeated the Germans and gave the USSR time to organize effectively, not least by allowing the very talented military leaders (some of them recently released from gulags) to do what they thought best. The years of 1942–45 was the only time when Stalin paused in his terror.

Once the Russian war had not been decided within three months, as Hitler had expected, Germany was lost, since it was neither equipped for nor could sustain a long war. In spite of its triumphs, it had, and produced, far fewer aircraft and tanks than even Britain and Russia without the USA. A new German offensive in 1942, after the gruelling winter, seemed as brilliantly successful as all the others, and pushed the German armies deep into the Caucasus and into the lower Volga valley, but it could no longer decide the war. The German armies were held, ground down and eventually surrounded and forced to surrender at Stalingrad (summer 1942–March 1943). After that the Russians in turn began the advance which only brought them into Berlin, Prague and Vienna by the end of the war. From Stalingrad on everyone knew that the defeat of Germany was only a question of time.

Meanwhile the war, still basically European, had become truly global. This was partly due to the stirrings of anti-imperialism among the subjects and dependents of Britain, still the geatest of world-wide empires, though they could still be suppressed without difficulty. The Hitler sympathisers among the Boers in South Africa could be interned – they re-emerged after the war as the architects of the Apartheid regime of 1948 – and Rashid Ali's seizure of power in Iraq in the spring of 1941 was quickly put down. Much more significant was that the triumph of Hitler in Europe left a partial imperial vacuum in Southeast Asia into which Japan now moved, by asserting a protectorate over the helpless relics of the French in Indochina. The USA regarded this extension of Axis power into Southeast Asia as intolerable, and put severe economic pressure on Japan, whose trade and supplies depended entirely on maritime communications. It was this conflict that led to war between the two countries. The Japanese attack on Pearl Harbor on 7 December 1941 made the war worldwide. Within a few months the Japanese had overrun all of Southeast Asia, continental and insular, threatening to invade India from Burma in the west, and the empty north of Australia from New Guinea.

Probably Japan could not have avoided war with the USA unless the country had given up the aim of establishing a powerful economic empire (euphemistically described as a 'Greater East Asian Co-Prosperity Sphere'), which was the very essence of its policy. However, having watched the consequences of the European powers' failure to resist Hitler and Mussolini, and its results, F.D. Roosevelt's USA could not be expected to react to Japanese expansion as Britain and France had reacted to German expansion. In any case, US public opinion regarded the Pacific (unlike Europe) as a normal field for US action, rather like Latin America. American 'isolationism' merely wanted to keep out of Europe. In fact, it was the Western (i.e. American) embargo on Japanese trade and freezing of Japanese assets, which forced Japan to take action, if the Japanese economy, which depended entirely on oceanic imports, was not to be strangled in short order. The gamble it took was dangerous, and proved suicidal. Japan would seize perhaps its only opportunity to establish its southern empire quickly; but since it calculated that this required the immobilization of the American navy, the only force that could intervene, it also meant that the USA with its overwhelmingly superior forces and resources would *immediately* be drawn into war. There was no way that Japan could win such a war.

The mystery is, why Hitler, already fully stretched in Russia, gratuitously declared war on the USA, thus giving Roosevelt's government the chance to enter the European war on the British side without meeting overwhelming political resistance at home. For there was very little doubt in Washington's mind that Nazi Germany constituted a much more serious, or, at any rate, a much more global danger to the US position – and the world – than Japan. The US therefore deliberately chose to concentrate on winning the war against Germany before that against Japan, and to concentrate its resources accordingly. The calculation was correct. It took another three-and-a-half years to defeat Germany, after which Japan was brought to its knees in three months. There is no adequate explanation of Hitler's folly, though we know him to have persistently, and dramatically, underestimated the capacity for action, not to mention the economic and technological potential, of the USA because he thought democracies incapable of action. The only democracy he took seriously was the British, which he rightly regarded as not entirely democratic.

The decisions to invade Russia and to declare war against the USA decided the result of the Second World War. This did not seem immediately obvious, since the Axis powers reached the peak of their success in mid-1942, and did not entirely lose the military initiative until 1943. Moreover, the Western Allies did not effectively re-enter the European

Continent untill 1944, for, while they successfully drove the Axis out of North Africa and crossed into Italy, they were successfully held at bay by the German army. In the meantime the Western Allies' only major weapon against Germany was airpower, and this, as subsequent research has shown, was spectacularly ineffective, except in killing civilians and destroying cities. Only the Soviet armies continued to advance, and only in the Balkans – mainly in Yugoslavia, Albania and Greece – did a largely communist-inspired armed resistance movement cause Germany, and even more Italy, serious military problems. Nevertheless, Winston Churchill was right when he confidently claimed after Pearl Harbor that victory by 'the proper application of overwhelming force' was certain (Kennedy, p. 347). From the end of 1942 on nobody doubted that the Grand Alliance against the Axis would win. The Allies began to concentrate on what do do with their foreseeable victory.

We need not follow the course of military events further, except to note that, in the West, German resistance proved very hard to overcome even after the Allies re-entered the Continent in force in June 1944, and that, unlike 1918, there was no sign of any German revolution against Hitler. Only the German generals, the heart of traditional Prussian military power and efficiency, plotted Hitler's downfall in July 1944, since they were rational patriots rather than enthusiasts for a Wagnerian *Götterdämmerung* in which Germany would be totally destroyed. They had no mass support, failed and were killed *en masse* by Hitler's loyalists. In the East there was even less sign of a crack in Japan's determination to fight to the end, which is why nuclear arms were dropped on Hiroshima and Nagasaki to ensure a rapid Japanese surrender. Victory in 1945 was total, surrender unconditional. The defeated enemy states were totally occupied by the victors. No formal peace was made, since no authorities independent of the occupying forces were recognized, at least in Germany and Japan. The nearest thing to peace negotiations were the series of conferences between 1943 and 1945 in which the main allied powers – the USA, the USSR and Great Britain – decided the division of the spoils of victory and (not too successfully) tried to determine their post-war relations with each other: in Teheran in 1943; in Moscow in the autumn of 1944; in Yalta in the Crimea in early 1945; and at Potsdam in occupied Germany in August 1945. More successfully, a series of inter-allied negotiations between 1943 and 1945 set up a more general framework for political and economic relations between states, including the establishment of the United Nations. These matters belong to another chapter (see chapter 9).

Even more than the Great War, the Second World War was therefore fought to a finish, without serious thought of compromise on either side, except by Italy, which changed sides and political regime in 1943 and was not treated entirely as an occupied territory, but as a defeated country with a recognized government. (It was helped by the fact that the Allies failed to drive the Germans, and a Fascist 'Social Republic' under Mussolini dependent on them, out of half of Italy for almost two years.) Unlike the First World War, this intransigence on both sides requires no special explanation. This was a war of religion, or, in modern terms, of ideologies, on both sides. It was also, and demonstrably, a fight for life for most of the countries concerned. The price of defeat by the German National Socialist regime, as demonstrated in Poland and the occupied parts of the USSR, and by the fate of the Jews, whose systematic extermination gradually became known to an incredulous world, was enslavement and death. Hence the war was waged without limit. The Second World War escalated mass war into total war.

Its losses are literally incalculable, and even approximate estimates are impossible, since the war (unlike the First World War) killed civilians as readily as people in uniform, and much of the worst killing took place in regions, or at times, when nobody was in a position to count, or cared to. Deaths directly caused by this war have been estimated at between three and five times the (estimated) figure for the First World War (Milward, 270; Petersen, 1986), and, in other terms, at between 10 and 20 per cent of the *total* population in the USSR, Poland and Yugoslavia; and between 4 and 6 per cent of Germany, Italy, Austria, Hungary, Japan and China. Casualties in Britain and France were far lower than in the First World War – about 1 per cent, but in the USA somewhat higher. Nevertheless, these are guesses. Soviet casualties have been estimated at various times, even officially, at seven millions, eleven millions, or of the order of twenty or even fifty millions. In any case, what does statistical exactitude mean, where the orders of magnitude are so astronomic? Would the horror of the holocaust be any less if historians concluded that it exterminated not six millions (the rough and almost certainly exaggerated original estimate) but five or even four? What if the nine hundred days of the German siege of Leningrad (1941–44) killed a million or only three quarters or half a million by starvation and exhaustion? Indeed, can we really *grasp* figures beyond the reality open to physical intuition? What does it mean to the average reader of this page that out of 5.7 million Russian prisoners of war in Germany 3.3 million died? (Hirschfeld, 1986.) The only certain fact about the casualties of the war is that, on the whole, they killed more men than women. In 1959 there were still, in the USSR, seven women between the ages of thirty-five and fifty for every four men (Milward, 1979, p. 212). Buildings could more easily be rebuilt after this war than surviving lives.

III

We take it for granted that modern warfare involves all citizens and mobilizes most of them; that it is waged with armaments which require a diversion of the entire economy to produce them, and which are used in unimaginable quantities; that it produces untold destruction and utterly dominates and transforms the life of the countries involved in it. Yet all these phenomena belong to the wars only of the twentieth century. There were, indeed, tragically destructive wars earlier, and even wars anticipating modern total war efforts, as in France during the Revolution. To this day the Civil War of 1861–65 remains the bloodiest conflict in US history, which killed as many men as all the later wars of the USA put together, including both world wars, Korea and Vietnam. Nevertheless, before the twentieth-century, wars embracing all society were exceptional. Jane Austen wrote her novels during the Napoleonic wars, but no reader who did not know this already would guess it, for the wars do not appear in her pages, even though a number of the young gentlemen who pass through them undoubtedly took part in them. It is inconceivable that any novelist could write about Britain in the twentieth-century wars in this manner.

The monster of twentieth-century total war was not born full-sized. Nevertheless, from 1914 on, wars were unmistakably mass wars. Even in the First World War Britain mobilized 12.5 per cent of its men for the forces, Germany 15.4 per cent, France almost 17 per cent. In the Second World War the percentage of the total active labour force that went into the armed forces was pretty generally in the neighborhood of 20 per cent (Milward, 1979, p. 216). We may note in passing that such a level of mass mobilization, lasting for a matter of years, cannot be maintained except by a modern high-productivity industrialized economy, and – or alternatively – an economy largely in the hands of the non-combatant parts of the population. Traditional agrarian economies cannot usually mobilize so large a proportion of their labour force except seasonally, at least in the temperate zone, for there are times in the agricultural year when all hands are needed (for instance to get in the harvest). Even in industrial societies so great a manpower mobilization puts enormous strains on the labour force, which is why modern mass wars both strengthened the powers of organized labour and produced a revolution in the employment of women outside the household: temporarily in the First World War, permanently in the Second World War.

Again, twentieth-century wars were mass wars in the sense that they used, and destroyed, hitherto inconceivable quantities of products in the course of fighting. Hence the German phrase *Materialschlacht* to describe the western battles of 1914–18 – battles of materials. Napoleon, luckily for the extremely restricted industrial capacity of France in his day, could win the battle of Jena in 1806 and thus destroy the power of Prussia with no more than 1,500 rounds of artillery. Yet even before the First World War France planned for a munitions output of 10–12,000 shells *a day*, and in the end its industry had to produce 200,000 shells *a day*. Even Tsarist Russia found that it produced 150,000 shells a day, or at the rate of four-and-a-half millions a month. No wonder that the processes of mechanical engineering factories were revolutionized. As for the less destructive implements of war, let us recall that during the Second World War the US army ordered over 519 million pairs of socks and over 219 million pairs of pants, whereas the German forces, true to bureaucratic tradition, in a single year (1943) ordered 4.4 million pairs of scissors and 6.2 million pads for the stamps of military offices (Milward, 1979, p. 68). Mass war required mass production.

But production also required organization and management – even if its object was the rationalized destruction of human lives in the most efficient manner, as in the German extermination camps. Speaking in the most general terms, total war was the largest enterprise hitherto known to man, which had to be consciously organized and managed.

This also raised novel problems. Military affairs had always been the special concern of governments, since these took over the running of permanent ('standing') armies in the seventeenth century, rather than subcontracting them from military entrepreneurs. In fact, armies and war soon became far larger 'industries' or complexes of economic activity than anything in private business, which is why in the nineteenth century they so often provided the expertise and the management skills for the vast private enterprises which developed in the industrial era, for instance railway projects or port installations. Moreover, almost all governments were in the business of manufacturing armaments and war material, although in the late nineteenth century a sort of symbiosis developed between government and specialized private armaments producers, especially in the high-tech sectors such as artillery and the navy, which anticipated what we now know as the 'military-industrial complex' (see *Age of Empire*, chapter 13). Nevertheless, the basic assumption between the era of the French revolution and the First World War was that the economy would, so far as possible, continue to operate in wartime as it had in peacetime ('business as usual'), though of course certain industries would clearly feel its impact – for instance the clothing industry, which would be required to produce military garments far beyond any conceivable peacetime capacity.

The governments' main problem, as they saw it, was fiscal: how to pay for wars. Should it be through loans, through direct taxation, and, in either case, on what precise terms? Consequently it was Treasuries or Ministries of Finance which were seen as the commanders of the war economy. The First World War, which lasted so much longer than governments had anticipated, and used up so many more men and armaments, made 'business as usual' and, with it, the domination of Ministries of Finance, impossible, even though Treasury officials (like the young Maynard Keynes in Britain) still shook their heads over the politicians' readiness to pursue victory without counting the financial costs. They were, of course, right. Britain waged both world wars far beyond its means, with lasting and negative consequences for its economy. Yet if war was to be waged at all on the modern scale, not only its costs had to be counted but its production – and in the end the entire economy – had to be managed and planned.

Governments only learned this by experience in the course of the First World War. In the Second World War they knew it from the outset, thanks largely to the experience of the First war, the lessons of which their officials had studied intensively. Nevertheless, it only gradually became clear how completely governments had to take over the economy, and how essential physical planning and the allocation of resources (other than by the usual economic mechanisms) now were. At the outset of the Second World War only two states, the USSR and, to a lesser extent, Nazi Germany, had any mechanism for physically controlling the economy, which is not surprising, since Soviet ideas of planning were originally inspired by, and to some extent based on, what the Bolsheviks knew of the German planned war economy of 1914–17 (see chapter 13). Some states, notably Britain and the USA, had not even the rudiments of such mechanisms.

It is, therefore, a strange paradox that among the government-run planned war economies of both wars, and in total wars that meant *all* war economies those of the Western democratic states – Britain and France in the First war; Britain and even the USA in the Second – proved far superior to Germany with its tradition and theories of rational-bureau-cratic administration. (For Soviet planning, see chapter 13.) We can only guess at the reasons, but there is no doubt about the facts. The German war economy was less systematic and effective in mobilizing all resources for war – of course, until after the strategy of lightning strikes failed, it did not have to – and it certainly took less care of the German civilian population. Inhabitants of Britain and France who survived the First World War unharmed were likely to be somewhat healthier than before the war, even when they were poorer, and their workers' real income had risen. Germans were hungrier, and their workers' real wages had fallen. Comparisons in the Second World War are more difficult, if only because France was soon eliminated, the USA was richer and under much less pressure, the USSR poorer and under much more. The German war economy had virtually all Europe to exploit but ended the war with far greater physical destruction than Western belligerents. Still, on the whole a poorer Britain, whose civilian consumption fell by over 20 per cent by 1943, ended the war with a slightly better-fed and healthier population, thanks to a war-planned economy systematically slanted towards equality and fairness of sacrifice, and social justice. The German system was, of course, inequitable on principle. Germany exploited both the resources and the manpower of occupied Europe, and treated the non-German populations as inferior, and, in extreme cases – Poles, but especially Russians and Jews – virtually as expendable slave-labour which did not even have to be kept alive. Foreign labour rose to form about one fifth of the labour force in Germany by 1944 – 30 per cent in the armaments industries. Even so, the most that can be claimed for Germany's own workers is that their real earnings stayed the same as in 1938. British child mortality and sickness rates fell progressively during the war. In occupied and dominated France, a country proverbially rich in food and out of the war after 1940, the average weight and fitness of the population at all ages declined.

Total war undoubtedly revolutionized management. How far did it revolutionize technology and production? Or, to put it another way, did it advance or retard economic development? It plainly advanced technology, since the conflict between advanced belligerents was not only one of armies but of competing technologies for providing them with effective weapons, and other essential services. But for the Second World War, and the fear that Nazi Germany might also exploit the discoveries of nuclear physics, the atom bomb would certainly not have been made, nor would the quite enormous expenditures needed to produce any kind of nuclear energy have been undertaken in the twentieth century. Other technological advances made, in the first instance, for purposes of war, have proved considerably more readily applicable in peace – one thinks of aeronautics and computers – but this does not alter the fact that war or the preparation for war has been a major device for accelerating technical progress by 'carrying' the development costs of technological innovations which would almost certainly not have been undertaken by anyone making peacetime cost-benefit calculations, or which would have been made more slowly and hesitantly (see chapter 9).

Still, the technological bent of war was not new. Moreover, the modern industrial economy was built on constant technological innovation, which would certainly have taken place, probably at an accelerating rate, even without wars (if we can make this unrealistic assumption for the sake of argument). Wars, especially the Second World War, greatly helped to diffuse technical expertise, and they certainly had a major impact on industrial organization and methods of mass production, but what they achieved was, by and large, an acceleration of change rather than a transformation.

Did war advance economic growth? In one sense it plainly did not. The losses of productive resources were heavy, quite apart from the fall in the working population. Twenty-five per cent of pre-war capital assets were destroyed in the USSR during the Second World War, 13 per cent in Germany, 8 per cent in Italy, 7 per cent in France, though only 3 per cent in Britain (but this must be offset by new wartime constructions). In the extreme case of the USSR, the net economic effect of the war was entirely negative. In 1945 the country's agriculture lay in ruins, as did the industrialization of the pre-war Five-Year Plans. All that remained was a vast and quite inadaptable armaments industry, a starving and decimated people and massive physical destruction.

On the other hand wars were clearly good to the US economy. Its rate of growth in both wars was quite extraordinary, especially in the Second World War when it grew at the rate of roughly 10 per cent per annum, faster than ever before or since. In both wars the USA benefited from being both remote from the fighting, and the main arsenal of its allies, and from the capacity of its economy to organize the expansion of production more effectively than any other. Probably the most lasting economic effect of both world wars was to give the US economy a global preponderance during the whole of the Short Twentieth Century, which only slowly began to fade towards the end of the century (see chapter 9). In 1914 it was already the largest industrial economy, but not yet the dominant economy. The wars, which strengthened it while, relatively or absolutely, weakening its competitors, transformed its economic situation.

If the USA (in both wars) and Russia (especially in the Second World

War represent the two extremes of the wars' economic effects, the rest of the world is situated somewhere between these extremes; but on the whole closer to the Russian than to the American end of the curve.

IV

It remains to assess the human impact of the era of wars, and its human costs. The sheer mass of casualties, to which we have already referred, are only one part of these. Curiously enough, except, for understandable reasons, in the USSR, the much smaller figures of the First World War were to make a much greater impact than the vast quantities of the Second World War, as witness the much greater prominence of memorials and the cult of the fallen of the First World War. The Second World War produced no equivalent to the monuments to 'the unknown soldier', and after it the celebration of 'armistice day' (the anniversary of 11 November 1918) gradually lost its inter-war solemnity. Perhaps ten million dead hit those who had never expected such sacrifice more brutally than fifty-four millions hit those who have already once experienced war as massacre.

Certainly both the totality of the war efforts and the determination on both sides to wage war without limit and at whatever cost, made its mark. Without it, the growing brutality and inhumanity of the twentieth century is difficult to explain. About this rising curve of barbarism after 1914 there is, unfortunately, no serious doubt. By the early twentieth century, torture had officially been ended throughout Western Europe. Since 1945 we have once again accustomed ourselves, without much revulsion, to its use in at least one third of the member-states of the United Nations, including some of the oldest and most civilized (Peters, 1985).

The growth of brutalization was due not so much to the release of the latent potential for cruelty and violence in the human being, which war naturally legitimizes, although this certainly emerged after the First World War among a certain type of ex-servicemen (veterans), especially in the strong-arm or killer squads and 'Free Corps' on the nationalist ultra-Right. Why should men who had killed and seen their friends killed and mangled, hesitate to kill and brutalize the enemies of a good cause?

One major reason was the strange democratisation of war. Total conflicts turned into 'people's wars', both because civilians and civilian life became the proper, and sometimes the main, targets of strategy, and because in democratic wars, as in democratic politics, adversaries are naturally demonized in order to make them properly hateful or at least despicable. Wars conducted on both sides by professionals, or specialists, especially those of similar social standing, do not exclude mutual respect and acceptance of rules, or even chivalry. Violence has its rules. This was still evident among fighter pilots in air forces in both wars, as witness Jean Renoir's pacifist film about the First World War, *La Grande Illusion*. Professionals of politics and diplomacy, when untrammeled by the demands of votes or newspapers, can declare war or negotiate peace with no hard feelings about the other side, like boxers who shake hands before they come out fighting, and drink with each other after the fight. But the total wars of our century were far removed from the Bismarckian or eighteenth-century pattern. No war in which mass national feelings are mobilized can be as limited as aristocratic wars. And, it must be said, in the Second World War the nature of Hitler's regime and the behaviour of the Germans, including the old non-Nazi German army, in eastern Europe, was such as to justify a good deal of demonization.

Another reason, however, was the new impersonality of warfare, which turned killing and maiming into the remote consequence of pushing a button or moving a lever. Technology made its victims invisible, as people eviscerated by bayonets, or seen through the sights of firearms could not be. Opposite the permanently fixed guns of the western front were not men but statistics – not even real, but hypothetical statistics, as the 'body-counts' of enemy casualties during US Vietnam War showed. Far below the aerial bombers were not people about to be burned and eviscerated, but targets. Mild young men, who would certainly not have wished to plunge a bayonet in the belly of any pregnant village girl, could far more easily drop high explosive on London or Berlin, or nuclear bombs on Nagasaki. Hard-working German bureaucrats who would certainly have found it repugnant to drive starving Jews into abattoirs themselves, could work out the railway timetables for a regular supply of death-trains to Polish extermination camps with less sense of personal involvement. The greatest cruelties of our century have been the impersonal cruelties of remote decision, of system and routine, especially when they could be justified as regrettable operational necessities.

So the world accustomed itself to the compulsory expulsion and killing on an astronomic scale, phenomena so unfamiliar that new words had to be invented for them: 'stateless' ('apatride') or 'genocide'. The First World War led to the killing of an uncounted number of Armenians by Turkey – the most usual figure is 1.5 millions – which can count as the first modern attempt to eliminate an entire population. It was later followed by the better-known Nazi mass-killing of about five million Jews – the numbers remain in dispute. (Hilberg, 1985). One First World War and the Russian revolution forced millions to move as refugees, or by compulsory 'exchanges of populations' between states, which amounted to the same. A total of 1.3 million Greeks were repatriated to Greece, mainly from Turkey; 400,000 Turks were decanted into the state which claimed them; some 200,000 Bulgarians moved into the diminished territory bearing their national name; while 1.5 or perhaps 2 million Russian nationals, escaping from the Russian revolution or on the losing side of the Russian civil war, found themselves homeless. It was mainly for these rather than the 320,000 Armenians fleeing genocide, that a new document was invented for those who, in an increasingly bureaucratized world, had no bureaucratic existence in any state: the so-called Nansen passport of the League of Nations, named after the great Norwegian arctic explorer who made himself a second career as a friend to the friendless. At a rough guess the years 1914–22 generated between four and five million refugees.

This first flood of human jetsam was as nothing to that which followed the Second World War, or to the inhumanity with which they were treated. It has been estimated that by May 1945 there were perhaps 40.5 million uprooted people in Europe, excluding non-German forced labourers and Germans who fled before the advancing Soviet armies (Kulischer, 1948, pp. 253–73). About thirteen million Germans were expelled from the parts of Germany annexed by Poland and the USSR, from Czechoslovakia and parts of south-eastern Europe where they had long been settled (Holborn, p. 363). They were taken in by the new German Federal Republic, which offered a home and citizenship to any German who returned there, as the new state of Israel offered a 'right of return' to any Jew. When, but in an epoch of mass flight, could such offers by states have been seriously made? Of the 11,332,700 'displaced persons' of various nationalities found in Germany by the victorious armies in 1945, ten millions soon returned to their homelands – but half of these were compelled to do so against their will (Jacobmeyer, 1986).

These were only the refugees of Europe. The decolonization of India in 1947 created fifteen million of them, forced to cross the new frontiers between India and Pakistan (in both directions), without counting the two millions killed in the accompanying civil strife. The Korean War, another by-product of The Second World War, produced perhaps five million displaced Koreans. After the establishment of Israel – yet another of the war's after-effects – about 1.3 million Palestinians were registered with the United Nations Relief and Work Agency (UNWRA); conversely by the early 1960s 1.2 million Jews had migrated to Israel, the majority of these also as refugees. In short, the global human catastrophe unleashed by the Second World War is almost certainly the largest in human history. Not the least tragic aspect of this catastrophe is that humanity has learned to live in a world in which killing, torture and mass exile have become everyday experiences which we no longer notice.

Looking back on the thirty-one years from the assassination of the Austrian Archduke in Sarajevo to the unconditional surrender of Japan, they must be seen as an era of havoc comparable to the Thirty Years' War of the seventeenth century in German history. And Sarajevo – the first Sarajevo – certainly marked the beginning of a general age of catastrophe and crisis in the affairs of the world, which is the subject of this and the next four chapters. Nevertheless, in the memory of the generations after 1945, the Thirty-one Years' War did not leave behind the same sort of memory as its more localised seventeenth-century predecessor.

This is partly because it formed a single era of war only in the historians' perspective. For those who lived through it, it was experienced as two distinct though connected wars, separated by an 'inter-war' period without overt hostilities, ranging from thirteen years for Japan (whose second war began in Manchuria in 1931) to twenty-three years for the USA (which did not enter the Second World War until December 1941). However, it is also because each of these wars had its own historical character and profile. Both were episodes of carnage without parallel, leaving behind the technological nightmare images that haunted the nights and days of the next generation: poison gas and aerial bombardment after 1918, the mushroom cloud of nuclear destruction after 1945. Both ended in breakdown and – as we shall see in the next chapter – social revolution over large regions of Europe and Asia. Both left the belligerents exhausted and enfeebled, except for the USA, which emerged from both undamaged and enriched, as the economic lord of the world. And yet, how striking the differences! The First World War solved nothing. Such hopes as it generated – of a peaceful and democratic world of nation-states under the League of Nations; of a return to the world economy of 1913; even (among those who hailed the Russian Revolution) of world capitalism overthrown within years or months by a rising of the oppressed, were soon disappointed. The past was beyond reach, the future postponed, the present bitter, except for a few fleeting years in the mid-1920s. The Second World War actually produced solutions, at least for decades. The dramatic social and economic problems of capitalism in its Age of Catastrophe seemed to disappear. The Western world economy entered its Golden Age; Western political democracy, backed by an extraordinary improvement in material life, was stable; war was banished to the Third World. On the other side, even revolution appeared to have found its way forward. The old colonial empires vanished or were shortly destined to go. A consortium of communist states, organized around the Soviet Union, now transformed into a superpower, seemed ready to compete in the race for economic growth with the West. This proved to be an illusion, but not until the 1960s did it begin to vanish. As we can now see, even the international scene was stabilized, though it did not seem so. Unlike after the Great War, the former enemies – Germany and Japan – reintegrated into the (Western) world economy, and the new enemies – the USA and the USSR – never actually came to blows.

Even the revolutions which ended both wars were quite different. Those after the First World War were, as we shall see, rooted in a revulsion against what most people who lived through it, had increasingly seen as a pointless slaughter. They were revolutions against the war. The revolutions after the Second World War grew out of the popular participation in a world struggle against enemies – Germany, Japan, more generally imperialism – which, however terrible, those who took part in it felt to be just. And yet, like the two World Wars, the two sorts of post-war revolution can be seen in the historian's perspective as a single process. To this we must now turn.

CHAPTER TWO
The World Revolution

At the same time [Bukharin] added, 'I do think we have entered upon a period of revolution which may last fifty years before the revolution is at last victorious in all Europe and finally in all the world.'

– Arthur Ransome, *Six Weeks in Russia in 1919* (Ransome, 1919, p. 54)

How terrible to read Shelley's poem (not to mention the Egyptian peasant songs of 3,000 years ago), denouncing oppression and exploitation. Will they be read in a future still filled with oppression and exploitation, and will people say: 'Even in those days . . .'

– Bertolt Brecht on reading Shelley's 'The Masque of Anarchy' in 1938 (Brecht, 1964)

Since the French Revolution there has arisen in Europe a Russian revolution, and this has once again taught the world that even the strongest of invaders can be repelled, once the fate of the Fatherland is truly entrusted to the poor, the humble, the proletarians, the labouring people.

From the wall newspaper of the *19 Brigata Eusebio Giambone* of the Italian Partisans, 1944 (Pavone, 1991, p. 406)

Revolution was the child of twentieth-century war: specifically the Russian revolution of 1917 which created the Soviet Union, transformed into a superpower by the second phase of the Thirty-one Years' War, but, more generally, revolution as a global constant in the century's history. War alone does not necessarily lead to crisis, breakdown and revolution in belligerent countries. In fact, before 1914 the opposite assumption held the field, at least about established regimens with traditional legitimacy. Napoleon I had complained bitterly that the Emperor of Austria could happily survive a hundred lost battles, as the king of Prussia survived military disaster and the loss of half his lands, whereas he himself, child of the French revolution, would be at risk after a single defeat. Yet the strains of twentieth-century total war on the states and peoples involved in it were so overwhelming and unprecedented that they were almost bound to stretch both to their limits, and, as like as not, to breaking-point. Only the USA came out of the world wars very much as it had gone into them, only rather stronger. For all others the end of wars meant upheaval.

It seemed obvious that the old world was doomed. The old society, the old economy, the old political systems had, as the Chinese phrase put it, 'lost the mandate of heaven'. Humanity was waiting for an alternative. Such an alternative was familiar in 1914. Socialist parties, resting on the support of the expanding working classes of their countries and inspired by a belief in the historic inevitability of their victory, represented this alternative in most countries of Europe (see *Age of Empire*, chapter 5). It looked as though only a signal was needed for the peoples to rise, to replace capitalism by socialism, and thus to transform the meaningless sufferings of world war into something more positive: the bloody birth-pains and convulsions of a new world. The Russian Revolution or, more precisely, the Bolshevik revolution of October 1917, set out to give the world this signal. It therefore became an event as central to the history of this century as the French revolution of 1789 was to the nineteenth. Indeed, it is not an accident that the history of the Short Twentieth Century, as defined in this book, virtually coincides with the lifetime of the state born of the October revolution.

However, the October revolution had far more profound and global repercussions than its ancestor. For, if the ideas of the French revolution have, as is now evident, outlasted Bolshevism, the practical consequences of 1917 were far greater and more lasting than those of 1789. The October revolution produced by far the most formidable organized revolutionary movement in modern history. Its global expansion has no parallel since the conquests of Islam in its first century. A mere thirty to forty years after Lenin's arrival at the Finland Station in Petrograd, one third of humanity found itself living under regimes directly derived from the 'Ten Days That Shook the World' (Reed, 1919), and Lenin's organizational model, the Communist Party. Most of them followed the USSR in a second wave of revolutions which emerged from the second phase of the long world war of 1914–45. The present chapter is about this two-part revolution, although it naturally concentrates on the original and formative revolution of 1917 and the special house-style it imposed on its successors.

In any case, it largely dominated these.

I

For a large part of the Short Twentieth Century, Soviet communism claimed to be an alternative and superior system to capitalism, and one destined by history to triumph over it. For much of this period even many of those who rejected its claims to superiority were far from convinced that it might not triumph. And – with the significant exception of the years from 1933 to 1945 (see chapter 5), the international politics of the entire Short Twentieth Century since the October revolution can best be understood as a secular struggle by the forces of the old order against social revolution, believed to be embodied in, allied with, or dependent on the fortunes of the Soviet Union and international communism.

As the Short Twentieth Century advanced, this image of world politics as a duel between the forces of two rival social systems (each, after 1945, mobilized behind a superpower wielding weapons of global destruction), became increasingly unrealistic. By the 1980s it had as little relevance to international politics as the Crusades. Yet we can understand how it came into being. For, more completely and uncompromisingly even than the French revolution in its Jacobin days, the October revolution saw itself less as a national than as an ecumenical event. It was made not to bring freedom and socialism to Russia, but to bring about the world proletarian revolution. In the minds of Lenin and his comrades, the victory of Bolshevism in Russia was primarily a battle in the campaign to win the victory of Bolshevism on a wider global scale, and barely justifiable except as such.

That Tsarist Russia was ripe for revolution, richly deserved a revolution, and indeed that such a revolution would certainly overthrow Tsarism, had been accepted by every sensible observer of the world scene since the 1870s (see *Age of Empire*, chapter 12). After 1905–6, when Tsarism had actually been brought to its knees by revolution, nobody seriously doubted it. There are some historians who, in retrospect, argue that Tsarist Russia, but for the accident of the First World War and the Bolshevik revolution, would have evolved into a flourishing liberal-capitalist industrial society, and was on the way to doing so, but one would need a microscope to detect prophesies to this effect made before 1914.

Indeed, the Tsarist regime had barely recovered from the 1905 revolution when, indecisive and incompetent as always, it found itself once again lashed by a rapidly rising wave of social discontent. But for the solid loyalty of the army, police and civil service in the last months before the outbreak of war, the country seemed once again on the verge of an eruption. Indeed, as in so many of the belligerent countries, mass enthusiasm and patriotism after the outbreak of war defused the political situation – though, in the case of Russia, not for long. By 1915 the problems of the Tsar's government once again seemed insurmountable. Nothing seemed less surprising and unexpected than the revolution of March 1917* which overthrew the Russian monarchy and which was universally hailed by all Western political opinion other than the most rock-ribbed traditionalist reactionaries.

And yet, with the exception of those romantics who saw a straight road leading from the collective practices of the Russian village community to a socialist future, it was equally taken for granted by all that a Russian revolution could not and would not be socialist. The conditions for such a transformation were simply not present in a peasant country that was a by-word for poverty, ignorance and backwardness and where the industrial proletariat, Marx's predestined gravedigger of capitalism, was only a minuscule, though strategically localized, minority. The Russian Marxist revolutionaries themselves shared this view. Taken by itself, the overthrow of Tsarism and the landlord system would, and could only be expected to, produce a 'bourgeois revolution'. The class struggle between bourgeoisie and proletariat (which, according to Marx, could have only one outcome), would then continue under the new political conditions. Of course, Russia did not exist in isolation, and a revolution in that enormous country, stretching from the borders of Japan to those of Germany, and whose government was one of the handful of 'great powers' that dominated the world situation, could not but have major international consequences. Karl Marx himself, at the end of his life, had hoped that a Russian revolution might act as a sort of detonator, setting off the proletarian revolution in the industrially more developed Western

---

* Since Russia still operated by the Julian calendar, which was thirteen days behind the Gregorian calendar adopted everywhere else in the Christian or Westernized world, the February revolution actually occurred in March, the October revolution on 7 November. It was the October revolution which reformed the Russian calendar, as it reformed Russian orthography, thus demonstrating the profundity of its impact. For it is well known that such small changes usually require socio-political earthquakes to bring them about. The most lasting and universal consequence of the French revolution is the metric system.

countries, where the conditions for a proletarian socialist revolution were present. As we shall see, towards the end of the First World War, it looked as though this was exactly what was going to happen.

There was only one complication. If Russia was not ready for the Marxists' proletarian socialist revolution, it was not ready for their liberal 'bourgeois revolution' either. Even those who wished to achieve no more than this, had to find a way of doing so which did not rely on the small and feeble forces of the Russian Liberal middle class, a tiny minority population lacking both moral standing, public support and an institutional tradition of representative government into which it could fit. The Kadets, the party of bourgeois liberalism, had less than 2.5 per cent of the deputies in the freely elected (and soon dissolved) Constitutional Assembly of 1917–18. Either a bourgeois-liberal Russia had to be won by the rising of peasants and workers who did not know or care what it was, under the leadership of revolutionary parties who wanted something else, or, and this was more likely, the forces making the revolution would go beyond its bourgeois-liberal stage to a more radical one ('permanent revolution', to use the phrase adopted by Marx and revived during the 1905 Revolution by the young Trotsky). In 1917 Lenin, whose hopes had not gone much beyond a bourgeois-democratic Russia in 1905, also concluded from the start that the liberal horse was not a runner in the Russian revolutionary race. This was a realistic assessment. However, in 1917 it was as clear to him as to all other Russian and non-Russian Marxists that the conditions for a *socialist* revolution were simply not present in Russia. For Marxist revolutionaries in Russia, their revolution *had* to spread elsewhere.

But nothing seemed more likely than that it would, because the Great War ended in widespread political breakdown and revolutionary crisis, particularly in the defeated belligerent states. In 1918 all the four rulers of the defeated powers (Germany, Austria-Hungary, Turkey and Bulgaria) lost their thrones, plus the Tsar of Russia, defeated by Germany, who had already gone in 1917. Moreover, social unrest, amounting almost to revolution in Italy, shook even the European belligerents on the winning side.

As we have seen, the societies of belligerent Europe began to buckle under the extraordinary pressures of mass war. The initial surge of patriotism that had followed the outbreak of war had subsided. By 1916 war-weariness was turning into sullen and silent hostility to an apparently endless and indecisive slaughter that nobody seemed willing to end. While the adversaries of the war in 1914 had felt helpless and isolated, by 1916 they could feel that they spoke for the majority. How dramatically the situation had changed was demonstrated when, on 28 October 1916, Friedrich Adler, son of the leader and founder of the Austrian socialist party, deliberately and in cold blood assassinated the Austrian prime minister, Count Stürgkh, in a Vienna café – this was the age of innocence before the security men – as a public gesture against the war.

Anti-war sentiment naturally raised the political profile of the socialists, who increasingly reverted to their movements' pre-1914 opposition to war. Indeed, some parties (e.g. in Russia, Serbia and Britain – the Independent Labour Party) never ceased to oppose it, and, even where socialist parties supported the war, its most vocal enemies were to be found in their ranks.* At the same time, and in all major belligerent countries, the organized labour movement in the vast armaments industries, became a centre of both industrial and anti-war militancy. The lower-echelon union activists in these factories, skilled men in a strong bargaining position ('shop stewards' in Britain; *'Betriebsobleute'* in Germany) became by-words for radicalism. The artificers and mechanics in the new high-tech navies, little different from floating factories, moved in the same direction. Both in Russia and in Germany the chief naval bases (Kronstadt, Kiel) were to become major centres of revolution, and later a French naval mutiny in the Black Sea was to halt French military intervention against the Bolsheviks in the Russian Civil War of 1918–20. Rebellion against the war thus acquired both focus and agency. No wonder the Austro–Hungarian censors, monitoring the correspondence of their troops, began to note a change in tone. 'If only the good Lord would bring us peace' turned into 'We've had enough' or even 'They say the socialists are going to make peace.'

It is, therefore, no surprise that, once again according to the Habsburg censors, the Russian revolution was the first political event since the outbreak of the war to echo in the letters even of peasants' and workers' wives. And no surprise that, especially after the October revolution brought Lenin's Bolsheviks to power, the desires for peace and social revolution merged: a third of the sample of censored letters between November 1917 and March 1918 expected to get peace from Russia, a third from revolution, and another 20 per cent from a combination of both. That a Russian revolution would have major international repercussions was always clear: even the first one, in 1905–6, had shaken

---

* In 1917 an important Independent Social Democratic Party of Germany (USPD) formally split on this issue from the majority of the Socialists (SPD) which continued to support the war.

the surviving ancient empires of its time, from Austria-Hungary via Turkey and Persia to China (see *The Age of Empire*, chapter 12). By 1917 all Europe had become a pile of social explosives ready for ignition.

II

Russia, ripe for social revolution, war-weary and on the verge of defeat, was the first of the regimes of central and eastern Europe to collapse under the stresses and strains of the First World War. The explosion was expected, though nobody could predict the timing and occasion of the detonation. A few weeks before the February revolution, Lenin in his Swiss exile had still wondered whether he would live to see it. In fact, the Tsar's rule collapsed when a demonstration of working-class women (on the socialist movement's customary 'Women's Day' – 8 March) combined with an industrial lock-out in the notoriously militant Putilov metalworks to produce a general strike and an invasion of the centre of the capital across the frozen river, essentially to demand bread. The fragility of the regime was revealed when the Tsar's troops, even the always loyal Cossacks, hesitated, then refused to attack the crowds and began to fraternize with them. When, after four chaotic days, they mutinied, the Tsar abdicated, to be replaced by a liberal 'provisional government', not without some sympathy or even assistance from Russia's Western allies, who were afraid that the desperate Tsar's regime might pull out of the war and sign a separate peace with Germany. Four spontaneous and leaderless days on the street put an end to an Empire.* More than this: so ready was Russia for social revolution that the masses of Petrograd immediately treated the fall of the Tsar as the proclamation of universal freedom, equality and direct democracy. Lenin's extraordinary achievement was to transform this uncontrollable anarchic popular surge into Bolshevik power.

So, instead of a liberal and constitutional Western-oriented Russia ready and willing to fight the Germans, what emerged was a revolutionary vacuum: a powerless 'provisional government' on one side, and, on the other, a multitude of grassroots 'councils' (Soviets) springing up

---

* The human cost, larger than the October revolution but relatively modest: 53 officers, 602 soldiers, 73 policemen and 587 citizens injured, wounded or killed. (W.H. Chamberlin, 1965, vol. I, p. 85).

spontaneously everywhere like mushrooms after the rains.* These actually held power, or at least veto-power, locally, but they had no idea what to do with it or what could or ought be done. The various revolutionary parties and organizations – Bolshevik and Menshevik Social Democrats, Social Revolutionaries, and numerous lesser factions of the Left, emerging from illegality – attempted to establish themselves in these assemblies, to coordinate them and to convert them to their policies, though initially only Lenin saw them as the alternative to the government ('All power to the Soviets'). However, it is clear that, when the Tsar fell, relatively few among the Russian people knew what the revolutionary party labels represented or, if they knew, could distinguish between their rival appeals. What they knew was that they no longer accepted authority – not even the authority of revolutionaries who claimed to know better than they.

The basic demand of the city poor was for bread, and, of the workers among them, for better wages and shorter hours. The basic demand of the 80 per cent of Russians who lived by agriculture, was, as always, for land. Both agreed that they wanted an end to the war, though the mass of peasant-soldiers who formed the army was at first not against fighting as such but against harsh discipline and the mistreatment of other ranks. These slogans, 'Bread, Peace, Land' won rapidly growing support for those who propagated them, notably Lenin's Bolsheviks, who grew from a small troop of a few thousands in March 1917 to a quarter of a million members by the early summer of that year. Contrary to the Cold War mythology, which saw Lenin essentially as an organizer of coups, the only real asset he and the Bolsheviks had was the ability to recognize what the masses wanted; to, as it were, lead by knowing how to follow. When, for instance, he recognized that, contrary to the socialist programme, the peasants wanted a division of the land into family farms, he did not hesitate for a moment to commit the Bolsheviks to this form of economic individualism.

Conversely, the Provisional Government and its supporters failed to recognize their inability to get Russia to obey its laws and decrees. When businessmen and managers tried to re-establish labour discipline, they merely radicalized the workers. When the Provisional Government insisted on launching the army into another military offensive in June 1917,

* Such 'councils', presumably rooted in the experience of Russian self-governing village communities, emerged as political entities among factory workers during the 1905 revolution. Since assemblies of directly elected delegates were familiar to organized workers everywhere, and appealed to their built-in sense of democracy, the term 'Soviet', sometimes but not always translated into the local languages (councils; räte) had a strong international appeal.

the army had had enough, and the peasant-soldiers went home to their villages to take part in dividing the land with their kin. Revolution spread along the lines of the railways that carried them back. The time was not yet ripe for an immediate fall of the Provisional Government, but from the summer on radicalization accelerated both in the army and in the main cities, increasingly to the benefit of the Bolsheviks. The peasantry gave overwhelming support to the heirs of the Narodniks (see *Age of Capital*, chapter 9), the Social Revolutionaries, though these developed a more radical left wing which drew closer to the Bolsheviks, and briefly joined them in government after the October revolution.

As the Bolsheviks – then essentially a workers' party – found itself the majority in the major Russian cities, and especially in the capital, Petrograd and in Moscow, and gained ground rapidly in the army, the Provisional Government's existence became increasingly shadowy; especially when it had to appeal to the revolutionary forces in the capital to defeat an attempted counter-revolutionary coup by a monarchist general in August. The radicalized groundswell of their followers pushed the Bolsheviks inevitably towards the seizure of power. In fact, when the moment came, power had not so much to be seized as to be picked up. It has been said that more people were injured in the making of Eisenstein's great film *October* (1927) than had been hurt during the actual taking of the Winter Palace on 7 November 1917. The Provisional Government, with no one left to defend it, merely dissolved into thin air.

From the moment that the fall of the Provisional Govenment became certain, to the present, the October revolution has been drenched in polemics. Most of them are misleading. The real issue is not whether, as anticommunist historians have argued, it was a putsch or coup by the fundamentally antidemocratic Lenin, but who or what should or could follow the fall of the Provisional Government. From early September Lenin tried to convince the hesitant elements in his party not only that power might easily escape them if not seized by planned action during the, possibly short, time when it was within their grasp, but – perhaps with equal urgency – to answer the question 'Can the Bolsheviks Retain State Power?' if they did seize it. What, indeed, could *anybody* do who tried to govern the volcanic eruption of revolutionary Russia? No party, other than Lenin's Bolsheviks, was prepared to envisage this responsibility on its own – and Lenin's pamphlet suggests that not all Bolsheviks were as determined as he. Given thc favourable political situation in Petrograd, Moscow and the northern armies, the purely short-term case for seizing power *now*, rather than waiting further on events, was indeed difficult to answer. The military counter-revolution had only begun. A desperate government, rather than giving way to the Soviet, might surrender Petrograd to the German army, already on the northern border of what is now Estonia, i.e. a few miles from the capital. Moreover, Lenin rarely hesitated to look the darkest facts in the face. If the Bolsheviks failed to seize the moment, 'a wave of real anarchy may become stronger *than we are*'. In the last analysis Lenin's argument could not but convince his party. If a revolutionary party did not seize power when the moment and the masses called for it, how did it differ from a non-revolutionary one?

It was the longer-term prospect that was problematic, even supposing that the power seized in Petrograd and Moscow could be extended to the rest of Russia and maintained there against anarchy and counter-revolution. Lenin's own programme of committing the new Soviet (i.e. primarily Bolshevik Party) government to the 'socialist transformation of the Russian Republic' was essentially a gamble on the conversion of the Russian Revolution into the world, or at least the European, revolution. Who – he said so often enough – could imagine that the victory of socialism 'can come about . . . except by the complete destruction of the Russian and European bourgeoisie?' In the meanwhile the primary, indeed the only, duty of the Bolsheviks was to hold on. The new regime did little about socialism except to declare that this was its object, to take over the banks and to declare 'workers' control' over the existing managements, i.e., to put the official stamp on what they had been doing anyway since the revolution, while urging them to keep production going. It had nothing further to tell them.*

The new regime did hold on. It survived a penal peace imposed by Germany at Brest-Litowsk, some months before the Germans were themselves defeated, and which detached Poland, the Baltic provinces, Ukraine and substantial parts of south and west Russia as well as, *de facto*, Transcaucasia (Ukraine and Transcaucasia were recovered). The Allies saw no reason to be more generous to the centre of world subversion. Various counter-revolutionary ('White') armies and regimes rose against the Soviets, financed by the Allies, who sent British, French, American, Japanese, Polish, Serb, Greek and Rumanian troops on to Russian soil. At the worst moments of the brutal and chaotic 1918–20 Civil War, Soviet Russia was reduced to a landlocked hulk of territory in North and Central Russia somewhere between the Ural region and the

---

* 'I said to them: do all you want to do, take all you want, we shall support you, but take care of production, see that production is useful. Take up useful work, you will make mistakes, but you will learn.' (Lenin: *Report on the Activities of the Council of People's Commissars*, 11/24 January 1918, Lenin, 1970, p. 551.)

present Baltic States, but for the tiny exposed finger of Leningrad, pointing at the Gulf of Finland. The only major assets the new regime possessed, as it improvised an eventually victorious Red army out of nothing, was the incompetence and division of the quarrelling 'White' forces, their capacity to antagonize the Great Russian peasantry, and the well-founded suspicion among the Western powers that their mutinous soldiers and sailors could not be safely ordered to fight the Bolsheviks. By late 1920 the Bolsheviks had won.

So, against expectations, Soviet Russia survived. The Bolsheviks maintained, indeed extended, their power not only (as Lenin noted with pride and relief after two months and fifteen days) longer than the Paris Commune of 1871, but through years of unbroken crisis and catastrophe, German conquest and a penal peace, regional breakaways, counter-revolution, civil war, foreign armed intervention, hunger and economic collapse. It could have no strategy or perspective beyond choosing, day by day, between the decisions needed for immediate survival and the ones which risked immediate disaster. Who could afford to consider the possible long-term consequences for the revolution of decisions which had to be taken *now*, or else there would be an end to the revolution and no further consequences to consider? One by one the necessary steps were taken. When the new Soviet Republic emerged from its agony, they were found to have led in a direction far removed from the one in the mind of Lenin at the Finland Station.

Still, the revolution survived. It did so for three major reasons: First, it possessed a uniquely powerful, virtually a state-building, instrument in the 600,000-strong centralized and disciplined Communist Party. Whatever its role before the revolution, this organizational model, tirelessly propagated and defended by Lenin since 1902, came into its own after it. Virtually all revolutionary regimes of the Short Twentieth Century were to adopt some variant of it. Second, it was quite evidently the *only* government able and willing to hold Russia together as a state, and therefore enjoyed considerable support from otherwise politically hostile patriotic Russians such as the officers without whom the new Red army could not have been built. For these, as for the retrospective historian, the choice in 1917–18 lay not between a liberal-democratic or a non-liberal Russia, but between Russia and the disintegration which was the fate of the other archaic and defeated empires, namely Austria-Hungary and Turkey. Unlike these, the Bolshevik revolution preserved most of the multinational territorial unity of the old Tsarist state at least for another seventy-four years. The third reason was that the revolution had allowed the peasantry to take the land. When it came to the point, the bulk of the

Great Russian peasants – core of the state as well as of its new army – thought their chances of keeping it were better under the Reds than if the gentry returned. This gave the Bolsheviks a decisive advantage in the civil war of 1918–20. As it turned out, the Russian peasants were too optimistic.

III

The world revolution, which justified Lenin's decision to commit Russia to socialism, did not take place, and with it Soviet Russia was committed to a generation of impoverished and backward isolation. The options for its future development were determined, or at least narrowly circumscribed (see chapters 13 and 16). Yet a wave of revolution swept across the globe in the two years after October, and the hopes of the embattled Bolsheviks did not seem unrealistic. '*Völker hört die Signale*' ('Peoples, hear the signals') was the first line of the refrain of the Internationale in German. The signals came, loud and clear, from Petrograd and, after their capital had been transferred to a safer location in 1918, Moscow;* they were heard wherever labour and socialist movements operated, irrespective of their ideology, and even beyond. 'Soviets' were formed by the tobacco workers in Cuba where few knew where Russia was. The years from 1917–19 in Spain came to be known as 'the Bolshevik biennium', though the local left was passionately anarchist, i.e. politically at the opposite pole from Lenin. Revolutionary student movements erupted in Peking (Beijing) in 1919 and Córdoba (Argentina) in 1918, soon to spread across Latin America and to generate local revolutionary marxist leaders and parties. The Indian nationalist militant M.N. Roy immediately fell under its spell in Mexico, where the local revolution, entering its most radical phase in 1917, naturally recognized its affinity with revolutionary Russia: Marx and Lenin became its icons, together with Moctezuma, Emiliano Zapata and assorted labouring Indians, and can still be seen on the great murals of its official artists. Within a few

* The capital city of Tsarist Russia was St Petersburg, which sounded too German in the First World War and was therefore changed to Petrograd. After Lenin's death it became Leningrad (1924), and during the fall of the USSR it returned to its original name. The Soviet Union (followed by its more slavish satellites) was unusually given to political toponymy, often complicated by the twists and turns of party fortunes. Thus Tsaritsyn on the Volga became Stalingrad, scene of an epic battle of the Second World War, but, after Stalin's death, Volgograd. At the time of writing it still had that name.

months Roy was in Moscow to play a major role in forming the new Communist International's policy for colonial liberation. Partly through resident Dutch socialists like Henk Sneevliet, the October revolution immediately made its mark on the Indonesian national liberation movement's main mass organization, Sarekat Islam. 'This action of the Russian people', wrote a provincial Turkish paper, 'someday in the future will turn into a sun and illuminate all humanity'. In the distant interior of Australia, tough (and largely Irish Catholic) sheep-shearers, with no discernible interest in political theory, cheered the Soviets as a workers' state. In the USA the Finns, long the most strongly socialist of immigrant communities, converted to communism en masse, filling the bleak mining settlements of Minnesota with meetings 'where the mentioning of the name of Lenin made the heart throb . . . In mystic silence, almost in religious ecstasy, did we admire everything that came from Russia' (Kivisto, 1983). In short, the October revolution was universally recognized as a world-shaking event.

Even many of those who saw the revolution at close quarters, a process less conducive to religious ecstasy, were converted, from prisoners-of-war who returned to their countries as convinced Bolsheviks and future communist leaders of their countries, like the Croat mechanic Josef Broz (Tito), to visiting journalists like the *Manchester Guardian*'s Arthur Ransome, not a notably political figure, best known for putting his passion for sailing into enchanting children's books. An even less Bolshevik figure, the Czech writer Jaroslav Hašek – future author of that masterpiece, *The Adventures of the Good Soldier Schwejk* – found himself, for the first time in his life, the militant of a cause, and it is claimed, even more astonishingly, sober. He took part in the civil war as a Red army commissar, after which he returned to his more familiar role as a Prague anarcho-bohemian and drunk, on the grounds that post-revolutionary Soviet Russia wasn't his style. But the revolution had been.

However, the events of Russia inspired not only revolutionaries but, more important, revolutions. In January 1918, within weeks of the taking of the Winter Palace, and while the Bolsheviks desperately tried to negotiate peace at all costs with the advancing German army a wave of mass political strikes and anti-war demonstrations swept through central Europe, starting in Vienna, spreading via Budapest and the Czech regions to Germany, and culminating in the revolt of the Austro-Hungarian navy's sailors in the Adriatic. As the last doubts about the defeat of the Central Powers disappeared, their armies finally broke. In September the Bulgarian peasant soldiers went home, proclaimed a Republic and marched on Sofia, though they were still disarmed with German help. In

October the Habsburg monarchy fell apart after the last lost battles on the Italian front. Various new nation-states were proclaimed in the (justified) hope that the victorious Allies would prefer them to the dangers of Bolshevik revolution. And indeed, the first Western reaction to the Bolsheviks' appeal to the peoples to make peace – and their publication of the secret treaties in which the Allies had carved up Europe among themselves – had been President Wilson's Fourteen Points, which played the nationalist card against Lenin's international appeal. A zone of small nation-states was to form a sort of quarantine belt against the Red virus. In early November mutinous sailors and soldiers spread the German revolution from the naval base of Kiel throughout the country. A Republic was proclaimed and the emperor retired to the Netherlands, to be replaced by a social-democratic ex-saddler as the head of state.

The revolution, which thus swept away all regimes from Vladivostok to the Rhine, was a revolt against the war and, for the most part, the achievement of peace defused much of the explosive it contained. Its social content was in any case vague, except among the peasant soldiers of the Habsburg, Romanov and Ottoman Empires and the lesser states of south-eastern Europe, and their families. There it consisted of four items: land, and suspicion of cities, or strangers (especially Jews) and or governments. This made peasants revolutionary but not Bolshevik in large parts of central and eastern Europe, though not in Germany (except for some of Bavaria), Austria, and parts of Poland. They had to be conciliated by a measure of land reform even in some conservative, indeed counter-revolutionary countries like Rumania and Finland. On the other hand, where they constituted the majority of the population, they practically guaranteed that socialists, let alone Bolshevik ones, would not win democratic general elections. This did not necessarily make peasant bastions of political conservatism, but it fatally handicapped democratic socialists; or else – as in Soviet Russia – pressed them into abolishing electoral democracy. For this reason the Bolsheviks, having demanded a Constituent Assembly (a familiar revolutionary tradition since 1789) dissolved it as soon as it met, a few weeks after October. And the establishment of new small nation-states along Wilsonian lines, though far from eliminating national conflicts in the zone of revolutions, also diminished the scope for Bolshevik revolution. That, indeed, had been the intention of the Allied peacemakers.

On the other hand, the impact of the Russian revolution on the European upheavals of 1918–19 was so patent, that there could hardly be much room in Moscow for scepticism about the prospect of a spreading revolution of the world proletariat. To the historian – even to some local revolutionaries – it seemed clear that imperial Germany was a state of considerable social and political stability, with a strong, but essentially moderate working-class movement, which would certainly not have experienced anything like armed revolution but for the war. Unlike Tsarist Russia or ramshackle Austria-Hungary; unlike Turkey, the proverbial 'sick man of Europe'; unlike the wild, gun-toting inhabitants of the mountains of the continent's south-east, who were capable of anything, it was not a country where upheavals were to be expected. And, indeed, compared to the genuinely revolutionary situations in defeated Russia and Austria-Hungary, the bulk of German revolutionary soldiers, sailors and workers remained as moderate and law-abiding as the, possibly apocryphal, jokes of Russian revolutionaries had always made them out to be ('Where there is a notice forbidding the public to step on the grass, German insurrectionaries will naturally walk only on the paths').

Yet this was the country where the revolutionary sailors carried the banner of the Soviets through the country, where the executive of a Berlin workers' and soldiers' soviet appointed a socialist government of Germany, where February and October seemed to be one, as effective power in the capital already appeared to be in the hands of radical socialists from the moment the emperor abdicated. This was an illusion, due to the total, but temporary, paralysis of the old army, state and power-structure under the double shock of utter defeat and revolution. After a few days the republicanised old regime was soon back in the saddle again, and no longer seriously troubled by the socialists, who even failed to gain a majority at the first elections, though these were held a few weeks after the revolution.* They were even less troubled by the newly improvised Communist Party, whose leaders, Karl Liebknecht and Rosa Luxemburg, were quickly murdered by free-lance army gunmen.

Nevertheless, the German revolution of 1918 confirmed the hopes of the Russian Bolsheviks, all the more because a shortlived Socialist republic was actually proclaimed in Bavaria in 1918, and, in the spring of 1919, after the assassination of its leader, a brief Soviet Republic was set up in Munich, the capital of German art, intellectual counter-culture and (politically less subversive) of beer. It overlapped with another and more serious attempt to carry Bolshevism westwards, the Hungarian Soviet

---

* The moderate majority social-democrats gained just under 38 per cent of the vote – their all-time high – the revolutionary Independent Social Democrats about 7.5 per cent of the vote.

Republic of March–July 1919.* Both were, of course, suppressed with the expected brutality. Moreover, disappointment with the Social Democrats rapidly radicalized German workers, many of whom transferred their loyalties to the Independent Socialists, and after 1920, to the Communist Party, which therefore became the largest such party outside Soviet Russia. Could not a German October revolution be expected after all? Even though 1919, the peak year of Western social unrest, had brought defeat to the only attempts to spread the Bolshevik revolution; even though the revolutionary wave was rapidly and visibly subsiding in 1920, the Bolshevik leadership in Moscow did not abandon the hope of German revolution until late in 1923.

On the contrary. It was in 1920 that the Bolsheviks committed themselves to what in retrospect seems a major error, the permanent division of the international labour movement. They did so by structuring their new international communist movement on the pattern of the Leninist vanguard party of an elite of fulltime 'professional revolutionaries'. The October revolution, as we have seen, had won wide sympathies in the international socialist movements, virtually all of which emerged from the world war both radicalized and enormously strengthened. With rare exceptions the socialist and labour parties contained large bodies of opinion that favoured joining the new Third or Communist International, which the Bolsheviks founded to replace the Second International (1889–1914), discredited and broken by the world war it had failed to resist.† Indeed, several, such as the Socialist Parties of France, Italy, Austria and Norway, and the Independent Socialists of Germany actually voted to do so, leaving the unreconstructed opponents of Bolshevism in a minority. Yet what Lenin and the Bolsheviks wanted was not an international movement of socialist sympathisers with the October revolution, but a corps of utterly committed and disciplined activists, a sort of global striking-force for revolutionary conquest. Parties unwilling to adopt the Leninist structure were refused admittance to or expelled from the new International, which could only be weakened by accepting such fifth columns of opportunism and reformism, not to mention what Marx had once called 'parliamentary cretinism'. In the imminent battle there could be a place only for soldiers.

* Its defeat spread a diaspora of political and intellectal refugees across the world, some of them with unexpected future careers, like the film-tycoon Sir Alexander Korda and the actor Bela Lugosi, best known as the star of the original horror film *Dracula*.

† The so-called First International was Karl Marx's own International Workingmen's Association of 1864–72.

The argument made sense on only one condition: that the world revolution was still in progress, and its battles were in immediate prospect. Yet while the European situation was far from stabilized, it was clear in 1920 that Bolshevik revolution was not on the agenda in the West, though it was also clear that in Russia the Bolsheviks were permanently established. No doubt, as the International met there seemed to be a chance that the Red Army, victorious in the Civil War, and now sweeping towards Warsaw, would spread the revolution westwards by armed force, as the by-product of a brief Russo–Polish War, provoked by the territorial ambitions of Poland. Restored to statehood after a century-and-a-half of non-existence, Poland now demanded its eighteenth century frontiers. These lay deep in Belorussia, Lithuania and the Ukraine. The Soviet advance, which has left a marvellous literary monument in Isaac Babel's *Red Cavalry*, was hailed by an unusually wide assortment of contemporaries ranging from the Austrian novelist Joseph Roth, later the elegist of the Habsburgs, to Mustafa Kemal, the future leader of Turkey. Yet the Polish workers failed to rise, and the Red army was turned back at the gates of Warsaw. Henceforth, in spite of appearances, all was to be quiet on the western front. Admittedly, the prospects of the revolution moved East into Asia, to which Lenin had always paid considerable attention. Indeed, from 1920 to 1927 the hopes of world revolution seemed to rest on the Chinese revolution, advancing under the Kuomintang, then the party of national liberation, whose leader Sun Yat-sen (1866–1925) welcomed both the Soviet model, Soviet military assistance and the new Chinese Communist Party as part of his movement. The Kuomintang-Communist alliance was to sweep north from its bases in South China in the great offensive of 1925–27, bringing most of China once again under the control of a single government for the first time since the fall of the Empire in 1911, before the leading Kuomintang general, Chiang Kai-shek, turned on the communists and slaughtered them. Yet even before this proof that even the East was not yet ripe for October, the promise of Asia could not conceal the failure of revolution in the West.

By 1921 this was undeniable. The revolution was in retreat in Soviet Russia, though politically Bolshevik power was unassailable (see p. 379). It was off the agenda in the West. The Third Congress of the Comintern recognized this without quite admitting it by calling for a 'united front' with the very socialists whom the Second had expelled from the army of revolutionary progress. Just what this meant was to divide the revolutionaries for the next generations. However, in any case it was too late. The movement was permanently split, the majority of left socialists, individuals and parties drifted back into the social-democratic movement, overwhelmingly led by anti-communist moderates. The new communist parties remained minorities of the European Left, and generally – with a few exceptions such as Germany, France or Finland – rather small, if impassioned minorities. Their situation was not to change until the 1930s (see chapter 5).

IV

Yet the years of upheaval left behind not only a single, huge but backward country now governed by communists and committed to the building of an alternative society to capitalism, but also a government, a disciplined international movement, and, perhaps equally important, a generation of revolutionaries committed to the vision of world revolution under the flag raised in October and under the leadership of the movement which, inevitably, had its headquarters in Moscow. (For several years it had been hoped soon to transfer it to Berlin, and German, not Russian, remained the official language of the International between the wars.) The movement may not have known quite how the world revolution was to advance after stabilisation in Europe and defeat in Asia, and the communists' scattered attempts at independent armed insurrection (Bulgaria and Germany in 1923, Indonesia in 1926, China in 1927 and – late and anomalous – Brazil in 1935) were disasters. Still, as the Great Slump and the rise of Hitler were soon to prove, the state of the world between the wars was hardly such as to discourage apocalyptic expectations (see chapters 3 to 5). This does not explain the sudden switch of the Comintern into the rhetorical mode of ultra-revolutionism and sectarian leftism between 1928 and 1934 since, whatever the rhetoric, in practice the movement neither expected nor prepared for taking power anywhere. The change, which proved politically calamitous, is rather to be explained by the internal politics of the Soviet Communist Party, as Stalin took control of it, and perhaps also as an attempt to compensate for the increasingly evident divergence between the interests of the USSR, as a state which inevitably had to coexist with other states – it began to win international recognition as a regime from 1920 – and the movement whose aim was to subvert and overthrow all other governments.

In the end the state interests of the Soviet Union prevailed over the world revolutionary interests of the Communist International, which Stalin reduced to an instrument of Soviet state policy under the strict control of the Soviet Communist Party, purging, dissolving and reforming its components at will. World revolution belonged to the rhetoric of the past, and indeed any revolution was tolerable only if a) it did not conflict with Soviet state interest and b) could be brought under direct Soviet control. Western governments who saw the advance of communist regimes after 1944 essentially as an extension of Soviet power certainly read Stalin's intentions correctly; but so did the unreconstructed revolutionaries who bitterly blamed Moscow for not wanting communists to take power and discouraged every attempt to do so, even those which proved successful, as in Yugoslavia and China (see chapter 5).

Nevertheless, until the end Soviet Russia remained, even in the eyes of many self-serving and corrupt members of its *nomenklatura*, something more than just another great power. Universal emancipation, the construction of a better alternative to capitalist society was, after all, its fundamental reason for existence. Why else should hard-faced Moscow bureaucrats have continued to finance and arm the guerrillas of the communist-allied African National Congress whose chances of overthrowing the *apartheid* system of South Africa seemed and were minimal for decades? (Curiously enough the Chinese Communist regime, though it criticised the USSR for betraying revolutionary movements after the break between the two countries, has no comparable record of practical support for Third World liberation movements.) Humanity, the USSR had learned long since, would not be transformed by Moscow-inspired world revolution. In the long twilight of the Brezhnev years even Nikita Khrushchev's sincerely held conviction that socialism would 'bury' capitalism by dint of its economic superiority faded away. It may well be that the terminal erosion of this belief in the system's universal vocation explains why, in the end, it disintegrated without resistance (see chapter 16).

None of these hesitations troubled the first generation of those inspired by the shining light of October to devote their lives to the world revolution. Like the early Christians, most pre-1914 socialists were believers in the great apocalyptic change which would abolish all that was evil and bring about a society without unhappiness, oppression, inequality and injustice. Marxism offered the hope of the millennium the guarantee of science and historic inevitability; the October revolution now offered the proof that the great change had begun.

The total number of these soldiers in the necessarily ruthless and disciplined army of human emancipation was perhaps no larger than a few tens of thousands; the number of the professionals of the international movement, 'changing countries more often than pairs of shoes' as Bertolt Brecht put it in a poem written in their honour, was perhaps no more than a few hundreds in all. They must not be confused with what the

Italians, in the days of their million-strong Communist Party, called 'the communist people', the millions of supporters and rank-and-file members for whom the dream of a new and *good* society was also real, though in practice theirs was no more than the old socialist movement's daily activism, and whose commitment was in any case one of class and community rather than of personal dedication. Yet though their numbers were small, the twentieth century cannot be understood without them.

Without the Leninist 'party of a new type' of 'professional revolution-aries' of which they were the cadres, it is inconceivable that in barely more than thirty years after October, one third of the human race would have found itself living under Communist regimes. What their faith, and their unqualified loyalty to the headquarters of world revolu-tion in Moscow, gave communists was the ability to see themselves (sociologically speaking) as parts of a universal church, not a sect. Moscow-oriented communist parties lost leaders by secession and purge, but until the heart had gone out of the movement after 1956 they did not split, unlike the fragmenting groups of the Marxist dissi-dents who followed Trotsky and the even more fissiparous 'Marxist-Leninist' conventicles of post-1960 Maoism. However small – and when Mussolini was overthrown in Italy in 1943 the Italian Communist Party consisted of about 5,000 men and women, mostly emerging from jail or exile – they were what the Bolsheviks had been in February 1917, the nucleus of an army of millions, potential rulers of a people and a state.

For this generation, especially those who had, however young, lived through the years of upheaval, revolution was what happened in their lifetimes; the days of capitalism were inevitably numbered. Contemporary history was the antechamber of ultimate victory for those who lived to see it, which would include only some soldiers of the revolution ('the dead on leave of absence' as the Russian communist Leviné put it shortly before being executed by those who overthrew the Munich Soviet of 1919). If bourgeois society itself had so much reason to doubt its future, why should they be confident of its survival? Their own lives demonstrated its reality.

Let us take the case of two young Germans temporarily linked as lovers, who were mobilized for life by the Bavarian Soviet revolution of 1919: Olga Benario, daughter of a prosperous Munich lawyer, and Otto Braun, a school-teacher. Olga was to find herself organizing revolution in the western hemisphere, attached and eventually married to Luís Carlos Prestes, the leader of a long insurrectionary march through the Brazilian backwoods who had talked Moscow into backing a rising in Brazil in

1935. The rising failed, and Olga was delivered by the Brazilian government to Hitler's Germany, where she eventually died in a concentration
camp. Meanwhile Otto, more successfully, set out to revolutionize the
East as Comintern military expert in China and, as it turned out, the only
non-Chinese to take part in the famous 'Long March' of the Chinese
communists before returning to Moscow and eventually to the GDR.
(The experience left him sceptical of Mao.) When, except in the first half
of the twentieth century, could two intertwined lives have taken these
shapes?

So, in the generation after 1917, Bolshevism absorbed all other social-
revolutionary traditions, or pushed them on to the margin of radical
movements. Before 1914 anarchism had been far more of a driving
ideology of revolutionary activists than Marxism over large parts of the
world. Marx, outside Eastern Europe, was seen rather as the guru of
mass parties whose inevitable, but not explosive, advance to victory he
had demonstrated. By the 1930s anarchism had ceased to exist as a
significant political force outside Spain, even in Latin America, where the
black-and-red had traditionally inspired more militants than the red flag.
(Even in Spain the Civil War was to destroy anarchism, whereas it made
the fortunes of the communists, hitherto relatively insignificant.) Indeed,
such social-revolutionary groups as existed outside Moscow-communism
henceforth took Lenin and the October revolution as their point of
reference, and were almost invariably headed or inspired by some dissident or expelled figure from the Comintern, which engaged in an
increasingly ruthless hunt for heretics, as Joseph Stalin established, and
later clamped, his grip on the Soviet Communist Party and the International. Few of these dissident Bolshevik centres amounted to much
politically. By far the most prestigious and famous of the heretics, the
exiled Leon Trotsky – co-leader of the October revolution and architect
of the Red army – utterly failed in his practical endeavours. His 'Fourth
International' intended to compete with the Stalinized Third International, was virtually invisible. When he was assassinated by order of
Stalin in his Mexican exile in 1940, his political significance was
negligible.

In short, to be a social revolutionary increasingly meant to be a
follower of Lenin and the October revolution, and increasingly a member
or supporter of some Moscow-aligned Communist party; all the more so
when, after the triumph of Hitler in Germany, these parties adopted the
policies of anti-fascist union which allowed them to emerge from sectarian
isolation and to win mass support among both workers and intellectuals
(see chapter 5). The young who thirsted to overthrow capitalism became

orthodox communists, and identified their cause with the Moscow-centred international movement; and Marxism, restored by October as the ideology of revolutionary change, now meant the Marxism of Moscow's Marx–Engels–Lenin Institute, which was now the global centre for the dissemination of the great classic texts. Nobody else within sight offered both to interpret the world and to change it, or looked better able to do so. This was to remain the case until after 1956, when the disintegration of both Stalinist orthodoxy in the USSR and of the Moscow-centred international communist movement brought the hitherto marginalized thinkers, traditions and organizations of left heterodoxy into the public sphere. Even so, they still lived under the gigantic shadow of October. Though anyone with the slightest knowledge of ideological history could recognize the spirit of Bakunin, or even Nechaev, rather than Marx in the student radicals of 1968 and after, it led to no significant revival of anarchist theory or movements. On the contrary, 1968 produced an enormous intellectual vogue for Marxism in theory – generally in versions which would have surprised Marx – and for a variety of 'Marxist–Leninist' sects and groups, united by the rejection of Moscow and the old communist parties as insufficiently revolutionary and Leninist.

Paradoxically, this virtually complete take-over of the social-revolutionary tradition occurred at a moment when the Comintern had plainly abandoned the original revolutionary strategies of 1917–23, or, rather, envisaged strategies for the transfer of power quite different from those of 1917 (see chapter 5). From 1935 on, the literature of the critical left was filled with accusations that Moscow's movements missed, rejected, nay betrayed the opportunities for revolution, because Moscow did not want it any more. Until the proudly 'monolithic' Soviet-centred movement began to break up from within, these arguments had little effect. So long as the communist movement retained its unity, cohesion and its striking immunity to fission, it was, for most of the world's believers in then need for global revolution, the only game in town. Moreover, who could possibly deny that the countries which broke with capitalism in the second great wave of world social revolution, from 1944 to 1949, did so under the auspices of the orthodox, Soviet-oriented communist parties? Not until after 1956 did the revolutionary-minded have a real choice between several such movements with some real claim to political or insurrectionary effectiveness. Even these – various brands of Trotskyism, Maoism and groups inspired by the Cuban revolution of 1959 (see chapter 15) – were still more or less Leninist in derivation. The old communist parties still remained much the largest groups on the far left, but by this time the heart had gone out of the old communist movement.

V

The force of the movements for world revolution lay in the communist form of organization, Lenin's 'party of a new type', a formidable innovation of twentieth-century social engineering, comparable to the invention of Christian monastic and other orders in the Middle Ages. It gave even small organizations disproportionate effectiveness, because the party could command extraordinary devotion and self-sacrifice from its members, more than military discipline and cohesiveness, and a total concentration on carrying out party decisions at all costs. This impressed even hostile observers profoundly. And yet, the relation between the 'vanguard party' model and the great revolutions it had been designed to make, and occasionally succeeded in making, was far from clear, although nothing was more evident than that the model came into its own *after* successful revolutions, or during wars. For the Leninist parties were essentially constructed as elites (vanguards) of leaders or rather, before revolutions had been won, 'counter-elites', and social revolutions, as 1917 showed, depend on what happens among the masses and in situations which neither elites nor counter-elites can fully control. As it happens, the Leninist model actually had considerable appeal for young members of the old elites, especially in the Third World, who joined such parties in disproportionate numbers, in spite of these parties' heroic, and relatively successful, efforts to promote true proletarians. The major expansion of Brazilian communism in the 1930s rested on the conversion of young intellectuals from families of the land-owning oligarchy and junior army officers (Martins Rodrigues, 1984, pp. 390–97).

On the other hand the feelings of the actual 'masses' (sometimes including the active supporters of the 'vanguards') was often at odds with their leaders' ideas, especially in times of genuine mass insurrection. Thus the rebellion of the Spanish generals against the Popular Front government in July 1936 immediately released social revolution in large regions of Spain. That the militants, especially the anarchist ones, should proceed to collectivise the means of production, was not surprising, though the Communist Party and the central government later opposed and where possible reversed this transformation, and its pros and cons continue to be discussed in the political and historical literature. However, the event also released the greatest of all the waves of iconoclasm and anticlerical homicide, since this form of activity first became part of Spanish popular agitations in 1835, when Barcelona citizens had reacted to an unsatisfactory bullfight by burning a number of churches. About seven thousand clerical persons – i.e. 12–13 per cent of the country's priests and monks, though only a negligible proportion of its nuns –were killed, while in a *single* diocese of Catalonia (Gerona) over six thousand images were destroyed (Hugh Thomas, 1977, pp. 270–71; M. Delgado, 1992, p. 56).

Two things are clear about this terrifying episode: it was denounced by the leaders or spokesmen of the Spanish revolutionary left, passionate anticlericals though they were, including the notoriously priest-hating anarchists; and for those who perpetrated it, as well as for many of those who watched it, *this* more than anything else, was what the revolution really meant: the reversal of the order of society and its values, not just for a brief symbolic moment, but for ever (M. Delgado, 1992, pp. 52–53). It was all very well for leaders to insist, as they always did, that the capitalist and not the priest was the principal enemy: in their bones the masses felt differently. (Whether popular politics in a less macho society than the Iberian would have been as murderously iconoclastic is a counterfactual question, but one on which serious research about women's attitudes might nevertheless throw some light.)

As it happens, the kind of revolution which sees the structure of political order and authority suddenly evaporate, leaving the man (and, so far as she was allowed, the woman) on the street to their own devices, proved to be rare in the twentieth century. Even the closest other example of a sudden collapse of established regimes, the Iranian revolution of 1979, was not quite so unstructured, in spite of the extraordinary unanimity of the Teheran mobilization of the masses against the Shah, much of which must have been spontaneous. Thanks to the structures of Iranian clericalism the new regime was already present in the ruin of the old, though it would not take its complete shape for a little while (see chapter 15).

In fact, the typical post-October revolution of the short Twentieth Century, leaving aside some localized explosions, was to be either initiated by an (almost always military) *coup*, capturing the capital, or as the final outcome of a lengthy and mostly rural armed struggle. Since junior officers – much more rarely non-commissioned officers – of radical and Left-wing sympathies were common in poor and backward countries, where the military life provided attractive career prospects for able and educated young men without family connections and wealth, such initiatives were typically found in countries like Egypt (the Free Officer revolution of 1952), and other countries in the Middle East (Iraq 1958, Syria at various times since the 1950s, and Libya in 1969). Military men are part of the fabric of Latin American revolutionary history, although they have rarely, or for very long, taken over national power for clearly

Left-wing causes. On the other hand, to most observers' surprise, in 1974 a military putsch by young officers disillusioned with and radicalized by long colonial rearguard wars, overthrew the oldest Right-wing regime then operating in the world: the 'revolution of carnations' in Portugal. The alliance between them, a strong Communist Party emerging from underground, and various radical Marxist groups, was soon divided and by-passed, to the relief of the European Community, which Portugal joined soon after.

The social structure, ideological traditions and political functions of the armed forces in developed countries made military men with political interests in these countries choose the right. Coups in alliance with communists, or even socialists, were not in their line. Admittedly in the liberation movements of the French Empire former soldiers of the native forces raised by France in its colonies – they had rarely been officers – came to play a prominent part (notably in Algeria). Their experience in and after the Second World War had been unsatisfactory, not only because of the usual discrimination, but also because the largely colonial soldiers in the forces of de Gaulle's Free France were, like the largely non-Gallic members of the armed resistance within France, quickly pushed into the shadows.

The Free French armies in the official victory parades after liberation were a great deal 'whiter' than the ones which had actually won the Gaullist battle honours. Nevertheless, on the whole the colonial armies of imperial powers, even when actually officered by natives of the colony, remained loyal, or rather unpolitical, even if we allow for the fifty thousand or so Indian soldiers who joined the Indian National Army under the Japanese (M. Echenberg, 1992, pp. 141–45; M. Barghava and A. Singh Gill, 1988, p. 10; T. R. Sareen, 1988, pp. 20–21).

VI

The road to revolution through long guerrilla war was discovered rather late by twentieth-century social revolutionaries; perhaps this was because historically this form of essentially rural activity had been overwhelmingly associated with movements of archaic ideologies easily confused by sceptical city observers with conservatism, or even with reaction and counter-revolution. After all, the powerful guerrilla wars of the French revolutionary and Napoleonic period had been invariably directed *against* and never *for* France and the cause of its revolution. The very word 'guerrilla' did not form part of Marxist vocabulary until after the Cuban revolution of 1959. The Bolsheviks, who had waged irregular as well as regular warfare during the Civil War, used the term 'partisan', which became standard in Soviet-inspired resistance movements during the Second World War. In retrospect it is surprising that guerrilla action played next to no part in the Spanish Civil War, though there should have been plenty of scope for it in republican areas occupied by the Franco forces. In fact, the communists organized some quite significant guerrilla nuclei from outside after the Second World War. Before that World War it was simply not part of the tool-kit of the prospective makers of revolutions.

Except in China, where the new strategy was pioneered by some (but by no means all) communist leaders – after the Kuomintang under Chiang Kai-shek turned on its former communist allies in 1927, and after the spectacular failure of communist insurrection in the cities (as in Canton, 1927). Mao Tse-tung, the chief champion of the new strategy – which was eventually to make him the leader of Communist China – not only recognized that, after more than fifteen years of revolution, large regions of China were outside the effective control of any central administration, but, as a devoted admirer of *The Water Margin*, the great classical novel of Chinese social banditry, that guerrilla tactics were a traditional part of Chinese social conflict. Indeed, no classically educated Chinese would miss the similarity between the establishment of Mao's first free guerrilla zone in the Kiangsi mountains in 1927, and the mountain fortress of the *Water Margin* heroes, whom the young Mao had called upon his fellow-students to imitate in 1917 (Schram, 1966, pp. 43–44).

The Chinese strategy, however heroic and inspiring, seemed unsuited to countries with functioning modern internal communications and governments in the habit of administering all their territory, however remote and physically difficult. As it happened, it did not prove successful in the short run even in China, where the national government, after several military campaigns, forced the communists in 1934 to give up their free soviet territories in the main regions of the country and to retreat, by means of the legendary Long March, to a remote and thinly-populated outlying border region of the north-west.

After the Brazilian rebel lieutenants like Luís Carlos Prestes moved from backwoods trekking to communism in the late 1920s, no Left-wing groups of importance chose the guerrilla road elsewhere, unless we count General César Augusto Sandino's fight against the American marines in Nicaragua (1927–33), which was to inspire the Sandinista revolution fifty years later. (Still, rather implausibly, the Communist International tried to present Lampião, the celebrated Brazilian social bandit and hero of a thousand chap-books, in this light.) Mao himself did not become the guiding star of revolutionaries until after the Cuban Revolution.

However, the Second World War produced a more immediate and general incentive to take the guerrilla road to revolution: the need to resist the occupation of most of continental Europe, including large parts of the European Soviet Union, by the armies of Hitler Germany and its allies. Resistance, and especially armed resistance, developed on a substantial scale after Hitler's attack on the USSR mobilized the various communist movements. When the German army was finally defeated, with varying contributions from the local resistance movements (see chapter 5), the regimes of occupied or fascist Europe disintegrated, and social-revolutionary regimes under communist control took over, or attempted to take over, in several countries where the armed resistance had been most effective (Yugoslavia, Albania and – but for the British, and eventually US-backed military support – Greece). They could probably also have taken over, though not for long, in Italy north of the Apennines, but, for reasons still debated on what remains of the revolutionary left, they did not try. The communist regimes which were established in East and South-east Asia after 1945 (in China, part of Korea and French Indochina) should also be regarded as children of wartime resistance; for even in China the massive advance of Mao's Red armies towards power only began after the Japanese army set out to take over the main body of China in 1937. The second wave of world social revolution emerged out of the Second World War, as the first had emerged out of the First – though in an utterly different way. This time it was the waging of war and not the revulsion against it which brought revolution to power.

The nature and policies of the new revolutionary regimes is considered elsewhere (see chapters 5 and 13). Here we are concerned with the process of revolution itself. The revolutions of the mid-century, which came at the victorious end of long wars, differed from the classical 1789 or 'October' scenario, or even from the slow-motion break-up of old regimes like imperial China and Porfirian Mexico (see *Age of Empire*, chapter 12) in two ways. First – and in this they resemble the result of successful military coups – there was no real doubt about who had made the revolution or exercised power: the political group(s) associated with the victorious armed forces of the USSR, since Germany, Japan and Italy would not have been defeated *only* by Resistance forces – not even in China. (The victorious Western armies were of course opposed to communist-dominated regimes.) There was no interregnum or power vacuum. Conversely, the only situations when strong Resistance forces failed to take over quickly after the collapse of the Axis powers, was where the Western Allies maintained a foothold in liberated countries (South Korea, Vietnam) or where the internal anti-Axis forces were themselves divided, as in China. There the communists after 1945 had still to establish themselves against a corrupt and rapidly weakening, but co-belligerent Kuomintang government; observed by a notably unenthusiastic USSR.

Second, the guerrilla road to power inevitably led out of the towns and industrial centres where the traditional force of socialist labour movements lay, and into the rural hinterland. More precisely, since guerrilla war is most easily maintained in bush, mountains, forests and on similar terrains, into sparsely-peopled territory remote from the main populations. In Mao's words, the countryside would surround the city before conquering it. In European resistance terms, urban insurrection – the rising of Paris in the summer of 1944; of Milan in the spring of 1945 – had to wait until the war was virtually over, at least in their region. What happened to Warsaw in 1944 was the penalty of premature city risings: they have only one shot in their magazine, though a big one. In short, for most of the population, even of a revolutionary country, the guerrilla road to revolution meant waiting for long periods for change to come from somewhere else without being able to do much. The actual effective resistance fighters, including all their infrastructure, were, inevitably, a fairly small minority.

On their territory, of course, the guerrillas could not function without mass backing; not least because in lengthy conflicts their forces would have to be largely recruited locally: thus (as in China) parties of industrial workers and intellectuals might be quietly transformed into armies of former peasants. Yet their relation to the masses was inevitably not as simple as is suggested by Mao's phrase about the guerrilla fish swimming in the people's water. In typical guerrilla country almost any harried group of outlaws which behaved itself, by local standards, was apt to enjoy widespread sympathy against invading foreign soldiers, or for that matter any agents of national government. However, the deep-rooted divisions within the countryside also meant that winning friends automatically risked acquiring enemies. The Chinese Communists who established their rural soviet areas in 1927–28 found, to their unjustified surprise, that converting one clan-dominated village helped to establish a network of 'red villages' based on connected clans, but also involved them in war against their traditional enemies, who formed a similar network of 'black villages'. 'In some cases', they complained, 'the class struggle was transformed into the fight of one village against another. There are cases when our troops had to besiege and destroy entire villages' (Räte-China, 1973, pp. 45–46). Successful guerrilla revolutionaries learned how to navigate such treacherous waters, but – as Milovan Djilas' memoir of the Yugoslav Partisan war makes clear, liberation was far more complex than a simple unanimous uprising of an oppressed people against foreign conquerors.

VII

These were not reflections likely to tarnish the satisfaction of communists who now found themselves at the head of all governments between the river Elbe and the China Seas. The world revolution, which had inspired them, had visibly advanced. Instead of a single, weak and isolated USSR, something like a dozen states had emerged, or were emerging, from the second great wave of global revolution, headed by one of the two powers in the world which deserved the name (the term superpower is recorded as early as 1944). Nor was the impetus of global revolution exhausted, for the decolonization of the old imperialist overseas possessions was still in full progress. Could it not be expected to lead to further advances of the cause of communism? Did not the international bourgeoisie itself fear for the future of what remained of capitalism, at least in Europe? Did not the French industrialist relatives of the young historian Le Roy Ladurie ask themselves, as they rebuilt their factories, whether in the end nationalization, or quite simply the Red Army, would not provide a final solution for their problems: sentiments which, he was to recall as an elderly conservative, confirmed his decision to join the French Communist Party in 1949? (Le Roy Ladurie, 1982, p. 37.) Did not a US Undersecretary of Commerce tell President Truman's administration in March 1947 that most European countries were standing on the very brink and may be pushed over at any time; others are gravely threatened? (Loth, 1988, p. 137.)

Such was the state of mind of the men and women who came out of illegality, battle and resistance, jail, concentration camp, or exile, to take over the responsibility for the future of countries, most of which lay in ruins. Perhaps some of them observed that, once again, capitalism had proved far easier to overthrow where it was weak or barely existed, than in its heartlands. And yet, could anyone deny that the world had shifted dramatically to the left? If the new communist rulers or co-rulers of their transformed states worried about anything immediately after the war, it was not about the future of socialism. It was about how to rebuild impoverished, exhausted and ruined countries, amid sometimes hostile populations, and about the danger of a war launched by the capitalist powers against the socialist camp before the rebuilding had made it safe. Paradoxically, the same fears haunted the sleep of Western politicians and ideologists. As we shall see, the Cold War which settled on the world after the second wave of world revolution was a contest of nightmares. Whether the fears of either East or West were justified, they were part of the era of world revolution born in October 1917. But that era itself was about to end, though it took another forty years before it was possible to write its epitaph.

Nevertheless it has changed the world, though not in the way that Lenin, and those who were inspired by the October Revolution, expected. Outside the Western hemisphere, the fingers of two hands are enough to count the few states of the world that have not gone through some combination of revolution, civil war, resistance to and liberation from foreign occupation, or the prophylactic decolonisation by empires doomed in an era of world revolution. (Britain, Sweden, Switzerland and perhaps Iceland are the only European cases.) Even in the western hemisphere, omitting the many violent changes of government always locally described as 'revolutions', major social revolutions – in Mexico, in Bolivia, the Cuban revolution and its successors – have transformed the Latin American scene.

The actual revolutions made in the name of communism have exhausted themselves, although it is too early for funeral orations about them, so long as the Chinese, one fifth of the human race, continue to live in a country governed by a Communist Party. Yet it is obvious that a return to the world of the *ancien regimes* of those countries is as impossible as it was in France after the revolutionary and Napoleonic era, or, for that matter, as the return of ex-colonies to pre-colonial life has proved to be. Even where the experience of communism has been reversed, the present of the ex-communist countries, and presumably their future, bear, and will continue to bear, the specific marks of the counter-revolution which replaced the revolution. There is no way in which the Soviet era can be written out of Russian or world history, as though it had not been. There is no way in which St Petersburg can return to 1914.

However, the indirect consequences of the era of upheaval after 1917 have been as profound as the direct consequences. The years after the Russian revolution opened the process of colonial emancipation and decolonisation and introduced both the politics of savage counter-revolution (in the form of fascism and other such movements – see chapter 4) and the politics of social-democracy to Europe. It is often forgotten, that until 1917 all labour and socialist parties (outside somewhat peripheral Australasia) chose to be in permanent opposition until the moment for socialism had come. The first social-democratic governments or coalition governments outside the Pacific were formed in 1917–19 (Sweden, Finland, Germany, Austria, Belgium), to be followed, within a few years, by Britain, Denmark and Norway. We tend to forget that the very moderation of such parties was largely a reaction to Bolshevism, as was the readiness of the old political system to integrate them.

In short, the history of the Short Twentieth Century cannot be understood without the Russian revolution and its direct and indirect effects. Not least because it proved to be the saviour of liberal capitalism, both by enabling the West to win the Second World War against Hitler's Germany and by providing the incentive for capitalism to reform itself and – paradoxically – through the Soviet Union's apparent immunity to the Great Depression, the incentive to abandon the belief in free market orthodoxy. As we shall see in the next chapter.

CHAPTER THREE
Into the Economic Abyss

No Congress of the United States ever assembled, on surveying the state of the Union, has met with a more pleasing prospect than that which appears at the present time ... The great wealth created by our enterprise and industry, and saved by our economy, has had the widest distribution among our own people, and has gone out in a steady stream to serve the charity and the business of the world. The requirements of existence have passed beyond the standard of necessity into the region of luxury. Enlarging production is consumed by an increasing demand at home and an expanding commerce abroad. The country can regard the present with satisfaction and anticipate the future with optimism.

President Calvin Coolidge, Message to Congress,
4 December 1928

Next to war, unemployment has been the most widespread, the most insidious, and the most corroding malady of our generation: it is the specific social disease of Western civilization in our time.

The Times, 23 January 1943

I

Let us suppose the First World War had been merely a temporary, if catastrophic, disruption of an otherwise stable economy and civilization. The economy would then have returned, after removing the debris of war, to something like normal and carried on from there. Rather in the same way as Japan buried the 300,000 dead of the 1923 earthquake, cleared the ruins which had made two or three millions homeless, and rebuilt a city like the old one, but rather more earthquake-proof. What would the inter-war world have been like under such circumstances? We cannot know, and it is pointless to speculate about what did not happen, and almost certainly could not have happened. The question is not useless, however, for it helps us to grasp the profound effect on the history of the twentieth century of the world economic breakdown between the wars.

But for it, there would certainly have been no Hitler. There would almost certainly have been no Roosevelt. It is extremely unlikely that the Soviet system would have been regarded as a serious economic rival and alternative to world capitalism. The consequences of the economic crisis in the non-European or non-Western world, which are sketched elsewhere, were patently dramatic. In short, the world of the second half of the twentieth century is incomprehensible without understanding the impact of the economic collapse. It is the subject of this chapter.

The First World War devastated only parts of the old world, mainly those in Europe. World revolution, the most dramatic aspect of the breakdown of nineteenth century bourgeois civilization, spread more widely: from Mexico to China and, in the form of movements for colonial liberation, from the Maghreb to Indonesia. However, it would have been perfectly easy to find parts of the globe whose citizens were remote from both, notably the United States of America, as well as large regions of sub-Saharan colonial Africa. Yet the First World War was followed by one kind of breakdown that was genuinely worldwide, at least wherever men and women were enmeshed in, or operated by, impersonal market transactions. Indeed, the proud USA itself, so far from being a safe haven from the convulsions of less fortunate continents, became the epicentre of this, the largest global earthquake ever to be measured on the economic historians' Richter Scale – the Great Inter-war Depression. In a sentence: between the wars the capitalist world economy appeared to collapse. Nobody quite knew how it might recover.

The operations of a capitalist economy are never smooth, and fluctuations of various length, often very severe, are integral parts of this way of running the affairs of the world. The so-called 'trade cycle' of boom and slump was familiar to all businessmen from the nineteenth century. It was expected to repeat itself, with variations, every seven to eleven years. A rather more lengthy periodicity had first begun to attract attention at the end of the nineteenth century, as observers looked back on the unexpected peripeties of the previous decades. A spectacular, record-breaking global boom from about 1850 to the early 1870s had been followed by twenty-odd years of economic uncertainties (economic writers, somewhat misleadingly, spoke of a Great Depression), and then another evidently secular forward surge of the world economy (see *Age of Capital, Age of Empire,* chapter 2). In the early 1920s a Russian economist, N.D. Kondratiev, later an early victim of Stalin, discerned a pattern of economic development since the late eighteenth century through a series of 'long waves' of from fifty to sixty years, though neither he nor anyone else could give a satisfactory explanation of these movements, and indeed sceptical statisticians have even denied their existence. They have since been universally familiar in the specialist literature under his name. Kondratiev, by the way, concluded at the time that the long wave of the world economy was due for its downturn*. He was right.

In the past, waves and cycles, long, medium and short, had been accepted by businessmen and economists rather as farmers accept the weather, which also has its ups and downs. There was nothing to be done about them: they created opportunities or problems, they could lead to bonanzas or bankruptcy for individuals or industries, but only socialists who, with Karl Marx, believed that cycles were part of a process by which capitalism generated what would in the end prove insuperable internal contradictions, thought they put the existence of the economic system as such at risk. The world economy was expected to go on growing and advancing, as it had patently done, except for the sudden and shortlived catastrophes of cyclical slumps, for over a century. What was novel about the new situation was that, probably for the first, and so far the only, time in the history of capitalism, its fluctuations seemed to be genuinely system-endangering. What is more, in important respects the secular rise of its curve seemed to break.

The history of the world economy since the Industrial Revolution had been one of accelerating technological progress, of continuous but uneven economic growth, and of increasing 'globalization', that is to say of an increasingly elaborate and intricate worldwide division of labour; an increasingly dense network of flows and exchanges that bound every part of the world economy to the global system. Technical progress continued and even accelerated in the Age of Catastrophe, both transforming, and being transformed by, the era of world wars. Although in the lives of most men and women the central economic experiences of the age were cataclysmic, culminating in the Great Slump of 1929–33, economic

---

* That good predictions have proved possible on the basis of Kondratiev Long Waves – this is not very common in economics – has convinced many historians and even some economists that there is something in them, even if we don't know what.

growth during these decades did not cease. It merely slowed down. In the largest and richest economy of the time, the USA, the average rate of growth of the GNP per head of the population between 1913 and 1938 was only a modest 0.8 per cent per year. World industrial production grew by just over 80 per cent in the twenty-five years after 1913, or at about half the rate of the previous quarter-century (W.W. Rostow; 1978, p. 662). As we shall see (chapter 9) the contrast with the post-1945 era was to be even more spectacular. Still, if some Martian had been observing the curve of economic movements from sufficiently far off to overlook the jagged fluctuations which human beings experienced on the ground, he, she or it would have concluded that the world economy was unquestionably continuing to expand.

Yet in one respect it patently was not. The globalization of the economy, it seemed, had stopped advancing in the inter-war years. Any way we measure it, the integration of the world economy stagnated or regressed. The pre-war years had been the greatest period of mass migration in recorded history, but now these streams dried out, or rather, were dammed by the disruptions of wars and political restrictions. In the last fifteen years before 1914 almost fifteen millions had landed in the USA. In the next fifteen years the flow shrunk to five-and-a-half millions; in the 1930s and the war years it came to an almost complete stop: less than three quarters of a million entered the USA (Historical Statistics I, p.105, Table C 89–101). Iberian migration, overwhelmingly to Latin America, fell from one-and-three-quarter millions in the decade 1911–20 to less than a quarter of a million in the 1930s. World trade recovered from the disruptions of war and post-war crisis to climb a little above 1913 in the late twenties, then fell during the slump, but at the end of the Age of Catastrophe (1948) it was not significantly higher in volume than before the First World War (W.W. Rostow 1978, p. 669). Between the early 1890s and 1913 it had more than doubled. Between 1948 and 1971 it would quintuple. This stagnation is all the more surprising, when we remember that the First World War produced a substantial number of new states in Europe and the Middle East. So many more miles of state borders should have led us to expect an automatic increase in interstate trade, as commercial dealings that had once taken place within the same country (say, Austria-Hungary or Russia) were now classified as international. (World trade statistics only measure trade that crosses frontiers.) Just so the tragic flood of post-war and post-revolution refugees, whose numbers were already to be measured in millions (see chapter 11) should have led us to expect a growth rather than a shrinking of global migration. During the Great Slump even the international flow of capital seemed to dry up. Between 1927 and 1933 international lending dropped by over 90 per cent.

Why this stagnation? Various reasons have been suggested, for instance that the largest of the world's national economies, the USA, was getting virtually self-sufficient, except in the supply of a few raw materials; it had never been particularly dependent on foreign trade. However, even countries which had been heavy traders, like Britain and the Scandinavian states, showed the same trend. Contemporaries focused on a more obvious cause for alarm, and they were almost certainly right. Each state now did its best to protect its economy against threats from outside, that is to say against a world economy that was visibly in major trouble.

Both businessmen and governments had originally expected that, after the temporary disruptions of the world war, somehow the world economy would return to the happy days before 1914, which they regarded as normal. And indeed the immediate post-war boom, at least in the countries not disrupted by revolution and civil war, looked promising, even though both business and governments shook their heads over the enormously strengthened power of labour and its unions, which looked like raising production costs via higher wages and shorter hours. Yet readjustment proved more difficult than expected. Prices and the boom collapsed in 1920. This undermined the power of labour – British unemployment never thereafter fell much below 10 percent and the unions lost half their members over the next twelve years – thus once again tilting the balance firmly towards the employers, but prosperity remained elusive.

The Anglo-Saxon world, the wartime neutrals and Japan did what they could to deflate, i.e. to get their economies back to the old and firm principles of stable currencies guaranteed by sound finance and the gold standard, which had been unable to resist the strains of war. Indeed, they more or less succeeded in doing so between 1922 and 1926. However, the great zone of defeat and convulsion from Germany in the West to Soviet Russia in the East saw a spectacular collapse of the monetary system, comparable only to that in part of the post-communist world after 1989. In the extreme case – Germany in 1923 – the currency unit was reduced to one million millionth of its 1913 value, that is to say in practice the value of money was reduced to zero. Even in less extreme cases, the consequences were drastic. The writer's grandfather, whose insurance policy matured during the Austrian inflation,* liked to tell the story of

---

* Over the nineteenth century, at the end of which prices were much lower than they had been at the beginning, people got so used to stable or falling prices, that the mere word *inflation* was enough to describe what we now call 'hyper-inflation'.

drawing this large sum in devalued currency, and finding it was just enough to buy himself a drink in his favourite café.

In short, private savings disappeared totally, thus creating an almost complete vacuum of working capital for business, which does much to explain the massive reliance of the German economy on foreign loans in the following years. This made it unusually vulnerable when the slump came. The situation in the USSR was hardly better, though wiping out private savings in monetary form had neither the same economic nor the same political consequences there. When the great inflation was ended in 1922–23, essentially by the decision of governments to stop printing paper money in unlimited quantities and to change the currency, people in Germany who had relied on fixed incomes and savings were wiped out, although at least a tiny fraction of the value of money had been saved in Poland, Hungary and Austria. However, the traumatic effect of the experience on the local middle and lower-middle classes may be imagined. It made central Europe ready for fascism. Devices for getting populations used to long periods of pathological price inflation (e.g. by the 'indexation' of wages and other incomes – the word was first used around 1960) were not invented until after the Second World War.*

By 1924 these post-war hurricanes had calmed down, and it seemed possible to look forward to a return to what an American president christened 'normalcy'. There was indeed something like a return to global growth, even though some of the producers of raw materials and foodstuffs, including notably North American farmers, were troubled because prices of primary products turned down again after a brief recovery. The roaring 1920s were not a golden age on the farms of the USA. Moreover, unemployment in most of Western Europe remained astonishingly, and by pre-1914 standards, pathologically, high. It is hard to remember that even in the boom years of the 1920s (1924–29) it averaged between 10 and 12 per cent in Britain, Germany and Sweden, and no less than 17–18 per cent in Denmark and Norway. Only the USA, with average unemployment of about 4 per cent, was an economy really under full steam. Both facts pointed to serious weaknesses in the economy. The sagging of primary prices (which were prevented from falling further by building up increasingly large stockpiles) simply demonstrated that the demand for them could not keep pace with the capacity to produce. Nor should we overlook the fact that the boom, such as it was, was largely fuelled by the enormous flows of international capital

---

* In the Balkans and the Baltic states governments never entirely lost control of inflation, though it was serious.

which swept across the industrial worlds in those years, and notably to Germany. That country alone, which took about half of all the world's capital exports in 1928, borrowed between 20,000 and 30,000 billion Marks, half of it probably on short term (Arndt, p. 47; Kindleberger, 1986). Once again this made the German economy highly vulnerable, as was proved when the American money was withdrawn after 1929.

It therefore came as no great surprise to anyone except the boosters of smalltown America, whose image became familiar to the Western world at this time through the American novelist Sinclair Lewis' *Babbitt* (1922), that the world economy was in trouble again a few years later. The Communist International had indeed predicted another economic crisis at the height of the boom, expecting it – or so its spokesmen believed or pretended to believe – to lead to a new round of revolutions. It actually produced the opposite at short notice. However, what nobody expected, probably not even the revolutionaries in their most sanguine moments, was the extraordinary universality and depth of the crisis which began, as even non–historians know, with the New York Stock Exchange crash of 29 October 1929. It amounted to something very close to the collapse of the capitalist world economy, which now seemed gripped in a vicious circle where every downward movement of the economic indices (other than unemployment, which moved to ever more astronomic heights) reinforced the decline in all the others.

As the admirable experts of the League of Nations observed, though nobody took much notice of them, a dramatic recession of the North American industrial economy, soon spread to the other industrial heartland, Germany (Ohlin, 1931). US industrial production fell by about a third from 1929 to 1931, German production by about the same, but these are smoothing averages. Thus in the USA, Westinghouse, the great electrical firm, lost two-thirds of its sales between 1929 and 1933, while its net income fell by 76 per cent in two years (Schatz, 1983, p. 60). There was a crisis in primary production, both of foodstuffs and raw materials, as their prices, no longer kept up by building stocks as before, went into free fall. The price of tea and wheat fell by two thirds, the price of raw silk by three quarters. This prostrated – to name but the countries listed by the League of Nations in 1931 – Argentina, Australia, the Balkan countries, Bolivia, Brazil, (British) Malaya, Canada, Chile, Colombia, Cuba, Egypt, Ecuador, Finland, Hungary, India, Mexico, the Netherlands Indies (the present Indonesia), New Zealand, Paraguay, Peru, Uruguay and Venezuela, whose international trade depended heavily on a few primary commodities. In short, it made the Depression global in the literal sense.

The economies of Austria, Czechoslovakia, Greece, Japan, Poland and Great Britain, extremely sensitive to the seismic shocks coming from the West (or East), were equally shaken. The Japanese silk industry had tripled its output in fifteen years to supply the vast and growing US market for silk stockings, which now disappeared temporarily – and so did the market for the 90 per cent of Japan's silk that then went to America. Meanwhile the price of the other great staple of Japanese agricultural production, rice, also plummeted, as it did in all the great rice-producing zones of South and East Asia. Since, as it happened, the wheat price collapsed even more completely than that of rice, and wheat was therefore cheaper, many Orientals are said to have switched from the one to the other. However, the boom in chapattis and noodles, if there was one, worsened the situation of farmers in rice-exporting countries like Burma, French Indochina and Siam (now Thailand) (Latham, 1981, p. 178). Farmers tried to compensate for falling prices by growing and selling more crops, and this made prices sink even further.

For farmers dependent on the market, especially the export market, this meant ruin, unless they could retreat to the traditional ultimate redoubt of the peasant, subsistence production. This was indeed still possible in much of the dependent world, and insofar as most Africans, South and East Asians and Latin Americans were still peasants, it undoubtedly cushioned them. Brazil became a byword for the waste of capitalism and the depth of the Depression, as its coffee-growers desperately tried to prevent the price-collapse by burning coffee instead of coal on their steam railroad engines. (Between two thirds and three quarters of the coffee sold on the world market came from that country.) Nevertheless the Great Slump was far more tolerable for the still overwhelmingly rural Brazilians than the economic cataclysms of the 1980s; especially since poor people's expectations of what they could get of an economy were still extremely modest.

Still, even in colonial peasant countries someone suffered, as is suggested by the drop of about two thirds in the importation of sugar, flour, canned fish and rice into the Gold Coast (now Ghana), where the bottom had fallen out of the (peasant-based) cocoa market, not to mention the 98 per cent drop in the imports of gin (Ohlin, 1931, p. 52).

For those who, by definition, had no control over or access to the means of production (unless they could go home to a peasant family in some village), namely the men and women hired for wages, the primary consequence of the slump was unemployment on an unimagined and unprecedented scale, and for longer than anyone had ever expected. At the worst period of the Slump (1932–33) 22–23 per cent of the British and

Belgian labour force, 24 per cent of the Swedish, 27 per cent of the US, 29 per cent of the Austrian, 31 per cent of the Norwegian, 32 per cent of the Danish and no less than 44 per cent of the German workers were out of jobs. What is equally to the point, even the recovery after 1933 did not reduce the average unemployment of the 1930s below 16–17 per cent in Britain and Sweden or below 20 per cent in the rest of Scandinavia, Austria and the USA. The only Western state which succeeded in eliminating unemployment was Nazi Germany between 1933 and 1938. There had been nothing like this economic catastrophe in the lives of working people for as long as anyone could remember.

What made it even more dramatic was that public provision for social security, including unemployment relief, was either non-existent, as in the USA, or, by late twentieth-century standards, extremely meagre, especially for the long-term unemployed. That is why security had always been such a vital concern of working people: protection against the terrible uncertainties of employment (i.e. wages), sickness or accident and the terrible certainties of an old age without earnings. That is why working people dreamed of seeing their children in modestly paid, but secure and pensionable jobs. Even in the country most fully covered by Unemployment Insurance schemes before the Slump (Great Britain) less than 60 per cent of the labour force were covered by it – and that only because Britain since 1920 had already been forced to adjust to mass unemployment. Elsewhere in Europe (except for Germany, where it was above 40 per cent) the proportion of working people with claims for unemployment relief ranged from zero to about one quarter (Flora, 1983, p. 461). People who had been used to fluctuating employment or to passing spells of cyclical unemployment were desperate when no job turned up anywhere, after their small savings had gone and their credit at the local grocer's shop had been exhausted.

Hence the central, the traumatic, impact of mass unemployment on the politics of the industrialized countries, for that is what first and foremost, the Great Slump meant, to the bulk of their inhabitants. What did it matter to them that economic historians (and indeed logic) can demonstrate that the majority of the nation's labour force, which was in employment even at the worst moments, was actually getting significantly better off, since prices were falling throughout the inter-war years, and the price of foodstuffs fell more rapidly than any other in the worst depression years. The image which dominated at the time was that of soup kitchens, of unemployed 'Hunger Marchers' from smokeless settlements where no steel or ships were made converging on capital cities to denounce those they held responsible. Nor did politicians fail to observe that up to 85 per cent of the membership of the German Communist Party, growing almost as fast as the Nazi Party in the slump years, and, in the last months before Hitler's accession to power, faster, were unemployed (Weber, I, p. 243).

Unemployment was conceived, not surprisingly, as a deep and potentially mortal wound in the body politic. 'Next to war' wrote an editorialist in the London *Times* in the middle of the Second World War, 'unemployment has been the most widespread, the most insidious, and the most corroding malady of our generation: it is the specific social disease of Western civilization in our time' (Arndt, 1944, p. 250). Never before in the history of industrialization could such a passage have been written. It explains more about post-war Western governments' policies than prolonged archival researches.

Curiously enough, the sense of catastrophe and disorientation caused by the Great Slump was perhaps greater among businessmen, economists and politicians than among the masses. Mass unemployment, the collapse of agrarian prices, hit them hard, but they had no doubt that some political solution for these unexpected injustices was available – on the left or on the right – in so far as poor people could ever expect their modest needs to be satisfied. It was precisely the absence of any solutions within the framework of the old liberal economy that made the predicament of the economic decision-makers so dramatic. To meet immediate, short-term crises, they had, as they saw it, to undermine the long-term basis of a flourishing world economy. At a time when world trade fell by 60 per cent in four years (1929–32), states found themselves building increasingly high barriers to protect their national markets and currencies against the world economic hurricanes, knowing quite well that this meant the dismantling of the world system of multilateral trade on which, they believed, world prosperity must rest. The keystone of such a system, the so-called 'most favoured nation status' disappeared from almost 60 per cent of 510 commercial agreements signed between 1931 and 1939 and, where it remained, it was usually in a limited form (Snyder, 1940).* Where would it end? Was there an exit from the vicious circle?

We shall consider the immediate political consequences of this, the most traumatic episode in the history of capitalism, below. However, its most significant long-term implication must be mentioned immediately. In a single sentence: the Great Slump destroyed economic liberalism for

---

* The 'most favoured nation' clause actually means the opposite of what it seems to mean, namely that the commercial partner will be treated on the same terms as the 'most favoured nation' – i.e. *no* nation will be most favoured.

half a century. In 1931–32 Britain, Canada, all of Scandinavia and the USA abandoned the gold standard, always regarded as the foundation of stable international exchanges and by 1936 they had been joined even by those impassioned believers in bullion, the Belgians and Dutch, and finally the very French.* Almost symbolically, Great Britain in 1931 abandoned Free Trade, which had been as central to the British economic identity since the 1840s as the American Constitution is to US political identity. Britain's retreat from the principles of free transactions in a single world economy dramatises the general rush into national self-protection at the time. More specifically, the Great Slump forced Western governments to give social considerations priority over economic ones in their state policies. The dangers of failing to do so – radicalization of the Left and, as Germany and other countries now proved, of the Right – were too menacing.

So governments no longer protected agriculture simply by tariffs against foreign competition, though, where they had done so before, they raised tariff barriers even higher. During the Depression they took to subsidising it by guaranteeing farm prices, buying up surpluses or paying farmers not to produce, as in the USA after 1933. The origins of the bizarre paradoxes of the European Community's 'Common Agricultural Policy', through which in the 1970s and 1980s increasingly exiguous minorities of farmers threatened to bankrupt the Community through the subsidies they enjoyed, go back to the Great Slump.

As for the workers, after the war 'full employment', i.e. the elimination of mass unemployment, became the keystone of economic policy in the countries of a reformed democratic capitalism, whose most celebrated prophet and pioneer, though not the only one, was the British economist John Maynard Keynes (1883–1946). The Keynesian argument for the benefits of eliminating permanent mass unemployment was economic as well as political. Keynesians held, correctly, that the demand which the incomes of fully employed workers must generate, would have the most stimulating effect on depressed economies. Nevertheless, the reason why this means of increasing demand was given such urgent priority – the British government committed itself to it even before the end of the Second World War – was that mass unemployment was believed to be politically and socially explosive, as indeed it had proved to be in the Slump. This belief was so powerful that, when many years later mass

* In the classical form a *gold standard* gives the unit of a currency, e.g. a dollar bill, the value of a particular weight of gold, for which, if necessary, the bank will exchange it.

unemployment returned, and especially during the serious depression of the early 1980s, obervers (including the present author) confidently expected social unrest to occur, and were surprised when it did not (see chapter 14).

This was, of course, largely due to another prophylactic measure taken during, after and as a consequence of the Great Slump: the installation of modern welfare systems. Who can be surprised that the US passed its Social Security Act in 1935? We have become so used to the universal prevalence of ambitious welfare systems in developed states of industrial capitalism – with some exceptions, such as Japan, Switzerland and the USA – that we forget how few 'welfare states' in the modern sense there were before the Second World War. Even the Scandinavian countries were only just beginning to develop them. Indeed, the very term welfare state did not come into use before the 1940s.

The trauma of the Great Slump was underlined by the fact that the one country that had clamorously broken with capitalism appeared to be immune to it: the Soviet Union. While the rest of the world, or at least liberal Western capitalism, stagnated, the USSR was engaged in massive ultra-rapid industrialization under its new Five Year Plans. From 1929 to 1940 Soviet industrial production tripled, at the very least. It rose from 5 per cent of the world's manufactured products in 1929 to 18 per cent in 1938, while during the same period the joint share of the USA, Britain and France, fell from 59 per cent to 52 per cent of the world's total. What was more, there was no unemployment. These achievements impressed foreign observers of all ideologies, including a small but influential flow of socio-economic tourists to Moscow in 1930–35, more than the visible primitiveness and inefficiency of the Soviet economy, or the ruthlessness and brutality of Stalin's collectivisation and mass repression. For what they were trying to come to terms with was not the actual phenomenon of the USSR but the breakdown of their own economic system, the depth of the failure of Western capitalism. What was the secret of the Soviet system? Could anything be learned from it? Echoing Russia's Five Year Plans, 'Plan' and 'Planning' became buzz-words in politics. Social Democratic parties adopted 'plans', as in Belgium and Norway. Sir Arthur Salter, a British civil servant of the utmost distinction and respectability, and a pillar of the Establishment, wrote a book, *Recovery* to demonstrate that a planned society was essential, if the country and the world were to escape from the vicious cycle of the Great Slump. Other British middle-of-the-road civil servants and functionaries set up a non-partisan think-tank called PEP (Political and Economic Planning). Young Conservative politicians like the future prime minister Harold Macmillan

(1894–1986) made themselves spokesmen for 'planning'. Even the very Nazis plagiarized the idea, as Hitler introduced a 'Four Year Plan' in 1933. (For reasons to be considered in the next chapter, the Nazis' own success in dealing with the Slump after 1933 had fewer international repercussions.)

II

Why did the capitalist economy between the wars fail to work? The situation of the USA is a central part of any answer to this question. For if the disruptions of war and post-war Europe, or at least the belligerent countries of Europe, could be made at least partly responsible for the economic troubles there, the USA had been far away from the war, though briefly, if decisively, involved in it. So far from disrupting its economy, the First World War I, like the Second World War, benefited it spectacularly. By 1913 the USA had already become the largest economy in the world, producing over one third of its industrial output – just under the combined total for Gemany, Great Britain and France. In 1929 it produced over 42 per cent of the total world output, as against just under 28 per cent for the three European industrial powers. (Hilgerdt, 1945, Table 1.14.) This is a truly astonishing figure. Concretely, while US steel production rose by about one quarter between 1913 and 1920, steel production in the rest of the world fell by about one third. (Rostow, 1978, p. 194, Table III. 33.) In short, after the end of the first World War the USA was in many ways as internationally dominant an economy as it once again became after the Second World War. It was the Great Slump which temporarily interrupted this ascendancy.

Moreover, the war had not only reinforced its position as the world's greatest industrial producer, but turned it into the world's greatest creditor. The British had lost about a quarter of their global investments during the war, mainly those in the USA, which they had to sell to buy war supplies; the French lost about half of theirs, mainly through revolution and breakdown in Europe. Meanwhile the Americans, who had begun the war as a debtor country, ended it as the main international lender. Since the USA concentrated its operations in Europe and the western hemisphere (the British were still by far the biggest investors in Asia and Africa) their impact on Europe was decisive.

In short, there is no explanation of the world economic crisis without the USA. It was, after all, both the premier exporting nation of the world in the 1920s and, after Great Britain, the premier importing nation. As for raw materials and foodstuffs, it imported almost 40 per cent of all the imports of the fifteen most commercial nations, a fact which goes a long way to explaining the disastrous impact of the slump on the producers of commodities like wheat, cotton, sugar, rubber, silk, copper, tin and coffee (Lary, pp. 28–29). By the same token, it was to become the principal victim of the Slump. If its imports fell by 70 per cent between 1929 and 1932, its exports fell at the same rate. World trade dipped by less than a third from 1929 to 1939, but US exports crashed by almost half.

This is not to underestimate the strictly European roots of trouble, which were largely political in origin. At the Versailles peace conference (1919) vast but undefined payments had been imposed on Germany as 'reparations' for the cost of the war and the damage done to the victorious powers. To justify these a clause had also been inserted into the peace treaty making Germany *solely* responsible for the war (the so-called 'war-guilt' clause) which was both historically doubtful and proved to be a gift to German nationalism. The amount Germany was to pay remained vague, as a compromise between the position of the USA, which proposed fixing Germany's payments according to the country's capacity to pay, and the other Allies – chiefly the French – who insisted on recovering the entire costs of the war. Their, or at least France's, real object was to keep Germany weak and to have a means of putting pressure on it. In 1921 the sum was fixed at 132 billion (thousand million) Gold Marks, i.e. \$33 billions at the time, which everyone knew to be a fantasy.

'Reparations' led to endless debates, periodic crises and settlements under American auspices, since the USA, to its former Allies' displeasure, wished to to link the question of Germany's debts to them, to that of their own wartime debts to Washington. These were almost as crazy as the sums demanded of the Germans, which amounted to one and a half times the entire national income of the country in 1929; the British debts to the US amounted to half the British national income; the French debts to two-thirds (Hill, 1988, pp. 15–16). A 'Dawes Plan' in 1924 actually fixed a real sum for Germany to pay annually; a 'Young Plan' in 1929 modified the repayment scheme and, incidentally, set up the Bank of International Settlements in Basel (Switzerland), the first of the international financial institutions which were to multiply after the Second World War. (At the time of writing it is still in business.) For practical purposes all payments, German and Allied, ceased in 1932. Only Finland ever paid its war debts to the USA.

Without going into the details, two questions were at issue. *First*, there was the point made by the young John Maynard Keynes, who wrote a savage critique of the Versailles conference in which he took part as a junior member of the British delegation: *The Economic Consequences of the Peace* (1920). Without a restoration of the German economy, he argued, the restoration of a stable liberal civilization and economy in Europe would be impossible. The French policy of keeping Germany feeble for the sake of French 'security' was counter-productive. In fact, the French were too weak to impose their policy, even when they briefly occupied the industrial heartland of West Germany in 1923 on the excuse that the Germans were refusing to pay. Eventually they had to tolerate a policy of German 'fulfilment' after 1924 which strengthened the German economy. But, *second*, there was the question of how reparations were to be paid. Those who wanted to keep Germany weak wanted cash rather than (as was rational) goods out of current production, or at least out of the income from German exports, since this would have strengthened the German economy against its competitors. In effect they forced Germany into heavy borrowing, so that such reparations as were paid came out of the massive (American) loans of the mid-1920s. For Germany's rivals this seemed to have the additional advantage that Germany ran into deep debt rather than expanding its exports to achieve an external balance. In fact, German imports soared. However, the whole arrangement, as we have already seen, made both Germany and Europe highly sensitive to the decline in American lending which began even before the crisis and the shutting of the American loan-tap, which followed the Wall Street Crisis of 1929. The entire house of cards of reparations collapsed during the Slump. By then the end of these payments had no positive effects on Germany or the world economy, because this had broken down as an integrated system and so, in 1931–33, had all arrangements for international payments.

However, wartime and post-war disruptions and political complications in Europe can only partly explain the severity of the inter-war economic breakdown. Speaking economically, we can look at it in two ways.

The first will see chiefly a striking and growing imbalance in the international economy, due to the asymmetry in development between the USA and the rest of the world. The world system, it can be argued, did not work, because, unlike Great Britain, which had been its centre before 1914, the USA did not much need the rest of the world, and therefore, again unlike Great Britain, which knew that the world payments system rested on the Pound Sterling and saw to it that it remained stable, the USA did not bother to act as a global stabilizer. The USA did not need the world much, because after the First World War it needed to import less capital, labour and (relatively speaking) fewer commodities than ever – except for some raw materials. Its exports, though internationally important – Hollywood virtually monopolised the international movie market – made a far smaller contribution to the national income than in any other industrial country. How significant this, as it were, withdrawal of the USA from the world economy was, may be debated. However, it is quite clear that this explanation of the Slump was one which influenced US economists and politicians in the 1940s, and helped to convince Washington in the war years to take over responsibility for the stability of the world economy after 1945 (Kindleberger, 1973).

The second perspective on the Depression fixes on the failure of the world economy to generate enough demand for a lasting expansion. The foundations of the prosperity of the 1920s, as we have seen, were weak, even in the USA, where farming was virtually already in depression, and money wages, contrary to the myth of the great jazz age, were not rising dramatically, and actually stagnant in the last mad years of the boom (Historical Statistics of the USA, I, p. 164, Table D722–727). What was happening, as often happens in free market booms, was that, with wages lagging, profits rose disproportionately and the prosperous got a larger slice of the national cake. But as mass demand could not keep pace with the rapidly increasing productivity of the industrial system in the heyday of Henry Ford, the result was over-production and speculation. This, in turn, triggered off the collapse. Once again, whatever the arguments among historians and economists, who still continue to debate the issue, contemporaries with a strong interest in government policies were deeply impressed with the weakness of demand; not least John Maynard Keynes.

When the collapse came, it was of course all the more drastic in the USA because in fact a lagging expansion of demand had been beefed up by means of an enormous expansion of consumer credit. (Readers who remember the later 1980s may find themselves on familiar territory.) Banks, already hurt by the speculative real-estate boom which, with the usual help of self-deluding optimists and mushrooming financial crookery,* had reached its peak some years before the Big Crash, loaded with bad debts, refused new housing loans or to refinance existing ones. This did not stop them from failing by the thousands,† while (in 1933) nearly half of all US home mortgages were in default and a thousand

---

* Not for nothing were 1920s the decade of psychologist Emile Coué (1857–1926) who popularised optimistic auto-suggestion by means of the slogan, constantly to be repeated: 'Every day in every way I am getting better and better.'

† The US banking system did not permit the European kind of giant bank with a nation-wide system of branches, and therefore consisted of relatively weak local or, best, state-wide banks.

properties a day were being foreclosed (Miles et al., 1991, p. 108). Automobile purchasers alone owed $1,400 million out of a total personal indebtedness of $6,500 million in short- and medium-term loans (Ziebura, p. 49). What made the economy so much more vulnerable to this credit boom was that customers did not use their loans to buy the traditional mass consumption goods which kept body and soul together, and were therefore pretty inelastic: food, clothing and the like. However poor one is, one can't reduce one's demand for groceries below a certain point; and that demand will not double if one's income doubles. Instead they bought the durable consumer goods of the modern consumer society which the USA was even then pioneering. But the purchase of cars and houses could be readily postponed, and, in any case, they had and have a very high income elasticity of demand.

So, unless a slump was expected to be brief, or was short, and confidence in the future was not undermined, the effect of such a crisis could be dramatic. Thus automobile production in the USA *halved* between 1929 and 1931 or, at a much lower level, the production of poor people's gramophone records ('race' records and jazz records addressed to a black public) virtually ceased for a while. In short, 'unlike railroads or more efficient ships or the introduction of steel and machine tools – which cut costs – the new products and way of life required high and expanding levels of income and a high degree of confidence about the future, to be rapidly diffused' (Rostow, 1978, p. 219). But that is exactly what was collapsing.

The worst cyclical slump sooner or later comes to an end, and after 1932 there were increasingly clear signs that the worst was over. Indeed, some economies roared ahead. Japan and, on a more modest scale, Sweden, reached almost twice the pre-slump level of production by the end of the 1930s, and by 1938 the German (though not the Italian) economy was 25 per cent above 1929. Even sluggish economies like the British showed plenty of signs of dynamism. Yet somehow the expected upsurge did not return. The world remained in depression. This was most visible in the greatest of all the economies, the USA, for the various experiments in stimulating the economy undertaken under President F.D. Roosevelt's 'New Deal' – sometimes inconsistently – did not really live up to their economic promise. A strong upsurge was followed, in 1937–38, by another economic crash, though on a rather more modest scale than after 1929. The leading sector of American industry, automobile production, never regained its 1929 peak. In 1938 it was little more than it had been in 1920 (Historical Statistics, II, p. 716). Looking back from the 1990s we are struck by the pessimism of intelligent commentators. Able and brilliant economists saw the future of capitalism, left to itself, as one of stagnation. This view, anticipated in Keynes' pamphlet against the Versailles peace treaty, naturally became popular in the USA after the Slump. Must not any mature economy tend to become a stagnating one? As the proponent of another pessimistic prognosis for capitalism, the Austrian economist Schumpeter, put it, 'In any prolonged period of economic malaise economists, falling in like other people with the humours of their time, proffer theories that pretend to show that depression has come to stay' (Schumpeter, 1954, p. 1172). Perhaps historians looking back on the period from 1973 to the end of the Short Twentieth Century from an equal distance, will be equally struck by the persistent reluctance of the 1970s and 1980s to envisage the possibility of a general depression of the world capitalist economy.

All this in spite of the fact that the 1930s were a decade of considerable technological innovation in industry, for instance, in the development of plastics. Indeed, in one field – entertainment and what later came to be called 'the media' – the inter-war years saw the major breakthrough, at least in the Anglo-Saxon world, with the triumph of mass radio, and the Hollywood movie industry, not to mention the modern rotogravure illustrated press (see chapter 6). Perhaps it is not quite so surprising that the giant movie theatres rose like dream palaces in the grey cities of mass unemployment, for cinema tickets were remarkably cheap, the youngest, as well as the oldest, disproportionately hit by unemployment then as later, had time to kill, and, as the sociologists observed, during the depression husbands and wives were more likely to share joint leisure activities than before (Stouffer, Lazarsfeld, pp. 55, 92).

III

The Great Slump confirmed intellectuals, activists and ordinary citizens in the belief that something was fundamentally wrong with the world they lived in. Who knew what could be done about it? Certainly few of those in authority over their countries, and certainly not those who tried to steer a course by the traditional navigational instruments of secular liberalism or traditional faith, and by the charts of the nineteenth century seas which were plainly no longer to be trusted. How much confidence did economists deserve, however brilliant, who demonstrated, with great lucidity, that the Slump in which even they lived, could not happen in a properly conducted free-market society, since (according to an economic law named after an early nineteenth century Frenchman) no overproduction was possible which did not very soon correct itself? In 1933 it was not easy to believe, for instance, that where consumer demand, and therefore consumption, fell in a depression, the rate of interest would fall by just as much as was needed to stimulate investment, so that the increased investment demand would exactly fill the gap left by the smaller consumer demand. As unemployment soared, it did not seem plausible to believe (as the British Treasury apparently did) that public works would not increase employment at all,because the money spent on them would merely be diverted from the private sector, which would otherwise have generated just as much employment. Economists who simply advised leaving the economy alone, governments whose first instincts, apart from protecting the gold standard by deflationary policies, was to stick to financial orthodoxy, balance budgets and cut costs, were visibly not making the situation better. Indeed, as the depression contin-ued, it was argued with considerable force not least by J.M. Keynes who consequently became the most influential economist of the next forty years – that they were making the depression worse. Those of us who lived through the years of the Great Slump still find it almost impossible to understand how the orthodoxies of the pure free market, then so obviously discredited, once again came to preside over a global period of depression in the late 1980s and 1990s, which, once again, they were equally unable to understand or to deal with. Still, this strange phenom-enon should remind us of the major characteristic of history which it exemplifies: the incredible shortness of memory of both the theorists and practitioners of economics. It also provides a vivid illustration of society's need for historians, who are the professional remembrancers of what their fellow-citizens wish to forget.

In any case, what was a 'free market economy' when an economy increasingly dominated by huge corporations made nonsense of the term 'perfect competition' and economists critical of Karl Marx could observe that he had been proved right, not least in his prediction of the growing concentration of capital (Leontiev, 1977, p. 78). One did not have to be a Marxist, or show an interest in Marx, to observe how unlike the economy of nineteenth century free competition inter-war capitalism was. Indeed, well before the Wall Street crash, an intelligent Swiss banker observed that the failure of economic liberalism (and, he added, pre-1917 socialism) to maintain themselves as universal programmes, explained the pressure towards autocratic economics – fascist, communist or under the auspices of large corporations independent of their shareholders (Somary, 1929, pp. 174, 193). And by the end of the 1930s the liberal orthodoxies of free-market competition were so far away that the world economy could be seen as a triple system composed of a market sector, an inter-governmental sector (within which planned or controlled economies such as Japan, Turkey, Germany and the Soviet Union conducted their transactions with each other) and a sector of international public or quasi-public authorities which regulated certain parts of the economy (e.g. by international commodity agreements) (Staley, 1939, p. 231).

It is therefore not surprising that the effects of the Great Slump on both politics and public thinking were dramatic and immediate. Unlucky the government which happened to be in office during the cataclysm, whether it was on the right, like Herbert Hoover's presidency in the USA (1928–32), or on the left, like Britain's and Australia's labour governments. The change was not always as immediate as in Latin America, where twelve countries changed government or regime in 1930–31, ten of them by military coup. Nevertheless, by the middle 1930s there were few states whose politics had not changed very substantially from what they had been before the Crash. In Europe and Japan there was a striking move to the right, except in Scandinavia, where Sweden entered its half-century of social-democratic rule in 1932, and in Spain, where the Bourbon monarchy gave way to an unhappy, and as it turned out shortlived, Republic in 1931. More of this in the next chapter, though it must be said immediately that the almost simultaneous victory of nationalist, warlike, and actively aggressive regimes in two major military powers – Japan (1931) and Germany (1933) – constituted the most far-reaching and sinister political consequence of the Great Depression. The gates to the Second World War were opened in 1931.

The strengthening of the radical Right was reinforced, at least during the worst period of the Slump, by the spectacular setbacks for the revolutionary Left. So far from initiating another round of social revolution, as the Communist International had expected, the Depression reduced the international communist movement outside the USSR to a state of unprecedented feebleness. This was admittedly due in some measure to the suicidal policy of the Comintern, which not only grossly underestimated the danger of National Socialism in Germany, but pursued a policy of sectarian isolation that seems quite incredible in retrospect, by deciding that its main enemy was the organized mass labour movement of social-democratic and labour parties (described as 'social-fascist').* Certainly by 1934, after Hitler had destroyed the German CP

---

* This went so far that in 1933 Moscow insisted that the Italian communist leader P. Togliatti withdraw the suggestion that, perhaps, social-democracy was not the primary danger, at least in Italy. By then Hitler had actually come to power. The Comintern did not change its line until 1934.

(KPD), once Moscow's hope of world revolution and still by far the largest and apparently most formidable and growing section of the International, when even the Chinese Communists, expelled from their rural guerrilla bases, were no more than a harried caravan on its Long March to some distant and safe refuge, very little seemed to be left of a significant organized international revolutionary movement, legal or even illegal. In the Europe of 1934 only the French Communist Party still had a genuine political presence. In Fascist Italy, ten years after the March on Rome and in the depth of the international slump, Mussolini felt sufficiently confident actually to release some imprisoned communists to celebrate that anniversary (Spriano, 1969, p. 397). All this was to change within a few years (see chapter 5). But the fact remains that the immediate result of the Slump, at all events in Europe, was the exact opposite of what social revolutionaries had expected.

Nor was this decline of the Left confined to the communist sector, for with Hitler's victory the German Social Democratic Party disappeared from sight, while a year later Austrian social democracy fell after a brief armed resistance. The British Labour Party had already become a victim of the Slump, or rather of its belief in nineteenth century economic orthodoxy, in 1931, and its trade unions, which had lost half their members since 1920, were weaker than they had been in 1913. Most of European socialism had its backs to the wall.

Outside Europe, however, the situation was different. The northern parts of the Americas moved quite markedly to the left, as the USA, under its new President Franklin D. Roosevelt (1933–45), experimented with a more radical New Deal, and Mexico, under President Lázaro Cardenas (1934–40) revived the original dynamism of the early Mexican Revolution, especially in the matter of agrarian reform. Quite powerful social/political movements arose on the crisis-stricken prairies of Canada. *Social Credit* and the Cooperative Commonwealth Federation (today's *New Democratic Party*), both on the Left by 1930s criteria.

It is not so easy to characterize the political impact of the slump on the remainder of Latin America, for if its governments or ruling parties fell like ninepins as the collapse in the world price of their export staples broke their finances, they did not all fall in the same direction. Still, more of them fell towards the Left than to the Right, even if only briefly. Argentina entered the era of military government after a lengthy period of civilian rule; and though fascist-minded leaders like General Uriburu (1930–32) were soon sidelined, it clearly moved to the Right, even if a traditionalist Right. Chile, on the other hand, used the Slump to overthrow one of its rare military president-dictators, before the era of General Pinochet, Carlos Ibañez (1927–31), and moved, in a stormy fashion, towards the Left. It actually passed through a momentary 'Socialist Republic' in 1932, under the splendidly named Colonel Marmaduke Grove, and later developed a successful Popular Front on the European model (see chapter 5). In Brazil the Slump ended the oligarchic 'old Republic' of 1889–1930 and brought to power Getulio Vargas, best described as a nationalist-populist (see page 135). He dominated his country's history for the next twenty years. The shift in Peru was much more clearly to the Left, though the most powerful of the new parties, the American Popular Revolutionary Alliance (APRA) – one of the few successful mass working-classed-based parties of the European type in the western hemisphere * – failed in its revolutionary ambitions (1930–32). The change in Colombia was even more clearly to the Left. The Liberals, under a reform-minded president much influenced by Roosevelt's New Deal took over after almost thirty years of Conservative rule. The radical shift was even more marked in Cuba, where Roosevelt's inauguration allowed the inhabitants of this offshore US protectorate to overthrow a hated and, even by the then prevailing Cuban standards, unusually corrupt President.

In the vast colonial sector of the world, the Slump brought a marked increase in anti-imperialist activity, partly because of the collapse of the commodity prices on which colonial economies (or at least their public finances and middle classes) depended, partly because the metropolitan countries themselves rushed to protect their agriculture and employment, irrespective of the effects of such policies on their colonies. In short, European states whose economic decisions were being determined by domestic factors, could not in the long term keep together empires with an infinite complexity of producer interests (Holland, 1985, p. 13) (see chapter 7).

For this reason, in most of the colonial world the Slump marked the effective beginning of indigenous political and social discontent, which could not but be directed against the (colonial) government, even where political nationalist movements did not emerge until after the Second World War. In both (British) West Africa and the Caribbean social unrest now made its appearance. It grew directly out of the crisis of local export crops (cocoa and sugar). However, even in countries with already developed anti-colonial national movements, the depression years brought a sharpening of conflict, particularly where political agitation had reached

* The others were the Chilean and Cuban Communist Parties.

the masses. These, after all, were the years of the expansion of the Moslem Brotherhood in Egypt (founded 1928) and of the second mobilisation of the Indian masses by Gandhi (1931) (see chapter 7). Perhaps the victory of the Republican ultras under De Valera in the Irish elections of 1932 should also be seen as a belated anti-colonial reaction to the economic breakdown.

Probably nothing demonstrates both the globality of the Great Slump and the profundity of its impact more than this rapid bird's eye view of the virtually universal political upheavals it produced within a period measured in months or single years, from Japan to Ireland, from Sweden to New Zealand, from Argentina to Egypt. Yet the depth of its impact is not to be judged only, or even mainly, by its short-term political effects, dramatic though these often were. It was a catastrophe which destroyed all hope of restoring the economy, and the society, of the long nineteenth century. The period 1929–33 was a canyon which henceforth made a return to 1913 not merely impossible, but unthinkable. Old-fashioned liberalism was dead or seemed doomed. Three options now competed for intellectual-political hegemony. Marxist communism was one. After all, Marx's own predictions seemed to be coming true, as the American Economic Association itself was told in 1938 and, even more impressively, the USSR appeared to be immune to the catastrophe. A capitalism shorn of its belief in the optimality of free markets and reformed by a sort of unofficial marriage or permanent liaison with the moderate social-democracy of non-communist labour movements was the second, and, after World War, proved to be the most effective. However, in the short run it was not so much a conscious programme or policy alternative as a sense that once the Slump was over, such a thing must never be allowed to happen again and, in the best of cases, a readiness to experiment stimulated by the evident failure of classical free-market liberalism. Thus the Swedish social-democratic policy after 1932 was a conscious reaction to the failures of the economic orthodoxy that had dominated the disastrous British Labour government of 1929–31, at all events in the opinion of one of its major architects, Gunnar Myrdal. An alternative theory to the bankrupt free market economics was only in the process of elaboration. J.M. Keynes' *General Theory of Employment, Interest and Money*, the most influential contribution to it, was not published until 1936. An alternative government practice, the macro-economic steering and management of the economy based on national income accounting did not develop until the Second World War and after, though, perhaps with an eye on the USSR, governments and other public entities in the 1930s increasingly took to seeing the national economy as a whole and estimating the size of its total product or income.*

The third option was fascism, which the slump transformed into a world movement, and, more to the point, a world danger. Fascism in its German version (National Socialism) benefited both from the German intellectual tradition which (unlike the Austrian one) had been hostile to the neoclassical theories of economic liberalism that had become the international orthodoxy since the 1880s, and from a ruthless government determined to get rid of unemployment at all costs. It dealt with the Great Slump, it must be said, rapidly and more successfully than any other (the record of Italian fascism was less impressive). However, this was not its major appeal in a Europe that had largely lost its bearings. But as the tide of fascism rose with the Great Slump, it became increasingly clear that in the Age of Catastrophe not only peace, social stability and the economy, but also the political institutions and intellectual values of nineteenth century liberal bourgeois society, were in retreat or collapse. To this process we must now turn.

---

* The first governments to do so were the USSR and Canada in 1925. By 1939 nine countries had official government statistics of national income, and the League of Nations had estimates for twenty-six in all. Immediately after the Second World War estimates were available for thirty-nine, in the middle 1950s for ninety-three, and since then national income figures, often with only the remotest connection with the realities of their people's livelihood, have become almost as standard for independent states as national flags.

Chapter Four
The Fall of Liberalism

In Nazism we have a phenomenon which seems scarcely capable of subjection to rational analysis. Under a leader who talked in apocalyptic tones of world power or destruction and a regime founded on an utterly repulsive ideology of race-hatred, one of the most culturally and economically advanced countries of Europe planned for war, launched a world conflagration which killed around 50 million people, and perpetrated atrocities – culminating in the mechanized mass murder of millions of Jews – of a nature and scale as to defy imagination. Faced with Auschwitz, the explanatory powers of the historian seem puny indeed.

– Ian Kershaw (1993, pp. 3–4)

To die for the Fatherland, for the Idea! . . . No, that is a cop-out. Even at the front killing's the thing . . . Dying is nothing, it's non-existent. Nobody can imagine his own death. Killing's the thing. That's the frontier to be crossed. Yes, that is a concrete act of your will. Because there you make your will live in another man's.

– From the letter of a young volunteer for the Fascist Social Republic of 1943–45 (Pavone, 1991, p.431)

I

Of all the developments in the Age of Catastrophe, survivors from the nineteenth century were perhaps most shocked by the collapse of the values and institutions of the liberal civilization whose progress their century had taken for granted, at any rate in 'advanced' and 'advancing' parts of the world. These values were a distrust of dictatorship and absolute rule; a commitment to constitutional government with or under freely elected governments and representative assemblies, which guaranteed the rule of law; and an accepted set of citizens' rights and liberties, including freedom of speech, publication and assembly. State and society should be informed by the values of reason, public debate, education, science and the improvability (though not necessarily the perfectibility) of the human condition. These values, it seemed clear, had made progress throughout the century, and were destined to advance further. After all, by 1914 even the two last autocracies of Europe, Russia and Turkey, had made concessions in the direction of constitutional government, and Iran had even borrowed a constitution from Belgium. Before 1914 these values had been challenged only by traditionalist forces like the Roman Catholic church, building defensive barricades of dogma against the superior forces of modernity; by a few intellectual rebels and prophets of doom, mainly from 'good families' and established centres of culture, and thus somehow part of the civilization they challenged; and the forces of democracy, on the whole a new and troubling phenomenon (see *Age of Empire*). The ignorance and backwardness of these masses, their commitment to the overthrow of bourgeois society by social revolution, and the latent human irrationality so easily exploited by demagogues, were indeed a cause for alarm. However, the most immediately dangerous of these new democratic mass movements, the socialist labour movements, were actually, both in theory and in practice, as passionately committed to the values of reason, science, progress, education and individual freedom as anyone. The German Social Democratic Party's May Day medal showed Karl Marx on one side, the Statue of Liberty on the other. Their challenge was to the economy, not to constitutional government and civility. It would not be easy to regard a government headed by Victor Adler, August Bebel or Jean Jaurès as the end of 'civilization as we know it'. In any case such governments seemed, as yet, remote.

Politically, indeed, the institutions of liberal democracy had advanced, and the eruption of barbarism in 1914–18 had, it seemed, only hastened this advance. Except for Soviet Russia, all the regimes emerging from the first World War, old and new, were, basically, elected representative parliamentary regimes, even Turkey. Europe, west of the Soviet border, consisted entirely of such states in 1920. Indeed, the basic institution of liberal constitutional government, elections to representative assemblies and/or presidents was almost universal in the world of independent states by this time, although we must remember that the sixty-five or so independent states of the inter-war period were primarily a European and American phenomenon: one third of the world's population lived under colonial rule. The only states which had no elections whatever in the period 1919–47 were isolated political fossils, namely Ethiopia, Mongolia, Nepal, Saudi Arabia and Yemen. Another five states had only *one* election during this period, which does not argue a strong inclination towards liberal democracy, namely Afghanistan, Kuomintang China, Guatemala, Paraguay and Thailand, then still known as Siam, but the very existence of elections is evidence of at least some penetration of liberal political ideas, at least in theory. One would not, of course, wish to suggest that the mere existence or frequency of elections proves more than this. Neither Iran, which had six elections after 1930, nor Iraq, which had three, could even then count as strongholds of democracy.

Still, representative electoral regimes were frequent enough. And yet the twenty years between Mussolini's so-called 'March on Rome' and the peak of the Axis success in the Second World War saw an accelerating, increasingly catastrophic, retreat of liberal political institutions.

In 1918–20 legislative assemblies were dissolved or became ineffective in two European states, in the 1920s in six, the 1930s in nine, while German occupation destroyed constitutional power in another five during the Second World War. In short, the only European countries with adequately democratic political institutions that functioned without a break during the entire inter-war period were Britain, Finland (only just), the Irish Free State, Sweden and Switzerland.

In the Americas, the other region of independent states, the situation was more mixed, but hardly suggested a general advance of democratic institutions. The list of *consistently* constitutional and non-authoritarian states in the western hemisphere was short: Canada, Colombia, Costa Rica, the USA and that now forgotten 'Switzerland of South America' and its only real democracy, Uruguay. The best we can say is that the movements between the end of the First World War and that of the Second World War were sometimes to the Left as well as to the Right. As for the rest of the globe, much of which consisted of colonies, and was thus non-liberal by definition, it plainly moved away from liberal constitutions, insofar as it had ever had them. In Japan a moderate Liberal regime gave way to a nationalist-militarist one in 1930/31. Thailand made some tentative steps towards constitutional government, and Turkey was taken over by the progressive military modernizer Kemal Atatürk in the early 1920s, not a man to let any elections stand in his way. In the three continents of Asia, Africa and Australasia only Australia and New Zealand were consistently democratic, for the majority of South Africans remained strictly outside the ambit of the white men's constitution.

In short, political liberalism was in full retreat throughout the Age of Catastrophe, a retreat which accelerated sharply after Adolf Hitler became Germany's chancellor in 1933. Taking the world as a whole, there had been perhaps thirty-five or more constitutional and elected governments in 1920 (depending on where we situate some Latin American republics). Until 1938 there were perhaps seventeen such states, in 1944 perhaps twelve out of the global total of sixty-four. The world trend seemed clear.

It may be worth reminding ourselves that in this period the threat to liberal institutions came exclusively from the political right, for between 1945 and 1989 it was assumed, almost as a matter of course, that it came essentially from communism. Until then the term 'totalitarianism', originally invented as a description or self-description of Italian Fascism, was applied virtually only to such regimes. Soviet Russia (from 1923: the USSR) was isolated and neither able nor, after the rise of Stalin, willing to extend communism. Social revolution under Leninist (or any) leadership ceased to spread after the initial post-war wave had ebbed. The (Marxist) social-democratic movements had turned into state-sustaining rather than subversive forces, and their commitment to democracy was unquestioned. In most countries' labour movements communists were minorities, and where they were strong, in most cases they were, or had been, or were about to be, suppressed. The fear of social revolution, and the communists' role in it, was realistic enough, as the second wave of revolution during and after the Second World War proved, but in the twenty years of liberal retreat not a single regime that could be reasonably called liberal-democratic had been overthrown from the left.* The danger came exclusively from the Right. And that Right represented not merely a threat to constitutional and representative government, but an ideological threat to liberal civilization as such, and a potentially world-wide *movement*, for which the label 'fascism' is both insufficient and not wholly irrelevant.

It is insufficient, because by no means all the forces overthrowing liberal regimes were fascist. It is relevant, because fascism, first in its original Italian form, later in its German form of National Socialism, both inspired other anti-liberal forces, supported them and lent the international Right a sense of historic confidence: in the 1930s it looked like the wave of the future. As has been said, by an expert in the field: 'It is no accident that . . . the eastern European royal dictators, bureaucrats,

---

* The closest to such an overthrow is the annexation of Estonia by the USSR in 1940, for at the time this small Baltic country, having passed through some authoritarian years, had again passed to a more democratic constitution.

and officers, and Franco (in Spain) should have mimicked fascism.' (Linz, 1975, p. 206).

The forces overthrowing liberal-democratic regimes were of three kinds, omitting the more traditional form of military coups installing Latin American dictators or *caudillos* which had no particular political colouring *a priori*. All were against social revolution, and indeed a reaction against the subversion of the old social order in 1917–20 was at the root of all of them. All were authoritarian and hostile to liberal political institutions, though sometimes for pragmatic reasons rather than on principle. Old-fashioned reactionaries might ban some parties, notably the communist, but not all. After the overthrow of the shortlived Hungarian soviet republic of 1919, Admiral Horthy, head of what he maintained was the kingdom of Hungary, though it no longer had either king or navy, governed an authoritarian state which remained parliamentary, but not democratic, in the old eighteenth century oligarchic sense. All tended to favour the military and foster the police, or other bodies of men capable of exercising physical coercion, since these were the most immediate bulwarks against subversion. Indeed, their support was often essential for the Right to come to power. And all tended to be nationalist, partly because of resentment against foreign states, lost wars, or insufficient empires, partly because waving national flags was a way to both legitimacy and popularity. Nevertheless, there were differences.

Old-fashioned authoritarians or conservatives – Admiral Horthy, Marshal Mannerheim of Finland, winner of the civil war of white vs. red in newly independent Finland; Colonel, later Marshal, Pilsudski, the liberator of Poland; King Alexander, formerly of Serbia, now of the newly united Yugoslavia; and General Francisco Franco of Spain – had no particular ideological agenda, other than anti-communism and the prejudices traditional to their class. They might find themselves allied to Hitler Germany and to fascist movements in their own countries, but only because in the inter-war conjuncture, the 'natural' alliance was one of all sectors of the political right. Of course national considerations might cut across this alliance. Winston Churchill, a strongly Right-wing Tory in this period, though an uncharacteristic one, expressed some sympathy for Mussolini's Italy, and could not bring himself to support the Spanish Republic against General Franco's forces, but Germany's threat to Britain made him into the champion of international anti-fascist union. On the other hand, such old reactionaries might also have to confront the opposition of genuinely fascist movements in their own countries, sometimes with substantial mass support.

A second strand of the Right produced what has been called 'organic statism' (Linz, 1975, pp. 277, 306–13) or conservative regimes, not so much defending a traditional order, but deliberately recreating its principles as a way of resisting both Liberal individualism and the challenge of labour and socialism. Behind it stood an ideological nostalgia for an imagined Middle Ages or feudal society, in which the existence of classes or economic groups was recognized, but the awful prospect of class struggle was kept at bay by the willing acceptance of social hierarchy, by a recognition that each social group or 'estate' had its part to play in an organic society composed of all, and should be recognized as a collective entity. This produced various brands of 'corporativist' theories which replaced liberal democracy by the representation of economic and occupational interest groups. This was sometimes described as 'organic' participation or democracy, and therefore better than the real kind, but in fact was invariably combined with authoritarian regimes and strong states ruled from above, largely by bureaucrats and technocrats. It invariably limited or abolished electoral democracy ('Democracy based on corporative correctives' in the phrase of the Hungarian premier Count Bethlen) (Ranki, 1971). The most complete examples of such corporate states were found in some Roman Catholic countries, notably the Portugal of Professor Oliveira Salazar, the longest-lived of all Europe's anti-liberal regimes of the right (1927–74), but also in Austria between the destruction of democracy and the invasion of Hitler (1934–38), and, to some extent, in Franco Spain.

Yet if reactionary regimes of this kind had origins and inspirations both older than fascism, and sometimes very different from it, no clear line separated the two, because both shared the same enemies, if not the same goals. Thus the Roman Catholic Church, profoundly and unswervingly reactionary as it was in the version officially consecrated by the first Vatican Council of 1870, was not fascist. Indeed, by its hostility to essentially secular states with totalitarian pretensions, it had to be opposed to fascism. Yet the doctrine of the 'corporate state', most fully exemplified in Catholic countries, had been largely elaborated in (Italian) fascist circles, though these, of course, drew on the Catholic tradition among others. Indeed, these regimes were sometimes actually called 'clerical fascist'. Fascists in Catholic countries might emerge directly out of integrist Catholicism, as in the *Rexist* movement of the Belgian Leon Degrelle. The ambiguity of the Church's attitude to Hitler's racism has been often noted; less often, the considerable help given after the war by persons within the Church, sometimes in important positions, to fugitive Nazis or fascists of various kinds, including many accused of horrifying war crimes. What linked the Church not only with old-fashioned reactionaries but with fascists, was a common hatred for the eighteenth century Enlightment, the French Revolution and all that in the Church's opinion derived from it: democracy, liberalism and, of course, most urgently, 'godless communism'.

In fact, the fascist era marked a turning-point in Catholic history largely because the Church's identification with a Right whose major international standard-bearers now were Hitler and Mussolini created substantial moral problems for socially-minded Catholics, not to mention, as fascism retreated towards inevitable defeat, substantial political problems for insufficiently anti-fascist hierarchies. Conversely, anti-fascism, or just patriotic resistance to the foreign conqueror, for the first time gave democratic Catholicism (Christian Democracy) legitimacy within the Church. Political parties mobilizing the Roman Catholic vote had come into existence, on pragmatic grounds, in countries where Catholics were a significant minority, normally to defend Church interests against secular states, as in Germany and the Netherlands. The Church resisted such concessions to the politics of democracy and liberalism in officially Catholic countries, although it was sufficiently worried by the rise of godless socialism to formulate – a radical innovation – a social policy in 1891, which stressed the need to give workers their due while maintaining the sacredness of family and private property, but *not* of capitalism as such.* This had provided a first foothold for social Catholics, or others prepared to organize such forms of worker defence as Catholic labour unions, also more inclined by such activities to the more liberal side of Catholicism. Except in Italy, where Pope Benedict XV (1914 – 22) briefly permitted a large (Catholic) Popular Party to emerge after the First World War, until fascism destroyed it, democratic and social Catholics remained politically marginal minorities. It was the advance of fascism in the 1930s which brought them into the open, even though the Catholics who declared their support for the Spanish Republic were a small, if intellectually distinguished band. The support of Catholics went overwhelmingly to Franco. It was the Resistance, which they could justify on grounds of patriotism rather than ideology, which gave them their chance, and victory which allowed them to take it. But the triumphs of political Christian Democracy in Europe, and some decades later in parts of Latin America, belong to a later period. In the period when liberalism fell, the Church, with rare exceptions, rejoiced at its fall.

* This was the Encyclical *Rerum Novarum*, supplemented forty years later, and not by chance in the depth of the Great Slump, by *Quadragesimo Anno*. It remains the cornerstone of the Church's social policy to this day, as witness Pope John Paul II's 1991 Encyclical *Centesimus Annus*, issued on the centenary of *Rerum Novarum*. However, the precise balance of condemnation has varied with political context.

II

There remain the movements which can be truly called fascist. The first of these was the Italian one which gave the phenomenon its name, the creation of a renegade socialist journalist, Benito Mussolini, whose first name, a tribute to the Mexican anti-clerical president Benito Juárez, symbolized the passionate anti-papalism of his native Romagna. Adolf Hitler himself acknowledged his debt to, and respect for, Mussolini, even when both Mussolini and fascist Italy had demonstrated their feebleness and incompetence in the Second World War. In return Mussolini took over from Hitler, rather late in the day, the anti-semitism which had been totally absent from his movement before 1938, and indeed from the history of Italy since its unification.* However, Italian Fascism alone did not exercise much international attraction, even though it tried to inspire and finance similar movements elsewhere, and showed some influence in unexpected quarters, as on Vladimir Jabotinsky, the founder of Zionist 'Revisionism', which became the government of Israel under Menachem Begin in the 1970s.

Without the triumph of Hitler in Germany in early 1933, fascism would not have become a general movement. In fact, all the fascist movements outside Italy that amounted to anything were founded after his arrival in power, notably the Hungarian Arrow Cross which scored 25 per cent of votes in the first secret ballot ever held in Hungary (1939), and the Rumanian Iron Guard, whose real support was even greater. Indeed, even movements virtually financed entirely by Mussolini, like the Croatian *Ustashi* terrorists of Ante Pavelich, did not gain much ground, and become ideologically fascisized until the 1930s, when part of them also looked for inspiration and finance to Germany. More than this, without Hitler's triumph in Germany, the idea of fascism as a *universal* movement, a sort of right-wing equivalent of international communism with Berlin as its Moscow, would not have developed. This did not produce a serious movement, but only, during the second World War, ideologically motivated collaborators with the Germans in occupied Europe. It was on this point that, notably in France, many on the traditional ultra-Right, however savagely reactionary, refused to follow:

---

* It should be said, in honour of Mussolini's countrymen, that during the war the Italian army flatly refused to deliver Jews for extermination to the Germans or anyone else in the areas it occupied – mainly south-eastern France and parts of the Balkans. Though the Italian administration also showed a conspicuous lack of zeal in the matter, about half of the small Italian Jewish population perished; some however, as anti-fascist militants rather than mere victims (Steinberg, 1990; Hughes, 1983).

they were nationalists or they were nothing. Some even joined the Resistance. Moreover, without the international standing of Germany as an evidently successful and rising world power, fascism would have had no serious impact outside Europe, nor indeed would non-fascist reactionary rulers have bothered to dress up as fascist sympathisers, as when Portugal's Salazar claimed in 1940 that he and Hitler were 'linked by the same ideology' (Delzell, 1970, p. 348).

What the various brands of fascism had in common, other than – after 1933 – a general sense of Germany hegemony, is not so easy to discern. Theory was not the strong point of movements devoted to the inadequacies of reason and rationalism and the superiority of instinct and will. They attracted all kinds of reactionary theorists in countries with an active conservative intellectual life – Germany is an obvious case in point – but these were decorative rather than structural elements of fascism. Mussolini could have readily dispensed with his house philosopher, Giovanni Gentile, and Hitler probably neither knew nor cared about the support of the philosopher Heidegger. Fascism cannot be identified either with a particular form of state organization, such as the corporate state – Nazi Germany lost interest in such ideas rapidly, all the more since they conflicted with the idea of a single undivided and total *Volksgemeinschaft*, or People's Community. Even so apparently central an element as racism was initially absent from Italian fascism. Conversely, of course, as we have seen, fascism shared nationalism, anti-communism, anti-liberalism etc. with other non-fascist elements on the right. Several of these, notably among the non-fascist French reactionary groups, also shared with it a preference for politics as street violence.

The major difference between the fascist and the non-fascist Right was that fascism existed by mobilizing masses from below. It belonged essentially to the era of democratic and popular politics which traditional reactionaries deplored and which the champions of the 'organic state' tried to by-pass. Fascism gloried in the mobilization of masses, and maintained it symbolically in the form of public theatre – the Nuremberg rallies, the masses on the Piazza Venezia looking up to Mussolini's gestures on his balcony – even when it came to power; as also did Communist movements. Fascists were the revolutionaries of counter-revolution: in their rhetoric, in their appeal to those who considered themselves victims of society, in their call for a total transformation of society, even in their deliberate adaptation of the symbols and names of the social revolutionaries, which is so obvious in Hitler's 'National *Socialist Workers Party*' with its (modified) red flag and its immediate institution of the Reds' First of May as an official holiday in 1933.

Similarly, though fascism also specialized in the rhetoric of return to the traditional past, and received much support from classes of people who would genuinely have preferred to wipe out the past century if they could, it was in no real sense a traditionalist movement like, say, the Carlists of Navarra, who formed one of the main bodies of Franco's support in the Civil War or Gandhi's campaigns for a return to hand-looms and village ideals. It stressed many traditional *values*, which is another matter. They denounced liberal emancipation – women should stay at home and bear a great many children – and they distrusted the corroding influence of modern culture, and especially of the modernist arts, which the German National Socialists described as 'cultural bolshevism' and degenerate. Yet the central fascist movements – the Italian and the German – did not appeal to those historic guardians of the conservative order, Church and King, but on the contrary sought to supplant them by an entirely non-traditional leadership principle embodied in self-made men legitimized by their mass support, and by secular ideologies, and sometimes cults.

The past to which they appealed was an artefact. Their traditions were invented. Even Hitler's racism was not the pride in an unbroken and unmixed line of kinship descent which provides genealogists with commissions from Americans who hope to prove their descent from some sixteenth-century Suffolk yeoman, but a late nineteenth-century post-Darwinian farrago claiming (and, alas, in Germany often receiving) the support of the new science of genetics, or more precisely of that branch of applied genetics ('eugenics') which dreamed of creating a human super-race by selective breeding and the elimination of the unfit. The race destined through Hitler to dominate the world did not even have a name until 1898 when an anthropologist coined the term 'Nordic'. Hostile as it was on principle to the heritage of the eighteenth-century Enlightenment and the French revolution, fascism could not formally believe in modernity and progress, but it had no difficulty in combining a lunatic set of beliefs with technological modernity in practical matters, except where it crippled its basic scientific research on ideological grounds (see chapter 18). Fascism was triumphantly anti-liberal. It also provided the proof that men can, without difficulty, combine crack-brained beliefs about the world with a confident mastery of contemporary high technology. The late twentieth century, with its fundamentalist sects wielding the weapons of television and computer-programmed fund-raising, have made us more familiar with this phenomenon.

Nevertheless, the combination of conservative values, the techniques of mass democracy, and an innovative ideology of irrationalist savagery, essentially centered in nationalism, must be explained. Such non-traditional movements of the radical Right had emerged in several European countries in the late nineteenth century in reaction against both liberalism (i.e. the accelerating transformation of societies by capitalism) and the rising socialist working-class movements, and, more generally, against the tide of foreigners that was sweeping across the world in the greatest mass migration of history up to that date. Men and women migrated not only across oceans and international frontiers, but from country to city; from one region of the same state to another – in short from 'home' to the land of strangers and, turning the coin round, as strangers into others' home. Almost fifteen out of every hundred Poles left their country for good plus half a million a year as seasonal migrants – overwhelmingly, as such migrants did, to join the working classes of the receiving countries. Anticipating the late twentieth century, the late nineteenth pioneered mass xenophobia, of which racism – the protection of the pure native stock against contamination, or even submersion, by the invading sub-human hordes – became the common expression. Its strength can be measured not only by the fear of Polish immigration which led the great German liberal sociologist Max Weber into temporary support for the Pangerman League, but by the increasingly febrile campaign against mass immigration in the USA, which eventually, during and after the First World War, led the country of the Statue of Liberty to bar its frontiers to those whom the Statue had been erected to welcome.

The common cement of these movements was the resentment of little men in a society that crushed them between the rock of big business on one side and the hard place of rising mass labour movements on the other. Or which, at the very least, deprived them of the respectable position they had occupied in the social order, and believed to be their due, or the social status in a dynamic society to which they felt they had a right to aspire. These sentiments found their characteristic expression in anti-semitism, which began to develop specific political movements based on hostility to the Jews in the last quarter of the nineteenth century in several countries. Jews were almost universally present, and could readily symbolize all that was most hateful about an unfair world, not least its commitment to the ideas of the Enlightenment and the French revolution which had emancipated them, and in doing so had made them so much more visible. They could serve as symbols of the hated capitalist/financier; of the revolutionary agitator; of the corroding influence of 'rootless intellectuals' and the new mass media; of the competition – how could it be otherwise than 'unfair?' – that gave them a disproportionate share of jobs in certain professions requiring education; and of the foreigner and outsider as such. Not to mention the accepted view among old-fashioned Christians that they had killed Jesus Christ.

Dislike of Jews was indeed pervasive in the Western world, and their position in nineteenth-century society was indeed ambiguous. Yet the fact that striking workers were apt, even when members of non-racist labour movements, to attack Jewish shopkeepers, and to think of their employers as Jews (often enough correctly, in large zones of central and eastern Europe), should not lead us into seeing them as proto-National Socialists, any more than the matter-of-course anti-semitism of Edwardian British liberal intellectuals, such as the Bloomsbury Group, made them into sympathisers of *political* anti-semites of the radical Right. The peasant anti-semitism of east-central Europe, where for practical purposes the Jew was the point of contact between the livelihood of the villager and the outside economy on which it depended, was certainly more permanent and explosive, and became more so as Slav, Magyar or Rumanian rural societies became increasingly convulsed by the incomprehensible earthquakes of the modern world. Among such dark people tales of Jews sacrificing Christian children could still be believed, and moments of social explosion would lead to *pogroms*, which reactionaries in the Tsar's Empire encouraged, especially after the assassination of Tsar Alexander II in 1881 by social revolutionaries. Here a straight road leads from original grassroots anti-semitism to the extermination of Jewry during the second World War. Certainly grassroots anti-semitism gave such East European Fascist movements as acquired a mass base – notably the Rumanian Iron Guard and the Hungarian Arrow Cross – their foundation. At all events, in the former territories of Habsburg and Romanov this connexion was much clearer than in the German Reich, where grassroots rural and provincial anti-semitism, though strong and deeply rooted, was also less violent: one might even say, more tolerant. Jews who escaped from newly occupied Vienna to Berlin in 1938 were astonished at the absence of street anti-semitism. Here violence came by decree from above, as in November 1938 (Kershaw, 1983). Yet even so, there is no comparison between the casual and intermittent savagery of the pogroms and what was to come a generation later. The handful of dead of 1881, the forty to fifty of the Kishinev pogrom of 1903, outraged the world – and justifiably – because in the days before the advance of barbarism, such a number of victims seemed intolerable to a world which expected civilization to advance. Even the much larger pogroms that accompanied the mass peasant risings of the 1905 Russian revolution had, by later standards, only modest casualties – perhaps eight hundred dead in all. This may be compared with the 3,800 Jews killed in Vilnius

(Vilna) by the Lithuanians in three days of 1941 as the Germans invaded the USSR, and before the systematic exterminations got under way.

The new movements in the radical Right which appealed to, but fundamentally transformed, these older traditions of intolerance, appealed particularly to the lower and middle groups of European societies, and were formulated as rhetoric and theory by nationalist intellectuals who emerged as a trend in the 1890s. The very term 'nationalism' was coined in that decade to describe these new spokesmen of reaction. Middle and lower-middle-class militancy took a turn to the radical Right chiefly in countries where the ideologies of democracy and liberalism were not dominant, or among classes which did not identify with them, that is to say, chiefly in countries which had not undergone a French revolution or its equivalent. Indeed, in the core countries of Western Liberalism – Britain, France, and the USA – the general hegemony of the revolutionary tradition prevented the emergence of any mass fascist movements of importance. It is a mistake to confuse the racism of American Populists or the chauvinism of French Republicans with proto-Fascism: these were movements of the Left.

This did not mean that, once the hegemony of Liberty, Equality and Fraternity no longer stood in the way, old instincts might not attach themselves to new political slogans. There is little doubt that the activists of the Swastika in the Austrian Alps were to be largely recruited from the sort of provincial professionals – veterinary surgeons, surveyors and the like – who had once been the local Liberals, an educated and emancipated minority in an environment dominated by peasant clericalism. Just so, in the later twentieth century, the disintegration of the classical proletarian labour and socialist movements left the instinctive chauvinism and racism of so many manual workers free play. Hitherto, while far from immune to such sentiments, they had hesitated to express them in public out of loyalty to parties passionately hostile to such bigotry. Since the 1960s Western xenophobia and political racism is found mainly among the manual labouring strata. However, in the decades when fascism was incubated, it belonged to those who did not get their hands dirty at work.

The middle and lower-middle strata remained the backbone of such movements thoughout the era of the rise of fascism. This is not seriously denied even by historians anxious to revise the consensus of 'virtually' every analysis of Nazi support produced between 1930 and 1980 (Childers, 1983; Childers, 1991, pp. 8, 14–15). To take merely one case among the many enquires into the membership and support of such movements inter-war Austria. Of the National Socialists elected as district councillors in Vienna in 1932, 18 per cent were self-employed, 56 per cent were white-collar, office workers and public employees, and 14 per cent were blue-collar. Of the Nazis elected in five Austrian assemblies outside Vienna in the same year, 16 per cent were self-employed and farmers, fifty-one were office-workers etc. and 10 per cent were blue-collars (Larsen et al., 1978, pp. 766–67).

This does not mean that Fascist movements could not acquire genuine mass support among the labouring poor. Whatever the composition of its cadres, the Rumanian Iron Guard's support came from the poor peasantry. The Hungarian Arrow Cross electorate was largely working-class (the Communist Party being illegal and the Socialdemocratic Party, always small, paying the price for its toleration by the Horthy regime) and, after the defeat of Austrian Socialdemocracy in 1934, there was a noticeable swing of workers to the Nazi Party, especially in the Austrian provinces. Moreover, once fascist governments with public legitimacy had established themselves, as in Italy and Germany, far more formerly socialist and communist workers than the Left tradition likes to dwell on, fell into line with the new regimes. Nevertheless, since fascist movements had trouble in appealing to the genuinely traditional elements in rural society (unless reinforced, as in Croatia, by organizations like the Roman Catholic Church), and were the sworn enemies of the ideologies and parties identified with the organised working classes, their core constituency was naturally to be found in the middle strata of society.

How far into the middle class the original appeal of fascism extended is a more open question. Certainly its appeal to middle-class youth was strong, especially to Continental European university students who, between the wars, were notoriously on the ultra-Right. Thirteen per cent of the members of the Italian Fascist movement in 1921 (i.e. before the 'March on Rome') were students. In Germany between 5 and 10 per cent of all students were party members as early as 1930, when the great majority of future Nazis had not begun to take an interest in Hitler (Kater, 1985, p. 467; Noelle/Neumann, 1967, p. 196). As we shall see, the element of middle-class ex-officers was strongly represented: the sort for whom the Great War, with all its horrors, marked a mountain-peak of personal achievement, from which the view showed only the disappointing lowlands of their future civilian life. These were, of course, segments of the middle strata particularly receptive to the appeals of activism. Broadly speaking, the appeal of the radical Right was the stronger, the greater the threat to the standing, actual or conventionally expected, of a middle-class occupation, as the framework buckled and broke that was supposed to hold their social order in place. In Germany the double blow of the Great Inflation which reduced the value of money to zero, and the subsequent Great Slump, radicalized even strata of the middle class such as middle and higher civil servants, whose position seemed secure, and who would, under less traumatic circumstances, have been happy to continue as old-style conservative patriots, nostalgic for Kaiser William, but willing to do their duty to a Republic headed by Field Marshal Hindenburg, had it not been visibly collapsing under their feet. Most nonpolitical Germans between the wars looked back to William's empire. As late as the 1960s, when most West Germans had (understandably) concluded that the best times in German history were *now*, 42 per cent of those over sixty years old still thought that the time before 1914 was better than the present, as against 32 per cent who were converted by the *Wirtschaftswunder* (Noelle/Neumann, 1967, p. 196). The voters of the bourgeois Centre and Right defected in massive numbers to the Nazi Party between 1930 and 1932. Yet these were not the builders of fascism.

Such conservative middle classes were, of course, potential supporters or even converts to fascism, because of the way the inter-war lines of political battle were drawn. The threat to liberal society and all its values seemed to come exclusively from the Right; the threat to the social order from the Left. Middle-class people chose their politics according to their fears. Traditional conservatives usually sympathized with the demagogues of fascism and were prepared to ally with them against the major enemy. Italian Fascism had a rather good press in the 1920s and even in the 1930s, except from Liberalism leftwards. 'But for the bold experiment of fascism the decade has not been fruitful in constructive statesmanship,' wrote John Buchan, the eminent British Conservative and thriller-writer. (A taste for writing thrillers has, alas, rarely gone with left-wing convictions.) (Graves/Hodge, 1941, p. 248.) Hitler was brought to power by a coalition of the traditional Right, which he subsequently swallowed. General Franco included the then not very significant Spanish *Falange* in his national front, because what he represented was the union of the entire Right against the spectres of 1789 and 1917, between which he did not make fine distinctions. He was lucky enough not actually to join in the Second World War on Hitler's side, but he sent a volunteer force, the 'Blue Division', to fight the godless communists in Russia side by side with the Germans. Marshal Pétain was certainly not a fascist or Nazi sympathiser. One reason why it was so difficult after the war to distinguish between wholehearted French fascists and pro-German collaborators on one hand, and the main body of support for Marshal Pétain's Vichy regime on the other, was that there was in fact no clear line. Those whose fathers had hated Dreyfus, the Jews and the bitch-Republic – some Vichy figures were old enough to have done so themselves – shaded insensibly into the zealots for a Hitlerian Europe. In short, the 'natural' alliance of the Right between the wars went from traditional conservatives *via* old-style reactionaries to the outer fringes of fascist pathology. The traditional forces of conservatism and counter-revolution were strong, but often inert. Fascism provided them both with a dynamic and, perhaps even more important, with the example of victory over the forces of disorder. (Was not the proverbial argument in favour of fascist Italy, that 'Mussolini made the trains run on time'?) Just as the dynamism of the communists exercised an attraction on the disoriented and rudderless Left after 1933, so the successes of fascism, especially after the National Socialist takeover in Germany, made it look like the wave of the future. The very fact that at this time fascism made a prominent, if brief, entrance on – of all countries – the political scene of Conservative Great Britain, demonstrates the power of this 'demonstration effect'. That it converted one of the most prominent of the nation's politicians and won the support of one of its major press-lords is more significant than the fact that Sir Oswald Mosley's movement was quickly abandoned by respectable politicians and Lord Rothermere's *Daily Mail* soon dropped its support of the British Union of Fascists. For Britain was still universally and rightly seen as a model of political and social stability.

III

The rise of the radical Right after the First World War was undoubtedly a response to the danger, indeed to the reality, of social revolution and working-class power in general, to the October revolution and Leninism in particular. Without these, there would have been no fascism, for though the demagogic Right-wing Ultras had been politically vocal and aggressive in a number of European countries since the end of the nineteenth century, they had almost invariably been kept well under control before 1914. To this extent apologists for fascism are probably right in holding that Lenin engendered Mussolini and Hitler. However, it is entirely illegitimate to exculpate fascist barbarism by claiming that it was inspired by and imitated the allegedly earlier barbarities of the Russian Revolution, as some German historians came close to doing in the 1980s (Nolte, 1987).

However, two important qualifications must be made to the thesis that the Right backlash was essentially a response to the revolutionary Left. First, it underestimates the impact of the First World War on an important stratum of, largely middle and lower middle-class, nationalist soldiers or young men who, after November 1918, resented their missed chance of heroism. The so-called 'front-line soldier' (*frontsoldat*) was to play a most important part in the mythology of radical-Right movements – Hitler was one himself – and it was to provide a substantial bloc of the first ultra-nationalist strong-arm squads, such as the officers who murdered the German communist leaders Karl Liebknecht and Rosa Luxemburg in early 1919, the Italian *squadristi* and German *freikorps*. Fifty-seven per cent of the early Italian fascists were ex-servicemen. As we have seen, the First World War was a machine for brutalizing the world, and these men gloried in the release of of their latent brutality.

The strong commitment of the Left, from the liberals onwards, to anti-war and anti-militarist movements, the huge popular revulsion against the mass killing of the First World War, led many to under-estimate the emergence of a relatively small, but absolutely numerous, minority for whom the experience of fighting, even under the condi-tions of 1914–18, was central and inspirational; for whom uniform and discipline, sacrifice – of self and others – and blood, arms and power were what made masculine life worth living. They did not write many books about the war, though (especially in Germany) one or two did. These Rambos of their time were natural recruits for the radical Right.

The second qualification is that the Right-wing backlash responded not against Bolshevism as such, but against all movements, and notably the organized working class, which threatened the existing order of society or could be blamed for its breakdown. Lenin was the symbol of this threat rather than the actual reality, which, for most politicians, was represented not so much by the socialist labour parties, whose leaders were moderate enough, but by the upsurge of working-class power, confidence and radicalism, which gave the old socialist parties a new political force and, in fact, made them the indispensable props of liberal states. It is no accident that in the immediate post-war years the central demand of socialist agitators since 1889 was conceded almost everywhere in Europe: the eight-hour day.

It was the threat implicit in the rise of labour's power which froze the blood of conservatives, rather than the mere transformation of labour union leaders and opposition orators into government ministers, though this was bitter enough. They belonged by definition to 'the Left'. In an era of social upheaval, no clear line divided them from the Bolsheviks. Indeed, many of the socialist parties would have happily joined the communists in the immediate post-war years, had these not rejected their affiliation. The man whom Mussolini had assassinated after his 'March on Rome' was not a CP leader but the Socialist, Matteotti. The traditional Right may have seen godless Russia as the embodiment of all that was evil in the world, but the rising of the Generals in 1936 was not directed against the communists as such if only because these were the smallest part of the Popular Front (see chapter 5). It was directed against a popular upsurge which, until the Civil War, favoured Socialists and Anarchists. It is an ex post facto rationalization which makes Lenin and Stalin the excuse for fascism.

And yet, what must be explained is why the Right-wing backlash after the First World War won its crucial victories in the form of fascism. For extremist movements of the ultra-Right had existed before 1914 – hysterically nationalist and xenophobic, idealising war and violence, intolerant and given to strong-arm coercion, passionately anti-liberal, anti-democratic, anti-proletarian, anti-socialist and anti-rationalist, dreaming of blood and soil and a return to the values which modernity was disrupting. They had some political influence, within the political Right, and in some intellectual circles, but nowhere did they dominate or control.

What gave them their chance after the First World War, was the collapse of the old regimes and, with them, of the old ruling classes and their machinery of power, influence and hegemony. Where these remained in good working order, there was no need for fascism. It made no progress in Britain, in spite of the brief flurry of nerves noted above. The traditional Conservative Right remained in control. It made no effective progress in France until after the defeat of 1940. Though the traditional French radical Right – the monarchist *Action Française* and Colonel La Rocque's *Croix de Feu* (Fiery Cross) – were ready enough to beat up Leftists, it was not strictly fascist. Indeed, some elements of it would even join the Resistance.

Again, fascism was not needed where a new nationalist ruling class or group could take over in newly independent countries. These men could be reactionary and might well opt for authoritarian government, for reasons to be considered below, but it was rhetoric that identified every turn to the antidemocratic Right in Europe between the wars with fascism. There were no fascist movements of importance in the new Poland, which was run by authoritarian militarists and in the Czech part of Czechoslovakia, which was democratic, nor in the (dominant) Serbian core of the new Yugoslavia. Where significant fascist or similar movements existed in countries whose rulers were old-fashioned Right-wingers or reactionaries – in Hungary, Rumania, Finland, even in Franco Spain, whose leader was not himself a fascist – they had little trouble in keeping them under control unless (as in Hungary in 1944) the Germans put the screw on them. This does not mean that minority nationalist movements in old or new states might not find fascism attractive, if only because they could expect financial and political support from Italy and, after 1933, from Germany. This was clearly so in (Belgian) Flanders, in Slovakia and in Croatia.

The optimal conditions for the triumph of the crazy ultra-Right were an old state and its ruling mechanisms which could no longer function; a mass of disenchanted, disoriented and discontented citizens who no longer knew where their loyalties lay; strong socialist movements threatening or appearing to threaten social revolution, but not actually in a position to achieve it; and a move of nationalist resentment against the peace treaties of 1918–20. These were the conditions in which helpless old ruling elites were tempted to have recourse to the ultra-radicals, as the Italian Liberals did to Mussolini's fascists in 1920–22 and as the German Conservatives did to Hitler's National Socialists in 1932–33. These, by the same token, were the conditions that turned movements of the radical Right into powerful organized and sometimes uniformed and paramilitary forces (*squadristi*; storm-troopers) or, as in Germany during the Great Slump, into massive electoral armies. However, in neither of the two fascist states did fascism 'conquer power', though in both Italy and Germany it made much of the rhetoric of 'capturing the street' and 'marching on Rome'. In both cases fascism came to power by the connivance of, indeed (as in Italy) on the initiative of, the old regime, that is to say in a 'constitutional' fashion.

The novelty of fascism was that, once in power, it refused to play the old political games, and took over completely where it could. The total transfer of power, or the elimination of all rivals, took rather longer in Italy (1922–28) than in Germany (1933–34) but, once it was achieved, there were no further internal political limits on what became, characteristically, the untrammeled dictatorship of a supreme populist 'leader' (*Duce*; *Führer*).

At this point we must briefly dismiss two equally inadequate theses about fascism, the one fascist, but taken over by many liberal historians, the other dear to orthodox Soviet Marxism. There was no 'fascist revolution' and neither was fascism the expression of 'monopoly capitalism' or big business.

Fascist movements had the elements of revolutionary movements, inasmuch as they contained people who wanted a fundamental transformation of society, often with a notably anti-capitalist and anti-oligarchic edge. However, the horse of revolutionary fascism failed either to start or to run. Hitler rapidly eliminated those who took the 'socialist' component in the name of the National Socialist German Workers' Party seriously – as he certainly did not. The utopia of a return to some kind of little man's Middle Ages, full of hereditary peasant-proprietors, artisan craftsmen like Hans Sachs and girls in blonde plaits, was not a programme that could be realized in major twentieth-century states (except in the nightmare version of Himmler's plans for a racially purified people), least of all in regimes which, like Italian and German Fascism, were committed in their way to modernisation and technological advance.

What National Socialism certainly achieved was a radical purging of the old Imperial elites and institutional structures. After all, the only group which actually launched a revolt against Hitler – and was consequently decimated – was the old aristocratic Prussian army in July 1944. This destruction of the old elites and the old frameworks, reinforced after the war by the policies of the occupying Western armies, was eventually to make it possible to build the Federal Republic on a much sounder basis than the Weimar Republic of 1918–33, which had been little more than the defeated empire minus the Kaiser. Nazism certainly had, and partly achieved, a social programme for the masses: holidays; sports; the planned 'people's car', which the world came to know after the Second World War as the *Volkswagen* 'beetle'. Its chief achievement, however, was to liquidate the Great Slump more effectively than any other government, for the anti-liberalism of the Nazis had the positive side that it did not commit them to an *a priori* belief in the free market. Nevertheless, Nazism was a revamped and revitalized old regime rather than a basically new and different one. Like the imperial and militarist Japan of the 1930s (which nobody would claim to have been a revolutionary system), it was a non-liberal capitalist economy which achieved a striking dynamization of its industrial system. The economic and other achievements of fascist Italy were considerably less impressive, as was demonstrated in the Second World War. Its war economy was unusually feeble. Talk of a 'fascist revolution' was rhetoric, though no doubt for many Italian rank-and-file fascists sincere rhetoric. It was much more openly a regime in the interests of the old ruling classes, having come into existence as a defence against post-1918 revolutionary unrest rather than, like in Germany, as a reaction to the traumas of the Great Slump and the inability of Weimar governments to cope with them. Italian fascism, which in one sense carried on the process of Italian unification from the nineteenth century, thus producing a stronger and more centralized government, had some significant achievements to its credit. It was, for instance, the only Italian regime successfully to suppress the Sicilian

Mafia and the Neapolitan Camorra. Yet its historical significance lay, not in its aims and achievements, but in its role as the global pioneer of a new version of the triumphant counter-revolution. Mussolini inspired Hitler, and Hitler never failed to acknowledge Italian inspiration and priority. On the other hand Italian fascism was, and for a long time remained, an anomaly among radical Right-wing movements in its toleration of, even a certain taste for, artistic avantgarde 'modernism', and in some other respects – notably, until Mussolini fell into line with Germany in 1938, a complete lack of interest in anti-semitic racism.

As for the 'monopoly capitalist' thesis, the point about really big business is that it can come to terms with any regime that does not actually expropriate it, and any regime must come to terms with it. Fascism was no more 'the expression of the interests of monopoly capital' than the American New Deal or British Labour governments, or the Weimar Republic. Big business in the early 1930s did not particularly want Hitler, and would have preferred more orthodox conservatism. It gave him little support until the Great Slump, and even then support was late and patchy. However, when he came to power, business collaborated wholeheartedly, up to the point of using slave labour and extermination camp labour for its operations during the Second World War. Large and small business, of course, benefited from the expropriation of the Jews.

It must nevertheless be said that fascism had some major advantages for business over other regimes. First, it eliminated or defeated Left-wing social revolution, and indeed seemed to be the main bulwark against it. Second, it eliminated labour unions and other limitations on the rights of management to manage its workforce. Indeed, the fascist 'leadership principle' was what most bosses and business executives applied to their subordinates in their own businesses and fascism gave it authoritative justification. Third, the destruction of labour movements helped to secure an unduly favourable solution of the Depression for business. Whereas in the USA the top 5 per cent of consuming units between 1929 and 1941 saw their share of total (national) income fall by 20 per cent (there was a similar but more modest egalitarian trend in Britain and Scandinavia), in Germany the top 5 per cent gained 15 per cent during the comparable period (Kuznets, 1956). Finally, as already noted, fascism was good at dynamising and modernising industrial economies – although actually not as good at adventurous and long-term techno-scientific planning as the Western democracies.

IV

Would fascism have become very significant in world history but for the Great Slump? Probably not. Italy alone was not a promising base from which to shake the world. In the 1920s no other European movement of radical Right counter-revolution looked as though it had much of a future, for much the same reason as insurrectionary attempts at communist social revolution failed: the post-1917 revolutionary wave had ebbed, and the economy seemed to recover. In Germany the pillars of imperial society, generals, civil servants and the rest, had indeed given some backing to the free-lance paramilitaries and other wild men of the Right after the November revolution, though (understandably) putting their main effort in keeping the new republic conservative, anti-revolutionary and, above all, a state capable of maintaining some international room for manoeuvre. However, when forced to choose, as during the Right-wing Kapp Putsch of 1920 and the Munich revolt of 1923, in which Adolf Hitler first found himself in the headlines, they unhesitatingly backed the status quo. After the economic upturn of 1924, the National Social Workers' Party was reduced to a rump of 2.5–3 per cent of the electorate, scoring little more than half of even the small and civilised German Democratic Party, little more than a fifth of the communists and well under a tenth of the Social Democrats in the elections of 1928. Yet two years later it had risen to over 18 per cent of the electorate, the second-strongest party in German politics. Four years later, in the summer of 1932, it was by far the strongest, with over 37 per cent of the total vote, though it did not maintain this support while democratic elections lasted. It was patently the Great Slump which turned Hitler from a phenomenon of the political fringe into the potential, and eventually the actual, master of the country.

However, even the Great Slump would not have given fascism either the force or the influence it plainly exercised in the 1930s, if it had not brought a movement of this kind to power in Germany, a state destined by its size, economic and military potential, and, not least, geographical position, to play a major political role in Europe under any form of government. Utter defeat in two world wars has, after all, not prevented Germany from ending the twentieth century as the dominant state on that continent. Just as, on the Left, the victory of Marx in the largest state of the globe ('one sixth of the world's land surface', as communists liked to boast between the wars) gave communism a major international presence, even at times when its political force outside the USSR was negligible, so the capture of Germany by Hitler appeared to confirm the success of Mussolini's Italy and to turn fascism into a powerful global political current. The successful policy of aggressive militarist expansionism by both states (see chapter 5) – reinforced by that of Japan – dominated the international politics of the decade. It was therefore natural that suitable states or movements should be attracted and influenced by fascism, should seek the support of Germany and Italy, and – given these countries' expansionism – should often receive it.

In Europe, for obvious reasons, such movements belonged overwhelmingly to the political Right. Thus within Zionism (which at this time was overwhelmingly a movement of Ashkenazic Jews living in Europe), that wing of the movement which looked towards Italian fascism, Vladimir Jabotinsky's 'Revisionists', were clearly seen and classified themselves on the Right, against the (predominant) socialist and liberal Zionist bodies. Yet the influence of fascism in the 1930s could not but be to some extent global, if only because it was associated with two dynamic and active powers. Yet outside Europe the conditions which created fascist movements in the home continent hardly existed. Hence, where fascist, or plainly fascist-influenced movements emerged, their political location and function was far more problematic.

Of course certain characteristics of European fascism found an echo overseas. It would have been surprising if the Mufti of Jerusalem and other Arabs resisting Jewish colonization in Palestine (and the British who protected it) had not found Hitler's anti-semitism to their liking, though it bore no relation to the traditional modes of Islamic coexistence with unbelievers of various kinds. Some upper-caste Hindus in India were, like modern Sinhalese extremists in Sri Lanka, conscious of their superiority as certified – indeed as the original – 'Aryans' to darker races on their own subcontinent. And the Boer militants who were interned as pro-Germans during the Second World War – some became their country's leaders in the era of apartheid after 1948 – also had ideological affinities with Hitler, both as convinced racists and through the theological influence of elitist ultra-Right-wing Calvinist currents in the Netherlands. Yet this hardly qualifies the basic proposition that fascism, unlike communism, was non-existent in Asia and Africa (except perhaps among some local European settlers) because it appeared to have no bearing on the local political situations.

This is broadly true even of Japan, though that country was allied to Germany and Italy, fought on the same side in the Second World War, and its politics were dominated by the Right. The affinities between the dominant ideologies of the eastern and western ends of the 'Axis' are indeed strong. The Japanese were second to none in their conviction of racial superiority and the need for racial purity in their belief in the military virtues of self-sacrifice, absolute obedience to orders, self-abnegation and stoicism. Every Samurai would have subscribed to the motto of Hitler's SS ('Meine Ehre ist Treue', best translated as 'Honour means blind subordination'). Theirs was a society of rigid hierarchy, of the total dedication of the individual (if such a term had any local meaning in the Western sense at all) to the nation and its divine Emperor, and the utter rejection of Liberty, Equality and Fraternity. The Japanese had no trouble in understanding the Wagnerian brand of myths about barbarian gods, pure and heroic medieval knights and the specifically German nature of mountain and forest, both filled with German *voelkisch* dreams. They had the same capacity to combine barbaric behaviour with a sophisticated aesthetic sensibility: the concentration camp torturer's taste for playing Schubert quartets. Insofar as fascism could have been translated into Zen terms, the Japanese might well have welcomed it, though they had no need of it. And indeed, among the diplomats accredited to the European fascist powers, but especially among the ultra-nationalist terror groups given to assassinating insufficiently patriotic politicians, and in the Kwantung army which was conquering, holding and enslaving Manchuria and China, there were Japanese who recognized these affinities and campaigned for closer identification with the European fascist powers.

Yet European fascism could not be reduced to an oriental feudalism with an imperial national mission. It belonged essentially to the era of democracy and the common man, while the very concept of a 'movement' of mass mobilization for novel, indeed for would-be revolutionary purposes, behind self-selected leaders, made no sense in Hirohito's Japan. The Prussian army and tradition, rather than Hitler, fitted their view of the world. In short, despite the similarities with German national socialism (the affinities with Italy were far less), Japan was not fascist.

As for the states and movements which looked for support from Germany and Italy, especially during the Second World War when the Axis looked very much like winning, ideology was not their major motive, though some of the minor nationalist regimes in Europe, whose position depended entirely on German backing, readily advertised themselves as more Nazi than the SS, notably the Croatian Ustashi state. Yet it would be absurd to think of the Irish Republican army or the Berlin-based Indian nationalists as in any sense 'fascist' because, in the Second World War as in the First, some of them negotiated for German support on the principle that 'my enemy's enemy is my friend'. Indeed, the Irish Republican leader Frank Ryan, who entered such negotiations, was ideologically so anti-fascist that he had actually joined the International Brigades to fight General Franco in the Spanish Civil War, before being captured by Franco's forces and sent to Germany. Such cases need not detain us.

However, there remains a continent on which the ideological impact of European fascism is undeniable: the Americas.

In North America men and movements inspired by Europe were not of great significance outside particular immigrant communities whose members brought the ideologies of the old country with them, as the Scandinavians and Jews had brought a proclivity towards socialism, or who retained some loyalty to the country of their origin. Thus the sentiments of Germany – and to a much smaller extent, Italian – Americans contributed to US isolationism, though there is no good evidence that they became fascists in large numbers. The paraphernalia of militias, coloured shirts and arms raised in salutes to leaders did not belong to the native Right-wing and racist mobilisations, of which the Ku Klux Klan was the most familiar. Anti-semitism was certainly strong, though its contemporary Right-wing US version – as in Father Coughlin's popular radio sermons out of Detroit – probably owed more to the Right-wing corporatism of European Catholic inspiration. It is characteristic of the USA in the 1930s that the most successful and possibly dangerous demagogic populism of the decade, Huey Long's conquest of Louisiana, came from what was, in American terms, a clearly radical and Left-wing tradition. It cut down democracy in the name of democracy and appealed, not to the resentments of a petty-bourgeoisie or the anti-revolutionary instincts of self-preservation of the rich, but to the egalitarianism of the poor. Nor was it racist. No movement whose slogan was 'Every Man a King' could belong in the fascist tradition.

It was in Latin America that European fascist influence was to be open and acknowledged, both on individual politicians, like Colombia's Jorge Eliézer Gaitán (1898–1948) and Argentina's Juan Domingo Perón (1895–1974), and on regimes, like Getulio Vargas' *Estado Novo* (New State) of 1937–45 in Brazil. In fact, and in spite of baseless US fears of Nazi encirclement from the south, the main effect of fascist influence in Latin America was domestic. Apart from Argentina, which clearly favoured the Axis – but did so before Perón took power in 1943 as well as after – the governments of the Western hemisphere joined the war on the US side, at least nominally. It is, however, true that in some South American countries their military had been modelled on the German system or trained by German or even Nazi cadres.

Fascist influence south of the Rio Grande is easily explained. Seen from the south, the US after 1914 no longer looked, as it had in the nineteenth century, like the ally of the domestic forces of progress and the diplomatic counterweight to the imperial or ex-imperial Spaniards, French and British. US imperial conquests from Spain in 1898, the Mexican revolution, not to mention the rise of the oil and banana industries, introduced an anti-Yankee anti-imperialism into Latin American politics, and one which the obvious taste of Washington in the first third of the century for gunboat diplomacy and landing marines did nothing to discourage. Víctor Raúl Haya de la Torre, founder of the anti-imperialist APRA (American Popular Revolutionary Alliance) whose ambitions were pan-Latin American, even if APRA only established itself in his native Peru, planned to have his insurrectionaries trained by the cadres of the celebrated anti-Yankee rebel Sandino in Nicaragua. (Sandino's long guerrilla war against US occupation after 1927 was to inspire the 'Sandinista' revolution in Nicaragua in the 1980s.) Moreover, the USA of the 1930s, enfeebled by the Great Slump, did not look anything like as formidable and dominant as before. Franklin D. Roosevelt's abandonment of the gunboats and marines of his predecessors could be seen not only as a 'good neighbour policy' but also (mistakenly) as a sign of weakness. Latin America in the 1930s was not inclined to look north.

But, seen from across the Atlantic, fascism undoubtedly looked like the success story of the decade. If there was a model in the world to be imitated by up-and-coming politicians of a continent that had always taken its inspiration from the culturally hegemonic regions, such potential leaders of countries always on the look-out for the recipe to become modern, rich and great, it was surely to be found in Berlin and Rome, since London and Paris no longer provided much political inspiration and Washington was out of action. (Moscow was still seen essentially as a model for social revolution, which restricted its political appeal.)

And yet, how different from their European models were the political activities and achievements of men who made no bones about their intellectual debt to Mussolini and Hitler! I still recall my shock at hearing the President of revolutionary Bolivia admitting it without hesitation in a private conversation. In Bolivia soldiers and politicians with their eye on Germany found themselves organizing the revolution of 1952 which nationalized the tin-mines and gave the Indian peasantry radical land reform. In Colombia the great people's tribune Jorge Eliecer Gaitán, so far from choosing the political Right, captured the leadership of the Liberal Party and would certainly as president have led it in a radical direction, had he not been assassinated in Bogotá on 9 April 1948, an event which provoked the *immediate* popular insurrection of the capital (including its police) and the proclamation of revolutionary communes in many a provincial municipality of the country. What Latin American leaders took from European fascism was its deification of populist leaders with a reputation for action. But the masses they wanted to mobilize, and found themselves mobilizing, were not those who feared for what they might lose, but those who had nothing to lose. And the enemies against whom they mobilized them were not foreigners and outgroups (even though the element of anti-semitism in Perónist, or other Argentine politics is undeniable), but 'the oligarchy' – the rich, the local ruling class. Perón found his core support in the Argentine working class, and his basic political machine in something like a labour party built around the mass labour union movement he fostered. Getulio Vargas in Brazil made the same discovery. It was the army that overthrew him in 1945 and, again, forced him into suicide in 1954. It was the urban working class, to which he had given social protection in return for political support, which mourned him as the father of his people. European fascist regimes destroyed labour movements, the Latin American leaders they inspired created them. Whatever the intellectual filiation, historically, we cannot speak of the same kind of movement.

V

Yet these movements too must be seen as part of the decline and fall of liberalism in the Age of Catastrophe. For if the rise and triumph of fascism was the most dramatic expression of the liberal retreat, it is a mistake, even in the 1930s, to see this retreat exclusively in terms of fascism. So at the conclusion of this chapter we must ask how it is to be explained. However, a common confusion which identifies fascism and nationalism must first be cleared away.

That fascist movements tended to appeal to nationalist passions and prejudices is obvious, though the semi-fascist corporate states, like Portugal and Austria 1934–38, being largely under Catholic inspiration, had to reserve their unqualified hatred for peoples and nations of another religion or godless ones. Moreover, simple nationalism was difficult for local fascist movements in countries conquered and occupied by Germany or Italy, or whose fortunes depended on the victory of those states against their own national governments. In suitable cases (Flanders, the Netherlands, Scandinavia) they could identify themselves with the Germans as part of a greater Teutonic racial group, but a more convenient stance (strongly backed by Dr Goebbels' propaganda during the war), was paradoxically *internationalist*. Germany was seen as the core and only guarantee of a future *European order*, with the usual appeals to Charlemagne and anti-communism; a phase in the development of the European idea on which historians of the post-war European Community do not much like to dwell. The non-German military units which fought under the German flag in the Second World War, mainly as part of the SS, usually stressed this transnational element.

On the other hand it ought to be equally obvious that not all nationalisms sympathized with fascism, and not only because the ambitions of Hitler, and to a lesser extent Mussolini, threatened a number of them – e.g. the Poles and the Czechs. Indeed, as we shall see (chapter 5) in a number of countries mobilisation against fascism was to produce a patriotism of the Left, especially during the war, when resistance to the Axis was conducted by 'national fronts' or governments spanning the entire political spectrum, excluding only fascists and their collaborators. Broadly speaking, whether a local nationalism found itself on the side of fascism depended on whether it had more to gain than to lose by the advance of the Axis, and whether its hatred of communism or some other state, nationality or ethnic group (the Jews, the Serbs) was greater than its dislike of Germans or Italians. Thus the Poles, though strongly anti-Russian and anti-Jewish, did not significantly collaborate with Nazi Germany, whereas the Lithuanians and some of the Ukrainians (occupied by the USSR from 1939–41) did.

Why did liberalism recede between the wars, even in states which did not accept fascism? Western radicals, socialists and communists who lived through this period were inclined to see the era of global crisis as the final agony of the capitalist system. Capitalism, they argued, could no longer afford the luxury of ruling through parliamentary democracy, and under liberal freedoms, which, incidentally, had provided the power-base for moderate, reformist labour movements. Faced with insoluble economic problems and/or an increasingly revolutionary working class, the bourgeoisie now had to fall back on force and coercion, that is to say, on something like fascism.

As both capitalism and liberal democracy were to make a triumphant comeback in 1945, it is easy to forget that there was a core of truth in this view, as well as rather too much agitational rhetoric. Democratic systems do not work unless there is a basic consensus among most citizens about the acceptability of their state and social system, or at least a readiness to bargain for compromise settlements. This, in turn, is much facilitated by prosperity. In most of Europe these conditions were simply not present between 1918 and the Second World War. Social cataclysm seemed to be impending or had happened. The fear of revolution was such that over most of eastern and south-eastern Europe as well as part of the Mediterranean, communist parties were barely ever allowed to emerge from illegality. The unbridgeable gap between the ideological Right and even the moderate Left wrecked Austrian democracy in 1930–34, though it has flourished in that country since 1945 under exactly the same two-party system of Catholics and Socialists (Seton Watson, 1962, p. 184). Spanish democracy broke under the same tensions in the 1930s. The contrast with the negotiated transition from the Franco dictatorship to a pluralist democracy in the 1970s is dramatic.

What chances of stability there were in such regimes could not survive the Great Depression. The Weimar Republic fell largely because the Great Slump made it impossible to keep the tacit bargain between state, employers and organized workers, which had kept it afloat. Industry and government felt they had no choice but to impose economic and social cuts and mass unemployment did the rest. In mid-1932 National Socialists and communists between them polled an absolute majority of all German votes, and the parties committed to the Republic were reduced to little more than a third. Conversely, it it is undeniable that the stability of democratic regimes after the second World War, not least that of the new German Federal Republic, rested on the economic miracles of those decades (see chapter 9). Where governments have enough to distribute to satisfy all claimants, and most citizens' standard of life is steadily rising in any case, the temperature of democratic politics rarely rises to fever-pitch. Compromise and consensus tended to prevail, as even the most impassioned believers in the overthrow of capitalism found the status quo less intolerable in practice than in theory, and even the most uncompromising champions of capitalism took social security systems and regular negotiations of wage rises and fringe benefits with labour unions for granted.

Yet, as the Great Slump itself showed, this is only part of the answer. A very similar situation – the refusal of the organized workers to accept Depression cuts – led to the collapse of parliamentary government and, eventually, to the nomination of Hitler as head of government in Germany, but in Britain merely to a sharp shift from a Labour to a (Conservative) 'National Government' within a stable and quite unshaken parliamentary system.* The Depression did not automatically lead to the

---

* A Labour government in 1931 split over this issue, some Labour leaders and their Liberal supporters went over to the Conservatives, who won the subsequent election by a landslide and remained comfortably in power until May 1940.

suspension or abolition of representative democracy, as is also evident from the political consequences in the USA (Roosevelt's New Deal) and Scandinavia (the triumph of social democracy). Only in Latin America, where government finances depended, for the most part, on the exports of one or two primary products, whose price collapsed suddenly and dramatically (see chapter 3), did the Slump produce the almost immediate and automatic fall of whatever governments were in being, mainly by military coups. It should be added that political change in the opposite direction also took place then in Chile and Colombia.

At bottom liberal politics was vulnerable because its characteristic form of government, representative democracy, was rarely a convincing way of running states, and the conditions of the Age of Catastrophe rarely guaranteed the conditions that made it viable, let alone effective.

The first of these conditions was that it should enjoy general consent and legitimacy. Democracy itself rests on this consent, but does not create it, except that in well-established and stable democracies the very process of regular voting has tended to give citizens – even those in the minority – a sense that the electoral process legitimizes the governments it produces. But few of the inter-war democracies were well-established. Indeed, until the early twentieth century democracy had been rare outside the USA and France (see *Age of Empire*, chapter 4). Indeed, at least ten of Europe's states after the First World War were either entirely new or so changed from their predecessors as to have no special legitimacy for their inhabitants. Even fewer democracies were stable. The politics of states in the Age of Catastrophe were, more often than not, the politics of crisis.

The second condition was a degree of compatibility between the various components of 'the people', whose sovereign vote was to determine the common government. The official theory of liberal bourgeois society did not recognize 'the people' as a set of groups, communities and other collectivities with interests as such, although anthropologists, sociologists and all practising politicians did. Officially the people, a theoretical concept rather than a real body of human beings, consisted of an assembly of self-contained individuals whose votes added up to arithmetical majorities. and minorities, which translated into elected assemblies as majority governments and minority oppositions. Where democratic voting crossed the lines between the divisions of the national population, or where it was possible to conciliate or defuse conflicts between them, democracy was viable. However, in an era of revolution and radical social tensions, class struggle translated into politics rather than class peace was the rule. Ideological and class intransigence could wreck democratic government. Moreover, the botched peace settlements after 1918 multiplied what we, at the end of the twentieth century, know to be the fatal virus of democracy, namely the division of the body of citizens exclusively along ethnic-national or religious lines (Glenny, 1992, pp. 146–48), as in ex-Yugoslavia and Northern Ireland. Three ethnic-religious communities voting as blocks, as in Bosnia; two irreconcilable communities, as in Ulster; sixty-two political parties each representing a tribe or clan, as in Somalia, cannot, as we know, provide the foundation for a democratic political system, but – unless one of the contending groups or some outside authority is strong enough to establish (non-democratic) dominance – only for instability and civil war. The fall of the three multinational empires of Austria-Hungary, Russia and Turkey replaced three supranational states whose governments were neutral as between the numerous nationalities over which they ruled, with a great many more multinational states, each identified with *one*, or at most with two or three, of the ethnic communities within their borders.

The third condition was that democratic governments did not have to do much governing. Parliaments had come into existence not so much to govern as to control the power of those who did, a function which is still obvious in the relations between the US Congress and the US presidency. They were devices designed as brakes which found themselves having to act as engines. Sovereign assemblies, elected on a restricted but expanding franchise, were, of course, increasingly common from the Age of Revolution on, but nineteenth-century bourgeois society assumed that the bulk of its citizens' lives would take place, not in the sphere of government, but in the self-regulating economy and in the world of private and unofficial associations ('civil society').* It side-stepped the difficulties of running governments through elected assemblies in two ways: by not expecting too much governing, or even legislation, from their parliaments, and by seeing that government – or rather administration – could be carried on regardless of their vagaries. As we have seen (see chapter 1) bodies of independent, permanently appointed public officials had become an essential device for the government of modern states. A parliamentary majority was essential only where major and controversial executive decisions had to be taken, or approved, and organizing or maintaining an adequate body of supporters was the major task of government leaders, since (except in the Americas) the executive in parliamentary regimes was

---

* The 1980s in West and East were to be full of nostalgic rhetoric seeking an entirely impracticable return to an idealized nineteenth-century constructed on these assumptions.

usually not directly elected. In states with a restricted suffrage (i.e. an electorate composed mainly of the wealthy, powerful or influential minority) this was made easier by a common consensus of what constituted their collective interest (the 'national interest'), not to mention the resources of patronage.

The twentieth century multiplied the occasions when it became essential for governments to govern. The kind of state which confined itself to providing the ground rules for business and civil society, and the police, prisons and armed forces to keep internal and external danger at bay, the 'nightwatchman state' of political wits, became as obsolete as the 'nightwatchmen' who inspired the metaphor.

The fourth condition was wealth and prosperity. The democracies of the 1920s broke under the tension of revolution and counter-revolution (Hungary, Italy, Portugal) or of national conflict (Poland, Yugoslavia); those of the thirties, under the tensions of the Slump. One has only to compare the political atmosphere of Weimar Germany and 1920s Austria with that of Federal Germany and post-1945 Austria to be convinced. Even national conflicts were less unmanageable, so long as each minority's politicians could feed at the state's common trough. That was the strength of the Agrarian Party in east-central Europe's only genuine democracy, Czechoslovakia: it offered benefits across national lines. In the 1930s, even Czechoslovakia could no longer hold together the Czechs, Slovaks, Germans, Hungarians and Ukrainians.

Under these circumstances democracy was, more likely than not, a mechanism for formalizing divisions between irreconcilable groups. Very often even in the best circumstances, it produced no stable basis for democratic government at all, especially when the theory of democratic representation was applied in the most rigorous versions of proportional representation.* Where, in times of crisis, no parliamentary majority was available, as in Germany (as distinct from Britain)† the temptation to look elsewhere was overwhelming. Even in stable democracies the political divisions the system implies are seen by many citizens as costs rather than benefits of the system. The very rhetoric of politics advertises candidates and party as the representative of the national rather than the

---

* The endless permutations of democratic electoral systems – proportional or otherwise – are all attempts to ensure or maintain stable majorities permitting stable governments in political systems which, by their very nature, make this difficult.

† In Britain the refusal to entertain any form of proportional representation ('winner takes all') favoured a two-party system, and marginalized other parties – since the First World War the once dominant Liberal Party, though it continued to

narrow party interest. In times of crisis the costs of the system seemed unsustainable, its benefits uncertain.

Under these circumstances it is easy to understand that parliamentary democracy in the successor states to the old empires, as well as in most of the Mediterranean and in Latin America, was a feeble plant growing in stony soil. The strongest argument in its favour, that, bad as it is, it is better than any alternative system, is itself half-hearted. Between the wars it only rarely sounded realistic and convincing. Even its champions spoke with muted confidence. Its retreat seemed to be inevitable, as even in the United States serious, but needlessly gloomy observers noted that 'It Can Happen Here' (Sinclair Lewis, 1935). Nobody seriously predicted or expected its post-war renaissance, still less its return, however brief, as the predominant form of government across the globe in the early 1990s. For those who looked back on the period between the wars at this time, the fall of liberal political systems seemed a brief interruption in their secular conquest of the globe. Unfortunately, as the new millennium approached, the uncertainties surrounding political democracy no longer seemed quite so remote. The world may be unhappily re-entering a period when its advantages no longer seem as obvious as they did between 1950 and 1990.

---

poll a steady 10 per cent of the national vote (this was still the case in 1992). In Germany the proportional system, though slightly favouring larger parties, produced none after 1920 with even one third of seats (except the Nazis in 1932) among five major and a dozen or so minor groupings. In the absence of a majority the constitution provided for (temporary) executive rule by emergency powers, i.e., the suspension of democracy.

CHAPTER FIVE

Against the Common Enemy

Tomorrow for the young the poets exploding like bombs,
The walks by the lake, the weeks of perfect communion;
　　Tomorrow the bicycle races
Through the suburbs on summer evenings. But to–day the struggle . . .

　　　　　　　　　　　　– W.H. Auden, 'Spain', 1937

Dear Mum, Of all people I know you are the one that will feel it
most, so my very last thoughts go to you. Don't blame anyone else
for my death, because I myself chose my fate.

　　I don't know what to write to you, because, even though I have a
clear head, I can't find the right words. I took my place in the
Army of Liberation, and I die as the light of victory is already
beginning to shine . . . I shall be shot very shortly with twenty three
other comrades.

　　After the war you must claim your rights to a pension. They will
let you have my things at the jail, only I am keeping Dad's
undervest, because I don't want the cold to make me shiver . . .

　　Once again I say goodbye. Courage!

　　　　　　　　　　　　　　　　　Your son.
　　　　　　　　　　　　　　　　　Spartaco

– Spartaco Fontanot, metalworker, twenty-two years old, member
　　of the French resistance group of Misak Manouchian, 1944
　　　　　　　　　　　　　　　　　(Lettere, p. 306)

I

Public opinion research is the child of America in the 1930s, for the
extension of the 'sample survey' of the market researchers into politics

essentially began with George Gallup in 1936. Among the early results of this new technique is one which would have amazed all US presidents before Franklin D. Roosevelt, and will amaze all readers who have grown up since the Second World War. When asked in January 1939 who Americans wanted to win, if a war broke out between the Soviet Union and Germany, 83 per cent favoured a Soviet victory against 17 per cent who were for Germany (Miller, 1989, pp. 283–84). In a century dominated by the confrontation between the anti-capitalist communism of the October revolution, represented by the USSR and anti-communist capitalism, of which the USA was the champion and chief exemplar, nothing looks more anomalous than this declaration of sympathy, or at least preference, for the home of world revolution over a strongly anti-communist country, whose economy was recognizably capitalist. All the more so as the Stalinist tyranny in the USSR was at that time, by general consent, at its worst.

The historic situation was certainly exceptional and comparatively short-lived. It lasted, at a maximum, from 1933 (when the USA recognized the USSR officially) until 1947 (when the two ideological camps confronted each other as enemies in the 'Cold War'), but more realistically, for the years from 1935 to 1945. In other words, it was determined by the rise and fall of Hitler Germany (1933–45) (see chapter 4), against which both the USA and the USSR made common cause, because they saw it as a greater danger than each of the two saw the other.

The reasons why they did so go beyond the range of conventional international relations or power politics, and this is what makes the anomalous alignment of states and movements which eventually fought and won the Second World War so significant. What eventually forged the union against Germany was the fact that it was not just any nation-state with reasons to feel discontented with its situation, but one whose policy and ambitions were determined by its ideology. In short, that it was a fascist power. So long as this was left aside or not appreciated, the ordinary calculations of *Realpolitik* held good. Germany could be opposed or conciliated, counter-balanced or, if need be, fought, depending on the interests of a country's state policy and the general situation. In fact, at one time or another between 1933 and 1941 all other major players in the international game treated Germany accordingly. London and Paris appeased Berlin (i.e. offered concessions at someone else's expense), Moscow exchanged a stance of opposition for one of helpful neutrality in return for territorial gains, and even Italy and Japan, whose interests aligned them with Germany, found that these interests also told them, in 1939, to stay out of the first stages of the Second World War. As it happened, the logic of Hitler's war drew all of them as well as the USA into it eventually.

But as the 1930s advanced it became increasingly clear that more was at issue than the relative balance of power between the nation-states constituting the international (i.e. primarily the European) system. Indeed, the politics of the West – from the USSR through Europe to the Americas – can be best understood, not through the contest of states, but as an international ideological civil war. As we shall see, this is not the best way to understand the politics of Afroasia and the Far East, which were dominated by the fact of colonialism (see chapter 7). And, as it turned out, the crucial lines in this civil war were not drawn between capitalism as such and communist social revolution, but between ideological families: on the one hand the descendants of the eighteenth-century Enlightenment and the great revolutions including, obviously, the Russian revolution; on the other, its opponents. In short, the frontier ran not between capitalism and communism, but between what the nineteenth century would have called 'progress' and 'reaction' – only that these terms were no longer quite apposite.

It was an international war, because it raised essentially the same issues in most Western countries. It was a civil war, because the lines between the pro- and anti-fascist forces ran through each society. Never has there been a period when patriotism, in the sense of automatic loyalty to a citizen's national government, counted for less. When the Second World War ended, the governments of at least ten old European countries were headed by men who, at its beginning (or, in the case of Spain, at the start of the Civil War), had been rebels, political exiles or, at the very least, persons who had regarded their own government as immoral and illegitimate. Men and women, often from the heart of their countries' political classes, chose loyalty to communism (i.e. to the USSR) over that to their own state. The 'Cambridge spies' and, probably to greater practical effect, the Japanese members of the Sorge spy ring, were only two groups out of many.* On the other hand, the special term 'quisling' was invented – based on the name of a Norwegian Nazi – to describe the political forces within states attacked by Hitler who chose, out of conviction rather than expediency, to join their country's enemy.

* It has been argued that Sorge's information, based on the most reliable sources, that Japan did *not* intend to attack the USSR in late 1941, enabled Stalin to transfer vital reinforcements to the Western Front at a time when the Germans were on the outskirts of Moscow (Deakin and Storry, 1964, chapter 13; Andrew and Gordievsky, 1991, pp. 281–82).

This was true even of people moved by patriotism rather than global ideology. For even traditional patriotism was now divided. Strongly imperialist and anti-communist Conservatives like Winston Churchill, and men of reactionary Catholic background like de Gaulle, chose to fight Germany, not because of any special animus against fascism, but because of '*une certaine idée de la France*' or 'a certain idea of England'. Yet even for such as these, their commitment could be part of an international *civil* war, since their concept of patriotism was not necessarily their governments'. In going to London and declaring, on 18 June 1940, that under him 'Free France' would continue to fight Germany, Charles de Gaulle was committing an act of rebellion against the legitimate government of France, which had constitutionally decided to end the war, and was almost certainly supported in its decision by the great majority of Frenchmen at the time. No doubt Churchill, in such a situation, would have reacted in the same manner. Had Germany won the war, he would have been treated by his government as a traitor, as the Russians who fought with the Germans against the USSR were treated by their country after 1945. Just so Slovaks and Croats, whose countries acquired their first taste of (qualified) state independence as satellites of Hitler Germany regarded the leaders of their wartime states retrospectively as patriotic heroes or fascist collaborators on ideological grounds: members of each people fought on both sides.*

What bonded all these national civil divisions into a single global war, both international and civil, was the rise of Hitler Germany. Or, more precisely, between 1931 and 1941 the march to conquest and war of the combination of states – Germany, Italy and Japan, of which Hitler Germany became the central pillar. And Hitler Germany was both more ruthlessly and manifestly committed to the destruction of the values and institutions of the 'Western civilisation' of the Age of Revolution, and capable of carrying out its barbaric project. Step by step the potential victims of Japan, Germany and Italy watched the states of what came to be called 'the Axis' push their conquests forward, towards the war which, from 1931 on, seemed unavoidable. As the phrase went, 'fascism means war'. In 1931 Japan invaded Manchuria and set up a puppet state there. In 1932 Japan occupied China north of the Great Wall and landed in Shanghai. In 1933 Hitler came to power in Germany, with a programme which he made no attempt to conceal. In 1934 a brief civil war in Austria

---

* However, this should not be used to justify the atrocities committed by either side which, certainly in the case of the Croat state of 1942–45, probably in the case of the Slovak state, were greater than their opponents', and in any case indefensible.

eliminated democracy in Austria, and introduced a semi-fascist regime distinguished chiefly by resisting integration into Germany and (with Italian backing at the time) defeating a Nazi coup which murdered the Austrian premier. In 1935 Germany denounced the peace treaties and re-emerged as a major military and naval power, re-acquiring (by plebiscite) the Saar region on its western frontier and, contemptuously resigning from the League of Nations. In the same year Mussolini, with equal contempt for international opinion, invaded Ethiopia, which Italy proceeded to conquer and occupy as a colony in 1936–37, after which the state also tore up its membership of the League. In 1936, Germany recovered the Rhineland and, with open assistance and intervention from both Italy and Germany, a military coup in Spain initiated a major conflict, the Spanish Civil War, about which more will be said below. The two fascist powers entered a formal alignment, the Rome–Berlin Axis, while Germany and Japan concluded an 'Anti-Comintern Pact'. In 1937, not surprisingly, Japan invaded China and set out on a course of open warfare which did not cease until 1945. In 1938 Germany plainly also felt the time for conquest had come. Austria was invaded and annexed in March, without military resistance, and, after various threats, the Munich agreement of October broke up Czechoslovakia and transferred large parts of it to Hitler, again peacefully. The remainder was occupied in March 1939, encouraging Italy, which had not demonstrated imperial ambitions for a few months, to occupy Albania. Almost immediately a Polish crisis, which arose once again out of German territorial demands, paralysed Europe. Out of it came the European war of 1939–41, which grew into the Second World War.

However, another thing wove the threads of national politics into a single international web: the consistent and increasingly spectacular feebleness of liberal-democratic states (which happened also to be the victor states of the First World War); their inability or unwillingness to act, singly or in conjunction, to resist the advance of their enemies. As we have seen, it was this crisis of liberalism which strengthened both the arguments and the forces of fascism and authoritarian government (see chapter 4). The Munich agreement of 1938 perfectly demonstrated this combination of confident aggression on one side, fear and concession on the other, which is why for generations the very word 'Munich' became a synonym, in Western political discourse, for craven retreat. The shame of Munich, which was felt almost immediately, even by those who signed the agreement, lay not simply in handing Hitler a cheap triumph, but in the palpable fear of war that preceded it, and the even more palpable sense of relief that it had been avoided at any cost. '*Bande de cons*' the

French premier Daladier is said to have muttered contemptuously when, having signed away the life of an ally of France, he expected to be hissed on his return to Paris, but met nothing but delirious cheers. The popularity of the USSR, and the reluctance to criticise what was happening there, was chiefly due to its consistent opposition to Nazi Germany, so different from the hesitations of the West. The shock of the pact with Germany in August 1939 was all the greater.

II

The mobilization of the full potential of support against fascism, i.e. against the German camp, therefore, was a triple call for union of all political forces which had a common interest in resisting the Axis advance; for an actual policy of resistance, and for governments prepared to carry out such a policy. In fact, it took more than eight years to achieve this mobilization – ten, if we date the start of the race to world war in 1931. For the response to all three calls was, inevitably, hesitant, muffled or mixed.

The call for anti-fascist unity was, in some ways, likely to win the most immediate response, since fascism publicly treated liberals of various kinds, socialists and communists, any kind of democratic regimes and soviet regimes as enemies to be equally destroyed. In the old English phrase, they had all to hang together if they did not want to hang separately. The communists, who hitherto had been the most divisive force on the Enlightenment Left, concentrating their fire (as is, alas, characteristic of political radicals) not against the obvious enemy but against the nearest potential competitor, above all the Social Democrats (see chapter 2) changed course within eighteen months of Hitler's accession to power and turned themselves into the most systematic and, as usual, the most efficient, champions of anti-fascist unity. This removed the major obstacle to unity on the Left, though not deeply rooted mutual suspicions.

Essentially the strategy put forward (in conjunction with Stalin) by the Communist International (which had chosen as its new General Secretary George Dimitrov, a Bulgarian whose brave public defiance of the Nazi authorities in the Reichstag fire trial of 1933 had electrified anti-fascists everywhere)* was one of concentric circles. The united forces of labour

---

* Within a month of Hitler's accession to power, the German parliament building in Berlin was mysteriously burned down. The Nazi government immediately accused the Communist Party and used the occasion to suppress it. The communists accused

(the 'United Front') would form the foundation of a wider electoral and political alliance with democrats and liberals (the 'Popular Front'). Beyond this, as the advance of Germany continued, the communists envisaged an even wider extension into a 'National Front' of all who, irrespective of ideology and political beliefs, regarded fascism (or the Axis powers) as the primary danger. This extension of the anti-fascist alliance beyond the political Centre to the Right – the French communists' 'hand stretched out to the Catholics', or the British ones' readiness to embrace the notoriously red-baiting Winston Churchill – met with more resistance, on the traditional Left until the logic of war finally imposed it. However, the union of Centre and Left made political sense, and 'Popular Fronts' were established in France (which pioneered this device) and Spain, which pushed back local offensives of the Right, and won dramatic election victories in Spain (February 1936) and France (May 1936).

These victories dramatized the costs of past disunion, because the united electoral lists of Centre and Left won substantial parliamentary majorities – but though they showed a striking shift of opinion *within* the Left, notably in France, in favour of the Communist Party, they did not indicate any serious widening of political support for anti-fascism. In fact, the triumph of the French Popular Front, which produced the first French government ever headed by a Socialist, the intellectual Léon Blum (1872–1950), was achieved by an increase of barely one per cent of the united Radical-Socialist-Communist vote of 1932, and the electoral triumph of the Spanish Popular Front by a slightly larger shift, but one that still left the new government with almost half the voters against it (and a Right somewhat stronger than before). Still, these victories pumped hope, even euphoria, into the local labour and socialist movements; more than can be said for the British Labour Party, shattered by slump and political crisis in 1931 – it was reduced to a rump of fifty – but which, four years later, had not quite recovered its pre-slump vote, or much more than half of its 1929 seats. Between 1931 and 1935 the Conservative vote merely fell from c. 61 per cent to c. 54 per cent. The so-called 'National' government of Britain, headed from 1937 on by Neville

---

the Nazis of having organized the fire for this purpose. An unbalanced Dutch loner of revolutionary sympathies, Van der Lubbe, as well as the leader of the communist parliamentary group and three Bulgarians working in Berlin for the Communist International, were arrested and tried. Van der Lubbe was certainly involved in the arson, the four arrested communists certainly not, nor obviously was the KPD. Current historical scholarship does not support the suggestion of a Nazi provocation.

Chamberlain, who became the synonym for the 'appeasement' of Hitler, rested on solid majority support. There is no reason to suppose that, had war not broken out in 1939 and had an election been held in 1940, as it would have had to have been, the Conservatives would not have won it again comfortably. Indeed, except for most of Scandinavia, where the Social Democrats gained ground strongly, there was no sign of any significant electoral shift to the Left in Western Europe in the 1930s, and some fairly massive shifts to the Right in those parts of eastern and south-eastern Europe in which elections were still held. There is a sharp contrast between the old and new worlds. Nothing like the dramatic shift from Republicans to Democrats in 1932 (their presidential vote rose from between fifteen and sixteen to almost twenty-eight millions in four years) occurred anywhere in Europe, but it must be said that, in electoral terms, Franklin D. Roosevelt reached his peak in 1932, even though (to everyone's surprise except the people's) he barely fell short of it in 1936.

Anti-fascism, therefore, organized the traditional adversaries of the Right, but did not swell their numbers; it mobilized minorities more easily than majorities. Among these minorities, intellectuals and those concerned with the arts were particularly open to its appeal (except for an international current of literature inspired by the nationalist and anti-democratic Right – see chapter 6), because the arrogant and aggressive hostility of National Socialism to the values of civilization as hitherto conceived was instantly obvious in the fields that concerned them. Nazi racism immediately led to the mass exodus of Jewish and Left-wing scholars who scattered across the remaining world of toleration. Nazi hostility to intellectual freedom almost immediately purged the German universities of perhaps one third of their teachers. The attacks on 'modernist' culture, the public burning of 'Jewish' and other undesirable books, began virtually as soon as Hitler entered government. However, while ordinary citizens might disapprove of the more brutal barbarities of the system – the concentration camps and the reduction of the German Jews (which included all those with at least one Jewish grandparent) to a segregated underclass without rights – a surprisingly large number saw them, at worst, as limited aberrations. After all, concentration camps were still primarily deterrents for potential communist opposition and jails for the cadres of subversion, an object with which many conventional conservatives had some sympathy, and when war broke out there were no more than about 8,000 persons in all of them. (Their expansion into an *univers concentrationnaire* of terror, torture and death for hundreds of thousands, even millions, happened during the war.) And, until the war, Nazi policy, however barbarous the treatment of the Jews, still appeared to envisage the 'final solution' of the 'Jewish problem' as mass expulsion rather than mass extermination. Germany itself appeared to the non-political observer as a stable, indeed an economically flourishing country with a popular government, though with some unattractive characteristics. Those who read books, including the Führer's own *Mein Kampf*, were more likely to recognize, in the bloodthirsty rhetoric of racist agitators and the localized torture and murder of Dachau or Buchenwald, the threat of an entire world built on the deliberate reversal of civilization. Western intellectuals (though at this time only a fraction of students, then overwhelmingly a contingent of sons and future entrants of the 'respectable' middle classes) were therefore the first social stratum mobilised en masse against fascism in the 1930s. It was still a rather small stratum, though an unusually influential one, not least because it included the journalists who, in the non-fascist countries of the West, played a crucial role in alerting even more conservative readers and decision-makers to the nature of National Socialism.

The actual policy of resistance to the rise of the fascist camp was, once again, simple and logical on paper. It was to unite all countries against the aggressors (the League of Nations provided a potential framework for this), to make no concessions to them, and, by the threat and, if necessary, the reality of common action, to deter or defeat them. The USSR's foreign commissar Maxim Litvinov (1876–1951) made himself the spokesman of this 'Collective Security'. Easier said than done. The major obstacle was that, then as now, even states which shared the fear and suspicion of the aggressors had other interests which divided them or could be used to divide them.

How far the most obvious division counted, that between the Soviet Union committed in theory to the overthrow of bourgeois regimes and the end of their empires everywhere, and the other states, now saw the USSR as the inspirer and instigator of subversion, is not clear. While governments – all the main ones after 1933 recognized the USSR – were always prepared to come to terms with it when it suited their purposes, some of their members and agencies continued to regard Bolshevism, at home and abroad, as the essential enemy, in the spirit of the post-1945 cold wars. The British Intelligence services were admittedly exceptional in concentrating against the Red menace to such an extent that they did not abandon it as their main target until the middle 1930s (Andrew, 1985, p. 530). Nevertheless many a good conservative felt, especially in Britain, that the best of all solutions would be a German–Soviet war, weakening, perhaps destroying, both enemies, and a defeat of Bolshevism by a weakened Germany would be no bad thing. The sheer reluctance of

Western governments to enter into effective negotiations with the Red state, even in 1938–39 when the urgency of an anti-Hitler alliance was no longer denied by anyone, is only too patent. Indeed, it was the fear of being left to confront Hitler alone which eventually drove Stalin, since 1934 the unswerving champion of an alliance with the West against him, into the Stalin–Ribbentrop Pact of August 1939, by which he hoped to keep the USSR out of the war while Germany and the Western powers would weaken one another, to the benefit of his state which, by the secret clauses of the pact, acquired a large part of the western territories lost by Russia after the revolution. The calculation proved wrong, but, like the abortive attempts to create a common front against Hitler, they demonstrate the divisions between states which made possible the extraordinary and virtually unresisted rise of Nazi Germany between 1933 and 1939.

Moreover, geography, history and economics gave governments different perspectives on the world. The continent of Europe as such was of little or no interest to Japan and the USA, whose policies were Pacific and American, and to Britain, still committed to a worldwide empire and a global maritime strategy, though too weak to maintain either. The countries of Eastern Europe were squeezed between Germany and Russia and this obviously determined their policies, especially when (as it turned out) the Western powers were unable to protect them. Several had acquired formerly Russian territories after 1917, and, though hostile to Germany, therefore resisted any anti-German alliance which would bring Russian forces back on their lands. And yet, as the Second World War was to demonstrate, the only effective anti-fascist alliance was one which included the USSR. As for economics, countries like Britain which knew they had waged a First World War beyond their financial capacities, recoiled from the costs of rearmament. In short, there was a wide gap between recognizing the Axis powers as a major danger and doing something about it.

Liberal democracy (which by definition did not exist on the fascist or authoritarian side) widened this gap. It slowed down or prevented political decision, notably in the USA, and unquestionably made it difficult, and sometimes impossible, to pursue unpopular policies. No doubt some governments used this to justify their own torpor, but the example of the USA shows that even a strong and popular president like F.D. Roosevelt was unable to carry his anti-fascist foreign policy against the opinion of the electorate. But for Pearl Harbor, and Hitler's declaration of war, the USA would almost certainly have continued to stay out of the Second World War. It is not clear under what circumstances it could have come in.

Yet what weakened the resolution of the crucial European democracies, France and Great Britain, was not so much the political mechanisms of democracy, as the memory of the First World War. This was a wound whose pain was felt both by voters and governments, because the impact of that war had been both unprecedented and universal. For both France and Britain it was, in human (though not in material) terms, far greater than the impact of the Second World War proved to be (see chapter 1). Another such war had to be avoided at almost all costs. It was certainly the last of all resorts of politics.

A reluctance to go to war must not be confused with a refusal to fight, though the potential military morale of the French, who had suffered more than any other belligerent country, was certainly weakened by the trauma of 1914–18. Nobody went into the Second World War singing, not even the Germans. On the other hand unqualified (non-religious) pacifism, though quite popular in Britain in the 1930s, was never a mass movement and faded away in 1940. In spite of the extensive tolerance for 'conscientious objectors' in the Second World War, the numbers who claimed the right to refuse to fight were small (Calvocoressi, 1987, p. 63).

On the non-communist Left, even more emotionally committed to hatred of war and militarism after 1918 than it had been (in theory) before 1914, peace at any price remained a minority position, even in France where it was strongest. In Britain George Lansbury, a pacifist who, by the accident of an electoral holocaust, found himself at the head of the Labour Party after 1931, was efficiently and brutally removed from leadership in 1935. Unlike the French socialist-headed Popular Front government of 1936–38, British Labour could be criticized, not for lack of firmness towards the fascist aggressors, but for refusing to support the necessary military measures to make resistance effective, such as rearmament and conscription. So, for the same reasons, could the communists, who were never tempted by pacifism.

The Left was indeed in a quandary. On the one hand the strength of anti-fascism was that it mobilized those who feared war, both the last and the unknown horrors of the next. That fascism meant war was a convincing reason for fighting it. On the other hand, resistance to fascism which did not envisage the use of arms could not succeed. What is more, the hope of bringing about the collapse of Nazi Germany, or even Mussolini's Italy, by collective but peaceable firmness, rested on illusions about Hitler and about the supposed forces of opposition within Germany. In any case we who lived through those times *knew* that there would be a war, even as we sketched out unconvincing scenarios for avoiding it. We – the historian may also appeal to his memory – *expected* to fight in the next war, and probably to die. And as anti-fascists we had no doubt that when it came to the point we had no choice but to fight.

Nevertheless, the political dilemma of the Left cannot be used to explain the failure of governments, if only because effective preparations for war did not depend on resolutions passed (or not passed) at party congresses; or even, for a period of several years, on the fear of elections. Yet governments, and in particular the French and the British, had also been indelibly scarred by the Great War. France had emerged from it bled white, and still potentially a smaller and a weaker power than a defeated Germany. France was nothing without allies against a revived Germany, and the only European countries which had an equal interest in allying with France, Poland and the Habsburg succession states, were plainly too weak for the purpose. The French put their money on a line of fortifications (the 'Maginot Line', named after a soon-forgotten minister) which, they hoped, would deter the attacking Germans by the prospect of losses like those of Verdun (see chapter 1). Beyond this they could only look to Britain and, after 1933, the USSR.

The British governments were equally conscious of fundamental weakness. Financially they could not afford another war. Strategically, they no longer had a navy capable of simultaneously operating in the three great oceans and in the Mediterranean. At the same time, the problem that really worried them was not what happened in Europe, but how to hold together, with patently insufficient forces, a global empire geographically larger than ever before, but also and visibly on the verge of decomposition.

Both states thus knew themselves to be too weak to defend a status quo largely established in 1919 to suit them. Both also knew that this status quo was unstable, and impossible to maintain. Neither had anything to gain from another war, and plenty to lose. The obvious and logical policy was to negotiate with a revived Germany in order to establish a more durable European pattern, and this, beyond any doubt, meant making concessions to Germany's growing power. Unfortunately the revived Germany was Adolf Hitler's.

The so-called policy of 'appeasement' has had such a bad press since 1939 that we must remember how sensible it seemed to so many Western politicians who were not viscerally anti-German or passionately anti-fascist on principle, and especially in Britain, where changes on the continental map, especially in 'far-off countries of which we know little' (Chamberlain on Czechoslovakia in 1938), did not raise the blood pressure. (The French were understandably far more nervous about *any* initiatives favouring Germany, which must sooner or later turn against themselves, but France was weak.) A Second World War, it could safely be predicted, would ruin the British economy, and disband large parts of the British Empire. Indeed, this is what happened. Though it was a price socialists, communists, colonial liberation movements and President F.D. Roosevelt were only too ready to pay for the defeat of fascism, let us not forget that it was excessive from the point of view of rational British imperialists.

Yet compromise and negotiation with Hitler's Germany were impossible, because the policy objectives of National Socialism were irrational and unlimited. Expansion and aggression were built into the system and, short of accepting German domination in advance, i.e. choosing not to resist the Nazi advance, war was unavoidable, sooner rather than later. Hence the central role of ideology in the formation of policy in the 1930s: if it determined the aims of Nazi Germany, it excluded *realpolitik* for the other side. Those who recognized that there could be no compromise with Hitler, which was a realistic assessment of the situation, did so for entirely unpragmatic reasons. They regarded fascism as intolerable on principle and *a priori*, or (as in the case of Winston Churchill) they were driven by an equally *a priori* idea of what their country and empire 'stood for', and could not sacrifice. The paradox of Winston Churchill was that this great romantic, whose political judgment had been almost consistently wrong on every matter since 1914 – including the assessment of military strategy on which he prided himself – was realistic on the one question of Germany.

Conversely, the political realists of appeasement were entirely unrealistic in their assessment of the situation, even when the impossibility of a negotiated settlement with Hitler became obvious to any reasonable observer in 1938–39. This was the reason for the black tragicomedy of March–September 1939, which ended in a war nobody wanted at a time and in a place nobody wanted it (not even Germany), and which actually left Britain and France without any idea of what, as belligerents, they were supposed to do, until the *blitzkrieg* of 1940 swept them aside. In the face of the evidence they themselves accepted, the appeasers in Britain and France still could not bring themselves to negotiate seriously for an alliance with the USSR, without which war could neither be postponed nor won, and without which the guarantees against German attack suddenly and heedlessly scattered around Eastern Europe by Neville Chamberlain – without, incredible as it may seem, consulting or even adequately *informing* the USSR – were waste paper. London and Paris did not want to fight, but at most to deter by a show of strength. This did not look plausible for a moment to Hitler, or for that matter to Stalin, whose negotiators asked vainly for proposals for joint strategic operations in the Baltic. Even as the German armies marched into Poland, Neville Chamberlain's government was still prepared to do a deal with Hitler, as Hitler had calculated he would (Watt, 1989, p. 215).

Hitler miscalculated, and the Western states declared war, not because their statesmen wanted it, but because Hitler's own policy after Munich cut the ground from under the appeasers' feet. It was he who mobilized the hitherto uncommitted masses against fascism. Essentially the German occupation of Czechoslovakia in March 1939 converted British public opinion to resistance, and in doing so forced the hand of a reluctant government; which in turn forced the hand of a French government that had no other option except to go along with its only effective ally. For the first time the fight against Hitler Germany united rather than divided the British, but – as yet – to no purpose. As the Germans quickly and ruthlessly destroyed Poland, and partitioned its remains with Stalin, who retreated into a doomed neutrality, a 'phony war' succeeded an implausible peace in the West.

No kind of *realpolitik* can explain the appeasers' policy after Munich. Once a war seemed sufficiently likely – and who in 1939 doubted this? – the only thing to do was to prepare for it as effectively as possible, and this was not done. For Britain, even Chamberlain's Britain, was certainly not prepared to accept a Hitler-dominated Europe before it happened, even if after the collapse of France there was some serious support for a negotiated peace – i.e. for accepting defeat. Even in France, where pessimism verging on defeatism was far more common among politicians and military men, the government did not intend to give up the ghost, or do so, until the army had collapsed in June 1940. Their policy was half-hearted, because they neither dared follow the logic of power-politics, nor the *a priori* convictions of resisters, to whom *nothing* could be more important than fighting fascism (as fascism or as Hitler Germany) or those of anti-communists, to whom 'Hitler's defeat would mean the collapse of the authoritarian systems which constitute the principle rampart against communist revolution' (Thierry Maulnier, 1938 in Ory, 1976, p. 24). It is not easy to say what determined these statesmen's actions, since they were moved not only by intellect, but by prejudices, preconceptions, hopes and fears which silently skewed their vision. There were the memories of the First World War and the self-doubt of politicians who saw their liberal democratic political systems and economies in what might well be final retreat; a state of mind more typical of the Continent than of Britain. There was the genuine uncertainty about whether, under such circumstances, the unpredictable results of a successful policy of resistance could justify the prohibitive costs that it might entail. For, after all, for most British and French politicians the best that could be achieved was to preserve a not very satisfactory and probably unsustainable status quo. And behind all this there was the question whether, if the status quo was doomed anyway, fascism was not better than the alternative, social revolution and Bolshevism. If the only kind of fascism on offer had been the Italian kind, few conservative or moderate politicians would have hesitated. Even Winston Churchill was pro-Italian. The problem was, that they faced not Mussolini but Hitler. Still, it is not without significance that the main hope of so many governments and diplomats of the 1930s, was to stabilize Europe by coming to terms with Italy, or at least to detach Mussolini from the alliance with his disciple. It did not work, even though Mussolini himself was sufficiently realistic to keep some freedom of action until, in June 1940, he then concluded, mistakenly but not altogether unreasonably, that the Germans had won and declared war himself.

III

The issues of the 1930s, whether fought out within states or between them, were thus transnational. Nowhere was this more immediately evident than in the Spanish Civil War of 1936–39, which became the quintessential expression of this global confrontation.

In retrospect it may seem surprising that this conflict *instantly* mobilized the sympathies of both Left and Right in Europe and the Americas, and notably of the Western world's intellectuals. Spain was a peripheral part of Europe, and its history had been persistently out of phase with the rest of the continent from which it was divided by the wall of the Pyrenees. It had kept out of all European wars since Napoleon, and was to keep out of the Second World War. Since the early nineteenth century its affairs had been of no real concern to European governments, though the USA had provoked a brief war against it in 1898 in order to rob it of the last remaining parts of the old worldwide empire of the sixteenth century, Cuba, Puerto Rico and the Philippines.* In fact, and contrary to the beliefs of this author's generation, the Spanish Civil War was not the first phase of the Second World War, and the victory of General Franco

---

* Spain retained a foothold in Morocco, disputed by the warlike local Berber tribesmen, who also provided the Spanish army with formidable fighting units, and some African territories further south, forgotten by everyone.

who, as we have seen, cannot even be described as a fascist, had no significant global consequences. It merely kept Spain (and Portugal) isolated from the rest of world history for another thirty years.

Yet it was no accident that the domestic politics of that notoriously anomalous and self-contained country became the symbol of a global struggle in the 1930s. They raised the fundamental political issues of the time: on the one side, democracy and social revolution, Spain being the only country in Europe where it was ready to erupt; on the other, a uniquely uncompromising camp of counter-revolution or reaction, inspired by a Catholic Church which rejected everything that had happened in the world since Martin Luther. Curiously enough, neither the parties of Muscovite communism nor those inspired by fascism were of serious significance there before the Civil War, for Spain went its own eccentric way both on the anarchist ultra-Left and on the Carlist ultra-Right.*

The well-meaning liberals, anti-clerical and masonic in the nineteenth-century manner of Latin countries, who took over from the Bourbons by a peaceful revolution in 1931, could neither contain the social ferment of the Spanish poor, in both cities and countryside, nor defuse it by effective social (i.e. primarily agrarian) reforms. In 1933 they were pushed aside by conservative governments whose policy of repressing agitations and local insurrections, such as the rising of the Asturian miners in 1934, simply helped to build up the potential revolutionary pressure. At this stage the Spanish Left discovered the Comintern's Popular Front, which was being urged on it from neighbouring France. The idea that all parties should form a single electoral front against the Right made sense to a Left that did not quite know what to do. Even the Anarchists, in this their last mass stronghold in the world, were inclined to ask their supporters to practise the bourgeois vice of voting in an election, which they had hitherto rejected as unworthy of the real revolutionary, though no anarchists actually sullied themselves by standing for election. In February 1936 the Popular Front won a small, but by no means sweeping majority of votes and, thanks to its coordination, a substantial majority of seats in the Spanish Parliament or *Cortes*. This victory produced not so much an effective government of the Left as a fissure through which the accumulated lava of social discontent could begin to spurt. This became increasingly evident in the next months.

At this stage, orthodox Right-wing politics having failed, Spain reverted

---

* Carlism was a fiercely monarchist and ultra-traditionalist movement with strong peasant support, mainly in Navarre. The Carlist fought civil wars in the 1830s and 1870s in support of one branch of the Spanish royal family.

to a form of politics it had pioneered, and which had become characteristic of the Iberian world: the *pronunciamento*, or military coup. But just as the Spanish Left found itself looking beyond national frontiers to Popular Frontism, so the Spanish Right was drawn to the fascist powers. This was not so much through the modest local fascist movement, the Falange, as through the Church and the monarchists, for whom there was little difference between the equally godless liberals and communists, and no possibility of compromise with either. Italy and Germany hoped to draw some moral and perhaps political benefit from a Right-wing victory. The Spanish generals who began seriously to plot a coup after the election needed financial support and practical help, which they negotiated with Italy.

However, moments of democratic victory and political mass mobilization are not ideal for military coups, which rely for success on the convention that civilians, not to mention uncommitted sections of the armed forces, accept the signals, just as military putschists whose signals are not accepted, quietly recognize their failure. The classic *pronunciamento* is a game best played at times when the masses are in recess or governments have lost legitimacy. These conditions were not present in Spain. The generals' coup of 17 July 1936 succeeded in some towns, and was met with passionate resistance from people and loyal forces in others. It failed to capture the two main cities of Spain, including the capital, Madrid. In parts of Spain it therefore precipitated the social revolution it had been intended to pre-empt. In all of Spain it became a long-drawn-out civil war between the legitimate and duly elected government of the Republic, now extended to include socialists, communists and even some anarchists, but uneasily cohabiting with the forces of mass rebellion which had defeated the coup, and the insurgent generals who presented themselves as nationalist crusaders against communism. The youngest, and most politically intelligent of the generals, Francisco Franco y Bahamonde (1892–1975) found himself the leader of a new regime, which in the course of the war became an authoritarian state, with a single party – a Right-wing conglomerate ranging from fascism to old monarchists and Carlist ultras, the absurdly named Spanish Traditionalist Falange. But both sides in the Civil War needed support. Both appealed to their potential backers.

The reaction of anti-fascist opinion to the rising of the generals was immediate and spontaneous, unlike the reaction of the non-fascist governments, which was distinctly more cautious, even when, like the USSR and the socialist-led Popular Front government that had just come to power in France, they were strongly for the Republic. (Italy and Germany immediately sent arms and men to their side.) France was anxious to help, and gave some (officially 'deniable') assistance to the Republic until urged into an official policy of 'non-intervention' by internal divisions and the British government, deeply hostile to what they saw as the advance of social revolution and bolshevism in the Iberian Peninsula. Middle-class and conservative opinion in the West generally shared this attitude, though (except for the Catholic Church and the pro-fascists) it did not passionately identify with the generals. Russia, though firmly on the Republican side, also joined the British-sponsored Non-Intervention Agreement, whose object, to prevent German and Italian help to the generals, nobody expected, or wanted, to achieve and which consequently 'graduated from equivocation to hypocrisy' (Thomas, 1977, p. 395). From September 1936 on, Russia wholeheartedly, if not quite officially, sent men and materials to support the Republic. Non-intervention, which meant merely that Britain and France refused to do anything about the massive intervention of the Axis powers in Spain, and in doing so abandoned the Republic, confirmed both fascists and anti-fascists in their contempt for the non-interveners. It also enormously raised the prestige of the USSR, the only power that helped the legitimate government of Spain, and of the communists inside and outside that country, not only because they organized this help, internationally, but also because they soon established themselves as the backbone of the Republic's military effort.

Yet even before the Soviets mobilized their resources, all from the liberals to the outer reaches of the Left immediately recognized the Spanish struggle as their own. As the finest British poet of the decade, W.H. Auden, wrote

> On that arid square, that fragment nipped off from hot
> Africa, soldered so crudely to inventive Europe;
> On that table-land scored by rivers,
> Our thoughts have bodies; the menacing shapes of our fever
> Are precise and alive.

What is more: there, and only there, was the endless and demoralizing retreat of the Left being halted by men and women who fought the advance of the Right in arms. Even before the Communist International began to organize the International Brigades (whose first contingents arrived at their future base in mid-October), indeed before the first organized volunteer columns appeared at the front (those of the Italian liberal-socialist movement *Giustizia e Libertá*), foreign volunteers already fought for the Republic in some quantities. Eventually over forty thousand young foreigners from over fifty nations* went to fight and many to die in a country about which most of them probably knew no more than what it looked like in a school atlas. It is significant that no more than a thousand foreign volunteers fought on the Franco side (Thomas, 1977, p. 980). For the benefit of readers who have grown up in the moral milieu of the late twentieth century, it must be added that these were neither mercenaries, nor, except in a very few cases, adventurers. They went to fight for a cause.

What Spain meant to liberals and those on the Left who lived through the 1930s, is now difficult to remember, though for many of us the survivors, now all past the Biblical life-span, it remains the only political cause which, even in retrospect, appears as pure and compelling as it did in 1936. It now seems to belong to a prehistoric past, even in Spain. Yet at the time it seemed to those who fought fascism to be the central front of their battle, because the only one in which action never ceased for over two-and-a-half years, the only one where they could participate as individuals, if not in uniform, then by collecting money, by helping refugees, and by the never-ending campaigns to put pressure on our own chicken-hearted governments. And the gradual, but apparently irreversible advance of the nationalist side, the foreseeable defeat and death of the Republic, merely made the need to forge a union against world fascism more desperately urgent.

For the Spanish Republic, in spite of all our sympathies and the (insufficient) help it received, fought a rearguard action against defeat from the start. In retrospect, it is clear that this was due to its own weaknesses. By the standards of the people's wars of the twentieth century, won or lost, the Republican war of 1936–39, with all its heroism, rates poorly; in part because it made no serious use of that powerful weapon against superior conventional forces, guerrilla warfare – a strange omission in the country which gave this form of irregular warfare its name. Unlike the Nationalists, who enjoyed a single military and political direction, the Republic remained politically divided, and – in spite of the communists' contribution – did not acquire a single military will and

---

* They included perhaps 10,000 French, 5,000 Germans and Austrians, 5,000 Poles and Ukrainians, 3,350 Italians, 2,800 from the USA, 2,000 British, 1,500 Yugoslavs, 1,500 Czechs, 1,000 Hungarians, 1,000 Scandinavians and a number of others. The 2–3,000 Russians can hardly be classed as volunteers. About 7,000 of these were said to be Jews (Thomas, 1977, p. 982–84; Paucker, 1991, p. 15).

strategic command, or not until it was too late. The best it could do was from time to time to throw back potentially fatal offensives by the other side, thus prolonging a war which might well have been effectively ended in November 1936 by the capture of Madrid.

At the time, the Spanish Civil War hardly looked like a good omen for the defeat of fascism. Internationally, it was a miniature version of a European war, fought between fascist and communist states, the latter notably more cautious and less determined than the former. The Western democracies remained sure about nothing except their non-involvement. Internally it was a war in which the mobilisation of the Right proved far more effective than that of the Left. It ended in total defeat, several hundred thousand dead, several hundreds of thousands of refugees in such countries as would receive them, including most of the surviving intellectual and artistic talents of Spain, which had, with the rarest exceptions, rallied to the Republic. The Communist International had mobilized all its formidable talents for the Spanish Republic. The future Marshal Tito, liberator and leader of Communist Yugoslavia, organized the flow of recruits to the International Brigades from Paris; Palmiro Togliatti, the Italian Communist leader, in effect ran the inexperienced Spanish Communist Party, and was among the last to escape from the country in 1939. It also failed, and knew it was failing, as did the USSR which detached some of its most impressive military minds for service in Spain (e.g. the future Marshals Konev, Malinovsky, Voronov and Rokossovsky and the future Commander of the Soviet navy, Admiral Kuznetsov).

IV

And yet, the Spanish Civil War anticipated and prepared the shape of the forces which were, within a few years of Franco's victory, to destroy fascism. It anticipated the politics of the Second World War, that unique alliance of national fronts ranging from patriotic conservatives to social revolutionaries, for the defeat of the national enemy, and simultaneously for social regeneration. For the Second World War was, for those on the winning side, not merely a struggle for military victory, but – even in Britain and the USA – for a better society. Nobody dreamed of a post-war return to 1939 – or even to 1928 or to 1918, as statesmen after the First World War had dreamed of a return to the world of 1913. A British government under Winston Churchill committed itself, in the midst of a desperate war, to a comprehensive welfare state and full employment. It was no accident that the Beveridge Report, which recommended all these, came out in as black a year as any in Britain's desperate war: 1942. The post-war plans of the USA dealt only incidentally with the problem of how to make another Hitler impossible. The real intellectual efforts of the post-war planners were devoted to learning the lessons of the Great Slump and the 1930s, so that these could not recur. As for the resistance movements in the countries defeated and occupied by the Axis, the inseparability of liberation and social revolution or at least major transformation, went without saying. Moreover, throughout formerly occupied Europe, east and west, the same kinds of governments emerged from victory: administrations of national union based on all the forces that had opposed fascism, without ideological distinction. For the first, and only, time in history, communist ministers sat beside conservative, liberal or social-democratic ministers in most European states, admittedly a situation not destined to last long.

Even though a common threat drew them together, this astonishing unity of opposites, Roosevelt and Stalin, Churchill and the British socialists, de Gaulle and the French communists, would have been impossible without a certain slackening of hostilities and mutual suspicions between the champions and the adversaries of the October revolution. The Spanish Civil War made this a great deal easier. Even anti-revolutionary governments could not forget that the Spanish government, under a Liberal president and prime minister, had complete constitutional and moral legitimacy when it appealed for aid against its insurgent generals. Even those democratic statesmen who betrayed it, out of fear for their own skins, had a bad conscience. Both the Spanish government and, more to the point, the communists who were increasingly influential in its affairs, insisted that social revolution was not their object, and, indeed, visibly did what they could to control and reverse it, to the horror of revolutionary enthusiasts. Revolution, both insisted, was not the issue: the defence of democracy was.

The interesting point is that this was not mere opportunism or, as the purists on the ultra-Left thought, treason to the revolution. It reflected a deliberate shift from an insurrectionary to a gradualist, from a confrontational to a negotiating, even a parliamentary, way to power. In the light of the Spanish people's reaction to the coup, which was undoubtedly revolutionary,* communists could now see how an essentially defensive tactic, imposed by the desperate situation of their movement after Hitler's

---

. * In the words of the Comintern, the Spanish revolution was 'an integral part of the anti-fascist struggle which rests on the widest social base. It is a popular

accession to power, opened perspectives of advance, i.e. a 'democracy of a new type', arising out of the imperatives of both wartime politics and economics. Landlords and capitalists who supported the rebels would lose their property; not as landlords and capitalists but as traitors. The government would have to plan and take over the economy; not for reasons for ideology but by the logic of war-economies. Consequently, if victorious, 'such a democracy of a new type cannot but be the enemy of the conservative spirit . . . It provides a guarantee for the further economic and political conquests of the Spanish working people' (ibid., p. 176).

The Comintern pamphlet of October 1936 thus described with considerable accuracy the shape of politics in the anti-fascist war of 1939–45. This was to be a war waged in Europe by all-embracing 'people's' or 'national front' governments or resistance coalitions, which was waged by state-managed economies and ended, in the occupied territories, with massive advances in the public sector, due to the expropriation of capitalists, not as such but as Germans or collaborators with the Germans. In several countries of central and eastern Europe the road led directly from anti-fascism to a 'new democracy' dominated, and eventually swallowed by, the communists, but until the outbreak of the Cold War, the object of these post-war regimes was, quite specifically, *not* the immediate conversion to socialist systems or the abolition of political pluralism and private property.* In Western countries the net social and economic consequences of war and liberation were not very different, though the political conjuncture was. Social and economic reforms were introduced, not (as after the First World War) in response to mass pressure and the fear of revolution, but by governments committed to them on principle – governments, partly of the old reformist kind, like the Democrats in the USA, the Labour Party, now in government in Britain; partly by parties of reform and national revival directly emerging from the various anti-fascist resistance movements. In short, the logic of the anti-fascist war led towards the Left.

---

revolution. It is a national revolution. It is an anti-fascist revolution.' (Ercoli, October 1936, cited in Hobsbawm, 1986, p. 175.)

  * As late as the foundation conference of the new cold war Communist Information Bureau (Cominform), the Bulgarian delegate, Vlko Tchervenkov, still described the perspectives of his country firmly in these terms. (Reale, 1954, pp. 66–67, 73–74).

V

In 1936 and even more in 1939 these implications of the Spanish war seemed remote, even unreal. After almost a decade of apparently total failure for the Comintern's line of anti-fascist unity, Stalin erased it from his agenda, at least for the time being, and not only came to terms with Hitler (though both sides knew that this could not last), but even instructed the international movement to abandon the anti-fascist strategy, a senseless decision perhaps best explained by his proverbial aversion to even the slightest risks.* Yet in 1941 the logic of the Comintern line came into its own. For as Germany invaded the USSR and brought the USA into the war – in short, as the struggle against fascism finally became a global war – the war became political as much as military. Internationally, it became an alliance between the capitalism of the USA and the communism of the Soviet Union. Within each country of Europe – but not, at the time, the world dependent on Western imperialism – it hoped to unite all who were ready to resist Germany or Italy, i.e. to form a Resistance coalition ranging across the political spectrum. Since all of belligerent Europe except Great Britain was occupied by the Axis powers, this war of the resisters was essentially one of civilians, or armed forces of former civilians, not recognized as such by the German and Italian armies: a savage struggle of partisans, which imposed political choices on all.

The history of European Resistance movements is largely mythological, since (except to some extent in Germany itself) the legitimacy of post-war regimes and governments essentially rested on their Resistance record. France is the extreme case, because there the governments after Liberation lacked all real continuity with the French government of 1940, which had made peace and cooperated with the Germans, and because organized, let alone armed, resistance had been rather weak, at any rate until 1944, and popular support for it had been patchy. Post-war France was rebuilt by General de Gaulle on the basis of the myth that, essentially, the eternal France had never accepted defeat. As he himself put it, 'Resistance was a bluff that came off' (Gillois, 1973, p. 164). It was an act of policy that the only fighters in the Second World War commemorated on French war memorials today are Resistance fighters, and those who joined de Gaulle's forces. However, France is by no means the only case of a state built on the Resistance mystique.

---

* Perhaps he was afraid that enthusiastic communist participation in a French or British anti-fascist war might be seen by Hitler as a sign of his secret bad faith, and thus an excuse to attack him.

Two things must be said about European Resistance movements. First, their military importance (with the possible exception of Russia) was negligible before Italy withdrew from the war in 1943, and not decisive anywhere except perhaps in parts of the Balkans. One must repeat that their major significance was political and moral. Thus Italian public life was transformed after over twenty years of fascism, which had enjoyed considerable support, even among intellectuals, by the unusally impressive and widespread mobilization of the Resistance in 1943–45, including an armed partisan movement in central and northern Italy of up to 100,000 combatants with forty-five thousand dead (Bocca, 1966, pp. 297–302, 385–89, 569–70; Pavone, 1991, p. 413). While Italians could thus put the memory of Mussolini's era behind them with a good conscience, Germans, who had remained solidly behind their government to the end, could not put a distance between themselves and the Nazi era of 1933–45. Their internal resisters, a minority of communist militants, Prussian military conservatives, with a scattering of religious and liberal dissenters, were dead or emerged from concentration camps. Conversely, of course, support for fascism or collaboration with the occupier virtually removed the people concerned from public life for a generation after 1945, though the Cold War against communism found plenty of employment for such persons in the underworld or half-world of Western military and intelligence operations.*

The second observation about the Resistance is that, for obvious reasons – though with one notable exception in Poland – its politics were skewed to the Left. In each country the fascist and radical Right and conservatives, the local rich and others whose main terror was social revolution, tended to sympathize, or at least not to oppose, the Germans; so did a number of regionalist or lesser nationalist movements; themselves traditionally on the ideological Right, some of which actually hoped to

---

* The secret anti-communist armed force known, after its existence was revealed by an Italian politician in 1990, as 'Stay Behind' (in Italy *Gladio* or 'the sword') was set up in 1949 to continue internal resistance in various European countries after a Soviet occupation, if such a situation arose. Its members were armed and paid by the USA, trained by the CIA and British secret and special forces, and its existence was concealed from the governments in whose territories they operated, apart from selected individuals. In Italy, and perhaps elsewhere, it originally consisted of last-ditch fascists who had been left behind as nuclei of resistance by the defeated Axis, who subsequently acquired a new value as fanatical anti-communists. In the 1970s, when invasion by the Red Army no longer seemed plausible even to American secret service operatives, the Gladiators found a new field of activity as Right-wing terrorists, sometimes masquerading as Left-wing terrorists.

benefit from their collaboration, notably Flemish, Slovak and Croat nationalism. So, it should not be forgotten, did the profoundly and intransigently anti-communist elements in the Catholic Church, and its armies of the conventionally pious, though Church politics were far too complex to be simply classified as 'collaborationist' anywhere. It follows that those from the political Right who chose resistance were inevitably uncharacteristic of their political constituency. Winston Churchill and General de Gaulle were not typical members of their ideological families, though it must be said that for more than one visceral Right-wing traditionalist of military instincts, a patriotism that did not defend the fatherland was unthinkable.

This explains, if any special explanation is needed, the extraordinary prominence of the communists in the resistance movements, and, consequently, their startling political advance during the war. The European communist movements reached the peak of their influence in 1945–47 for this reason, except in Germany, where they did not recover from the brutal decapitation of 1933, and the heroic but suicidal attempts at resistance in the next three years. Even in countries far from social revolution, like Belgium, Denmark and the Netherlands, communist parties scored 10–12 per cent of the vote – a multiple of what they had ever scored before, forming the third- or fourth-largest blocs in their countries' parliaments. In France they emerged as the largest party of all in the 1945 elections, larger, for the first time, than their old rivals the socialists. In Italy their record was even more startling. A small, harried and notoriously unsuccessful band of illegal cadres before the war – they were actually threatened with dissolution by the Comintern in 1938 – they emerged from two years of resistance as a mass party of eight hundred thousand members, soon (1946) to reach almost two millions. As for the countries where the war against the Axis had been waged essentially by the armed internal resistance – Yugoslavia, Albania and Greece – the partisan forces had been dominated by the communists, so much so that the British government under Churchill, who lacked the slightest sympathy for communism, transferred its support and aid from the royalist Mihailović to the communist Tito, when it became clear that one was incomparably more dangerous to the Germans than the other.

The communists took to resistance, not only because Lenin's 'vanguard party' structure was designed to produce a force of disciplined and selfless cadres whose very purpose was efficient action, but because extreme situations, such as illegality, repression and war, were precisely what these bodies of 'professional revolutionaries' had been designed for. Indeed, they 'alone had foreseen the possibility of resistance war' (M.R.D.

Foot, 1976, p. 84). In this they differed from the mass socialist parties, which found it almost impossible to operate in the absence of the legality – elections, public meetings and the rest – which defined and determined their activities. Faced with a fascist take-over or German occupation, social-democratic parties tended to go into hibernation, from which, in the best of cases they emerged, like the German and Austrian ones, at the end of the dark era, with most of their old support and ready to resume politics. While not absent from the resistance, they were, for structural reasons, under-represented. In the extreme case of Denmark a Social Democratic government was actually in office when Germany occupied the country *and remained in office* throughout the war, though presumably lacking in sympathy for the Nazis. (It took some years to recover from this episode.)

Two other characteristics helped the communists to prominence in the resistance: their internationalism and the passionate, quasi-millennial conviction with which they dedicated their lives to the cause (see chapter 2). The first allowed them to mobilize men and women more open to the anti-fascist appeal than to any patriotic call, e.g. in France the Spanish Civil War refugees who provided most of the armed partisan resistance in the south-west of that country – perhaps twelve thousand fighters before D-Day (Pons Prades, 1975, p. 66) – and the other refugees and working-class immigrants from seventeen nations who, under the acronym MOI (*Main d'Oeuvre Immigrée*), did some of the Party's most dangerous work, such as the Manouchian group (Armenians and Polish Jews) which attacked German officers in Paris.* The second generated that combination of bravery, self-sacrifice and ruthlessness which impressed even the adversaries, and which that work of marvellous honesty, the Yugoslav Milovan Djilas' *Wartime* (Djilas, 1977), brings out so vividly. The communists, in the opinion of a politically moderate historian, were 'among the bravest of the brave' (Foot, 1976, p. 86), and though their disciplined organization gave them the best survival chances in prisons and concentration camps, their losses were heavy. Suspicion of the French CP, whose leadership was disliked even among other communists, could not entirely deny its claim to be *le parti des fusillés*, which had at least fifteen thousand of its militants executed by the enemy (Jean Touchard, 1977, p. 258). Not surprisingly, they had a powerful appeal to

---

* One of the author's friends, who eventually became deputy commander of MOI under the Czech Artur London, was an Austrian Jew of Polish origin, whose resistance task was to organize anti-Nazi propaganda among the German troops in France.

brave men and women, especially the young, and perhaps especially in countries where mass support for the active resistance had been scarce, as in France or Czechoslovakia. They also appealed strongly to intellectuals, the group most readily mobilized under the banner of anti-fascism, and who formed the core of the non-party (but generically Left-wing) resistance organizations. The love affair of French intellectuals with Marxism, the domination of Italian culture by people associated with the Communist Party, both of which lasted for a generation, were products of the resistance. Whether the intellectuals themselves launched themselves into resistance, like the leading post-war publisher who notes with pride that *all* members of his firm took up arms as partisans, or became communist sympathisers because they or their families had *not* been actual resisters – they might even have been on the other side – they all felt the pull of the Party.

Except in their Balkan guerrilla strongholds, the communists made no attempt to establish revolutionary regimes. It is true that they were in no position to do so anywhere west of Trieste even had they wanted to make a bid for power, but also that the USSR, to which their parties were utterly loyal, strongly discouraged such unilateral bids for power. The communist revolutions actually made (Yugoslavia, Albania, later China) were made *against* Stalin's advice. The Soviet view was that, both internationally and within each country, post-war politics should continue within the framework of the all-embracing anti-fascist alliance, i.e. it looked forward to a long-term coexistence, or rather symbiosis, of capitalist and communist systems, and further social and political change, presumably occurring by shifts within the 'democracies of a new type' which would emerge out of the wartime coalitions. This optimistic scenario soon disappeared into the night of Cold War, so completely that few remember that Stalin urged the Yugoslav communists to keep the monarchy or that in 1945 British communists were opposed to the break-up of the Churchill wartime coalition, i.e. to the electoral campaign which was to bring the Labour government to power. Nevertheless, there is no doubt that Stalin meant all this seriously, and tried to prove it by dissolving the Comintern in 1943, and the Communist Party of the USA in 1944.

Stalin's decision, expressed in the words of an American communist leader 'that we will not raise the issue of socialism in such a form and manner as to endanger or weaken . . . unity' (Browder, 1944, in J. Starobin, 1972, p. 57) made his intentions clear. For practical purposes, as dissident revolutionaries recognized, it was a permanent goodbye to world revolution. Socialism would be confined to the USSR and the area assigned by diplomatic negotiation as its zone of influence, i.e. basically that occupied by the Red Army at the end of the war. Even within that zone of influence it would remain an undefined prospect for the future rather than an immediate programme for the new 'people's democracies'. History, which takes little notice of policy intentions, went another way – except in one respect. The division of the globe, or a large part of it, into two zones of influence, negotiated in 1944–45, remained stable. Neither side overstepped the line dividing them more than momentarily for thirty years. Both withdrew from open confrontation, thus guaranteeing that cold world wars never became hot ones.

VI

Stalin's brief dream of post-war US–Soviet partnership did not actually strengthen the global alliance of liberal capitalism and communism against fascism. Rather it demonstrated its strength and width. It was, of course, an alliance against a military threat, and one which would never have come into existence but for the series of Nazi Germany's aggressions, culminating in the invasion of the USSR and the declaration of war against the US. Nevertheless, the very nature of war confirmed the 1936 insights into the implications of the Spanish Civil War: the unity of military and civilian mobilization and social change. On the allied side – more than on the fascist side – it was a war of reformers, partly because not even the most confident capitalist power could hope to win a long war without abandoning 'business as usual', partly because the very fact of the Second World War dramatized the failures of the inter-war years, of which the failure to unite against the aggressors was merely one minor symptom.

That victory and social hope went together is also clear from what we know of the development of public opinion in the belligerent or liberated countries in which there was freedom to express it except, curiously enough, in the USA, where the years since 1936 saw a marginal erosion of the Democratic presidential vote, but a marked revival of the Republicans: this was a country dominated by its domestic concerns and far more remote from the sacrifices of war than any other. Where there were genuine elections, they showed a sharp shift to the Left. The most dramatic case was the British, where the elections of 1945 defeated the universally loved and admired war-leader, Winston Churchill, and brought to power the Labour Party with a 50 per cent increase in its vote. In the next five years it presided over a period of unprecedented social reforms. Both the major parties had been equally involved in the war effort. The electorate chose the one which promised both victory and social transformation. The phenomenon was general in warring Western Europe, though neither its scale nor its radicalism should be exaggerated, as its public image tended to be, by the temporary elimination of the former fascist or collaborationist Right.

The situation in the parts of Europe liberated by guerrilla revolution or the Red Army is more difficult to judge, if only because mass genocide, mass population displacement and mass expulsion or forced emigration make it impossible to compare the pre-war and post-war countries bearing their old names. Throughout this area the bulk of the inhabitants of the countries invaded by the Axis saw themselves as its victims, with the exception of the politically divided Slovaks and Croats, who acquired nominally independent states under German auspices; the majority peoples in Germany's allied states, Hungary and Rumania; and, of course, the large German diaspora. This did not mean that they sympathised with communist-inspired resistance movements – except perhaps for the Jews, persecuted by everyone else – still less (except for traditionally russophile Balkan slavs) with Russia. The Poles were overwhelmingly both anti-German and anti-Russian, not to mention antisemitic. The small Baltic peoples, occupied by the USSR in 1940, were both anti-Russian, anti-semitic and pro-German, while they had the choice in 1941–45. Neither communists nor resistance were to be found in Romania, and little enough in Hungary. On the other hand, both communism and pro-Russian sentiment were strong in Bulgaria, though resistance had been patchy, and in Czechoslovakia the CP, always a mass party, emerged as the largest party by far in genuinely free elections. Soviet occupation soon made such political differences academic. Guerrilla victories are not plebiscites, but there is little doubt that most Yugoslavs welcomed the triumph of Tito's partisans, except the German minority, the supporters of the Croatian Ustashi regime, on whom the Serbs took savage revenge for earlier massacres, and a traditionalist core in Serbia, where Tito's movement, and consequently anti-German warfare, had never flourished.* Greece remained proverbially divided, in spite of the refusal of Stalin to assist the Greek communist and pro-red forces against the British who supported their opponents. Only experts in

---

* However, the Serbs in Croatia and Bosnia, as well as the Montenegrins (who provided 17 per cent of the officers for the Partisan army) were strongly for Tito, as were important sections of Croats – Tito's own people – and the Slovenes. Most of the fighting took place in Bosnia.

kinship studies would care to hazard a guess about the political sentiments of the Albanians after the communists triumphed. However, in all these countries an era of massive social transformation was about to begin.

Oddly enough, the USSR was (with the USA) the only belligerent country in which the war brought no significant social and institutional change. It began and ended the conflict under Joseph Stalin (see chapter 13). However, it is clear that the war imposed enormous strains on the stability of the system, especially in the harshly repressed countryside. But for the ingrained belief of National Socialism in the Slavs as a race of sub-human helots, the German invaders could have won lasting support among many Soviet peoples. Conversely, the real foundation of Soviet victory was the patriotism of the majority nationality of the USSR, the Great Russians, always the core of the Red Army, to which the Soviet regime appealed in its moment of crisis. Indeed, the Second World War became officially known in the USSR as 'the Great Patriotic War', and rightly so.

VII

At this point the historian must make a major leap to avoid falling into the pit of a purely occidental analysis. For very little of what has been written in this chapter so far applies to the greater part of the globe. It is not quite irrelevant to the conflict between Japan and continental East Asia, since Japan, dominated by the politics of the ultra-nationalist Right, was allied with Nazi Germany, and the main forces of resistance in China were the communists. It applies to some extent in Latin America, a great importer of fashionable European ideologies like fascism or communism, and especially to Mexico, reviving its great revolution in the 1930s under President Lázaro Cardenas (1934–40) and passionately taking sides for the Spanish Republic in the Civil War. In fact, after its defeat Mexico remained the only state which continued to recognize the Republic as the legitimate government of Spain. However, for most of Asia, Africa and the Islamic world, fascism, whether as an ideology or as the policy of an aggressor state, was not and never became the main, let alone the only enemy. This was 'imperialism' or 'colonialism', and the imperialist powers were, overwhelmingly, the liberal democracies: Britain, France, the Netherlands, Belgium and the USA. Moreover, all imperial powers, with the single exception of Japan, were white.

Logically the enemies of the imperial power were also potential allies in the fight for colonial liberation. Even Japan, which, as the Koreans,

Taiwanese, Chinese and others could tell, had its own ruthless brand of colonialism, could appeal to anti-colonial forces in South-east and South Asia as a champion of non-whites against whites. The anti-imperial struggle and the anti-fascist struggle, therefore, tended to pull in opposite directions. Thus Stalin's pact with the Germans in 1939, which disrupted the Western Left, allowed Indian or Vietnamese communists to concentrate happily on opposing the British and French; whereas the German invasion of the USSR in 1941 forced them, as good communists, to put the defeat of the Axis first, i.e. to put the liberation of their own countries much lower on the agenda. This was not merely unpopular, but strategically senseless at a time when the colonial empires of the West were at their most vulnerable, if not actually collapsing. And, indeed, local leftists who did not feel bound by the iron hoops of Comintern loyalty exploited the opportunity. The Indian National Congress launched the Quit India movement in 1942, while the Bengali radical Subhas Bose recruited an Indian Liberation Army for the Japanese from among the Indian army prisoners of war taken during the lightning initial advances. Anti-colonial militants in Burma and Indonesia saw matters the same way. The *reductio ad absurdum* of this anti-colonialist logic was the attempt by an extremist Jewish fringe group in Palestine to negotiate with the *Germans* (via Damascus, then under the Vichy French) for help in liberating Palestine from the British, which they regarded as the top priority for Zionism. (A militant of the group involved in this mission eventually became prime minister of Israel: Yitzhak Shamir.) Such approaches evidently did not imply any ideological sympathy for fascism, though Nazi anti-semitism might appeal to Palestinian Arabs at odds with Zionist settlers, and some groups in South Asia might recognize themselves in the superior Aryans of Nazi mythology. But these were special cases (see chapters 12 and 15).

What needs explaining is why, after all, anti-imperialism and the colonial liberation movements inclined overwhelmingly to the Left, and thus found themselves, at least at the end of the war, converging with the global anti-fascist mobilisation. The fundamental reason is that the Western Left was the nursery of anti-imperialist theory and policies, and that support for colonial liberation movements came overwhelmingly from the international Left, and especially (since the Bolsheviks' 1920 Congress of the Eastern Peoples in Baku) from the Comintern and the USSR. Moreover, the activists and future leaders of independence movements, who belonged chiefly to the Western-educated elites of their countries, found themselves more at ease in the non-racist and anti-colonial milieu of local liberals, democrats, socialists and communists than in any other, when they came to their metropoles. They were in any case almost all modernizers, whom the nostalgic medievalist myths, Nazi ideology and the racist exclusiveness of their theories, reminded of just those 'communalist' and 'tribalist' tendencies which, in their opinion, were symptoms of their countries' backwardness which were exploited by imperialism.

In short, an alliance with the Axis, on the principle that 'my enemy's enemies are my friends', could only be tactical. Even in South-east Asia, where Japanese rule was less repressive than the old colonialists', and exercised by non-whites against whites, it could only have been short-lived, since Japan, quite apart from its pervasive racism, had no interest in liberating colonies as such. (In fact, it was short-lived, because Japan was soon defeated.) Fascism or the Axis nationalisms held no particular attraction. On the other hand a man like Jawaharlal Nehru who (unlike the communists) did not hesitate to launch himself into the Quit India rebellion in 1942, the crisis year of the British Empire, never ceased to believe that a free India would build a socialist society, and that the USSR would be an ally in this endeavour, perhaps even – with all qualifications – an example.

That the leaders and spokesmen for colonial liberation were, so often, minorities untypical of the population they set out to emancipate actually made convergence with anti-fascism easier, for the bulk of the colonial populations were moved, or at least mobilisable, by feelings and ideas to which (but for its commitment to racial superiority) fascism might have made some appeal: traditionalism; religious and ethnic exclusiveness; a suspicion of the modern world. In fact, these sentiments were not yet mobilized to any substantial extent or, if mobilized, they did not yet become politically dominant. Islamic mass mobilization did develop very strongly in the Moslem world between 1918 and 1945. Thus Hassan al-Banna's Muslim Brotherhood (1928), a fundamentalist movement strongly hostile to liberalism and communism, became the main standard-bearer of Egyptian mass grievances in the 1940s, and its potential affinities with the Axis ideologies were more than tactical, especially given its hostility to Zionism. Yet the movements and politicians which actually came to the top in Islamic countries, sometimes carried on the backs of the fundamentalist masses, were secular and modernizing. The Egyptian colonels who were to make the revolution of 1952, were emancipated intellectuals, who had been in contact with the small Egyptian communist groups, whose leadership, incidentally, was largely Jewish (Perrault, 1987). On the Indian subcontinent, Pakistan (a child of the 1930s and 1940s) has been correctly described as 'the program of secularized

elites who were forced by the [territorial] disunity of the Muslim population and by competition with the Hindu majorities to call their political
society 'Islamic' rather than nationally separatist (Lapidus, 1988, p. 738).
In Syria the running was made by the Ba'ath Party, founded in the
1940s by two Paris-educated schoolteachers who, with all their Arab
mysticism, were ideologically anti-imperialist and socialist. The Syrian
constitution contains no mention of Islam. Iraqi politics (until the Gulf
War of 1991) was determined by various combinations of nationalist
officers, communists and Ba'athists, all devoted to Arab unity and
socialism (at least in theory), but distinctly not to the Law of the Koran.
Both for local reasons and because the Algerian revolutionary movement
had a wide mass base (not least among the large emigration of labourers
to France) there was a strong Islamic element in the Algerian revolution.
However, the revolutionaries specifically agreed (in 1956) that 'theirs was
a struggle to destroy an anachronistic colonization but not a war of
religion' (Lapidus, 1988, p. 693) and proposed to form a social and
democratic republic, which became constitutionally a one-party socialist
republic. Indeed, the period of anti-fascism is the only one in which
actual communist parties acquired substantial support and influence
within some parts of the Islamic world, notably in Syria, Iraq and Iran.
It was only much later that the secular and modernizing voices of
political leadership were drowned and silenced by the mass politics of
fundamentalist revival (see chapters 12 and 15).

In spite of their conflicts of interest, which were to re-emerge after the
war, the anti-fascism of the developed Western countries and the anti-
imperialism of their colonies found themselves converging towards what
both envisaged as a post-war future of social transformation. The USSR
and local communism helped to bridge the gap, since they meant anti-
imperialism to one world, total commitment to victory to the other.
However, unlike the European theatres of war, the non-European ones
did not bring the communists major political triumphs, except in the
special cases where (as in Europe) anti-fascism and national/social liberation coincided: in China and Korea, where the colonialists were the
Japanese, and in Indochina (Vietnam, Cambodia, Laos), where the
immediate enemy of freedom remained the French, whose local administration had subordinated itself to the Japanese, when these overran
South-east Asia. These were the countries where communism was destined to triumph in the post-war era, under Mao, Kim Il Sung and Ho
Chi Minh. Elsewhere the leaders of the states about to be decolonised
came from movements, generally of the Left, but less hampered in 1941–
45 by the need to give the defeat of the Axis priority over all else. Still,

even these could not but look at the world situation after the Axis defeat with some optimism. The two super-powers were no friends to the old colonialism, at least on paper. A known anti-colonialist party had come to power in the heart of the largest empire of all. The force and legitimacy of the old colonialism had been severely undermined. The chances for freedom seemed better than ever before. This proved to be the case, but not without some savage rearguard actions by the old empires.

VIII

So the defeat of the Axis – more precisely, of Germany and Japan – left little grief behind, except in Germany and Japan itself, whose people had fought, with stubborn loyalty and formidable efficiency, to the last day. In the end fascism had mobilized nothing outside its core countries except a scattering of ideological minorities of the radical right, most of whom would have remained on the political fringes in their own countries, a few nationalist groups who expected to achieve their objects by a German alliance, and a lot of the flotsam and jetsam of war and conquest, recruited into the savage auxiliary soldiery of the Nazi occupation. The Japanese mobilized nothing but, momentarily, a sympathy for yellow rather than white skins. The major appeal of European fascism, that it provided a safeguard against working-class movements, socialism, communism and the godless devil's headquarters in Moscow that inspired them all, had won it a good deal of support among the conservative rich, though big-business support was always pragmatic rather than principled. It was not an appeal that would outlive failure and defeat. In any case, the net effect of twelve years of National Socialism was that large parts of Europe now lay at the mercy of the Bolsheviks.

So fascism dissolved like a clump of earth thrown into a river, and virtually disappeared from the political scene for good except in Italy, where a modest neo-fascist movement (the *Movimento Sociale Italiano*) honouring Mussolini has a permanent presence in Italian politics. This was not due merely to the exclusion from politics of persons formerly prominent in fascist regimes, though by no means from the state services and from public life, and still less from economic life. It was not even due to the trauma of good Germans (and, in a different way, loyal Japanese) whose world collapsed in the physical and moral chaos of 1945, and for whom mere fidelity to their old beliefs was actually counterproductive. It stood in the way of adjusting themselves to a new, initially incomprehensible, life under the occupying powers who imposed their institutions and ways on them: who laid the rails along which their trains would henceforth necessarily have to roll. National Socialism had nothing to offer to the post-1945 German except memories. It is typical that in a strongly National Socialist part of Hitler's Germany, namely in Austria (which, by a twist of international diplomacy found itself classified among the innocent rather than the guilty), post-war politics soon reverted to exactly what it had been before democracy was abolished in 1933, with the exception of a slight shift to the Left (see Flora, 1983, p. 99). Fascism disappeared with the world crisis that had allowed it to emerge. It had never been, even in theory, a universal programme or political project.

On the other hand anti-fascism, however heterogeneous and impermanent its mobilisation, succeeded in uniting an extraordinary range of forces. What is more, this unity was not negative but positive and, in certain respects, lasting. Ideologically, it was based on the shared values and aspirations of the Enlightenment and the Age of Revolution: progress by the application of reason and science; education and popular government; no inequalities based on birth or origin; societies looking to the future rather than the past. Some of these similarities existed purely on paper, though it is not entirely insignificant that political entities as remote from Western, or indeed any, democracy as Mengistu's Ethiopia, Somalia before the fall of Siad Barre, Kim Il Sung's North Korea, Algeria and communist East Germany chose to give themselves the official title of Democratic or People's (Popular) Democratic Republic. It is a label which inter-war fascist, authoritarian and even traditional conservative regimes between the wars would have rejected with contempt.

In other respects common aspirations were not so remote from common reality. Western constitutional capitalism, communist systems and the third world were equally committed to equal rights for all races and both sexes, i.e. they all fell short of the common target, but not in ways that systematically distinguished one lot from another.* They were all secular states. More to the point, after 1945 they were virtually all states which, deliberately and actively, rejected the supremacy of the market and believed in the active management and planning of the economy by the state. Difficult though it might be to recall in the age of neoliberal economic theology, between the early 1940s and the 1970s the most prestigious and formerly influential champions of complete market freedom, e.g. Friedrich von Hayek, saw themselves and their like as prophets

* Notably all forgot the major part played by women in war, resistance and liberation.

in the wilderness vainly warning a heedless Western capitalism that it was rushing along the 'Road to Serfdom' (Hayek, 1944). In fact, it was advancing into an era of economic miracles (see chapter 9). Capitalist governments were convinced that only economic interventionism could prevent a return to the economic catastrophes between the wars, and avoid the political dangers of people radicalized to the point of choosing communism, as they had once chosen Hitler. Third-world countries believed only public action could lift their economies out of backwardness and dependency. In the decolonised world, following the inspiration of the Soviet Union, they were to see the way forward as socialism. The Soviet Union and its newly extended family believed in nothing but central planning. And all three regions of the world advanced into the post-war world with the conviction that victory over the Axis, achieved by political mobilisation and revolutionary policies as well as by blood and iron, opened a new era of social transformation.

In a sense they were right. Never has the face of the globe and human life been so dramatically transformed as in the era which began under the mushroom clouds of Hiroshima and Nagasaki. But as always history took only marginal notice of human intentions, even those of the national decision-makers. The real social transformation was neither intended nor planned. And in any case, the first contingency they had to face was the almost immediate breakdown of the great anti-fascist alliance. As soon as there was no longer a fascism to unite against, capitalism and communism once again got ready to face each other as one another's mortal enemies.

CHAPTER SIX
The Arts 1914–1945

The surrealists' Paris, too, is a little 'universe'. . . . In the larger one, the cosmos, things look no different. There, too, are crossroads where ghostly signals flash from the traffic, and inconceivable analogies and connections between events are the order of the day. It is the region from which the lyric poetry of Surrealism reports.

– Walter Benjamin, 'Surrealism', from *One Way Street* (1979, p. 231)

The New Architecture seems to be making little progress in the USA . . . The advocates of the new style are full of earnestness, and some of them carry on in the shrill pedagogical manner of believers in the Single Tax . . . but, save on the level of factory design, they do not seem to be making many converts.

– H.L. Mencken, 1931

I

Why brilliant fashion-designers, a notoriously non-analytic breed, sometimes succeed in anticipating the shape of things to come better than professional predictors, is one of the most obscure questions in history; and, for the historian of culture, one of the most central. It is certainly crucial to anyone who wants to understand the impact of the age of cataclysms on the world of high culture, the elite arts, and, above all, the avantgarde. For it is generally accepted that these arts anticipated the actual breakdown of liberal-bourgeois society by several years (see *Age of Empire*, chapter 9). By 1914 virtually everything that can take shelter under the broad and rather undefined canopy of 'modernism' was already in place: cubism; expressionism; futurism; pure abstraction in painting;

functionalism and flight from ornament in architecture; the abandonment of tonality in music; the break with tradition in literature.

A large number of names who would be on most people's list of eminent 'modernists' were all mature and productive or even famous in 1914.* Even T.S. Eliot, whose poetry was not published until 1917 and after, was by then clearly a part of the London avant-garde scene [as a contributor (with Pound) to Wyndham Lewis's *Blast*]. These children of, at the latest, the 1880s, remained icons of modernity forty years later. That a number of men and women who only began to emerge after the war would also make most high-culture shortlists of eminent 'modernists' is less surprising than the domination of the older generation.† (Thus even Schönberg's successors – Alban Berg and Anton Webern – belong to the generation of the 1880s.)

In fact, the only formal innovations after 1914 in the world of the 'established' avantgarde seem to have been two: *Dadaism*, which shaded over into or anticipated *surrealism* in the western half of Europe, and the Soviet-born *constructivism* in the East. Constructivism, an excursion into skeletal three-dimensional and preferably moving constructions which have their nearest real-life analogue in some fairground structures (giant wheels, big dippers etc.), was soon absorbed into the main stream of architecture and industrial design, largely through the Bauhaus (of which more below). Its most ambitious projects, such as Tatlin's famous rotating leaning tower in honour of the Communist International, never got built, or else lived evanescent lives as the decor of early Soviet public ritual. Novel as it was, constructivism did little more than extend the repertoire of architectural modernism.

Dadaism took shape among a mixed group of exiles in Zurich (where another group of exiles under Lenin awaited the revolution) in 1916, as an anguished but ironic nihilist protest against world war and the society that had incubated it: including its art. Since it rejected all art, it had no formal characteristics, although it borrowed a few tricks from the pre-1914 cubist and futurist avant-gardes, including notably *collage*, or sticking together bits and pieces, including parts of pictures. Basically anything that might cause apoplexy among conventional bourgeois art-lovers was acceptable Dada. Scandal was its principle of cohesion. Thus

* Matisse and Picasso; Schönberg and Stravinsky; Gropius and Mies van der Rohe; Proust, James Joyce, Thomas Mann and Franz Kafka; Yeats, Ezra Pound, Alexander Blok and Anna Akhmatova.

† Among others, Isaac Babel (1894); Le Corbusier (1897); Ernest Hemingway (1899); Bertolt Brecht, Garcia Lorca and Hanns Eisler (all born 1898); Kurt Weill (1900); Jean Paul Sartre (1905); and W.H. Auden (1907).

Marcel Duchamp's (1887–1968) exhibition of a public urinal as 'ready-made art' in New York in 1917 was entirely in the spirit of Dada, which he joined on his return from the USA; but his subsequent quiet refusal to have anything further to do with art – he preferred to play chess – was not. For there was nothing quiet about Dada.

Surrealism, while equally devoted to the rejection of art as hitherto known, equally given to public scandal and (as we shall see) even more attracted to social revolution, was more than a negative protest; as might be expected from a movement essentially centred in France, a country where every fashion requires a theory. Indeed, we can say that, as Dada foundered in the early 1920s with the era of war and revolution that had given it birth, surrealism emerged from it as what has been called 'a plea for the revival of the imagination, based on the Unconscious as revealed by psychoanalysis, together with a new emphasis on magic, accident, irrationality, symbols and dreams (Willett, 1978).'

In some ways it was a romantic revival in twentieth-century costume (see *Age of Revolution*, chapter 14), but with more sense of absurdity and fun. Unlike the mainstream 'modernist' avant-gardes, but like Dada, surrealism had no interest in formal innovation as such: whether the Unconscious expressed itself in a random stream of words ('automatic writing') or in the meticulous nineteenth-century academician's style in which Salvador Dali (1904–89) painted his deliquescent watches in desert landscapes, was of no interest. What counted was to recognize the capacity of the spontaneous imagination, unmediated by rational control systems, to produce cohesion out of the incoherent, an apparently necessary logic out of the plainly illogical or even impossible. René Magritte's (1898–1967) *Castle in the Pyrenees*, carefully painted in the manner of a picture-postcard, emerges from the top of a huge rock, as though it had grown there. Only the rock, like a giant egg, is floating through the sky above the sea, painted with equal realistic care.

Surrealism was a genuine addition to the repertoire of avant-garde arts, its novelty attested by the ability to produce shock, incomprehension, or what amounted to the same thing, a sometimes embarrassed laughter, even among the older avant-garde. This was my own, admittedly juvenile, reaction to the 1936 International Surrealist Exhibition in London, and later to a surrealist painter friend in Paris, whose insistence on producing the exact equivalent in oils of a photograph of human entrails I found hard to understand. Nevertheless, in retrospect it must be seen as a remarkably fertile movement, though chiefly in France and countries such as the Hispanic ones, where French influence was strong. It influenced first-rate poets in France (Eluard, Aragon); in Spain (García

1. Sarajevo: the Archduke Franz Ferdinand of Austria and his wife leaving the Town Hall of Sarajevo on their way to their assassination, which sparked off the First World War (28 June 1914).

2. The killing fields of France, seen by the dying: Canadian soldiers among shell-craters, 1918.

3. The killing fields of France, seen by the survivors: war cemetery, Chalons-sur-Marne.

4. Russia, 1917: soldiers with revolutionary banners ('Workers of all lands, unite!').

5. October revolution: image of Lenin ('great leader of the proletariat'). The workers' banner reads 'All power to the Soviets'.

6. World revolution, as seen on a Soviet May Day Poster, *c*.1920. The red flag circling the globe is inscribed 'workers of all lands unite!'.

7. The traumatic post-war inflation, whose memory still haunts Germany: A German banknote for twenty million marks (July 1923).

8. Gateway to the Great Depression: the Wall Street crash of 1929.

9. Men without work: British unemployed in the 1930s.

10. The two leaders of fascism: Adolf Hitler (1889-1945) and Benito Mussolini (1883-1945) had much to smile about in 1938.

11. The Duce: young Italian fascists marching past Mussolini.

12. The Führer: Nazi rally at Nuremberg.

13. Spanish Civil war 1936-39: anarchist militia in Barcelona, 1936, on an improvised armoured vehicle.

14. Fascism triumphant? Adolf Hitler, conqueror of Europe, 1940-41, in occupied Paris.

15. Second World War: the bombs. US Boeing 'Flying Fortresses' raid Berlin.

16. Second World War: the tanks. Soviet armoured vehicles attacking in the greatest tank battle of history, Kursk 1943.

17. War of the non-combatants: London burning, 1940.

18. War of the non-combatants: Dresden burned, 1945.

19. War of the non-combatants: Hiroshima after the atom bomb, 1945.

20. War of the resisters: Josip Broz (Marshal Tito), 1892–1980, during the partisan struggle for the liberation of Yugoslavia.

21. Empire before the fall: a British wartime poster.

22. Empire falling: Algiers about to win independence from France, 1961.

23. After Empire: Premier Indira Gandhi (1917–1984) heading the annual Independence Day parade in New Delhi.

24. (*left*) US Cruise missile.

25. (*below*) A silo for the Soviet SS missiles.

26. Two worlds divided: the Berlin Wall (1961-89), separating capitalism and 'real socialism', near the Brandenburg Gate.

27. Third World in ferment: Fidel Castro's rebel army enters liberated Santa Clara before taking power in Cuba on 1 January 1959.

28. The *guerrilleros*: insurrectionaries in El Salvador in the 1980s, preparing hand grenades.

29. From Third World guerrillas to First World students: demonstration against the US war in Vietnam, Grosvenor Square, London, 1968.

30. Social revolution in the name of God: Iran 1979, the first major twentieth-century social upheaval rejecting both the traditions of 1789 and 1917.

31. Cold War ended: the man who ended it, Michael Sergeyevich Gorbachov, General Secretary of the Communist Party of the Soviet Union (1985-91).

32. Cold War ended: the Berlin Wall falls, 1989.

33. Fall of European Communism: Stalin removed in Prague.

Lorca); Eastern Europe and Latin America (César Vallejo in Peru, Pablo Neruda in Chile); and indeed some of it still echoes through 'magical realist' writing in that continent much later. Its images and visions – Max Ernst (1891–1976), Magritte, Joan Miró (1893–1983), yes, even Salvador Dali – have become part of ours. And, unlike most earlier Western avant-gardes, it actually fertilized the central art of the twentieth century, that of the camera. It is no accident that the cinema is indebted to surrealism not only for Luis Buñuel (1900–83) but also for the central scriptwriter of the French cinema in this era, Jacques Prévert (1900–77), while photo-journalism is indebted to it for Henri Cartier-Bresson (1908–).

Yet, taken all in all, these were amplifications of the avantgarde revolution in the high arts which had already taken place before the world whose collapse it expressed actually went to pieces. Three things can be noted about this revolution in the era of cataclysms: the avant-garde became, as it were, part of established culture; it became at least partly absorbed into the fabric of everyday life; and – perhaps above all – it became dramatically politicized, perhaps more so than the high arts in any period since the Age of Revolution. And yet, we must never forget that, throughout this period, it remained isolated from the tastes and concerns of the mass of even the Western public, though it now impinged on it more than that public generally recognized. Except for a somewhat larger minority than before 1914, it was not what most people actually and consciously enjoyed.

To say that the new avant-garde became central to the established arts is not to claim that it displaced the classic and the fashionable, but that it supplemented both, and became the proof of a serious interest in cultural matters. The international operatic repertoire remained essentially what it had been in the Age of Empire, with composers born in the early 1860s (Richard Strauss, Mascagni) or even earlier (Puccini, Leoncavallo, Janacek) at the outer limits of 'modernity', as, broadly speaking, it still remains.*

Yet the traditional partner of opera, namely ballet, was transformed into a consciously avant-garde medium by the great Russian impresario Sergei Diaghilev (1872–1929) mainly during the First World War. After his 1917 Paris production of *Parade* (designs by Picasso, music by Satie, libretto by Jean Cocteau, programme notes by Guillaume Apollinaire),

* It is significant that, with comparatively rare exceptions – Alban Berg, Benjamin Britten – the major creations for the musical stage after 1918, for instance *The Threepenny Opera*, *Mahagonny*, *Porgy and Bess* – were not written for official opera houses.

décors by the likes of the cubists Georges Braque (1882–1963) and Juan Gris (1887–1927); music by, or rewritten by Stravinsky, de Falla, Milhaud and Poulenc became *de rigeur*, while both styles of dancing and choreography were modernized accordingly. Before 1914, at least in Britain, the 'Post-Impressionist Exhibition' had been jeered by a philistine public, while Stravinsky caused scandal wherever he went, as did the Armory Show in New York and elsewhere. After the war, the philistines fell silent before the provocative displays of 'modernism', deliberate declarations of independence from the discredited pre-war world, manifestos of cultural revolution. And, through the modernist ballet, exploiting its unique combination of snob appeal, the magnetism of vogue (plus the new *Vogue*) and elite artistic status, the avant-garde broke out of its stockade. Thanks to Diaghilev, wrote a characteristic figure in the British cultural journalism of the 1920s, 'the crowd has positively enjoyed decorations by the best and most ridiculed living painters. He has given us Modern Music without tears and Modern Painting without laughter' (Mortimer, 1925).

Diaghilev's ballet was merely one medium for the diffusion of the avant-garde arts which, in any case, varied from one country to the next. Nor, indeed, was the same avant-garde diffused throughout the Western world for, in spite of the continued hegemony of Paris over large regions of elite culture, reinforced after 1918 by the influx of American expatriates (the generation of Hemingway and Scott Fitzgerald), there was actually no longer a unified high culture in the old world. In Europe Paris competed with the Moscow-Berlin axis, until the triumphs of Stalin and Hitler silenced or dispersed the Russia or German avant-gardes. The fragments of the former Habsburg and Ottoman Empires went their own way in literature, isolated by languages which nobody seriously or systematically attempted to translate until the era of the anti-fascist diaspora in the 1930s. The extraordinary flowering of poetry in the Spanish language on both sides of the Atlantic had next to no international impact until the Spanish Civil War of 1936–39 revealed it. Even the arts least hampered by the tower of Babel, those of sight and sound, were less international than might be supposed, as a comparison of the relative standing of, say, Hindemith in and outside Germany or of Poulenc in and outside France shows. Educated English art-lovers entirely familiar with even the lesser members of the inter-war École de Paris, might not even have heard the names of German expressionist painters as important as Nolde and Franz Marc.

There were really only two avant-garde arts which all flag-carriers of artistic novelty in all relevant countries could be guaranteed to admire, and both came out of the new world rather than the old: films and jazz. The cinema was co-opted by the avant-garde some time during the First World War, having previously been unaccountably neglected by it (see *Age of Empire*). It not merely became essential to admire this art, and notably its greatest personality, Charlie Chaplin (to whom few self-respecting modern poets failed to address a composition), but avant-garde artists themselves launched themselves into film-making, most notably in Weimar Germany and Soviet Russia, where they actually dominated production. The canon of 'art-films' which the highbrow film-buffs were expected to admire in small specialized movie-temples during the age of cataclysms, from one side of the globe to the other, consisted essentially of such avant-garde creations: Sergei Eisenstein's (1898–1948) *Battleship Potemkin* of 1925 was generally regarded as the all-time masterpiece. The Odessa Steps sequence of this work, which no one who ever saw it – as I did in a Charing Cross avant-garde cinema in the 1930s – will ever forget, has been described as 'the classic sequence of silent cinema and possibly the most influential six minutes in cinema history' (Manvell, 1944, pp. 47–48).

From the mid-1930s, intellectuals favoured the populist French cinema of René Clair; Jean Renoir (not uncharacteristically the painter's son); Marcel Carné; Prévert, the ex-surrealist; and Auric, the ex-member of the avant-garde musical cartel '*Les Six*'. These, as non-intellectual critics liked to point out, were less enjoyable, though no doubt artistically more high-class than the great bulk of what the hundreds of millions (including the intellectuals) watched every week in increasingly gigantic and luxurious picture-palaces, namely the production of Hollywood. On the other hand the hard-headed showmen of Hollywood were almost as quick as Diaghilev to recognize the avant-garde contribution to profitability. 'Uncle' Carl Laemmle, the boss of Universal Studios, perhaps the least intellectually ambitious of the Hollywood majors, took care to supply himself with the latest men and ideas on his annual visits to his native Germany, with the result that the characteristic product of his studios, the horror movie (Frankenstein, Dracula etc.) was sometimes a fairly close copy of German expressionist models. The flow of central-European directors, like Lang, Lubitsch and Wilder, across the Atlantic – and practically all of them can be regarded as highbrows in their native grounds – was to have a considerable impact on Hollywood itself, not to mention that of technicians like Karl Freund (1890–1969) or Eugen Schufftan (1893–1977). However, the course of the cinema and the popular arts will be considered below.

The 'jazz' of the 'Jazz Age', i.e. some kind of combination of American Negroes, syncopated rhythmic dance-music and an instrumentation which was unconventional by traditional standards, almost certainly aroused universal approval among the avant-garde, less for its own merits than as yet another symbol of modernity, the machine age, a break with the past – in short, another manifesto of cultural revolution. The staff of the Bauhaus had itself photographed with a saxophone. A genuine passion for the sort of jazz which is now recognized as the major contribution of the USA to twentieth-century music, remained rare among established intellectuals, avant-garde or not, until the second half of the century. Those who developed it, as I did after Duke Ellington's visit to London in 1933, were a small minority.

Whatever the local variant of modernism, between the wars it became the badge of those who wanted to prove that they were both cultured and up to date. Whether or not one actually liked, or even had read, seen or heard, works by the recognized OK names – say, among literary English schoolboys of the first half of the 1930s, T.S. Eliot, Ezra Pound, James Joyce and D.H. Lawrence – it was inconceivable not to talk knowledge-ably about them. What is perhaps more interesting, each country's cultural vanguard rewrote or revalued the past to fit in with contemporary requirements. The English were firmly told to forget about Milton and Tennyson, but to admire John Donne. The most influential British critic of the period, F.R. Leavis of Cambridge, even devised a canon, or 'great tradition', of English novels which was the exact opposite of a real tradition, since it omitted from the historical succession anything the critic did not like, such as all of Dickens, with the exception of one novel hitherto regarded as one of the master's minor works, *Hard Times*.*

For lovers of Spanish painting, Murillo was now out, but admiration for El Greco was compulsory. But above all, anything to do with the Age of Capital and the Age of Empire (other than its avant-garde art) was not only rejected: it became virtually invisible. This was not only demon-strated by the vertical fall in the prices of nineteenth-century academic painting (and the corresponding but still modest rise of the Impressionists and later modernists): they remained practically unsaleable until the 1960s. The very attempts to recognize any merit in Victorian building had about them an air of deliberate provocation of *real* good taste, associated with camp reactionaries. The present author, grown up among the great architectural monuments of the liberal bourgeoisie which encir-cle Vienna's old 'inner city', learned, by a sort of cultural osmosis, that they were to be regarded as either inauthentic or pompous or both. Such

* To be fair, Dr Leavis eventually, if somewhat grudgingly, found less inadequate words of appreciation for this great writer.

buildings were not actually torn down *en masse* until the 1950s and 1960s, the most disastrous decade in modern architecture, which is why a Victorian Society to protect buildings of the 1840–1914 period was not set up in Britain until 1958 (more than twenty years after a Georgian Group, to protect the less outcast eighteenth-century heritage).

The impact of the avant-garde on the commercial cinema already suggests that 'modernism' began to make its mark on everyday life. It did so obliquely, through productions which the broad public did not consider to be 'art', and consequently to be judged by *a priori* criteria of aesthetic value: primarily through publicity, industrial design, commercial print and graphics, and genuine objects. Thus among champions of modernity Marcel Breuer's (1902–81) famous tubular chair (1925–29) carried an enormous ideological and aesthetic charge (Giedion, 1948, pp. 488–95). Yet it was to make its way through the modern world not as a manifesto, but as the modest but universally useful movable stacking chair. But there can be no doubt at all that, within less than twenty years of the outbreak of the First World War, metropolitan life all over the Western world was visibly marked by modernism, even in countries like the USA and Great Britain, which appeared entirely unreceptive to it in the 1920s. Streamlining, which swept through the American design of both suitable and unsuitable products from the early 1930s, echoed Italian futurism. The Art Deco style (derived from the Paris Exposition of Decorative Arts of 1925) domesticated modernist angularity and abstraction. The modern paperback revolution in the 1930s (Penguin Books) carried the banner of the avant-garde typography of Jan Tschichold (1902–74). The direct assault of modernism was still deflected. Not until after the Second World War did the so-called International Style of modernist architecture transform the city scene, though its chief propagandists and practitioners – Gropius, Le Corbusier, Mies van der Rohe, Frank Lloyd Wright, etc. – had long been active. Some exceptions apart, the bulk of public building, including public housing projects by municipalities of the Left, which might have been expected to sympathize with the socially conscious new architecture, showed little sign of its influence except an apparent dislike for decoration. Most of the massive rebuilding of working-class 'Red Vienna' in the 1920s was undertaken by architects who figure barely, if at all, in most histories of architecture. But the lesser equipment of everyday life was rapidly reshaped by modernity.

How far this was due to the heritage of the arts-and-crafts and *art nouveau* movements, in which vanguard art had committed itself to daily use; how far to the Russian constructivists, some of whom deliberately set out to revolutionize mass production design; how far to the genuine suitability of modernist purism for modern domestic technology (e.g. kitchen design) we must leave to art history to decide. The fact remains that a short-lived establishment, which began very much as a political and artistic avant-garde centre, came to set the tone of both architecture and the applied arts of two generations. This was the Bauhaus, or art and design school of Weimar and later Dessau in Central Germany (1919–33), whose existence coincided with the Weimar Republic – it was dissolved by the National Socialists shortly after Hitler took power. The list of names associated with the Bauhaus in one way or another reads like a *Who's Who* of the advanced arts between the Rhine and the Urals: Gropius and Mies van der Rohe; Lyonel Feininger, Paul Klee and Wassily Kandinsky; Malevich, El Lissitzky, Moholy-Nagy, etc. Its influence rested not only on these talents but – from 1921 – on a deliberate turn away from the old arts-and-crafts and (avant-garde) fine arts tradition to designs for practical use and industrial production: car bodies (by Gropius), aircraft seats, advertising graphics (a passion of the Russian constructivist El Lissitzky), not forgetting the design of the one and two million Mark banknotes during the great German hyper-inflation of 1923.

The Bauhaus – as its problems with unsympathetic politicians shows – was considered deeply subversive. And, indeed, political commitment of one kind or another dominates the 'serious' arts in the Age of Catastrophe. In the 1930s it reached even Britain, still a haven of social and political stability amid European revolution, and the USA, remote from war but not from the Great Slump. That political commitment was by no means only to the Left, though radical art-lovers found it hard, especially when young, to accept that creative genius and progressive opinions should not go together. Yet, especially in literature, deeply reactionary convictions, sometimes translated into fascist practice, were common enough in Western Europe. The poets T.S. Eliot and Ezra Pound in Britain and exile; William Butler Yeats (1865–1939) in Ireland; the novelists Knut Hamsun (1859–1952) in Norway, an impassioned collaborator of the Nazis, D.H. Lawrence (1885–1930) in Britain and Louis Ferdinand Céline in France (1884–1961) are obvious examples. The brilliant talents of the Russian emigration cannot, of course, be automatically classified as 'reactionary', although some of them were, or became, so; for a refusal to accept Bolshevism united émigrés of widely different political views.

Nevertheless, it is probably safe to say that in the aftermath of world war and the October revolution, and even more in the era of anti-fascism of the 1930s and 1940s, it was the Left, often the revolutionary Left, that primarily attracted the avant-garde. Indeed, war and revolution politicized a number of notably non-political pre-war avant-garde movements in France and Russia. (Most of the Russian avant-garde, however, showed no initial enthusiasm for October.) As Lenin's influence brought Marxism back to the Western world as the only important theory and ideology of social revolution, so it assured the conversion of avant-gardes to what the National Socialists, not incorrectly, called 'cultural Bolshevism' (*Kulturbolschewismus*). Dada was for revolution. Its successor, surrealism, had difficulty only in deciding which brand of revolution it was for, the majority of the sect choosing Trotsky over Stalin. The Moscow–Berlin axis which shaped so much of Weimar culture rested on common political sympathies. Mies van der Rohe built a monument to the murdered Spartacist leaders Karl Liebknecht and Rosa Luxemburg for the German Communist Party. Gropius, Bruno Taut (1880–1938), Le Corbusier, Hannes Meyer and an entire 'Bauhaus Brigade' accepted Soviet commissions – admittedly at a time when the Great Slump made the USSR not merely ideologically but also professionally attractive to Western architects. Even the basically not very political German cinema was radicalized, as witness the wonderful director G.W. Pabst (1885–1967), a man visibly more interested in presenting women rather than public affairs, and later quite prepared to work under the Nazis. Yet in the last Weimar years he was the author of some of the most radical films, including Brecht-Weill's *Threepenny Opera*.

It was the tragedy of modernist artists, Left or Right, that the much more effective political commitment of their own mass movements and politicians – not to mention their adversaries – rejected them. With the partial exception of Futurist-influenced Italian fascism, the new authoritarian regimes of both Right and Left preferred old-fashioned and gigantic monumental buildings and vistas in architecture, inspirational representations in both painting and sculpture, elaborate performances of the classics on stage, and ideological acceptability in literature. Hitler, of course, was a frustrated artist who eventually found a competent young architect to realize his gigantic conceptions, Albert Speer. However, neither Mussolini nor Stalin nor General Franco, all of whom inspired their own architectural dinosaurs, began life with such personal ambitions. Neither the German nor the Russian avant-garde, therefore, survived the rise of Hitler and Stalin, and the two countries, spearhead of all that was advanced and distinguished in the arts of the 1920s, almost disappear from the cultural scene.

In retrospect we can see better than contemporaries could what a cultural disaster the triumph of both Hitler and Stalin proved to be, that is to say, how much the avant-garde arts were rooted in the revolutionary soil of central and eastern Europe. The best wine of the arts seemed to grow on the lava-streaked slopes of volcanos. It was not merely that the cultural authorities of politically revolutionary regimes gave more official recognition, i.e. material backing, to artistic revolutionaries than the conservative ones they replaced, even if their political authorities showed no enthusiasm. Anatol Lunacharsky, the 'Commissar for Enlightenment', encouraged the avant-garde, though Lenin's taste in the arts was quite conventional. The social-democratic government of Prussia, before it was expelled in 1932 from office (unresistingly) by the authorities of the more right-wing German Reich, encouraged the radical conductor Otto Klemperer to turn one of the Berlin opera houses into a showcase of all that was advanced in music between 1928 and 1931. However, in some undefinable way, it also seems that the times of cataclysm heightened the sensibilities, sharpened the passions of those who lived through them, in Central and Eastern Europe. Theirs was a harsh not a happy vision, and its very harshness and the tragic sense that infused it was what sometimes gave talents which were not in themselves outstanding a bitter denunciatory eloquence, for instance B. Traven, an insignificant anarchist bohemian emigrant once associated with the short-lived Munich Soviet Republic of 1919, who took to writing movingly about sailors and Mexico (Huston's *Treasure of the Sierra Madre* with Bogart is based on him). Without it he would have remained in deserved obscurity. Where such an artist lost the sense that the world was intolerable, as the savage German satirist George Grosz did on emigrating to the USA after 1933, nothing remained but technically competent sentimentality.

The central European avant-garde art of the Age of Cataclysm rarely articulated hope, even though its politically revolutionary members were committed to an upbeat vision of the future by their ideological convictions. Its most powerful achievements, most of them dating from the years before Hitler's and Stalin's supremacy – 'I can't think what to say about Hitler',* quipped the great Austrian satirist Karl Kraus, whom the First World War had left far from speechless (Kraus, 1922) – come out of apocalypse and tragedy: Alban Berg's opera *Wozzek* (first performed 1926); Brecht and Weill's *Threepenny Opera* (1928) and *Mahagonny* (1931); Brecht-Eisler's *Die Massnahme* (1930); Isaac Babel's stories *Red Cavalry* (1926); Eisenstein's film *Battleship Potemkin* (1925); or Alfred Döblin's *Berlin-Alexanderplatz* (1929). As for the collapse of the

---

* '*Mir fällt zu Hitler nichts ein.*' This did not prevent Kraus, after a lengthy silence, writing some hundred pages on the subject, which nevertheless exceeded his grasp.

Habsburg Empire, it produced an extraordinary outburst of literature, ranging from the denunciation of Karl Kraus's *The Last Days of Humanity* (1922) through the ambiguous buffoonery of Jaroslav Hašek's *Good Soldier Schwejk* (1921) to the melancholy threnody of Josef Roth's *Radetzkymarsch* (1932) and the endless self-reflection of Robert Musil's *Man without Qualities* (1930). No set of political events in the twentieth century has had a comparably profound impact on the creative imagination, although in their own ways the Irish revolution and civil war (1916–22) through O'Casey and, in a more symbolic mode, through its muralists, the Mexican revolution (1910–20) – but not the Russian revolution – inspired the arts in their respective countries. An empire destined to collapse as a metaphor for a Western elite culture itself undermined and collapsing: these images had long haunted the dark corners of the Central European imagination. The end of order found expression in the great poet Rainer Maria Rilke's (1875–1926) *Duino Elegies* (1913–23). Another Prague writer in the German language presented an even more absolute sense of the incomprehensibility of the human predicament, both singular and collective: Franz Kafka (1883–1924), almost all of whose work was published posthumously.

This, then, was art created

> in the days the world was falling
> the hour the earth's foundations fled

to cite the classical scholar and poet A.E. Housman, who was far from the avant-garde (Housman, 1988, p. 138). This was art whose view was that of the 'angel of history', whom the German-Jewish marxist Walter Benjamin (1892–1940) claimed to recognize in Paul Klee's picture *Angelus Novus*:

> His face is turned towards the past. Where we see a chain of events before us, *he* sees a single catastrophe which keeps piling wreckage upon ruin till they reach his feet. If only he could stay to wake the dead and to piece together the fragments of what has been broken! But a storm blows from the direction of Paradise, catching his wings with such force that the Angel can no longer close them. This storm drives him irresistibly into the future, to which his back is turned, while the pile of debris at his feet grows into the sky. This storm is what we call progress (Benjamin, 1971, pp. 84–85).

West of the zone of collapse and revolution the sense of a tragic and ineluctable cataclysm was less, but the future seemed equally enigmatic. In spite of the trauma of the First World War, continuity with the past was not so obviously broken until the 1930s, the decade of the Great Slump, fascism and the steadily approaching war.* Even so, in retrospect the mood of the Western intellectuals seems less desperate and more hopeful than that of the central Europeans, now scattered and isolated from Moscow to Hollywood, or the captive East Europeans silenced by failure and terror. They still felt themselves to be defending values threatened, but not yet destroyed, to revitalize what was living in their society, if need be by transforming it. As we shall see (chapter 18), much of the Western blindness to the faults of the Stalinist Soviet Union was due to the conviction that, after all, it represented the values of the Enlightenment against the disintegration of reason; of 'progress' in the old and simple sense, so much less problematic than Walter Benjamin's 'wind blowing from Paradise'. It was only among ultra-reactionaries that we find the sense of the world as an incomprehensible tragedy, or rather, as in the greatest British novelist of the period, Evelyn Waugh (1903–66), as a black comedy for stoics; or, as in the French novelist Louis Ferdinand Céline (1894–1961), a nightmare even for cynics. Though the finest and most intelligent of the young British avant-garde poets of the time, W.H. Auden (1907–73), had a sense of history as tragedy – *Spain*, *Musée des Beaux Arts* – the mood of the group of which he was the centre found the human predicament acceptable enough. The most impressive British artists of the avant-garde, the sculptor Henry Moore (1898–1986) and the composer Benjamin Britten (1913–76), give the impression that they would have been quite ready to let the world crisis pass them by, had it not intruded. But it did.

The avant-garde arts were still a concept confined to the culture of Europe and its outliers and dependencies, and even there the pioneers on the frontier of artistic revolution still often looked longingly at Paris and even – to a lesser but surprising extent – at London.† It did not yet look to New York. What this means is that the non-European avant-garde

---

* Indeed, the major literary echoes of the First World War only began to reverberate towards the end of the 1920s when Erich Maria Remarque's *All Quiet on the Western Front* (1929, Hollywood film 1930) sold two-and-a-half million copies in eighteen months in twenty-five languages.

† The Argentinian writer Jorge Luis Borges (1899–1986) was notoriously anglophile and anglo-oriented; the extraordinary Alexandrian Greek poet C.P. Cavafy (1863–1933) actually had English as his first language, as – at least for writing purposes – had Fernando Pessoa (1888–1935), the greatest Portuguese poet of the century. Kipling's influence on Bertolt Brecht is well known.

barely existed outside the western hemisphere, where it was firmly anchored to both artistic experiment and social revolution. Its best-known representatives at this time, the mural painters of the Mexican revolution, disagreed only about Stalin and Trotsky, but not about Zapata and Lenin, whom Diego Rivera (1886–1957) insisted on including in a fresco destined for the new Rockefeller Center in New York (a triumph of art-deco second only to the Chrysler Building) to the displeasure of the Rockefellers.

Yet for most artists in the non-Western world the basic problem was modernity not modernism. How were their writers to turn spoken vernaculars into flexible and comprehensive literary idioms for the contemporary world, as the Bengalis had done since the mid-nineteenth century in India? How were men (perhaps, in these new days, even women) to write poetry in Urdu, instead of the classical Persian hitherto obligatory for such purposes; in Turkish instead of in the classical Arabic which Atatürk's revolution threw into the dustbin of history with the *fez* and the woman's veil? What, in countries of ancient cultures, were they to do with or about their traditions; arts which, however attractive, did not belong to the twentieth century? To abandon the past was revolutionary enough to make the Western revolt of one phase of modernity against another appear irrelevant or even incomprehensible. All the more so when the modernizing artist was at the same time a political revolutionary, as was more than likely. Chekhov and Tolstoy might seem more apposite models than James Joyce for those who felt their task – and their inspiration – was to 'go to the people' and to paint a realistic picture of their sufferings and to help them rise. Even the Japanese writers, who took to modernism from the 1920s (probably through contact with Italian Futurism), had a strong and from time to time dominant socialist or communist 'proletarian' contingent (Keene, 1984, chapter 15). Indeed, the first great Chinese modern writer, Lu Hsün (1881–1936), deliberately rejected Western models and looked to Russian literature where 'we can see the kindly soul of the oppressed, their sufferings and struggles' (Lu Hsün, 1975, p. 23).

For most of the creative talents of the non-European world who were neither confined within their traditions nor simple Westernizers, the major task seemed to be to discover, to lift the veil from, and to present the contemporary reality of their peoples. Realism was their movement.

II

In a way, this desire united the arts of East and West. For the twentieth century, it was increasingly clear, was the century of the common people, and dominated by the arts produced by and for them. And two linked instruments made the world of the common man visible as never before and capable of documentation: reportage and the camera. Neither was new (see *Age of Capital*, chapter 15; *Age of Empire*, chapter 9) but both entered a self-conscious golden age after 1914. Writers, especially in the USA, not only saw themselves as recorders or reporters, but wrote for newspapers and indeed were or had been newspapermen: Ernest Hemingway (1899–1961), Theodore Dreiser (1871–1945), Sinclair Lewis (1885–1951). 'Reportage' – the term first appears in French dictionaries in 1929 and in English ones in 1931 – became an accepted genre of socially-critical literature and visual presentation in the 1920s, largely under the influence of the Russian revolutionary avant-garde who extolled fact against the pop entertainment which the European Left had always condemned as the people's opium. The Czech communist journalist Egon Erwin Kisch, who gloried in the name of 'Reporter in a Rush' (*Der rasende Reporter*, 1925, was the title of the first of a series of his reportages) seems to have given the term currency in central Europe. It spread, mainly via the cinema, through the Western avant-garde. Its origins are clearly visible in the sections headed 'Newsreel' and 'the Camera Eye' – an allusion to the avant-garde film documentarist Dziga Vertov – with which the narrative is intercut in John Dos Passos' (1896–1970) trilogy *USA*, written in that novelist's Left-wing period. In the hands of the avant-garde Left 'documentary film' became a self-conscious movement, but in the 1930s even the hard-headed professionals of the news and magazine business claimed a higher intellectual and creative status by upgrading some movie newsreels, usually undemanding space-fillers, into the more grandiose 'March of Time' documentaries, and borrowing the technical innovations of the avant-garde photographers as pioneered in the communist AIZ of the 1920s to create a golden age of the picture-magazine: *Life* in the USA, *Picture Post* in Britain, *Vu* in France. However, outside the Anglo-Saxon countries it only began to flourish massively after the Second World War.

The new photo-journalism owed its merits not only to the talented men – even some women – who discovered photography as a medium, to the illusory belief that 'the camera cannot lie', i.e. that it somehow represented 'real' truth, and to the technical improvements that made unposed pictures easy with the new miniature cameras (the Leica launched in 1924), but perhaps most of all to the universal dominance of the cinema. Men and women learned to see reality through camera lenses. For while there was growth in the circulation of the printed word (now also increasingly interwoven with rotogravure photos in the tabloid press), it lost ground to the film. The Age of Catastrophe was the age of the large cinema screen. In the late 1930s for every British person who bought a daily newspaper, two bought a cinema ticket (Stevenson, pp. 396, 403). Indeed, as depression deepened and the world was swept by war, Western cinema attendances reached their all-time peak.

In the new visual media, avant-garde and mass arts fertilized one another. Indeed, in the old Western countries the domination of the educated strata and a certain elitism penetrated even the mass medium of film, producing a golden age for the German silent film in the Weimar era, for the French sound film in the 1930s, and for the Italian film as soon as the blanket of fascism which covered its talents had been lifted. Of these perhaps the populist French cinema of the 1930s was most successful in combining what intellectuals wanted from culture with what the larger public wanted from entertainment. It was the only highbrow cinema which never forgot the importance of the story, especially about love and crime, and the only one capable of making good jokes. Where the avant-garde (political or artistic) had its own way entirely, as in the documentary movement or agitprop art, its work rarely reached beyond small minorities.

However, the avant-garde input is not what makes the mass arts of the period significant. It is their increasingly undeniable cultural hegemony even though, as we have seen, outside the USA they still had not quite escaped from the supervision of the educated. The arts (or rather entertainments) which became dominant were those aimed at the broadest masses rather than at the large, and growing, middle-class and lower-middle class public with traditional tastes. These still dominated the European 'boulevard' or 'West End' stage or its equivalents, at least until Hitler dispersed the manufacturers of such products, but their interest is slight. The most interesting development in this middlebrow region was the extraordinary, explosive growth of a genre that had shown some signs of life before 1914, but no hint of its subsequent triumphs: the detective puzzle story, now mainly written at book-length. The genre was primarily British – perhaps a tribute to A. Conan Doyle's Sherlock Holmes, who became internationally known in the 1890s – and, more surprisingly, largely female or academic. Its pioneer, Agatha Christie (1891–1976) remains a bestseller to this day. The international versions of this genre were still largely, and evidently, inspired by the British model, i.e. they were almost exclusively about murder treated as a parlour game requiring some ingenuity, rather like the high-class crossword puzzles with enigmatic clues which were an even more exclusively British speciality. The genre is best seen as a curious invocation to a social order threatened but not yet breached. Murder, which now became the central, almost the only crime to mobilize the detective, irrupts into a characteristically ordered environment – the country house, or some familiar professional milieu – and is traced to one of those rotten apples which confirm the soundness of the rest of the barrel. Order is restored through reason as applied to the problem by the detective who himself (he was still overwhelmingly male) represents the milieu. Hence perhaps the insistence on the *private* investigator, unless the policeman himself is, unlike most of his kind, a member of the upper and middle classes. It was a deeply conservative, though still self-confident genre, unlike the contemporary rise of the more hysterical secret agent thriller (also mainly British), a genre with a great future in the second half of the century. Its authors, men of modest literary merits, often found a suitable metier in their country's secret service.*

By 1914 mass media on the modern scale could already be taken for granted in a number of Western countries. Nevertheless, their growth in the age of cataclysms was spectacular. Newspaper circulation in the USA rose much faster than population, doubling between 1920 and 1950. By that time something between 300 and 350 papers were sold for every 1,000 men, women and children in the typical 'developed' country, though the Scandinavians and Australians consumed even more newsprint, and the urbanized British, possibly because their press was national rather than localized, bought an astonishing six hundred copies per thousand of the population (UN *Statistical Yearbook*, 1948). The press appealed to the literate, although in countries of mass schooling it did its best to satisfy the incompletely literate by means of pictures and comic strips, not yet admired by the intellectuals, and by developing a highly-coloured, attention-grabbing, pseudo-demotic idiom avoiding words of too many syllables. Its influence on literature was not negligible. The cinema, on the other hand, made small demands on literacy, and after it learned to talk in the late 1920s, practically none on the English-speaking public.

---

* The literary ancestors of the modern 'hard-boiled' thriller or 'private eye' story were much more demotic. Dashiell Hammett (1894–1961) began as a Pinkerton operative and published in pulp magazines. For that matter the only writer to turn the detective story into genuine literature, the Belgian Georges Simenon (1903–89), was an autodidact hack writer.

However, unlike the press, which in most parts of the world interested only a small elite, films were almost from the start an international mass medium. The abandonment of the potentially universal language of the silent film with its tested codes for cross-cultural communication probably did much to make spoken English internationally familiar and thus helped to establish the language as the global pidgin of the later twentieth century. For, in the golden age of Hollywood, films were essentially American – except in Japan, where about as many full-size movies were made as in the USA. As for the rest of the world, on the eve of the Second World War Hollywood produced about as many films as all other industries combined, even if we include India which already produced about 170 a year for an audience as large as Japan's and almost as large as the USA's. In 1937 it turned out 567 films, or rather more than ten a week. The difference between the hegemonic capacity of capitalism and bureaucratized socialism is that between this figure and the forty-one films the USSR claimed to have produced in 1938. Nevertheless, for obvious linguistic reasons, so extraordinary a global predominance of a single industry could not last. In any case it did not survive the disintegration of the 'studio system' which reached its peak in this period as a machine for mass-producing dreams, but collapsed shortly after the Second World War.

The third of the mass media was entirely new: radio. Unlike the other two, it rested primarily on the private ownership of what was still a sophisticated piece of machinery, and was thus confined essentially to the comparatively prosperous 'developed' countries. In Italy the number of radio sets did not exceed that of automobiles until 1931 (Isola, 1990). The greatest densities of radio-sets were to be found, on the eve of the Second World War, in the USA, Scandinavia, New Zealand and Britain. However, in such countries it advanced at a spectacular rate, and even the poor could afford it. Of Britain's nine million sets in 1939, half had been bought by people earning between £2.5 and £4 per week – a modest income – and another two million by people earning less than this (Briggs, II, p. 254). It is perhaps not surprising that the radio audience doubled in the years of the Great Slump, when its rate of growth was faster than before or later. For radio transformed the life of the poor, and especially of housebound poor women, as nothing else had ever done. It brought the world into their room. Henceforth the loneliest need never again be entirely alone. And the entire range of what could be said, sung, played or otherwise expressed in sound, was now at their disposal. Is it surprising that a medium unknown when the First World War ended had captured ten million households in the USA by the year of the stock exchange crash, over twenty-seven millions by 1939, over forty millions by 1950?

Unlike film, or even the revolutionized mass press, radio did not transform the human ways of perceiving reality in any profound way. It did not create new ways of seeing or establishing relations between sense impressions and ideas (see *Age of Empire*). It was merely the medium, not the message. But its capacity for speaking simultaneously to untold millions, each of whom felt addressed as an individual, made it an inconceivably powerful tool of mass information and, as both rulers and salesmen immediately recognized, for propaganda and advertisement. By the early 1930s the President of the USA had discovered the potential of the radio 'fireside chat', and the king of Britain that of the royal Christmas broadcast (1932 and 1933 respectively). In the Second World War, with its endless demand for news, radio came into its own as a political instrument and as a medium of information. The number of radio sets in continental Europe increased substantially in all countries except some of the worst victims of battle (Briggs, III, Appendix C). In several cases it doubled or more than doubled. In most of the non-European countries the rise was even steeper. Commerce, though from the start it ruled the airwaves over the USA, had a harder conquest elsewhere, since by tradition governments were reluctant to give up control over so powerful a medium for influencing citizens. The BBC maintained its public monopoly. Where commercial broadcasting was tolerated, it was nevertheless expected to defer to the official voice.

It is difficult to recognize the innovations of radio culture, since so much that it pioneered has become part of the furniture of everyday life – the sports commentary, the news bulletin, the celebrity guest show, the soap opera, or indeed the serial programme of any kind. The most profound change it brought was simultaneously to privatize and to structure life according to a rigorous timetable, which henceforth ruled not only the sphere of labour but that of leisure. Yet curiously this medium – and, until the rise of video and VCR its successor, television – though essentially centered on individual and family, created its own public sphere. For the first time in history people unknown to each other who met knew what each had in all probability heard (or, later, seen) the night before: the big game, the favourite comedy show, Winston Churchill's speech, the contents of the news bulletin.

The art most significantly affected by radio was music, since it abolished the acoustic or mechanical limitations on the range of sounds. Music, the last of the arts to break out of the bodily prison that confines oral communication, had already entered the era of mechanical reproduction before 1914 with the gramophone, although this was hardly yet within reach of the masses. The years between the wars certainly brought both gramophones and records within the range of the masses, though the virtual collapse of the record-market for 'race records', i.e. typical poor people's music during the American slump, demonstrates the fragility of this expansion. Yet the record, though its technical quality improved after about 1930 had its limits, if only of length. Moreover, its range depended on its sales. Radio, for the first time, enabled music to be heard at a distance at more than five minutes' unbroken length, and by a theoretically limitless number of listeners. It thus became both a unique popularizer of minority music (including classical music) and by far the most powerful means for selling records, as indeed it still remains. Radio did not change music – it certainly affected it less than the theatre or the movies, which also soon learned to reproduce sound – but the role of music in contemporary life, not excluding its role as aural wallpaper for everyday living, is inconceivable without it.

The forces which dominated the popular arts were thus primarily technological and industrial: press, camera, film, record and radio. Yet since the later nineteenth century an authentic spring of autonomous creative innovation had been visibly welling up in the popular and entertainment quarters of some great cities (see *Age of Empire*). It was far from exhausted, and the media revolution carried its products far beyond their original milieus. Thus the Argentine tango formalized, and especially amplified from dance into song, probably reached its peak of achievement and influence in the 1920s and 1930s, and when its greatest star Carlos Gardel (1890–1935) died in an air crash in 1935, he was mourned all over Spanish America, and (thanks to records) turned into a permanent presence. The samba, destined to symbolize Brazil as the tango did Argentina, is the child of the democratization of the Rio carnival in the 1920s. However, the most impressive and, in the long run, influential development of this sort was the development of jazz in the USA, largely under the impact of the migration of Negroes from the southern states to the big cities of middle west and north-east: an autonomous art music of professional (mainly black) entertainers.

The impact of some of these popular innovations or developments was as yet restricted outside their native milieus. It was also as yet less revolutionary than it became in the second half of the century, when – to take the obvious example – an idiom directly derived from the American Negro blues became, as rock-and-roll, a global language of youth culture. Nevertheless, though – with the exception of film – the impact both of mass media and popular creation was more modest than it became in the second half of the century (this will be considered below); it was already enormous in quantity and striking in quality, especially in the USA which began to exercise an unchallengeable hegemony in these fields, thanks to its extraordinary economic preponderance, its firm commitment to commerce and democracy and, after the Great Slump, the influence of Rooseveltian populism. In the field of popular culture the world was American or it was provincial. With one exception, no other national or regional model established itself globally, though some had substantial regional influence (for instance, Egyptian music within the Islamic world) and an occasional exotic touch entered global commercial popular culture from time to time, as in the Caribbean and Latin American components of dance-music. The unique exception was sport. In this branch of popular culture – and who, having seen the Brazilian team in its days of glory will deny it the claim to art? – US influence remained confined to the area of Washington's political domination. As cricket is played as a mass sport only where once the Union Jack flew, so baseball made little impact except where US marines had once landed. The sport the world made its own was association football, the child of Britain's global economic presence, which had introduced teams named after British firms or composed of expatriate Britons (like the São Paulo Athletic Club) from the polar ice to the Equator. This simple and elegant game, unhampered by complex rules and equipment, and which could be practised on any more or less flat open space of the required size, made its way through the world entirely on its merits and, with the establishment of the World Cup in 1930 (won by Uruguay) became genuinely international.

And yet, by our standards, mass sports, though now global, remained extraordinarily primitive. Their practitioners had not yet been absorbed by the capitalist economy. The great stars were still amateurs, as in tennis (i.e. assimilated to traditional bourgeois status), or professionals paid a wage not all that much higher than a skilled industrial worker's, as in British football. They had still to be enjoyed face-to-face, for even radio could only translate the actual sight of the game or race into the rising decibels of a commentator's voice. The age of television and sportsmen paid like filmstars was still a few years away. But, as we shall see (chapters 9–11) not all that many.

CHAPTER SEVEN
End of Empires

He became a terrorist revolutionary in 1918. His *guru* was present at his wedding night and he never lived with his wife for ten years till her death in 1928. It was an iron rule for the revolutionaries that they should keep aloof from women ... He used to tell me how India would become free by fighting the way the Irish fought. It was when I was with him that I read Dan Breen's *My Fight for Irish Freedom*. Dan Breen was Masterda's ideal. He named his organisation the Indian 'Republican Army, Chittagong branch' after the Irish Republican Army.

– Kalpana Dutt (1945, pp. 16–17)

The heaven-born breed of colonial administrators tolerated and even encouraged the bribery-corruption system because it provided a cheap machinery for the exercise of control over restless and often dissident populations. For what it means in effect is that what a man wants (e.g. to win his lawsuit, to get a government contract, to be given a birthday honour or to get an official job) can be achieved by doing a favour to the man with power to give or with-hold. The 'favour' done need not be a gift of money (that is crude and few Europeans in India soiled their hands that way). It could be a gift of friendship and respect, lavish hospitality, or the gift of funds to a 'good cause', but above all, loyalty to the Raj.

– M. Carritt (1985, pp. 63–64)

In the course of the nineteenth century a few countries – mostly those bordering on the northern Atlantic – conquered the rest of the non-

European globe with ridiculous ease. Insofar as they did not bother to occupy and rule it, the countries of the West established an even more unchallenged superiority by means of their economic and social system and its organization and technology. Capitalism and bourgeois society transformed and ruled the world and provided the model – until 1917 the *only* model – for those who did not want to be devoured or swept aside by the juggernaut of history. After 1917 Soviet communism provided an alternative model, but essentially a model of the same type, except that it dispensed with private enterprise and liberal institutions. The twentieth-century history of the non-Western or more exactly non-north-Western world is therefore essentially determined by its relations with the countries which had established themselves in the nineteenth century as the lords of human kind.

To this extent the history of the Short Twentieth Century remains geographically skewed, and can only be written as such, by the historian who wants to concentrate on the dynamics of global transformation. This does not mean that one shares the condescending and only too often ethnocentric or even racist sense of superiority, and the entirely unjustified self-satisfaction which is still common in the favoured countries. Indeed, this historian is passionately opposed to what E.P. Thompson has called 'the enormous condescension' towards the world's backward and poor. Nevertheless, the fact remains that the dynamics of the greater part of the world's history in the Short Twentieth Century are derived, not original. They consist essentially in the attempts by the elites of non-bourgeois societies to imitate the model pioneered in the West, which was essentially seen as that of societies generating progress, the form of wealth power and culture, by economic and techno-scientific 'development' in a capitalist or socialist variant.* There was no operational model other than 'westernisation' or 'modernisation' or whatever one chose to call it. Conversely, only political euphemism separates the various synonyms of 'backwardness' (as Lenin had no hesitation in describing the situation of his own country and 'the colonial and backward countries') which international diplomacy has scattered round

* It is worth observing that the simple dichotomy 'capitalist'/'socialist' is political rather than analytical. It reflects the emergence of mass political labour movements whose socialist ideology was, in practice, little more than the concept of the present society ('capitalism') turned inside out. This was reinforced, after October 1917, by the long Red/anti-Red Cold War of the Short Twentieth Century. Instead of classifying the economic systems of, say, the USA, South Korea, Austria, Hong Kong, West Germany and Mexico under the same heading of 'capitalism', it would be perfectly possible to classify them under several.

a decolonized world ('under-developed', 'developing' etc.).

The operational model of 'development' could be combined with various other sets of beliefs and ideologies, so long as these did not interfere with it, i.e. so long as the country concerned did not, say, ban the construction of airports on the ground that they had not been authorised by Koran or Bible, or conflicted with the inspiring tradition of medieval knighthood, or were incompatible with the depth of the Slav soul. On the other hand, where such sets of belief were opposed to the process of 'development' *in practice* and not merely in theory they guaranteed failure and defeat. However strong and sincere the belief that magic would turn machine-gun bullets aside, it worked too rarely to make much difference. Telephone and telegraph were better means of communication than the holy man's telepathy.

This is not to dismiss the traditions, beliefs or ideologies, unchanging or modified, by which societies coming into contact with the new world of 'development' judged it. Both traditionalism and socialism concurred in detecting the empty moral space at the centre of triumphant economic – and political – capitalist liberalism, as it destroyed all bonds between individuals except those based on Adam Smith's 'propensity to barter' and to pursue their personal satisfactions and interests. As a moral system, a way of ordering the place of human beings in the world, as a way of recognizing what and how much 'development' and 'progress' destroyed, the pre- or non-capitalist ideologies and value-systems were often superior to the beliefs that gunboats, merchants, missionaries and colonial administrators brought with them. As a means of mobilizing the masses in traditional societies against modernization, either capitalist or socialist, or more precisely against the outsiders who imported it, they could under some circumstances be quite effective, although in fact none of the successful movements of liberation in the backward world before the 1970s was inspired or achieved by traditional or neo-traditional ideologies. This is in spite of the fact that one such movement, the shortlived Khilafat agitation in British India (1920–21), which demanded the preservation of the Turkish Sultan as Caliph of all the faithful, the maintenance of the Ottoman Empire in its 1914 frontiers, and of Moslem control over the Holy Places of Islam (including Palestine), probably forced mass non-cooperation and civil disobedience on a hesitant Indian National Congress (Minault, 1982). The most characteristic mass mobilizations under the auspices of religion – 'Church' retained its hold over the common people better than 'King' – were rearguard actions, though sometimes stubborn and heroic ones like the peasant resistance to the secularising Mexican revolution under the banner of 'Christ the King'

(1926–32), described by its chief historian in epic terms as 'the Christiad' (Meyer, 1973–79). Fundamentalist religion as a major force of successful mass mobilization belongs to the last decades of the twentieth century, which have even witnessed a bizarre return to fashion among some intellectuals of what their educated grandfathers would have described as superstition and barbarism.

Conversely, the ideologies, the programmes, even the methods and forms of political organization which inspired the emancipation of dependent countries from dependency, backward ones from backwardness, were Western: liberal; socialist; communist and/or nationalist; secularist and suspicious of clericalism; using the devices developed for the purposes of public life in bourgeois societies – press, public meetings, parties, mass campaigns, even when the discourse adopted was, and had to be, in the religious vocabulary used by the masses. What this meant was that the history of the makers of the Third World transformations of this century is the history of elite minorities, and sometimes relatively minute ones, for – quite apart from the absence of the institutions of democratic politics almost everywhere – only a tiny stratum possessed the requisite knowledge, education or even elementary literacy. After all, before independence, over 90 per cent of the population of the Indian subcontinent was illiterate. The number of those literate in a Western language (i.e. English) was even more exiguous – say half a million out of three hundred millions or so before 1914, or one in six hundred.* Even the by far most education-hungry region (West Bengal) at the time of independence (1949–50) had only 272 college students to every 100,000 of the population, five times as high as in the North Indian heartland. The role played by these numerically insignificant minorities was enormous. The thirty-eight thousand Parsi men of Bombay Presidency, one of the main administrative divisions of British India, at the end of the nineteenth century, more than one quarter of whom were literate *in English*, not surprisingly became the elite of traders, industrialists and financiers throughout the subcontinent. The 100 advocates to the High Court of Bombay admitted between 1890 and 1900 contained two major national leaders of independent India (Mohandas Karamchand Gandhi and Vallabhai Patel) and the future founder of Pakistan, Muhammad Ali Jinnah (Seal, 1968, p. 884; Misra, 1961, p. 328). The all-purpose function of such Western-educated elites may be illustrated by one Indian family of this writer's acquaintance. The father, a landowner and prosperous lawyer

---

* Based on the data for those undergoing Western-type secondary schooling (Anil Seal, 1971, pp. 21–22).

and social figure under the British, became a diplomat and eventually state governor after 1947. The mother was the first woman minister in the Indian National Congress provincial governments of 1937. Of the four children (all educated in Britain), three joined the Communist Party, one became Commander-in-Chief of the Indian army; another eventually became a member of the Assembly for the party; a third – after chequered political fortunes – a minister in Mrs Gandhi's government; while the fourth made his way into business.

None of this means that the Westernising elites necessarily accepted all the values of the states and cultures they took as their models. Their personal views might range from 100 per cent assimilationism to a deep distrust of the West, combined with the conviction that only by adopting its innovations could the specific values of the native civilization be preserved or restored. The object of the most wholehearted and successful project of 'modernization', Japan since the Meiji Restoration, was not to Westernize, but on the contrary to make traditional Japan viable. In the same way, what Third-World activists read into the ideologies and programmes they made their own was not so much the ostensible text as their own subtext. Thus in the period of independence, socialism (i.e. the Soviet communist version) appealed to decolonized governments, not only because the cause of anti-imperialism had always belonged to the metropolitan Left, but even more because they saw the USSR as the model for overcoming backwardness by means of planned industrialization, a matter of far more urgent concern to them than the emancipation of whatever could be described in their countries as 'the proletariat' (see pp. 350 and 376). Similarly while the Brazilian Communist Party never wavered in its commitment to Marxism, a particular kind of developmental nationalism became 'a fundamental ingredient' in Party policy from the early 1930s, even when it conflicted with labour interests considered separately from others' (Martins Rodrigues, p. 437). Nevertheless, whatever the conscious or unconscious objectives of those who shaped the history of the backward world, modernization, that is to say, the imitation of Western-derived models, was the necessary and indispensable way to achieve them.

This was all the more obvious, since the perspectives of the Third World elites and those of the mass of their populations differed very substantially, except insofar as white (i.e. North Atlantic) racism provided a common bond of resentment which could be shared by maharajahs and sweepers. Even so, it might well be less felt by men, and especially women, who were used to inferior status within any society, irrespective of its members' skin-colour. Outside the Islamic world, the case where a common religion provided such a bond – in this case of immutable superiority to the unbelievers – was unusual.

II

The world economy of capitalism in the Age of Empire penetrated and transformed virtually all parts of the globe, even if, after the October Revolution, it temporarily stopped at the frontiers of the USSR. That is why the Great Slump of 1929–33 was to be such a landmark in the history of anti-imperialism and Third World liberation movements. Whatever the economy, the wealth, the cultures and political systems of countries had been before they came within reach of the North Atlantic octopus, they were all sucked into the world market, insofar as they were not dismissed by Western businessmen and governments as economically uninteresting, even if colourful, like the Beduin of the great deserts before the discovery of oil or natural gas in their inhospitable habitat. Their value to the world market was essentially as suppliers of primary products – the raw materials for industry and energy and the products of farming and livestock rearing – and as an outlet for northern capital investment, mainly in government loans and the infrastructures of transport, communications and cities, without which the resources of dependent countries could not be effectively exploited. In 1913 over three quarters of all British overseas investment – and the British exported more capital than the rest of the world put together – was in government stocks, railways, ports and shipping (Brown, 1963, p. 153).

The industrialization of the dependent world was still part of no one's game-plan, even in countries like those of the southern cone of Latin America, where it seemed logical to process such locally produced foodstuffs as meat into more easily transportable form as tins of corned beef. After all, canning sardines and bottling port wine had not industrialized Portugal, nor was it intended that it should. In fact, the basic pattern in the minds of most northern governments and entrepreneurs was one in which the dependent world paid for its imports of their manufactures by the sale of its primaries. This had been the foundation of the British dominated world economy in the pre-1914 period (*Age of Empire*, chapter 2), although, with the exception of the countries of so-called 'settler capitalism', the dependent world was not a particularly rewarding export market for manufacturers. The three hundred million inhabitants of the Indian subcontinent, the four hundred million Chinese, were too poor and supplied too many of their everyday needs locally to buy much from anyone. Fortunately for the British in their age of economic hegemony, their seven hundred million penniesworth added up to enough to keep the Lancashire cotton industry in business. Its interest, like that of all northern producers, was obviously to make the dependent market, such as it was, completely dependent on their production, i.e. to agrarianize it.

Whether or not they had this object, they could not succeed, partly because the local markets created by the very absorption of economies into a world market society, a society of buying and selling, stimulated local consumer-goods production, which it was cheaper to set up locally, and partly because many of the economies in the dependent regions, especially in Asia, were highly complex structures with long histories of manufacture, considerable sophistication and impressive technical and human resources and potential. So the giant entrepôt port cities which came to be the characteristic links between the North and the dependent world – from Buenos Aires and Sydney to Bombay, Shanghai and Saigon – developed local industry in the shelter of their temporary protection from imports, even if that was not the intention of their rulers. It would hardly take much to make local textile producers in Ahmedabad or Shanghai, whether native or agents for some foreign firm, supply the Indian or Chinese market close by, with the cotton goods hitherto imported from distant and high-cost Lancashire. In fact, this is what happened in the aftermath of the First World War, and it broke the neck of the British cotton industry.

And yet, when we consider how logical Marx's prediction of the eventual spread of the industrial revolution to the rest of the world seemed, it is astonishing how little industry had left the world of developed capitalism before the end of the era of empires, and indeed before the 1970s. In the late 1930s the only major change in the world map of industralization was that due to the Soviet Five-Year Plans (see chapter 2). As late as 1960 the old heartlands of industrialization in Western Europe and North America produced over 70 per cent of gross world output and almost 80 per cent of the world's 'value added in manufacturing', i.e. industrial output (Harris, 1987, pp. 102–3). The really dramatic shift away from the old West – including the major rise of the Japanese industry, which in 1960 turned out only something like 4 per cent of world industrial production – came in the last third of the century. Not until the 1970s did economists begin to write books on 'the new international division of labour', i.e. the beginning of the deindustrialization of the old heartlands.

Evidently imperialism, the old 'international division of labour', had a built-in tendency to reinforce the industrial monopoly of the old core countries. To this extent the inter-war Marxists, joined later by the post-1945 'dependency theorists' of various brands, had clear grounds for their attacks on imperialism as a mode of ensuring the continued backwardness of the backward countries. Yet paradoxically it was the relative immaturity of the development of the capitalist world economy, and, more exactly, of the technology of transport and communication, which kept industry located in its original homelands. There was nothing in the logic of profit-making enterprise and capital accumulation to keep the manufacture of steel in Pennsylvania or the Ruhr for ever, although it is no cause for surprise that governments of industrial countries, especially if inclined to protectionism or with large colonial empires, should do their best to stop potential competitors from harming the homeland's industry. But even imperial governments could have reasons to industralize their colonies, even though the only case where they did so systematically was Japan, which developed heavy industries in Korea (annexed in 1911) and, after 1931, in Manchuria and Taiwan because these resource-rich colonies were sufficiently close to the exiguous and notoriously raw-material-poor homeland to serve Japanese national industrialization directly. Yet even in the greatest of colonies, the discovery, during the First World War, that India had not been in a position to manufacture enough for industrial self-sufficiency and military defence led to a policy of government protection and direct participation in the country's industrial development (Misra, 1961, pp. 239, 256). If war brought the drawbacks of insufficient colonial industry home even to imperial administrators, the slump of 1929–33 put them under financial pressure. As agricultural revenues fell, the income of colonial government had to be shored up by higher duties on manufactured goods, including the home country's own, British, French or Dutch. For the first time Western firms, which had hitherto imported freely, had a strong incentive to set up local production facilities in these marginal markets (Holland, 1985, p. 13). Still, even allowing for war and slump, the dependent world in the first half of the Short Twentieth Century remained overwhelmingly agrarian and rural. That is why the 'great leap forward' of the world economy in the third quarter of the century was to prove so dramatic a turning-point in its fortunes.

III

Practically all parts of Asia, Africa and Latin/Caribbean America were and felt themselves to be dependent on what happened in a few states of the northern hemisphere, but (outside the Americas) most of them were also owned, administered or otherwise dominated and commanded by them. This applied even to those left with their own native authorities (e.g. as 'protectorates' or princely states), for it was well understood that the 'advice' of the British or French representative at the court of the local emir, bey, rajah, king or sultan, was compelling. It was true even in formally independent states like China, where foreigners enjoyed extra-territorial rights and supervision over some of the central functions of sovereign states, such as revenue collection. In these areas the problem of getting rid of foreign rule was bound to arise. This was not so in Central and South America, which consisted almost wholly of sovereign states, even though the USA – but no one else – was inclined to treat the smaller Central American ones as *de facto* protectorates, especially in the first and last thirds of the century.

The colonial world has been so completely transformed into a collection of nominally sovereign states since 1945 that it must seem, in retrospect, that this was not only inevitable but what the colonial peoples had always wanted. This is almost certainly true in those countries which looked back on a long history as political entities, the great Asian empires – China, Persia, the Ottomans – and perhaps one or two other countries like Egypt; especially when they were built round a substantial '*staatsvolk*' or 'state people' like the Han Chinese or the believers in Shiite Islam as virtually the national religion of Iran. In such countries popular sentiment against foreigners could be easily politicized. It is no accident that China, Turkey and Iran have all three been the scene of important autochthonous revolutions. However, such cases were exceptional. More often, the very concept of a permanent territorial political entity, with fixed frontiers separating it from other such entities, and subject exclusively to one permanent authority, i.e. the idea of the independent sovereign state which we take for granted, was meaningless to people, at least (even in areas of permanent and fixed agriculture) above the village level. Indeed, even where a clearly self-described or recognized 'people' existed, which Europeans liked to describe as a 'tribe', the idea that it could be territorially separated from other people with whom it coexisted and intermingled and divided functions was difficult to grasp, because it made little sense. In such regions the only foundation for such independ-ent states of the twentieth-century type were the territories into which imperial conquest and rivalry had divided them, usually without any reference to local structures. The post-colonial world is thus almost entirely divided by the frontiers of imperialism.

Moreover, those inhabitants of the Third World who most resented the Westerners (whether as unbelievers, as bringers of all manner of disruptive and godless modern innovations, or simply out of resistance to any change in ordinary people's ways of life, which they, not unjustifiably, supposed would be for the worse), were equally opposed to the elites' justified conviction that modernization was indispensable. This made a common front against the imperialists difficult, even in colonial countries where all members of the subject people bore the common burden of the colonialists' contempt for the inferior race.

The major task of middle-class nationalist movements in such countries was how to acquire the support of the essentially traditionalist and anti-modern masses without jeopardizing their own modernizing project. The dynamic Bal Ganghadar Tilak (1856–1920), in the early days of Indian nationalism, was right in supposing that the best way to win mass support, even among the lower middle classes – and not only in his native part of western India – was by defending the sanctity of cows and the marriage of ten-year-old girls, and asserting the spiritual superiority of the ancient Hindu or 'Aryan' civilization and its religion to modern 'Western' civilization and its native admirers. The first important phase of Indian nationalist militancy, from 1905 to 1910, was largely conducted in such 'nativist' terms, not least among the young terrorists of Bengal. Eventually Mohandas Karamchand Gandhi (1869-1948) was to succeed in mobilizing the villages and bazaars of India in their tens of millions by very much the same appeal to nationalism as Hindu spirituality, though taking care not to break the common front with the modernisers (of whom, in a real sense, he was one – see *Age of Empire*, chapter 13), and to avoid the antagonism to Mohammedan India, which was always implicit in a militantly Hindu approach to nationalism. He invented the politician as saint, revolution by the collective act of passivity ('non-violent non-cooperation'), and even social modernization, such as the rejection of the caste system, by exploiting the reforming potential contained within the endlessly changing and all-embracing ambiguities of an evolving Hinduism. He succeeded beyond anyone's wildest hopes (or fears). And yet, as he himself recognized at the end of his life, before being assassinated by a militant in the Tilak tradition of Hindu exclusive-ness, he had failed in his fundamental endeavour. In the long run it was impossible to reconcile what moved the masses and what had to be done. In the end, free India was to be governed by those who 'did not look back to a revival in India of ancient times', who 'had no sympathy or understanding of them . . . looked to the West and felt greatly attracted by Western progress' (Nehru, 1936, pp. 23–24). Yet, at the time this book is written, the tradition of Tilak's anti-modernism, now represented by the militant BJP Party, remained as the major focus of popular opposition, and – then as now – it is the major divisive force in India, not only among the masses, but also among the intellectuals. Mahatma Gandhi's brief attempt at a Hinduism both populist and progressive has sunk from sight.

A similar pattern emerged in the Moslem world, although there (except after successful revolutions) all modernisers always had to pay their respects to universal popular piety, whatever their private beliefs. However, unlike India, the attempts to read a reforming or modernising message into Islam were not designed to mobilize the masses and did not do so. The disciples of Jamal al-Din al Afghani (1839–97) in Iran, Egypt and Turkey; of his follower Mohammed Abduh (1849–1905) in Egypt; of the Algerian Abdul Hamid Ben Badis (1889–1940) were not to be found in the villages but in schools and colleges, where the message of resistance to the European powers would in any case have found sympathetic audiences.* Nevertheless, the real revolutionaries of the Islamic world, and those who came to the top there were, as we have seen (chapter 5), non-Islamic secular modernisers: men like Kemal Atatürk, who substituted the bowler hat for the Turkish fez (itself a nineteenth-century innovation), roman letters for the Islam-tainted arabic script and, in fact, broke the links between Islam, State and Law. Nevertheless, as recent history again confirms, mass mobilization was most easily achieved on the basis of anti-modern mass piety ('Islamic fundamentalism'). In short, a profound conflict separated the modernisers, who were also the nationalists (an entirely untraditional concept), and the common people of the Third World.

Anti-imperialist and anti-colonial movements before 1914 were, therefore, less prominent than one might think in the light of almost total liquidation of the Western and Japanese colonial empires within half a century of the outbreak of the first World War. Even in Latin America hostility to economic dependency in general and to the USA in particular, the only imperial state which insisted on a military presence in the region, was not then an important asset in local politics. The only empire that faced serious problems in some areas – i.e.

---

* In French North Africa rural piety was dominated by various Sufi holy men ('Marabouts') who were the particular target of the reformers' denunciation.

problems which could not be handled by police operations – was the British. By 1914 it had already conceded internal autonomy to the colonies of mass white settlement, known from 1907 as 'dominions' (Canada, Australia, New Zealand, South Africa) and it was committed to autonomy ('Home Rule') for ever-troublesome Ireland. In India and Egypt it was already clear that imperial interests and local demands for autonomy, even for independence, might require political solutions. After 1905 one could even speak of some element of mass support for the nationalist movement in India and Egypt.

However, the First World War was the first set of events which seriously shook the structure of world colonialism, as well as destroying two empires (the German and the Ottoman, whose former possessions were divided, mainly between the British and the French) and temporarily knocking out a third, Russia (which recovered its Asian dependencies within a few years). The strains of the war on the dependencies, whose resources Britain needed to mobilize, generated unrest. The impact of the October Revolution and the general collapse of old regimes, followed by *de facto* Irish independence for the twenty-six Southern Counties (1921), made foreign empires look mortal for the first time. At the end of the war an Egyptian party, Said Zaghlul's *Wafd* ('delegation'), inspired by President Wilson's rhetoric, for the first time demanded complete independence. Three years of struggle (1919–22) forced the British to transform their protectorate into a semi-independent Egypt under British control, a formula which Britain also found convenient for the management of all but one of the Asian areas it took over from the Turkish Empire: Iraq and Transjordan. (The exception was Palestine, which they administered directly, vainly trying to reconcile the promises made during the war both to Zionist Jews, in return for support against Germany, and Arabs, in return for support against the Turks.)

It was less easy for Britain to find a simple formula for maintaining control over the largest colony of all, India, where the slogan of 'self-rule' (*Swaraj*), adopted by the Indian National Congress for the first time in 1906, now edged increasingly towards complete independence. The revolutionary years 1918–22 transformed mass nationalist politics in the subcontinent, partly by turning the Moslem masses against the British, partly by the lapse into bloodthirsty hysteria of a British general in the turbulent year 1919, who massacred an unarmed crowd in an exitless enclosure, killing several hundreds (the 'Amritsar Massacre'), but chiefly by the combination of a wave of workers' strikes combined with the mass civil disobedience called for by Gandhi and a radicalized Congress. For a moment an almost millennial mood seized the liberation movement: Gandhi announced that *Swaraj* would be won by the end of 1921. The government did 'not seek to minimise in any way the fact that great anxiety is caused by the situation', as the towns were paralysed by non-cooperation, the countryside in large areas of North India, Bengal, Orissa and Assam was in uproar and 'a large proportion of the Mohammedan population throughout the country are embittered and sullen' (Cmd 1586, 1922, p. 13). From now on India became intermittently ungovernable. Probably it was only the hesitation of most Congress leaders, including Gandhi, to plunge their country into the savage darkness of an uncontrollable insurrection by the masses, their own lack of confidence, and the conviction of most nationalist leaders, shaken but not utterly destroyed, that the British were genuinely committed to Indian reform that saved the British Raj. After Gandhi called off the campaign of civil disobedience early in 1922, on the grounds that it had led to the massacre of policemen in one village, it can reasonably be claimed that British rule in India depended on his moderation – far more than on police and army.

The conviction was not unjustified. While there was a powerful bloc of diehard imperialism in Britain, of which Winston Churchill made himself the spokesman, the effective view of the British ruling class after 1919 was that some form of Indian self-rule similar to 'dominion status' was ultimately unavoidable, and the future of Britain in India depended on coming to terms with the Indian elite, including the nationalists. An end to unilateral British rule in India was henceforth only a question of time. Since India was the core of the entire British Empire, the future of that Empire as a whole, therefore, now seemed uncertain, except in Africa and the scattered islands of the Caribbean and Pacific, where paternalism still ruled unchallenged. Never had a larger area of the globe been under the formal or informal control of Britain than between the two world wars, but never before had the rulers of Britain felt less confident about maintaining their old imperial supremacy. This was one major reason why, when the position became unsustainable after the Second World War, the British, by and large, did not resist decolonisation. It is perhaps also the reason why other empires, notably the French – but also the Dutch – fought with arms to maintain their colonial positions after 1945. Their empires had not been shaken by the First World War. The only major headache of the French was that they had not yet completed their conquest of Morocco, but the warlike Berber clansmen of the Atlas mountains were essentially a military rather than a political problem and, in fact, a rather greater one for Spain's Moroccan colony, where a local highland intellectual, Abd-el-Krim, proclaimed a Rif Republic in 1923. Enthusiastically backed by French communists and others on the Left, Abd-el-Krim was defeated in 1926 with French help, after which the mountain Berbers returned to their habitual pursuits of fighting in the French and Spanish colonial armies abroad, and resisting any kind of central government at home. A modernizing anti-colonial movement in the French Islamic colonies and in French Indochina did not develop until well after the First World War, except for modest anticipations in Tunisia.

IV

The years of revolution had shaken primarily the British Empire, but the Great Slump of 1929–33 shook the entire dependent world. For practically all of it the era of imperialism had been one of almost continuous growth, unbroken even by the world war from which most of them remained remote. Of course, many of its inhabitants were not yet much involved in the expanding world economy, or did not feel themselves to be involved in any very novel way, for what did it matter to poor men and women who had dug and carried loads since the beginning of time in what exact global context they did so? Still, the imperialist economy brought substantial changes to the lives of ordinary people, especially in the regions of export-oriented primary production. Sometimes these changes had already surfaced in the sort of politics native or foreign rulers recognized. Thus, as the Peruvian *haciendas* were transformed, between 1900 and 1930, into coastal sugar factories and highland commercial sheep ranches, and the trickle of Indian labour migration to coast and city became a flow, new ideas seeped into the traditional hinterlands. By the early 1930s Huasicancha, an 'especially remote' community some 3,700 metres up the inaccessible Andean slopes, was already debating which of two national radical parties would best represent its interests (Smith, 1989, esp. p. 175). Yet far more often nobody except the locals as yet knew or cared much how they changed.

What, for instance, did it mean for economies which had hardly used money, or had used it only for a limited range of purposes, to move into an economy where it was the universal means of exchange, as happened in the Indo-Pacific seas? The meaning of goods, services and transactions between people was transformed, and so consequently were the moral values of the society, and, indeed, its form of social distribution. Among the matrilineal rice-growing peasants of Negri Sembilan (Malaysia) the ancestral lands, cultivated mainly by the women, could only be inherited by or through women, but the new plots cleared in the jungle by the men, and on which supplementary crops were grown, such as fruit and vegetables, could be transmitted directly to men. But with the rise of rubber, a far more profitable crop than rice, the balance between the sexes changed, as inheritance from male to male gained ground. And this in turn strengthened the patriarchally-minded leaders of orthodox Islam, who were in any case trying to super-impose orthodoxy on local customary law, not to mention the local ruler and his kinfolk, another island of patrilineal descent in the local matrilineal lake (Firth, 1954). The dependent world was full of such changes and transformations in communities of people whose direct contact with the wider world was minimal – perhaps in this instance, only through a Chinese trader, himself in most cases originally a peasant or artisan emigrant from Fukien, whose culture had accustomed him to consistent effort, but above all to sophistication in matters of money, but otherwise equally far from the world of Henry Ford and General Motors (Freedman, 1959).

And yet, the world economy as such seemed remote, because its immediate, recognizable impact was not cataclysmic, except perhaps in the rapidly-growing cheap-labour industrial enclaves of such regions as India and China, where labour conflict, even labour organization on the Western models, spread from 1917, and in the gigantic port and industrial cities through which the dependent world communicated with the world economy that determined their fortunes: Bombay, Shanghai (whose population grew from 200,000 in the mid-nineteenth century to three-and-a-half millions in the 1930s), Buenos Aires or, on a smaller scale, Casablanca, whose population reached 250,000, less than thirty years after it opened as a modern port (Bairoch, 1985, pp. 517, 525).

The Great Slump changed all this. For the first time the interests of dependent and metropolitan economies clashed visibly, if only because the prices of primary products, on which the Third World depended, collapsed so much more dramatically than those of the manufactured goods which they bought from the West (chapter 3). For the first time colonialism and dependency became unacceptable even to those who had hitherto benefited from it. 'Students rioted in Cairo, Rangoon and Djakarta (Batavia), not because they felt that some political millennium was in striking distance, but because depression had suddenly knocked away the supports which had made colonialism so acceptable to the generation of their parents' (Holland 1985, p. 12). More than this: for the first time (other than during wars) the lives of ordinary people were shaken by earthquakes plainly not of natural origin, and which called for protest rather than prayer. A mass basis for political mobilization came into existence, especially where peasants had come to be heavily involved in the world-market cash-crop economy, as on the West African coast and in South-east Asia. At the same time the Slump destabilized both the national and international politics of the dependent world.

The 1930s were, therefore, a crucial decade for the Third World, not so much because the Slump led to political radicalization but rather because it established contact between the politicised minorities and the common people of their countries. This was so even in countries like India, where the nationalist movement already had mobilized mass support. A second wave of mass non-cooperation in the early 1930s, a new compromise constitution conceded by the British, and the first nation-wide provincial elections in 1937 demonstrated the nationwide support of Congress, its members in the Ganges heartland rising from about sixty thousand in 1935 to one-and-a-half millions at the end of the 1930s (Tomlinson, 1976, p. 86). It was even more obvious in hitherto less mobilized countries. The outlines of the mass politics of the future began to emerge, dimly or clearly: Latin American populism based on authoritarian leaders seeking the support of urban workers; political mobilization by labour union leaders with a future as party leaders, as in the British Caribbean; a revolutionary movement with a strong base among labour migrants to and returners from, France, as in Algeria; a communist-based national resistance with strong agrarian links, as in Vietnam. At the very least, as in Malaya, the depression years fractured the bonds between colonial authorities and peasant masses, leaving a space for the rise of future politics.

By the end of the 1930s the crisis of colonialism had spread to other empires, although two of them, the Italian (which had just conquered Ethiopia) and the Japanese (which was trying to conquer China), were still expanding, though not for long. In India the new Constitution of 1935, an unhappy compromise with the rising forces of Indian nationalism, proved to be a major concession to it through the almost nationwide electoral triumph of Congress. In French North Africa serious political movements emerged for the first time in Tunisia, in Algeria – there were even some stirrings in Morocco – whilst mass agitation under communist leadership, orthodox and dissident, became substantial for the first time in French Indochina. The Dutch managed to keep control in Indonesia, a region which 'feels the movements in the East as not many other countries do' (Van Asbeck, 1939), not because it was quiet, but mainly because the forces of opposition – Islamic, communist and secular nationalist – were divided among themselves and against each other. Even in what colonial ministries regarded as the somnolent Caribbean, a series of strikes in the oil fields of Trinidad and the plantations and cities of Jamaica between 1935 and 1938 turned into riots and island-wide clashes, revealing a hitherto unrecognized mass disaffection.

Only sub-Saharan Africa still remained quiescent, although even there the Slump years brought the first mass labour strikes after 1935, starting on the central African copper-belt, and London began to urge colonial governments to create labour departments, take steps to improve workers' conditions and stabilize labour forces, recognizing the current system of rural men's migration from village to mine as socially and politically destabilizing. The strike-wave of 1935–40 was Africa-wide. But it was not yet political in an anti-colonial sense, unless we count as political the spread of black-oriented African churches and prophets and of such rejectors of wordly governments as the (American-derived) millennial Watchtower movement on the Copper-belt. For the first time colonial governments began to reflect on the destabilising effect of economic change on rural African society – which was actually passing through a notable era of prosperity – and to encourage research on this topic by social anthropologists.

However, politically, danger seemed remote. In the countryside this was the golden age of the white administrator, with or without the compliant 'chief', sometimes created for this purpose where colonial administration was 'indirect'. In the cities a dissatisfied class of educated urban Africans was already sufficiently large in the mid-1930s to maintain a flourishing political press, such as the *African Morning Post* on the Gold Coast (Ghana), the *West African Pilot* in Nigeria, and the *Éclaireur de la Côte d'Ivoire* on the Ivory Coast ('it led a campaign against senior chiefs and the police; it demanded measures of social reconstruction; it urged the cause of the unemployed and of the African farmers hit by the economic crisis') (Hodgkin, 1961, p. 32). The leaders of local political nationalism were already emerging, influenced by ideas from the Black movement in the USA, from the France of the Popular Front era, the ideas circulating in the West African Students Union in London, even from the communist movement.* Some of the future presidents of the future African republics were already on the scene – Kenya's Jomo Kenyatta (1889–1978); Dr Namdi Azikiwe, later president of Nigeria.

* However, not a single leading African figure became, or remained, communist.

None of this as yet caused sleepless nights in European colonial ministries.

Did the universal end of colonial empires, though probable, actually seem imminent in 1939? Not if the present writer's memory of a 'school' for British and 'colonial' student communists in that year is any guide. And nobody was likely to have higher expectations at that time than impassioned and hopeful young Marxist militants. What transformed the situation was the Second World War. Though it was far more than this, it was unquestionably an inter-imperialist war, and, until 1943, the great colonial empires were on the losing side. France collapsed ignominiously, and many of its dependencies survived by permission of the Axis powers. The Japanese overran what there was of the British, Dutch, and other Western colonies in South-east Asia and the western Pacific. Even in North Africa the Germans occupied what they chose to control up to a few score miles west of Alexandria. At one point the British seriously considered withdrawing from Egypt. Only Africa south of the deserts remained under firm Western control, and indeed the British managed to liquidate the Italian Empire in the Horn of Africa with little trouble.

What fatally damaged the old colonialists was the proof that white men and their states could be defeated, shamefully and dishonourably, and the the old colonial powers were patently too weak, even after a victorious war, to restore their old positions. The test of the British Raj in India was not the major rebellion organized by Congress in 1942 under the slogan 'Quit India', for they suppressed it without serious difficulty. It was that, for the first time, up to fifty-five thousand Indian soldiers defected to the enemy to form an 'Indian National Army' under a Left-wing Congress leader, Subhas Chandra Bose, who had decided to seek Japanese support for Indian independence (Bhargava/Singh Gill, 1988, p. 10; Sareen, 1988, pp. 20–21). Japanese policy, possibly under the influence of the navy, more sophisticated than the soldiers, exploited the skin-colour of its people to claim merit as a liberator of colonies, with substantial success (except among the overseas Chinese and in Vietnam, where it maintained the French administration). An 'Assembly of Greater East Asiatic Nations'* was even organized in Tokyo in 1943, attended by the 'presidents' or 'prime ministers' of Japanese-sponsored China, India, Thailand, Burma and Manchuria (but not Indonesia, which was offered even Japanese 'independence' only when the war was lost). The colonial

---

* The term 'Asian' only came into currency after the Second World War, for reasons which are obscure.

nationalists were too realistic to be pro-Japanese, though they appreciated the support from Japan, especially when this was substantial, as in Indonesia. When the Japanese were about to lose, they turned against them, but they never forgot how weak the old Western empires had proved to be. Nor did they overlook the fact that the two powers which had actually defeated the Axis, Roosevelt's USA and Stalin's USSR, were both, for different reasons, hostile to the old colonialism, even though American anti-communism soon made Washington the defender of conservatism in the Third World.

V

Not surprisingly, the old colonial systems first broke in Asia. Syria and Lebanon (formerly French) became independent in 1945; India and Pakistan in 1947; Burma, Ceylon (Sri Lanka), Palestine (Israel) and the Dutch East Indies (Indonesia) in 1948. In 1946 the USA had granted formal status of independence to the Philippines, which it had occupied since 1898. The Japanese Empire had, of course, disappeared in 1945. Islamic North Africa was already shaking, but still held. Most of sub-Saharan Africa and the islands of the Caribbean and Pacific remained relatively quiet. Only in parts of South-east Asia was this political decolonisation seriously resisted, notably in French Indochina (the present Vietnam, Cambodia and Laos) where the communist resistance had declared independence after liberation under the leadership of the noble Ho Chi Minh. The French, supported by the British and later the USA, conducted a desperate rearguard action to reconquer and hold a country against the victorious revolution. They were defeated and forced to withdraw in 1954, but the USA prevented the unification of the country and maintained a satellite regime in the southern part of a divided Vietnam. After this in turn looked like collapsing, the USA waged ten years of major war in Vietnam itself, until it was finally defeated and forced to withdraw in 1975, having dropped more high explosive on the unhappy country than had been used in the whole of the Second World War.

Resistance in the rest of South-east Asia was patchier. The Dutch (who turned out to be rather better than the British in decolonizing their Indian empire without partitioning it) were too weak to maintain adequate military power in the huge Indonesian archipelago, most of whose islands would have been quite prepared to keep them as counterweight to the predominance of the fifty-five million-strong Javanese. They gave up when they discovered that the USA did not consider Indonesia an essential front against world communism, unlike Vietnam. Indeed, so far from being under communist leadership, the new Indonesian nationalists had just put down an insurrection by the local Communist Party in 1948, an event which convinced the USA that Dutch military power would be better employed in Europe against the supposed Soviet threat than to maintain their empire. So the Dutch gave up, only maintaining a colonial foothold in the western half of the great melanesian island of New Guinea, until this also was transferred to Indonesia in the 1960s. The British in Malaya found themselves caught between the traditional sultans who had done well out of empire and two different and mutually suspicious bodies of inhabitants, the Malays and the Chinese, each radicalized in different ways; the Chinese by the Communist Party which had gained much influence as the only body of resisters to the Japanese. Once the Cold War had broken out no question of allowing communists, let alone Chinese ones, into power or office in an ex-colony could arise, but after 1948 it took the British twelve years, fifty thousand troops, sixty thousand police and a home guard of two hundred thousand to defeat a primarily Chinese guerrilla insurrection and war. It may well be asked whether Britain would have paid the costs of these operations so willingly if Malaya's tin and rubber had not been such reliable dollar earners, thus guaranteeing the stability of sterling. However, the decolonisation of Malaya would in any case have been a rather complex affair and was not achieved to the satisfaction of Malay conservatives and Chinese millionaires until 1957. In 1965 the mainly Chinese island of Singapore broke away to constitute itself an independent, and very rich, city state.

Unlike the French and the Dutch, Britain had learned by long experience in India that once a serious nationalist movement existed the only way to hold on to the advantages of empire was to let go of formal power. The British withdrew from the Indian subcontinent in 1947 before their inability to control it became patent, and without the slightest resistance. Ceylon (renamed Sri Lanka in 1972) and Burma were also given their independence, the former to its welcome surprise, the latter with more hesitation, since the Burmese nationalists, though led by an Anti-fascist People's Freedom League, had also cooperated with the Japanese. Indeed they were so hostile to Britain that, alone of all de-colonized British possessions, Burma immediately refused to join the British Commonwealth, the non-committal association by which London tried to maintain at least the memory of the British Empire. In this it anticipated even Ireland, which declared itself a Republic outside the Commonwealth in the same year. All the same, while the rapid and peaceful retreat of Britain from the largest block of humanity ever subdued and administered by a foreign conqueror was a credit to the British Labour government which came to power at the end of the Second World War, it was far from an unqualified success. It was achieved at the cost of a bloodstained partition of India into a Muslim Pakistan and a non-denominational, but overwhelmingly Hindu India, in the course of which perhaps several hundred thousand people were massacred by religious opponents and several more millions were driven from their ancestral homes into what was now a foreign country. This had not been part of the plan of either Indian nationalism or Muslim movements or of the imperial rulers.

How the idea of a separate 'Pakistan', whose very concept and name was only invented by some students in 1932–33, became reality by 1947 is a question that continues to haunt both scholars and dreamers about the 'if onlys' of history. Since, as we can see with the wisdom of hindsight, the partition of India along religious lines established a sinister precedent for the world's future, it needs some explanation. In a sense it was nobody's or everybody's fault. In the elections under the 1935 Constitution, Congress had triumphed, even in most Moslem areas, and the national party claiming to represent the minority community, the Moslem League, had done rather poorly. The rise of a secular and non-sectarian, Indian National Congress naturally made many Muslims, most of them (like most Hindus) still non-voters, nervous of Hindu power, since the majority of the Congress leaders in a predominantly Hindu country were likely to be Hindus. Instead of recognizing these fears and giving Muslims special representation, the elections seemed to strengthen Congress claims to be the *only* national party, representing both Hindus and Muslims. This is what caused the Muslim League under its formidable leader, Muhammad Ali Jinnah, to break with Congress and to set out on what became the road to potential separatism. However, not until 1940 did Jinnah drop his opposition to a separate Muslim state.

It was the war that broke India in two. In one sense it was the last great triumph of the British Raj – and at the same time its last exhausted gasp. For the last time the Raj mobilized the men and the economy of India for a British war, on an even greater scale than in 1914–18, this time against the opposition of the masses now behind a party of national liberation, and – unlike the First World War – against imminent military invasion from Japan. The achievement was astonishing, but the costs were high. Congress opposition to the war kept its leaders out of politics and, after 1942, in jail. The strains of the war economy alienated important bodies of the Raj's political supporters among the Muslims, notably in the Punjab, and thus sent them to the Moslem League, which now became a mass force at the very moment when the government in Delhi, fearing the Congress's ability to sabotage the war effort, deliberately and systematically exploited Hindu–Moslem rivalry to immobilize the national movement. This time it can be truly said that Britain 'divided to rule'. In its last desperate effort to win the war, the Raj destroyed not only itself but its moral legitimation: the achievement of a single Indian subcontinent in which all its multiple communities could coexist in relative peace under a single because impartial administration and law. When the war ended, the engine of communal politics could no longer be put into reverse.

By 1950 Asian decolonization was complete, except in Indochina. Meanwhile the region of western Islam, from Persia (Iran) to Morocco, was transformed by a series of popular movements, revolutionary coups and insurrections, starting with the nationalization of the Western oil companies in Iran (1951) and the swing to populism of that country under Dr Muhammad Mussadiq (1880–1967) supported by the then powerful Tudeh (Communist) Party. (Not surprisingly communist parties in the Middle East acquired some influence in the aftermath of the great Soviet victory.) Mussadiq was to be overthrown by an Anglo-American secret service coup in 1953. The revolution of the Free Officers in Egypt (1952) led by Gamal Abdel Nasser (1918–70) and the subsequent overthrow of Western client regimes in Iraq (1958) and Syria could not be so reversed, though the British and French, combining with the new anti-Arab state of Israel, tried their best to overthrow Nasser in the Suez War of 1956 (see p. 359). However, the French bitterly resisted the rising for national independence in Algeria (1954–62), one of those territories, like South Africa and – in a different manner – Israel, where the coexistence of an indigenous population with a large body of European settlers made the problem of decolonisation particularly intractable. The Algerian war was thus a conflict of peculiar brutality which helped to institutionalize torture in the armies, police and security forces of countries that purported to be civilized. It popularized the subsequently widespread and infamous use of torture by electric shocks applied to tongues, nipples and genitalia, and led to the overthrow of the Fourth Republic (1958) and almost to that of the Fifth (1961), before Algeria won the independence which General de Gaulle had long recognized as inevitable. Meanwhile the French government had quietly negotiated the autonomy and (1956) independence of the two other North African protectorates; Tunisia (which became a republic) and Morocco (which remained a monarchy). In the same year the British quietly let go of the Sudan, which had become untenable when they lost control over Egypt.

It is not clear when the old empires realized that the Age of Empire was definitely at an end. Certainly, in retrospect, the attempt by Britain and France to reassert themselves as global imperial powers in the Suez adventure of 1956 seems more doomed than it evidently did to the governments of London and Paris, who planned a military operation to overthrow the revolutionary Egyptian government of Colonel Nasser, in conjunction with Israel. The episode was a catastrophic failure (except from the point of view of Israel), all the more ridiculous for the combination of indecision, hesitation and unconvincing disingenuousness by the British prime minister, Anthony Eden. The operation, barely launched, was called off under the pressure of the USA, pushed Egypt towards the USSR, and ended for good what has been called 'Britain's Moment in the Middle East', the epoch of unquestioned British hegemony in that region since 1918.

At all events, by the late 1950s it had become clear to the surviving old empires that formal colonialism had to be liquidated. Only Portugal continued to resist its dissolution since its backward, politically isolated and marginalized metropolitan economy could not afford neo-colonialism. It needed to exploit its African resources and, since its economy was uncompetitive, could do so only through direct control. South Africa and Southern Rhodesia, the African states with substantial white-settler populations (except for Kenya) also refused to go along with policies which would inevitably produce African-dominated regimes, and Southern Rhodesia even declared white-settler independence (1965) from Britain to avoid this fate. However, Paris, London and Brussels (the Belgian Congo) decided that the voluntary grant of formal independence with economic and cultural dependence was preferable to lengthy struggles likely to end in independence under Left-wing regimes. Only in Kenya was there a substantial popular insurrection and guerrilla war, though one largely confined to sections of one local people, the Kikuyu (the so-called Mau Mau movement, 1952–56). Elsewhere the policy of prophylactic decolonization was pursued successfully, except in the Belgian Congo, where it almost immediately collapsed into anarchy, civil war and international power politics. In British Africa the Gold Coast (now Ghana), which already had a mass party under a talented African politician and pan-African intellectual, Kwame Nkrumah, was granted independence in 1957. In French Africa Guinea was pitchforked into an early and impoverished independence in 1958 when its leader, Sekou Touré, refused to join a 'French Community' offered by de Gaulle, which combined autonomy with strict dependence on the French economy, and was therefore – first among black African leaders – forced to look for help to Moscow. Almost all the remaining British, French and Belgian colonies in Africa were turned loose in 1960–62, the rest shortly after. Only Portugal and the independent settler states resisted the trend.

The larger British Caribbean colonies were quietly decolonized in the 1960s, the smaller islands at intervals between then and 1981, the Indian and Pacific islands in the late 1960s and 1970s. In fact, by 1970 no territories of any significant size remained under direct administration by the former colonialist powers or their settler regimes, except in Central and Southern Africa – and, of course, in embattled Vietnam. The imperial era was at an end. Less than three quarters of a century earlier, it had seemed indestructible. Even thirty years earlier, it covered most of the peoples of the globe. An irrecoverable part of the past, it became part of the sentimentalised literary and cinematic memories of the former imperial states, as a new generation of indigenous writers from formerly colonial countries began to produce a literature which began with the age of independence.

PART TWO
THE GOLDEN AGE

CHAPTER EIGHT
Cold War

Although Soviet Russia intends to spread her influence by all possible means, world revolution is no longer part of her programme and there is nothing in the internal conditions within the Union which might encourage a return to the old revolutionary traditions. Any comparison between the German menace before the war and a Soviet menace today, must allow for ... fundamental differences ... There is, therefore, infinitely less danger of a sudden catastrophe with the Russians than with the Germans.

> – Frank Roberts, British Embassy, Moscow, to Foreign Office, London, 1946 (Jensen, 1991, p.56)

The war economy provides comfortable niches for tens of thousands of bureaucrats in and out of military uniform who go to the office every day to build nuclear weapons or to plan nuclear war; millions of workers whose jobs depend on the system of nuclear terrorism; scientists and engineers hired to look for that final 'technological breakthrough' that can provide total security; contractors unwilling to give up easy profits; warrior intellectuals who sell threats and bless wars.

> – Richard Barnet (1981, p. 97)

I

The forty-five years from the dropping of the atom bombs to the end of the Soviet Union do not form a single homogeneous period in world history. As we shall see in the following chapters, they fall into two halves, the decades on either side of the watershed of the early 1970s (see chapters 9 and 14). Nevertheless, the history of the entire period was welded into a single pattern by the peculiar international situation which dominated it until the fall of the USSR: the constant confrontation of the two superpowers which emerged from the Second World War the so-called 'Cold War'.

The Second World War had barely ended when humanity plunged into what can reasonably be regarded as a Third World War, though a very peculiar one. For, as the great philosopher Thomas Hobbes observed, 'War consisteth not in battle only, or the act of fighting: but in a tract of time, wherein the will to contend by battle is sufficiently known' (Hobbes, chapter 13). The Cold War between the two camps of the USA and the USSR, which utterly dominated the international scene in the second half of the Short Twentieth Century, was unquestionably such a tract of time. Entire generations grew up under the shadow of global nuclear battles which, it was widely believed, could break out at any moment, and devastate humanity. Indeed, even those who did not believe that either side intended to attack the other found it hard not to be pessimistic, since Murphy's Law is one of the most powerful generalizations about human affairs ('If it can go wrong, sooner or later it will'). As time went on, more and more things were there which could go wrong, both politically and technologically, in a permanent nuclear confrontation based on the assumption that only the fear of 'mutually assured destruction' (correctly concentrated into the acronym MAD) would prevent one side or the other from giving the ever-ready signal for the planned suicide of civilization. It did not happen, but for some forty years it looked a daily possibility.

The peculiarity of the Cold War was that, speaking objectively, no imminent danger of world war existed. More than this: in spite of the apocalyptic rhetoric on both sides, but especially on the American side, the governments of both the superpowers accepted the global distribution of force at the end of the Second World War, which amounted to a highly uneven but essentially unchallenged balance of power. The USSR controlled, or exercised predominant influence in one part of the globe – the zone occupied by the Red Army and/or other communist armed forces at the end of the war, and did not attempt to extend its range of influence further by military force. The USA exercised control and predominance over the rest of the capitalist world as well as the western hemisphere and the oceans, taking over what remained of the old imperial hegemony of the former colonial powers. In return, it did not intervene in the zone of accepted Soviet hegemony.

In Europe the demarcation lines had been drawn in 1943–45, both by agreement at various summit meetings between Roosevelt, Churchill and Stalin, and by virtue of the fact that only the Red Army could actually defeat Germany. There were a few uncertainties, notably about Germany and Austria, which were solved by the partition of Germany along the lines of the Eastern and Western occupation forces, and the withdrawal of all ex-belligerents from Austria. The latter became a sort of second Switzerland – a small country committed to neutrality, envied for its persistent prosperity and therefore described (correctly) as 'boring'. The USSR accepted West Berlin as a Western enclave inside its German territory with reluctance, but was not prepared to fight the issue.

The situation outside Europe was less clear-cut, except for Japan, where the USA from the start established a completely unilateral occupation that excluded not only the USSR but any other co-belligerent. The problem was that the end of the old colonial empires was predictable, and indeed in 1945 plainly imminent on the Asian continent, but the future orientation of the new post colonial states was by no means clear. As we shall see (chapters 12 and 15) this was the zone in which the two superpowers continued, throughout the Cold War, to compete for support and influence, and hence the major zone of friction between them, and indeed the one where armed conflict was most likely, and actually broke out. Unlike Europe, not even the limits of the area under future communist control could be predicted, let alone agreed by negotiation in advance, however provisionally and ambiguously. Thus the USSR did not much want a communist take over in China,* but it took place nevertheless.

However, even in what soon came to be called the 'Third World', the conditions for international stability began to emerge within a few years, as it became clear that most of the new post-colonial states, however unsympathetic to the USA and its camp, were non-communist, indeed mostly anti-communist in their domestic politics, and 'non-aligned' (i.e. outside the Soviet military bloc) in international affairs. In short, the 'communist camp' showed no sign of significant expansion between the

---

* There was a spectacular lack of reference – in any context – to China in Zhdanov's report on the world situation which opened the founding conference of the Communist Information Bureau (Cominform) in September 1947, though Indonesia and Vietnam were classified as 'joining the anti-imperialist camp' and India, Egypt and Syria as 'sympathising' with it (Spriano, 1983, 286). As late as April 1949, when Chiang-Kai-shek abandoned his capital in Nanking, the Soviet ambassador – *alone* among the diplomatic corps – joined him in his retreat to Canton. Six months later Mao proclaimed the People's Republic (Walker, 1993, p. 63).

Chinese revolution and the 1970s, by which time Communist China was no longer in it (see chapter 16).

In effect, the world situation became reasonably stable soon after the war and remained so until the middle 1970s, when the international system and its component units entered another period of lengthy political and economic crisis. Until then both the superpowers accepted the uneven division of the world, made every effort to settle demarcation disputes without an open clash between their armed forces that might lead to a war between them, and, contrary to ideology and Cold War rhetoric, worked on the assumption that long-term peaceful coexistence between them was possible. Indeed, when it came to the point, both trusted one another's moderation, even at times when they were officially on the brink of, or even engaged in, war. Thus during the Korean War of 1950–53, in which the Americans were officially involved, but not the Russians, Washington knew perfectly well that up to 150 Chinese planes were actually Soviet planes flown by Soviet pilots (Walker, 1993, pp. 75–77). The information was kept dark, because it was correctly assumed that the last thing Moscow wanted was war. During the Cuban missile crisis of 1962, as we now know (Ball, 1992; Ball 1993), the main concern on both sides was how to prevent warlike gestures from being misinterpreted as actual moves to war.

Until the 1970s this tacit agreement to treat the Cold War as a Cold Peace held good. The USSR knew (or rather learned) as early as 1953 that the US calls to 'roll back' communism were mere radio histrionics, when Soviet tanks were quietly allowed to re-establish communist control against a serious working-class revolt in East Germany. From then on, as the Hungarian revolution of 1956 confirmed, the West would keep out of the region of Soviet domination. The Cold War that actually tried to live up to its own rhetoric of a struggle for supremacy or annihilation was not the one in which basic decisions were taken by governments, but the shadowy contest between their various acknowledged and unacknowledged secret services, which in the West produced that most characteristic spin-off of the international tension, the fiction of espionage and covert killing. In this genre the British, through Ian Fleming's James Bond and John Le Carré's sour-sweet heroes – both had served their time in the British secret services – maintained a steady superiority, thus compensating for their country's decline in the world of real power. However, except in some of the weaker countries of the Third World, the operations of KGB, CIA and their like were trivial in terms of real power politics, though often dramatic.

Was there, under these circumstances, a real danger of world war at any time during this long period of tension – except, of course, by the sort of accident which inevitably threatens those who skate long enough on sufficiently thin ice? It is hard to say. Probably the most explosive period was that between the formal enunciation of the 'Truman Doctrine' in March 1947 ('I believe that it must be the policy of the United States to support free peoples who are resisting attempted subjugation by armed minorities or by outside pressures') and April 1951, when the same US president dismissed General Douglas MacArthur, commander of the US forces in the Korean War (1950–53), who pushed military ambition too far. This was the period when the American fear of social disintegration or revolution within the non-Soviet parts of Eurasia were not wholly fantastic – after all, in 1949 the communists took over China. Conversely, the USSR found itself faced with a US which enjoyed the monopoly of nuclear arms and multiplied militant and threatening declarations of anti-communism, while the first cracks appeared in the solidity of the Soviet bloc as Tito's Yugoslavia broke away (1948). Moreover, from 1949 on China was under a government which did not merely plunge readily into a major war in Korea, but – unlike all other governments – was willing to envisage actually fighting and surviving a nuclear holocaust.* Anything might happen.

Once the USSR acquired nuclear weapons – four years after Hiroshima in the case of the atom bomb (1949), nine months after the USA in the case of the hydrogen bomb (1953) – both superpowers plainly abandoned war as an instrument of policy against one another, since it was the equivalent of a suicide pact. Whether they seriously envisaged nuclear action against third parties – the USA in Korea in 1951, and to save the French in Vietnam in 1954; the USSR against China in 1969 – is not quite clear, but in any case the weapons were not used. However, both used the nuclear threat, almost certainly without intending to carry it out, on some occasions: the USA to speed peace negotiations in Korea and Vietnam (1953, 1954), the USSR to force Britain and France to withdraw from Suez in 1956. Unfortunately, the very certainty that neither superpower would actually *want* to press the nuclear button tempted both sides into using nuclear gesticulation for purposes of negotiation or (in the USA) for domestic politics, confident that the

* Mao is reported to have told the Italian leader Togliatti: 'Who told you that Italy must survive? Three hundred million Chinese will be left, and that will be enough for the human race to continue.' 'Mao's blithe readiness to accept the inevitability of a nuclear war and its possible utility as a way to bring about the final defeat of capitalism, stunned his comrades from other countries' in 1957 (Walker, 1993, p. 126).

other did not want war either. This confidence proved justified, but at the cost of racking the nerves of generations. The Cuban missile crisis of 1962, an entirely unnecessary exercise of this kind, almost plunged the world into an unnecessary war for a few days, and actually frightened even the top decision-makers into rationality for a while.*

II

How then are we to explain the forty years of an armed and mobilized confrontation, based on the always implausible, and in this case plainly baseless, assumption that the globe was so unstable that a world war might break out at any moment, and was held at bay only by unceasing mutual deterrence? In the first instance, the Cold War was based on a Western belief, absurd in retrospect but natural enough in the aftermath of the Second World War, that the Age of Catastrophe was by no means at an end; that the future of world capitalism and liberal society was far from assured. Most observers expected a serious post-war economic crisis, even in the USA, on the analogy of what had happened after the First World War. A future Nobel prize economist in 1943 spoke of the possibility, in the USA, of 'the greatest period of unemployment and industrial dislocation which any economy has ever faced' (Samuelson, 1943, p. 51). Indeed, the post-war plans of the US government were far more concretely concerned with preventing another Great Slump than with preventing another war, a matter to which Washington gave only divided and provisional attention before victory (Kolko, 1969, pp. 244–46).

If Washington expected 'the great post-war troubles' which undermined 'stability – social, political and economic – in the world' (Dean Acheson, cited in Kolko, 1969, p. 485), it was because at the end of the war the belligerent countries, with the exception of the USA, were a field of ruins inhabited by what seemed to Americans hungry, desperate, and probably radicalized peoples, only too ready to listen to the appeal of social revolution and economic policies incompatible with the inter-

---

* The Soviet leader N.S. Khrushchev decided to place Soviet missiles in Cuba to offset the American missiles already in place across the Soviet border in Turkey. (Burlatsky, 1992). The USA forced him to withdraw them by the threat of war, but also withdrew its missiles from Turkey. The Soviet missiles, as President Kennedy was told at the time, made no difference to the strategic balance, though a considerable difference to presidential public relations (Ball, 1992, p. 18; Walker, 1988). The US missiles withdrawn were described as 'obsolescent'.

national system of free enterprise, free trade and investment by which the USA and the world were to be saved. Moreover, the pre-war international system had collapsed, leaving the USA facing an enormously strengthened Communist USSR across large stretches of Europe and even vaster stretches of the non-European world, whose political future seemed quite uncertain – except that in this explosive and unstable world anything that happened was more likely than not to weaken both capitalism and the USA, and to strengthen the power which had come into existence by and for revolution.

The immediate post-war situation in many of the liberated and occupied countries seemed to undermine the situation of moderate politicians, with little to support them except the Western allies, and beset within and outside their governments by the communists, who emerged from the war everywhere far stronger than at any time in the past, and sometimes as the largest parties and electoral forces of their countries. The (socialist) premier of France came to Washington to warn that, without economic support, he was likely to fall to the communists. The terrible harvest of 1946, followed by the appalling winter of 1946–47, made both European politicians and American presidential advisers even more nervous.

Under the circumstances it is not surprising that the wartime alliance between the major capitalist and the socialist power now at the head of its own zone of influence should have broken down, as even less heterogeneous coalitions so often do at the end of wars. However, this is clearly not enough to explain why US policy – Washington's allies and clients, with the possible exception of Britain, were considerably less overheated – should have been based, at least in its public statements, on a nightmare scenario of the Muscovite super-power poised for the immediate conquest of the globe, and directing a godless 'communist world conspiracy' ever ready to overthrow the realms of freedom. It is even more inadequate to explain the campaign rhetoric of a J.F. Kennedy in 1960, at a time when what the British premier Harold Macmillan called 'our modern free society – the new form of capitalism' (Horne, 1989, vol. II, p. 283) could not conceivably have been said to be in any immediate trouble.*

Why could the outlook of 'the State Department professionals' in the aftermath of the war be described as 'apocalyptic'? (Hughes, 1969, p. 28).

* 'The enemy is the communist system itself – implacable, insatiable, unceasing in its drive for world domination ... This is not a struggle for supremacy of arms alone. It is also a struggle for supremacy between two conflicting ideologies: freedom under God versus ruthless, godless tyranny' (Walker, 1993, p. 132).

Why did even the calm British diplomat who rejected any comparison of the USSR with Nazi Germany then report from Moscow that the world was 'now faced with the danger of a modern equivalent of the religious wars of the sixteenth century, in which Soviet communism will struggle with Western social democracy and the American version of capitalism for domination of the world'? (Jensen, 1991, pp. 41, 53–54; Roberts, 1991.) For it is now evident, and was reasonably probable even in 1945–47 that the USSR was neither expansionist – still less aggressive – nor counting on any further extension of the communist advance beyond what is assumed had been agreed at the summits of 1943–45. Indeed, where Moscow controlled its client regimes and communist movements, these were specifically committed to *not* building states on the model of the USSR, but mixed economies under multi-party parliamentary democracies, which were specifically distinguished from 'the dictatorship of the proletariat', and 'still more' of a single party. These were described in inner-party documents as 'neither useful nor necessary' (Spriano, 1983, p. 265). (The only communist regimes that refused to follow this line were those whose revolutions, actively discouraged by Stalin, escaped from Moscow's control, e.g. Yugoslavia.) Moreover, though this has not been much noticed, the Soviet Union demobilized its troops – its major military asset – almost as fast as the USA, reducing the Red Army from a 1945 peak strength of almost twelve millions to three millions by late 1948 (*New York Times*, 24/10/1946; 24/10/1948).

On any rational assessment, the USSR presented no immediate danger to anyone outside the reach of the Red Army's occupation forces. It emerged from war in ruins, drained and exhausted, its peacetime economy in shreds, its government distrustful of a population much of which, outside Great Russia, had shown a distinct and understandable lack of commitment to the regime. On its western fringe, it continued to have trouble with Ukrainian and other nationalist guerrillas for some years. It was ruled by a dictator who had demonstrated that he was as risk-averse outside the territory he controlled directly as he was ruthless within it: J.V. Stalin (see chapter 13). It needed all the economic aid it could get, and, therefore, had no short-term interest in antagonising the only power that could give it, the USA. No doubt Stalin, as a communist, believed that capitalism would inevitably be replaced by communism, and to this extent any coexistence of the two systems would not be permanent. However, Soviet planners did not see capitalism as such in crisis at the end of the Second World War. They had no doubt that it would continue for a long time under the hegemony of the USA, whose enormously increased wealth and power was only too obvious (Loth, 1988, pp. 36–

37). That, in fact, is what the USSR suspected and was afraid of.* Its basic posture after the war was not aggressive but defensive.

However, a policy of confrontation on both sides arose out of their situation. The USSR, conscious of the precariousness and insecurity of its position, faced the world power of the USA, conscious of the precariousness and insecurity of central and western Europe, and the uncertain future of much of Asia. Confrontation would probably have developed even without ideology. George Kennan, the American diplomat who in early 1946 formulated the 'containment' policy which Washington adopted with enthusiasm, did not believe that Russia was crusading for communism, and – as his subsequent career proved – was far from an ideological crusader (except possibly against democratic politics, of which he had a low opinion). He was merely an able Russian expert of the old school of diplomatic power-politics – there were many such in European foreign offices – who saw Russia, Tsarist or Bolshevik, as a backward and barbarous society ruled by men moved by a 'traditional and instinctive Russian sense of insecurity', always cutting itself off from the outside world, always under autocrats, always seeking 'security' only in patient and deadly struggle for total destruction of rival power, never in compacts and compromises with it; always, consequently, responding only to 'the logic of force', never to reason. Communism, of course, in his opinion made the old Russia more dangerous by reinforcing the most brutal of great powers with the most ruthless of utopian, i.e. world-conquering, ideologies. But the implication of the thesis was that the only 'rival power' to Russia's, namely the USA, would have had to 'contain' its pressure by uncompromising resistance even if it had not been communist.

Conversely, from Moscow's point of view, the only rational strategy for defending and exploiting a vast but fragile new position of international power, was exactly the same: no compromise. Nobody knew better than Stalin how weak a hand he had to play. There could be no negotiation on the positions offered by Roosevelt and Churchill at the time when the Soviet effort was essential to defeat Hitler, and was still believed to be essential to defeat Japan. The USSR might be ready to retreat from any exposed position beyond that fortified by what it considered to have been agreed at the summit meetings of 1943–45, and especially Yalta – for instance on the borders of Iran and Turkey in

---

* They would have been even more suspicious had they known that the US joint chiefs of staff produced a plan to atom-bomb the twenty chief Soviet cities within ten weeks of the end of the war (Walker, 1993, pp. 26–27).

1945–46 – but any attempt to re-open Yalta could only be met by a flat refusal. Indeed, the 'No' of Stalin's foreign minister Molotov at all international meetings after Yalta became notorious. The Americans had the power; though only just. Until December 1947 there were no planes to transport the twelve available atom bombs or military capable of assembling them (Moisi, 1981, pp. 78–79). The USSR had not. Washington would give nothing away except against concessions, but these were precisely what Moscow could not afford to make, even in return for desperately needed economic aid, which in any case the Americans did not want to give them, claiming to have 'mislaid' the Soviet request for a post-war loan, made before Yalta.

In short, while the USA was worried about the danger of a possible Soviet world supremacy some time in the future, Moscow was worried about the actual hegemony of the USA now, over all parts of the globe not occupied by the Red Army. It would not take much to turn an exhausted and impoverished USSR into yet another client region of the US economy, stronger at the time than all the rest of the world put together. Intransigence was the logical tactic. Let them call Moscow's bluff.

Yet the politics of mutual intransigence, even of permanent power-rivalry, do not imply the daily danger of war. Nineteenth-century British foreign secretaries, who took it for granted that the expansionist urges of Tsarist Russia must be continuously 'contained' in the Kennanite manner, knew perfectly well that moments of open confrontation were rare, and war crises even rarer. Still less does mutual intransigence imply the politics of life-or-death struggle or religious war. However, two elements in the situation helped to move confrontation from the realm of reason to that of emotion. Like the USSR, the USA was a power representing an ideology, which most Americans sincerely believed to be the model for the world. Unlike the USSR, the USA was a democracy. Unfortunately it must be said that the second of these was probably the more dangerous.

For the Soviet government, though it also demonized the global antagonist, did not have to bother about winning votes in Congress, or in presidential and congressional elections. The US government did. For both purposes an apocalyptic anti-communism was useful, and therefore tempting, even for politicians who were not sincerely convinced of their own rhetoric, or, like President Truman's Secretary of State for the Navy, James Forrestal (1882–1949) clinically mad enough to commit suicide because he saw the Russians coming from his window in the hospital. An external enemy who threatened the USA was convenient for

American governments which had concluded, correctly, that the USA was now a world power – in fact, the greatest world power by far – and which still saw 'isolationism' or a defensive protectionism as its major domestic obstacle. If America itself was not safe, then there could be no withdrawal from the responsibilities – and rewards – of world leadership, as after the First World War. More concretely, public hysteria made it easier for presidents to raise the vast sums required for American policy from a citizenry notorious for its disinclination to pay taxes. And anti-communism was genuinely and viscerally popular in a country built on individualism and private enterprise where the nation itself was defined in exclusively ideological terms ('Americanism') which could be virtually defined as the polar opposite of communism. (Nor should we forget the votes of immigrants from Sovietised Eastern Europe.) It was not the American government which initiated the squalid and irrational frenzy of the anti-Red witch-hunt, but otherwise insignificant demagogues – some of them, like the notorious Senator Joseph McCarthy, not even particularly anti-communist – who discovered the political potential of wholesale denunciation of the enemy within.* The bureaucratic potential had long since been discovered by J. Edgar Hoover (1895–1972), the virtually irremoveable chief of the Federal Bureau of Investigations (FBI). What one of the main architects of the Cold War called 'the attack of the Primitives' (Acheson, 1970, p. 462) both facilitated and constrained Washington policy by pushing it to extremes, especially in the years following the victory of the communists in China, for which Moscow was naturally blamed.

At the same time the schizoid demand of the vote-sensitive politicians for a policy that should both roll back the tide of 'communist aggression', save money and interfere as little as possible with Americans' comfort, committed Washington, and with it the rest of the alliance, not only to an essentially nuclear strategy of bombs rather than men, but to the ominous strategy of 'massive retaliation', announced in 1954. The potential aggressor was to be threatened with nuclear weapons even in the case of a limited conventional attack. In short, the USA found itself committed to an aggressive stance, with minimal tactical flexibility.

Both sides thus found themselves committed to an insane arms race to mutual destruction, and to the sort of nuclear generals and nuclear intellectuals whose profession required them not to notice this insanity.

* The only politician of real substance who emerged from the underworld of the witch-hunters was Richard Nixon, the most unpleasant individual among post-war American presidents (1968–74).

Both also found themselves committed to what the retiring President Eisenhower, a moderate military man of the old school who found himself presiding over this descent into lunacy, without being quite infected by it, called 'the military-industrial complex', i.e. the increasingly vast agglomeration of men and resources which lived by the preparation of war. It was a larger vested interest than ever before in times of stable peace between the powers. As might be expected, both military-industrial complexes were encouraged by their governments to use their excess capacity to attract and arm allies and clients, and, not least, to win profitable export markets, while keeping their most up-to-date armaments to themselves; and, of course, their nuclear weapons. For in practice the superpowers retained their nuclear monopoly. The British acquired bombs of their own in 1952, ironically with the object of lessening their dependence on the USA; the French (whose nuclear arsenal was actually independent of the USA) and the Chinese in the 1960s. While the Cold War lasted, none of these counted. In the course of the 1970s and 1980s some other countries acquired the capacity to make nuclear weapons, notably Israel, South Africa, and probably India, but such nuclear proliferation did not become a serious international problem until after the end of the bi-polar superpower world order in 1989.

So who was responsible for the Cold War? Since the debate on this question was for long an ideological tennis-match between those who put the blame exclusively on the USSR and the (mainly, it must be said, American) dissidents who said it was primarily the fault of the USA, it is tempting to join the historical mediators who put it down to mutual fear escalating from confrontation until the two 'armed camps began to mobilize under their two opposing banners' (Walker, 1993, p. 55). This is plainly true, but it is not the whole truth. It explains what has been called the 'congealing' of the fronts in 1947–49; the step-by-step partition of Germany, from 1947 to the building of the Berlin Wall in 1961; the failure of the anti-communists on the Western side to avoid complete involvement in the US-dominated military alliance (except for General de Gaulle in France); and the failure of those on the Eastern side of the divide to escape complete subordination to Moscow (except for Marshall Tito in Yugoslavia). But it does not explain the apocalyptic *tone* of the Cold War. That came from America. All Western European governments, with or without large communist parties, were without exception whole-heartedly anti-communist, and determined to protect themselves against possible Soviet military attack. None would have hesitated if asked to choose between the USA and the USSR, even those committed by history, policy or negotiation to neutrality. Yet the 'communist world conspiracy' was not a serious part of the domestic politics of any of those who had some claim to being political democracies, at least after the immediate post-war years. Among democratic countries it was *only* in the USA that presidents were elected (like John F. Kennedy in 1960) against communism, which in terms of domestic politics was as insignificant in that country as Buddhism in Ireland. If anyone put the crusading element into the *realpolitik* of international power confrontation, and kept it there, it was Washington. In fact, as the rhetoric of J. F. Kennedy's electioneering demonstrates with the clarity of good oratory, the issue was not the academic threat of communist world domination, but the maintenance of a real US supremacy.* It must, however, be added that the governments of the NATO alliance, though far from happy about American policy, were ready to accept American supremacy as the price of protection against the military power of an abhorrent political system, while that system continued in existence. They were as unprepared as Washington to trust the USSR. In short, 'containment' was everyone's policy; the destruction of communism was not.

III

Though the most obvious face of the Cold War was military confrontation and an ever-more frenetic nuclear arms race in the West, this was not its major impact. The nuclear arms were not used. Nuclear powers engaged in three major wars (but not against each other). Shaken by the communist victory in China, the US and its allies (disguised as the United Nations) intervened in Korea in 1950 to prevent the communist regime in the North of that divided country from spreading to the South. The result was a draw. They did so again with the same object in Vietnam, and lost. The USSR withdrew in 1988 after eight years of providing military support for a friendly government in Afghanistan against American-backed and Pakistan-supplied guerrillas. In short, the expensive high-technology hardware of superpower competition proved indecisive. The constant threat of war produced international peace movements, essentially directed against nuclear arms, which from time to time became mass movements in parts of Europe and were regarded by the Cold War crusaders as secret weapons of the communists. The movements for

* 'We will mould our strength and become first again. Not first if. Not first but. But first period. I want the world to wonder not what Mr Khrushchev is doing. I want them to wonder what the United States is doing' (Beschloss, 1991, p. 28).

nuclear disarmament were not decisive either, although a specific anti-war movement, that of young Americans against being conscripted for the Vietnam War (1965–75), proved more effective. At the end of the Cold War these movements left behind a memory of good causes and some curious peripheral relics, such as the adoption of the anti-nuclear logo by the post-1968 counter-cultures and an ingrained prejudice among environmentalists against any kind of nuclear energy.

Much more obvious were the political consequences of the Cold War. Almost immediately it polarized the world controlled by the superpowers into two sharply divided 'camps'. The governments of national anti-fascist unity which had led all Europe out of the war (except, significantly, the three main belligerent states, USSR, USA and Britain), split into homogeneous pro-communist and anti-communist regimes in 1947–48. In the West the Communists disappeared from governments to become permanent political outcasts. The USA planned military intervention if they won the 1948 elections in Italy. The USSR followed suit by eliminating the non-communists from their multi-party 'people's democracies' which were henceforth re-classified as 'dictatorships of the proletariat', i.e. of the Communist Parties. A curiously restricted and Eurocentric Communist International (the 'Cominform' or Communist Information Bureau) was set up to confront the USA, but quietly dissolved in 1956 when international temperatures had cooled. Direct Soviet control was firmly clamped on all of Eastern Europe except, oddly enough, Finland, which was at the Soviets' mercy and dropped its strong Communist Party from its government in 1948. Why Stalin refrained from installing a satellite government there remains obscure. Perhaps the high probability that the Finns would once again take up arms (as they had done in 1939–40 and 1941–44) dissuaded him, for he certainly did not want to run the risk of a war that might get out of hand. He tried but failed to impose Soviet control on Tito's Yugoslavia, which consequently broke with Moscow in 1948, without joining the other side.

The politics of the Communist bloc were henceforth predictably monolithic, although the brittleness of the monolith became increasingly obvious after 1956 (see chapter 16). The politics of the US-aligned states of Europe were less monochromatic since virtually all local parties except the communists were united in their dislike of the Soviets. In terms of foreign policy it did not matter who was in office. However, the USA simplified matters in two ex-enemy countries, Japan and Italy, by creating what amounted to a permanent single-party system. In Tokyo it encouraged the foundation of the Liberal-Democratic Party (1955), and in Italy, by insisting on the total exclusion of the natural opposition party from power, because it happened to be communist, it handed the country over to the Christian Democrats, supplemented as occasion required by a selection of dwarf parties – Liberals, Republicans etc. From the early 1960s the only other party of substance, the socialists, joined the government coalition, having disengaged themselves from a long alliance with the communists after 1956. The consequence in both these countries was both to stabilize the communists (in Japan, the socialists) as the major party of opposition, and to install a government regime of institutional corruption on a scale so sensational that, when finally revealed in 1992–93, it shocked even the Italians and Japanese. Both government and opposition, thus frozen into immobility, collapsed with the super-power balance that had kept it in being.

Although the USA soon reversed the reforming anti-monopolist policies which its Rooseveltian advisers had initially imposed on occupied Germany and Japan, fortunately for the peace of mind of America's allies, the war had eliminated National Socialism, fascism, overt Japanese nationalism and much of the right-wing and nationalist sector of the political spectrum from the acceptable public scene. It was therefore impossible as yet to mobilize these unquestionably effective anti-communist elements for the struggle of the 'free world' against 'totalitarianism', as the restored German big business corporations and the Japanese *zaibatsu* could be.* The political base of Western Cold War governments therefore ranged from the pre-war social-democratic Left to the pre-war moderate non-nationalist Right. Here the parties linked to the Catholic Church proved particularly useful, since the anti-communist and conservative credentials of the Church were second to none, but its 'Christian-Democratic' parties (see chapter 4) had both a solid anti-fascist record and a (non-socialist) social programme. These parties thus played a central role in Western politics after 1945, temporarily in France, more permanently in Germany, Italy, Belgium and Austria (see also p. 283).

However, the effect of the Cold War on the international politics of Europe was more striking than on the Continent's domestic politics. It created the 'European Community' with all its problems; an entirely unprecedented form of political organization, namely a permanent (or at least a long-lasting) arrangement to integrate the economies, and to some extent the legal systems, of a number of independent nation-states. Initially (1957) formed by six states (France, the German Federal Republic, Italy, the Netherlands, Belgium and Luxemburg), by the end of the

---

* However, former fascists were systematically used from the start by intelligence services and in other functions not in the public view.

Short Twentieth Century, when the system began to totter, like all other products of the Cold War, it had been joined by another six (Britain, Ireland, Spain, Portugal, Denmark, Greece), and was in theory committed to even closer political, as well as economic integration. This was to lead to permanent federal or confederal political union for 'Europe'.

The 'Community' was, like so many other things in post-1945 Europe, created both by and against the USA. It illustrates both the power and ambiguity of that country and its limits; but it also illustrates the strength of the fears that held the anti-Soviet alliance together. These were not only fears of the USSR. So far as France was concerned, Germany remained the chief danger, and the fear of a revived giant power in Central Europe was shared, to a lesser extent, by the other ex-belligerent or occupied states of Europe, all of whom now found themselves locked into the NATO alliance with both the USA and an economically revived and re-armed Germany, though fortunately a truncated one. There were also, of course, fears of the USA, an indispensable ally against the USSR, but a suspect because unreliable one, not to mention one which, not surprisingly, was apt to put the interests of the American world supremacy above all else – including those of America's allies. One must not forget that in all the calculations about the post-war world, and in all post-war decisions, 'the premise of all policy makers was American economic pre-eminence' (Maier, 1987, p. 125).

Fortunately for America's allies, the west European situation in 1946–47 seemed so tense that Washington felt that the development of a strong European, and a little later, a strong Japanese economy was the most urgent priority, and the Marshall Plan, a massive design for European recovery, was launched accordingly, in June 1947. Unlike earlier aid, which was clearly part of aggressive economic diplomacy, it mostly took the form of grants rather than loans. Again, fortunately for them, the original American plan for a post-war world economy of free trade, free convertibility and free markets, dominated by the USA proved quite unrealistic, if only because the desperate payments difficulties of Europe and Japan, thirsting for ever-scarcer dollars, meant that there was no immediate prospect for liberalizing trade and payments. Nor was the US in a position to impose on the European states its ideal of a single European plan, preferably leading to a single Europe modelled on the USA in its political structure as well as in its flourishing free enterprise economy. Neither the British, who still saw themselves as a world power, nor the French, who dreamed of a strong France and a weak and partitioned Germany, liked it. However, for the Americans an effectively restored Europe, part of the anti-Soviet military alliance which was the logical complement of the Marshall Plan – the North Atlantic Treaty Organization (NATO) of 1949 – had realistically to rest on a German economic strength reinforced by German re-armanent. The best the French could do was to so entangle West German and French affairs that conflict between the two old adversaries would be impossible. The French therefore proposed their own version of European union, the 'European Coal and Steel Community' (1951), which developed into the 'European Economic Community or Common Market (1957), later simply the 'European Community' and, from 1993, 'European Union'. Its headquarters were in Brussels, but Franco–German unity was its core. The European Community was established as an *alternative* to the US plan for European integration. Once again, the end of the Cold War was to undermine the foundation on which the European Community and the Franco–German partnership had been built; not least by unbalancing both through the German reunification of 1990 and the unpredicted economic troubles it brought.

However, even though the USA was unable to impose its politico-economic plans on the Europeans in detail, it was strong enough to dominate their international behaviour. The policy of the alliance against the USSR was the USA's, and so were its military plans. Germany was re-armed, hankerings after European neutralism were firmly suppressed, and the only attempt by Western powers to engage in a world policy independent of the USA's, namely the Anglo-French Suez war against Egypt of 1956, was aborted under American pressure. The most that an allied or client state could allow itself to do was to refuse complete integration into the military alliance without actually leaving it (like General de Gaulle).

And yet, as the Cold War era stretched out, there was a growing gap between the overwhelming military, and therefore political, domination of the alliance by Washington, and the USA's gradually weakening economic predominance. The economic weight of the world economy was now shifting from the USA to the European and Japanese economies, which the USA felt it had rescued and rebuilt (see chapter 9). The dollars, so scarce in 1947, had flowed out of the USA in a growing torrent, accelerated – especially in the 1960s – by the American penchant for deficit financing of the enormous costs of their global military activities, notably the Vietnam War (after 1965), as well as the most ambitious social welfare programme in US history. The dollar, keystone of the post-war world economy planned and guaranteed by the USA, grew weaker. In theory backed by the bullion of Fort Knox, which had held almost three quarters of the world's gold reserves, in practice it consisted increasingly of floods of paper or book-entries – but since the stability of the dollar was guaranteed by its link to a given quantity of gold, cautious Europeans, headed by the ultra-cautious and bullion-minded French, preferred to exchange potentially devalued paper for solid ingots. Gold therefore poured out of Fort Knox, its price rising as the demand for it rose. For most of the sixties the stability of the dollar, and with it of the international payment system, was no longer based on the USA's own reserves but on the willingness of European central banks – under US pressure – not to cash in their dollars for gold, and to join in a 'Gold Pool' to stabilize the price of gold in the market. It did not last. In 1968 the 'Gold Pool', now drained, was dissolved. *De facto*, the convertibility of the dollar ended. It was formally abandoned in August 1971, and with it the stability of the international payments system, and its control by the USA or any other single national economy came to an end.

When the Cold War ended, so little was left of the US economic hegemony that even the military hegemony could no longer be financed out of the country's own resources. The 1991 Gulf War against Iraq, an essentially US military operation, was paid for, willingly or reluctantly, by other countries which supported Washington. This was one of the rare wars out of which a major power actually made a profit. Fortunately for everyone concerned, except the unhappy inhabitants of Iraq, it was over within a matter of days.

IV

Some time in the early 1960s the Cold War appeared to move a few tentative steps in the direction of sanity. The dangerous years from 1947 to the dramatic events of the Korean War (1950–53) had passed without a world explosion. So had the seismic upheavals which shook the Soviet bloc after Stalin's death (1953), especially in the middle fifties. So far from fighting off social crisis, the countries of western Europe began to notice that they were actually living through an era of unexpected and general prosperity, which will be discussed more fully in the next chapter. In the traditional jargon of old-style diplomats, slackening tension was 'détente'. The word now became familiar.

It had first surfaced in the last years of the 1950s, when N.S. Khrushchev established his supremacy in the USSR after post-Stalinist alarums and excursions (1958–64). This admirable rough diamond, a believer in reform and peaceful coexistence, who incidentally emptied

Stalin's concentration camps, dominated the international scene in the next few years. He was also perhaps the only peasant boy ever to rule a major state. However, détente had first to survive what looked like an unusually tense spell of confrontations between Khrushchev's taste for bluff and impulsive decisions and the gesture politics of John F. Kennedy (1960–63), the most overrated US president of the century. The two superpowers were thus led by two high-risk operators at a time when – it is hard to recall – the capitalist West felt itself to be losing ground to the communist economies, which had grown faster than its own in the 1950s. Had they not just demonstrated a (short-lived) technological superiority to the USA by the dramatic triumph of Soviet satellites and cosmonauts? Moreover, had not – to everyone's surprise – communism just triumphed in Cuba, a country only a few dozen miles from Florida? (see chapter 15).

Conversely, the USSR was worried not only by Washington's ambiguous, but often only too bellicose rhetoric, but by the fundamental rupture with China, which now accused Moscow of going soft on capitalism, thus forcing the pacifically-minded Khrushchev into a more uncompromising public stance towards the West. At the same time the sudden acceleration of decolonisation and Third World revolution (see chapters 7, 12 and 15) seemed to favour the Soviets. A nervous but confident USA thus confronted a confident but nervous USSR over Berlin, over the Congo, over Cuba.

In fact, the net result of this phase of mutual threats and brinkmanship was a relatively stabilized international system, and a tacit agreement of the two superpowers not to frighten each other and the world, symbolized by the installation of the telephone 'hot line' which now (1963) came to link the White House with the Kremlin. The Berlin Wall (1961) closed the last undefined border between East and West in Europe. The USA accepted a communist Cuba on its doorstep. The small flames of liberation and guerrilla war lit by the Cuban revolution in Latin America, and by the wave of decolonization in Africa, did not turn into forest fires, but seemed to flicker out (see chapter 15). Kennedy was assassinated in 1963; Khrushchev sent packing in 1964 by the Soviet Establishment, which preferred a less impetuous approach to politics. The sixties and early seventies actually saw some significant steps to control and limit nuclear arms: test-ban treaties, attempts to stop nuclear proliferation (accepted by those who already had nuclear weapons or never expected to have them, but not by those building their own new nuclear arsenals like China, France and Israel), a Strategic Arms Limitation Treaty (SALT) between, the USA and the USSR, even some agreement about each side's Anti-Ballistic Missiles (ABMs). More to the point, trade between the USA and the USSR, politically strangled by both sides for so long, began to flourish as the 1960s turned into the 1970s. The prospects looked good.

They were not. In the middle 1970s the world entered what has been called the Second Cold War (see chapter 15). It coincided with a major change in the world economy, the period of long-term crisis which was to characterize the two decades beginning in 1973, and reached a climax in the early 1980s (chapter 14). However, initially the change in the economic climate was not much noticed by the players in the super-power game, except for the sudden jump in energy prices brought about by the successful coup of the oil-producers cartel, OPEC, one of several developments which seemed to suggest a weakening of the international domination of the USA. Both superpowers were reasonably happy about the soundness of their economies. The USA was plainly less affected by the new economic slow-down than Europe; the USSR – whom the gods wish to destroy they first make complacent – felt that everything was going its way. Leonid Brezhnev, Khrushchev's successor, who presided over the twenty years of what Soviet reformers were to call 'the era of stagnation', seemed to have some cause for optimism, not least because the oil crisis of 1973 had just quadrupled the international market value of the gigantic new deposits of oil and natural gas which had been discovered in the USSR since the middle 1960s.

Yet, economics apart, two inter-related developments now seemed to shift the balance of the superpowers. The first was what looked like defeat and destabilisation in the USA, as that country launched itself into a major war. The Vietnam war demoralized and divided the nation, amid televised scenes of riot and anti-war demonstrations; destroyed an American president; led to a universally predicted defeat and retreat after ten years (1965–75); and, what was even more to the point, demonstrated the isolation of the USA. For not a single one of America's European allies sent even nominal contingents of troops to fight alongside the US forces. Why the USA came to embroil itself in a doomed war, against which both its allies, neutrals, and even the USSR had warned it,* is almost impossible to understand, except as part of that dense cloud of

---

* 'If you want to, go ahead and fight in the jungles of Vietnam. The French fought there for seven years and still had to quit in the end. Perhaps the Americans will be able to stick it out for a little longer, but eventually they will have to quit too.' – Krushchev to Dean Rusk in 1961 (Beschloss, 1991, p. 649).

incomprehension, confusion and paranoia through which the main actors in the Cold War tapped their way.

And, if Vietnam was not enough to demonstrate America's isolation, the 1973 Yom Kippur war between Israel, which the US had allowed to become its closest ally in the Middle East, and the Soviet-supplied forces of Egypt and Syria, made it even more evident. For when a hard-pressed Israel, short of planes and ammunition, appealed to the USA to rush supplies, the European allies, with the single exception of that last hold-out of pre-war fascism, Portugal, refused even to allow US planes to use the US air bases on their soil for this purpose. (The supplies reached Israel via the Azores.) The US believed – one does not quite see why – that its own vital interests were at stake. Indeed, the US Secretary of State, Henry Kissinger (whose President, Richard Nixon, was otherwise engaged vainly trying to fend off impeachment), actually declared the first nuclear alert since the Cuban missile crisis, an action characteristic in its brutal insincerity of this able and cynical operator. It did not sway America's allies, who were far more concerned with their oil supplies from the Middle East than with supporting some regional ploy of the USA which Washington claimed unconvincingly to be essential to the global struggle against communism. For, through OPEC, the Arab states of the Middle East had done what they could to impede support for Israel by cutting oil supplies and threatening oil embargoes. In doing so they discovered their ability to multiply the world price of oil. And the foreign ministries of the world could not fail to notice that there was nothing the all-powerful USA did, or could immediately do, about that.

Vietnam and the Middle East weakened the USA, though it did not in itself alter the global balance of superpower, or the nature of the confrontation in the various regional theatres of the Cold War. However, between 1974 and 1979 a new wave of revolutions surged across a large part of the globe (see chapter 15). This, the third round of such upheavals in the Short Twentieth Century, actually looked as though it might shift the superpower balance away from the USA, since a number of regimes in Africa, Asia and even on the very soil of the Americas were attracted to the Soviet side and – more concretely – provided the USSR with military, and especially naval, bases outside its landlocked heartlands. It was the coincidence of this third wave of world revolution with the moment of public American failure and defeat which produced the Second Cold War. But it was also the coincidence of both with the optimism and self-satisfaction of Brezhnev's USSR in the 1970s, which made it certain. This phase of conflict was waged by a combination of local wars in the Third World, fought indirectly by the USA, which now avoided the Vietnam error of committing its own troops, and by an extraordinary acceleration of the nuclear arms race; the former less evidently irrational than the latter.

Since the situation in Europe had been so clearly stabilized – not even the Portuguese revolution of 1974 nor the end of the Franco regime in Spain changed it – and the lines had been so clearly drawn, in effect both superpowers had shifted their competition to the Third World. Détente in Europe had given the USA under Nixon (1968–74) and Kissinger the opportunity to score two major successes: the expulsion of the Soviets from Egypt and, much more significant, the informal recruitment of China into the anti-Soviet alliance. The new wave of revolutions, all of which were likely to be against the conservative regimes of which the USA had made itself the global defender, gave the USSR the chance to recover the initiative. As the collapsing Portuguese African empire (Angola, Mozambique, Guinea-Cape Verde) came under communist rule and the revolution which overthrew the Ethiopian emperor turned eastwards; as the rapidly growing Soviet navy acquired major new bases on either side of the Indian Ocean; as the Shah of Iran fell, a mood close to hysteria gripped American public and private debate. How else (except, in part, by a staggering ignorance of Asian topography) are we to explain the American view, seriously put forward at the time, that the entry of Soviet troops into Afghanistan marked the first step of a Soviet advance that would soon reach the Indian Ocean and the Persian Gulf* (see p. 479).

The unjustified self-satisfaction of the Soviets encouraged such gloom. Long before American propagandists explained, ex post facto, how the USA had set out to win the Cold War by bankrupting its antagonist, the Brezhnev regime had begun to bankrupt itself by plunging into an armaments programme which raised defence expenditure by an annual average of 4–5 per cent (in real terms) for twenty years after 1964. The race had been pointless, though it gave the USSR the satisfaction of being able to claim that it reached parity with the US in missile launchers by 1971, 25 per cent superiority by 1976 (it remained far below America in the number of warheads). Even the small Soviet nuclear arsenal had deterred the USA during the Cuba crisis, and both sides had long been able to reduce one another to multiple layers of rubble. The systematic Soviet effort to build a navy with worldwide presence on – or,

---

* The suggestion that the Nicaraguan Sandinistas brought military danger to within a few days' truck-drive of the Texan frontier was another, and characteristic, piece of school-atlas geopolitics.

rather, since its main strength was in nuclear submarines, under – the oceans, was not much more sensible in strategic terms, but at least it was comprehensible as a political gesture by a global superpower, which claimed the right to the global showing of the flag. Yet the very fact that the USSR no longer accepted its regional confinement struck American Cold warriors as plain proof that western supremacy would end, if not reasserted by a show of power. The increasing confidence which led Moscow to abandon the post-Khrushchev caution in international affairs confirmed them.

The hysteria in Washington was not, of course, based on realistic reasoning. In real terms US power, as distinct from US prestige, remained decisively greater than Soviet power. As for the economies and the technology of the two camps, Western (and Japanese) superiority was beyond calculation. The Soviets, crude and inflexible, might by titanic efforts have managed to build the best economy of the 1890s vintage anywhere in the world (to cite Jowitt, 1991, p. 78), but what did it help the USSR that by the middle 1980s it produced 80 per cent more steel, twice as much pig-iron and five times as many tractors than the USA, when it had failed to adapt to an economy that depended on silicone and software? (see chapter 16). There was absolutely no evidence, or likelihood, that the USSR wanted a war (except perhaps against China), let alone that it was planning a military attack on the West. The feverish scenarios of nuclear attack which came from the mobilized Western cold warriors and government publicity in the early 1980s were self-generated. They actually had the effect of convincing the Soviets that a pre-emptive nuclear attack by the West on the USSR was possible, or even – as at moments in 1983 – impending (Walker, 1993, chapter 11), and of setting off the largest mass European anti-nuclear peace movement of the Cold War, the campaign against the deployment of a new range of missiles in Europe.

Historians of the twenty-first century, remote from the living memories of the 1970s and 1980s, will puzzle over the apparent insanity of this outburst of military fever, the rhetoric of apocalypse, and the often bizarre international behaviour of US governments, especially in the early years of President Reagan (1980–88). They will have to appreciate the depth of the subjective traumas of defeat, impotence and public ignominy which had lacerated the US political establishment in the 1970s, and which were made even more painful by the apparent disarray of the American presidency during the years when Richard Nixon (1968–74) had to resign over a sleazy scandal, followed by two negligible successors. They culminated in the humiliating episode of US diplomats held hostage in revolutionary Iran, Red revolution in a couple of small central American states and a second international oil crisis, as OPEC once again raised their price to an all-time peak.

The policy of Ronald Reagan, elected to the presidency in 1980, can be understood only as an attempt to wipe out the stain of felt humiliation by demonstrating the unchallengeable supremacy and invulnerability of the USA, if need be by gestures of military power against sitting targets, like the invasion of the small Caribbean island of Grenada (1983), the massive naval and air attack on Libya (1986) and the even more massive and pointless invasion of Panama (1989). Reagan, perhaps just because he was a run-of-the-mill Hollywood actor, understood the mood of his people and the depth of the wounds to its self-esteem. In the end the trauma was only healed by the final, unpredicted and unexpected collapse of the great antagonist, which left the USA alone as a global power. Even then, we may detect in the Gulf War of 1991 against Iraq a belated compensation for the awful moments in 1973 and 1979 when the greatest power on the earth could find no response to a consortium of feeble Third World states which threatened to strangle its oil supplies.

The crusade against the 'Evil Empire' to which – at least in public – President Reagan's government devoted its energies, was thus designed as therapy for the USA rather than as a practical attempt to re-establish the world power balance. This had, in fact, been done quietly in the later 1970s, when NATO – under a Democratic US president and Social-Democratic Labour governments in Germany and Britain – had begun its own rearmament, and the new Left-wing states in Africa had been kept in check from the beginning by US-backed movements or states, fairly successfully in Central and southern Africa, where the US could act together with the formidable *apartheid* regime of the Republic of South Africa, less so in the Horn of Africa. (In both areas the Russians had the invaluable assistance of expeditionary forces from Cuba, testifying to Fidel Castro's commitment to Third World revolution as well as to his alliance with the USSR.) The Reaganite contribution to the Cold War was of a different kind.

It was not so much practical as ideological – part of the Western reaction to the troubles of the era of troubles and uncertainties into which the world had seemed to drift after the end of the Golden Age (see chapter 14). A lengthy period of centrist and moderately social-democratic rule ended, as the economic and social policies of the Golden Age seemed to fail. Governments of the ideological right, committed to an extreme form of business egoism and *laissez-faire*, came to power in several countries around 1980. Among these Reagan and the confident and formidable Mrs Thatcher in Britain (1979–90) were the most prominent. For this new Right the state-sponsored welfare capitalism of the 1950s and 1960s, no longer buttressed, since 1973, by economic success, had always looked like a sub-variety of that socialism ('the road to serfdom', as the economist and ideologue von Hayek called it) of which they saw the USSR as the logical end-product. The Reaganite Cold War was directed not only against the 'evil empire' abroad, but against the memory of Franklin D. Roosevelt at home: against the Welfare State as well as any other intrusive state. Its enemy was liberalism (the 'L-word' used to good effect in presidential election campaigns) as much as communism.

Since the USSR was to collapse just after the end of the Reagan era, American publicists were naturally to claim that it had been overthrown by a militant campaign to break and destroy it. The USA had waged and won the Cold War and utterly defeated its enemy. We need not take this crusaders' version of the 1980s seriously. There is no sign that the US government expected or envisaged the impending collapse of the USSR or was in any way prepared for it when it happened. While it certainly hoped to put the Soviet economy under pressure, it was informed (mistakenly) by its own intelligence that it was in good shape and capable of sustaining the arms race with the USA. In the early 1980s the USSR was still seen (also mistakenly) as engaged on a confident global offensive. In fact, President Reagan himself, whatever the rhetoric put before him by his speech writers, and whatever went on in his not always lucid mind, actually believed in the coexistence of the USA and the USSR, but one which should not be based on an abhorrent balance of mutual nuclear terror. What he dreamed of was a world entirely without nuclear arms. And so, as became clear at their strange and excited summit meeting in the sub-arctic gloom of autumnal Iceland in 1986, did the new General Secretary of the Communist Party of the Soviet Union, Mikhail Sergeyevich Gorbachev.

The Cold War ended when one or both the superpowers recognized the sinister absurdity of the nuclear arms race, and when one or both accepted the other's sincerity in wishing to end it. It was probably easier for a Soviet leader to take this initiative than for an American, because the Cold War had never been seen by Moscow in the crusading terms common in Washington, perhaps because an excited public opinion did not have to be considered. On the other hand, just for this reason, it would be harder for a Soviet leader to convince the West that he meant business. That is why the world owes so enormous a debt to Mikhail Gorbachev, who not only took this initiative but succeeded, singlehanded, in convincing the US government and others in the West that he meant what he said. However, let us not underestimate the contribution of President Reagan whose simple-minded idealism broke through the unusually dense screen of ideologists, fanatics, careerists, desperados and professional warriors around him to let himself be convinced. For practical purposes the Cold War ended at the two summits of Reykjavik (1986) and Washington (1987).

Did the end of the Cold War entail the end of the Soviet system? The two phenomena are historically separable, though obviously connected. The Soviet type of socialism had claimed to be a global alternative to the capitalist world system. Since capitalism had not collapsed, or looked like collapsing – though one wonders what would have happened if all the socialist and Third World debtors had united in 1981 to default simultaneously on their Western loans – the prospects of socialism as a world alternative depended on its ability to compete with the world capitalist economy, as reformed after the Great Slump and the Second World War, and as transformed by the 'post-industrial' revolution of communications and information technology in the 1970s. That socialism was falling behind at an accelerating rate was patent after 1960. It was no longer competitive. Insofar as this competition took the form of a confrontation of two political, military and ideological superpowers, the inferiority became ruinous.

Both superpowers overstretched and distorted their economies by a massive and enormously expensive competitive arms race, but the world capitalist system could absorb the three trillion dollars of debt – essentially for military spending – into which the 1980s plunged the USA, till then the world's greatest creditor-state. There was nobody, at home or abroad, to take the equivalent strain on Soviet expenditure, which, in any case, represented a far higher proportion of Soviet production – perhaps a quarter – than the 7 per cent of the titanic US GDP which went on war outlays in the mid-1980s. The USA, by a combination of historical luck and policy, had seen its dependencies turn into economies so flourishing that they outweighed its own. By the end of the 1970s the European Community and Japan together were 60 per cent larger than the US economy. On the other hand, the Soviets' allies and dependents never walked on their own feet. They remained a constant and vast annual drain of tens of billions of dollars on the USSR. Geographically and demographically, the backward countries of the world, whose revolutionary mobilizations, Moscow hoped, would one day outweigh the global predominance of capitalism, represented 80 per cent of the world. In economic terms, they were peripheral. As for technology, as Western superiority grew almost exponentially, there was no contest. In short, the Cold War, from the start, was a war of unequals.

But it was not the hostile confrontation with capitalism and its super-power that undermined socialism. It was rather the combination of its own increasingly evident and crippling economic defects and the accelerating invasion of the socialist economy by the far more dynamic, advanced and dominant capitalist world economy. Insofar as the rhetoric of the Cold War saw capitalism and socialism, 'the free world' and 'totalitarianism', as two sides of an unbridgeable canyon, and rejected any attempt to bridge it,* one might even say that, short of the mutual suicide of nuclear war, it guaranteed the survival of the weaker contestant. For, barricaded behind iron curtains, even the inefficient and slackening centrally planned command economy was viable – perhaps sagging slowly, but in no way likely to collapse in short order.† It was the interaction of Soviet-type economics with the capitalist world economy from the 1960s on which made socialism vulnerable. When socialist leaders in the 1970s chose to exploit the newly available resources of the world market (oil prices, easy loans etc.) instead of facing the hard problem of reforming their economic system, they dug their own graves (see chapter 16). The paradox of the Cold War was that what defeated and in the end wrecked the USSR was not confrontation but détente.

Yet in one sense the Washington Cold War ultras were not entirely wrong. The real Cold War, as we can easily see in retrospect, ended at the Washington summit of 1987, but it could not be universally *recognized* as being at an end until the USSR had visibly ceased to be a superpower, or indeed any kind of power. Forty years of fear and suspicion, of the sowing and harvesting of military-industrial dragons' teeth, could not be so easily reversed. The wheels of the war-making machine services went on turning on both sides. Professionally paranoic secret services went on suspecting every move by the other side as an astute trick to disarm the enemy's vigilance, the better to defeat him. It was the collapse of the Soviet Empire in 1989, the disintegration and dissolution of the USSR itself in 1989-91, which made it impossible to pretend, let alone to believe, that nothing had changed.

* cf the American use of the term 'Finlandization' as a term of abuse.

† To take the extreme case, the little communist mountain republic of Albania was poor and backward, but viable during the thirty or so years when it virtually sealed itself off from the world. Only when the walls sheltering it from the world economy were razed did it collapse into a pile of economic rubble.

V

But what exactly had changed? The Cold War had transformed the international scene in three respects. First, it had entirely eliminated, or overshadowed, all but one of the rivalries and conflicts that shaped world politics before the Second World War. Some disappeared because the empires of the imperial era vanished, and with them the rivalries of colonial powers over dependent territories under their rule. Others went, because all the 'great powers' except two that had been relegated to the second or third divisions of international politics, and their relations with each other were no longer autonomous, or indeed of more than local interest. France and (West) Germany buried the old hatchet after 1947 not because Franco–Germany conflict had become unthinkable – French governments thought about it all the time – but because their common membership of the US camp and the hegemony of Washington over western Europe would not allow Germany to get out of hand. Even so, it is astonishing how rapidly the major preoccupation of states after large wars disappeared from sight: namely the winners' worry about the recovery plans of the losers, and the losers' plans how to reverse their defeat. Few in the West were seriously preoccupied by the dramatic return to great-power status of West Germany and Japan, armed, though non-nuclear, so long as both were, in effect, subordinate members of the US alliance. Even the USSR and its allies, though denouncing the German danger, of which they had bitter experience, did so for propaganda rather than out of real fear. What Moscow was afraid of was not the German armed forces, but the NATO missiles on German soil. But after the Cold War other power conflicts could emerge.

Second, the Cold War had frozen the international situation, and in doing so had stabilized what was an essentially unfixed and provisional state of affairs. Germany was the most obvious example. For forty-six years it remained divided – *de facto* if not, for long periods, *de jure* – into four sectors: the West, which became the Federal Republic in 1949; the middle, which became the German Democratic Republic in 1954; and the East, beyond the Oder–Neisse line, which expelled most of its Germans and became part of Poland and the USSR. The end of the Cold War and the disintegration of the USSR reunited the two western sectors and left the Soviet-annexed parts of East Prussia detached and isolated, separated from the rest of Russia by the now independent state of Lithuania. It left the Poles with German promises to accept the 1945 frontiers, which did not reassure them. Stabilization did not mean peace. Except in Europe, the Cold War was not an era when fighting was forgotten. There was hardly a year between 1948 and 1989 without a fairly serious armed conflict somewhere. Nevertheless, conflicts were controlled, or stifled, by the fear that they might provoke an open – i.e. a nuclear – war between the superpowers. Iraq's claims against Kuwait – the small, oil-rich British protectorate at the top of the Persian Gulf, independent since 1961 – were old and constantly reasserted. They did not lead to war until the Persian Gulf had ceased to be an almost automatic flashpoint of superpower confrontation. Before 1989 it is certain that the USSR, which was the chief armourer of Iraq, would have strongly discouraged any Baghdad adventurism in this area.

The development of the domestic politics of states was not, of course, frozen in the same manner – except where such changes would shift, or look like shifting, the allegiance of a state to its dominant superpower. The US were not more inclined to tolerate communists or philo-communists in office in Italy, Chile or Guatemala than the USSR was prepared to abdicate its right to send troops into brother-states with dissident governments, like Hungary and Czechoslovakia. It is true that the USSR tolerated far less variety in its friendly and satellite regimes, but on the other hand its capacity to assert itself within them was much less. Even before 1970 it had completely lost what control it ever had over Yugoslavia, Albania and China; it had to tolerate some very individualist behaviour from the leaders of Cuba and Romania; and, as for the Third World countries it supplied with arms, and which shared its hostility to American imperialism, community of interests apart, it had no real hold over them at all. Hardly any of them even tolerated the legal existence of local communist parties. Nevertheless, the combination of power, political influence, bribery and the logic of bi-polarity and anti-imperialism kept the divisions of the world more or less stable. Except for China, no important state really changed sides unless by a home-grown revolution, which the superpowers could neither bring about nor prevent, as the USA discovered in the 1970s. Even those US allies which found their policies increasingly constrained by the alliance, like the German governments after 1969 in the matter of *Ostpolitik*, did not pull out of an increasingly troublesome alignment. Politically impotent, unstable and indefensible political entities incapable of survival in a real international jungle – the region between the Red Sea and Persian Gulf was full of them – somehow remained in being. The shadow of the mushroom cloud guaranteed the survival not of liberal democracies in western Europe, but of regimes like Saudi Arabia and Kuwait. The Cold War was the best time in which to be a mini-state – as after the Cold War the difference between problems solved and problems shelved became obvious.

Third, the Cold War had filled the world with arms to a degree that beggars belief. This was the natural result of forty years when major industrial states had constantly competed to arm themselves against a war that might break out at any moment; forty years of superpowers competing to win friends and influence people by distributing arms all over the globe, not to mention forty years of constant 'low intensity' warfare with occasional outbreaks of major conflict. Economies largely militarized, and in any case with enormous and influential military-industrial complexes, had an economic interest in selling their products abroad, if only to comfort their governments with proof that they were not *only* swallowing the astronomic and economically unproductive military budgets which kept them going. The unprecedented global fashion for military governments (see chapter 12) provided a grateful market, fed not only by superpower largesse, but – since the oil-price revolution – by local revenues multiplied beyond the imagination of earlier Third World sultans and sheikhs. Everybody exported arms. Socialist economies and some declining capitalist states like Britain had little else to export that was competitive on the world market. The trade in death was not only in the large chunks of hardware which governments alone could use. An age of guerrilla warfare and terrorism also developed a large demand for light, portable and adequately destructive and murderous devices, and the underworlds of the late twentieth-century cities could provide a further civilian market for such products. In such milieux the Uzi machine-gun (Israeli), the Kalashnikov rifle (Russian) and Semtex explosive (Czech) became household names.

In this manner the Cold War perpetuated itself. The little wars that had once set clients of one superpower against those of the other continued after the old conflict ended on a local basis, resisting those who had launched them and now wanted to end them. The UNITA rebels in Angola remained in the field against the government, although the South Africans and the Cubans had withdrawn from the unhappy country and although the USA and the United Nations had disavowed them and recognized the other side. They would not run short of arms. Somalia, armed first by the Russians when the emperor of Ethiopia was on the side of the US, then by the US, when revolutionary Ethiopia turned to Moscow, entered the post Cold War world as a famine-stricken territory of anarchic clan warfare, short of everything except an almost unlimited supply of guns, ammunition, land-mines and military transport. The US and the UN mobilized to bring food and peace. It proved harder than flooding the country with guns. In Afghanistan the USA had distributed the hand-held 'Stinger' anti-aircraft missiles and launchers wholesale to the anti-communist tribal guerrillas, calculating, correctly, that these would offset the Soviet command of the air. When the Russians withdrew, the war continued as though nothing had changed, except that, in the absence of planes, the tribesmen could now themselves exploit the flourishing demand for Stingers, which they sold profitably on the international arms market. In despair the US offered to buy them back itself at the rate of $100,000 a piece, with spectacular lack of success (*International Herald Tribune*, p. 24, 5/7/93; *Repubblica* 6/4/94). As Goethe's sorcerer's apprentice exclaimed: '*Die ich rief die Geister, werd' ich nun nicht los.*'

The end of the Cold War suddenly removed the props which had held up the international structure and, to an extent not yet appreciated, the structures of the world's domestic political systems. And what was left was a world in disarray and partial collapse, because there was nothing to replace them. The idea, briefly entertained by American spokesmen, that the old bi-polar order could be replaced by a 'new world order' based on the single superpower which remained in being, and therefore looked stronger than ever, rapidly proved unrealistic. There could be no return to the world before the Cold War, because too much had changed, too much had disappeared. All landmarks were fallen, all maps had to be altered. Politicians and economists used to one kind of world even found it difficult or impossible to appreciate the nature of the problems of another kind. In 1947 the USA had recognized the need for an immediate and gigantic project to restore the West European economies, because the supposed danger to these economies – communism and the USSR – was easily defined. The economic and political consequences of the collapse of the Soviet Union and Eastern Europe were even more dramatic than the troubles of western Europe, and would prove even more far-reaching. They were predictable enough in the late 1980s and even visible – but none of the wealthy economies of capitalism treated this impending crisis as a global emergency requiring urgent and massive action because its *political* consequences were not so easily specified. With the possible exception of West Germany, they reacted sluggishly – and even the Germans totally misunderstood and understimated the nature of the problem, as their troubles with the annexation of the former German Democratic Republic were to demonstrate.

The consequences of the end of the Cold War would probably have been enormous in any case, even had it not coincided with a major crisis in the world economy of capitalism and with the final crisis of the Soviet Union and its system. Since the historian's world is what happened and not what might have happened if things had been different, we need not consider the possibility of other scenarios. The end of the Cold War proved to be not the end of an international conflict, but the end of an era: not only for the East, but for the entire world. There are historic moments which may be recognized, even by contemporaries, as marking the end of an age. The years around 1990 clearly were such a secular turning-point. But, while everyone could see that the old had ended, there was utter uncertainty about the nature and prospects of the new.

Only one thing seemed firm and irreversible amid these uncertainties: the extraordinary, unprecedented, fundamental changes which the world economy, and consequently human societies, had undergone in the period since the Cold War began. These will, or should, have a far larger place in the history books of the third millennium than the Korean war, the Berlin and Cuba crises, and the Cruise missiles. To these transformations we must now turn.

CHAPTER NINE
The Golden Years

It is in the past forty years that Modena has really seen the great leap forward. The era from Italian Unification until then had been a long age of waiting, or of slow and intermittent modifications, before transformation accelerated to the speed of lightning. People now came to enjoy a standard of living previously confined to a tiny elite.

– G. Muzzioli (1993, p. 323)

No hungry man who is also sober can be persuaded to use his last dollar for anything but food. But a well-fed, well-clad, well-sheltered and otherwise well-tended person can be persuaded as between an electric razor and an electric toothbrush. Along with prices and costs, consumer demand becomes subject to management.

– J.K. Galbraith, *The New Industrial State* (1967, p. 24)

I

Most human beings operate like historians: they only recognize the nature of their experience in retrospect. In the course of the 1950s many people, especially in the increasingly prosperous 'developed' countries, became aware that times were indeed strikingly improved, especially if their memories reached back to the years before the Second World War. A British Conservative premier fought and won a general election in 1959 on the slogan 'You've never had it so good', a statement that was undoubtedly correct. Yet it was not until the great boom was over, in the disturbed seventies, waiting for the traumatic eighties, that observers – mainly, to begin with, economists – began to realize that the world, particularly the world of developed capitalism, had passed through an altogether exceptional phase of its history; perhaps a unique one. They looked for names to describe it: the 'thirty glorious years' of the French (*les trente glorieuses*); the quarter-century Golden Age of the Anglo-Americans (Marglin and Schor, 1990). The gold glowed more brightly against the dull or dark background of the subsequent decades of crisis.

There are several reasons why it took so long to recognize the exceptional nature of the era. For the USA, which dominated the world economy after the second World War, it was not all that revolutionary. It merely continued the expansion of the war years which, as we have seen, had been uniquely kind to that country. It had suffered no damage, increased its GNP by two thirds (Van der Wee, 1987, p. 30) and ended the war with almost two thirds of the world's industrial production. Moreover, just because of the size and advance of the US economy, its actual performance during The Golden Years was not as impressive as the rate of growth of other countries, which started from a much smaller base. Between 1950 and 1973 it grew more slowly than any other industrial country except Britain and, what is more to the point, its growth was no higher than in the most dynamic earlier periods of its development. In all other industrial countries, including even sluggish Britain, the Golden Age broke all previous records (Maddison, 1987, p. 650). In fact, for the USA this was, economically and technologically, a time of relative dropping back rather than of advance. The gap in productivity per man-hour between it and other countries diminished, and if in 1950 it enjoyed a national wealth (GDP) per capita double that of France and Germany, over five times that of Japan, and more than half as large again as Britain, the other states were fast catching up and continued to do so in the 1970s and 1980s.

Recovering from the war was the overwhelming priority for the European countries and Japan, and for the first years after 1945 they measured their success simply by how close they had come to a target set by reference to the past, not the future. In the non-communist states recovery also meant putting the fear of social revolution and communist advance, heritage of war and resistance, behind them. While most countries (other than Germany and Japan) were back to their pre-war levels by 1950, the early Cold War and the persistence of powerful communist parties in France and Italy discouraged euphoria. In any case, the material benefits of growth took some time to make themselves felt. In Britain it was not until the middle 1950s that they became palpable. No politician before then could have won an election on Harold Macmillan's slogan. Even in so spectacularly prosperous a region as Italy's Emilia-

Romagna, the benefits of the 'affluent society' did not become general until the 1960s (Francia, Muzzioli, 1984, pp. 327-29). Moreover, the secret weapon of a society of *popular* affluence, namely full employment, did not become general until the 1960s, when the average of west European unemployment stood at 1.5 per cent. In the 1950s Italy still had almost 8 per cent out of work. In short, not until the 1960s did Europe come to take its extraordinary prosperity for granted. By then, indeed, sophisticated observers began to assume that, somehow, everything in the economy would go onwards and upwards for ever. 'There is no special reason to doubt that the underlying trends of growth in the early and middle 1970s will continue much as in the 1960s,' wrote a United Nations report in 1972. 'No special influence can now be foreseen which would at all drastically change the external environment of European economies.' The club of advanced capitalist industrial economies, the OECD (Organization for Economic Cooperation and Development) revised its forecasts for future growth upwards as the 1960s advanced. By the early 1970s they were expected to be ('in the medium term') over 5 per cent (Glyn, Hughes, Lipietz, Singh, 1990, p. 39). It was not to be.

It is now evident that the Golden Age essentially belonged to the developed capitalist countries, which, throughout these decades, represented about three quarters of the world's production and over 80 per cent of its manufacturing exports (OECD, Impact, 1979 pp. 18–19). One further reason why this specificity of the era was only slowly recognized was that in the 1950s the economic upsurge seemed quite world-wide and independent of economic regimes. Indeed, initially it looked as though the newly expanded socialist part of the world had the advantage. The growth-rate of the USSR in the 1950s was faster than any Western country's, and the economies of Eastern Europe grew almost as rapidly – faster in hitherto backward countries, slower in the already industrialized or partly industrialized ones. Communist East Germany, however, lagged behind non-communist Federal Germany. Even though the Eastern Bloc of Europe lost pace in the 1960s, its GDP per capita over the whole of the Golden Age still grew slightly faster (or, in the case of the USSR just less) than that in the major capitalist industrial countries (IMF, 1990, p. 65). Still, in the 1960s it became clear that capitalism was forging ahead rather than socialism.

Nevertheless, the Golden Age was a worldwide phenomenon, even though general affluence never came within sight of the majority of the world's population – those who lived in countries for whose poverty and backwardness the experts of the UN tried to find diplomatic euphemisms. Though the population of the Third World grew at a spectacular rate – the numbers of Africans, East Asians and South Asians more than doubled in the thirty-five years after 1950, the number of Latin Americans rose even faster (World Resources, 1986, p. 11). The 1970s and 1980s once again grew familiar with mass famine, its classic image, the starving exotic child observed after supper on every Western TV screen. During the Golden decades there was no mass starvation, except as the product of wars and political madness, as in China (see pp. 466–7) Indeed, as population multiplied, life expectancy stretched out by an average of seven years – even by seventeen years if we compare the later 1930s with the later 1960s (Morawetz, 1977, p. 48). This means that food production rose faster than population, as it did both in the developed and in every major area of the non-industrial world. In the 1950s it rose by more than 1 per cent a year per capita in every region of the 'developing world' except Latin America, and even there it grew per capita, though more modestly. In the 1960s it still rose in all parts of the non-industrial world, but (once again with the exception of Latin America, this time ahead of the rest), only very slightly. Nevertheless, the total food production of the poor world in both the 1950s and 1960s rose faster than in the developed world.

In the 1970s the disparities between different parts of the poor world make such global figures useless. By then some regions, such as the Far East and Latin America, were drawing well ahead of their population growth, whereas Africa was falling behind by more than 1 per cent a year. In the 1980s the poor world's food production per capita did not grow at all outside South and East Asia (but even here some countries produced less per head than in the 1970s – Bangladesh, Sri Lanka, the Philippines. Certain regions stayed well below their 1970 levels, or even continued to fall, notably Africa, Central America and the Asian Near East (Van der Wee, 1987, p. 106; FAO, *The State of Food*, 1989, Annex, Table 2, pp. 113–15).

Meanwhile the problem of the developed world was that it produced so much surplus food that it did not know what to do with it and, in the 1980s, decided to grow substantially less, or else (as in the European Community) to dump its 'butter mountains' and 'milk lakes' below cost, thus undercutting producers in the poor countries. It became cheaper to buy Dutch cheese on Caribbean islands than in the Netherlands. Curiously, the contrast between food surpluses on one side, hungry people on the other, which had so outraged the world during the Great Depression of the 1930s, caused less comment in the late twentieth century. It was an aspect of the growing divergence between the rich and the poor world which became increasingly evident from the 1960s.

The industrial world was, of course, expanding everywhere: in the capitalist and socialist regions and in the 'Third World'. In the old West there were dramatic examples of industrial revolution, such as Spain and Finland. In the world of 'really existing socialism' (see chapter 13) purely agrarian countries like Bulgaria and Rumania acquired massive industrial sectors. In the Third World the most spectacular development of the so-called 'newly industrialising countries' (NICs) occurred after the Golden Age, but everywhere the number of countries depending primarily on agriculture, at least for financing their imports from the rest of the world, diminished sharply. By the later 1980s a mere fifteen states paid for half their imports or more from farm exports. With one exception (New Zealand), all were in sub-saharan Africa and Latin America (FAO, *The State of Food*, 1989, Annex, Table 11, pp. 149–51).

The world economy was thus growing at an explosive rate. By the 1960s it was plain that there had never been anything like it. World output of manufactures quadrupled between the early 1950s and the early 1970s and, what is even more impressive, world trade in manufactured products grew tenfold. As we have seen, world agricultural output also shot up, if not so spectacularly. It did so not so much (as so often in the past) by bringing new land into cultivation, but rather by raising its productivity. Grain yields per hectare almost doubled between 1950–52 and 1980–82 – and more than doubled in North America, Western Europe and East Asia. World fisheries meanwhile trebled their catches before falling again (World Resources, 1986, pp. 47, 142).

One by-product of this extraordinary explosion was as yet barely noticed, though in retrospect it already looked menacing: pollution and ecological deterioration. During the Golden Age it attracted little attention, except from wild life enthusiasts and other protectors of human and natural rarities, because the dominant ideology of progress took it for granted that the growing domination of nature by man was the very measure of humanity's advance. Industrialization in the socialist countries was for this reason particularly blind to the ecological consequences of its massive construction of a rather archaic industrial system based on iron and smoke. Even in the West, the old nineteenth century businessman's motto 'Where there's muck, there's brass' (i.e. pollution means money), was still convincing, especially for road-builders and real-estate 'developers' who rediscovered the unbelievable profits to be made in an era of secular boom from speculation which could not go wrong. All one had to do was to wait for the value of the right building site to rise into the stratosphere. A single well-sited building could now make a man a multimillionaire virtually without cost, since he could borrow on the security of his future construction and borrow further as its value (built or unbuilt, occupied or empty) continued to go up. Eventually, as usual, there was a crash – the Golden Age ended like earlier booms in a real-estate-cum-banking collapse – but until then city centres, large and small, were ripped out and 'developed' across the world, incidentally destroying medieval cathedral cities like Worcester in Britain or Spanish colonial capitals like Lima in Peru. Since the authorities in both East and West also discovered that something like factory methods could be used to construct public housing quickly and cheaply, filling the outskirts of cities with blankly menacing high-rise apartment blocks, the 1960s will probably go down as the most disastrous decade in the history of human urbanization.

In fact, far from worrying about the environment, there seemed to be grounds for self-satisfaction, as the results of nineteenth century pollution yielded to twentieth century technology and ecological conscience. Did not the simple banning of coal fires in London from 1953 abolish, at one stroke, the impenetrable fog so familiar from Charles Dickens' novels, which had periodically blanketed the city? Were not, some years later, salmon once again swimming up the once dead river Thames? Cleaner, smaller, quieter factories distributed themselves around the countryside instead of the vast smoke-swathed plants that had previously signified 'industry'. Airports replaced railway stations as the quintessential buildings representing transport. As the countryside emptied, people, or at least middle-class people moving into abandoned villages and farmsteads, could feel themselves closer than ever to nature.

Yet there is no denying that the impact of human activities on nature, primarily urban and industrial but also, it was eventually realized, agricultural, increased steeply from the middle of the century. This was largely due to the enormous increase in the use of fossil fuels (coal, oil, natural gas, etc.), whose potential exhaustion had worried earlier gazers into the future from the mid-nineteenth century on. New sources were discovered faster than they could be used. That total energy consumption shot up – it actually tripled in the USA between 1950 and 1973 (Rostow, 1978, p. 256; Table III, p. 58) is far from surprising. One of the reasons why the Golden Age was golden was that the price of a barrel of Saudi oil averaged less than $2 throughout the entire period from 1950 to 1973, thus making energy ridiculously cheap, and getting cheaper all the time. Ironically, it was only after 1973, when the oil-producers' cartel OPEC finally decided to charge what the traffic would bear (see pp. 473–4), that ecology-watchers took serious note of the effects of the consequent explosion in petrol-driven traffic, which was already darkening the skies above the great cities in the motorized, and in particular the American, parts of the world. Smog was the immediate worry and understandably so. However, carbon dioxide emissions warming the atmosphere almost tripled between 1950 and 1973, that is to say the concentration of this gas in the atmosphere increased by a little less than 1 per cent a year (World Resources, Table 11.1, p. 318; 11.4, p. 319; V. Smil, 1990 p. 4, Fig. 2). The production of chlorofluorcarbons, chemicals which affect the ozone layer, rose almost vertically. At the end of the war they had barely been used, but by 1974 over 300,000 tons of one compound and over 400,000 tons of another were being released into the atmosphere each year (World Resources, Table 11.3, p. 319). The rich Western countries naturally generated the lion's share of this pollution, though the unusually filthy industrialization of the USSR produced almost as much carbon dioxide as the USA; almost five times as much in 1985 as in 1950. (Per capita, of course, the USA remained a long way ahead.) Only Britain actually lowered the amount emitted per inhabitant over this period (Smil, 1990, Table I, p. 14).

II

Initially this astonishing explosion of the economy seemed merely a gigantic version of what had gone before; as it were, a globalization of the state of the pre-1945 USA, taking that country as the model of a capitalist industrial society. So, to some extent, it was. The age of the automobile had long arrived in North America, but after the war it came to Europe and later more modestly to the socialist world and the Latin American middle classes, while cheap fuel made the truck and the bus the major means of transport over most of the globe's land-mass. If the rise of Western affluent society could be measured by the multiplication of private cars – from Italy's 469,000 in 1938 to the same country's fifteen millions in 1975 (Rostow, 1978, p. 212; UN Statistical Yearbook, 1982, Table 175, p. 960) – the economic development of many a Third-World country could be recognized by the rate at which the number of its trucks grew.

Much of the great world boom was thus a catching up, or in the USA a continuation of old trends. The model of Henry Ford's mass production spread across the oceans to new auto industries, while in the USA the Fordist principle was extended to new kinds of production, from house-building to junk food (McDonald's was a post-war success story). Goods and services previously confined to minorities were now produced for a mass market, as in the field of mass travel to sunny beaches. Before the war never had more than 150,000 North Americans travelled to Central America and the Caribbean in any year, but between 1950 and 1970 their numbers grew from three hundred thousand to seven millions (US Hist Statistics I, p. 403). The European figures were, not surprisingly, even more spectacular. Spain, which had virtually no mass tourism until the later 1950s, welcomed over fifty-four millions of foreigners per year at the end of the 1980s, a number only slightly surpassed by Italy's fifty-five millions (Stat.Jahrbuch, 1990, p. 262). What had once been luxury, became the expected standard of comfort, at all events in the rich countries: the refrigerator, the private washing machine, the telephone. By 1971 there were over 270 million telephones in the world, i.e. overwhelmingly in North America and Western Europe, and their spread was accelerating. Ten years later their numbers had almost doubled. In the developed market economies there was more than one phone for every two inhabitants (UN World Situation, 1985, Table 19, p. 63). In short, it was now possible for the average citizen in those countries to live as only the very wealthy had lived in their parents' day – except, of course, that mechanization had now replaced personal servants.

However, what strikes us most about the period is the extent to which the economic surge seemed powered by technological revolution. To this extent it multiplied not only improved products of the old kind, but quite unprecedented ones, including many which had been virtually unimagined before the war. Some revolutionary products, such as the synthetic materials known as 'plastics' had been developed between the wars or even begun to enter commercial production, like nylon (1935), polystyrene and polythene. Some, like television and recording on magnetic tape, were then barely out of the experimental stage. The war, with its demands on high technology, prepared a number of revolutionary processes for later civilian use, though rather more on the British side (subsequently taken up by the USA) than among the science-minded Germans: radar, the jet engine, and various ideas and techniques which prepared the ground for post-war electronics and information technology. Without them the transistor (invented 1947) and the first civilian digital computers (1946) would certainly have appeared considerably later. Perhaps fortunately, nuclear energy, first mobilized during the war for destruction, remained largely outside the civilian economy, except as a (so far) marginal contribution to the world's generation of electrical energy – about 5 per cent in 1975. Whether these innovations were based on inter-war or post-war science, on inter-war technical or even commercial pioneering or on the great post-1945 forward rush – the integrated circuits developed in the 1950s, the lasers of the 1960s, or the various spin-offs from space rocketry – hardly matters for our purpose. Except in one sense. More than any previous period, the Golden Age rested on the most advanced and often esoteric scientific research, which now found practical application within a few years. Industry and even agriculture for the first time moved decisively beyond the technology of the nineteenth century (see chapter 18).

Three things about this technological earthquake strike the observer. *First*, it utterly transformed everyday life in the rich world and even, to a lesser extent, in the poor world, where radio could now reach the remotest villages thanks to the transistor and the miniaturized long-life battery, where the 'green revolution' transformed rice and wheat cultivation and plastic sandals replaced bare feet. Any European reader of this book who makes a quick inventory of his or her personal possessions, can verify this. Most of the contents of the refrigerator or freezer (neither of which most family homes would have owned in 1945) is novel: freeze-dried food, factory-farmed poultry produce, meat stuffed with enzymes and various chemicals to change its taste, or even constructed by the 'simulation of boneless high-quality cuts' (Considine, 1982, pp. 1164 ff.) not to mention products imported fresh by air from halfway across the globe, as would then have been impossible.

Compared to 1950 the share of natural or traditional materials – wood, metal treated in old-fashioned ways, natural fibres or fillings, even ceramics – in our kitchens, household furnishings and personal clothing has gone down dramatically, although the hype surrounding everything produced by the personal hygiene and beauty industry was such that it obscured (by systematically exaggerating) the degree of novelty of its enormously increased and diversified output. For technological revolution entered consumer consciousness to such an extent that novelty became the main sales appeal for everything from synthetic detergents (which came into their own in the 1950s) to laptop computers. The assumption was that 'new' equalled not just better, but utterly revolutionized.

As for the products visibly representing technological novelty, their list is endless, and needs no comment: television; vinyl records (LPs came in 1948); followed by tapes (tape cassettes came in the 1960s) and compact discs; small portable transistor radios – the present writer got his first as a present from a Japanese friend in the late 1950s – digital watches, pocket calculators, battery and then solar-powered; and then the rest of domestic electronics, photo and video equipment. Not the least significant thing about these innovations is the systematic process of miniaturisation of such products, i.e. *portability*, which vastly extended their potential range and market. However, the technological revolution was perhaps symbolized just as much as superficially unchanged products which had, since the Second World War, been transformed from top to bottom, such as pleasure sailing boats. Their masts and hulls, their sails and rigging, their navigational equipment had little or nothing in common with inter-war vessels except shape and function.

Second, the more complex the technology involved, the more complex was the road from discovery or invention to production, and the more elaborate and expensive the process of traversing it. 'Research and Development' (R & D) became central to economic growth and, for this reason, the already enormous advantage of the 'developed market economies' over the rest was reinforced. (As we shall see in chapter 16, technological innovation did not flourish in the socialist economies.) The typical 'developed country' had upwards of a thousand scientists and engineers for every million of its population in the 1970s, but Brazil had about 250, India 130, Pakistan about sixty, Kenya and Nigeria about thirty, (UNESCO, 1985, Table 5.18). Moreover, the process of innovation became so continuous that the cost of developing new products became an increasingly large and indispensable share of the cost of production. In the extreme case of the armaments industries, where, admittedly, money was no object, new devices, had barely become fit for practical use before they were scrapped for even more advanced (and, of course, vastly more expensive) pieces of equipment, to the considerable financial benefit of the corporations concerned. In the more mass-market-oriented industries such as pharmaceutical chemicals, a new and genuinely needed drug, especially when protected from competition by patent rights, could make several fortunes, which were explained away by its producers as absolutely essential for further research. Less easily protected innovators had to clean up more quickly, for as soon as other products entered the market, the price dropped through the floor.

Third, the new technologies were, overwhelmingly, capital-intensive and (except for the highly skilled scientists and technicians) labour-saving, or even labour-replacing. The major characteristic of the Golden Age was that it needed constant and heavy investment and, increasingly, that it did not need people, except as consumers. However, the impetus and speed of the economic surge was such that, for a generation, this was not obvious. On the contrary, the economy grew so fast that, even in the industrial countries, the industrial working class maintained or even increased its share of the occupied population. In all advanced countries but the USA, the reserve lakes of labour filled during pre-war depression and post-war demobilization were drained, new supplies of labour were sucked in from the native countryside and from foreign immigration, and married women, hitherto kept outside the labour market, entered it in growing numbers. Nevertheless, the ideal to which the Golden Age aspired, though it was only gradually realized, was production, or even service, without humans: automated robots assembling cars, silent voids filled with banks of computers controlling the output of power, trains without drivers. Human beings were essential to such an economy only in one respect: as buyers of goods and services. Here lay its central problem. In the Golden Age it still seemed unreal and remote, like the future death of the universe by entropy about which Victorian scientists had warned the human race.

On the contrary. All the problems which had haunted capitalism in its era of catastrophe appeared to dissolve and to disappear. The terrible and inevitable cycle of boom and slump, so murderous between the wars became a succession of mild fluctuations thanks to – or so the Keynesian economists who now advised governments were convinced – their intelligent macro-economic management. Mass unemployment? Where was it to be found in the developed world in the 1960s, when Europe averaged 1.5 per cent of its labour force out of work and Japan 1.3 per cent (Van der Wee, 1987, p. 77)? Only in North America was it not yet eliminated. Poverty? Of course most of humanity remained poor, but in the old heartlands of industrial labour what meaning could the *Internationale's* 'Arise, ye starvelings from your slumbers' have for workers who now expected to have their car and spend their annual paid vacation on the beaches of Spain? And, if they fell upon hard times, would not an increasingly universal and generous Welfare State provide them with protection, undreamed of before, against the hazards of ill-health, misfortune, even the dreaded old age of the poor? Their incomes rose year by year, almost automatically. Would they not go on rising for ever? The range of goods and services offered by the productive system, and available to them, made former luxuries part of everyday consumption. It widened year by year. What more, in material terms, could humanity want except to extend the benefits already enjoyed by the favoured peoples of some countries to the unhappy inhabitants of those parts of the world, admittedly still the majority of mankind, who had not yet entered upon 'development' and 'modernization'?

What problems remained to be solved? An extremely intelligent and prominent British socialist politician wrote in 1956:

Traditionally socialist thought has been dominated by the economic problems posed by capitalism, poverty, mass unemployment, squalor, instability, and even the possibility of the collapse of the whole system . . . Capitalism had been reformed out of all recognition. Despite occasional minor recessions and balance of payments crises, full employment and at least a tolerable degree of stability are likely to be maintained. Automation can be expected steadily to solve any remaining problems of under-production. Looking ahead, our present rate of growth will give us a national output three times as high in fifty years (Crosland, 1957, p. 517).

III

How are we to explain this extraordinary and quite unexpected triumph of a system which, for half a lifetime, had seemed on the verge of ruin? What needs explaining, of course, is not the mere fact of a lengthy period of economic expansion and well-being, following on a similar period of economic and other troubles and disturbances. Such a succession of 'long waves' of about half a century in length has formed the basic rhythm of the economic history of capitalism since the late eighteenth century. As we have seen (chapter 2), the Age of Catastrophe had drawn attention to this pattern of secular fluctuations, whose nature remains obscure. They are generally known by the name of the Russian economist Kondratiev. In the long perspective, the Golden Age was just another Kondratiev upswing, like the great Victorian boom of 1850–73 – curiously the dates almost coincide at a century's distance – and the *belle époque* of the late Victorians and Edwardians. Like earlier such upswings, it was preceded and followed by 'downswings'. What needs explaining is not this, but the extraordinary scale and depth of this secular boom, which is a sort of pendant to the extraordinary scale and depth of the preceding era of crises and depressions.

There are no really satisfactory explanations for the sheer scale of this 'Great Leap Forward' of the capitalist world economy, and consequently for its unprecedented social consequences. Of course other countries had enormous scope for catching up with the model economy of early twentieth-century industrial society, the USA, a country devastated by neither war, defeat nor victory, though briefly shaken by the Great Slump. Other countries did indeed systematically try to imitate the USA, a process which speeded up economic development, since it is always easier to adapt an existing technology than to invent a new one.

That, as the Japanese example was to show, could come later. However, there was clearly more to the Great Leap than this. There was a substantial restructuring and reform of capitalism and a quite spectacular advance in the globalization and internationalization of the economy.

The first produced a 'mixed economy', which both made it easier for states to plan and manage economic modernization, and which also enormously increased demand. The great post-war economic success stories of capitalist countries, with the rarest exceptions (Hong Kong), are stories of industralization backed, supervised, steered, and sometimes planned and managed by governments: from France and Spain in Europe to Japan, Singapore and South Korea. At the same time the political commitment of governments to full employment and – to a lesser extent – to the lessening of economic inequality, i.e. a commitment to welfare and social security, for the first time provided a mass consumer market for luxury goods which could now become accepted as necessities. The poorer people are, the higher the proportion of their income they must spend on indispensable essentials such as food (a sensible observation known as 'Engel's Law'). In the 1930s, even in the rich USA about a third of household expenditure still went on food, but by the early 1980s only 13 per cent. The rest was available for other expenditures. The Golden Age democratized the market.

The second multiplied the productive capacity of the world economy by making possible a far more elaborate and sophisticated international division of labour. Initially this was largely confined to the collective of the so-called 'developed market economies', i.e. the countries in the US camp. The socialist part of the world was largely separate (see chapter 13), and the most dynamic developers in the Third World in the 1950s opted for a segregated and planned industrialization by substituting their own production for imported manufactures. The core countries of Western capitalism, of course, traded with the overseas world, and very advantageously too, since the terms of trade favoured them – i.e. they could get their raw materials and foodstuffs more cheaply. Still, what really exploded was the trade in industrial products, mainly between the industrial core countries. World trade in manufactures multiplied over tenfold in the twenty years after 1953. Manufactures, which had formed a fairly constant share of world trade since the nineteenth century at a little less than half, now shot up to over 60 per cent (W.A. Lewis, 1981). The Golden Age remained anchored to the economies of the core capitalist countries – even in purely quantitative terms. In 1975 the Big Seven of capitalism alone (Canada, the USA, Japan, France, Federal Germany, Italy and Great Britain) contained three quarters of all the passenger cars on the globe and almost as high a proportion of its telephones (UN *Statistical Yearbook*, 1982, pp. 955 ff, 1018 ff). Nevertheless, the new industrial revolution could not be confined to any region.

The restructuring of capitalism and the advance in economic internationalisation were central. It is not so clear that technological revolution explains the Golden Age, though there was plenty of it. As has been shown, much of the new industrialization of these decades was the spread of old industrializations based on old technologies to new countries: the nineteenth-century industrialization of coal, iron and steel to the socialist agrarian countries; the twentieth-century American industries of oil and internal combustion engines to European ones. The impact of the high-research-generated technology on civilian industry probably did not become massive until the Crisis Decades after 1973, when the major breakthrough of information technology and genetic engineering took place, as well as a number of other leaps into the unknown. Perhaps the chief innovations which began to transform the world almost as soon as the war ended were chemical and pharmaceutical. Their impact on the demography of the Third World was immediate (see chapter 12). Their cultural effects were a little more delayed, but not much, for the Western sexual revolution of the 1960s and 1970s was made possible by antibiotics – unknown before the Second World War – which appeared to remove the major risks from sexual promiscuity by making venereal diseases easily curable, and by the birth-control pill which became widely available in the 1960s. (The risk was to return to sex in the 1980s with AIDS.)

All the same, an innovating high technology soon became so much part of the great boom that it must form part of any explanation, even if we do not regard it as decisive in its own right.

Post-war capitalism was unquestionably, as the Crosland quotation put it, a system 'reformed out of all recognition' or, in the words of the British premier Harold Macmillian, a 'new' version of the old system. What happened was far more than a return of the system from some avoidable interwar 'errors' to its 'normal' record of 'both . . . maintaining a high level of employment and . . . enjoying some non-negligible rate of economic growth' (H.G. Johnson, 1972, p. 6). Essentially it was a sort of marriage between economic liberalism and social democracy (or, in American terms, Rooseveltian New Deal policy), with substantial borrowings from the USSR, which had pioneered the idea of economic planning. That is why the reaction against it by the theological free marketeers was to be so impassioned in the 1970s and 1980s, when the policies based on this marriage were no longer protected by economic success. Men like the Austrian economist Friedrich von Hayek (1899–1992) had never been pragmatists, ready (if reluctant) to be persuaded that economic activities which interfered with *laissez-faire* worked; though of course they denied, with subtle arguments, that they could work. They were believers in the equation 'Free Market = Freedom of the Individual' and consequently condemned any departure from it as, to quote the title of his 1944 book, '*The Road to Serfdom*'. They had stood by the purity of the market in the Great Slump. They continued to condemn the policies which made the Golden Age golden, as the world grew richer and capitalism (plus political liberalism) flourished again on the basis of mixing markets and governments. But between the 1940s and the 1970s nobody listened to such Old Believers.

Nor can we doubt that capitalism was deliberately reformed, largely by the men who were in a position to do so in the USA and Britain, during the last war years. It is a mistake to suppose that people never learn from history. The inter-war experience, and especially the Great Slump, had been so catastrophic that nobody could possibly dream, as plenty of men in public life had done after the First World War, of returning as soon as possible to the time before the air-raid sirens had begun to sound. All the men (women were hardly yet accepted into the first division of public life) who sketched out what they hoped would be the post-war principles of the world economy and the future of the global economic order, had lived through the Great Slump. Some, like J.M. Keynes, had been in public life since before 1914. And if the economic memory of the 1930s was not enough to sharpen their appetite for reforming capitalism, the fatal political risks of not doing so were patent to all who had just fought Hitler's Germany, the child of the Great Slump, and were confronted with the prospect of communism and Soviet power advancing westwards across the ruins of capitalist economies that did not work.

Four things seemed clear to these decision-makers. The inter-war catastrophe, which must on no account be allowed to return, had been due largely to the breakdown of the global trading and financial system and the consequent fragmentation of the world into would-be autarchic national economies or empires. The global system had once been stabilized by the hegemony, or at least the centrality of the British economy and its currency, the pound sterling. Between the wars Britain and sterling were no longer strong enough to carry this load, which could now only be taken over by the USA and the dollar. (The conclusion, naturally, aroused more genuine enthusiasm in Washington than elsewhere.) Third, the Great Slump had been due to the failure of the unrestricted free market. Henceforth the market would have to be supplemented by, or to work within the framework of, public planning and economic management. Finally, for social and political reasons, mass unemployment must not be allowed to return.

Decision-makers outside the Anglo-Saxon countries could do little about the reconstruction of the world trading and financial system, but found the rejection of the old free market liberalism congenial enough. Strong state-guidance and state-planning in economic matters were not new in several countries, from France to Japan. Even the state ownership and management of industries was familiar enough, and had been widely extended in Western countries after 1945. It was in no sense a particular issue between socialists and anti-socialists, although the general leftward swing of wartime Resistance politics gave it more prominence than it would have had before the war, as for instance in the French and Italian Constitutions of 1946–47. Thus, even after fifteen years of socialist government, Norway in 1960 had a proportionately (and of course absolutely) smaller public sector than West Germany, which was not a country given to nationalization.

As for the socialist parties and labour movements which were so prominent in Europe after the war, they fitted in readily with the new reformed capitalism, because for practical purposes they had no economic policy of their own, except for the communists, whose policy consisted in gaining power and then following the model of the USSR. The pragmatic Scandinavians left their private sectors intact. The British Labour government of 1945 did not, but did nothing whatever to reform it, and showed a lack of interest in planning that was quite startling, especially when contrasted with the enthusiastic planned modernisation of contemporary (and non-socialist) French governments. In effect, the Left concentrated on improving the conditions of their working-class constituencies and social reforms for this purpose. Since they had no alternative solutions except to call for the abolition of capitalism, which no social-democratic government knew how to, or tried to, abolish, they had to rely on a strong wealth-creating capitalist economy to finance their aims. In effect, a reformed capitalism which recognized the importance of labour and social-democratic aspirations suited them well enough.

In short, for a variety of reasons the politicians, officials and even many of the businessmen of the post-war West were convinced that a return to *laissez-faire* and the unreconstructed free market were out of the question. Certain policy objectives – full employment, the containment of communism, the modernization of lagging or declining or ruined economies – had absolute priority and justified the strongest government presence. Even regimes dedicated to economic and political liberalism now could, and had to, run their economies in ways which would once have been rejected as 'socialist'. After all, that is how Britain and even the USA had run their war-economies. The future lay with the 'mixed economy'. Though there were moments when the old orthodoxies of fiscal rectitude, stable currencies and stable prices still counted, even these were no longer absolutely compelling. Since 1933 the scarecrows of inflation and deficit finance no longer kept the birds away from the economic fields, but the crops still seemed to grow.

These were not minor changes. They led a US stateman of ironclad capitalist credentials – Averell Harriman – in 1946 to tell his country-men: 'People in this country are no longer scared of such words as "planning"... people have accepted the fact the government has got to plan as well as individuals in this country' (Maier, 1987, p. 129). They made it natural for a champion of economic liberalism and admirer of the US economy, Jean Monnet (1888–1979) to become a passionate backer of French economic planning. They turned Lionel (Lord) Robbins, a free market economist who had once defended orthodoxy against Keynes and run a seminar jointly with Hayek at the London School of Economics, into a director of the semi-socialist British war economy. For thirty years or so there was a consensus among 'western' thinkers and decision-makers, notably in the USA, which determined what other countries on the non-communist side could do, or rather what they could not do. All wanted a world of rising production, growing foreign trade, full employ-ment, industrialization and modernization, and all were prepared to achieve it, if need be, through systematic government control and the management of mixed economies, and by co-operating with organized labour movements so long as they were not communist. The Golden Age of capitalism would have been impossible without this consensus that the economy of private enterprise ('free enterprise' was the preferred name)* needed to be saved from itself to survive.

However, though capitalism certainly reformed itself, we must make a clear distinction between the general readiness to do the hitherto unthink-able and the actual effectiveness of the specific new recipes which the chefs of the new economic restaurants were creating. This is hard to judge. Economists, like politicians, are always inclined to put down success to the sagacity of their policies, and, during the Golden Age,

---

* The word 'capitalism', like 'imperialism', was avoided in public discourse, since it had negative associations in the public mind. Not until the 1970s do we find politicians and publicists proudly declaring themselves 'capitalist', slightly anticipated from 1965 in the motto of the business magazine *Forbes* which, reversing a jargon phrase of American communists, began to describe itself as a 'capitalist tool'.

when even weak economies like the British flourished and grew, there seemed plenty of scope for self-congratulation. Still, deliberate policy undoubtedly scored some striking successes. In 1945–46 France, for instance, set out quite consciously on a course of economic planning to modernize the French Industrial economy. This adaptation of Soviet ideas to a capitalist mixed economy must have had some effect, since between 1950 and 1979 France, hitherto a by-word for economic retardation, caught up more successfully than any other of the chief industrial countries with US productivity, more so even than Germany (Maddison, 1982, p. 46). Nevertheless, we must leave the economists, a notably contentious tribe, to argue out the merits and demerits and the efficacy of the various policies of the various governments (mostly associated with the name of J.M. Keynes, who had died in 1946).

IV

The difference between broad intention and detailed application is particularly clear in the reconstruction of the international economy, for here the 'lesson' of the Great Slump (the word constantly appears in the discourse of the 1940s) were at least partly translated into concrete institutional arrangements. US supremacy was, of course, a fact. The political pressure for action came from Washington, even when many of the ideas and initiatives came from Britain, and where opinions differed, as between Keynes and the American spokesman Harry White,* over the new International Monetary Fund (IMF), the US view prevailed. Yet the original plan for the new liberal economic world order envisaged it as part of a new international political order, also planned during the last war years as the United Nations, and it was not until the original model of the UN collapsed in the Cold War that the only two international institutions actually set up under the Bretton Woods Agreements of 1944, the World Bank ('International Bank for Reconstruction and Development') and the IMF, both still in existence, became *de facto* subordinated to US policy. They were to foster long-term international investment and maintain exchange stability as well dealing with balance-of-payments problems. Other points on the international programme did not generate special institutions (e.g. for controlling the price of primary commodities and for international measures to maintain full employment), or were

---

* Ironically, White later became a victim of the US witch-hunt as an alleged secret Communist Party sympathiser.

only incompletely implemented. The proposed International Trade Organization ended up as the much more modest General Agreement on Tariffs and Trade (GATT), a framework for reducing trade barriers by periodic bargaining.

In short, insofar as the planners of the brave new world tried to construct a set of working institutions to give their projects reality, they failed. The world did not emerge from the war in the shape of a working international system of multilateral free trade and payments, and the American moves to establish it broke down within two years of victory. And yet, unlike the United Nations, the international system of trade and payments worked, though not in the way originally predicted or intended. In practice the Golden Age was the era of free trade, free capital movements and stable currencies that had been in the minds of the wartime planners. No doubt this was due primarily to the overwhelming economic dominance of the USA and of the dollar, which functioned all the better as a stabilizer because it was linked to a specific quantity of gold until the system broke down in the late 1960s and early 1970s. One must constantly bear in mind that in 1950 the USA alone contained 60 per cent or so of all the capital stock of all the advanced capitalist countries, produced 60 per cent or so of all their output, and even at the peak of the Golden Age (1970) still held over 50 per cent of the total capital stock of all these countries and produced almost half their output (Armstrong, Glyn, Harrison, 1991, p. 151).

It was also due to the fear of communism. For, contrary to American convictions, the chief obstacle to a free-trading international capitalist economy was not the protectionist instincts of foreigners, but the combination of traditional US high tariffs at home and the drive for a vast expansion of American exports, which the wartime planners in Washington regarded as 'essential to the attainment of full and effective employment in the USA (Kolko, 1969, p. 13). Aggressive expansion was plainly in the minds of American policy-makers as soon as the war was over. It was the Cold War which encouraged them to take a longer view, by persuading them that helping their future competitors to grow as rapidly as possible was politically urgent. It has even been argued that, in this manner, the Cold War was the major engine of the great global boom (Walker, 1993). This is probably an exaggeration, but the gigantic largesse of Marshall Aid (see pp. 240–1) certainly helped the modernization of such recipients as wanted to use it for this purpose – as Austria and France did systematically – and American aid was decisive in speeding up the transformation of West Germany and Japan. No doubt these two countries would have become great economic powers in any case. The mere fact that, as defeated states, they were not masters of their foreign policy gave them an advantage, since it did not tempt them into pouring more than a minimum of resources into the barren hole of military spending. Nevertheless, we have only to ask what would have happened to the German economy if its recovery had depended on the Europeans, who feared its revival. How fast would the Japanese economy have recovered, if the USA had not found itself building up Japan as the industrial base for the Korean War and again the Vietnam War after 1965? America funded the doubling of Japan's manufacturing output between 1949 and 1953, and it is no accident that 1966–70 were the years of peak Japanese growth – no less than 14.6 per cent per annum. The role of the Cold War is thus not to be underestimated, even if the long-term economic effect of the vast diversion of resources by states into competitive armaments was damaging. In the extreme case of the USSR it was probably fatal. However, even the USA traded off military strength against growing economic weakness.

A capitalist world economy thus developed round the USA. It raised fewer obstacles to the international movements of factors of production than any other since the mid-Victorian period, with one exception: international migration was slow to recover from inter-war strangulation. This was partly an optical illusion. The great Golden Age boom was fuelled not only by the labour of the formerly unemployed, but by vast flows of internal migration – from country to city, from farming (especially out of regions of poor upland soils), from poorer to richer regions. So Italian southerners flooded into the factories of Lombardy and Piedmont and four hundred thousand Tuscan share-croppers left their holdings in twenty years. The industrialization of eastern Europe was essentially such a process of mass migration. Moreover, some of these internal migrants were actually international migrants, except that they had originally arrived in the receiving country, not as seekers for employment, but as part of the terrible mass exodus of refugees and expelled populations after 1945.

Nevertheless, it is notable that in an era of spectacular economic growth and increasing labour shortage, and in a Western world dedicated to free movements in the economy, governments resisted free immigration, and, when they found themselves actually permitting it (as in the case of the Caribbean and other inhabitants of the British Commonwealth, who had the right to settle because they were legally British), put a stop to it. In many cases such immigrants, mostly from the less developed Mediterranean countries, were only allowed conditional and temporary residence, so that they could be easily re-patriated, although the expansion of the European Economic Community to include several emigrant countries (Italy, Spain, Portugal, Greece) made this harder. Still, by the early 1970s about seven-and-a-half millions had migrated into the developed European countries (Potts, 1990, pp. 146–47). Even in the Golden Age immigration was a politically sensitive issue. In the difficult decades after 1973 it was to lead to a sharp rise in public xenophobia in Europe.

However, the world economy in the Golden Age remained *international* rather than *transnational*. Countries traded with each other to an ever greater extent. Even the USA, which had been largely self-supplying before the Second World War, quadrupled its exports to the rest of the world between 1950 and 1970, but it also became a massive importer of consumer goods from the late 1950s on. In the late 1960s it even began to import automobiles (Block, 1977, p. 145). Yet, though the industrial economies increasingly bought and sold each others' production, the bulk of their economic activities remained home-centred. At the peak of the Golden Age the USA exported only just under 8 per cent of its GDP, and, more surprisingly, export-oriented Japan only a little more (Marglin and Schor, p. 43, Table 2.2).

Nevertheless, an increasingly *transnational* economy began to emerge, especially from the 1960s on, that is to say, a system of economic activities for which state territories and state frontiers are not the basic framework, but merely complicating factors. In the extreme case, a 'world economy' comes into existence which actually has no specifiable territorial base or limits, and which determines, or rather sets limits to, what even the economies of very large and powerful states can do. Some time in the early 1970s such a transnational economy became an effective global force. It continued to grow, if anything more rapidly than before, during the Crisis Decades after 1973. Indeed its emergence largely created the problems of these decades. Of course it went hand in hand with a growing *internationalization*. Between 1965 and 1990 the percentage of the world's product which went in exports was to double (World Development, 1992, p. 235).

Three aspects of this transnationalization were particularly obvious: transnational firms (often known as 'multinationals'), the new international division of labour and the rise of offshore finance. The last of these was not only one of the earliest forms of transnationalism to develop, but also the one which demonstrates most vividly the way in which the capitalist economy escaped from national, or any other, control.

The term 'offshore' entered civilian public vocabulary some time in the 1960s to describe the practice of registering the legal seat of businesses in some, usually tiny and fiscally generous territory which permitted entrepreneurs to avoid the taxes and other constraints imposed on them by their own country. For every serious state or territory, however committed to the freedom of profit-making, had by the mid-century established certain controls and restrictions on the conduct of legitimate business in the interests of its people. A suitably complex and ingenious combination of the legal loopholes in the corporate and labour laws of kindly mini-territories – for instance Curaçao, the Virgin Islands and Liechtenstein – could do wonders for a firm's balance-sheet. For 'the essence of offshoreness lies in turning an enormous number of loopholes into a viable but unregulated corporate structure' (Raw, Page and Hodgson, 1972, p. 83). For obvious reasons offshoreness lent itself particularly to financial transactions, although Panama and Liberia had long subsidized their politicians by the income from registering the merchant ships of other countries whose owners found their native labour and safety regulations too onerous.

Sometime in the 1960s a little ingenuity turned the old international financial centre, the City of London, into a major global offshore centre by the invention of 'Eurocurrency' i.e. mainly 'Eurodollars'. Dollars held on deposit in non-US banks and not repatriated, mainly to avoid the restrictions of US banking law, became a negotiable financial instrument. These free-floating dollars, accumulating in huge quantities thanks to the growing American investments abroad and the enormous political and military expenditures of the US government, became the foundation of an entirely uncontrolled global market, mainly in short-term loans. Its rise was quite dramatic. The net Eurocurrency market rose from perhaps fourteen billion dollars in 1964 to perhaps 160 billions in 1973 and almost five hundred billions five years later, when this market became the main mechanism for recycling the Klondike of oil-profits which the OPEC countries suddenly found themselves wondering how to spend and invest (see p. 473). The USA was the first country to find itself at the mercy of these vast, multiplying floods of unattached capital that washed round the globe from currency to currency, looking for quick profits. Eventually all governments were to be its victims, since they lost control over exchange rates and the world money supply. By the early 1990s even joint action by leading central banks proved impotent.

That firms based in one country, but operating in several, should expand their activities, was natural enough. Nor were such 'multinationals' new. The US corporations of this kind raised their foreign affiliates from about seven-and-a-half thousand in 1950 to over twenty-three thousand in 1966, mostly in western Europe and the western hemisphere (Spero, 1977, p. 92). However, increasingly other countries firms followed. The German chemical corporation Hoechst, for instance, established or associated itself with 117 plants in forty-five countries, in all but six cases after 1950 (Fröbel, Heinrichs, Kreye, 1986, Tabelle IIIA, p. 281 ff.). The novelty lay rather in the sheer scale of operations of these transnational entities. By the early 1980s US transnational corporations accounted for over three quarters of their country's exports and almost half its imports, and such corporations (both British and foreign) were responsible for over 80 per cent of British exports (UN Transnational, 1988, p. 90).

In one sense these are irrelevant figures, since the main function of such corporations was 'to internalize markets across national frontiers', i.e. to make themselves independent of the state and its territory. Much of what the statistics (which are still basically collected country by country) show as imports or exports is in fact *internal* trade within a transnational entity such as General Motors, which operated in forty countries. The ability to operate in this manner naturally reinforced the tendency for capital to concentrate, familiar since Karl Marx. By 1960 it was already estimated that the sales of the two hundred largest firms in the (non-socialist) world were the equivalent of 17 per cent of the GNP of that sector of the world, and by 1984 they were said to amount to 26 per cent.* Most of such transnationals were based in substantial 'developed' states. In fact, 85 per cent of the 'big 200' were based in the USA, Japan, Britain and Germany, with firms from eleven other countries making up the rest. Yet, even if the links of such super-giants with their native governments were likely to close, by the end of the Golden Age it is doubtful whether any of them, except the Japanese ones and some essentially military firms, could be confidently described as *identified* with their government's or nation's interests. It was no longer as clear as it had once seemed that, in the words of a Detroit tycoon who entered the US government, 'What's good for General Motors is good for the USA'. How could it be, when their operations in the home country were merely those in one market of the hundred in which, say, Mobil Oil was active, or the 170 in which Daimler-Benz was present? Business logic would force an international oil firm to calculate its strategy and policy towards its native country in exactly the same way as towards Saudi Arabia or Venezuela, namely in terms of profit and loss on one hand, of the comparative power of company and government on the other.

The tendency for business transactions and business enterprises – and by no means only those of a few score of giants – to emancipate

---

* Such estimates are to be used with care, and are best treated simply as orders of magnitude.

themselves from the traditional nation state, became even more marked as industrial production began, slowly at first but with growing speed, to move out of the European and North American countries that had pioneered industralization and capitalist development. These countries remained the powerhouse of Golden Age growth. In the middle 1950s the industrial countries had sold about three-fifths of their manufactured exports to each other, in the early 1970s, three quarters. However, then things began to change. The developed world began to export somewhat more of its manufactures to the rest of the world, but – more significantly – the Third World began to export manufactures to the developed industrial countries on a substantial scale. As the traditional primary exports of backward regions lost ground (except, after the OPEC revolution, mineral fuels) they began, patchily but rapidly, to industralize. Between 1970 and 1983 the Third World's share of global industrial exports, hitherto stable at about 5 per cent, more than doubled (Fröbel et al, 1986, p. 200).

A new international division of labour therefore began to undermine the old one. The German firm Volkswagen set up car factories in Argentina, Brazil (three plants), Canada, Ecuador, Egypt, Mexico, Nigeria, Peru, South Africa and Yugoslavia – as usually, mainly after the mid-1960s. New Third-World industries supplied not only the swelling local markets, but also the world market. They could do this, both by exporting articles completely produced by local industry (such as textiles, most of which had by 1970 already emigrated from the old countries to the 'developing' ones), and *by becoming part of a transnational process of manufacture.*

This was the decisive innovation of the Golden Age, though it did not fully come into its own until later. It could not have happened but for the revolution in transport and communication, which made it possible and economically feasible to split the production of a single article between, say, Houston, Singapore and Thailand, air-freighting the partly completed product between these centres and controlling the entire process centrally by modern information technology. Major electronics producers began to globalize themselves from the mid-1960s. The line of production now moved not through gigantic hangars on a single site, but across the globe. Some of them stopped in the extra-territorial 'free production zones' or offshore plants which now began to spread, overwhelmingly in poor countries with cheap and mainly young women's labour, another and new device for escaping the control of a single state. Thus one of the earliest, Manaus, deep in the Amazonian jungle, manufactured textiles, toys, paper goods, electronics and digital watches for US, Dutch and Japanese firms.

All this produced a paradoxical change in the political structure of the world economy. As the globe became its real unit, the national economies of the large states found themselves giving way to such offshore centres, mostly situated in the small or tiny mini-states which had conveniently multiplied as the old colonial empires fell apart. At the end of the Short Twentieth Century the world, according to the World Bank, contained seventy-one economies with populations of less than two-and-a-half millions (eighteen of them with populations of less than 100,000), that is to say, two fifths of all the political units officially treated as 'economies' (World Development, 1992). Until the Second World War such units had been regarded as economic jokes, and indeed not real states at all.* They were and are certainly incapable of defending their nominal independence in the international jungle, but in the Golden Age it became evident that they could flourish as well as, and sometimes better than, large national economies by providing services directly to the global economy. Hence the rise of new city states (Hong Kong, Singapore), a form of polity last seen to flourish in the Middle Ages; patches of Persian Gulf desert were transformed into major players on the global investment market (Kuwait), and of the many offshore refuges from state law.

This situation was to provide the multiplying ethnic movements of late twentieth century nationalism with unconvincing arguments for the viability of an independent Corsica or Canary Islands. Unconvincing, because the only independence achieved by secession was that of separation from the nation state with which such territories had previously been associated. Economically, separation would almost certainly make them more dependent on the transnational entities which increasingly determined such matters. The most convenient world for multinational giants is one populated by dwarf states or no states at all.

V

It was natural that industry should shift from high-cost to cheap labour locations as soon as this became technically possible and cost-effective, and the (hardly surprising) discovery that some non-white labour forces were at least as skilled and educated as white ones was to be an additional bonus for high-tech industries. Yet there was a particularly convincing reason why the Golden Age boom should lead to a shift away from the core countries of the old industralization. This was the peculiar 'Keyne-

* Not until the early 1990s were the ancient statelets of Europe – Andorra, Liechtenstein, Monaco, San Marino – treated as potential members of the United Nations.

sian' combination of economic growth in a capitalist economy based on the mass consumption of a fully employed and increasingly well-paid and well-protected labour force.

This combination was, as we have seen, a political construct. It rested on an effective policy consensus between Right and Left in most 'Western' countries, the extreme fascist-ultranationalist right having been eliminated from the political scene by the Second World War, the extreme communist left by the Cold War. It was also based on a tacit or explicit consensus between employers and labour organizations to keep labour demands within limits that did not eat into the profits, and the future prospects of profits high enough to justify the huge investments without which the spectacular growth of Golden Age labour productivity could not have taken place. Indeed, in the sixteen most industrial of the market economies investment grew at an annual rate of 4.5 per cent, about three times as fast as during the years from 1870 to 1913, even allowing for the rather less impressive rate in North America, which pushed the general average down (Maddison, 1982, Table 5.1, p. 96). *De facto*, the arrangement was triangular, with governments, formally or informally, presiding over the institutionalized negotiations between capital and labour, who were now habitually described, at least in Germany, as the 'social partners'. After the end of the Golden Age these arrangements were savagely assailed by the rising free-market theologians under the name of 'corporatism', a word which had half-forgotten and entirely irrelevant associations with inter-war fascism (see p. 114).

This was a deal acceptable to all sides. Employers, who hardly minded high wages during a long boom with high profits, welcomed the predictability which made forward planning easier. Labour got regularly rising wages and fringe benefits, and a steadily extended and more generous Welfare State. Government got political stability, weakening communist parties (except in Italy) and predictable conditions for the macro-economic management which all states now practised. And the economies of the industrial capitalist countries did splendidly, if only because for the first time (outside North America and, perhaps Australasia) an economy of mass consumption came into existence on the basis of full employment and regularly rising real incomes, buttressed by social security, which in time was paid for by rising public revenues. Indeed, in the euphoric 1960s some incautious governments went so far as to guarantee the unemployed – who were then few – 80 per cent of their former wage.

Until the late 1960s the politics of the Golden Age reflected this state of affairs. The war was followed everywhere by strongly reformist governments, Rooseveltian in the USA, socialist-dominated or social-democratic in virtually all ex-belligerent Western Europe except in occupied West Germany (where there were neither independent institutions nor elections until 1949). Even the communists were in government until 1947 (see p. 238). The radicalism of the Resistance years affected even the emerging conservative parties – the West German Christian Democrats thought capitalism was bad for Germany as late as 1949 (Leaman, 1988) – or at least made it hard to swim against the tide. The British Conservative party claimed credit for the reforms of the Labour government of 1945.

Somewhat surprisingly, reformism soon retreated, though not the consensus. The great boom of the 1950s was presided over, almost everywhere, by governments of moderate conservatives. In the USA (from 1952) in Britain (from 1951), in France (except for brief episodes of coalition), West Germany, Italy and Japan, the Left was entirely out of power, though Scandinavia remained social democratic and socialist parties were in government coalitions in other small countries. There can be no doubt about the recession of the Left. This was not due to any massive loss of support by the socialists or even the communists in France and Italy where they were the major working-class party.* Nor, except perhaps in Germany, where the Social Democratic Party (SPD) was 'unsound' on German unity, and in Italy where it remained allied to the communists, was it due to the Cold War. Everybody, except for the communists, was reliably anti-Russian. The mood of the booming decade was against the Left. This was not a time for change.

In the 1960s the centre of gravity of the consensus shifted towards the Left; perhaps partly due to the increasing retreat of economic liberalism before Keynesian management, even in anti-collectivist hold-outs like Belgium and West Germany, perhaps in part because the elderly gentlemen who had presided over the stabilization and revival of the capitalist system left the scene – Dwight Eisenhower (born 1890) in 1960, Konrad Adenauer (b. 1876) in 1965, Harold Macmillan (b. 1894) in 1964. Eventually (1969) even the great General de Gaulle (b. 1890) departed. A certain rejuvenation of politics took place. In fact, the peak years of the Golden Age seemed to be as congenial to the moderate Left, once again in government in many west European states, as the 1950s had been

---

* However, all Left parties were electoral minorities, though large ones. The highest vote scored by such a party was 48.8 per cent by the British Labour Party in 1951, ironically in an election won by the Conservatives with a slightly smaller vote, thanks to the vagaries of the British electoral system.

uncongenial. This drift to the Left was partly due to electoral shifts, as in West Germany, Austria and Sweden, and anticipated even more striking shifts in the 1970s and early 1980s, when both the French socialists and the Italian communists reached their all-time peaks, but essentially voting patterns remained stable. Electoral systems exaggerated relatively minor shifts.

However, there is a clear parallelism between the shift to the Left and the most significant public developments of the decade, namely the appearance of welfare states in the literal meaning of the word, that is to say states in which welfare expenditures – income maintenance, care, education, etc. – became the *greater part* of total public expenditure, and people engaged in welfare activities formed the largest body of all public employment, e.g. in the middle of the 1970s 40 per cent in Britain and 47 per cent in Sweden (Therborn, 1983). The first welfare states in this sense appeared round 1970. Of course the decline of military expenditure during the détente years automatically raised the proportion of spending under other headings, but the example of the USA shows that there was a real change. In 1970, while the Vietnam War was at its height, the number of school employees in the USA for the first time became significantly larger than the number of 'military and civilian defense personnel' (Statistical History 1976, II, pp. 1102, 1104, 1141). By the end of the 1970s all advanced capitalist states had become such 'welfare states', with six states spending more than 60 per cent of total public outlays for welfare (Australia, Belgium, France, West Germany, Italy, Netherlands). This was to produce considerable problems after the end of the Golden Age.

Meanwhile the politics of 'developed market economies' seemed tranquil, if not somnolent. What was there to get impassioned about, except communism, the dangers of nuclear war and the crises imported into their affairs by imperial activities abroad, such as the Suez adventure of 1956 in Britain, the Algerian war in France (1954–61) and, after 1965, the Vietnam War in the USA? That was the reason why the sudden and almost worldwide spurt of student radicalism in and around 1968 took politicians and older intellectuals so much by surprise.

It was a sign that the Golden Age balance could not last. Economically this balance depended on a coordination between the growth of productivity and earnings which kept profits stable. A sag in the continuous rise of productivity and/or a disproportionate rise in wages would result in destabilization. It depended on what had been so dramatically absent between the wars, a balance between the growth of production and the ability of consumers to buy it. Wages had to rise fast enough to keep the market buoyant, but not fast enough to squeeze profits. But how to control wages in an era of labour shortage or, more generally, prices in a time of exceptionally booming demand? How, in other words, to control inflation, or at least keep it within bounds? Lastly, the Golden Age depended on the overwhelming political and economic dominance of the USA which acted – sometimes without meaning to – as the stabilizer and guarantor of the world economy.

In the course of the 1960s, all these showed signs of wear and tear. The hegemony of the USA declined and, as it slipped, the gold-dollar based world monetary system broke down. There were some signs of slow-down in labour productivity in several countries, and certainly signs that the great labour reservoir of internal migration which had fed the industrial boom was close to exhaustion. After twenty years, a new generation had become adult, for whom inter-war experience – mass unemployment, insecurity, stable or falling prices – were history and not part of experience. They had adjusted their expectations to the only experience of their age group, that of full employment and continuous inflation (Friedman, 1968, p. 11). Whatever the specific situation which triggered the 'worldwide wage explosion' at the end of the 1960s – labour shortage, growing efforts by employers to hold down real wages or, as in France and Italy, the great student rebellions, all of them rested on the discovery by a generation of workers who had got used to having or finding work, that the regular and welcome rises so long negotiated by their unions were actually much less than could be screwed out of the market. Whether or not we detect a return to class struggle in this recognition of market realities (as many in the post-1968 'new Left' held), there is no doubt about the striking change of mood between the moderation and calm of wage negotiations before 1968 and the last years of the Golden Age.

Since it was directly relevant to the way the economy worked, the shift in labour's mood was far more significant than the great burst of student unrest in and around 1968, though the students provided more dramatic material for the media and far more food for the commentators. The student rebellion was a phenomenon outside economics and politics. It mobilized a particular minority sector of the population, as yet barely recognized as a special group in public life, and – since most of its members were still being educated – largely outside the economy, except as purchasers of rock records: the (middle-class) youth. Its cultural significance was far greater than its political significance, which was fleeting – unlike analogous movements in Third World and dictatorial countries (see pp 332 and 444). Yet it served as a warning, a sort of *memento mori* to a generation that half-believed it had solved the problems of Western society for good. The major texts of Golden Age reformism Crosland's *The Future of Socialism*; J.K. Galbraith's *The Affluent Society*; Gunnar Myrdal's *Beyond the Welfare State*; and Daniel Bell's *The End of Ideology*, all written between 1956 and 1960, rested on the presumption of the growing internal harmony of a society that was now basically satisfactory, if improvable, that is to say, on confidence in the economy of organized social consensus. That consensus did not survive the 1960s.

So 1968 was neither an end nor a beginning, but only a signal. Unlike the wage explosion, the collapse of the Bretton Woods international financial system in 1971, the commodities boom of 1972–3 and the OPEC oil crisis of 1973, it does not figure much in the explanation of economic historians about the end of the Golden Age. Its end was not quite unexpected. The expansion of the economy in the early 1970s, accelerated by a rapidly rising inflation, by massive rises in the world's money supplies and the vast American deficit, became hectic. In the economists' jargon, the system became 'overheated'. In the twelve months from July 1972, the real GDP in the OECD countries rose by 7.5 per cent, and real industrial production by 10 per cent. Historians who had not forgotten the way the great mid-Victorian boom ended, might well have wondered whether the system was not riding for a fall. They would have been right, though I do not think anyone predicted the fall of 1974, Nor, perhaps, took it as seriously as it turned out to be, for, though the GNP of the advanced industrial countries actually *dropped* substantially – such a thing had not happened since the war – people still thought of economic crises in terms of 1929, and there was no sign of catastrophe. As usual, the immediate reaction of shocked contemporaries, was to look for special reasons for the collapse of the old boom, 'an unusual bunching of unfortunate disturbances unlikely to be repeated on the same scale, the impact of which was compounded by some avoidable errors', to quote the OECD (McCracken, 1977, p. 14). The more simple-minded put it all down to the greed of the OPEC oil sheikhs. Any historian who puts major changes in the configuration of the world economy down to bad luck and avoidable accidents should think again. And this was a major change. The world economy did not recover its old stride after the crash. An era was at an end. The decades since 1973 were to be once again an age of crisis.

The Golden Age lost its gilt. Nevertheless, it had begun, indeed it had largely achieved the most dramatic, rapid and profound revolution in human affairs of which history has record. To this we must now turn.

CHAPTER TEN
The Social Revolution 1945–1990

LILY: My grandmother'd tell us things about the Depression. You can read about it too.

ROY: They're always tellin' us that we should be glad we got food and all that, 'cause back in the Thirties they used to tell us people were starving and got no jobs and all that stuff.

* * *

BUCKY: I never had a Depression, so it don't bother me really.

ROY: From what you hear, you'd hate to live in that time.

BUCKY: Well, I ain't livin' in that time.

– Studs Terkel, *Hard Times* (1970, pp. 22–23)

When [General de Gaulle] took power there were a million television sets in France . . . When he left there were ten million . . . The state is always a show-biz affair. But yesterday's theatre-state was a very different matter from the TV-state that exists today.

– Regis Debray (1994, p. 34)

I

When people face what nothing in their past has prepared them for they grope for words to name the unknown, even when they can neither define nor understand it. Some time in the third quarter of the century we can see this process at work among the intellectuals of the West. The keyword was the small preposition 'after', generally used in its latinate form 'post' as a prefix to any of the numerous terms which had, for some generations, been used to mark out the mental territory of twentieth-century life. The world, or its relevant aspects, became post-industrial, post-imperial, post-modern, post-structuralist, post-Marxist, post-Guten-berg, or whatever. Like funerals, these prefixes took official recognition of death without implying any consensus or indeed certainty about the nature of life after death. In this way the greatest and most dramatic, rapid and universal social transformation in human history entered the consciousness of reflective minds who lived through it. This transforma-tion is the subject of the present chapter.

The novelty of this transformation lies both in its extraordinary speed and in its universality. True, the developed parts of the world, i.e. for practical purposes the central and western parts of Europe and North America, plus a thin layer of the cosmopolitan rich and mighty elsewhere, had long lived in a world of constant change, technological transformation and cultural innovation. For them the revolution of global society meant an acceleration or intensification of movement to which they were already accustomed in principle. After all, New Yorkers of the mid-1930s already looked up to a skyscraper, the Empire State Building (1934), whose height was not exceeded until the 1970s, and then only by a modest thirty metres or so. It took a while to notice, and even longer to take the measure of, the transformation of quantitative material growth into the qualitative upheavals of life, even in these parts of the world. But for most of the globe the changes were both sudden and seismic. For 80 per cent of humanity the Middle Ages ended suddenly in the 1950s; or perhaps better still, they were *felt* to end in the 1960s.

In many ways those who actually lived through these transformations on the spot did not grasp their full extent, since they experienced them incrementally, or as changes in the lives of individuals which, however dramatic, are not conceived as permanent revolutions. Why should the decision of country folk to look for work in the city imply in their minds any more lasting transformation than joining the armed forces or some branch of the war economy did for British or German men and women in the two world wars? They did not intend to change their way of life for good, even if it turned out that they did. It is those who see them from outside, re-visiting the scenes of such transformations at intervals, who recognize how much has changed. How utterly different, for instance, the Valencia of the early 1980s was from the same city and region in the early 1950s, when the present writer had last seen that part of Spain. How disoriented a Sicilian peasant Rip Van Winkle felt – actually, a local bandit absent in jail for a couple of decades from the mid-1950s – when he returned to the environs of Palermo which had in the meantime become unrecognizable by urban real-estate development. 'Where once there were vineyards, now there are *palazzi*', he told me, head-shaking in disbelief. Indeed, the speed of change was such that historical time could be measured in even shorter intervals. Less than ten years (1962–71) separated a Cuzco where, outside the confines of the city, most Indian men still wore traditional costume from a Cuzco where a substantial proportion of them already wore *cholo*, i.e. European clothes. At the end of the 1970s stall holders in the food-market of a Mexican village already figured out their customers' costs on small Japanese pocket calculators, unknown there at the start of the decade.

There is no way in which readers not old and mobile enough to have seen history move in this manner since 1950, can expect to duplicate these experiences, although since the 1960s, when young westerners discovered that travel to Third World countries was both feasible and fashionable, all it has taken to watch global transformation is an open pair of eyes. In any case, historians cannot remain content with images and anecdotes, however significant. They need to specify and to count.

The most dramatic and far-reaching social change of the second half of this century, and the one which cuts us off for ever from the world of the past, is the death of the peasantry. For since the neolithic era most human beings had lived off the land and its livestock or harvested the sea as fishers. With the exception of Britain, peasants and farmers remained a massive part of the occupied population even in industrialized countries until well into the twentieth century. So much so that in the present writer's student days, the 1930s, the refusal of the peasantry to fade away was still currently used as an argument against Karl Marx's prediction that they would. After all, on the eve of the Second World War, there was only one industrial country, in addition to Britain, where agriculture and fisheries employed less than 20 per cent of the population, namely Belgium. Even in Germany and the USA, the greatest industrial economies, where the agricultural population had indeed been declining steadily, it still amounted to roughly a quarter; in France, Sweden and Austria it was still between 35 and 40 per cent. As for backward agrarian countries – say, in Europe, Bulgaria or Rumania – something like four out of every five inhabitants worked on the land.

Yet consider what happened in the third quarter of the century. It is perhaps not too surprising that by the early 1980s less than three out of every 100 Britons or Belgians were in agriculture, so that the average Briton was far more likely in the course of everyday life to encounter a person who had once farmed in India or Bangladesh than one who actually farmed in the United Kingdom. The farming population of the USA had fallen to the same percentage, but, given its long-term steep decline, this was less astonishing than the fact that this tiny fraction of the labour force was in a position to flood the USA and the world with untold quantities of food. What few would have expected in the 1940s was that by the early 1980s *no* country west of the 'Iron curtain' borders had more than 10 per cent of its population engaged in farming, except the Irish Republic (which was only a little above this figure), and the Iberian states. But the very fact that in Spain and Portugal people in agriculture, who had formed just under half the population in 1950, were reduced to 14.5 per cent and 17.6 per cent respectively thirty years later speaks for itself. The Spanish peasantry was halved in the twenty years after 1950, the Portuguese in the twenty years after 1960 (ILO, 1990, Table 2A; FAO, 1989).

These are spectacular figures. In Japan, for instance, farmers were reduced from 52.4 per cent of the people in 1947 to 9 per cent in 1985, i.e. between the time that a young soldier returned from the battles of the Second World War and the time he retired from his subsequent civilian career. In Finland – to take an actual life-history known to the writer – a girl born as a farmer's daughter and who became a farmer's working wife in her first marriage, could, before she had got far into middle age, have transformed herself into a cosmopolitan intellectual and political figure. But then, in 1940 when her father died in the winter war against Russia, leaving mother and infant on the family holding, 57 per cent of Finns were farmers and foresters. By the time she was forty-five less than 10 per cent were. What is more natural than that, under such circumstances, Finns should begin on farms and end in very different circumstances?

Yet if Marx's prediction that industrialization would eliminate the peasantry was at last evidently coming true in countries of headlong industrialization, the really extraordinary development was the decline of the farming population in countries whose obvious lack of such development the United Nations tried to disguise by a variety of euphemisms for the words 'backward' and 'poor'. At the very moment when hopeful young leftists were quoting MaoTse-tung's strategy for the triumph of revolution by mobilizing the countless rural millions against the encircled urban strongholds of the status quo, these millions were abandoning their villages and moving into the cities themselves. In Latin America the percentage of peasants halved in twenty years in Colombia (1951–73), in Mexico (1960–80) and – almost – in Brazil (1960–1980). It fell by two thirds, or almost two thirds, in the Dominican Republic (1960–81), Venezuela (1961–81) and Jamaica (1953–81). All these – except Venezuela – were countries in which at the end of the Second World War peasants had formed half, or an absolute majority of, the occupied population. But as early as the 1970s there was, in Latin America – outside the mini-states of the central American landstrip and Haiti – *no* country in which peasants were not a minority. The situation was similar in the countries of western Islam. Algeria slimmed its agriculturals from 75 per cent of the population to 20 per cent; Tunisia from 68 per cent to 23 per cent in just over thirty years Morocco, less dramatically, lost its peasant majority in ten (1971–82). Syria and Iraq still had about half their people on the land in the mid–1950s. Within about twenty years the first had halved this percentage, the second reduced it to less than one third. Iran dropped from about 55 per cent of peasants in the mid-1950s to 29 per cent in the mid-1980s.

Meanwhile, of course, the peasants of agrarian Europe stopped tilling the land. By the 1980s even the ancient strongholds of peasant agriculture in the east and south-east of the continent had no more than a third or so of their labour force in farming (Romania, Poland, Yugoslavia, Greece), and some had considerably less, notably Bulgaria (16.5 per cent in 1985). Only one peasant stronghold remained in or around the neighbourhood of Europe and the Middle East – Turkey, where the peasantry declined, but, in the mid-1980s, still remained an absolute majority.

Only three regions of the globe remained essentially dominated by their villages and fields: sub-Saharan Africa, South and continental South-east Asia, and China. In these regions alone was it still possible to find countries which the decline of the cultivators had apparently passed by – where those who grew crops and looked after animals remained throughout the stormy decades a steady proportion of the population – over 90 per cent in Nepal, about 70 per cent in Liberia, about 60 per cent in Ghana, or even – a somewhat surprising fact – 70 per cent or so in India through the twenty-five years after independence, and barely less (66.4 per cent) even in 1981. Admittedly these regions of peasant dominance still represented half the human race at the end of our period. However, even they were crumbling at the edges under the pressures of economic development. The solid peasant block of India was surrounded by countries whose farming populations were visibly declining quite fast: Pakistan, Bangladesh and Sri Lanka, where peasants had long ceased to be a majority; as they had, by the 1980s, in Malaysia, the Philippines and Indonesia and, of course, in the new industrial states of East Asia, Taiwan and South Korea, which had more than 60 per cent of its people in the fields as recently as 1961. Moreover in Africa the peasant predominance of several southern countries was a Bantustan illusion. Farming, mostly conducted by the women, was the visible side of an economy which actually depended largely on the remittances of male migrant labour to the white cities and mines in the south.

The strange thing about this massive and silent exodus from the land in the greater part of the world's land mass and even more of its islands* is that it was only partly due to agricultural progress, at least in the former peasant areas. As we have seen (see chapter 9), the developed industrial countries with one or two exceptions, also transformed themselves into the major producers of agricultural goods for the world market, and they did so while reducing their actual farming population to a steadily diminishing, and sometimes an absurdly tiny percentage of their people. This was plainly achieved by an extraordinary spurt in capital-intensive productivity per head of the agriculturists. Its most immediately visible aspect was the sheer quantity of machinery which the farmer in rich and developed countries now had at his (or her) disposal and which realized the great dreams of plenty through mechanized agriculture that inspired all those symbolic bare-chested tractor-drivers in the propaganda photos of the young Soviet republic, and which Soviet agriculture so signally failed to live up to. Less visible, but equally significant, were the increasingly impressive achievements of agricultural chemistry, selective breeding and bio-technology. Under these conditions farming simply no longer needed the numbers of hands and arms without which, in pre-technological days, a harvest could not be got in, nor indeed the number of regular farm families and their permanent servants. And where they were needed, modern transport made it unnecessary to keep them in the country. Thus in the 1970s sheep farmers in Perthshire (Scotland) found it cost-effective to import expert specialist shearers from New Zealand for the (short) local shearing season which, naturally, did not coincide with that in the southern hemisphere.

In the poor regions of the world the agricultural revolution was not absent, though it was patchier. Indeed, but for irrigation and the input of *science* through the so-called 'green revolution',† controversial though the long-term consequences of both may be, large parts of South and South-east Asia would have been unable to feed a rapidly multiplying population. Yet, on the whole, the countries of the Third World, and parts of the (formerly or still socialist) Second World, no longer fed themselves, let alone produced the major exportable food surplus that might be expected from agrarian countries. At best they were encouraged to concentrate on specialized export crops for the market of the developed world, while

* About the three-fifths of the land area of the globe, omitting the uninhabited continent of Antarctica.

† The systematic introduction in parts of the Third World of new high-yielding crop varieties grown by methods specifically suited to them. Mainly since the 1960s.

their peasants, when not buying the dumped surpluses of export food from the North, went on hoeing and ploughing in the old, labour-intensive manner. There were no good reasons why they should have left an agriculture which needed their labour, except perhaps the population explosion which might make land scarcer. But the regions out of which the peasants flooded were often, as in Latin America, quite thinly settled and tended to have open frontiers to which a small proportion of the countrymen migrated as squatters and free settlers, often, as in Colombia and Peru, providing the political base for local guerrilla movements. Conversely, the Asian regions in which the peasantry maintained itself best was perhaps the most densely settled zone in the world with densities per square mile ranging from 250 to 2,000 (the average for South America is 41.5).

When the land empties the cities fill up. The world of the second half of the twentieth century became urbanized as never before. By the mid-1980s 42 per cent of its population were urban, and, but for the weight of the enormous rural populations of China and India, which kept three quarters of Asians countrymen, it would have been a majority (Population, 1984, p. 214). But even in the rural heartlands people shifted from country to city, and especially to the great city. Between 1960 and 1980 the urban population of Kenya doubled, though in 1980 it had only reached 14.2 per cent; but almost six out of every ten townsmen now lived in Nairobi, whereas twenty years earlier only four out of ten had done so. In Asia the multi-million city mushroomed, generally a capital. Seoul, Teheran, Karachi, Jakarta, Manila, New Delhi, Bangkok, all had between roughly 5 and 8.5 million inhabitants in 1980 and were expected to have between 10 and 13.5 million in the year 2000. In 1950 not one of them (except Jakarta) had more than about one-and-a-half millions each (World Resources, 1986). Indeed, by far the most gigantic urban agglomerations at the end of the 1980s were to be found in the Third World: Cairo, Mexico City, São Paulo and Shanghai, whose populations were counted in eight figures. For, paradoxically, while the developed world remained far more urbanized than the poor world (except for parts of Latin America and the Islamic zone), its own giant cities were dissolving. They had reached their peak in the early twentieth century, before the flight to suburbs and satellite out-of-town communities gained speed, and the old city centres became hollow shells at night when the workers, shoppers and seekers after entertainment had gone home. While Mexico City almost quintupled in the thirty years after 1950, New York, London and Paris slowly drifted out of, or to the lower edges of, the big league of cities.

Yet, in a curious way, both the old and the new worlds converged. The typical 'great city' of the developed world became a region of linked urban settlements, generally focused on some central area or areas of business or administration recognizable from the air as a sort of mountain range of high-rise buildings and skyscrapers, except where (as in Paris) such building was not permitted.* Their interconnection, or perhaps the breakdown of private motor-traffic under the pressure of massive automobile ownership, was demonstrated, from the 1960s, by a new revolution in public transport. Never, since the first construction of urban street-car and underground railway systems in the late nineteenth century, had so many new subway and rapid suburban transit systems been built in so many places: from Vienna to San Francisco, from Seoul to Mexico. At the same time decentralization spread, as most component communities or suburban complexes developed their own shopping and leisure services, notably through the (American-pioneered) peripheral 'shopping malls'.

On the other hand the Third-World city, though also bound together by (usually obsolete and inadequate) public transport systems and a myriad of broken-down private buses and 'collective taxis', could not but be scattered and unstructured, if only because there is no way in which agglomerations to ten to twenty million people cannot be so, especially if much of their component settlements have begun life as low-built shanty-towns, as like as not established by groups of squatters on some unused open space. The inhabitants of such cities may have to spend several hours a day travelling to and from employment (for regular work is precious), and they may be willing to make pilgrimages of equal length to places of public ritual like Rio de Janeiro's Maracaná Stadium (two hundred thousand seats), where Cariocas worship the divinities of *futebol*, but in fact, both Old and New World conurbations were increasingly collections of nominally – or, in the case of the West, often formally – autonomous communities, though in the rich West, at least on the outskirts, they contained far more green spaces than in the poor or overcrowded East and South. While in the slums and shanty-towns humans lived in symbiosis with the hardy rat and roach, the strange no-man's land between town and country that surrounded what was left of

---

* Such high-rise centres, the natural consequence of high land-prices in such districts, had been extremely unusual before 1950. New York was virtually unique. They became common from the 1960s, even low-slung, decentralized cities like Los Angeles, acquiring such a 'downtown'.

the 'inner cities' of the developed world was colonized by the fauna of the wilds: weasel, fox and raccoon.

II

Almost as dramatic as the decline and fall of the peasantry, and much more universal, was the rise of the occupations which required secondary and higher education. Universal primary education, i.e. basic literacy, was indeed the aspiration of virtually all governments, so much so that by the late 1980s only the most honest or helpless states admitted to having as many as half their population illiterate, and only ten – all but Afghanistan in Africa – were prepared to concede that less than 20 per cent of their population could read and write. And literacy made striking progress, not least in the revolutionary countries under communist rule whose achievements in this respect were indeed most impressive, even when the claims to have 'liquidated' illiteracy within some implausibly short spell of time were sometimes optimistic. Yet, whether or not mass literacy was general, the demand for places in secondary and especially in higher education multiplied at an extraordinary rate. And so did the numbers of people who had undergone it or were undergoing it.

This explosion of numbers was particularly dramatic in university education, hitherto so unusual as to be demographically negligible, except in the USA. Before the Second World War even Germany, France and Britain, three of the largest, most developed, and educated countries with a total population of 150 millions, contained no more than 150,000 or so university students between them, or one tenth of one per cent of their joint populations. Yet by the late 1980s students were counted in millions in France, the Federal Republic of Germany, Italy, Spain and the USSR (to name only European countries), not to mention Brazil, India, Mexico, the Philippines and, of course, the USA, which had been the pioneer of mass college education. By this time in educationally ambitious countries, students formed upwards of 2.5 per cent of the *total* population – men, women and children – or even, in exceptional cases, above 3 per cent. It was not uncommon for 20 per cent of the twenty to twenty-four age-group to be in formal education. Even the academically most conservative countries – Britain and Switzerland – had risen to 1.5 per cent. Moreover some of the relatively largest student bodies were to be found in economically far from advanced countries: Ecuador (3.2 per cent), the Philippines (2.7 per cent) or Peru (2 per cent).

All this was not merely new, but quite sudden. 'The most striking fact from the study of Latin American university students in the middle 1960s is that they were so few in number' (Liebman, Walker, Glazer, 1972, p. 35), US scholars wrote during that decade, convinced that this echoed the basic elitist-European model of higher education south of the Rio Grande. And this in spite of the fact that their numbers had been growing by about 8 per cent a year. In fact, not until the 1960s was it undeniable that students had become, both socially and politically, a far more important force than ever before, for in 1968 the worldwide uprisings of student radicalism spoke louder than statistics. But these also became impossible to overlook. Between 1960 and 1980, to stick to well-schooled Europe, the number of students tripled or quadrupled in the most typical country, except where it multiplied by four to five, as in Federal Germany, Ireland and Greece; by five to seven, as in Finland, Iceland, Sweden and Italy; and seven to nine-fold, as in Spain and Norway (Burloiu, Unesco, 1983, pp. 62–63). At first sight it seems curious that, on the whole, the rush into the universities was less marked in the socialist countries, in spite of their pride in mass education, though the case of Mao's China is aberrant. The Great Helmsman virtually abolished all higher education during the Cultural Revolution (1966–76). As the troubles of the socialist systems grew in the 1970s and 1980s, they fell further behind the West. Hungary and Czechoslovakia had a smaller percentage of their populations in higher education than practically all other European states.

Does it seem quite as curious at second sight? Perhaps not. The extraordinary growth of higher education which, by the early 1980s, produced at least seven countries with more than 100,000 *teachers* at university level, was due to consumer pressure, to which socialist systems were not geared to respond. It was obvious to planners and governments that the modern economy required far more administrators, teachers and technical experts than in the past, who had to be trained somewhere – and universities or similar institutions of higher education had, by ancient tradition, functioned largely as training-schools for public service and the specialised professions. But while this, as well as a general democratic bias, justified a substantial expansion of higher education, the scale of the student explosion far exceeded what rational planning might have envisaged.

In fact, where families had the choice and the chance, they rushed their children into higher education, because it was by far the best way of winning them a better income, but, above all, higher social status. Of the Latin American students interviewed by US investigators in the mid-1960s in various countries, between 79 and 95 per cent were convinced that study would put them into a higher social class within ten years. Only between 21 and 38 per cent felt that it would win them a much higher economic status than their family's (Liebman, Walker, Glazer, 1972). In fact, of course, it would almost certainly give them a higher income than non-graduates, and, in countries of small education, where the certificate of graduation guaranteed a place in the state machine, and therefore power, influence, and financial extortion, it could be the key to real wealth. Most students, of course, came from families that were better off than most – how otherwise could they have afforded to pay for some years' study by young adults of working age? – but not necessarily rich. Often the sacrifices their parents made were real. The Korean educational miracle, it was said, rested on the carcases of cows sold by small farmers to push their children into the honoured and privileged ranks of scholars. (In eight years – 1975–83 – Korean students rose from 0.8 per cent to almost 3 per cent of the population.) No one who has the experience of being the first in his family to go to university full-time will have any difficulty in understanding their motivations. The great world boom made it possible for countless modest families – white-collar employees and public officials, shopkeepers and small business-men, farmers, in the West, even prosperous skilled workers – to afford full-time study for their children. The Western welfare state, starting with the US subsidies for ex-service students after 1945, provided substantial student aid in one way or another, though most students still expected a distinctly unluxurious life. In democratic and egalitarian countries, something like a right for graduates of secondary schools to move to higher things was often accepted, to the point where in France selective admission to a state university was still regarded as constitu-tionally impossible in 1991. (No such right existed in the socialist countries.) As young men and women surged into higher education, governments – for, outside the USA, Japan and a few other countries, universities were overwhelmingly public rather than private institutions – multiplied new establishments to take them in, especially in the 1970s when the number of the world's universities more than doubled.* And, of course, the newly independent ex-colonies which multiplied during the 1960s insisted on their own institutions of higher education as a symbol of independence, as they insisted on a flag, an airline or an army.

* Here again, the socialist world was under smaller pressure.

These masses of young men and women and their teachers, counted in millions or at least in hundreds of thousands in all except the very smallest or the exceptionally backward states, increasingly concentrated in large and often isolated campuses or 'university cities', were a novel factor in both culture and politics. They were transnational, moving and communicating ideas and experiences across frontiers with ease and speed, and were probably more at ease than governments with the technology of communications. As the 1960s revealed, they were not only politically radical and explosive, but uniquely effective in giving national, even international, expression to political and social discontent. In dictatorial countries they usually provided the *only* bodies of citizens capable of collective political action, and it is far from insignificant that, while other Latin American student populations swelled, their number in the military dictator Pinochet's Chile after 1973 was made to drop: from 1.5 to 1.1 per cent of the population. And if there was a single moment in the golden years after 1945 which corresponds to the world simultaneous upheaval of which the revolutionaries had dreamed after 1917, it was surely 1968, when students rebelled from the USA and Mexico in the West to socialist Poland, Czechoslovakia and Yugoslavia, largely stimulated by the extraordinary outbreak of May 1968 in Paris, epicentre of a Continent-wide student uprising. It was far from revolution, though it was considerably more than the 'psychodrama' or 'street theatre' which unsympathetic senior observers like Raymond Aron dismissed. After all, 1968 ended the era of General de Gaulle in France, the era of Democratic presidents in the USA, the hopes of liberal communism in communist central Europe and (through the silent after-effects of the student massacre of Tlatelolco) it marked the beginning of a new era in Mexican politics.

The reason why 1968 (with its prolongation into 1969 and 1970) was not the revolution, and never looked as though it would or could be, was that students alone, however numerous and mobilizable, could not make one alone. Their political effectiveness rested on their ability to act as signals and detonators for larger but less easily combustible groups. Since the 1960s students have sometimes succeeded in doing so. They sparked off enormous working-class strike-waves in France and Italy in 1968 and 1969, but, after twenty years of unparalleled improvement for wage-earners in economies of full employment, revolution was the last thing in the minds of the proletarian masses. Not until the 1980s – and then in non-democratic countries as widely different as China, South Korea and Czechoslovakia – did student rebellions look like realizing their potential for detonating revolution, or at least to force governments to treat them like a serious public danger by massacring them on a large scale, as in Tiananmen Square, Beijing. After the failure of the great dreams of 1968, some student radicals did indeed attempt to make revolution on their own by small-group terrorism, but, though such movements received a great deal of publicity (thus achieving at least one of their major objectives), they rarely had any serious political impact. Where they threatened to have, they were fairly rapidly suppressed once the authorities decided to act: in the 1970s with unexampled brutality and systematic torture in 'dirty wars' in South America, with bribery and backstairs negotiations in Italy. The only significant survivors of these initiatives in the last decade of the century were the Basque nationalist terrorist ETA and the theoretically communist peasant guerrilla *Sendero Luminoso* in Peru, an undesired gift of the staff and students of the University of Ayacucho to their countrymen.

Nevertheless, this leaves us with a slightly puzzling question: why did the movement of this new social group of students, alone among the new or old social actors of the golden era, opt for a radicalism of the Left? For (if we leave aside rebels against the communist regimes) even nationalist student movements tended to stitch the red badge of Marx, Lenin or Mao somewhere on their banners until the 1980s.

In some ways this inevitably takes us well beyond social stratification, for the new student body was, by definition, also an age-group of youth, i.e. a temporary halting place on the human passage through life, and it also contained a rapidly growing, and disproportionately large, component of women, suspended between the impermanence of their age and the permanence of their sex. Later we shall consider the development of special youth cultures, which linked students to others of their generation, and the new women's consciousness, which also reached out beyond the universities. Youth groups, not yet settled in established adulthood, are the traditional locus for high spirits, riot and disorder, as even medieval university rectors knew, and revolutionary passions are more common at eighteen than at thirty-five, as generations of bourgeois parents in Europe had told generations of sceptical sons and (later) daughters. In fact, this belief was so ingrained in Western cultures that the Establishment in several countries – perhaps mostly Latin ones on either side of the Atlantic – entirely discounted student militancy, even to the point of armed guerrilla struggle, in the younger generation. If anything, it was a sign of a spirited rather than a torpid personality. Students from San Marcos in Lima (Peru), as the joke went, 'did their revolutionary service' in some ultra-Maoist sect before settling down to a solid and unpolitical middle-class profession – while such a thing as normal life still continued in that unhappy country (Lynch, 1990). Mexican students soon learned *a.* that the state and party apparatus essentially recruited its cadres from the universities, and *b.* that the more revolutionary they were as students, the better the jobs they were likely to be offered after graduation. But even in respectable France, the ex-Maoist of the early 1970s who made a brilliant career in the state service became familiar.

Nevertheless, this does not explain why bodies of young people who were obviously on the way to a far better future than their parents, or, at any rate, than most non-students, should have – with rare exceptions – been attracted by political radicalism.* Indeed, a high proportion of them probably were not, preferring to concentrate on getting the degrees which guaranteed their future, though they were less noticeable than the smaller – but still numerically large – number of the politically active, especially when these dominated the visible parts of university life, by means of public demonstrations ranging from graffiti- and poster-filled walls to meetings, marches and pickets. Still, even this degree of Left-wing radicalization was new in the developed countries, though not in the backward and dependent ones. Before the Second World War, the great majority of students in central and western Europe and North America had been non-political or Right-wing.

The sheer explosion of student numbers suggests a possible answer. The number of French students at the end of the Second World War was less than 100,000. By 1960 it was over 200,000 and within the next ten years it tripled to 651,000 (Flora, p. 582; *Deux Ans*, 1990, p. 4). (During these ten years the number of students in the humanities multiplied by almost three-and-a-half, the number of students in the social sciences by four.) The most immediate and direct consequence was an inevitable tension between these masses of mainly first-generation students now suddenly pouring into universities, and institutions which were neither physically nor organizationally and intellectually prepared for such an influx. Moreover, as a growing proportion of the age-group had the chance to study – in France it was 4 per cent in 1950, 15½ per cent in 1970 – going to university ceased to be an exceptional privilege which was

---

* Among these rare exceptions we note Russia where, unlike all the other communist countries of Eastern Europe and China, students as a group were neither prominent nor influential in the years of the break-up of communism. The democratic movement in Russia has been described as 'a revolution of the forty-year-olds' watched by a de-politicized and demoralized youth (Riordan, 1991).

its own reward, and the constraints it imposed on young (and generally impecunious) adults were more resented. Resentment of one kind of authority, the university's, easily broadened out into resentment of any authority, and therefore (in the West) inclined students to the Left. It is not at all surprising that the 1960s became the decade of student unrest *par excellence*. Special reasons intensified it in this or that country – hostility to the Vietnam War in the USA (i.e. to military service), racial resentment in Peru (Lynch, 1990, pp. 32–37) – but the phenomenon was too general to need special ad hoc explanations.

And yet, in a more general, less definable, sense this new mass of students stood, as it were, at an awkward angle to the rest of society. Unlike other and older-established classes or social groupings, they had no established place in it or pattern of relations to it – for how could the new student armies be compared to the relatively tiny pre-war bodies (forty thousand in well-educated 1939 Germany) – who were merely a junior phase of middle-class life? In many ways the very existence of the new masses implied questions about the society that had engendered them; and from questions to criticism is but one step. How did they fit into it? What sort of society was it? The very youth of the student body, the very width of the generation gap between these children of the post-war world and the parents who remembered and compared, made their questions more urgent, their attitude more critical. For the discontents of the young were not blanketed by the consciousness of living through times of staggering improvement, far better times than their parents had ever expected to see. The new times were the only ones that young men and women who went to college knew. On the contrary, they felt things could be different and better, even when they did not quite know how. Their elders, used to, or at least remembering, times of hardship and unemployment, did not expect mass radical mobilizations at a time when, surely, the economic incentive for them in the developed countries was less than ever before. But the explosion of student unrest erupted at the very peak of the great global boom, because it was directed, however vaguely and blindly, against what they saw as characteristic of *this* society, not against the fact that the older society might not have improved quite enough. But, paradoxically, the fact that the impetus for the new radicalism came from groups unaffected by economic discontent, stimulated even the groups used to mobilize on an economic basis to discover that, after all, they could ask for far more from the new society than they had imagined. The most immediate effect of the European student rebellion was a wave of working-class strikes for higher wages and better conditions.

III

Unlike countryside and college populations, the industrial working classes experienced no demographic earthquakes, until in the 1980s they began to decline quite noticeably. This is surprising, considering how much talk there was, even from the 1950s on, about a 'post-industrial society'; considering how revolutionary, indeed, were the technical transformations of production, most of which economized, by-passed or eliminated human labour; and considering how obviously the political parties and movements which based themselves on the working class were in crisis after 1970 or thereabouts. Yet the widespread impression that somehow the old industrial working class was dying out was statistically mistaken, at least on a global scale.

With the one major exception of the USA, where the percentage of people employed in manufacturing began to decline from 1965, and very obviously after 1970, the industrial working classes remained pretty stable throughout the golden years even in the old industrial countries,* at about one third of the occupied population. In fact in eight out of twenty-one OECD countries – the the club of the most developed – it continued to rise between 1960 and 1980. Naturally it rose in the newly industrialized parts of (non-communist) Europe, and then remained stable until 1980, while in Japan it increased dramatically, remaining fairly stable in the 1970s and 1980s. In the communist countries undergoing rapid industrialization, notably in Eastern Europe, proletarians multiplied faster than ever, as indeed they did in those parts of the Third World which entered on their own industrialization – Brazil, Mexico, India, Korea and others. In short, at the end of the golden years there were certainly far more workers in the world in absolute figures, and almost certainly a higher proportion of manufacturing employees in the global population, than ever before. With very few exceptions, such as Britain, Belgium and the USA, in 1970 workers probably formed a larger proportion of the total occupied population than they had in the 1890s in all countries where vast mass socialist parties had suddenly emerged at the end of the nineteenth century on the basis of proletarian consciousness. Only in the 1980s and 1990s can we detect signs of a major contraction of the working class.

The illusion of a collapsing working class was due to the shifts within it, and within the process of production, rather than to demographic haemorrhage. The old industries of the nineteenth and early twentieth

---

* Belgium, (West) Germany, Britain, France, Sweden, Switzerland.

centuries declined, and their very visibility in the past, when they had often symbolized 'industry' as a whole, made their decline particularly dramatic. Coal-miners, once counted in hundreds of thousands, in Britain even in millions, became less common than university graduates. The US steel industry now employed fewer people than McDonald's hamburger restaurants. Even when such traditional industries did not disappear, they shifted from old to new industrial countries. Textiles, clothing and footwear migrated massively. The number of people employed in the textile and clothing industries within the German Federal Republic fell by more than half between 1960 and 1984, but in the early 1980s for every 100 German workers the German clothing industry employed thirty-four workers abroad. Even in 1966 it had been less than three. Iron and steel and ship-building virtually disappeared from the lands of early industrialization, but surfaced in Brazil and Korea, in Spain, Poland and Romania. Old industrial areas became 'rustbelts' – a term invented in the USA in the 1970s – or even entire countries identified with an earlier phase of industry, such as Great Britain, were largely de-industrialized, turning into living or dying museums of a vanished past, which entrepreneurs exploited, with some success, as tourist attractions. As the last coal-mines disappeared from South Wales, where over 130,000 had earned their living as miners at the start of the Second World War, surviving elderly men descended into dead pits to demonstrate to tourist parties what they had once done down there in the eternal darkness.

And even when new industries replaced old ones, they were not the same industries, often enough not in the same places, and more likely than not, differently structured. The jargon of the 1980s which talked about 'Post-Fordism' suggests as much.* The huge mass-production plant built around the conveyor belt, the city or region dominated by a single industry, as Detroit or Turin were by automobiles; the local working class united, welded together by residential segregation and workplace, into a multi-headed unity – these seemed to have been characteristics of the classic industrial era. It was an unrealistic image, but represented more than a symbolic truth. Where the old industrial structures flourished in the late twentieth century, as in newly industrializing Third World countries or socialist industrial economies, caught in their (deliberately) Fordist time-warp, the similarities to the inter-war, or

* The phrase, which emerged from attempts to rethink Left-wing analyses of industrial society, was popularized by Alain Lipietz, who took the term 'Fordism' from the Italian Marxist thinker Gramsci.

even the pre-1914 Western industrial world were evident – even to the emergence of powerful labour organizations in great industrial centres based on big auto-works (as in São Paulo), or shipyards (as in Gdansk). Just so the United Auto Workers' and Steel Workers' unions had emerged from the great strikes of 1937 in what is now the rustbelt of the US Middle West. Conversely, while the large mass-production firm and the large plant survived into the 1990s, though automated and altered, the new industries *were* very different. The classic 'post-Fordist' industrial regions – for instance the Veneto, Emilia-Romagna and Tuscany in North and Central Italy – lacked the great industrial cities, the dominant firms, the huge plants. They were mosaics or networks of enterprises ranging from the cottage workshop to the modest (but high-tech) manufactory, spread across town and country. How would the city of Bologna like it, its mayor was asked by one of the largest firms in Europe, if one of its major factories were to be sited there? The mayor* politely fended off the suggestion. His city and region, prosperous, sophisticated and, as it happens, communist, knew how to handle the economic and social situation of the new agro-industrial economy: let Turin and Milan cope with the problems of their kinds of industrial city.

Of course eventually – and very plainly in the 1980s – the working classes visibly became the victims of the new technologies; especially the unskilled and semi-skilled men and women of the mass production lines, who could most easily be replaced by automated machinery. Or rather, as the great global boom decades of the 1950s and 1960s gave way to an era of world economic difficulties in the 1970s and 1980s, industry no longer expanded at the old rate which had swelled workforces even as production became more labour-saving (see chapter 14). The economic crises of the early 1980s recreated mass unemployment for the first time in forty years, at all events in Europe.

In some ill-advised countries the crisis produced a veritable industrial holocaust. Britain lost 25 per cent of its manufacturing industry in 1980–84. Between 1973 and the late 1980s the total number employed in manufacturing in the six old-industrial countries of Europe fell by seven millions, or about a quarter, about half of which was lost between 1979 and 1983. By the late 1980s, as the working classes in the old industrial countries eroded and the new ones rose, the workforce employed in manufactures settled down at about a quarter of all civilian employment in all western developed regions, except the USA, where by that time it was well below 20 per cent (Bairoch, 1988). It was a long way from the

* He told me so himself.

old Marxist dream of populations gradually proletarianized by the development of industry until most people would be (manual) workers. Except in the rarest cases, of which Britain was the most notable, the industrial working class had always been a minority of the working population. Nevertheless, the apparent crisis of the working class and its movements, especially in the old industrial world, was patent long before there was – speaking globally – any question of a serious decline.

It was a crisis not of the class, but of its consciousness. At the end of the nineteenth century (see *Age of Empire*, chapter 5) the very miscellaneous and far from homogeneous populations who earned their living in the developed countries by selling their manual labour for wages learned to see themselves as a single working class, and to regard that fact as by far the most important thing about their situation as human beings in society. Or at least enough of them came to this conclusion to make parties and movements which appealed to them essentially as workers (as indicated by their very name – Labour Party, Parti Ouvrier, etc.) into huge political forces within a matter of a few years. They were, of course, united not only by wages and getting their hands dirty at work. They belonged, overwhelmingly, to the poor and the economically insecure, for, though the essential pillars of labour movements were far from destitution or pauperism, what they expected and got from life was modest, and well below what the middle classes expected. Indeed, the economy of consumer durables for the masses had passed them by everywhere before 1914, and everywhere except North America and Australasia between the wars. A British communist organizer sent to the arms factories of wartime Coventry, as militant as they were prosperous, came back open-mouthed: 'Do you realize', he told his London friends, myself among them, 'that up there the comrades have *cars*?'

They were united also by massive social segregation, by separate lifestyles or even clothing, and by the constriction of life-chances which separated them from the socially more mobile, if economically also hard-pressed, white-collar strata. Workers' children did not expect to go, and rarely went, to university. Most of them did not expect to go to school at all after the minimum school-leaving age (usually fourteen). In the pre-war Netherlands 4 per cent of the ten to nineteen-year-olds went to secondary schools beyond this age, and in democratic Sweden and Denmark an even smaller proportion. Workers lived differently from others, with different expectations of life, in different places. As one of the earliest of their (British) university-educated sons put it in the 1950s, when this segregation was still fairly obvious: 'such people have their own recognizable styles of housing ... their houses are usually rented, not owned (Hoggart, 1958, p. 8).'*

They were united, finally, by the central element of their life, collectivity: the domination of 'us' over 'I'. What gave labour movements and parties their original strength was the justified conviction of workers that people such as they could not improve their lot by individual action, but only by collective action, preferably through organizations, whether by mutual aid, striking or voting. And, conversely, that the numbers and peculiar situation of manual wage-workers put collective action within their grasp. Where workers saw private escape-routes from their class, as in the USA, their class-consciousness, though far from absent, was less of a uniquely defining characteristic of their identity. But 'we' dominated 'I', not only for instrumental reasons, but because – with the major, and often tragic exception of the married working-class housewife, imprisoned behind her four walls – working-class life had to be largely public, because the private space was so inadequate. And even the housewife shared in the public life of market, street, and neighbouring parks. Children had to play on street or in parks. Young men and women had to dance and court outside. Men socialized in 'public houses'. Until the radio, which transformed the life of the housebound working-class woman between the wars – and then only in a few favoured countries – all forms of entertainment beyond the private party had to be public, and in poorer countries even television was, in its early years, something watched in some public space. From football match to political meeting or holiday outing, life was something experienced, for most pleasurable purposes, en masse.

In most respects this conscious working-class cohesiveness reached its peak, in older developed countries, at the end of the Second World War. During the golden decades almost all elements of it were undermined. The combination of secular boom, full employment and a society of genuine mass consumption utterly transformed the lives of working-class people in the developed countries, and continued to transform it. By the standards of their parents, and indeed, if old enough, by their own memories, they were no longer poor. Lives immeasurably more prosperous than any non-Americans or non-Australians had ever expected were privatised by both money technology and the logic of the market: television made it unnecessary to go to the football match, just as TV

---

* Cf also: 'The predominance of industry, with its abrupt division between workers and management, tends to encourage the different classes to live apart, so that a particular district of a town becomes a reservation or ghetto' (Allen, 1968, pp. 32–33).

and videos have made it unnecessary to go to the cinema, or telephones to gossip with friends on the piazza or at the market. Trade unionists or party members who had once turned up for branch meetings or public political occasions because, among other things, they were also a form of diversion or entertainment, could now think of more attractive ways of spending their time, unless abnormally militant. (Conversely, face-to-face contact ceased to be an effective form of electoral campaigning, although it continued out of tradition and in order to cheer up the increasingly untypical party activists.) Prosperity and privatisation broke up what poverty and collectivity in the public place had welded together.

It was not that workers became unrecognisable as such, although, strangely, as we shall see, the new independent youth culture (see p. 324 ff.) from the late 1950s on took its fashions in both clothes and music from the working-class young. It was rather that some sort of affluence was now within the reach of most, and the difference between the owner of a Volkswagen Beetle and the owner of a Mercedes was far less than that between the owner of any car and the owner of no car, especially if the more expensive cars were (in theory) available on monthly instalments. Workers, especially in the last years of youth before marriage and household expenses dominated the budget, could now be luxury spenders, and the industrialization of the couture and beauty business from the 1960s on immediately responded. Between the top and the bottom end of the high-tech luxury markets which now developed – e.g. between the most expensive Hasselblad camera and the cheapest Olympus or Nikon that produced results while conferring status – there was only a difference of degree. In any case, starting with television, entertainments hitherto only available as personal services to millionaires were now in the most modest of living-rooms. In short, full employment and a consumer society aimed at a genuine mass market placed most of the working class in the old developed countries, at least for part of their lives, well above the threshold below which their fathers, or they themselves, had once lived: where income is primarily spent on basic necessities.

Moreover, several significant developments widened the cracks between different sections of the working classes, though this did not become evident until the end of full employment, during the economic crisis of the 1970s and 1980s, and until the pressure of neo-liberalism on the welfare policies and 'corporatist' systems of industrial relations which had given substantial shelter to the weaker sections of the workers. For the top end of the working class – the skilled and supervisory – adjusted more easily to the era of modern high-tech production, * and their position was such that they could actually benefit from a free market, even as their less favoured brothers lost ground. Thus in Mrs Thatcher's Britain, admittedly an extreme case, as government and union protection was dismantled, the bottom fifth of the workers actually became worse off compared to the rest of the workers than they had been a century earlier. And as the top 10 per cent of workers, with gross earnings three times as high as those in the bottom tenth, congratulated themselves on their improvement, they were increasingly likely to reflect that, as national and local tax-payers, they were subsidizing what came, in the 1980s, to be called by the sinister term 'the underclass', who lived on the public welfare system which they themselves could, they hoped, do without except in emergencies. The old Victorian division between the 'respectable' and the 'unrespectable' poor revived, perhaps in a more embittered form, for in the glorious days of the global boom, when full employment seemed to take care of most of labour's material needs, welfare payments had been raised to generous levels which, in the new days of mass welfare demands, seemed to enable an army of the 'unrespectable' to live far better on 'welfare' than the old Victorian pauper 'residuum'. And far better than, in the opinion of hardworking tax-payers, they had a right to.

The skilled and respectable thus found themselves, perhaps for the first time, potential supporters of the political right,† all the more since the traditional labour and socialist organizations naturally remained committed to redistribution and welfare, especially as the numbers of those needing public protection grew. The Thatcher governments in Britain relied for their success essentially on the secession of skilled workers from Labour. Desegregation, or rather a shift in segregation, promoted this crumbling of the labouring block. Thus the skilled and upwardly mobile moved out of the inner cities – especially as industries moved into periphery and country, leaving the old solid inner-city working-class districts, or 'red belts', to be ghettoised or gentrified, while the new satellite towns or greenfield industries generated no single-class concentrations on the same scale. In the inner cities, public housing projects, once

* Thus in the USA 'craftsmen and foremen' declined from 16 per cent of the total occupied population to 13 per cent between 1950 and 1990, whereas 'laborers' declined from 31 per cent to 18 per cent in the same period.

† 'The socialism of redistribution, of the Welfare State . . . was dealt a hard blow with the economic crisis of the seventies. Important sectors of the middle class as well as sectors of the better-paid workers, broke their links with the alternatives of democratic socialism and lent their votes to form new majorities for conservative governments' (Programma 2000, 1990).

built for the solid core of the working class, indeed with a natural bias towards those able to pay rent regularly, now turned into settlements of the marginal, the socially problematic and welfare-dependent.

At the same time mass migration brought a phenomenon hitherto confined, at least since the end of the Habsburg Empire, only to the USA and to a lesser extent France: ethnic and racial diversification of the working class and its consequence, conflicts within it. The problem lay not so much in ethnic diversity, even though the immigration of people of a different colour, or (like North Africans in France) likely to be classified as such, brought out an always latent racism even in countries that had been regarded as immune to it, such as Italy and Sweden. The weakening of traditional socialist labour movements made this easier, since these had been passionately opposed to such discrimination, and thus damped down the more anti-social expression of racist feelings within their constituency. However, leaving pure racism aside, traditionally – and even in the nineteenth century – labour migration had rarely led to that direct competition between different ethnic groups which divides working classes, since each particular group of migrants tended to find its own niche or niches in the economy, which it then colonized or even monopolized. Immigrant Jews in most western countries moved en masse into the garment industry, but not into, say, motor manufacturing. To cite an even more specialized case, the staff of Indian restaurants in both London and New York, and no doubt wherever this form of Asian cultural expansion has reached outside the Indian subcontinent, was even in the 1990s primarily recruited from emigrants from one particular district of Bangladesh (Sylhet). Or else immigrant groups found themselves concentrated in particular districts or plants or workshops or grades of the same industry, leaving the rest to others. In such a 'segmented labour market' (to use the jargon term), solidarity between different ethnic groups of workers was easier to develop and maintain, since the groups did not compete, and variations in their conditions could not – or only rarely – be ascribed to the self-interest of other groups of workers. *

For a variety of reasons, among them the fact that immigration in postwar Western Europe was largely a state-sponsored response to labour shortage, the new immigrants entered the same labour market as the natives, and with the same rights, except where they were officially

---

* Northern Ireland, where Catholics were systematically pushed out of the skilled industrial occupations which increasingly became Protestant monopolies, is an exception.

segregated from them as a class of temporary and therefore inferior 'guest-workers'. Both cases generated tension. Men and women with formally inferior rights hardly saw their interests as identical with people enjoying superior status. Conversely, French or British workers, even when they did not mind working side by side and on the same terms with Moroccans, West Indians, Portuguese or Turks, were by no means so ready to see foreigners promoted above them, especially those regarded as collectively inferior to the national-born. Moreover, and for similar reasons, there were tensions between different groups of immigrants, even when all resented the natives' treatment of outsiders.

In short, whereas in the period when classic labour parties and movements had been formed all sections of the workers (unless divided by unusually insuperable national or religious barriers) could reasonably assume that the same policies, strategies and institutional changes would benefit each, this was no longer automatically the case. At the same time both the changes in production, the emergence of the 'two-thirds society' (see p. 340) and the changing, and increasingly fuzzy frontier between what was 'manual' and what was 'non-manual' work, diffused and dissolved the formerly clear outlines of 'the proletariat'.

IV

One major change which affected the working class, as well as most other parts of developed societies, was the strikingly greater part played in it by women; and notably – a new and revolutionary phenomenon – of married women. The change was indeed dramatic. In 1940 married women who lived with their husbands and worked for pay formed less than 14 per cent of the total female population of the USA. In 1980 they formed over half: the percentage just about doubled between 1950 and 1970. That women entered the labour market in growing numbers was not, of course, new. From the end of the nineteenth century on, office work and shops and certain kinds of services, e.g. telephone exchanges and the caring professions, were powerfully feminised, and these tertiary occupations expanded and swelled at the (relative and eventually absolute) expense of both primary and secondary ones, that is to say, agriculture and industry. In fact this rise of the tertiary sector was one of the most striking tendencies of the twentieth century. It is less easy to generalize about women in manufacturing industries. In the old industrial countries the labour-intensive industries in which women had been characteristically concentrated, such as textiles and clothing, were on the decline; but so, in the new rustbelt regions and countries, were the heavy and mechanical industries with their overwhelmingly masculine, not to say macho composition – mines, iron and steel, shipbuilding, car and trucks manufacture. On the other hand, in newly developing countries, and in the enclaves of manufacture developing in the Third World, labour-intensive industries thirsty for female labour (which was traditionally less well-paid and less rebellious than male hands) flourished. The share of women in the local workforce therefore rose, though the case of Mauritius where it jumped from about 20 per cent in the early 1970s to over 60 per cent in the mid-1980s is rather extreme. Whether it grew (but less than the service sector) or remained stable in the developed industrial countries depended on national circumstances. In practice the distinction between women in manufacture and in the tertiary sector was not significant, since the bulk of them in both were in subaltern positions, and several of the feminized service occupations, notably those in the public and social services, were strongly unionized.

Women also, and in strikingly growing numbers, entered higher education, which was now the most obvious entrance gate to the (senior) professions. Immediately after the Second World War they constituted between 15 and 30 per cent of all students in most of the developed countries, except for Finland – a beacon of female emancipation – where they already formed almost 43 per cent. Even in 1960 nowhere in Europe and North America did they provide half of the students, though Bulgaria – another, and less widely advertised pro-feminine country – already almost reached that figure. (The socialist states were on the whole quicker to foster women's study – the GDR outdistanced the Federal Republic – but otherwise their feminist record was patchy.) However, in 1980 half or more than half of all students were women in the USA, Canada and six socialist countries, headed by the GDR and Bulgaria, and in only four European countries did women by then constitute less than 40 per cent (Greece, Switzerland, Turkey and the UK). In a word, higher study was now as common among girls as among boys.

The mass entry of married women – i.e. largely mothers – into the labour market and the striking expansion of higher education formed the background, at least in the typical developed Western countries, to the impressive revival of feminist movements from the 1960s on. Indeed the women's movements are inexplicable without these developments. Since women in so many parts of Europe and North America had achieved the great aim of the vote and equal civic rights in the aftermath of the First World War and the Russian Revolution (*Age of Empire*, chapter 8), feminist movements had moved out of the sunlight into the shadows, even where the triumph of fascist and reactionary regimes had not destroyed them. They remained in the shadows, in spite of the victory of anti-fascism and (in Eastern Europe and parts of East Asia) revolution, which extended the rights won after 1917 to most countries that had not yet enjoyed them, most obviously by giving votes to the women of France and Italy in Western Europe, and indeed to women in all newly communist countries, in almost all former colonies and (in the first ten post-war years) in Latin America. Indeed, where elections were held at all, women everywhere in the world had acquired voting rights by the 1960s, except in some Islamic states and, rather curiously, in Switzerland.

Yet these changes were neither achieved by feminist pressures, nor did they have any immediate notable repercussion on the situation of women; even in the relatively few countries where voting had political effects. However, from the 1960s, starting in the USA but spreading rapidly through the rich Western countries and beyond into the elites of educated women in the dependent world – but not, initially, into the heartlands of the socialist world – we find a striking revival of feminism. While these movements belonged, essentially, to the educated middle-class milieu, it is likely that in the 1970s and especially the 1980s a politically and ideologically less specific form of women's consciousness spread among the masses of the sex (which ideologists now insisted should be called a 'gender') far beyond anything achieved by the first wave of feminism. Indeed women as a group now became a major political force, as they had not done before. The first, and perhaps most striking example of this new gender-consciousness was the revolt of the traditionally faithful women in Roman Catholic countries against unpopular doctrines of the Church, as shown notably in the Italian referenda in favour of divorce (1974) and of more liberal abortion laws (1981); and later in the election to the presidency of pious Ireland of Mary Robinson, a woman lawyer very much associated with the liberalization of the Catholic moral code (1990). By the early 1990s a striking divergence of political opinions between the sexes was recorded in a number of countries by public opinion surveys. No wonder that politicians began to court this new women's consciousness, especially on the Left where the decline of working-class consciousness deprived parties of some of their older constituencies.

However, the very width of the new consciousness of femaleness and its interests makes simple explanations in terms of the changing role of women in the economy inadequate. In any case, what changed in the social revolution was not only the nature of women's own activities in society, but also the roles played by women or the conventional expectations of what those roles should be, and in particular the assumptions about the *public* roles of women and their public prominence. For while major changes, such as the massive entry of married women into the labour market might be expected to produce concomitant or consequential changes, they need not do so – as witness the USSR where (after the initial utopian-revolutionary aspirations of the 1920s had been abandoned) married women generally found themselves carrying the double load of old household responsibilities and new wage-earning responsibilities without any change in relations between the sexes or in the public or private spheres. In any case the reasons why women in general, and especially married women, plunged into paid work had no necessary connection with their view of women's social position and rights. It might be due to poverty, to employers' preference for female over male workers as being cheaper and more biddable, or simply to the growing number – especially in the dependent world – of female-headed families. The mass labour migration of men, as from the countryside into the cities of South Africa, or from parts of Africa and Asia into the Persian Gulf states, inevitably left the women to head the family economy at home. Nor should we forget the appalling and sex-discriminating killings of the great wars, which left post-1945 Russia with five women for every three men.

None the less, the signs of significant, even revolutionary, changes in women's expectations about themselves and the world's expectations about their place in society, are undeniable. The new prominence of some women in politics was obvious, though it cannot be used in any way as a direct index of the situation of women as a whole in the countries concerned. After all, the percentage of women in the elected parliaments of macho Latin America (11 per cent) in the 1980s was considerably higher than the percentage of women in the equivalent assemblies of the demonstrably more 'emancipated' North America. Again, a substantial proportion of the women who now, for the first time, found themselves heading states and governments in the dependent world did so through family inheritance: Indira Gandhi (India 1966–84) and Benazir Bhutto (Pakistan 1988–90; 1994) and Aung San Suu Kyi, who would have been chief of Burma but for the military veto, as daughters; Sirimavo Bandaranaike (Sri Lanka, 1960–65; 1970–77) and Corazon Acquino (Philippines, 1986–92) and Isabel Perón (Argentina, 1974–76) as widows. This was in itself no more revolutionary than the succession of Maria Theresa or Victoria to the throne of the Habsburg and British Empires long before. Indeed, the contrast between the female rulers of such countries as India, Pakistan and the Philippines, and the exceptionally depressed and oppressed state of women in their parts of the world underlines their untypicality.

And yet, before the Second World War, the succession of *any* woman to the leadership of *any* republic under *any* circumstances would have been regarded as politically unthinkable. After 1945 it became politically possible – Sirimavo Bandaranaike in Sri Lanka became the world's first woman premier in 1960 – and by 1990 women were or had been heads of government in sixteen states (World's Women, p. 32). In the 1990s even the woman who had got to the top as a career politician was an accepted if uncommon part of the landscape: as prime minister in Israel (1969); Iceland (1980); Norway (1981); not least in Great Britain (1979); in Lithuania (1990); and France (1991); in the shape of Doi, accepted leader of the main (socialist) opposition party, in the far from feminist Japan (1986). The political world was indeed changing fast, even though the public recognition of women (if only as a political pressure group) still usually took the form, even in many of the most 'advanced' countries, of symbolic or token representation on public bodies.

However, it makes little sense to generalize globally about the role of women in the public sphere, and the corresponding public aspirations of women's political movements. The dependent world, the developed world and the socialist or ex-socialist world are only marginally comparable. In the Third World, as in Tsarist Russia, the great mass of lower-class and poorly educated women remained outside the public sphere, in the modern 'Western' sense, though some of these countries developed, and some already had, a small stratum of exceptionally emancipated and 'advanced' women, mainly wives, daughters and other female kin of the established indigenous upper classes and bourgeoisies, analogous to the corresponding female intelligentsia and activists of Tsarist Russia. Such a stratum had existed in the Indian Empire even in colonial times, and seems to have emerged in several of the less rigorist Islamic countries – notably Egypt, Iran, Lebanon and the Maghreb – until the rise of Moslem fundamentalism pushed women into obscurity again. For these emancipated minorities a public space existed on the upper social levels of their own countries, where they could act and feel at home in much the same way as they (or their opposite numbers) could in Europe and North America, though probably they were slower to abandon the sexual conventions and traditional family obligations of their culture than Western women, or at least non-Catholic ones.* In this respect emancipated

---

* It can hardly be an accident that the rates of divorce and re-marriage in Italy, Ireland, Spain and Portugal were spectacularly lower in the 1980s than in the rest of

women in the 'Westernised' dependent countries were far more favourably situated than their sisters in, say, the non-socialist Far East, where the force of traditional roles and conventions to which even elite women had to conform, was enormous and stifling. Educated Japanese or Korean women who found themselves in the emancipated West for a few years often dreaded the return to their own civilizations, and to an as yet only marginally eroded sense of women's subordination.

In the socialist world the situation was paradoxical. Practically all women were in the paid labour force in Eastern Europe – or at least it contained almost as many women as men (90 per cent), a far higher proportion than anywhere else. Communism as an ideology had been passionately committed to women's equality and liberation, in every sense including the erotic, in spite of Lenin's own dislike of casual sexual promiscuity.* (However, both Krupskaya and Lenin were among the rare revolutionaries who specifically favoured the sharing of housework between the sexes.) Moreover, the revolutionary movement, from the Narodniks through the Marxists, had welcomed women, especially intellectual ones, with exceptional warmth, and had provided exceptional scope for them, as was still evident in the 1970s when they were disproportionately represented in some of the Left-wing terrorist movements. Yet, with rather rare exceptions (Rosa Luxemburg, Ruth Fischer, Anna Pauker, La Pasionaria, Federica Montseny) they were not prominent in the first political ranks of their parties, or indeed at all,† and in the new communist-governed states they became even less visible. Indeed, women in leading political functions virtually disappeared. As we have seen, one or two countries, notably Bulgaria and the German Democratic Republic, clearly gave their women unusually good chances of public prominence, as indeed of higher education, yet, on the whole, the public position of

---

the West European and North American zone. Divorce rates: 0.58 per 1,000 population, against 2.5 for a mean of nine other countries (Belgium, France, Federal Germany, Netherlands, Sweden, Switzerland, UK, Canada, USA). Remarriages (per cent of all marriages): 2.4 against 18.6 for a mean of nine countries.

* Thus the right to abortion, forbidden by the German Civil Code, was an important issue for agitation by the German Communist Party, which is why the German Democratic Republic was to enjoy a far more liberal abortion law than the (Christian-Democrat-influenced) German Federal Republic, thus complicating the legal problems of German unification in 1990.

† In the KPD, 1929, out of sixty-three members and candidate members of the Central Committee there were six women. Out of 504 leading party members 1924–29, just 7 per cent were women.

women in communist countries was not notably different from that in developed capitalist ones, and, where it was, it did not necessarily bring advantages. When women streamed into a profession opened to them, as in the USSR, where the medical profession became largely feminized in consequence, it lost status and income. As against Western feminists, most married Soviet women, long used to a lifetime of paid work, dreamed of the luxury of staying at home and doing only one job.

Indeed, the original revolutionary dream of transforming the relations between the sexes and of altering the institutions and habits that embodied the old masculine domination generally ran into the sand, even where – as in the early years of the USSR, but not, in general, in the new European communist regimes after 1944 – it was seriously pursued. In backward countries, and most communist regimes were established in such countries, it was blocked by the passive non-cooperation of traditional populations, who insisted that in practice, whatever the law said, women were treated as less than men. The heroic efforts at female emancipation were not, of course, in vain. To give women equal legal and political rights, to insist on their access to education and men's work and men's responsibilities, even to unveil them and allow them to come and go freely in public, are not small changes, as anyone can verify who compares women's predicament in countries where religious fundamentalism rules or is re-imposed. Moreover, even in those communist countries where female reality lagged rather far behind theory, even at times when governments imposed a virtual moral counter-revolution, seeking to re-install the family and women as basically child-bearers (as in the USSR in the 1930s), the sheer freedom of personal choice available to them under the new system, including the freedom of sexual choice, was incomparably greater than it could have been before the new regime. Its real limits were not so much legal or conventional as material, like the shortage of devices for birth-control for which, as for other gynaecological needs, the planned economy made only the faintest provision.

Still, whatever the achievements and failures of the socialist world, it did not generate specifically feminist movements, and could indeed hardly have done so, given the virtual impossibility of any political initiatives not sponsored by state and party before the mid-1980s. However, it is unlikely that the issues which preoccupied feminist movements in the West would have found much echo in the communist states before then.

Initially these issues in the West, and notably in the USA, which pioneered the revival of feminism, were mainly concerned with problems affecting middle-class women, or in the form which chiefly affected them. This is fairly evident if we look at the occupations in the USA where feminist pressure achieved its major breakthrough, and which, presumably, reflect the concentration of its efforts. By 1981 women had not only virtually eliminated men from office and white-collar occupations, most of which were indeed subaltern though respectable, but they formed almost 50 per cent of real-estate agents and brokers and almost 40 per cent of bank officers and financial managers, and they had established a substantial, though still inadequate presence in the intellectual professions, although the traditional professions of law and medicine still confined them to modest bridgeheads. But if 35 per cent of college and university teachers, over a quarter of computer specialists, and 22 per cent of those in the natural sciences were now women the masculine monopolies of manual labour, skilled and unskilled, remained virtually undented: only 2.7 per cent of truck-drivers, 1.6 per cent of electricians and 0.6 per cent of automobile mechanics were female. Their resistance to the female influx was certainly no weaker than that of doctors and lawyers, who had made way for 14 per cent of them; but it is not unreasonable to suppose that the pressure to conquer these bastions of masculinity was less.

Even a cursory reading of the American pioneers of the new feminism in the 1960s suggests a distinct class perspective on women's problems (Friedan, 1963; Degler, 1987). They were heavily concerned with the question 'how a woman could combine career or job with marriage and family' one which was central only to those who have this choice, which did not then exist for most of the world's women and for all the poor ones. They were, with entire justification, concerned with *equality* between men and women, a concept that became the chief tool for the legal and institutional advance of Western women, since the word 'sex' was inserted into the American Civil Rights Act of 1964, which was originally intended to prohibit only racial discrimination. But 'equality' or rather 'equal treatment' and 'equal opportunity' assume that there are no significant differences between men and women, social or otherwise, and for most of the world's women, and especially the poor, it seemed obvious that part of the social inferiority of women was due to their difference as a sex from men and might therefore require sex-specific remedies – for instance special provisions for pregnancy and maternity or special protection against attacks by the physically stronger and more aggressive sex. US feminism was slow to address such vital interests of working-class women as maternity leave. A later phase of feminism did indeed learn to insist on gender difference as well as gender inequality, even though the use of a liberal ideology of abstract indivdualism and the tool of 'equal rights' law was not readily compatible with the recognition that women were not, and ought not necessarily to be, like men, and the other way round.*

Moreover, in the 1950s and 1960s the very demand to break out of the domestic sphere into the paid labour market had a strong ideological charge among the prosperous, educated middle-class married women which it did not have for others, for its motivations in these milieux were seldom economic. Among the poor, or those with tight budgets, married women went out to work after 1945 because, to put it crudely, children no longer did so. Child labour in the West had almost vanished, while on the contrary, the need to give children an education that would improve their prospects, put a greater financial burden on their parents for longer than in the past. In short, as has been said, 'in the past children had worked so that their mothers could remain at home fulfilling domestic and reproductive responsibilities. Now when families needed additional income, mothers worked instead of children' (Tilly/Scott, 1987, p. 219). This could hardly have been possible without fewer children, even though a substantial mechanisation of household chores (notably by means of the domestic washing machines) and the rise of prepared and ready-cooked foods also made it easier. But for married middle-class women whose husbands earned an income suitable to their status, going out to work rarely made much of an addition to the family income, if only because women were paid so much less than men in the jobs then available for them. It might make no significant net contribution to the family when enough paid help to look after household and children had to be hired (in the form of cleaners and, in Europe, *au pair* girls) to enable the woman to earn an outside income.

If there was an incentive for married women to go outside the home in those circles, it was the demand for freedom and autonomy: for the

* Thus 'affirmative action', i.e. giving a group *preferential* treatment in access to some social resource or activity, is consistent with equality only on the assumption that it is a temporary measure, to be phased out when equal access has been achieved on its own merits; i.e. that on the assumption that preferential treatment is merely the removal of an unfair handicap on entrants to the same race. This is obviously sometimes the case. But where we deal with permanent differences it cannot be to the point. It is absurd, even at first sight, to give men priority in entering courses on coloratura singing or to insist that it is theoretically desirable, on demographic grounds, that 50 per cent of army generals should be women. On the other hand it is entirely legitimate to give every man with the wish and potential qualification to sing *Norma*, and every woman with the wish and potential to lead an army, their chance to do so.

married woman to be a person in her own right and not an appendage of husband and household, someone judged by the world as an individual and not a member of a species ('just a housewife and mother'). Income came into it not because it was needed, but because it was something that a woman could spend or save without asking her husband first. Of course, as two-income middle-class households became more common, family budgets were increasingly calculated in terms of two incomes. Indeed, as higher education for middle-class children became almost universal, and parents might have to make financial contributions to their offspring into the late twenties or even later, paid work for middle-class married women ceased to be primarily a declaration of independence and became what it had long been for the poor, a way of making ends meet. Nevertheless, the consciously emancipatory element in it did not disappear, as the growth of 'commuting marriages' showed. For the costs (and not only the financial ones) of marriages in which each spouse worked in often widely distant locations were high, though the revolution in transport and communications made it increasingly common in professions such as the academic, from the 1970s on. Yet where once middle-class wives (though not children above a certain age) had almost automatically followed wherever husbands' new jobs took them, it now became almost unthinkable, at least in middle-class intellectual circles, to disrupt the woman's own career, and her right to decide where she wanted to conduct it. At last, it seemed, men and women treated one another as equals in this respect.*

Nevertheless, in the developed countries of the world, middle-class feminism, or the movement of educated or intellectual women, broadened out into a sort of generic sense that the time for women's liberation, or at least women's self-assertion, had come. This was because the specific early middle-class feminism, though sometimes not directly relevant to the concerns of the rest of Western femininity, raised questions that concerned all: and these questions became urgent as the social upheaval we have sketched generated a profound, and in many ways sudden, moral and cultural revolution, a dramatic transformation of the conventions of social and personal behaviour. Women were crucial to this cultural revolution, since it pivoted on, and found expression in, changes in the traditional family and household of which they had always been the central element.

To this we must now turn.

---

* Though rarer, cases where the husband faced the problem of following where his wife's new job took her also became more frequent. Any academic of the 1990s could think of some examples within his or her personal acquaintance.

CHAPTER ELEVEN
Cultural Revolution

In the film, Carmen Maura plays a man who's had a transsexual operation and, due to an unhappy love-affair with his/her father, has given up men to have a lesbian (I guess) relationship with a woman, who is played by a famous Madrid transvestite.

– Film-review in the *Village Voice*, Paul Berman (1987, p. 572)

Successful demonstrations are not necessarily those which mobilize the greatest number of people, but those which attract the greatest interest among journalists. Exaggerating only slightly, one might say that fifty clever folk who can make a successful 'happening' get five minutes on TV, can have as much political effect as half a million demonstrators.

– Pierre Bourdieu (1994)

I

The best approach to this cultural revolution is therefore through family and household, i.e. through the structure of relations between the sexes and generations. In most societies this had been impressively resistant to sudden change, though this does not mean that such structures were static. Moreover, in spite of appearances to the contrary, patterns were world-wide, or at least had basic similarities over very wide areas, although it has been suggested, on socio-economic and technological grounds, that there is a major difference between Eurasia (including both sides of the Mediterranean) on one hand, and the rest of Africa on the other (Goody, 1990, XVII). Thus polygyny, which is said to have been almost completely absent or had become so in Eurasia, except for specially privileged groups and in the Arab world, flourished in Africa, where more than a quarter of all marriages are said to be polygamous (Goody, 1990, p. 379).

Nevertheless, across all variations the vast majority of humanity shared a number of characteristics, such as the existence of formal marriage with privileged sex-relations for the spouses ('adultery' is universally treated as an offence); the superiority of husbands to wives ('patriarchy') and of parents to children, as well as of senior to junior generations; family households consisting of several people, and the like. Whatever the extent and complexity of the kinship network and the mutual rights and obligations within it, a nuclear residence – a couple plus children – was generally present somewhere, even when the co-resident or co-operating group or household was much larger. The idea that the nuclear family, which became the standard model in nineteenth and twentieth century Western society, had in some way evolved out of much larger family and kinship units, as part of the growth of bourgeois or any other individualism, rests on a historical misunderstanding, not least of the nature of social co-operation and its rationale in preindustrial societies. Even in so communist an institution as the Balkan Slavs' *zadruga* or joint family, 'every woman works for her family in the narrow sense of the word, namely her husband and children, but also, when it is her turn, for the unmarried members of the community and the orphans' (Guidetti/Stahl, 1977, p. 58). The existence of such a family and household nucleus does not, of course, mean that the kin groups or communities within which it is to be found are in other respects similar.

Yet in the second half of the twentieth century these basic and long-lasting arrangements began to change with express speed, at all events in the 'developed' Western countries, though unevenly, even within these regions. Thus in England and Wales – admittedly a rather dramatic example – in 1938 there was one divorce for every fifty-eight weddings (Mitchell, 1975, p. 30–32), but in the mid-1980s one for every 2.2 new weddings (*UN Yearbook*, 1987). Moreover, we can see the acceleration of this trend in the freewheeling 1960s. At the end of the 1970s there were more than ten divorces for every thousand married couples in England and Wales, or five times as many as in 1961 (*Social Trends*, 1980, p. 84).

This trend was by no means confined to Britain. Indeed, the spectacular change is most clearly seen in countries with strongly compelling traditional moralities such as Catholic ones. In Belgium, France and the Netherlands the crude divorce rate (annual number of divorces per thousand population) roughly trebled between 1970 and 1985. However, even in countries with a tradition of emancipation in these matters, like

Denmark and Norway, they could double or almost double in the same period. Clearly something unusual was happening to Western marriage. The women attending a gynaecological clinic in California in the 1970s showed 'a substantial decrease in formal marriage, a reduction in the wish for children . . . and an attitudinal shift towards acceptance of a bi-sexual adaptation' (Esman, 1990, p. 67). It is unlikely that such a reaction from a cross-section of women would have been recorded anywhere, even in California, before that decade.

The number of people living alone (i.e. not as a member of any couple or larger family) also began to shoot up. In Britain they stayed much the same for the first third of the century at about 6 per cent of all households, drifting upwards fairly gently thereafter. Yet between 1960 and 1980 the percentage almost doubled from 12 per cent to 22 per cent of all households and by 1991 it was more than one-quarter (Abrams, Carr Saunders, *Social Trends*, 1993, p. 26). In many Western big cities they formed about half of all households. Conversely, the classical Western nuclear family, the married couple with children, was in patent retreat. In the USA such families fell from 44 per cent of all households to 29 per cent in twenty years (1960–80); in Sweden, where almost half of all births in the mid-1980s were to unmarried women (Worlds Women, p. 16), from 37 per cent to 25 per cent. Even in the developed countries where they had still formed half or more than half of all households in 1960 (Canada, Federal Germany, Netherlands, Britain) the nuclear family was now a distinct minority.

In particular cases, it ceased to be even nominally typical. Thus in 1991 58 per cent of all black families in the USA were headed by a single woman and 70 per cent of all children were born to single mothers. In 1940 only 11.3 per cent of 'non-white' families had been headed by single mothers, and even in cities, only 12.4 per cent (Franklin Frazier, 1957, p. 317). Even in 1970 the figure had only been 33 per cent (*New York Times*, 5.10.92).

The crisis of the family was linked with quite dramatic changes in the public standards governing sexual behaviour, partnership and procreation. These were both official and unofficial, and the major change in both is datable, and coincides with the 1960s and 1970s. Officially this was an extraordinary era of liberalisation both for heterosexuals (i.e. mainly for women, who had enjoyed so much less freedom than men) and homosexuals, as well as for other forms of cultural-sexual dissidence. In Britain most homosexuality was de-criminalized in the second half of the 1960s, a few years later than the USA, where the first state to make sodomy legal (Illinois) did so in 1961 (Johansson/Percy, p. 304, 1349). In the

Pope's own Italy divorce became legal in 1970, a right confirmed by referendum in 1974. The sale of contraceptives and birth-control information was legalized in 1971, and in 1975 a new family code replaced the old one which had survived from the fascist period. Finally, abortion became legal in 1978, confirmed by referendum in 1981.

Though permissive laws undoubtedly made hitherto forbidden acts easier, and gave far more publicity to these matters, the law recognized rather than created the new climate of sexual relaxation. That in the 1950s only 1 per cent of British Women had cohabited for any length of time with their future husband before marriage was not due to legislation, and neither was the fact that in the early 1980s 21 per cent of them did so (Gillis, 1985, p. 307). Things now became permissible which had hitherto been prohibited, not only by law and religion, but also by customary morality, convention and neighbourhood opinion.

These tendencies did not, of course, affect all parts of the world evenly. While divorce increased in all countries where it was available (assuming, for the moment, that formal dissolution of mariage by official action had the same meaning in all of them), marriage had clearly become much less stable in some. In the 1980s it remained much more permanent in (non-communist) Roman Catholic countries. Divorce was far less common in the Iberian peninsula and in Italy and even rarer in Latin America; even in countries priding themselves on their sophistication: one divorce per twenty-two weddings in Mexico, per thirty-three in Brazil (but one per 2.5 in Cuba). South Korea remained unusually traditional for so fast-moving a country (one per eleven weddings), but in the early 1980s even Japan had a divorce rate less than one quarter of the French and far below the readily divorcing British and Americans. Even within the (then) socialist world there were variations, though smaller than in capitalism, except for the USSR which was second only to the USA in its citizens' readiness to break up their marriages (UN World Social Situation, 1989, p. 36). Such variations cause no surprise. What was and is far more interesting is that, large or small, the same transformations can be traced across the entire 'modernizing' globe. Nowhere was this more striking than in the field of popular, or more specifically of youth culture.

II

For if divorce, illegitimate, births and the rise of the single-parent (i.e. overwhelmingly the single-mother) household indicated a crisis in the relation between the sexes, the rise of a specific, and extraordinarily powerful youth culture indicated a profound change in the relation between the generations. Youth, as self-conscious group stretching from puberty – which in developed countries occurred several years earlier than in previous generations (Tanner, 1962, p. 153) – to the middle twenties, now became an independent social agent. The most dramatic political developments, particularly in the 1960s and 1970s, were the mobilizations of the age-band which, in less politicized countries, made the fortunes of the record industry, 75–80 per cent of whose output – namely rock music – was sold almost wholly to customers between the ages of fourteen and twenty-five (Hobsbawm, 1993, p. xxviii–xxix). The political radicalization of the 1960s, anticipated by smaller contingents of cultural dissidents and drop-outs under various labels, belonged to these young people, who rejected the status of children, or even adolescents (i.e. not-quite-mature adults), while denying full humanity to any generation above the age of thirty, except for the occasional guru.

Except in China, where the ancient Mao mobilized the youth levies to terrible effect (see chapter 16) the young radicals were led – insofar as they accepted leaders – by members of their peer-group. This was patently true of the world-wide student movements, but where these sparked off mass labour uprisings, as in France and Italy in 1968–69, the initiative there also came from young workers. Nobody with even minimal experience of the limitations of real life, i.e. no genuine adult, could have drafted the confident but patently absurd slogans of the Parisian May days of 1968 or the Italian 'hot autumn' of 1969: '*tutto e subito*', we want everything and we want it now (Albers/Goldschmidt/Oehlke, pp. 59, 184).

The new 'autonomy' of youth as a separate social stratum was symbolized by a phenomenon which, on this scale, probably had no parallel since the romantic era of the early nineteenth century: the hero whose life and youth ended together. This figure, anticipated in the 1950s by the film star James Dean, was common, perhaps even ideal-typical, in what became the characteristic cultural expression of youth – rock music. Buddy Holly, Janis Joplin, Brian Jones of the *Rolling Stones*, Bob Marley, Jimi Hendrix and a number of other popular divinities fell victim to a life-style designed for early death. What made such deaths symbolic was that youth, which they represented, was impermanent by definition. To be an actor can be a lifetime career, but not to be a *jeune premier*.

Nevertheless, though the membership of youth is always changing – a student 'generation' notoriously lasts a bare three or four years – its ranks are always being re-filled. The emergence of the adolescent as self-conscious social actor was increasingly recognized, enthusiastically by the manufacturers of consumer goods, sometimes less willingly by his or her seniors, as they found the space expanding between those who were willing to accept the label 'child' and those who insisted on that of 'adult'. In the mid-sixties even Baden Powell's own movement, the English Boy Scouts, dropped the first part of their name as a concession to the mood of the times, and exchanged the old scout sombrero for the less obtrusive beret (Gillis, 1974, p. 197).

Age groups are nothing new in societies, and even in bourgeois civilization a stratum of those who are sexually mature but still engaged in physical and intellectual growth, and lack the experience of adult life, had been recognized. That this group was becoming younger in age as puberty began and maximum heights were reached earlier (Floud et al, 1990) did not in itself change the situation. It merely caused tension between the young and their parents and teachers who insisted on treating them as less grown-up than they felt themselves to be. Bourgeois milieux had expected that their young men – as distinct from their young women – passed through a period of turbulence and 'sowing their wild oats' on the way to 'settling down'. The novelty of the new youth culture was threefold.

First, 'youth' was seen not as a preparatory stage of adulthood but, in some sense, as the final stage of full human development. As in sport, the human activity in which youth is supreme, and which now defined the ambitions of more human beings than any other, life clearly went downhill after the age of thirty. At best, after that age it held little more of interest. That this did not, in fact, correspond to a social reality in which (except for sport, some forms of entertainment and perhaps pure mathematics) power, influence and achievement as well as wealth rose with age, was one more proof of the unsatisfactory way the world was organized. For, until the 1970s, the post-war world was actually governed by a gerontocracy to a greater extent than in most earlier periods, namely by men – hardly as yet by women – who had been adults at the end, or even at the beginning, of the First World War. This applied both to the capitalist world (Adenauer, de Gaulle, Franco, Churchill) and to the communist world (Stalin and Khrushchev, Mao, Ho-Chi-Minh, Tito), as well as to the large post-colonial states (Gandhi, Nehru, Sukarno). A leader below forty was a rarity even in revolutionary regimes emerging from military coups, a type of political change usually made by relatively junior officers because these have less to lose than senior ones. Hence much of the international impact of Fidel Castro, who captured power at the age of thirty-two.

Nevertheless, silent and perhaps not always conscious concessions to the juvenescence of society were made by the establishments of the old, and not least by the flourishing industries of cosmetics, hair-care and personal hygiene, which benefited disproportionately from the accumulating wealth of a few developed countries.* From the end of the 1960s there was a tendency to lower the voting age to eighteen – e.g. in the USA, Britain, Germany and France – and also some sign of a lowering of the age of consent for (heterosexual) sexual intercourse. Paradoxically, as the expectation of life lengthened, the percentage of the old increased and, at least among the favoured upper and middle classes, senile decline was postponed, retirement was reached sooner and, in times of difficulty, 'early retirement' became a favourite method of cutting labour costs. Business executives over forty who lost their jobs found it as hard as manual and white-collar workers to find new ones.

The second novelty of the youth culture follows from the first: it was or became dominant in the 'developed market economies', partly because it now represented a concentrated mass of purchasing power, partly because each new generation of adults had been socialized as part of a self-conscious youth culture and bore the marks of this experience, and not least because the amazing speed of technological change actually gave youth a measurable advantage over more conservative, or at least more inadaptable age. Whatever the age-structure of the management of IBM or Hitachi, new computers were designed, new software devised, by people in their twenties. Even when such machines and programmes had been hopefully made idiot-proof, the generation that had not grown up with them was acutely aware of its inferiority to the generations that had. What children could learn from parents became less obvious than what parents did not know and children did. The role of generations was reversed. Blue jeans, the deliberately demotic wear pioneered on American college campuses by students who did *not* wish to look like their elders, came to appear, on weekdays and holidays, or even, in 'creative' or other hip occupations at work, below many a grey head.

The third peculiarity of the new youth culture in urban societies was its astonishing internationalism. Blue jeans and rock music became the

---

* Of the global 'personal products' market in 1990, 34 per cent was in non-communist Europe, 30 per cent in North America and 19 per cent in Japan. The remaining 85 per cent of the world's population divided 16–17 per cent among its (richer) members (*Financial Times*, 11/4/1991).

marks of 'modern' youth, of the minorities destined to become majorities, in every country in which they were officially tolerated and in some where they were not, as in the USSR from the 1960s on (Starr, 1990, chapters 12 to 13). The English language of rock lyrics was often not even translated. This reflected the overwhelming cultural hegemony of the USA in popular culture and life-styles, although it should be noted that the heartlands of Western youth culture themselves were the opposite of culturally chauvinist, especially in their musical tastes. They welcomed styles imported from the Caribbean, Latin America and, from the 1980s, increasingly Africa.

This cultural hegemony was not new, but its *modus operandi* had changed. Between the wars its chief vector had been the American film industry, the only one with a mass global distribution. It was seen by a public of hundreds of millions which reached its maximum size just after the Second World War. With the rise of television, of international film production and with the end of the Hollywood studio system, the American industry lost some of its predominance and more of its public. In 1960 it produced no more than one sixth of the world film output even without counting Japan and India (*UN Statistical Yearbook*, 1961), although eventually it was to recover much of its hegemony. The USA never managed to establish a comparable hold on the vast and linguistically more diversified markets of television. Its youth styles spread directly, or through amplification of their signals *via* the cultural halfway house of Britain, by a sort of informal osmosis. It spread through records and later tapes, whose major medium of promotion, then as before and since, was old-fashioned radio. It spread through the world distribution of images; through the personal contacts of international youth tourism, which distributed small but growing and influential streams of young men and women in jeans across the globe; through the world network of universities, whose capacity for rapid international communication became obvious in the 1960s. Not least, it spread through the force of fashion in the consumer society which now reached the masses, magnified by pressure within peer-groups. A global youth culture had come into being.

Could it have emerged in any earlier period? Almost certainly not. Its constituency would have been far smaller, relatively and absolutely, for the lengthening of full-time education, and especially the creation of vast populations of young men and women living together as an age-group in universities, dramatically expanded it. Moreover, even the adolescents who entered the full-time labour market at school-leaving age (between fourteen and sixteen in the typical 'developed' country) had far more independent spending power than their predecessors, thanks to the prosperity and full employment of the Golden Age; and thanks to the greater prosperity of their parents, who had less need of their children's contribution to the family budget. It was the discovery of this youth market in the mid-1950s which revolutionized the pop music business and, in Europe, the mass-market end of the fashion industries. The British 'teen-age boom' which began at this time, was based on the urban concentrations of relatively well-paid girls in the expanding offices and shops, often with more to spend than the boys, and in those days less committed to the traditional male patterns of expenditure on beer and cigarettes. The boom 'first revealed its strength in fields where girls' purchases were pre-eminent, like blouses, skirts, cosmetics and pop records' (Allen, 1968, pp. 62-63), not to mention pop concerts, of which they were the most prominent and audible attenders. The power of young money may be measured by the sales of records in the USA which rose from $277 millions in 1955 when rock appeared, to six hundred millions in 1959 and two thousand millions in 1973 (Hobsbawm, 1993, p. xxix). Every member of the five to nineteen-year age-group in the USA spent at least five times as much on records in 1970 as in 1955. The richer the country, the greater the record business: youngsters in the USA, Sweden, West Germany, the Netherlands and Britain spent between seven and ten times as much per head as those in poorer but rapidly developing countries like Italy and Spain.

Independent market power made it easier for youth to discover material or cultural symbols of identity. However, what sharpened the outlines of that identity was the enormous historical gap which separated the generations born before, say, 1925 from those born after, say, 1950; a gap far greater than that between parents and children in the past. Most parents with teen-age children became acutely aware of it in and after the 1960s. The young lived in societies sundered from their past, whether transformed by revolution, as in China, Yugoslavia or Egypt; by conquest and occupation, as in Germany and Japan; or by colonial liberation. They had no memory of the era before the deluge. Except perhaps through the shared experience of a great national war, such as bonded old and young together for a while in Russia and Britain, they had no way of understanding what their elders had experienced or felt – even when these were prepared to talk about the past, as most German, Japanese and French ones were reluctant to do. How could a young Indian, to whom Congress was a government or a political machine, understand one for whom it had been the expression of a nation struggling to be free? How, even, could the brilliant young Indian economists who swept the world's university departments understand their own teachers, for whom the height of ambition in the colonial period had been simply to become 'as good as' their metropolitan models?

The Golden Age widened this gap, at least until the 1970s. How could boys and girls, growing up in an era of full employment, understand the experience of the 1930s, or, conversely, an older generation understand the young for whom a job was not a safe haven after stormy seas (especially a secure one with pension rights), but something that could be got at any time and abandoned any time a person felt like going to Nepal for a few months? This version of the generation gap was not confined to the industrial countries, for the dramatic decline of the peasantry created a similar chasm between rural and ex-rural, manual and mechanized generations. French history professors, brought up in a France where every child came from a farm or passed its vacations there, discovered they had to explain to students in the 1970s what milkmaids had done and what a farmyard with a dungheap looked like. What is more, this generation gap affected even those – the majority of the world's inhabitants – whom the great political events of the century had passed by or who had no particular opinions about them, except insofar as they affected their private lives.

But, of course, whether or not these events had passed them by, the majority of the world's population was now younger than ever. Over the greater part of the Third World where the demographic transition from high to low birthrates had not yet taken place, anything between two fifths and half the inhabitants at any moment of the second half of the century were likely to be less than fourteen years old. However strong their family ties, however powerful the web of tradition that enmeshed them, there could not but be a vast gap between their understanding of life, their experiences and expectations, and those of older generations. The South African political exiles who returned to their country in the early 1990s had a different understanding of what it meant to fight for the African National Congress from the youthful 'comrades' who carried the same flag in the African townships. Conversely, what could the majority in Soweto, born long after Nelson Mandela entered jail, make of him other than as a symbol or an icon? In many ways in such countries the generation gap was even greater than in the West, where permanent institutions and political continuity bound old and young together.

III

Youth culture became the matrix of the cultural revolution in the wider sense of a revolution in manners and customs, in ways of spending leisure and in the commercial arts, which increasingly formed the atmosphere that urban men and women breathed. Two of its characteristics are therefore relevant. It was both demotic and antinomian, especially in matters of personal conduct. Everyone was to 'do their own thing' with minimal outside restraint, although in practice peer pressure and fashion actually imposed as much uniformity as before, at least within peer-groups and subcultures.

That the upper social strata should let themselves be inspired by what they found among 'the people' was not a novelty in itself. Even if we leave aside Queen Marie Antoinette playing at milkmaids, the romantics had adored rural folk culture, folk music and folk dance, their hipper intellectuals (Baudelaire) had fancied the urban *nostalgie de la boue* (the longing for the gutter), and many a Victorian had found that sex with someone from the lower orders, gender depending on taste, was unusually rewarding. (Such feelings were far from extinct in the late twentieth century.) In the Age of Empire cultural influences for the first time began to move systematically upward (see *Age of Empire*, chapter 9) both through the powerful impact of the newly developing plebeian arts and through the cinema, the mass market entertainment par excellence. Yet most of the popular and commercial entertainments between the wars remained in many ways under middle-class hegemony or were brought under its umbrella. The classic Hollywood movie industry was, above all, *respectable*; its social ideal that of the US version of solid 'family values', its ideology that of patriotic oratory. Whenever, in the pursuit of the box-office queue, it discovered a genre incompatible with the moral universe of the fifteen 'Andy Hardy' films (1937–47) which won an Academy Award for 'furthering the American way of life' (Halliwell, 1988, p. 321), as for instance in the early gangster movies which risked idealizing delinquents, the moral order was soon restored, insofar as it was not already in the safe hands of the Hollywood Production Code (1934–66), which limited the permissible time for screen kisses (with mouth shut) to a maximum of thirty seconds. The greatest triumphs of Hollywood – say, *Gone With The Wind* – were based on novels designed for middle-class middlebrow reading, and belonged to that cultural universe as firmly as Thackeray's *Vanity Fair* or Edmond Rostand's *Cyrano de Bergerac*. Only the anarchic and demotic genre of vaudeville and circus-born film comedy resisted gentrification for a while, although in the 1930s even it retreated under the pressure of a brilliant boulevard genre, the Hollywood 'crazy comedy'.

Again, the triumphant Broadway 'musical' of the inter-war years, and the dance-tunes and ballads which studded it, were a bourgeois genre, though one unthinkable without the influence of jazz. They were written for a middle-class New York public with librettos and song-lyrics plainly addressed to an adult audience that saw itself as one of emancipated urban sophisticates. A rapid comparison of the lyrics of Cole Porter with those of the Rolling Stones will make the point. Like the golden age of Hollywood, the golden Age of Broadway rested on a symbiosis of the plebeian and the respectable, but it was not demotic.

The novelty of the 1950s was that the upper-and middle-class young, at least in the Anglo-Saxon world which increasingly set the global tone, began to accept the music, the clothes, even the language of the urban lower classes, or what they took to be such, as their model. Rock music was the most startling example. In the mid-1950s it suddenly broke out of the ghetto of 'Race' or 'Rhythm and Blues' catalogues of American record companies, aimed at poor US blacks, to become the universal idiom of the young, and notably of the *white* young. Young working-class dandies in the past had sometimes taken their styles from high fashion in the upper social strata or from such middle-class subcultures as the artistic boheme; working-class girls even more so. Now a curious reversal seemed to take place. The fashion market for the plebeian young established its independence and began to set the tone for the patrician market. As blue jeans (for both sexes) advanced, Paris *haute couture* retreated, or rather accepted defeat by using its prestigious names to sell mass-market products, directly or under licence. Nineteen sixty-five, by the way, was the first year when the French women's clothing industry produced more trousers than skirts (Veillon, p. 6). Young aristocrats began to shed the accents which, in Britain, had infallibly identified members of their class and began to talk an approximation to London working-class speech.* Respectable young men and, increasingly, young women, began to copy what had once been a strictly unrespectable macho fashion among manual workers, soldiers and the like, the casual use of obscenities in conversation. Literature kept pace: a brilliant theatrical critic brought the word 'fuck' to the radio public. For the first time in the history of the fairy tale, Cinderella became the belle of the ball by *not* wearing splendid clothes.

This demotic turn in the tastes of the middle- and upper-class young in the Western world, which even had some parallels in the Third World

* The young men at Eton began to do so at the end of the 1950s, according to a vice-provost of that elite institution.

with the Brazilian intellectuals' championship of the *samba*,* may or may not have something to do with the rush of middle-class students into revolutionary politics and ideology a few years later. Fashion is often prophetic, nobody knows how. It was almost certainly reinforced among male youth by the public emergence, in the new climate of liberalism, of a homosexual subculture of singular importance as trend-setters in fashion and in the arts. However, perhaps it is not necessary to assume more than that the demotic style was a convenient way of rejecting the values of parental generations or, more precisely, a language in which the young could grope for ways of dealing with a world to which their seniors' rules and values no longer seemed relevant.

The essential antinomianism of the new youth culture came out most clearly at the moments when it found intellectual expression, as in the instantly famous posters of the Paris May days of 1968: 'It is forbidden to forbid', and the American pop radical Jerry Rubin's maxim that one should never trust anyone who had not done time (in jail) (Wiener, 1984, p. 204). Contrary to first appearances, these were not political statements in the traditional sense – even in the narrow sense of aiming to abolish repressive laws. This was not their object. They were public announcements of private feelings and desires. As a slogan of May 1968 put it: 'I take my desires for reality, for I believe in the reality of my desires' (Katsiaficas, 1987, p. 101). Even when such desires came together in public manifestations, groups and movements; even in what looked like, and sometimes had the effect of, mass rebellion, subjectivity was at their core. 'The personal is political' became an important slogan of the new feminism, perhaps the most lasting result of the years of radicalization. It meant more than simply that political commitment had personal motivations and satisfactions, and that the criterion of political success was how it affected people. In some mouths it simply meant 'I shall call anything that worries me, political', as in the title of a 1970s book, *Fat Is a Feminist Issue* (Orbach, 1978).

The May 1968 slogan 'When I think of revolution I want to make love' would have puzzled not only Lenin, but also Ruth Fischer, the militant young Viennese communist whose championship of sexual promiscuity Lenin attacked (Zetkin, 1968, pp. 28ff). Yet, conversely, even for the typically politically conscious neo-Marxist-Leninist radical of the 1960s and 1970s, Brecht's Comintern agent who, like the commercial

---

* Chico Buarque de Holanda, the major figure on the Brazilian pop music scene, was the son of an eminent progressive historian who had been a central figure in his country's intellectual-cultural revival in the 1930s.

traveller 'made love with other things on his mind' ('*Der Liebe pflegte ich achtlos*' – Brecht, 1976, II, p. 722) would have been incomprehensible. For them the important thing was surely not what revolutionaries hoped to achieve by their actions, but what they did and how they felt while doing it. Making love and making revolution could not be clearly separated.

Personal liberation and social liberation thus went hand in hand; the most obvious ways of shattering the bonds of state, parental and neighbours' power, law and convention, being sex and drugs. The former, in all its manifold forms, did not have to be discovered. What the melancholy conservative poet meant by the line 'Sexual intercourse began in 1963' (Larkin, 1988, p. 167) was not that this activity was uncommon before the 1960s or even that he had not practised it, but that it changed its public character with – his examples – the Lady Chatterley trial and 'the Beatles' first LP'. Where an activity had formerly been prohibited, such gestures against older ways were easy. Where it had previously been tolerated, officially or unofficially, as for instance lesbian relationships had, the fact that it *was* a gesture had to be specially established. A public commitment to the hitherto prohibited or unconventional ('coming out') therefore became important. Drugs, on the other hand, except for alcohol and tobacco, had hitherto been confined to small subcultures of high, low and marginal society, and did not benefit from permissive legislation. They spread not only as a gesture of rebellion, for the sensations they made possible could be sufficient attraction. Nevertheless, drug use was by legal definition an outlaw activity, and the very fact that the drug most popular among the Western young, marihuana, was probably more harmless than alcohol or tobacco, made smoking it (typically, a social activity) not merely an act of defiance but of superiority over those who banned it. On the wilder shores of the American 1960s, where rock fans and student radicals met, the line between getting stoned and building barricades often seemed hazy.

The newly extended field of publicly acceptable behaviour, including the sexual, probably increased experimentation and the frequency of behaviour hitherto considered unacceptable or deviant, and certainly increased its visibility. Thus in the USA the public emergence of an openly practised homosexual subculture, even in the two trend-setting cities of San Francisco and New York, which influenced one another, did not occur until well into the 1960s, its emergence as a political pressure group in these two cities not until the 1970s (Duberman et al, 1989, p. 460). However, the major significance of these changes was that, implicitly or explicitly, they rejected the long-established and historical ordering of human relations in society, which the social conventions and prohibitions expressed, sanctioned and symbolized.

What is even more significant is that this rejection was not in the name of some other pattern of ordering society, though the new libertarianism was given ideological justification by those who felt it needed such labels,* but in the name of the unlimited autonomy of individual desire. It assumed a world of self-regarding individualism pushed to its limits. Paradoxically the rebels against the conventions and restrictions shared the assumptions on which mass consumer society was built, or at least the psychological motivations which those who sold consumers goods and services found most effective in selling them.

The world was now tacitly assumed to consist of several billion human beings defined by their pursuit of individual desire, including desires hitherto prohibited or frowned on, but now permitted – not because they had now become morally acceptable but because so many egos had them. Thus until the 1990s official liberalization stopped short of legalizing drugs. These continued to be prohibited with varying degrees of severity and a high degree of inefficacy. For from the later 1960s an enormous market for cocaine developed with great rapidity, primarily among the prosperous middle classes of North America and, a little later, Western Europe. This, like the somewhat earlier and more plebeian growth in the market for heroin (also primarily North American) turned crime for the first time into genuinely big business (Arlacchi, 1983, pp. 215, 208).

IV

The cultural revolution of the later twentieth century can thus best be understood as the triumph of the individual over society, or rather, the breaking of the threads which in the past had woven human beings into social textures. For such textures had consisted not only of the actual relations between human beings and their forms of organization but also of the general models of such relations and the expected patterns of people's behaviour towards each other; their roles were prescribed, though not always written. Hence the often traumatic insecurity when

---

* However, there was next to no revival of the one ideology which believed that spontaneous, unorganized, anti-authoritarian and libertarian action would bring about a new, just and stateless society, namely Bakuninite or Kropotkinite *anarchism*; even though this corresponded far more closely to the actual ideas of most student rebels of the 1960s and 1970s than the then fashionable Marxism.

older conventions of behaviour were either overturned or lost their rationale, or the incomprehension between those who felt this loss and those too young to have known anything but anomic society.

Thus a Brazilian anthropologist in the 1980s described the tension of a middle-class male, raised in his country's Mediterranean culture of honour and shame, faced with the increasingly common contingency of a group of robbers who asked for his money and threatened to rape his girl-friend. Under such circumstances a gentleman had always been expected to defend the woman, if not the money, at the cost of his life; a lady, to prefer death to a fate proverbially 'worse than death'. Yet in the reality of late twentieth century big cities it was unlikely that resistance would save either the woman's 'honour' or the money. The rational policy in such circumstances was to yield, so as to prevent the aggressors from losing their tempers and committing real mayhem or even murder. As for female honour, traditionally defined as virginity before marriage and total marital fidelity thereafter, what exactly was being defended in the light of the assumptions about, and the realities of, sexual behaviour by both men and women which were current among the educated and emancipated in the 1980s? And yet, as the anthropologist's enquiries showed, not surprisingly this did not make the predicament less traumatic. Less extreme situations could produce comparable insecurity and mental suffering – for instance ordinary sexual encounters. The alternative to an old convention, however unreasonable, might turn out to be not some new convention or rational behaviour, but no rules at all, or at least no consensus about what should be done.

Over most of the world the old social textures and conventions, though undermined by a quarter of a century of unparalleled social and economic transformation, were strained, but not yet in disintegration. This was fortunate for most of humanity, especially the poor, since the network of kin, community and neighbourhood was essential to economic survival and especially to success in a changing world. In much of the Third World it functioned as a combination of information service, labour exchange, a pool of labour and capital, a savings mechanism and a social security system. Indeed, without cohesive families the economic successes of some parts of the world – e.g. the Far East – are difficult to explain.

In the more traditional societies the strains would show chiefly inasmuch as the triumph of the business economy undermined the legitimacy of the hitherto accepted social order based on inequality, both because aspirations became more egalitarian and because the functional justifications of inequality were eroded. Thus the wealth and profligacy of Indian rajahs (like the known immunity to taxation of the British family's royal wealth, which was not challenged until the 1990s), had not been envied or resented by their subjects, as a neighbour's might have been. They belonged to, and were marks of, their special role in the social – perhaps even in the cosmic – order, which in some sense was believed to maintain, to stabilize and certainly to symbolize, their realm. In a somewhat different mode, the considerable privileges and luxuries of Japanese business tycoons were less unacceptable, so long as they were seen not as individually appropriated wealth, but essentially as adjuncts to their official positions in the economy, rather like the luxuries of British cabinet ministers – limousines, official residences, etc – which are withdrawn within hours of their ceasing to occupy the post to which they are attached. The actual distribution of incomes in Japan, as we know, was considerably less unequal than in Western business societies. Yet anyone who observed the Japanese situation in the 1980s, even from afar, could hardly avoid the impression that during this boom decade the sheer accumulation of personal wealth and its public display made the contrast between the conditions under which the ordinary Japanese lived at home – so much more modestly than their Western homologues – and the condition of the Japanese rich far more visible. Perhaps for the first time they were no longer sufficiently protected by what had been seen as the legitimate privileges that go with service to state and society.

In the West, the decades of social revolution had created far greater havoc. The extremes of such breakdown are most easily visible in the public ideological discourse of the occidental *fin de siècle*, especially in the kind of public statements which, while laying no claim to analytical depth, were formulated in terms of widely held beliefs. One thinks of the argument, at one time common in some feminist circles, that women's domestic work should be calculated (and where necessary, paid) at a market rate, or the justification of abortion reform in terms of an abstract and unlimited 'right to choose' of the individual (woman).* The pervasive influence of neo-classical economics, which in secular Western societies increasingly took the place of theology, and (via the cultural hegemony of the USA) the influence of the ultra-individualist American jurisprudence,

---

* The legitimacy of a claim must be distinguished clearly from the arguments used to justify it. The relation of husband, wife and children in a household has not the faintest resemblance to that of buyers and sellers in a market, however notional. Nor is the decision to have or not to have a child, even if taken unilaterally, one which concerns exclusively the individual who takes that decision. This statement of the obvious is perfectly compatible with the desire to transform women's household role or favour the right of abortion.

encouraged such rhetoric. It found political expression in the British premier Margaret Thatcher's: 'There is no society, only individuals.'

Yet, whatever the excesses of theory, practice was often equally extreme. Sometime in the 1970s, social reformers in the Anglo-Saxon countries, rightly shocked (as enquirers periodically were) by the effects of institutionalization on the mentally ill or impaired, successfully campaigned to have as many of them as possible let out of confinement 'to be cared for in the community'. But in the cities of the West there no longer was a community to care for them. There was no kin. Nobody knew them. There were only the streets of cities like New York filled with homeless beggars with plastic bags who gestured and talked to themselves. If they were lucky or unlucky (it depended on the point of view) they eventually moved from the hospitals that had expelled them to the jails which, in the USA, became the main receptacle of the social problems of American society, especially its black part. In 1991 15 per cent of what was proportionately the largest prison population in the world – 426 prisoners per 100,000 population – were said to be mentally ill (Walker, 1991; Human Development, 1991, p. 32, Fig. 2.10).

The institutions most severely undermined by the new moral individualism were the traditional family and traditional organized churches in the West, which collapsed dramatically in the last third of the century. The cement that had held the communities of Roman Catholics together crumbled with astonishing speed. In the course of the 1960s attendance at Mass in Quebec (Canada) fell from 80 to 20 per cent and the traditionally high French-Canadian birth-rate fell below the Canadian average (Bernier/Boily, 1986). Women's liberation, or more precisely women's demand for birth-control, including abortion and the right to divorce, drove perhaps the deepest wedge between the Church and what had in the nineteenth century become the basic stock of the faithful (see *Age of Capital*), as became increasingly evident in notoriously Catholic countries like Ireland and the Pope's own Italy, and even – after the fall of communism – in Poland. Vocations for the priesthood and other forms of the religious life fell steeply, as did the willingness to live lives of celibacy, real or official. In short, for good or ill, the Church's moral and material authority over the faithful disappeared into the black hole that opened between its rules of life and morality and the reality of late-twentieth-century behaviour. Western Churches with a less compelling hold over their members, including even some of the older Protestant sects, declined even more rapidly.

The material consequences of the loosening of traditional family ties were perhaps even more serious. For, as we have seen, the family was not

only what it had always been, a device for reproducing itself, but also a device for social cooperation. As such it had been essential for maintaining both the agrarian and the early industrial economies, the local and the global. This was partly because no adequate *impersonal* capitalist business structure had been developed before the concentration of capital and the rise of big business began to generate the modern corporate organization at the end of the nineteenth century, that 'visible hand' (Chandler, 1977) which was to supplement Adam Smith's 'invisible hand' of the market.*
But an even stronger reason was that the market by itself makes no provision for that central element in any system of private profit-seeking, namely trust; or, its legal equivalent, the performance of contracts. This required either state power (as the seventeenth-century political theorists of individualism knew well) or the ties of kin or community. Thus international trading, banking and finance, fields of sometimes physically remote activities, large rewards and great insecurity, had been most successfully conducted by kin-related bodies of entrepreneurs, preferably from groups with special religious solidarities like Jews, Quakers, or Huguenots. Indeed, even in the late twentieth century, such links were still indispensable in criminal business, which was not only against the law but outside its protection. In a situation where nothing else guaranteed contracts, only kin and the threat of death could do so. The most successful Calabrian *mafia* families therefore consisted of a substantial group of brothers (Ciconte, 1992, pp. 361–62).

Yet just these non-economic group bonds and solidarities were now being undermined, as were the moral systems that went with them. These had also been older than modern bourgeois industrial society, but they had also been adapted to form an essential part of it. The old moral vocabulary of rights and duties, mutual obligations, sin and virtue, sacrifice, conscience, rewards and penalties, could no longer be translated into the new language of desired gratification. Once such practices and institutions were no longer accepted as part of a way of ordering society that linked people to each other and ensured social cooperation and reproduction, most of their capacity to structure human social life vanished. They were reduced simply to expressions of individuals' preferences, and claims that the law should recognize the supremacy of these

---

* The operational model of really large enterprise before the era of corporate capitalism ('monopoly capitalism') was not drawn from private business experience, but from state or military bureaucracy – cf. the uniforms of railway employees. Often, indeed, it was, and had to be, directly conducted by the state or other non-profit- maximizing public authorities, like the postal and most telegraph and telephone services.

preferences.* Uncertainty and unpredictability impended. Compass needles no longer had a North, maps became useless. This is what became increasingly evident in the most developed countries from the 1960s on. It found ideological expression in a variety of theories, from extreme free-market liberalism to 'postmodernism' and its like, which tried to sidestep the problem of judgment and values altogether, or rather to reduce them to the single denominator of the unrestricted freedom of the individual.

Initially, of course, the advantages of wholesale social liberalization had seemed enormous to all except ingrained reactionaries, and its costs minimal; nor did it seem to imply economic liberalization. The great tide of prosperity washing across the populations of the favoured regions of the world, reinforced by the increasingly comprehensive and generous public social security systems, appeared to remove the debris of social disintegration. Being a single parent (i.e. overwhelmingly a single mother) was still by far the best guarantee of a life of poverty, but in modern welfare states it also guaranteed a minimum of livelihood and shelter. Pensions, welfare services and, in the end, geriatric wards took care of the isolated old, whose sons and daughters could not, or no longer felt the obligation to, look after parents in their decline. It seemed natural to deal with other contingencies that had once been part of the family order in the same way, for instance by shifting the burden of caring for infants from mothers to public crèches and nurseries, as socialists, concerned with the needs of wage-earning mothers, had long demanded.

Both rational calculation and historical development seemed to point in the same direction as various kinds of progressive ideology, including all those which criticized the traditional family because it perpetuated the subordination of women or of children and adolescents, or on more general libertarian grounds. Materially, public provision was obviously superior to that which most families could provide for themselves, either because of poverty or for other reasons. That the children in democratic states emerged from the world wars actually healthier and better fed than before, proved the point. That welfare states survived in the richest countries at the end of the century, in spite of systematic attacks on them by free-market governments and ideologists, confirmed it. Moreover, it was a commonplace among sociologists and social anthropologists that in

* This is the difference between the language of (legal or constitutional) 'rights', which became central to the society of uncontrolled individualism, at all events in the USA, and the old moral idiom in which rights and obligations were the two sides of the same coin.

general the role of kinship 'diminishes with the importance of governmental institutions'. For better or worse, it declined with 'the growth of economic and social individualism in industrial societies' (Goody, 1968, p. 402–3). In short, as had long been predicted, *Gemeinschaft* was giving way to *Gesellschaft*; communities to individuals linked in anonymous societies.

The material advantages of a life in a world in which community and family declined were, and remain, undeniable. What few realized was how much of modern industrial society up to the mid-twentieth century had relied on a symbiosis between old community and family values and the new society, and therefore how dramatic the effects of their spectacularly rapid disintegration were likely to be. This became evident in the era of neo-liberal ideology, when the macabre term 'the underclass' entered, or re-entered the socio-political vocabulary around 1980.* These were the people who, in developed market societies after the end of full employment, could not manage or did not want to make a living for themselves and their families in the economy of the market (supplemented by the social security system), which seemed to work well enough for two thirds of most of the inhabitants of such countries, at all events until the 1990s (hence the phrase 'the Two-Thirds Society' coined in that decade by a worried German Social-Democratic politician, Peter Glotz). The very word 'underclass', like the old 'underworld', implied an exclusion from 'normal' society. Essentially such 'underclasses' relied on public housing and public welfare, even when they supplemented their income by forays into the black or grey economy or into 'crime', i.e. those parts of the economy not reached by the government's fiscal systems. However, since these were the strata where family cohesion had largely broken down, even their incursions into the informal economy, legal or illegal, were marginal and unstable. For, as the Third World and its new mass immigration to the Northern countries proved, even the unofficial economy of shanty-towns and illegal immigrants works well only with kinship networks.

The poor parts of the native-born urban Negro population in the USA, that is to say, the majority of US Negroes,† became the standard

---

* The late-nineteenth-century equivalent for this in Britain had been 'the residuum'.

† The description officially preferred at the time of writing is 'African-American'. However, these names change – in the author's lifetime there have been several such changes ('Coloured', 'Negro', 'Black') – and will go on changing. I use the term which probably had currency longer than any other among those who wished to show respect to the descendants of African slaves in the Americas.

example of such an 'underclass', a body of citizens virtually extruded from official society, forming no real part of it or – in the case of many of its young males – of the labour market. Indeed, many of its young, especially the males, virtually considered themselves an outlaw society or anti-society. The phenomenon was not confined to people of any skin-colour. With the decline and fall of the labour-employing industries of the (nineteenth and early twentieth) century, such 'underclasses' began to appear in a number of countries. Yet in the housing projects built by socially responsible public authorities for all who could not afford market rents or house purchase, but now inhabited by 'the underclass', there was no community either, and little enough regular kin mutuality. Even 'neighbourliness', the last relic of community, could hardly survive the universal fear, generally of wild adolescent males, now increasingly armed, that stalked these Hobbesian jungles.

Only in those parts of the world that had not yet entered the universe where human beings lived side by side but not as social beings did community survive to some extent, and with it a social order, though, for most human beings, a desperately poor one. Who could talk of a minority 'underclass' in a country like Brazil where, in the mid-1980s, the top 20 per cent of the population received over 60 per cent of their country's income while the bottom 40 per cent received 10 per cent or even less? (UN World Social Situation, 1984, p. 84). It was generally a life of unequal status as well as income. Yet, for the most part, it still lacked the pervasive insecurity of urban life in the 'developed' societies, their old guides to behaviour dismantled, and replaced by an uncertain void. The sad paradox of the twentieth century *fin de siècle* was that, by all the measurable criteria of social well-being and stability, living in socially retrograde but traditionally structured Northern Ireland, unemployed and after twenty unbroken years of something like civil war, was better, and actually safer, than living in most of the great cities of the United Kingdom.

The drama of collapsed traditions and values lay not so much in the material disadvantages of doing without the social and personal services once supplied by family and community. These could be replaced in the prosperous welfare states, although not in the poor parts of the world, where the great majority of humanity still had little to rely on except kin, patronage and mutual aid (for the socialist sector of the world, see chapters 13 and 16). It lay in the disintegration both of the old value systems and the customs and conventions which controlled human behaviour. This loss was felt. It was reflected in the rise of what came to be called (again in the USA where the phenomenon became noticeable from the end of the 1960s) 'identity politics', generally ethnic/national or religious, and of militantly nostalgic movements seeking to recover a hypothetical past age of unproblematic order and security. Such movements were cries for help rather than carriers of programmes – calls for some 'community' to belong to in an anomic world; some family to belong to in a world of social isolates; some refuge in the jungle. Every realistic observer and most governments knew that crime was not diminished or even controlled by executing criminals or by deterrence through long penal sentences, but every politician knew the enormous, emotionally loaded strength, rational or not, of the mass demand of ordinary citizens to *punish* the anti-social.

These were the political dangers of the fraying and snapping of the old social textures and value systems. However, as the 1980s advanced, generally under the banner of pure market sovereignty, it became increasingly obvious that it also constituted a danger to the triumphant capitalist economy.

For the capitalist system, even while built on the operations of the market, had relied on a number of proclivities which had no intrinsic connection with that pursuit of the individual's advantage which, according to Adam Smith, fuelled its engine. It relied on 'the habit of labour', which Adam Smith assumed to be one of the fundamental motives of human behaviour, on the willingness of human beings to postpone immediate gratification for a long period, i.e. to save and invest for future rewards, on pride in achievement, on customs of mutual trust, and on other attitudes which were not implicit in the rational maximisation of anyone's utilities. The family became an integral part of early capitalism because it supplied it with a number of these motivations. So did 'the habit of labour', the habits of obedience and loyalty, including the loyalty of executives to their firm, and other forms of behaviour which could not readily be fitted into rational choice theory based on maximisation. Capitalism could function in the absence of these, but, when it did, it became strange and problematic even for businessmen themselves. This happened during the fashion for piratical 'take-overs' of business corporations and other financial speculations which swept the financial districts of ultra-free-market states like the USA and Britain in the 1980s, and which virtually broke all links between the pursuit of profit and the economy as a system of production. That is why capitalist countries which had not forgotten that growth is not achieved by profit maximisation alone (Germany, Japan, France), made such raiding difficult or impossible.

Karl Polanyi, surveying the ruins of nineteenth-century civilization during the Second World War, pointed out how extraordinary and unprecedented were the assumptions on which it had been constructed: those of the self-regulating and universal system of markets. He argued that Adam Smith's 'propensity to barter, truck and exchange one thing for another' had inspired 'an industrial system ... which practically and theoretically, implied that the human race was swayed in all its economic activities, if not also in its political, intellectual and spiritual pursuits, by that one particular propensity.' (Polanyi, 1945, pp. 50–51). Yet Polanyi exaggerated the logic of capitalism in his time, just as Adam Smith had exaggerated the extent to which, taken by itself, the pursuit by all men of their economic advantage would automatically maximize the wealth of nations.

As we take for granted the air we breathe, and which makes possible all our activities, so capitalism took for granted the atmosphere in which it operated, and which it had inherited from the past. It only discovered how essential it had been, when the air became thin. In other words, capitalism had succeeded because it was not just capitalist. Profit maximization and accumulation were necessary conditions for its success but not sufficient ones. It was the cultural revolution of the last third of the century which began to erode the inherited historical assets of capitalism and to demonstrate the difficulties of operating without them. It was the historic irony of the neo-liberalism that became fashionable in the 1970s and 1980s, and looked down on the ruins of the communist regimes, that it triumphed at the very moment when it ceased to be as plausible as it had once seemed. The market claimed to triumph as its nakedness and inadequacy could no longer be concealed.

The main force of the cultural revolution was naturally felt in the urbanised 'industrial market economies' of the old capitalist heartlands. However, as we shall see, the extraordinary economic and social forces released in later twentieth century also transformed what now came to be called the 'Third World'.

CHAPTER TWELVE
The Third World

[I suggested that], without books to read, life in the evenings on their [Egyptian] country estates must hang heavily, and that an easy chair and a good book on a cool veranda would make life much more agreeable. My friend said at once: 'You don't think that a landlord in the district could sit out on a veranda after dinner with a bright light over his head, do you, and not get shot?' I might have thought of that myself.

– Russell Pasha, 1949

Whenever village conversation was steered to the subject of mutual help and the offer of cash loans as part of such help to fellow villagers, it rarely failed to raise statements bemoaning the decreasing cooperation between villagers ... Such statements were always accompanied with reference to the fact that people in the village are becoming increasingly calculating in their approach to money matters. Villagers would then unfailingly hark back to what was termed as the 'old days' when people were always ready to offer aid.

– M. b.Abdul Rahim, 1973 (in Scott, 1985, p. 188)

I

Decolonization and revolution dramatically transformed the political map of the globe. The number of internationally recognized independent states in Asia quintupled. In Africa, where there had been one in 1939, there were now about fifty. Even in the Americas, where early nineteenth-century decolonization had left behind twenty or so Latino republics, decolonization added another dozen. However, the important thing about them was not their number, but their enormous and growing demographic weight and pressure they represented collectively.

This was the consequence of an astonishing demographic explosion in the dependent world after the Second World War, which changed, and continues to change, the balance of world population. Since the first industrial revolution, possibly since the sixteenth century, this had been moving in favour of the 'developed' world, i.e. of populations in or originating from Europe. From less than 20 per cent of the global population in 1750, these had risen to constitute about one third of humanity by 1900. The Age of Catastrophe froze the situation, but since the middle of the century, world population has grown at a rate beyond all precedent, and most of this has come from the regions once ruled by, or about to be conquered by, a handful of empires. If we take the membership of the rich countries in the OECD as representing the 'developed world', their collective population at the end of the 1980s represented a mere 15 per cent of humanity; an inevitably declining share (but for immigration), since several of the 'developed' countries were no longer giving birth to enough children to reproduce themselves.

This demographic explosion in the poor countries of the world, which first caused serious international worry at the end of the 'golden age', is probably the most fundamental change in the Short Twentieth Century, even if we assume that global population will be eventually stabilized at ten billions (or whatever the current guess may be) some time in the twenty-first century.* A world population that doubled in the forty years since 1950, or a population like that of Africa which can expect to double in less than thirty years, is entirely without historical precedent, as are the practical problems it must raise. One has merely to consider the social and economic situation of a country 60 per cent of whose people are less than fifteen years old.

The demographic explosion in the poor world was so sensational because the basic birth-rates in these countries were usually far higher than those of the corresponding historical period in the 'developed' countries, and because the enormous rates of mortality, which used to keep down the population, dropped like a stone since the 1940s – four or five times as fast as the corresponding drop in nineteenth-century Europe

* If the spectacular acceleration of growth we have experienced during this century were to continue, a catastrophe would seem to be unavoidable. Humanity reached its first billion about two hundred years ago. The next billion took 120 years to reach, the third thirty-five years, the fourth fifteen years. At the end of the 1980s it stood at 5.2 billions and was expected to exceed six billions by 2000.

(Kelley, 1988, p. 168). For, while in Europe this fall had to wait for the gradual improvement of living and environmental standards, modern technology swept through the world of the poor countries like a hurricane in the 'Golden Age', in the form of modern drugs and the transport revolution. From the 1940s on, medical and pharmaceutical innovation for the first time was in a position to save lives on a massive scale (e.g. by DDT and antibiotics), which it had previously never been able to, except perhaps in the case of smallpox. So, as birth-rates stayed high, or even rose in times of prosperity, death-rates plummeted – in Mexico they dropped by more than half in the twenty-five years after 1944 – and the population shot up, even though neither the economy nor its institutions had necessarily changed much. One incidental consequence of this was to widen the gap between the rich and poor, the advanced and backward countries, even when the economies of both regions grew at the same rate. To distribute a GDP twice as large as thirty years ago in a country whose population was stable is one thing; to distribute it among a population which (like Mexico) had doubled in thirty years is quite another.

It is important to begin any account of the Third World with some consideration of its demography, since the population explosion is the central fact of its existence. Past history in the developed countries suggests that, sooner or later it will also undergo what the experts call 'the demographic transition', by stabilizing its population on the basis of a low birth-rate and a low death-rate, i.e. of giving up having more than one or two children. However, while there is indeed evidence that the 'demographic transition' was in the process of taking place in several countries, notably in East Asia, at the end of the Short Twentieth Century the bulk of the poor countries had not advanced very far along that road, except in the ex-Soviet bloc. This was one reason for their continued poverty. Several countries with a giant population were so troubled about the tens of millions of additional mouths that asked to be fed every year that from time to time their governments engaged in ruthless coercion to impose birth control or some other kind of family limitation on their citizens (notably the sterilisation campaign in India in the 1970s and the 'one-child' policy of China). It is unlikely that the population problem in any country will be solved by these means.

II

However, as they emerged into the post-war and post-colonial world, these were not the first concerns of the states of the poor world. What shape should they take?

Not surprisingly they adopted, or were urged into, political systems derived from their old imperial masters or those who had conquered them. The minority, emerging out of social revolution or (what amounted to the same thing) lengthy wars of liberation, were more likely to follow the model of the Soviet revolution. In theory, therefore, the world was increasingly filled with what purported to be parliamentary republics with contested elections, plus a minority of 'people's democratic republics' under a single guiding party. (In theory everybody henceforth was democratic, though only the communist or social-revolutionary regimes insisted on being 'popular' and/or 'democratic' in their official title.*)

In practice these labels indicated at most where such new states wished to situate themselves internationally. They were in general as unrealistic as the official constitutions of the Latin American republics had long tended to be, and for the same reasons: in most cases they lacked the material and political conditions to live up to them. This was so even in the new states of the communist type, though their basically authoritarian structure and the device of a single 'leading party' made them rather less unsuitable to states of a non-Western background than were liberal republics. Thus one of the few unshakeable and unshaken political principles of communist states was the supremacy of the (civilian) party over the military. Yet in the 1980s, among revolutionary-inspired states, Algeria, Benin, Burma, the Congo Republic, Ethiopia, Madagascar and Somalia – plus the somewhat eccentric Libya – were under the rule of soldiers who had come to power by coups, as were both Syria and Iraq both under governments of the Ba'ath Socialist Party, though in rival versions.

Indeed, the prevalence of, or the tendency to lapse into, military regimes united Third World states of whatever constitutional and political affiliation. If we omit the main body of Third World communist regimes (North Korea, China, the Indochinese republics and Cuba), and the long-established regime sprung from the Mexican Revolution, it is difficult to think of any republics which have not known at least episodes of

---

* Before the collapse of communism the following states had the words 'people's', 'popular', 'democratic' or 'socialist' in their official names: Albania, Angola, Algeria, Bangladesh, Benin, Burma, Bulgaria, Cambodia, China, Congo, Czechoslovakia, Ethiopia, German Democratic Republic, Hungary, North Korea, Laos, Libya, Madagascar, Mongolia, Mozambique, Poland, Romania, Somalia, Sri Lanka, USSR, Vietnam, PDR Yemen, and Yugoslavia. Guyana announced itself as a 'cooperative republic'.

military regimes since 1945. (The few monarchies, with some exceptions (Thailand), seem to have been safer.) India, of course, remains at the time of writing by far the most impressive example of a Third World state that has both maintained unbroken civilian supremacy and an unbroken succession of government by regular and relatively honest popular election, though whether this justifies the label 'the world's greatest democracy' depends on how precisely we define Lincoln's 'government of the people, for the people, by the people'.

We have become so accustomed to military coups and regimes in the world – even in Europe – that it is worth reminding ourselves that on the present scale they are a distinctly new phenomenon. In 1914 not a single internationally sovereign state had been under military rule, except in Latin America, where military *coups d'état* were part of tradition, and even there, at that time, the only major republic that was not under civilian rule was Mexico, which was in the middle of a revolution and civil war. There were plenty of militarist states, of states in which the military carried more than its share of political weight, and several states in which the bulk of the officer-corps was out of sympathy with its government – France being an obvious example. Nevertheless, the instinct and the habit of soldiers in properly conducted and stable states was to obey and keep out of politics; or, more precisely, to participate in politics only in the manner of another group of officially voiceless personages, ruling-class women, namely behind the scenes and by intrigue.

The politics of military coup were therefore the product of the new era of uncertain or illegitimate government. The first serious discussion of the subject, by an Italian journalist with memories of Machiavelli, Curzio Malaparte's *Coup d'État*, appeared in 1931, halfway through the years of catastrophe. In the second half of the century, while the superpower balance appeared to stabilize frontiers and, to a lesser extent, regimes, armed men became ever more commonly involved in politics, if only because the globe was now filled with up to two hundred states, most of which were new and therefore lacked any traditional legitimacy, and most of which were saddled with political systems more likely to produce political breakdown than effective government. In such situations the armed forces were often the only bodies capable of political or any other action on a state-wide basis. Moreover, since the international Cold War between the superpowers was largely conducted through the armed forces of client or allied states, these were subsidized and armed by the appropriate superpower or, in some cases, first by one and then by the other superpower, as in Somalia. There was more scope in politics for the men in tanks than ever before.

In the core countries of communism they were kept under control by the presumption of civilian supremacy through the party, although in his last lunatic years Mao Tse-tung came close to abandoning it at moments. In the core countries of the Western alliance the scope for military politics remained restricted by the absence of political instability or the effective mechanisms for keeping it under control. Thus after General Franco's death in Spain a transition to liberal democracy was negotiated efficiently under the aegis of the new king, and a putsch by the unreconstructed Francoist officers in 1981 was quickly stopped in its tracks by the king's refusal to accept it. In Italy, where the USA maintained a local coup potential against the possibility of participation in government by the large local Communist Party, civilian government remained in being, even though the 1970s produced various and still unexplained flurries of action in the obscure depth of the military, secret service and terrorist underworlds. Only where the traumas of decolonization (i.e. defeat by colonial insurrectionaries) proved intolerable, were Western officers tempted into military coups – as in France during the losing struggle to hold Indochina and Algeria in the 1950s, and (with Left-wing political orientation) in Portugal as the African empire collapsed in the 1970s. In both cases the armed forces were soon brought under civilian control again. The only military regime actually backed by the USA in Europe was that installed in 1967 (probably on local initiative) by a particularly witless group of ultra-Right-wing Greek colonels in a country where civil war between communists and their opponents (1944–49) had left bitter memories on both sides. The regime, distinguished by a taste for the systematic torture of its opponents, collapsed after seven years under the weight of its own political stupidity.

Conditions for military intervention in the Third World were far more inviting, especially in new, feeble and often tiny states where a few hundred armed men, reinforced or sometimes even replaced by foreigners, could carry decisive weight, and where inexperienced or incompetent governments were quite likely to produce recurrent states of chaos, corruption and confusion. The typical military ruler in most African countries was not an aspirant dictator, but someone genuinely trying to clear up such messes, hoping – too often in vain – that civilian government would soon take over again. Generally he failed in both endeavours, which is why few military chieftains lasted very long. In any case, the slightest hint that local government might fall into the hands of the communists virtually guaranteed American support.

In short, military politics, like military intelligence, tended to fill the void left by the absence of ordinary politics or intelligence. It was not any particular brand of politics, but a function of the surrounding instability and insecurity. However, it became increasingly pervasive in the Third World because virtually all the countries of the ex-colonial or dependent part of the globe were now committed, in one way or another, to policies which required them to have exactly those stable, functioning and efficient states which so few of them had. They were committed to economic independence and 'development'. In the aftermath of the second round of world war, world revolution and its consequence, global decolonization, it seemed that there was no future for the old programme of prosperity as primary-producers for the world market of the imperialist countries: the programme of the Argentine and Uruguayan *estancieros*, hopefully imitated by Mexico's Porfirio Díaz and Peru's Leguía. In any case it had ceased to look plausible since the Great Slump. Moreover, both nationalism and anti-imperialism called for policies less dependent on the old empires, and the example of the USSR provided an alternative model of 'development'. Never did that example look more impressive than in the years after 1945.

The more ambitious states therefore called for an end to agrarian backwardness by systematic industrialization, whether on the centrally-planned Soviet model or by import substitution. Both, in different ways, rested on state action and state control. Even the less ambitious, who did not dream of a future of great tropical steelworks, powered by huge hydro-electric installations overshadowed by titanic dams, wanted to control and develop their own national resources themselves. Oil had been traditionally produced by private Western corporations, usually with the closest relations to imperial powers. Governments, following the example of Mexico in 1938, now took to nationalizing them and operating them as state enterprises. Those which refrained from nationalization discovered (especially after 1950 when ARAMCO offered Saudi Arabia the hitherto unimaginable deal of a 50/50 revenue split) that physical possession of oil and gas gave them the whip-hand in negotiations with the foreign corporations. In practice the Organization of Petrol Exporting Countries (OPEC), which eventually held the world to ransom in the 1970s, became possible because the ownership of the world's oil had shifted from companies to a relatively few producer-governments. In short, even those governments of decolonized or dependent states which were quite happy with relying on foreign capitalists old or new ('neo-colonialism' in contemporary Left-wing terminology), did so within a state-controlled economy. Probably the most successful of such states until the 1980s was the former French Ivory Coast.

Probably the least successful were new countries which underestimated the constraints of backwardness – lack of skilled and experienced experts, administrators and economic cadres; illiteracy; unfamiliarity or lack of sympathy with programmes of economic modernization – especially when their governments set themselves targets which even developed countries found difficult, such as centrally state-planned industrialization. Ghana, with Sudan the first sub-Saharan African state to be granted independence, thus threw away currency reserves of two hundred millions, accumulated thanks to high cocoa prices and wartime earnings – higher than the sterling balances of independent India – in an attempt to build an industrialized state-controlled economy, not to mention Kwame Nkrumah's plans for pan-African union. The results were disastrous, and made worse by the collapse of cocoa prices in the 1960s. By 1972 the great projects had failed, the domestic industries in the small country could survive only behind high tariff walls, price controls and import licences, which led to a flourishing black economy and generalized corruption that has remained ineradicable. Three quarters of all wage-earners were employed in the public sector, while subsistence agriculture (as in so many other African states) was neglected. After Nkrumah's overthrow by the usual military coup (1966) the country continued on its disillusioned way amid a succession of usually disappointed military, and occasionally civilian governments.

The dismal record of sub-Saharan Africa's new states should not lead us to underestimate the substantial achievements of better-placed ex-colonial or dependent countries, who chose the road of state-planned or state-sponsored economic development. What came to be known from the 1970s in international functionaries' jargon as the NICs (Newly Industrializing Countries) were all, with the exception of the city-state of Hong Kong, based on such policies. As anyone with the slightest knowledge of Brazil and Mexico will testify, they produced bureaucracy, spectacular corruption and much waste – but also a 7 per cent annual rate of growth in both countries for decades: in short, both achieved the desired transition to modern industrial economies. In fact, Brazil became for a time the eighth-largest industrial country of the non-communist world. Both countries had a sufficiently vast population to provide a substantial home market, so that industrialization by import substitution made sense, at least for quite a long time. Public spending and activities sustained high demand at home. At one time the Brazilian public sector handled about half the gross domestic product and represented nineteen out of the twenty largest companies, while in Mexico it employed a fifth of the total workforce and paid two fifths of the national wage-bill (Harris, 1987, pp. 84–85). State-planning in the Far East tended to rely less on direct public enterprise and more on favoured business groups dominated by government control of credit and investment, but the dependence of economic development on the state was the same. Planning and state initiative was the name of the game everywhere in the world in the 1950s and 1960s and in the NICs until the 1990s. Whether this form of economic development produced satisfactory or disappointing results depended on local conditions and human errors.

III

Development, state-controlled or not, was not of immediate interest to the great majority of the inhabitants of the Third World who lived by growing their own food; for even in countries or colonies whose public revenues relied on the income from one or two major export crops – coffee, bananas or cocoa – these were usually concentrated in a few restricted areas. In sub-Saharan Africa and most of South and South-east Asia as well as in China, the mass of people continued to live by agriculture. Only in the western hemisphere and in the dry lands of western Islam did the countryside as yet drain into the giant cities, turning rural into urban societies in a couple of dramatic decades (see chapter 10). In fertile and not too densely populated regions, like much of black Africa, most people would have managed pretty well if left to themselves. Most of its inhabitants did not need their states, which were usually too weak to do much harm, and, if they grew too troublesome, could probably be by-passed by a retreat into village self-sufficiency. Few continents started the era of independence with greater advantages, which were soon to be thrown away. Most Asian and Islamic peasants were much poorer, or at least worse fed – sometimes, as in India, desperately and historically poor – and the pressure of men and women on limited lands was already more severe. Nevertheless, it seemed to a good many of them that the best solution to their problems was not to get involved with those who told them that economic development would bring untold wealth and prosperity, but to keep them at bay. Long experience had shown them and their ancestors before them, that no good came from outside. Generations of silent calculation had taught them that minimizing risks was a better policy than maximising profits. This did not keep them entirely outside the ambit of a global economic revolution which reached even the more isolated among them in the form of plastic sandals, petrol-cans, ancient trucks and – of course – government offices with pieces of paper in them, but it tended to divide humanity in such areas into those who operated in and through the world of writing and offices and the rest. In most of the rural Third World the central distinction was between 'coast' and 'interior' or city and backwoods.*

The trouble was that, since modernity and government went together, 'the interior' was governed by 'the coast', the backwoods by the city, the illiterate by the educated. In the beginning was the word. The House of Assembly of what would shortly become the independent state of Ghana, included among its 104 members sixty-eight who had had some form of post-primary education. The 106 members of the Legislative Assembly for the Telengana (South India) contained ninety-seven with secondary or higher education, including fifty graduates. In both these regions the great majority of the inhabitants at the time were illiterate (Hodgkin, 1961, p. 29; Gray, 1970, p. 135). What is more, anyone wishing to be active in the *national* government of Third World states needed to be literate not only in the common language of the region (which was not necessarily that of his or her community) but in one of the small number of international languages (English, French, Spanish, Arabic, Mandarin Chinese), or at least the regional lingua franca which new governments tended to develop into written 'national' languages (Swahili, Bahasa, Pidgin). The only exception was in those parts of Latin America where the written official languages (Spanish and Portuguese) coincided with the spoken language of the majority. Out of the candidates for public office in Hyderabad (India) in the general election of 1967 only three (out of thirty-four) spoke no English (Bernstorff, 1970, p. 146).

Even the more remote and backward people therefore increasingly recognized the advantages of superior education, even when they could not themselves share them; perhaps especially when they could not. In a literal sense, knowledge meant power, most obviously in countries where the state appeared to its subjects to be a machine that extracted their resources and then distributed these resources to state employees. Education meant a post, often a guaranteed post,† in the public service, with luck a career, which enabled men to extract bribes and commissions and to provide jobs for family and friends. A village in, say, Central Africa, which invested in the education of one of its young men, hoped for a

---

* Similar divisions were to be found in some of the backward regions of socialist states, e.g. in Soviet Kazakhstan, where the indigenous inhabitants showed no interest in abandoning farming and livestock, leaving industrialization and cities to a correspondingly large body of (Russian) immigrants.

† E.g. until the mid-1980s in Benin, Congo, Guinea, Somalia, Sudan, Mali, Rwanda and the Central African Republic (World Labour, 1989, p. 49).

return in the form of income and protection for the whole community from the government post which education would guarantee. In any case the successful civil servant was the best-paid man in the population. In a country like Uganda in the 1960s he could expect a (legal) salary 112 times the average per capita income of his countrymen (as against a comparable ratio of 10:1 in Great Britain) (UN *World Social Situation*, 1970, p. 66).

Where it seemed that poor people from the countryside might themselves share in the advantages of education, or provide them for their children (as in Latin America, the Third World region closest to modernity and most distant from colonialism), the desire to learn was virtually universal. 'They all want to learn something,' a Chilean communist organizer among the Mapuche Indians told the author in 1962. 'I'm not an intellectual, and I can't teach them school knowledge, so I teach them how to play football.' This thirst for knowledge explains much of the amazing mass migration from village to city which emptied the countryside of the South American continent from the 1950s on. For all enquiries concur that the attraction of the city lay not least in the better chances of education and training for the children. There they 'could become something else'. Schooling naturally opened the best prospects, but in backward agrarian regions even so simple a skill as being able to drive a motor vehicle could be the key to a better life. It was the first thing that an emigrant from a Quechua village in the Andes taught the cousins and nephews from home who joined him in the city, hoping to make their own way into the modern world, for had not his employment as an ambulance driver proved to be the foundation of his own family's success? (Julca, 1992).

Probably it was not until the 1960s or later that rural people outside parts of Latin America began systematically to see modernity as a promise rather than a threat. And yet there was one aspect of the policy of economic development which might have been expected to appeal to them since it directly affected the three fifths or more of human beings who lived by agriculture: land reform. This general slogan of politics in agrarian countries might cover anything from the break-up of large landholdings and their re-distribution to peasants and landless labourers to the abolition of feudal tenures or servitudes; rent reduction and tenancy reforms of various kinds to revolutionary land nationalization and collectivization.

There has probably never been more of it than in the decade after the end of the Second World War, for it was practised along the entire spectrum of politics. Between 1945 and 1950 almost half of the human race found themselves living in countries undergoing some kind of land reform – of the communist type in Eastern Europe and, after 1949 China, as a consequence of decolonization in the former British Indian empire and as a consequence of Japan's defeat, or rather American occupation policy, in Japan, Taiwan and Korea. The Egyptian revolution of 1952 extended its range to the western Islamic world: Iraq, Syria and Algeria followed the Cairo example. The Bolivian revolution of 1952 introduced it into South America, though Mexico since the revolution of 1910, or, more precisely, since its revival in the 1930s, had long championed *agrarismo*. Still, in spite of an increasing flood of political declarations and statistical enquiry on the subject, Latin America had too few revolutions, decolonisations or lost wars to have much actual land reform, until Fidel Castro's Cuban revolution (which introduced it on that island) put the matter on the political agenda.

For the modernizers the case for land reform was political (gaining peasant support for revolutionary regimes or for those which could pre-empt revolution or the like), ideological ('giving the land back to the toilers' etc.), and sometimes economic, although most revolutionaries or reformers did not expect too much from a mere distribution of land to a traditional peasantry and the landless or land-poor. Indeed, farm output fell drastically in Bolivia and Iraq immediately after these countries' respective land reforms in 1952 and 1958, though in fairness one should add that, where peasant skill and productivity were already high, land reform could quickly release a great deal of productive potential hitherto held in reserve by sceptical villagers, as in Egypt, Japan and, most strikingly, Taiwan (Land Reform, 1968, pp. 570–75). The case for maintaining a large peasantry in being was and is non-economic, since in the history of the modern world the enormous rise in agrarian output has gone together with an equally spectacular decline in the number and proportion of agriculturists; most dramatically so since the Second World War. Land reform could and did, however, demonstrate that peasant farming, especially by larger, modern-minded farmers, could be as efficient as, and more flexible than the traditional landed estate, the imperialist plantation, and, indeed, ill-judged modern attempts to conduct agriculture on a quasi-industrial basis, such as Soviet-type giant state farms and the British scheme for producing ground-nuts in Tanganyika (the present Tanzania) after 1945. Crops like coffee, or even sugar and rubber, once thought of as essentially plantation-produced, are so no longer, even if the plantation still maintains a clear advantage over small-scale and unskilled producers in some cases. Still, the major advances of Third World agriculture since the war, the 'Green revolution' of new scientifically selected crops, have been achieved by business-minded farmers, as in the Punjab.

However, the strongest economic case for land reform rests not on productivity but on equality. On the whole economic development has tended, first to increase and later to diminish the inequality of national income distribution over the long haul, although economic decline and a theological belief in the free market have lately begun to reverse this here and there. Equality at the end of the Golden Age was greater in the developed Western countries than in the Third World. Yet while income inequality was at its highest in Latin America, followed by Africa, it was unusually low in a number of Asian countries, where a very radical land reform had been imposed under the auspices, or by, the American occupying forces: Japan, South Korea and Taiwan. (None, however, were as egalitarian as the socialist countries of Eastern Europe or, at the time, Australia.) (Kakwani, 1980.) Observers of the industrialising triumphs of these countries have naturally speculated how far they have been assisted by the social or economic advantages of this situation, just as observers of the much more fitful advance of the Brazilian economy, always on the verge of but never achieving its destiny as the USA of the southern hemisphere, have wondered how far it has been held back by the spectacular inequality of its income distribution – which inevitably restricts the domestic market for industry. Indeed, the striking social inequality of Latin America can hardly be unconnected with the equally striking absence of systematic agrarian reform from so many of its countries.

Land reform was undoubtedly welcomed by the peasantry of the Third World, at least until it was transformed into collective farming or cooperative production, as it usually was in communist countries. However, what the modernisers saw in it was not what it meant to the peasants, who were uninterested in macro–economic problems, who saw national politics in a different perspective from the city reformers, and whose demand for land was not based on general principle but on specific claims. Thus the radical land reform instituted by a government of reformist generals in Peru in 1969, which destroyed the country's system of large estates (*haciendas*) at one blow, failed for this reason. For the Indian highland communities, which had lived in unstable coexistence with the vast Andean livestock ranches to whom they supplied labour, reform simply meant the just return to the 'native communities' of the common lands and pastures once alienated from them by the landlords, whose boundaries were accurately remembered over the centuries, and whose loss they had never accepted (Hobsbawm, 1974). They were not interested in the maintenance of the old enterprise as a productive unit (now under the ownership of the *comunidades* and its former workforce), in cooperative experiments, or in other agrarian novelties, other than the traditional mutual aid within the – far from egalitarian – community. After the reform the communities went back to 'invading' the lands of the cooperativized estates (of which they were now co-proprietors), as though nothing had changed in the conflict between estate and community (and between communities in dispute about their lands) (Gómez Rodríguez, pp. 242–55). As far as they were concerned, nothing had changed. The land reform closest to the peasant ideal was probably the Mexican one of the 1930s, which gave the common land inalienably to village communities to organize as they wished (*ejidos*) and assumed peasants were engaged in subsistence agriculture. It was a huge political success, but economically irrelevant to subsequent Mexican agrarian development.

IV

It is not surprising that the dozens of post-colonial states which emerged after the Second World War, together with most of Latin America, which also plainly belonged to the regions dependent on the old imperial and industrial world, soon found themselves grouped together as the 'Third World' – the term is said to have been coined in 1952 (Harris, 1987, p.18) – by contrast with the 'First World' of the developed capitalist countries and the 'Second World' of the communist ones. In spite of the evident absurdity of treating Egypt and Gabon, India and Papua-New Guinea as societies of the same kind, this was not wholly implausible, inasmuch as all were poor (compared to the 'developed' world), * all were dependent, all had governments that wanted to 'develop', and none believed, in the aftermath of the Great Slump and the Second World War, that the capitalist world market (i.e. the economists' doctrine of 'comparative advantage') or spontaneous private enterprise at home would achieve this end. Moreover, as the iron grille of the Cold War was clamped across the globe, all who had any freedom of action wanted to avoid joining either of the two alliance systems, i.e. to keep out of the Third World War which everyone feared.

* With the rarest exceptions, notably Argentina, which though rich, never recovered from the decline and fall of the British Empire, which had given it prosperity as a food exporter until 1929.

This does not mean that the 'non-aligned' were equally opposed to both sides in the Cold War. The inspirers and champions of the movement (usually called after its first international conference in 1955 at Bandung in Indonesia), were radical colonial ex-revolutionaries – Jawaharlal Nehru of India, Sukarno of Indonesia, Colonel Gamal Abdel Nasser of Egypt, and a dissident communist, President Tito of Yugoslavia. All these, like so many of the ex-colonial regimes, were or claimed to be socialist in their own (i.e. non-Soviet) way, including the Royal Buddhist socialism of Cambodia. All had some sympathies for the Soviet Union or were at least ready to accept economic and military help from it; not surprisingly, since the United States had abandoned its old anti-colonial traditions at a moment's notice after the world divided, and visibly looked for support among the most conservative elements of the Third World: Iraq (before the 1958 revolution), Turkey, Pakistan and the Shah's Iran, which formed the Central Treaty Organization (CENTO); Pakistan, the Philippines and Thailand in the South-east Asia Treaty Organization (SEATO), both designed to complete the anti-Soviet military system whose main pillar was NATO (neither amounted to much). When the essentially Afro-Asian non-aligned group became tri-continental after the Cuban revolution of 1959, its Latin American members not surprisingly came from the republics of the western hemisphere least sympathetic to the Big Brother of the North. Nevertheless, unlike the US sympathisers in the Third World, who might actually join the western alliance system, the non-communist Bandung states had no intention of being involved in a global superpower confrontation, since, as the Korean and the Vietnam War and the Cuban missile crisis proved, they were the perpetual potential front line in such a conflict. The more the actual (European) border between the two camps was stabilized, the more likely, if the guns were to fire, the bombs to drop, it would be in some Asian mountains or African bush.

Yet though the superpower confrontation dominated, and to some extent stabilized, inter-state relations world-wide, it did not entirely control them. There were two regions in which indigenous Third World tensions, essentially unconnected with the Cold War, created permanent conditions for conflict which periodically erupted in war: the Middle East and the northern part of the Indian subcontinent. (Both, not by chance, were the heirs to imperial schemes of partition.) The latter conflict zone was more easily insulated from the global Cold War, in spite of Pakistan's attempts to involve the Americans, which failed until the Afghan War of the 1980s (see chapters 8 and 16). Hence the West heard little and remembers even less of the three regional wars: the Sino–Indian War of

1962 over the ill-defined border between the two countries, won by China; the Indo–Pakistan War of 1965 (handily won by India); and the second Indo–Pakistan conflict of 1971, arising out of the breakaway of East Pakistan (Bangladesh), which India supported. USA and USSR tried to act as benevolent neutrals and mediators. The situation in the Middle East could not be so isolated, because several of America's allies were directly involved: Israel, Turkey and the Shah's Iran. Moreover, as the succession of local revolutions, military and civilian, proved – from Egypt in 1952 via Iraq and Syria in the 1950s and 1960s; South Arabia in the 1960s and 1970s, to Iran itself in 1979 – the region was and remains socially unstable.

These regional conflicts had no essential connection with the Cold War: the USSR had been among the first to recognize the new state of Israel, which later established itself as the main ally of the USA, and the Arab or other Islamic states, Right or Left, were united in repressing communism within their frontiers. The main force of disruption was Israel, where the Jewish settlers built a larger Jewish state than had been envisaged under the British partition (driving out seven hundred thousand non-Jewish Palestinians, perhaps a larger number than the Jewish population in 1948) (Calvocoressi, 1989, p. 215), fighting one war per decade for the purpose (1948, 1956, 1967, 1973, 1982). In the course of these wars, which can best be compared with the wars fought by the Prussian king Frederick II in the eighteenth century to win recognition for his possession of Silesia, which he had robbed from his neighbour, Austria, Israel also turned itself into the most formidable military force in the region and acquired nuclear arms, but failed to establish a stable basis of relations with its neighbour states, let alone with the permanently embittered Palestinians within its extended frontiers or in the diaspora of the Middle East. The collapse of the USSR removed the Middle East from the front line of the Cold War, but left it as explosive as before.

Three lesser centres of conflict helped to keep it so: the eastern Mediterranean, the Persian Gulf and the border region between Turkey, Iran, Iraq and Syria where the Kurds attempted vainly to win the national independence which President Wilson had incautiously urged them to demand in 1918. Unable to find a permanent backer among the powerful states, they disturbed the relations between all their neighbours, who massacred them by all available means, including in the 1980s poison gas, insofar as not resisted by the proverbial skill of the Kurds as mountain guerrilla fighters. The eastern Mediterranean remained relatively quiet, since both Greece and Turkey were members of NATO, even though the conflict between the two led to a Turkish invasion of Cyprus, which was partitioned in 1974. On the other hand the rivalry between the western powers, Iraq and Iran, for positions in the Persian Gulf was to lead to the savage eight-year war between Iraq and revolutionary Iran 1980–88 and, after the end of the Cold War, between the USA and its allies and Iraq in 1991.

One part of the Third World remained fairly remote from both global and local international conflicts until after the Cuban revolution: Latin America. Except for small patches on the mainland (the Guyanas, Belize – then known as British Honduras and the smaller islands of the Caribbean), it had been decolonized long ago. Culturally and linguistically its populations were Western, inasmuch as the great bulk of even its poor inhabitants were Roman Catholics and, but for some areas of the Andes and continental central America, spoke or understood a culture-language shared by Europeans. While the region had inherited an elaborate racial hierarchy from the Iberian conquerors, it also inherited from an overwhelmingly male conquest a tradition of massive miscegenation. There were few genuine whites, except in the southern cone of South America (Argentina, Uruguay, southern Brazil) populated by European mass immigration, where there were very few natives. In both cases achievement and social status cancelled out race. Mexico elected a recognizably Zapotec Indian, Benito Juárez, as president as early as 1861. At the time of writing Argentina has as president a Lebanese Muslim immigrant and Peru a Japanese immigrant. Both choices were still unthinkable in the USA. To this day Latin America still remains outside the vicious circle of ethnic politics and ethnic nationalism which ravages the other continents.

Moreover, while most of the continent clearly recognized itself to be what was now called a 'neocolonial' dependency on a single dominant imperial power, the USA was realistic enough not to send gunboats and marines into the larger states – it did not hesitate to use them against the small ones – and the Latin governments from the Rio Grande to Cape Horn knew perfectly well that the wise thing was to keep on the right side of Washington. The Organization of American States (OAS), founded in 1948, its headquarters in Washington, was not a body inclined to disagree with the USA. When Cuba made its revolution, the OAS expelled it.

V

And yet, at the very moment when the Third World and the ideologies based on it were at their peak, the concept began to crumble. In the 1970s it became increasingly evident that no single name or label could adequately cover a set of increasingly divergent countries. The term was still convenient to distinguish poor countries of the world from the rich, and insofar as the gap between the two zones, often now called 'the North' and 'the South', was visibly widening, there was much point to the distinction. The gap in per capita GNP between the 'developed' and the backward world (i.e. the OECD countries and the 'low and middle economies')* continued to widen: the first group averaged 14.5 times the GNP per capita of the second in 1970 but over twenty-four times the poor countries' GNP per capita in 1990 (*World Tables*, 1991, Table 1). However, the Third World is demonstrably no longer a single entity.

What split it was primarily economic development. The triumph of OPEC in 1973 produced, for the first time, a body of Third World states, mostly backward by any criteria and hitherto poor, which now emerged as world-scale super-millionaires, especially when they consisted of smallish thinly inhabited stretches of sand or forest ruled by (usually Muslim) sheikhs or sultans. It was plainly impossible to class, say, the United Arab Emirates, each of whose half-million inhabitants (1975) had, in theory, a share of the GNP worth over $13,000 – almost double the GNP per capita of the USA at this date (*World Tables*, 1991, pp. 596, 604) – in the same pigeon-hole as, say, Pakistan, which then enjoyed a GNP per capita of $130. Oil states with a large population did not do so well, but it nevertheless became evident that states dependent on the export of a single primary commodity, however disadvantaged in other respects, could become extremely rich, even if this easy money also, almost invariably, tempted them into throwing it out of the window.† By the early 1990s even Saudi Arabia had managed to run into debt.

In the second place, part of the Third World was visibly and rapidly becoming industrialized and joining the First World, even though it

* The OECD, which comprises most of the 'developed' capitalist countries, includes Belgium, Denmark, the German Federal Republic, France, Great Britain, Ireland, Iceland, Italy, Luxemburg, Netherlands, Norway, Sweden, Switzerland, Canada and the USA, Japan and Australia. For political reasons this organization, set up during the Cold War, also included Greece, Portugal, Spain and Turkey.

† This is not a Third World phenomenon. When informed of the wealth of the British North Sea oil fields, a cynical French politician is said to have remarked prophetically: 'They will waste it and run into a crisis.'

remained much poorer. South Korea, as spectacular an industrial success story as any in history, had a GNP per capita (1989) barely higher than that of Portugal, the poorest by far of the members of the European Community (World Bank Atlas , 1990, p. 7). Once again, qualitative differences apart, South Korea is no longer comparable with, say, Papua-New Guinea, although the GNP per capita of the two countries was exactly the same in 1969 and remained of the same order of magnitude until the middle of the 1970s: it is now about five times as large (World Tables, 1991, pp. 352, 456). As we have seen, a new category, the NICs, entered the international jargon. There was no precise definition, but practically all lists include the four 'Pacific tigers' (Hong Kong, Singapore, Taiwan and South Korea), India, Brazil and Mexico, but the process of Third World industrialization is such that Malaya and the Philippines, Colombia, Pakistan and Thailand as well as some others have also been included. Actually, a category of new and rapid industrializers crosses the borders of the three worlds, for strictly it should also include such 'industrialized market economies' (i.e. capitalist countries) as Spain and Finland, and most of the ex-socialist states of Eastern Europe; not to mention, since the late 1970s, Communist China.

In fact, in the 1970s observers began to draw attention to a 'new international division of labour', i.e. a massive shift of industries producing for the world market from the first generation of industrial economies, which had previously monopolized them, to other parts of the world. This was partly due to the deliberate transfer by firms from the old industrial world of part or all of their production or supplies to the Second and Third Worlds, eventually followed by some transfers of even very sophisticated processes in high-tech industries, such as research and development. The revolution in modern transport and communications made genuinely worldwide production both possible and economic. It was also due to the deliberate efforts of Third World governments to industrialize by conquering export markets, if need be (but preferably not) at the expense of the old protection of home markets.

This economic globalization, which can be verified by anyone who checks the national origins of products sold in any North American shopping mall, developed slowly in the 1960s and accelerated strikingly during the decades of the world's economic troubles after 1973. How rapidly it advanced may once again be illustrated by South Korea which, at the end of the 1950s, still had almost 80 per cent of its working population in agriculture, from which it derived almost three quarters of its national income (Rado, 1962, pp. 740, 742–43). It inaugurated the first of its Five-Year development plans in 1962. By the late 1980s it got only

10 per cent of its GDP from agriculture and had become the eighth-largest industrial economy of the non-communist world.

In the third place, a number of countries emerged (or rather were submerged) at the bottom of the international statistics, which even international euphemism found it difficult to describe simply as 'developing', since they were plainly both poor and increasingly lagging. A sub-group of low-income developing countries was tactfully established to distinguish the three billion human beings whose GNP per capita (had they received it) would have worked out at an average of $330 in 1989, from the five hundred luckier millions in less destitute countries, like the Dominican Republic, Ecuador and Guatemala, whose average GNP was about three times as high and the even more luxurious members of the next group (Brazil, Malaysia, Mexico and the like) which averaged about eight times as much. (The eight hundred or so millions in the most prosperous group enjoyed a theoretical GNP allocation per head of $18,280 or fifty-five times as much as the bottom three-fifths of humanity (World Bank Atlas, 1990, p. 10). In effect, as the world economy became genuinely global and, especially after the fall of the Soviet region, more purely capitalist and business-dominated, investors and entrepreneurs discovered that large parts of it were of no profitable interest to them, unless, perhaps, they could bribe its politicians and civil servants into wasting the money extracted from their unfortunate citizens on armaments or prestige projects.*

A disproportionately large number of these countries were to be found in the unhappy continent of Africa. The end of the Cold War deprived such states of the economic (i.e. largely military) aid which had turned some of them, like Somalia, into armed camps and eventual battlefields.

Moreover, as divisions among the poor increased, so globalization brought movements most obviously of human beings that crossed the dividing lines between regions and classifications. From the rich countries tourists flowed into the Third World as never before. In the middle of the 1980s (1985), to take only some Muslim countries, the sixteen millions of Malaysia received three million tourists per year; the seven million Tunisians two millions; the three million Jordanians two millions (Din, 1989, p. 545). From the poor countries the streams of labour migration into the rich swelled into huge torrents, insofar as they were

---

* 'As a rule of thumb 5 per cent of $200,000 will win the help of a senior official below top rank. The same percentage of $2m and you are dealing with the permanent secretary. At $20m enter the minister and senior staff, while a cut from $200m "justifies the serious attention of the head of state"' (Holman, 1993).

not dammed back by political barriers. By 1968 migrants from the Maghreb (Tunisia, Morocco and, above all, Algeria) already formed almost a quarter of all foreigners in France (in 1975 5.5 per cent of the Algerian population emigrated) and one third of all immigrants to the USA came from Latin America – at that time still overwhelmingly from Central America (Potts, 1990, pp. 145, 146, 150). Nor did this migration move only towards the old industrial countries. The number of foreign workers in the oil-producing states of the Middle East and Libya shot up from 1.8 to 2.8 millions in a mere five years (1975–80) (Population, 1984, p. 109). Most of them came from the region, but a large body came from South Asia and even further afield. Unfortunately in the grim 1970s and 1980s labour migration became increasingly hard to separate from the torrents of men, women and children who fled from, or were uprooted by, famine, political or ethnic persecution, war and civil war, thus facing the countries of the First World, equally committed (in theory) to helping refugees and (in practice) to preventing immigration from poor countries, with severe problems of political and legal casuistry. With the exception of the USA, and to a lesser extent Canada and Australia, which encouraged or permitted mass immigration from the Third World, they opted to keep them out under the pressure of a growing xenophobia among their native populations.

VI

The astonishing 'great leap forward' of the (capitalist) world economy, and its growing globalization not only divided and disrupted the concept of a Third World, it also brought virtually all its inhabitants consciously into the modern world. They did not necessarily like it. Indeed, many 'fundamentalist' and other nominally traditionalist movements which now gained ground in several Third World countries, especially, but not exclusively, in the Islamic region, were specifically revolts against modernity, though this is certainly not true of all movements to which this imprecise label is attached.* But they knew themselves to be part of a world which was not like their fathers'. It came to them in the form of the dusty backroads bus or truck; the petrol pump; the battery-powered

* Thus conversion to 'fundamentalist' Protestant sects, which is common in Latin America, is, if anything, a 'modernist' reaction against the ancient status quo represented by local Catholicism. Other 'fundamentalisms' are analagous to ethnic nationalism, e.g. in India.

transistor radio, which brought the world to them – perhaps even to the illiterates in their own unwritten dialect or language, though this was probably the privilege of the urban immigrant. But in a world where country people migrated to the cities in their millions, and even in rural Africa countries with urban populations of a third or more becoming common – Nigeria, Zaire, Tanzania, Senegal, Ghana, Ivory Coast, Chad, Central African Republic, Gabon, Benin, Zambia, Congo, Somalia, Liberia – almost everybody had worked in the city, or had a relative who lived there. Village and city were henceforth interwoven. Even the most remote now lived in a world of plastic sheeting, Coca-Cola bottles, cheap digital watches and artificial fibres. By a strange inversion of history the back country of the Third World even began to commercialize its skills in the First World. On city street-corners of Europe small groups of peripatetic Indians from the South American Andes played their melancholy flutes and on the pavements of New York, Paris and Rome black pedlars from West Africa sold trinkets to the natives as the natives' ancestors had done on their trading voyages to the Dark Continent.

Almost certainly the big city was the crucible of change, if only because it was modern by definition. 'In Lima', as an upwardly mobile migrant from the Andes used to tell his children, 'there's more progress, there's much more stimulation' (*más roce*) (Julca, 1992). However much the migrants used the tool-kit of traditional society to construct their urban existence, building and structuring the new shanty-towns like the old rural communities, too much in the city was novel and unprecedented, too many of its mores conflicted with those of the olden days. Nowhere was this more dramatic than in the expected behaviour of young women, whose break with tradition was deplored from Africa to Peru. In a traditional *huayno* song from Lima ('*La gringa*') an immigrant boy complains:

> When you came from your homeland, you came as a country girl
> Now you are in Lima you comb your hair in a city way
> You even say, wait 'please'. I'm going to dance the twist
> . . .
> Don't be pretentious, be less proud
> . . .
> Between your hair and my hair, there is no difference.
> (Mangin, 1970, pp. 31–32.)*

---

* Or, from Nigeria in the image of a new type of African girl in the market literature of Onitsha: 'The girls are no longer the traditional, quiet, modest playthings

Yet from the city the consciousness of modernity spread to the countryside (even where rural life was not itself transformed by new crops, new technology, and new forms of organization and marketing) through the dramatic 'green revolution' of grain-crop farming by scientifically designed crop varieties in parts of Asia, which spread from the 1960s on, or, a little later, by the development of new export crops for the world market, made possible both by the mass air-freighting of perishables (tropical fruit, flowers) and new consumer tastes in the 'developed' world (cocaine). The effect of such rural changes is not to be underestimated. Nowhere did the old ways and the new come into more frontal collision than on the Amazonian frontier of Colombia, which in the 1970s became a staging-post for the transport of Bolivian and Peruvian coca, and the location of the laboratories processing it into cocaine. This happened a few years after it had been settled by peasant frontier colonists escaping from state and landlords, and who were defended by those recognized protectors of the peasant way of life, the (communist) guerrillas of the FARC. Here the market, in its most ruthless form, clashed with those who lived by subsistence farming and what men could get with a gun, a dog and a fishing-net. How could a patch of yucca and bananas compete against the temptation to cultivate a crop commanding bonanza prices – even though unstable ones – and the old way of life against the airstrips and the boomtown settlements of the drug-makers and traffickers and their freewheeling gunmen, bars and brothels? (Molano, 1988.)

The countryside was indeed being transformed, but even its transformations depended on the city civilization and its industries, for often enough its very economy depended on the earnings of the emigrants, as in the so-called 'black homelands' of apartheid South Africa, which generated only 10-15 per cent of their inhabitants' income, the remainder coming from the earnings of migrant workers in the white territories (Ripken and Wellmer, 1978, pp. 196). Paradoxically, in the Third World as in parts of the First, the city could become the saviour of a rural economy which, but for its impact, might have been abandoned by people who had learned from migrant experience – their own or their neighbours' – that men and women had alternatives. They discovered that it was not inevitable that they should slave a lifetime away scratching a wretched livelihood from marginal, exhausted and stony land, as their ancestors had done. Plenty of rural settlements across the globe, in romantic, and

of their parents. They write love letters. They are coy. They demand presents from their boy-friends and victims. They even deceive men. They are no longer the dumb creatures to be won through their parents' (Nwoga, 1965, pp. 178–79).

therefore agriculturally marginal landscapes, were emptied of all except the elderly from the 1960s on. Yet a highland community whose emigrants discovered a niche in the economy of the big city which they could occupy – in this case selling fruit, or, more precisely, strawberries in Lima – could maintain or revitalize its pastoral character by a shift from farm-income to non-farm-income operating through a complicated symbiosis of migrant and resident households (Smith, 1989, chapter 4). It is perhaps significant that, in this particular case, which has been unusually well studied, the migrants rarely became workers. They chose to fit into the great network of the Third World 'informal economy' as petty traders. For the major social change in the Third World was probably that carried by the new and growing middle and lower-middle classes of migrants engaged in some method, or more likely multiple methods, of earning money, and the major form of its economic life was – especially in the poorest countries – the informal economy which escaped official statistics.

So, some time in the last third of the century the wide trench that separated the small modernising or Westernized ruling minorities of Third World countries from the mass of their peoples began to be filled by the general transformation of their societies. We do not yet know how or when this happened or what forms the new consciousness of this transformation took, for most of these countries still lacked even adequate government statistical services or the machinery of market and public opinion research, or the academic social science departments with research students to keep busy. In any case, what happens at the grassroots of societies is difficult to discover even in the best-documented countries, until it has happened, which is why the early stages of new social and cultural fashions among the young are unpredictable, unpredicted and often unrecognized even by those who live by making money out of them, like the popular culture industry, let alone by the parental generation. Yet clearly something was stirring in Third World cities below the level of elite consciousness, even in an apparently completely stagnant country like the Belgian Congo (now Zaire), for how else can we explain that the type of popular music developed there in the inert 1950s became the most influential in Africa in the 1960s and 1970s (Manuel, 1988, pp. 86, 97–101)? For that matter, how can we explain the rise of political consciousness which causes the Belgians to send the Congo off to independence in 1960 virtually at a moment's notice, though until then this colony, almost equally hostile to native education as to native political activity, looked, to most observers, as 'likely to remain as shut off from the rest of the world as Japan before the Meiji restoration' (Calvocoressi, 1989, p. 377)?

Whatever the stirrings in the 1950s, by the 1960s and 1970s the signs of major social transformation were quite evident in the western hemisphere, and undeniable in the Islamic world and the major countries of South and Southeast Asia. Paradoxically, they were probably least visible in the parts of the socialist world which corresponded to the Third World, e.g. in Soviet central Asia and the Caucasus. For it is not often recognized that communist revolution was an engine of conservation. While it set out to transform a specified number of aspects of life – state power, property relations, economic structure and the like – it froze others in their pre-revolutionary shapes, or at any rate protected them against the universal continuous subversion of change in capitalist societies. In any case its strongest weapon, sheer state power, was less effective at transforming human behaviour than either the positive rhetoric about 'the new socialist man' or the negative rhetoric about 'totalitarianism' liked to think. Uzbeks and Tadjiks who lived north of the Soviet–Afghan border were almost certainly more literate and more secularized and better-off than those who lived south of it, but they may not have differed as much in their mores as seventy years of socialism would have led one to expect. Blood-feud was probably not a major preoccupation of the authorities in the Caucasus since the 1930s (though during collectivisation the death of a man in a *kolkhoz* threshing-machine accident led to a feud which entered the annals of Soviet jurisprudence), but in the early 1990s observers warned of 'the danger of national self-extermination [in Chechnia] since the majority of the Chechen families have been dragged into a vendetta type relationship' (Trofimov/Djangava, 1993).

The cultural consequences of this social transformation await the historian. They cannot be considered here, though it is clear that, even in very traditional societies, the network of mutual obligation and customs came under increasing strain. 'The extended family in Ghana and across Africa' it was observed (Harden, 1990, p. 67) 'functions under immense stress. Like a bridge that has borne too much high-speed traffic for too many years, its foundations are cracking . . . The rural old and the urban young are separated by hundreds of miles of bad roads and centuries of development.'

Politically it is easier to assess the paradoxical consequences. For, with the entry of the masses of the population, or at least the young and city people, into a modern world, the monopoly of the small, Westernized elites who shaped the first generation of post-colonial history was being challenged. And with them, the programmes, the ideologies, the very vocabulary and syntax of the public discourse, on which the new states rested. For the new urban and urbanised masses, even the new massive middle classes, however educated, were not, and by virtue of sheer numbers, could not be, the old elites, whose members could hold their own with the colonialists or with their fellow-graduates from European or American schools. Often – this was very obvious in South Asia – they resented them. In any case, the masses of the poor did not share the belief in the Western nineteenth-century aspiration of secular progress. In the western Islamic countries the conflict between the old secular leaders and the new Islamic mass democracy became patent, and explosive. From Algeria to Turkey the values which, in the countries of Western liberalism, are associated with constitutional government and the rule of law, as for instance the rights of women, were being protected – insofar as they existed – against democracy by the military force of the liberators of their nations, or their heirs.

The conflict was not confined to Islamic countries, nor the reaction against the old values of progress to the masses of the poor. The Hindu exclusivism of the BJP party in India had substantial support among the new business and middle classes. The impassioned and savage ethno-religious nationalism which in the 1980s turned peaceful Sri Lanka into a killing field, comparable only to El Salvador, occurred, unexpectedly, in a prosperous Buddhist country. It was rooted in two social transformations: the profound identity crisis of villages whose social order had gone to pieces, and the rise of a mass stratum of better-educated youth (Spencer, 1990). Villages transmuted by in-and out-migration, divided by the widening differences between rich and poor that the cash economy brought, racked with the instability brought by the unevenness of an education-based social mobility, the fading of the physical and linguistic markers of caste and status which separated people but also left no doubt about their positions – these inevitably lived in anxiety about their community. This has been used to explain, among other things, the appearance of novel symbols and rituals of a togetherness which was itself novel, such as the sudden development of congregational forms of Buddhist worship in the 1970s, replacing older private and household forms of devotion; or the institution of school sports days opened with the national anthem played on borrowed tape cassettes.

These were the politics of a changing and inflammable world. What made them less predictable was that in many countries of the Third World nationwide politics in the sense invented and recognized in the West since the French Revolution had never existed, or had not been allowed to function. Where there was a long tradition of politics with some kind of mass roots, or even a substantial acceptance among the passive citizens of the legitimacy of the 'political classes' who conducted their affairs, a degree of continuity could be maintained. Colombians, as readers of García Márquez know, continued to be born little liberals or little conservatives, as they had for more than a century, though they might change the content of the bottles with these labels. The Indian National Congress changed, split and reformed in the half-century since independence, but until the 1990s Indian general elections – with only fleeting exceptions – continued to be won by those who appealed to its historic aims and traditions. Though communism disintegrated elsewhere, the deep-rooted Left-wing tradition of Hindu (West) Bengal, as well as competent administration maintained the Communist Party (Marxist) in almost permanent government in the state where the national struggle against Britain had meant not Gandhi nor even Nehru, but the terrorists and Subhas Bose.

Moreover, structural change might itself lead politics in directions familiar in the history of the First World. 'Newly industrializing countries' were likely to develop industrial working classes who demanded workers' rights and labour unions, as the record of Brazil and South Korea showed, as indeed did that of Eastern Europe. They did not have to develop political labour-cum-people's parties reminiscent of the mass social democratic movements of pre-1914 Europe, although it is not insignificant that Brazil generated just such a successful national party in the 1980s, the Workers' Party (PT). (But the tradition of the workers' movement in its home base, the automobile industry of São Paulo, was a combination of populist labour law and communist factory militants, and that of the intellectuals who flocked to support it was solidly Left, as was the ideology of the Catholic clergy, whose support helped to put it on its feet.)* Again, the rapid industrial growth tended to generate large and educated professional classes which, though far from subversive, would have welcomed the civic liberalization of authoritarian industrializing regimes. Such longings for liberalization were to be found, in the 1980s, in different contexts and with varying results, in Latin America and the Far-Eastern NICs (South Korea and Taiwan), as well as within the Soviet block.

Nevertheless, there were vast areas of the Third World where the political consequences of social transformation were indeed impossible to

---

* Except for the socialist orientation of the one, the anti-socialist ideology of the other, the similarities between the Brazilian Workers' Party and the contemporary Polish Solidarity movement were striking: a bona fide proletarian leader – a shipyard electrician and skilled auto-worker – a brains trust of intellectuals and strong Church backing. They are even greater if we remember that the PT sought to replace the communist organization, which opposed it.

foresee. All that was certain, was the instability and inflammability of that world, to which the half-century since the Second World War had borne witness.

We must now turn to that part of the world which, for most of the Third World after decolonisation, appeared to provide a more suitable and encouraging model for progress than the West: the 'Second World' of the socialist systems modelled on the Soviet Union.

CHAPTER THIRTEEN
'Real Socialism'

The October Revolution did not only produce a world-historical division by establishing the first post-capitalist state and society, but it also divided Marxism and socialist politics ... After the October Revolution, socialist strategies and perspectives began to be based upon political example instead of upon analyses of capitalism.

> – Göran Therborn (1985, p. 227)

Economists today ... understand much better than before the real versus the formal modes of the economy's functioning. They know about the 'second economy', maybe even a third one too, and about a welter of informal but widespread practices without which nothing works.

> – Moshe Lewin in Kerblay (1983, p. xxii)

I

When the dust of the battles of war and civil war had settled in the early 1920s, and the blood of the corpses and wounds had congealed, most of what had before 1914 been the Orthodox Russian Empire of the Tsars emerged intact as an empire, but under the government of the Bolsheviks and dedicated to the construction of world socialism. It was the only one of the antique dynastic-cum-religious empires to survive the First World War, which shattered both the Ottoman Empire, whose sultan was khalif of all faithful Muslims, and the Habsburg Empire which maintained a special relationship with the Roman Church. Both broke up under the pressures of defeat. That Russia survived as a single multi-ethnic entity stretching from the Polish border in the west to the Japanese border in

the east was almost certainly due to the October revolution, for the
tensions which had broken up the earlier empires elsewhere emerged
or re-emerged in the Soviet Union at the end of the 1980s, when the
communist system that had held the union together since 1917 effectively abdicated. Whatever the future was to bring, what emerged in
the early 1920s was a single state, desperately impoverished and backward –far more backward even than Tsarist Russia – but of enormous
size: 'one sixth of the world's surface', as communists liked to boast
between the wars – dedicated to a society different from and opposed to
capitalism.

In 1945 the borders of the region that seceded from world capitalism
were dramatically extended. In Europe they now included the entire area
east of a line running, roughly, from the river Elbe in Germany to the
Adriatic sea, and the entire Balkan peninsula except Greece and the small
part of Turkey that remained on that continent. Poland, Czechoslovakia,
Hungary, Yugoslavia, Romania, Bulgaria and Albania now moved into
the socialist zone, as well as that part of Germany occupied by the Red
Army after the war and transformed into a 'German Democratic Republic'
in 1954. Most of the areas lost by Russia in the aftermath of war and
revolution after 1917 and one or two territories previously belonging to
the Habsburg Empire were also recuperated or acquired by the Soviet
Union between 1939 and 1945. Meanwhile a vast new extension of the
future socialist region took place in the Far East with the transfer of
power to communist regimes in China (1949) and, partly, in Korea (1945)
and what had been French Indochina (Vietnam, Laos, Cambodia) in the
course of a thirty years' war (1945–75). There were a few further
extensions of the communist region somewhat later, both in the western
hemisphere – Cuba (1959) and in Africa in the 1970s – but substantially
the socialist sector of the globe had taken shape by 1950. Thanks to the
enormous numbers of the Chinese people, it now included about one
third of the world's population, though the average size of the socialist
states other than China, the USSR and Vietnam (fifty-eight millions)
was not particularly large. Their populations ranged from the 1.8 million
of Mongolia to the thirty-six millions of Poland.

This was the part of the world whose social systems some time in the
1960s came to be called, in the terminology of Soviet ideology, the
countries of 'really existing socialism'; an ambiguous term which implied
or suggested that there might be other and better kinds of socialism, but
in practice this was the only kind actually functioning. This was also the
region whose social and economic systems as well as whose political
regimes collapsed totally in Europe as the 1980s gave way to the 1990s.

In the East the political systems maintained themselves for the time being, though the actual economic restructuring they undertook in varying degrees amounted to a liquidation of socialism as hitherto understood by those regimes, notably in China. The scattered regimes elsewhere imitating or inspired by 'really existing socialism' in other parts of the world had either collapsed or were probably not destined for a long life.

The first thing to observe about the socialist region of the globe was that for most of its existence it formed a separate and largely self-contained sub-universe both economically and politically. Its relations with the rest of the world economy, capitalist or dominated by the capitalism of the developed countries, were surprisingly scanty. Even at the height of the great boom in international trade during the Golden Years, only something like 4 per cent of the exports of the developed market economies went to the 'centrally planned economies' and by the 1980s the share of Third World exports going to them was not much more. The socialist economies sent rather more of their modest exports to the rest of the world but even so two thirds of their international trade in the 1960s (1965) was within their own sector* (UN International Trade, 1983, vol. 1, p. 1046).

There was, for obvious reasons, little movement of people from the 'first' to the 'second' world, though some East European states began to encourage mass tourism from the 1960s. Emigration to non-socialist countries as well as temporary travel were strictly controlled, and at times virtually impossible. The political systems of the socialist world, essentially modelled on the Soviet system, had no real equivalent elsewhere. They were based on a strongly hierarchical and authoritarian single party which monopolized state power – in fact it sometimes virtually substituted itself for the state – operating a centrally planned command economy and (at least in theory) imposing a single mandatory Marxist-Leninist ideology on its country's inhabitants. The segregation or self-segregation of the 'socialist camp' (as Soviet terminology came to call it from the late 1940s) gradually crumbled in the 1970s and 1980s. Nevertheless, the sheer degree of mutual ignorance and incomprehension that persisted between the two worlds was quite extraordinary, especially when we bear in mind that this was a period when both travel and communication of information were utterly revolutionized. For long periods very little information about these countries was allowed out and very little about other parts of the world was permitted to enter. In return, even non-expert educated

* The data refer strictly speaking, to the USSR and its associated states, but it will serve as an order of magnitude.

and sophisticated citizens of the First World often found they could not make sense of what they saw or heard in countries whose past and present was so different from their own and whose languages were often beyond their reach.

The fundamental reason for the separation of the two 'camps' was no doubt political. As we have seen, after the October revolution Soviet Russia saw world capitalism as the enemy to be overthrown as soon as practicable by world revolution. That revolution did not take place and Soviet Russia was isolated, surrounded by a capitalist world, many of whose most powerful governments wanted to prevent the establishment of this centre of global subversion, and, later, to eliminate it as soon as possible. The mere fact that the USSR did not acquire official diplomatic recognition of its existence by the USA until 1933 demonstrates its initial outlaw status. Moreover, even when the always realistic Lenin was prepared, and indeed anxious, to make the most far-reaching concessions to foreign investors in return for their assistance in Russia's economic development, in practice he found no takers. Thus the young USSR was necessarily launched on a course of self-contained development, in virtual isolation from the rest of the world economy. Paradoxically this was soon to provide it with its most powerful ideological argument. It seemed immune to the gigantic economic depression which devastated the capitalist economy after the Wall Street crash of 1929.

Politics once again helped to isolate the Soviet economy in the 1930s and, even more dramatically, the expanded Soviet sphere after 1945. The Cold War froze both the economic and the political relations between the two sides. For practical purposes all economic relations between them other than the most trivial (or the unavowable) had to pass through the state controls imposed by both. Trade between the blocs was a function of political relations. Not until the 1970s and 1980s were there signs that the separate economic universe of the 'socialist camp' was being integrated into the wider world economy. In retrospect we can see that this was the beginning of the end for 'really existing socialism'. Yet there is no theoretical reason why the Soviet economy, as it emerged from revolution and civil war, could not have evolved in a far closer relationship with the rest of the world economy. Centrally planned and Western-type economies can be closely linked, as shown by the case of Finland, which at one point (1983) took over a quarter of its imports from the USSR and sent a similar proportion of its exports there. However, the 'socialist camp' that concerns the historian is the one which actually emerged, not what might have been.

The central fact of Soviet Russia was that its new rulers, the Bolshevik

Party, had never expected it to survive in isolation, let alone to become the nucleus of a self-contained collectivist economy ('socialism in one country'). None of the conditions which Marx or any of his followers had hitherto considered essential to the establishment of a socialist economy were present in this enormous hulk of a territory which was virtually a synonym for economic and social backwardness in Europe. The founders of Marxism assumed that the function of a Russian revolution could only be to spark off the revolutionary explosion in the more advanced industrial countries where the preconditions for the construction of socialism were present. As we have seen this was exactly what looked like happening in 1917–18, and it appeared to justify Lenin's highly controversial decision – at least among Marxists – to set the course of the Russian Bolsheviks for Soviet power and socialism. In Lenin's view, Moscow would only be the temporary headquarters of socialism until it could move to its permanent capital in Berlin. It is no accident that the official language of the Communist International, set up as the general staff of world revolution in 1919, was – and remained – not Russian but German.

When it became clear that Soviet Russia was to be, for the time being, which would certainly not be short, the only country in which proletarian revolution had triumphed, the logical, indeed the only persuasive policy for the Bolsheviks, was to transform it from a backward into an advanced economy and society as soon as possible. The most obvious known way to do this was to combine an all-out offensive against the cultural backwardness of the notoriously 'dark', ignorant, illiterate and superstitious masses with an all-out drive for technological modernization and industrial revolution. A Soviet-based communism therefore became primarily a programme for transforming backward countries into advanced ones. This concentration on ultra-rapid economic growth was not without its appeal even in the developed capitalist world in its age of catastrophe, desperately seeking for a way to recover its economic dynamism. It was even more directly relevant to the problems of the world outside Western Europe and North America, most of which could recognize its own image in the agrarian backwardness of Soviet Russia. The Soviet recipe for economic development – centralized state economic planning aimed at the ultra-rapid construction of the basic industries and infrastructure essential to a modern industrial society – seemed designed for them. Moscow was not only a more attractive model than Detroit or Manchester because it stood for anti-imperialism, but it also seemed a more suitable model, especially for countries lacking both in private capital and a large body of private and profit-oriented industry. 'Socialism' in this sense inspired a number of newly independent ex-colonial countries after the

Second World War whose governments rejected the communist political system (see chapter 12). Since the countries joining that system were also backward and agrarian, with the exception of Czechoslovakia, the future German Democratic Republic and, to a lesser extent, Hungary, the Soviet economic recipe also seemed to suit them, and their new rulers launched themselves into the task of economic construction with genuine enthusiasm. Moreover, the recipe seemed to be effective. Between the wars, and especially during the 1930s, the rate of growth of the Soviet economy outpaced all other countries except Japan, and in the first fifteen years after the Second World War the economies of the 'socialist camp' grew considerably faster than those of the West, so much so that Soviet leaders like Nikita Khrushchev sincerely believed that, the curve of their growth continuing upwards at the same rate, socialism would outproduce capitalism within a foreseeable future; as indeed did the British premier Harold Macmillan. More than one economic observer in the 1950s wondered whether this might not happen.

Curiously enough no discussion of 'planning', which was to be the central criterion of socialism, nor of rapid industrialization with priority for the heavy industries, was to be found in the writings of Marx and Engels, though planning is implicit in a socialized economy. But socialists, Marxist or otherwise, before 1917 had been too busy opposing capitalism to give much thought to the nature of the economy that would replace it, and after October Lenin himself, dipping, as he himself put it, one foot into the deep waters of socialism, made no attempt to dive into the unknown. It was the crisis of the Civil War that brought matters to a head. It led to the nationalisation of all industries in mid-1918, and to the 'War Communism' by means of which an embattled Bolshevik state organized its life-and-death struggle against counter-revolution and foreign intervention, and tried to raise the resources for it. All war economies, even in capitalist countries, involve planning and control by the state. In fact, the specific inspiration for Lenin's idea of planning was the German war economy of 1914–18 (which, as we have seen, was probably not the best model of its period and kind). Communist war economies were naturally inclined on grounds of principle to replace private by public property and management, and to dispense with the market and the price-mechanism, especially as none of these were of much use to improvise a national war effort at a moment's notice, and there were indeed communist idealists, like Nikolai Bukharin, who saw the civil war as the opportunity to establish the main structures of a Communist Utopia, and the grim economy of crisis, permanent and universal shortage, and the non-monetary allocation of rationed basic necessities to the people in kind – bread, clothes, bus-tickets – as a spartan pre-view of that social ideal. In fact, as the Soviet regime emerged victorious from the struggles of 1918–20 it was evident that War Communism, however necessary for the time being, could not continue, partly because the peasants would rebel against the military requisitioning of their grain, which had been its base, and the workers against its hardships, partly because it provided no effective means for restoring an economy which had been virtually destroyed: iron and steel production was down from 4.2 million tons in 1913 to two hundred thousand in 1920.

With his habitual realism Lenin introduced the New Economic Policy in 1921, which in effect reintroduced the market and, indeed, in his own words, retreated from War Communism to 'State Capitalism'. Yet it was at this very moment, when Russia's already retrograde economy had fallen to 10 per cent of its pre-war size (see chapter 2), that the need to industrialize massively, and to do so by government planning, became the obvious priority task for the Soviet government. And while the New Economic Policy dismantled War Communism, state control and compulsion remained as the only known model of an economy of socialized ownership and management. The first planning institution, the State Commission for the Electrification of Russia (GoELRo), in 1920 aimed, naturally enough, at modernizing technology, but the State Planning Commission set up in 1921 (Gosplan) had more universal objectives. It remained in being under that name until the end of the USSR. It became the ancestor and inspirer of all state institutions designed to plan, or even to exercise macro-economic supervision over, the economies of twentieth-century states.

The New Economic Policy (NEP) was the subject of impassioned debate in Russia in the 1920s and again in the early Gorbachev years of the 1980s, but for the opposite reasons. In the 1920s it was clearly recognized as a defeat for communism, or at least a diversion of the columns marching towards socialism from the main highway to which, in one way or another, the way back had to be found. Radicals, such as the followers of Trotsky, wanted a break with NEP as soon as possible and a massive drive for industrialization, which was the policy eventually adopted under Stalin. Moderates, headed by Bukharin, who had put the ultra-radicalism of the War Communist years behind him, were keenly aware of the political and economic constraints under which the Bolshevik government had to operate in a country more overwhelmingly dominated by peasant agriculture than before the revolution. They favoured a gradual transformation. Lenin's own views could not be adequately expressed after paralysis hit him in 1922 – he survived only until early

1924 – but, while he could express himself, he seems to have favoured gradualism. On the other hand, the debates of the 1980s were retrospective searches for an historical socialist alternative to the Stalinism which actually succeeded NEP: a different road to socialism from the one actually envisaged by Bolshevik Right and Left in the 1920s. In retrospect Bukharin became a sort of proto-Gorbachev.

These debates are no longer relevant. Looking back we can see that the original justification for the decision to establish socialist power in Russia disappeared when 'proletarian revolution' failed to conquer Germany. Worse than this, Russia survived the Civil War in ruins and far more backward than it had been under Tsarism. True, Tsar, nobility, gentry and bourgeoisie had gone. Two millions emigrated, incidentally depriving the Soviet state of a large section of its educated cadres. But so had the industrial development of the Tsarist era, and most of the industrial workers who provided the social and political base for the Bolshevik party. Revolution and civil war had killed or dispersed them or transferred them from factories into the offices of state and party. What remained was a Russia even more firmly anchored in the past, the immobile, unshiftable mass of peasants in the restored village communities, to whom the revolution had (against earlier Marxist judgment) given the land, or rather whose occupation and distribution of the land in 1917–18 it had accepted as the necessary price of victory and survival. In many ways NEP was a brief golden age of peasant Russia. Suspended above this mass was the Bolshevik Party no longer representing anyone. As Lenin recognized with his usual lucidity, all it had going for it was the fact that it was, and was likely to remain, the accepted and established government of the country. It had nothing else. Even so, what actually governed the country was an undergrowth of smaller and larger bureaucrats, on average even less educated and qualified than before.

What options had this regime, which was, moreover, isolated and boycotted by foreign governments and capitalists, mindful of the expropriation of Russian assets and investments by the Revolution? NEP was indeed brilliantly successful in restoring the Soviet economy from the ruin of 1920. By 1926 Soviet industrial production had more or less recovered its pre-war level, though this did not mean much. The USSR remained as overwhelmingly rural as in 1913 (82 per cent of the population in both cases) (Bergson/Levine, 1983, p. 100; Nove, 1969), and indeed only 7.5 per cent were employed outside agriculture. What this mass of peasants wanted to sell to the cities; what it wanted to buy from them; how much of its income it wanted to save; and how many of the many millions who chose to feed themselves in the villages rather than face city poverty wanted to leave the farms: this determined Russia's economic future, for, apart from the state's tax income, the country had no other available source of investment and labour. Leaving aside all political considerations, a continuation of NEP, modified or not, would at best produce a modest rate of industrialisation. Moreover, until there was a great deal more industrial development, there was little that the peasants could buy in the city to tempt them to sell their surplus rather than to eat and drink it in the villages. This (known as the 'scissors crisis') was to be the noose that eventually strangled NEP. Sixty years later a similar but proletarian 'scissors' undermined Gorbachev's *perestroika*. Why, Soviet workers were to argue, should they raise their productivity to earn higher wages unless the economy produced the consumer goods to buy with these higher wages? But how were these goods to be produced unless Soviet workers raised their productivity?

It was therefore never very likely that NEP – i.e. balanced economic growth based on a peasant market economy steered by the state which controlled its commanding heights – would prove a lasting strategy. For a regime committed to socialism the political arguments against it were in any case overwhelming. Would it not put the small forces committed to this new society at the mercy of petty commodity production and petty enterprise which would regenerate the capitalism just overthrown? And yet, what made the Bolshevik Party hesitate was the prospective cost of the alternative. It meant industrialisation by force: a second revolution, but this time not rising from below but imposed by state power from above.

Stalin, who presided over the ensuing iron age of the USSR, was an autocrat of exceptional, some might say unique, ferocity, ruthlessness and lack of scruple. Few men have manipulated terror on a more universal scale. There is no doubt that under some other leader of the Bolshevik Party the sufferings of the peoples of the USSR would have been less, the number of victims smaller. Nevertheless, any policy of rapid modernization in the USSR, under the circumstances of the time, was bound to be ruthless and, because imposed against the bulk of the people and imposing serious sacrifices on them, to some extent coercive. And the centralised command economy which conducted this drive through its 'plans' was, equally inevitably, closer to a military operation than to an economic enterprise. On the other hand, like military enterprises which have genuine popular moral legitimacy, the breakneck industrialisation of the first Five-Year Plans (1929–41) generated support by the very 'blood, toil, tears and sweat' it imposed on the people. As Churchill knew, sacrifice itself can motivate. Difficult though it may be to believe, even the Stalinist system, which once again turned peasants into serfs attached to the land and made important parts of the economy dependent on a prison labour force of between four and thirteen millions (the Gulags) (Van der Linden, 1993) almost certainly enjoyed substantial support, though clearly not among the peasantry (Fitzpatrick, 1994).

The 'planned economy' of the Five-Year Plans which took the place of NEP in 1928 was necessarily a crude instrument – far cruder than the sophisticated calculations of the Gosplan's pioneer economists of the 1920s, which were in turn far cruder than the planning instruments available to governments and large corporations in the later twentieth century. Essentially its business was to create new industries rather than to run them, and it chose to give immediate priority to the basic heavy industries and energy-production which were the foundation of any large industrial economy: coal, iron and steel, electricity, oil, etc. The USSR's exceptional wealth in suitable raw materials made this choice both logical and convenient. As in a war economy – and the Soviet planned economy was a kind of war economy – targets for production can, and indeed often must, be set without considering cost and cost-effectiveness, the test being whether they can be met and when. As in all such life-or-death efforts, the most effective method of fulfilling targets and meeting deadlines is giving urgent orders which produce all-out rushes. Crisis is its form of management. The Soviet economy settled down as a set of routines broken by frequent, almost institutionalized 'shock efforts' in response to orders from above. Nikita Krushchev was later desperately to look for a way of making the system work in some other way than as a response to 'shouting' (Khruschev, 1990, p. 18). Stalin, earlier, had exploited 'storming' by deliberately setting unrealistic targets which encouraged superhuman efforts.

Moreover, the targets once set had to be understood, and carried out down to the remotest outpost of production in inner Asia – by administrators, managers, technicians and workers who, at least in the first generation, were inexperienced, ill-educated and used to wooden ploughs rather than machines. (The cartoonist David Low, visiting the USSR in the early 1930s, drew a sketch of a collective farm-girl 'absent-mindedly trying to milk a tractor'.) This eliminated the last elements of sophistication, except at the very top which, for that very reason, carried the responsibility of an increasingly total centralization. As Napoleon and his chief-of-staff had once had to compensate for the technical deficiencies of his marshals, essentially untrained fighting officers promoted from the ranks, so all decisions were increasingly concentrated at the apex of the Soviet system. Gosplan's overcentralization compensated for the shortage of managers. The drawback of this procedure was an enormous bureaucratisation of the economic apparatus as well as of all other parts of the system.*

So long as the economy remained at the semi-subsistence level and had merely to lay the foundation for modern industry, this rough-and-ready system, developed mainly in the 1930s, worked. It even developed its own flexibility, in an equally crude manner. Setting one lot of targets did not necessarily get into the immediate way of setting other targets, as it would in the sophisticated labyrinth of a modern economy. In fact, for a backward and primitive country isolated from foreign help, command industrialization, with all its waste and inefficiencies, worked impressively. It turned the USSR into a major industrial economy in a few years and one capable, as Tsarist Russia had not been, of surviving and winning the war against Germany in spite of the temporary loss of areas containing a third of her population and, in many industries, half the industrial plant. One must add that in few other regimes could or would the people have borne the unparalleled sacrifices of this war effort (see Milward 1979, pp. 92–97), or, indeed, those of the 1930s. Yet, if the system kept the consumption of the population at rock-bottom – in 1940 the economy produced only a little over one pair of footwear in all for each inhabitant of the USSR – it guaranteed them that social minimum. It gave them work, food, clothes and housing at controlled (i.e. subsidized) prices and rents, pensions, health care and a rough equality until the system of rewards by special privileges for the '*nomenklatura*' got out of hand after Stalin's death. Much more generously, it gave education. The transformation of a largely illiterate country into the modern USSR was, by any standards, a towering achievement. And for millions from the villages to whom, even in the harshest of times, Soviet development meant the opening of new horizons, the escape from darkness and ignorance to the city, light and progress, not to mention personal advancement and careers, the case for the new society was entirely convincing. In any case, they knew no other.

However, this success story did not include agriculture and those who lived by it, for industrialization rested on the backs of an exploited peasantry. There is very little to be said in favour of the Soviets' peasant and agricultural policy except perhaps that the peasants were not the only ones to carry the burden of 'socialist primitive accumulation' (the phrase

---

* 'If sufficiently clear instructions are to be issued for every major product group and for every producing unit, and in the absence of multi-level planning, then the centre cannot but be saddled with a colossal burden of work' (Dyker, 1985, p. 9).

of a follower of Trotsky who favoured it)* as has been claimed. The workers also carried part of the burden of generating resources for investing in the future.

The peasants – the majority of the population – were not only legally and politically inferior in status, at least until the (entirely inoperative) 1936 Constitution; they were not only taxed more highly and received inferior security, but the basic agricultural policy that replaced NEP, namely compulsory collectivisation in cooperative or state farms, was and remained disastrous. Its immediate effect was to lower grain output and almost halve livestock, thus producing a major famine in 1932–33. Collectivisation led to a drop in the already low productivity of Russian farming, which did not regain the NEP level until 1940 or, allowing for the further disasters of the Second World War, 1950 (Tuma, 1965, p. 102). The massive mechanizations which tried to compensate for this fall was also, and has remained, massively inefficient. After a promising post-war period when Soviet agriculture even produced a modest surplus of grain for export, though the USSR never even looked like becoming a major exporter as Tsarist Russia had been, Soviet farming ceased to be able to feed the population. From the early 1970s on it relied, sometimes to the extent of a quarter of its needs, on the world grain market. But for the slight relaxation of the collective system, which allowed peasants to produce for the market from small private plots – they covered about 4 per cent of the farmed area in 1938 – the Soviet consumer would have eaten little but black bread. In short, the USSR exchanged an inefficient peasant agriculture for an inefficient collective agriculture at vast cost.

As so often, this reflected the social and political conditions of Soviet Russia, rather than the inherent nature of the Bolshevik project. Cooperation and collectivisation, combined in varying degrees with private cultivation – or even, as in the Israeli *kibbuzim*, more communist than anything in the USSR – can be successful, while pure peasant farming has often been better at extracting subsidies from governments than profits from the soil.† However, in the USSR there is no doubt at all that the agrarian policy was a failure. And one only too often copied, at

* In Marx's terms, 'primitive accumulation' by expropriation and pillage was necessary to enable capitalism to acquire the original capital which subsequently undertook its own endogenous accumulation.

† Thus in the first half of the 1980s, Hungary, with a largely collectivised farming, exported more agricultural products than France from an agricultural area little more than a quarter of the French, and about twice as much (in value) as Poland did from an agricultural area almost three times the size of the Hungarian. Polish farming, like French, was not collective. (FAO Production, 1986, FAO Trade, vol. 40, 1986.)

least initially, by subsequent socialist regimes.

The other aspect of Soviet development for which very little can be said is the enormous and overblown bureaucratization which a centralized command government engendered, and with which even Stalin was unable to cope. Indeed, it has been seriously suggested that the Great Terror of the later 1930s was Stalin's desperate method to 'overcome the bureaucratic maze and its skilful dodging of most government controls or injunctions' (Lewin, 1991, p. 17), or at least to prevent it from taking over as an ossified ruling class, as was eventually to happen under Brezhnev. Every attempt to make the administration more flexible and efficient merely swelled it and made it more indispensable. In the last years of the 1930s it grew at two-and-a-half times the rate of employment in general. As war approached, there was more than one administrator for every two blue-collar workers (Lewin, 1991). Under Stalin the top layer of these leading cadres were, as has been said, 'uniquely powerful slaves, always on the brink of catastrophe. Their power and privileges were shadowed by a constant *memento mori*.' After Stalin, or rather after the last of the 'great bosses', Nikita Khrushchev, was removed in 1964, there was nothing in the system to prevent stagnation.

The third drawback of the system, and the one which in the end sank it, was its inflexibility. It was geared to constant growth in the output of products whose character and quality had been predetermined, but it contained no built-in mechanism for varying either quantity (except upward) or quality, or for innovation. In fact, it did not know what to do about inventions, and did not use them in the civilian economy, as distinct from the military-industrial complex.* As for the consumers, they were provided for neither by a market, which would have indicated their preferences, nor by any bias in their favour within the economic or, as we shall see, the political system. On the contrary, the system's original bias towards maximum growth of capital goods was reproduced by the planning machine. The most that one might claim is that, as the economy grew, it provided more consumer goods even while industrial structure kept on favouring capital goods. Even so, the system of distribution was so bad, and, above all, the system of organizing services so non-existent, that the rising standard of living in the USSR – and improvement from the 1940s to the 1970s was very striking – could function effectively only with the help of, or by means of, an extensive 'second' or

---

* 'As little as one-third of all inventions find an application in the economy and even in these cases their diffusion is rare' (Vernikov, 1989, p. 7). The data appear to refer to 1986.

'black' economy, which grew rapidly, particularly from the end of the 1960s. Since unofficial economies by definition escape from official documentation, we can only guess at its size – but in the late 1970s it was estimated that the Soviet urban population spent about twenty billion roubles on private consumer, medical and legal services, plus about another seven billions in 'tips' to ensure service (Alexeev, 1990). This would at the time have been a sum comparable to the total of imports of the country.

In short, the Soviet system was designed to industrialize a very backward and undeveloped country as rapidly as possible, on the assumption that its people would be content with a standard of living guaranteeing a social minimum and a standard of material living somewhat above subsistence – how much depended on what trickled down from the general growth of an economy geared to further industrialization. Inefficient and wasteful though it was, it achieved these objects. In 1913 the Tsarist Empire, with 9.4 per cent of the world's population, produced 6 per cent of the world's total of 'national incomes' and 3.6 per cent of its industrial output. In 1986 the USSR, with less than 6 per cent of the global population produced 14 per cent of the globe's 'national income' and 14.6 per cent of its industrial output. (But it produced only a slightly higher share of the world's agricultural output.) (Bolotin, 1987, pp. 148– 52.) Russia had been transformed into a major industrial power, and indeed its status as a superpower, maintained for almost half a century, rested on this success. However, and contrary to the expectations of the communists, the engine of Soviet economic development was so constructed as to slow down rather than speed up when, after the vehicle had advanced a certain distance, the driver stepped on the accelerator. Its dynamism contained the mechanism of its own exhaustion. This was the system which, after 1944, became the model for the economies under which a third of the human race lived.

However, the Soviet revolution also developed a very special political system. The European popular movements of the Left, including the Marxist labour and socialist movements to which the Bolshevik party belonged, drew on two political traditions: electoral, and sometimes even direct democracy, and the centralized action-oriented revolutionary efforts inherited from the Jacobin phase of the French Revolution. The mass labour and socialist movements which emerged almost everywhere in Europe at the end of the nineteenth century, whether as parties, labour unions, cooperatives or a combination of all these, were strongly democratic both in their internal structure and their political aspirations. In fact, where constitutions based on a wide franchise did not yet exist, they were the chief forces pressing for them and, unlike the anarchists, the Marxists were fundamentally committed to *political* action. The political system of the USSR, which was also later transferred to the socialist world, broke sharply with the democratic side of socialist movements, though maintaining an increasingly academic commitment to it in theory.* It even moved far beyond the Jacobin heritage, which, whatever its commitment to revolutionary rigour and ruthless action, did not favour individual dictatorship. In short, as the Soviet economy was a command economy, so Soviet politics was command politics.

This evolution reflected partly the history of the Bolshevik Party, partly the crises and urgent priorities of the young Soviet regime and partly the peculiarities of the drunkard cobbler's ex-seminarist son from Georgia who became the autocrat of the USSR under the self-chosen political name 'the man of steel', namely J.V. Stalin (1879–1953). Lenin's model of the 'Vanguard Party', a uniquely efficient disciplined cadre of professional revolutionaries, geared to carrying out the tasks assigned to them by a central leadership, was potentially authoritarian, as numerous other equally revolutionary Russian Marxists had pointed out from the start. What was to stop 'substitutism' of the party for the masses it claimed to lead? Of its (elected) committees for the members, or rather the regular congresses expressing their views? Of the actual operational leadership for the central committee, and eventually by the (in theory elected) unique leader who in practice replaced all of these? The danger, as it turned out, was no less real because Lenin neither wanted to nor was in a position to be a dictator, or because the Bolshevik Party, like all organizations of the ideological Left, behaved much less like a military staff and much more like an endless debating society. It became more immediate after the October Revolution, as the Bolsheviks turned from a body of a few thousand illegals into a mass party of hundreds of thousands, eventually of millions of professional mobilizers, administrators, executives and controllers, who swamped the 'Old Bolsheviks' and other pre-1917 socialists who had joined them, such as Leon Trotsky. They shared none of the old political culture of the Left. All they knew was that the party was right and that decisions made by superior authority must be carried out if the revolution was to be saved.

* Thus the authoritarian centralism so characteristic of communist parties retained the official name of 'democratic centralism', and the 1936 Soviet Constitution is, on paper, a typical democratic constitution, with as much room for multiparty elections as, say, the American constitution. Nor was this pure window-dressing, since much of it was drafted by Nikolai Bukharin, who, as an old pre-1917 Marxist revolutionary, undoubtedly believed that this type of constitution suited a socialist society.

Whatever the pre-revolutionary attitude of the Bolsheviks to democracy in and outside the party, to free speech, civil liberties and toleration, the circumstances of the years 1917–21 imposed an increasingly authoritarian mode of government on (and within) a party committed to any action that was (or seemed) necessary to maintain the fragile and struggling Soviet power. It had not actually begun as a one-party government, nor one rejecting opposition, but it won the Civil War as a single-party dictatorship buttressed by a powerful security apparatus, and using terror against counter-revolutionaries. Equally to the point, the party itself abandoned internal democracy, as the collective discussion of alternative policies was banned (in 1921). The 'democratic centralism' which governed it in theory became mere centralism. It ceased to operate by its own party constitution. The annual meetings of party congresses became less regular, until under Stalin they became unpredictable and occasional. The NEP years relaxed the non-political atmosphere, but not the feeling that the party was a beleaguered minority which might have history on its side, but was working against the grain of the Russian masses and the Russian present. The decision to launch the industrial revolution from above, automatically committed the system to imposing authority, perhaps even more ruthlessly than in the Civil War years, because its machinery for exercising power continuously was now much greater. It was then that the last elements of a separation of powers, the modest even if diminishing room for manoeuvre of the Soviet government as distinct from the party, came to an end. The single political leadership of the party now concentrated absolute power in its hands, subordinating all else.

It was at this point that the system became an autocracy under Stalin, and one seeking to impose total control over all aspects of its citizens' lives and thoughts, all their existence being, so far as possible, subordinated to the achievement of the system's objectives, as defined and specified by the supreme authority. This was certainly not envisaged by Marx and Engels, nor did it develop in the second (Marxist) International and most of its parties. Thus Karl Liebknecht, who, with Rosa Luxemburg, became the leader of the German communists and was assassinated with her in 1919 by reactionary officers, did not even claim to be a Marxist, though he was the son of a founder of the German Social-democratic Party. The Austro-Marxists, though, as their name suggests, committed to Marx, made no bones about going their own various ways, and even when a man was branded an official heretic, as Eduard Bernstein was for his 'revisionism', it was taken for granted that he was a legitimate social-democrat. Indeed, he continued as an official editor of the works of Marx and Engels. The idea that a socialist state should force every citizen to think the same, let alone to endow its leaders collectively with something like papal infallibility (that any single person should exercise this function was unthinkable), would not have crossed the mind of any leading socialist before 1917.

One might at most claim that Marxist socialism was for its adherents a passionate personal commitment, a system of hope and belief, which had some characteristics of a secular religion (though not more than the ideology of non-socialist crusading groups) and, perhaps more to the point, that, once it became a mass movement, subtle theory inevitably became at best a catechism; at worst, a symbol of identity and loyalty, like a flag, which must be saluted. Such mass movements, as intelligent central European socialists had long noted, also tended to admire, even to worship, leaders, though it must be said that the well-known tendency to argument and rivalry within Left-wing parties would usually keep this under some control. The construction of the Lenin mausoleum on the Red Square, where the preserved body of the great leader would for ever be visible to the faithful, did not derive from anything in even the Russian revolutionary tradition, but was an obvious attempt to mobilize the appeal of Christian saints and relics to a backward peasant people for the benefit of the Soviet regime. One might also claim that in the Bolshevik Party constructed by Lenin, orthodoxy and intolerance were to some extent implanted not as values in themselves but for pragmatic reasons. Like a good general – and Lenin was fundamentally a planner of action – he did not want arguments in the ranks which would prevent practical effectiveness. Moreover, like other practical geniuses, he was convinced that he knew best, and had little time for other opinions. In theory, he was an orthodox, even a fundamentalist, Marxist because it was clear to him that any monkeying with the text of a theory whose essence was revolution was likely to encourage compromisers and reformists. In practice, he unhesitatingly modified Marx's views and added to them freely, always defending his literal loyalty to the master. Since, for most of the years before 1917, he led, and represented an embattled minority on the Russian Left, and even within Russian social democracy, he acquired a reputation for intolerance of dissent, but he had as little hesitation in welcoming his opponents, once the situation had changed, as he had in denouncing them, and, even after October, he never relied on his authority within the party, but invariably on argument. Nor, as we have seen, did his positions ever make their way unchallenged. Had he lived, Lenin would no doubt have gone on denouncing opponents, and, as in the civil war, his pragmatic intolerance would know no limits. Yet there is no evidence that he envisaged, or would even have tolerated, the sort of secular version of a universal and compulsory state-cum-private religion which developed after his death. Stalin may not have founded it consciously. He may merely have gone with what he saw as the main-stream of a backward peasant Russia and its autocratic and orthodox tradition. But it is unlikely that, without him, it would have developed, and certain that it would not have been imposed on, or copied by other socialist regimes.

Yet one thing must be said. The possibility of dictatorship is implicit in any regime based on a single, irremovable party. In a party organized on the centralized hierarchical basis of Lenin's Bolsheviks, it becomes a probability. And irremovability was merely another name for the total conviction of the Bolsheviks that the Revolution must not be reversed, and that its fate was in their hands and in nobody else's. Bolsheviks argued that a bourgeois regime might safely envisage the defeat of a Conservative administration and the succession of a Liberal, since this would not change the bourgeois character of society, but it would and could not tolerate a communist regime, for the same reason that a communist one could not tolerate being overthrown by any force that would restore the old order. Revolutionaries, including revolutionary socialists, are not democrats in the electoral sense, however sincerely convinced of acting in the interests of 'the people'. Nevertheless, even if the assumption that the party was a political monopoly with a 'leading role' made a democratic Soviet regime as unlikely as a democratic Catholic Church, it did not imply personal dictatorship. It was Joseph Stalin who turned communist political systems into non-hereditary monarchies.*

In many ways Stalin, tiny,† cautious, insecure, cruel, nocturnal and endlessly suspicious, seems a figure out of Suetonius' *Lives of the Caesars* rather than out of modern politics. Outwardly unimpressive and indeed forgettable, 'a grey blur' as a contemporary observer called him in 1917 (Sukhanov), he conciliated and manoeuvred where he had to, until he reached the top; but, of course, his very considerable gifts had got him

---

* The similarity with monarchy is indicated by the tendency of some such states actually to move in the direction of hereditary succession, a development which would have seemed absurdly unthinkable to earlier socialists and communists. North Korea and Romania were two cases in point.

† The present writer, who saw Stalin's embalmed body in the Red Square mausoleum before it was removed in 1957 can remember the shock of seeing a man so tiny and yet so all-powerful. Significantly, all films and photographs concealed the fact that he was only 5 ft 3 ins tall.

close to the top even before the revolution. He was a member of the first government after revolutionary government as Commissar for nationalities. When he finally became the unchallenged leader of the party and (in effect) of the state, he lacked the palpable sense of personal destiny, the charisma and self-confidence which made Hitler the founder and accepted master of his party and kept his entourage loyal to him without coercion. Stalin ruled his party, as everything else within reach of his personal power, by terror and fear.

In turning himself into something like a secular Tsar, defender of the secular Orthodox faith, the body of whose founder, transformed into a secular saint, awaited the pilgrims outside the Kremlin, Stalin showed a sound sense of public relations. For a collection of peasant and animal-herding peoples mentally living in the Western equivalent of the eleventh century, this was almost certainly the most effective way of establishing the legitimacy of the new regime, just as the simple, unqualified, dogmatic catechisms to which he reduced 'Marxism-Leninism' were ideal for introducing ideas to the first generation of literates.* Nor can his terror simply be seen as the assertion of a tyrant's unlimited personal power. There is no doubt that he enjoyed that power, the fear that he inspired, the ability to give life or death, just as there is no doubt that he was quite indifferent to the material rewards that someone in his position could command. Yet, whatever his personal psychological kinks, Stalin's terror was, in theory, as rationally instrumental a tactic as was his caution where he lacked control. Both, in fact, were based on the principle of avoiding risks, which, in turn, reflected that very lack of confidence in his ability to assess situations ('to make a Marxist analysis', in the Bolshevik jargon) which had distinguished Lenin. His terrifying career makes no sense except as a stubborn, unbroken, pursuit of that utopian aim of a communist society to whose reassertion he devoted the last of his publications, a few months before his death (Stalin, 1952)

Power in the Soviet Union was all that the Bolsheviks had gained by the October Revolution. Power was the only tool they could wield to change society. This was beset by constant, and in one way or another, constantly renewed, difficulties. (This is the meaning of Stalin's otherwise absurd thesis that the class struggle would become more intense decades after 'the proletariat had taken power'.) Only the determination to use power consistently and ruthlessly to eliminate all possible obstacles to the process could guarantee eventual success.

.* And not only these. The 1939 *Short History* of the Soviet Communist Party, whatever its lies and intellectual limitations, was pedagogically a masterly text.

Three things drove a policy based on this assumption towards a murderous absurdity.

First, Stalin's belief that in the last analysis only he knew the way forward and was sufficiently determined to pursue it. Plenty of politicians and generals have this sense of indispensability, but only those with absolute power are in a position to compel others to share this belief. Thus the great purges of the 1930s which, unlike earlier forms of terror, were directed against the party itself and especially its leadership, began after many hardened Bolsheviks, including those who had supported him against the various oppositions of the 1920s and genuinely backed the Geat Leap Forward of Collectivisation and Five Year Plan, found the ruthless cruelties of the period and the sacrifices it imposed, more than they would willingly accept. No doubt many of them remembered Lenin's refusal to back Stalin as his successor because of his excessive brutality. The seventeenth Congress of the CPSU(b) revealed a substantial opposition to him. Whether it actually constituted a threat to his power we shall never know, for between 1934 and 1939 four or five million party members and officials were arrested on political grounds, four or five hundred thousand of them were executed without trial, and the next (eighteenth) Party Congress which met in the spring of 1939, contained a bare thirty-seven survivors of the 1827 delegates who had been present at the seventeenth in 1934 (Kerblay, 1983, p. 245).

What gave this terror an unprecedented inhumanity was that it recognized no conventional or other limits. It was not so much the belief that a great end justifies all the means necessary to achieve it (though it is possible that this was Mao Tse-tung's belief), or even the belief that the sacrifices imposed on the present generation, however large, are as nothing to the benefits which will be reaped by the endless generations of the future. It was the application of the principle of total war to all times. Leninism, perhaps because of the powerful strain of voluntarism which made other Marxists distrust Lenin as a 'Blanquist' or 'Jacobin', thought essentially in military terms, as his own admiration for Clausewitz would indicate, even if the entire vocabulary of Bolshevik politics did not bear witness to it. 'Who whom?' was Lenin's basic maxim: the struggle as a zero-sum game in which the winner took, the loser lost, all. As we know, even the liberal states waged both world wars in this spirit, and recognized absolutely no limit on the suffering they were prepared to impose on the the population of 'the enemy', and, in the First World War, even on their own armed forces. Indeed, even the victimisation of entire blocks of people, defined on *a priori* grounds, became part of warfare: such as the internment during the Second World War of all US citizens of Japanese origins or of all resident Germans and Austrians in Britain on the grounds that they might contain some potential agents of the enemy. This was part of that relapse of nineteenth-century civil progress into a renaissance of barbarism, which runs like a dark thread through this book.

Fortunately, in constitutional and preferably democratic states under the rule of law and with a free press, there are some countervailing forces. In systems of absolute power there are none, even though eventually conventions of power-limitation may develop, if only for the sake of survival and because the use of total power may be self-defeating. Paranoia is its logical end-product. After Stalin's death a tacit understanding among his successors decided to put an end to the era of blood, although (until the Gorbachev era) it was left to dissidents within and scholars or publicists abroad to estimate the full human cost of the Stalin decades. Henceforth Soviet politicians died in their beds, and sometimes at an advanced age. As the Gulags emptied in the late 1950s, the USSR remained a society which treated its citizens badly by Western standards, but it ceased to be a society which imprisoned and killed its citizens on a uniquely massive scale. Indeed, by the 1980s it had a distinctly smaller proportion of its inhabitants in jail than the USA (268 prisoners per 100,000 population against 426 per 100,000 in the USA) (Walker 1991). Moreover, in the 1960s and 1970s the USSR actually became a society in which the ordinary citizen probably ran a smaller risk of being deliberately killed by crime, civil conflict or the state than a substantial number of other countries in Asia, Africa and the Americas. Nevertheless, it remained a police state, an authoritarian society and, by any realistic standards, an unfree one. Only officially authorized or permitted information was available to the citizen – any other kind remained at least technically punishable by law until Gorbachev's policy of *glasnost* ('openness') – and freedom of travel and settlement depended on official permission, an increasingly nominal restriction within the USSR, but a very real one where frontiers had to be crossed even into another friendly 'socialist' country. In all these respects the USSR remained distinctly inferior to Tsarist Russia. Moreover, even though for most everyday purposes the rule of law operated, the powers of administrative, i.e. arbitrary, imprisonment or internal exile remained.

It will probably never be possible to calculate the human cost of Russia's iron decades adequately, since even such official statistics of execution and Gulag populations as exist or might become available cannot cover all the losses, and estimates vary enormously depending on the assumption made by the estimators. 'By a sinister paradox' it has been said, 'we are better informed as to losses to Soviet livestock in this period than about the number of the regime's opponents who were exterminated' (Kerblay, 1983, p. 26). The suppression of the 1937 census alone introduces almost insuperable obstacles. Still, whatever assumptions are made,* the number of direct and indirect victims must be measured in eight rather than seven digits. In these circumstances it does not much matter whether we opt for a 'conservative' estimate nearer to ten than to twenty millions or a larger figure: none can be anything but shameful and beyond palliation, let alone justification. I add, without comment, that the total population of the USSR in 1937 was said to have been 164 millions, or 16.7 millions less than the demographic forecasts of the Second Five-Year Plan (1933–38).

Brutal and dictatorial though it was, the Soviet system was not 'totalitarian', a term which became popular among critics of communism after the Second World War, having been invented in the 1920s by Italian fascism to describe its objects. Hitherto it had been used almost exclusively to criticize both it and German National Socialism. It stood for an all-embracing centralized system which not only imposed total physical control over its population but, by means of its monopoly of propaganda and education, actually succeeded in getting its people to internalize its values. George Orwell's *1984* (published in 1949) gave this Western image of the totalitarian society its most powerful form: a society of brainwashed masses under the watchful eye of 'Big Brother', from which only the occasional lonely individual dissented.

This is certainly what Stalin would have *wanted* to achieve, though it would have outraged Lenin and other Old Bolsheviks, not to mention Marx. Insofar as it aimed at the virtual deification of the leader (what was later shyly euphemized as 'the cult of personality'), or at least at establishing him as a compendium of virtues, it had some success, which Orwell satirized. Paradoxically, this owed little to Stalin's absolute power. The communist militants outside the 'socialist' countries who wept genuine tears as they learned of his death in 1953 – and many did – were voluntary converts to the movement they believed him to have symbolized and inspired. Unlike most foreigners, all Russians knew well enough how much suffering had been, and still was, their lot. Yet in some sense by virtue merely of being a strong and legitimate ruler of the Russian lands and a modernizer of these lands, he represented something of themselves: most recently as their leader in a war which was, for Great Russians at least, a genuinely national struggle.

* For the uncertainties of such procedures see Kosinski, 1987, pp. 151–52.

Yet, in every other respect, the system was not 'totalitarian', a fact which throws considerable doubt on the usefulness of the term. It did not exercise effective 'thought control', let alone ensure 'thought conversion', but in fact depoliticized the citizenry to an astonishing degree. The official doctrines of Marxism-Leninism left the bulk of the population virtually untouched, since it had no apparent relevance to them, unless they were interested in a career in which such esoteric knowledge was expected. After forty years of education in a country dedicated to Marxism, passers-by on Marx Square in Budapest were asked who Karl Marx was. They were told:

> He was a Soviet philosopher; Engels was his friend. Well, what else can I say? He died at an old age. (Another voice): Of course, a politician. And he was, you know, he was what's his name's – Lenin's, Lenin, Lenin's works – well he translated them into Hungarian (Garton Ash, 1990, p. 261).

For the majority of Soviet citizens most public statements about politics and ideology coming from on high were probably not consciously absorbed at all, unless they bore directly on their everyday problems – which they rarely did. Only the intellectuals were forced to take them seriously in a society built on and around an ideology that claimed to be rational and 'scientific'. Yet, paradoxically, the very fact that such systems needed intellectuals, and gave those who did not publicly dissent from it substantial privileges and advantages, created a social space outside the state's control. Only terror as ruthless as Stalin's could completely silence the unofficial intellect. In the USSR it re-emerged as soon as the ice of fear began to thaw – *The Thaw* (1954) was the title of an influential *roman à thèse* by Ilya Ehrenburg (1891–1967), a talented survivor – in the 1950s. In the 1960s and 1970s dissent, both in the uncertainly tolerated form of communist reformers and in the form of total intellectual, political and cultural dissidence, dominated the Soviet scene, though officially the country remained 'monolithic' – a favourite Bolshevik term. This was to become evident in the 1980s.

II

The communist states which came into being after the Second World War, i.e. all except the USSR, were controlled by communist parties formed or shaped in the Soviet, i.e. Stalinist, mould. This was true even to some extent of the Chinese Communist Party, which had established real autonomy from Moscow in the 1930s under Mao Tse-tung. It was, perhaps, less true of later recruits to the 'socialist camp' from the Third World – Fidel Castro's Cuba, and various more shortlived African, Asian and Latin American regimes which arose in the 1970s, and which also tended to assimilate themselves officially to the established Soviet pattern. In all of them we find one-party political systems with highly centralized authority structures; officially promulgated cultural and intellectual truth determined by political authority; central state-planned economies; even, the most obvious relic of the Stalinist heritage, strongly profiled supreme leaders. Indeed, in the states directly occupied by the Soviet army, including the Soviet security services, local governments were compelled to follow the Soviet example, for instance by organizing show trials and purges of local communists on the Stalin model, a matter for which the native communist parties showed no spontaneous enthusiasm. In Poland and East Germany they even managed to avoid these caricatures of the judicial process altogether, and no leading communist was killed or handed over to the Soviet security services, although, in the aftermath of the break with Tito prominent local leaders in Bulgaria (Traicho Kostov) and Hungary (Laszlo Rajk) were executed and in Stalin's last year a particularly implausible mass trial of leading Czech communists, with a markedly anti-semitic tinge, decimated the old leadership of the local party. It may or may not have had some connection with the increasingly paranoiac behaviour of Stalin himself as he deteriorated both physically and mentally and planned to eliminate even his most loyal supporters

The new regimes of the 1940s, though in Europe all were made possible by the victory of the Red Army, were only in four cases imposed exclusively by the force of that army: in Poland; the occupied part of Germany; Romania (where the local communist movement consisted at best of a few hundred people, most of them not ethnic Romanians); and, in substance, Hungary. In Yugoslavia and Albania it was very much home-grown, in Czechoslovakia the communist party's 40 per cent of the vote in 1947 almost certainly reflected genuine strength at the time, and in Bulgaria communist influence was reinforced by the Russophile sentiment so universal in that country. Communist power in China, Korea and former French Indochina – or rather, after the Cold War division, in the northern parts of those countries – owed nothing to Soviet arms, though after 1949 the smaller communist regimes benefited, for a while, from Chinese support. The subsequent additions to the 'socialist camp', starting with Cuba, had made their own way there, although struggling guerrilla liberation movements in Africa could count on serious support from the Soviet bloc.

Yet, even in the states where communist power was imposed only by the Red Army, the new regime initially enjoyed a temporary legitimacy and, for a time, some genuine support. As we have seen (chapter 5), the idea of building a new world on what was so visibly the total ruin of the old, inspired many of the young and the intellectuals. However unpopular party and government, the very energy and determination which both brought to the task of post-war reconstruction commanded a broad, if reluctant, assent. Indeed, the success of the new regimes in this task was hard to deny. In the more backward agrarian states, as we have seen, the communist commitment to industrialization, that is, to progress and modernity, re-echoed far beyond the party's ranks. Who could doubt that countries like Bulgaria or Yugoslavia were advancing far more rapidly than had seemed likely, or even possible before the war? Only where a primitive and ruthless USSR had occupied and forcibly absorbed less backward regions, or, at any rate, regions with developed cities, as in the areas transferred in 1939–40, and in the Soviet zone of Germany (after 1954 the German Democratic Republic), which continued for some time after 1945 to be pillaged by the USSR for its own reconstruction, did the balance look entirely negative.

Politically, the communist states, home-grown or imposed, began by forming a single bloc under the leadership of the USSR, which, on grounds of anti-Western solidarity, was supported even by the communist regime which took full control of China in 1949, though Moscow's influence over the Chinese Communist Party had been tenuous ever since Mao Tse-tung became its unchallengeable leader in the middle 1930s. Mao went his own way amid professions of loyalty to the USSR, and Stalin, as a realist, was careful not to strain his relations with the effectively independent giant eastern brother-party. When in the later 1950s Nikita Khrushchev did strain them the result was an acrimonious breach, as China challenged Soviet leadership of the international communist movement, though not very successfully. Stalin's attitude to the states and communist parties in the parts of Europe occupied by the Soviet armies was less conciliatory, partly because his armies were still present in Eastern Europe, but also because he thought he could rely on the genuine local communist loyalty to Moscow, and to himself personally. He was almost certainly surprised in 1948 when the Yugoslav communist leadership, so loyalist that Belgrade had been made the headquarters of the reconstructed Cold War Communist International (the 'Communist Information Bureau' or Cominform) only a few months earlier, pushed their resistance to Soviet directives to the point of an open breach, and when Moscow's appeal to the loyalty of good communists over the head of Tito met with next to no serious response in Yugoslavia. Characteristically his reaction was to extend purges and show-trials to the remaining satellite communist leaderships.

Nevertheless, the Yugoslav secession left the rest of the communist movement unaffected. The political crumbling of the Soviet bloc began with Stalin's death in 1953, but especially with the official attacks on the Stalinist era in general and, more cautiously, on Stalin himself, at the Twentieth Congress of the CPSU in 1956. Although aimed at a highly restricted domestic Soviet audience – foreign communists were excluded from Khrushchev's secret speech – the news soon got out that the Soviet monolith had split. The effects within the Soviet-dominated region of Europe was immediate. Within a few months a new, reforming communist leadership in Poland was peacefully accepted by Moscow (probably with the help of advice from the Chinese), and a revolution broke out in Hungary. Here the new government under another communist reformer, Imre Nagy, announced the end of one-party rule, which the Soviets might conceivably have tolerated – opinions among them were divided – but also the withdrawal of Hungary from the Warsaw Pact and its future neutrality, which they would not tolerate. The revolution was suppressed by the Russian army in November 1956.

That this major crisis within the Soviet bloc was not exploited by the Western alliance (except for purposes of propaganda) demonstrated the stability of East–West relations. Both sides tacitly accepted the boundaries of each other's zones of influence, and during the 1950s and 1960s no indigenous revolutionary changes appeared on the globe to disturb this balance, except in Cuba.*

In regimes where politics was so obviously in control, no sharp line between political and economic developments can be drawn. Thus the governments of Poland and Hungary could not but make economic concessions to peoples who had so clearly demonstrated their lack of enthusiasm for communism. In Poland agriculture was de-collectivized, though this did not make it notably more efficient, and, more to the point, the political force of a working class, much strengthened by the

---

* The revolutions of the 1950s in the Middle East, Egypt in 1952, and Iraq in 1958, contrary to Western fears, did not change the balance, in spite of providing much scope for USSR diplomatic success, chiefly because the local regimes eliminated their own communists ruthlessly, where they were influential, as in Syria and Iraq.

rush into heavy industrialization, was henceforth tacitly acknowledged. After all, it was an industrial movement in Poznan which had initiated the events of 1956. From then until the triumph of Solidarity at the end of the 1980s, Polish politics and economics were dominated by the confrontation of irresistible mass, the regime, and immovable object, the working class, which, initially without organization, was eventually organized into a classical labour movement, allied as usual with intellectuals, and eventually formed a political movement, just as Marx had predicted. Only the ideology of this movement, as Marxists had to note with melancholy, was not anti-capitalist but anti-socialist. Typically these confrontations were about the periodic attempts of Polish governments to cut down the heavy subsidies on basic living-costs by raising prices. These then led to strikes, followed typically (after a crisis in the government) by retreat. In Hungary the leadership imposed by the Soviets after the defeat of the 1956 revolution was more genuinely reformist and effective. It set out under János Kádár (1912–89) systematically (and possibly with tacit support from influential quarters in the USSR) to liberalize the regime, conciliate the opposition and, in effect, to achieve the objectives of 1956 within the limits of what the USSR would regard as acceptable. In this it was notably successful until the 1980s.

This was not the case in Czechoslovakia, politically inert since the ruthless purges of the early 1950s, but cautiously and tentatively beginning to de-Stalinize. For two reasons this process snowballed in the second half of the 1960s. The Slovaks (including the Slovak component of the CP), never entirely at ease in the bi-national state, provided backing for potential opposition in the party. It is no accident that the man elected to the general secetaryship in a party coup in 1968 was a Slovak, Alexander Dubček.

However, quite separately, pressure to reform the economy, and introduce some rationality and flexibility into the Soviet-type command system, became increasingly hard to resist in the 1960s. As we shall see, it was by then felt throughout the communist bloc. Economic decentralization, which was not in itself politically explosive, became so when combined with the demand for intellectual and, even more, for political liberalization. In Czechoslovakia this demand was all the stronger, not only because Stalinism had been particularly harsh and long-lasting, but also because so many of its communists (especially intellectuals, sprung from a party with genuine mass support both before and after the Nazi occupation) were profoundly shocked by the contrast between the communist hopes they still retained and the reality of the regime. As so often in Nazi-occupied Europe, where the party became the heart of the resistance movement, it attracted young idealists whose commitment at such a time was a guarantee of selflessness. What, other than hope and possible torture and death, could someone expect who, like a friend of the present writer, joined the party in Prague in 1941?

As always – as was indeed inevitable, given the structure of communist states – reform came from above, i.e. from within the party. The 'Prague Spring' of 1968, preceded and accompanied by politico-cultural ferment and agitation, coincided with the general outburst of global student radicalism which is discussed elsewhere (see chapter 10): one of the rare movements which crossed oceans and the borders of social systems, and produced simultaneous social movements, mainly student-centred, from California and Mexico to Poland and Yugoslavia. The 'Action Programme' of the Czechoslovak CP might or might not have been – just – acceptable to the Soviets, though it moved the one-party dictatorship rather dangerously towards a pluralist democracy. However, the cohesion, perhaps the very existence of the East European Soviet bloc seemed to be at stake, as the 'Prague Spring' revealed, and increased, the cracks within it. On the one side hard-line regimes without mass support, such as Poland and East Germany, feared internal destabilization from the Czech example, which they criticized bitterly; on the other, the Czechs were supported enthusiastically by most European communist parties, by the reforming Hungarians and, from outside the bloc, by the independent communist regime of Tito in Yugoslavia, as well as by Rumania which, since 1965, had begun to mark its distance from Moscow on nationalist grounds under a new leader, Nicolae Ceauşescu (1918–89). (In internal matters Ceauşescu was anything but a communist reformer.) Both Tito and Ceauşescu visited Prague and received hero's welcomes from the public. Hence Moscow, though not without divisions and hesitation, decided to overthrow the Prague regime by military force. This proved to be the virtual end of the Moscow-centred international communist movement, already cracked by the 1956 crisis. However, it held the Soviet bloc together for another twenty years, but henceforth only by the threat of Soviet military intervention. In the last twenty years of the Soviet bloc, even the leadership of the ruling communist parties appear to have lost any real belief in what they were doing.

Meanwhile, and quite independently of politics, the need to reform or change the economic system of Soviet-type central planning became increasingly urgent. On the one hand, the developed non-socialist economies grew and flourished as never before (see chapter 9), widening the already considerable gap between the two systems. This was particularly obvious in Germany, where both systems coexisted in different parts of the same country. On the other hand, the rate of growth of the socialist economies, which had surpassed the Western economies up to the latter part of the 1950s, began visibly to slacken off. The Soviet GNP, which grew at a rate of 5.7 per cent per annum in the 1950s (almost as fast as in the first twelve years of industrialization, 1928–40), fell to 5.2 per cent in the 1960s, 3.7 per cent in the first half of the 1970s, 2.6 per cent in the second half of that decade and 2 per cent in the last five years before Gorbachev (1980–85) (Ofer, 1987, p. 1778). The record of Eastern Europe was similar. Attempts to make the system more flexible, essentially by decentralization, were made in the 1960s almost everywhere in the Soviet bloc, not least in the USSR itself under premier Kosygin in the 1960s. With the exception of the Hungarian reforms, they were not notably successful, and, in several cases, they hardly got off the ground or (as in Czechoslovakia) were not allowed to for political reasons. A somewhat eccentric member of the family of socialist systems, Yugoslavia, was not notably more successful when, out of hostility to Stalinism, it replaced the centrally planned state economy with a system of autonomous cooperative enterprises. As the world economy entered a new period of uncertainties in the 1970s, nobody in East or West any longer expected the 'really existing' socialist economies to overtake and surpass, or even to keep pace with the non-socialist ones. However, though more problematic than before, their future did not seem a cause for immediate worry. This was soon to change.

PART THREE
THE LANDSLIDE

CHAPTER FOURTEEN
The Crisis Decades

I was asked the other day about United States competitiveness and
I replied that I don't think about it at all. We at NCR think of
ourselves as a globally competitive company that happens to be
headquartered in the United States.

> – Jonathan Schell, *NY Newsday* 1993

At a particularly neuralgic level, one of the results (of mass unemployment) could be the progressive alienation from the rest of society of
the young who, according to contemporary surveys, still *want* jobs,
however difficult they may be to obtain, and still *hope* for meaningful
careers. More broadly, there must be some danger that the coming
decade will be a society in which not merely are 'we' progressively
divided from 'they' (the two divisions representing, very roughly,
the labour force and management), but in which the majority
groups are increasingly splintered, with the young and the relatively
unprotected at odds with the better protected and more experienced
members of the work force.

> – The Secretary-General of OECD, (Investing, 1983, p. 15)

I

The history of the twenty years after 1973 is that of a world which lost its
bearings and slid into instability and crisis. And yet, until the 1980s it
was not clear how irretrievably the foundations of the Golden Age had
crumbled. Until after one part of the world – the USSR and the Eastern
Europe of 'real socialism' – had collapsed entirely, the global nature of the
crisis was not recognized, let alone admitted in the developed non-
communist regions. Even so, for many years economic troubles were

still 'recessions'. The half-century's taboo on the use of the terms 'depression' or 'slump', that reminder of the Age of Catastrophe, was not completely broken. Simply to use the word might conjure up the thing, even if the 'recessions' of the 1980s were 'the most serious for fifty years' – a phrase which carefully avoided specifying the actual period, the 1930s. The civilization that had elevated the word-magic of the advertisers into a basic principle of the economy, was caught in its own mechanism of delusion. Not until the early 1990s do we find admissions – as, for instance, in Finland – that the economic troubles of the present were actually worse than those of the 1930s.

In many ways this was puzzling. Why should the world economy have become less stable? As economists observed, the elements stabilizing the economy were now actually stronger than before, even though free-market governments, like those of Presidents Reagan and Bush in the USA, Mrs Thatcher and her successor in Britain, tried to weaken some of them (World Economic Survey, 1989, pp. 10–11). Computerized inventory control, better communications and quicker transport reduced the importance of the volatile 'inventory cycle' of the old mass production which produced enormous stocks 'just in case' they were needed at times of expansion, and then stopped dead while stocks were sold off in times of contraction. The new method, pioneered by the Japanese, and made possible by the technologies of the 1970s was to carry far smaller inventories, produce enough to supply dealers 'just in time', and in any case with a far greater capacity to vary output at short notice to meet changing demands. This was the age not of Henry Ford but of Benetton. At the same time the sheer weight of government consumption and of that part of private income which came from government ('transfer payments' such as social security and welfare) also stabilized the economy. Between them they amounted to about a third of GDP. If anything both increased in the crisis era, if only because the cost of unemployment, pensions and health care rose. As this era was still continuing at the end of the Short Twentieth Century, we may have to wait for some years before the economists are able to use the historians' ultimate weapon, hindsight, to find a persuasive explanation.

Of course the comparison of the economic troubles of the 1970s–90s with those between the wars is flawed, even though the fear of another Great Slump haunted these decades. 'Can it happen again?' was a question asked by many, especially after a new, dramatic American (and global) stock exchange crash in 1987 and a major international exchange crisis in 1992 (Temin, 1993, p. 99). The Crisis Decades after 1973 were no more a

'Great Depression' in the sense of the 1930s than the decades after 1873 had been, even though they were also given that name at the time. The global economy did not break down, even momentarily, although the Golden Age ended in 1973–75 with something very like a classical cyclical slump, which reduced industrial production in the 'developed market economies' by 10 per cent in one year and international trade by 13 per cent (Armstrong, Glyn, 1991, p. 225). Economic growth in the developed capitalist world continued, though at a distinctly slower pace than during the Golden Age, except for some of the (mainly Asian) 'newly industrializing countries' or NICs (see chapter 12), whose industrial revolutions had only begun in the 1960s. The growth of the collective GDP of the advanced economies until 1991 was barely interrupted by short periods of stagnation in the recession years 1973–75 and 1981–83 (OECD, 1993, pp. 18–19). International trade in the products of industry, the motor of world growth, continued, and in the boom years of the 1980s even accelerated to a rate comparable with the Golden Age. At the end of the Short Twentieth Century the countries of the developed capitalist world were, taken as a whole, far richer and more productive than in the early 1970s, and the global economy of which they still formed the central element was vastly more dynamic.

On the other hand, the situation in particular regions of the globe was considerably less rosy. In Africa, in Western Asia and in Latin America the growth of GDP per capita ceased. Most people actually became poorer in the 1980s and output fell for most years of the decade in the first two of these regions, for some years in the last (UN, World Economic Survey, 1989, pp. 8, 26). Nobody seriously doubted that for these parts of the world the 1980s were an era of severe depression. As for the former area of Western 'real socialism', after 1989 their economies, which had continued in modest growth during the 1980s, collapsed utterly. In this region the comparison of the crisis after 1989, with the Great Slump was perfectly apposite, although it underestimated the devastation of the early 1990s. Russia's GDP fell by 17 per cent in 1990–91, by 19 per cent in 1991–92 and by 11 per cent in 1992–93. Though some stabilization began in the early 1990s, Poland had lost over 21 per cent of its GDP in 1988–92, Czechoslovakia almost 20 per cent, Romania and Bulgaria 30 per cent or more. Their industrial production in mid-1992 was between half and two thirds that of 1989 (*Financial Times*, 24/2/94; EIB papers, November 1992, p. 10).

This was not the case in the East. Nothing was more striking than the contrast between the disintegration of the economies of the Soviet region and the spectacular growth of the Chinese economy in the same period.

In that country, and indeed in much of South-east and East Asia, which emerged in the 1970s as the most dynamic economic region of the world economy, the term 'Depression' had no meaning – except, curiously enough, in the Japan of the early 1990s. However, though the capitalist world economy flourished, it was not at ease. The problems which had dominated the critique of capitalism before the war, and which the Golden Age had largely eliminated for a generation – 'poverty, mass unemployment, squalor, instability' (see p. 268) – reappeared after 1973. Growth was, once again, interrupted by severe slumps, as distinct from 'minor recessions', in 1974–75, 1980–82 and at the end of the 1980s. Unemployment in Western Europe rose from an average of 1.5 per cent in the 1960s to 4.2 per cent in the 1970s (Van der Wee, p. 77). At the peak of the boom in the late 1980s it averaged 9.2 per cent in the European Community, in 1993, 11 per cent. Half of the unemployed (1986–87) had been out of work for more than a year, one third for more than two years (Human Development, 1991, p. 184). Since the potential working population was no longer being swelled, as in the Golden Age, by the flood of growing post-war babies, and since young people, in good times and bad, tended to have much higher unemployment rates than older workers, one would have expected permanent unemployment to shrink, if anything.*

As for poverty and squalor, in the 1980s even many of the richest and most developed countries found themselves, once again, getting used to the everyday sight of beggars on the streets, and the even more shocking spectacle of the homeless sheltering in doorways in cardboard boxes, insofar as they were not removed from visibility by the police. On any night of 1993 in New York twenty-three thousand men and women slept on the street or in public shelters, a small part of the 3 per cent of the population of the city which had, at one time or another in the five years before then, no roof over their heads (*New York Times*, 16/11/93). In the United Kingdom (1989) 400,000 people were officially classed as 'homeless' (UN Human Development, 1992, p. 31). Who, in the 1950s, or even the early 1970s, would have expected this?

The re-appearance of homeless paupers was part of the striking growth

---

* Between 1960 and 1975 the population aged fifteen to twenty-four rose by some twenty-nine millions in the 'developed market economies', but between 1970 and 1990 only by about six millions. Incidentally, the rates of youth unemployment in the Europe of the 1980s were startlingly high, except in social-democratic Sweden and West Germany. They ranged (1982–88) from over 20 per cent for Britain to over 40 per cent for Spain and 46 per cent for Norway (UN World Survey, 1989, pp. 15–16).

of social and economic inequality in the new era. By world standards the rich 'developed market economies' were not – or not yet – particularly unfair in the distribution of their income. In the most inegalitarian among them – Australia, New Zealand, the USA, Switzerland – the top 20 per cent of the households enjoyed an income, on average, between eight and ten times that of the bottom fifth, and the top 10 per cent usually took home between 20 and 25 per cent of their country's total income; only the top Swiss, New Zealanders, and the rich of Singapore and Hong Kong took home much more. This was as nothing compared to the inequality of countries like the Philippines, Malaysia, Peru, Jamaica or Venezuela, where they received over a third of their country's total income, let alone Guatemala, Mexico, Sri Lanka and Botswana, where they took home over 40 per cent, not to mention the world contender for the championship of economic inequality, Brazil.* In that monument to social injustice the lowest 20 per cent of the population divided 2½ per cent of the nation's total income among themselves, while the top 20 per cent enjoyed almost two-thirds of it. The top 10 per cent alone appropriated almost half (UN World Development, 1992, pp. 276–77; Human Development, 1991, pp. 152–53, 186).†

Nevertheless, during the Crisis Decades inequality unquestionably increased in the 'developed market economies', and all the more so since the almost automatic rise in real incomes to which the working classes had got used in the Golden Age had now come to an end. The extremes of poverty and wealth both grew, as did the range of income distribution in between. Between 1967 and 1990 the number of American Negroes earning less than $5,000 (1990) and the number of those earning more than $50,000 both grew at the expense of the intermediate incomes (*New York Times*, 25/9/92). Since the rich capitalist countries were far richer than ever before, and their people, on the whole, were now cushioned by the generous welfare and social security systems of the Golden Age (see p. 284), there was less social unrest than might have been expected, but government finances found themselves squeezed between enormous social welfare payments, which climbed faster than state revenues in

* The actual champions, i.e. those with a Gini coefficient of more than 0.6 were some much smaller countries, also in the Americas. The Gini co-efficient, a convenient measure of inequality, measures inequality of a scale from 0.0 – an equal distribution of income – to 1.0 – maximum inequality. The coefficient for Honduras in 1967–85 was 0.62, for Jamaica 0.66 (UN Human Development, 1990, pp. 158–59).

† Comparable data for some of the most inegalitarian countries are not available. The list would certainly also include several other African and Latin American states and, in Asia, Turkey and Nepal.

economies growing more slowly than before 1973. In spite of substantial efforts, hardly any national governments in the rich – and mainly democratic – countries, and certainly not those most hostile to public social welfare, managed to reduce the vast proportion of their expenditure for these purposes, or even to keep it in check.*

Nobody in 1970 had expected, let alone intended, all this to happen. By the early 1990s a mood of insecurity and resentment had begun to spread even through much of the rich countries. As we shall see, it contributed to the breakdown of traditional political patterns in them. Between 1990 and 1993 few attempts were made to deny that even the developed capitalist world was in depression. Nobody seriously claimed to know what to do about it, other than to hope it would pass. Nevertheless, the central fact about the Crisis Decades is not that capitalism no longer worked as well as it had done in the Golden Age, but that its operations had become uncontrollable. Nobody knew what to do about the vagaries of the world economy or possessed instruments to manage them. The major instrument for doing so in the Golden Age, government policy, national or internationally coordinated, no longer worked. The crisis decades were the era when the national state lost its economic powers.

This was not immediately obvious, because – as usual – most politicians, economists and businessmen failed to recognize the permanence of the shift in the economic conjuncture. The policies of most governments in the 1970s, and the politics of most states, assumed that the troubles of the 1970s were only temporary. A year or two would bring a return to the old prosperity and the old growth. There was no need to change the policies that had served so well for a generation. Essentially the story of that decade was one of governments buying time – in the case of third-world and socialist states often by going heavily into what they hoped was short-term debt – and applying the old recipes of Keynesian economic management. As it happened, in most advanced capitalist countries social-democratic governments were in office in much of the 1970s, or returned to office after unsuccessful conservative interludes (as in Britain in 1974 and the USA in 1976). These were not likely to abandon the policies of the Golden Age.

---

* In 1972 fourteen such states spent a mean of 48 per cent of their central government expenditure on housing, social security, welfare and health. In 1990 they spent a mean of 51 per cent. The states concerned are: Australia and New Zealand, the US and Canada, Austria, Belgium, Britain, Denmark, Finland, (Federal) Germany, Italy, the Netherlands, Norway and Sweden (calculated from UN World Development, 1992, Table 11).

The only alternative offered was that propagated by the minority of ultra-liberal economic theologians. Even before the crash, the long-isolated minority of believers in the unrestricted free market had begun their attack on the domination of the Keynesians and other champions of the managed mixed economy and full employment. The ideological zeal of the old champions of individualism was now reinforced by the apparent impotence and failure of conventional economic policies, especially after 1973. The newly created (1969) Nobel Prize for economics backed the neo-liberal trend after 1974 by awarding it to Friedrich von Hayek (see p. 271) in 1974, and, two years later, to an equally militant champion of economic ultra-liberalism, Milton Friedman.* After 1974 the free marketeers were on the offensive, although they did not come to dominate government policies until the 1980s, with the exception of Chile, where a terrorist military dictatorship allowed US advisers to install an unrestricted free market economy thus, incidentally, demonstrating that there was no intrinsic connection between the free market, after the overthrow of a popular government in 1973 and political democracy. (To be fair to Professor von Hayek, unlike the run-of-the-mill Cold War propagandists of the West, he did not claim that there was.)

The battle between Keynesians and neo-liberals was neither a purely technical confrontation between professional economists, nor a search for ways of dealing with novel and troubling economic problems. (Who, for instance, had so much as considered the unpredicted combination of economic stagnation and rapidly rising prices, for which the jargon term 'stagflation' had to be invented in the 1970s?) It was a war of incompatible ideologies. Both sides put forward economic arguments. The Keynesians claimed that high wages, full employment and the Welfare State created the consumer demand that had fuelled expansion, and that pumping more demand into the economy was the best way to deal with economic depressions. The neo-liberals argued that Golden Age economics and politics prevented the control of inflation and the cutting of costs in both government and private business, thus allowing profits, the real motor of economic growth in a capitalist economy, to rise. In any case, they held, that Adam Smith's 'hidden hand' of the free market was bound to produce the greatest growth of the 'Wealth of Nations' and the best sustainable distribution of wealth and income within it; a claim which the Keynesians denied. Yet economics in both cases rationalized an ideological

* The prize was instituted in 1969 and before 1974 had been awarded to men distinctly *not* associated with *laissez-faire* economics.

commitment, an *a priori* view of human society. Neo-liberals distrusted and disliked social-democratic Sweden, a spectacular economic success-story of the twentieth century, not because it was to run into trouble in the Crisis Decades – as did other types of economy – but because it was based on 'the famed Swedish economic model with its collectivist values of equality and solidarity' (*Financial Times*, 11/11/90). Conversely Mrs Thatcher's government in Britain was unpopular on the Left, even during its years of economic success, because it was based on an a-social, indeed an anti-social egoism.

These were positions barely accessible to argument. Suppose, for instance, it could be shown that the supply of blood for medical use was best obtained by buying it off anyone willing to sell a pint of his or her blood at the market price. Would this have weakened the argument for the British system of unpaid voluntary donors, so eloquently and power-fully put forward by R.M. Titmuss in '*The Gift Relationship*' (Titmuss, 1970)? Surely not, although Titmuss had also shown that the British way of giving blood was as efficient and safer than the commercial way.*
Other things being equal, for many of us a society in which citizens are prepared to give selfless help to unknown fellow-humans, however symbolically, is better than one in which they won't. In the early 1990s the Italian political system was shattered by a voters' rebellion against its endemic corruption, not because many Italians had actually suffered from it – a large number of them, perhaps a majority had benefited from it – but on moral grounds. The only political parties not swept away by the moral avalanche were those not involved in the system. Champions of absolute individual freedom were unmoved by the evident social injustices of unrestricted market capitalism, even when (as in Brazil for most of the 1980s) it did not produce economic growth. Conversely, believers in equality and social fairness (like the present author) welcomed the chance to argue that even capitalist economic success might rest most firmly on a relatively egalitarian distribution of income, as in Japan (see p. 356).†

* This was confirmed in the early 1990s when the blood-transfusion services of some countries, but not Britain, discovered that patients had been infected by commercially acquired blood contaminated by the HIV/Aids virus.

† The richest 20 per cent of the population in the 1980s had 4.3 times the total income of the poorest 20 per cent, which was less than the figure in any other (capitalist) industrial country, even Sweden. The average for the eight most industrial-ized countries of the European Community was 6, the figure for the USA 8.9 (Kidron/Segal, 1991, pp. 36–37). To put it another way: the USA in 1990 had ninety-three dollar billionaires, the European Community fifty-nine, not counting the thirty-three domiciled in Switzerland and Lichtenstein. Japan had nine (ibid.).

That each side also translated its fundamental beliefs into pragmatic arguments, e.g. about whether the allocation of resources through free-market pricing was or was not optimal, was secondary. But, of course, both sides had to produce policies to deal with the economic slow-down.

In this respect the supporters of Golden Age economics were not very successful. This was partly because they were constrained by their political and ideological commitment to full employment, welfare states and the post-war consensus politics. Or rather, they were squeezed between the demands of capital and labour, when Golden Age growth no longer allowed both profits and non-business incomes to rise without getting in each other's way. In the 1970s and 1980s Sweden, the social-democratic state *par excellence*, maintained full employment with remark-able success by industrial subsidies, work-spreading and expanding state and public employment dramatically, thus making possible a notable extension of the welfare system. Even so, the policy could only be maintained by holding down the living standards of employed workers, penal tax-rates on high incomes and heavy deficits. In the absence of a return to the days of the Great Leap Forward, these could only be temporary measures, and from the mid-1980s on they were reversed. At the end of the Short Twentieth Century the 'Swedish Model' was in retreat even in its own country.

However, the model was also, and perhaps even more fundamentally, undermined by the globalization of the economy after 1970, which put the governments of all states – except perhaps the USA, with its enormous economy – at the mercy of an uncontrollable 'world market'. (Moreover, it was an undeniable fact that 'the market' was very much more likely to distrust Left governments than conservative ones.) In the early 1980s even a country as large and wealthy as France, then under a socialist government, found it impossible to pump up its economy unilaterally. Within two years of President Mitterand's triumphant elec-tion France faced a balance-of-payments crisis, was forced to devalue its currency, and to replace Keynesian demand stimulation by 'austerity with a human face'.

On the other hand, the neo-liberals were also at a loss, as was to become obvious at the end of the 1980s. They had little trouble attacking the rigidities, inefficiencies and economic wastages so often sheltering under Golden Age government policies once these were no longer kept afloat by the ever-rising tide of Golden Age prosperity, employment and government revenues. There was considerable scope for applying the neo-liberal cleansing-agent to the encrusted hull of many a good ship

'Mixed Economy' with beneficial results. Even the British Left was eventually to admit that some of the ruthless shocks imposed on the British economy by Mrs Thatcher had probably been necessary. There were good grounds for some of the disillusion with state-managed industries and public administration that became so common in the 1980s.

Nevertheless, the mere belief that business was good and government bad (in President Reagan's words 'government was not the solution but the problem') was not an alternative economic policy. Nor, indeed, could it be for a world in which, even in the Reaganite USA, central government expenditure amounted to about a quarter of the Gross National Product, and, indeed, in the developed countries of the European Community, averaged over 40 per cent of GNP (UN World Development, 1992, p. 239). Such enormous chunks of the economy could be managed in a businesslike manner and with a due sense of costs and benefits (as was not always the case), but they did not and could not operate like markets even when ideologists made them pretend to. In any case most neo-liberal governments were obliged to manage and steer their economies, while claiming that they were only encouraging market forces. Moreover, there was no way in which the weight of the state could be reduced. After fourteen years in power the most ideological of free-market regimes, Thatcherite Britain, actually taxed its citizens somewhat more heavily than they had been taxed under Labour.

In fact, there was no single or specific neo-liberal economic policy, except after 1989 in the former socialist states of the Soviet region, where some predictably disastrous attempts were made, on the advice of Western economic whiz-kids, to transfer the operations of the economy to the free market from one day to the next. The greatest of neo-liberal regimes, President Reagan's USA, though officially devoted to fiscal conservatism (i.e. balanced budgets), and Milton Friedman's 'monetarism', in fact used Keynesian methods to spend its way out of the depression of 1979–82 by running a gigantic deficit and engaging in an equally gigantic armaments build-up. So far from leaving the value of the dollar entirely to monetary rectitude and the market, Washington after 1984 returned to deliberate management through diplomatic pressure (Kuttner, 1991, pp. 88–94). As it happened, the regimes most deeply committed to *laissez-faire* economics were also sometimes, and notably in the case of Reagan's USA and Thatcher's Britain, profoundly and viscerally nationalist and distrustful of the outside world. The historian cannot but note that the two attitudes are contradictory. In any case, neo-liberal triumphalism did not survive the world economic setbacks of the early 1990s, nor perhaps the unexpected discovery that the most dynamic and rapidly growing economy of the globe after the fall of Soviet communism, was that of Communist China, leading Western business-school lectures and the authors of management manuals, a flourishing genre of literature, to scan the teachings of Confucius for the secrets of entrepreneurial success.

What made the economic problems of the Crisis Decades unusually troubling, and socially subversive, was that conjunctural fluctuations coincided with structural upheavals. The world economy facing the problems of the 1970s and 1980s was no longer that of the Golden Age, although it was, as we have seen, the predictable product of that era. Its system of production had been transformed by technological revolution and it had been globalized or 'transnationalized' to an extraordinary extent, and with dramatic consequences. Moreover, by the 1970s it became impossible to overlook the revolutionary social and cultural consequences of the Golden Age, discussed in earlier chapters, as well as its potential ecological consequences.

The best way to illustrate these is through work and unemployment. The general tendency of industrialization has been to replace human skill by the skill of machines, human labour by mechanical forces, thus throwing people out of work. It was assumed, correctly, that the vast growth of the economy made possible by this constant industrial revolution would automatically create more than enough new jobs to replace the lost old ones, although opinions differed about how large a body of unemployed workers was necessary for the efficient operation of such an economy. The Golden Age had apparently confirmed this optimism. As we have seen (see chapter 10), the growth of industry was so great that the number and proportion of industrial workers even in the most industrialized countries did not seriously drop. Yet the Crisis Decades began to shed labour at a spectacular rate, even in plainly expanding industries. Between 1950 and 1970 the number of long-distance telephone operators in the USA dropped by 12 per cent, as the number of calls grew five-fold; but between 1970 and 1980 it fell by 40 per cent while calls tripled (Technology, 1986, p. 328). The number of workers diminished, relatively, absolutely and, in any case, rapidly. The rising unemployment of these decades was not merely cyclical but structural. The jobs lost in bad times would not come back when times improved: they would never come back.

This was not only because the new international division of labour transferred industries from old regional countries and continents to new ones, turning the old centres of industry into 'rust-belts', or, in some ways, even more spectrally, into urban landscapes like face-lifts from which all trace of former industry had been removed. The rise of new industrial countries is indeed striking. In the mid-1980s seven of such countries in the Third World alone already consumed 24 per cent of the world's steel and produced 15 per cent of it – still as good an index of industrialization as any.* Moreover, in a world of free economic flows across state borders – except, characteristically, of migrants seeking work – labour-intensive industries naturally migrated from high-wage to low-wage countries, that is to say, from the rich core countries of capitalism like the USA to countries of the periphery. Every worker employed at Texan rates in El Paso was an economic luxury, if a worker, even an inferior one, was available at one tenth of the wage across the river in Mexican Juárez.

Yet even the pre-industrial and the new early industrial countries, were governed by the iron logic of mechanization, which sooner or later made even the cheapest human being more expensive than a machine capable of his or her work, and by the equally iron logic of genuine world-wide free-trading competition. Cheap as labour was in Brazil, compared to Detroit and Wolfsburg, the São Paulo automobile industry faced the same problems of increasing labour redundancy through mechanization as in Michigan and Lower Saxony; or so the author was told by its trade union leaders in 1992. The performance and productivity of machinery could be constantly, and for practical purposes, endlessly raised by technological progress, and its cost could be dramatically reduced. Not so that of human beings, as a comparison of the improvements in the speed of air transport and the 100-metre world record demonstrates. In any case the cost of human labour cannot, for any length of time, be reduced below the cost of keeping human beings alive at the minimum level regarded as acceptable in their society, or indeed at any level. Human beings are not efficiently designed for a capitalist system of production. The higher the technology, the more expensive the human component of production compared to the mechanical.

The historic tragedy of the Crisis Decades was that production now visibly shed human beings faster than the market economy generated new jobs for them. Moreover, this process was accelerated by global competition, by the financial squeeze on governments, which – directly or indirectly – were the largest single employers, and, not least, after 1980, by the then prevailing free-market theology which pressed for the transfer of employment to profit-maximising forms of enterprise, especially to private firms which, by definition, considered no interest but their own

.* China, South Korea, India, Mexico, Venezuela, Brazil and Argentina (Piel, 1992, pp. 286–89).

pecuniary one. This meant, among other things, that governments and other public entities ceased to be what has been called 'the employer of last resort' (World Labour, 1989, p. 48). The decline of trade unions, weakened both by economic depression and by the hostility of neo-liberal governments, accelerated this process, since the protection of jobs was one of their most cherished functions. The world economy was expanding, but the automatic mechanism by which its expansion generated jobs for men and women who entered the labour market without special qualifications was visibly breaking down.

To put the matter another way. The peasantry, which had formed the majority of the human race throughout recorded history, had been made redundant by agricultural revolution, but the millions no longer needed on the land had in the past been readily absorbed by labour-hungry occupations elsewhere, which required only a willingness to work, the adaptation of country skills, like digging and building walls, or the capacity to learn on the job. What would happen to the workers in those occupations when they in turn become unnecessary? Even if some could be re-trained for the high-grade jobs of the information age which continued to expand (most of which increasingly demanded a higher education), there were not enough of these to compensate (*Technology*, 1986, pp. 7–9, 335). What, for that matter, would happen to the peasants of the Third World who still flooded out of their villages?

In the rich countries of capitalism, they now had welfare systems to fall back on, although those who became permanently welfare-dependent were both resented and despised by those who thought of themselves as earning a living by work. In the poor countries they joined the large and obscure 'informal' or 'parallel' economy in which men, women and children lived, nobody quite knew how, by a combination of small jobs, services, expedients, buying, selling and taking. In the rich countries they began to form or re-form an increasingly separate and segregated 'underclass' whose problems were *de facto* regarded as insoluble, but secondary, since they formed only a permanent minority. The ghetto society of the native Negro population in the USA* became the textbook example of such a social underworld. Not that the 'black economy' was absent in the First World. Researchers were surprised to discover that in the early 1990s the twenty-two million households of Britain between them held

---

* Black immigrants into the USA from the Caribbean and Hispanic America behaved, essentially, like other immigrant communities, and did not allow themselves to be extruded from the labour market to anything like the same extent.

over £10 billions in cash, or an average of £460 per household, a figure said to be so high because the 'black economy deals largely in cash' (*Financial Times*, 18/10/93).

II

The combination of depression and a massively restructured economy designed to expel human labour created a sullen tension that penetrated the politics of the Crisis Decades. A generation had got accustomed to full employment or the confidence that the sort of work a person wanted was sure to be available somewhere soon. While the Slump of the early 1980s had already brought insecurity back into the lives of workers in manufacturing industries, it was not until the Slump of the early 1990s that large sections of the white-collar and professional classes in countries like Great Britain felt that neither their jobs nor their futures were safe: almost half of all people in the most prosperous parts of the country thought they might lose theirs. These were times when people, their old ways of life already undermined and crumbling in any case (see chapter 10 and 11), were likely to lose their bearings. Was it an accident that 'of the ten largest mass murders in American history . . . eight have occurred since 1980', typically the acts of middle-aged white men in their thirties and forties, 'after a prolonged period of being lonely, frustrated and full of rage', and often precipitated by a catastrophe in their lives such as losing their job or divorce?* Was even 'the growing culture of hate in the United States', which may have encouraged them, an accident (Butterfield, 1991)? This hate certainly became audible in the lyrics of popular music in the 1980s, and evident in the growingly overt cruelty of film and TV programmes.

This sense of disorientation and insecurity produced significant tectonic cracks and shifts in the politics of the developed countries, even before the end of the Cold War destroyed the international balance on which the stability of several Western parliamentary democracies had rested. In times of economic troubles voters are notoriously inclined to blame whatever party or regime is in power, but the novelty of the Crisis Decades was that the reaction against governments did not necessarily benefit the established forces of opposition. The major losers were the

---

* 'This is especially true . . . for some of the millions of people who have picked up in mid-life and moved. They get there and if they lose their job there, they really have no one to turn to.'

social-democratic or labour parties of the West, whose main instrument of satisfying their supporters – economic and social action by national governments – lost its force, while the central block of these supporters, the working class, broke into fragments (see chapter 10). In the new transnational economy, domestic wages were far more directly exposed to foreign competition than before, and the ability of governments to shelter them was far less. At the same time in a period of depression the interests of various parts of the traditional social-democratic constituency diverged: those whose jobs were (relatively) safe; those who were insecure; those in the old and unionised regions and industries; those in the less threatened new industries in new and non-union areas; and the universally unpopular victims of bad times who sank into the 'underclass'. Moreover, since the 1970s a number of (mainly young and/or middle-class) supporters abandoned the main parties of the Left for more specialized campaigning movements – notably 'the environment', women's movements and other so-called 'new social movements' – thus weakening them. In the early 1990s labour and social-democratic governments became as uncommon as they had been in the 1950s, for even administrations nominally headed by socialists abandoned their traditional policies, willingly or not.

The new political forces which stepped into this void were a mixed assortment, ranging from the xenophobic and racist on the right, via secessionist parties (mainly, but not only ethnic/nationalist) to the various 'Green' parties and other 'new social movements' which claimed a place on the Left. Several of these established a significant presence in their country's politics, sometimes a regional dominance, though by the end of the Short Century none had actually replaced the old political establishments. The support of others fluctuated wildly. Most of the influential ones rejected the universalism of democratic and citizen politics for the politics of some group identity, and consequently shared a visceral hostility to foreigners and outsiders, and to the all-inclusive nation-state of the American and French revolutionary tradition. We shall consider the rise of the new 'identity politics' below.

However, the importance of these movements lay not so much in their positive content, as in their rejection of the 'old politics'. Several of the most formidable rested essentially on this negative claim, for instance the separatist Northern League in Italy, the 20 per cent of the US electorate which supported a wealthy Texan maverick for President in 1992, or, for that matter, the electors of Brazil and Peru who actually elected men to the presidency in 1989 and 1990 on the grounds that they must be trustworthy as they had never heard of them before. In Britain only the systematically unrepresentative electoral system prevented the emergence of a massive third party at various times since the early 1970s, when the Liberals, alone or in combination or after fusion with a moderate Social Democratic breakaway from the Labour Party, gained almost as much support as – or even more support than – one or other of the two major parties. Since the early 1930s, another depression period, there had been nothing like the dramatic collapse of electoral support in the late 1980s and early 1990s for established parties with long records in government – the Socialist Party in France (1990), the Conservative Party in Canada (1993), the Italian government parties (1993). In short, during the Crisis Decades the hitherto stable structures of politics in the democratic capitalist countries began to fall apart. What is more, the new political forces which showed the greatest potential for growth were those which combined populist demagogy, highly visible personal leadership and hostility to foreigners. Survivors from the inter-war era had reasons for feeling discouraged.

III

It was not much noticed that, again from around 1970, a similar crisis had begun to undermine the 'Second World' of the 'centrally planned economies'. It was first concealed, later underlined, by the inflexibility of their political systems, so that the change, when it came, was sudden, as in the late 1970s, after the death of Mao in China, and in 1983–85, after the death of Brezhnev in the USSR (see chapter 16). Economically, it was clear from the middle 1960s that centrally state-planned socialism badly needed reform. From the 1970s on there were strong signs of actual regression. This was the very moment when these economies were exposed, like everyone else – even if perhaps not to the same extent – to the uncontrollable movements and unpredictable fluctuations of the transnational world economy. The massive entry of the USSR on the international grain market, and the impact of the oil crises of the 1970s dramatized the ending of the 'socialist camp' as a virtually self-contained regional economy protected from the vagaries of the world economy (see pp. 374).

East and West were curiously bonded together not only by the transnational economy, which neither could control, but by the strange interdependence of the Cold War power system. This, as we have seen (see chapter 8), stabilized both superpowers and the world between them, and was in turn to throw both into disorder when it collapsed. The disorder was not merely political, but economic. For, with the sudden collapse of the Soviet political system, the inter-regional division of labour and the network of mutual dependence which had developed in the Soviet sphere also collapsed, forcing countries and regions that were geared to it to come to terms singly with a world market for which they were not equipped. But the West was equally unprepared to integrate the remains of the old communist 'parallel world system' into its own world market, even when it wanted to, as the European Community did not.* Finland, one of the spectacular economic success stories of post-war Europe, was plunged into a major slump by the collapse of the Soviet economy. Germany, the greatest economic power of Europe, was to impose tremendous strains on its own economy, and on Europe as a whole, simply because its government (against warnings by its bankers, it must be said) completely underestimated the difficulty and costs of absorbing a relatively tiny part of the socialist economy, the sixteen-million-strong German Democratic Republic. These, however, were unpredicted consequences of the Soviet break-up, which almost nobody expected until it actually happened.

Nevertheless, in the meantime, as in the West, unthinkable thoughts became thinkable in the East; invisible problems became visible. Thus in both East and West the defence of the environment became an important campaigning issue in the 1970s, whether the issue was the defence of whales or the preservation of Lake Baikal in Siberia. Given the restrictions on public debate, we cannot exactly trace the development of critical thoughts in these societies, but by 1980 first-class and formerly reforming communist economists within the regime, like János Kornai in Hungary, were publishing notably negative analyses of the socialist economic systems, and the ruthless probes into the defects of the Soviet social system, which became known in the mid-eighties, had clearly been long gestating among the academics of Novosibirsk and elsewhere. When leading communists actually gave up their belief in socialism is even harder to establish, for after 1989–91 such people had some interest in retrospectively ante-dating their conversion. What was true in economics was even more patently true in politics, as Gorbachev's *perestroika* was to show, at any rate in the Western socialist countries. With all their historic admiration for and attachment to Lenin, there is little doubt that many reform communists would have wanted to abandon much of

---

* I recall the cry of anguish of a Bulgarian at an international colloquium in 1993: 'What do you want us to do? We lost our markets in the former socialist countries. The European Community does not want to take our exports. As loyal members of the UN we can't even sell to Serbia now, because of the Bosnian blockade. Where do we go?'

the political heritage of Leninism, though few (outside the Italian Communist Party, to which reformers in the East felt attracted) were prepared to say so.

What most reformers in the socialist world would have wanted, was to transform communism into something like Western social democracy. Stockholm was their model rather than Los Angeles. There is no sign that Hayek and Friedman had many secret admirers in Moscow or Budapest. It was their bad luck that the crisis of the communist systems coincided with the crisis of Golden Age capitalism, which was also the crisis of social democratic systems. It was their even worse luck that the sudden collapse of communism made a programme of gradual transformation appear both undesirable and impractical, and that it occurred when the root-and-branch radicalism of the pure free-market ideologists was (briefly) triumphant in the capitalist West. This therefore became the theoretical inspiration of post-communist regimes, though in practice it proved as unrealisable there as anywhere else.

However, though in many ways the crises in East and West ran parallel and were linked into a single global crisis by both politics and economics, they differed in two major respects. For the communist system, which at least in the Soviet sphere, was inflexible and inferior, it was a matter of life and death, which it did not survive. Survival of the economic system was never at issue in the developed countries of capitalism, and, in spite of the crumbling of their political systems, neither, as yet, was the viability of these systems. This may explain, though it cannot justify, the implausible claim by an American writer that, with the end of communism, the future history of humanity would be that of liberal democracy. Only in one vital respect were these systems at risk: their future existence as single territorial states was no longer guaranteed. However, in the early 1990s, not a single one of the Western nation-states threatened with secessionist movements had actually broken up.

During the Age of Catastrophe, the end of capitalism had seemed near. The Great Slump could be described, like the title of a contemporary book, as *This Final Crisis* (Hutt, 1935). Few were seriously apocalyptic about the immediate future of developed capitalism, although a French historian and art dealer firmly predicted the end of Western civilization in 1976 on the not untenable ground that the momentum of the US economy, which had carried the rest of the capitalist world forward in the past, was now a spent force (Gimpel, 1992). He therefore expected the current depression to 'continue well into the next millennium'. It is only fair to add that, until the middle or even late 1980s, few were apocalyptic about the prospects of the USSR either.

However, precisely because of the greater and more uncontrollable dynamism of the capitalist economy, the social texture of Western societies had been far more profoundly undermined than that of socialist ones, and consequently in this respect the crisis of the West was more severe. The social fabric of the USSR and Eastern Europe went to pieces as a result of the system's collapse and not as a precondition of it. Where comparisons were possible, as between West and East Germany, it seemed that the values and habits of traditional Germany had been better preserved under the lid of communism than in the Western region of economic miracles. The Jewish emigrants from the USSR to Israel revived the classical music scene there, since they came from a country where going to live concerts was still a normal part of cultured behaviour, at any rate for Jews. The concert public had not yet been reduced, in effect, to a small and mainly middle-aged or elderly minority.* The inhabitants of Moscow and Warsaw were less worried by what troubled those of New York or London: a visibly rising crime rate, public insecurity, and the unpredictable violence of anomic youths. There was, obviously, little public flaunting of the kind of behaviour which outraged the socially conservative or conventional, even in the West, who saw it as evidence of the breakdown of civilization, and darkly muttered 'Weimar'.

How much of this difference between East and West was due to the greater wealth of Western societies and the far more rigid control of the state in the East is difficult to establish. In some respects East and West had evolved in the same direction. In both, families became smaller, marriages broke up more freely than elsewhere, the populations of states – or, at any rate, of their more urbanized and industrialized regions – reproduced themselves barely if at all. In both, so far as we can tell, the hold of traditional Western religions was drastically weakened, although it was claimed by religious enquirers that there was a revival of religious belief in post-Soviet Russia, though not in religious attendance. As events after 1989 showed, Polish women became as reluctant to let the Catholic Church dictate their mating habits as Italian women, although in the communist era Poles had shown a passionate attachment to the Church on nationalist and anti-Soviet grounds. Plainly the communist regimes provided less social space for subcultures, countercultures and under-worlds of all kinds, and repressed dissidence. Moreover, peoples which had passed through the periods of genuinely ruthless and wholesale

---

* In New York, one of the world's two major musical centres, the concert public for classical music was said in the early 1990s to rest on twenty to thirty thousand people out of a population of ten millions.

terror, which studded the history of most such states, were likely to keep their heads down even when the exercise of power became gentler. Nevertheless, the relative tranquility of socialist life was not due to fear. The system insulated its citizens from the full impact of the Western social transformations because it insulated them from the full impact of Western capitalism. What change they underwent, came through the state or through their response to the state. What the state did not set out to change stayed much as it had been before. The paradox of communism in power was that it was conservative.

IV

About the vast area of the Third World (including those parts of it which were now industrializing) it is hardly possible to generalize. Insofar as its problems can be surveyed as a whole, I have tried to do so in chapters 7 and 12. The Crisis Decades, as we have seen, affected its regions in very different ways. How are we to compare South Korea, where the ownership of television sets went from 6.4 per cent of the population to 99.1 per cent in the fifteen years from 1970 to 1985 (Jon, 1993), with a country like Peru, where over half the population was below the poverty line – more than in 1972 – and the per capita consumption was falling (Anuario, 1989), let alone with the ravaged countries of sub-Saharan Africa? The tensions within a subcontinent like India were those of a growing economy and a society in transformation. Those in areas like Somalia, Angola and Liberia were those of countries in dissolution, in a continent about whose future few were optimistic.

Only one generalization was fairly safe: since 1970 almost all the countries in this region had plunged deeply into debt. In 1990 they ranged from the three giants of international debt ($60 to 110 billions) – Brazil, Mexico and Argentina – through the other twenty-eight who owed over $10 billions each, down to the minnows who owed a billion or two. The World Bank (which had reason to know) counted only seven among the ninety-six 'low' and 'middle-income' economies it monitored who had external debts substantially below a billion dollars – countries like Lesotho and Chad – and even these were many times as large as they had been twenty years earlier. In 1970 there had been only twelve countries with a debt over $1 billion, and none with debts over $10 billions. In more realistic terms, by 1980 six countries had a debt virtually as large as their entire GNP, or bigger; 1990 twenty-four countries owed more than they produced, including, taking the region as a whole, *all* of sub-Saharan Africa. The relatively most heavily indebted countries were not surprisingly to be found in Africa (Mozambique, Tanzania, Somalia, Zambia, Congo, the Ivory Coast), some disrupted by war, some by the collapse of the price of their exports. However, the countries which had to bear the heaviest cost of servicing these vast debts, that is to say, where this amounted to a quarter or more of the country's total exports, were more evenly spread. Indeed, among the regions of the world, sub-saharan Africa was rather below this figure, better off in this respect than South Asia, Latin America and the Caribbean, and the Middle East.

Practically none of this money was ever likely to be repaid, but so long as the banks continued to earn interest on it – an average of 9.6 per cent in 1982 (UNCTAD) – they did not mind. There was a moment of genuine panic in the early 1980s when, starting with Mexico, the major Latin American debtors could no longer pay, and the Western banking system was on the verge of collapse, since several of the largest banks had lent their money with such abandon in the 1970s (when the petro-dollars flooded in, clamouring for investment) that they would now be technically bankrupt. Fortunately for the economy of the rich countries, the three Latin giants of debt failed to act together, separate arrangements for re-scheduling the debts were made and the banks, supported by governments and international agencies, had time in which gradually to write off their lost assets and to maintain technical solvency. The debt crisis remained, but was no longer potentially fatal. This was probably the most dangerous moment for the capitalist world economy since 1929. Its full story has not yet been written.

While their debts mounted, the assets or potential assets of the poor states did not. The capitalist world economy, which judges exclusively by profit or potential profit, clearly decided to write off a large part of the Third World in the Crisis Decades. Of the forty-two 'low-income economies' in 1970, nineteen had zero net foreign investments. In 1990 direct foreign investors had lost total interest in twenty-six. Indeed there was substantial investment (more than $500 million) in only fourteen out of almost 100 low- and middle-income countries outside Europe, and massive investment (from about one billion or so upwards) in only eight, of which four were in East and South-east Asia (China, Thailand, Malaysia, Indonesia), and three in Latin America (Argentina, Mexico, Brazil).* The increasingly integrated transnational world economy did not entirely overlook the outcast regions. The smaller and more scenic among them

---

* The other investment attractor was, somewhat surprisingly, Egypt.

had potential as tourist paradises and offshore refuges from government control, and the discovery of some suitable resource on some hitherto uninteresting territory might well change the situation. However, on the whole a large part of the world was dropping out of the world economy. After the collapse of the Soviet bloc, this also looked like being the case with the area between Trieste and Vladivostok. In 1990 the only former socialist states of Eastern Europe which attracted any net foreign investment were Poland and Czechoslovakia (UN World Development, 1992, Tables 21, 23, 24). Within the vast area of the former USSR there were clearly resource-rich districts or republics which attracted serious money, and zones which were left to their own miserable devices. One way or another, most of the former Second World was being assimilated to Third World status.

The main effect of the Crisis Decades was thus to widen the gap between rich and poor countries. The real GDP per capita of sub-Saharan Africa declined from 14 per cent of that of the industrial countries to 8 per cent between 1960 and 1987, that of the 'least developed' countries (which included both African and non-African countries) from 9 per cent to 5 per cent.* (UN *Human Development*, 1991, Table 6.)

V

As the transnational economy established its grip over the world, it undermined a major, and since 1945, virtually universal, institution: the territorial nation-state, since such a state could no longer control more than a diminishing part of its affairs. Organizations whose field of action was effectively bounded by the frontiers of their territory, like trade unions, parliaments and national public broadcasting systems, therefore lost, as organizations not so bounded, like transnational firms, the international currency market and the globalized media and communications of the satellite era, gained. The disappearance of the superpowers, which could at any rate control their satellite states, was to reinforce this tendency. Even the most irreplaceable function nation-states had developed during the century, that of redistributing their income among their

---

* The 'least developed nations' is a category established by the UN. Mostly they have less than $300 per annum GNP per head. 'Real GDP per capita' is a way of expressing this figure in terms of what it could purchase locally, instead of simply in terms of official exchange rates, according to a scale of 'international purchasing power parities'.

populations through the 'transfer payments' of the welfare, educational and health services and other fund allocations, could no longer be territorially self-contained in theory, though most of it had to remain so in practice, except where supra-national entities like the European Community or Union supplemented it in some respects. During the heyday of the free-market theologians, the state was further undermined by the tendency to dismantle activities hitherto conducted by public bodies on principle, leaving them to 'the market'.

Paradoxically, but perhaps not surprisingly, this weakening of the nation-state went with a new fashion for cutting up the old territorial nation-states into what claimed to be (smaller) new ones, mostly based on the demand of some group to ethnic-linguistic monopoly. To begin with, the rise of such autonomist and separatist movements, mainly after 1970, was primarily a Western phenomenon, observable in Britain, Spain, Canada, Belgium, even in Switzerland and Denmark, but also, from the early 1970s, in the least centralized of socialist states, Yugoslavia. The crisis of communism spread it to the East, where more new and nominally national states were to be formed after 1991 than at any other time during the twentieth century. Until the 1990s it left the western hemisphere south of the Canadian border virtually unaffected. In the areas where the 1980s and 1990s brought the collapse and disintegration of states, as in Afghanistan and parts of Africa, the alternative to the old state was not so much a partition into new states as anarchy.

The development was paradoxical, since it was perfectly plain that the new mini-nation-states suffered from precisely the same drawbacks as the older ones, only, being smaller, more so. It was less surprising than it seemed, simply because the only actual state model available in the late twentieth century, was that of the bounded territory with its own autonomous institutions – in short the nation-state model of the Age of Revolution. Moreover, since 1918 all regimes had been committed to the principle of 'national self-determination', which had been increasingly defined in ethnic-linguistic terms. In this respect Lenin and President Wilson were at one. Both the Europe of the Versailles peace treaties and what became the USSR were conceived of as collections of such nation-states. In the case of the USSR (and Yugoslavia, which later followed its example) these were unions of such states which, however, in theory – though not in practice – retained their right to secession.* When such

* In this they differed from the states of the USA which, since the end of the American Civil War in 1865, have not had the right to secession, except possibly for Texas.

unions broke up, it would naturally be along the pre-determined fracture lines.

However, in fact the new separatist nationalism of the Crisis Decades was quite a different phenomenon from the nation-state creation of the nineteenth and early twentieth century. It was indeed, a combination of three phenomena. One was the resistance of existing nation-states against their demotion. This became increasingly clear in the 1980s with the attempts by members or potential members of the European Community, sometimes of widely differing political complexions, like Norway and Mrs Thatcher's Britain, to retain their regional autonomy within the all-European standardization in matters which they thought important. However, it was significant that the main traditional prop of nation-state self-defence, namely protectionism, was incomparably weaker in the Crisis Decades than it had been in the Age of Catastrophe. Global free trade remained the ideal and, to a surprising extent, the reality – more so than ever after the fall of the state-command economies – even though several states developed unacknowledged methods for protecting themselves against foreign competition. The Japanese and the French were said to be expert at this, but probably the Italians' success in keeping a lion's share of their home market for automobiles in Italian hands (i.e. Fiat) was the most striking. Nevertheless, these were rearguard actions, though increasingly hard-fought and sometimes successful ones. They were probably contested most bitterly where the issue was not simply economic but one of cultural identity. The French, and to a lesser extent the Germans, fought to maintain the vast subsidies for their peasants, not only because farmers had vital votes, but also because they genuinely felt that the destruction of peasant farming, however inefficient or uncompetitive, would mean the destruction of a landscape, a tradition, a part of the nation's character. The French, supported by the other Europeans, resisted the US demand for free trade in films and audio-visual products, not simply because this would have swamped their public and private screens with American products, since an American-based (though by now internationally owned and controlled) entertainment industry had re-established a potential world monopoly on the scale of the old Hollywood power. They also, and justly, felt that it was intolerable that pure calculations of comparative costs and profitability should lead to the end of film production in the French language. Whatever the economic arguments, there were things in life which had to be protected. Would any government seriously consider tearing down Chartres Cathedral or the Taj Mahal if it could be shown that building a luxury hotel, shopping mall and conference centre on the site (assuming it were to be sold to private buyers) would make a greater net addition to the country's GNP than could be yielded by the existing tourist traffic? The question has only to be formulated to be answered.

The second is best described as the collective egoism of wealth, and reflected the growing economic disparities within continents, countries and regions. Old fashioned nation-state governments, centralized or federal, as well as supra-national entities like the European Community, had accepted responsibility for developing their entire territories, and therefore, to some extent, for equalizing burdens and benefits across the whole of them. This meant that the poorer and more backward regions were subsidized (via some central distributive mechanism) by the richer and more advanced, or even given preference in investment in order to diminish their lag. The European Community was realistic enough only to admit states to membership whose backwardness and poverty would not put too great a strain on the rest, a realism totally absent from the North American Free Trade Area of 1993 which yoked the USA and Canada (1990 GNP per capita of about $20,000) with Mexico with one-eighth of this per capita GNP.* The reluctance of rich areas to subsidize poorer ones had long been familiar to students of local government, especially in the USA. The problem of the 'inner city', inhabited by the poor, and with a tax-base shrinking because of the flight to the suburbs, was largely due to this. Who wanted to pay for the poor? Rich suburbs in Los Angeles like Santa Monica and Malibu opted out of the city, and in the early 1990s Staten Island voted to secede from New York for the same reason.

Some of the separatist nationalism of the Crisis Decades plainly fed on this collective egoism. The pressure for breaking up Yugoslavia came from 'European' Slovenia and Croatia; and for splitting Czechoslovakia from the vociferously 'Western' Czech Republic. Catalonia and the Basque country were the wealthiest and most 'developed' parts of Spain, and the only signs of significant separatism in Latin America came from the richest state of Brazil, Rio Grande do Sul. The purest example of this phenomenon was the sudden rise in the late 1980s of the Lombard League (later: Northern League) which aimed at the secession of the region centred on Milan, the 'economic capital' of Italy, from Rome, the political capital. The rhetoric of the League, with its references to a glorious medieval past and the Lombard dialect, was the usual one of

---

* The poorest member of the European Union, Portugal, had a 1990 GNP of one-third of the Community's average.

nationalist agitation, but the real issue was the rich region's wish to keep its resources to itself.

The third element was perhaps chiefly a response to the 'cultural revolution' of the second half of the century, that extraordinary dissolution of traditional social norms, textures and values, which left so many of the inhabitants of the developed world orphaned and bereft. Never was the word 'community' used more indiscriminately and emptily than in the decades when communities in the sociological sense became hard to find in real life – 'the intelligence community', 'the public relations community', the 'gay community'. The rise of 'identity groups' – human ensembles to which a person could 'belong', unequivocally and beyond uncertainty and doubt, was noted from the late 1960s by writers in the always self-observing USA. Most of these, for obvious reasons, appealed to a common 'ethnicity', although other groups of people seeking collective separatism used the same nationalist language (as when homosexual activists spoke of 'the queer nation').

As the emergence of this phenomenon in the most systematically multi-ethnic of states suggests, the politics of identity groups had no intrinsic connexion with the 'national self-determination', i.e. the desire to create territorial states, identical with a particular 'people', which was the essence of nationalism. Secession made no sense for US Negroes or Italians, nor was it part of their ethnic politics. Ukrainian politics in Canada were not Ukrainian but Canadian.* Indeed, the essence of ethnic or similar politics in urban, i.e. almost by definition heterogeneous societies, was to compete with other such groups for a share of the resources of the non-ethnic state, by using the political leverage of group loyalty. The politicians elected for the New York municipal constituencies, gerrymandered in order to provide specific representation for Latino, Oriental and homosexual voting blocs, wanted more out of New York City, not less.

What ethnic identity politics had in common with *fin-de-siècle* ethnic nationalism was the insistence that one's group identity consisted in some existential, supposedly primordial, unchangeable and therefore permanent personal characteristic shared with other members of the group, and with

---

* At most, local immigrant communities could develop what has been called 'long-distance nationalism' on behalf of their original or chosen homelands, generally representing the extremes of nationalist politics in those countries. The North American Irish and Jews were the original pioneers in this field, but the global diasporas created by migration multiplied such organizations, e.g. among Sikh migrants from India. Long-distance nationalism came into its own with the collapse of the socialist world.

no one else. Exclusiveness was all the more essential to it, since the actual differences which marked human communities off from each other were attenuated. Young American Jews searched for their 'roots' when the things which stamped them indelibly as Jews were no longer effective markers of Jewry; not least the segregation and discrimination of the years before the Second World War. Though Quebec nationalism insisted on separation because it claimed to be a 'distinct society', it actually emerged as a significant force precisely when Quebec ceased to be the 'distinct society' it had so patently and unmistakably been until the 1960s (Ignatieff, 1993, pp. 115–17). The very fluidity of ethnicity in urban societies made its choice as the only criterion of the group arbitrary and artificial. In the USA, except for Blacks, Hispanics, and those of English and German origins, at least 60 per cent of American-born women of *all* ethnic origins married outside their group (Lieberson, Waters, 1988, p. 173). Increasingly one's identity had to be constructed by insisting on the non-identity of others. How otherwise could the neo-Nazi skinheads in Germany, wearing the uniforms, hair-styles and musical tastes of the cosmopolitan youth culture, establish their essential Germanness, except by beating up local Turks and Albanians? How, except by eliminating those who did not 'belong' could the 'essentially' Croat or Serb character of some region be established in which, for most of history, a variety of ethnicities and religions had lived as neighbours?

The tragedy of this exclusionary identity politics, whether or not it set out to establish independent states, was that it could not possibly work. It could only pretend to. The Italian-Americans from Brooklyn, who (perhaps increasingly) insisted on their Italianness and talked to one another in Italian, apologising for their lack of fluency in what they supposed to be their native language,* worked in an American economy to which Italianness as such was irrelevant, except as a key to a relatively modest niche market. The pretence that there was a Black, or Hindu, or Russian, or female truth incomprehensible and therefore essentially incommunicable to those outside the group, could not survive outside institutions whose only function was to encourage such views. Islamic fundamentalists who studied physics did not study Islamic physics; Jewish engineers did not learn Chassidic engineering; even the most culturally nationalist Frenchmen or Germans learned that operating in the global village of the scientists and technical experts who made the world work required

---

* I have overheard such conversations in a New York department store. Their immigrant parents or grandparents had almost certainly not spoken Italian, but Neapolitan, Sicilian or Calabrian.

communication in a single global language analogous to medieval Latin, which happened to be based on English. Even a world divided into theoretically homogeneous ethnic territories by genocide, mass expulsion and 'ethnic cleansing' was inevitably heterogenised again by mass movements of people (workers, tourists, businessmen, technicians), of styles and by the tentacles of the global economy. That, after all, is what happened to the countries of Central Europe, 'ethnically cleansed' during and after the Second World War. That is what would inevitably happen again in an increasingly urbanized world.

Identity politics and *fin-de-siècle* nationalism were thus not so much programmes, still less effective programmes for dealing with the problems of the late twentieth century, but rather emotional reactions to these problems. And yet, as the century drew to its end, the absence of institutions and mechanisms actually capable of dealing with these problems became increasingly evident. The nation-state was no longer capable of dealing with them. Who or what was?

Various devices had been invented for this purpose since the United Nations had been set up in 1945 on the assumption, immediately disappointed, that USA and USSR would continue to agree sufficiently to take global decisions. About the best that could be said for this organization is that, unlike its predecessor, the League of Nations, it remained in being throughout the second half of the century, and indeed became a club whose membership, increasingly, proved that a state had been formally accepted as internationally sovereign. It had, by the nature of its constitution, no powers or resources independent of those assigned to it by member-nations, and hence no powers of independent action.

The sheer need for global co-ordination multiplied international organizations faster than ever in the crisis decades. By the mid-1980s there were 365 inter-governmental ones and no less than 4,615 non-governmental ones, or more than twice as many as in the early 1970s (Held, 1988, p. 15). Moreover, global action on problems such as conservation and the environment was increasingly recognized to be urgent. However, unfortunately, the only formal procedures for achieving it, namely by international treaties separately signed and ratified by sovereign nation-states, were slow, clumsy and inadequate, as was demonstrated by the efforts to preserve the Antarctic continent and permanently to ban the hunting of whales. The very fact that in the 1980s the government of Iraq killed thousands of its citizens by poison gas, thus breaking one of the few genuinely universal international conventions, the Geneva Protocol of 1925 against the use of chemical warfare, underlined the weakness of available international instruments.

Nevertheless, two ways of securing international action were available, and the Crisis Decades saw both substantially reinforced. One was the voluntary abdication of national power to supra-national authorities by middle-sized states which no longer felt strong enough to stand on their own in the world. The European Economic Community (re-named the European Community in the 1980s and the European Union in the 1990s) doubled its size in the 1970s and prepared to expand it even further in the 1990s, while reinforcing its authority over the affairs of its member-states. The fact of this double extension was unquestionable, though it was to provoke considerable national resistance, both by member-governments and public opinion in their countries. The strength of the Community/Union lay in the fact that its un-elected central authority in Brussels took independent policy initiatives and was virtually immune to the pressures of democratic politics, except very indirectly, through the periodic meetings and negotiations of representatives of its (elected) member-governments. This state of affairs enabled it to function as an effective supra-national authority, subject only to specific vetos.

The other instrument of international action was equally, if not more, protected against nation-states and democracies. This was the authority of the international financial bodies set up in the aftermath of the Second World War, mainly the International Monetary Fund and the World Bank (see pp. 274ff.). Backed by the oligarchy of the major capitalist countries which, under the vague label of the 'Group of Seven' became increasingly institutionalized from the 1970s, they acquired increasing authority during the Crisis Decades, as the uncontrollable vagaries of the global exchanges, debt crisis of the Third World and, after 1989, the collapse of the Soviet bloc economies made a growing number of countries dependent on the willingness of the rich world to grant them loans. These loans were increasingly made conditional on the local pursuit of economic policies agreeable to the global banking authorities. The triumph of neo-liberal theology in the 1980s was, in effect, translated into policies of systematic privatisation and free-market capitalism which were imposed on governments too bankrupt to resist them, whether they were immediately relevant to their economic problems or not (as in post-Soviet Russia). It is interesting, but, alas, pointless to speculate on what J.M. Keynes and Harry Dexter White would have thought about this transformation of the institutions they had constructed with very different objects in mind, not least the object of full employment in their respective countries.

Still, these were effective international authorities, at all events for the imposition of policies by the rich on the poor countries. At the end of the century it remained to be seen what the consequences of these policies were, and what their effects on world development would be.

Two vast regions of the world were about to test them. One was the region of the USSR and its associated European and Asian economies, which, after the fall of the western communist systems, now lay in ruins. The other was the storehouse of social explosive which filled so much of the Third World. As we shall see in the next chapter, it had, since the 1950s, formed the major element of political instability on the globe.

CHAPTER FIFTEEN
Third World and Revolution

In January 1974 General Beleta Abebe stopped over in the Gode
barracks on his way to an inspection . . . The next day an incredible
report came to the Palace: the general has been arrested by the
soldiers, who are forcing him to eat what they eat. Food so
obviously rotten that some fear the general will fall ill and die. The
Emperor [of Ethiopia] sends in the airborne unit of his Guard,
which liberates the general and takes him to the hospital.

> – Ryszard Kapuściński, *The Emperor* (1983, p. 120)

We killed all the cattle [of the university's experimental farm] that
we could. But while we were killing them, the peasant women
started to cry: those poor beasts, why are they killing them like that,
what have they done? When the ladies (*señoras*) began to cry, oh
poor thing, we gave up, but we had already killed about a quarter,
like eighty head. We wanted to kill the lot, but we couldn't because
the peasant women started to cry.

When we'd been there for a while, a gentleman on his horse, over
towards Ayacucho, he'd gone to tell them what had happened. So,
the next day, it was on the news on the *La Voz* radio station. Just
then we were on the way back, and some comrades had those little
radios, so we listened, and, well, that made us feel good, didn't it?

> – A young member of *Sendero Luminoso, Tiempos*,
> (1990, p. 198)

I

However we interpret the changes in the Third World and its gradual
decomposition and fission, all of it differed from the First World in one

fundamental respect. It formed a worldwide zone of revolution – whether just achieved, impending or possible. The First World was, by and large, politically and socially stable when the global Cold War began. Whatever simmered under the surface of the Second World was held down by the lid of party power and potential Soviet military intervention. On the other hand, very few Third World states of any size passed through the period from 1950 (or the date of their foundation) without revolution; military coups to suppress, prevent or advance revolution; or some other form of internal armed conflict. The main exceptions up to the date of writing are India, and a few colonies ruled by long-lived and authoritarian paternalists, like Dr Banda of Malawi (the former colony of Nyasaland) and the (until 1994) indestructible M. Felix Houphouet-Boigny of the Ivory Coast. This persistent social and political instability of the Third World provided its common denominator.

This instability was equally evident to the USA, protector of the global status quo, which identified it with Soviet communism, or at least regarded it as a permanent and potential asset for the other side in the great global struggle for supremacy. Almost from the start of the Cold War, the USA set out to combat this danger by all means, from economic aid and ideological propaganda through official and unofficial military subversion to major war; preferably in alliance with a friendly or bought local regime, but if need be without local support. This is what kept the Third World a zone of war, when the First and Second Worlds settled down to the longest era of peace since the nineteenth century. Before the collapse of the Soviet system it was estimated that about nineteen – perhaps even twenty – millions had been killed in over one hundred 'major wars and military actions and conflicts' between 1945 and 1983, virtually all in the Third World: over nine million in East Asia; three-and-a-half million in Africa; two-and-a-half in South Asia; rather over half a million in the Middle East, without counting the most murderous of its wars, the Iran-Iraq conflict of 1980–88 which had barely begun; and rather less in Latin America (UN World Social Situation, 1985, p. 14). The Korean War of 1950–53, whose dead have been estimated at between three and four million (in a country of thirty million) (Halliday/Cumings, 1988, pp. 200–1) and the thirty years of Vietnam wars (1945–1975) were much the largest, and the only ones in which American forces themselves were directly engaged on a large scale. In each about fifty thousand Americans were killed. The losses of the Vietnamese and other Indochinese peoples are difficult to estimate, but the most modest estimate runs to two million. However, some of the indirectly fought anti-communist wars were of comparable barbarity, especially in Africa, where about one million-and-a-half are said to have died between 1980 and 1988 in the wars against the governments of Mozambique and Angola (joint population c. twenty-three million), with twelve million displaced from their homes or threatened by hunger (UN, Africa, 1989, p. 6).

The revolutionary potential of the Third World was equally evident to the communist regimes, if only because, as we have seen, the leaders of colonial liberation tended to see themselves as socialists, engaged on the same sort of project of emancipation, progress and modernization as the Soviet Union, and along the same lines. If educated in the Western style, they might even think of themselves as inspired by Lenin and Marx, though powerful communist parties in the Third World were uncommon, and (outside Mongolia, China and Vietnam) none became the main force in the movements of national liberation. However, several new regimes appreciated the usefulness of the Leninist type of party, and built or borrowed their own, as Sun Yat-sen had done in China after 1920. Some communist parties which acquired particular strength and influence were sidelined (as in Iran and Iraq in the 1950s) or eliminated by massacre, as in Indonesia in 1965, where something like half a million communists or supposed communists were killed after what was said to be a pro-communist military coup – probably the largest political butchery in history.

For several decades the USSR took an essentially pragmatic view of its relations with Third World revolutionary, radical and liberation movements, since it neither intended nor expected to enlarge the region under communist government beyond the range of Soviet occupation in the West, or of Chinese intervention (which it could not entirely control) in the East. This did not change even in the Khrushchev period (1956–64), when a number of home-grown revolutions, in which communist parties played no significant part, came to power under their own steam, notably in Cuba (1959) and Algeria (1962). African decolonisation also brought to power national leaders who asked for nothing better than the title of anti-imperialist, socialist and friend of the Soviet Union, especially when the latter brought technical and other aid not tainted by the old colonialism: Kwame Nkrumah in Ghana, Sekou Touré in Guinea, Modibo Keita in Mali, and the tragic Patrice Lumumba in the Belgian Congo, whose murder made him a Third World icon and martyr. (The USSR renamed the Peoples' Friendship University it established for Third World students in 1960, 'Lumumba University'.) Moscow sympathized with such new regimes and helped them, though soon abandoning excessive optimism about the new African states. In the ex-Belgian Congo it gave armed support to the Lumumbist side against the clients or puppets of the USA and the Belgians in the civil war (with interventions by a military force of the United Nations, equally disliked by both superpowers) that followed the precipitate granting of independence to the vast colony. The results were disappointing.* When one of the new regimes, Fidel Castro's in Cuba, actually declared itself to be officially communist, to everyone's surprise, the USSR took it under its wing, but not at the risk of permanently jeopardising its relations with the USA. Nevertheless, there is no real evidence that it planned to push forward the frontiers of communism by revolution until the middle 1970s, and even then the evidence suggests that the USSR made use of a favourable conjuncture it had not set out to create. Khrushchev's hopes, older readers may recall, were that capitalism would be buried by the economic superiority of socialism.

Indeed, when Soviet leadership of the international communist movement was challenged in 1960 by China, not to mention by various dissident Marxists, in the name of revolution, Moscow's parties in the Third World maintained their chosen policy of studied moderation. Capitalism was not the enemy in such countries, insofar as it existed, but the pre-capitalism, local interests and the (US) imperialism that supported them. Armed struggle was not the way forward, but a broad popular or national front in which the 'national' bourgeoisie or petty-bourgeoisie were allies. In short, Moscow's Third World strategy continued the Comintern line of the 1930s against all denunciations of treason to the cause of the October revolution (see chapter 5). This strategy, which infuriated those who preferred the way of the gun, sometimes looked like winning, as in Brazil and in Indonesia in the early 1960s, and in Chile in 1970. Perhaps not surprisingly, when it got to this point, it was stopped short by military coups followed by terror, as in Brazil after 1964, in Indonesia in 1965 and in Chile in 1973.

Nevertheless, the Third World now became the central pillar of the hope and faith of those who still put their faith in social revolution. It represented the great majority of human beings. It seemed to be a global volcano waiting to erupt, a seismic field whose tremors announced the major earthquakes to come. Even the analyst of what he called 'the end of ideology' in the stabilized, liberal, capitalist West of the Golden Age (Bell, 1960) admitted that the age of millennial and revolutionary hope

* A brilliant Polish journalist, then reporting from the (theoretically) Lumumbist province, has given the most vivid account of the tragic Congolese anarchy (Kapuszin-ski, 1990).

A CHANGING WORLD

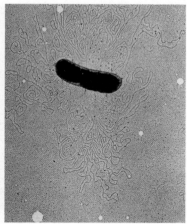

34. The pattern of the old: agricultural terracing in the Liping valley, Guizhou, China.

35. The pattern of the new: Electron micrograph of an intestinal bacterium spewing forth its chromosomes (x 55,000 magnification).

FROM THE OLD TO THE NEW

36. The world that ended after 8,000 years: Chinese peasant, ploughing.

37. The ancient world meets the new: Turkish immigrant couple in West Berlin.

38. The emigrants: West Indians, arriving hopefully in 1950s London.

39. Refugees: Africa at the end of the century

40. City Life: the old – Ahmedabad (India).

41. (*left*) City Life: the new –
Chicago.

43. (*opposite above left*) Transport:
rail, the nineteenth-century heritage –
Augsburg, Germany.

44. (*opposite above right*) Transport:
the internal combustion engine triumphed in the twentieth century.
Motorways, cars, and pollution in
Houston, Texas.

42. City Life – underground: rush hour in Shinjuku, Tokyo.

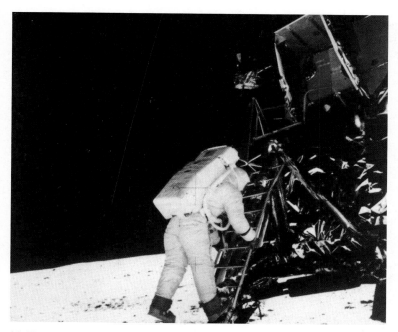

45. Transport beyond the earth. The first moon landing, 1969.

46. People in production: a 1930s cannery – Amarillo, Texas.

47. Production without people: Dungeness nuclear power station.

48. Where people once produced: de-industrialisation in North England (Middlesbrough).

DAILY LIFE TRANSFORMED

49. Revolution in the Kitchen: the refrigerator.

50. Revolution in the living room: the television set.

53. Old regime – civilian version: Neville Chamberlain (1869-1940), British premier 1937-40, fishing.

54. (*left*) Old regime – uniformed version: Louis (Francis Albert Victor Nicholas), 1st Earl Mountbatten of Burma (1900-79), last Viceroy of India.

51. (*opposite below left*) Shopping transformed: the supermarket.

52. (*opposite below right*) Leisure transformed: miniaturisation and mobility – the portable radio-cassette player.

55. New regime – the leader as revolutionary: Lenin speaking from the back of a truck, 1917.

56. New regime – the leader as revolutionary: Gandhi leaving an East End settlement in 1931 to negotiate with the British government.

57. (*left*) Stalin (Josif Vissarionovich Djugashvili, 1879-1953).

58. (*below*) Hitler's birthday parade, 1939.

59. (*left*) 'Chairman Mao' of China: Mao Tse-tung (1893-1976), as seen by Andy Warhol.

60. (*below*) The corpse of Ayatollah Khomeini, (1900-89), leader of revolutionary Iran, lies in state in Teheran.

61. (*left*) The artist as rebel after 1917. George Grosz, (1893–1959), savages the German ruling class.

62. (*below*) The 1930s – the proletariat: British shipyard workers march on London.

63. The 1960s – the students: Demonstration against the Vietnam War, Berkeley, California. Note the prominence of women.

LOOKING FORWARD

ONLY ONE LAUNCHED A CAMPAIGN THAT CONQUERED THE WORLD.

How did Coke succeed where history's most ambitious leaders failed? By choosing the right weapon. Advertising.

This ad is brought to you in the interest of advertising by The Richards Group and Adweek.

64. End of the century: claims to world conquest.

65. After the Gulf War, 1991.

66. After the Free Market: homeless.

67. Before freedom: waiting to vote in South Africa, 1994.

68. Sarajevo eighty years after 1914.

was not dead there. Nor was the Third World important only to the old revolutionaries of the October tradition, or to romantics, recoiling from the tawdry if prosperous mediocrity of the 1950s. The entire Left, including humanitarian liberals and moderate social democrats, needed something more than social security legislation and rising real wages. The Third World could preserve its ideals; and parties belonging to the great tradition of the Enlightenment need ideals as well as practical politics. They cannot survive without them. How otherwise can we explain the genuine passion for giving aid to Third World countries in those strong-holds of non-revolutionary progress, the Scandinavian countries, the Netherlands and the (Protestant) World Council of Churches, which was the late-twentieth-century equivalent of the support of missionary endeav-our in the nineteenth? In the later twentieth century it led European liberals to support or sustain Third World revolutionaries and revolutions.

II

What struck both the opponents of revolution and the revolutionaries was that, after 1945, the primary form of revolutionary struggle in the Third World, i.e. anywhere in the world, now seemed to be guerrilla warfare. A 'chronology of major guerrilla wars' compiled in the middle 1970s listed thirty-two since the end of the Second World War. All but three (the Greek civil war of the late forties, the Cyprus struggle against Britain in the 1950s and Ulster (1969–), were outside Europe and North America (Laqueur 1977, p. 442). The list could have been easily prolonged. The image of revolution as emerging exclusively from the hills was not quite accurate. It underestimated the role of Left-wing military coups, which admittedly seemed implausible in Europe until a dramatic example of the species occurred in Portugal in 1974, but which were common enough in the Islamic world and not unexpected in Latin America. The Bolivian revolution of 1952 was made by a conjunction of miners and army insurrectionaries; the most radical reform of Peruvian society by a military regime in the late 1960s and 1970s. It also underestimated the revolutionary potential of old-fashioned urban mass actions, which was to be demonstrated by the Iranian revolution of 1979 and thereafter in Eastern Europe. However, in the third quarter of the century all eyes were on the guerrillas. Their tactics, moreover, were strongly propagated by ideologues on the radical Left, critical of Soviet policy. Mao Tse-tung (after his split with the USSR) and, after 1959, Fidel Castro, or rather his comrade, the handsome and peripatetic Che Guevara (1928-67), inspired these activists. The Vietnamese communists, though by far the most formidable and successful practitioners of the guerrilla strategy, and internationally much admired for defeating both the French and the might of the USA, did not encourage their admirers to take sides in the internecine ideological feuds of the Left.

The 1950s were full of Third World guerrilla struggles, practically all in those colonial countries in which, for one reason or another, the former colonial powers or local settlers resisted peaceful decolonisation – Malaya, Kenya (the Mau Mau movement) and Cyprus in the dissolving British Empire; the much more serious wars in Algeria and Vietnam in the dissolving French one. Oddly it was a relatively small movement – certainly smaller than the Malayan insurgency (Thomas, 1971, p. 1040) – untypical but successful, which put the guerrilla strategy on the world's front pages: the revolution that took over the Caribbean island of Cuba on 1 January 1959. Fidel Castro (1927–) was a not uncharacteristic figure in Latin American politics: a strong and charismatic young man of good landowning family, whose politics were hazy, but who was determined to demonstrate personal bravery and to be a hero of whatever cause of freedom against tyranny presented itself at a suitable moment. Even his slogans ('Fatherland or Death' – originally 'Victory or Death' – and 'We shall be victorious') belong to an older era of liberation: admirable but lacking in precision. After an obscure period among the pistol-packing gangs of Havana University student politics, he chose rebellion against the government of General Fulgencio Batista (a familiar and tortuous figure in Cuban politics since his debut in an army coup in 1933 as the then Sergeant Batista), who had taken power again in 1952 and abrogated the Constitution. Fidel's approach was activist: an attack on an army barracks in 1953, jail, exile, and the invasion of Cuba by a guerrilla force which, on its second attempt, established itself in the mountains of the remotest province. The ill-prepared gamble paid off. In purely military terms the challenge was modest. Che Guevara, the Argentinian doctor and highly gifted guerrilla leader, set out to conquer the rest of Cuba with 148 men, rising to 300 by the time he had virtually done so. Fidel's own guerrillas only captured their first town of 1,000 inhabitants in December 1958 (Thomas, 1971, pp. 997, 1020, 1024). The most that he demonstrated by 1958 – though that was much – was that an irregular force could control a large 'liberated territory' and defend it against an offensive by an admittedly demoralized army. Fidel won because the Batista regime was fragile, lacking all real support, except that motivated by convenience and self-interest, and led by a man grown lazy by long corruption. It collapsed as soon as the opposition of all political classes from the democratic bourgeoisie to the communists united against him and the dictator's own agents, soldiers, policemen and torturers concluded that his time had run out. Fidel proved that it had run out, and, naturally enough, his forces inherited the government. A bad regime which few supported had been overthrown. The victory of the rebel army was genuinely felt by most Cubans as a moment of liberation and infinite promise, embodied in its young commander. Probably no leader in the Short Twentieth Century, an era full of charismatic figures on balconies and before microphones, idolized by the masses, had fewer sceptical or hostile listeners than this large, bearded, unpunctual man in crinkled battle-dress who spoke for hours at a time, sharing his rather unsystematic thoughts with the attentive and unquestioning multitudes (including the present writer). For once revolution was experienced as a collective honeymoon. Where would it lead? It had to be somewhere better.

Latin American rebels in the 1950s inevitably found themselves drawing not only on the rhetoric of their historic liberators, from Bolívar to Cuba's own José Martí, but on the anti-imperialist and social-revolutionary tradition of the post-1917 Left. They were both for 'agrarian reform', whatever that meant (see p. 354), and, at least implicitly, against the USA, especially in poor central America, so far from God, so near to the USA, in the phrase of the old Mexican strong-man Porfirio Díaz. Though radical, neither Fidel nor any of his comrades were communists nor (with two exceptions) even claimed to have Marxist sympathies of any kind. In fact, the Cuban Communist Party, the only such mass party in Latin America apart from the Chilean one, was notably unsympathetic until parts of it joined him rather late in his campaign. Relations beween them were distinctly frosty. The US diplomats and policy advisers constantly debated whether the movement was or was not pro-communist – if it were, the CIA, which had already overthrown a reforming government in Guatemala in 1954, knew what to do – but clearly concluded that it was not.

However, everything was moving the Fidelist movement in the direction of communism, from the general social-revolutionary ideology of those likely to undertake armed guerrilla insurrections to the passionate anti-communism of the USA in the decade of Senator McCarthy, which automatically inclined the anti-imperialist Latin rebels to look more kindly on Marx. The global Cold War did the rest. If the new regime antagonized the USA, which it was almost certain to do, if only by threatening American investments, it could rely on the almost guaranteed sympathy and support of the USA's great antagonist. Moreover,

Fidel's form of government by informal monologues before the millions, was not a way to run even a small country or a revolution for any length of time. Even populism needs organization. The Communist Party was the only body on the revolutionary side which could provide him with it. The two needed one another and converged. However, by March 1960, well before Fidel had discovered that Cuba was to be socialist and he himself was a communist, though very much in his own manner, the USA had decided to treat him as such, and the CIA was authorized to arrange for his overthrow (Thomas, 1971, p. 1271). In 1961 they tried by an invasion of exiles at the Bay of Pigs, and failed. A Communist Cuba survived seventy miles from Key West, isolated by the US blockade and increasingly dependent on the USSR.

No revolution could have been better designed to appeal to the Left of the western hemisphere and the developed countries, at the end of a decade of global conservatism; or to give the guerrilla strategy better publicity. The Cuban revolution had everything: romance, heroism in the mountains, ex-student leaders with the selfless generosity of their youth – the eldest were barely past thirty – a jubilant people, in a tropical tourist paradise pulsing with rumba rhythms. What is more, it could be hailed by all Left revolutionaries.

In fact, it was more likely to be hailed by the critics of Moscow, long dissatisfied with the Soviets' priority for peaceful coexistence between it and capitalism. Fidel's example inspired the militant intellectuals everywhere in Latin America, a continent of ready trigger-fingers and a taste for unselfish bravery, especially in heroic postures. After a while Cuba came to encourage continental insurrection, urged on by Guevara, the champion of pan-Latin American revolution and of the creation of 'two, three, many Vietnams'. A suitable ideology was provided by a brilliant young French Leftist (who else?) who systematized the idea that, in a continent ripe for revolution, all that was needed was the import of small groups of armed militants into suitable mountains to form 'focuses' (*focos*) for mass liberation struggle (Debray, 1965).

All over Latin America enthusiastic groups of young men launched themselves into uniformly doomed guerrilla struggles under the banner of Fidel, or Trotsky or Mao Tse-tung. Except in Central America and Colombia, where there was an old base for peasant support for armed irregulars, most such enterprises collapsed almost immediately, leaving behind the corpses of the famous – Che Guevara himself in Bolivia; the equally handsome and charismatic priest-rebel Father Camilo Torres in Colombia – and the unknown. It was a spectacularly misconceived strategy, all the more so because, given the right conditions, effective and lasting guerrilla movements in many of these countries *were* possible, as the (official communist) FARC (Armed Forces of the Colombian Revolution) proved in Colombia from 1964 to the time of this writing, and the (Maoist) Shining Path movement (*Sendero Luminoso*) proved in Peru in the 1980s.

However, even when peasants took to the guerrilla road, guerrillas were seldom – the Colombian FARC are a rare exception – a peasant movement. They were overwhelmingly carried into the Third World countryside by young intellectuals, initially drawn from their countries' established middle classes, later reinforced by the new generation of student sons and (more rarely) daughters of the rising rural petty-bourgeoisie. This was also true when the guerrilla tactic was transferred from the rural back country to the world of the big cities, as some parts of the revolutionary Third World Left (e.g. in Argentina, Brazil and Uruguay and in Europe) began to do from the late 1960s.* As it happens, urban guerrilla operations are much easier to mount than rural ones, since they need not rely on mass solidarity or connivance, but can exploit the anonymity of the big city plus the purchasing power of money and a minimum of, mostly middle-class, sympathisers. These 'urban-guerrilla' or 'terrorist' groups found it easier to produce dramatic publicity coups, and spectacular killings (as of Admiral Carrero Blanco, Franco's intended successor, by the Basque ETA in 1973; of the Italian premier Aldo Moro by the Italian Red Brigades in 1978), not to mention money-raising raids, than to revolutionize their countries.

For even in Latin America the major forces for political change were civilian politicians – and armies. The wave of Right-wing military regimes which began to flood large parts of South America in the 1960s – military government had never gone out of fashion in Central America, except for revolutionary Mexico and little Costa Rica, which actually abolished its army after a revolution in 1948 – were not primarily responding to armed rebels. In Argentina they overthrew the populist chieftain Juan Domingo Perón (1895–1974) whose force lay in the organization of labour and the mobilization of the poor (1955), after which they found themselves resuming power at intervals, since the Perónist mass movement proved indestructible and no stable civilian

---

* The major exception are the activists of what may be called 'ghetto' guerrilla movements, such as the Provisional IRA in Ulster, the short-lived US 'Black Panthers' and the Palestinian guerrillas, children of the diaspora of refugee camps, who may come largely or wholly from among the children of the street and not the seminar; especially where the ghettos contain no significant middle class.

alternative could be constructed. When Perón returned from exile in 1972, this time with much of the local Left hanging to his coat-tails, once again to demonstrate the predominance of his supporters, the military took over again with blood, torture and patriotic rhetoric, until dislodged after the defeat of their armed forces in the brief, pointless but decisive Anglo–Argentinian war of 1982.

The armed forces took over in Brazil in 1964 against a very similar enemy: the heirs of the great Brazilian populist leader Getulio Vargas (1883–1954), moving towards the political Left in the early 1960s and offering democratisation, land reform and scepticism about US policy. The small guerrilla attempts of the late 1960s, which provided an excuse for the ruthless repressions of the regime, never represented the slightest real challenge to it; but it must be said that after the early 1970s the regime began to relax and returned the country to civilian rule by 1985. In Chile the enemy was the united Left of socialists, communists and other progressives – what European (and for that matter Chilean) tradition knew as a 'popular front' (see chapter 5). Such a front had already won elections in Chile in the 1930s, when Washington was less nervous and Chile was a byword for civilian constitutionalism. Its leader, the socialist Salvador Allende, was elected President in 1970, his government was destabilised and, in 1973, overthrown by a military coup strongly backed, perhaps even organized, by the USA, which introduced Chile to the characteristic features of 1970s military regimes – executions or massacres, official and para-official, systematic torture of prisoners, and the mass exile of political opponents. The military chief General Pinochet remained in power for seventeen years, which he used to impose a policy of economic ultra-liberalism on Chile, thus demonstrating, among other things, that political liberalism and democracy are not natural partners of economic liberalism.

Possibly the military take-over in revolutionary Bolivia after 1964 had some connexion with American fears of Cuban influence in that country, where Che Guevara himself died in a half-baked attempt at guerrilla insurrection, but Bolivia is not a place readily controlled for any length of time by any local soldier, however brutal. The military era ended after fifteen years filled with a rapid succession of generals, increasingly eyeing the profits of the drug trade. Though in Uruguay the military took a particularly intelligent and effective 'urban guerrilla' movement as an excuse for the usual killings and tortures, it was the rise of a 'Broad Left' popular front, competing with the traditional two-party system, that probably explains the military takeover of 1972 in the only South American country which could be described as a genuine lasting democracy. The Uruguayans retained enough of their tradition eventually to vote down the handcuffed constitution offered them by their military rulers and in 1985 returned to civilian rule.

Though it had already achieved, and was likely to achieve more dramatic successes in Latin America, Asia and Africa, in the developed countries the guerrilla road to revolution made little sense. However, it is not surprising that, through its guerrillas, rural and urban, the Third World inspired the growing number of youthful rebels and revolutionaries, or merely the cultural dissidents of the First World. Rock music reporters compared the juvenile masses at the Woodstock music festival (1969) to 'an army of peaceful guerrillas' (Chapple and Garofalo, 1977, p. 144). Images of Che Guevara were carried like icons by student demonstrators in Paris and Tokyo, and his bearded, bereted and unquestionably manly features fluttered even non-political hearts in the counter-culture. No name (except that of the philosopher Marcuse) is mentioned more often than his in a well-informed survey of the global 'New Left' of 1968 (Katsiaficas, 1987), even if, in practice, the name of the Vietnamese leader Ho-Chi-Minh ('Ho Ho Ho-Chi-Minh') was chanted even more frequently in the demonstrations of the First World Left. For it was support for Third World guerrillas, and, in the USA after 1965, resistance against being sent to fight against them, which mobilized the Left more than anything else, except hostility to nuclear arms. *The Wretched of the Earth*, written by a Caribbean psychologist who had taken part in the Algerian war of liberation, became an enormously influential text among intellectual activists who were thrilled by its praise of violence as a form of spiritual liberation for the oppressed.

In short, the image of guerrillas with coloured skins amid tropical vegetation was an essential part, perhaps the chief inspiration, of the First World radicalisation of the 1960s. 'Third Worldism', the belief that the world would be emancipated by means of the liberation of its impoverished and agrarian 'periphery', exploited and pressed into 'dependency' by the 'core countries' of what a growing literature called 'the world system', captured much of the theorists of the First World Left. If, as the 'world system' theorists implied, the roots of the world's troubles lay not in the rise of modern industrial capitalism, but in the conquest of the Third World by European colonialists in the sixteenth century, then the reversal of this historical process in the twentieth century offered the powerless revolutionaries of the First World a way out of their impotence. No wonder that some of the most powerful arguments to this effect came from American Marxists, who could hardly count on a victory of socialism by forces indigenous to the USA.

III

Nobody in the flourishing countries of industrial capitalism took the classic prospect of social revolution by insurrection and mass action seriously any more. And yet, at the very peak of Western prosperity, at the very core of capitalist society, governments suddenly, unexpectedly and, at first sight, inexplicably found themselves facing something that not only looked like old-fashioned revolution, but also disclosed the weaknesses of apparently firm regimes. In 1968–69 a wave of rebellion swept across all three worlds, or large parts of them, carried essentially by the new social force of students, whose numbers were now counted by the hundreds of thousands in even medium-sized Western countries, and would soon be counted in millions (see chapter 10). Moreover, their numbers were reinforced by three political characteristics which multiplied their political effectiveness. They were easily mobilized in the enormous knowledge-factories which contained them, while leaving them much more free time than workers in giant plants. They were usually to be found in capital cities, under the eyes of politicians and the cameras of the media. And, being members of the educated classes, often children of the established middle class, and – almost everywhere but especially in the Third World – the recruiting ground for the ruling elite of their societies, they were not so easy to shoot down as the lower orders. In Europe, west and east, there were no serious casualties, not even in the vast riots and street-combats of Paris in May 1968. The authorities took care that there should be no martyrs. Where there was a major massacre, as in Mexico City in 1968 – the official count was twenty-eight dead and two hundred wounded when the army dispersed a public meeting (González Casanova, 1975, vol. II, p. 564) – the subsequent course of Mexican politics was permanently changed.

The student rebellions were thus disproportionately effective, especially where, as in France in 1968 and in the 'hot autumn' of Italy in 1969, they released huge waves of working-class strikes which temporarily paralysed the economy of entire countries. And yet, of course, they were not genuine revolutions nor likely to develop into such. For the workers, where they took part in them, they were merely the opportunity to discover the industrial bargaining-power they had accumulated without noticing over the past twenty years. They were not revolutionaries. The First World students were rarely interested in such trifling matters as overthrowing governments and seizing power, although in fact the French ones came quite close to bringing down General de Gaulle in May 1968 and certainly shortened his reign (he retired a year later), and the American student anti-war protest unseated President L.B. Johnson in the same year. (Third World students were closer to the realities of power: Second World students knew that they were necessarily remote from them.) The Western student rebellion was more of a cultural revolution, a rejection of everything in society represented by 'middle-class' parental values, and has been discussed as such in chapters 10 to 11.

Nevertheless, it helped to politicize a substantial number of the rebel student generation, who naturally turned towards the accepted inspirers of radical revolution and total social transformation – Marx, the non-Stalinist icons of the October revolution, and Mao. For the first time since the anti-fascist era, Marxism, no longer confined to Moscow orthodoxy, attracted large numbers of young Western intellectuals. (It had, of course, never ceased to attract them in the Third World.) It was a peculiar seminar-oriented Marxism, combined with a variety of other then current academic fashions, and sometimes with other ideologies, nationalist or religious, for it came out of the classroom, not the experience of working lives. Indeed, it had little relation to the practical political behaviour of these new disciples of Marx, which usually called for the kind of radical militancy that has no need for analysis. When the utopian expectations of the original rebellion had evaporated, many returned to, or rather turned to, the old parties of the Left, which (like the French Socialist Party, reconstructed at this period, or the Italian Communist Party) were revived partly by the infusion of young enthusiasm. Since the movement was largely one of intellectuals, many were recruited to the academic profession. In the USA, this consequently acquired an unprecedented contingent of politico-cultural radicals. Others saw themselves as revolutionaries in the October tradition and joined or recreated the small, disciplined, preferably clandestine 'vanguard' organizations of cadres along Leninist lines, either to infiltrate mass organizations or for terrorist purposes. Here the West converged with the Third World, which was also full of bodies of illegal fighters hoping to offset mass defeat by small-group violence. The various Italian 'Red Brigades' of the 1970s were probably the most important among the European groups of Bolshevik provenance. A curious clandestine world of conspiracy emerged in which direct-action groups of nationalist and social revolutionary ideology, sometimes both, were linked in an international network that consisted of various – generally tiny – 'Red Armies', Palestinian, Basque insurrectionaries, the IRA and the rest, overlapping with other illegal networks, infiltrated by intelligence services, protected and where necessary assisted by Arab or eastern states.

It was a milieu ideally suited to the writers of secret-service and terror thrillers, for whom the 1970s were a golden age. It was also the darkest era of torture and counter-terror in the history of the West. This was the blackest period so far recorded in the modern history of torture, of nominally unidentifiable 'death squadrons' or kidnapping and death gangs in unmarked cars who 'disappeared' people, but whom everyone knew to be part of army and police, of armed services, police and intelligence or security services that made themselves virtually independent of government, let alone of democratic control, of unspeakable 'dirty wars'.* This was observable even in a country of old and powerful traditions of law and constitutional procedure like Great Britain, when the early years of the conflict in Northern Ireland led to some serious abuses, which attracted the attention of Amnesty International's report on torture (1975). It was probably at its worst in Latin America. Though it was not much noticed, the socialist countries were barely affected by this sinister fashion. Their ages of terror were behind them, and they had no terrorist movements in their borders, only tiny groups of public dissidents who knew that, in their circumstances, the pen was mightier than the sword, or rather the typewriter (plus Western public protest) than the bomb.

The student revolt of the late 1960s was the last hurrah of the old world revolution. It was revolutionary in both the ancient utopian sense of seeking a permanent reversal of values, a new and perfect society, and in the operational sense of seeking to achieve it by action on streets and barricades, by bomb and mountain ambush. It was global, not only because the ideology of the revolutionary tradition, from 1789 to 1917, was universal and internationalist – even so exclusively nationalist a movement as the Basque separatist ETA, a typical product of the 1960s, claimed to be in some sense Marxian – but because, for the first time, the world, or at least the world in which student ideologists lived, was genuinely global. The same books appeared, almost simultaneously, in the student bookshops in Buenos Aires, Rome and Hamburg (in 1968 almost certainly including Herbert Marcuse). The same tourists of revolution crossed oceans and continents from Paris to Havana to São Paulo to Bolivia. The first generation of humanity to take rapid and cheap global air travel and telecommunications for granted, the students of the late

---

* The best estimate of the number of people 'disappeared' or murdered in the Argentinian 'dirty war' of 1976–82 is about ten thousand. (Las Cifras, 1988, p. 33.)

1960s, had no difficulty in recognizing what happened at the Sorbonne, in Berkeley, in Prague, as part of the same event in the same global village in which, according to the Canadian guru Marshall McLuhan (another fashionable name of the 1960s), we all lived.

And yet this was not the world revolution as the generation of 1917 had understood it, but the dream of something that no longer existed: often enough not much more than the pretence that behaving as though the barricades were up would somehow cause them to rise, by sympathetic magic. The intelligent conservative Raymond Aron even described the 'events of May 1968' in Paris, not quite inaccurately, as street theatre or psychodrama.

Nobody any longer expected social revolution in the Western world. Most revolutionaries no longer even regarded the industrial working class, Marx's 'gravedigger of capitalism', as fundamentally revolutionary, unless by loyalty to the orthodox doctrine. In the western hemisphere, whether among the theoretically committed ultra-Left of Latin America or among the untheoretical student rebels of North America, the old 'proletariat' was even dismissed as an enemy of radicalism, whether as a favoured labour aristocracy or as patriotic supporters of the Vietnam War. The future of revolution lay in the (now rapidly emptying) peasant hinterlands of the Third World, but the very fact that their inhabitants had to be shaken out of their passivity by armed apostles of revolt from far away, led by Castros and Guevaras, suggested a certain flagging in the old belief that historic inevitability guaranteed the 'damned of the earth', of whom the Internationale sang, would break their chains alone.

Moreover, even where revolution was a reality, or a probability, was it any longer genuinely worldwide? The movements in which the revolutionaries of the 1960s put their hopes were the opposite of ecumenical. The Vietnamese, the Palestinians, the various guerrilla movements for colonial liberation, were concerned purely with their own national affairs. They were linked to the wider world only insofar as they were led by communists who had such wider commitments, or insofar as the bipolar structure of the Cold War world system automatically made them the friends of their enemy's enemy. How inessential the old ecumenism had become, was demonstrated by Communist China, which, in spite of a rhetoric of global revolution, pursued a relentlessly self-centred national policy that was to take it, in the 1970s and 1980s, into a policy of alignment with the USA against Communist USSR and into actual armed conflict with both the USSR and Communist Vietnam. Revolution aiming beyond national borders survived only in the attenuated form of regional movements: pan-African, pan-Arabic and especially pan-Latin American. Such movements had a certain reality, at least for intellectual militants who spoke the same language (Spanish, Arabic) and moved freely from country to country, as exiles or planners of revolt. One could even claim that some of them – notably the Fidelista version – contained genuinely globalist elements. After all, Che Guevara himself fought for a while in the Congo, and Cuba was to send its troops to assist revolutionary regimes in the Horn of Africa and in Angola in the 1970s. And yet, outside the Latin American Left, how many really expected even an all-African or all-Arabic triumph of socialist emancipation? Did not the break-up of the short lived United Arab Republic of Egypt and Syria, with a loosly attached Yemen (1958–61), and the constant frictions between the equally pan-Arab and socialist Baath party regimes in Syria and Iraq demonstrate the fragility, even the political unreality, of supranational revolutions?

Indeed, the most dramatic proof of the fading of world revolution, was the disintegration of the international movement dedicated to it. After 1956 the USSR and the international movement under its leadership, lost their monopoly of the revolutionary appeal, and of the theory and ideology that unified it. There were now many different species of Marxists, several of Marxist-Leninists, and even two or three different brands among those few communist parties which, after 1956, maintained the picture of Joseph Stalin on their banners (the Chinese, the Albanians, the very different C.P. [Marxist] which split from the orthodox Indian Communist Party).

What remained of the Moscow-centred international communist movement disintegrated between 1956 and 1968, as China broke with the USSR in 1958–60 and called, with little success, for the secession of states from the Soviet bloc and the formation of rival communist parties, as (mainly Western) communist parties, headed by the Italians, began openly to distance themselves from Moscow, and as even the original 'socialist camp' of 1947 was now split into states with varying degrees of loyalty to the USSR, ranging from the totally committed Bulgarians* to the totally independent Yugoslavia. The Soviet invasion of Czechoslovakia, in 1968, for the purpose of replacing one form of communist policy by another, finally nailed down the coffin of 'proletarian internationalism'. Thereafter it became normal for even Moscow-aligned communist parties to criticise the USSR in public and to adopt policies at variance with those of Moscow ('Eurocommunism'). The end of the international

---

* It appears that Bulgaria actually asked for incorporation into the USSR as a Soviet Republic, but was refused on grounds of international diplomacy.

communist movement was also the end of any kind of socialist or social-revolutionary internationalism, for the dissident and anti-Muscovite forces developed no effective international organizations other than rival sectarian synods. The only body which still faintly recalled the tradition of ecumenical liberation was the old, or rather revived, Socialist International (1951), which now represented government and other parties, mostly Western, that had formally abandoned revolution, world-wide or not, and, in most cases, even the belief in the ideas of Marx.

IV

However, if the tradition of social revolution in the mode of October 1917 was exhausted – or even, as some argued, its parent tradition of revolution in the mode of the French Jacobins of 1793 – the social and political instability which generated revolutions remained. The volcano had not ceased to be active. As the Golden Age of world capitalism came to an end in the early 1970s, a new wave of revolution swept across large parts of the world, to be followed in the 1980s by the crisis of the Western communist systems, which led to their breakdown in 1989.

Though they occurred overwhelmingly in the Third World, the revolutions of the 1970s formed a geographically and politically ill-assorted ensemble. They began, surprisingly enough, in Europe with the overthrow in April 1974 of the Portuguese regime of the longest-lived Rightwing system of the Continent, and, shortly after, the collapse of a much briefer ultra-Right-wing military dictatorship in Greece (see p. 349). After General Franco's long-awaited death in 1975, the peaceful transition of Spain from authoritarianism to parliamentary government completed this return to constitutional democracy in southern Europe. These transformations could still be considered as the liquidation of unfinished business left over from the era of European fascism and the Second World War.

The coup of radical officers which revolutionised Portugal was engendered in the long and frustrating wars against African colonial liberation guerrillas, which the Portuguese army had been waging since the early 1960s, though without major troubles, except in the small colony of Guinea-Bissau, where perhaps the ablest of all African liberation leaders, Amilcar Cabral, had fought them to a standstill by the end of the 1960s. African guerrilla movements had multiplied in the 1960s, following the Congo conflict and the hardening of South African *apartheid* policy (the creation of the black 'homelands'; the Sharpeville massacre), but without significant success, and weakened by both inter-tribal and Soviet–Chinese rivalries. With increasing Soviet help – China was otherwise occupied with the bizarre cataclysm of Mao's 'Great Cultural Revolution' – they revived in the early 1970s, but it was the Portuguese revolution that enabled the colonies finally to win their independence in 1975. Mozambique and Angola were soon plunged into a far more murderous civil war again by the joint intervention of South Africa and the USA.

However, as the Portuguese Empire collapsed, a major revolution broke out in the oldest independent African country, the famine-stricken Ethiopia, where the Emperor was overthrown (1974) and eventually replaced by a Leftist military junta strongly aligned with the USSR, which therefore switched its support in this region from the military dictatorship of Siad Barre in Somalia (1969–91), also then advertising its enthusiasm for Marx and Lenin. Within Ethiopia the new regime was challenged, and was eventually to be overthrown in 1991 by equally Marxist-inclined regional liberation or secession movements.

These changes created a fashion for regimes dedicated, at least on paper, to the cause of socialism. Dahomey declared itself a People's Republic under the usual military leader and changed its name to Benin; the island of Madagascar (Malagasy) declared its commitment to socialism, also in 1975, after the usual military coup; Congo (not to be confused with its giant neighbour, the former Belgian Congo, now renamed Zaire under the sensationally rapacious pro-American militarist Mobutu) stressed its character as a People's Republic, also under the military; and in Southern Rhodesia (Zimbabwe) the eleven-year attempt to establish a white-ruled independent state came to an end in 1976 under growing pressure from two guerrilla movements, divided by tribal identity and political orientation (Russian and Chinese respectively). In 1980 Zimbabwe became independent under one of the guerrilla leaders.

While on paper these movements belonged to the old revolutionary family of 1917, in reality they clearly belonged to a different species, inevitably so given the differences between the societies for which Marx's and Lenin's analyses had been designed, and those of sub-Saharan post-colonial Africa. The only African country in which some of the conditions of such an analysis applied was the economically developed and industrialized settler capitalism of South Africa, where a genuine mass liberation movement crossing tribal and racial frontiers came into existence – the African National Congress – with the help of the organization of a genuine mass trade union movement and an effective Communist Party. After the end of the Cold War even the *apartheid* regime was forced into retreat by it. Still, even here the movement was disproportionately strong among certain African tribes, relatively much weaker among others (e.g.

the Zulus), a situation exploited by the *apartheid* regime to some effect. Everywhere else, except for the small and sometimes tiny cadre of the educated and Westernized urban intellectuals, 'national' or other mobilizations were essentially based on tribal loyalties or alliances, a situation which was to enable the imperialists to mobilize other tribes against the new regimes – as notably in Angola. The only relevance of Marxism-Leninism to these countries was a recipe for forming disciplined cadre parties and authoritarian governments.

The US withdrawal from Indochina reinforced the advance of communism. All of Vietnam was now under unchallenged communist government, and similar governments now took over in Laos and Cambodia, in the latter case under the leadership of the 'Red Khmer' party, a particularly murderous combination of the Paris café Maoism of their leader Pol Pot (1925–) and the armed backwoods peasantry bent on destroying the degenerate civilization of the cities. The new regime killed its citizens in numbers enormous even by the standards of our century – they cannot have eliminated much less than 20 per cent of the population – until it was driven from power by a Vietnamese invasion which restored a human government in 1978. After this – in one of the more depressing episodes of diplomacy – both China and the US bloc continued to support the remains of the Pol Pot regime on anti-Soviet and anti-Vietnamese grounds.

The late 1970s saw the wave of revolution send its sprays directly over the USA, as Central America and the Caribbean, Washington's unquestioned zone of domination, seemed to veer to the Left. Neither the Nicaraguan revolution of 1979, which overthrew the Somoza family, kingpins of US control in the small republics of the region, nor the growing guerrilla movement in El Salvador, nor even the troublesome General Torrijos, who sat by the Panama Canal, weakened US dominance seriously, any more than the Cuban revolution had done; still less the revolution on the tiny island of Grenada in 1983 against which President Reagan mobilized all his armed might. And yet the success of such movements contrasted strikingly with their failure in the 1960s, and caused an atmosphere little short of hysteria in Washington during the period of President Reagan (1980–88). Nevertheless, these were undoubtedly revolutionary phenomena, though of a familiar Latin American type; the major novelty, both puzzling and troubling to those of the old Left-wing tradition, which had been basically secular and anticlerical, was the appearance of Marxist-Catholic priests who supported or even participated in and led insurrections. The tendency, legitimized by a 'theology of liberation' backed by an episcopal conference in Colombia (1968), had emerged after the Cuban Revolution* and found powerful intellectual support in the most unexpected quarter, the Jesuits, and less unexpected opposition in the Vatican.

While the historian sees how far from the October revolution even those revolutions of the 1970s were, which claimed an affinity to it, the governments of the USA inevitably regarded them essentially as part of a global offensive by the communist superpower. This was partly due to the supposed rule of the zero-sum game of the Cold War. The loss of one player must be the gain of the other, and, since the USA had aligned itself with the conservative forces in most of the Third World, and more than ever in the 1970s, it found itself on the losing side of revolutions. Moreover, Washington thought it had some cause for nervousness about the progress of the Soviet nuclear armament. In any case, the Golden Age of world capitalism, and the centrality of the dollar in it, was at an end. The position of the US as a superpower was inevitably weakened by the universally predicted defeat in Vietnam, from which the greatest military power on earth was forced finally to withdraw in 1975. Since Goliath had been felled by the slingshot of David, there had not been such a debacle. Is it too much to suppose, especially in the light of the Gulf War against Iraq in 1991, that a more confident USA would, in 1973, have taken the coup of OPEC so unresistingly? What was OPEC other than a group of mostly Arab states of no political significance apart from their oil wells and not yet armed to the teeth thanks to the high oil prices they could now extort?

The USA inevitably saw any weakening in its global supremacy as a challenge to it, and as a sign of Soviet thirst for world domination. The revolutions of the 1970s therefore led to what has been called 'the Second Cold War' (Halliday, 1983), which was, as usual, fought by proxy between the two sides, mainly in Africa and later in Afghanistan, where the Soviet army itself became involved outside its frontiers for the first time since the Second World War. Yet we cannot dismiss the assertion that the USSR itself felt that the new revolutions allowed it to shift the global balance slightly in its favour – or, more precisely, to offset at least part of the major diplomatic loss it suffered in the 1970s by the setbacks in China and Egypt, whose alignments Washington managed to shift. The USSR kept out of the Americas, but it intervened elsewhere, especially in Africa, to a far greater extent than before, and with some

---

* The present writer recalls hearing Fidel Castro himself, in one of his great public monologues in Havana, expressing his astonishment at this development, as he urged his listeners to welcome these surprising new allies.

success. The mere fact that the USSR allowed or encouraged Fidel Castro's Cuba to send troops to help Ethiopia against the new US client-state Somalia (1977), and Angola against the US-backed rebel movement UNITA and the South African army, speaks for itself. Soviet statements now spoke of 'socialist-oriented states' in addition to fully communist ones. Angola, Mozambique, Ethiopia, Nicaragua, South Yemen and Afghanistan attended the funeral of Brezhnev in 1982 under this heading. The USSR had neither made these revolutions nor controlled them, but it visibly welcomed them as allies with some alacrity.

Nevertheless, the next succession of regimes to collapse or be overthrown demonstrated that neither Soviet ambition nor the 'communist world conspiracy' could be made responsible for these upheavals, if only because, from 1980 on, it was the Soviet system itself that began to be destabilized, and, at the end of the decade, it disintegrated. The fall of 'really existing socialism' and the question how far it can be treated as revolutions will be discussed in another chapter. However, even the major revolution which preceded the eastern crises, though a greater blow to the USA than any of the other changes of regime in the 1970s, had nothing to do with the Cold War.

This was the overthrow of the Shah of Iran in 1979, the greatest by far of the revolutions of the 1970s, and which will enter history as one of the major social revolutions of the twentieth century. It was the response to the programme of lightning modernization and industrialization (not to mention armament) undertaken by the Shah on the basis of the solid support of the USA and the country's oil-wealth, its value multiplied after 1973 by the OPEC price revolution. No doubt, apart from other signs of the megalomania usual among absolute rulers with a formidable and dreaded secret police, he hoped to become the dominant power in western Asia. Modernization meant agrarian reform as the Shah saw it, which turned large numbers of share-croppers and tenants into large numbers of sub-economic smallholders or unemployed labourers who migrated to the cities. Teheran grew from 1.8 millions (1960) to six millions. The capital-intensive high-tech agribusinesses favoured by the government made more labour surplus, but did not help the per capita production of agriculture, which declined in the 1960s and 1970s. By the late 1970s Iran was importing most of its food from abroad.

Increasingly, therefore, the Shah relied on industrialisation financed by oil, and, unable to compete in the world, promoted and protected at home. The combination of a declining agriculture, an inefficient industry, massive foreign imports – not least of arms – and the oil boom produced inflation. It is possible that the standard of living of most Iranians not directly involved in the modern sector of the economy, and or the growing and flourishing urban business classes, actually dipped in the years before the revolution.

The energetic cultural modernization of the Shah also turned against him. His (and the Empress's) genuine support for an improvement in the position of women was unlikely to be popular in a Muslim country, as the Afghan communists also were to discover. And his equally genuine enthusiasm for education increased mass literacy (but about half the population remained illiterate) and produced a large body of revolutionary students and intellectuals. Industrialization strengthened the strategic position of the working-class, especially in the oil industry.

Since the Shah had been put back on the throne in 1953 by a CIA-organized coup against a large popular movement, he did not have much accumulated capital of loyalty and legitimacy to draw on. His very dynasty, the Pahlavis, could look back only to a coup by its founder, Reza Shah, a soldier in the Cossack Brigade, who took the imperial title in 1925. Still, in the 1960s and 1970s the old communist and National opposition was kept down by the secret police, regional and ethnic movements were repressed, as were the usual Leftist guerrilla groups, whether orthodox Marxist or Islamic-Marxist. These could not provide the spark for the explosion, which – a return to the ancient tradition of revolution from Paris in 1789 to Petrograd in 1917 – was essentially a movement of the urban masses. The countryside remained quiet.

The spark came from the peculiar speciality of the Iranian scene, the organized and politically active Islamic clergy which occupied a public position that had no real parallel elsewhere in the Muslim world, or even within its Shiite sector. They, with the bazaar merchants and artisans, had in the past formed the activist element in Iranian politics. They now mobilized the new urban plebs, a vast body with more than adequate reasons for opposition.

Their leader, Ayatollah Ruholla Khomeini, aged, eminent and vindictive, had been in exile since the middle 1960s when he had led demonstrations against a proposed referendum on land reform and police repression of clerical activities in the holy city of Qum. Thence he denounced the monarchy as un-Islamic. From the early 1970s he began to preach a total Islamic form of government, the duty of the clergy to rebel against despotic authorities and, in effect, to take power: in short, an Islamic revolution. This was a radical innovation, even for politically activist Shiite clergymen. These sentiments were communicated to the masses by means of the post-Koranic device of tape-cassettes, and the masses listened. The young religious students in the holy city acted in 1978 by demonstrating against an alleged assassination by the secret police, and were shot down. Further demonstrations mourning the martyrs were organized, and these were to be repeated every forty days. They grew, until by the end of the year millions went on the street to demonstrate against the regime. The guerrillas went into action again. The oil workers shut down the oil fields in a crucially effective strike, the bazaaris their shops. The country was at a standstill and the army failed or refused to suppress the uprising. On 16 January 1979 the Shah went into exile and the Iranian revolution had won.

The novelty of this revolution was ideological. Virtually all the phenomena commonly recognized as revolutionary up to that date had followed the tradition, ideology and, in general, the vocabulary of Western revolution since 1789; more precisely: of some brand of the secular Left, mainly socialist or communist. The traditional Left was indeed present and active in Iran, and its part in the overthrow of the Shah, e.g. by means of the workers' strikes, was far from insignificant. Yet it was almost immediately eliminated by the new regime. The Iranian revolution was the first made and won under the banner of religious fundamentalism and which replaced the old regime by a populist theocracy whose professed programme was a return to the seventh century AD, or rather, since we are in an Islamic milieu, the situation after the *hijra* when the Holy Koran was written down. For revolutionaries of the old kind this was as bizarre a development as if Pope Pius IX had taken the lead in the Roman revolution of 1848.

This does not mean that henceforth religious movements were to fuel revolutions, even though from the 1970s on in the Islamic world they undoubtedly became a mass political force among the middle classes and intellectuals of their countries' swelling populations, and took an insurrectionary turn under the influence of the Iranian revolution. Islamic fundamentalists revolted and were savagely put down in Ba'athist Syria, stormed the holiest of shrines in pious Saudi Arabia, and assassinated the President of Egypt (under the leadership of an electrical engineer), all in 1979–82.* No single doctrine of revolution replaced the old revolutionary tradition of 1789/1917, nor any single dominant project for changing the world, as distinct from overthrowing it.

It does not even mean that the old tradition disappeared from the

---

* Other apparently religious movements of violent politics which gained ground in this period lack, and indeed deliberately exclude the universalist appeal, and are best seen as subvarieties of ethnic mobilization, e.g. the militant Buddhism of the Sinhalese in Sri Lanka, and the Hinduist and Sikh extremisms in India.

political scene, or lost all force to overthrow regimes, though the fall of Soviet communism virtually eliminated it as such over a large part of the world. The old ideologies retained substantial influence in Latin America, where the most formidable insurrectionary movement of the 1980s, the Peruvian *Sendero Luminoso*, or Shining Path, flaunted its Maoism. They were alive in Africa and India. Moreover, to the surprise of those brought up on Cold War commonplaces, the 'vanguard' ruling parties of the Soviet type survived the fall of the USSR, especially in backward countries and in the Third World. They won bona fide elections in the southern Balkans, and demonstrated in Cuba and Nicaragua, in Angola, even, after the withdrawal of the Soviet army, in Kabul, that they were more than simple clients of Moscow. Still, even here the old tradition was eroded, and often virtually destroyed from within, as in Serbia, where the Communist Party transformed itself into a party of Greater Serb chauvinism, or in the Palestinian movement, where a leadership of the secular Left was increasingly undermined by the rise of Islamic fundamentalism.

V

The revolutions of the late twentieth century thus had two characteristics: the atrophy of the established tradition of revolution was one; the revival of the masses was another. As we have seen (see chapter 2), few revolutions since 1917–18 had been made at the grass roots. Most had been made by the activist minorities of the committed and organized, or imposed from above, as by army coups or military conquest; which does not mean that they had not, in suitable circumstances, been genuinely popular. Except where they came with foreign conquerors, they could rarely have established themselves otherwise. Yet in the late twentieth century the 'masses' returned to the scene in major rather than supporting roles. Minority activism, in the form of rural or urban guerrillas and terrorism, continued, and indeed became endemic in the developed world, and in significant parts of South Asia and the Islamic zone. International terrorist incidents, as counted by the US State Department, rose almost continuously from 125 in 1968 to 831 in 1987, the number of their victims rose from 241 to 2,905 (UN World Social Situation, 1989, p. 165).

The list of political assassinations grew longer – Presidents Anwar Sadat of Egypt (1981); Indira Gandhi (1984) and Rajiv Gandhi of India (1991), to name but some. The activities of the Provisional Irish Republican Army in the United Kingdom and of the Basque ETA in Spain are characteristic of this type of small-group violence, which had the advantage that it could be conducted by a few hundred, or even a few dozen activists, with the help of the extremely powerful, cheap and portable explosives and armaments that a flourishing international arms traffic now scattered wholesale over the globe. They were a symptom of the growing barbarisation of all three worlds, and added to the pollution by generalized violence and insecurity of the atmosphere which urban humanity at the end of the millennium learned to breathe. However, its contribution to political revolution was small.

Not so, as the Iranian revolution showed, the readiness of people in their millions to come out on the streets. Or, as in East Germany ten years later, the decision of citizens of the German Democratic Republic – unorganized, spontaneous, though decisively facilitated by the decision of Hungary to open its frontiers – to vote against their regime with their feet and cars by migrating to West Germany. Within two months about 130,000 had done so (Umbruch, 1990, pp. 7–10), before the Berlin Wall fell. Or, as in Romania, where television for the first time caught the moment of revolution, in the sagging face of the dictator as the crowd convoked by the regime on the public square began to boo rather than to cheer. Or in the occupied parts of Palestine, when the mass non-cooperation movement of the *intifada*, which began in 1987, demonstrated that henceforth only active repression, not passivity or even tacit acceptance, sustained Israeli occupation. Whatever stimulated hitherto inert populations into action – modern communications like TV and tape-recorders made it hard to insulate even the most secluded from the world's affairs – it was the readiness of the masses to come out that decided matters.

These mass actions did not and could not overthrow regimes by themselves. They might even have been stopped short by coercion and guns, as the mass mobilization for democracy in China was, in 1989, by the massacre of Tiananmen Square in Beijing. (Still, vast though it was, this student and urban movement represented only a modest minority in China and, even so, it was large enough to cause the regime serious hesitation.) What such mobilization of the masses achieved was to demonstrate a regime's loss of legitimacy. In Iran, as in Petrograd 1917, the loss of legitimacy was demonstrated in the most classical fashion by the refusal of army and police to obey orders. In Eastern Europe it convinced old regimes already demoralized by the refusal of Soviet help that their time had run out. It was a textbook demonstration of Lenin's maxim that voting with citizens' feet could be more effective than voting in elections. Of course the mere clump of the massed citizens' feet alone could not make revolutions. They were not armies, but crowds, or statistical aggregates of individuals. They required leaders, political structures or strategies to be effective. What mobilized them in Iran was a campaign of political protest by adversaries of the regime; but what turned that campaign into a revolution was the readiness of the millions to join it. Just so earlier massive examples of such direct mass intervention responded to a political call from above – whether from the Indian National Congress to abstain from cooperation with the British in the 1920s and 1930s (see chapter 7) or from the supporters of President Perón to demand the release of their arrested hero on the famous 'Day of Loyalty' in the Plaza de Mayo of Buenos Aires (1945). Moreover, what counted was not sheer numbers, but numbers acting in a situation which made them operationally effective.

We do not yet understand why voting with massed feet became so much more significant a part of politics in the last decades of the century. One reason must be that in this period the gap between rulers and ruled widened almost everywhere, though in states which provided political mechanisms for discovering what their citizens thought, and ways for them to express political preferences from time to time, this was unlikely to produce revolution or complete loss of contact. Demonstrations of almost unanimous non-confidence were most likely to occur in regimes which had either lost or (like Israel in the occupied territories) never had legitimacy, especially when they concealed this from themselves.* Still, massive demonstrations of rejection for existing political or party systems became common enough even in established and stable parliamentary-democratic systems, as witness the Italian political crisis of 1992–93, and the rise of new and large electoral forces in several countries, whose common denominator was simply that they were *not* identified with any of the old parties.

However, there is another reason for the revival of the masses: the urbanization of the globe, and especially the Third World. In the classic era of revolution, from 1789 to 1917, old regimes were overthrown in the great cities, but new ones were made permanent by the inarticulate plebiscites of the countryside. The novelty of the post-1930s phase of revolutions was that they were made in the countryside and, once victorious, imported into the cities. In the late twentieth century, a few retrograde regions apart, revolution once more came from the city, even in the Third World. It had to, both because a majority of the inhabitants

---

* Four months before the collapse of the German Democratic Republic local elections in that state had given the ruling party a vote of 98.85 per cent.

of any large state now lived there, or seemed likely to, and because the big city, seat of power, could survive and defend itself against rural challenge, thanks not least to modern technology, so long as its authorities did not lose the loyalty of their populations. The war in Afghanistan (1979–88) demonstrated that a city-based regime could maintain itself in classic guerrilla country, bristling with rural insurrectionaries, supported, financed and equipped with modern high-technology weaponry, even after the withdrawal of the foreign army on which it had relied. The government of President Najibullah, to everyone's surprise, survived some years after the Soviet army left; and when it fell, it was not because Kabul could no longer resist the rural armies, but because a section of its own professional warriors decided to change sides. After the Gulf War of 1991, Saddam Hussein maintained himself in Iraq, against major insurrections in the north and south of his country, and in a state of military weakness, essentially because he did not lose Baghdad. Revolutions in the late twentieth century have to be urban if they are to win.

Will they continue to occur? Will the four great twentieth-century waves of 1917–20, 1944–62, 1974–78 and 1989– be followed by further bouts of breakdown and overthrow? No one who looks back on a century in which no more than a handful of states existing at present have come into being or survived without passing through revolution, armed counter-revolution, military coups or armed civil conflict* would bet much money on the universal triumph of peaceful and constitutional change, as predicted in 1989 by some euphoric believers in liberal democracy. The world which enters the third millennium is not a world of stable states or stable societies.

However, if it is virtually certain that the world, or at least a great part of it, will be full of violent changes, the nature of these changes is obscure. The world at the end of the Short Twentieth Century is in a state of social breakdown rather than revolutionary crisis, though it naturally contains countries in which like Iran in the 1970s, the conditions are present for the overthrow of hated regimes that have lost legitimacy, by popular upsurge under the leadership of forces capable of replacing them: for instance, at the time of writing, Algeria and, before the

* Omitting the mini-states of less than half-a-million inhabitants, the only consistently 'constitutional' states are the USA, Australia, Canada, New Zealand, Ireland, Sweden, Switzerland and Great Britain (excluding Northern Ireland). States occupied during and after the Second World War have not been classified as enjoying unbroken constitutionality, but, at a pinch, a few ex-colonies or backwaters which never knew military coups or domestic armed challenge could also be regarded as 'non-revolutionary' – e.g. Guyana, Bhutan and the United Arab Emirates.

abdication of the apartheid regime, South Africa. (It does not follow that revolutionary conditions potential or actual, will produce successful revolutions.) Nevertheless, this sort of focused discontent with the status quo is today less common than an unfocused rejection of the present, an absence or distrust of political organization, or simply a process of disintegration to which the domestic and international politics of states adjust, as best they can.

It is also full of violence – more violence than in the past – and, what is perhaps equally relevant, full of arms. In the years before Hitler came to power in Germany and Austria, acute though racial tensions and hatreds were, it is difficult to imagine that they would have taken the form of neo-Nazi teenage skinheads burning down a house inhabited by immigrants, killing six members of a Turkish family. Yet in 1993 such an incident shocks but no longer surprises when it occurs in the heart of tranquil Germany, incidentally in a city (Solingen) with one of the oldest traditions of working-class socialism in the country.

Moreover, the accessibility of highly destructive weaponry and explosives today is such that the usual state monopoly of armaments in developed societies can no longer be taken for granted. In the anarchy of poverty and greed which replaced the former Soviet bloc, it was no longer even inconceivable that nuclear arms, or the means of making them, could get into the hands of bodies other than governments.

The world of the third millennium will therefore almost certainly continue to be one of violent politics and violent political changes. The only thing uncertain about them is where they will lead.

CHAPTER SIXTEEN
End of Socialism

[The] health [of revolutionary Russia], however, is subject to one indispensable condition: that never (as one day happened even to the Church) should a black market of power be opened. Should the European correlation of power and money penetrate Russian too, then perhaps not the country, perhaps not even the Party, but Communism in Russia would be lost.

– Walter Benjamin, (1979, pp. 195–6)

It is not true any more that a single official creed is the only operative guide to action. More than one ideology, a mixture of modes of thinking and frames of references, coexist and not only in society at large but also inside the Party and inside the leadership ... A rigid and codified 'Marxism-Leninism' could not, except in official rhetoric, respond to the regime's real needs.

– M. Lewin in Kerblay, (1983, p. xxvi)

The key to achieving modernization is the development of science and technology ... Empty talk will get our modernization programme nowhere; we must have knowledge and trained personnel ... Now it appears that China is fully twenty years behind the developed countries in science, technology and education ... As early as the Meiji restoration the Japanese began to expend a great deal of effort on science, technology and education. The Meiji Restoration was a kind of modernization drive undertaken by the emerging Japanese bourgeoisie. As proletarians we should, and can, do better.

– Deng Xiaoping, 'Respect Knowledge, Respect Trained Personnel', 1977

I

One socialist country in the 1970s was particularly worried by its relative economic backwardness, if only because its neighbour, Japan, was the most spectacularly successful of the capitalist states. Chinese communism cannot be regarded simply as a subvariety of Soviet communism, still less as part of the Soviet satellite system. For one thing, it triumphed in a country with a far larger population than the USSR, or for that matter any other state. Even allowing for the uncertainties of Chinese demography, something like one out of every five human beings was a Chinese living on mainland China. (There was also a substantial Chinese diaspora in East and South-east Asia.) Moreover, China was not only nationally far more homogeneous than most other countries – about 94 per cent of its population were Han Chinese – but had formed a single, though intermittently disrupted, political unit probably for a minimum of two thousand years. Even more to the point, for most of these two millennia the Chinese Empire, and probably most of its inhabitants who had a view on these matters, had considered China to be the centre and model of world civilization. With minor exceptions *all* other countries in which communist regimes triumphed, from the USSR on, were and saw themselves as culturally backward and marginal, relative to some more advanced and paradigmatic centre of civilization. The very stridency with which the USSR insisted, in the Stalin years, on its lack of intellectual and technological dependence on the West, and on the indigenous source of all the leading inventions from telephones to aircraft, was a telling symptom of this sense of inferiority.*

Not so China, which, quite correctly, saw its classical civilization, art, script and social value-system as the acknowledged inspiration and model for others – not least for Japan itself. It certainly had no sense whatever of any intellectual and cultural inferiority, either collectively or of individual Chinese compared to any other people. The very fact that China had no neighbouring states which could even faintly threaten her, and, thanks to adopting fire-arms, no longer had any difficulty in fending off the barbarians on its frontier, confirmed sense of

---

* The intellectual and scientific achievements of Russia between c. 1830 and 1930 were indeed extraordinary, and included some striking technological innovations, which backwardness rarely allowed to be economically developed. Yet the brilliance and world significance of a few Russians only makes the broad inferiority of Russia to the West more obvious.

superiority, even as it made the empire unprepared for Western imperial expansion. The technological inferiority of China which became only too evident in the nineteenth century, because it was translated into military inferiority, was not due to technical or educational incapacity, but to the very sense of self-sufficiency and self-confidence of traditional Chinese civilization. This made it reluctant to do what the Japanese did after the Meiji Restoration of 1868: plunge into 'modernization' by adopting European models wholesale. This could and would be done only on the ruins of the ancient Chinese Empire, guardian of the old civilization, and through social revolution, which was at the same time a cultural revolution against the Confucian system.

Chinese communism, therefore, was both social and, if the word does not beg questions, national. The social explosive which fuelled communist revolution was the extraordinary poverty and oppression of the Chinese people, initially of the labouring masses in the great coastal cities of central and south China which formed enclaves of foreign imperialist control and sometimes modern industry – Shanghai, Canton, Hong Kong – later of the peasantry which formed 90 per cent of the country's vast population. Its condition was far worse than even the Chinese urban population, whose consumption, per capita, was something like two-and-a-half times higher. The sheer poverty of China is hard for Western readers to imagine. Thus at the time of the communist take-over (1952 data) the average Chinese lived essentially on half a kilogram of rice or grains a day, and consumed rather less than 0.08 kilos of tea *a year*. He or she acquired a new pair of footwear once every five years or so (China Statistics, 1989, Tables 3.1, 15.2, 15.5).

The national element in Chinese communism operated both through the intellectuals of upper- and middle-class origin who provided most of the leadership of all twentieth-century Chinese political movements, and through the feeling, undoubtedly widespread among the Chinese masses, that the barbarian foreigners meant no good to such Chinese individuals as they had dealings with, and to China as a whole. Since China had been attacked, defeated, partitioned and exploited by every foreign state within reach since the middle of the nineteenth century, this assumption was not implausible. Mass anti-imperialist movements with a traditional ideology were already familiar before the end of the Chinese Empire, for instance the so-called Boxer Rising of 1900. There is little doubt that resistance to the Japanese conquest of China is what turned the Chinese communists from a defeated force of social agitators, which they were in the middle 1930s, into the leaders and representatives of the entire Chinese people. That they also called for the social liberation of the Chinese poor made their appeal for national liberation and regeneration sound more convincing to the (mainly rural) masses.

In this they had the advantage over their rivals, the (older) Kuomintang Party, which had attempted to rebuild a single, powerful, Chinese republic out of the scattered warlord-led fragments of the Chinese Empire after its fall in 1911. The short-term objectives of the two parties did not seem incompatible, the political base of both was in the more advanced cities of South China (where the Republic established its capital) and their leadership consisted of very much the same sort of educated elite, allowing for a certain bias towards businessmen in one, peasants and workers in the other. Both, for instance, contained virtually the same percentage of men drawn from the traditional landlords and scholar-gentry, the elites of imperial China, although the communists tended to have more leaders with a higher education of the Western type (North/Pool, 1966, pp. 378–82). Both movements came out of the anti-imperial movement of the 1900s, reinforced by the 'May movement', the national upsurge among students and teachers in Peking after 1919. Sun Yat-sen, the Kuomintang leader, was a patriot, democrat and socialist, who relied for advice and support on Soviet Russia – the only revolutionary and anti-imperialist power – and found the Bolshevik model of the single state-party more suited than Western models for his task. In fact, the communists became a major force largely through this Soviet tie-up, which allowed them to be integrated into the official national movement, and, after Sun's death in 1925, to share in the great northern advance by which the Republic extended its influence into the half of China it did not control. Sun's successor, Chiang Kai-shek (1887–1975), never managed to establish complete control over the country, even though in 1927 he broke with the Russians and suppressed the communists, whose main body of mass support at that time was among the small urban working class.

The communists, forced to turn their main attention to the countryside, now waged a peasant-based guerrilla war against the Kuomintang, on the whole – thanks, not least, to their own divisions and confusions and the remoteness of Moscow from Chinese realities – with little success. In 1934 their armies were forced to retreat to a remote corner of the far north-west in the heroic 'Long March'. These developments made Mao Tse-tung, who had long favoured the rural strategy, into the undisputed leader of the Communist Party in its exile in Yenan, but did not offer any immediate prospects of communist advance. On the contrary, the Kuomintang steadily extended their control over most of the country until the Japanese invasion of 1937.

Yet the Kuomintang's lack of a genuine mass appeal to the Chinese, as well as its abandonment of the revolutionary project, which was at the same time a project of modernization and regeneration, made them no match for their communist rivals. Chiang Kai-shek never became an Ataturk – another head of a modernizing, anti-imperialist, national revolution who found himself making friends with the young Soviet Republic, using the local communists for his own purposes and turning away from them, though less stridently than Chiang. Like Ataturk, he had an army: but it was not an army with national loyalty, let alone the revolutionary morale of the communist armies, but a force recruited from among men for whom, in times of trouble and social collapse, a uniform and a gun are the best way to get by, and officered by men who knew – as did Mao Tse-tung himself – that at such times 'power grew from the barrel of a gun', and so did profit and wealth. He had a good deal of urban middle-class support, and perhaps even more support from the wealthy overseas Chinese: but 90 per cent of Chinese, and almost all the country's territory, were outside the cities. They were controlled, if at all, by local notables and men of power, from warlords with their armed men to gentry families and relics of the imperial power-structure, with whom the Kuomintang came to terms. When the Japanese set out to conquer China seriously, the Kuomintang armies could not prevent them from almost immediately overrunning the coastal cities, where its genuine strength lay. In the rest of China, they became what they had always potentially been, another corrupt landlord-warlord regime, resisting the Japanese ineffectively, if at all. Meanwhile the communists effectively mobilized mass resistance to the Japanese in the occupied areas. When they took over China in 1949, having almost contemptuously swept aside the Kuomintang forces in a brief civil war, they were, for all except the fleeing remnants of the Kuomintang power, the legitimate government of China, true successors to the imperial dynasties after a forty-years interregnum. And they were all the more readily accepted as such because, from their experience as a Marxist–Leninist party, they were able to forge a nation-wide disciplined organization capable of bringing government policy from the centre to the remotest villages of the giant country – as, in the mind of most Chinese, a proper empire should do. *Organisation*, rather than doctrine, was the chief contribution of Lenin's Bolshevism to changing the world.

Yet, of course, they were more than the empire revived, even though they undoubtedly benefited from the enormous continuities of Chinese history, which established both how ordinary Chinese expected to relate to any government enjoying the 'mandate of heaven', and how those who administered China expected to think about their tasks. There is no other country in which political debates within a communist system would have been conducted by reference to what a loyal mandarin said to the Ming Emperor Chia-ching in the sixteenth century.* That is what a hard-nosed old China-watcher – the London *Times* correspondent – meant in the 1950s by the claim, shocking to those who heard it at the time, like the present writer, that there would be no communism left in the twenty-first century, except in China, where it would survive as the national ideology. For most Chinese this was a revolution which was primarily a restoration: of order and peace; of welfare; of a system of government whose civil servants found themselves appealing to precedents from the T'ang dynasty; of the greatness of a great empire and civilization.

And, for the first few years, that is what most Chinese seemed to be getting. Peasants raised their output of food-grains by more than 70 per cent between 1949 and 1956 (China Statistics, 1989, p. 165), presumably because they were not yet interfered with too much, and while China's intervention in the Korean War of 1950–52 created a serious panic, the ability of the Chinese communist army first to defeat, then to hold at bay the mighty USA could hardly fail to impress. Planning for industrial and educational development began in the early 1950s. Yet very soon the new People's Republic, under the now unchallenged and unchallengeable Mao, began to enter two decades of largely arbitrary catastrophes provoked by the great helmsman. From 1956 the rapidly deteriorating relations with the USSR, which ended in the clamorous breach between the two communist powers in 1960, led to the withdrawal of the important technical and other material aid from Moscow. However, this complicated rather than caused the calvary of the Chinese people, which was marked by three main stations of the cross: the ultra-rapid collectivisation of peasant farming in 1955–57; the 'Great Leap Forward' of industry in 1958, followed by the great famine of 1959–61, probably the greatest famine of the twentieth century,† and the ten years of 'Cultural Revolution' which ended with Mao's death in 1976.

* Cf. the article 'Hai Tui reprimands the Emperor' in the *People's Daily* in 1959. The same author (Wu Han) composed a libretto for a classical Peking opera, *The Dismissal of Hai Tui*, in 1960, which, some years later, provided the occasion that sparked off the 'Cultural Revolution' (Leys, 1977, pp. 30, 34).

† According to official Chinese statistics, the country's population in 1959 was 672.07 millions. At the natural growth rate of the preceding seven years, which was

These cataclysmic plunges were, it is generally agreed, due largely to Mao himself, whose policies were often received with reluctance in the party leadership, and sometimes – most notably in the case of the 'Great Leap Forward' – with frank opposition, which he overcame only by launching the 'Cultural Revolution'. Yet they cannot be understood without a sense of the peculiarities of Chinese communism, of which Mao made himself the spokesman. Unlike Russian communism, Chinese communism had virtually no direct relations with Marx and Marxism. It was a post-October movement which came to Marx *via* Lenin, or more precisely Stalin's 'Marxism–Leninism'. Mao's own knowledge of Marxist theory seems to have been almost entirely derived from the Stalinist *History of the CPSU [b]: Short Course* of 1939. And yet below the Marxist-Leninist top-dressing, there was – and this is very evident in the case of Mao, who never travelled outside China until he became head of state, and whose intellectual formation was entirely home-grown – a very Chinese utopianism. This naturally had points of contact with Marxism: all social-revolutionary utopias have something in common, and Mao, no doubt in complete sincerity, seized on those aspects of Marx and Lenin which fitted into his vision and used them to justify it. Yet his view of an ideal society united by a total consensus, and in which, it has been said, 'the individual's total self-abnegation and total immersion in the collectivity (are) ultimate goods ... a kind of collectivist mysticism', is the opposite of classical Marxism which, at least in theory and as the ultimate object, envisaged the complete liberation and self-fulfilment of the individual (Schwartz, 1966). The characteristic emphasis on the power of spiritual transformation to bring this about by remoulding man, though it seizes on Lenin's, and later Stalin's belief in consciousness and voluntarism, went far beyond it. With all his belief in the role of political action and decision, Lenin never lost sight of the fact – how could he have done? – that practical circumstances imposed severe constraints on the effectiveness of action, and even Stalin recognized that his power had limits. Yet without the belief that 'subjective forces' were all-powerful, that men *could* move mountains and storm heaven if they wanted to, the lunacies of the Great Leap Forward are inconceivable. Experts told you what could and could not be done, but revolutionary fervour alone could

---

at least 20 per thousand per year (actually a mean of 21.7 per 000), one would have expected the Chinese population in 1961 to have been 699 millions. In fact, it was 658.59 millions or *forty millions* less than might have been expected (China Statistics, 1989, Tables T 3.1 and T 3.2).

overcome all material obstacles, and mind transform matter. Hence to be
'Red' was not so much more important than to be expert, but its
alternative. A unanimous surge of enthusiasm in 1958 would industrialize
China *immediately*, leaping across the ages into the future when communism would *immediately* come into full operation. The countless little
low-quality backyard furnaces by which China was to double its steel
output within one year – and did actually more than treble it by 1960,
before it fell back by 1962 to less than it had been before the Great Leap –
represented one side of the transformation. The 24,000 'peoples communes'
of farmers, set up in a mere two months of 1958, represented the other side.
They were completely communist, not only in that all aspects of peasant life
were collectivized, including family life – communal nurseries and messhalls
freeing women from household and child care, and sending them, regi-
mented, into the fields – but the free supply of six basic services were to
replace wages and money income. These six services were food, medical
care, education, funerals, haircuts and movies. Patently, this did not
work. Within months, faced with passive resistance, the extremer aspects
of the system were abandoned, though not before it had (like Stalin's
collectivisation) combined with nature to produce the famine of 1960–61.

   In one way this belief in the capacity of willed transformation rested
on a more specific Maoist belief in 'the people', ready to be transformed
and hence to take part, creatively and with all the traditional Chinese
intelligence and ingenuity, in the great march forward. It was the
essentially romantic view of an artist, though, one gathers from those who
can judge the poetry and calligraphy he liked to practice, not a very good
one. ('Not as bad as Hitler's painting, but not as good as Churchill's', in
the view of the British orientalist Arthur Waley, using painting as an
analogy for poetry.) It led him, against the sceptical, and realistic advice
of other communist leaders, to call on the intellectuals of the old elite to
contribute their gifts freely in the 'Hundred Flowers' campaign of 1956–
57, on the assumption that the revolution, and perhaps he himself, had
already transformed them. ('Let a hundred flowers bloom, let a hundred
schools of thought contend'.) When, as less inspirational comrades had
foreseen, this outburst of free thought proved lacking in unanimous
enthusiasm for the new order, Mao's native distrust of intellectuals as
such was confirmed. It was to find spectacular expression in the ten years
of the Great Cultural Revolution, when higher education virtually came
to a complete stop, and such intellectuals as already existed were massively
regenerated by compulsory physical labour in the countryside.* Neverthe-

---

* In 1970 the total number of students in all China's 'Institutions of Higher

less, Mao's belief in the peasants, who were urged to solve all the problems of production during the Great Leap on the principle of 'letting all schools [i.e. of local experience] contend' remained unaffected. For – and this was yet another aspect of Mao's thought which found support in what he read into the Marxist dialectic – Mao was fundamentally convinced of the importance of struggle, conflict and high tension as something that was not only essential to life but prevented the relapse into the weaknesses of the old Chinese society, whose very insistence on unchanging permanence and harmony had been its weakness. The revolution, communism itself, could only be saved from degeneration into stasis by a constantly renewed struggle. Revolution could never end.

The peculiarity of the Maoist policy was that it was 'at once an extreme form of Westernisation and a partial reversion to traditional patterns', on which, indeed, it largely relied, for the old Chinese Empire was characterised, at least in the periods when the emperor's power was strong and secure, and therefore legitimate, by the autocracy of the ruler and the acquiescence and obedience of the subjects (Hu, 1966, p. 241). The mere fact that 84 per cent of Chinese peasant households had allowed themselves to be quietly collectivised within a single year (1956), apparently without any of the consequences of Soviet collectivisation, speaks for itself. Industrialization, on the heavy-industry-inflected Soviet model, was the unconditional priority. The murderous absurdities of the Great Leap were due primarily to the conviction, which the Chinese regime shared with the Soviet, that agriculture must both supply industrialization and maintain itself without the diversion of resources from industrial to farming investment. Essentially this meant substituting 'moral' for 'material' incentives, which meant, in practice, the almost unlimited amount of human muscle-power available in China for the technology that was not available. At the same time the countryside remained the foundation of Mao's system, as it had ever since the guerrilla epoch, and, unlike the USSR, the Great Leap model made it the preferred locus of industrialization also. Unlike the USSR, China experienced no mass urbanization under Mao. Not until the 1980s did the rural population fall below 80 per cent.

Learning' was 48,000; in the country's technical schools (1969) 23,000; and in its Teachers' Training Colleges (1969) 15,000. The absence of any data about postgraduates suggests that there was no provision for them at all. In 1970 a grand total of 4,260 young persons began to study the natural sciences at Institutions of Higher Learning, and a grand total of ninety began to study the social sciences. This in a country of, at the time, 830 million people (China Statistics, Tables T17.4, T17.8, T17.10).

However much we may be shocked by the record of the twenty Maoist years, a record combining mass inhumanity and obscurantism with the surrealist absurdities of the claims made on behalf of the divine leader's thoughts, we should not allow ourselves to forget that, by the standards of the poverty-stricken Third World, the Chinese people were doing well. At the end of the Mao period the average Chinese food consumption (in calories) ranked just above the median of all countries, above fourteen countries in the Americas, thirty-eight in Africa, and just about in the middle of the Asian ones – well above all South and South-east Asia, except Malaysia and Singapore (Taylor/Jodice, 1983, Table 4.4). The average expectation of life at birth rose from thirty-five years in 1949 to sixty-eight in 1982, mainly owing to a dramatic and – except for the famine years – continuous fall in the mortality rate (Liu, 1986, p. 323–24). Since the Chinese population, even allowing for the great famine, grew from *c.* 540 to *c.* 950 millions between 1949 and Mao's death, it is evident that the economy managed to feed them – a little above the level of the early 1950s – and it slightly improved their supply of clothing (China Statistics, Table T15.1). Education, even at the elementary level, suffered both from the famine, which cut attendance down by twenty-five millions and from the Cultural Revolution, which reduced it by fifteen millions. Nevertheless, there is no denying that in the year of Mao's death six times as many children went to primary school as when he came to power – i.e. a 96 per cent enrolment rate, compared to less than 50 per cent even in 1952. Admittedly, even in 1987 more than a quarter of the population over the age of twelve remained illiterate and 'semi-illiterate' – among women this figure was as high as 38 per cent – but we should not forget that literacy in Chinese is unusually difficult, and only a fairly small proportion of the 34 per cent born before 1949 could have been expected to have acquired it fully (China Statistics, pp. 69, 70–72, 695). In short, while the achievement of the Maoist period might not impress sceptical Western observers – there were many who lacked scepticism – it would certainly have appeared impressive to say, Indian or Indonesian ones, and it might not have looked particularly disappointing to the 80 per cent of rural Chinese, isolated from the world, whose expectations were those of their fathers.

Nevertheless, it was undeniable that internationally China had lost ground since the revolution, and notably in relation to its non-communist neighbours. Its rate of economic growth per capita, though impressive in the Mao years (1960–75), was less than that of Japan, Hong Kong, Singapore, South Korea and Taiwan – to name the East Asian countries which Chinese observers would certainly keep an eye on. Vast though it was, its total GNP was just about the same size as Canada's, less than Italy's, and a mere quarter of Japan's (Taylor/Jordice, Tables 3.5, 3.6). The disastrous zigzag course steered by the Great Helmsman since the middle 1950s had continued only because Mao, in 1965, with military backing, launched an anarchic, initially student, movement of young 'Red Guards' against the party leadership which had quietly sidelined him, and intellectuals of any kind. This was the Great Cultural Revolution which devastated China for some time, until Mao called in the army to restore order, and in any case found himself obliged to restore some kind of party control. Since he was plainly on his last legs, and Maoism without him had very little real support, it did not survive his death in 1976, and the almost immediate arrest of the 'Gang of Four' ultra-Maoists, headed by the leader's widow, Jiang Quing. The new course, under the pragmatical Deng Xiaoping, began immediately.

II

Deng's new course in China was the frankest public recognition that dramatic changes in the structure of 'really existing socialism' were needed, but as the 1970s turned into the 1980s it was increasingly evident that something was seriously wrong with all socialist systems that claimed to have come into being. The slowing-down of the Soviet economy was palpable: the rate of growth of almost everything that counted, and could be counted in it, fell steadily from one five-year period to the next after 1970: gross domestic product, industrial output, farming output, capital investment, productivity of labour, real income per head. If not actually regressing, the economy was advancing at the pace of an increasingly tired ox. Moreover, so far from becoming one of the industrial giants of world trade, the USSR appeared to be internationally regressing. In 1960 its major exports had been machinery, equipment, means of transport, and metals or metal articles, but in 1985 it relied for its exports primarily (53 per cent) on energy (i.e. oil and gas). Conversely, almost 60 per cent of its imports consisted of machinery, metals etc. and industrial consumer articles (SSSR, 1987, pp. 15–17, 32–33). It had become something like an energy-producing colony of more advanced industrial economies – i.e. in practice largely its own Western satellites, notably Czechoslovakia and the German Democratic Republic, whose industries could rely on the unlimited and undemanding market of the USSR without doing much to improve their own deficiencies.*

* 'It seemed to the economic policy-makers at that time that the Soviet market was

In fact, by the 1970s it was clear that not only economic growth was lagging, but even the basic social indicators such as mortality were ceasing to improve. This undermined confidence in socialism perhaps more than anything else, since its ability to improve the lives of ordinary people through greater social justice did not depend primarily on its ability to generate greater wealth. That the average expectation of life at birth in the USSR, Poland and Hungary remained virtually unchanged during the last twenty years before the collapse of communism – indeed from time to time it actually dipped – was cause for serious worry, for in most other countries it continued to rise (including, it ought to be said, in Cuba and the Asian communist countries about which we have data). In 1969 Austrians, Finns and Poles could expect to die at the same average age (70.1 years), but in 1989 Poles had a life expectancy about four years shorter than Austrians and Finns. This may have made people healthier, as demographers suggested, but only because in socialist countries people died who might have been kept alive in capitalist ones (Riley, 1991). Reformers in the USSR and elsewhere did not fail to observe these trends with growing anxiety (World Bank Atlas, 1990, pp. 6–9 and World Tables, 1991, passim).

About this time another symptom of recognized decline in the USSR is reflected in the rise of the term *nomenklatura* (it appears to have reached the West via dissident writings). Until then the officer-corps of party *cadres*, which constituted the command system of the Leninist states, had been regarded abroad with respect and a reluctant admiration, although defeated oppositionists at home, like the Trotskyites and – in Yugoslavia – Milovan Djilas (Djilas, 1957), had pointed out its potential for bureaucratic degeneration and personal corruption. Indeed, in the 1950s, even into the 1960s, the general tone of Western, and especially US comment had been that here – in the organizational system of the communist parties and its body of monolithic, selfless cadres, loyally (if brutally) carrying out 'the line' – was the secret of communism's global advance (Fainsod, 1956; Brzezinski, 1962; Duverger, 1972).

On the other hand, the term *nomenklatura*, practically unknown before 1980, except as part of CPSU administrative jargon, came to suggest precisely the weaknesses of the self-serving party bureaucracy of the Brezhnev era: a combination of incompetence and corruption. And,

---

inexhaustible and that the Soviet Union could secure the necessary quantity of energy and raw materials for a continuous extensive economic growth' (D. Rosati and K. Mizsei, 1989, p. 10).

indeed, it became increasingly evident that the USSR itself operated primarily through a system of patronage, nepotism and payment.

With the exception of Hungary, serious attempts to reform the socialist economies in Europe had been, in effect, abandoned in despair after the Prague spring. As for the occasional attempts to revert to the old command economies, in a Stalinist form (as in Ceauşescu's Romania), or in the Maoist form which substituted voluntarism and putative moral zeal for economics (as with Fidel Castro), the less said about them the better. The Brezhnev years were to be called the 'era of stagnation' by the reformers, essentially because the regime had stopped trying to do anything serious about a visibly declining economy. Buying wheat on the world market was easier than trying to cure the apparently growing inability of Soviet agriculture to feed the people of the USSR. Lubricating the rusty engine of the economy by means of a universal and omnipresent system of bribery and corruption was easier than to clean and re-tune, let alone to replace it. Who knew what would happen in the long run? In the short run it seemed more important to keep the consumers happy, or, at any rate to keep their discontent within limits. Hence probably in the first half of the 1970s most inhabitants of the USSR were and felt better off than at any other time within living memory.

The trouble for 'really existing socialism' in Europe was that, unlike the inter-war USSR, which was virtually outside the world economy and therefore immune to the Great Slump, now socialism was increasingly involved in it, and therefore not immune to the shocks of the 1970s. It is an irony of history that the 'real socialist' economies of Europe and the USSR, as well as parts of the Third World, became the real victims of the post-Golden Age crisis of the global capitalist economy, whereas the 'developed market economies', though shaken, made their way through the difficult years without major trouble, at least until the early 1990s. Until then some, indeed, like Germany and Japan, barely faltered in their forward march. 'Real socialism', however, now confronted not only its own increasingly insoluble systemic problems, but also those of a changing and problematic world economy into which it was increasingly integrated. This may be illustrated by the ambiguous example of the international oil crisis which transformed the world energy market after 1973: ambiguous because its effects were potentially both negative and positive. Under pressure from the global oil-producers' cartel, OPEC (the Organization of Petrol-Exporting Countries), the oil price, low and, in real terms actually falling since the war, more or less quadrupled in 1973 and more or less trebled again at the end of the 1970s, in the aftermath of the Iranian Revolution. Indeed, the actual range of fluctuations was even more dramatic: in 1970 oil was selling at an average price of $2.53 a barrel, but in late 1980 a barrel was worth about $41.

The oil crisis had two apparently fortunate consequences. For oil producers, of whom the USSR happened to be one of the most important, it turned black liquid into gold. It was like a guaranteed weekly winning ticket to the lottery. The millions simply rolled in without effort, postponing the need for economic reform and, incidentally, enabling the USSR to pay for its rapidly growing imports from the capitalist West with exported energy. Between 1970 and 1980 Soviet exports to the 'developed market economies' rose from just under 19 per cent of total exports to 32 per cent (SSSR, 1987, p. 32). It has been suggested that it was this enormous and unforeseen bonanza that tempted Brezhnev's regime into a more active international policy of competing with the USA in the middle 1970s, as revolutionary unrest once again swept the Third World (see chapter 15), and into the suicidal course of trying to match American arms superiority (Maksimenko, 1991).

The other apparently fortunate consequence of the oil crises was the flood of dollars which now spurted from multi-billionaire OPEC states, often with tiny populations, and which was distributed by the international banking system in the form of loans to anyone who wanted to borrow. Few developing countries resisted the temptation to take the millions thus shovelled into their pockets, and which were to provoke the world debt crisis of the early 1980s. For the socialist countries which succumbed to it – notably Poland and Hungary – loans seemed a providential way of simultaneously paying for investment in accelerating growth and raising their people's standard of living.

This only made the crisis of the 1980s more acute, for the socialist economies – and notably the free-spending Polish one – were too inflexible to utilize the influx of resources productively. The mere fact that oil consumption in Western Europe (1973–85) fell by 40 per cent in response to the rise in prices, but in the USSR and Eastern Europe by only little more than 20 per cent in the same period, speaks for itself (Köllö, 1990, p. 39). That Soviet production costs increased sharply, while the Romanian oil fields dried up, makes the failure to economize energy even more striking. By the early 1980s Eastern Europe was in an acute energy crisis. This in turn produced shortages of food and manufactured goods (except where, as in Hungary, the country plunged even more heavily into debt, accelerating inflation and lowering real wages). This was the situation in which 'really existing socialism' in Europe entered what proved to be its final decade. The only immediate effective way of dealing with such a crisis was the traditional Stalinist recourse to strict central orders and restrictions, at least where central planning was still operational (as it no longer quite was in Hungary and Poland). It worked, between 1981 and 1984. Debt fell by 35–70 per cent (except in these two countries). This even encouraged illusory hopes of a return to dynamic economic growth without basic reforms, which 'brought about a Great Leap Back to the debt crisis and further deterioration of economic perspectives' (Köllö, p. 41). This was the moment when Mikhail Sergeyevitch Gorbachev became the leader of the USSR.

III

At this point we must revert from the economics to the politics of 'really existing socialism', since politics, both high and low, were to bring about the Euro–Soviet collapse of 1989–1991.

Politically, Eastern Europe was the Achilles heel of the Soviet system, and Poland (plus, to a lesser extent, Hungary) its most vulnerable spot. After the Prague Spring it was clear, as we have seen, that the satellite communist regimes had lost all legitimacy as such in most of the region.* They were maintained in being by state coercion, backed by the threat of Soviet intervention, or, at best – as in Hungary – by giving the citizenry material conditions and relative freedom far superior to the East-European average, but which the economic crisis made it impossible to maintain. However, with one exception, no serious form of organized political or other public opposition was possible. In Poland the conjunction of three factors produced this possibility. The country's public opinion was overwhelmingly united not only by a dislike of the regime but by an anti-Russian (and anti-Jewish) and consciously Roman Catholic, Polish nationalism; the Church retained independent nationwide organization; and its working class had demonstrated its political power by massive strikes at intervals since the middle 1950s. The regime had long resigned itself to tacit toleration or even retreat – as when the strikes of 1970 forced the abdication of the then communist leader – so long as opposition was unorganized, though its room for manoeuvre shrank dangerously. But from the middle of the 1970s it had to face both a politically organized labour movement backed by a brains trust of politically sophisticated

---

* The less developed parts of the Balkan peninsula – Albania, southern Yugoslavia, Bulgaria – may be an exception, since communists still won the first multi-party elections after 1989. However, even here the weakness of the system soon became patent.

dissident intellectuals, mainly ex-Marxists, and also by an increasingly aggressive Church, encouraged in 1978 by the election of the first Polish pope in history, Karol Wojtyla (John Paul II).

In 1980 the triumph of the trade union movement Solidarity as, in effect, a national public opposition movement armed with the weapon of the mass strike, demonstrated two things: that the Communist Party regime in Poland was at the end of its tether; but also that it could not be overthrown by mass agitation. In 1981 Church and State quietly agreed to pre-empt the danger of armed Soviet intervention (which was seriously considered), by a few years of martial law under the commander of the armed forces, which could plausibly claim both communist and national legitimacy. Order was re-established with little trouble by the police rather than by the army, but in effect the government, as helpless as ever to cope with the economic problems, had nothing to set against an opposition which remained in being as the organized expression of the nation's public opinion. Either the Russians decided to intervene, or, sooner rather than later, the regime had to abandon the key position of communist regimes, the one-party system under the 'leading role' of the state party, i.e. to abdicate. But, as the rest of the satellite governments nervously watched the unfolding of this scenario while mostly and vainly trying to stop their people from also doing so, it became increasingly evident that the Soviets were no longer prepared to intervene.

In 1985 a passionate reformer, Mikhail Gorbachev, came to power as General Secretary of the Soviet Communist Party. This was no accident. Indeed, but for the death of the desperately ill General Secretary and former chief of the Security apparatus, Yuri Andropov (1914–84) who had actually made the decisive break with the Brezhnev era in 1983, the era of change would have begun a year or two earlier. It was entirely evident to all other communist governments, in and out of the Soviet orbit, that major transformations were at hand, though quite unclear, even to the new General Secretary, what they would bring.

The 'era of stagnation' (*zastoi*) which Gorbachev denounced had, in fact, been an era of acute political and cultural ferment among the Soviet elite. This included not only the relatively tiny group of self-co-opted Communist Party chieftains at the top of the Union hierarchy, the only place where real political decisions were, or could be, made, but the relatively vast group of educated and technically trained middle classes as well as the economic managers who actually kept the country going: academics, technical intelligentsia, experts and executives of various kinds. In some ways Gorbachev himself represented this new educated cadre generation – he studied law, whereas the classical way up for the old Stalinist cadre had been (and still surprisingly often remained) from the factory floor via an engineering or agronomical degree into the apparatus. The depth of this ferment is not to be measured by the size of the actual group of public dissidents which now appeared – a few hundreds at most. Banned or semi-legalized (through the influence of brave editors like that of the famous 'thick journal' *Novy Mir*), criticism and self-criticism pervaded the cultural milieu of the metropolitan USSR under Brezhnev, including important sectors of party and state, notably in the security and foreign services. The enormous and sudden response to Gorbachev's call for *glasnost* ('openness' or 'transparency') can hardly be explained otherwise.

Yet the response of the political and intellectual strata must not be taken as the response of the mass of Soviet peoples. For these, unlike the peoples of most European communist states, the Soviet regime was legitimate and entirely accepted, if only because they knew no other and could have known no other (except under German occupation in 1941–44, which was hardly attractive). Every Hungarian over the age of sixty in 1990 had some adolescent or adult memory of the pre-communist era, but no inhabitant of the original USSR under the age of eighty-eight could have had such first-hand experience. And if the government of the Soviet state had an unbroken continuity stretching back to the end of the Civil War, the country itself had an unbroken, or virtually unbroken, continuity stretching back even longer, except for the territories along the western border acquired or re-acquired in 1939–40. It was the old Tsarist Empire under new management. That, incidentally, is why before the late 1980s there was no sign of serious political separatism anywhere except in the Baltic countries (which had been independent states from 1918 to 1940), in the western Ukraine (which had been part of the Habsburg and not the Russian Empire before 1918), and perhaps in Bessarabia (Moldavia), which had been part of Rumania from 1918 to 1940. Even in the Baltic States there was little more open dissidence than in Russia (Lieven, 1993).

Moreover, the Soviet regime was not merely home-grown and domestically rooted – as time went on even the party, originally much stronger among Great Russians than other nationalities, recruited much the same percentage of inhabitants in the European and Transcaucasian republics – but the people itself, in ways difficult to specify, fitted themselves into it, as the regime adjusted to them. As the dissident satirist Zinoviev pointed out, there really was a 'new Soviet man', even if he corresponded to his (or, insofar as she was considered, which was hardly at all, her) official public image no more than anything else did in the USSR. He/she was at ease in the system (Zinoviev, 1979). It provided a guaranteed livelihood and comprehensive social security at a modest but real level, a socially and economically egalitarian society and at least one of the traditional aspirations of socialism, Paul Lafargue's 'Right to Idleness' (Lafargue, 1883). Moreover, for most Soviet citizens the Brezhnev era spelled not 'stagnation' but the best times they and their parents, or even grandparents, had ever known.

Small wonder that radical reformers found themselves up against Soviet humanity as well as Soviet bureaucracy. In the characteristic tone of irritated anti-plebeian elitism, one reformer wrote:

> Our system has generated a category of individuals supported by society, and more interested in taking than in giving. This is the consequence of a policy of so-called egalitarianism which has . . . totally invaded Soviet society . . . That society is divided into two parts, those who decide and distribute and those who are commanded and who receive, constitutes one of the major brakes on the development of our society. *Homo sovieticus* . . . is both ballast and brake. On the one hand, he is opposed to reform, on the other he constitutes the base of support for the existing system (Afanassiev, 1991, pp. 13–14).

Socially and politically, most of the USSR was a stable society, no doubt partly by virtue of ignorance of other countries maintained by authority and censorship, but by no means only for this reason. Is it an accident that there had been no equivalent of the 1968 student rebellion in the USSR, unlike Poland, Czechoslovakia and Hungary? That even under Gorbachev the reform movement did not mobilize the young to any great extent (outside some western nationalist regions)? That it was, as the saying went, 'a rebellion of the thirty- and forty-year-olds', i.e. of the generation born after the end of the war but before the not uncomfortable torpor of the Brezhnev years? Wherever the pressure to change came from in the USSR, it was not from the grass-roots.

In fact it came, as it had to come, from the top. Precisely how an obviously passionate and sincere communist reformer came to be Stalin's successor at the head of the Soviet CP on 15 March 1985 still remains unclear, and will remain so until Soviet history in the last decades becomes a subject for history rather than accusation and self-exculpation. In any case, what matters are not the ins and outs of politics in the Kremlin, but the two conditions which allowed someone like Gorbachev to come to power. First, the growing, and increasingly unconcealed, corruption of the Communist Party leadership in the Brezhnev era could not but outrage that section of the party which still believed in its ideology, in however oblique a fashion. And a Communist Party, however degenerate, without some leaders who are socialists is no more likely than a Catholic Church without some bishops and cardinals who are Christians, both being based on genuine systems of belief. Second, the educated and technically competent strata which actually kept the Soviet economy running were keenly aware that without drastic, indeed fundamental change it would inevitably founder sooner or later, not only because of the built-in inefficiency and inflexibility of the system, but because its weaknesses were compounded by the demands of a status as a military superpower, which a declining economy simply could not support. The military strain on the economy had actually increased dangerously since 1980 when, for the first time in many years, the Soviet armed forces found themselves involved directly in a war. They sent a force into Afghanistan to establish some sort of stability in that country, which since 1978 had been governed by a local communist People's Democratic Party, split into conflicting factions, both of which antagonized local landlords, Moslem clergy and other believers in the status quo by such godless activities as land reform and rights for women. The country had been quietly in the Soviet sphere of influence since the early 1950s, without raising Western blood-pressure noticeably. However, the USA chose or purported to regard the Soviet move as a major military offensive directed against the 'free world'. It therefore (via Pakistan) poured money and advanced armaments without limits into the hands of fundamentalist Moslem mountain warriors. As was to be expected, the Afghan government with heavy Soviet support, had little trouble in holding the major cities of the country, but the cost to the USSR was inordinately high. Afghanistan became – as some people in Washington undoubtedly intended it to be – the Soviet Union's Vietnam.

But what could the new Soviet leader do to change the situation in the USSR, other than to end, as soon as possible, the Second Cold War confrontation with the USA which was haemorrhaging the economy? This, of course, was Gorbachev's immediate objective, and his greatest success, for, within a surprisingly short period, he convinced even sceptical Western governments that this was indeed the Soviet intention. It won him a huge and lasting popularity in the West, which contrasted strikingly with the growing lack of enthusiasm for him in the USSR, to which he eventually fell victim in 1991. If any single man ended some forty years of global cold war it was he.

The aims of communist economic reformers since the 1950s had been to make the centrally planned command economies more rational and flexible by the introduction of market pricing and calculations of profit and loss in enterprises. The Hungarian reformers had gone some way in this direction, and, but for the Soviet occupation of 1968, the Czech reformers would have gone even further: both hoping that this would also make it easier to liberalize and democratize the political system. This was also Gorbachev's position* which he naturally saw as a way of restoring or establishing a better socialism than the 'really existing' one. It is possible, but very unlikely that any influential reformer in the USSR envisaged the abandonment of socialism, if only because this seemed quite impracticable politically, although elsewhere trained economists who had been associated with reform began to conclude that the system, whose defects were first systematically analysed in public from within in the 1980s, could not be reformed from within.†

IV

Gorbachev launched his campaign to transform Soviet socialism with the two slogans of *perestroika*, or restructuring (of both economy and political structure), and *glasnost*, or freedom of information.‡

There was what turned out to be an insoluble conflict between them. The only thing that made the Soviet system work, and could conceivably transform it, was the command structure of party/state inherited from the Stalinist days. This was a familiar situation in Russian history even in the days of the Tsars. Reform came from the top. But the party/state structure was at the same time the chief obstacle to transforming a system which it had created, to which it had adjusted, in which it had a large vested interest, and to which it found it hard to conceive an alternative.§

---

* He had publicly identified himself with the extremely 'broad' and virtually social-democratic position of the Italian Communist Party even before his official election (Montagni, 1989, p. 85).

† The crucial texts here are by the Hungarian Janos Kornai, notably *The Economics of Shortage* (Amsterdam, 1980).

‡ It is an interesting sign of the interpenetration of official reformers and dissident thinking in the Brezhnev years, that *glasnost* was what the writer Alexander Solzhenitsyn had called for in his open letter to the Congress of the Union of Soviet Writers in 1967, before his expulsion from the USSR.

§ As a Chinese communist bureaucrat told the writer in 1984 in the midst of a similar 'restructuring': 'We are reintroducing elements of capitalism into our system, but how can we know what we are letting ourselves in for? Since 1949 nobody in China, except perhaps some old men in Shanghai, has had any experience of what capitalism is.'

It was far from the only obstacle, and reformers, not only in Russia, have always been tempted to blame 'the bureaucracy' for the failure of their country and people to respond to their initiatives, but it is undeniable that large parts of the party/state apparatus greeted any major reform with inertia concealing hostility. *Glasnost* was intended to mobilize support within and outside the apparatus against such resistance. But its logical consequence was to undermine the only force which could act. As has been suggested above, the structure of the Soviet system and its *modus operandi* were essentially military. Democratizing armies does not improve their efficiency. On the other hand, if a military system is not wanted, care must be taken that a civilian alternative is available before it is destroyed, otherwise reform produces not reconstruction but collapse. The USSR under Gorbachev fell into this widening chasm between *glasnost* and *perestroika*.

What made the situation worse was that in the minds of the reformers, *glasnost* was a far more specific programme than *perestroika*. It meant the introduction, or re-introduction, of a constitutional and democratic state based on the rule of law and the enjoyment of civil liberties as commonly understood. This implied the separation of party and state, and (contrary to all development since the rise of Stalin) the shift of the locus of effective government from party to state. This in turn implied the end of the single-party system, and of the party's 'leading role'. It also, obviously, meant the revival of the Soviets at all levels, in the form of genuinely elected representative assemblies, culminating in a Supreme Soviet which would be a genuinely sovereign legislative assembly, granting power to, but capable of controlling a strong executive. That, at least, was the theory.

In fact, the new constitutional system was eventually installed. The new economic system of *perestroika* was barely sketched out in 1987–88 by the half-hearted legalization of petty private enterprise ('cooperatives') – i.e. of much of the 'second economy' – and by the decision in principle to allow permanently loss-making state enterprises to go bankrupt. In fact, the gap between the rhetoric of economic reform and the reality of an economy visibly running down widened day by day.

This was desperately dangerous. For constitutional reform merely dismantled one set of political mechanisms and replaced it with another. It left open the question of what the new institutions would do, though the processes of decision would presumably be more cumbersome in a democracy than in a military command system. For most people the difference would merely be that, in one case, they had a genuine electoral choice every so often and had the choice in between of listening to opposition politicians criticising the government. On the other hand, the criterion of *perestroika* was and had to be not how the economy was run in principle but how it performed every day, in ways that could easily be specified and measured. It could only be judged by results. For most Soviet citizens this meant by what happened to their real incomes, to the effort needed to earn them, to the quantity and range of the goods and services within their reach, and the ease with which they could acquire them. But while it was very clear what the economic reformers were against and wished to abolish, their positive alternative, a 'socialist market economy' of autonomous and economically viable enterprises, public, private and cooperative, macro-economically steered by 'the centre of economic decision-making', was little more than a phrase. It simply meant that the reformers wished to have the advantages of capitalism without losing those of socialism. Nobody had the slightest idea of how, in practice, the transition from a centralized state command economy to the new system was to be made and – equally to the point – how what would inevitably remain a dual state and non-state economy for the foreseeable future would actually work. The appeal of the ultra-radical Thatcherite or Reaganite free-market ideology to young intellectual reformers was that it promised to provide a drastic but also an *automatic* solution for these problems. (As might have been foreseen, it did not.)

Probably the nearest thing to a model of transition for the Gorbachev reformers was the vague historical memory of the New Economic Policy of 1921–28. This had, after all, 'yielded spectacular results in revitalizing agriculture, trade, industry, finances, for several years after 1921' and had restored a collapsed economy to health because it 'relied on market forces' (Vernikov, 1989, p. 13). Moreover, a very similar policy of market liberalization and decentralization had, since the end of Maoism, produced dramatic results in China, whose rate of GNP growth in the 1980s, surpassed only by South Korea, averaged almost 10 per cent per annum (World Bank Atlas, 1990). Yet there was no comparison between the desperately poor, technologically backward and overwhelmingly rural Russia of the 1920s and the highly urbanized and industrialized USSR of the 1980s, whose most advanced industrial sector, the military-industrial-scientific complex (including the space programme), in any case depended on a market consisting of a single customer. It is safe to say that *perestroika* would have worked rather better if Russia in 1980 had still been (like China at that date) a country of 80 per cent villagers, whose idea of wealth beyond the dreams of avarice would be a television set. (Even in the early 1970s some 70 per cent of the Soviet population watched television for an average of one-and-a-half hours a day) (Kerblay, pp. 140–41).

Nevertheless, the contrast between Soviet and Chinese *perestroika* is not entirely explained by such time-lags, nor even by the obvious fact that the Chinese were careful to keep their central command system intact. How far they benefited from the cultural traditions of the Far East, which turned out to favour economic growth irrespective of social systems, must be left for twenty-first-century historians to investigate.

Did anyone in 1985 seriously suppose that, six years later, the USSR and its Communist Party, would have ceased to exist, and indeed that all other communist regimes in Europe would have disappeared? To judge by the complete lack of preparation of Western governments for the sudden collapse of 1989–91, the predictions of the imminent demise of the West's ideological enemy were no more than the small change of public rhetoric. What drove the Soviet Union with accelerating speed towards the precipice, was the combination of *glasnost* that amounted to the disintegration of authority, with a *perestroika* that amounted to the destruction of the old mechanisms that made the economy work, without providing any alternative; and consequently the increasingly dramatic collapse of the citizens' standard of living. The country moved towards a pluralist electoral politics at the very moment that it subsided into economic anarchy: for the first time since the inception of planning, Russia in 1989 no longer had a Five-Year Plan (Di Leo, 1992, p. 100 n). It was an explosive combination, for it undermined the shallow foundations of the USSR's economic and political unity.

For the USSR had increasingly evolved towards a structural decentralization, its elements held together primarily by the all-Union institutions of party, army, security forces and the central plan, and never more rapidly than in the long Brezhnev years. *De facto* much of the Soviet Union was a system of autonomous feudal lordships. Its local chieftains – the Party Secretaries of the Union republics with their subordinate territorial commanders, and the managers of the great and lesser production units, who kept the economy in operation – were united by little more than their dependency on the central party apparatus in Moscow, which nominated, transferred, deposed and coopted, and by the need to 'fulfil the plan' elaborated in Moscow. Within these very broad limits the territorial chieftains had considerable independence. Indeed the economy would not have functioned at all but for the development, by those who actually had to run institutions with real functions, of a network of lateral relations independent of the centre. This system of deals, barter arrangements and exchanges of favours with other cadres in similar positions was another 'second economy' within the nominally planned whole. One might add that, as the USSR became a more complex industrial and urban society, the cadres in charge of the actual production, distribution, and general care of the citizenry had diminished sympathy for the ministries and the purely party figures who were their superiors, but whose concrete functions were no longer clear, apart from that of feathering their nests, as many of them did in the Brezhnev period, often in the most spectacular manner. Revulsion against the increasingly monumental and all-pervasive corruption of the *nomenklatura* was the initial fuel for the process of reform, and Gorbachev had fairly solid support for *perestroika* from the economic cadres, especially those from the military-industrial complex, who genuinely wanted to improve the management of a stagnant and, in scientific and technical terms, paralytic economy. No one knew better than they how bad things really had become. Moreover, they did not need the party to carry on their activities. If the party bureaucracy were to disappear, they would still be there. They were indispensable, it was not. Indeed, they *were* still there after the collapse of the USSR, now organized as a pressure group in the new (1990) 'Industrial-Scientific Union' (NPS) and its successors, after the end of communism, as the (potentially) legal owners of the enterprises which they had commanded without legal property rights before.

Nevertheless, corrupt, inefficient and largely parasitic as the party command system had been, it remained essential in an economy based on command. The alternative to party authority was not the constitutional and democratic authority, but, in the short run, no authority. This is indeed what happened. Gorbachev, like his successor, Yeltsin, shifted his power-base from party to state, and, as constitutional president, legally accumulated powers to rule by decree, in some instances powers greater in theory than any earlier Soviet leader had formally enjoyed, even Stalin (Di Leo, 1992, p. 111). Nobody took any notice, outside the newly established democratic, or rather constitutional-public assemblies, the People's Congress and the Supreme Soviet (1989). Nobody governed or, rather, obeyed in the Soviet Union any more.

Like a crippled giant tanker moving towards the reefs, a rudderless Soviet Union therefore drifted towards disintegration. The lines along which it was to fracture were already drawn: on the one hand the system of territorial power-autonomy largely embodied in the state's federal structure, on the other the autonomous economic complexes. Since the official theory on which the Union had been constructed was one of territorial autonomy for national groups, both in the fifteen Union Republics and in the autonomous regions and areas within each,* national-

---

* In addition to the RSFSR (Russian Federation), by far the largest territorially

ist fracture was potentially built into the system, although, with the exception of the three small Baltic States, separatism was not even thought of before 1988, when the first nationalist 'fronts' or campaign organizations were founded in response to *glasnost* (in Estonia, Latvia, Lithuania and Armenia). However, at this stage, even in the Baltic States, they were directed not so much against the centre as against the insufficiently Gorbachevist local communist parties, or, as in Armenia, against neighbouring Azerbaijan. The object was not yet independence, although nationalism was rapidly radicalised in 1989–90 under the impact of the rush into electoral politics, and the struggle between radical reformers and the organized resistance of the old party establishment in the new assemblies, as well as the frictions between Gorbachev and his resentful victim, rival and eventual successor, Boris Yeltsin.

Essentially the radical reformers looked for support against the entrenched party hierarchies to the nationalists in the republics and, in doing so, strengthened these. In Russia itself, the appeal to Russian interests against the peripheral republics, subsidized by Russia and increasingly felt to be better off than Russia, was a powerful weapon in the radicals' struggle to eject the party bureaucracy, entrenched in the central state apparatus. For Boris Yeltsin, an old party boss from the command society, who combined the gifts of getting on in the old politics (toughness and cunning) with the gifts for getting on in the new (demagogy, joviality and a sense of the media), the way to the top lay through the capture of the Russian Federation, thus allowing him to by-pass the institutions of Gorbachev's Union. Hitherto, in effect, the Union and its chief component, the RSFSR, had not been clearly distinct. In transforming Russia into a Republic like the others, Yeltsin *de facto* favoured the disintegration of the Union, which a Russia under his control would in effect supplant. This is, indeed, what happened in 1991.

Economic disintegration helped to advance political disintegration, and was nourished by it. With the end of the Plan, and of party orders from the centre, there was no effective *national* economy, but a rush, by any community, territory, or other unit that could manage it, into self-protection and self-sufficiency, or bilateral exchanges. The commanders of the great provincial company towns, always used to such arrangements, bartered industrial products for foodstuffs with the heads of the regional collective farms, as – a dramatic example – the Leningrad Party chief,

---

and demographically, there were also Armenia, Azerbaijan, Byelorussia, Estonia, Georgia, Kazakhstan, Kyrghyzstan, Latvia, Lithuania, Moldavia, Tadjikistan, Turkmenistan, Ukraine and Uzbekistan.

Gidaspov, dealt with an acute grain shortage in his city by a phone-call to Nazarbayev, the Kazakhstan Party boss, who arranged a swap of cereals for footwear and steel (Yu Boldyrev, 1990). But even this kind of transaction between two of the top figures in the old party hierarchy in effect treated the national system of distribution as irrelevant. 'Particularisms, autarchies, relapses into primitive practices seemed to be the real results of the laws which had liberalized local economic forces' (Di Leo, p. 101).

The point of no return was reached in the second half of 1989, bicentenary of the outbreak of the French Revolution, whose non-existence or irrelevance to twentieth-century politics French 'revisionist' historians were busy trying to demonstrate at the time. The political breakdown followed (as in eighteenth century France) the calling of the new democratic, or largely democratic assemblies in the summer of that year. The economic breakdown became irreversible in the course of a few crucial months between October 1989 and May 1990. However, the eyes of the world at this time were fixed on a related, but secondary phenomenon: the sudden, and once again unpredicted, dissolution of the satellite communist regimes in Europe. Between August 1989 and the end of that year communist power abdicated or ceased to exist in Poland, Czechoslovakia, Hungary, Romania, Bulgaria and the German Democratic Republic – without so much as a shot being fired, except in Romania. Shortly thereafter the two Balkan states which were not Soviet satellites, Yugoslavia and Albania, also ceased to be communist regimes. The German Democratic Republic was soon to be annexed to Western Germany, and Yugoslavia was soon to break up into civil war. The process was watched not only on the television screens of the Western world, but also, with great care, by the communist regimes in other continents. Though they ranged from the radically reformist (at least in economic matters), as in China, to the implacably old-style centralist, as in Cuba (chapter 15), all presumably had doubts about the Soviet plunge into unrestricted *glasnost*, and the weakening of authority. When the movement for liberalization and democracy spread from the USSR to China, the Beijing government decided, in mid-1989, after some obvious hesitations and lacerating internal disagreements, to re-establish its authority in the most unambiguous manner, by what Napoleon, who also used the army to suppress public agitation during the French Revolution, had called 'a whiff of grapeshot'. The troops cleared a mass student demonstration from the capital's main square, at a heavy cost in lives, probably – though no reliable data were available at the time of writing – several hundreds. The massacre of Tienanmen Square horrified Western public opinion, and undoubtedly lost the Chinese Communist Party most of what little legitimacy it may still have had among the younger generations of Chinese intellectuals, including party members, but it left the Chinese regime free to continue the policy of successful economic liberalisation without immediate political problems. The collapse of communism after 1989 was confined to the USSR and the states in its orbit (including Outer Mongolia, which had chosen Soviet protection over Chinese domination between the world wars). The three surviving Asian communist regimes (China, North Korea and Vietnam) as well as remote and isolated Cuba, were not immediately affected.

V

It seemed natural, particularly in the bicentenary year of 1789, to describe the changes of 1989–90 as the East European revolutions, and, insofar as events which lead to the complete overthrow of regimes are revolutionary, the word is apposite, but misleading. For none of the regimes in Eastern Europe were *over-thrown*. None, except Poland, contained any internal force, organized or not, which constituted a serious threat to them, and the fact that Poland contained a powerful political opposition actually guaranteed that the system there was not destroyed from one day to the next, but replaced by a negotiated process of compromise and reform, not unlike the way in which Spain made the transition to democracy after the death of General Franco in 1975. The most immediate threat to those in the Soviet orbit came from Moscow, which made it clear that it would no longer rescue them by military intervention, as in 1956 and 1968, if only because the end of the Cold War made them strategically less necessary to the USSR. If they wanted to survive, in Moscow's opinion, they would be well advised to follow the line of liberalization, reform and flexibility of the Polish and Hungarian communists, but, by the same token, Moscow would not compel the hardliners in Berlin and Prague. They were on their own.

The very withdrawal of the USSR underlined their bankruptcy. They remained in power merely by virtue of the void they had created around them, which had left no alternative to the status quo except (where this was possible) emigration or (for a few) the formation of marginal dissident groups of intellectuals. The bulk of the citizens had accepted things as they were, because they had no alternative. People of energy, talent and ambition worked within the system, since any position requiring these things, and indeed any public expression of talent, was within the system or by its permission, even in entirely non-political fields like pole-vaulting and chess. This applied even to the licensed opposition, mainly in the arts, which was allowed to develop in the decline of the systems, as dissident writers who had chosen not to emigrate, discovered to their cost after the fall of communism, when they were treated as collaborators.* No wonder that most people opted for the quiet life, which included the formal gestures of support for a system nobody except primary school-children believed in, such as voting or demonstrating, even when the penalties for dissidence were no longer terrifying. One of the reasons why the old regime was denounced with such fury after its fall, especially in hardline countries like Czechoslovakia and the ex-GDR, was that

'the great majority voted in the sham elections to avoid unpleasant consequences, though not very serious ones; they took part in the obligatory marches ... The police informers were easily recruited, won over by miserable privileges, often agreeing to serve as the result of very mild pressure' (Kolakowski, 1992, pp. 55–56).

Yet hardly anyone believed in the system or felt any loyalty to it, not even those who governed it. They were no doubt surprised when the masses finally abandoned their passivity and demonstrated their dissi-dence – the moment of amazement has been caught forever on the videotape of President Ceauşescu, in December 1989, confronting a crowd that booed instead of loyally applauding – but they were surprised, not by the dissidence, only by the action. At that moment of truth, no East European government ordered its forces to fire. All abdicated quietly, except in Romania, and even there resistance was brief. Perhaps they could not have regained control, but nobody even tried. No groups of communist ultras anywhere prepared to die in the bunker for their faith, or even for the far-from-unimpressive record of forty years' commu-nist rule in a number of these states. What should they have defended? Economic systems whose inferiority to their Western neighbours leaped to the eye, which were running down, and which had proved to be unreformable, even where serious and intelligent efforts at reform had been made? Systems which had plainly lost the justification that had sustained their communist cadres in the past, namely that socialism was superior to capitalism and destined to replace it? Who could any longer believe that, though it had not looked implausible in the 1940s or even

---

* Even so passionate an opponent of communism as the Russian writer Alexander Solzhenitsyn had his career as a writer established through the system, which permitted/encouraged the publication of his first novels for reformist purposes.

1950s? Since communist states were no longer even united, and sometimes actually fought each other with arms (e.g. China and Vietnam in the early 1980s), one could no longer even speak of a single 'socialist camp'. All that remained of the old hopes was the fact that the USSR, the country of the October revolution, was one of the two global superpowers. Except perhaps for China, all communist governments, and a good many communist parties and states or movements in the Third World, knew well enough how much they owed to the existence of this counterweight to the economic and strategic predominance of the other side. But the USSR was visibly shedding a politico-military burden it could no longer carry, and even communist states which were in no sense dependencies of Moscow (Yugoslavia, Albania) could not but realize how profoundly its disappearance would weaken them.

In any case, in Europe as in the USSR, the communists, who had once been sustained by the old convictions, were now a generation of the past. In 1989 few under sixty could have shared the experience that linked communism and patriotism in several countries, namely the Second World War and Resistance, and few under fifty could even have first-hand memories of that time. The legitimizing principle of states was, for most people, official rhetoric or senior citizens' anecdotage.* Even party members among the less-than-elderly were likely to be not communists in the old sense, but men and women (alas, far too few women) who made careers in countries that happened to be under communist rule. When times changed, and if they were allowed to, they were ready at a moment's notice to change their coats. In short, those who ran the Soviet satellite regimes had lost their faith in their own systems, or had never had it. While the systems were operational, they operated them. When it became clear that the USSR itself was cutting them adrift, the reformers (as in Poland and Hungary) tried to negotiate a peaceful transition, the hardliners (as in Czechoslovakia and the GDR) to stand pat until it became evident that the citizens no longer obeyed, even if the army and police still did. In both cases they went quietly when they realised that their time was up, thus taking an unconscious revenge on the propagandists of the West who had argued that this was precisely what 'totalitarian' regimes could never conceivably do.

They were replaced, briefly, by the men and (once again, far too rarely) women who had represented dissidence or opposition, and who

* This was obviously not the case in Third-world communist states like Vietnam, where liberation struggles had continued until the middle 1970s, but there the civil divisions of the liberation wars were probably also more vivid in people's minds.

had organized, or perhaps better, successfully called for the mass demonstrations which gave the signal for the old regimes' peaceful abdication.
Except in Poland, where Church and the trade unions formed the
backbone of opposition, they consisted of a few often very brave intellectuals, a stage-army of leaders which briefly found itself at the head of
peoples: often, as in the 1848 revolutions which come to the historian's
mind, academics or from the world of the arts. For a moment dissident
philosophers (Hungary) or medieval historians (Poland) were considered
as presidents or prime ministers, and a dramatist, Vaclav Havel, actually
became President of Czechoslovakia, surrounded by an eccentric body of
advisers ranging from a scandal-loving American rock musician to a
member of the Habsburg high aristocracy (Prince Schwarzenberg). There
was a tidal wave of talk about 'civil society', i.e. the ensemble of
voluntary citizens' organizations or private activities, taking the place of
authoritarian states, and about the return to the principles of revolutions
before Bolshevism had distorted them.* Alas, as in 1848, the moment of
freedom and truth did not last. Politics, and those who ran the affairs of
state reverted to those who usually occupy such functions. The *ad hoc*
'fronts' or 'civic movements' crumbled as rapidly as they had risen.

This also proved to be the case in the USSR, where the collapse of
party and state proceeded more slowly until August 1991. The failure of
perestroika and the consequent rejection of Gorbachev by the citizenry
were increasingly obvious, though not appreciated in the West, where his
popularity remained justifiably high. It reduced the leader of the USSR
to a series of backstairs manoeuvres and shifting alliances with the
political groups and power groups that had emerged from the parliamen-
tarisation of Soviet politics, which made him equally distrusted by the
reformers who had initially rallied round him – whom he had indeed
made into a state-changing force – and the fragmented party bloc whose
power he had broken. He was and will go into history as a tragic figure,
a communist 'Tsar-Liberator' like Alexander II (1855–81) who destroyed
what he wanted to reform and was destroyed in the process.†

* The author recalls one of those discussions at a Washington conference in 1991,
brought down to earth by the Spanish ambassador to the USA, who remembered
the young (at that time mainly liberal communist) students and ex-students feeling
much the same after General Franco's death in 1975. 'Civil society', he thought,
merely meant that young ideologues who actually found themselves, for a moment,
speaking for the whole people, were tempted to see this as a permanent situation.

† Alexander II (1855–81) freed the serfs and undertook a number of other
reforms, but was assassinated by members of the revolutionary movement, which for
the first time became a force in his reign.

Charming, sincere, intelligent and genuinely moved by the ideals of a communism which he saw corrupted since the rise of Stalin, Gorbachev was, paradoxically, too much of an organization man for the hurly-burly of democratic politics he created; too much of a committee man for decisive action; too remote from the experiences of urban and industrial Russia, which he had never managed, to have the old party boss's sense of grass-roots realities. His trouble was not so much that he had no effective strategy for reforming the economy – nobody had even after his fall – as that he was remote from the everyday experience of his country.

The contrast with another of the post-war generation of leading Soviet communists in their fifties is instructive. Nursultan Nazarbayev, who took charge of the Asian republic of Kazakhstan in 1984 as part of the reform drive, had (like many other Soviet politicians, and unlike Gorbachev and practically any statesmen in non-socialist countries) come into full-time public life from the factory floor. He shifted from party to state, becoming President of his Republic, pushed forward the required reforms, including decentralization and the market, and survived both the fall of Gorbachev, of the party of the Union, none of which he welcomed. After the fall he remained one of the most powerful men in the shadowy 'Community of Independent States'. But Nazarbayev, always the pragmatist, had systematically pursued a policy of optimising the position of his fief (and its population), and had taken the utmost care that market reforms should not be socially disruptive. Markets yes, uncontrolled price-rises decidedly no. His own preferred strategy was bilateral trade deals with other Soviet (or ex-Soviet) republics – he favoured a Central Asian Soviet common market – and joint ventures with foreign capital. He had no objection to radical economists, for he hired some from Russia, or even non-communist ones, for he brought in one of the brains of the South Korean economic miracle, which showed a realistic sense of how really successful post-Second World War capitalist economies actually worked. The road to survival and perhaps to success was paved less with good intentions than with the hard cobbles of realism.

The last years of the Soviet Union were a slow-motion catastrophe. The fall of the European satellites in 1989, and Moscow's reluctant acceptance of German reunification, demonstrated the collapse of the Soviet Union as an international power, let alone as a superpower. Its utter inability to play any role in the Persian Gulf crisis of 1990–91 merely underlined this. Internationally speaking, the USSR was like a country comprehensively defeated, as after a major war – only without a war. Nevertheless, it retained the armed forces and the military-industrial complex of the former superpower, a situation that imposed severe limits on its politics. However, though the international debacle encouraged secessionism in the republics where nationalist sentiment was strong, notably the Baltic States and Georgia – Lithuania tested the waters with a provocative declaration of total independence in March 1990* – the disintegration of the Union was not due to nationalist forces.

It was due essentially to the disintegration of central authority, which forced every region or sub-unit of the country to look after itself, and, not least, to save what it could from the ruins of an economy sliding into chaos. Hunger and shortage lie behind everything that happened in the last two years of the USSR. Despairing reformers, mainly from among the academics who had been such obvious beneficiaries of *glasnost*, were pushed into an apocalyptic extremism: nothing could be done until the old system and everything about it was destroyed utterly. In economic terms, the system must be completely pulverised by total privatisation and the introduction of a 100 per cent free market immediately and at whatever cost. Dramatic plans for doing this in a matter of weeks or months (there was a 'programme of five hundred days') were proposed. These policies were not based on any knowledge of free markets or capitalist economies, though they were vigorously recommended by visiting American and British economists and financial experts, whose opinions were not, in turn, based on any knowledge of what actually went on in the Soviet economy. Both were correct in supposing that the existing system, or rather, while it existed, the command economy, was far inferior to economies based primarily on private property and private enterprise, and that the old system, even in a modified form, was doomed. Yet both failed to confront the real problem of how a centrally planned command economy was, in practice, to be transformed into some version or another of a market-dynamised economy. Instead they repeated first-year-economics-course demonstrations of the virtues of the market in the abstract. It would, they argued, automatically fill the shelves of shops with goods withheld by producers at affordable prices, once supply and demand were allowed free play. Most of the long-suffering citizens of the USSR knew that this would not happen, and when, after it ceased to exist, the shock liberation treatment was briefly applied, it did not. Moreover, no serious observer of the country believed that in the year

---

* Armenian nationalism, though provoking the breakdown of the Union by reclaiming the region of Mountain Karabakh from Azerbaijan, was not crazy enough to *desire* the disappearance of the USSR, but for whose existence there would be no Armenia.

2000 the state and public sector of the Soviet economy would not still be substantial. The disciples of Friedrich Hayek and Milton Friedman condemned the very idea of such a mixed economy. They had no advice to offer about how it was to be operated, or transformed.

Yet, when it came, the final crisis was not economic but political. For virtually the entire Establishment of the USSR, from the party, the planners and scientists, the state, to the armed forces the security apparatus and the sporting authorities, the idea of a total break-up of the USSR was unacceptable. Whether it was desired, or even conceived of by any large body of Soviet citizens outside the Baltic States, even after 1989, we cannot tell, but it is not likely: whatever reservations we have about the figures, 76 per cent of voters in a referendum of March 1991 voted for maintaining the USSR, 'as a renovated Federation of sovereign and equal Republics, in which the rights and liberty of every person of whatever nationality are fully safeguarded' (*Pravda*, 25/1/91). It was certainly not officially part of any major Union politician's policy. Yet the dissolution of the centre seemed inevitably to strengthen the centrifugal forces and to make the break-up inevitable, not least because of the policy of Boris Yeltsin, whose star rose as Gorbachev's waned. By now the Union was a shadow, the republics the only reality. At the end of April, Gorbachev, supported by the nine major republics,* negotiated a 'Treaty of Union' which, somewhat in the manner of the Austro-Hungarian Compromise of 1867, was intended to preserve the existence of a central federal power (with a directly elected federal president), in charge of the armed forces, foreign policy, the coordination of financial policy and of economic relations with the rest of the world. The Treaty was to come into force on 20 August.

For most of the old party and Soviet establishment, this treaty was yet another of Gorbachev's paper formulas, doomed like all the others. Hence they regarded it as the gravestone of the Union. Two days before the Treaty was due to come into force, virtually all the heavyweights of the Union, ministers of defence and interior, head of the KGB, vice-president and prime minister of the USSR and pillars of the party, proclaimed that an Emergency Committee would take over power in the absence of the President and General Secretary (under house arrest on vacation). It was not so much a coup – nobody was arrested in Moscow, not even the broadcasting stations were taken over – as a proclamation that the machinery of real power was once again in operation, in the

* i.e. all except the three Baltic states, Moldavia and Georgia, as well as, for obscure reasons, Kyrghyzstan.

confident hope that the citizenry would welcome, or at least quietly accept, the return to order and government. It was not defeated by a revolution or rising of the people either, for the population of Moscow remained quiet, and the call for a strike against the coup went unheeded. As in so much of Soviet history, it was a drama played by a small body of actors over the heads of the long-suffering people.

But not quite. Thirty, even ten years earlier, the mere proclamation of where power really lay would have been enough. Even as it was, most citizens of the USSR kept their heads down: 48 per cent of the people (according to a poll) and – less surprisingly – 70 per cent of party committees, supported the 'coup' (Di Leo, 1992, pp. 141, 143n). Equally to the point, more governments abroad than cared to admit it, expected the coup to succeed.* Yet the old-style reassertion of the power of party/state relied on universal and automatic assent rather than counting heads. By 1991 there was neither central power nor universal obedience. A genuine coup might well have succeeded over most of the territory and population of the USSR, and, whatever the divisions and uncertainties within the armed forces and security apparatus, enough reliable troops for a successful *putsch* in the capital could probably have been found. But the symbolic reassertion of authority was no longer enough. Gorbachev was right: *perestroika* had defeated the conspirators by changing society. It had also defeated him.

A symbolic coup could be defeated by a symbolic resistance, for the last thing the plotters were prepared for or wanted was a civil war. Indeed, their gesture was intended to stop what most people feared: a slide into such a conflict. So, while the shadowy institutions of the USSR fell into line with the plotters, the barely less shadowy institutions of the Russian Republic under Boris Yeltsin, just elected as its President by a substantial majority of voters, did not. The plotters had nothing to do except throw in their hand, after Yeltsin, surrounded by some thousands of supporters come to defend his headquarters, defied the embarrassed tanks camped in front of it, for the benefit of the world's television screens. Bravely, but also safely, Yeltsin, whose political gifts and capacity for decision contrasted dramatically with Gorbachev's style, immediately seized his opportunity to dissolve and expropriate the Communist Party and take over for the Russian Republic what remained of

---

* On the first day of the 'coup' the Finnish government's official news digest reported the news of President Gorbachev's arrest briefly without comment halfway down page 3 of a four-page bulletin. It only began to express opinions when the attempt had evidently failed.

the assets of the USSR, which was formally ended a few months later. Gorbachev himself was pushed into oblivion. The world, which had been ready to accept the coup, now accepted the much more effective counter-coup of Yeltsin, and treated Russia as the natural successor to the dead USSR in the United Nations and elsewhere. The attempt to save the old structure of the Soviet Union had destroyed it more suddenly and irrevocably than anyone had expected.

However, it had solved none of the problems of economy, state and society. In one respect it had made them worse, for the other republics were now afraid of their big brother Russia as they had not been of the non-national USSR, especially since Russian nationalism was the best card Yeltsin could play to conciliate the armed forces, whose core had always been among the Great Russians. Since most of the republics contained large minorities of ethnic Russians, Yeltsin's hint that the frontiers between the republics might have to be renegotiated, accelerated the rush total separation: the Ukraine immediately declared its independence. For the first time populations used to the impartial oppression of all (including Great Russians) by central authority had cause to fear oppression from Moscow in the interests of one nation. In fact, this put paid to the hope of maintaining even a semblance of union, for the shadowy 'Commonwealth of Independent States' which succeeded the USSR soon lost all reality, and even the last survivor of the Union, the (extremely successful) United Team which competed at the 1992 Olympic Games, beating the United States, did not seem destined for a long life. Thus the destruction of the USSR achieved the reversal of almost four hundred years of Russian history, and the return of the country to something like the dimensions and international standing of the era before Peter the Great (1672–1725). Since Russia, whether under the Tsars or as the USSR, had been a great power since the middle of the eighteenth century, its disintegration left an international void between Trieste and Vladivostok, which had not previously existed in modern world history, except briefly during the Civil War of 1918–20: a vast zone of disorder, conflict and potential catastrophe. This was the agenda for the world's diplomats and military men at the end of the millennium.

VI

Two observations may conclude this survey. The first is to note how superficial the hold of communism proved to be over the enormous area it had conquered more rapidly than any other ideology since Islam in its first century. Though a simplistic version of Marxism–Leninism became the dogmatic (secular) orthodoxy for all citizens between the Elbe and the China Seas, it disappeared from one day to the next with the political regimes that had imposed it. Two reasons may be suggested for this historically rather startling phenomenon. Communism was not based on mass conversion, but was a faith of cadres or (in Lenin's terms) 'vanguards'. Even Mao's famous phrase about successful guerrillas moving among the peasantry like fish in water, implies the distinction between the active element (the fish) and the passive (the water). Unofficial labour and socialist movements (including some mass communist parties) might be coextensive with their community or constituency, as in coalmining villages. On the other hand, all ruling communist parties were, by choice and definition, minority elites. The assent to communism of 'the masses' depended not on their ideological or other convictions but on how they judged what life under communist regimes did for them, and how they compared their situation with others'. Once it ceased to be possible to insulate populations from contact with, or even knowledge about, other countries, these judgments were sceptical. Again, communism was essentially an instrumental faith: the present having value purely as a means of reaching an undefined future. Except in rare cases – for instance patriotic wars, where victory justifies present sacrifices – such a set of beliefs is better suited to sects or elites than to universal churches, whose field of operation, whatever their promise of ultimate salvation, is and must be the everyday range of human life. Even the cadres of communist parties began to concentrate on the ordinary satisfactions of life once the millennial aim of earthly salvation, to which they had dedicated their lives, moved into an undefined future. And – typically enough – when this happened, the party provided no guidance for their behaviour. In short, by the nature of its ideology communism asked to be judged by success, and had no reserves against failure.

But why did it fail, or rather break down? It is the paradox of the USSR that, in its death, it provided one of the strongest arguments for the analysis of Karl Marx, which it had claimed to exemplify. Marx wrote in 1859:

> In the social production of their means of existence human beings enter into definite, necessary relations independent of their will, productive relationships which correspond to a definite stage in the development of their material productive forces ... At a certain stage of their development the material productive forces of society come into contradiction with the existing productive relationships,

or, what is but a legal expression for these, with the property relationships within which they had moved before. From forms of development of the productive forces these relationships are transformed into their fetters. We then enter an era of social revolution.

Rarely has there been a clearer example of Marx' forces of production coming into conflict with the social, institutional and ideological superstructure which had transformed backward agrarian economies into advanced industrial ones – up to the point where they turn from forces into fetters of production. The first result of the 'era of social revolution' thus initiated was the disintegration of the old system.

But what would replace it? Here we can no longer follow the nineteenth-century optimism of Marx, who argued that the overthrow of the old system must lead to a better one, because 'mankind always sets itself only such problems as it can solve'. The problems which 'mankind', or rather the Bolsheviks, set themselves in 1917 were not soluble in the circumstances of their time and place, or only very incompletely soluble. And today it would take a high degree of confidence to argue that in the foreseeable future a solution is visible for the problems arising out of the collapse of Soviet communism, or that any solution that may arise within the next generation will strike the inhabitants of the former USSR and the communist Balkans as an obvious improvement.

With the collapse of the USSR the experiment of 'really existing socialism' came to an end. For, even where communist regimes survived and succeeded, as in China, they abandoned the original ideal of a single, centrally controlled and state-planned economy based on a completely collectivised state – or cooperatively owned economy virtually without a market. Will this experiment ever be renewed? Clearly not in the form developed in the USSR, or probably in any form, except in conditions of something like a total war economy, or some other analogous emergency.

This is because the Soviet experiment was designed not as a global alternative to capitalism, but as a specific set of responses to the particular situation of a vast and spectacularly backward country at a particular and unrepeatable historical conjuncture. The failure of revolution elsewhere left the USSR committed to build socialism alone, in a country in which, by the universal consensus of Marxists in 1917, including the Russian ones, the conditions for doing so were simply not present. The attempt to do so produced remarkable achievements – not least the ability to defeat Germany in the Second World War – but at quite enormous and intolerable human cost, and at the cost of what proved eventually to be a dead-end economy and a political system for which there was nothing to be said. (Had not George Plekhanov, the 'father of Russian Marxism', predicted that the October revolution could lead at best to a 'Chinese Empire coloured red'?) The other 'really existing' socialism, emerging under the wings of the Soviet Union, operated under the same disadvantages, though to a lesser extent, and with – compared to the USSR far less human suffering. A revival or rebirth of this pattern of socialism is neither possible, desirable, nor – even assuming conditions were to favour it – necessary.

How far the failure of the Soviet experiment throws doubt on the entire project of traditional socialism, an economy essentially based on the social ownership and planned management of the means of production, distribution and exchange, is another question. That such a project is economically rational in theory has been accepted by economists since before the First World War, though, curiously enough, the theory was worked out not by socialists but by non-socialist pure economists. That it would have practical drawbacks, if only through bureaucratisation, was obvious. That it had to work, at least partly, through *prices*, both market pricing and realistic 'accounting prices', was also clear if socialism was to take account of the wishes of consumers rather than telling them what was good for them. In fact, socialist economists in the West who thought about these matters in the 1930s, when the subject was naturally much debated, assumed a combination of planning, preferably decentralized, with prices. To demonstrate the feasibility of such a socialist economy is not, of course, to demonstrate its necessary superiority to, say, some socially juster version of the Golden Age mixed economy, still less, that people would prefer it. It is merely to separate the question of socialism in general from that of the specific experience of 'really existing socialism'. The failure of Soviet socialism does not reflect on the possibility of other kinds of socialism. Indeed, the very inability of the dead-end economy of Soviet-type central command-planning to reform itself into 'market socialism', as it wanted to, demonstrates the gap between the two kinds of development.

The tragedy of the October revolution was precisely that it could only produce its kind of ruthless, brutal, command socialism. One of the most sophisticated socialist economists of the 1930s, Oskar Lange, returned from the USA to his native Poland to build socialism, until he came to a London hospital to die. On his death-bed he talked to the friends and admirers who came to visit him, including myself. This, as I recall, is what he said:

If I had been in Russia in the 1920s, I would have been a

Bukharinite gradualist. If I had advised on Soviet industrialization, I would have recommended a more flexible and limited set of targets, as indeed the able Russian planners did. And yet, as I think back, I ask myself, again and again: was there an alternative to the indiscriminate, brutal, basically unplanned rush forward of the first Five-Year Plan? I wish I could say there was, but I cannot. I cannot find an answer.

CHAPTER SEVENTEEN
The Avant-garde Dies –
The Arts After 1950

Art as an investment is a conception scarcely older than the early 1950s.

> – G. Reitlinger, *The Economics of Taste*, vol. 2 (1982, p. 14)

The great big white goods, the things that keep our economy going – refrigerators, stoves, all the things that used to be porcelain and white – they're now tinted. This is new. There's pop art that goes along with them. Very nice. Mandrake the Magician coming off the wall at you as you open your refrigerator to get your orange juice.

> – Studs Terkel, *Division Street: America* (1967, p. 217)

I

It is the practice of historians – including this one – to treat the development of the arts, however obvious and profound their roots in society, as in some way separable from their contemporary context, as a branch or type of human activity subject to its own rules, and capable of being judged accordingly. Yet in the era of the most revolutionary transformations of human life so far recorded, even this ancient and convenient principle of structuring a historical survey becomes increasingly unreal. Not only because the boundary between what is and is not classifiable as 'art' 'creation' or artifice became increasingly hazy, or even disappeared altogether, or because an influential school of literary critics at the *fin de siècle* thought it impossible, irrelevant and undemocratic to decide whether Shakespeare's *Macbeth* was better or worse than *Batman*. It was also because the forces determining what happened within the arts, or what old-fashioned observers would have called by that name, were overwhelmingly exogenous. As might have been expected in an era of extraordinary techno-scientific revolution, they were predominantly technological.

Technology revolutionized the arts most obviously by making them omnipresent. Radio had already brought sounds – words and music – into most households in the developed world, and continued its penetration of the backward world. But what made it universal was the transistor, which made it both small and portable, and the long-life electric battery which made it independent of official (i.e. mainly urban) networks of electric power. The gramophone or record-player was already ancient, and, though technically improved, remained comparatively cumbersome. The long-playing record (1948), which established itself rapidly in the 1950s (Guiness, 1984, p. 193) benefited the lovers of classical music, whose compositions, unlike those of popular music, had rarely tried to keep within the three- or five-minute limit of the 78 rpm disc, but what made self-chosen music genuinely transportable was the tape-cassette, playable on the increasingly small and portable and battery-powered recorder/players, which swept the world in the 1970s and had the additional advantage of being readily copied. By the 1980s music could be everywhere: privately accompanying every possible activity through earphones attached to pocket-sized devices pioneered (as so often) by the Japanese, or projected only too publicly from the large portable 'ghetto-blasters' (for loudspeakers had not yet been successfully miniaturized). This technological revolution had political as well as cultural consequences. In 1961 President de Gaulle appealed successfully to French conscripts against their commanders' military coup, because soldiers could hear him on portable radios. In the 1970s the speeches of Ayatollah Khomeini, exiled leader of the future Iranian revolution, were readily transported into Iran, copied and diffused.

Television never became as readily portable as radio – or at least it lost far more by reduction than sound – but it domesticated the moving image. Moreover, while a TV set remained a far more expensive and physically clumsy device than a radio set, it soon became almost universally and constantly accessible even to the poor in some backward countries, wherever an urban infrastructure existed. In the 1980s some 80 per cent of the population of a country like Brazil had access to television. This is more surprising than that in the USA the new medium replaced both radio and films as the standard form of popular entertainment in the 1950s, and in prosperous Britain in the 1960s. The mass demand for it was overwhelming. In the advanced countries it began (via the video-cassette player, which still remained a rather expensive device) to bring the whole range of the filmed image into the domestic small screen. While the repertoire produced for the big screen generally suffered from being miniaturized, the VCR had the advantage of giving the viewer a theoretically almost unlimited choice of what to see and when to see it. With the spread of domestic computers, the small screen seemed about to become the individual's major visual link with the outside world.

Yet technology not only made the arts omnipresent, but transformed their perception. It is barely possible for someone who has been brought up in the age when electronic and mechanically generated music is the standard sound heard on live and recorded pop music, when any child can freeze frames, and repeat a sound or visual passage as once only textual passages could be re-read, when theatrical illusion is as nothing to what technology can do in television commercials, including telling a dramatic narrative in thirty seconds, to recapture simple linearity or sequentiality of perception in the days before modern high-tech made it possible to move within seconds through the full range of available television channels. Technology transformed the world of the arts, though that of the popular arts and entertainments earlier and more completely than that of the 'high arts', especially the more traditional ones.

II

But what had happened to these?

At first sight the most striking thing about the development of the high arts in the world after the Age of Catastrophe was a marked geographical shift away from the traditional (European) centres of elite culture, and – given the era of unprecedented global prosperity – an enormous rise in the financial resources available to support them. Closer scrutiny, as we shall see, was to prove less encouraging.

That 'Europe' (by which most people in the West between 1947 and 1989 meant 'Western Europe') was no longer the major home of the high arts became a commonplace observation. New York prided itself on having replaced Paris as the centre of the visual arts, by which it meant the art market or the place where living artists became the highest-priced commodities. More significantly, the jury of the Nobel Prize for literature, a body whose sense of politics is usually more interesting than its literary judgments, began to take non-European literature seriously from the 1960s on, having previously neglected it almost completely, except for North America (which got prizes regularly from 1930, when Sinclair Lewis became its first laureate). No serious reader of novels could, by the

1970s, fail to have made contact with the brilliant school of Latin American writers. No serious film-buff could fail to admire, or at least to talk as though he or she admired the great Japanese film directors who, starting with Akira Kurosawa (1910–) in the 1950s, conquered the international film festivals, or the Bengali Satyadjit Ray (1921–92). Nobody was surprised when in 1986 the first sub-Saharan African, the Nigerian Wole Soyinka (1934–), got a Nobel Prize.

The shift away from Europe was even more obvious in the most visually insistent art, namely architecture. As we have already seen, the modern movement in architecture had actually built very little between the wars. After the war, when it came into its own, the 'international style' achieved both its largest and most numerous monuments in the USA, which developed it further and eventually, mainly via the American-owned networks of hotels which settled on the world from the 1970s on like spiderwebs, exported a peculiar form of dream-palace for travelling business executives and prosperous tourists. In their most characteristic versions they were easily recognizable by a sort of central nave or giant conservatory, generally with indoor trees, plants and fountains; transparent elevators visibly gliding up the insides or outsides of walls; glass everywhere and theatrical lighting. They were to be for late twentieth-century bourgeois society what the standard opera house had been for its nineteenth-century predecessor. But the modern movement created equally prominent monuments elsewhere: Le Corbusier (1887–1965) constructed an entire capital city in India (Chandigarh); Oscar Niemeyer (1907–) much of another in Brazil (Brasilia); while perhaps the most beautiful of the great products of the modern movement – also built by public commission rather than private patronage or profit – is to be found in Mexico City, the National Museum of Anthropology (1964).

It seemed equally evident that the old European centres of the arts were showing signs of battle-fatigue, with the possible exception of Italy, where the mood of anti-fascist self-liberation, largely under communist leadership, inspired a decade or so of cultural renaissance which made its main international impact through the Italian 'neo-realist' films. The French visual arts did not maintain the reputation of the inter-war school of Paris, which was in itself little more than an afterglow of the era before 1914. The major reputations of French fiction writers were intellectual rather than literary: as inventors of gimmicks (like the '*nouveau roman*' of the 1950s and 1960s) or as non-fiction writers (like J.-P. Sartre), rather than for their creative work. Had any post-1945 'serious' French novelist established any international reputation as such by the 1970s? Probably not. The British artistic scene had been considerably livelier, not least because London after 1950 transformed itself into one of the world's major centres for musical and theatrical performance, and also produced a handful of avant-garde architects whose adventurous projects gained them more fame abroad – in Paris or Stuttgart – than at home. Nevertheless, if post-Second World War Britain occupied a less marginal place in the West European arts than between the wars, its record in the field where the country had always been strong, literature, was not particularly impressive. In poetry, the post-war writers of little Ireland could more than hold their own against the UK. As for Federal Germany, the contrast between that country's resources and achievements, and indeed between its glorious Weimar past and its Bonn present, was striking. It was not entirely explained by the disastrous effects and after-effects of the twelve Hitler years. It is significant that in the fifty post-war years several of the best talents active in West German literature were not natives but immigrants from further east (Celan, Grass and various incomers from the GDR).

Germany, of course, was divided between 1945 and 1990. The contrast between the two parts – one militantly democratic-liberal, market-oriented and Western, the other a textbook version of communist centralization – illustrates a curious aspect of the migration of high culture: its relative flowering under communism, at least at certain periods. This plainly does not apply to all arts, nor, of course, to states under the iron heel of a genuinely murderous dictatorship, like Stalin's and Mao's, or of lesser megalomaniac tyrannies, like Ceaușescu's in Romania (1961–89) or Kim Il Sung's in North Korea (1945–1994).

Moreover, insofar as arts depended upon public, i.e. central government, patronage, the standard dictatorial preference for pompous gigantism reduced the artists' choice, as did the official insistence on a sort of upbeat sentimental mythology known as 'socialist realism'. It is possible that the wide open spaces lined with neo-Victorian towers so characteristic of the 1950s may one day find admirers – one thinks of Smolensk Square in Moscow – but the discovery of their architectural merits must be left to the future. On the other hand it must be admitted that, where communist governments did not insist on telling artists exactly what to do, their generosity in subsidising cultural activities (or, as others might put it, their defective sense of accountancy) was helpful. It is presumably not an accident that the West imported the typical avant-garde opera producer of the 1980s from East Berlin.

The USSR remained culturally fallow, at least in comparison with its pre-1917 glories and even the ferment of the 1920s, except perhaps for the writing of poetry, the art most capable of being practised in private and the one where the great twentieth-century Russian tradition maintained its continuity best after 1917 – Akhmatova (1889–1966), Tsvetayeva (1892–1941), Pasternak (1890–1960), Blok (1880–1921), Mayakovsky (1893–1930), Brodsky (1940–), Voznesensky (1933–), Akhmadulina (1937–). Its visual arts suffered particularly from the combination of a rigid orthodoxy, both ideological, aesthetic and institutional, and total isolation from the rest of the world. The passionate cultural nationalism which began to emerge in parts of the USSR during the Brezhnev period – orthodox and slavophil in Russia (Solzhenitsyn (1918–), mythical-medievalist in Armenia (e.g. in the films of Sergei Paradjanov (1924–) – derived largely from the fact that those who rejected anything recommended by the system and the party, as so many intellectuals did, had no other traditions to draw on but the local conservative ones. Moreover, the intellectuals in the USSR were spectacularly isolated not only from the system of government but also from the bulk of ordinary Soviet citizens who, in some obscure way, accepted its legitimacy and adjusted to the only life they knew, and which, in the 1960s and 1970s, was actually improving quite noticeably. They hated the rulers and despised the ruled, even when (like the neo-slavophils) they idealized the Russian soul in the shape of a Russian peasant who no longer existed. It was not a good atmosphere for the creative artist, and the dissolution of the apparatus of intellectual coercion, paradoxically, turned talents from creation to agitation. The Solzhenitsyn who is likely to survive as a major twentieth-century writer is the one who still had to preach by writing novels (*A Day in the Life of Ivan Denisovich*, *The Cancer Ward*) because he as yet lacked the freedom to write sermons and historical denunciations.

The situation in Communist China until the late 1970s was dominated by ruthless repression, underlined by rare momentary relaxation ('let a hundred flowers bloom') which served to identify the victims of the next purges. The regime of Mao Tse-tung reached its climax in the 'Cultural Revolution' of 1966–76, a campaign against culture, education and intelligence without parallel in twentieth-century history. It virtually shut down secondary and university education for ten years, brought the practice of (Western) classical and other music to a halt, where necessary by destroying its instruments, and reduced the national repertoire of stage and film to half-a-dozen politically correct pieces (as judged by the Great Helmsman's wife, once a second-rank Shanghai film actress), which were endlessly repeated. Given both this experience and the ancient Chinese tradition of imposing orthodoxy, which was modified but not abandoned in the post-Mao era, the light shining out of Communist China in the arts remained dim.

On the other hand, creativity flourished under the communist regimes of Eastern Europe, at least once orthodoxy was even slightly relaxed, as happened during de-Stalinisation. The film industry in Poland, Czechoslovakia and Hungary, hitherto not much heard of even locally, burst into unexpected bloom from the late fifties on, and for a while became one of the most distinguished sources of interesting movies anywhere. Until the collapse of communism, which also entailed the collapse of the mechanisms for cultural production in the countries concerned, even the revival of repression (after 1968 in Czechoslovakia, after 1980 in Poland) did not halt it, though the rather promising start of the East German film industry in the early 1950s had been brought to a stop by political authority. That an art so dependent on heavy state investment should have flourished artistically under communist regimes is more surprising than that creative literature should, for, after all, even under intolerant governments, books can be written 'for the bottom drawer' or for circles of friends.* However narrow the public for which they originally wrote, several of the writers won international admiration – the East Germans, who produced substantially more interesting talent than the prosperous Federal Republic, and the Czechs of the 1960s whose writings only reached the West via internal and external emigration after 1968.

What all these talents had in common was something that few writers and film-makers in the developed market-economies enjoyed, and Western theatre folk (a group given to uncharacteristic political radicalism dating back, in the USA and Britain, to the 1930s) dreamed about: the sense of being needed by their public. Indeed, in the absence of real politics and a free press, practitioners of the arts were the *only* ones who spoke for what their people, or at least the educated among them, thought and felt. These feelings were not confined to artists in communist regimes, but in other regimes where intellectuals were at odds with the prevalent political system, and, though not totally unrestricted, were free enough to express themselves in public. Apartheid in South Africa inspired its adversaries to more good literature than had come out of that subcontinent before. That most Latin American intellectuals south of Mexico between the 1950s and the 1990s were likely, at some point in their lives, to be political refugees, is not irrelevant to the cultural achievements of that part of the Western hemisphere. The same was true of Turkish intellectuals.

---

* However, the processes of copying remained incredibly laborious, since no technology later than the manual typewriter and carbon paper were available. For political reasons the pre-*perestroika* communist world did not use the xerox.

Nevertheless, there was more to the ambiguous flowering of some arts in Eastern Europe than their function as a tolerated opposition. Most of their younger practitioners had been inspired by the hope that their countries, even under unsatisfactory regimes, would in some way enter a new era after the horrors of wartime; some, more than cared to be reminded of it, had actually felt the wind of utopia in the sails of youth, at least in the first few post-war years. A few continued to be inspired by their times: Ismail Kadaré (1930–), perhaps the first Albanian novelist to make a mark on the outside world, became the mouth-piece not so much of Enver Hoxha's hardline regime as of a small mountain country which, under communism, won a place in the world for the first time (he emigrated in 1990). Most of the others sooner or later moved into varying degrees of opposition – yet, often enough, rejecting the only alternative offered to them (whether across the West German border or by Radio Free Europe), in a world of binary and mutually exclusive opposites. And even where, as in Poland, rejection of the existing regime became total, all but the youngest knew enough about their country's history since 1945 to pick shades of grey as well as the propagandist's black and white. That is what gives a tragic dimension to the films of Andrzej Wajda (1926–), their ambiguity to the Czech film-makers of the 1960s, then in their thirties, and the writers of the GDR – Christa Wolf (1929–), Heiner Müller (1929–) – disillusioned but not oblivious of their dreams.

Paradoxically, artists and intellectuals in both the (socialist) Second World and the various parts of the Third World enjoyed both prestige and relative prosperity and privilege, at least between bouts of persecution. In the socialist world they might be among the richest citizens and enjoy that rarest of all freedoms in those collective prison-houses, the right to travel abroad, or even to have access to foreign literature. Under socialism their political influence was zero, but in the various third worlds (and, after the fall of communism, briefly in the former world of 'really existing socialism') being an intellectual or even an artist was a public asset. In Latin America leading writers, almost irrespective of their political opinions, could expect diplomatic posts, preferably in Paris, where the location of UNESCO gave each country that wanted to several chances to place citizens in the neighbourhood of Left Bank cafés. Professors had always expected spells as cabinet ministers, preferably of economics, but the fashion of the late 1980s for persons connected with the arts to stand as presidential candidates (as a good novelist did in Peru), or actually to become presidents (as in post-communist Czecho-slovakia and Lithuania) seemed new, though it had precedents in earlier times among new states, both European and African, which were likely to give prominence to those few of their citizens who were known abroad, i.e. most likely concert pianists, as in 1918 Poland, French poets, as in Senegal, or dancers, as in Guinea. Still, novelists, dramatists, poets and musicians were political non-starters in most developed Western countries under any circumstances, even in intellectually-minded ones, except perhaps as potential Ministers of Culture (André Malraux in France, Jorge Semprún in Spain).

The public and private resources devoted to the arts were inevitably far greater than before in an era of unprecedented prosperity. Thus even the British government, never in the forefront of public patronage, spent well over £1 billion sterling on the arts in the late 1980s, whereas in 1939 it had been £900,000 (*Britain: An Official Handbook*, 1961, p. 222; 1990, p. 426). Private patronage was less important, except in the USA, where billionaires, encouraged by suitable fiscal concessions, supported education, learning and culture on a more munificent scale than anywhere else, partly out of a genuine appreciation of the higher things in life, especially among first-generation tycoons; partly because, in the absence of a formal social hierarchy, what might be called Medici-status was the next best thing. Increasingly the big spenders did not merely donate their collections to national or civic galleries (as in the past), but insisted on founding their own museums named after themselves, or at least their own wings or sectors of museums in which their own collections were presented in the form laid down by their owners and donors.

As for the art market, from the 1950s on it discovered that almost half a century of depression was lifting. Prices, especially of French Impressionists, post-Impressionists and the most eminent Parisian early modernists, rose into the sky, until in the 1970s the international art market, whose location shifted first to London and then to New York, had equalled the all-time records (in real terms) of the Age of Empire, and in the mad bull market of the 1980s soared beyond them. The price of Impressionists and post-Impressionists multiplied twenty-three-fold between 1975 and 1989 (Sotheby, 1992). However, comparisons with earlier periods were henceforth impossible. True, the rich still collected – old money, as a rule, preferring old masters, new money going for novelty – but increasingly art-purchasers bought for investment, as once men had bought speculative gold mining shares. The British Rail Pensions Fund, which (on the best advice) made a lot of money out of art, cannot be thought of as an art lover, and the ideal-typical art transaction of the late 1980s was one in which a Western Australian instant tycoon bought a Van Gogh for £31 million, a large part of which had been lent him by the auctioneers, both presumably hoping for further price rises which would make the picture a more valuable collateral for bank loans, and raise the dealer's future profits. As it happens, both were disappointed: Mr Bond of Perth went bankrupt and the speculative art boom collapsed in the early 1990s.

The relation between money and the arts is always ambiguous. It is far from clear that the major achievements of the arts in the second half of the century owed much to it; except in architecture, where, on the whole, big is beautiful, or, at any rate, more likely to get into the guidebooks. On the other hand, another kind of economic development unquestionably affected most of the arts profoundly; their integration into academic life, in the institutions of superior education whose extraordinary expansion we have noticed elsewhere (chapter 10). This development was both general and specific. Speaking generally, the decisive development of twentieth-century culture, the rise of a revolutionary popular entertainment industry geared to the mass market, reduced the traditional forms of high art to elite ghettoes, and from the middle of the century their inhabitants were essentially people who had enjoyed a higher education. The public of theatre and opera, the readers of their country's literary classics and the sort of poetry and prose taken seriously by the critics, the visitors to museums and art galleries belonged overwhelmingly to those who had at least completed secondary education – except in the socialist world where the profit-maximising entertainment industry was kept at bay – until, after its fall, it was no longer kept at bay. The common culture of any late twentieth-century urbanized country was based on the mass entertainment industry – cinema, radio, television, pop music – in which the elite shared, certainly from the triumph of rockmusic onwards, and to which intellectuals no doubt gave a highbrow twist to make it suitable for elite taste. Beyond this, segregation was increasingly complete, for the bulk of the public to which the mass market industry appealed only encountered by occasional accident, the genres that high-culture buffs raved about, as when a Puccini aria sung by Pavarotti found itself associated with the World Football Cup in 1990, or when brief themes from Handel or Bach appeared incognito in television commercials. If one did not want to join the middle classes one did not bother about seeing Shakespeare plays. Conversely, if one did, the most obvious means being to pass the requisite exams at secondary school, one could not avoid seeing them: they were the subject of examinations. In extreme cases, of which class-divided Britain was a notable example, newspapers addressed respectively to the educated and the uneducated virtually inhabited different universes.

More specifically, the extraordinary expansion of higher education increasingly provided employment, and constituted the market for men and women with inadequate commercial appeal. This was most dramatically exemplified in literature. Poets taught, or at least were resident at colleges. In some countries the occupation of novelist and professor overlapped to such an extent that an entirely new genre appeared in the 1960s and, since vast numbers of potential readers were familiar with the milieu, flourished: the campus novel which, apart from the usual subject-matter of fiction, the relation between the sexes, dealt with matters of more esoteric interest, such as academic exchanges, international colloquia, university gossip and the peculiarities of students. More dangerously, academic demand encouraged the production of creative writing that lent itself to seminar dissection, and therefore benefited by complexity, if not incomprehensibility, following the example of the great James Joyce, whose later work had as many commentators as genuine readers. Poets wrote for other poets, or for students expected to discuss their works. Protected by academic salaries, grants and obligatory reading lists, the non-commercial creative arts could hope, if not necessarily to flourish, then at least to survive in comfort. Alas, another by-product of the growth of academia undermined their position, for the glossators and scholiasts made themselves independent of their subject by claiming that the text was only what the reader made of it. The critic who interpreted Flaubert, they argued, was as much the creator of Madame Bovary as the author, perhaps – since that novel survived only through others' readings, mainly for academic purposes – even more than the author. This theory had long been hailed by avant-garde theatrical producers (anticipated by the actor-managers and film-moguls of old) for whom Shakespeare or Verdi were basically raw material for their own adventurous and preferably provocative interpretations. Triumphant though these sometimes were, they actually underlined the growing esotericism of the highbrow arts, for they were themselves commentaries upon and critiques of earlier interpretations, and not fully comprehensible except to initiates. The fashion spread even to the populist genre of films, where sophisticated directors advertised their cinematic erudition to the elite which understood their allusions while keeping the masses (and hopefully the box office) happy with blood and sperm.*

Is it possible to guess how the cultural histories of the twenty-first

---

* Thus Brian de Palma's *The Untouchables* (1987), ostensibly a rousing cops-and-robbers film about Al Capone's Chicago (though actually a pastiche of the original genre), contains a literal quote from Eisenstein's *Battleship Potemkin*, incomprehensible to all who had not seen the famous passage of the pram careering down the Odessa steps.

century will assess the artistic achievements of the high arts of the second half of the twentieth? Obviously not, but they will hardly fail to notice the decline, at least regionally, of characteristic genres that had flourished greatly in the nineteenth century, and survived into the first half of the twentieth. Sculpture is an example that springs to mind, if only because the main expression of this art, the public monument, virtually died out after the First World War, except in dictatorial countries, where, by general consent, quality did not equal quantity. It is impossible to avoid the impression that painting was not what it had been even between the wars. At all events it would be difficult to draw up a list of painters of 1950–1990 who would be accepted as major figures (e.g. worthy of inclusion in museums other than the artist's own country) comparable to such a list for the inter-war period. That, we may remind ourselves, would have included at the very least Picasso (1881–1973), Matisse (1869–1954), Soutine (1894–1943), Chagall (1889–1985) and Rouault (1871–1958) from the École de Paris; Klee (1879–1940), perhaps two or three Russians and Germans, and one or two Spaniards and Mexicans. How would a later twentieth-century list compare with these, even if it included several leaders of the New York School of 'abstract expressionists', Francis Bacon and couple of Germans?

In classical music, once again, the decline in the old genres was concealed by the enormous increase in their performance, but mainly in the form of a repertoire of dead classics. How many new operas, written after 1950, had established themselves in the international, or even any national, repertoires, which endlessly recycled the products of composers of whom the youngest had been born in 1860? Except for Germany and Britain (Henze, Britten and at best two or three others), very few composers even created grand operas. The Americans (e.g. Leonard Bernstein, 1918–90) preferred the less formal genre of the musical. How many composers other than the Russians any longer wrote symphonies, regarded as the crown of instrumental achievement in the nineteenth century?* Musical talent, which continued in plentiful and distinguished supply, simply tended to abandon the traditional forms of expression, even though these overwhelmingly dominated the high-art market

A similar retreat from the nineteenth-century genre is obvious in the novel. Naturally it continued to be written in vast quantities, bought and read. Yet if we look for the great novels and the great novelists of the second half of the century, the ones which took an entire society or

---

* Prokofiev wrote seven and Shostakovich fifteen, and even Stravinsky wrote three: but all these belonged, or had been formed in the first part of the century.

historical era as their subject, we find them outside the central regions of Western culture – except, once again, for Russia, where the novel re-surfaced, with the early Solzhenitsyn, as the major creative mode of coming to terms with the experience of Stalinism. We may find novels of the great tradition in Sicily (Lampedusa's *The Leopard*), in Yugoslavia (Ivo Andrić, Miroslav Krleža) and Turkey. We shall certainly find them in Latin America, whose fiction, hitherto unknown outside the countries concerned, captured the literary world from the 1950s on. The novel most unhesitatingly and instantly recognized as a masterpiece all over the globe came from Colombia, a country that most educated people in the developed world had trouble even identifying on a map before it became identified with cocaine: Gabriel García Márquez's *A Hundred Years of Solitude*. Perhaps the remarkable rise of the Jewish novel in several countries, notably the USA and Israel, reflects the exceptional trauma of its people's experience under Hitler, with which, directly or indirectly, Jewish writers felt they had to come to terms.

The decline of the classical genres of high art and literature was certainly not due to any shortage of talent. For even if we know little about the distribution of exceptional gifts among human beings and its variation, it is safer to assume that there are rapid changes in the incentives to express them, or in the outlets for expressing them, or in the encouragement to do so in some particular manner, rather than in the quantity of available talent. There is no good reason to assume that Tuscans today are less talented, or even have a less developed aesthetic sense than in the century of the Florentine Renaissance. Talent in the arts abandoned the old ways of seeking expression because new ways were available or attractive, or rewarding, as when, even between the wars, young avant-garde composers might be tempted, like Auric and Britten, to write soundtracks for films rather than string quartets. A great deal of routine painting and drawing was replaced by the triumph of the camera, which, to take one example, took over the representation of fashion almost completely. The serial novel, already a dying breed between the wars, gave way in the age of television to the screen serial. The film, which allowed far greater scope for individual creative talent after the collapse of the Hollywood studio system of factory production, and as the mass cinema audience melted into its homes to watch television and later video, took the place once occupied by both novel and drama. For every culture-lover who could fit two plays to the names of even five living playwrights, there were fifty who could reel off all the leading movies of a dozen or more film-directors. Nothing was more natural than this. Only the social status associated with old-fashioned 'high culture' prevented an even more rapid decline of its traditional genres.*

However, there were two even more important factors which now undermined classical high culture. The first was the universal triumph of the society of mass consumption. From the 1960s on the images which accompanied human beings in the Western world – and increasingly in the urbanized Third World – from birth to death were those advertising or embodying consumption or dedicated to commercial mass entertainment. The sounds which accompanied urban life, in and outdoors, were those of commercial pop music. Compared to these the impact of the 'high arts' on even the most 'cultured' was occasional at best, especially since the technology-based triumph of sound and image put severe pressure on what had been the major medium for the continuous experience of high culture, namely the printed word. Except for light entertainment – mainly love-stories for women, thrillers of various kinds for men and perhaps, in the era of liberalization, some erotica or pornography – people who read books seriously for other than professional, educational or other instructional purposes, were a smallish minority. Though the educational revolution expanded their numbers absolutely, ease of reading declined in countries of theoretically universal literacy, when print ceased to be the main gate to the world beyond mouth-to-ear communication. After the 1950s even the children of the educated classes in the rich Western world did not take to reading as spontaneously as their parents had done.

The words which dominated Western consumer societies were no longer the words of holy books, let alone of secular writers, but the brand-names of goods or whatever else could be bought. They were printed on T-shirts, attached to other garments like magical charms by means of which the wearer acquired the spiritual merit of the (generally youthful) life-style which these names symbolized and promised. The images that became the icons of such societies were those of mass entertainment and mass consumption: stars and cans. It is not surprising that in the 1950s, in the heartland of consumer democracy, the leading school of painters abdicated before image-makers so much more powerful than old-fashioned art. 'Pop Art' (Warhol, Lichtenstein, Rauschenberg, Oldenburg), spent its time reproducing, with as much accuracy and insensitivity as possible, the visual trappings of American commercialism: soup cans, flags, Coca-Cola bottles, Marilyn Monroe.

* A brilliant French sociologist analysed the use of culture as a class-marker in a book entitled *La Distinction* (Bourdieu, 1979).

Negligible as art (in the nineteenth-century sense of the word), this fashion nevertheless recognized that the triumph of the mass market was, in some profound ways, based on satisfying the spiritual as well as the material needs of consumers, a fact of which advertising agencies had long been vaguely aware when they geared their campaigns to selling 'not the steak but the sizzle', not soap but the dream of beauty, not tins of soup but family happiness. What became increasingly clear in the 1950s was that this had what could be called an aesthetic dimension, a grass-roots creativity, occasionally active but mainly passive, which producers had to compete to supply. The baroque excesses of 1950s Detroit automobile design had exactly this in view; and in the 1960s a few intelligent critics began to investigate what had previously been over-whelmingly dismissed and rejected as 'commercial' or just aesthetically null, namely what actually attracted men and women on the street (Banham, 1971). The older intellectuals, now increasingly described as 'elitist' (a word adopted with enthusiasm by the new radicalism of the 1960s), had looked down on the masses whom they saw as passive recipients of what big business wanted them to buy. Yet the 1950s demonstrated most dramatically through the triumph of rock-and-roll, an adolescents' idiom derived from the self-made urban blues of North American black ghettoes, that the masses themselves knew, or at least recognized what they liked. The recording industry, which made its fortunes from rock music, did not create let alone plan it, but took it over from the amateurs and small street-corner operators who discovered it. No doubt rock music was corrupted in the process. 'Art' (if that was the right word) was seen to come from the soil rather than from exceptional flowers growing out of it. Moreover, as the populism shared by both the market and anti-elitist radicalism held, the important thing about it was not to distinguish between good and bad, elaborate and simple, but at most between what appealed to more and fewer people. This did not leave much space for the old-fashioned concept of the arts.

Yet an even more powerful force undermined the high arts: the death of 'modernism' which had, since the late nineteenth century, legitimated the practice of non-utilitarian artistic creation and certainly had provided the justification for the artists' claim to freedom from all constraints. Innovation had been its core. On the analogy of science and technology, 'Modernity' tacitly assumed that art was progressive and therefore today's style was superior to yesterday's. It had been, by definition, the art of the *avant-garde*, a term which entered critical vocabulary in the 1880s, i.e. of minorities which in theory looked forward one day to capturing the majority, but in practice were happy as yet not to have done so.

Whatever its specific form, 'modernism' rested on the rejection of nineteenth-century bourgeois-liberal conventions in both society and art, and on the perceived need to create an art in some way suited to the technologically and socially revolutionary twentieth century, to which the arts and lifestyles of Queen Victoria, the Emperor William and President Theodore Roosevelt were so plainly unsuited (see *Age of Empire*, chapter 9). Ideally the two objectives went together: Cubism was both a rejection and critique of Victorian representative painting and an alternative to it, as well as a collection of 'works of art' by 'artists' in its and their own right. In practice they did not have to coincide, as the (deliberate) artistic nihilism of Marcel Duchamp's urinal and Dada had demonstrated long ago. These were not intended to be any kind of art, but anti-art. Again, ideally the social values which 'modernist' artists looked for in the twentieth century and the ways of expressing these in word, sound, image and shape should melt into each other, as they very largely did in modernist architecture, which was essentially a style for building social utopias in forms allegedly suited to it. Once again, in practice form and substance were not logically connected. Why, for instance, should Le Corbusier's 'radiant city' (*cité radieuse*) consist of high-rise buildings with flat roofs rather than pitched ones?

Nevertheless, as we have seen, in the first half of the century 'modernism' worked, the feebleness of its theoretical foundations unnoticed, the short distance to the limits of development permitted by its formulas (e.g. twelve-tone music or abstract art) not yet quite traversed, its fabric uncracked as yet by inner contradictions or potential fissures. Formal avant-garde innovation and social hope were still welded together by the experience of world war, world crisis and potential world revolution. The era of anti-fascism postponed reflection. Modernism still belonged to avant-garde and opposition, except among the industrial designers and advertising agencies. It had not won.

Except in the socialist regimes it shared the victory over Hitler. Modernism in art and architecture conquered the USA, filling the galleries and prestige corporation offices with 'abstract expressionists', and the business districts of American cities with the symbols of the 'international style' – elongated rectangular boxes standing on end, not so much scraping the sky as flattening their roofs against it: with great elegance, as in Mies van der Rohe's Seagram building, or just very high, like the World Trade Center (both in New York). On the old Continent, to some extent following the American trend, which now inclined to associate modernism with 'Western values', abstraction (non-figurative art') in the visual arts and modernism in architecture became part, sometimes the dominant part of the established cultural scene, even reviving in countries like Britain, where it had seemed to stagnate.

Yet from the end of the 1960s a marked reaction against it became increasingly manifest and, in the 1980s, fashionable under such labels as 'postmodernism'. It was not so much a 'movement' as a denial of any pre-established criteria of judgment and value in the arts, or indeed of the possibility of such judgments. In architecture, where this reaction first and most visibly made itself felt, it surmounted skyscrapers with Chippendale pediments, all the more provocative for having been built by the very co-inventor of the term 'international style', Philip Johnson (1906–). Critics for whom the spontaneously shaped Manhattan skyline had once been the model of the modern city-scape, discovered the virtues of the totally unstructured Los Angeles, a desert of detail without shape, the paradise (or hell) of those who 'did their own thing'. Irrational though they were, aesthetic-moral rules had governed modern architecture, but henceforth anything went.

The achievement of the modern movement in architecture had been impressive. It had, since 1945, built the airports that bound the world together, its factories, its office buildings and such public buildings as still needed to be erected – capital cities in the Third World, museums, universities and theatres in the First. It had presided over the massive and global rebuilding of cities in the 1960s, for even in the socialist world its technical innovations, which lent themselves to cheap and rapid construction of mass housing, left their mark. It had, without serious doubt, produced a substantial number of very beautiful buildings or even masterpieces, though also a number of ugly ones and very many more faceless and inhuman ant-boxes. The achievements of post-war modernist painting and sculpture were incomparably less and usually much inferior to their inter-war predecessors, as a comparison of Parisian art in the 1950s with that of the 1920s immediately demonstrates. It consisted largely of a series of increasingly desperate gimmicks by which artists sought to give their work an immediately recognizable individual trademark, a succession of manifestos of despair or abdication in the face of the floods of non-art which submerged the old-style artist (pop art, Dubuffet's *art brut* and the like), the assimilation of doodles and other bits and pieces, or of gestures reducing the sort of art which was primarily bought for investment and its collectors *ad absurdum*, as by adding an individual's name to piles of brick or soil ('minimal art') or by preventing it from becoming such a commodity through making it too short-lived to be permanent ('performance art').

The smell of impending death rose from these avant-gardes. The future was no longer theirs, though nobody knew whose it was. More than ever, they knew themselves to be on the margin. Compared to the real revolution in perception and representation achieved via technology by the money-makers, the formal innovations of studio bohemians had always been child's play. What were the Futurists' imitations of speed on canvas compared to real speed, or even to mounting a film camera on a locomotive footplate, which anyone could do? What were concert experiments with electronic sound in modernist compositions, which every impresario knew to be box office poison, compared to rock music which made electronic sound into the music of the millions? If all 'high arts' were segregated in ghettos, could the avant-gardes fail to observe that their own sections of the ghetto were tiny and diminishing, as any comparison of the sales of Chopin and Schoenberg confirmed? With the rise of pop art, even the major rampart of modernism in the visual arts, abstraction, lost its hegemony. Representation once again became legitimate.

'Postmodernism' therefore attacked both self-confident and exhausted styles, or rather the ways of conducting both activities which had to go on, in one style or another, like building and public works, and those which were not in themselves indispensable, like the artisan production of easel paintings to be sold singly. Hence it would be misleading to analyse it primarily as a trend within the arts, like the development of the earlier avant-gardes. Actually, we know that the term 'postmodernism' spread to all manner of fields that had nothing to do with the arts. By the 1990s there were 'postmodern' philosophers, social scientists, anthropologists, historians and other practitioners of disciplines that had not previously tended to borrow their terminology from the arts avant-garde, even when they happened to be associated with them. Literary criticism, of course, adopted it with enthusiasm. In fact 'postmodern' fashions, pioneered under various names ('deconstruction', 'post-structuralism' etc.) among the French-speaking intelligentsia, made their way into (US departments of literature and thence into the rest of the humanities and social sciences.

All 'postmodernisms' had in common an essential scepticism about the existence of an objective reality, and/or the possibility of arriving at an agreed understanding of it by rational means. All tended to a radical relativism. All, therefore, challenged the essence of a world that rested on the opposite assumptions, namely the world transformed by science and the technology based upon it, and the ideology of progress which reflected it. We shall consider the development of this strange, yet not unexpected contradiction in the next chapter. Within the more restricted field of the high arts, the contradiction was not so extreme since, as we have seen (*Age of Empire*, chapter 9), the modernist avant-gardes had already extended the limits of what could claim to be 'art' (or, at any rate, yield products that could be sold or leased or otherwise profitably separated from their creators as 'art') almost to infinity. What 'postmodernism' produced was rather a (largely generational) gap between those who were repelled by what they saw as the nihilist frivolity of the new mode and those who thought taking the arts 'seriously' was just one more relic of the obsolete past. What, they argued, was wrong with 'the refuse dumps of civilization . . . camouflaged with plastic' which so outraged the social philosopher Jürgen Habermas, last outpost of the famous Frankfurt School? (Hughes, 1988, p. 146).

'Postmodernism' was therefore not confined to the arts. Nevertheless, there were probably good reasons why the term should have first emerged from the art scene. For the very essence of the avant-garde arts was the search for ways of expressing what could not possibly be expressed in terms of the past, namely the reality of the twentieth century. This was one of the two branches of that century's great dream, the other being the search for the radical transformation of that reality. Both were revolutionary in different senses of the word, but both were about the same world. Both coincided to some extent in the 1880s and 1890s, and again between 1914 and the defeat of fascism, when creative talents were so often revolutionary, or at least radical, in both senses – usually but by no means always on the Left. Both were to fail, although in fact both have modified the world of 2000 so profoundly that their marks cannot conceivably be effaced.

In retrospect it is clear that the project of avant-garde revolution was doomed to failure from the outset, both by virtue of its intellectual arbitrariness and by the nature of the mode of production the creative arts represented in a liberal bourgeois society. Almost any of the numerous manifestos by means of which avant-garde artists have announced their intentions in the course of the past hundred years demonstrate the lack of coherence between ends and means, the object and the methods of achieving it. A particular version of novelty is not the necessary consequence of choosing to reject the old. Music which deliberately avoids tonality is not necessarily Schönberg's serial music, based on the permutations of the twelve notes of the chromatic scale; nor is this the only basis for serial music; nor is serial music necessarily atonal. Cubism, however attractive, had no theoretical rationale whatever. Indeed, the very decision to abandon traditional procedures and rules for new ones may be as arbitrary as the choice of particular novelties. The equivalent of 'modernism' in chess, the so-called 'hyper-modern' school of players of the 1920s

(Réti, Grünfeld, Nimzowitsch, *et al.*) did not propose to change the rules of the game, as some did. They merely reacted against convention (the 'classical' school of Tarrasch) by exploiting paradox – choosing unconventional openings ('After 1, P-K4 White's game is in the last throes') and observing rather than occupying the centre. Most writers, and certainly most poets, in practice did the same. They went on accepting the traditional procedures, e.g. rhymed and metred verse where it seemed appropriate, and broke with convention in other ways. Kafka was not less 'modern' than Joyce because his prose was less adventurous. Moreover, where modernist style claimed to have an intellectual rationale, e.g. as expressing the era of the machine or of (later) the computer, the connection was purely metaphorical. In any case, the attempt to assimilate 'the work of art in the era of its technical reproducibility' (Benjamin, 1961) to the old model of the individual creative artist recognizing only his personal inspiration was bound to fail. Creation was now essentially cooperative rather than individual, technological rather than manual. The young French film critics who, in the 1950s, developed a theory of film as the work of a single creative *auteur*, the director, on the basis, of all things, of a passion for the Hollywood B-movies of the 1930s and 1940s, were absurd because coordinated cooperation and division of labour was and is the essence of those whose business is to fill the evenings on public and private screens, or to produce some other regular succession of works for mental consumption, such as newspapers or magazines. The talents that went into the characteristic forms of twentieth-century creation, which were mainly products for, or by-products of the mass market, were not inferior to those of the classic nineteenth-century bourgeois model, but they could no longer afford the classical artist's role of the loner. Their only direct link with their classic predecessors was through that limited sector of the classic 'high arts' which had always operated through collectives: the stage. If Akira Kurosawa (1910–), Lucchino Visconti (1906–76) or Sergei Eisenstein (1898–1948) – to name only three unquestionably very great artists of the century, all with a theatrical background – had wished to create in the manner of Flaubert, Courbet or even Dickens, none of them would have got very far.

Yet, as Walter Benjamin observed, the era of 'technical reproducibility' transformed not only the way in which creation took place – thus making the film, and all that derived from it (television, video) into the central art of the century – but also the way in which human beings perceived reality and experienced creative works. This was no longer by means of those acts of secular worship and prayer for which the museums, galleries, concert halls and public theatres, that were so typical of nineteenth-century bourgeois civilisation, provided the churches. Tourism, which now filled these establishments with foreigners rather than natives, and education were the last strongholds of this sort of art-consumption. The numbers undergoing these experiences were, of course, enormously larger than ever before, but even most of these who, after elbowing themselves to within sight of the *Primavera* in the Florence Uffizi, stood in silent awe, or who were moved as they read Shakespeare as part of the examination syllabus, usually lived in a different multifarious and motley universe of perception. Sense impressions, even ideas, were apt to reach them simultaneously from all sides – through the combination of headlines and pictures, text and advertisement on the newspaper page, the sound in the earphone as the eye scanned the page, through the juxtaposition of image, voice, print and sound – all, as like as not, taken in peripherally, unless, for a moment, something concentrated attention. This had long been the way in which city people experienced the street, in which popular fairground and circus entertainment operated, familiar to artists and critics since the days of the Romantics. The novelty was that technology had drenched everyday life in private as well as in public with art. Never had it been harder to avoid aesthetic experience. The 'work of art' was lost in the flow of words, of sounds, of images, in the universal environment of what would once have been called art.

Could it still be so called? For those who cared for such things, great and lasting works could still be identified, though in the developed parts of the world the works exclusively created by a single individual and identifiable only with him or her became increasingly marginal. And so, with the exception of buildings, did single works of creation or construction that were not designed for reproduction. Could it still be judged and graded by the standards which had governed the assessment of these matters in the great days of bourgeois civilization? Yes and no. Measuring merit by chronology had never suited the arts: creative works had never been better merely because they were old, as was thought in the Renaissance, or because they were more recent than others, as the avant-gardes held. The latter criterion became absurd in the later twentieth century, when it merged with the economic interests of consumer industries, which made their profits out of a short fashion-cycle, and instant mass sales of articles for intensive but brief use.

On the other hand it was still both possible and necessary to apply the distinction between what was serious and what was trivial, between good and bad, professional and amateur in the arts, and all the more necessary because a number of interested parties denied such distinctions, on the grounds that the only measure of merit was the sales figure, or that they were elitist, or that, as postmodernism argued, no objective distinctions could be made at all. Indeed, only the ideologists and salesmen held such absurd views in public, and in their private capacity even most of these knew that they distinguished between good and bad. In 1991 a highly successful British mass market jeweller created a scandal by telling a conference of businessmen that his profits came from selling crap to people who had no taste for anything better. He, unlike postmodern theorists, knew that judgments of quality were part of life.

But if such judgments were still possible, were they still relevant to the world in which, for most urban citizens, the spheres of life and art, of emotion generated from within and emotion generated from without, or work and leisure, were increasingly indistinguishable? Or rather, were they still relevant outside the specialized enclosures of school and academia in which so much of the traditional arts were seeking refuge? It is difficult to say, because the very attempt to answer or to formulate such a question may beg it. It is quite easy to write the history of jazz or to discuss its achievements in terms quite similar to those applicable to classical music, allowing for the considerable difference in the social milieu, and the public and the economics of this form of art. It is by no means clear that such a procedure makes any sense for rock music, even though this is also derived from American black music. What the achievements of Louis Armstrong or Charlie Parker are, and their superiority over other contemporaries is or can be made clear. On the other hand it seems far more difficult for someone who has not fused a particular sound with his or her life, to pick out this or that rock group from the huge flood of sound which has swept down the valley of this music for the past forty years. Billie Holiday has (at least, until the time of writing) been able to communicate with listeners who were born many years after she died. Can anyone who was not a contemporary of the Rolling Stones develop anything like the passionate enthusiasm which this group aroused in the middle 1960s? How much of the passion for some sound or image today is based on association: not because the song is admirable but because 'this is our song'? We cannot tell. The role, or even the survival, of living arts in the twenty-first century are obscure until we can.

This is not the case with the roles of the sciences.

CHAPTER EIGHTEEN
Sorcerers and Apprentices –
The Natural Sciences

Do you think there is a place for philosophy in today's world?

Of, course, but only if it is based on the current state of scientific knowledge and achievement . . . Philosophers cannot insulate themselves against science. Not only has it enlarged and transformed our vision of life and the universe enormously: it has also revolutionized the rules by which the intellect operates.

– Claude Lévi-Strauss (1988)

The standard text in gas dynamics written by its author while on a Guggenheim Fellowship has been described by him as having had its form dictated by the needs of industry. Within this framework, confirming Einstein's theory of general relativity came to be seen as a critical step toward improving 'ballistic missile accuracy by accounting for minute gravitational effects'. Increasingly post-war physics narrowed its concentration into those areas thought to have military applications.

– Margaret Jacob (1993, pp. 66–7)

I

No period in history has been more penetrated by and more dependent on the natural sciences than the twentieth century. Yet no period, since Galileo's recantation, has been less at ease with it. This is the paradox with which the historian of the century must grapple. But before I try to do so, the dimensions of the phenomenon must be recognised.

In 1910 all the German and British physicists and chemists put together amounted to perhaps eight thousand people. In the late 1980s the number of scientists and engineers actually engaged in research and experimental development in the world was estimated at about five *millions*, of whom almost one million were in the USA, the leading scientific power, and a slightly larger number in the states of Europe.* Though scientists continued to form a tiny fraction of the population, even in the developed countries, their numbers continued to rise quite dramatically, more or less doubling in the twenty years after 1970, even in the most advanced economies. However, by the late 1980s they formed the tip of a much larger iceberg of what could be called potential scientific and technological manpower, which essentially reflected the educational revolution of the second half of the century (see chapter 10). It represented perhaps 2 per cent of the global population, and perhaps 5 per cent of the North American population (UNESCO, 1991, Table 5.1). The actual scientists were increasingly selected by means of an advanced 'doctoral thesis' which became the ticket of entry to the profession. In the 1980s the typical advanced Western country generated something like the 130–140 such science doctorates per year for each million of its inhabitants (Observatoire, 1991). Such countries also spent, mainly from public funds – even in the most capitalist countries – quite astronomic sums on such activities. Indeed, the most expensive forms of 'big science' were beyond the scope of any single country except (until the 1990s) the USA.

There was, however, one major novelty. In spite of the fact that 90 per cent of scientific papers (whose numbers doubled every ten years) appeared in four languages (English, Russian, French and German), Eurocentric science ended in the twentieth century. The Age of Catastrophe, and especially the temporary triumph of fascism, transferred its centre of gravity to the USA, where it has remained. Between 1900 and 1933 only seven science Nobel Prizes were awarded to the USA, but between 1933 and 1970 seventy-seven. The other countries of European settlement also established themselves as independent centres of research – Canada, Australia, the often under-rated Argentina† – though some, for reasons of size or politics, exported most of their major scientists (New Zealand, South Africa). At the same time the rise of non-European scientists, especially those from East Asia and the Indian subcontinent, was striking. Before the end of the Second World War only one Asian had won a science Nobel prize (C. Raman in physics, 1930); since 1946 such prizes

* The even larger number in the then USSR (about 1.5 millions) was probably not entirely comparable (UNESCO, 1991, Tables 5.2, 5.4, 5.16).

† Three Nobel prizes, all since 1947.

have been awarded to more than ten workers with obviously Japanese, Chinese, Indian and Pakistani names, and this clearly under-estimates the rise of Asian science as much as the pre-1933 record under-estimated the rise of US science. However, at the end of the century there were still parts of the world which generated notably few scientists in absolute terms and even more markedly in relative terms, e.g. most of Africa and Latin America.

Yet it is a striking fact that (at least) a third of the Asian laureates do not appear under their own country of origin, but as US scientists. (Indeed, of the US laureates twenty-seven are first-generation immigrants.) For, in an increasingly globalized world, the very fact that the natural sciences speak a single universal language and operate under a single methodology has paradoxically helped to concentrate them in the relatively few centres with adequate resources for their development, i.e. in a few highly developed rich states, and above all in the USA. The brains of the world, which in the Age of Catastrophe fled from Europe for political reasons, have since 1945 drained from poorer to richer countries mainly for economic ones.* This is natural, since in the 1970s and 1980s the developed capitalist countries spent almost three-quarters of all the world's outlays on research and development, whereas the poor countries ('developing') spent no more than 2–3 per cent (UN World Social Situation 1989, p. 103).

Yet, even within the developed world, science gradually lost dispersion, partly because of the concentration of people and resources – for reasons of efficiency – partly because the enormous growth in higher education inevitably created a hierarchy or, rather, an oligarchy among its institutes. In the 1950s and 1960s half the doctorates in the United States came from the fifteen most prestigious university graduate schools, to which the ablest young scientists consequently flocked. In a democratic and populist world, scientists were an elite, concentrated in a relatively few subsidized centres. As a species, they occurred in groups, for communication ('someone to talk to') was central to their activities. As time went on, these activities became ever more incomprehensible to non-scientists, though laymen tried desperately to understand, with the help of a large literature of popularisation, sometimes written by the best scientists themselves. Indeed, as specialization grew, even scientists increasingly

---

* A small temporary drain out of the USA during the McCarthyite years may be noted, and larger occasional political flights from the Soviet region (Hungary 1956, Poland and Czechoslovakia 1968, China and the USSR at the end of the 1980s), as well as a steady drain from the German Democratic Republic to West Germany.

required journals to explain to each other what was happening outside their own field.

That the twentieth century depended on science hardly needs proof. 'Advanced' science, that is to say, the kind of knowledge which could neither be acquired by everyday experience, nor practised nor even understood without many years of schooling, culminating in esoteric postgraduate training, had only a comparatively narrow range of practical applications until the end of the nineteenth century. The physics and mathematics of the seventeenth century governed the engineers, while, by the middle of Victoria's reign, chemical and electrical discoveries of the late eighteenth and early nineteenth centuries were already essential to industry and communications, and the explorations of professional scientific researchers were recognized as the necessary spearhead of even technological advance. In short, science-based technology was already at the core of the nineteenth-century bourgeois world, even though practical people did not quite know what to do with the triumphs of scientific theory except, in suitable cases, to turn them into ideology: as the eighteenth century had done with Newton and the late nineteenth century did with Darwin. Nevertheless, vast areas of human life continued to be ruled by little more than experience, experiment, skill, trained common sense and, at most, the systematic diffusion of knowledge about the best available practices and techniques. This was plainly the case in farming, building and medicine, and indeed over a vast range of activities which supplied human beings with their needs and luxuries.

Some time in the last third of the century this had begun to change. In the Age of Empire not only do the outlines of modern high technology begin to be visible – one has only to think of automobiles, aviation, radio and film – but so do those of modern scientific theory: relativity, the quantum, genetics. Moreover, the most esoteric and revolutionary discoveries of science were now seen to have immediate technological potential, from wireless telegraphy to the medical use of X-rays, both based on discoveries of the 1890s. Nevertheless, while the high science of the Short Twentieth Century was already visible before 1914, and while the high technology of the later century was already implicit in it, high science was not yet something without which everyday life *everywhere* on the globe was inconceivable.

This is the case as the millennium draws to its close. As we have seen (see chapter 9), technology based on advanced scientific theory and research, dominated the economic boom of the second half of the twentieth century, and no longer only in the developed world. Without state-of-the-art genetics India and Indonesia could not have produced enough food for their exploding populations, and by the end of the century biotechnology had become a significant element in both agriculture and medicine. The point about such technologies is that they were based on discoveries and theories so far from the world of the ordinary inhabitant of even the most sophisticated of developed countries that barely a few dozen or, at most, a few hundred persons in the world could initially grasp that they had practical implications. When the German physicist Otto Hahn discovered nuclear fission in 1937 even some of the scientists most active in the field, such as the great Niels Bohr (1885– 1962), doubted that it had practical applications in peace or war, at all events for the foreseeable future. And if the physicists who understood its potential had not told their generals and politicians, these would certainly have remained in ignorance, unless they were themselves postgraduate physicists, which was very unlikely. Again, Alan Turing's celebrated paper of 1935, which was to provide the foundation of modern computer theory, was originally written as a speculative exploration for mathematical logicians. The war gave him and others the occasion to translate theory into the beginnings of practice for the purpose of code-breaking, but when it appeared nobody except a handful of mathematicians even read, let alone took notice of Turing's paper. Even in his own college this clumsy-looking pale-faced genius, then a junior fellow with a taste for jogging, who posthumously became a sort of icon among homosexuals, was not a figure of any prominence; at least I do not remember him as such.* Even when scientists were plainly engaged in trying to solve problems of acknowledged capital importance, only a small huddle of brains in an isolated intellectual corner recognized what they were up to. Thus the present author was a Fellow of a Cambridge college at the very time when Crick and Watson were preparing their triumphant discovery of the structure of DNA (the 'Double Helix'), immediately recognized as

---

* Turing committed suicide in 1954, after having been convicted of homosexual behaviour, then officially a crime, and believed to be a medically or psychologically curable pathological condition. He could not stand the compulsory 'cure' imposed on him. He was not so much a victim of the criminalisation of (male) homosexuality in Britain before the 1960s as of his own failure to recognize it. His sexual proclivities had raised no problem whatever in the milieu of boarding school, King's College, Cambridge, and among the notorious collection of anomalies and eccentrics in the wartime code-breaking establishment at Bletchley, in which he had passed his life before going to Manchester after the war. Only a man who did not quite recognize the world most people lived in would have gone to the police to complain that a (temporary) boy-friend had robbed his apartment, thus giving the police the opportunity to catch two legal delinquents at the same time.

one of the crucial breakthroughs of the century. Yet, though I even recall meeting Crick socially at the time, most of us were simply not aware that these extraordinary developments were being hatched within a few tens of yards of my college gates, in laboratories we passed regularly and pubs where we drank. It was not that we took no interest in such matters. Those who pursued them simply saw no point in telling us about them, since we could not have contributed to their work, or probably even understood exactly what their difficulties were.

Nevertheless, however esoteric and incomprehensible the innovations of science, once made they were almost immediately translated into practical technologies. Thus transistors emerged as a by-product of researches in solid-state physics, i.e. the electro-magnetic properties of slightly imperfect crystals in 1948 (their inventors were given Nobel prizes within eight years), as did lasers (1960), which came not from optical studies but from work to make molecules vibrate in resonance with an electric field (Bernal, 1967, p. 563). Their inventors were also quickly recognized by Nobel prizes, as was – belatedly – the Cambridge and Soviet physicist Peter Kapitsa (1978) for work in low-temperature physics which produced superconductors. The experience of wartime research in 1939–46, which demonstrated – at least to the Anglo-Americans – that an overwhelming concentration of resources could solve the most difficult technological problems within an improbably short time,[*] encouraged technological pioneering regardless of cost, for purposes of war or national prestige (e.g. the exploration of cosmic space). This, in turn, accelerated the transformation of laboratory science into technology, some of which proved to have a wide potential for everyday use. Lasers are an example of this speed. First seen in the laboratory in 1960, they had by the early 1980s reached the consumer in the form of the compact disc. Biotechnology was even quicker off the mark. Recombinant DNA techniques, i.e. techniques for combining genes from one species with those of another, were first recognized as adequately practicable in 1973. Less than twenty years later biotechnology was a staple of medical and agricultural investment.

Moreover, thanks largely to the astonishing explosion of information

---

[*] Essentially it is now clear that Nazi Germany failed to make a nuclear bomb not because German scientists did not know how it could be made, or try to make it, with different degrees of reluctance, but because the German war-machine was unwilling or unable to devote the necessary resources to it. They abandoned the effort and switched to what seemed the more cost-effective concentration on rocketry, which promised quicker returns.

theory and practice, new scientific advances were translated, with ever-diminishing time-lags, into a technology that required no understanding whatever by the end-users. The ideal result was an entirely idiot-proof set of buttons or a keyboard which only required pressing in the right places to activate a self-acting, self-correcting and, so far as possible, decision-taking procedure which required no further inputs from the limited and unreliable skills and intelligence of the average human being. Indeed, ideally the procedure could be programmed to do without human intervention entirely, except when something went wrong. The supermarket check-out of the 1990s typified this elimination of the human element. It required no more of the human operator than to recognize the notes and coins of the local currency and to key in the quantity offered by the customer. An automatic scanner translated the bar-code on the purchase into a price, added up all the purchase prices, deducted the total from the amount offered by the customer and told the operator how much change to give. The procedure for ensuring the performance of all these activities is extraordinarily complex, resting as it does on a combination of enormously sophisticated hardware and very elaborate programming. Yet, unless or until something went wrong, such miracles of late twentieth-century scientific technology required no more of the operators than the recognition of the cardinal numbers, a minimal attention span and a rather greater capacity for concentrated tolerance of boredom. It did not even require literacy. So far as most operators were concerned, the forces which told them to inform the customer that he or she had to pay £2.15 and instructed them to offer £7.85 as change for a £10 note, were as irrelevant as they were incomprehensible. They did not have to understand anything about them to operate them. The sorcerer's apprentice no longer had to worry about his or her lack of knowledge.

For practical purposes the situation of the supermarket check-out operator represented the human norm of the late twentieth century; the operation of miracles of avant-garde scientific technology which we do not need to understand or modify, even if we know, or think we know, what is going on. Someone else will do or has done it for us. For, even if we suppose ourselves to be experts in one special field or another – i.e. the sort of person who could put the device right if it went wrong, or could design or construct it – faced with most of the other everyday products of science and technology, we are ignorant and uncomprehending laymen and lay women. And even if we were not, our understanding of what makes the thing we use work, and of the principles behind it, is largely irrelevant knowledge, as the technical process for manufacturing playing cards is to the (honest) poker-player. Fax machines are designed to be used by people who have no idea why the machine in London reproduces a text fed into it in Los Angeles. They do not function better when operated by professors of electronics.

Thus science, through the technology-saturated fabric of human life, demonstrates its miracles daily to the late twentieth-century world. It is as indispensable and omnipresent – for even the remoter corners of humanity know the transistor radio and the electronic calculator – as Allah is to the pious Moslem. We may debate when this capacity of certain human activities to produce superhuman results became part of the common consciousness, at least in the urban parts of 'developed' industrial societies. It certainly did so after the explosion of the first nuclear bomb in 1945. However, there can be no doubt that the twentieth century was the one in which science transformed both the world and our knowledge of it.

We should have expected the ideologies of the twentieth century to glory in the triumphs of science, which are the triumphs of the human mind, as the secular ideologies of the nineteenth century had done. Indeed, we should have expected even the resistance of traditional religious ideologies, the great redoubts of nineteenth-century resistance to science, to weaken. For not only did the hold of traditional religions slacken over most of the century, as we shall see, but religion itself became as dependent on high-science-based technology as any other human activity in the developed world. At a pinch, a bishop or imam or holy man in the 1900s could have conducted their activities as though Galileo, Newton, Faraday or Lavoisier had not existed, i.e. on the basis of fifteenth-century technology, and such nineteenth-century technology has raised no problems of compatability with theology or holy texts. It became far harder to overlook the conflict between science and holy writ in an age when the Vatican was obliged to communicate by satellite and to test the authenticity of the Turin shroud by radio-carbon dating: when the Ayatollah Khomeini spread his words from abroad into Iran by means of tape cassettes, and when states dedicated to the laws of the Koran were also engaged in trying to equip themselves with nuclear weapons. The *de facto* acceptance of the most sophisticated contemporary science, *via* the technology which depended on it, was such that in *fin-de-siècle* New York the sales of super-high-tech electronic and photographic goods became largely the specialty of Chassidim, a brand of eastern messianic Judaism chiefly known, apart from their extreme ritualism and insistence on wearing a version of eighteenth-century Polish costume, by a preference for ecstatic emotion over intellectual enquiry. In some ways the superiority of 'science' was even accepted officially. The Protestant fundamentalists in the USA who rejected the theory of evolution as unscriptural (the world having been created in its present version in six days) demanded that Darwin's teaching should be replaced, or at least countered by the teaching of what they described as 'creation science'.

And yet, the twentieth century was not at ease with the science which was its most extraordinary achievement, and on which it depended. The progress of the natural sciences took place against a background glow of suspicion and fear, occasionally flaring up into flames of hatred and rejection of reason and all its products. And in the undefined space between science and anti-science, among the searchers for ultimate truth by absurdity and the prophets of a world composed exclusively of fictions, we increasingly find that characteristic and largely Anglo-American product of the century, and especially of its second half, 'science fiction'. The genre, anticipated by Jules Verne (1828–1905) was initiated by H.G. Wells (1866–1946) at the very end of the nineteenth century. While its more juvenile forms, such as the familiar TV and wide-screen space-westerns with cosmic capsules as horses and death-rays as six-shooters, continued the old tradition of fantastic adventures with high-tech gadgets, in the second half of the century the more serious contributions to the genre veered towards a gloomy or at least an ambiguous view of the human condition and its prospects.

The suspicion and fear of science was fuelled by four feelings: that science was incomprehensible; that both its practical and moral consequences were unpredictable and probably catastrophic; and that it underlined the helplessness of the individual, and undermined authority. Nor should we overlook the sentiment that, to the extent that science interfered with the natural order of things, it was inherently dangerous. The first two feelings were shared by both scientists and laymen, the last two belonged mainly to outsiders. Lay individuals could only react against their sense of impotence by seeking out things which 'science could not explain' along the lines of Hamlet's 'There are more things on heaven and earth . . . than are dreamed of in your philosophy', by refusing to believe that they could ever be explained by 'official science', by hungering to believe in the inexplicable *because* it seemed absurd. At least in an unknown and unknowable world everyone would be equally powerless. The greater the palpable triumphs of science, the greater the hunger to seek the inexplicable. Shortly after the Second World War, which culminated in the atom bomb, Americans (1947), later followed as usual by their cultural followers the British, took to observing the mass arrival of 'unidentified flying objects', plainly inspired by science fiction. These, it was firmly believed, came from extra-terrestrial civilizations different from and superior to ours. The more enthusiastic observers had actually seen their strangely shaped denizens emerging from these 'flying saucers', and one or two even claimed to have been given rides by them. The phenomenon became world-wide, although a distribution-map of the landings of these extra-terrestrials would show a heavy preference for landing on or circling over Anglo-Saxon territories. Any scepticism about UFOs was put down to the jealousy of narrow-minded scientists helpless to explain phenomena beyond their narrow horizons, perhaps even to a conspiracy of those who kept the common man in intellectual bondage to conceal superior wisdom from him.

These were not the beliefs in magic and miracles of traditional societies, for which such interventions in reality were part of very incompletely controllable lives, and much less amazing than, say, the sight of an airplane or the experience of speaking into a telephone. Nor were they part of the universal and permanent fascination of human beings with the monstrous, the freakish and the marvellous to which popular literature bears witness since the invention of printing, from broadsheet woodcut to US supermarket check-out magazine. They were a rejection of the claims and the rule of science, sometimes consciously so, as in the extraordinary (and once again US-centred) rebellion of fringe groups against the practice of putting fluoride into the water supply after it had been discovered that an intake of this element would dramatically reduce dental decay in modern urban populations. It was passionately resisted not merely in the name of the freedom to choose caries but (by its more extreme opponents) as a dastardly plot to enfeeble human beings by compulsory poisoning. And in this reaction, vividly brought to life in Stanley Kubrik's film *Dr Strangelove* (1963), suspicion of science as such merged with fear of its practical consequences.

The built-in valetudinarianism of North American culture also spread such fears, as life was increasingly submerged by modern technology, including medical technology, with its risks. The unusual fondness of the USA for letting litigation answer all matters in human dispute, allows us to monitor these fears (Huber, 1990, pp. 97–118). Did spermicides cause birth defects? Did electric power – lines cause medical harm to people who lived near them? The gap between experts, who had some criterion for judgment, and lay persons, who had only hope or fear, was widened by the difference between dispassionate assessment, which might well judge a small degree of risk to be a price worth paying for a large degree of benefit, and individuals who, understandably, desired zero risk (at least in theory).*

---

* The difference between theory and practice in this area is enormous, since people who are prepared to run quite significant risks in practice (e.g. being in a car

In effect, such fears were the fears of the unknown menace of science by men and women who only knew that they lived under its dominion; fears whose intensity and focus differed according to the nature of their views, and fears about contemporary society (Fischhof et al., 1978, pp. 127–52).*

However, in the first half of the century, the major hazards to science came not from those who felt humbled by its unlimited and uncontrollable powers but from those who thought they could control them. The only two types of political regimes (apart from the then rare reversions to religious fundamentalism) which interfered with scientific research *on principle* were both deeply committed to technical progress without limit and, in one case, to an ideology which identified it with 'science' and hailed the conquest of the world by reason and experiment. Yet in different ways both Stalinism and German National Socialism rejected science even as they used it for technological purposes. What they objected to was its challenge to world-views and values expressed in *a priori* truths.

Thus neither regime felt at ease with post-Einsteinian physics. The Nazis rejected it as 'Jewish' and the Soviet ideologists as insufficiently 'materialist' in Lenin's sense of the word, though both tolerated it in practice, since modern states could not do without the physicists who were post-Einsteinians to a man or woman. The National Socialists, however, deprived themselves of the flower of continental Europe's physical talent by driving Jews and ideological opponents into exile, incidentally destroying the early twentieth-century German scientific supremacy in the process. Between 1900 and 1933 twenty-five out of sixty-six Nobel prizes in Physics and Chemistry had gone to Germany, but since 1933 only about one in ten. Neither regime was in tune with the biological sciences either. Nazi Germany's racial policies horrified serious geneticists, who – largely because of racists' enthusiasm for eugenics – had begun after the First World War to put some distance between themselves and policies of human genetic selection and breeding

---

on a motorway or using the subway in New York) may insist on avoiding aspirin on the grounds that it has side-effects in some rather rare cases.

* Participants rated the risks and benefits of twenty-five technologies: refrigerators, photocopy machines, contraceptives, suspension bridges, nuclear power, electronic games, diagnostic X-rays, nuclear weapons, computers, vaccinations, water fluoridation, roof-top solar collectors, lasers, tranquillizers, Polaroid photographs, fossil electric power, motor vehicles, movie special effects, pesticides, opiates, food preservatives, open-heart surgery, commercial aviation, genetic engineering and windmills. (Also Wildavsky, 1990, pp. 41–60.)

(which included the killing of the 'unfit'), although it must be sadly admitted that there was a good deal of support for National Socialist racism among German biologists and medical men (Proctor, 1988). The Soviet regime, under Stalin, found itself at odds with genetics both for ideological reasons and because state policy was committed to the principle that, with sufficient effort, *any* change was achievable, whereas science pointed out that, in the field of evolution in general and agriculture in particular this was not the case. In other circumstances the controversy among evolutionary biologists between the followers of Darwin (for whom inheritance was genetic) and those of Lamarck (who had believed in the inheritance of characteristics acquired and practised during a creature's lifetime) would have been left to be settled in seminars and laboratories. Indeed, it was regarded by most scientists as settled in favour of Darwin, if only because no satisfactory evidence for the inheritance of acquired characteristics had ever been found. Under Stalin, a fringe biologist, Trofim Denisovich Lysenko (1898–1976), won the support of the political authorities with the argument that farm output could be multiplied by Lamarckian procedures which short-circuited the relatively slow processes of orthodox plant – and animal-breedings. In those days it was unwise to disagree with authority. Academician Nikolai Ivanovich Vavilov (1885–1943), the most famous of Soviet geneticists, died in a labour camp for disagreeing with Lysenko (a view shared by the rest of serious Soviet geneticists), though it was not until after the Second World War that Soviet biology was officially committed to the obligatory rejection of genetics, as understood in the rest of the world, at least until after the dictator's demise. The effect of such policies on Soviet science was, predictably, disastrous.

Regimes of the National Socialist and Soviet communist type, utterly different as they were in many respects, shared the belief that their citizens were supposed to assent to a 'true doctrine', but one formulated and imposed by the secular politico/ideological authorities. Hence the ambiguity and uneasiness about science, which was felt in so many societies, found *official* expression in such states, unlike in political regimes which were agnostic about their citizens' individual beliefs, as secular governments had learned to be during the long nineteenth century. In fact, the rise of regimes of secular orthodoxy was, as we have seen (see chapters 4 and 13), a by-product of the Age of Catastrophe, and they did not last. In any case, the attempt to force science into ideological strait-jackets was plainly counter-productive, where it was seriously made (as in Soviet biology), or ridiculous, where science was left to go its own way, while the superiority of ideology was merely asserted (as in both German and Soviet physics).* The official imposition of criteria for scientific theory in the later twentieth century was once again left to regimes based on religious fundamentalism. Nevertheless, the uneasiness persisted, not least because science itself became increasingly incredible and uncertain. But until the second half of the century it was not due to fear of the practical results of science.

True, scientists themselves knew better and earlier than anyone else what the potential consequences of their discoveries might be. Ever since the time the first atom bomb became operational (1945) some of them had warned their masters in government of the destructive forces the world now had at its disposal. Yet the idea that science equals potential catastrophe essentially belonged to the second half of the century: in its first phase – the nightmare of nuclear war – to the era of superpower confrontation after 1945; in its later and more universal phase, to the era of crisis that opened in the 1970s. However, the Age of Catastrophe, perhaps because it strikingly slowed down world economic growth, was still one of scientific complacency about man's ability to control the powers of nature, or, at worst, about nature's ability to adjust to the worst that man could do.† On the other hand, what made scientists themselves uneasy then was their own uncertainty about what to make of their theories and findings.

II

Some time during the Age of Empire the links had snapped between the findings of scientists and the reality based on, or imaginable by sense experience; and so did the links between science and the sort of logic based on, or imaginable by common sense. The two breaks reinforced one another, since the progress of the natural sciences became increasingly dependent on people writing equations (i.e. mathematical sentences) on pads of paper, rather than experimenting in laboratories. The twentieth century was to be the century of the theoreticians telling the practitioners what they were to look for and should find in the light of their theories; in other words, the century of the mathematicians. Molecular biology, in

* Thus in Nazi Germany Werner Heisenberg was allowed to teach relativity, but on condition that the name of Einstein should not be mentioned (Peierls, 1992, p. 44).

† 'One may sleep in peace with the consciousness that the Creator has put some foolproof elements into his handiwork, and that man is powerless to do it any titanic damage,' wrote Robert Millikan of Caltech (Nobel Prize, 1923) in 1930.

which, good authority informs me, there is as yet very little theory, is an exception. Not that observation and experiment were secondary. On the contrary, their technology was more profoundly revolutionized than at any time since the seventeenth century by new devices and new techniques, several of which were to be given the ultimate scientific accolade of Nobel prizes.* To give only one example, the limitations of merely optical magnification were overcome by the electron microscope (1937) and the radio telescope (1957), with the result that a far deeper observational penetration into the molecular and even atomic realm and into the remotenesses of the universe became possible. In recent decades the automation of routine, and increasingly more complex forms of laboratory activity and calculation, as by computers, has further and enormously raised the powers of experimenters, observers, and increasingly of the model-building theorists. In some fields, notably in astronomy, this led to the making of discoveries, sometimes by accident, which subsequently compelled theoretical innovation. Modern cosmology is at bottom the result of two such discoveries: Hubble's observation that the universe must be expanding, based on the analysis of the spectra of galaxies (1929); and Penzias' and Wilson's discovery of the cosmic background radiation (radio noise) in 1965. Nevertheless, while science is and must be a collaboration between theorists and practitioners, in the Short Twentieth Century the theorists were in the driving seat.

For the scientists themselves, the break with sense experience and common sense meant a break with the traditional certainties of their field and its methodology. Its consequences can be most vividly illustrated by following the unquestioned queen of sciences in the first half of the century, physics. Indeed, inasmuch as this discipline is still the one concerned both with the smallest elements of all matter, live or dead, and with the constitution and structure of the largest ensemble of matter, namely the universe, physics remained the central pillar of the natural sciences even at the end of the century, though in the second half it had increasing competition from the life sciences, transformed after the 1950s by the revolution in molecular biology.

No field of the sciences seemed more firm, coherent, and methodologically certain than the Newtonian physics whose foundations were undermined by the theories of Planck and Einstein and the transformation of atomic theory that followed on the discovery of radioactivity in the 1890s.

---

* Well over twenty Nobel prizes in Physics and Chemistry since the First World War have been given wholly or partly for new research methods, devices and techniques.

It was objective, i.e. it could be adequately observed, subject to technical limitations in the observing apparatus (e.g. of the optical microscope or telescope). It was unambiguous: an object or phenomenon was either one thing or something else, and the distinction between these was clear. Its laws were universal, equally valid at the cosmic and the microcosmic level. The mechanism linking phenomena were understandable (i.e. capable of being expressed as 'cause and effect'). Consequently, the entire system was in principle determinist, and the purpose of the laboratory experiment was to demonstrate this determinacy by eliminating, so far as possible, the complex muddle of ordinary life which concealed it. Only a fool or a child would claim that the flight of birds and butterflies negated the laws of gravitation. Scientists knew quite well that there were 'non-scientific' statements, but these were not their concern as scientists.

All these characteristics were put into question between 1895 and 1914. Was light a continuous wave motion or an emission of discrete particles (photons) as Einstein held, following Planck? Sometimes it was best to treat it as one, sometimes as the other, but how, if at all, were they connected? What was light 'really'? As the great Einstein himself stated, twenty years after having created the puzzle: 'We now have two theories of light, both indispensable, but, it must be admitted, without any logical connection between them, despite twenty years of colossal effort by theoretical physicists.' (Holton, 1970, p. 1017). What was happening inside the atom, which was now seen to be not (as its original Greek name implied) the smallest possible, and therefore indivisible, unit of matter, but a complex system consisting of a variety of even more elementary particles? The first assumption, after Rutherford's great discovery of the atomic nucleus in 1911 in Manchester – a triumph of the experimental imagination and the foundation of modern nuclear physics and of what eventually became 'big science' – was that electrons circulated in orbits round this nucleus in the manner of a miniaturized solar system. Yet when the structure of individual atoms was investigated, notably that of hydrogen by Niels Bohr, who knew about Max Planck's 'quanta', in 1912–13, the results showed, once again, a profound conflict between what his electrons did and – his own words – 'the admirably coherent group of conceptions which have been rightly termed the classical theory of electrodynamics' (Holton, 1970, p. 1028). Bohr's model worked, i.e. it had brilliant explanatory and predictive force, but it was 'quite irrational and absurd' from the point of view of classical Newtonian mechanics, and in any case disclaimed any idea of what actually happened inside the atom as the electron 'leaped' or otherwise got from one orbit to another, or what happened between the moment when it was discovered in one and when it appeared in another.

What, indeed, happened to the certainties of science itself, as it became clear that the very process of observing phenomena at the subatomic level actually changes them: for this reason the more precisely we want to know the position of a sub-atomic particle, the more uncertain must be its velocity. It has been said of any means of detailed observation to find out where an electron 'really' is: 'To look at it means to knock it out' (Weisskopf, 1980, p. 37). This was the paradox which a brilliant young German physicist, Werner Heisenberg, in 1927 generalized into the famous 'uncertainty principle' that bears his name. The very fact that the name concentrates on *uncertainty* is significant, since it indicates what was worrying the explorers of the new scientific universe as they left the certainties of the old one behind them. It was not that they themselves were uncertain or produced doubtful results. On the contrary, their theoretical predictions, however implausible and bizarre, were verified by humdrum observation and experiment, from the time Einstein's theory of general relativity (1915) appeared to be verified in 1919 by a British eclipse expedition which found that light from some distant stars was deflected towards the sun, as predicted by the theory. For practical purposes particle physics was as subject to regularity and as predictable as Newtonian physics, though in a different way; and in any case at the supra-atomic level Newton and Galileo remained completely valid. What made scientists nervous was that they did not know how to fit the old and the new together.

Between 1924 and 1927 the dualities which so troubled physicists in the first quarter of the century were eliminated, or rather side-stepped, by a brilliant coup of mathematical physics, the construction of 'quantum mechanics', almost simultaneously devised in a number of countries. The true 'reality' within the atom was not wave or particle, but indivisible 'quantum states' which were potentially manifested as either or both. It was pointless to regard it as continuous or discontinuous movement, because we cannot, now or ever, follow the path of the electron step by step. Classical physical concepts such as position, velocity or momentum simply do not apply beyond certain points, marked out by Heisenberg's 'uncertainty principle'. But, of course, beyond these points other concepts apply, which produce far from uncertain results. These arise from the specific patterns produced by the 'waves' or vibrations of (negatively charged) electrons, kept within the confined space of the atom near the (positive) nucleus. Successive 'quantum states' within this confined space produce well-defined patterns of different frequencies which, as Schrödinger showed in 1926, could be calculated, as could the energy corresponding to each ('wave mechanics'). These electron patterns had quite remarkable predictive and explanatory power. Thus many years later, when plutonium was first produced in nuclear reactions at Los Alamos, on the way to constructing the first atomic bomb, the quantities were so small that its properties could not be observed. However, from the number of electrons in the atom of this element, and from the patterns of these ninety-four electrons vibrating round the nucleus, *and from nothing else*, scientists predicted (correctly) that plutonium would turn out to be a brown metal with a specific mass of about twenty grams per cubic centimetre, and possess a certain electric and thermal conductivity and elasticity. Quantum mechanics also explained why atoms (and the molecules and higher combinations based on them) remain stable, or rather what extra input of energy would be necessary to change them. Indeed it has been said that

> even the phenomena of life – the shape of DNA and the fact that different nucleotides are resistant to thermal motion at room temperature – are based on those primal patterns. The fact that every spring the same flowers emerge is based on the stability of the patterns of the different nucleotides (Weisskopf, 1980, pp. 35–38).

Yet this great and astonishingly fruitful advance in the exploration of nature was achieved on the ruins of all that had been considered certain and adequate in scientific theory, and by a willed suspension of disbelief, which not only the older scientists found troublesome. Consider the 'antimatter' which Paul Dirac proposed from Cambridge, after he discovered (1928) that his equations had solutions corresponding to electron states with an energy *less* than the zero energy of empty space. The concept of 'antimatter', meaningless in everyday terms, was happily manipulated by physicists thereafter (Steven Weinberg, 1977, pp. 23–4). The mere word itself implied a deliberate refusal to allow the progress of theoretical calculation to be diverted by any preconceived notion of reality: whatever reality turned out to be, it would catch up with the equations. And yet, it was not easy to accept this, even for scientists who had long put behind them the great Rutherford's view that no physics could be good unless it could be explained to a barmaid.

There were pioneers of the new science who simply found it impossible to accept the end of the old certainties, not least its founders, Max Planck and Albert Einstein himself, who expressed his suspicion of purely probabilistic laws rather than determinist causality in a well-known phrase: 'God does not play dice'. He had no valid arguments, but 'an inner voice tells me that Quantum mechanics is not the real truth' (cited in M. Jammer, 1966, p. 358). More than one of the quantum revolutionaries themselves had dreamed of eliminating the contradictions by subsuming one side under the other: Schrödinger hoped his 'wave mechanics' had dissolved the supposed 'jumps' of electrons from one atomic orbit to another, into the *continuous* process of energy change, and, in doing so, preserve classical space, time and causality. Reluctant pioneer revolutionaries, notably Planck and Einstein, sighed with relief, but in vain. The ballgame was new. The old rules no longer held good.

Could physicists learn to live with permanent contradiction? Niels Bohr thought they could and must. There was no way of expressing the wholeness of nature in a single description, given the nature of human language. There could be no single, directly comprehensive model. The only way of seizing reality was by reporting it in different ways, and putting them all together to complement each other in an 'exhaustive overlay of different descriptions that incorporate apparently contradictory notions' (Holton, 1970, p. 1018). This was Bohr's principle of 'complementarity', a metaphysical concept akin to relativity which he derived from writers far removed from physics, and regarded as having universal applicability. Bohr's 'complementarity' was not intended to advance the research of the atomic scientists, but rather to comfort them by justifying their confusions. Its appeal lies outside the field of reason. For while we all, and not least intelligent scientists, know that there are different ways of perceiving the same reality, sometimes non-comparable or even contradictory, but all needed to grasp it in its totality, we still have no idea how we connect them. The effect of a Beethoven sonata can be analysed physically, physiologically and psychologically, and it can also be absorbed by listening to it: but how are these modes of understanding connected? Nobody knows.

Nevertheless, the uneasiness remained. On the one hand there was the mid-1920s synthesis of the new physics, which provided an extraordinarily effective way of breaking into the bank-vaults of nature. The basic concepts of the quantum revolution were still being applied in the late twentieth century. Unless we follow those who see the non-linear analysis, made possible by computing, as a radically new departure, there has been no revolution in physics since 1900–27, but only vast evolutionary advances within the same conceptual framework. On the other hand, there was generalized incoherence. In 1931 that incoherence was extended to the ultimate redoubt of certainty, mathematics. An Austrian mathematical logician, Kurt Gödel, proved that a system of axioms can never be based on itself. If it is to be shown as being consistent, statements from outside the system must be used. In the light of 'Gödel's theorem', a non-contradictory internally consistent world could not even be thought of.

Such was the 'crisis in physics', to cite the title of a book by a young British Marxist autodidact intellectual who was killed in Spain, Christopher Caudwell (1907–37). It was not only a 'crisis of the foundations', as the period 1900–30 has been called in mathematics (see *Age of Empire*, chapter 10) but also of the scientists' general world picture. Indeed, as the physicists learned to shrug their shoulders about philosophical questions, while they plunged into the new territory opening before them, the second aspect of the crisis became ever more obtrusive. For in the 1930s and 1940s the structure of the atom became more complicated year by year. Gone was the simple duality of positive nucleus and negative electron(s). Atoms were now inhabited by a growing fauna and flora of elementary particles, some of them very strange indeed. Chadwick of Cambridge discovered the first of these in 1932, the electrically neutral neutrons – though others, such as the massless and electrically neutral neutrino, had already been predicted on theoretical grounds. These subatomic particles, almost all shortlived and fleeting, multiplied, particularly under the bombardment of the high-energy accelerators of 'big science' which became available after the Second World War. By the end of the 1950s there were more than a hundred of them, and no end was in sight. The picture was still further complicated, from the early 1930s, by the discovery of two unknown and obscure forces at work within the atom, in addition to the electrical ones that bonded nucleus and electrons together. The so-called 'strong force' bonded neutron and positively charged proton together in the atomic nucleus, and the so-called 'weak force' was responsible for certain kinds of particle decay.

Now in the conceptual debris on which the twentieth-century sciences were built, one basic and essentially aesthetic assumption was not challenged. Indeed, as uncertainty clouded all the others, it became increasingly central to scientists. Like the poet Keats, they believed that 'Beauty is truth, truth beauty', though their criterion of beauty was not his. A beautiful theory, which was in itself a presumption of truth, must be elegant, economical and general. It must unify and simplify, as the great triumphs of scientific theory had hitherto done. The scientific revolution of Galileo and Newton's time had shown that the same laws govern heaven and earth. Chemical revolution had reduced the endless variety of forms in which matter appeared to ninety-two systematically connected elements. The triumph of nineteenth-century physics had been to show that electricity, magnetism and optical phenomena had the same roots.

Yet the new revolution in science produced not simplification but complication. Einstein's marvellous relativity theory, which described gravitation as a manifestation of the curvature of spacetime, actually introduced a troubling duality into nature: 'on the one hand was the stage – the curved spacetime, gravity; on the other hand the actors – the electrons, the protons, the electromagnetic fields – and there was no link between them' (Steven Weinberg, 1979, p. 43). For the last forty years of his life Einstein, the Newton of the twentieth century, laboured to produce a 'unified field theory' which would unify electromagnetism with gravitation, but he failed – and now there were two more apparently unconnected classes of force in nature with no apparent relations with electromagnetism and gravitation. The multiplication of subatomic particles, however exciting, could only be a temporary, a preliminary truth because, however pretty in detail, there was no beauty in the new atom as there had once been in the old. Even the pure pragmatist of the era for which the only criterion of a hypothesis was that it worked, had at least sometimes to dream of a noble, beautiful and general 'theory of everything' (to use the phrase of a Cambridge physicist (Stephen Hawking). But it appeared to recede into the distance, although from the 1960s on physicists began, once again, to discern the possibility of such a synthesis. Indeed, by the 1990s there was a widespread belief among physicists that they were nearly down to some really basic level, and that the multiplicity of elementary particles could be reduced to a relatively simple and coherent grouping.

At the same time on the undefined borders between such widely disparate subjects as meteorology, ecology, non-nuclear physics, astronomy, fluid dynamics and various branches of mathematics independently pioneered in the Soviet Union and (slightly later) in the West, and aided by the extraordinary development of computers as an analytical tool and a visual inspiration, a new branch of synthesis was emerging – or re-emerging – under the somewhat misleading name of 'chaos theory'. For what it revealed was not so much the unpredictable results of perfectly determinist scientific procedures, but the extraordinary universality of the shapes and patterns of nature in its most disparate and apparently unconnected manifestations.* Chaos theory helped to put a new spin, as it were, on old causality. It broke the links between causality and predictability, for its essence was not that events were fortuitous but

---

* The development of 'chaos theory' in the 1970s and 1980s has something in common with the emergence in the early nineteenth century of a 'romantic' school of science, mainly centred in Germany ('*Naturphilosophie*') in reaction against the 'classical' mainstream, centred in France and Britain. It is interesting that two

that the effects which followed specifiable causes could not be predicted. It reinforced another development, pioneered among palaeontologists, and of considerable interest to historians. This suggests that chains of historical or evolutionary development are perfectly coherent and capable of explanation *after* the fact, but that eventual results cannot be predicted from the outset, because, if the same course was set again, any early change, however slight and without apparent importance at the time, 'and evolution cascades into a radically different channel' (Gould, 1989, p. 51). The political, economic and social consequences of this approach may be far-reaching.

Furthermore, there was the sheer absurdity of much of the new physicists' world. So long as it was confined within the atom, it did not directly affect ordinary life, which even scientists live, but at least one new and unassimilated discovery could not be so quarantined. This was the extraordinary fact, predicted by some on the basis of relativity theory, but observed by the American astronomer E. Hubble in 1929, that the entire universe appeared to be expanding at a dizzying rate. This expansion, which even many scientists found hard to swallow, some devising alternative 'steady state' theories of the cosmos, was verified by other astronomical data in the 1960s. It was impossible not to speculate where this expansion was taking it (and us), when and how it began, and therefore about the history of the universe, starting with the initial 'Big Bang'. This produced the flourishing field of cosmology, the part of twentieth-century science most readily turned into bestsellers. It also enormously increased the element of history in natural sciences hitherto (except for geology and its by-products) proudly uninterested in it, and incidentally diminished the identification of 'hard' science with experiment, i.e. with reproduction of natural phenomena. For how could events unrepeatable by definition be repeated? The expanding universe thus added to the confusion of both scientists and lay persons.

This confusion confirmed those who lived through the Age of Catastrophe, and knew or thought about such matters, in their conviction that an old world had ended, or, at the very least, was in terminal upheaval, but that the contours of the new one were not yet clearly discernible. The great Max Planck had no doubt of the link between the crisis in science and in outside life:

---

eminent pioneers of the new research (Feigenbaum, Libchaber – see Gleick, pp. 163, 197) were actually inspired by reading Goethe's passionately anti-Newtonian theory of colours, and his treatise on *The Transformation of Plants*, which may be regarded as a prospectively anti-Darwinian/evolutionary theory (For *Naturphilosophie*, see *Age of Revolution*, chapter 15).

We are living in a very singular moment of history. It is a moment of crisis in the literal sense of that word. In every branch of our spiritual and material civilization we seem to have arrived at a critical turning point. This spirit shows itself not only in the actual state of public affairs, but also in the general attitude towards fundamental values in personal and social life . . . Now the iconoclast has invaded the temple of science. There is scarcely a scientific axiom that is not nowadays denied by somebody. And at the same time almost any nonsensical theory would be almost sure to find believers and disciples somewhere or other (Planck, 1933, p. 64).

Nothing was more natural than that a middle-class German brought up in the nineteenth century certainties should express such sentiments in the days of the Great Slump, and Hitler's rise to power.

Nevertheless, gloom was the opposite of what most scientists felt. They agreed with Rutherford who told the British Association (1923) that 'we are living in the heroic age of physics' (Howarth, 1978, p. 92). Every issue of the scientific journals, every colloquium – for most scientists loved, more than ever, to combine cooperation and competition – brought new, exciting and profound advances. The scientific community was still small enough, at least in spearhead subjects like nuclear physics and crystallography, to offer almost every young researcher the prospect of stardom. To be a scientist was to be envied. Certainly those of us who were students in Cambridge, which produced most of the thirty British Nobel prizes of the first half of the century – which, for practical purposes, *was* British science at this time – knew what we would have wanted to study, if our mathematics had been good enough.

Indeed, the natural sciences could look forward to nothing except further triumph and intellectual advance, which made the patchiness, the imperfections and improvisations of current theory tolerable, since they were bound to be only temporary. Why should people who got Nobel prizes for work done in their mid-twenties lack confidence about the future?* And yet, how could even the men (and the occasional rare woman) who continued to prove the reality of the shaken idea of 'progress' in their field of human activity remain immune to the epoch of crisis and catastrophe in which they lived?

They could not and did not. The Age of Catastrophe was therefore

---

* The physics revolution of 1924–28 was made by men born in 1900–2 (Heisenberg, Pauli, Dirac, Fermi, Joliot). Schrödinger, de Broglie and Max Born were in their thirties.

also one of the comparatively rare ages of politicised scientists, and not only because the mass migration of racially and ideologically unacceptable scientists from large zones of Europe demonstrated that scientists could not take their personal immunity for granted. At all events, the typical British scientist of the 1930s was a member of the (Left-wing) Cambridge Scientists' Anti-War Group, confirmed in his or her radicalism by the undisguised radical sympathies of their seniors, whose distinction ranged from the Royal Society to the Nobel prize: Bernal (crystallography), Haldane (genetics), Needham (chemical embryology),* Blackett (physics), Dirac (physics) and the mathematician G.H. Hardy, who considered that only two others in the twentieth century were in the class of his Australian cricketing hero Don Bradman: Lenin and Einstein. The typical young American physicist of the 1930s was more than likely to be in political trouble in the post-war years of the Cold War for his pre-war or continuing radical sympathies, like Robert Oppenheimer (1904–67), the chief architect of the atom bomb, and Linus Pauling the chemist, (1901–) who won two Nobel prizes, including one for Peace and a Lenin prize. The typical French scientist was a sympathiser with the Popular Front of the 1930s and an active supporter of the Resistance during the war; not many Frenchmen were the latter. The typical refugee scientist from central Europe could hardly not be hostile to fascism, however uninterested in public affairs. Scientists who stayed in or were prevented from leaving fascist countries or the USSR could not avoid their government's politics either, whether or not they sympathised with them, if only because public gestures were imposed on them, like the Hitler salute in Germany, which the great physicist Max von Laue (1897–1960) avoided by carrying something in both hands whenever he left his house. Unlike the social or human sciences, such politicisation was unusual in the natural sciences, whose subject does not require or (except in parts of the life sciences) even suggest views about human affairs, though it often suggests views about God.

However, scientists were more directly politicised by their well-founded belief that laymen, including politicians, had no idea of the extraordinary potential that modern science, properly used, put at the disposal of human society. Both the collapse of the world economy and the rise of Hitler seemed to confirm this in different ways. (Conversely, the official Marxist devotion of the Soviet Union and its ideology to the natural sciences, misled many Western scientists at this time into seeing it as a regime suited to realizing this potential.) Technocracy and radicalism

* He later became the eminent historian of science in China.

converged, because at this point it was the political Left, with its ideological commitment to science, rationalism and progress (lampooned by conservatives with the new term 'scientism')* which naturally represented adequate recognition and support for 'The Social Function of Science', to cite the title of a highly influential book-cum-manifesto of the time (Bernal, 1939) characteristically written by a brilliant and militantly Marxist physicist. It was equally characteristic that the French Popular Front government of 1936–39 established the first Undersecretaryship for Scientific Research (occupied by the Nobel Laureate Irène Joliot-Curie), and developed what is still the main mechanism for funding French research, the CNRS (*Centre National de la Recherche Scientifique*). Indeed, it became increasingly obvious, at least to scientists, that not only public funding but publicly organized research was needed. British government scientific services, which in 1930 employed a grand total of 743 scientists, could not be adequate – thirty years later it employed over seven thousand (Bernal, 1967, p. 931).

The era of politicized science reached its climax in the Second World War, the first conflict since the Jacobin era of the French revolution when scientists were systematically and *centrally* mobilized for military purposes; probably more effectively on the side of the Allies than of Germany, Italy and Japan, because they never expected to win rapidly with immediately available resources and methods (see chapter 1). Tragically, nuclear warfare itself was the child of anti-fascism. A mere war between nation-states would almost certainly not have moved the spearhead nuclear physicists, themselves largely refugees or exiles from fascism, to urge the British and American governments to build an atom bomb. And the very horror of these scientists at their achievement, their desperate last-minute struggles to prevent the politicians and generals from actually using the bomb, and later to resist the construction of a hydrogen bomb, bears witness to the strength of *political* passions. Indeed, insofar as anti-nuclear campaigns after the Second World War had weighty support in the scientific community, it was among the members of the politicised anti-fascist generations.

At the same time the war finally convinced governments that the commitment of hitherto unimaginable resources to scientific research was both practicable and, in future, essential. No economy except that of the USA's could have found the two billion dollars (wartime value) to build the atom bomb during the war; but it is also true that no government at all would, before 1940, have dreamed of spending even a small fraction of

* The word appears for the first time in 1936 in France (Guerlac, 1951, pp. 93–4).

this money on a speculative project based on some incomprehensible calculations by wild-haired academics. After the war the sky, or rather the size of the economy alone, became the limit on government scientific outlays and employment. In the 1970s the US government funded two-thirds of the basic research costs in that country, which then ran at almost five billion dollars *a year*, and it employed something like one million scientists and engineers (Holton, 1978, pp. 227–28).

III

The political temperature of science dropped after the Second World War. Radicalism in the laboratories receded rapidly in 1947–49 when views regarded as baseless and bizarre elsewhere became mandatory for scientists in the USSR. Even most hitherto loyal communists found Lysenkoism (see p. 533) impossible to swallow. Moreover, it became increasingly evident that the regimes modelled on the Soviet system were neither materially nor morally attractive, at least to most scientists. On the other hand, in spite of much propaganda, the Cold War between the West and the Soviet bloc never generated anything like the political passions once roused among scientists by fascism. Perhaps because of the traditional affinity between liberal and Marxist rationalism, perhaps because the USSR, unlike Nazi Germany, never looked as though it were in a position to conquer the West, even if it had wanted to, which there was good reason to doubt. For most Western scientists the USSR, its satellites and Communist China were bad states whose scientists were to be pitied, rather than evil empires calling for a crusade.

In the developed West the natural sciences remained politically and ideologically quiescent for a generation, enjoying their intellectual triumphs and the vastly expanded resources now available for their researches. In fact, the munificent patronage of governments and large corporations encouraged a breed of researchers who took their paymasters' policies for granted and preferred not to think about the wider implications of their work, especially when these were military. At most, the scientists in such sectors protested against not being allowed to publish their research results. Indeed, most members of what was now a very large army of Ph.Ds, employed in the National Aeronautics and Space Administration (NASA), which was established to face the Soviet challenge in 1958, had no more interest in querying the rationale of their activities than members of any other army. In the later 1940s men and women still agonized over the question whether to join government

establishments specialising in chemical and biological war research.*
There is no evidence that subsequently such establishments had any
trouble in recruiting their staff.

Somewhat unexpectedly, it was in the Soviet region of the globe that
science became, if anything, more political as the second half of the
century advanced. It was no accident that the major national (and
international) spokesman for dissidence in the USSR was to be a
scientist, Andrei Sakharov (1921–89), the physicist who had been chiefly
responsible in the late 1940s for the construction of the Soviet hydrogen
bomb. Scientists were members *par excellence* of that new, large, educated
and technically trained professional middle class, which was the main
achievement of the Soviet system, but at the same time the class most
directly aware of its weaknesses and limitations. They were more essential
to it than their opposite numbers in the West, since they and they alone
enabled an otherwise backward economy to face the USA as a
superpower. Indeed, they demonstrated their indispensability by allowing
the USSR for a short time to overtake the West in the highest of
technologies, that of outer space. The first man-made satellite (Sputnik,
1957), the first manned space flight by man and woman (1961, 1963), and
the first space-walks were all Russian. Concentrated in research institutes
or special 'science cities', articulate, necessarily conciliated and allowed
some degree of freedom by the post-Stalin regime, it is not surprising
that critical opinions were generated in the milieu of research, whose
social prestige was in any case higher than that of any other Soviet
occupation.

IV

Can it be said that these fluctuations in political and ideological temperature affected the progress of the natural sciences? Plainly far less than was
the case in the social and human sciences, let alone the ideologies and
philosophies. The natural sciences could reflect the century scientists
lived in only within the confines of the empiricist methodology that
necessarily became standard in an era of epistemological uncertainty: that
of hypotheses verifiable – or, in the terms of Karl Popper (1902–), which
many scientists made their own, falsifiable – by practical tests. This imposed limits on ideologizing. Economics, though subject to the requirements

---

* I recall the embarrassment at this time of a (formerly pacifist, later communist)
biochemist friend who had taken such a post in the relevant British establishment.

of logic and consistency, has flourished as a form of theology – probably, in the Western world, as the most influential branch of secular theology – because it can be, and usually is, so formulated as to lack this control. Physics cannot. So, while it is easy to show that the conflicting schools and changing fashions in economic thought directly reflect contemporary experience and ideological debate, this is not so in cosmology.

Yet science did echo its times, even though it is undeniable that some important movements in science are endogenous. Thus it was almost inevitable that the disordered multiplication of sub-atomic particles, particularly after it accelerated in the 1950s, should lead theorists to seek for simplification. The (initially) arbitrary nature of the new and hypothetical 'ultimate' particle, of which protons, electrons, neutrons and the rest were now said to be composed, is indicated by its very name, taken from James Joyce's *Finnegan's Wake*: the *quark* (1963). It was soon divided into three or four sub-species (with their 'anti-quarks'), described as 'up', 'down', 'sideways' or 'strange', and quarks with 'charm', each of them endowed with a property called 'colour'. None of these words had anything like their usual meanings. As usual, successful predictions on the basis of this theory were made, thus concealing the fact that no experimental evidence for the existence of quarks of any kind had been found by the 1990s.* Whether these new developments constituted a simplification of the sub-atomic maze or an additional layer of complexity, must be left to suitably qualified physicists to judge. However, the sceptical, if admiring, lay observer may sometimes be reminded of the titanic labours of intelligence and ingenuity expended at the end of the nineteenth century to maintain scientific belief in the 'aether' before the work of Planck and Einstein banished it into the museum of pseudo-theories together with the 'phlogiston' (see *Age of Empire*, chapter 10).

The very lack of contact of such theoretical constructs with the reality they set out to explain (except as falsifiable hypotheses) opened them to influences from the outside world. Was it not natural that, in a century so dominated by technology, mechanical analogies should help to shape them again, though in the form of the techniques of communication and control in both animals and machines, which from 1940 on generated a body of theory known under various names (cybernetics, general systems theory, information theory, etc.)? Electronic computers, which developed

---

* John Maddox comments that it depends what one means by 'found'. Particular effects of quarks have been identified, but, it appears, they are not found 'bare' but only as pairs or triples. What puzzles physicists is not whether quarks are there, but why they are never alone.

at a dizzying speed after the Second World War, especially after the discovery of the transistor, had an enormous capacity for simulation, which made it far easier than before to evolve mechanical models of what had hitherto been regarded as the physical and mental operations of organisms, including the human. Late twentieth century scientists talked about the brain as though it were essentially an elaborate information processing system, and one of the familiar philosophical debates of the second half of the century was whether, and, if so, how, human intelligence could be distinguished from 'artificial intelligence', i.e. what, if anything, in the human mind was not theoretically programmable in a computer. That such technological models have advanced research is not in question. Where would the study of the nervous system (i.e. the study of the electric nerve impulses) be without that of electronics? Yet at bottom these are reductionist analogies, which may well some day look as dated as the eighteenth century description of human movement in terms of a system of levers.

Such analogies were useful in the formulation of particular models. Yet beyond these, the life experience of scientists could not but affect their way of looking at nature. Ours has been a century when, to quote one scientist reviewing another, 'the conflict between gradualists and catastrophism pervades human experience' (Steve Jones, 1992, p. 12). And so, not surprisingly, it came to pervade science.

In the nineteenth century of bourgeois improvement and progress, continuity and gradualism dominated the paradigms of science. Whatever nature's mode of locomotion, it was not allowed to jump. Geological change and the evolution of life on earth had proceeded without catastrophes and by tiny increments. Even the foreseeable end of the universe in some remote future would be gradual, by the insensible but inevitable transformation of energy into heat, according to the second law of thermodynamics (the 'heat death of the universe'). Twentieth-century science has developed a very different image of the world.

Our universe was born, fifteen million years ago, in a massive super-explosion and according to the cosmological speculations at the time of writing may end in an equally dramatic manner. Within it the life history of stars, and hence of their planets, is, like the universe, full of cataclysms: novas, supernovas, red giants, dwarfs, black holes and the rest – none recognized or regarded as more than peripheral astronomic phenomena before the 1920s. Most geologists long resisted the idea of large lateral displacements, such as the continents shifting all over the globe in the course of the earth's history, though the evidence for it was really rather strong. They did so on grounds which were largely ideological, to judge by the extraordinary bitterness of the controversy against the main proponent of 'continental drift', Alfred Wegener. At all events, the argument that it could not be true because no geophysical mechanism to bring about such movements was known was no more convincing *a priori* in view of the evidence than Lord Kelvin's nineteenth-century argument that the timescale then postulated by geologists must be wrong, because physics, as then understood, made the earth much younger than geology required. Yet since the 1960s the previously unthinkable has become the everyday orthodoxy of geology: a globe of shifting, sometimes rapidly shifting giant plates ('plate tectonics').*

Perhaps even more to the point is the return of direct catastrophism to both geology and evolutionary theory via palaeontology, since the 1960s. Once again the *prima facie* evidence has long been familiar: every child knows about the extinction of dinosaurs at the end of the Cretaceous period. Such was the force of the Darwinian belief that evolution was *not* the result of catastrophes (or creation) but of slow and tiny changes operating throughout geological history, that this apparent biological cataclysm attracted little attention. Geological time was simply regarded as long enough to allow for any observed evolutionary changes. Is it surprising, in an era when human history was so plainly cataclysmic, that evolutionary discontinuities should attract attention again? One might even go further. The mechanism most favoured by both geological and palaeontological catastrophists at the time of writing is bombardment from outer space, i.e. the collision of the earth is with one or more very large meteorites. According to some calculations an asteroid large enough to destroy civilisation, i.e. the equivalent to eight million Hiroshimas, is likely to arrive every three hundred thousand years. Such scenarios have always been part of fringe pre-history, but would any serious scientist before the epoch of nuclear war have thought in such terms? Such theories of evolution as slow change interrupted from time to time by relatively sudden change ('punctuated equilibrium') remained controversial in the 1990s, but now they were part of a debate *within* the scientific community. Again, the lay observer cannot but notice the emergence, within the field of thought remotest from flesh-and-blood human life, of two mathematical sub-fields known respectively as 'catastrophe theory'

---

* The *prima facie* evidence consisted mainly of a) the 'fit' of the coastlines of remote continents – notably the west coasts of Africa and the east coasts of South America; b) the similarity of the geological strata in such cases and c) the geographical distribution of certain types of land animals and plants. I can remember my surprise at the total refusal of a geophysical colleague in the 1950s – shortly before the breakthrough of plate tectonics – even to consider that this needed explaining.

(from the 1960s) and 'chaos theory' (1980s) (see pp. 541ff.). The one, a development of topology pioneered in France in the 1960s, claimed to investigate the situations when gradual change produced sudden ruptures, i.e. the interrelation between continuous and discontinuous change; the other (of American origin) modelled the uncertainty and unpredictability of situations in which apparently tiny events (the fluttering of a butterfly's wings) could be shown to lead to huge results elsewhere (a hurricane). Those who lived through the later decades of the century had no difficulty in understanding why such images as chaos and catastrophe should come into the minds of scientists and mathematicians also.

V

However, from the 1970s on, the outside world began to impinge on the laboratories and seminar rooms more indirectly, but also more powerfully, through the discovery that science-based technology, its power multiplied by global economic explosion, looked like producing fundamental and perhaps irreversible changes to the planet Earth, or at least to the Earth as a habitat for living organisms. This was even more disquieting than the prospect of the man-induced catastrophe of nuclear war which haunted imaginations and consciences during the long Cold War; for a Soviet-US world nuclear war was avoidable and, as it turned out, was avoided. It was not so easy to escape by-products of science-linked economic growth. Thus in 1973 two chemists, Rowland and Molina, first noticed that fluorocarbons (widely used in refrigeration and the newly popular aerosols) depleted the ozone in the earth's atmosphere. It could hardly have been noticed much earlier, since the release of such chemicals (CFC 11 and CFC 12) had not totalled forty thousand tons before the early 1950s. (But between 1960 and 1972 over 3.6 million tons of them had entered the atmosphere.* Yet by the early 1990s the existence of large 'ozone holes' in the atmosphere was layman's knowledge, and the only question was how rapidly the depletion of the ozone layer would proceed, and how soon it would go beyond the earth's powers of natural recuperation. If CFCs were got rid of, nobody doubts that it would reappear. The 'greenhouse effect', i.e. the uncontrollable warming of the global temperature through the release of man-produced gases, which began to be seriously discussed around 1970, became a major preoccupation of

* UN *World Resources*, 1986, Table 11.1, p. 319.

both specialists and politicians in the 1980s (Smil, 1990); the danger was real, though sometimes much exaggerated.

At about the same time the word 'ecology', coined in 1873 for the branch of biology that dealt with the interrelationships of organisms and their environment, acquired its now familiar quasi-political meaning (E.M. Nicholson, 1970).* These were the natural consequences of the secular economic superboom (see chapter 9).

These worries would be enough to explain why politics and ideology began, once again, to surround the natural sciences in the 1970s. However, they began to penetrate even parts of the sciences themselves in the form of debates about the need for practical and moral limitations on scientific enquiry.

Never since the end of theological hegemony had such issues been seriously raised. Not surprisingly, they emerged from that part of the natural sciences which had always had, or seemed to have, direct implications for human affairs: genetics and evolutionary biology. For within ten years of the Second World War, the life sciences were revolutionized by the astonishing advances of molecular biology, which revealed the universal mechanism of inheritance, the 'genetic code'.

The revolution in molecular biology was not unexpected. After 1914 it could be taken for granted that life had to be, and could be, explained in terms of physics and chemistry and not in terms of some essence peculiar to living beings.† Indeed, biochemical models of the possible origin of life on earth, starting with sunlight, methane, ammonia and water, were first suggested in the 1920s (largely with anti-religious intentions) in Soviet Russia and Britain, and put the subject on the serious scientific agenda. Hostility to religion, by the way, continued to animate researchers in this field: both Crick and Linus Pauling are cases in point (Olby, 1970, p. 943). The major thrust of biological research had for decades been biochemical, and increasingly physical, since the recognition that protein molecules could be crystallized, and therefore analysed crystallographically. It was known that one substance, deoxyribonucleic acid (DNA) played a central, possibly the central role in heredity: it seemed to be the

---

* 'Ecology . . . is also the main intellectual discipline and tool which enables us to hope that human evolution can be mutated, can be shifted on to a new course, so that man will cease to knock hell out of the environment on which his own future depends.'

† 'How can the events in space and time which take place within the spatial boundary of a living organism be accounted for by physics and chemistry?' (E. Schrödinger, 1944, p. 2).

basic component of the gene, the unit of inheritance. The problem of how the gene 'cause(d) the synthesis of another structure like itself, in which even the mutations of the original gene are copied' (Muller, 1951, p. 95), i.e. how heredity operated, was already under serious investigation in the late 1930s. After the war it was clear that, in Crick's words, 'great things were just around the corner'. The brilliance of Crick and Watson's discovery of the double-helical structure of DNA and of the way it explained 'gene copying' by an elegant chemico-mechanical model is not diminished by the fact that several workers were converging on the same result in the early 1950s.

The DNA revolution, 'the greatest single discovery in biology' (J.D. Bernal), which dominated the life-sciences in the second half of the century, was essentially about genetics and, since twentieth-century Darwinism is exclusively genetic, about evolution.* Both these are notoriously touchy subjects, both because scientific models are themselves frequently ideological in such fields – we remember Darwin's debt to Malthus (Desmond/Moore, chapter 18) – and because they frequently feed back into politics ('social Darwinism'). The concept of 'race' illustrates this interplay. The memory of Nazi racial policies made it virtually unthinkable for liberal intellectuals (which included most scientists) to operate with this concept. Indeed, many doubted that it was legitimate even to enquire systematically into the genetically determined differences between human groups, for fear that the results might provide encouragement for racist opinions. More generally, in the Western countries the post-fascist ideology of democracy and equality revived the old debates of 'nature v. nurture', or heredity v. environment. Plainly the human individual was shaped both by heredity and environment, by genes and culture. Yet conservatives were only too willing to accept a society of irremovable, i.e. genetically determined inequalities, while the Left, committed to equality, naturally held that all inequalities could be removed by social action: they were at bottom environmentally determined. The controversy flared up over the question of human intelligence, which (because of its implications for selective or universal schooling) was highly political. It raised far wider issues than those of race, though it bore on these also. How wide they were, emerged with the revival

---

* It was also 'about' the essentially mathematical-mechanical variant of experimental science, which is perhaps why it has met with less than 100 per cent enthusiasm in some less readily quantifiable or experimental life sciences, such as zoology and palaeontology. (See R.C. Lewontin, *The Genetic Basis of Evolutionary Change.*)

of the feminist movement (see chapter 10), several of whose ideologists came close to claiming that *all* mental differences between men and women were essentially culture-determined, i.e. environmental. Indeed, the fashionable substitution of the term 'gender' for 'sex' implied the belief that 'woman' was not so much a biological category as a social role. A scientist who tried to investigate such sensitive subjects knew himself to be in a political minefield. Even those who entered it deliberately, like E.O. Wilson of Harvard (b. 1929), the champion of 'socio-biology', shied away from plain speech.*

What made the atmosphere more explosive, was that scientists themselves, especially on the more obviously social wing of the life sciences – evolutionary theory, ecology, ethology or the study of animal social behaviour and the like – were only too apt to use anthropomorphic metaphors or draw human conclusions. Sociobiologists, or those who popularized their findings, suggested that the (male) traits inherited from the millennia during which primitive man had been selected to adapt, as a hunter, to a more predatory existence in open habitats (Wilson, ibid.) still dominated our social existence. Not only women but also historians were irritated. Evolutionary theorists analysed natural selection, in the light of the great biological revolution, as the struggle for existence of 'The Selfish Gene' (Dawkins, 1976). Even some who sympathised with the hard version of Darwinism wondered what real bearing genetic selection had on debates about human egoism, competition and cooperation. Science was once more beleaguered by critics, though – significantly – it was no longer seriously under fire from traditional religion, apart from intellectually negligible fundamentalist groups. The clergy now accepted the hegemony of the laboratory, drawing what theological comfort it could from scientific cosmology, whose 'Big Bang' theories could, with

---

* 'My overall impression of the available information is that *Homo Sapiens* is a typical animal species with reference to the quality and magnitude of the genetic diversity affecting behavior. If the comparison is correct, the psychic unity of humankind has been reduced in status from a dogma to a testable hypothesis. This is not an easy thing to say in the present political ambience of the United States, and it is regarded as punishable heresy in some sectors of the academic community. But the idea needs to be faced squarely if the social sciences are to be entirely honest . . . It will be better for scientists to study the subject of genetic behavioral diversity than to maintain a conspiracy of silence out of good intentions' (Wilson, 1977, 'Biology and the Social Sciences', p. 133).

The plain meaning of this convoluted passage is: there are races and for genetic reasons they are permanently unequal in certain specifiable respects.

the eye of faith, be presented as proof that a God had created the world. On the other hand the Western cultural revolution of the 1960s and 1970s produced a strong neo-romantic and irrationalist attack on the scientific view of the world, which could readily shift from a radical to a reactionary key.

Unlike the outlying trenches of the life-sciences, the main fortress of pure research in the 'hard' sciences was little disturbed by such snipings until it became evident by the 1970s that research could not be divorced from the social consequences of the technologies it now, and almost immediately, generated. It was the prospect of 'genetic engineering' – logically of humans as well as other forms of life – which really raised the immediate question of whether limits on scientific research should be envisaged. For the first time such opinions were heard among scientists themselves, notably in the biological field, for by now some of the essential elements of the Frankensteinian technologies were not separable from pure research and subsequent to it, but – as in the Genome project, the plan to map all the genes in human heredity – they *were* the basic research. These criticisms undermined what all scientists had hitherto regarded, and most scientists continued to regard as the basic principle of science, namely that, with the most marginal concessions to the moral beliefs of society,* science should pursue truth wherever that pursuit led them. They had no responsibility for what non-scientists did with their results. That, as one American scientist observed in 1992, 'no prominent molecular biologist of my acquaintance is without a financial stake in the biotechnology business' (Lewontin, 1992, p. 37; pp. 31–40); that – to cite another – 'the issue (of ownership) is at the heart of everything we do' (ibid, p. 38), made the claim of purity even more dubious.

What was now at issue was not the pursuit of truth, but the impossibility of separating it from its conditions and consequences. At the same time the debate was essentially between pessimists and optimists about the human race. For the basic assumption of those who envisaged restraints or self-limitation on scientific enquiry was that humanity, as at present organized, was not capable of handling the earth-transforming powers it had, or even of recognizing the risks it was running. For even those sorcerers who resisted all limits on their enquiries did not trust their apprentices. The arguments for unlimited enquiry 'pertain to basic scientific research, not to the technological applications of science, some of which ought to be restrained' (Baltimore, 1978).

And yet, such arguments were beside the point. For, as all scientists

---

* Such as, notably, the restriction of experiment on human beings.

knew, scientific research was *not* unlimited and free, if only because it required resources which were in limited supply. The question was not whether anyone should tell researchers what to do or not to do, but who imposed such limits and directions, and by what criteria. For most scientists, whose institutions were directly or indirectly paid for out of public funds, these controllers of research were governments, whose criteria, however sincere their devotion to the values of free enquiry, were not those of a Planck or a Rutherford or an Einstein.

Theirs were, by definition, not the priorities of 'pure' research, especially when that research was expensive; and, after the end of the great global boom, even the richest governments, their revenue no longer climbing ahead of their expenditure, had to budget. Nor were they, or could they be, the priorities of 'applied' research, which employed the great majority of scientists, for these were set not in terms of the 'advance of knowledge' in general (though this might well result), but by the need to achieve certain practical results – for instance a cure for cancer or AIDS. Researchers in these fields pursued not necessarily what interested them, but what was socially useful or economically profitable, or at least what money was available for, even when they hoped it would lead them back to the path of fundamental research. Under the circumstances it was windy rhetoric to claim that restraints on research were intolerable because man was by nature a species that needed 'to satisfy our curiosity, exploration and experimentation' (Lewis Thomas in Baltimore, p. 44) or that the peaks of knowledge must be climbed, in the classic mountaineer's phrase, 'because they are there'.

The truth is that 'science' (by which most people meant the 'hard' natural sciences) was too big, too powerful, too indispensable to society in general and its paymasters in particular to be left to its own devices. The paradox of its situation was that, in the last analysis, the huge powerhouse of twentieth-century technology, and the economy it made possible, increasingly depended on a relatively minuscule community of people for whom these titanic consequences of their activities were secondary, and often trivial. For them the ability of men to travel to the moon or to bounce the images of a Brazilian football match off a satellite so that it could be watched on a screen in Düsseldorf, was far less interesting than the discovery of some cosmic background noise which was identified during the search for phenomena that troubled communication, but confirmed a theory about the origins of the universe. Yet, like the ancient Greek mathematician Archimedes, they knew that they lived in and helped to shape a world that could not understand and did not care about what they did. Their call for the freedom of research was like Archimedes' *cri-de-coeur* to the invading soldiers, against whom he had devised military engines for his city of Syracuse, and who took no notice of them as they killed him: 'For God's sake, don't ruin my diagrams.' It was understandable, but not necessarily realistic.

Only the world-changing powers to which they had the key protected them, for these appeared to depend on allowing an otherwise incomprehensible and privileged elite – incomprehensible, until late in the century, even in its relative lack of interest in the external signs of wealth and power – to go its own way. All twentieth-century states which had done otherwise had cause to regret it. All states therefore supported science, which, unlike the arts and most of the humanities, could not effectively function without such support, while avoiding interference so far as possible. But governments are not concerned with ultimate truth (except those of ideology or religion) but with instrumental truth. At most they may foster 'pure' (i.e. at the moment useless) research because it might one day yield something useful, or for reasons of national prestige, in which the pursuit of Nobel prizes preceded that of Olympic medals and still remains more highly valued. Such were the foundations on which the triumphant structures of scientific research and theory were erected, by which the twentieth century will be remembered as an age of human progress and not primarily of human tragedy.

CHAPTER NINETEEN
Towards the Millennium

We are at the beginning of a new era, characterised by great insecurity, permanent crisis and the absence of any kind of *status quo* ... We must realise, that we find ourselves in one of those crises of world history which Jakob Burckhardt described. It is no less significant than the one after 1945, even if the initial conditions for surmounting it seem better today. There are no victors and no defeated powers today, not even in eastern Europe.

– M. Stürmer in Bergedorf (1993, p. 59)

Although the earthly ideal of Socialism-Communism has collapsed, the problems it purported to solve remain: the brazen use of social advantage and the inordinate power of money, which often direct the very course of events. And if the global lesson of the twentieth century does not serve as a healing inoculation, then the vast red whirlwind may repeat itself in entirety.

– Alexander Solzhenitsyn in *New York Times*, 28 November 1993

It is a privilege for a writer to have experienced the end of three states: the Weimar republic, the fascist state and the GDR. I don't suppose I'll live long enough to see the end of the Federal Republic.

– Heiner Müller, (1992, p. 361)

I

The Short Twentieth Century ended in problems, for which nobody had, or even claimed to have, solutions. As the citizens of the *fin-de-siècle* tapped their way through the global fog that surrounded them, into the third millennium, all they knew for certain was that an era of history had ended. They knew very little else.

Thus, for the first time in two centuries, the world of the 1990s entirely lacked any international system or structure. The very fact that, after 1989, dozens of new territorial states appeared without any independent mechanism for determining their borders – without even third parties accepted as sufficiently impartial to act as general mediators – speaks for itself. Where was the consortium of great powers which had once established, or at least formally ratified disputed frontiers? Where the victors of the First World War who supervised the re-drawing of the map of Europe and the world, fixing a borderline here, insisting on a plebiscite there? (Where, indeed, were those working international conferences so familiar to the diplomats of the past, so different from the brief public-relations and photo-exercise summits which had now taken their place?)

What, indeed, were international powers, old or new, at the end of the millennium? The only state left that would have been recognized as a great power, in the sense in which the word had been used in 1914, was the USA. What this meant in practice was quite obscure. Russia had been reduced to the size it had been in the mid-seventeenth century. Never since Peter the Great had it been so negligible. Britain and France had been reduced to purely regional status, which was not concealed by the possession of nuclear arms. Germany and Japan were certainly economic 'great powers', but neither had seen the need to back their enormous economic resources with military muscle, in the traditional manner, even when they became free to do so, though nobody knew what they might want to do in the unknown future. What was the international political status of the new European Union, which aspired to a common political policy but proved spectacularly incapable of even pretending to have one, unlike in economic matters? It was not even clear whether all but a few states, large or small, old or young, would exist in their present form by the time the twenty-first century reached its first quarter.

If the nature of the players on the international scene was unclear, so was the nature of the dangers that confronted the world. The Short Twentieth Century had been one of world wars, hot or cold, conducted by great powers and their allies with increasingly apocalyptic scenarios of mass destruction, culminating in the, fortunately avoided, nuclear holocaust of the superpowers. This danger had clearly disappeared. Whatever the future would bring, the very disappearance or transformation of all but one of the old actors in the world drama, meant that a Third World War of the old kind was among the least likely prospects.

Patently this did not mean that the age of wars was at an end. The 1980s had already demonstrated by means of the British–Argentinian war of 1983 and the Iran–Iraq war of 1980–88 that wars which had nothing to do with the global superpower confrontation were a permanent possibility. The years after 1989 saw more military operations in more parts of Europe, Asia and Africa than anyone could remember, though not all of them were officially classified as wars: in Liberia, Angola, the Sudan and the Horn of Africa, in ex-Yugoslavia, in Moldova, in several countries of the Caucasus and Transcaucasus, in the ever-explosive Middle East, in ex-Soviet Central Asia and Afghanistan. Since it was often not clear who was fighting whom and why in the increasingly frequent situations of national breakdown and disintegration, these activities did not readily fit under any of the classic headings of 'war', international or civil. Yet the inhabitants of the region concerned could hardly feel themselves to be living in times of peace, especially when, as in Bosnia, Tadzhikistan or Liberia, they had been living in unquestionable times of peace not so long ago. Besides, as the Balkans in the early 1990s demonstrated, there was no sharp line between regional internecine struggles and a more recognizable war of the old type, into which they could quite easily turn. In short, the global danger of war had not disappeared. It had merely changed.

No doubt the inhabitants of stable, strong and favoured states (the European Union as distinct from the adjoining zone of troubles; Scandinavia as distinct from the ex-Soviet shores of the Baltic Sea) might think themselves immune to such insecurity and carnage in the unhappy parts of the Third World and the ex-socialist world, but, if they did so, they were mistaken. The crisis in the affairs of the traditional nation-states was enough to make them vulnerable. Quite apart from the possibility that some states might in turn split or break up, a major, and not often recognized innovation of the second half of the century weakened them, if only by depriving them of the monopoly of effective force, which had been the criterion of state power in all regions of permanent settlement. This was the democratisation or privatisation of the means of destruction, which transformed the prospect of violence and wreckage *anywhere* on the globe.

It was now possible for quite small groups of political or other dissidents to disrupt and destroy anywhere, as the mainland activities of the IRA in Britain and the attempt to blow up the World Trade Center in New York (1993) showed. Up to the end of the Short Century, the costs of these activities, except to the insurance companies, were modest, since non-state terrorism, contrary to common assumptions, was much less indiscriminate than the bombardments of official warfare, if only because its aim (where it had one) was mainly political rather than military. Moreover, except for explosive charges, it usually operated with hand-held arms more suitable for small-scale killing than for mass murder. However, there was no reason why even nuclear arms, and the material and know-how for their manufacture, all widely available on the world market, could not be adapted for small-group use.

Moreover, the democratisation of the means of destruction raised the costs of keeping unofficial violence under control quite dramatically. Thus the British government, faced with actual combatant forces among the Catholic and Protestant para-militaries of Northern Ireland of no more than a few hundreds, maintained itself in being in the province by the constant presence of something like twenty thousand trained troops, eight thousand armed police and an expenditure of £3 billion a year. What was true of small rebellions or other forms of domestic violence was even more true of small conflicts outside a country's borders. There were not many international situations in which even quite rich states would be prepared to incur such costs without limit.

Several situations in the immediate aftermath of the Cold War dramatized this unsuspected limitation on state power, notably Bosnia and Somalia. They also threw light on what looked like becoming perhaps the major cause of international tension in the new millennium, namely that which arose out of the rapidly widening gap between the rich and the poor parts of the world. Each resented the other. The rise of Islamic fundamentalism was patently a movement not only against the ideology of modernization by Westernization, but against the 'West' itself. Not by accident did the activists of such movements pursue their ends by disrupting the visits of Western tourists, as in Egypt, or murdering local Western residents in substantial numbers, as in Algeria. Conversely, the most jagged edge of popular xenophobia in the rich countries was directed against foreigners from the Third World, and the European Union dammed its borders against the flood of the Third World's labour-seeking poor. Even within the USA, signs of serious opposition to that country's *de facto* tolerance of unlimited immigration began to appear.

And yet, politically and in military terms, each side lay beyond the power of the other. In almost any conceivable open conflict between states of the North and South, the overwhelming technical superiority and wealth of the North was bound to win, as the Gulf War of 1991 demonstrated conclusively. Even the possession of a few nuclear missiles by some Third World country – assuming it also had the means of maintaining and delivering them – was most unlikely to be an effective deterrent, since Western states, as Israel and the Gulf War coalition proved in Iraq, were both ready and able to undertake pre-emptive strikes against potential enemies too weak to be really threatening as yet. From a military point of view the First World could safely treat the Third as what Mao had called a 'paper tiger'.

Yet it had become increasingly clear over the last half of the Short Twentieth Century that the First World could win battles but not wars against the Third, or rather that winning wars, even if possible, could not guarantee control of such territories. The major asset of imperialism had disappeared, namely the readiness of colonial populations, once con-quered, to let themselves be quietly administered by a handful of occupiers. Ruling Bosnia-Hercegovina had been no problem for the Habsburg Empire, but in the early 1990s all governments were advised by their military advisers that the pacification of that unhappy war-torn country would require the presence, for an indefinite period, of several hundreds of thousands of troops, i.e. a mobilization comparable to that of a major war. Somaliland had always been a difficult colony, and had once even briefly required the intervention of a British force headed by a Major-General, and yet it had not crossed the minds of London or Rome that even Muhammad ben Abdallah, the celebrated 'Mad Mullah', raised permanently unmanageable problems for the British and Italian colonial governments. Yet in the early 1990s the USA and the rest of the UN forces of occupation of several tens of thousands withdrew ignomini-ously when confronted with the option of an indefinite occupation without clear ends. Even the might of the great USA blenched when faced in neighbouring Haiti – a traditional satellite and dependent of Washington – by a local general, heading the local, American-armed and shaped army, who refused to allow an elected and (reluctantly) American-backed president to return, and challenged the USA to occupy Haiti. The USA refused to occupy Haiti once again, as it had done from 1915 until 1934, not because the one thousand or so uniformed thugs of the Haitian army constituted a serious military problem, but because it simply did not know any longer how to settle the Haitian problem by outside force.

In short, the century ended in a global disorder whose nature was un-clear, and without an obvious mechanism for either ending it or keeping it under control.

II

The reason for this impotence lay not only in the genuine profundity and complexity of the world's crisis, but also in the apparent failure of all programmes, old and new, for managing or improving the affairs of the human race.

The Short Twentieth Century had been an era of religious wars, though the most militant and bloodthirsty of its religious were secular ideologies of nineteenth-century vintage, such as socialism and nationalism, whose god-equivalents were either abstractions or politicians venerated in the manner of divinities. Probably the extremes of such secular devotion were already in decline even before the end of the Cold War, including the various political cults of personality, or, rather, they had been reduced from universal churches to a scattering of rival sects. Nevertheless, their strength had lain not so much in their ability to mobilize emotions akin to those of traditional religion – ideological liberalism hardly even tried – but in their promise to provide lasting solutions to the problems of a world in crisis. Yet just this was what they now failed to provide as the century ended.

The collapse of the USSR naturally drew attention primarily to the failure of Soviet communism, that is to say, of the attempt to base an entire economy on universal state-ownership of the means of production and all-encompassing central planning, without any effective recourse to market or pricing mechanisms. All other historic forms of the socialist ideal had assumed an economy based on the social ownership of all means of production, distribution and exchange (though not necessarily central state ownership), and the elimination of private enterprise and resource allocation by a competitive market. Hence this failure also undermined the aspirations of non-communist socialism, Marxist or otherwise, even though no such regimes or governments had actually claimed to establish socialist economies. Whether, or in which of its forms, Marxism, the intellectual justification and inspiration of communism, would continue remained a matter of debate. However, clearly, if Marx would live on as a major thinker, which could hardly be doubted, none of the versions of Marxism formulated since the 1890s as doctrines of political action and aspiration for socialist movements were likely to do so in their original forms.

On the other hand, the counter-utopia to the Soviet one was also demonstrably bankrupt. This was the theological faith in an economy in which resources were allocated *entirely* by the totally unrestricted market, under conditions of unlimited competition, a state of affairs believed to produce not only the maximum of goods and services, but also the maximum of happiness and the only kind of society deserving the name of 'freedom'. No such purely *laissez-faire* society had ever existed. Unlike the Soviet utopia, fortunately no attempt to institute the ultra-liberal utopia in practice had been made before the 1980s. It had survived most of the Short Twentieth Century as a principle for criticizing both the inefficiencies of existing economies and the growth of state power and bureaucracy. The most consistent attempt to do so in the West, Mrs Thatcher's regime in Britain, whose economic failure was generally admitted by the time of her overthrow, had to operate with a certain gradualism. However, when attempts were made to institute such *laissez-faire* economies to replace the former Soviet-socialist economies at short notice by means of the 'shock therapies' recommended by Western advisers, the results were economically dreadful and both socially and politically disastrous. The theories on which the neo-liberal theology was based, while elegant, had little relation to reality.

The failure of the Soviet model confirmed supporters of capitalism in their conviction that no economy without a stock exchange could work; the failure of the ultra-liberal model confirmed socialists in the more justified belief that human affairs, including the economy, were too important to be left to the market. It also supported the supposition of sceptical economists that there was no visible correlation between a country's economic success or failure and the distinction of its economic theorists.* However, it may well be that the debate which confronted capitalism and socialism as mutually exclusive and polar opposites will be seen by future generations as a relic of the twentieth-century ideological Cold Wars of Religion. It may turn out to be as irrelevant to the third millennium as the debate between Catholics and various reformers in the sixteenth and seventeenth centuries on what constituted true Christianity proved to be in the eighteenth and nineteenth.

More serious than the evident breakdown of the two polar extremes was the disorientation of what might be called the intermediate or mixed

---

* If anything, it might even suggest an inverse correlation. Austria was not a by-word for economic success in the days (before 1938) when it possessed one of the most distinguished schools of economic theorists; it became one after the Second World War when it was hard to think of any economist resident in that country with a reputation outside it. Germany, which refused even to recognize the internationally recognized brand of economic theory in its universities, did not appear to suffer. How many Korean or Japanese economists are cited in the average issue of the *American Economic Review*? However, Scandinavia, social-democratic, prosperous and full of the most internationally respected economic theorists since the late nineteenth century, could be cited on the other side of the argument.

programmes and policies which had presided over the most impressive economic miracles of the century. These had pragmatically combined public and private, market and planning, state and business, as the occasion and local ideology warranted. The problem here lay not in the application of some intellectually attractive or impressive theory, whether or not this was defensible in the abstract, for the strength of these programmes had been practical success rather than intellectual coherence. It was the erosion of that practical success. The Crisis Decades demonstrated the limitations of the various Golden Age policies, but without – as yet – generating convincing alternatives. They also revealed the unpredicted but dramatic social and cultural consequences of the era of economic world revolution since 1945, as well as their potentially catastrophic ecological consequences. In short, they revealed that human collective institutions had lost control over the collective consequences of human action. Indeed, one of the intellectual attractions which helps to explain the brief vogue for the neo-liberal utopia was precisely that it purported to by-pass collective human decisions. Let every individual pursue his or her satisfaction without restraint, and, whatever the result was, it was the best that could be achieved. Any alternative course it was implausibly argued, was worse.

If the programmatic ideologies born of the Age of Revolution and the nineteenth century found themselves at a loss at the end of the twentieth century, the most ancient guides to the perplexed of this world, the traditional religions, provided no plausible alternative. The Western ones were in disarray, even in the few countries – headed by that strange anomaly, the USA – where membership of churches and frequent attendance at religious rituals were still habitual (Kosmin/Lachmann, 1993). The decline of the various Protestant denominations accelerated. Churches and chapels, constructed at the beginning of the century, stood empty at its end, or were sold to be used for some other purpose, even in countries like Wales, where they had helped to shape the national identity. From the 1960s on, as we have seen, the decline of Roman Catholicism became precipitous. Even in the ex-communist countries, where the Church had enjoyed the advantage of symbolizing opposition to deeply unpopular regimes, the post-communist Catholic sheep showed the same tendency to stray from their shepherd as elsewhere. Religious observers sometimes believed they could detect a return to religion in the post-Soviet region of Orthodox Christianity, but at the end of the century the evidence for this unlikely, though not impossible development was not strong. A diminishing number of men and women listened to the various doctrines of these Christian denominations, whatever their merits.

The decline and fall of the traditional religions was not compensated, at least in the urban society of the developed world, by the growth of militantly sectarian religion, or by the rise of novel cults and cult communities, still less by the evident desire of so many men and women to take refuge from a world they could neither understand nor control in a variety of beliefs whose very irrationality constituted their strength. The public visibility of such sects, cults and beliefs should not distract attention from the relative weakness of their support. Not more than 3–4 per cent of British Jews belonged to any of the ultra-orthodox sects or groups. Not more than 5 per cent of the US adult population belonged to the militant and missionary sects (Kosmin, Lachmann, 1993, pp. 15–16).*

In the Third World and on its fringes the situation was indeed different, always excepting the vast population of the Far East, whom the Confucian tradition had kept immune to official religion for some millennia, though not to unofficial cults. Here, indeed, one might have expected the religious traditions which constituted popular ways of thinking about the world to become prominent on the public scene, as the common people became established actors on that scene. This is what happened in the last decades of the century, as the secularized and modernizing elite minorities who had led their countries into the modern world were marginalized (see chapter 12). The appeal of politicized religion was all the greater because the old religions were, almost by definition, enemies to the Western civilization which was the agent of social disruption, and to the rich and godless countries that looked, more than ever, like the exploiters of the poor world's poverty. That the local targets of such movements were the Westernized rich with their Mercedes and emancipated women, added a tinge of class struggle to such movements. They became familiarly (but misleadingly) known as 'fundamentalism' in the West. Whatever the fashionable name, such movements looked back, as it were *ex officio*, to some simpler and stabler and more comprehensible age of the imagined past. Since there was no way back to such an era, and since these ideologies could have nothing of relevance to say about the actual problems of societies utterly unlike those of, say, pastoral nomads in the ancient Middle East, they provided no guidance to these problems. They were symptoms of what the Viennese wit Karl Kraus called psychoanalysis: 'the disease of which they purport to be the cure'.

---

* I have counted in those describing themselves as Pentecostal, Churches of Christ, Jehovah's Witnesses, Seventh Day Adventists, Assemblies of God, Holiness Churches, 'Born Again' and 'Charismatic'.

This was also the case of the amalgam of slogans and emotions – it can hardly be called an ideology – which flourished on the ruins of the old institutions and ideologies, much in the way weeds had colonized the bombed ruins of European cities after the Second World War bombs fell. This was xenophobia and identity politics. To reject an unacceptable present is not necessarily to formulate, let alone to provide a solution to its problems (see chapter 14/vi). Indeed, the closest thing to a political programme reflecting such an approach, the Wilsonian–Leninist 'right to national self-determination' for supposedly homogeneous ethnic-linguistic-cultural 'nations', was patently being reduced to a savage and tragic absurdity as the new millennium approached. In the early 1990s, perhaps for the first time, rational observers irrespective of politics (other than those of some specific group of nationalist activism) began publicly to propose the abandonment of the 'right of self-determination'.*

Not for the first time, the combination of intellectual nullity with strong, even desperate, mass emotion, was politically powerful in times of crisis, insecurity, and – over large parts of the globe – disintegrating states and institutions. Like the movements of inter-war resentment which had generated fascism, the religio-political protests of the Third World and the hunger for a secure identity and social order in a disintegrating world (the call for 'community' was habitually joined with the call for 'law and order') provided the humus in which effective political forces could grow. These in turn could overthrow old regimes and become new ones. However, they were no more likely to produce solutions for the new millennium than fascism had been to produce solutions for the Age of Catastrophe. At the end of the Short Twentieth Century it was not even clear whether they were capable of generating organized national mass movements of the kind which had made some fascisms politically formidable even before they acquired the decisive weapon of state power. Their major asset was probably an immunity to academic economics and the anti-state rhetoric of a liberalism identified

* Cf. the 1949 forecast of an exiled anti-communist Russian, Ivan Ilyin (1882–1954), who predicted the consequences of attempting an impossible 'rigorous ethnic and territorial sub-division' of post-Bolshevik Russia. 'On the most modest assumptions we would have a score of separate 'states', none with an uncontested territory, nor governments with authority, nor laws, nor tribunals, nor army, nor an ethnically defined population. A score of empty labels. And slowly, in the course of the following decades, new states would form, by separation or disintegration. Each of them would wage a long struggle with its neighbours for territory and population, in what would amount to an endless series of civil wars within Russia' (cited in Chiesa, 1993, pp. 34, 36–37).

with the free market. If politics were to dictate re-nationalizing an industry, they would not be put off by arguments to the contrary, especially when they could not understand them. And yet, if they were ready to do anything, they knew no more than anyone else what should be done.

III

Neither, of course, does the author of this book. And yet, some long-term tendencies of development were so plain that they allow us to sketch both an agenda of some of the world's major problems, and at least some of the conditions for their solution.

The two central, and, in the long run, decisive, problems were demographic and ecological. The world's population, exploding in size since the middle of the twentieth century, was generally expected to stabilize at about ten billion human beings, or five times its 1950 numbers, some time around 2030, essentially by a decline in the Third World's birth-rate. If this forecast were to prove wrong, all bets on the future would be off. Even if it proved roughly realistic, it would raise the problem, not hitherto ever faced on a global scale, of how to maintain a stable world population or, more likely, a world population fluctuating round a level or slightly rising (or falling) trend. (A dramatic fall in the global population, improbable but not inconceivable, would introduce yet further complexities.) However, stable or not, the predictable movements of the world's population were certain to increase the disequilibria between its different regions. On the whole, as in the Short Twentieth Century, the rich and developed countries would be those whose population would be the first to stabilize, or even no longer to reproduce itself, as several such countries in the 1990s no longer did.

Surrounded by poor countries with vast armies of the young, clamouring for the modest jobs in the rich world which make men and women rich by the standards of El Salvador or Morocco, these countries of many senior citizens and few children would face the choice of allowing massive immigration (which produced political troubles at home), barricading themselves against the immigrants whom they needed (which might be impracticable in the long run), or finding some other formula. The most likely was to permit temporary and conditional immigration, which did not give the foreigners the social and political rights of citizens, i.e. to create essentially inegalitarian societies. These could range from the societies of frank *apartheid* like those of South Africa and Israel (declining in some parts of the world but by no means excluded in others), to the informal toleration of immigrants who made no claims on the receiving country, because they saw it simply as a place in which to earn money from time to time, while basically remaining rooted in their own homeland. Later twentieth-century transport and communications, as well as the enormous gap between the incomes that could be earned in rich and poor countries, made this sort of dual existence more possible than before. Whether it could in the long or even the medium run, render the frictions between natives and foreigners less incendiary, remains in dispute between the eternal optimists and the illusionless sceptics.

There can be little doubt that these frictions will be a major factor in the politics, national or global, of the next decades.

The ecological problems, though in the long run decisive, were not so immediately explosive. This is not to underestimate them, even though, from the time they entered public consciousness and public debate in the 1970s, they tended to be mistakenly discussed in terms of an imminent apocalypse. However, the fact that the 'greenhouse effect' may not cause the average sea-level to rise high enough by the year 2000 to drown all of Bangladesh and the Netherlands, or that the loss of an unknown number of species every day is not unprecedented, was no cause for complacency. A rate of economic growth like that of the second half of the Short Twentieth Century, if maintained indefinitely (assuming this to be possible), must have irreversible and catastrophic consequences for the natural environment of this planet, including the human race which is part of it. It will not destroy the planet or make it absolutely uninhabitable, but it will certainly change the pattern of life on the biosphere, and may well make it uninhabitable by the human species as we know it in anything like its present numbers. Moreover, the rate at which modern technology has increased the capacity of our species to transform the environment is such that, even if we assume that it does not accelerate, the time available to deal with the problem must be measured in decades rather than centuries.

About the answer to this approaching ecological crisis only three things can be said with reasonable certainty. First, that it must be global rather than local, even though clearly more time would be gained if the greatest single source of global pollution, the 4 per cent of the world's population who inhabit the USA, were to be charged a realistic price for the petrol they consume. Second, that the objective of ecological policy must be both radical and realistic. Market solutions, i.e. including the costs of environmental externalities in the price consumers pay for their goods and services, are neither. As the example of the USA shows, even a modest attempt to raise an energy tax in that country can raise insuperable political difficulties. The record of oil prices since 1973 proves that, in a free market society, the effect of multiplying energy costs twelve- to fifteenfold in six years, was not to diminish energy use but to make it more efficient, while encouraging massive investment in new and environmentally dubious sources of irreplaceable fossil fuel. These in turn would lower the price again and encourage more wasteful use. On the other hand, proposals like a world of zero growth, let alone fantasies like a return to the alleged primitive symbiosis between man and nature, while radical, were completely impracticable. Zero growth under existing conditions would freeze the present inequalities between the world's countries, a situation more tolerable to the average inhabitant of Switzerland than to the average inhabitant of India. It is no accident that the main support for ecological policies comes from the rich countries and from the comfortable rich and middle classes in all countries (except for businessmen who hope to make money by polluting activities). The poor, multiplying and under-employed, wanted more 'development' not less.

Yet, rich or not, the supporters of ecological policies were right. The rate of development must be reduced to what was 'sustainable' in the medium run – the term was conveniently meaningless – and, in the long run, a balance would have to be struck between humanity, the (renewable) resources it consumed and the effect of its activities on the environment. Nobody knew and few dared to speculate how this was to be done, and at what level of population, technology and consumption such a permanent balance would be possible. Scientific expertise could no doubt establish what needed to be done to avoid an irreversible crisis, but the problem of establishing such a balance was not one of science and technology, but political and social. One thing, however, was undeniable. It would be incompatible with a world economy based on the unlimited pursuit of profit by economic enterprises dedicated, by definition, to this object and competing with each other in a global free market. From the environmental point of view, if humanity was to have a future, the capitalism of the Crisis Decades could have none.

IV

Considered in isolation, the problems of the world economy were, with one exception, less serious. Even left to itself, it would continue to grow. If there was anything in the Kondratiev periodicity (see p. 87), it was due to enter another era of prosperous expansion before the end of the millennium, although this might be hampered for a while by the after-effects of the disintegration of Soviet socialism, by the collapse of parts of the world into anarchy and warfare, and perhaps by an excessive dedication to global free trade, about which economists tend to be more starry-eyed than economic historians. Nevertheless, the scope for expansion was enormous. The Golden Age, as we have seen, was primarily the great leap forward of the 'developed market economies', perhaps twenty countries inhabited by about six hundred millions (1960). Globalization and the international redistribution of production would continue to bring most of the rest of the world's six thousand million into the global economy. Even congenital pessimists had to admit that this was an encouraging prospect for business.

The major exception was the, apparently irreversible, widening of the chasm between the rich and poor countries of the world, a process somewhat accelerated by the disastrous impact of the 1980s in much of the Third World, and the pauperization of many ex-socialist countries. Short of a spectacular fall in the growth-rate of the Third World population, the gap looked like continuing to widen. The belief, following neoclassical economics, that unrestricted international trade would allow the poorer countries to come closer to the rich, runs counter to historical experience as well as common sense.* A world economy developing by the generation of such growing inequalities was, almost inevitably, accumulating future troubles.

However, in any case economic activities do not and cannot exist in isolation from their context and consequences. As we have seen, three aspects of the late twentieth-century world economy gave cause for alarm. First, technology continued to squeeze human labour out of the production of goods and services, without providing either enough work of the same kind for those it jettisoned, or the guarantee of a rate of economic growth sufficient to absorb them. Very few observers seriously expected even a temporary return to the full employment of the Golden Age in the West. Second, while labour remained a major factor of production, the globalization of the economy shifted industry from its old centres in the rich countries with high-cost labour to countries whose main advantage, other things being equal, was cheap hands and heads.

* The examples of successful export-led Third World industrialization usually quoted – Hong Kong, Singapore, Taiwan and South Korea – represent less than 2 per cent of the Third World population.

One or both of two consequences must follow: the transfer of jobs from high-wage to low-wage regions and (on free-market principles) the fall of wages in high-wage regions under the pressure of global wage competition. Old industrial countries like Britain could therefore move in the direction of becoming cheap-labour economies themselves, though with socially explosive results and unlikely to compete on this basis with the NICs. Historically such pressures had been countered by state action – e.g. by protectionism. However, and this was the third worrying aspect of the *fin-de-siècle* world economy, its triumph and that of a pure free market ideology, weakened, or even removed most instruments for managing the social effects of economic upheavals. The world economy was an increasingly powerful and uncontrolled engine. Could it be controlled, and, if so, by whom?

This raised both economic and social problems, though obviously far more immediately troubling ones in some countries (e.g. Britain) than in others (e.g. South Korea).

The economic miracles of the Golden Age had rested on rising real incomes in the 'developed market economies', for mass-consumption economies need mass consumers with enough income for high-technology consumer durables.* Most of these incomes had been earned as wages in high-wage labour markets. These were now at risk, though mass consumers were more essential to the economy than ever. Of course, in the rich countries the mass market had been stabilized by the shift of labour from industry to tertiary occupations, which had, in general, much stabler employment, and by the vast growth in transfer incomes (mostly social security and welfare). These represented something like 30 per cent of the joint GNP of the Western developed countries in the late 1980s. In the 1920s they had probably stood at less than 4 per cent of GNP (Bairoch, 1993, p. 174). This may well explain why the Wall Street stock exchange collapse of 1987, the largest since 1929, did not lead to a world capitalist slump like that of the 1930s.

However, precisely these two stabilizers were now being undermined. As the Short Twentieth Century ended, Western governments and economic orthodoxy agreed that the cost of public social security and welfare was too high and must be reduced, and mass reduction of employment in the hitherto stablest sectors of tertiary occupations –

---

* It is not widely realized that all developed countries except the USA sent a *smaller* share of their exports to the Third World in 1990 than in 1938. The Western ones (including the USA) sent less than one fifth of their exports there in 1990 (Bairoch, 1993, Table 6.1, p. 75).

public employment, banking and finance, the technologically redundant mass office-work – became common. These were not immediate dangers to the global economy, so long as the relative decline in the old markets was compensated by expansion in the rest of the world or, so long as the global number of those with rising real incomes grew faster than the rest. To put it brutally, if the global economy could discard a minority of poor countries as economically uninteresting and irrelevant, it could also do so with the very poor within the borders of any and all its countries, so long as the number of potentially interesting consumers was sufficiently large. Seen from the impersonal heights from which business economists and corporate accountants survey the scene, who needed the 10 per cent of the US population whose real hourly earnings since 1979 had *fallen* by up to 16 per cent?

Again, taking the global perspective which is implict in the model of economic liberalism, inequalities of development are irrelevant unless it can be shown that they produce globally more negative than positive results.* From this point of view there is no economic reason why, if comparative costs say so, France should not shut down its entire agriculture and import all its foodstuffs, or why, if this were technically possible, as well as cost-effective, all the world's TV programmes should not be made in Mexico City. However, this is not a view that can be held without reservations by those who live in the national economy, as well as in the global one; that is to say, by all national governments and most of the inhabitants of their countries. Not least, because we cannot avoid the social and political consequences of worldwide upheavals.

Whatever the nature of these problems, an unrestricted and uncontrolled global free-market economy could provide no solution for them. If anything, it was likely to make developments such as the growth of permanent unemployment and underemployment worse, since the rational choice of profit-making businesses was *a*. to cut down the number of its employees as much as possible, human beings being more expensive than computers, and *b*. to cut down social security (or any other) taxes as far as possible. Nor was there any good reason to suppose that the global free-market economy would solve them. Until the 1970s national and world capitalism had never operated under such conditions or, if they had, had not necessarily benefited. For the nineteenth century it is at least arguable that 'contrary to the classical model, free trade coincided with and was probably the main cause of depression and protectionism

* As a matter of fact, this can often be shown.

was probably the main cause of development for most of today's developed countries' (Bairoch, 1993, p. 164). As for the twentieth century, its economic miracles were not achieved by *laissez-faire* but against it.

It was therefore likely that the fashion for economic liberalization and 'marketization', which had dominated the 1980s, and reached a peak of ideological complacency after the collapse of the Soviet system, would not last long. The combination of the world crisis of the early 1990s, and the spectacular failure of such policies when applied as 'shock therapy' in the ex-socialist countries, already caused second thoughts among some former enthusiasts – who would have expected economic consultants in 1993 to announce 'Perhaps Marx was right after all'? However, two major obstacles stood in the way of a return to realism. The first was the absence of a credible political threat to the system, such as communism and the existence of the USSR, or – in a different way – the Nazi conquest of Germany had once seemed to be. These, as this book has tried to show, had provided the incentive for capitalism to reform itself. The collapse of the USSR, the decline and fragmentation of the working class and its movements, the military insignificance in conventional war of the Third World, the reduction of the really poor in the developed countries to a minority 'underclass' – all these diminished the incentive for reform. Nevertheless, the rise of movements of the ultra-Right, and the unexpected revival of support for the heirs of the old regime in the ex-communist countries, were warning signals, and, by the early 1990s, once again seen to be such. The second was the very process of globalization, reinforced by the dismantling of the national mechanisms for protecting the victims of the free global economy from the social costs of what was proudly described as 'the system of wealth creation ... now everywhere regarded as the most effective that humanity has yet devised.'

For, as the same editorial of the *Financial Times* (24/12/93) admitted

It remains, however, an imperfect force ... About two thirds of the world's population have gained little or no substantial advantage from rapid economic growth. In the developed world, the lowest quartile of income earners have witnessed trickle-up rather than trickle-down.

As the millennium approached, it became increasingly evident that the central task of the time was not to gloat over the corpse of Soviet communism, but to consider, once again, the built-in defects of capitalism. What changes in the system would their removal require? Would it still be the same system after their removal? For, as Joseph Schumpeter had observed, apropos of the cyclical fluctuations of the capitalist economy, they 'are not, like tonsils, separate things that can be treated by themselves, but are, like the beat of the heart, of the essence of the organism that displays them' (Schumpeter, 1939, I, v).

V

The immediate reaction of Western commentators to the collapse of the Soviet system was that it ratified the permanent triumph of both capitalism and liberal democracy, two concepts which the less sophisticated of North American world-watchers tended to confuse. Though capitalism was certainly not in the best of shape at the end of the Short Twentieth Century, Soviet-type communism was unquestionably dead, and quite unlikely to revive. On the other hand, no serious observer in the early 1990s could be as sanguine about liberal democracy as about capitalism. The most that could be predicted with some confidence (except, perhaps, for the more divinely inspired fundamentalist regimes) was that practically all states would continue to declare their profound attachment to democracy, organize elections of some kind, with some toleration for a sometimes notional opposition, while putting their own gloss on the meaning of the term.*

Indeed, the most obvious thing about the political situation of the world's states was its instability. In most of them the chances of survival for the existing regime over the next ten or fifteen years were, on the most optimistic calculation, not good. Even where countries had a relatively predictable system of government, as, for instance, Canada, Belgium or Spain, their existence as single states in ten or fifteen years might be uncertain, and, consequently, so would be the nature of their possible successor regimes, if any. In short, politics was not a field that encouraged futurology.

Nevertheless, some features of the global political landscape stood out. The first, as already noted, was the weakening of the nation-state, the central institution of politics since the Age of Revolution, both by virtue of its monopoly of public power and law, and because it constituted the

---

* Thus a Singaporean diplomat argued that developing countries might benefit from a 'postponement' of democracy, but that, when it arrived, it would be less permissive than the Western type; more authoritarian, stressing the common good rather than individual rights; often with a single dominant party; and nearly always a centralized bureaucracy and 'strong state'.

effective field of political action for most purposes. The nation-state was eroded in two ways, from above and below. It was rapidly losing power and function to various supra-national entities, and, indeed, absolutely, inasmuch as the disintegration of large states and empires produced a multiplicity of smaller ones, too weak to defend themselves in an era of international anarchy. It was also, as we have seen, losing its monopoly of effective power and its historic privileges within its borders, as witness the rise of private security or protection and the rise of private courier services to compete with the post, hitherto virtually everywhere managed by a state ministry.

These developments did not make the state either redundant or ineffective. Indeed, in some respects its capacity to monitor and control the affairs of its citizens was reinforced by technology, since virtually all their financial and administrative transactions (other than small cash payments) were now likely to be recorded by some computer, and all their communications (except for most face-to-face conversations in the open air) could now be intercepted and recorded. And yet, its posture had changed. From the eighteenth century until the second half of the twentieth, the nation-state had extended its range, powers and functions almost continuously. This was an essential aspect of 'modernization'. Whether governments were liberal, conservative, social-democratic, fascist or communist, at the peak of this trend, the parameters of citizens' lives in 'modern' states were almost exclusively determined (except during inter-state conflict) by the activities or inactivities of that state. Even the impact of global forces, such as world economic booms and slumps, came to them filtered through their state's policy and institutions.* By the end of the century the nation-state was on the defensive against a world economy it could not control; against the institutions it had constructed to remedy its own international weakness, such as the European Union; against its apparent financial incapacity to maintain the services to its citizens so confidently undertaken a few decades ago; against its real incapacity to maintain what, by its own criteria, was its major function: the maintenance of public law and order. The very fact that, during the era of its rise, the state had taken over and centralized so many functions,

* Thus Bairoch suggests that the reason why the Swiss GNP per capita fell in the 1930s while that of the Swedes rose – in spite of the fact that the great slump had been much less severe in Switzerland – is 'largely explained by the wide range of socio-economic measures taken by the Swedish government and the lack of intervention by the Swiss federal authorities' (Bairoch, 1993, p. 9).

and set itself such ambitious standards of public order and control, made its inability to maintain them doubly painful.

And yet, the state, or some other form of public authority representing the public interest, was more indispensable than ever if the social and environmental iniquities of the market economy were to be countered, or even – as the reform of capitalism in the 1940s had shown – if the economic system was to operate satisfactorily. Without some state allocation and redistribution of the national income, what, for instance, would happen to the peoples of the old developed countries, whose economy rested on a relatively shrinking foundation of income earners, squeezed between the rising numbers of those not needed for labour by the high-tech economy, and a swelling proportion of the non-earning old? It was absurd to argue that the citizens of the European Community, whose per capita share of the joint national income had increased by 80 per cent from 1970 to 1990, could not 'afford' the level of income and welfare in 1990 that had been taken for granted in 1970 (World Tables, 1991, pp. 8–9). But these could not exist without the state. Suppose – the scenario is not utterly fantastic – present trends continued, and led to economies in which one quarter of the population worked gainfully, and three quarters did not, but after twenty years the economy produced a national income per capital twice as large as before. Who, except public authority, would and could ensure a minimum of income and welfare for all? Who could counter the tendencies to inequality so strikingly visible in the Crisis Decades? To judge by the experience of the 1970s and 1980s, not the free market. If these decades proved anything it was that the major political problem of the world, and certainly of the developed world, was not how to multiply the wealth of nations, but how to distribute it for the benefit of their inhabitants. This was so even in poor 'developing' countries which needed more economic growth. Brazil, a monument to social neglect, had a GNP per capita almost two-and-a-half times as large as Sri Lanka in 1939, and over six times as large at the end of the 1980s. In Sri Lanka, which had subsidized basic foodstuffs and given free education and health care until the later 1970s, the average newborn could expect to live several years longer than the average Brazilian, and to die as an infant at about half the Brazilian rate in 1969, at a third of the Brazilian rate in 1989 (World Tables, pp. 144–47, 524–27). The percentage of illiteracy in 1989 was almost twice as great in Brazil as on the Asian island.

Social distribution and not growth would dominate the politics of the new millennium. Non-market allocation of resources, or, at least, a ruthless limitation of market allocation, was essential to head off the impending ecological crisis. One way or another, the fate of humanity in the new millennium would depend on the restoration of public authorities.

VI

This leaves us with a double problem. What would be the nature and scope of the decision-making authorities – supranational, national, subnational and global, alone or in combination? What would be their relation to the people about whom these decisions are made?

The first was, in a sense, a technical question, since the authorities were already in existence, and in principle – though by no means in practice – so were models of the relationship between them. The expanding European Union provided plenty of relevant material, even if every specific proposal for dividing labour between global, supranational, national and subnational authorities was likely to be bitterly resented by someone or other. The existing global authorities were no doubt too specialized in their functions, though they tried to extend their range by imposing political and ecological policies on countries that needed to borrow money. The European Union stood alone, and, being the child of a specific and probably unrepeatable historical conjuncture, was likely to remain alone, unless something similar was to be reconstituted from fragments of the former USSR. The pace at which supranational decision-making would advance, could not be predicted. Nevertheless, it would certainly advance, and one could see how it might operate. It operated already, through the global bank-managers of the great international lending-agencies, representing the joint resources of the oligarchy of the richest countries, which also happened to include the most powerful ones. As the gap between the rich and poor grew, the scope for exercising such global power looked like increasing. The trouble was that, since the 1970s, the World Bank and the International Monetary Fund, politically backed by the USA, had pursued a policy systematically favouring free-market orthodoxy, private enterprise and global free trade, which suited the late twentieth-century US economy as well as it had the mid-nineteenth-century British one, but not necessarily the world. If global decision-making was to realize its potential, such policies would have to be changed. This did not look an immediate prospect.

The second problem was not technical at all. It arose out of the dilemma of a world committed, at the end of the century, to a particular brand of political democracy, but also faced with policy problems, to

which the election of presidents and pluri-party assemblies were irrelevant, even when it did not complicate their solutions. More generally, it
was the dilemma of the role of the common people in what had been
called, correctly, at least by pre-feminist standards, 'the century of the
common man'. It was the dilemma of an age when government could –
some would say: must – be 'of the people' and 'for the people', but could
not in any operational sense be 'by the people', or even by representative
assemblies elected among those who competed for its vote. The dilemma
was not new. The difficulties of democratic politics (discussed for the
inter-war years in an earlier chapter) had been familiar to political
scientists and satirists since the politics of universal suffrage became more
than a peculiarity of the USA.

The democratic predicament was more acute now, both because public
opinion, monitored by polls, magnified by the omnipresent media, was
now constantly inescapable, and because public authorities had to take far
more decisions to which public opinion was no sort of guide. Often they
might have to be decisions which might well be opposed by the majority
of the electorate, each voter disliking their prospective effect on his or her
private affairs, though perhaps believing them to be desirable in the
general interest. Thus at the end of the century politicians in some
democratic countries had come to the conclusion that any proposal to
raise taxes for any purpose meant electoral suicide. Elections therefore
became contests in fiscal perjury. At the same time voters and parliaments
were constantly faced with decisions on matters about which non-experts
– that is to say, the vast majority both of the electors and the elected –
had no qualifications to express an opinion, for instance the future of the
nuclear industry.

There had been moments, even in democratic states, when the citizen
body was so identified with the purposes of a government enjoying
legitimacy and public trust that a sense of the common interest prevailed,
as in Britain during the Second World War. There had been other
situations which made possible a basic consensus between the main
political rivals, once again leaving governments free to pursue the general
aims of policies, about which there was no major disagreement. As we
have seen, this was the case in a number of Western countries during the
Golden Age. Governments had also, often enough, been able to rely on a
consensus of peer judgment among their technical and scientific advisers,
indispensable to administrations of laymen. When they spoke with the
same voice, or, at any rate, their consensus overrode dissidents, policy
controversy narrowed. It is when they do not, that lay decision-makers
grope through darkness, like juries faced with rival psychologists called

by prosecution and defence, neither of whom there is strong reason to believe.

But, as we have seen, the Crisis Decades had undermined political consensus and generally accepted truths in intellectual matters, especially in fields with a bearing on policy. As for undivided peoples firmly identified with their governments (or the other way round), they were thin on the ground in the 1990s. True, there were still many countries whose citizens accepted the idea of a strong, active and socially responsible state that deserved some freedom of action, because it served the common welfare. Unfortunately the actual governments of the *fin-de-siècle* rarely looked like this ideal. As for the countries in which government as such was suspect, they were those which modelled themselves on the USA's pattern of individualist anarchism, tempered by litigation and pork-barrel politics, and the much more numerous ones where the state was so weak or so corrupt that citizens did not expect it to produce any public good at all. These were common in parts of the Third World, but, as Italy in the 1980s showed, not unknown in the First.

Hence the most untroubled decision-makers were those who escaped democratic politics altogether: private corporations, supranational authorities and, of course, non-democratic regimes. Within democratic systems it was not so easy to shelter decision-making from politicians, although central banks were removed from their grasp in some countries and conventional wisdom wanted this example followed elsewhere. Increasingly, however, governments took to by-passing both the electorate and its representative assemblies, if possible, or at least to taking decisions first and then challenging both to reverse a *fait accompli*, relying on the volatility, divisions or inertness of public opinion. Politics increasingly became an exercise in evasion, as politicians were afraid to tell voters what they did not want to hear. After the end of the Cold War, unavowable actions were no longer so easily hidden behind the iron curtain of 'national security'. Almost certainly this strategy of evasion would continue to gain ground. Even in democratic countries more and more decision-making bodies would be withdrawn from electoral control, except in the most indirect sense that the governments which appointed such bodies had themselves, at one time, been elected. Centralizing governments, such as those of Britain in the 1980s and early 1990s, were particularly inclined to multiply such *ad hoc* authorities not answering to an electorate and nicknamed 'quangos'. Even countries without an effective division of powers found this tacit demotion of democracy convenient. In countries like the USA it was indispensable, since the built-in conflict between executive and legislature made it almost impossible to take decisions under normal circumstances, except behind the scenes.

By the century's end large numbers of citizens were withdrawing from politics, leaving the affairs of state to the 'political class' – the phrase seems to have originated in Italy – who read each others' speeches and editorials, a special-interest group of professional politicians, journalists, lobbyists and others whose occupations ranked at the bottom of the scale of trustworthiness in sociological enquiries. For many people the political process was irrelevant, or merely something that affected their personal lives favourably or not. On the one hand, wealth, the privatisation of life and entertainment, and consumer egoism, made politics less important and less attractive. On the other hand, those who reckoned to get little out of elections, turned their backs on them. Between 1960 and 1988 the proportion of blue-collar workers who cast their vote in American presidential elections, fell by one third (Leighly, Naylor, 1992, p. 731). The decline of the organized mass parties, class-based, ideological or both, eliminated the major social engine for turning men and women into politically active citizens. For most people even the collective identification with their country now came more easily through the national sports, teams and non-political symbols than through the institutions of the state.

One might have supposed that de-politicisation would leave the authorities freer to take decisions. In fact, it had the opposite effect. The minorities which went on campaigning, sometimes for specific issues of public interest, more often for some sectional interest, could interfere with the smooth processes of government just as effectively, perhaps even more effectively, than all-purpose political parties, since, unlike these, each pressure group could concentrate its energy on pursuing a single objective. Moreover, the increasingly systematic tendency of governments to sidestep the electoral process, magnified the political function of the mass media, which now reached into every household, providing by far the most powerful means of communication from the public sphere to the private men, women and children. Their capacity to discover and publish what authority wished to keep quiet, and to give expression to public feelings which were not, or could no longer be, articulated by the formal mechanisms of democracy, made them into major actors on the public scene. Politicians used them and were frightened of them. Technical progress made them increasingly difficult to control, even in highly authoritarian countries. The decline of state power made them harder to monopolize in non-authoritarian ones. As the century ended it became evident that the media were a more important component of the political process than parties and electoral systems, and likely to remain so –

unless politics took a sharp turn away from democracy. However, while they were enormously powerful as a counterweight to government secrecy, they were in no sense a means of democratic government.

Neither the media, nor assemblies elected by the politics of universal suffrage, nor 'the people' itself could actually govern in any realistic sense of the word. On the other hand, government, or any analogous form of public decision-making, could no longer govern against the people or even without it, any more than 'the people' could live without or against government. For better or worse, in the twentieth century the common people entered history as actors in their own collective right. Every regime except theocracy now derived its authority from them, even those who terrorized and killed their citizens on a large scale. The very concept of what it was once fashionable to call 'totalitarianism' implied populism, for if it did not matter what 'the people' thought about those who ruled in its name, why bother to make them think the thoughts deemed appropriate by their rulers? Governments which derived their authority from the unquestioning obedience to some divinity, to tradition, or from the deference of lower to higher ranks in a hierarchical society, were on the way out. Even Islamic 'fundamentalism', the most flourishing brand of theocracy, advanced not by the will of Allah, but by the mass mobilization of the common people against unpopular governments. Whether 'the people' had the right to elect its government or not, its interventions in public affairs, active or passive, were decisive.

Indeed, just because the twentieth century had plenty of examples of incomparably ruthless regimes, and those seeking to impose minority power on majorities by force – as in *apartheid* South Africa – it demonstrated the limits of sheer coercive power. Even the most ruthless and brutal rulers were well aware that unlimited power alone could not supplant the political assets and skills of authority: a public sense of the regime's legitimacy, a degree of active popular support, the ability to divide and rule, and – especially in times of crisis – the citizens' willing obedience. When, as in 1989, this obedience was visibly withdrawn from Eastern European regimes, these regimes abdicated, even though they still had the full backing of their civil functionaries, armed forces and security services. In short, contrary to appearances, the twentieth century showed that one can rule against all the people for some of the time, some of the people all the time, but not all the people all the time. Admittedly, this was no comfort to permanently oppressed minorities or to peoples who suffered during a generation or more of virtually universal oppression.

Yet all this did not answer the question what the relation between decision-makers and peoples should be. It merely underlined the difficulty of the answer. The policies of authorities had to take account of what people, or at least majorities of citizens, wanted or did not want, even if it was not their purpose to reflect popular wishes. At the same time they could not govern simply on the basis of asking them. Moreover, unpopular decisions were harder to impose on masses than on power-groups. It was far easier to impose mandatory standards of emission on a few giant auto-producers than to persuade millions of motorists to halve their petrol consumption. Every European government discovered that the results of leaving the future of the European Community to popular votes were unfavourable, or at best unpredictable. Every serious observer knew that many of the policy decisions that would have to be taken in the early twenty-first century, would be unpopular. Perhaps another tension-relax-ing era of general prosperity and improvement, like the Golden Age, would soften the citizens' mood, but neither a return to the 1960s nor a relaxation of the social and cultural insecurities and tensions of the Crisis Decades were to be expected.

If voting by universal suffrage remained the general rule – as was probable – there seemed to be two main options. Where decision-making was not already outside politics, it would increasingly side-step the electoral process, or rather the constant monitoring of government insepa-rable from it. Authorities which had themselves to be elected would also, increasingly, hide, octopus-like, behind clouds of obfuscation to confuse their electorates. The other option was to recreate the sort of consensus which allowed authorities substantial freedom of action, at least so long as the bulk of citizens did not feel too much cause for discontent. An old-established political model for this had been available since Napoleon III in the mid-nineteenth century: the democratic election of a saviour of the people or a nation-saving regime – i.e. 'plebiscitary democracy'. Such a regime might or might not have come to power constitutionally, but, if ratified by a reasonably honest election with a choice of rival candidates, and some voice for an opposition, it satisfied the *fin-de-siècle* criteria of democratic legitimacy. But it offered no encouraging prospect for the future of parliamentary democracy of the liberal kind.

VII

What I have written cannot tell us whether and how humanity can solve problems it faces at the end of the millennium. Perhaps it can help us understand what these problems are, and what the conditions for their solution must be, but not how far these conditions are present, or in the process of coming into being. It can tell us how little we know, and how extraordinarily poor has been the understanding of men and women who took the major public decisions in the century; how little of what happened, especially in the second half of that century, was expected and still less predicted by them. It can confirm what many have always suspected, that history – among many other and more important things – is the record of the crimes and follies of mankind. It is no help to prophesy.

So it would be foolish to end this book with predictions of what a landscape will look like which has already been left unrecognizable by the tectonic upheavals of the Short Twentieth Century, and will be left even more unrecognizable by those which are even now taking place. There is less reason to feel hopeful about the future than in the middle 1980s, when the present author concluded his trilogy on the history of the 'long nineteenth century' (1789–1914) with the words:

> The evidence that the world in the twenty-first century will be better is not negligible. If the world succeeds in not destroying itself [i.e. by nuclear war], the probability will be quite strong.

Nevertheless, even a historian whose age precludes him from expecting dramatic changes for the better in what remains of his lifetime, cannot reasonably deny the possibility that in another quarter- or half-century things may look more promising. In any case it is highly likely that the present phase of post-Cold War breakdown will be temporary, even though it already looks like lasting rather longer than the phases of breakdown and disruption which followed the two 'hot' world wars. However, hopes or fears are not predictions. We know that behind the opaque cloud of our ignorance and the uncertainty of detailed outcomes, the historical forces that shaped the century, are continuing to operate. We live in a world captured, uprooted and transformed by the titanic economic and techno-scientific process of the development of capitalism, which has dominated the past two or three centuries. We know, or at least it is reasonable to suppose, that it cannot go on *ad infinitum*. The future cannot be a continuation of the past, and there are signs, both externally, and, as it were, internally, that we have reached a point of historic crisis. The forces generated by the techno-scientific economy are now great enough to destroy the environment, that is to say, the material foundations of human life. The structures of human societies themselves, including even some of the social foundations of the capitalist economy, are on the point of being destroyed by the erosion of what we have inherited from the human past. Our world risks both explosion and implosion. It must change.

We do not know where we are going. We only know that history has brought us to this point and – if readers share the argument of this book – why. However, one thing is plain. If humanity is to have a recognizable future, it cannot be by prolonging the past or the present. If we try to build the third millennium on that basis, we shall fail. And the price of failure, that is to say, the alternative to a changed society, is darkness.

References

Abrams, 1945: Mark Abrams, *The Condition of the British People, 1911-1945* (London, 1945)

Acheson, 1970: Dean Acheson, *Present at the Creation: My Years in the State Department* (New York, 1970)

Afanassiev, 1991: Juri Afanassiev, in M. Paquet ed. *Le court vingtième siècle*, *preface* d'Alexandre Adler (La Tour d'Aigues, 1991)

Agosti/Borgese, 1992: Paola Agosti, Giovanna Borgese, *Mi pare un secolo: Ritratti e parole di centosei protagonisti del Novecento* (Turin, 1992)

Albers/Goldschmidt/Oehlke, 1971: *Klassenkämpfe in Westeuropa* (Hamburg, 1971)

Alexeev, 1990: M. Alexeev, book review in *Journal of Comparative Economics* vol.14, pp. 171–73 (1990)

Allen, 1968: D. Elliston Allen, *British Tastes: An enquiry into the likes and dislikes of the regional consumer* (London, 1968)

Amnesty, 1975: Amnesty International, *Report on Torture* (New York, 1975)

Andrić, 1990: Ivo Andrić, *Conversation with Goya: Bridges, Signs* (London, 1990)

Andrew, 1985: Christopher Andrew, *Secret Service: The Making of the British Intelligence Community* (London, 1985)

Andrew/Gordievsky, 1991: Christopher Andrew and Oleg Gordievsky, *KGB: The Inside Story of its Foreign Operations from Lenin to Gorbachev* (London, 1991)

Anuario, 1989: *Comisión Economica para America Latina y el Caribe, Anuario Estadístico de America Latina y el Caribe: Edición 1989* (Santiago de Chile, 1990)

Arlacchi, 1983: Pino Arlacchi, *Mafia Business* (London, 1983)

Armstrong, Glyn, Harrison: Philip Armstrong, Andrew Glyn, John Harrison, *Capitalism Since 1945* (Oxford, 1991 edn)

Arndt, 1944: H.W. Arndt, *The Economic Lessons of the 1930s* (London, 1944)

Asbeck, 1939: Baron F.M. van Asbeck, *The Netherlands Indies' Foreign Relations* (Amsterdam, 1939)

Atlas, 1992: A. Fréron, R.Hérin, J. July eds, *Atlas de la France Universitaire* (Paris, 1992)

Auden: W.H. Auden, *Spain* (London, 1937)

Babel, 1923: Isaac Babel, *Konarmiya* (Moscow, 1923); *Red Cavalry* (London, 1929)

Bairoch, 1985: Paul Bairoch, *De Jéricho à Mexico: villes et économie dans l'histoire* (Paris, 1985)

Bairoch, 1988: Paul Bairoch, *Two major shifts in Western European Labour Force: the Decline of the Manufacturing Industries and of the Working Class* (mimeo) (Geneva, 1988)

Bairoch, 1993: Paul Bairoch, *Economics and World History: Myths and Paradoxes* (Hemel Hempstead, 1993)

Ball, 1992: George W. Ball, 'JFK's Big Moment' in *New York Review of Books*, pp. 16–20 (13 February 1992)

Ball 1993: George W. Ball, 'The Rationalist in Power' in *New York Review of Books* 22 April 1993, pp. 30–36

Baltimore, 1978: David Baltimore, 'Limiting Science: A Biologist's Perspective' in *Daedalus* 107/2 spring 1978, pp. 37–46

Banham, 1971: Reyner Banham, *Los Angeles* (Harmondsworth, 1973)

Banham, 1975: Reyner Banham, in C.W.E. Bigsby ed. *Superculture: American Popular Culture and Europe*, pp. 69–82 (London, 1975)

Banks, 1971: A.S. Banks, *Cross-Polity Time Series Data* (Cambridge MA and London, 1971)

Barghava/Singh Gill, 1988: Motilal Barghava and Americk Singh Gill, *Indian National Army Secret Service* (New Delhi, 1988)

Barnet, 1981: Richard Barnet, *Real Security* (New York, 1981)

Becker, 1985: J.J. Becker, *The Great War and the French People* (Leamington Spa, 1985)

Bédarida, 1992: François Bédarida, *Le génocide et la nazisme: Histoire et témoignages* (Paris, 1992)

Beinart, 1984: William Beinart, 'Soil erosion, conservationism and ideas about development: A Southern African exploration, 1900–1960' in *Journal of Southern African Studies* 11, 1984, pp. 52–83

Bell, 1960: Daniel Bell, *The End of Ideology* (Glencoe, 1960)

Bell, 1976: Daniel Bell, *The Cultural Contradictions of Capitalism* (New York, 1976)

Benjamin, 1961: Walter Benjamin, '*Das Kunstwerk im Zeitalter seiner Reproduzierbarkeit*' in *Illuminationen: Ausgewählte Schriften*, pp. 148–184 (Frankfurt, 1961)

Benjamin, 1971: Walter Benjamin, *Zur Kritik der Gewalt und andere Aufsätze*, pp. 84–85 (Frankfurt 1971)

Benjamin, 1979: Walter Benjamin, *One-Way Street, and Other Writings* (London, 1979)

Bergson/Levine, 1983: A. Bergson and H.S. Levine eds. *The Soviet Economy: Towards the Year 2000* (London, 1983)

Berman: Paul Berman, 'The Face of Downtown' in *Dissent* autumn 1987, pp. 569–73

Bernal, 1939: J.D. Bernal, *The Social Function of Science* (London, 1939)

Bernal, 1967: J.D. Bernal, *Science in History* (London, 1967)

Bernier/Boily: Gérard Bernier, Robert Boily et al., *Le Québec en chiffres de 1850 à nos jours*, p. 228 (Montreal, 1986)

Bernstorff, 1970: Dagmar Bernstorff, 'Candidates for the 1967 General Election in Hyderabad' in E. Leach and S.N. Mukhejee eds, *Elites in South Asia* (Cambridge, 1970)

Beschloss, 1991: Michael R. Beschloss, *The Crisis Years: Kennedy and Khrushchev 1960–1963* (New York, 1991)

Beyer, 1981: Gunther Beyer, 'The Political Refugee: 35 Years Later' in *International Migration Review* vol. XV, pp. 1–219

Block, 1977: Fred L. Block, *The Origins of International Economic Disorder: A Study of United States International Monetary Policy from World War II to the Present* (Berkeley, 1977)

Bobinska/Pilch 1975: Celina Bobinska, Andrzej Pilch, *Employment-seeking Emigrations of the Poles World-Wide XIX and XX C.* (Cracow, 1975)

Bocca, 1966: Giorgio Bocca, *Storia dell'Italia Partigiana Settembre 1943–Maggio 1945* (Bari, 1966)

Bokhari, 1993: Farhan Bokhari, 'Afghan border focus of region's woes' in *Financial Times, 12 August 1993*

Boldyrev, 1990: Yu Boldyrev in *Literaturnaya Gazeta*, 19 December 1990, cited in Di Leo, 1992

Bolotin, 1987: B. Bolotin in *World Economy and International Relations* No. 11, 1987, pp. 148–52 (in Russian)

Bourdieu, 1979: Pierre Bourdieu, *La Distinction: Critique Sociale du Jugement* (Paris, 1979), English trs: *Distinction: A Social Critique of the Judgment of Taste* (Cambridge MA, 1984)

Bourdieu, 1994: Pierre Bourdieu, Hans Haacke, *Libre-Echange* (Paris, 1994)

Britain: *Britain: An Official Handbook* 1961, 1990 eds. (London, Central Office for Information)

Briggs, 1961: Asa Briggs, *The History of Broadcasting in the United Kingdom* vol. 1 (London, 1961); vol.2 (1965); vol.3 (1970); vol.4 (1979)

Brown, 1963: Michael Barratt Brown, *After Imperialism* (London, Melbourne, Toronto, 1963)

Brecht, 1964: Bertolt Brecht, Über Lyrik (Frankfurt, 1964)

Brecht, 1976: Bertolt Brecht, *Gesammelte Gedichte*, 4 vols (Frankfurt, 1976)

Brzezinski 1962: Z.Brzezinski, *Ideology and Power in Soviet Politics* (New York, 1962)

Brzezinski, 1993: Z. Brzezinski, *Out of Control: Global Turmoil on the Eve of the Twenty-first Century* (New York, 1993)

Burks, 1961: R.V.Burks, *The Dynamics of Communism in Eastern Europe* (Princeton, 1961)

Burlatsky, 1992: Fedor Burlatsky, 'The Lessons of Personal Diplomacy' in *Problems of Communism*, vol. XVI (41), 1992

Burloiu, 1983: Petre Burloiu, *Higher Education and Economic Development in Europe 1975–80* (UNESCO, Bucharest, 1983)

Butterfield 1991: Fox Butterfield, 'Experts Explore Rise in Mass Murder' in *New York Times* 19 October 1991, p. 6

Calvocoressi, 1987: Peter Calvocoressi, *A Time for Peace: Pacifism, Internationalism and Protest Forces in the Reduction of War* (London, 1987)

Calvocoressi, 1989: Peter Calvocoressi, *World Politics Since 1945* (London, 1989 edn)

Carritt, 1985: Michael Carritt, *A Mole in the Crown* (Hove, 1980)

Carr-Saunders, 1958: A. M. Carr-Saunders, D. Caradog Jones, C. A. Moser, *A Survey of Social Conditions in England and Wales* (Oxford, 1958)

Catholic: *The Official Catholic Directory* (New York, annual)

Chamberlin, 1933: W. Chamberlin, *The Theory of Monopolistic Competition* (Cambridge MA, 1933)

Chamberlin, 1965: W.H. Chamberlin, *The Russian Revolution, 1917-1921*, 2 vols (New York, 1965 edn).

Chandler, 1977: Alfred D. Chandler Jr, *The Visible Hand: The Managerial Revolution in American Business* (Cambridge MA, 1977)

Chapple/Garofalo, 1977: S. Chapple and R. Garofalo, *Rock'n Roll Is Here to Pay* (Chicago, 1977)

Chiesa, 1993: Giulietta Chiesa, '*Era una fine inevitabile?*' in *Il Passagio: rivista di dibattito politico e culturale*, VI, July-October, pp. 27–37

Childers, 1983: Thomas Childers, *The Nazi Voter: The Social Foundations of Fascism in Germany, 1919-1933* (Chapel Hill, 1983)

Childers, 1991: 'The *Sonderweg* controversy and the Rise of German Fascism' in (unpublished conference papers) *Germany and Russia in the 20th Century in Comparative Perspective*, pp. 8, 14–15 (Philadelphia 1991)

China Statistics, 1989: State Statistical Bureau of the People's Republic of China, *China Statistical Yearbook 1989* (New York, 1990)

Ciconte, 1992: Enzo Ciconte, '*Ndrangheta dall' Unita a oggi* (Barri, 1992)

Cmd 1586, 1992: British Parliamentary Papers cmd 1586: *East India* (*Non-Co-operation*), XVl, p. 579, 1922. (Telegraphic Correspondence regarding the situation in India.)

Considine, 1982: Douglas M. Considine and Glenn Considine, *Food and Food Production Encyclopedia* (New York, Cincinnati etc., 1982). Article in 'meat', section, 'Formed, Fabricated and Restructured Meat Products'.

Crosland, 1957: Anthony Crosland, *The Future of Socialism* (London, 1957)

Dawkins, 1976: Richard Dawkins, *The Selfish Gene* (Oxford, 1976)

Deakin/Storry, 1966: F.W. Deakin and G.R. Storry, *The Case of Richard Sorge* (London, 1966)

Debray, 1965: Régis Debray, *La révolution dans la révolution* (Paris, 1965)

Debray, 1994: Régis Debray, *Charles de Gaulle: Futurist of the Nation* (London, 1994)

Degler, 1987: Carl N. Degler, 'On re-reading "The Woman in America"' in *Daedalus*, autumn 1987

Delgado, 1992: Manuel Delgado, *La Ira Sagrada: Anticlericalismo, iconoclastia y antiritualismo en la España contemporanea* (Barcelona, 1992)

Delzell, 1970: Charles F. Delzell ed., *Mediterranean Fascism, 1919-1945* (New York, 1970)

Deng, 1984 Deng Xiaoping, *Selected Works of Deng Xiaoping* (*1975–1984*) (Beijing, 1984)

Desmond/Moore: Adrian Desmond and James Moore, *Darwin* (London, 1991)

Destabilization, 1989: United Nations Inter-Agency Task Force, Africa Recovery Programme/Economic Commission for Africa, *South African Destabilization The Economic Cost of Frontline Resistance to Apartheid* (New York, 1989)

Deux Ans, 1990: *Ministère de l'Education Nationale:Enseignement Supérieur*, Deux Ans d'Action, 1988–1990 (Paris, 1990)

Di Leo, 1992: Rita di Leo, *Vecchi quadri e nuovi politici: Chi commanda davvero nell'ex-Urss?* (Bologna, 1992)

Din, 1989: Kadir Din, 'Islam and Tourism' in *Annals of Tourism Research*, vol. 16/4, 1989, pp. 542 ff.

Djilas, 1957: Milovan Djilas, *The New Class* (London, 1957)

Djilas, 1962: Milovan Djilas, *Conversations with Stalin* (London, 1962)

Djilas, 1977: Milovan Djilas, *Wartime* (New York, 1977)

Drell, 1977: Sidney D. Drell, 'Elementary Particle Physics' in *Daedalus* 106/3, summer 1977, pp. 15–32

Duberman et al, 1989: M. Duberman, M. Vicinus and G. Chauncey, *Hidden From History: Reclaiming the Gay and Lesbian Past*, New York, 1989

Dutt, 1945: Kalpana Dutt, *Chittagong Armoury Raiders: Reminiscences* (Bombay, 1945)

Duverger, 1972: Maurice Duverger, *Party Politics and Pressure Groups: A Comparative Introduction* (New York, 1972)

Dyker, 1985: D.A. Dyker, *The Future of the Soviet Economic Planning System* (London, 1985)

Echenberg, 1992: Myron Echenberg, *Colonial Conscripts: The* Tirailleurs Sénégalais *in French West Africa, 1857-1960* (London, 1992)

EIB Papers, 1992: European Investment Bank, Cahiers BEI/EIB Papers, J. Girard, *De la recession à la reprise en Europe Centrale et Orientale,* pp. 9–22, (Luxemburg, 1992)

Encyclopedia Britannica, article 'war' (11th edn, 1911).

Ercoli, 1936: Ercoli, *On the Peculiarity of the Spanish Revolution* (New York, 1936); reprinted in Palmiro Togliatti, *Opere* IV/i, pp. 139–54 (Rome, 1979)

Esman, 1990: Aaron H. Esman, *Adolescence and Culture* (New York, 1990)

Estrin/Holmes, 1990: Saul Estrin and Peter Holmes, 'Indicative Planning in Developed Economies' in *Journal of Comparative Economics* 14/4 December 1990, pp. 531–54

Eurostat: *Eurostat. Basic Statistics of the Community* (Office for the Official Publications of the European Community, Luxemburg, annual since 1957)

Evans, 1989: Richard Evans, *In Hitler's Shadow: West German Historians and the Attempt to Escape from the Nazi Past* (New York, 1989)

Fainsod, 1956: Merle Fainsod, *How Russia Is Ruled* (Cambridge MA, 1956)

FAO, 1989: FAO (UN Food and Agriculture Organization), *The State of Food and Agriculture: world and regional reviews, sustainable development and natural resource management* (Rome, 1989)

FAO Production: FAO *Production Yearbook,* 1986

FAO Trade: FAO *Trade Yearbook* vol. 40, 1986

Fitzpatrick, 1994: Sheila Fitzpatrick, *Stalin's Peasants* (Oxford, 1994)

Firth, 1954: Raymond Firth, 'Money, Work and Social Change in Indo-Pacific Economic Systems' in *International Social Science Bulletin,* vol. 6, 1954, pp. 400–10

Fischhof et al., 1978: B. Fischhof, P. Slovic, Sarah Lichtenstein, S. Read, Barbara Coombs, 'How Safe is Safe Enough? A Psychometric Study of Attitudes towards Technological Risks and Benefits' in *Policy Sciences 9,* 1978, pp. 127–152

Flora, 1983: Peter Flora et.al., *State, Economy and Society in Western Europe 1815-1975: A Data Handbook in Two Volumes* (Frankfurt, London, Chicago, 1983)

Floud et al., 1990: Roderick Floud, Annabel Gregory, Kenneth Wachter, *Height, Health and History: Nutritional Status in the United Kingdom 1750-1980* (Cambridge, 1990)

Fontana, 1977: Alan Bullock and Oliver Stallybrass eds., *The Fontana Dictionary of Modern Ideas* (London, 1977 edn)

Foot, 1976: M.R.D. Foot, *Resistance: An Analysis of European Resistance to Nazism 1940–1945* (London, 1976)

Francia, Muzzioli, 1984: Mauro Francia, Giuliano Muzzioli, *Cent'anni di cooperazione: La cooperazione di consumo modenese aderente alla Lega dalle origini all'unificazione* (Bologna, 1984)

Frazier, 1957: Franklin Frazier, *The Negro in the United States* (New York, 1957 edn)

Freedman, 1959: Maurice Freedman, 'The Handling of Money: A Note on the Background to the Economic Sophistication of the Overseas Chinese' in *Man*, vol. 59, 1959, pp. 64–65

Friedan, 1963: Betty Friedan, *The Feminine Mystique* (New York, 1963)

Friedman 1968: Milton Friedman, 'The Role of Monetary Policy' in *American Economic Review*, vol. LVIII, no. 1, March 1968, pp. 1–17

Fröbel, Heinrichs, Kreye, 1986: Folker Fröbel, Jürgen Heinrichs, Otto Kreye, *Umbruch in der Weltwirtschaft* (Hamburg, 1986)

Galbraith, 1974: J.K. Galbraith, *The New Industrial State* (2nd edn, Harmondsworth, 1974)

Gallagher, 1971: M.D. Gallagher, 'Léon Blum and the Spanish Civil War' in *Journal of Contemporary History*, vol. 6, no. 3, 1971, pp. 56–64

Garton Ash, 1990: Timothy Garton Ash, *The Uses of Adversity: Essays on the Fate of Central Europe* (New York, 1990)

Gatrell/Harrison, 1993: Peter Gatrell and Mark Harrison, 'The Russian and Soviet Economies in Two World Wars: A Comparative View' in *Economic History Review* XLVI, 3, 1993, pp. 424–52

Giedion, 1948: S. Giedion, *Mechanisation Takes Command* (New York, 1948)

Gillis, 1974: John R. Gillis, *Youth and History* (New York, 1974)

Gillis, 1985: John Gillis, *For Better, For Worse: British Marriages 1600 to the Present* (New York, 1985)

Gillois, 1973: André Gillois, *Histoire Secrète des Français à Londres de 1940 à 1944* (Paris, 1973)

Gimpel, 1992: 'Prediction or Forecast? Jean Gimpel interviewed by Sanda Miller' in *The New European*, vol. 5/2, 1992, pp. 7–12

Ginneken/Heuven, 1989: Wouter van Ginneken and Rolph van der Heuven, 'Industrialisation, employment and earnings (1950–87): An international survey' in *International Labour Review*, vol. 128, 1989/5, pp. 571–99

Gleick, 1988: James Gleick, *Chaos: Making a New Science* (London, 1988)

Glenny 1992: Misha Glenny, *The Fall of Yugoslavia: The Third Balkan War* (London, 1992)

Glyn, Hughes, Lipietz, Singh, 1990: Andrew Glyn, Alan Hughes, Alan Lipietz, Ajit Singh, *The Rise and Fall of the Golden Age* in Marglin and Schor, 1990, pp. 39–125

Gómez Rodríguez, 1977: Juan de la Cruz Gómez Rodríguez, '*Comunidades de pastores y reforma agraria en la sierra sur peruana*' in Jorge A. Flores Ochoa, *Pastores de puna* (Lima, 1977)

González Casanova 1975: Pablo González Casanova, coord. *Cronología de la violencia política en America Latina* (1945–1970), 2 vols (Mexico DF, 1975)

Goody, 1968: Jack Goody, 'Kinship: descent groups' in *International Encyclopedia of Social Sciences*, vol. 8, pp. 402–3 (New York, 1968)

Goody, 1990: Jack Goody, *The Oriental, the Ancient and the Primitive: Systems of Marriage and the Family in the Pre-Industrial Societies of Eurasia* (Cambridge, 1990)

Gopal, 1979: Sarvepalli Gopal, *Jawaharlal Nehru: A Biography, vol, II, 1947–1956* (London, 1979)

Gould, 1989: Stephen Jay Gould, *Wonderful Life: The Burgess Shale and the Nature of History* (London, 1990)

Graves/Hodge, 1941: Robert Graves, and Alan Hodge, *The Long Week-End: A Social History of Great Britain 1918–1939* (London, 1941)

Gray, 1970: Hugh Gray, 'The landed gentry of Telengana' in E. Leach and S.N. Mukherjee eds. *Elites in South Asia* (Cambridge, 1970)

Guerlac, 1951: Henry E. Guerlac, 'Science and French National Strength' in Edward Meade Earle ed., *Modern France: Problems of the Third and Fourth Republics* (Princeton, 1951)

Guidetti/Stahl, 1977: M. Guidetti and Paul M. Stahl eds., *Il sangue e la terra: Comunità di villagio e comunità familiari nell Europea dell 800* (Milano, 1977)

Guinness, 1984: Robert and Celia Dearling, *The Guinness Book of Recorded Sound* (Enfield, 1984)

Haimson, 1964/5: Leopold Haimson, 'The Problem of Social Stability in Urban Russia 1905–1917' in *Slavic Review*, December 1964, pp. 619–64; March 1965, pp. 1–22

Halliday, 1983: Fred Halliday, *The Making of the Second Cold War* (London, 1983)

Halliday/Cumings, 1988: Jon Halliday and Bruce Cumings, *Korea: The Unknown War* (London, 1988)

Halliwell, 1988: *Leslie Halliwell's Filmgoers' Guide Companion* 9th edn, 1988, p. 321

Hànak, 1970: Peter Hànak, '*Die Volksmeinung während des letzten Kriegsjahres in Österreich-Ungarn*' in *Die Auflösung des Habsburgerreiches. Zusammenbruch und*

Neuorientierung im Donauraum, Schriftenreihe des österreichischen Ost- und Südosteuropainstituts vol. III, Vienna, 1970, pp. 58–66

Harden, 1990: Blaine Harden, *Africa, Despatches from a Fragile Continent* (New York, 1990)

Harff/Gurr, 1988: Barbara Harff and Ted Robert Gurr, 'Victims of the State: Genocides, Politicides and Group Repression since 1945 in *International Review of Victimology*, I, 1989, pp. 23–41

Harff/Gurr, 1989: Barbara Harff and Ted Robert Gurr, 'Toward Empirical Theory of Genocides and Politicides:Identification and Measurement of Cases since 1945,' *International Studies Quarterly*, 32, 1988, pp. 359–71

Harris, 1987: Nigel Harris, *The End of the Third World* (Harmondsworth, 1987)

Hayek, 1944: Friedrich von Hayek, *The Road to Serfdom* (London, 1944)

Heilbroner, 1993: Robert Heilbroner, *Twenty-first Century Capitalism* (New York, 1993)

Hilberg 1985: Raul Hilberg, *The Destruction of the European Jews* (New York, 1985)

Hill, 1988: Kim Quaile Hill, *Democracies in Crisis: Public policy responses to the Great Depression* (Boulder and London, 1988)

Hilgerdt: See League of Nations, 1945

Hirschfeld, 1986: G. Hirschfeld ed., *The Policies of Genocide: Jews and Soviet Prisoners of War in Nazi Germany* (Boston, 1986)

Historical Statistics of the United States: Colonial Times to 1970, part 1c, 89–101, p. 105 (Washington DC, 1975)

Hobbes: Thomas Hobbes, Leviathan (London, 1651)

Hobsbawm 1974: E.J. Hobsbawm, 'Peasant Land Occupations' in *Past & Present*, 62, February 1974, pp. 120–52

Hobsbawm, 1986: E.J. Hobsbawm, 'The Moscow Line' and international Communist policy 1933–47' in Chris Wrigley ed. *Warfare, Diplomacy and Politics: Essays in Honour of A.J.P. Taylor*, pp. 163–88 (London, 1986)

Hobsbawm, 1987: E.J. Hobsbawm, *The Age of Empire 1870–1914* (London, 1987)

Hobsbawm, 1990: E.J. Hobsbawm, *Nations and Nationalism Since 1780: Programme, Myth, Reality* (Cambridge, 1990)

Hobsbawm, 1993: E.J. Hobsbawm, *The Jazz Scene* (New York, 1993)

Hodgkin, 1961: Thomas Hodgkin, *African Political Parties: An introductory guide* (Harmondsworth, 1961)

Hoggart, 1958: Richard Hoggart, *The Uses of Literacy* (Harmondsworth, 1958)

Holborn, 1968: Louise W.Holborn, 'Refugees I: World Problems' in *International Encyclopedia of the Social Sciences* vol. XIII, p. 363

Holland, R.F., 1985: R.F. Holland, *European Decolonization 1918–1981: An introductory survey* (Basingstoke, 1985)

Holman, 1993: Michael Holman, 'New Group Targets the Roots of Corruption' in *Financial Times*, 5 May 1993

Holton, 1970: G. Holton, 'The Roots of Complementarity' in *Daedalus*, autumn 1978, p.1017

Holton, 1972: Gerald Holton ed., *The Twentieth-Century Sciences: Studies in the Biography of Ideas* (New York, 1972)

Horne, 1989: Alistair Horne, *Macmillan*, 2 vols (London, 1989)

Housman, 1988: A.E. Housman, *Collected Poems and Selected Prose* edited and with an introduction and notes by Christopher Ricks (London, 1988)

Howarth, 1978: T.E.B. Howarth, *Cambridge Between Two Wars* (London, 1978)

Hu, 1966: C.T. Hu, 'Communist Education: Theory and Practice' in R. Mac-Farquhar ed., *China Under Mao: Politics Takes Command* (Cambridge MA, 1966)

Huber, 1990: Peter W.Huber, 'Pathological Science in Court' in *Daedalus*, vol. 119, no. 4, autumn 1990, pp. 97–118

Hughes, 1969: H. Stuart Hughes, 'The second year of the Cold War: A Memoir and an Anticipation' in *Commentary*, August 1969

Hughes 1983: H. Stuart Hughes, *Prisoners of Hope: The Silver Age of the Italian Jews 1924–1947* (Cambridge MA, 1983)

Hughes, 1988: H. Stuart Hughes, *Sophisticated Rebels* (Cambridge and London, 1988)

Human Development: United Nations Development Programme (UNDP) *Human Development Report*, (New York, 1990, 1991, 1992)

Hutt, 1935: Allen Hutt, *This Final Crisis* (London, 1935)

Ignatieff, 1993: Michael Ignatieff, *Blood and Belonging: Journeys into the New Nationalism* (London, 1993)

ILO, 1990: *ILO Yearbook of Labour Statistics: Retrospective edition on Population Censuses 1945–1989* (Geneva, 1990)

IMF, 1990: International Monetary Fund, Washington: *World Economic Outlook: A Survey by the Staff of the International Monetary Fund*, Table 18: Selected Macro-economic Indicators 1950–1988 (IMF, Washington, May 1990)

Investing: *Investing in Europe's Future* ed. Arnold Heertje for the European Investment Bank (Oxford, 1983)

Isola, 1990: Gianni Isola, *Abbassa la tua radio, per favore. Storia dell'ascolto radiofonico nell'Italia fascista* (Firenze, 1990)

Jacobmeyer, 1985: Wolfgang Jacobmeyer, *Vom Zwangsarbeiter zum heimatlosen Ausländer: Die Displaced Persons in Westdeutschland, 1945–1951* (Gottingen, 1985)

Jacob, 1993: Margaret C. Jacob, 'Hubris about Science' in *Contention*, vol. 2, no. 3 (Spring 1993)

Jammer, 1966: M. Jammer, *The Conceptual Development of Quantum Mechanics* (New York, 1966)

Jayawardena, 1993: Lal Jayawardena *The Potential of Development Contracts and Towards sustainable Development Contracts, UNU/WIDER: Research for Action* (Helsinki, 1993)

Jensen, 1991: K.M. Jensen ed., *Origins of the Cold War: The Novikov, Kennan and Roberts 'Long Telegrams' of 1946,* United States Institute of Peace (Washington 1991)

Johansson/Percy 1990: Warren Johansson and William A. Percy ed., *Encyclopedia of Homosexuality*, 2 vols (New York and London, 1990)

Johnson, 1972: Harry G. Johnson, *Inflation and the Monetarist Controvery* (Amsterdam, 1972)

Jon, 1993: Jon Byong-Je, *Culture and Development: South Korean experience*, International Inter-Agency Forum on Culture and Development, September 20–22 1993, Seoul

Jones, 1992: Steve Jones, review of David Raup, *Extinction: Bad Genes or Bad Luck?* in *London Review of Books*, 23 April 1992

Jowitt, 1991: Ken Jowitt, 'The Leninist Extinction' in Daniel Chirot ed., *The Crisis of Leninism and the Decline of the Left* (Seattle, 1991)

Julca, 1993: Alex Julca, From the highlands to the city (unpublished paper, 1993)

Kakwani, 1980: Nanak Kakwani, *Income Inequality and Poverty* (Cambridge, 1980)

Kapuściński 1983: Ryszard Kapuściński, *The Emperor* (London, 1983)

Kapuściński, 1990: Ryszard Kapuściński, *The Soccer War* (London, 1990)

Kater, 1985: Michael Kater, '*Professoren und Studenten im dritten Reich*' in *Archiv f. Kulturgeschichte* 67/1985, no. 2, p. 467

Katsiaficas, 1987: George Katsiaficas, *The Imagination of the New Left: A global analysis of 1968* (Boston, 1987)

Kedward, 1971: R.H. Kedward, *Fascism in Western Europe 1900–1945* (New York, 1971)

Keene, 1984: Donald Keene, *Japanese Literature of the Modern Era* (New York, 1984)

Kelley, 1988: Allen C. Kelley, 'Economic Consequences of Population Change in the Third World' in *Journal of Economic Literature*, XXVI, December 1988, pp.1685–1728

Kennedy, 1987: Paul Kennedy, *The Rise and Fall of the Great Powers* (New York, 1987)

Kerblay, 1983: Basile Kerblay, *Modern Soviet Society* (New York, 1983)

Kershaw, 1983: Ian Kershaw, *Popular Opinion and Political Dissent in the Third Reich: Bavaria 1933–1945* (Oxford, 1983)

Kershaw, 1993: Ian Kershaw, *The Nazi Dictatorship: Perspectives of Interpretation*, 3rd edn (London, 1993)

Khrushchev, 1990: Sergei Khrushchev, *Khrushchev on Khrushchev: An Inside Account of the Man and His Era* (Boston, 1990)

Kidron/Segal, 1991: Michael Kidron and Ronald Segal, *The New State of the World Atlas*, 4th ed (London, 1991)

Kindleberger, 1973: Charles P. Kindleberger, *The World in Depression 1919–1939* (London and New York, 1973)

Kivisto, 1983: Peter Kivisto, 'The Decline of the Finnish–American Left 1925–1945' in *International Migration Review*, XVII, 1, 1983

Kolakowski, 1992: Leszek Kolakowski, 'Amidst Moving Ruins' in *Daedalus* 121/2, spring 1992

Kolko, 1969: Gabriel Kolko, *The Politics of War: Allied diplomacy and the world crisis of 1943–45* (London, 1969)

Köllö, 1990: Janos Köllö, 'After a dark golden age – Eastern Europe' in *WIDER Working Papers* (duplicated), Helsinki, 1990

Kornai: Janos Kornai, *The Economics of Shortage* (Amsterdam, 1980)

Kosinski, 1987: L.A. Kosinski, review of Robert Conquest, *The Harvest of Sorrow: Soviet Collectivisation and the Terror Famine*' in *Population and Development Review*, vol. 13, no. 1, 1987

Kosmin/Lachman, 1993: Barry A. Kosmin and Seymour P. Lachman, *One Nation Under God: Religion in Contemporary American Society* (New York, 1993)

Kraus, 1922: Karl Kraus, *Die letzten Tage der Menschheit: Tragödie in fünf Akten mit Vorspiel und Epilog* (Wien-Leipzig, 1922)

Kulischer, 1948: Eugene M. Kulischer *Europe on the Move: War and Population Changes 1917–1947* (New York, 1948)

Kuttner, 1991: Robert Kuttner, *The End of Laissez-Faire: National Purpose and the Global Economy after the Cold War* (New York, 1991)

Kuznets, 1956: Simon Kuznets, 'Quantitative Aspects of the Economic Growth of Nations' in *Economic Development and Culture Change*, vol. 5, no. 1, 1956, pp. 5–94

Kyle, 1990: Keith Kyle, *Suez* (London, 1990)

Ladurie, 1982: Emmanuel Le Roy Ladurie, *Paris–Montpellier: PC-PSU 1945–1963* (Paris, 1982)

Lafargue: Paul Lafargue, *Le droit à la paresse* (Paris, 1883); *The Right to Be Lazy and Other Studies* (Chicago, 1907)

Land Reform: Philip M. Raup, 'Land Reform' in art. 'Land Tenure', *International Encyclopedia of Social Sciences*, vol. 8, pp. 571–75 (New York, 1968)

Lapidus, 1988: Ira Lapidus, *A History of Islamic Societies* (Cambridge, 1988)

Laqueur, 1977: Walter Laqueur, *Guerrilla: A historical and critical study* (London, 1977)

Larkin, 1988: Philip Larkin, *Collected Poems* ed. and with an introduction by Anthony Thwaite (London, 1988)

Larsen E., 1978: Egon Larsen, *A Flame in Barbed Wire: The Story of Amnesty International* (London, 1978)

Larsen S. et al., 1980: Stein Ugevik Larsen, Bernt Hagtvet, Jan Petter, My Klebost et. al., *Who Were the Fascists?* (Bergen–Oslo–Tromsö, 1980)

Lary, 1943: Hal B. Lary and Associates, *The United States in the World Economy: The International Transactions of the United States during the Interwar Period*, US Dept of Commerce (Washington, 1943)

Las Cifras, 1988: *Asamblea Permanente para los Derechos Humanos, La Cifras de la Guerra Sucia* (Buenos Aires, 1988)

Latham, 1981: A.J.H. Latham, *The Depression and the Developing World, 1914–1939* (London and Totowa NJ, 1981)

League of Nations, 1931: *The Course and Phases of the World Depression* (Geneva, 1931; reprinted 1972)

League of Nations, 1945: *Industrialisation and Foreign Trade* (Geneva, 1945)

Leaman, 1988: Jeremy Leaman, *The Political Economy of West Germany 1945–1985* (London, 1988)

Leighly, Naylor, 1992: J.E. Leighly and J. Naylor, 'Socioeconomic Class Bias in Turnout 1964–1988: the voters remain the same' in *American Political Science Review*, 86/3 September, 1992, pp. 725–36

Lenin, 1970: V.I. Lenin, *Selected Works in 3 Volumes* (Moscow, 1970: 'Letter to the Central Committee, the Moscow and Petrograd Committees and the Bolshevik Members of the Petrograd and Moscow Soviets', October 1/14 1917, V.I. Lenin op. cit, vol. 2, p. 435; Draft Resolution for the Extraordinary All-Russia Congress of Soviets of Peasant Deputies, November 14/27, 1917, V.I. Lenin, loc. cit, p. 496; Report on the activities of the Council of People's Commissars, January 12/24 1918, loc. cit., p. 546

Leontiev, 1977: Wassily Leontiev, 'The Significance of Marxian Economics for Present-Day Economic Theory' in *Amer. Econ. Rev. Supplement* vol. XXVIII, 1 March 1938, republished in *Essays in Economics: Theories and Theorizing*, vol. 1, p. 78 (White Plains, 1977)

Lettere: P. Malvezzi and G. Pirelli eds *Lettere di Condannati a morte della Resistenza europea*, p. 306 (Turin, 1954)

Lévi-Strauss: Claude Lévi-Strauss, Didier Eribon, *De Près et de Loin* (Paris, 1988)

Lewin, 1991: Moshe Lewin, 'Bureaucracy and the Stalinist State' unpublished paper in *Germany and Russia in the 20th Century in Comparative Perspective* (Philadelphia, 1991)

Lewis, 1981: Arthur Lewis, 'The Rate of Growth of World Trade 1830–1973' in Sven Grassman and Erik Lundberg eds, *The World Economic Order:Past and Prospects* (London, 1981)

Lewis, 1938: Cleona Lewis, *America's Stake in International Investments* (Brookings Institution, Washington, 1938)

Lewis, 1935: Sinclair Lewis, *It Can't Happen Here* (New York, 1935)

Lewontin, 1973: R.C. Lewontin, *The Genetic Basis of Evolutionary Change* (New York, 1973)

Lewontin, 1992: R.C. Lewontin, 'The Dream of the Human Genome' in *New York Review of Books*, 28 May 1992, pp. 32–40

Leys,1977: Simon Leys, *The Chairman's New Clothes: Mao and the Cultural Revolution* (New York, 1977)

Lieberson, Waters, 1988: Stanley Lieberson and Mary C. Waters, *From many strands: Ethnic and Racial Groups in Contemporary America* (New York, 1988)

Liebman/Walker/Glazer: Arthur Liebman, Kenneth Walker, Myron Glazer, *Latin American University Students: A six-nation study* (Cambridge MA, 1972)

Lieven, 1993: Anatol Lieven, *The Baltic Revolution: Estonia, Latvia, Lithuania and the Path to Independence* (New Haven and London, 1993)

Linz, 1975: Juan J. Linz, 'Totalitarian and Authoritarian Regimes' in Fred J. Greenstein and Nelson W. Polsby eds, *Handbook of Political Science*, vol. 3, *Macropolitical Theory* (Reading MA, 1975)

Liu, 1986: Alan P.L. Liu, *How China Is Ruled* (Englewood Cliffs, 1986)

Loth, 1988: Wilfried Loth, *The Division of the World 1941–1955* (London, 1988)

Lu Hsün: as cited in Victor Nee and James Peck eds, *China's Uninterrupted Revolution: From 1840 to the Present*, p. 23 (New York, 1975)

Lynch, 1990: Nicolas Lynch Gamero, *Los jovenes rojos de San Marcos: El radicalismo universitario de los años setenta* (Lima, 1990)

McCracken, 1977: Paul McCracken et al., *Towards Full Employment and Price Stability* (Paris, OECD 1977)

Macluhan, 1962: Marshall Macluhan, *The Gutenberg Galaxy* (New York, 1962)

Macluhan, 1967: Marshall Macluhan and Quentin Fiore, *The Medium is the Massage* (New York, 1967)

McNeill, 1982: William H. McNeill, *The Pursuit of Power:Technology, Armed Force and Society since AD 1000* (Chicago, 1982)

Maddison, 1969: Angus Maddison, *Economic Growth in Japan and the USSR* (London, 1969)

Maddison, 1982: Angus Maddison, *Phases of Capitalist Economic Development* (Oxford, 1982)

Maddison, 1987: Angus Maddison, 'Growth and Slowdown in Advanced Capitalist Economies: Techniques of Quantitative Assessment' in *Journal of Economic Literature*, vol. XXV, June 1987

Maier, 1987: Charles S. Maier, *In Search of Stability: Explorations in Historical Political Economy* (Cambridge, 1987)

Maksimenko, 1991: V.I. Maksimenko, 'Stalinism without Stalin: the mechanism of "*zastoi*"' unpublished paper in *Germany and Russia in the 20th Century in Comparative Perspective*' (Philadelphia 1991)

Mangin, 1970: William Mangin ed., *Peasants in Cities: Readings in the Anthropology of Urbanization* (Boston, 1970)

Manuel, 1988: Peter Manuel, *Popular Musics of the Non-Western World: An Introductory Survey* (Oxford, 1988)

Marglin and Schor, 1990: S. Marglin and J. Schor eds, *The Golden Age of Capitalism* (Oxford, 1990)

Marrus, 1985: Michael R. Marrus, *European Refugees in the Twentieth Century* (Oxford, 1985)

Martins Rodrigues, 1984: '*O PCB: os dirigentes e a organização*' in *O Brasil Republicano*, vol. X, *tomo* III of Sergio Buarque de Holanda ed., *Historia Geral da Civilizacão Brasilesira* pp. 390–97 (Saõ Paulo, 1960–84)

Mencken, 1959: Alistair Cooke ed. *The Viking Mencken* (New York, 1959)

Jean A. Meyer, *La Cristiada*, 3 vols (Mexico D.F., 1973–79); English: *The Cristero Rebellion: The Mexican People between Church and State 1926–1929* (Cambridge, 1976)

Meyer-Leviné, 1973: Rosa Meyer-Leviné, *Leviné: The Life of a Revolutionary* (London, 1973)

Miles et al., 1991: M. Miles, E. Malizia, Marc A. Weiss, G. Behrens, G. Travis, *Real Estate Development: Principles and Process* (Washington DC, 1991)

Miller, 1989: James Edward Miller, 'Roughhouse diplomacy: the United States confronts Italian Communism 1945–1958' in *Storia delle relazioni internazionali*, V/1989/2, pp. 279–312

Millikan, 1930: R.A. Millikan, 'Alleged Sins of Science, in *Scribners Magazine* 87(2), 1930, pp. 119–30

Milward, 1979: Alan Milward, *War, Economy and Society 1939–45* (London, 1979)

Milward, 1984: Alan Milward, *The Reconstruction of Western Europe 1945–51* (London, 1984)

Minault, 1982: Gail Minault, *The Khilafat Movement: Religious Symbolism and Political Mobilization in India* (New York, 1982)

Misra, 1961: B.B. Misra, *The Indian Middle Classes: Their Growth in Modern Times* (London, 1961)

Mitchell/Jones: B.R. Mitchell and H.G. Jones *Second Abstract of British Historical Statistics* (Cambridge, 1971)

Mitchell, 1975: B.R. Mitchell, *European Historical Statistics* (London, 1975)

Moisi, 1981: D. Moisi ed., *Crises et guerres au XXe siècle* (Paris, 1981)

Molano, 1988: Alfredo Molano, '*Violencia y colonización*' in *Revista Foro: Fundación Foro Nacional por Colombia*, 6 June 1988 pp. 25–37

Montagni, 1989: Gianni Montagni, *Effetto Gorbaciov: La politica internazionale degli anni ottanta. Storia di quattro vertici da Ginevra a Mosca* (Bari, 1989)

Morawetz, 1977: David Morawetz, *Twenty-five Years of Economic Development 1950–1975* (Johns Hopkins, for the World Bank, 1977)

Mortimer, 1925: Raymond Mortimer, '*Les Matelots*' in *New Statesman*, 4 July 1925, p. 338

Muller, 1951: H. J. Muller in L.C. Dunn ed. *Genetics in the 20th Century: Essays on the Progress of Genetics During the First Fifty Years* (New York, 1951)

Müller, 1992: Heiner Müller, *Krieg ohne Schlacht: Leben in zwei Diktaturen* (Cologne, 1992)

Muzzioli, 1993: Giuliano Muzzioli, *Modena* (Bari, 1993)

Nehru, 1936: Jawaharlal Nehru, *An Autobiography, with musings on recent events in India* (London, 1936)

Nicholson, 1970: E.M. Nicholson cited in *Fontana Dictionary of Modern Thought*: 'Ecology' (London, 1977)

Noelle/Neumann, 1967: Elisabeth Noelle and Erich Peter Neumann eds, *The Germans: Public Opinion Polls 1947–1966* p. 196 (Allensbach and Bonn, 1967)

Nolte, 1987: Ernst Nolte, *Der europäische Bürgerkrieg, 1917–1945: Nationalsozialismus und Bolschewismus* (Stuttgart, 1987)

North/Pool, 1966: Robert North and Ithiel de Sola Pool, 'Kuomintang and Chinese Communist Elites' in Harold D. Lasswell and Daniel Lerner eds, *World Revolutionary Elites: Studies in Coercive Ideological Movements* (Cambridge MA, 1966)

Nove, 1969: Alec Nove, *An Economic History of the USSR* (London, 1969)

Nwoga, 1970: Donatus I. Nwoga, 'Onitsha Market Literature' in *Mangin*, 1970

Observatoire, 1991: *Comité Scientifique auprès du Ministère de l'Education Nationale*, unpublished paper, *Observatoire des Thèses* (Paris, 1991)

OECD Impact: OECD: *The Impact of the Newly Industrializing Countries on Production and Trade in Manufactures: Report by the Secretary-General* (Paris, 1979)

OECD National Accounts: *OECD National Accounts 1960–1991*, vol. 1 (Paris, 1993)

Ofer, 1987: Gur Ofer, 'Soviet Economic Growth, 1928-1985' in *Journal of Economic Literature*, XXV/4, December 1987, p. 1778

Ohlin, 1931: Bertil Ohlin, for the League of Nations, *The Course and Phases of the World Depression* (1931; reprinted Arno Press, New York, 1972)

Olby, 1970: Robert Olby, 'Francis Crick, DNA, and the Central Dogma' in Holton 1972, pp. 227-80

Orbach, 1978: Susie Orbach, *Fat is a Feminist Issue: the anti-diet guide to permanent weight loss* (New York and London, 1978)

Ory, 1976: Pascal Ory, *Les Collaborateurs: 1940–1945* (Paris, 1976)

Paucker, 1991: Arnold Paucker, *Jewish Resistance in Germany: The Facts and the Problems* (*Gedenkstaette Deutscher Widerstand*, Berlin, 1991)

Pavone, 1991: Claudio Pavone, *Una guerra civile: Saggio storico sulla moralità nella Resistenza* (Milan, 1991)

Peierls, 1992: Peierls, Review of D.C. Cassidy, *Uncertainty: The Life of Werner Heisenberg'* in *New York Review of Books*, 23 April 1992, p. 44

People's Daily, 1959: 'Hai Jui reprimands the Emperor' in *People's Daily* Beijing, 1959, cited in Leys, 1977

Perrault, 1987: Gilles Perrault, *A Man Apart: The Life of Henri Curiel* (London, 1987)

Peters, 1985: Edward Peters, *Torture* (New York, 1985)

Petersen, 1986: W. and R. Petersen, *Dictionary of Demography*, vol. 2, art: 'War' (New York–Westport–London, 1986)

Piel, 1992: Gerard Piel, *Only One World: Our Own To Make And To Keep* (New York, 1992)

Planck, 1933: Max Planck, *Where Is Science Going?* with a preface by Albert Einstein; translated and edited by James Murphy (New York, 1933)

Polanyi, 1945: Karl Polanyi, *The Great Transformation* (London, 1945)

Pons Prades, 1975: E. Pons Prades, *Republicanos Españoles en la 2a Guerra Mundial* (Barcelona, 1975)

Population, 1984: UN Dept of International Economic and Social Affairs: *Population Distribution, Migration and Development. Proceedings of the Expert Group, Hammamet (Tunisia) 21–25 March 1983* (New York, 1984)

Potts, 1990: Lydia Potts, *The World Labour Market: A History of Migration* (London and New Jersey, 1990)

Pravda, 25 January 1991.

Proctor, 1988. Robert N. Proctor, *Racial Hygiene: Medicine Under the Nazis* (Cambridge MA, 1988)

Programma 2000: PSOE (Spanish Socialist Party), *Manifesto of Programme: Draft for Discussion*, January 1990 (Madrid, 1990)

Prost: A Prost, '*Frontières et espaces du privé*' in *Histoire de la Vie Privée de la Première Guerre Mondiale à nos Jours* vol. 5, pp.13–153 Paris, 1987

Rado, 1962: A. Rado ed., *Welthandbuch: internationaler politischer und wirt-schaftlicher Almanach 1962* (Budapest, 1962)

Ranki, 1971: George Ranki in Peter F. Sugar ed., *Native Fascism in the Successor States: 1918–1945* (Santa Barbara, 1971)

Ransome, 1919: Arthur Ransome, *Six Weeks in Russia in 1919* (London, 1919)

Räte-China, 1973: Manfred Hinz ed., *Räte-China: Dokumente der chinesischen Revolution* (1927–31) (Berlin, 1973)

Raw, Page, Hodgson 1972: Charles Raw, Bruce Page, Godfrey Hodgson, *Do You Sincerely Want To Be Rich?* (London, 1972)

Reale, 1954: Eugenio Reale, *Avec Jacques Duclos au Banc des Accusés à la Réunion Constitutive du Cominform* (Paris, 1958)

Reed, 1919: John Reed *Ten Days That Shook The World* (New York, 1919 and numerous editions)

Reinhard et al, 1968: M. Reinhard, A. Armengaud, J. Dupaquier, *Histoire Générale de la population mondiale*, 3rd edn (Paris, 1968)

Reitlinger, 1982: Gerald Reitlinger, *The Economics of Taste: The Rise and Fall of Picture Prices 1760–1960* 3 vols (New York, 1982)

Riley, 1991: C. Riley, 'The Prevalence of Chronic Disease During Mortality Increase: Hungary in the 1980s' in *Population Studies*, 45/3 November 1991, pp. 489–97

Riordan, 1991: J. Riordan, *Life After Communism*, inaugural lecture, University of Surrey (Guildford, 1991)

Ripken/Wellmer, 1978: Peter Ripken and Gottfried Wellmer, *'Bantustans und ihre Funktion für das südafrikanische Herrschaftssystem'* in Peter Ripken, *Südliches Afrika: Geschichte, Wirtschaft, politische Zukunft*, pp. 194–203, Berlin, 1978

Roberts, 1991: Frank Roberts, *Dealing with the Dictators: The Destruction and Revival of Europe 1930–1970* (London, 1991)

Rozsati/Mizsei, 1989: D. Rosati and K. Mizsei, *Adjustment through opening of socialist economies* in UNU/WIDER, Working Paper 52 (Helsinki, 1989)

Rostow, 1978: W.W. Rostow, *The World Economy:History and Prospect* (Austin, 1978)

Russell Pasha 1949: Sir Thomas Russell Pasha, *Egyptian Service, 1902–1946* (London, 1949)

Samuelson, 1943: Paul Samuelson, 'Full employment after the war' in S. Harris ed., *Post-war Economic Problems*, pp. 27–53 (New York, 1943)

Sareen, 1988: T.R. Sareen, *Select Documents on Indian National Army* (New Delhi, 1988)

Sassoon, 1947: Siegfried Sassoon, *Collected Poems* (London, 1947)

Schatz, 1983: Ronald W. Schatz, *The Electrical Workers. A History of Labor at General Electric and Westinghouse* (University of Illinois Press, 1983)

Schell, 1993: Jonathan Schell 'A Foreign Policy of Buy and Sell' (*New York Newsday*, 21 November 1993)

Schram, 1966: Stuart Schram, *Mao Tse Tung* (Baltimore, 1966))

Schrödinger, 1944: Erwin Schrödinger, *What Is Life: The Physical Aspects of the Living Cell* (Cambridge, 1944)

Schumpeter, 1939: Joseph A. Schumpeter, *Business Cycles* (New York and London, 1939)

Schumpeter, 1954: Joseph A. Schumpeter, *History of Economic Analysis* (New York, 1954)

Schwartz, 1966: Benjamin Schwartz, 'Modernisation and the Maoist Vision' in Roderick MacFarquhar ed., *China Under Mao: Politics Takes Command* (Cambridge MA, 1966)

Scott, 1985. James C. Scott, *Weapons of the Weak: Everyday Forms of Peasant Resistance* (New Haven and London 1985)

Seal, 1968: Anil Seal, *The Emergence of Indian Nationalism: Competition and Collaboration in the later Nineteenth Century* (Cambridge, 1968)

Sinclair, 1982: Stuart Sinclair, *The World Economic Handbook* (London, 1982)

Singer, 1972: J. David Singer, *The Wages of War 1816–1965: A Statistical Handbook* (New York, London, Sydney, Toronto, 1972)

Smil, 1990: Vaclav Smil, 'Planetary Warming: Realities and Responses' in *Population and Development Review,* vol. 16, no.1, March 1990

Smith, 1989: Gavin Alderson Smith, *Livelihood and Resistance: Peasants and the Politics of the Land in Peru* (Berkeley, 1989)

Snyder, 1940: R.C. Snyder, 'Commercial policy as reflected in Treaties from 1931 to 1939' in *American Economic Review*, 30, 1940, pp. 782–802

Social Trends: UK Central Statistical Office, *Social Trends 1980* (London, annual)

Solzhenitsyn, 1993: Alexander Solzhenitsyn in *New York Times* 28 November 1993

Somary, 1929: Felix Somary, *Wandlungen der Weltwirtschaft seit dem Kriege* (Tübingen, 1929)

Sotheby: *Art Market Bulletin*, A Sotheby's Research Department Publication, End of season review, 1992

Spencer, 1990: Jonathan Spencer, *A Sinhala Village in Time of Trouble: Politics and Change in Rural Sri Lanka* (New Delhi, 1990)

Spero, 1977: Joan Edelman Spero, *The Politics of International Economic Relations* (New York, 1977)

Spriano, 1969: Paolo Spriano, *Storia del Partito Comunista Italiano* Vol. II (Turin, 1969)

Spriano, 1983: Paolo Spriano, *I comunisti europei e Stalin* (Turin, 1983)

SSSR, 1987: *SSSR v Tsifrakh v 1987*, pp. 15–17, 32–33

Staley, 1939: Eugene Staley, *The World Economy in Transition* (New York, 1939)

Stalin, 1952: J.V. Stalin, *Economic Problems of Socialism in the USSR* (Moscow, 1952)

Starobin, 1972: Joseph Starobin, *American Communism in Crisis* (Cambridge MA, 1972)

Starr, 1983: Frederick Starr, *Red and Hot: The Fate of Jazz in the Soviet Union 1917–1980* (New York, 1983)

Stat. Jahrbuch: Federal Republic Germany, Bundesamt für Statistik, *Statistisches Jahrbuch für das Ausland* (Bonn, 1990)

Steinberg, 1990: Jonathan Steinberg, *All or Nothing: The Axis and the Holocaust 1941–43* (London, 1990)

Stevenson, 1984: John Stevenson, *British Society 1914–1945* (Harmondsworth, 1984)

Stoll, 1990: David Stoll, *Is Latin America Turning Protestant: The Politics of Evangelical Growth* (Berkeley, Los Angeles, Oxford, 1992)

Stouffer/Lazarsfeld, 1937: S. Stouffer and P. Lazarsfeld, *Research Memorandum on the Family in the Depression*, Social Science Research Council (New York, 1937)

Stürmer, 1993: Michael Stürmer in '*Orientierungskrise in Politik und Gesellschaft? Perspektiven der Demokratie an der Schwelle zum 21. Jahrhundert*' in (*Bergedorfer Gesprächskreis, Protokoll Nr 98* Hamburg-Bergedorf, 1993)

Stürmer, 1993: Michael Stürmer, *99 Bergedorfer Gesprächskreis* (22–23 May, Ditchley Park): *Wird der Westen den Zerfall des Ostens überleben? Politische und ökonomische Herausforderungen für Amerika und Europa* (Hamburg, 1993)

Tanner, 1962: J.M. Tanner, *Growth at Adolescence*, 2nd edn (Oxford, 1962)

Taylor/Jodice, 1983: C.L. Taylor and D.A. Jodice, *World Handbook of Political and Social Indicators*, 3rd edn (New Haven and London, 1983)

Taylor, 1990: Trevor Taylor, 'Defence industries in international relations' in *Rev. Internat. Studies* 16, 1990, pp. 59–73

Technology, 1986: US Congress, Office of Technology Assessment, *Technology and Structural Unemployment: Reemploying Displaced Adults* (Washington DC, 1986)

Temin, 1993: Peter Temin, 'Transmission of the Great Depression' in *Journal of Economic Perspectives*, vol. 7/2, spring 1993, pp. 87–102)

Terkel, 1967: Studs Terkel, *Division Street: America* (New York, 1967)

Terkel, 1970: Studs Terkel, *Hard Times: An Oral History of the Great Depression* (New York, 1970)

Therborn, 1984: Göran Therborn, 'Classes and States, Welfare State Developments 1881–1981' in *Studies in Political Economy: A Socialist Review*, no. 13, spring 1984, pp. 7–41

Therborn, 1985: Göran Therborn, 'Leaving the Post Office Behind' in M. Nikolic ed. *Socialism in the Twenty-first Century* pp. 225–51 (London, 1985)

Thomas 1971: Hugh Thomas, *Cuba or the Pursuit of Freedom* (London 1971)

Thomas, 1977: Hugh Thomas, *The Spanish Civil War* (Harmondsworth, 1977 edition)

Tiempos, 1990: Carlos Ivan Degregori, Marfil Francke, José López Ricci, Nelson Manrique, Gonzalo Portocarrero, Patricia Ruíz Bravo, Abelardo Sánchez León, Antonio Zapata, *Tiempos de Ira y Amor: Nuevos Actores para viejos problemas*, DESCO (Lima, 1990)

Tilly/Scott, 1987: Louise Tilly and Joan W. Scott, *Women, Work and Family* (second edition, London, 1987)

Titmuss: Richard Titmuss, *The Gift Relationship: From Human Blood to Social Policy* (London, 1970)

Tomlinson, 1976: B.R.Tomlinson, *The Indian National Congress and the Raj 1929–1942: The Penultimate Phase* (London, 1976)

Touchard, 1977: Jean Touchard, *La gauche en France* (Paris, 1977)

Townshend, 1986: Charles Townshend, 'Civilization and Frightfulness: Air Control in the Middle East Between the Wars' in C. Wrigley ed. (see Hobsbawm, 1986)

Trofimov/Djangava, 1993: Dmitry Trofimov and Gia Djangava, *Some reflections on current geopolitical situation in the North Caucasus* (London, 1993, mimeo)

Tuma, 1965: Elias H. Tuma, *Twenty-six Centuries of Agrarian Reform: A comparative analysis* (Berkeley and Los Angeles, 1965)

Umbruch: See Fröbel, Heinrichs, Kreye, 1986

Umbruch, 1990: Federal Republic of Germany: *Umbruch in Europa: Die Ereignisse im 2. Halbjahr 1989. Eine Dokumentation, herausgegeben vom Auswärtigen Amt* (Bonn, 1990)

UN Africa, 1989: UN Economic Commission for Africa, Inter-Agency Task Force, Africa Recovery Programme, *South African Destabilization: The Economic Cost of Frontline Resistance to Apartheid* (New York, 1989)

UN Dept of International Economic and Social Affairs, 1984: See Population, 1984

UN International Trade: UN *International Trade Statistics Yearbook*, 1983

UN Statistical Yearbook (annual)

UN Transnational, 1988: United Nations Centre on Transnational Corporations, *Transnational Corporations in World Development: Trends and Prospects* (New York, 1988)

UN World Social Situation, 1970: UN, Department of Economic and Social Affairs, *1970 Report on the World Social Situation* (New York, 1971)

UN World Social Situation 1985: UN Dept of International Economic and Social Affair: *1985 Report on the World Social Situation* (New York, 1985)

UN World Social Situation 1989: UN Dept of International Economic and Social Affairs: *1989 Report on the World Social Situation* (New York, 1989)

UN World's Women: UN Social Statistics and Indicators Series K no. 8: *The World's Women 1970–1990: Trends and Statistics* (New York, 1991)

UNCTAD: UNCTAD (UN Commission for Trade and Development) *Statistical Pocket Book 1989* (New York, 1989)

UNESCO: UNESCO *Statistical Yearbook*, for the years concerned.

US Historical Statistics: US Dept of Commerce. Bureau of the Census, *Historical Statistics of the United States: Colonial Times to 1970*, 3 vols (Washington, 1975)

Van der Linden, 1993: 'Forced labour and non-capitalist industrialization: the case of Stalinism' in Tom Brass, Marcel van der Linden, Jan Lucassen, *Free and Unfree Labour* (IISH, Amsterdam, 1993)

Van der Wee: Herman Van der Wee, *Prosperity and Upheaval: The World Economy 1945–1980* (Harmondsworth, 1987)

Veillon 1992: Dominique Veillon, '*Le quotidien*' in *Ecrire l'histoire du temps présent. En hommage á Francois Bédarida: Actes de la journée d études de l'IHTP*, pp. 315–28 (Paris CNRS, 1993)

Vernikov, 1989: Andrei Vernikov, 'Reforming Process and Consolidation in the Soviet Economy', *WIDER Working Papers WP 53* (Helsinki, 1989)

Walker, 1988: Martin Walker, 'Russian Diary' in the *Guardian*, 21 March 1988, p. 19

Walker, 1991: Martin Walker, 'Sentencing system blights land of the free' in the *Guardian*, 19 June 1991, p. 11

Walker, 1993: Martin Walker, *The Cold War: And the Making of the Modern World* (London, 1993)

Ward, 1976: Benjamin Ward, 'National Economic Planning and Politics' in Carlo Cipolla ed., *Fontana Economic History of Europe: The Twentieth Century*, vol. 6/1 (London, 1976)

Watt, 1989: D.C. Watt, *How War Came* (London, 1989)

Weber, 1969: Hermann Weber, *Die Wandlung des deutschen Kommunismus: Die Stalinisierung der KPD in der Weimarer Republik* 2 vols (Frankfurt, 1969)

Weinberg, 1977: Steven Weinberg, 'The Search for Unity: Notes for a History of Quantum Field Theory' in *Daedalus*, autumn 1977

Weinberg, 1979: Steven Weinberg, 'Einstein and Spacetime Then and Now' in *Bulletin, American Academy of Arts and Sciences*, xxxiii. 2 November 1979

Weisskopf, 1980: V. Weisskopf, 'What Is Quantum Mechanics?' in *Bulletin, American Academy of Arts & Sciences*, vol. xxxiii, April 1980

Wiener, 1984: Jon Wiener, *Come Together: John Lennon in his Time* (New York, 1984)

Wildavsky, 1990: Aaron Wildavsky and Karl Dake, 'Theories of Risk Perception: Who Fears What and Why?' in *Daedalus*, vol. 119, no. 4, autumn 1990, pp. 41–60

Willett, 1978: John Willett, *The New Sobriety: Art and Politics in the Weimar Period* (London, 1978)

Wilson, 1977: E.O. Wilson, 'Biology and the Social Sciences' in *Daedalus 106/4*, autumn 1977, pp. 127–40

Winter, 1986: Jay Winter, *War and the British People* (London, 1986)

'Woman', 1964: 'The Woman in America' in *Daedalus* 1964

The World Almanack (New York, 1964, 1993)

World Bank Atlas: *The World Bank Atlas 1990* (Washington, 1990)

World Development: World Bank: *World Development Report* (New York, annual)

World Economic Survey, 1989: UN Dept of International Economic and Social Affairs, *World Economic Survey 1989: Current Trends and Policies in the World Economy* (New York, 1989)

World Labour, 1989: International Labour Office (ILO), *World Labour Report 1989* (Geneva, 1989)

World Resources, 1986: *A Report by the World Resources Institute and the International Institute for Environment and Development* (New York, 1986)

World Tables, 1991: The World Bank: *World Tables 1991* (Baltimore and Washington, 1991)

World's Women: see UN World's Women

Zetkin, 1968: Clara Zetkin, 'Reminiscences of Lenin' in *They Knew Lenin: Reminiscences of Foreign Contemporaries* (Moscow, 1968)

Ziebura, 1990: Gilbert Ziebura, *World Economy and World Politics 1924–1931: From Reconstruction to Collapse* (Oxford, New York, Munich, 1990)

Zinoviev, 1979: Aleksandr Zinoviev, *The Yawning Heights* (Harmondsworth, 1979)

Further Reading

Here are some suggestions for non-historians who want to know more.

The basic facts of twentieth-century world history can be found in a good college textbook, such as R.R. Palmer and Joel Colton, *A History of the Modern World* (6th edn 1983 or later), which has the advantage of excellent bibliographies. There are good single-volume surveys of some regions and continents, but not of others. Ira Lapidus, *A History of Islamic Societies* (1988), Jack Gray, *Rebellions and Revolutions: China from the 1800s to the 1980s* (1990), Roland Oliver and Anthony Atmore, *Africa since 1800* (1981) and James Joll, *Europe since 1870* (the most recent edition) are useful. Peter Calvocoressi, *World Politics since 1945* (6th edn 1991) is quite excellent for its period. It should be read against the background of Paul Kennedy, *The Rise and Fall of the Great Powers* (1987) and Charles Tilly, *Coercion, Capital and European States AD 900–1990* (1990).

Still within the compass of single volumes, W.W. Rostow, *The World Economy: History and Prospect* (1978), though debatable and far from bedside reading, provides a vast stock of information. Much to the point is Paul Bairoch, *The Economic Development of the Third World since 1900* (1975), as is David Landes, *The Unbound Prometheus* (1969) on the development of technology and industry.

Several works of reference are listed in the reference notes. Among statistical compendia, note the *Historical Statistics of the United States: Colonial Times to 1970* (3 vols, 1975), B.R. Mitchells's *European Historical Statistics* (1980), his *International Historical Statistics* (1986) and P. Flora, *State, Economy and Society in Western Europe 1815–1975* (2 vols, 1983). Chambers *Biographical Dictionary* is wide-ranging and convenient. For those who like maps, information is available in the imaginative *Times Atlas of World History* (1978), the brilliantly devised Michael Kidron and Ronald Segal, *The New State of the World Atlas* (4th edn, 1991) and the (economic and social) *World Bank Atlas*, annually since 1968. Among the numerous other map compendia, note Andrew Wheatcroft, *The World Atlas of Revolution* (1983), Colin McEvedy & R. Jones, *An Atlas of World Population History* (1982 edn) and Martin Gilbert, *Atlas of the Holocaust* (1972).

Maps are perhaps even more useful for the historical study of particular regions, among them G. Blake, John Dewdney, Jonathan Mitchell, *The*

Cambridge Atlas of the Middle East and North Africa (1987), Joseph E. Schwarzberg, *A Historical Atlas of South Asia* (1978), J.F. Adeadjayi and M. Crowder, *Historical Atlas of Africa* (1985) and Martin Gilbert, *Russian History Atlas* (1993 edn). There are good, up-to-date multi-volume histories of several of the world's regions and continents, but, oddly enough, not (in English) of Europe, nor of the world – except in economic history. The Penguin *History of the World Economy in the Twentieth Century* in five volumes is of remarkably high quality: Gerd Hardach, *The First World War 1914–1918*; Derek Aldcroft, *From Versailles to Wall Street, 1919–1929*; Charles Kindleberger, *The World in Depression 1929–1939*; Alan Milward's superb *War, Economy and Society, 1939–45*; and Herman Van der Wee, *Prosperity and Upheaval: The World Economy 1945–1980*.

Of the regional works, the twentieth-century volumes of the *Cambridge Histories* of *Africa* (vols 7–8), of *China* (vols 10–13) and of (Leslie Bethell ed.) *Latin America* (vols 6–9) are state-of-the art historiography, though for sampling rather than continuous reading. The enterprising *New Cambridge History of India* is unfortunately not sufficiently advanced as yet.

Marc Ferro, *The Great War* (1973) and Jay Winter, *The Experience of World War I* (1989) can guide readers into the First World War; Peter Calvocoressi, *Total War* (1989 edn), Gerhard L. Weinberg, *A World at Arms: a Global History of World War II* (1994) and Alan Milward's book into the Second World War. Gabriel Kolko, *Century of War: Politics, Conflict and Society since 1914* (1994) covers both wars and their revolutionary aftermath. For the world revolution, John Dunn, *Modern Revolutions* (2nd edn, 1989) and Eric Wolf, *Peasant Wars of the Twentieth Century* (1969) cover the whole range – or almost – including Third World revolutions. See also William Rosenberg and Marilyn Young, *Transforming Russia and China: Revolutionary Struggle in the Twentieth Century* (1982). E.J. Hobsbawm, *Revolutionaries* (1973), especially chapters 1–8, introduces the history of revolutionary movements.

The Russian revolution, drowned in monographs, as yet lacks the bird's-eye syntheses available for the French revolution. It continues to be rewritten. Leon Trotsky, *A History of The Russian Revolution* (1932) is the view from the (marxist) top; W.H. Chamberlin, *The Russian Revolution 1917–21* (2 vols, 1965 reprint) from the contemporary observer. Marc Ferro, *The Russian Revolution of February 1917* (1972) and *October 1917* (1979) are a fine introduction. The numerous volumes of E.H. Carr's monumental *History of Soviet Russia* (1950–78) are best used for reference. They only reach 1929. Alec Nove, *An Economic History of the USSR* (1972) and *The Economics of Feasible Socialism* (1983) are good introductions to the operations of 'really existing socialism'. Basile Kerblay, *Modern Soviet Society* (1983) is as close to a dispassionate survey of its results in the USSR as we have so far got. F. Fejtö has written contemporary histories of the 'people's democracies'. For China, Stuart Schram, *Mao Tse-tung* (1967) and John K. Fairbank, *The Great Chinese Revolution 1800–1985* (1986); see also Jack Gray, already cited.

The world economy is covered by the Penguin History series already cited, P. Armstrong, A. Glyn and J. Harrison, *Capitalism since 1945* (1991) and S. Marglin and J. Schor eds, *The Golden Age of Capitalism* (1990). For the period before 1945 the publications of the League of Nations, and for the period since 1960 those of the World Bank, OECD and IMF, are indispensable.

For the politics of inter-war and the crisis of liberal institutions one might suggest Charles S. Maier, *Recasting Bourgeois Europe* (1975), F.L. Carsten, *The Rise of Fascism* (1967), H. Rogger and E. Weber eds, *The European Right: a Historical Profile* (1965) and Ian Kershaw, *The Nazi Dictatorship: Problems and Perspectives* (1985). For the spirit of anti-fascism, P. Stansky and W. Abrahams, *Journey to the Frontier: Julian Bell and John Cornford* (1966). For the outbreak of war, Donald Cameron Watt, *How War Came* (1989). The best conspectus of the Cold War so far is Martin Walker, *The Cold War and the Making of the Modern World* (1993) and the clearest introduction to its later phases, F. Halliday, *The Making of the Second Cold War* (2nd edn, 1986). See also J.L. Gaddis, *The Long Peace: Inquiries into the History of the Cold War* (1987). For the reshaping of Europe, Alan Milward, *The Reconstruction of Western Europe 1945–51* (1984). For consensus politics and the welfare state, P. Flora and A.J. Heidenheimer eds, *Development of Welfare States in America and Europe* (1981) and D.W. Urwin, *Western Europe since 1945: a Short Political History* (revised edn, 1989). See also J. Goldthorpe ed., *Order and Conflict in Contemporary Capitalism* (1984). For the USA, W. Leuchtenberg, *A Troubled Feast: American Society since 1945* (1973).

For the end of empires, Rudolf von Albertini, *Decolonization: the Administration and Future of Colonies, 1919–1960* (1961) and the excellent R.F. Holland, *European Decolonization 1918–1981* (1985). The best way to point readers in the direction of Third World history is to name a handful of otherwise unrelated works about it. Eric Wolf's *Europe and the People without History* (1983) is fundamental, though it only deals marginally with our century. So, in a different way, both about capitalism and communism, is Philip C.C. Huang, *The Peasant Family and Rural Development in the Yangzi Delta, 1350–1988* (1990), to which Robin Blackburn has drawn my attention. It may be compared with Clifford Geertz's classic *Agricultural Involution* (1963), which is about Indonesia. On the urbanization of the Third World, part 4 of Paul Bairoch, *Cities and Economic Development* (1988) is essential. On politics, Joel S. Migdal, *Strong Societies and Weak States* (1988) is full of examples and ideas, some of them convincing.

For the sciences, Gerald Holton ed., *The Twentieth-Century Sciences* (1972) is a starting-point, for intellectual developments in general, George Lichtheim, *Europe in the Twentieth Century* (1972). A fine introduction to the avant-garde arts is John Willett, *Art and Politics in the Weimar Period: The New Sobriety, 1917–1933* (1978).

There are as yet no properly historical treatments of the social and cultural revolutions of the second half of the century, though the mass of comment and documentation is vast, and sufficiently accessible to let many of us form our own opinions (see the reference notes). Readers should not be misled by the confident tone of the literature (including my own observations) into confusing opinion with established truth.

Index

Now you can order superb titles directly from Abacus

☐	The Age of Revolution	Eric Hobsbawm	£12.99
☐	The Age of Capital	Eric Hobsbawm	£12.99
☐	The Age of Empire	Eric Hobsbawm	£12.99
☐	The New Century	Eric Hobsbawm	£7.99
☐	Revolutionaries	Eric Hobsbawm	£10.99
☐	Uncommon People	Eric Hobsbawm	£9.99
☐	Bandits	Eric Hobsbawm	£10.99
☐	The Scramble for Africa	Thomas Pakenham	£14.99
☐	The Boer War	Thomas Pakenham	£12.99
☐	The Rise and Fall of the British Empire	Lawrence James	£12.99

The prices shown above are correct at time of going to press. However, the publishers reserve the right to increase prices on covers from those previously advertised, without further notice.

――――――――――――― ⟨ABACUS⟩ ―――――――――――――

Please allow for postage and packing: **Free UK delivery.**
Europe; add 25% of retail price; Rest of World; 45% of retail price.

To order any of the above or any other Abacus titles, please call our credit card orderline or fill in this coupon and send/fax it to:

Abacus, P.O. Box 121, Kettering, Northants NN14 4ZQ
Fax: 01832 733076   Tel: 01832 737526
Email: aspenhouse@FSBDial.co.uk

☐ I enclose a UK bank cheque made payable to Abacus for £ . . . .
☐ Please charge £ . . . . . . to my Visa, Delta, Maestro.

Expiry Date ☐☐☐☐   Maestro Issue No. ☐☐

NAME (BLOCK LETTERS please) . . . .

ADDRESS . . . .

. . . .

. . . .

Postcode . . . . Telephone . . . .

Signature . . . .

Please allow 28 days for delivery within the UK. Offer subject to price and availability.

CHAPTERS INTO VERSE

Chapters into Verse

*Poetry in English
Inspired by The Bible*

VOLUME TWO:
Gospels to Revelation

Assembled and Edited by
ROBERT ATWAN &
LAURANCE WIEDER

Oxford   New York
OXFORD UNIVERSITY PRESS
1993

Oxford University Press

Oxford   New York   Toronto
Delhi   Bombay   Calcutta   Madras   Karachi
Kuala Lumpur   Singapore   Hong Kong   Tokyo
Nairobi   Dar es Salaam   Cape Town
Melbourne   Auckland   Madrid

and associated companies in
Berlin   Ibadan

Copyright © 1993 by Robert Atwan and Laurance Wieder

Published by Oxford University Press, Inc.,
200 Madison Avenue, New York, New York 10016

Oxford is a registered trademark of Oxford University Press

Library of Congress Cataloging-in-Publication Data
Chapters into verse : poetry in English inspired by the Bible /
assembled and edited by Robert Atwan and Laurance Wieder.
p.   cm.
Contents: v. 1. Genesis to Malachi — v. 2. Gospels to Revelation.
ISBN 0-19-506913-7 (v. 1). — ISBN 0-19-508305-9 (v. 2)
1. Bible—History of Biblical events—Poetry. 2. Religious
poerty, English.   3. Religious poetry, American.   I. Atwan, Robert, 1940—.
II. Wieder, Laurance, 1946– .
PR1191.C44 1993
821.008'0382—dc20   92-37206

The following pages are regarded as an extension
of the copyright page.

4 6 8 9 7 5 3

Printed in the United States of America
on acid-free paper

ACKNOWLEDGMENTS

We are grateful to many friends and colleagues for the help they gave us throughout the stages of this vast undertaking. We thank Rev. Lawrence E. Frizzell, Professor of Jewish-Christian Studies at Seton Hall University, for the initial inspiration that brought *Chapters into Verse* to life. We wish to thank, too, those people who offered us many valuable suggestions along the way: George Dardess, Glen Hartley, Michael Heyward, Ron Horning, Gen Kanai, Kenneth Koch, Christina Moustakis, Joyce Carol Oates, Charles O'Neill, Alicia Ostriker, Peggy Rosenthal, David Shapiro, J. O. Tate, and Edward W. Tayler. Michael McSpedon and Francis P. J. DiCesare II helped us with research and manuscript preparation. We appreciate the help and guidance we received from the staff at Oxford University Press, particularly from Elizabeth Maguire, our editor, and Susan Chang. We are especially grateful to Jack Roberts, who patiently went through the enormous first draft of the manuscript and helped us scale it down to publishable size. Finally, we dedicate this book to our families: for Helene, Gregory and Emily Atwan; for Andrea and Aiah Wieder.

CONTENTS

The Beloved

The Crucified

INTRODUCTION

There are no songs comparable to the songs of Zion; no orations equal to those of the prophets; and no politics like those which the Scriptures teach.

John Milton

Ezra Pound once tweaked T. S. Eliot for preferring Moses to the Muses. Pound's witty remark reminds us of English poetry's two great heritages: the classical and the scriptural or (as Matthew Arnold named them) the Hellenic and the Hebraic. Poetry inspired by classical Greek and Latin models has dominated the poetic landscape for so many centuries that most readers now consider it the only literary tradition. Although the scriptural tradition in English poetry is every bit as venerable as the classical, it has never received the attention accorded its chosen twin. Like Ishmael and Esau, it has led a shadow existence. We hope that this collection will finally bring the scriptural tradition out of the shadows and into the light.

Chapters into Verse, therefore, is more than just another anthology of English-language poetry. It is (so far as we know) the first collection ever assembled of poems inspired by the Bible. Its two volumes survey and define a literary legacy that has lived and at times flourished in the wilderness, unremarked by the reigning literary culture. All of the poems selected for both the *Old Testament* and *New Testament* editions respond to specific passages of scripture. Arranged in Biblical order, from "Genesis" to "Malachi" (in Volume One), from "Matthew" to "Revelation" (Volume Two), every poem is preceded by at least the kernel of the appropriate chapter and verse. Whenever possible, we print a poem's Biblical source in full; at other times, to save space, we have excerpted chapter and verse so that readers will have in front of them the salient passage(s) for context and comparison. Whenever a poet responds to an extensive Biblical episode, we provide as much text as is convenient, expecting that readers will turn to their own Bibles for further illumination.

We think that this arrangement lets the reader experience not merely an isolated poem or favorite Biblical quotation; it places the dialogue between individual poet and sacred text in plain view. Each poem, as it retells, contemplates, expands, debates with, praises, voices, or reimagines the language and events of the Bible, becomes as well an exegesis of the text. *Chapters into Verse* can thus be read as a poetic commentary upon the scriptures. The authority of this commentary derives from the individual poet's imaginative insight—from an intuitive precision and expressive vitality—rather than from scholarship or sectarian politics or established religion.

The collection covers an enormous range of literary styles, historical periods, and religious backgrounds. Poets from much of the English-speaking world are present, representing a diversity of countries, cultures, communities, and idioms—from the English metaphysical poets of the seventeenth century to the African-American voices of the Harlem Renaissance, from the Scots dialect of Robert Burns to the jaunty music of Australian Victor Daley. Whether writing in the King's English, another English, or their own invented language, the poets of the scriptural also employ the whole range of verse forms and personal tones familiar to readers of English literature: from lyric to dramatic, from blank verse to highly-wrought rhyme, from ridicule to reverence, from the majestic to the demotic, from epic to epigrammatic.

Although each volume of *Chapters into Verse* contains a wide variety of poetic forms, readers may discover that—aside from theological dissimilarities—there are some notable differences between the two books. Poets attracted to the Old Testament apparently prefer a larger scope and a more impassioned, or rhapsodic, language: they will exult in the glory of the creation, reimagine the songs of Moses, of Deborah, David, Solomon, Hezekiah; they will compose dramas, chivalric romances, verse essays, and epics. The poetry of the New Testament is largely lyrical and meditative, verse that seems better suited to the more inward and private response encouraged by the spiritual quest of Jesus. The Old Testament, on the other hand, invites a more public, less personal and introspective, poetry. In addition, far more of the Old Testament poetry is composed of paraphrase, a difference explained by the fact that the Hebrew Scripture is in many ways a poetic work, with approximately one-third of its text taken up with psalms, songs, lamentations, and various forms of narrative or prophetic verse. In contrast, the New Testament is essentially a prose work, encompassing many types of prose forms—biographies, encomiums, sayings, parables, letters, epistles, rabbinical stories, and episodic narratives.

This major literary distinction between the Old and New Testaments has clearly stimulated different poetic responses to the sacred texts. The Old Testament, for example, undoubtedly presents a special challenge to poets because of the extraordinary poetry it already contains; poets responding to the Hebrew Scriptures need to be fearless—as was William Blake—about competition. Walt Whitman, truly one of the fearless, claimed that he was "a thorough believer in the Hebrew Scriptures." Boldly intending his *Leaves of Grass* to be a "new Bible" for a new era, Whitman nevertheless prophesied that "No true Bard will ever contravene the Bible." Recognizing a scriptural tradition, he saw the unspoken covenant that existed between the books of the Bible and the work of poets. "If the time ever comes," he wrote, "when iconoclasm does its extremest in one direction against the books of the Bible in its present form, the collection must still survive in another, and dominate just as much as hitherto, or more than hitherto, through its divine and primal poetic structure."

To be included in *Chapters into Verse*, a poem had to meet two criteria: it had to possess real literary merit (as distinct from admirable sentiment, or propriety, or didactic fervor) and it had to derive from a specific scriptural source. As a result, some prominent figures who never or rarely partook of poetic inspiration from scripture are missing from this anthology, among them Geoffrey Chaucer, William Shakespeare, Andrew Marvell, Percy Bysshe Shelley, Edgar Allan Poe, and Wallace Stevens. In their place will be found such less familiar names as Francis Quarles, Michael Drayton, Thomas Stanley, Anne Finch, Countess of Winchilsea, Christopher Smart, P. Hately Waddell, and, starting in the twentieth century, such Jewish poets as Charles Reznikoff and Delmore Schwartz.

The decision to use the King James Bible was made not so much by us as by the authors we included. So many important poets since the seventeenth century have relied on this Bible's resonant style, regardless of their religious or historical backgrounds, that it made no literary or editorial sense for us to use any other version or translation. Aside from its theological importance, The King James Bible is itself a monumental literary achievement. Built on a foundation laid by William Tyndale, Miles Coverdale, and the learned committee in Geneva, its language informs both the literature and the everyday chatter of the English-speaking world, an influence rivalled by no other vernacular bible. Thomas Macaulay called the King James Bible "a book which, if everything else in our language should perish, would alone suffice to show the whole extent of its beauty and power." Much of that beauty and power emerges in this collection.

The history of the Bible in English runs parallel to the development of English poetry. John Wycliffe, who made an English Bible from the Latin Vulgate, was a contemporary of Friar Herebert. The first translation from the original tongues into English was undertaken by the unfortunate English Catholic priest, William Tyndale. He perished at the stake after falling into the hands of the Inquisition in the 1540s, the same decade that saw the deaths of the first English sonneteers, Sir Thomas Wyatt and Henry Howard, Earl of Surrey. Besides Englishing Petrarch, Wyatt also translated the Seven Penitential Psalms before his execution for leading a rebellion against the Catholic Queen Mary Tudor; Surrey verse-paraphrased Ecclesiastes. The Geneva Bible, issued by a committee of Calvinists in 1560, was for almost a century the Bible of English Protestants, whose cause found a champion and martyr in the ideal courtier and poet, Sir Philip Sidney. Sidney and his sister Mary Herbert, Countess of Pembroke, are mostly remembered for the crypto-Virgilian pastoral, *The Countess of Pembroke's Arcadia*. But as Sidney noted in his *An Apologie for Poetrie*, the Psalmist David was first a shepherd, then a king, and so the original pastoral poet. Before he died, Sidney translated the first forty-three Psalms; his sister took up the task, and triumphantly completed the Sidney Psalter. Other Renaissance poets, perhaps uncertain which camp (England or Rome, high or low, Hellenic or Hebraic) would prevail, pursued the double career: Sir John Davies and Thomas Campion, among many, made Psalms; Edmund Spenser epitomised the Book of Revelation in unrhymed sonnets; Michael Drayton translated the songs of the Patriarchs and Prophets, and John Donne the Lamentations of Jeremy. By the time James I's committee dedicated the official English Bible in 1611, Shakespeare's life was nearly over and John Milton was about to be born.

By the eighteenth century, literature and scripture had pretty much parted company. The Augustan poets, for the most part, eschewed religious themes, while the religious poets either used verse as sectarian propaganda or aimed it at a popular and sentimental audience. Isaac Watts, John Keble, and Charles Wesley, the most popular religious poets of their time, are largely remembered now for their contributions to the Protestant Hymnal. Of the eighteenth-century literary poets, both Christopher Smart, author of "A Song to David" and a translator of the Psalms, and William Cowper, who wrote the Olney Hymns, suffered bouts of depression and religious mania which gave a pretext for literary criticism to dismiss their religious verse.

Even William Blake, perhaps the last great poet to take the workings of the divine as his whole theme, has sometimes been prey to unconvinced readers' suspicions that his inspiration partakes more of madness than of the sacred breath. Oddly, the worldly Lord Byron actively engaged the scriptural tradition: his Hebrew Melodies are psalms in the Scots ballad tradition of Robert Burns and Thomas Moore. In the 1870s, P. Hately Waddell, a disciple of Robert Burns, published *The Psalms: frae Hebrew intil Scottis*, a work every bit the equal of the Scots Chaucerian Gawin Douglas' *Aeneid of Virgil*, which Ezra Pound called "the most beautiful book in the language."

It may surprise readers who regard the twentieth century as all Muses and no Moses to find so many modern poets in this collection. Not all literary modernists threw away their Bibles, as Wallace Stevens did in 1907 ("I'm glad the silly thing is gone," he wrote). Some, such as Charles Reznikoff, arranged and paraphrased the Jewish Bible. Perhaps the greatest heir of the poets of the New England Puritans (who called themselves Israel), Robert Frost wrote plain-style poetry that responded to scripture in profound and moral music. D. H. Lawrence knew his King James intimately (he wrote a book on Revelation), and quarreled with the New Testament intensely. Many of his poems read as though they were written directly in the margins of his Bible. Every bit as feisty as Lawrence, Laura (Riding) Jackson regarded herself as "religious in my devotion to poetry. But in saying this I am thinking of religion as it is a dedication to, a will to know and make known, the ultimate knowledge, a will to think, to be, with truth, to voice, to live articulately by, the essentialities of existence." In her Biblical poems, she continued that

ongoing debate with the creation which informs the lyric dissents of
Anne Bradstreet, Emily Dickinson, and Marianne Moore.

The past fifty years have seen at least three entirely new transla-
tions of the Bible from original tongues, and poets' versions of
"Genesis," "Job," and the "Book of Psalms." Sparked by a renewed
interest in Biblical scholarship, especially recent research into the
Hebrew Bible, many contemporary poets are rediscovering the scriptural tradition. That tradition is also being reinvigorated by the work
of women poets from many religious backgrounds who are viewing
the Bible from new perspectives.

The range of literary styles and historical periods covered in
Chapters into Verse compelled us to make several editorial decisions
regarding the texts of older poems. At first we thought we should
retain the flavor of the archaic spelling, punctuation and typographi-
cal conventions of sixteenth-, seventeenth-, and eighteenth-century
poetry, but upon reflection that notion struck us as fussy. We wanted
the poetry to be as clear as possible, to present the fewest barriers to
direct, unmediated reading. So we decided to exhibit the older
poetry entirely in contemporary dress, with no quaint frills or peculiar decoration or typographic bombast. We found that outright
modernization transforms many inaccessible-looking texts into
poems that seem breathtakingly fresh. To avoid clutter on the page,
we kept notes and glosses to a minimum.

This volume of *Chapters into Verse* contains poems from every
period of English literature, from Friar William Herebert's four-
teenth-century paraphrase on a passage from Isaiah to John Ash-
bery's postmodern meditation on Job. Nearly every book of the Old
Testament is also represented in this volume. Indeed, when we were
finally able to sort through the heap of material amassed during our
research, we found that only Amos and Obadiah lacked for corresponding poems. So much of the Old Testament has been rendered
in poets' paraphrases, that we easily might have collaged a nearly
complete English verse version of Hebrew Scripture. As might be
expected, the "Book of Psalms" has inspired poets in every century,
as has the "Song of Songs." We did not anticipate, however, that the
five chapters of "Lamentations" could be presented each by a different poet. Further, we might have embellished the poets' text with an
elegy by Francis Quarles upon every verse. Considerations of space,
tempered in some cases by mercy toward the reader, prevented such

an encyclopedic approach. Poets' versions and paraphrases of the Psalms easily fill an entire volume of their own, and we have omitted them here. Considerations of space, too, prevented us from including long poems (such as Christopher Smart's "Song of David") that did not lend themselves to excerpting. Even so, we believe that the historic scope and literary depth of the scriptural tradition is evident in these pages.

A Note on the New Testament Volume

Because the New Testament relates the life of Jesus in four (often overlapping) accounts, we decided it would be more efficient to "harmonize" the gospels into a single narrative. Events told in common were represented by what we considered the most direct and clearest version; details peculiar to each account were fitted into the mosaic whenever possible; obscurities and contradictions, such as where and when Peter denied Christ, were left standing.

CHAPTERS INTO VERSE

Matthew, Mark, Luke, and John,
Bless the bed that I lie on:

Four corners to my bed,
Four angels round my head;
One to watch and one to pray
And two to bear my soul away

TRADITIONAL NURSERY RHYME,
The White Paternoster
(17th Century)

EXTRACTS

To the Christians

7·3·09

FRANCIS LAUDERDALE ADAMS

Take, then, your paltry Christ,
  Your gentleman God.
We want the carpenter's son,
  With his saw and hod.

We want the man who loved
  The poor and oppressed,
Who hated the rich man and king
  And the scribe and the priest.

We want the Galilean
  Who knew cross and rod.
It's your 'good taste' that prefers
  A bastard God!

The Carpenter's Son

7·3·09

JOHN BERRYMAN

The child stood in the shed. The child went mad,
later, & saned the wisemen. People gathered
as he conjoined the Jordan joint
and he spoke with them until he got smothered
amongst their passion for   mysterious healing had.
They could not take his point:

—Repent, & love, he told them frightened throngs,
and it is so he did. Did some of them?
Which now comes hard to say.
The date's in any event a matter of wrongs
later upon him, lest we would not know him,
medieval, on Christmas Day.

Pass me a cookie. O one absolutely did
lest we not know him. Fasten to your fire

the blessing of the living God.
It's far to seek if it will do as good
whether in our womanly or in our manlihood,
this great man sought his retire.

from *Milton, a Poem in 2 Books*

Preface

William Blake

The Stolen and Perverted Writings of Homer and Ovid, of Plato and
Cicero, which all Men ought to contemn, are set up by artifice against
the Sublime of the Bible; but when the New Age is at leisure to
Pronounce, all will be set right, and those Grand Works of the more
ancient and consciously and professedly Inspired Men will hold their
proper rank, and the Daughters of Memory shall become the Daughters
of Inspiration. Shakespeare and Milton were both curbed by the general
malady and infection from the silly Greek and Latin slaves of the Sword.

Rouze up, O Young Men of the New Age! For we have Hirelings in
the Camp, the Court and the University, who would, if they could, for
ever depress Mental and prolong Corporeal War. Painters! on you I call.
Sculptors! Architects! Suffer not the fashionable Fools to depress your
powers by the prices they pretend to give for contemptible works, or the
expensive advertizing boasts that they make of such works; believe Christ
and his Apostles that there is a Class of Men whose whole delight is in
Destroying. We do not want either Greek or Roman Models if we are
but just and true to our own Imaginations, those Worlds of Eternity in
which we shall live forever in Jesus our Lord.

Satire VIII

Joseph Hall

Hence ye profane: mell not with holy things
That Sion muse from Palestina brings.
Parnassus is transformed to Sion hill,
And Jewry-palms her steep ascents done fill.
Now good Saint Peter weeps pure Helicon,
And both the Maries make a Music moan:
Yea and the prophet of heavenly lyre,

Great Solomon, sings in the English choir,
And is become a newfound sonnetist,
Singing his love, the holy spouse of Christ:
Like as she were some light-skirts of the rest,
In mightiest ink-hornisms he can thither wrest.
Ye Sion Muses shall by my dear will,
For this your zeal, and far-admired skill,
Be straight transported from Jerusalem,
Unto the holy house of Bethlehem.

THE RESPECTABLE BURGHER

On 'The Higher Criticism'

THOMAS HARDY

Since Reverend Doctors now declare
That clerks and people must prepare
To doubt if Adam ever were;
To hold the flood a local scare;
To argue, through the stolid stare,
That everything had happened ere
The prophets to its happening sware;
That David was no giant-slayer,
Nor one to call a God-obeyer
In certain details we could spare,
But rather was a debonair
Shrewd bandit, skilled as a banjo-player:
That Solomon sang the fleshly Fair,
And gave the Church no thought whate'er,
That Esther, with her royal wear,
And Mordecai, the son of Jair,
And Joshua's triumphs, Job's despair,
And Balaam's ass's bitter blare;
Nebuchadnezzar's furnace-flare,
And Daniel and the den affair,
And other stories rich and rare,
Were writ to make old doctrine wear
Something of a romantic air:
That the Nain widow's only heir,
And Lazarus with cadaverous glare
(As done in oils by Piombo's care)

Did not return from Sheol's lair:
That Jael set a fiendish snare,
That Pontius Pilate acted square,
That never a sword cut Malchus' ear;
And (but for shame I must forbear)
That —— —— did not reappear! . . .
– Since thus they hint, nor turn a hair,
All churchgoing I will forswear,
And sit on Sundays in my chair,
And read that moderate man Voltaire.

THE H. SCRIPTURES II

GEORGE HERBERT

Oh that I knew how all thy lights combine,
    And the configurations of their glory!
    Seeing not only how each verse doth shine,
But all the constellations of the story.

This verse marks that, and both do make a motion
    Unto a third, that ten leaves off doth lie:
    Then as dispersed herbs do watch a potion,
These three make up some Christian's destiny:

Such are thy secrets, which my life makes good,
    And comments on thee: for in every thing
    Thy words do find me out, and parallels bring,
And in another make me understood.

    Stars are poor books, and oftentimes do miss:
    This book of stars lights to eternal bliss.

O GRANT. . .

JOHN KEATS

O grant that like to Peter I
May like to Peter B,

And tell me, lovely Jesus, Y
This Peter went to C.

O grant me like to Peter I
May like to Peter B,
And tell me, lovely Jesus, Y
Old Jonah went to C.

JESUS

7.7.09

JAMES McAULEY

Touching Ezekiel his workman's hand
Kindled the thick and thorny characters;
And seraphim that seemed a thousand eyes,
Flying leopards, wheels and basilisks,
Creatures of power and of judgment, soared
From his finger-point, emblazoning the skies.

Then turning from the book he rose and walked
Among the stones and beasts and flowers of earth;
They turned their muted faces to their Lord,
Their real faces, seen by God alone;
And people moved before him undisguised;
He thrust his speech among them like a sword.

And when a dove came to his hand he knew
That hell was opening behind its wings.
He thanked the messenger and let it go;
Spoke to the dust, the fishes and the twelve
As if they understood him equally,
And told them nothing that they wished to know.

ON THE GOSPEL

FRANCIS QUARLES

When two Evangelists shall seem to vary
In one discourse, they're diverse, not contrary;
One truth doth guide them both, one spirit doth
Direct them; doubt not, to believe them both.

H. Scriptures

Henry Vaughan

Welcome dear book, soul's joy, and food! The feast
　　Of spirits, Heaven extracted lies in thee;
　　Thou art life's charter, the dove's spotless nest
Where souls are hatched unto Eternity.

In thee the hidden stone, the manna lies,
　　Thou art the great elixir, rare, and choice;
　　The key that opens to all mysteries,
The Word in characters, God in the voice.

O that I had deep cut in my hard heart
　　Each line in thee! Then would I plead in groans
　　Of my Lord's penning, and by sweetest art
Return upon himself the Law, and stones.
　　　　Read here, my faults are thine. This book, and I
　　　　Will tell thee so; *Sweet Savior thou didst die!*

N T

Charles Wesley

　　Matthew, and Mark, and Luke, and John:
　　The Acts, and Romans follow on:
　　Cor. Galat. Eph. Phipp. Col°.
　　Thess. Tim. and Tit. and Philemo:
　　Heb. James and Peter, John and Jude,
　　With Revelation to conclude.

To Him that was Crucified

Walt Whitman

My spirit to yours dear brother,
Do not mind because many sounding your name do not understand you,
I do not sound your name, but I understand you,

I specify you with joy O my comrade to salute you, and to salute those
    who are with you, before and since, and those to come also
That we all labor together transmitting the same charge and succession,
We few equals indifferent of lands, indifferent of times,
We, enclosers of all continents, all castes, allowers of all theologies,
Compassionaters, perceivers, rapport of men,
We walk silent among disputes and assertions, but reject not the
    disputers nor any thing that is asserted,
We hear the bawling and din, we are reached at by divisions, jealousies,
    recriminations on every side,
They close peremptorily upon us to surround us, my comrade,
Yet we walk unheld, free, the whole earth over, journeying up and down
    till we make our ineffaceable mark upon time and the diverse eras,
Till we saturate time and eras, that the men and women of races, ages to
    come, may prove brethren and lovers as we are.

The Gospels According to
MATTHEW, MARK, LUKE, *and* JOHN
Harmonized

PROLOGUE

**JOHN 1:1–5 In the beginning was the Word, and the Word was with
God, and the Word was God. The same was in the beginning with God.
All things were made by him; and without him was not any thing made
that was made. In him was life; and the life was the light of men. And the
light shineth in darkness; and the darkness comprehended it not.**

IN THE BEGINNING

713·09

DYLAN THOMAS

In the beginning was the three-pointed star,
One smile of light across the empty face;
One bough of bone across the rooting air,
The substance forked that marrowed the first sun;
And, burning ciphers on the round of space,
Heaven and hell mixed as they spun.

In the beginning was the pale signature,
Three-syllabled and starry as the smile;
And after came the imprints on the water,
Stamp of the minted face upon the moon;
The blood that touched the crosstree and the grail
Touched the first cloud and left a sign.

In the beginning was the mounting fire
That set alight the weathers from a spark,
A three-eyed, red-eyed spark, blunt as a flower;
Life rose and spouted from the rolling seas,
Burst in the roots, pumped from the earth and rock
The secret oils that drive the grass.

In the beginning was the word, the word
That from the solid bases of the light
Abstracted all the letters of the void;
And from the cloudy bases of the breath
The word flowed up, translating to the heart
First characters of birth and death.

In the beginning was the secret brain.
The brain was celled and soldered in the thought
Before the pitch was forking to a sun;
Before the veins were shaking in their sieve,
Blood shot and scattered to the winds of light
The ribbed original of love.

JOHN 1:14   **And the Word was made flesh, and dwelt among us,**

A WORD MADE FLESH IS SELDOM

EMILY DICKINSON

A Word made Flesh is seldom
And tremblingly partook
Nor then perhaps reported
But have I not mistook
Each one of us has tasted
With ecstasies of stealth
The very food debated
To our specific strength –

A Word that breathes distinctly
Has not the power to die
Cohesive as the Spirit
It may expire if He–
"Made Flesh and dwelt among us"
Could condescension be
Like this consent of Language
This loved Philology.

[handwritten: Emily D. never quite speaks to one.]

THE BODY OF GOD

D. H. LAWRENCE

[handwritten: 7.16]

God is the great urge that has not yet found a body
but urges towards incarnation with the great creative urge.
And becomes at last a clove carnation: lo! that is god!
and becomes at last Helen, or Ninon: any lovely and generous woman
at her best and her most beautiful, being god, made manifest,
any clear and fearless man being god, very god.

There is no god
apart from poppies and the flying fish,
men singing songs, and women brushing their hair in the sun.
The lovely things are god that has come to pass, like Jesus came.
The rest, the undiscoverable, is the demiurge.

[handwritten: Not quite — You refuse to get it, D.H. It's imaginative! I would think that makes sense.]

JOHN 1:14   (and we beheld his glory, the glory as of the only begotten of the Father,) full of grace and truth.

from THE EVERLASTING GOSPEL

WILLIAM BLAKE

[handwritten: 7.16 True]

The Vision of Christ that thou dost see
Is my Vision's Greatest Enemy:
Thine has a great hook nose like thine,
Mine has a snub nose like to mine:
Thine is the friend of All Mankind.

Mine speaks in parables to the Blind:
Thine loves the same world that mine hates,
Thy Heaven doors are my Hell Gates.
Socrates taught what Meletus
Loathed as a Nation's bitterest Curse.
And Caiphas was in his own Mind
A benefactor to Mankind:
Both read the Bible day and night,
But thou readst black where I read white.

THE BIRTH

MATTHEW 1:17 So all the generations from Abraham to David are fourteen generations; and from David until the carrying away into Babylon are fourteen generations; and from the carrying away into Babylon unto Christ are fourteen generations.

THE HARP

RALPH KNEVET

Some may occasion snatch to carp,
Saying that I have sung to Nero's harp,
And therefore am for David's most unfit,
Which piety requires, as well as wit:
But thus, I my defence prepare,
Showing how I have travelled far,
And by the streams of Babylon have sate,
Where I deplored my sad, and wretched state;
Upon a willow there I hung
That harp, to which I whilome sung:
This tree, which neither blossoms yields, nor fruit,
Did with this instrument unhappy suit:
There let it hang, consume, and rot
Since I a better harp have got,
Which doth in worth as far surpass the other,
As Abel in devotion, did his brother.

LUKE 1:26–27 And in the sixth month the angel Gabriel was sent from God unto a city of Galilee, named Nazareth, To a virgin espoused to a man whose name was Joseph, of the house of David; and the virgin's name was Mary.

THE VIRGIN

7/21/09

LAURA (RIDING) JACKSON

My flesh is at a distance from me.
Yet approach and touch it:
It is as near as anyone can come.

This vestiary stuff
Is a true relic,
Though I have never worn it,
Though I shall never be dead.

And the possession?
The violence will be over,
A forgotten passion,
Before I learn of it.

LUKE 1:28   **And the angel came in unto her, and said, Hail, thou that art highly favoured, the Lord is with thee: blessed art thou among women.**

AVE MARIA GRATIA PLENA

Note

⟶ OSCAR WILDE

7/21/09

Was this His coming! I had hoped to see
A scene of wondrous glory, as was told
Of some great God who in a rain of gold
Broke open bars and fell on Danaë:
Or a dread vision as when Semele,
Sickening for love and unappeased desire,
Prayed to see God's clear body, and the fire
Caught her brown limbs and slew her utterly.
With such glad dreams I sought this holy place,
⟶ And now with wondering eyes and heart I stand
Before this supreme mystery of Love:
Some kneeling girl with passionless pale face,
An angel with a lily in his hand,
And over both the white wings of a Dove.

There is another depiction — neither of these
But — perhaps: We can look (seem) this pale.

LUKE 1:29 And when she saw him, she was troubled at his saying, and cast in her mind what manner of salutation this should be.

The Annunciation

Edwin Muir

The angel and the girl are met.
Earth was the only meeting place.
For the embodied never yet
Travelled beyond the shore of space.
The eternal spirits in freedom go.
See, they have come together, see,
While the destroying minutes flow,
Each reflects the other's face
Till heaven in hers and earth in his
Shine steady there. He's come to her
From far beyond the farthest star,
Feathered through time. Immediacy
Of strangest strangeness is the bliss
That from their limbs all movement takes.
Yet the increasing rapture brings
So great a wonder that it makes
Each feather tremble on his wings

Outside the window footsteps fall
Into the ordinary day
And with the sun along the wall
Pursue their unreturning way
That was ordained in eternity.
Sound's perpetual roundabout
Rolls its numbered octaves out
And hoarsely grinds its battered tune.
But through the endless afternoon
These neither speak nor movement make,
But stare into their deepening trance
As if their gaze would never break.

LUKE 1:30–35 And the angel said unto her, Fear not, Mary: for thou hast found favour with God. And, behold, thou shalt conceive in thy womb, and bring forth a son, and shalt call his name JESUS. He shall be

great, and shall be called the Son of the Highest: and the Lord God shall
give unto him the throne of his father David: And he shall reign over the
house of Jacob for ever; and of his kingdom there shall be no end.
  Then said Mary unto the angel, How shall this be, seeing I know not
a man?
  And the angel answered and said unto her, The Holy Ghost shall
come upon thee, and the power of the Highest shall overshadow thee:

ON THE MARRIAGE OF A VIRGIN

DYLAN THOMAS

Waking alone in a multitude of loves when morning's light
Surprised in the opening of her nightlong eyes
His golden yesterday asleep upon the iris
And this day's sun leapt up the sky out of her thighs
Was miraculous virginity old as loaves and fishes,
Though the moment of a miracle is unending lightning
And the shipyards of Galilee's footprints hide a navy of doves.

No longer will the vibrations of the sun desire on
Her deepsea pillow where once she married alone,
Her heart all ears and eyes, lips catching the avalanche
Of the golden ghost who ringed with his streams her mercury bone,
Who under the lids of her windows hoisted his golden luggage,
For a man sleeps where fire leapt down and she learns through his arm
That other sun, the jealous coursing of the unrivalled blood.

? [handwritten annotation]

Not accessible [handwritten annotation]

LUKE 1:35   therefore also that holy thing which shall be born of thee
shall be called the Son of God.

ANNUNCIATION

JOHN DONNE

Salvation to all that will is nigh;
That All, which always is All every where,
Which cannot sin, and yet all sins must bear,
Which cannot die, yet cannot choose but die,

Lo, faithful Virgin, yields himself to lie
In prison, in thy womb; and though he there
Can take no sin, nor thou give, yet he will wear
Taken from thence, flesh, which death's force may try.
Ere by the spheres time was created, thou
Wast in his mind, who is thy Son, and Brother;
Whom thou conceiv'st, conceived; yea thou art now
Thy Maker's maker, and thy Father's mother;
Thou hast light in dark; and shut'st in little room,
Immensity cloistered in thy dear womb.

LUKE 1:38   And Mary said, Behold the handmaid of the Lord; be it unto me according to thy word. And the angel departed from her.

MARY AND GABRIEL

RUPERT BROOKE

Young Mary, loitering once her garden way,
Felt a warm splendour grow in the April day,
As wine that blushes water through. And soon,
Out of the gold air of the afternoon,
One knelt before her: hair he had, or fire,
Bound back above his ears with golden wire,
Baring the eager marble of his face.
Not man's or woman's was the immortal grace
Rounding the limbs beneath that robe of white,
And lighting the proud eyes with changeless light,
Incurious. Calm as his wings, and fair,
That presence filled the garden.
                            She stood there,
Saying, "What would you, Sir?"
                            He told his word,
"Blessed art thou of women!" Half she heard,
Hands folded and face bowed, half long had known,
The message of that clear and holy tone,
That fluttered hot sweet sobs about her heart;
Such serene tidings moved such human smart.
Her breath came quick as little flakes of snow.
Her hands crept up her breast. She did but know
It was not hers. She felt a trembling stir

Within her body, a will too strong for her
That held and filled and mastered all. With eyes
Closed, and a thousand soft short broken sighs,
She gave submission; fearful, meek, and glad. . . .

      She wished to speak. Under her breasts she had
Such multitudinous burnings, to and fro,
And throbs not understood; she did not know
If they were hurt or joy for her; but only
That she was grown strange to herself, half lonely,
All wonderful, filled full of pains to come
And thoughts she dare not think, swift thoughts and dumb,
Human, and quaint, her own, yet very far,
Divine, dear, terrible, familiar . . .
Her heart was faint for telling; to relate
Her limbs' sweet treachery, her strange high estate,
Over and over, whispering, half revealing,
Weeping; and so find kindness to her healing.
'Twixt tears and laughter, panic hurrying her,
She raised her eyes to that fair messenger.
He knelt unmoved, immortal; with his eyes
Gazing beyond her, calm to the calm skies;
Radiant, untroubled in his wisdom, kind.
His sheaf of lilies stirred not in the wind.
How should she, pitiful with mortality,
Try the wide peace of that felicity
With ripples of her perplexed shaken heart,
And hints of human ecstasy, human smart,
And whispers of the lonely weight she bore,
And how her womb within was hers no more
And at length hers?
                        Being tired, she bowed her head;
And said, "So be it!"
                        The great wings were spread
Showering glory on the fields, and fire.
The whole air, singing, bore him up, and higher,
Unswerving, unreluctant. Soon he shone
A gold speck in the gold skies; then was gone.

The air was colder, and grey. She stood alone.

LUKE 1:46–55   And Mary said, My soul doth magnify the Lord, And my
spirit hath rejoiced in God my Saviour. For he hath regarded the low
estate of his handmaiden: for, behold, from henceforth all generations
shall call me blessed. For he that is mighty hath done to me great things;
and holy is his name. And his mercy is on them that fear him from generation to generation. He hath shewed strength with his arm; he hath
scattered the proud in the imagination of their hearts. He hath put down
the mighty from their seats, and exalted them of low degree. He hath
filled the hungry with good things; and the rich he hath sent empty away.
He hath holpen his servant Israel, in remembrance of his mercy; As he
spake to our fathers, to Abraham, and to his seed for ever.

THE SONG OF THE VIRGIN MARY

MILES COVERDALE

My soul doth magnify the Lord,
My spirit rejoiceth greatly
In God my Savior and his word;
For he hath seen the low degree
Of me his handmaiden truly.
Behold now, after this day,
All generations shall speak of me,
And call me blessed alway.

For he that is only of might
Hath done great things for me;
And holy is his name by right:
As for his endless mercy,
It endureth perpetually,
In every generation,
On them that fear him unfeignedly
Without dissimulation.

He showeth strength with his great arm,
Declaring himself to be of power;
He scattereth the proud to their own harm,
Even with the wicked behavior
Of their own hearts every hour
He putteth down the mighty
From their high seat and great honor,
Exalting them of low degree.

The hungry filleth he with good,
And letteth the rich go empty,

Where his own people want no food:
He thinketh upon his mercy,
And helpeth his servant truly,
Even Israel, as he promised
Unto our fathers perpetually,
Abraham and to his seed.

**LUKE 1:56–60   Now Elisabeth's full time came that she should be deliv-
ered; and she brought forth a son. And her neighbours and her cousins
heard how the Lord had shewed great mercy upon her; and they rejoiced
with her. And it came to pass, that on the eighth day they came to cir-
cumcise the child; and they called him Zacharias, after the name of his
father. And his mother answered and said, Not so; but he shall be called
John.**

THE NATIVITY OF ST. JOHN THE BAPTIST

CHRISTOPHER SMART

Great and bounteous Benefactor,
    We thy generous aid adjure,
Shield us from the foul exactor,
    And his sons, that grind the poor.

Lo the swelling fruits of summer,
    With inviting colours dyed,
Hang, for every casual comer,
    O'er the fence projecting wide.

See the corn for plenty waving,
    Where the lark secured her eggs—
In the spirit then be saving,
    Give the poor that sings and begs.

Gentle nature seems to love us
    In each fair and finished scene,
All is beauteous blue above us,
    All beneath is cheerful green.

Now when warmer rays enlighten
    And adorn the lengthened time,

When the views around us brighten,
　　Days a ripening from their prime,

She that was as barren reckoned,
　　Had her course completely run,
And her dumb-struck husband beckoned
　　For a pen to write a son.

John, the child of Zacharias.
　　Just returning to his earth,
Prophet of the Lord Messias,
　　And fore-runner of his birth.

He too martyred, shall precede him,
　　Ere he speed to heaven again,
Ere the traitors shall implead him,
　　And the priest his God arraign.

John beheld the great and holy,
　　Hailed the love of God supreme;
O how gracious, meek, and lowly,
　　When baptized in Jordan's stream!

If from honour so stupendous
　　He the grace of power derived,
And to tyrants was tremendous,
　　That at fraud and filth connived;

If he led a life of rigour,
　　And th' abstemious vow obeyed;
If he preached with manly vigour,
　　Practised sinners to dissuade;

If his voice by fair confession
　　Christ's supremacy avowed;
If he checked with due suppression
　　Self-incitements to be proud.

Vice conspiring to afflict him
　　To the death that ends the great,
Offered him a worthy victim
　　For acceptance in the height.

LUKE 1:67–69   And his father Zacharias was filled with the Holy Ghost, and prophesied, saying, Blessed be the Lord God of Israel; for he hath visited and redeemed his people, And hath raised up an horn of salvation for us in the house of his servant David;

To St John Baptist

Henry Constable

As Anne long barren, Mother did become
    of him, who last was Judge in Israel:
    Thou last of prophets born like Samuel
    didst from a womb past hope of issue come.
His mother silent spake: thy father dumb
    recovering speech, God's wonder did foretell:
    he after death a prophet was in hell:
    and thou unborn within thy mother's womb:
He did annoint the king, whom God did take
    from charge of sheep, to rule his chosen land:
    But that high king who heaven and earth did make
Received a holier liquour from thy hand,
    When God his flock in human shape did feed,
    as Israel's king kept his in shepherd's weed.

MATTHEW 1:18   Now the birth of Jesus Christ was on this wise: When as his mother Mary was espoused to Joseph, before they came together, she was found with child of the Holy Ghost.

I Sing of a Maiden

Anonymous

I sing of a maiden
    That is makeless:
King of all kings
    To her son she ches.

He came also still
    Where his mother was
As dew in April
    That falleth on the grass.

He came also still
    To his mother's bower
As dew in April
    That falleth on the flower.

He came also still
    Where his mother lay
As dew in April
    That falleth on the spray.

Mother and maiden
    Was never none but she—
Well may such a lady
    God's mother be.

ANA-
{MARY
ARMY}
GRAM

GEORGE HERBERT

How well her name an *Army* doth present,
And whom the *Lord of Hosts* did pitch his tent!

**MATTHEW 1:24   Then Joseph being raised from sleep did as the angel
of the Lord had bidden him, and took unto him his wife:**

JOSEPH

G. K. CHESTERTON

If the stars fell; night's nameless dreams
    Of bliss and blasphemy came true,
If skies were green and snow were gold,
    And you loved me as I love you;

O long light hands and curled brown hair,
    And eyes where sits a naked soul;
Dare I even then draw near and burn
    My fingers in the aureole?

Yes, in the one wise foolish hour
    God gives this strange strength to a man.
He can demand, though not deserve,
    Where ask he cannot, seize he can.

But once the blood's wild wedding o'er,
    Were not dread his, half dark desire,
To see the Christ-child in the cot,
    The Virgin Mary by the fire?

MATTHEW 1:25   And knew her not till she had brought forth her first-born son:

A STICK OF INCENSE

WILLIAM BUTLER YEATS

Whence did all that fury come?
From empty tomb or Virgin womb?
Saint Joseph thought the world would melt
But liked the way his fingers smelt.

LUKE 2:1–3   And it came to pass in those days, that there went out a decree from Caesar Augustus that all the world should be taxed. (And this taxing was first made when Cyrenius was governor of Syria.) And all went to be taxed, every one into his own city.

CHRISTMAS DAY: THE FAMILY SITTING

JOHN MEADE FALKNER

In the days of Caesar Augustus
    There went forth this decree:

Si quis rectus et justus
    Liveth in Galilee,
Let him go up to Jerusalem
    And pay his scot to me.

There are passed one after the other
    Christmases fifty-three,
Since I sat here with my mother
    And heard the great decree:
How they went up to Jerusalem
    Out of Galilee.

They have passed one after the other,
    Father and mother died,
Brother and sister and brother
    Taken and sanctified.
I am left alone in the sitting,
    With none to sit beside.

On the fly-leaves of these old prayer-books
    The childish writings fade,
Which show that once they were their books
    In the days when prayer was made
For other kings and princesses,
    William and Adelaide.

The pillars are twisted with holly,
    And the font is wreathed with yew.
Christ forgive me for folly,
    Youth's lapses—not a few,
For the hardness of my middle life,
    For age's fretful view.

Cotton-wool letters on scarlet,
    All the ancient lore,
Tell how the chieftains starlit
    To Bethlehem came to adore;
To hail Him King in the manger,
    Wonderful, Counsellor.

The bells ring out in the steeple
    The gladness of erstwhile,
And the children of other people
    Are walking up the aisle;

They brush my elbow in passing,
   Some turn to give me a smile.

Is the almond-blossom bitter?
   Is the grasshopper heavy to bear?
Christ make me happier, fitter
   To go to my own over there:
Jerusalem the Golden,
   What bliss beyond compare!

My Lord, where I have offended
   Do Thou forgive it me.
That so when, all being ended,
   I hear Thy last decree,
I may go up to Jerusalem
   Out of Galilee.

LUKE 2:4–7 And Joseph also went up from Galilee, out of the city of Nazareth, into Judaea, unto the city of David, which is called Bethlehem; (because he was of the house and lineage of David:) To be taxed with Mary his espoused wife, being great with child. And so it was, that, while they were there, the days were accomplished that she should be delivered. And she brought forth her firstborn son, and wrapped him in swaddling clothes, and laid him in a manger; because there was no room for them in the inn.

NATIVITY

JOHN DONNE

Immensity cloistered in thy dear womb,
Now leaves his well-beloved imprisonment,
There he hath made himself to his intent
Weak enough, now into our world to come;
But Oh, for thee, for him, hath th' Inn no room?
Yet lay him in this stall, and from the Orient,
Stars, and wisemen will travel to prevent
Th' effect of Herod's jealous general doom.
Seest thou, my Soul, with thy faith's eyes, how he
Which fills all place, yet none holds him, doth lie?
Was not his pity towards thee wondrous high,
That would have need to be pitied by thee?

utterly lovely

Kiss him, and with him into Egypt go,
With his kind mother, who partakes thy woe.

UPON CHRIST HIS BIRTH

SIR JOHN SUCKLING

Strange news! a city full? will none give way
To lodge a guest that comes not every day?
No inn, nor tavern void? yet I descry
One empty place alone, where we may lie:
In too much fullness is some want: but where?
Men's empty hearts: let's ask for lodging there.
But if they not admit us, then we'll say
Their hearts, as well as inns, are made of clay.

SALUS MUNDI

MARY COLERIDGE

I saw a stable, low and very bare,
    A little child in a manger.
The oxen knew him, had Him in their care,
    To men He was a stranger.
The safety of the world was lying there,
    And the world's danger.

THE NATIVITY

C. S. LEWIS

Among the oxen (like an ox I'm slow)
I see a glory in the stable grow
Which, with an ox's dullness might at length
    Give me an ox's strength.

Among the asses (stubborn I as they)
I see my Saviour where I looked for hay;
So may my beastlike folly learn at least
    The patience of a beast.

Among the sheep (I like a sheep have strayed)
I watch the manger where my Lord is laid;
Oh that my baa-ing nature would win thence
    Some woolly innocence!

CHRISTMAS MOURNING

VASSAR MILLER

On Christmas Day I weep
Good Friday to rejoice.
I watch the Child asleep.
Does He half dream the choice
The Man must make and keep?

At Christmastime I sigh
For my Good Friday hope.
Outflung the Child's arms lie
To span in their brief scope
The death the Man must die.

Come Christmastide I groan
To hear Good Friday's pealing.
The Man, racked to the bone,
Has made His hurt my healing,
Has made my ache His own.

Slay me, pierced to the core
With Christmas penitence
So I who, new-born, soar
To that Child's innocence,
May wound the Man no more.

LUKE 2:8–11   And there were in the same country shepherds abiding in the field, keeping watch over their flock by night. And, lo, the angel of the

Lord came upon them, and the glory of the Lord shone round about
them: and they were sore afraid. And the angel said unto them, Fear not:
for, behold, I bring you good tidings of great joy, which shall be to all
people. For unto you is born this day in the city of David a Saviour,
which is Christ the Lord.

'UNTO US A CHILD IS BORN'

WILLIAM DUNBAR

Rorate coeli desuper.
Heavens distill your balmy showers,
For now is risen the bright day star
From the rose Mary, flower of flowers;
The clear son whom no cloud devours,
Surmounting Phoebus in the east,
Is coming of his heavenly towers
Et nobis Puer natus est.

Archangels, angels, and donations,
Thrones, potentates, and martyrs sere,
And all ye heavenly operations,
Star, planet, firmament, and spear,
Fire, earth, air, and water clear,
To him give loving, most and least,
That come in to so meek manner
Et nobis Puer natus est.

Sinners, be glad and penance do
And thank your maker heartfully,
For he that ye might not come to,
To you is come full humbly;
Your souls with his blood to buy
And loose you of the fiend's arrest,
And only of his own mercy
Pro nobis Puer natus est.

All clergy do to him incline
And bow unto that balm benign,
And do your observance divine
To him that is of kings is king;
Incense his altar, read and sing
In holy kirk, with mind digest,
Him honor, author all things
Qui nobis Puer est.

Celestial fowls in the air,
Sing with your notes upon high,
In firths and in forests fair
Be mirthfull now, at all your might;
For passed is your dully night,
Aurora has the clouds dispersed,
The sun is risen with gladsome light,
Et nobis Puer natus est.

Now spring up, flowers, from the root,
Revert you upward naturally,
In honor of the blessed fruit
That raised up from the rose Mary;
Lay out your leaves lustily,
From deed take life now at the least
In worship of that Prince worthy
Qui nobis Puer natus est.

Sing heaven imperial most of height,
Regions of air make harmony;
All fish in flood and fowl of flight
Be mirthful and make melody;
All *Gloria in excelsis* cry,
Heaven, earth, sea, man, bird, and beast:
He that is crowned above the sky
Pro nobis Puer natus est.

LUKE 2:12   And this shall be a sign unto you; Ye shall find the babe wrapped in swaddling clothes, lying in a manger.

THE SHEPHERDS

HENRY VAUGHAN

Sweet, harmless lives! (on whose holy leisure
    Waits innocence and pleasure,)
Whose leaders to those pastures, and clear springs,
    Were patriarchs, saints, and kings,
How happened it that in the dead of night
    You only saw true light,
While Palestine was fast asleep, and lay
    Without one thought of day?

Was it because those first and blesséd swains
    Were pilgrims on those plains
When they received the promise, for which now
    'Twas there first shown to you?
'Tis true, he loves that dust whereon they go
    That serve him here below,
And therefore might for memory of those
    His love there first disclose;
But wretched Salem once his love, must now
    No voice, nor vision know,
Her stately piles with all their height and pride
    Now languished and died,
And Beth'lems humble cots above them stepped
    While all her seers slept;
Her cedar, fir, hewed stones and gold were all
    Polluted through their fall,
And those once sacred mansions were now
    Mere emptiness and show,
This made the Angel call at reeds and thatch,
    Yet where the shepherds watch,
And God's own lodging (though he could not lack,)
    To be a common rack;
No costly pride, no soft-clothed luxury
    In those thin cells could lie,
Each stirring wind and storm blew through their cots
    Which never harbored plots,
Only content, and love, and humble joys
    Lived there without all noise,
Perhaps some harmless cares for the next day
    Did in their bosoms play,
As where to lead their sheep, what silent nook,
    What springs or shades to look,
But that was all; And now with gladsome care
    They for the town prepare,
They leave their flock, and in a busy talk
    All towards Beth'lem walk
To see their souls' great shepherd, who was come
    To bring all stragglers home,
Where now they find him out, and taught before
    That Lamb of God adore,
That Lamb whose days great kings and prophets wished
    And longed to see, but missed.
The first light they beheld was bright and gay
    And turned their night to day,

But to this later light they saw in him,
    Their day was dark, and dim.

LUKE 2:13–15   **And suddenly there was with the angel a multitude of the heavenly host praising God, and saying, Glory to God in the highest, and on earth peace, good will toward men. And it came to pass, as the angels were gone away from them into heaven, the shepherds said one to another, Let us now go even unto Bethlehem, and see this thing which is come to pass, which the Lord hath made known unto us.**

NEW HEAVEN, NEW WAR

ROBERT SOUTHWELL

Come to your heaven, you heavenly choirs,
Earth hath the heaven of your desires.
Remove your dwelling to your God;
A stall is now his best abode.
Since men their homage do deny,
Come, angels, all their fault supply.

His chilling cold doth heat require;
Come, seraphims, in lieu of fire.
This little ark no cover hath;
Let cherubs' wings his body swathe.
Come, Raphael, this babe must eat;
Provide our little Toby meat.

Let Gabriel be now his groom,
That first took up his earthly room.
Let Michael stand in his defense,
Whom love hath linked to feeble sense.
Let graces rock when he doth cry,
And angels sing his lullaby.

The same you saw in heavenly seat
Is he that now sucks Mary's teat;
Agnize your king a mortal wight,
His borrowed weed lets not your sight.
Come, kiss the manger where he lies,
That is your bliss above the skies.

This little babe, so few days old,
Is come to rifle Satan's fold;
All hell doth at his presence quake,
Though he himself for cold do shake,
For in this weak unarméd wise
The gates of hell he will surprise.

With tears he fights and wins the field;
His naked breast stands for a shield;
His battering shot are babish cries,
His arrows looks of weeping eyes,
His martial ensigns cold and need
And feeble flesh his warrior's steed.

His camp is pitchéd in a stall,
His bulwark but a broken wall,
The crib his trench, hay stalks his stakes
Of shepherds he his muster makes;
And thus, as sure his foe to wound
The angels' trumps alarum sound.

My soul, with Christ join thou in fight
Stick to the tents that he hath pight;
Within his crib is surest ward,
This little babe will be thy guard.
If thou wilt foil thy foes with joy
Then flit not from this heavenly boy.

[handwritten margin note: This is surely about Rhyme & we that we.]

LUKE 2:16   **And they came with haste, and found Mary, and Joseph, and the babe lying in a manger.**

A HYMN ON THE NATIVITY OF MY SAVIOR

BEN JONSON

I sing the birth, was born tonight,
The author both of life, and light;
        The angels so did sound it,
And like the ravished shepherds said,
Who saw the light, and were afraid,
        Yet searched, and true they found it.

The Son of God, th' Eternal King,
That did us all salvation bring,
    And freed the soul from danger;
He whom the whole world could not take,
The Word, which heaven, and earth did make,
    Was now laid in a manger.

The Father's wisdom willed it so,
The Son's obedience knew no No,
    Both wills were in one stature,
And as that wisdom had decreed,
The Word was now made Flesh indeed,
    And took on him our nature.

What comfort by him do we win?
Who made himself the prince of sin,
    To make us heirs of glory?
To see this babe, all innocence;
A martyr born in our defence;
    Can man forget this story?

CHRISTUS NATUS EST

COUNTEE CULLEN

In Bethlehem
On Christmas morn,
The lowly gem
Of love was born.
Hosannah! *Christus natus est.*

Bright in her crown
Of fiery star,
Judea's town
Shone from afar:
Hosannah! *Christus natus est.*

While beasts in stall,
On bended knee,
Did carol all
Most joyously:
Hosannah! *Christus natus est.*

For bird and beast
He did not come,
But for the least
Of mortal scum.
Hosannah! *Christus natus est.*

Who lies in ditch?
Who begs his bread?
Who has no stitch
For back or head?
Hosannah! *Christus natus est.*

Who wakes to weep,
Lies down to mourn?
Who in his sleep
Withdraws from scorn?
Hosannah! *Christus natus est.*

Ye outraged dust,
On field and plain,
To feed the lust
Of madmen slain:
Hosannah! *Christus natus est.*

The manger still
Outshines the throne;
Christ must and will
Come to his own.
Hosannah! *Christus natus est.*

LUKE 2:18–19   And all they that heard it wondered at those things which were told them by the shepherds. But Mary kept all these things, and pondered them in her heart.

THE MOTHER OF GOD

WILLIAM BUTLER YEATS

The threefold terror of love; a fallen flare
Through the hollow of an ear;
Wings beating about the room;

The terror of all terrors that I bore
The Heavens in my womb.

Had I not found content among the shows
Every common woman knows,
Chimney corner, garden walk,
Or rocky cistern where we tread the clothes
And gather all the talk ?

What is this flesh I purchased with my pains,
This fallen star my milk sustains,
This love that makes my heart's blood stop
Or strikes a sudden chill into my bones
And bids my hair stand up?

LUKE 2:20–21   And the shepherds returned, glorifying and praising God for all the things that they had heard and seen, as it was told unto them. And when eight days were accomplished for the circumcising of the child, his name was called JESUS, which was so named of the angel before he was conceived in the womb.

To his Savior. The New years gift.

Robert Herrick

That little pretty bleeding part
    Of foreskin send to me:
And I'll return a bleeding heart,
    For New-year's gift to thee.

Rich is the gem that thou didst send,
    Mine's faulty too, and small:
But yet this gift Thou wilt commend,
    Because I send Thee *all*.

Upon the Circumcision

John Milton

Ye flaming powers, and winged warriors bright,
That erst with music and triumphant song

First heard by happy watchful shepherds' ear,
So sweetly sung your joy the clouds along
Through the soft silence of the listening night,
Now mourn, and, if sad share with us to bear
Your fiery essence can distill no tear,
Burn in your sighs, and borrow
Seas wept from our deep sorrow:
He, who with all Heaven's heraldry whilere
Entered the world, now bleeds to give us ease;
Alas, how soon our sin
     Sore doth begin
         His Infancy to seize!
O more exceeding love or law more just?
Just law indeed, but more exceeding love!
For we by rightful doom remediless
Were lost in death, till he that dwelt above
High-throned in secret bliss, for us frail dust
Emptied his glory, even to nakedness;
And that great Covenant which we still transgress
Entirely satisfied,
And the full wrath beside
Of vengeful Justice bore for our excess,
And seals obedience first with wounding smart
This day; but Oh! ere long
Huge pangs and strong
     Will pierce more near his heart.

LUKE 2:25–35   And, behold, there was a man in Jerusalem, whose name was Simeon; and the same man was just and devout, waiting for the consolation of Israel: and the Holy Ghost was upon him. And it was revealed unto him by the Holy Ghost, that he should not see death, before he had seen the Lord's Christ. And he came by the Spirit into the temple: and when the parents brought in the child Jesus, to do for him after the custom of the law, Then took he him up in his arms, and blessed God, and said, Lord, now lettest thou thy servant depart in peace, according to thy word: For mine eyes have seen thy salvation, Which thou hast prepared before the face of all people; A light to lighten the Gentiles, and the glory of thy people Israel. And Joseph and his mother marvelled at those things which were spoken of him. And Simeon blessed them, and said unto Mary his mother, Behold, this child is set for the fall and rising again of many in Israel; and for a sign which shall be spoken against; (Yea, a sword shall pierce through thy own soul also,) that the thoughts of many hearts may be revealed.

A Song for Simeon

T. S. Eliot

Lord, the Roman hyacinths are blooming in bowls and
The winter sun creeps by the snow hills;
The stubborn season has made stand.
My life is light, waiting for the death wind,
Like a feather on the back of my hand.
Dust in sunlight and memory in corners
Wait for the wind that chills towards the dead land.

Grant us thy peace.
I have walked many years in this city,
Kept faith and fast, provided for the poor,
Have given and taken honour and ease.
There went never any rejected from my door.
Who shall remember my house, where shall live my children's children
When the time of sorrow is come?
They will take to the goat's path, and the fox's home,
Fleeing from the foreign faces and the foreign swords.

Before the time of cords and scourges and lamentation
Grant us thy peace.
Before the stations of the mountain of desolation,
Before the certain hour of maternal sorrow,
Now at this birth season of decease,
Let the Infant, the still unspeaking and unspoken Word,
Grant Israel's consolation
To one who has eighty years and no to-morrow.

According to thy word.
They shall praise Thee and suffer in every generation
With glory and derision,
Light upon light, mounting the saints' stair.
Not for me the martyrdom, the ecstasy of thought and prayer,
Not for me the ultimate vision.
Grant me thy peace.
(And a sword shall pierce thy heart,
Thine also).
I am tired with my own life and the lives of those after me,
I am dying in my own death and the deaths of those after me.
Let thy servant depart,
Having seen thy salvation.

MATTHEW 2:7–9 Then Herod, when he had privily called the wise men, enquired of them diligently what time the star appeared. And he sent them to Bethlehem, and said, Go and search diligently for the young child; and when ye have found him, bring me word again, that I may come and worship him also. When they had heard the king, they departed; and, lo, the star, which they saw in the east, went before them, till it came and stood over where the young child was.

THE MAGI

WILLIAM BUTLER YEATS

Now as at all times I can see in the mind's eye,
In their stiff, painted clothes, the pale unsatisfied ones
Appear and disappear in the blue depth of the sky
With all their ancient faces like rain-beaten stones,
And all their helms of silver hovering side by side,
And all their eyes still fixed, hoping to find once more,
Being by Calvary's turbulence unsatisfied,
The uncontrollable mystery on the bestial floor.

MATTHEW 2:10–11 When they saw the star, they rejoiced with exceeding great joy. And when they were come into the house, they saw the young child with Mary his mother, and fell down, and worshipped him: and when they had opened their treasures, they presented unto him gifts; gold, and frankincense, and myrrh.

TO HIS SAVIOR, A CHILD; A PRESENT, BY A CHILD

ROBERT HERRICK

Go pretty child, and bear this flower
Unto thy little Savior;
And tell him, by that bud now blown,
He is the Rose of Sharon known:
When thou hast said so, stick it there
Upon his bib, or stomacher:
And tell him, (for good handsell too)
That thou hast brought a whistle new,
Made of a clean strait oaten reed,
To charm his cries, (at time of need:)

Tell him, for coral, thou hast none;
But if thou hadst, he should have one;
But poor thou art, and known to be
Even as moneyless, as he.
Lastly, if thou canst win a kiss
From those mellifluous lips of his;
Then never take a second on,
To spoil the first impression.

THE GIFT

WILLIAM CARLOS WILLIAMS

As the wise men of old brought gifts
    guided by a star
        to the humble birthplace

of the god of love,
    the devils
        as an old print shows
retreated in confusion.

    What could a baby know
        of gold ornaments
or frankincense and myrrh,
    of priestly robes
        and devout genuflections?

But the imagination
    knows all stories
        before they are told
and knows the truth of this one
    past all defection.

The rich gifts
    so unsuitable for a child
        though devoutly proffered,
stood for all that love can bring.
    The men were old
        how could they know

of a mother's needs
    or a child's
        appetite?

But as they kneeled
        the child was fed.
                They saw it
and gave praise!
                A miracle

had taken place,
        hard gold to love,
a mother's milk!
                before
                        their wondering eyes.

The ass brayed
        the cattle lowed.
                It was their nature.

All men by their nature give praise.
        It is all
                they can do.

The very devils
        by their flight give praise.
                What is death,
beside this?
        Nothing. The wise men
                came with gift

and bowed down
        to worship
                this perfection.

**MATTHEW 2:12   And being warned of God in a dream that they should
not return to Herod, they departed into their own country another way.**

THE THREE KINGS

HENRY WADSWORTH LONGFELLOW

Three Kings came riding from far away,
        Melchior and Gaspar and Baltasar;
Three Wise Men out of the East were they.

And they travelled by night and they slept by day
    For their guide was a beautiful, wonderful star.

The star was so beautiful, large, and clear,
    That all the other stars of the sky
Became a white mist in the atmosphere.
And by this they knew that the coming was near
    Of the Prince foretold in prophecy.

Three caskets they bore on their saddlebows,
    Three caskets of gold with golden keys;
Their robes were of crimson silk with rows
Of bells and pomegranates and furbelows,
    Their turbans like blossoming almond-trees.

And so the Three Kings rode into the West,
    Through the dusk of night, over hill and dell,
And sometimes they nodded with beard on breast,
And sometimes talked, as they paused to rest,
    With the people they met at some wayside well.

"Of the child that is born," said Baltasar,
    "Good people, I pray you, tell us the news;
For we in the East have seen his star,
And have ridden fast, and have ridden far,
    To find and worship the King of the Jews."

And the people answered, "You ask in vain;
    We know of no king but Herod the Great!"
They thought the Wise Men were men insane,
As they spurred their horses across the plain,
    Like riders in haste, and who cannot wait.

And when they came to Jerusalem,
    Herod the Great, who had heard this thing,
Sent for the Wise Men and questioned them;
And said, "Go down unto Bethlehem,
    And bring me tidings of this new king."

So they rode away; and the star stood still,
    The only one in the gray of morn;
Yes, it stopped,—it stood still of its own free will,
Right over Bethlehem on the hill,
    The city of David, where Christ was born.

And the Three Kings rode through the gate and the guard,
    Through the silent street, till their horses turned
And neighed as they entered the great inn yard;
But the windows were closed and the doors were barred,
    And only a light in the stable burned.

And cradled there in the scented hay,
    In the air made sweet by the breath of kine,
The little child in the manger lay,
The child that would be king one day
    Of a kingdom not human but divine.

His mother Mary of Nazareth
    Sat watching beside his place of rest,
Watching the even flow of his breath,
For the joy of life and the terror of death
    Were mingled together in her breast.

They laid their offerings at his feet:
    The gold was their tribute to a King,
The frankincense, with its odor sweet,
Was for the Priest, the Paraclete,
    The myrrh for the body's burying.

And the mother wondered and bowed her head,
    And sat as still as a statue of stone;
Her heart was troubled yet comforted,
Remembering what the Angel had said
    Of an endless reign and of David's throne.

Then the Kings rode out of the city gate,
    With a clatter of hoofs in proud array;
But they went not back to Herod the Great,
For they knew his malice and feared his hate,
    And returned to their homes by another way.

**MATTHEW 2:13–15   And when they were departed, behold, the angel of
the Lord appeareth to Joseph in a dream, saying, Arise, and take the
young child and his mother, and flee into Egypt, and be thou there until I
bring thee word: for Herod will seek the young child to destroy him.
When he arose, he took the young child and his mother by night, and
departed into Egypt: And was there until the death of Herod: that it**

might be fulfilled which was spoken of the Lord by the prophet, saying, Out of Egypt have I called my son.

HOLY FAMILY

MURIEL RUKEYSER

A long road and a village.
A bloody road and a village.
A road away from war.
Born, born, we know how it goes.

A man and woman riding.
Riding, the new-born child.
White sky, clever and wild.
Born, born, we know how it goes.

A child rides into the forest
on its mother's arms.
The air screams the alarms.
Born, born, we know how it goes.

The wheel goes back.
How is it with the child ?
How is it with the world?
Born, born, we know how it goes.

Never look at the child.
Give it to bloody ground.
By this dream we are bound.
Born, born, we know how it goes.

Riding between these hills,
woman and man alone
enter the battle-line.
Born, born, we know how it goes.

They childless disappear
among the fighting men.
Two thousand years until they come again.
Born, born, we know how it goes.

THE FLIGHT IN THE DESERT

WILLIAM EVERSON

The last settlement scraggled out with a barbed wire fence
And fell from sight. They crossed coyote country:
Mesquite, sage, the bunchgrass knotted in patches;
And there the prairie dog yapped in the valley;
And on the high plateau the short-armed badger
Delved his clay. But beyond that the desert,
Raw, unslakable, its perjured dominion wholly contained
In the sun's remorseless mandate, where the dim trail
Died ahead in the watery horizon: God knows where.

And there the failures: skull of the ox,
Where the animal terror trembled on in the hollowed eyes;
The catastrophic wheel, split, sandbedded;
And the sad jawbone of a horse. These the denials
Of the retributive tribes, fiercer than pestilence,
Whose scrupulous realm this was.

Only the burro took no notice: the forefoot
Placed with the nice particularity of one
To whom the evil of the day is wholly sufficient.
Even the jocular ears marked time.
But they, the man and the anxious woman,
Who stared pinch-eyed into the settling sun,
They went forward into its denseness
All apprehensive, and would many a time have turned
But for what they carried. That brought them on.
In the gritty blanket they bore the world's great risk,
And knew it; and kept it covered, near to the blind heart,
That hugs in a bad hour its sweetest need,
Possessed against the drawn night
That comes now, over the dead arroyos,
Cold and acrid and black.

This was the first of his goings forth into the wilderness of the world.
There was much to follow: much of portent, much of dread.
But what was so meek then and so mere, so slight and strengthless,
(Too tender, almost, to be touched)—what they nervously guarded
Guarded them. As we, each day, from the lifted chalice,
That strengthless Bread the mildest tongue subsumes,
To be taken out in the blatant kingdom

Where Herod sweats, and his deft henchmen
Riffle the tabloids—that keeps us.

Over the campfire the desert moon
Slivers the west, too chaste and cleanly
To mean hard luck. The man rattles the skillet
To take the raw edge off the silence;
The woman lifts up her heart; the Infant
Knuckles the generous breast, and feeds.

MATTHEW 2:16 Then Herod, when he saw that he was mocked of the wise men, was exceeding wroth, and sent forth, and slew all the children that were in Bethlehem, and in all the coasts thereof, from two years old and under, according to the time which he had diligently enquired of the wise men.

LULLA, MY SWEET LITTLE BABY

WILLIAM BYRD

Lulla, la lulla, lulla lullaby.
My sweet little baby, what meanest thou to cry?
Be still, my blessed babe, though cause thou hast to mourn,
Whose blood most innocent to shed the cruel king hath sworn.
And lo, alas, behold what slaughter he doth make,
Shedding the blood of infants all, sweet Savior, for thy sake
A King is born, they say, which King this king would kill.
Oh woe, and woeful heavy day, when wretches have their will!

Lulla, la lulla, lulla lullaby.
My sweet little baby, what meanest thou to cry?
Three kings this King of kings to see are come from far,
To each unknown, with offerings great, by guiding of a star.
And shepherds heard the song which angels bright did sing,
Giving all glory unto God for coming of this King,
Which must be made away, King Herod would him kill.
Oh woe, and woeful heavy day, when wretches have their will!

Lulla, la lulla, lulla lullaby.
My sweet little baby, what meanest thou to cry?
Lo, my little babe, be still, lament no more;
From fury thou shalt step aside, help have we still in store.

We heavenly warning have some other soil to seek,
From death must fly the Lord of life, as lamb both mild and meek.
Thus must my babe obey the king that would him kill.
Oh woe, and woeful heavy day, when wretches have their will!

   Lulla, la lulla, lulla lullaby.
  My sweet little baby, what meanest thou to cry?
But thou shalt live and reign as Sibyls have foresaid,
As all the prophets prophesy, whose mother, yet a maid
And perfect virgin pure, with her breasts shall upbreed
Both God and man, that all hath made, the Son of heavenly seed,
Whom caitiffs none can 'tray, whom tyrants none can kill.
Oh joy, and joyful happy day, when wretches want their will!

MATTHEW 2:17–18   Then was fulfilled that which was spoken by Jeremy the prophet, saying, In Rama was there a voice heard, lamentation, and weeping, and great mourning, Rachel weeping for her children, and would not be comforted, because they are not.

To the Infant Martyrs

Richard Crashaw

Go smiling souls, your new built cages break,
In Heaven you'll learn to sing ere here to speak,
Nor let the milky fonts that bathe your thirst,
   Be your delay;
The place that calls you hence, is at the worst
   Milk all the way.

A Curse on Herod

Amy Witting

May you live forever. In that eternity
may birdcries from the playground ring in your ear
incessantly. When you plan your forays, may
on your terrible blueprints starfish prints appear.

May short fierce arms be locked about your knees
wherever you turn, and small fists drag at your hem

while voices whine of weewee and icecream. These
are your children. You have made them. Care for them.

May you have no rest. May you wake at night with a cry
chilled by a nightmare that you can't dispel.
May the bogeyman be thirty inches high
and immortal. These are your children. Guard them well.

May they weary you till death appears to be
brighter than the walking doll or the tin drum,
the loveliest present on the Christmas tree—
but to the bad children, Christmas does not come.

**LUKE 2:40–42   And the child grew, and waxed strong in spirit, filled
with wisdom: and the grace of God was upon him.**

    **Now his parents went to Jerusalem every year at the feast of the
passover. And when he was twelve years old, they went up to Jerusalem
after the custom of the feast.**

CHRIST'S CHILDHOOD

ROBERT SOUTHWELL

Till twelve years' age, how Christ His childhood spent
    All earthly pens unworthy were to write;
Such acts to mortal eyes he did present,
    Whose worth not men but angels must recite:
No nature's blots, no childish faults defiled,
Where grace was guide, and God did play the child.

In springing locks lay couchèd hoary wit,
    In semblance young, a grave and ancient port;
In lowly looks high majesty did sit,
    In tender tongue, sound sense of sagest sort:
Nature imparted all that she could teach,
And God supplied where nature could not reach.

His mirth, of modest mean a mirror was,
    His sadness, tempered with a mild aspect;
His eye, to try each action was a glass,
    Whose looks did good approve and bad correct;
His nature's gifts, his grace, his word and deed,
Well showed that all did from a God proceed.

LUKE 2:46–50   **And it came to pass, that after three days they found him in the temple, sitting in the midst of the doctors, both hearing them, and asking them questions. And all that heard him were astonished at his understanding and answers. And when they saw him, they were amazed: and his mother said unto him, Son, why hast thou thus dealt with us? behold, thy father and I have sought thee sorrowing. And he said unto them, How is it that ye sought me? wist ye not that I must be about my Father's business? And they understood not the saying which he spake unto them.**

TEMPLE

JOHN DONNE

With his kind mother who partakes thy woe,
Joseph turn back; see where your child doth sit,
Blowing, yea blowing out those sparks of wit,
Which himself on the Doctors did bestow;
The Word but lately could not speak, and lo,
It suddenly speaks wonders, whence comes it,
That all which was, and all which should be writ,
A shallow seeming child, should deeply know?
His godhead was not soul to his manhood,
Nor had time mellowed him to this ripeness,
But as for one which hath a long task, 'tis good,
With the sun to begin his business,
He in his age's morning thus began
By miracles exceeding power of man.

from THE EVERLASTING GOSPEL

WILLIAM BLAKE

Was Jesus Humble? or did he
Give any Proofs of Humility?
Boast of high Things with Humble tone
And give with Charity a Stone?
When but a Child he ran away
And left his Parents in dismay.
When they had wandered three days long
These were the words upon his tongue:
"No Earthly Parents I confess:

"I am doing my Father's business."
When the rich learned Pharisee
Came to consult him secretly,
Upon his heart with Iron pen
He wrote, "Ye must be born again."
He was too proud to take a bribe;
He spoke with authority, not like a Scribe.
He says with most consummate Art,
"Follow me, I am meek and lowly of heart,"
As that is the only way to escape
The Miser's net and the Glutton's trap.
What can be done with such desperate Fools
Who follow after the Heathen Schools?
I was standing by when Jesus died;
What I called Humility, they called Pride.
He who loves his Enemies betrays his Friends;
This surely is not what Jesus intends,
But the sneaking Pride of Heroic Schools,
And the Scribes' and Pharisees' Virtuous Rules;
For he acts with honest, triumphant Pride,
And this is the cause that Jesus died.
He did not die with Christian ease,
Asking pardon of his Enemies:
If he had, Caiphas would forgive;
Sneaking submission can always live.
He had only to say that God was the devil,
And the devil was God, like a Christian Civil:
Mild Christian regrets to the devil confess
For affronting him thrice in the Wilderness;
Like dr. Priestly and Bacon and Newton—
Poor Spiritual Knowledge is not worth a button!
He had soon been bloody Caesar's Elf;
And at last he would have been Caesar himself.
For thus the Gospel Sir Isaac confutes:
"God can only be known by his Attributes;
"And as for the Indwelling of the Holy Ghost
"Or of Christ and his Father, it's all a boast
"And Pride and Vanity of the imagination,
"That disdains to follow this World's Fashion."
To teach doubt and Experiment
Certainly was not what Christ meant.
What was he doing all that time,
From twelve years old to manly prime?
Was he then Idle, or the Less

About his Father's business?
Or was his wisdom held in scorn
Before his wrath began to burn
In Miracles throughout the Land,
That quite unnerved Caiaphas' hand?
If he had been Antichrist, Creeping Jesus,
He'd have done any thing to please us—
Gone sneaking into Synagogues
And not used the Elders and Priests like dogs,
But Humble as a Lamb or Ass
Obeyed himself to Caiaphas.
God wants not Man to Humble himself:
This is the trick of the ancient Elf.
This is the Race that Jesus ran:
Humble to God, Haughty to Man,
Cursing the Rulers before the People
Even to the temple's highest Steeple
And when he Humbled himself to God,
Then descended the Cruel Rod.
"If thou humblest thyself, thou humblest me;
"Thou also dwellst in Eternity.
"Thou art a Man, God is no more,
"Thy own humanity learn to adore,
"For that is my Spirit of Life.
"Awake, arise to Spiritual Strife
"And thy Revenge abroad display
"In terrors at the Last Judgment day.
"God's Mercy and Long Suffering
"Is but the Sinner to Judgment to bring.
"Thou on the Cross for them shalt pray
"And take Revenge at the Last Day."
Jesus replied and thunders hurled:
"I never will Pray for the World.
"Once I did so when I prayed in the Garden;
"I wished to take with me a Bodily Pardon."
Can that which was of woman born
In the absence of the Morn,
When the Soul fell into Sleep
And Archangels round it weep,
Shooting out against the Light
Fibres of a deadly night,
Reasoning upon its own dark fiction,
In doubt which is Self Contradiction?
Humility is only doubt,

And does the Sun and Moon blot out,
Rooting over with thorns and stems
The buried Soul and all its Gems.
This Life's dim Window of the Soul
Distorts the Heavens from Pole to Pole
And leads you to Believe a Lie
When you see with, not through, the Eye
That was born in a night to perish in a night,
When the Soul slept in the beams of Light.

THE CALL

MARK 1:2–6 Behold, I send my messenger before thy face, which shall prepare thy way before thee. The voice of one crying in the wilderness, Prepare ye the way of the Lord, make his paths straight. John did baptize in the wilderness, and preach the baptism of repentance for the remission of sins. And there went out unto him all the land of Judaea, and they of Jerusalem, and were all baptized of him in the river of Jordan, confessing their sins. And John was clothed with camel's hair, and with a girdle of a skin about his loins; and he did eat locusts and wild honey;

FOR THE BAPTIST

WILLIAM DRUMMOND OF HAWTHORNDEN

The last and greatest herald of Heaven's King,
Girt with rough skins, hies to the deserts wild,
Among that savage brood the woods forth bring,
Which he than man more harmless found and mild:
His food was blossoms, and what young doth spring,
With honey that from virgin hives distilled;
Parched body, hollow eyes, some uncouth thing
Made him appear, long since from Earth exiled.
There burst he forth; All ye, whose hopes rely
On God, with me amidst these deserts mourn,
Repent, repent, and from old errors turn.
Who listened to his voice, obeyed his cry?
        Only the echoes which he made relent,
        Rung from their marble caves, repent, repent.

MATTHEW 3:11–12 I indeed baptize you with water unto repentance: but he that cometh after me is mightier than I, whose shoes I am not worthy to bear: he shall baptize you with the Holy Ghost, and with fire:

Whose fan is in his hand, and he will thoroughly purge his floor, and
gather his wheat into the garner; but he will burn up the chaff with
unquenchable fire.

MIDNIGHT

HENRY VAUGHAN

When to my eyes
(Whilst deep sleep others catches,)
Thine host of spies
The stars shine in their watches,
I do survey
Each busy ray,
And how they work, and wind,
And wish each beam
My soul doth stream,
With the like ardor shined;
What emanations,
Quick vibrations
And bright stars are there?
What thin ejections,
Cold affections,
And slow motions here?

Thy heavens (some say,)
Are a fiery-liquid light,
Which mingling aye
Streams, and flames thus to the sight.
Come then, my God!
Shine on this blood,
And water in one beam,
And thou shalt see
Kindled by thee
Both liquors burn, and stream.
O what bright quickness,
Active brightness,
And celestial flows
Will follow after
On that water,
Which thy spirit blows!

MATTHEW 3:13–17   Then cometh Jesus from Galilee to Jordan unto John, to be baptized of him. But John forbad him, saying, I have need to be baptized of thee, and comest thou to me? And Jesus answering said unto him, Suffer it to be so now: for thus it becometh us to fulfil all righteousness. Then he suffered him. And Jesus, when he was baptized, went up straightway out of the water: and, lo, the heavens were opened unto him, and he saw the Spirit of God descending like a dove, and lighting upon him: And lo a voice from heaven, saying, This is my beloved Son, in whom I am well pleased.

MY BAPTISMAL BIRTH-DAY

SAMUEL TAYLOR COLERIDGE

God's child in Christ adopted,—Christ my all,—
What that earth boasts were not lost cheaply, rather
Than forfeit that blessed name, by which I call
The Holy One, the Almighty God, my Father?—
Father! in Christ we live, and Christ in Thee—
Eternal Thou, and everlasting we.
The heir of heaven, henceforth I fear not death:
In Christ I live! in Christ I draw the breath
Of the true life!—Let then earth, sea, and sky
Make war against me! On my heart I show
Their mighty master's seal. In vain they try
To end my life, that can but end its woe.—
Is that a death-bed where a Christian lies?—
Yes! but not his—'tis Death itself there dies.

LUKE 4:1   And Jesus being full of the Holy Ghost returned from Jordan, and was led by the Spirit into the wilderness, MATTHEW 4:2   And when he had fasted forty days and forty nights, he was afterward an hungred.

IN THE WILDERNESS

ROBERT GRAVES

Christ of His gentleness
Thirsting and hungering,
Walked in the wilderness;
Soft words of grace He spoke

Unto lost desert-folk
That listened wondering.
He heard the bitterns call
From ruined palace-wall,
Answered them brotherly.
He held communion
With the she-pelican
Of lonely piety.
Basilisk, cockatrice,
Flocked to His homilies,
With mail of dread device,
With monstrous barbèd slings,
With eager dragon-eyes;
Great bats on leathern wings
And poor blind broken things
Foul in their miseries.
And ever with Him went,
Of all His wanderings
Comrade, with ragged coat,
Gaunt ribs—poor innocent—
Bleeding foot, burning throat,
The guileless old scapegoat;
For forty nights and days
Followed in Jesus' ways,
Sure guard behind Him kept,
Tears like a lover wept.

MATTHEW 4:3–8 And when the tempter came to him, he said, If thou
be the Son of God, command that these stones be made bread. But he
answered and said, It is written, Man shall not live by bread alone, but by
every word that proceedeth out of the mouth of God.

Then the devil taketh him up into the holy city, and setteth him on a
pinnacle of the temple, And saith unto him, If thou be the Son of God,
cast thyself down: for it is written, He shall give his angels charge concerning thee: and in their hands they shall bear thee up, lest at any time
thou dash thy foot against a stone. Jesus said unto him, It is written
again, Thou shalt not tempt the Lord thy God. Again, the devil taketh
him up into an exceeding high mountain, and sheweth him all the kingdoms of the world, and the glory of them; LUKE 4:6 And the devil said
unto him, All this power will I give thee, and the glory of them: for that is
delivered unto me; and to whomsoever I will I give it. . . MATTHEW 4:9
. . . if thou wilt fall down and worship me. LUKE 4:8 And Jesus answered
and said unto him, Get thee behind me, Satan: for it is written, Thou
shalt worship the Lord thy God, and him only shalt thou serve.

from *Paradise Regained, Bk IV*

John Milton

ll. 155-232; 285-352
To whom the Tempter impudent replied.
I see all offers made by me how slight
Thou valu'st, because offered, and reject'st:
Nothing will please the difficult and nice,
Or nothing more than still to contradict:
On th' other side know also thou, that I
On what I offer set as high esteem,
Nor what I part with mean to give for naught;
All these which in a moment thou beholdst,
The kingdoms of the world to thee I give;
For given to me, I give to whom I please,
No trifle; yet with this reserve, not else,
On this condition, if thou wilt fall down,
And worship me as thy superior Lord,
Easily done, and hold them all of me;
For what can less so great a gift deserve?
Whom thus our Savior answered with disdain.
I never liked thy talk, thy offers less,
Now both abhor, since thou hast dared to utter
Th'abominable terms, impious condition;
But I endure the time, till which expired,
Thou hast permission on me. It is written
The first of all Commandments, Thou shalt worship
The Lord thy God, and only him shalt serve;
And dar'st thou to the Son of God propound
To worship thee accursed, now more accursed
For this attempt bolder than that on Eve,
And more blasphemous? which expect to rue.
The kingdoms of the world to thee were given,
Permitted rather, and by thee usurped,
Other donation none thou canst produce:
If given, by whom but by the King of Kings,
God over all supreme? If given to thee,
By thee how fairly is the giver now
Repaid? But gratitude in thee is lost
Long since. Wert thou so void of fear or shame,
As offer them to me the Son of God,
To me my own, on such abhorred pact,
That I fall down and worship thee as God?

Get thee behind me; plain thou now appearst
That Evil one, Satan for ever damned.
          To whom the Fiend with fear abashed replied.
Be not so sore offended, Son of God,
Though Sons of God both angels are and men;
If I to try whether in higher sort
Than these thou bearst that title, have proposed
What both from men and angels I receive,
Tetrarchs of fire, air, flood, and on the earth
Nations besides from all the quartered winds,
God of this world invoked and world beneath;
Who then thou art, whose coming is foretold
To me so fatal, me it most concerns.
The trial hath endamaged thee no way,
Rather more honor left and more esteem;
Me naught advantaged, missing what I aimed.
Therefore let pass, as they are transitory,
The kingdoms of this world; I shall no more
Advise thee, gain them as thou canst, or not.
And thou thyself seemst otherwise inclined
Than to a worldly crown, addicted more
To contemplation and profound dispute,
As by that early action may be judged,
When slipping from thy mother's eye thou wentst
Alone into the temple; there wast found
Among the gravest Rabbis disputant
On points and questions fitting Moses' Chair,
Teaching not taught; the childhood shows the man,
As morning shows the day. Be famous then
By wisdom; as thy empire must extend,
So let extend thy mind o'er all the world,
In knowledge, all things in it comprehend.
All knowledge is not couched in Moses' Law,
The *Pentateuch* or what the Prophets wrote;
The Gentiles also know, and write, and teach
To admiration, led by nature's light
And with the Gentiles much thou must converse,
Ruling them by persuasion as thou meanst,
Without their learning how wilt thou with them,
Or they with thee hold conversation meet? . . .

          To whom our Savior sagely thus replied.
Think not but that I know these things; or think
I know them not; not therefore am I short

Of knowing what I ought: he who receives
Light from above, from the fountain of light,
No other doctrine needs, though granted true;
But these are false, or little else but dreams,
Conjectures, fancies, built on nothing firm.
The first and wisest of them all professed
To know this only, that he nothing knew;
The next to fabling fell and smooth conceits;
A third sort doubted all things, though plain sense;
Others in virtue placed felicity,
But virtue joined with riches and long life;
In corporal pleasure he, and careless ease;
The Stoic last in philosophic pride,
By him called virtue; and his virtuous man,
Wise, perfect in himself, and all possessing
Equal to God, oft shames not to prefer,
As fearing God nor man, contemning all
Wealth, pleasure, pain or torment, death and life,
Which when he lists, he leaves, or boasts he can,
For all his tedious talk is but vain boast,
Or subtle shifts conviction to evade.
Alas! what can they teach, and not mislead;
Ignorant of themselves, of God much more,
And how the world began, and how man fell
Degraded by himself, on grace depending?
Much of the Soul they talk, but all awry,
And in themselves seek virtue, and to themselves
All glory arrogate, to God give none,
Rather accuse him under usual names,
Fortune and Fate, as one regardless quite
Of mortal things. Who therefore seeks in these
True Wisdom, finds her not, or by delusion
Far worse, her false resemblance only meets,
An empty cloud. However, many books
Wise men have said are wearisome; who reads
Incessantly, and to his reading brings not
A spirit and judgment equal or superior
(And what he brings, what needs he elsewhere seek)
Uncertain and unsettled still remains,
Deep versed in books and shallow in himself,
Crude or intoxicate, collecting toys,
And trifles for choice matters, worth a sponge;
As children gathering pebbles on the shore.
Or if I would delight my private hours

With music or with poem, where so soon
As in our native language can I find
That solace? All our law and story strewed
With hymns, our psalms with artful terms inscribed
Our hebrew songs and harps in Babylon,
That pleased so well our victors' ear, declare
That rather Greece from us these arts derived;
Ill imitated, while they loudest sing
The vices of their deities, and their own
In fable, hymn, or song, so personating
Their gods ridiculous, and themselves past shame.
Remove their swelling epithets thick laid
As varnish on a harlot's cheek, the rest,
Thin sown with aught of profit or delight,
Will far be found unworthy to compare
With Sion's songs, to all true tastes excelling,
Where God is praised aright, and godlike men,
The Holiest of Holies, and his Saints;
Such are from God inspired, not such from thee;
Unless where moral virtue is expressed
By light of nature, not in all quite lost.

JOHN 1:29   The next day John seeth Jesus coming unto him, and saith, Behold the Lamb of God, which taketh away the sin of the world.

THE LAMB

WILLIAM BLAKE

Little Lamb, who made thee?
  Dost thou know who made thee?
Gave thee life, and bid thee feed
By the stream and o'er the mead;
Gave thee clothing of delight,
Softest clothing, wooly, bright;
Gave thee such a tender voice,
Making all the vales rejoice?
  Little Lamb, who made thee?
  Dost thou know who made thee?

Little Lamb, I'll tell thee
Little Lamb, I'll tell thee:

He is callèd by thy name,
For he calls himself a Lamb.
He is meek, and he is mild;
He became a little child.
I a child, and thou a lamb,
We are callèd by his name.
　　Little Lamb, God bless thee!
　　Little Lamb, God bless thee!

JOHN 2:1–10　And the third day there was a marriage in Cana of Galilee; and the mother of Jesus was there: And both Jesus was called, and his disciples, to the marriage. And when they wanted wine, the mother of Jesus saith unto him, They have no wine. Jesus saith unto her, Woman, what have I to do with thee? mine hour is not yet come. His mother saith unto the servants, Whatsoever he saith unto you, do it. And there were set there six waterpots of stone, after the manner of the purifying of the Jews, containing two or three firkins apiece. Jesus saith unto them, Fill the waterpots with water. And they filled them up to the brim. And he saith unto them, Draw out now, and bear unto the governor of the feast. And they bare it. When the ruler of the feast had tasted the water that was made wine, and knew not whence it was: (but the servants which drew the water knew;) the governor of the feast called the bridegroom, And saith unto him, Every man at the beginning doth set forth good wine; and when men have well drunk, then that which is worse: but thou hast kept the good wine until now.

THE WEDDING FEAST

EDGAR LEE MASTERS

Said the chief of the marriage feast to the groom,
　　Whence is this blood of the vine?
Men serve at first the best, he said,
　　And at the last, poor wine.

Said the chief of the marriage feast to the groom,
　　When the guests have drunk their fill
They drink whatever wine you serve,
　　Nor know the good from the ill.

How have you kept the good till now
　　When our hearts nor care nor see?

Said the chief of the marriage feast to the groom,
    Whence may this good wine be?

Said the chief of the marriage feast, this wine
    Is the best of all by far.
Said the groom, there stand six jars without
    And the wine fills up each jar.

Said the chief of the marriage feast, we lacked
    Wine for the wedding feast.
How comes it now one jar of wine
    To six jars is increased?

Who makes our cup to overflow?
    And who has the wedding blessed?
Said the groom to the chief of the feast, a stranger
    Is here as a wedding guest.

Said the groom to the chief of the wedding feast,
    Moses by power divine
Smote water at Meribah from the rock,
    But this man makes us wine.

Said the groom to the chief of the wedding feast,
    Elisha by power divine
Made oil for the widow to sell for bread,
    But this man, wedding wine.

He changed the use of the jars, he said,
    From an outward rite and sign:
Where water stood for the washing of feet,
    For heart's delight there's wine.

So then 'tis he, said the chief of the feast,
    Who the wedding feast has blessed?
Said the groom to the chief of the feast, the stranger
    Is the merriest wedding guest.

He laughs and jests with the wedding guests,
    He drinks with the happy bride.
Said the chief of the wedding feast to the groom
    Go bring him to my side.

Jesus of Nazareth came up,
    And his body was fair and slim.

Jesus of Nazareth came up,
    And his mother came with him.

Jesus of Nazareth stands with the dancers
    And his mother by him stands.
The bride kneels down to Jesus of Nazareth
    And kisses his rosy hands.

The bridegroom kneels to Jesus of Nazareth
    And Jesus blesses the twain.
I go a way, said Jesus of Nazareth,
    Of darkness, sorrow and pain.

After the wedding feast is labor,
    Suffering, sickness, death,
And so I make you wine for the wedding,
    Said Jesus of Nazareth.

My heart is with you, said Jesus of Nazareth,
    As the grape is one with the vine.
Your bliss is mine, said Jesus of Nazareth,
    And so I make you wine.

Youth and love I bless, said Jesus,
    Song and the cup that cheers.
The rosy hands of Jesus of Nazareth
    Are wet with the young bride's tears.

Love one another, said Jesus of Nazareth,
    Ere cometh the evil of years.
The rosy hands of Jesus of Nazareth
    Are wet with the bridegroom's tears.

Jesus of Nazareth goes with his mother,
    The dancers are dancing again.
There's a woman who pauses without to listen,
    'Tis Mary Magdalen.

Forth to the street a Scribe from the wedding
    Goes with a Sadducee.
Said the Scribe, this shows how loose a fellow
    Can come out of Galilee!

JOHN 2:11 This beginning of miracles did Jesus in Cana of Galilee, and manifested forth his glory; and his disciples believed on him.

CANA

THOMAS MERTON

Once when our eyes were clean as noon, our rooms
Filled with the joys of Cana's feast:
For Jesus came, and His disciples, and His Mother,
And after them the singers
And some men with violins.

Once when our minds were Galilees,
And clean as skies our faces,
Our simple rooms were charmed with sun.

Our thoughts went in and out in whiter coats than God's disciples',
In Cana's crowded rooms, at Cana's tables.

Nor did we seem to fear the wine would fail:
For ready, in a row, to fill with water and a miracle,
We saw our earthen vessels, waiting empty.
What wine those humble waterjars foretell!

Wine for the ones who, bended to the dirty earth,
Have feared, since lovely Eden, the sun's fire,
Yet hardly mumble, in their dusty mouths, one prayer.

Wine for old Adam, digging in the briars!

THE SIGNS

JOHN 3:2 There was a man of the Pharisees, named Nicodemus, a ruler of the Jews: The same came to Jesus by night, and said unto him, Rabbi, we know that thou art a teacher come from God: for no man can do these miracles that thou doest, except God be with him.

THE NIGHT

HENRY VAUGHAN

Through that pure Virgin-shrine,
That sacred veil drawn o'er thy glorious noon

That men might look and live as glow-worms shine,
    And face the moon:
      Wise Nicodemus saw such light
      As made him know his God by night.

      Most blessed believer he!
Who in that land of darkness and blind eyes
Thy long expected healing wings could see,
    When thou didst rise,
      And what more can be done,
      Did at midnight speak with the sun!

      O who will tell me, where
He found thee at that dead and silent hour!
What hallowed solitary ground did bear
    So rare a flower
      Within whose sacred leafs did lie
      The fulness of the Deity.

      No mercy-seat of gold,
No dead and dusty cherub, nor carved stone,
But his own living works did my Lord hold
    And lodge alone;
      Where trees and herbs did watch and peep
      And wonder, while the Jews did sleep.

      Dear night! this worlds defeat;
The stop to busy fools; cares check and curb;
The day of spirits; my souls calm retreat
    Which none disturb!
      Christ's* progress, and his prayer time;
      The hours to which high Heaven doth chime.

      Gods silent, searching flight:
When my Lords head is filled with dew, and all
His locks are wet with the clear drops of night;
    His still, soft call;
      His knocking time; The souls dumb watch,
      When spirits their fair kindred catch.

      Were all my loud, evil days
Calm and unhaunted as is thy dark tent,

* *Mark, chap.* 1. 35. *S. Luke, chap.* 21. 37. [Vaughan's note.]

Whose peace but by some angels wing or voice
Is seldom rent;
Then I in Heaven all the long year
Would keep, and never wander here.

But living where the sun
Doth all things wake, and where all mix and tire
Themselves and others, I consent and run
To every mire,
And by this worlds ill-guiding light,
Err more than I can do by night.

There is in God (some say)
A deep, but dazzling darkness; As men here
Say it is late and dusky, because they
See not all clear;
O for that night! where I in him
Might live invisible and dim.

**JOHN 3:8   The wind bloweth where it listeth, and thou hearest the sound
thereof, but canst not tell whence it cometh, and whither it goeth: so is
every one that is born of the Spirit.**

THE WIND

CHRISTINA GEORGINA ROSSETTI

Who has seen the wind?
Neither I nor you.
But when the leaves hang trembling,
The wind is passing through.
Who has seen the wind?
Neither you nor I.
But when the trees bow their heads,
The wind is passing by.

**JOHN 3:16–19   For God so loved the world, that he gave his only begot-
ten Son, that whosoever believeth in him should not perish, but have
everlasting life. For God sent not his Son into the world to condemn the**

world; but that the world through him might be saved. He that believeth on him is not condemned: but he that believeth not is condemned already, because he hath not believed in the name of the only begotten Son of God. And this is the condemnation, that light is come into the world, and men loved darkness rather than light, because their deeds were evil.

But Men Loved Darkness Rather Than Light

Richard Crashaw

The world's light shines; shine as it will,
The world will love its darkness still:
I doubt though when the world's in Hell,
It will not love its darkness half so well.

JOHN 4:15–18   The woman saith unto him, Sir, give me this water, that I thirst not, neither come hither to draw.

Jesus saith unto her, Go, call thy husband, and come hither.

The woman answered and said, I have no husband. Jesus said unto her, Thou hast well said, I have no husband:

For thou hast had five husbands; and he whom thou now hast is not thy husband: in that saidst thou truly.

The Man Who Married Magdalene

Variation on a Theme by Louis Simpson

Anthony Hecht

Then said the Lord, dost thou well to be angry? (Jonah 4:4)

I have been in this bar
For close to seven days.
The dark girl over there,
For a modest dollar, lays.

And you can get a blow-job
Where other men have pissed,
In the little room that's sacred
To the Evangelist –

If you're inclined that way.
For myself, I drink and sleep.
The floor is knotty cedar
But the beer is flat and cheap.

And you can bet your life
I'll be here another seven.
Stranger, here's to my wife,
Who died and went to heaven.

She was a famous beauty,
But *our very breath is loaned.*
The rabbi's voice was fruity,
And since then I've been stoned –

A royal, nonstop bender.
But your money's no good here;
Put it away. Bartender,
Give my friend a beer.

I dreamed the other night
When the sky was full of stars
That I stood outside a gate
And looked in through the bars.

Two angels stood together.
A purple light was shed
From their every metal feather.
And then one of them said,

"It was pretty much the same
For years and years and years,
But since the Christians came
The place is full of queers.

Still, let them have their due.
Things here are fall less solemn.
Instead of each beardy Jew
Muttering, 'Shalom, Shalom,'

There's a down-to-earth, informal
Fleshiness to the scene;
It's healthier, more normal,
If you know what I mean.

Such as once went to Gehenna
Now dance among the blessed.
But Mary Magdalena,
She had it the best."

And he nudged his feathered friend
And gave him a wicked leer,
And I woke up and fought back
The nausea with a beer.

What man shall understand
The Lord's mysterious way?
My tongue is thick with worship
And whiskey, and some day

I will come to in Bellevue,
And make psalms unto the Lord.
But verily I tell you,
She hath her reward.

THE MASTER

JOHN 5:1–9   After this there was a feast of the Jews; and Jesus went up to Jerusalem. Now there is at Jerusalem by the sheep market a pool, which is called in the Hebrew tongue Bethesda, having five porches. In these lay a great multitude of impotent folk, of blind, halt, withered, waiting for the moving of the water. For an angel went down at a certain season into the pool, and troubled the water: whosoever then first after the troubling of the water stepped in was made whole of whatsoever disease he had. And a certain man was there, which had an infirmity thirty and eight years. When Jesus saw him lie, and knew that he had been now a long time in that case, he saith unto him, Wilt thou be made whole? The impotent man answered him, Sir, I have no man, when the water is troubled, to put me into the pool: but while I am coming, another steppeth down before me. Jesus saith unto him, Rise, take up thy bed, and walk. And immediately the man was made whole, and took up his bed, and walked:

NOCTURNE AT BETHESDA

ARNA BONTEMPS

I thought I saw an angel flying low,
I thought I saw the flicker of a wing
Above the mulberry trees; but not again.

Bethesda sleeps. This ancient pool that healed
A host of bearded Jews does not awake.
This pool that once the angels troubled does not move.
No angel stirs it now, no Saviour comes
With healing in His hands to raise the sick
And bid the lame man leap upon the ground.

The golden days are gone. Why do we wait
So long upon the marble steps, blood
Falling from our open wounds? and why
Do our black faces search the empty sky?
Is there something we have forgotten? some precious thing
We have lost, wandering in strange lands?

There was a day, I remember now,
I beat my breast and cried, "Wash me God,
Wash me with a wave of wind upon
The barley; O quiet One, draw near, draw near!
Walk upon the hills with lovely feet
And in the waterfall stand and speak.

"Dip white hands in the lily pool and mourn
Upon the harps still hanging in the trees
Near Babylon along the river's edge,
But oh, remember me, I pray, before
The summer goes and rose leaves lose their red."

The old terror takes my heart, the fear
Of quiet waters and of faint twilights.
There will be better days when I am gone
And healing pools where I cannot be healed.
Fragrant stars will gleam forever and ever
Above the place where I lie desolate.

Yet I hope, still I long to live.
And if there can be returning after death
I shall come back. But it will not be here;
If you want me you must search for me
Beneath the palms of Africa. Or if
I am not there then you may call to me
Across the shining dunes, perhaps I shall
Be following a desert caravan.

I may pass through centuries of death
With quiet eyes, but I'll remember still
A jungle tree with burning scarlet birds.

There is something I have forgotten, some precious thing.
I shall be seeking ornaments of ivory,
I shall be dying for a jungle fruit.

You do not hear, Bethesda.
O still green water in a stagnant pool!
Love abandoned you and me alike.
There was a day you held a rich full moon
Upon your heart and listened to the words
Of men now dead and saw the angels fly.
There is a simple story on your face;
Years have wrinkled you. I know, Bethesda!
You are sad. It is the same with me.

MATTHEW 4:17–22   From that time Jesus began to preach, and to say, Repent: for the kingdom of heaven is at hand.

And Jesus, walking by the sea of Galilee, saw two brethren, Simon called Peter, and Andrew his brother, casting a net into the sea: for they were fishers. And he saith unto them, Follow me, and I will make you fishers of men. And they straightway left their nets, and followed him. And going on from thence, he saw other two brethren, James the son of Zebedee, and John his brother, in a ship with Zebedee their father, mending their nets; and he called them. And they immediately left the ship and their father, and followed him.

from JUBILATE AGNO

CHRISTOPHER SMART

Let Peter rejoice with the Moonfish who keeps up the life in the waters
    by night.
Let Andrew rejoice with the Whale, who is arrayed in beauteous blue
    and is a combination of bulk and activity.
Let James rejoice with the Skuttle-Fish, who foils his foe by the effusion
    of his ink.
Let John rejoice with Nautilus who spreads his sail and plies his oar, and
    the Lord is his pilot.
Let Philip rejoice with Boca, which is a fish that can speak.
Let Bartholemew rejoice with the Eel, who is pure in proportion to
    where he is found and how he is used.
Let Thomas rejoice with the Sword-Fish, whose aim is perpetual and
    strength insuperable.

Let Matthew rejoice with Uranoscopus, whose eyes are lifted up to God.

Let James the less, rejoice with the Haddock, who brought the piece of
    money for the Lord and Peter.

Let Jude bless with the Bream, who is of melancholy from his depth and
    serenity.

Let Simon rejoice with the Sprat, who is pure and innumerable.

Let Matthias rejoice with the Flying-Fish, who has a part with the birds,
    and is sublimity in his conceit.

Let Stephen rejoice with Remora – The Lord remove all obstacles to his
    glory.

Let Paul rejoice with the Seal, who is pleasant and faithful, like God's
    good Englishman.

Let Agrippa, which is Agricola, rejoice with Elops, who is a choice fish.

Let Joseph rejoice with the Turbut, whose capture makes the poor
    fisher-man sing.

Let Mary rejoice with the Maid – blessed be the name of the
    Immaculate Conception.

Let John, the Baptist, rejoice with the Salmon – blessed be the name of
    the Lord Jesus for infant Baptism.

Let Mark rejoice with the Mullet, who is John Dore, God be gracious to
    him and his family.

Let Barnabas rejoice with the Herring – God be gracious to the Lord's
    fishery.

Let Cleopas rejoice with the Mackerel, who cometh in a shoal after a
    leader.

**MATTHEW 9:12–13 They that be whole need not a physician, but they
that are sick. But go ye and learn what that meaneth, I will have mercy,
and not sacrifice: for I am not come to call the righteous, but sinners to
repentance.**

MATTHEW 9. 12

FRANCIS QUARLES

Always pruning, always cropping?
    Is her brightness still obscured?
Ever dressing, ever topping?
    Always curing, never cured?
        Too much snuffing makes a waste;
        When the spirits bend too fast,
        They will shrink at every blast.

You that always are bestowing
    Costly pains in life repairing,
Are but always overthrowing
    Nature's work by overcaring:
        Nature meeting with her foe,
        In a work she hath to do,
        Takes a pride to overthrow.

Nature knows her own perfection,
    And her pride disdains a tutor,
Can not stoop to Art's correction,
    And she scorns a coadjutor;
        Saucy Art should not appear
        Till she whisper in her ear:
        Hagar flees, if Sarah bear.

Nature worketh for the better,
    If not hindered that she cannot;
Art stands by as her abettor,
    Ending nothing she began not;
        If distemper chance to seize,
        Nature foiled with the disease,
        Art may help her if she please.

But to make a trade of trying
    Drugs and doses; always pruning;
Is to die for fear of dying;
    He's untuned, that's always tuning.
        He that often loves to lack
        Dear-bought drugs hath found a knack
        To foil the man, and feed the quack.

O the sad, the frail condition
    Of the pride of Nature's glory!
How infirm his composition!
    And at best how transitory!
        When his riot doth impair
        Nature's weakness, then his care
        Adds more ruin by repair.

Hold thy hand, health's dear maintainer,
Life perchance may burn the stronger:
Having substance to sustain her,
She untouched, may last the longer:
When the artist goes about
To redress her flame, I doubt,
Oftentimes he snuffs it out.

LUKE 6:12   And it came to pass in those days, that he went out into a mountain to pray, and continued all night in prayer to God.

JESUS PRAYING

HARTLEY COLERIDGE

He sought the mountain and the loneliest height,
For He would meet his Father all alone,
And there, with many a tear and many a groan,
He strove in prayer throughout the long, long night.
Why need He pray, who held by filial right,
O'er all the world alike of thought and sense,
The fullness of his Sire's omnipotence?
Why crave in prayer what was his own by might?
Vain is the question,—Christ was man in deed,
And being man, his duty was to pray.
The Son of God confessed the human need,
And doubtless asked a blessing every day,
Nor ceases yet for sinful man to plead,
Nor will, till heaven and earth shall pass away.

LUKE 6:13–16   And when it was day, he called unto him his disciples: and of them he chose twelve, whom also he named apostles; Simon, (whom he also named Peter,) and Andrew his brother, James and John, Philip and Bartholomew, Matthew and Thomas, James the son of Alphaeus, and Simon called Zelotes, And Judas the brother of James, and Judas Iscariot, which also was the traitor. MATTHEW 10:1   And when he had called unto him his twelve disciples, he gave them power against unclean spirits, to cast them out, and to heal all manner of sickness and all manner of disease.

STARLIGHT LIKE INTUITION PIERCED THE TWELVE

DELMORE SCHWARTZ

The starlight's intuitions pierced the twelve,
The brittle night sky sparkled like a tune
Tinkled and tapped out on the xylophone.
Empty and vain, a glittering dune, the moon
Arose too big, and, in the mood which ruled,
Seemed like a useless beauty in a pit;
And then one said, after he carefully spat:
"No matter what we do, he looks at it!

"I cannot see a child or find a girl
Beyond his smile which glows like that spring moon."
"—Nothing no more the same," the second said,
"Though all may be forgiven, never quite healed
The wound I bear as witness, standing by;
No ceremony surely appropriate,
Nor secret love, escape or sleep because
No matter what I do, he looks at it——"

"Now," said the third, "no thing will be the same:
I am as one who never shuts his eyes,
The sea and sky no more are marvellous,
And I no longer understand surprise!"
"Now," said the fourth, "nothing will be enough
—I heard his voice accomplishing all wit:
No word can be unsaid, no deed withdrawn
—No matter what is said, he measures it!"

"Vision, imagination, hope or dream,
Believed, denied, the scene we wished to see?
It does not matter in the least: for what
Is altered, if it is not true? That we
Saw goodness, as it is—this is the awe
And the abyss which we will not forget,
His story now the sky which holds all thought:
No matter what I think, I think of it!"

"And I will never be what once I was,"
Said one for long as narrow as a knife,

"And we will never be what once we were;
We have died once; this is a second life."
"My mind is spilled in moral chaos," one
Righteous as Job exclaimed, "now infinite
Suspicion of my heart stems what I will
—No matter what I choose, he stares at it!"

"I am as one native in summer places
—Ten weeks' excitement paid for by the rich;
Debauched by that and then all winter bored,"
The sixth declared. "His peak left us a ditch!"
"He came to make this life more difficult,"
The seventh said, "No one will ever fit
His measure's heights, all is inadequate:
No matter what I do, what good is it?"

"He gave forgiveness to us: what a gift!"
The eighth chimed in. "But now we know how much
Must be forgiven. But if forgiven, what?
The crime which was will be; and the least touch
Revives the memory: what is forgiveness worth?"
The ninth spoke thus: "Who now will ever sit
At ease in Zion at the Easter feast?
No matter what the place, he touches it!"

"And I will always stammer, since he spoke,"
One, who had been most eloquent, said, stammering.
"I looked too long at the sun; like too much light,
So too much goodness is a boomerang,"
Laughed the eleventh of the troop. "I must
Try what he tried: I saw the infinite
Who walked the lake and raised the hopeless dead:
No matter what the feat, he first accomplished it!"

So spoke the twelfth; and then the twelve in chorus:
"Unspeakable unnatural goodness is
Risen and shines, and never will ignore us;
He glows forever in all consciousness;
Forgiveness, love, and hope possess the pit,
And bring our endless guilt, like shadow's bars:
No matter what we do, he stares at it!
What pity then deny? what debt defer?

We know he looks at us like all the stars,
And we shall never be as once we were,
This life will never be what once it was!"

MATTHEW 10:5–10 These twelve Jesus sent forth, and commanded them, saying, Go not into the way of the Gentiles, and into any city of the Samaritans enter ye not: But go rather to the lost sheep of the house of Israel. And as ye go, preach, saying, The kingdom of heaven is at hand. Heal the sick, cleanse the lepers, raise the dead, cast out devils: freely ye have received, freely give. Provide neither gold, nor silver, nor brass in your purses, Nor scrip for your journey, neither two coats, neither shoes, nor yet staves:

THE PASSIONATE MAN'S PILGRIMAGE

SIR WALTER RALEIGH?

Supposed to be written by one at the point of death

Give me my scallop shell of quiet,
My staff of faith to walk upon,
My scrip of joy, immortal diet,
My bottle of salvation:
My gown of glory, hope's true gage,
And thus I'll take my pilgrimage.

Blood must be my body's balmer,
No other balm will there be given
Whilst my soul like a white palmer
Travels to the land of heaven,
Over the silver mountains,
Where spring the nectar fountains:
And there I'll kiss
The bowl of bliss,
And drink my eternal fill
On every milken hill.
My soul will be a dry before,
But after it, will ne'er thirst more.

And by the happy blissful way
More peaceful pilgrims I shall see,
That have shook off their gowns of clay,
And go apparelled fresh like me.
I'll bring them first
To slake their thirst,
And then to taste those nectar suckets
At the clear wells
Where sweetness dwells,
Drawn up by saints in crystal buckets.

And when our bottles and all we,
Are filled with immortality:
Then the holy paths we'll travel
Strewed with rubies thick as gravel,
Ceilings of diamonds, sapphire floors,
High walls of coral and pearl bowers.

From thence to heaven's bribeless hall
Where no corrupted voices brawl,
No conscience molten into gold,
Nor forged accusers bought and sold,
No cause deferred, nor vain spent journey,
For there Christ is the King's Attorney:
Who pleads for all without degrees,
And he hath angels, but no fees.

When the grand twelve million jury,
Of our sins and sinful fury,
Gainst our souls black verdicts give,
Christ pleads his death, and then we live,
Be thou my speaker taintless pleader,
Unblotted lawyer, true proceeder,
Thou movest salvation even for alms:
Not with a bribed lawyer's palms.

And this is my eternal plea,
To him that made Heaven, Earth and Sea,
Seeing my flesh must die so soon,
And want a head to dine next noon,
Just at the stroke when my veins start and spread
Set on my soul an everlasting head.
Then am I ready like a palmer fit,
To tread those blessed paths which before I writ.

LUKE 6:24–25 **But woe unto you that are rich! for ye have received your consolation. Woe unto you that are full! for ye shall hunger. Woe unto you that laugh now! for ye shall mourn and weep.**

LUKE 6. 25

FRANCIS QUARLES

The world's a popular disease, that reigns
Within the froward heart and frantic brains
Of poor distempered mortals; oft arising
From ill digestion, through th' unequal poising
Of ill-weighed elements; whose light directs
Malignant humors to malign effects.
One raves, and labors with a boiling liver;
Rends hair by handfuls, cursing Cupid's quiver:
Another with a bloody-flux of oaths
Vows deep revenge: one dotes; the other loathes:
One frisks and sings, and vies a flagon more
To drench dry cares, and makes the welkin roar:
Another droops; the sunshine makes him sad;
Heaven cannot please: One's moped; the t'other's mad:
One hugs his gold; another lets it fly:
He knowing not for whom; nor t'other why.
One spends his day in plots, his night in play;
Another sleeps and slugs both night and day:
One laughs at this thing; t'other cries for that:
But neither one nor t'other knows for what.
Wonder of wonders! What we ought t' evite
As our disease, we hug as our delight:
'T is held a symptom of approaching danger,
When disacquainted sense becomes a stranger,
And takes no knowledge of an old disease;
But when a noisome grief begins to please
The unresisting sense, it is a fear
That death has parleyed, and compounded there:
As when the dreadful Thunderer's awful hand
Pours forth a vial on th' infected land;
At first th' affrighted mortals quake and fear,
And every noise is thought the Thunderer:
But when the frequent soul-departing bell
Has paved their ears with her familiar knell,
It is reputed but a nine days wonder,
They neither fear the Thunderer nor his thunder:

So when the world (a worse disease) began
To smart for sin, poor new created man
Could seek for shelter, and his generous son
Knew by his wages what his hands had done;
But bold-faced mortals in our blushless times
Can sin and smile, and make a sport of crimes,
Transgress of custom, and rebel in ease;
We false-joyed fools can triumph in disease,
And (as the careless pilgrim, being bit
By the tarantula, begins a fit
Of life-concluding laughter) waste our breath
In lavish pleasure, 'til we laugh to death.

MATTHEW 5:13–16   **Ye are the salt of the earth: but if the salt have lost his savour, wherewith shall it be salted? it is thenceforth good for nothing, but to be cast out, and to be trodden under foot of men. Ye are the light of the world. A city that is set on an hill cannot be hid. Neither do men light a candle, and put it under a bushel, but on a candlestick; and it giveth light unto all that are in the house. Let your light so shine before men, that they may see your good works, and glorify your Father which is in heaven.**

THE CANDLE INDOORS

GERARD MANLEY HOPKINS

Some candle clear burns somewhere I come by.
I muse at how its being puts blissful back
With yellowy moisture mild night's blear-all black,
Or to-fro tender trambeams truckle at the eye.
By that window what task what fingers ply,
I plod wondering, a-wanting, just for lack
Of answer the eagerer a-wanting Jessy or Jack
There/ God to aggrándise, God to glorify. –

Come you indoors, come home; your fading fire
Mend first and vital candle in close heart's vault:
You there are master, do your own desire;
What hinders? Are you beam-blind, yet to a fault
In a neighbour deft-handed? are you that liar
And, cast by conscience out, spendsavour salt?

MATTHEW 5:17–20   Think not that I am come to destroy the law, or
the prophets: I am not come to destroy, but to fulfil. For verily I say unto
you, Till heaven and earth pass, one jot or one tittle shall in no wise pass
from the law, till all be fulfilled. Whosoever therefore shall break one of
these least commandments, and shall teach men so, he shall be called
the least in the kingdom of heaven: but whosoever shall do and teach
them, the same shall be called great in the kingdom of heaven. For I say
unto you, That except your righteousness shall exceed the righteousness
of the scribes and Pharisees, ye shall in no case enter into the kingdom
of heaven.

PROGRESS

MATTHEW ARNOLD

The Master stood upon the mount, and taught.
He saw a fire in his disciples' eyes;
'The old law,' they said, 'is wholly come to naught!
        Behold the new world rise!'

'Was it,' the Lord then said, 'with scorn ye saw
The old law observed by Scribes and Pharisees?
I say unto you, see *ye* keep that law
        More faithfully than these!

'Too hasty heads for ordering worlds, alas!
Think not that I to annul the law have willed;
No jot, no tittle from the law shall pass,
        Till all hath been fulfilled.'

So Christ said eighteen hundred years ago.
And what then shall be said to those to-day,
Who cry aloud to lay the old world low
        To clear the new world's way?

'Religious fervours! ardour misapplied!
Hence, hence,' they cry, 'ye do but keep man blind!
But keep him self-immersed, preoccupied,
        And lame the active mind!'

Ah! from the old world let some one answer give:
'Scorn ye this world, their tears, their inward cares?
I say unto you, see that *your* souls live
        A deeper life than theirs!

'Say ye: The spirit of man has found new roads,
And we must leave the old faiths, and walk therein?—
Leave then the Cross as ye have left carved gods,
      But guard the fire within!

'Bright, else, and fast the stream of life may roll,
And no man may the other's hurt behold;
Yet each will have one anguish—his own soul
      Which perishes of cold.'

Here let that voice make end; then let a strain,
From a far lonelier distance, like the wind
Be heard, floating through heaven, and fill again
      These men's profoundest mind:

'Children of men! the unseen Power, whose eye
For ever doth accompany mankind,
Hath looked on no religion scornfully
      That men did ever find.

'Which has not taught weak wills how much they can?
Which has not fallen on the dry heart like rain?
Which has not cried to sunk, self-weary man:
      Thou must be born again!

'Children of men! not that your age excel
In pride of life the ages of your sires,
But that you think clear, feel deep, bear fruit well,
      The Friend of man desires.'

**MATTHEW 6:9–13 Our Father which art in heaven, Hallowed be thy
name. Thy kingdom come. Thy will be done in earth, as it is in heaven.
Give us this day our daily bread. And forgive us our debts, as we forgive
our debtors. And lead us not into temptation, but deliver us from evil:
For thine is the kingdom, and the power, and the glory, for ever. Amen.**

Our Father

JAMES SCHUYLER

This morning view
is very plain: thou art
in Heaven: modern

brick, plate glass, unhallowèd,
as yet, by time,
yet Thy Name
blesses all: silver tanks
of propane gas, the sky,
Thy will,
is lucent blue, French
gray and cream,
is done: the night
on earth
no longer needs
the one white street globe light
as the light, it is
in Heaven.
Give us this day
—and a Friday
13th, August '71,
at that:
our daily bread
and breakfast
(Product 19,
an egg, perchance: the hen-fruit,
food and symbol)
and forgive us our
trespasses
too numerous
to name as we
forgive our debtors: "pay
me when you can:
I don't take
interest"
how green
the grass! so many
flowering weeds
Your free
will has freely
let us name: dandy-
lion (*pisse-en-lit*)
and, clover
(O Trinity)
it is
a temptation
to list them all,

all I know, that is:
the temptation
to show off—to
make a show
of knowing more,
than, in fact, I
know, is very real:
as real as a twelve-
pane window sash
one pane slivered
by a crack, a flash,
a mountain line
that stays
to praise
Thee,
Your Name and Your
      Creation
let me surrender
ever—
poets do: it
is their way
and deliver me
from evil
and the Three
Illusions
of the Will—
for the power
that flows electrically
in me is thine
O glorious central,
O plant,
O dynamo!
and the glory
of this cool a.m.
now
all
silver, blue
and white.

MATTHEW 6:25–28   Therefore I say unto you, Take no thought for your
life, what ye shall eat, or what ye shall drink; nor yet for your body, what
ye shall put on. Is not the life more than meat, and the body than rai-

ment? Behold the fowls of the air: for they sow not, neither do they reap, nor gather into barns; yet your heavenly Father feedeth them. Are ye not much better than they? Which of you by taking thought can add one cubit unto his stature? And why take ye thought for raiment? Consider the lilies of the field, how they grow; they toil not, neither do they spin:

THE HABIT OF PERFECTION

GERARD MANLEY HOPKINS

Elected Silence, sing to me
And beat upon my whorlèd ear,
Pipe me to measures still and be
The music that I care to hear.

Shape nothing, lips; be lovely-dumb:
It is the shut, the curfew sent
From there where all surrenders come
Which only makes you eloquent.

Be shellèd, eyes, with double dark
And find the uncreated light:
This ruck and reel which you remark
Coils, keeps, and teases simple sight.

Palate, the hutch of tasty lust,
Desire not to be rinsed with wine:
The can must be so sweet, the crust
So fresh that come in fasts divine!

Nostrils, your careless breath that spend
Upon the stir and keep of pride,
What relish shall the censers send
Along the sanctuary side!

O feel-of-primrose hands, O feet
That want the yield of plushy sward,
But you shall walk the golden street
And you unhouse and house the Lord.

And, Poverty, be thou the bride
And now the marriage feast begun,
And lily-coloured clothes provide
Your spouse not laboured-at nor spun.

MATTHEW 6:29 And yet I say unto you, That even Solomon in all his glory was not arrayed like one of these.

FOR DAUGHTERS OF MAGDALEN

COUNTEE CULLEN

Ours is the ancient story:
    Delicate flowers of sin,
Lilies, arrayed in glory,
    That would not toil or spin.

MATTHEW 6:30 Wherefore, if God so clothe the grass of the field, which to day is, and to morrow is cast into the oven, shall he not much more clothe you, O ye of little faith?

A PARAPHRASE
OF THE LATTER PART OF THE SIXTH CHAPTER
OF ST. MATTHEW

JAMES THOMSON

When my breast labors with oppressive care,
And o'er my cheek descends the falling tear;
While all my warring passions are at strife,
Oh, let me listen to the words of Life!
Raptures deep-felt his doctrine did impart,
And thus he raised from earth the drooping heart:—

'Think not, when all your scanty stores afford
Is spread at once upon the sparing board—
Think not, when worn the homely robe appears,
While on the roof the howling tempest bears—
What farther shall this feeble life sustain,
And what shall clothe these shivering limbs again.
Say, does not life its nourishment exceed?
And the fair body its investing weed?
Behold! and look away your low despair—
See the light tenants of the barren air:
To them nor stores nor granaries belong,

Nought but the woodland and the pleasing song;
Yet your kind heavenly Father bends his eye
On the least wing that flits along the sky.
To him they sing when Spring renews the plain,
To him they cry in Winter's pinching reign;
Nor is their music, nor their plaint in vain.
He hears the gay and the distressful call,
And with unsparing bounty fills them all.
    Observe the rising lily's snowy grace;
Observe the various vegetable race;
They neither toil nor spin, but careless grow;
Yet see how warm they blush! how bright the glow!
What regal vestments can with them compare?
What king so shining, and what queen so fair?
    If ceaseless thus the fowls of heaven he feeds,
If o'er the fields such lucid robes he spreads;
Will he not care for you, ye faithless, say?
Is he unwise? or are ye less than they?'

MATTHEW 7:2 For with what judgment ye judge, ye shall be judged: and with what measure ye mete, it shall be measured to you again.

JUDGE NOT

THEODORE ROETHKE

Faces greying faster than loam-crumbs on a harrow;
Children, their bellies swollen like blown-up paper bags,
Their eyes rich as plums, staring from newsprint,—
These images haunted me noon and midnight.
I imagined the unborn, starving in wombs, curling;
I asked: May the blessings of life, O Lord, descend on the living.

Yet when I heard the drunkards howling,
Smelled the carrion at entrances,
Saw women, their eyelids like little rags,
I said: On all these, Death, with gentleness, come down.

MATTHEW 7:13–14 Enter ye in at the strait gate: for wide is the gate, and broad is the way, that leadeth to destruction, and many there be

which go in thereat: Because strait is the gate, and narrow is the way, which leadeth unto life, and few there be that find it.

H. BAPTISM II

GEORGE HERBERT

Since, Lord, to thee
A narrow way and little gate
Is all the passage, on my infancy
Thou didst lay hold, and antedate
My faith in me.

\   O let me still
Write thee great God, and me a child:
Let me be soft and supple to thy will,
Small to my self, to others mild,
Be hither ill.

Although by stealth
My flesh get on; yet let her sister
My soul bid nothing, but preserve her wealth:
The growth of flesh is but a blister;
Childhood is health.

MATTHEW 7:21–29   Not every one that saith unto me, Lord, Lord, shall enter into the kingdom of heaven; but he that doeth the will of my Father which is in heaven. Many will say to me in that day, Lord, Lord, have we not prophesied in thy name? and in thy name have cast out devils? and in thy name done many wonderful works? And then will I profess unto them, I never knew you: depart from me, ye that work iniquity. Therefore whosoever heareth these sayings of mine, and doeth them, I will liken him unto a wise man, which built his house upon a rock: And the rain descended, and the floods came, and the winds blew, and beat upon that house; and it fell not: for it was founded upon a rock. And every one that heareth these sayings of mine, and doeth them not, shall be likened unto a foolish man, which built his house upon the sand: And the rain descended, and the floods came, and the winds blew, and beat upon that house; and it fell: and great was the fall of it.

And it came to pass, when Jesus had ended these sayings, the people were astonished at his doctrine: For he taught them as one having authority, and not as the scribes.

Across the Sea, Along the Shore

Arthur Hugh Clough

Across the sea, along the shore,
In numbers more and ever more,
From lonely hut and busy town,
The valley through, the mountain down,
What was it ye went out to see,
Ye silly folk of Galilee?
The reed that in the wind doth shake?
The weed that washes in the lake?
The reeds that waver, the weeds that float?—
A young man preaching in a boat.

What was it ye went out to hear
By sea and land from far and near?
A teacher? Rather seek the feet
Of those who sit in Moses' seat.
Go humbly seek, and bow to them,
Far off in great Jerusalem.
From them that in her courts ye saw,
Her perfect doctors of the law,
What is it came ye here to note?—
A young man preaching in a boat.

A prophet! Boys and women weak!
    Declare, or cease to rave;
Whence is it he hath learned to speak?
    Say, who his doctrine gave?
A prophet? Prophet wherefore he
    Of all in Israel tribes?—
He teacheth with authority,
    And not as do the Scribes.

LUKE 7:18–24 **And the disciples of John shewed him of all these things. And John calling unto him two of his disciples sent them to Jesus, saying, Art thou he that should come? or look we for another? When the men were come unto him, they said, John Baptist hath sent us unto thee, saying, Art thou he that should come? or look we for another? And in that same hour he cured many of their infirmities and plagues, and of evil spirits; and unto many that were blind he gave sight. Then Jesus answer-**

ing said unto them, Go your way, and tell John what things ye have seen and heard; how that the blind see, the lame walk, the lepers are cleansed, the deaf hear, the dead are raised, to the poor the gospel is preached. And blessed is he, whosoever shall not be offended in me. And when the messengers of John were departed, he began to speak unto the people concerning John, What went ye out into the wilderness for to see? A reed shaken with the wind?

JOHN

JONES VERY

What went ye out to see? a shaken reed?
In him whose voice proclaims "prepare the way;"
Behold the oak that stormy centuries feed!
Though but the buried acorn of My day;
What went ye out to see? a kingly man?
In the soft garments clothed that ye have worn;
Behold a servant whom the hot suns tan,
His raiment from the rough-haired camel torn;
Ye seek ye know not what; blind children all,
Who each his idle fancy will demand;
Nor heed my true-sent prophet's warning call,
That you may learn of me the new command,
And see the Light that cometh down from heaven,
Repent! and see, while yet its light is given.

LUKE 7:36–38   And one of the Pharisees desired him that he would eat with him. And he went into the Pharisee's house, and sat down to meat. And, behold, a woman in the city, which was a sinner, when she knew that Jesus sat at meat in the Pharisee's house, brought an alabaster box of ointment, And stood at his feet behind him weeping, and began to wash his feet with tears, and did wipe them with the hairs of her head, and kissed his feet, and anointed them with the ointment.

SAINT MARY MAGDALENE OR THE WEEPER

RICHARD CRASHAW

Lo where a wounded heart with bleeding eyes conspire.
Is she a flaming fountain, or a weeping fire?

Hail Sister Springs,
Parents of silver-forded
Ever bubbling things!
Thawing Crystal! Snowy Hills!
Still spending, never spent; I mean
Thy fair eyes sweet Magdalene.

Heavens thy fair eyes be,
Heavens of ever-falling stars,
Tis seed-time still with thee
And stars thou sow'st whose harvest dares
Promise the earth; to countershine
What ever makes Heaven's fore-head fine.

But we are deceived all,
Stars they are indeed too true,
For they but seem to fall
As Heaven's other spangles do:
It is not for our Earth and us,
To shine in things so precious.

Upwards thou dost weep,
Heavens bosom drinks the gentle stream.
Where th' milky rivers meet,
Thine crawls above and is the cream.
Heaven, of such fair floods as this,
Heaven the Crystal Ocean is.

Every morn from hence,
A brisk Cherub something sips
Whose soft influence
Adds sweetness to his sweetest lips.
Then to his Music, and his song
Tastes of this breakfast all day long.

When some new bright guest
Takes up among the stars a room,
And Heaven will make a feast,
Angels with their bottles come;
And draw from these full eyes of thine,
Their master's water, their own wine.

The dew no more will weep,
The primroses pale cheek to deck,
The dew no more will sleep,
Nuzzled in the lilies' neck.

Much rather would it tremble here,
And leave them both to be thy tear.

Not the soft gold which
Steals from the amber-weeping
Makes sorrow half so rich.
As the drops distilled from thee.
Sorrow's best jewels lie in these
Caskets, of which Heaven keeps the keys.

When Sorrow would be
In her brightest majesty,
(For she is a Queen)
Then is she dressed by none but thee.
Then, and only then she wears
Her richest pearls, I mean thy tears.

Not in the evening's eyes
When they red with weeping are,
For the sun that dies,
Sits sorrow with a face so fair.
Nowhere but here did ever meet
Sweetness so sad, sadness so sweet.

Sadness all the while
She sits in such a throne as this,
Can do nought but smile,
Nor believes she sadness is.
Gladness itself would be more glad
To be made so sweetly sad.

There is no need at all
That the balsam-sweating bough
So coyly should let fall,
His medicinable tears; for now
Nature hath learned t'extract a dew,
More sovereign and sweet from you.

Yet the poor drops weep,
Weeping is the ease of woe,
Softly let them creep
Sad that they are vanquished so,
They, though to others no relief
May balsam be for their own grief.

Golden though he be,
Golden Tagus murmurs though,
Might he flow from thee
Content and quiet would he go,
Richer far does he esteem
Thy silver, then his golden stream.

Well does the May that lies
Smiling in thy cheeks, confess,
The April in thine eyes,
Mutual sweetness they express.
No April e'er lent softer showers,
Nor May returned fairer flowers.

Thus dost thou melt the year
Into a weeping motion,
Each minute waiteth here;
Takes his tear and gets him gone;
By thine eyes tinct ennobled thus
Time lays him up: he's precious.

Time as by thee he passes,
Makes thy ever-watery eyes
His hour-glasses.
By them his steps he rectifies.
The sands he used no longer please,
For his own sands he'll use thy seas.

Does thy song lull the air?
Thy tears just cadence still keeps time.
Does thy sweet breathed Prayer
Up in clouds of incense climb?
Still at each sigh, that is each stop:
A bead, that is a tear doth drop.

Does the Night arise?
Still thy tears do fall, and fall.
Does night loose her eyes?
Still the fountain weeps for all.
Let night or day do what they will
Thou hast thy task, thou weepest still.

Not, so long she lived,
Will thy tomb report of thee
But *so long she grieved,*
Thus must we date thy memory.

Others by days, by months, by years
Measure their ages, thou by tears.

     Say watery Brothers
Ye simpering sons of those fair eyes,
     Your fertile Mothers.
What hath our world that can entice
You to be born? what is't can borrow
You from her eyes swoll'n wombs of sorrow.

     Whither away so fast?
O whither? for the sluttish Earth
     Your sweetness cannot taste
Nor does the dust deserve your birth.
Whither hast ye then? o say
Why ye trip so fast away?

     We go not to seek
The darlings of Aurora's bed,
     The rose's modest cheek
Nor the violet's humble head.
No such thing; we go to meet
A worthier object, Our Lord's feet.

LUKE 7:44 And he turned to the woman, and said unto Simon, Seest thou this woman? I entered into thine house, thou gavest me no water for my feet: but she hath washed my feet with tears, and wiped them with the hairs of her head.

FOR THE MAGDALENE

WILLIAM DRUMMOND OF HAWTHORNDEN

These eyes (dear Lord) once brandons of desire,
Frail scouts betraying what they had to keep,
Which their own heart, then others set on fire,
Their traitorous black before thee here out-weep:
These locks, of blushing deeds the fair attire,
Smooth-frizzled waves, sad shelfs which shadow deep,
Soul-stinging serpents in gilt curls which creep,
To touch thy sacred feet do now aspire.

In seas of care behold a sinking bark,
By winds of sharp remorse unto thee driven,
O let me not exposed be ruin's mark,
My faults confessed (Lord) say they are forgiven.
>   Thus sighed to Jesus the Bethanian fair,
>   His tear-wet feet still drying with her hair.

MATTHEW 12:27–32   And if I by Beelzebub cast out devils, by whom do your children cast them out? therefore they shall be your judges. But if I cast out devils by the Spirit of God, then the kingdom of God is come unto you. Or else how can one enter into a strong man's house, and spoil his goods, except he first bind the strong man? and then he will spoil his house. He that is not with me is against me; and he that gathereth not with me scattereth abroad. Wherefore I say unto you, All manner of sin and blasphemy shall be forgiven unto men: but the blasphemy against the Holy Ghost shall not be forgiven unto men. And whosoever speaketh a word against the Son of man, it shall be forgiven him: but whosoever speaketh against the Holy Ghost, it shall not be forgiven him, neither in this world, neither in the world to come.

The Unpardonable Sin

Vachel Lindsay

This is the sin against the Holy Ghost:—
To speak of bloody power as right divine,
And call on God to guard each vile chief's house,
And for such chiefs, turn men to wolves and swine:—

To go forth killing in White Mercy's name,
Making the trenches stink with spattered brains,
Tearing the nerves and arteries apart,
Sowing with flesh the unreaped golden plains

In any Church's name to sack fair towns,
And turn each home into a screaming sty,
To make the little children fugitive,
And have their mothers for a quick death cry,—

This is the sin against the Holy Ghost:
This is the sin no purging can atone:—
To send forth rapine in the name of Christ:—
To set the face and make the heart a stone.

LUKE 8:5–8 A sower went out to sow his seed: and as he sowed, some
fell by the way side; and it was trodden down, and the fowls of the air
devoured it. And some fell upon a rock; and as soon as it was sprung up,
it withered away, because it lacked moisture. And some fell among
thorns; and the thorns sprang up with it, and choked it. And other fell on
good ground, and sprang up, and bare fruit an hundredfold. And when he
had said these things, he cried, He that hath ears to hear, let him hear.

THE SOWER

WILLIAM COWPER

Ye sons of earth prepare the plough,
　　Break up your fallow ground!
The Sower is gone forth to sow,
　　And scatter blessings round.

The seed that finds a stony soil,
　　Shoots forth a hasty blade;
But ill repays the sower's toil,
　　Soon withered, scorched, and dead.

The thorny ground is sure to balk
　　All hopes of harvest there;
We find a tall and sickly stalk,
　　But not the fruitful ear.

The beaten path and high-way side
　　Receive the trust in vain;
The watchful birds the spoil divide,
　　And pick up all the grain.

But where the Lord of grace and power
　　Has blessed the happy field;
How plenteous is the golden store
　　The deep-wrought furrows yield!

Father of mercies we have need
　　Of thy preparing grace;
Let the same hand that gives the seed,
　　Provide a fruitful place.

MATTHEW 13:10–13   And the disciples came, and said unto him, Why speakest thou unto them in parables? He answered and said unto them, Because it is given unto you to know the mysteries of the kingdom of heaven, but to them it is not given. For whosoever hath, to him shall be given, and he shall have more abundance: but whosoever hath not, from him shall be taken away even that he hath. Therefore speak I to them in parables: because they seeing see not; and hearing they hear not, neither do they understand.

On the holy Scriptures

Francis Quarles

Why did our blessed Savior please to break
His sacred thoughts in parables; and speak
In dark enigmas? Whosoe'er thou be
That findst them so, they were not spoke to thee:
In what a case is he, that haps to run
Against a post, and cries, *How dark's the sun?*
Or he, in summer, that complains of frost?
The Gospel's hid to none, but who are lost:
The Scripture is a ford, wherein, 'tis said,
An elephant shall swim; a lamb may wade.

MARK 4:26–29   And he said, So is the kingdom of God, as if a man should cast seed into the ground; And should sleep, and rise night and day, and the seed should spring and grow up, he knoweth not how. For the earth bringeth forth fruit of herself; first the blade, then the ear, after that the full corn in the ear. But when the fruit is brought forth, immediately he putteth in the sickle, because the harvest is come.

The Seed growing secretly

Henry Vaughan

If this world's friends might see but once
What some poor man may often feel,
Glory, and gold, and crowns and thrones
They would soon quit and learn to kneel.

My dew, my dew! my early love,
My souls bright food, thy absence kills!

Hover not long, eternal Dove!
Life without thee is loose and spills.

Something I had, which long ago
Did learn to suck, and sip, and taste,
But now grown sickly, sad and slow,
Doth fret and wrangle, pine and waste.

O spread thy sacred wings and shake
One living drop! one drop life keeps!
If pious griefs Heaven's joys awake,
O fill his bottle! thy child weeps!

Slowly and sadly doth he grow,
And soon as left, shrinks back to ill;
O feed that life, which makes him blow
And spread and open to thy will!

For thy eternal, living wells
None stained or withered shall come near:
A fresh, immortal green there dwells,
And spotless white is all the wear.

Dear, secret Greenness! nursed below
Tempests and winds, and winter-nights,
Vex not, that but one sees thee grow,
That One made all these lesser lights.

If those bright joys he singly sheds
On thee, were all met in one crown,
Both sun and stars would hide their heads;
And moons, though full, would get them down.

Let glory be their bait, whose minds
Are all too high for a low cell:
Though hawks can prey through storms and winds,
The poor bee in her hive must dwell.

Glory, the crowds cheap tinsel still
To what most takes them, is a drudge;
And they too oft take good for ill,
And thriving vice for virtue judge.

What needs a conscience calm and bright
Within it self an outward test?
Who breaks his glass to take more light,
Makes way for storms into his rest.

Then bless thy secret growth, nor catch
At noise, but thrive unseen and dumb;
Keep clean, bear fruit, earn life and watch,
Till the white winged Reapers come!

MATTHEW 13:31–32   Another parable put he forth unto them, saying, The kingdom of heaven is like to a grain of mustard seed, which a man took, and sowed in his field: Which indeed is the least of all seeds: but when it is grown, it is the greatest among herbs, and becometh a tree, so that the birds of the air come and lodge in the branches thereof.

The Kingdom of Heaven compared to a Grain of Mustard-seed

Christopher Smart

Then did he to the throng around
Another parable propound.
So fares it with the heavenly reign
As mustard-seed, of which a grain
Was taken in a farmer's hand
And cast into a piece of land.
This grain, the least of all that's sown,
When once to full perfection grown,
Outstrips all herbs to that degree
Till it at length becomes a tree,
And all the songsters of the air
Take up an habitation there.

Christ laid (at first an infant boy)
The basis of eternal joy;
And from humility, his plan,
Arose the best and greatest man,
The greatest man that ever trod
On earth was Christ th' eternal God,
Which as the branch of Jesse's root

Ascends to bear immortal fruit.
From contradiction, sin and strife,
He spreads abroad the tree of life;
And there his servants shall partake
The mansions, that the branches make;
There saints innumerable throng,
Assert their seat, and sing their song.

MATTHEW 13:46   Again, the kingdom of heaven is like unto a merchant man, seeking goodly pearls: Who, when he had found one pearl of great price, went and sold all that he had, and bought it.

THE PEARL. MATTH. 13

GEORGE HERBERT

I know the ways of learning; both the head
And pipes that feed the press, and make it run;
What reason hath from nature borrowed,
Or of it self, a good housewife, spun
In laws and policy; what the stars conspire,
What willing nature speaks, what forced by fire;
Both th' old discoveries, and the new-found seas,
The stock and surplus, cause and history:
All these stand open, or I have the keys:
             Yet I love thee.

I know the ways of honor, what maintains
The quick returns of courtesy and wit:
In vies of favors whether party gains,
When glory swells the heart, and moldeth it
To all expressions both of hand and eye,
Which on the world a true-love-knot may tie,
And bear the bundle, wheresoe'er it goes:
How many drams of spirit there must be
To sell my life unto my friends or foes:
             Yet I love thee.

I know the ways of pleasure, the sweet strains,
The lullings and the relishes of it;
The propositions of hot blood and brains;

What mirth and music mean; what love and wit
Have done these twenty hundred years, and more;
I know the projects of unbridled store:
My stuff is flesh, not brass; my senses live,
And grumble oft, that they have more in me
Than he that curbs them being but one to five:
           Yet I love thee.

I know all these, and have them in my hand:
Therefore not sealed, but with open eyes
I fly to thee, and fully understand
Both the main gale, and the commodities;
And at what rate and price I have thy love;
With all the circumstances that may move:
Yet through the labyrinths, not my groveling wit,
But thy silk twist let down from heaven to me,
Did both conduct and teach me, how by it
           To climb to thee.

MATTHEW 14:1–7   At that time Herod the tetrarch heard of the fame of Jesus, And said unto his servants, This is John the Baptist; he is risen from the dead; and therefore mighty works do show forth themselves in him. For Herod had laid hold on John, and bound him, and put him in prison for Herodias' sake, his brother Philip's wife. For John said unto him, It is not lawful for thee to have her. And when he would have put him to death, he feared the multitude, because they counted him as a prophet. But when Herod's birthday was kept, the daughter of Herodias danced before them, and pleased Herod. Whereupon he promised with an oath to give her whatsoever she would ask.

THE DAUGHTER OF HERODIAS

HENRY VAUGHAN

Vain, sinful Art! who first did fit
Thy lewd loathed motions unto sounds,
And made grave music like wild wit
Err in loose airs beyond her bounds?

What fires hath he heaped on his head?
Since to his sins (as needs it must,)
His art adds still (though he be dead,)
New fresh accounts of blood and lust.

Leave then* young Sorceress; the ice
Will those coy spirits cast asleep,
Which teach thee now to please† his eyes
Who doth thy loathsome mother keep.

But thou hast pleased so well, he swears,
And gratifies thy sin with vows:
His shameless lust in public wears,
And to thy soft arts strongly bows.

Skillful Enchantress and true bred!
Who out of evil can bring forth good?
Thy mother's nets in thee were spread,
She tempts to incest, thou to blood.

Portrait (II)

E. E. CUMMINGS

Babylon slim
-ness of
evenslicing
eyes are chisels

scarlet Goes
with her
whitehot
face,gashed

by hair's blue cold

jolts of
lovecrazed abrupt

flesh split "Pretty
Baby"
to
numb rhythm before christ

---

*Her name was Salome; in passing over a frozen river, the ice broke under her, and chopped off her head. [Vaughan's note.]
†Herod Antipas. [Vaughan's note.]

MATTHEW 14:8–11 **And she, being before instructed of her mother, said, Give me here John Baptist's head in a charger. And the king was sorry: nevertheless for the oath's sake, and them which sat with him at meat, he commanded it to be given her. And he sent, and beheaded John in the prison. And his head was brought in a charger, and given to the damsel: and she brought it to her mother.**

SALOME

CHARLES LAMB

Once on a charger there was laid,
And brought before a royal maid,
As price of attitude and grace,
A guiltless head, a holy face.

It was on Herod's natal day,
Who o'er Judea's land held sway.
He married his own brother's wife,
Wicked Herodias. She the life
Of John the Baptist long had sought,
Because he openly had taught
That she a life unlawful led,
Having her husband's brother wed.

This was he, that saintly John,
Who in the wilderness alone
Abiding, did for clothing wear
A garment made of camel's hair;
Honey and locusts were his food,
And he was most severely good.
He preached penitence and tears,
And waking first the sinner's fears,
Prepared a path, made smooth a way,
For his diviner Master's day.

Herod kept in princely state
His birthday. On his throne he sate,
After the feast, beholding her
Who danced with grace peculiar;
Fair Salome, who did excel
All in that land for dancing well.
The feastful monarch's heart was fired,
And whatsoe'er thing she desired,

Though half his kingdom it should be,
He in his pleasure swore that he
Would give the graceful Salome.
The damsel was Herodias' daughter:
She to the queen hastes, and besought her
To teach her what great gift to name.
Instructed by Herodias, came
The damsel back: to Herod said,
"Give me John the Baptist's head;
And in a charger let it be
Hither straightway brought to me."
Herod her suit would fain deny,
But for his oath's sake must comply.

When painters would by art express
Beauty in unloveliness,
Thee, Herodias' daughter, thee,
They fittest subject take to be.
They give thy form and features grace;
But ever in thy beauteous face
They show a steadfast cruel gaze,
An eye unpitying; and amaze
In all beholders deep they mark,
That thou betrayest not one spark
Of feeling for the ruthless deed,
That did thy praiseful dance succeed.
For on the head they make you look,
As if a sullen joy you took,
A cruel triumph, wicked pride,
That for your sport a saint had died.

MATTHEW 14:12 **And his disciples came, and took up the body, and buried it, and went and told Jesus.**

On S. John the Baptist

Thomas Stanley

Marino
As the youthful morning's light,
Chasing the dark shades of night,

By its blushes doth betray,
The approaching of the day:
So this Star that doth forerun
The day of our salvation;
Dyed in's purple blood, doth rise,
And the sun appearing, dies.

MATTHEW 14:15–21 And when it was evening, his disciples came to him, saying, This is a desert place, and the time is now past; send the multitude away, that they may go into the villages, and buy themselves victuals. But Jesus said unto them, They need not depart; give ye them to eat. And they say unto him, We have here but five loaves, and two fishes. He said, Bring them hither to me. And he commanded the multitude to sit down on the grass, and took the five loaves, and the two fishes, and looking up to heaven, he blessed, and brake, and gave the loaves to his disciples, and the disciples to the multitude. And they did all eat, and were filled: and they took up of the fragments that remained twelve baskets full. And they that had eaten were about five thousand men, beside women and children.

BUSINESS REVERSES

EDGAR LEE MASTERS

Everything! Counter and scales—
    I'll take whatever you give.
I'm through and off to Athens,
    Where a man like me can live.

And Hipparch, the baker, is going;
    My chum, who came with me
To follow the crowds who follow
    The prophet of Galilee.

We two were there at Damsacus
    Dealing in figs and wine.
Nice little business! Some one
    Said: "Here, I'll give you a line!

"Buy fish, and set up a booth,
    Get a tent and make your bread.
There are thousands come to listen,
    They are hungry, and must be fed."

And so we went. Believe me,
    There were crowds, and hungry, too.
Five thousand stood in the desert
    And listened the whole day through.

Famished? Well, yes. The disciples
    Were saying to send them away
To buy their bread in the village,
    But the prophet went on to say:

"Feed them yourselves, O you
    Of little faith." But they said:
"We have just two little fishes
    And five little loaves of bread."

We heard it, me and Hipparch,
    And rubbed our hands. You see
We were there to make some money
    In the land of Galilee.

We had stock in plenty. We waited.
    I wiped the scales, and my chum
Restacked the loaves. We bellowed,
    But no one seemed to come.

"Fresh fish!" I bawled my lungs out:
    "Nice bread!" poor Hipparch cried,
But what did they do? Sat down there
    In fifties, side by side,

In ranks, the whole five thousand.
    Then—well, the prophet spoke,
And broke the two little fishes,
    And the five little loaves he broke,

And fed the whole five thousand.
    Why, yes! So gorged they slept.
And we stood beaten and bankrupt.
    Poor Hipparch swore and wept.

They gathered up twelve baskets
    Full from the loaves of bread;
Two fishes made twelve baskets
    Of fragments after they fed.

And we—what was there to do
> But dump our stock on the sand?
That's what we got for our labor
> And thrift, in such a land.

We met a man near Damascus
> Who had joined the mystagogues.
He said: "I was wicked as you men
> Until I lost my hogs."

Now Hipparch and I are going
> To Athens, beautiful, free.
No more adventures for us two
> In the land of Galilee.

MATTHEW 14:22–25   And straightway Jesus constrained his disciples to get into a ship, and to go before him while he sent the multitudes away. And when he had sent the multitudes away, he went up into a mountain apart to pray: and when the evening was come, he was there alone. But the ship was now in the midst of the sea, tossed with waves: for the wind was contrary. And in the fourth watch of the night Jesus went unto them, walking on the sea.

IN THE TWENTIETH CENTURY

JAMES MCAULEY

Christ, you walked on the sea,
But cannot walk in a poem,
Not in our century.

There's something deeply wrong
Either with us or with you.
Our bright loud world is strong

And better in some ways
Than the old haunting kingdoms:
I don't reject our days.

But in you I taste bread,
Freshness, the honey of being,
And rising from the dead:

Like yolk in a warm shell—
Simplicities of power,
And water from a well.

We live like diagrams
Moving on a screen.
Somewhere a door slams

Shut, and emptiness spreads.
Our loves are processes
Upon foam-rubber beds.

Our speech is chemical waste;
The words have a plastic feel,
An antibiotic taste.

And yet we dream of song
Like parables of joy.
There's something deeply wrong.

Like shades we must drink blood
To find the living voice
That flesh once understood.

MATTHEW 14:26   And when the disciples saw him walking on the sea, they were troubled, saying, It is a spirit; and they cried out for fear.

WALKING ON WATER

JAMES DICKEY

Feeling it with me
On it, barely float, the narrow plank on the water,
I stepped from the clam-shell beach,
Breaking in nearly down through the sun
Where it lay on the sea,
And poled off, gliding upright
Onto the shining topsoil of the bay.

Later, it came to be said
That I was seen walking on water,

Not moving my legs
Except for the wrong step of sliding:
A child who leaned on a staff,
A curious pilgrim hiking
Between two open blue worlds,

My motion a miracle,
Leaving behind me no footprint,
But only the shimmering place
Of an infinite step upon water,
In which sat still and were shining
Many marsh-birds and pelicans.
Alongside my feet, the shark

Lay buried and followed,
His eyes on my childish heels.
Thus, taking all morning to stalk
From one littered beach to another
I came out on land, and dismounted
Making marks in the sand with my toes
Which truly had walked there, on water,

With the pelicans beating their shadows
Through the mirror carpet
Down, and the shark pursuing
The boy on the burning deck
Of a bare single ship-wrecked board.
Shoving the plank out to sea, I walked
Inland, on numb sparkling feet,

With the sun on the sea unbroken,
Nor the long quiet step of the miracle
Doing anything behind me but blazing,
With the birds in it nodding their heads
That must ponder that footstep forever
Rocking, or until I return
In my ghost, which shall have become, then,

A boy with a staff,
To loose them, beak and feather, from the spell
Laid down by a balancing child,
Unstable, tight-lipped, and amazed,
And, under their place of enthrallment,
A huge, hammer-headed spirit
Shall pass, as if led by the nose into Heaven.

MARK 6:50   For they all saw him, and were troubled. And immediately he talked with them, and saith unto them, Be of good cheer: it is I; be not afraid.

GALILEE SHORE

ALLEN GINSBERG

With the blue-dark dome old-starred at night, green boat-lights purring
     over water,
a faraway necklace of cliff-top Syrian electrics,
bells ashore, music from a juke-box trumpeted,
shadow of death against my left breast prest
—cigarette, match-flare, skull wetting its lips—

Fisherman-nets over wood walls, light wind in dead willow branch
on a grassy bank—the saxophone relaxed and brutal, silver horns echo—
Was there a man named Solomon? Peter walked here? Christ on this
     sweet water?
Blessings on thee Peacemaker!
                English spoken
on the street bearded Jews' sandals & Arab white head cloth—
the silence between Hebrew and Arabic—
the thrill of the first Hashish in a holy land—
Over hill down the valley in a blue bus, past Cana no weddings—
I have no name I wander in a nameless countryside—
young boys all at the movies seeing a great Western—
art gallery closed, pipe razor & tobacco on the floor.

To touch the beard of Martin Buber
to watch a skull faced Gershom Scholem lace his shoes
to pronounce Capernaum's name & see stone doors of a tomb
to be meek, alone, beside a big dark lake at night—
to pass thru Nazareth dusty afternoon, and smell the urine down near
     Mary's well
to watch the orange moon peep over Syria, weird promise—
to wait beside Galilee—night with Orion, lightning, negro voices,
     Burger's Disease, a glass of lemon tea—feel my left hand on my
     shaved chin—
all you have to do is suffer the metaphysical pain of dying.
Art is just a shadow, like cows or tea—
keep the future open, make no dates it's all here
with moonrise and soft music on phonograph memory—
Just think how amazing! someone getting up and walking on the water.

MATTHEW 14:28–29   And Peter answered him and said, Lord, if it be thou, bid me come unto thee on the water. And he said, Come. And when Peter was come down out of the ship, he walked on the water, to go to Jesus.

THE DRUNKEN FISHERMAN

ROBERT LOWELL

Wallowing in this bloody sty,
I cast for fish that pleased my eye
(Truly Jehovah's bow suspends
No pots of gold to weight its ends);
Only the blood-mouthed rainbow trout
Rose to my bait. They flopped about
My canvas creel until the moth
Corrupted its unstable cloth.

A calendar to tell the day;
A handkerchief to wave away
The gnats; a couch unstuffed with storm
Pouching a bottle in one arm;
A whiskey bottle full of worms;
And bedroom slacks: are these fit terms
To mete the worm whose molten rage
Boils in the belly of old age?

Once fishing was a rabbit's foot—
O wind blow cold, O wind blow hot,
Let suns stay in or suns step out:
Life danced a jig on the sperm whale's spout—
The fisher's fluent and obscene
Catches kept his conscience clean.
Children, the raging memory drools
Over the glory of past pools.

Now the hot river, ebbing, hauls
Its bloody waters into holes;
A grain of sand inside my shoe
Mimics the moon that might undo
Man and Creation too; remorse
Stinking, has puddled up its source;
Here tantrums thrash to a whale's rage.
This is the pot-hole of old age.

Is there no way to cast my hook
Out of this dynamited brook?
The Fisher's sons must cast about
When shallow waters peter out.
I will catch Christ with a greased worm,
And when the Prince of Darkness stalks
My bloodstream to its Stygian term. . .
On water the Man-Fisher walks.

**MATTHEW 14:30–32   But when he saw the wind boisterous, he was
afraid; and beginning to sink, he cried, saying, Lord, save me. And
immediately Jesus stretched forth his hand, and caught him, and said
unto him, O thou of little faith, wherefore didst thou doubt? And when
they were come into the ship, the wind ceased.**

E TENEBRIS

OSCAR WILDE

Come down, O Christ, and help me! reach thy hand,
        For I am drowning in a stormier sea
        Than Simon on thy lake of Galilee:
The wine of life is spilt upon the sand,
My heart is in some famine-murdered land
        Whence all good things have perished utterly,
        And well I know my soul in Hell must lie
If I this night before God's throne should stand.
"He sleeps perchance, or rideth to the chase,
        Like Baal, when his prophets howled that name
        From morn to noon on Carmel's smitten height."
Nay, peace, I shall behold, before the night,
        The feet of brass, the robe more white than flame,
The wounded hands, the weary human face.

THE BELOVED

**JOHN 6:47–51   Verily, verily, I say unto you, He that believeth on me
hath everlasting life. I am that bread of life. Your fathers did eat manna
in the wilderness, and are dead. This is the bread which cometh down
from heaven, that a man may eat thereof, and not die. I am the living
bread which came down from heaven: if any man eat of this bread, he
shall live for ever: and the bread that I will give is my flesh, which I will
give for the life of the world.**

MEDITATION EIGHT

EDWARD TAYLOR

I kenning through astronomy divine
    The world's bright battlement, wherein I spy
A golden path my pencil cannot line
    From that bright throne unto my threshold lie.
    And while my puzzled thoughts about it pore,
    I find the Bread of Life in't at my door.

When that this Bird of Paradise put in
    This wicker cage (my corpse) to tweedle praise
Had pecked the fruit forbid: and so did fling
    Away its food, and lost its golden days,
    It fell into celestial famine sore,
    And never could attain a morsel more.

Alas! alas! poor bird, what wilt thou do?
    This creatures' field no food for souls e'er gave:
And if thou knock at angels' doors, they show
    An empty barrel: they no soul bread have.
    Alas! poor bird, the world's white loaf is done,
    And cannot yield thee here the smallest crumb.

In this sad state, God's tender bowels run
    Out streams of grace: And he to end all strife,
The purest wheat in Heaven, his dear-dear Son
    Grinds, and kneads up into this Bread of Life:
    Which Bread of Life from Heaven down came and stands
    Dished in thy table up by angels' hands.

Did God mold up this bread in Heaven, and bake,
    Which from his table came, and to thine goeth?
Doth he bespeak thee thus: This soul bread take;
    Come, eat thy fill of this, thy God's white loaf?
    It's food too fine for angels; yet come, take
    And eat thy fill! It's Heaven's sugar cake.

What grace is this knead in this loaf? This thing
    Souls are but petty things it to admire.
Ye Angels, help: This fill would to the brim
    Heaven's whelmed-down crystal meal Bowl, yea and higher.
    This Bread of Life dropped in thy mouth doth cry:
    Eat, eat me, Soul, and thou shalt never die.

THE GIVEN FLESH RETURNS NOTHING BUT BREAD

AILEEN KELLY

The given flesh returns nothing but bread.
Quick breath is clothed in words, fold upon fold,
And after all, what's said is barely said.

Articulate skeleton fleshed in song and wed
To fire and flight; portioned, appraised and sold
The given flesh returns nothing but bread.

Starved night's afoot before the day's abed.
Love milled between two skins strikes hot or cold
And, after all, what's said is barely said.

Ploughed to blank earth the urgent, generous dead
Surge through green shoots to freight the season's gold:
The given flesh returns, nothing but bread.

Pent love and flight and song—stunned heart, hard head
Forbidding—break out lightwards unparoled;
And after all, what's said is barely said.

Word upon breakers cast, unheard, half-read,
Rises a silent harvest ocean-fold:
The given flesh returns nothing but bread.

And after all what's said is barely said.

**MATTHEW 16:18–19   And I say also unto thee, That thou art Peter, and
upon this rock I will build my church; and the gates of hell shall not prevail against it. And I will give unto thee the keys of the kingdom of heav-
en: and whatsoever thou shalt bind on earth shall be bound in heaven:
and whatsoever thou shalt loose on earth shall be loosed in heaven.**

WHEN IN MY PILGRIMAGE

ANONYMOUS

When in my pilgrimage I reach
The river that we all must cross

And land upon that farther beach
Where earthly gains are counted loss,

May I not earthly loss repair?
Well, if those fish should rise again,
There shall be no more parting there—
Celestial gut will stand the strain.

And, issuing from the portal, one
Who was himself a fisherman
Will drop his keys and, shouting, run
To help me land leviathan.

MATTHEW 16:22–23 Then Peter took him, and began to rebuke him, saying, Be it far from thee, Lord: this shall not be unto thee. But he turned, and said unto Peter, Get thee behind me, Satan: thou art an offence unto me: for thou savourest not the things that be of God, but those that be of men.

"RETRO ME, SATHANA"

DANTE GABRIEL ROSSETTI

Get thee behind me. Even as heavy-curled,
     Stooping against the wind a charioteer
     Is snatched from out his chariot by the hair,
So shall Time be; and as the void car, hurled
Abroad by reinless steeds, even so the world:
     Yea, even as chariot-dust upon the air,
     It shall be sought and not found anywhere.

Get thee behind me, Satan. Oft unfurled,
Thy perilous wings can beat and break like lath
     Much mightiness of men to win thee praise.
     Leave these weak feet to tread in narrow ways.
Thou still, upon the broad vine-sheltered path,
Mayst wait the turning of the phials of wrath
     For certain years, for certain months and days.

MATTHEW 16:27–28 **For the Son of man shall come in the glory of his Father with his angels; and then he shall reward every man according to his works. Verily I say unto you, There be some standing here, which shall not taste of death, till they see the Son of man coming in his kingdom.**

DO PEOPLE MOULDER EQUALLY

EMILY DICKINSON

Do People moulder equally,
They bury, in the Grave?
I do believe a Species
As positively live

As I, who testify it
Deny that I – am dead –
And fill my Lungs, for Witness –
From Tanks – above my Head –

I say to you, said Jesus –
That there be standing here –
A Sort, that shall not taste of Death –
If Jesus was sincere –

I need no further Argue –
That statement of the Lord
Is not a controvertible –
He told me, Death was dead –

LUKE 9:28–31 **And it came to pass about an eight days after these sayings, he took Peter and John and James, and went up into a mountain to pray. And as he prayed, the fashion of his countenance was altered, and his raiment was white and glistering. And, behold, there talked with him two men, which were Moses and Elias: Who appeared in glory, and spake of his decease which he should accomplish at Jerusalem.**

THE TRANSFIGURATION

EDWIN MUIR

So from the ground we felt that virtue branch
Through all our veins till we were whole, our wrists

As fresh and pure as water from a well,
Our hands made new to handle holy things,
The source of all our seeing rinsed and cleansed
Till earth and light and water entering there
Gave back to us the clear unfallen world.
We would have thrown our clothes away for lightness,
But that even they, though sour and travel stained,
Seemed, like our flesh, made of immortal substance,
And the soiled flax and wool lay light upon us
Like friendly wonders, flower and flock entwined
As in a morning field. Was it a vision?
Or did we see that day the unseeable
One glory of the everlasting world
Perpetually at work, though never seen
Since Eden locked the gate that's everywhere
And nowhere? Was the change in us alone,
And the enormous earth still left forlorn,
An exile or a prisoner? Yet the world
We saw that day made this unreal, for all
Was in its place. The painted animals
Assembled there in gentle congregations,
Or sought apart their leafy oratories,
Or walked in peace, the wild and tame together,
As if, also for them, the day had come.
The Shepherds' hovels shone clean at the heart
As on the starting-day. The refuse heaps
Were grained with that fine dust that made the world;
For he had said, 'To the pure all things are pure'.
And when we went into the town, he with us,
The lurkers under doorways, murderers,
With rags tied round their feet for silence, came
Out of themselves to us and were with us,
And those who hide within the labyrinth
Of their own loneliness and greatness came,
And those tangled in their own devices,
The silent and the garrulous liars, all
Stepped out of their dungeons and were free.
Reality or vision, this we have seen.
If it had lasted but another moment
It might have held for ever! But the world
Rolled back into its place, and we are here,
And all that radiant kingdom lies forlorn,
As if it had never stirred; no human voice
Is heard among its meadows, but it speaks

To itself alone, alone it flowers and shines
And blossoms for itself while time runs on.

But he will come again, it's said, though not
Unwanted and unsummoned; for all things,
Beasts of the field, and woods, and rocks, and seas,
And all mankind from end to end of the earth
Will call him with one voice. In our own time,
Some say, or at a time when time is ripe.
Then he will come, Christ the uncrucified
Christ the discrucified, his death undone,
His agony unmade, his cross dismantled—
Glad to be so—and the tormented wood
Will cure its hurt and grow into a tree
In a green springing corner of young Eden,
And Judas damned take his long journey backward
From darkness into light and be a child
Beside his mother's knee, and the betrayal
Be quite undone and never more be done.

**MATTHEW 18:2–3   And Jesus called a little child unto him, and set him
in the midst of them, And said, Verily I say unto you, Except ye be converted, and become as little children, ye shall not enter into the kingdom
of heaven.**

INNOCENCE

THOMAS TRAHERNE

But that which most I wonder at, which most
I did esteem my bliss, which most I boast
And ever shall enjoy, is that within
    I felt no stain, nor spot of sin.

    No darkness then did overshade,
    But all within was pure and bright,
    No guilt did crush nor fear invade,
    But all my soul was full of light.

A joyful sense and purity
    Is all I can remember.
The very night to me was bright,
'Twas Summer in December.

A serious meditation did employ
My soul within, which, taken up with joy,
Did seem no outward thing to note, but fly
    All objects that do feed the eye.

    While it those very objects did
    Admire, and prize, and praise, and love,
    Which in their glory most are hid,
    Which presence only doth remove.

    Their constant daily presence I
        Rejoicing at, did see;
    And that which takes them from the eye
    Of others, offered them to me.

No inward inclination did I feel
To avarice or pride: my soul did kneel
In admiration all the day. No lust, nor strife,
    Polluted then my infant life.

    No fraud nor anger in me moved,
    No malice, jealousy or spite;
    All that I saw I truly loved.
    Contentment only and delight

    Were in my soul. O Heaven! what bliss
        Did I enjoy and feel!
    What powerful delight did this
    Inspire! for this I daily kneel.

Whether it be that nature is so pure,
And custom only vicious, or that sure
God did by miracle the guilt remove,
    And make my soul to feel his love,

    So early; Or that 'twas one day
    Where in this happiness I found,

Whose strength and brightness so do ray,
That still it seems me to surround:

What e'er it is, it is a light
    So endless unto me
That I a world of true delight
Did then and to this day do see.

That prospect was the Gate of Heaven, that day
The ancient Light of Eden did convey
Into my soul: I was an Adam there,
    A little Adam in a sphere

Of joys! O there my ravished sense
Was entertained in paradise,
And had a sight of innocence,
Which was beyond all bound and price.

An antepast of Heaven sure!
    I on the Earth did reign.
Within, without me, all was pure.
I must become a Child again.

MATTHEW 18:9   And if thine eye offend thee, pluck it out, and cast it from thee: it is better for thee to enter into life with one eye, rather than having two eyes to be cast into hell fire.

A SHROPSHIRE LAD: POEM 45

A. E. HOUSMAN

If it chance your eye offend you,
    Pluck it out, lad, and be sound:
'Twill hurt, but here are salves to friend you,
    And many a balsam grows on ground.

And if your hand or foot offend you,
    Cut it off, lad, and be whole;

But play the man, stand up and end you,
When your sickness is your soul.

JOHN 7:1–8:11 . . . Jesus went unto the mount of Olives. **And early in the morning he came again into the temple, and all the people came unto him; and he sat down, and taught them. And the scribes and Pharisees brought unto him a woman taken in adultery; and when they had set her in the midst, They say unto him, Master, this woman was taken in adultery, in the very act. Now Moses in the law commanded us, that such should be stoned: but what sayest thou? This they said, tempting him, that they might have to accuse him. But Jesus stooped down, and with his finger wrote on the ground, as though he heard them not. So when they continued asking him, he lifted up himself, and said unto them, He that is without sin among you, let him first cast a stone at her. And again he stooped down, and wrote on the ground. And they which heard it, being convicted by their own conscience, went out one by one, beginning at the eldest, even unto the last: and Jesus was left alone, and the woman standing in the midst. When Jesus had lifted up himself, and saw none but the woman, he said unto her, Woman, where are those thine accusers? hath no man condemned thee? She said, No man, Lord. And Jesus said unto her, Neither do I condemn thee: go, and sin no more.**

from THE EVERLASTING GOSPEL

WILLIAM BLAKE

Was Jesus Chaste? or did he
Give any Lessons of Chastity?
The morning blushed fiery red:
Mary was found in Adulterous bed;
Earth groaned beneath, and Heaven above
Trembled at discovery of Love.
Jesus was sitting in Moses' Chair,
They brought the trembling Woman There.
Moses commands she be stoned to death,
What was the sound of Jesus' breath?
He laid His hand on Moses' Law:
The Ancient Heavens, in Silent Awe
Writ with Curses from Pole to Pole,
All away began to roll:

The Earth trembling and Naked lay
In secret bed of Mortal Clay,
On Sinai felt the hand divine
Putting back the bloody shrine,
And she heard the breath of God
As she heard by Eden's flood:
"Good and Evil are no more!
"Sinai's trumpets, cease to roar!
"Cease, finger of God, to write!
"The Heavens are not clean in thy Sight.
"Thou art Good, and thou Alone;
"Nor may the sinner cast one stone.
"To be Good only, is to be
"A God or else a Pharisee.
"Thou Angel of the Presence Divine
"That didst create this Body of Mine,
"Wherefore has thou writ these Laws
"And Created Hell's dark jaws?
"My Presence I will take from thee:
"A Cold Leper thou shalt be.
"Though thou wast so pure and bright
"That Heaven was Impure in thy Sight,
"Though thy Oath turned Heaven Pale,
"Though thy Covenant built Hell's Jail,
"Though thou didst all to Chaos roll
"With the Serpent for its soul,
"Still the breath Divine does move
"And the breath Divine is Love.
"Mary, Fear Not! Let me see
"The Seven Devils that torment thee:
"Hide not from my Sight thy Sin,
"That forgiveness thou mayst win.
"Has no Man Condemned thee?"
"No Man, Lord." "Then what is he
"Who shall Accuse thee? Come Ye forth,
"Fallen fiends of Heavenly birth
"That have forgot your ancient love
"And driven away my trembling Dove.
"You shall bow before her feet;
"You shall lick the dust for Meat;
"And though you cannot Love, but Hate,
"Shall be beggars at Love's Gate.
"What was thy love? Let me see it;
"Was it love or Dark Deceit?"

"Love too long from Me has fled;
" 'Twas dark deceit, to Earn my bread;
" 'Twas Covet, or 'twas Custom, or
"Some trifle not worth caring for;
"That they may call a shame and Sin
"Love's temple that God dwelleth in,
"And hide in secret hidden Shrine
"The Naked Human form divine,
"And render that a Lawless thing
"On which the Soul Expands its wing.
"But this, O Lord, this was my Sin
"When first I let these Devils in
"In dark pretence to Chastity:
"Blaspheming Love, blaspheming thee.
"Thence Rose Secret Adulteries,
"And thence did Covet also rise.
"My sin thou hast forgiven me,
"Canst thou forgive my Blasphemy?
"Canst thou return to this dark Hell,
"And in my burning bosom dwell?
"And canst thou die that I may live?
"And canst thou Pity and forgive?"
Then Rolled the shadowy Man away
From the Limbs of Jesus, to make them his prey,
An Ever devouring appetite
Glittering with festering Venoms bright,
Crying, "Crucify this cause of distress,
"Who don't keep the secrets of Holiness!
"All Mental Powers by Diseases we bind,
"But he heals the deaf and the Dumb and the Blind.
"Whom God has afflicted for Secret Ends,
"He comforts and Heals and calls them Friends."
But, when Jesus was Crucified,
Then was perfected his glittering pride:
In three Nights he devoured his prey,
And still he devours the Body of Clay;
For dust and Clay is the Serpent's meat,
Which never was made for Man to Eat.

LUKE 10:1–4 After these things the Lord appointed other seventy also, and sent them two and two before his face into every city and place, whither he himself would come. Therefore said he unto them, The har-

vest truly is great, but the labourers are few: pray ye therefore the Lord
of the harvest, that he would send forth labourers into his harvest. Go
your ways: behold, I send you forth as lambs among wolves. Carry neither purse, nor scrip, nor shoes: and salute no man by the way.

SALUTATION

ROBERT HERRICK

Christ, I have read, did to His chaplains say,
Sending them forth, *Salute no man by th' way:*
Not, that He taught His ministers to be
Unsmooth, or sour, to all civility;
But to instruct them, to avoid all snares
Of tardiation in the Lord's affairs.
Manners are good: but till his errand ends,
Salute we must, nor strangers, kin, or friends.

LUKE 10:17–19   And the seventy returned again with joy, saying, Lord,
even the devils are subject unto us through thy name. And he said unto
them, I beheld Satan as lightning fall from heaven. Behold, I give unto
you power to tread on serpents and scorpions, and over all the power of
the enemy: and nothing shall by any means hurt you.

SEE LUCIFER LIKE LIGHTNING FALL

JOHN KEBLE

See Lucifer like lightning fall,
        Dashed from his throne of pride;
While, answering Thy victorious call,
        The Saints his spoils divide;
This world of Thine, by him usurped too long,
Now opening all her stores to heal Thy servants' wrong.

So when the first-born of Thy foes
        Dead in the darkness lay,
When Thy redeemed at midnight rose
        And cast their bonds away,
The orphaned realm threw wide her gates, and told
Into freed Israel's lap her jewels and her gold.

And when their wondrous march was o'er,
    And they had won their homes,
Where Abraham fed his flock of yore,
    Among their fathers' tombs;—
A land that drinks the rain of Heaven at will,
Whose waters kiss the feet of many a vine-clad hill;—

Oft as they watched, at thoughtful eve,
    A gale from bowers of balm
Sweep o'er the billowy corn, and heave
    The tresses of the palm,
Just as the lingering sun had touched with gold,
Far o'er the cedar shade, some tower of giants old;

It was a fearful joy, I ween,
    To trace the Heathen's toil,
The limpid wells, the orchards green,
    Left ready for the spoil,
The household stores untouched, the roses bright
Wreathed o'er the cottage walls in garlands of delight,

And now another Canaan yields
    To Thine all-conquering ark;—
Fly from the "old poetic" fields,
    Ye Paynim shadows dark!
Immortal Greece, dear land of glorious lays,
Lo! here the "unknown God" of thy unconscious praise!

The olive wreath, the ivied wand,
    "The sword in myrtles dressed,"
Each legend of the shadowy strand
    Now wakes a vision blessed;
As little children lisp, and tell of Heaven,
So thoughts beyond their thought to those high Bards were given.

And these are ours: Thy partial grace
    The tempting treasure lends:
These relics of a guilty race
    Are forfeit to Thy friends:
What seemed an idol hymn, now breathes of Thee,
Tuned by Faith's ear to some celestial melody.

There's not a strain to Memory dear,
    Nor flower in classic grove,

There's not a sweet note warbled here,
But minds us of Thy Love.
O Lord, our Lord, and spoiler of our foes,
There is no light but Thine: with Thee all beauty glows.

LUKE 10:30–34   **And Jesus answering said, A certain man went down from Jerusalem to Jericho, and fell among thieves, which stripped him of his raiment, and wounded him, and departed, leaving him half dead. And by chance there came down a certain priest that way: and when he saw him, he passed by on the other side. And likewise a Levite, when he was at the place, came and looked on him, and passed by on the other side. But a certain Samaritan, as he journeyed, came where he was: and when he saw him, he had compassion on him, And went to him, and bound up his wounds, pouring in oil and wine, and set him on his own beast, and brought him to an inn, and took care of him.**

A MAN WHO HAD FALLEN AMONG THIEVES

E. E. CUMMINGS

a man who had fallen among thieves
lay by the roadside on his back
dressed in fifteenthrate ideas
wearing a round jeer for a hat

fate per a somewhat more than less
emancipated evening
had in return for consciousness
endowed him with a changeless grin

whereon a dozen staunch and leal
citizens did graze at pause
then fired by hypercivic zeal
sought newer pastures or because

swaddled with a frozen brook
of pinkest vomit out of eyes
which noticed nobody he looked
as if he did not care to rise

one hand did nothing on the vest
its wideflung friend clenched weakly dirt

while the mute trouserfly confessed
a button solemnly inert.

Brushing from whom the stiffened puke
i put him all into my arms
and staggered banged with terror through
a million billion trillion stars

LUKE 10:38–42   Now it came to pass, as they went, that he entered into a
certain village: and a certain woman named Martha received him into
her house. And she had a sister called Mary, which also sat at Jesus' feet,
and heard his word. But Martha was cumbered about much serving, and
came to him, and said, Lord, dost thou not care that my sister hath left
me to serve alone? bid her therefore that she help me. And Jesus
answered and said unto her, Martha, Martha, thou art careful and troubled about many things: But one thing is needful: and Mary hath chosen
that good part, which shall not be taken away from her.

THE SONS OF MARTHA

RUDYARD KIPLING

The Sons of Mary seldom bother, for they have inherited that good part;
But the Sons of Martha favour their Mother of the careful soul and the
    troubled heart.
And because she lost her temper once, and because she was rude to the
    Lord her Guest,
Her Sons must wait upon Mary's Sons, world without end, reprieve, or
    rest.

It is their care in all the ages to take the buffet and cushion the shock.
It is their care that the gear engages; it is their care that the switches
    lock.
It is their care that the wheels run truly; it is their care to embark and
    entrain,
Tally, transport, and deliver duly the Sons of Mary by land and main.

They say to mountains, " Be ye removed." They say to the lesser floods,
    "Be dry."
Under their rods are the rocks reproved—they are not afraid of that
    which is high.

Then do the hill-tops shake to the summit—then is the bed of the deep
    laid bare,
That the Sons of Mary may overcome it, pleasantly sleeping and
    unaware.

They finger death at their gloves' end where they piece and repiece the
    living wires.
He rears against the gates they tend: they feed him hungry behind their
    fires.
Early at dawn, ere men see clear, they stumble into his terrible stall,
And hale him forth like a haltered steer, and goad and turn him till
    evenfall.

To these from birth is Belief forbidden; from these till death is Relief
    afar.
They are concerned with matters hidden—under the earth-line their
    altars are—
The secret fountains to follow up, waters withdrawn to restore to the
    mouth,
And gather the floods as in a cup, and pour them again at a city's
    drouth.

They do not preach that their God will rouse them a little before the
    nuts work loose.
They do not teach that His Pity allows them to drop their job when they
    dam'-well choose.
As in the thronged and the lighted ways, so in the dark and the desert
    they stand,
Wary and watchful all their days that their brethren's days may be long
    in the land.

Raise ye the stone or cleave the wood to make a path more fair or flat—
Lo, it is black already with blood some Son of Martha spilled for that!
Not as a ladder from earth to Heaven, not as a witness to any creed,
But simple service simply given to his own kind in their common need.

And the Sons of Mary smile and are blessed—they know the Angels are
    on their side
They know in them is the Grace confessed, and for them are the
    Mercies multiplied.
They sit at the Feet—they hear the Word— they see how truly the
    Promise runs.
They have cast the burden upon the Lord, and—the Lord He lays it on
    Martha's Sons!

LUKE 11:27   And it came to pass, as he spake these things, a certain woman of the company lifted up her voice, and said unto him, Blessed is the womb that bare thee, and the paps which thou hast sucked.

BLESSED BE THE PAPS

RICHARD CRASHAW

Suppose he had been tabled at thy teats,
    Thy hunger feels not what he eats:
He'll have his teat ere long (a bloody one)
    The Mother then must suck the Son.

LUKE 12:37   Blessed are those servants, whom the lord when he cometh shall find watching: verily I say unto you, that he shall gird himself, and make them to sit down to meat, and will come forth and serve them.

LOVE III

GEORGE HERBERT

Love bade me welcome yet my soul drew back,
    Guilty of dust and sin.
But quick-eyed Love, observing me grow slack
    From my first entrance in,
Drew nearer to me, sweetly questioning,
    If I lacked any thing.

A guest, I answered, worthy to be here:
    Love said, You shall be he.
I the unkind, ungrateful? Ah my dear,
    I cannot look on thee.
Love took my hand, and smiling did reply,
    Who made the eyes but I?

Truth Lord, but I have marred them: let my shame
    Go where it doth deserve.
And know you not, says Love, who bore the blame?
    My dear, then I will serve.
You must sit down, says Love, and taste my meat:
    So I did sit and eat.

LUKE 13:1–5 There were present at that season some that told him of
the Galilaeans, whose blood Pilate had mingled with their sacrifices. And
Jesus answering said unto them, Suppose ye that these Galilaeans were
sinners above all the Galilaeans, because they suffered such things? I tell
you, Nay: but, except ye repent, ye shall all likewise perish. Or those
eighteen, upon whom the tower in Siloam fell, and slew them, think ye
that they were sinners above all men that dwelt in Jerusalem? I tell you,
Nay: but, except ye repent, ye shall all likewise perish.

THE FALLEN TOWER OF SILOAM

ROBERT GRAVES

Should the building totter, run for an archway!
We were there already—already the collapse
Powdered the air with chalk, and shrieking
Of old men crushed under the fallen beams
Dwindled to comic yelps. How not terrible
When the event outran the alarm
And suddenly we were free—

Free to forget how grim it stood,
That tower, and what great fissures ran
Up the west wall, how rotten the under-pinning
At the south-eastern angle. Satire
Had whirled a gentle wind around it,
As if to buttress the worn masonry;
Yet we, waiting, had abstained from satire.

It behoved us, indeed, as poets
To be silent in Siloam, to foretell
No visible calamity. Though kings
Were crowned and gold coin minted still and horses
Still munched at nose-bags in the public sheets,
All such sad emblems were to be condoned:
An old-wives' tale, not ours.

LUKE 13:6–9 He spake also this parable; A certain man had a fig tree
planted in his vineyard; and he came and sought fruit thereon, and found
none. Then said he unto the dresser of his vineyard, Behold, these three
years I come seeking fruit on this fig tree, and find none: cut it down; why
cumbereth it the ground? And he answering said unto him, Lord, let it

alone this year also, till I shall dig about it, and dung it: And if it bear
fruit, well: and if not, then after that thou shalt cut it down.

CONTRITION

RALPH KNEVET

My heart is broken (oh my God)
Break me not like a potters vessel,
Bruise me not with an iron rod,
But form me by thy holy chisel,
That I a statue may become,
Fit to adorn thy heavenly room.

The fig tree yields a fruit that's sweet,
Yet is unprofitable wood;
For sculptor's art it is unmeet,
And neither serves for saint, or rood:
For Vulcan's use it is unfit,
His bellows do no good on it.

But I that wretched tree am, which
The hunger of my Christ deceives,
He fruit expects, but I am rich
In nothing but vain spreading leaves,
Nor am I wood so fit, and apt
That of me can a saint be shaped.

Yea, I am that same fig tree vain,
Which in Christ's vineyard planted was,
Dressed many years with care, and pain,
Yet only serve to fill a place:
I therefore fear the axes wound,
Because I cumber but the ground.

(Lord) in me repair (by thy grace)
The image Thou didst first create:
Though Adam's sin did it deface,
Yet mine, did it more vitiate:
Vouchsafe t'amend it with thy hand,
Then in thy gallery it may stand.

LUKE 14:12–14 Then said he also to him that bade him, When thou makest a dinner or a supper, call not thy friends, nor thy brethren, neither thy kinsmen, nor thy rich neighbours; lest they also bid thee again, and a recompence be made thee. But when thou makest a feast, call the poor, the maimed, the lame, the blind: And thou shalt be blessed; for they cannot recompense thee: for thou shalt be recompensed at the resurrection of the just.

HIS METRICAL PRAYER

JAMES GRAHAM, MARQUIS OF MONTROSE

(On the eve of his own execution)

Let them bestow on ev'ry airth a limb;
Open all my veins, that I may swim
To Thee my Savior, in that crimson lake;
Then place my par-boiled head upon a stake;
Scatter my ashes, throw them in the air:
Lord (since Thou knowst where all these atoms are)
I'm hopeful, once Thou'lt recollect my dust,
And confident Thou'lt raise me with the just.

LUKE 14:34–15:15 . . . And he said, A certain man had two sons: And the younger of them said to his father, Father, give me the portion of goods that falleth to me. And he divided unto them his living. And not many days after the younger son gathered all together, and took his journey into a far country, and there wasted his substance with riotous living. And when he had spent all, there arose a mighty famine in that land; and he began to be in want. And he went and joined himself to a citizen of that country; and he sent him into his fields to feed swine.

THE PRODIGAL SON

ROBERT BLY

The Prodigal Son is kneeling in the husks.
He remembers the man about to die
who cried, "Don't let me die, Doctor!"
The swine go on feeding in the sunlight.

When he folds his hands, his knees on corncobs,
he sees the smoke of ships
floating off the isles of Tyre and Sidon,
and father beyond father beyond father.

An old man once, being dragged across the floor
by his shouting son, cried:
"Don't drag me any farther than that crack on the floor—
I only dragged my father that far!"

My father is seventy five years old.
How difficult it is,
bending the head, looking into the water.
Under the water there's a door the pigs have gone through.

**LUKE 15:16–24   And he would fain have filled his belly with the husks
that the swine did eat: and no man gave unto him. And when he came to
himself, he said, How many hired servants of my father's have bread
enough and to spare, and I perish with hunger! I will arise and go to my
father, and will say unto him, Father, I have sinned against heaven, and
before thee, And am no more worthy to be called thy son: make me as
one of thy hired servants. And he arose, and came to his father. But when
he was yet a great way off, his father saw him, and had compassion, and
ran, and fell on his neck, and kissed him. And the son said unto him,
Father, I have sinned against heaven, and in thy sight, and am no more
worthy to be called thy son. But the father said to his servants, Bring
forth the best robe, and put it on him; and put a ring on his hand, and
shoes on his feet: And bring hither the fatted calf, and kill it; and let us
eat, and be merry: For this my son was dead, and is alive again; he was
lost, and is found. And they began to be merry.**

THE PRODIGAL

ELIZABETH BISHOP

The brown enormous odor he lived by
was too close, with its breathing and thick hair,
for him to judge. The floor was rotten; the sty
was plastered halfway up with glass-smooth dung.
Light-lashed, self-righteous, above moving snouts,
the pigs' eyes followed him, a cheerful stare—
even to the sow that always ate her young—

till, sickening, he leaned to scratch her head.
But sometimes mornings after drinking bouts
(he hid the pints behind a two-by-four),
the sunrise glazed the barnyard mud with red;
the burning puddles seemed to reassure.
And then he thought he almost might endure
his exile yet another year or more.

But evenings the first star came to warn.
The farmer whom he worked for came at dark
to shut the cows and horses in the barn
beneath their overhanging clouds of hay,
with pitchforks, faint forked lightnings, catching light,
safe and companionable as in the Ark.
The pigs stuck out their little feet and snored.
The lantern—like the sun, going away—
laid on the mud a pacing aureole.
Carrying a bucket along a slimy board,
he felt the bats' uncertain staggering flight,
his shuddering insights, beyond his control,
touching him. But it took him a long time
finally to make his mind up to go home.

LUKE 16:19–28 . . . There was a certain rich man, which was clothed in purple and fine linen, and fared sumptuously every day: And there was a certain beggar named Lazarus, which was laid at his gate, full of sores, And desiring to be fed with the crumbs which fell from the rich man's table: moreover the dogs came and licked his sores. And it came to pass, that the beggar died, and was carried by the angels into Abraham's bosom: the rich man also died, and was buried; And in hell he lift up his eyes, being in torments, and seeth Abraham afar off, and Lazarus in his bosom. And he cried and said, Father Abraham, have mercy on me, and send Lazarus, that he may dip the tip of his finger in water, and cool my tongue; for I am tormented in this flame. But Abraham said, Son, remember that thou in thy lifetime receivedst thy good things, and likewise Lazarus evil things: but now he is comforted, and thou art tormented. And beside all this, between us and you there is a great gulf fixed: so that they which would pass from hence to you cannot; neither can they pass to us, that would come from thence. Then he said, I pray thee therefore, father, that thou wouldest send him to my father's house: For I have five brethren; that he may testify unto them, lest they also come into this place of torment.

To "A Certain Rich Man"

Alice Meynell

Thou wouldst not part thy spoil
Gained from the beggar's want, the weakling's toil,
Nor spare a jot of sumptuousness or state
For Lazarus at the gate.

And in the appalling night
Of expiation, as in day's delight,
Thou heldst thy niggard hand; it would not share
One hour of thy despair.

Those five—thy prayer for them!
O generous! who, condemned, wouldst not condemn,
Whose ultimate human greatness proved thee so
A miser of thy woe.

LUKE 16:29–31 Abraham saith unto him, They have Moses and the prophets; let them hear them. And he said, Nay, father Abraham: but if one went unto them from the dead, they will repent. And he said unto him, If they hear not Moses and the prophets, neither will they be persuaded, though one rose from the dead.

To Dives

Hilaire Belloc

Dives, when you and I go down to Hell
Where scribblers end and millionaires as well,
We shall be carrying on our separate backs
Two very large but very different packs;
And as you stagger under yours, my friend,
Down the dull shore where all our journeys end
And go before me (as your rank demands)
Toward the infinite flat underlands,
And that dear river of forgetfulness—
Charon, a man of exquisite address
(For as your wife's progenitors could tell,
They're very strict on etiquette in Hell),

Will, since you are a lord, observe, "My lord,
We cannot take these weighty things aboard!"
Then down they go, my wretched Dives, down—
The fifteen sorts of boots you kept for town,
The hat to meet the Devil in; the plain
But costly ties; the cases of champagne;
The solid watch, and seal, and chain, and charm;
The working model of a Burning Farm
(To give the little Belials); all the three
Biscuits for Cerberus; the guarantee
From Lambeth that the rich can never burn,
And even promising a safe return;
The admirable overcoat, designed
To cross Cocytus—very warmly lined;
Sweet Dives, you will leave them all behind
And enter Hell as tattered and as bare
As was your father when he took the air
Behind a barrow-load in Leicester Square.
Then turned to me, and noting one that brings
With careless step a mist of shadowy things;
Laughter and memories, and a few regrets,
Some honor, and a quantity of debts,
A doubt or two of sorts, a trust in God,
And (what will seem to you extremely odd)
His father's granfer's father's father's name,
Unspoilt, untitled, even spelt the same;
Charon, who twenty thousand times before
Has ferried Poets to the ulterior shore,
Will estimate the weight I bear and cry—
"Comrade!" (He has himself been known to try
His hand at Latin and Italian verse
Much in the style of Vergil—only worse)
"We let such vain imaginaries pass!"
Then tell me, Dives, which will look the ass—
You, or myself? Or Charon? Who can tell?
They order things so damnably in Hell.

JOHN 11:30–35 Now Jesus was not yet come into the town, but was in that place where Martha met him. The Jews then which were with her in the house, and comforted her, when they saw Mary, that she rose up hastily and went out, followed her, saying, She goeth unto the grave to weep there. Then when Mary was come where Jesus was, and saw him, she fell down at his feet, saying unto him, Lord, if thou hadst been here, my brother had not died. When Jesus therefore saw her weeping, and the Jews also weeping which came with her, he groaned in the spirit, and was troubled. And said, Where have ye laid him? They said unto him, Lord, come and see.

Jesus wept.

THE CONVERT

G. K. CHESTERTON

After one moment when I bowed my head
And the whole world turned over and came upright,
And I came out where the old road shone white,
I walked the ways and heard what all men said,
Forests of tongues, like autumn leaves unshed
Being not unlovable but strange and light;
Old riddles and new creeds, not in despite
But softly, as men smile about the dead.

The sages have a hundred maps to give
That trace their crawling cosmos like a tree,
They rattle reason out through many a sieve
That stores the sand and lets the gold go free:
And all these things are less than dust to me
Because my name is Lazarus and I live.

JOHN 11:43–44 And when he thus had spoken, he cried with a loud voice, Lazarus, come forth. And he that was dead came forth, bound hand and foot with graveclothes: and his face was bound about with a napkin. Jesus saith unto them, Loose him, and let him go.

ON LAZARUS RAISED FROM DEATH

HENRY COLMAN

Where am I, or how came I here, hath death
        Bereaved me of my breath,
            Or do I dream?
Nor can that be, for sure I am

These are no ensigns of a living man,
                    Beside, the stream
                    Of life did fly
From hence, and my blessed soul did soar on
              And well remember I,
              My friends on either hand
                    Did weeping stand
                    To see me die;
Most certain then it is my soul was fled
Forth of my clay, and I am buried.

These linens plainly show this cave did keep
              My flesh in its dead sleep,
                    And yet a noise
        Me-thought I heard, of such strange force
As would have raised to life the dullest corse,
                    So sweet a voice
                    As spite of death
Distilled through every vein a living breath,
              And sure I heard it charge
              Me by my name, even thus
                    O Lazarus
                    Come forth at large,
And so nought hinders, I will straightway then
Appear, (though thus dressed) ere it call again.

Was't my Redeemer called, no marvel then
              Though dead, I live again,
                    His word alone
        Can raise a soul, though dead in sin,
Ready the grave of hell to tumble in
                    High as the Throne;
                    In all things he
Is the true powerful Eternity:
              Since thou hast pleased to raise
              My body then, let my spirit
                    Heaven inherit
                    And thee praise.
And let thy miracle upon my clay
Prepare, and fit me 'gainst the reckoning day.

An Epistle Containing the Strange Medical Experience of Karshish, the Arab Physician

Robert Browning

Karshish, the picker-up of learning's crumbs,
The not-incurious in God's handiwork
(This man's-flesh he hath admirable made,
Blown like a bubble, kneaded like a paste,
To coop up and keep down on earth a space
That puff of vapour from his mouth, man's soul)
– To Abib, all-sagacious in our art,
Breeder in me of what poor skill I boast,
Like me inquisitive how pricks and cracks
Befall the flesh through too much stress and strain,
Whereby the wily vapour fain would slip
Back and rejoin its source before the term,
And aptest in contrivance (under God)
To baffle it by deftly stopping such: –
The vagrant Scholar to his Sage at home
Sends greeting (health and knowledge, fame with peace)
Three samples of true snakestone – rarer still,
One of the other sort, the melon-shaped,
(But fitter, pounded fine, for charms than drugs)
And writeth now the twenty-second time.

My journeyings were brought to Jericho:
Thus I resume. Who studious in our art
Shall count a little labour unrepaid?
I have shed sweat enough, left flesh and bone
On many a flinty furlong of this land.
Also, the country-side is all on fire
With rumours of a marching hitherward:
Some say Vespasian cometh, some, his son.
A black lynx snarled and pricked a tufted ear;
Lust of my blood inflamed his yellow balls:
I cried and threw my staff and he was gone.
Twice have the robbers stripped and beaten me,
And once a town declared me for a spy;
But at the end, I reach Jerusalem,
Since this poor covert where I pass the night,
This Bethany, lies scarce the distance thence

A man with plague-sores at the third degree
Runs till he drops down dead. Thou laughest here!
'Sooth, it elates me, thus reposed and safe,
To void the stuffing of my travel-scrip
And share with thee whatever Jewry yields.
A viscid choler is observable
In tertians, I was nearly bold to say;
And falling-sickness hath a happier cure
Than our school wots of: there's a spider here
Weaves no web, watches on the ledge of tombs,
Sprinkled with mottles on an ash-grey back;
Take five and drop them . . . but who knows his mind,
The Syrian runagate I trust this to?
His service payeth me a sublimate
Blown up his nose to help the ailing eye.
Best wait: I reach Jerusalem at morn,
There set in order my experiences,
Gather what most deserves, and give thee all –
Or I might add, Judea's gum-tragacanth
Scales off in purer flakes, shines clearer-grained,
Cracks 'twixt the pestle and the porphyry,
In fine exceeds our produce. Scalp-disease
Confounds me, crossing so with leprosy –
Thou hadst admired one sort I gained at Zoar –
But zeal outruns discretion. Here I end.

Yet stay: my Syrian blinketh gratefully,
Protesteth his devotion is my price –
Suppose I write what harms not, though he steal?
I half resolve to tell thee, yet I blush,
What set me off a-writing first of all.
An itch I had, a sting to write, a tang!
For, be it this town's barrenness – or else
The Man had something in the look of him –
His case has struck me far more than 'tis worth.
So, pardon if – (lest presently I lose
In the great press of novelty at hand
The care and pain this somehow stole from me)
I bid thee take the thing while fresh in mind,
Almost in sight – for, wilt thou have the truth?
The very man is gone from me but now,
Whose ailment is the subject of discourse.
Thus then, and let thy better wit help all!

'Tis but a case of mania – subinduced
By epilepsy, at the turning-point
Of trance prolonged unduly some three days:
When, by the exhibition of some drug
Or spell, exorcization, stroke of art
Unknown to me and which 'twere well to know,
The evil thing out-breaking all at once
Left the man whole and sound of body indeed, –
But, flinging (so to speak) life's gates too wide,
Making a clear house of it too suddenly,
The first conceit that entered might inscribe
Whatever it was minded on the wall
So plainly at that vantage, as it were,
(First come, first served) that nothing subsequent
Attaineth to erase those fancy-scrawls
The just-returned and new-established soul
Hath gotten now so thoroughly by heart
That henceforth she will read or these or none.
And first – the man's own firm conviction rests
That he was dead (in fact they buried him)
– That he was dead and then restored to life
By a Nazarene physician of his tribe:
– 'Sayeth, the same bade 'Rise,' and he did rise.
'Such cases are diurnal,' thou wilt cry.
Not so this figment! – not, that such a fume,
Instead of giving way to time and health,
Should eat itself into the life of life,
As saffron tingeth flesh, blood, bones and all!
For see, how he takes up the after-life.
The man – it is one Lazarus, a Jew,
Sanguine, proportioned, fifty years of age,
The body's habit wholly laudable,
As much, indeed, beyond the common health
As he were made and put aside to show.
Think, could we penetrate by any drug
And bathe the wearied soul and worried flesh,
And bring it clear and fair, by three days' sleep!
When has the man the balm that brightens all?
This grown man eyes the world now like a child.
Some elders of his tribe, I should premise,
Led in their friend, obedient as a sheep,
To bear my inquisition. While they spoke,
Now sharply, now with sorrow, – told the case, –
He listened not except I spoke to him,

But folded his two hands and let them talk,
Watching the flies that buzzed: and yet no fool.
And that's a sample how his years must go.
Look, if a beggar, in fixed middle-life,
Should find a treasure, – can he use the same
With straitened habits and with tastes starved small,
And take at once to his impoverished brain
The sudden element that changes things,
That sets the undreamed-of rapture at his hand
And puts the cheap old joy in the scorned dust?
Is he not such an one as moves to mirth –
Warily parsimonious, when no need,
Wasteful as drunkenness at undue times?
All prudent counsel as to what befits
The golden mean, is lost on such an one:
The man's fantastic will is the man's law.
So here – we call the treasure knowledge, say,
Increased beyond the fleshly faculty –
Heaven opened to a soul while yet on earth,
Earth forced on a soul's use while seeing heaven:
The man is witless of the size, the sum,
The value in proportion of all things,
Or whether it be little or be much.
Discourse to him of prodigious armaments
Assembled to besiege his city now,
And of the passing of a mule with gourds –
'Tis one! Then take it on the other side,
Speak of some trifling fact, – he will gaze rapt
With stupor at its very littleness,
(Far as I see) as if in that indeed
He caught prodigious import, whole results;
And so will turn to us the bystanders
In ever the same stupor (note this point)
That we too see not with his opened eyes.
Wonder and doubt come wrongly into play,
Preposterously, at cross-purposes.
Should his child sicken unto death, – why, look
For scarce abatement of his cheerfulness,
Or pretermission of the daily craft!
While a word, gesture, glance from that same child
At play or in the school or laid asleep,
Will startle him to an agony of fear,
Exasperation, just as like. Demand
The reason why – ' 'tis but a word,' object –

'A gesture' – he regards thee as our lord
Who lived there in the pyramid alone,
Looked at us (dost thou mind?) when, being young,
We both would unadvisedly recite
Some charm's beginning, from that book of his,
Able to bid the sun throb wide and burst
All into stars, as stars grown old are wont.
Thou and the child have each a veil alike
Thrown o'er your heads, from under which ye both
Stretch your blind hands and trifle with a match
Over a mine of Greek fire, did ye know!
He holds on firmly to some thread of life –
(It is the life to lead perforcedly)
Which runs across some vast distracting orb
Of glory on either side that meagre thread,
Which, conscious of, he must not enter yet –
The spiritual life around the earthly life:
The law of that is known to him as this,
His heart and brain move there, his feet stay here.
So is the man perplexed with impulses
Sudden to start off crosswise, not straight on,
Proclaiming what is right and wrong across,
And not along, this black thread through the blaze –
'It should be' balked by 'here it cannot be.'
And oft the man's soul springs into his face
As if he saw again and heard again
His sage that bade him 'Rise' and he did rise.
Something, a word, a tick o' the blood within
Admonishes: then back he sinks at once
To ashes, who was very fire before,
In sedulous recurrence to his trade
Whereby he earneth him the daily bread;
And studiously the humbler for that pride,
Professedly the faultier he knows
God's secret, while he holds the thread of life.
Indeed the especial marking of the man
Is prone submission to the heavenly will –
Seeing it, what it is, and why it is.
'Sayeth, he will wait patient to the last
For that same death which must restore his being
To equilibrium, body loosening soul
Divorced even now by premature full growth:
He will live, nay, it pleaseth him to live
So long as God please, and just how God please.

He even seeketh not to please God more
(Which meaneth, otherwise) than as God please.
Hence, I perceive not he affects to preach
The doctrine of his sect whate'er it be,
Make proselytes as madmen thirst to do:
How can he give his neighbour the real ground,
His own conviction? Ardent as he is –
Call his great truth a lie, why, still the old
'Be it as God please' reassureth him.
I probed the sore as thy disciple should:
'How, beast,' said I, 'this stolid carelessness
Sufficeth thee, when Rome is on her march
To stamp out like a little spark thy town,
Thy tribe, thy crazy tale and thee at once?'
He merely looked with his large eyes on me.
The man is apathetic, you deduce?
Contrariwise, he loves both old and young,
Able and weak, affects the very brutes
And birds – how say I? flowers of the field –
As a wise workman recognizes tools
In a master's workshop, loving what they make.
Thus is the man, as harmless as a lamb:
Only impatient, let him do his best,
At ignorance and carelessness and sin –
An indignation which is promptly curbed:
As when in certain travels I have feigned
To be an ignoramus in our art
According to some preconceived design,
And happed to hear the land's practitioners
Steeped in conceit sublimed by ignorance,
Prattle fantastically on disease,
Its cause and cure – and I must hold my peace!

Thou wilt object – Why have I not ere this
Sought out the sage himself, the Nazarene
Who wrought this cure, inquiring at the source,
Conferring with the frankness that befits?
Alas! it grieveth me, the learned leech
Perished in a tumult many years ago,
Accused, – our learning's fate, – of wizardry,
Rebellion, to the setting up a rule
And creed prodigious as described to me.
His death, which happened when the earthquake fell
(Prefiguring, as soon appeared, the loss

To occult learning in our lord the sage
Who lived there in the pyramid alone)
Was wrought by the mad people – that's their wont!
On vain recourse, as I conjecture it,
To his tried virtue, for miraculous help –
How could he stop the earthquake? That's their way!
The other imputations must be lies:
But take one, though I loathe to give it thee,
In mere respect for any good man's fame.
(And after all, our patient Lazarus
Is stark mad; should we count on what he says?
Perhaps not: though in writing to a leech
'Tis well to keep back nothing of a case.)
This man so cured regards the curer, then,
As – God forgive me! who but God himself,
Creator and sustainer of the world,
That came and dwelt in flesh on it awhile!
– 'Sayeth that such an one was born and lived,
Taught, healed the sick, broke bread at his own house,
Then died, with Lazarus, for aught I know,
And yet was . . . what I said nor choose repeat,
And must have so avouched himself, in fact,
In hearing of this very Lazarus
Who saith – but why all this of what he saith?
Why write of trivial matters, things of price
Calling at every moment for remark?
I noticed on the margin of a pool
Blue-flowering borage, the Aleppo sort,
Aboundeth, very nitrous. It is strange!

Thy pardon for this long and tedious case,
Which, now that I review it, needs must seem
Unduly dwelt on, prolixly set forth!
Nor I myself discern in what is writ
Good cause for the peculiar interest
And awe indeed this man has touched me with.
Perhaps the journey's end, the weariness
Had wrought upon me first. I met him thus:
I crossed a ridge of short sharp broken hills
Like an old lion's cheek teeth. Out there came
A moon made like a face with certain spots
Multiform, manifold and menacing:
Then a wind rose behind me. So we met
In this old sleepy town at unaware,

The man and I. I send thee what is writ.
Regard it as a chance, a matter risked
To this ambiguous Syrian – he may lose,
Or steal, or give it thee with equal good.
Jerusalem's repose shall make amends
For time this letter wastes, thy time and mine;
Till when, once more thy pardon and farewell!

The very God! think, Abib; dost thou think?
So, the All-Great, were the All-Loving too –
So, through the thunder comes a human voice
Saying, 'O heart I made, a heart beats here!
Face, my hands fashioned, see it in myself!
Thou hast no power nor mayst conceive of mine,
But love I gave thee, with myself to love,
And thou must love me who have died for thee!'
The madman saith He said so: it is strange.

LADY LAZARUS

SYLVIA PLATH

I have done it again.
One year in every ten
I manage it——

A sort of walking miracle, my skin
Bright as a Nazi lampshade,
My right foot

A paperweight,
My face a featureless, fine
Jew linen.

Peel off the napkin
O my enemy.
Do I terrify?——

Soon, soon the flesh
The grave cave ate will be
At home on me

And I a smiling woman.
I am only thirty.
And like the cat I have nine times to die.

This is Number Three.
What a trash
To annihilate each decade.

What a million filaments.
The peanut-crunching crowd
Shoves in to see

Them unwrap me hand and foot——
The big strip tease.
Gentleman, ladies,

These are my hands,
My knees.
I may be skin and bone,

Nevertheless, I am the same, identical woman.
The first time it happened I was ten.
It was an accident.

The second time I meant
To last it out and not come back at all.
I rocked shut

As a seashell.
They had to call and call
And pick the worms off me like sticky pearls.

Dying
Is an art, like everything else.
I do it exceptionally well.

I do it so it feels like hell.
I do it so it feels real.
I guess you could say I've a call.

It's easy enough to do it in a cell.
It's easy enough to do it and stay put.
It's the theatrical

Comeback in broad day
To the same place, the same face, the same brute
Amused shout:

"A miracle!"
That knocks me out.
There is a charge

For the eyeing of my scars, there is a charge
For the hearing of my heart——
It really goes.

And there is a charge, a very large charge,
For a word or a touch
Or a bit of blood

Or a piece of my hair
So, so, Herr Doktor.
So, Herr Enemy.

I am your opus,
I am your valuable,
The pure gold baby

That melts to a shriek.
I turn and burn.
Do not think I underestimate your great concern.

Ash, ash—
You poke and stir.
Flesh, bone, there is nothing there——

A cake of soap,
A wedding ring,
A gold filling.

Herr God, Herr Lucifer,
Beware
Beware.

Out of the ash
I rise with my red hair
And I eat men like air.

LUKE 17:20–21 . . . And when he was demanded of the Pharisees, when the kingdom of God should come, he answered them and said, The kingdom of God cometh not with observation: Neither shall they say, Lo here! or, lo there! for, behold, the kingdom of God is within you.

A LOSS OF SOMETHING EVER FELT I–

EMILY DICKINSON

A loss of something ever felt I –
The first that I could recollect
Bereft I was – of what I knew not
Too young that any should suspect

A Mourner walked among the children
I notwithstanding went about
As one bemoaning a Dominion
Itself the only Prince cast out –

Elder, Today, a session wiser
And fainter, too, as Wiseness is –
I find myself still softly searching
For my Delinquent Palaces –

And a Suspicion, like a Finger
Touches my Forehead now and then
That I am looking oppositely
For the site of the Kingdom of Heaven –

LUKE 18:9–14 . . . And he spake this parable unto certain which trusted in themselves that they were righteous, and despised others: Two men went up into the temple to pray; the one a Pharisee, and the other a publican. The Pharisee stood and prayed thus with himself, God, I thank thee, that I am not as other men are, extortioners, unjust, adulterers, or even as this publican. I fast twice in the week, I give tithes of all that I possess. And the publican, standing afar off, would not lift up so much as his eyes unto heaven, but smote upon his breast, saying, God be merciful to me a sinner. I tell you, this man went down to his house justified rather than the other: for every one that exalteth himself shall be abased; and he that humbleth himself shall be exalted.

Two went up into the Temple to pray

RICHARD CRASHAW

Two went to pray? o rather say
One went to brag, th'other to pray:

One stands up close and treads on high,
Where th'other dares not send his eye.

One nearer to God's altar trod,
The other to the altar's God.

MATTHEW 19:29   **And every one that hath forsaken houses, or brethren,
or sisters, or father, or mother, or wife, or children, or lands, for my
name's sake, shall receive an hundredfold, and shall inherit everlasting
life.**

Upon the first sight of New-England

June 29, 1638

THOMAS TILLAM

Hail holy-land wherein our holy lord
Hath planted his most true and holy word
Hail happy people who have dispossessed
Your selves of friends, and means, to find some rest
For your poor wearied souls, oppressed of late
For Jesus-sake, with envy, spite, and hate
To you that blessed promise truly's given
Of sure reward, which you'll receive in heaven
Methinks I hear the Lamb of God thus speak
Come my dear little flock, who for my sake
Have left your country, dearest friends, and goods
And hazarded your lives o'th' raging floods
Possess this country; free from all annoy
Here I'll be with you, here you shall enjoy
My sabbaths, sacraments, my ministry
And ordinances in their purity
But yet beware of Satan's wily baits
He lurks amongst you, cunningly he waits

To catch you from me; live not then secure
But fight 'gainst sin, and let your lives be pure
Prepare to hear your sentence thus expressed
Come ye my servants of my father blessed

LUKE 13:23–24   Then said one unto him, Lord, are there few that be saved? And he said unto them, Strive to enter in at the strait gate: for many, I say unto you, will seek to enter in, and shall not be able.

To Heaven

Robert Herrick

Open thy gates
To him, who weeping waits
        And might come in,
But that held back by sin.
        Let mercy be
So kind, to set me free,
        And I will strait
Come in, or force the gate.

MARK 10:46   And they came to Jericho: and as he went out of Jericho with his disciples and a great number of people, blind Bartimaeus, the son of Timaeus, sat by the highway side begging.

Blind Bartimæus

Henry Wadsworth Longfellow

Blind Bartimæus at the gates
Of Jericho in darkness waits;
He hears the crowd—he hears a breath
Say, "It is Christ of Nazareth!"
And calls, in tones of agony,
"Jesus, have mercy now on me!"

The thronging multitudes increase;
Blind Bartimæus, hold thy peace!

But still, above the noisy crowd,
The beggar's cry is shrill and loud;
Until they say, "He calleth thee!"
"Fear not, arise, He calleth thee!"

Then saith the Christ, as silent stands
The crowd, "What wilt thou at my hands?"
And he replies, "O give me light!
Rabbi, restore the blind man's sight!"
And Jesus answers, "Go in peace,
Thy faith from blindness gives release!"

Ye that have eyes, yet cannot see,
In darkness and in misery,
Recall those mighty Voices Three,
"Jesus, have mercy now on me!
Fear not, arise, and go in peace!
Thy faith from blindness gives release!"

THE CRUCIFIED

LUKE 19:32–35   And they that were sent went their way, and found even as he had said unto them. And as they were loosing the colt, the owners thereof said unto them, Why loose ye the colt? And they said, The Lord hath need of him. And they brought him to Jesus: and they cast their garments upon the colt, and they set Jesus thereon.

A GLOZE UPON THIS TEXT, *Dominus iis opus habet.*

GEORGE GASCOIGNE

My reckless race is run, green youth and pride be past,
My riper mellowed years begin to follow on as fast.
My glancing looks are gone, which wonted were to pry,
In every gorgeous garish glass, that glistered in mine eye.
My sight is now so dim, it can behold none such,
No mirror but the merry mean, can please my fancy much.
And in that noble glass, I take delight to view,
The fashions of the wonted world, compared by the new.
For mark who list to look, each man is for himself.
And beats his brain to hoard and heap, this trash and worldly pelf.
Our hands are closed up, great gifts go not abroad,
Few men will lend a lock of hay, but for to gain a load.
Give Gave is a good man, what need we lash it out,
The world is wondrous fearful now, for danger bids men doubt.

And ask how chanceth this? or what means all this meed?
Forsooth the common answer is, because *the Lord hath need.*
A noble jest by guess, I find it in my glass,
The same freehold our savior Christ, conveyed to his ass.
A text to try the truth, and for this time full fit,
For where should we our lessons learn, but out of holy writ?
First mark our only God, which ruleth all the roost,
He sets aside all pomp and pride, wherein fond worldlings boast.
His train is not so great, as filthy Satan's band,
A smaller herd may serve to feed, at our great master's hand.
Next mark the heathens' gods, and by them shall we see,
They be not now so good fellows, as they were wont to be.
Jove, Mars, and Mercury, Dame Venus and the rest,
They banquet not as they were wont, they know it were not best.
So kings and princes both, have left their halls at large,
Their privy chambers cost enough, they cut off every charge.
And when an office falls, as chance sometimes may be,
First keep it close a year or twain, then geld it by the fee.
And give it out at last, but yet with this proviso,
(A bridle for a brainsick jade) *durante bene placito.*
Some think these ladders low, to climb aloft with speed:
Well let them creep at leisure then, for sure *the Lord hath need.*
Dukes, earls, and barons bold, have learned like lesson now,
They break up house and come to court, they live not by the plow.
Percase their rooms be scant, not like their stately bower,
A field bed in a corner couched, a pallet on the floor.
But what for that? no force, they make thereof no boast,
They feed them selves with delicates, and at the prince's cost.
And as for all their men, their pages and their swains,
They choke them up with chines of beef, to multiply their gains.
Themselves lie near to look, when any leaf doth fall,
Such crumbs were wont to feed poor grooms, but now ye Lords lick all.
And why? oh sir, because, both dukes and lords have need,
I mock not I, my text is true, believe it as your creed.
Our prelates and our priests, can tell this text with me,
They can hold fast their fattest farms, and let no lease go free.
They have both wife and child, which may not be forgot,
The scriptures say *the Lord hath need*, and therefore blame them not.
Then come a little lower, unto the country knight,
The squire and the gentleman, they leave the country quite,
Their halls were all too large, their tables were too long,
The clouted shoes came in so fast, they kept too great a throng,
And at the porter's lodge, where lubbers wont to feed,
The porter learns to answer now, hence hence *the Lord hath need.*

His guests came in too thick, their diet was too great,
Their horses eat up all the hay, which should have fed his neat:
Their teeth were far too fine, to feed on pork and souse,
Five flocks of sheep could scarce maintain good mutton for his house.
And when this count was cast, it was no biding here,
Unto the good town is he gone, to make his friends good cheer.
And welcome there that will, but shall I tell you how:
At his own dish he feedeth them, that is the fashion now,
Side boards be laid aside, the tables end is gone,
His cook shall make you noble cheer, but hostler hath he none.
The chargers now be changed, wherein he wont to eat,
An old fruit dish is big enough to hold a joint of meat.
A salad or a sauce, to taste your cates with all,
Some strange device to feed men's eyes, men's stomachs now be small.
And when the tenants come to pay their quarter's rent,
They bring some fowl at Midsummer, a dish of fish in Lent,
At Christmas a capon, at Michelmas a goose:
And somewhat else at Newyear's tide, for fear their lease fly loose.
Good reason by my troth, when gentlemen lack groats,
Let plowmen pinch it out for pence, and patch their russet coats:
For better farmers fast, than manor houses fall,
The Lord hath need, then says the text, bring old Ass colt and all.
Well lowest now at last, let see the country lout,
And mark how he doth swink and sweat, to bring this gear about:
His feastings be but few, cast whipstocks clout his shoon,
The wheaten loaf is locked up as soon as dinner's done:
And where he wont to keep a lubber, two or three,
Now hath he learned to keep no more, but Sim his son and he,
His wife and Maude his maid, a boy to pitch the cart,
And turn him up at Hollontide, to feel the winter smart:
Dame Alyson his wife doth know the price of meal,
Her bride cakes be not half so big as she was wont to steal:
She wears no silver hooks, she is content with worse,
Her pendants and her silver pins she putteth in her purse.
Thus learn I by my glass, that merry mean is best,
And he most wise that finds the mean, to keep himself at rest.
Perchance some open mouth will mutter now and then,
And at the market tell his mate, our landlords a zore man:
He racketh up our rents, and keeps the best in hand,
He makes a wondrous deal of good out of his own mesne land:
Yea let such pelters prate, saint *Needam* be their speed,
We need no text to answer them, but this, *the Lord hath need.*

Ever or never

JOHN 12:12–13   On the next day much people that were come to the feast, when they heard that Jesus was coming to Jerusalem, Took branches of palm trees, and went forth to meet him,

THE DONKEY

G. K. CHESTERTON

When fishes flew and forests walked
    And figs grew upon thorn,
Some moment when the moon was blood,
    Then surely I was born;

With monstrous head and sickening cry
    And ears like errant wings,
The devil's walking parody
    On all four-footed things.

The tattered outlaw of the earth,
    Of ancient crooked will;
Starve, scourge, deride me: I am dumb,
    I keep my secret still.

Fools! For I also had my hour;
    One far fierce hour and sweet:
There was a shout about my ears,
    And palms before my feet!

MATTHEW 21:9   And the multitudes that went before, and that followed, cried, saying, Hosanna to the son of David: Blessed is he that cometh in the name of the Lord; Hosanna in the highest.

HOSANNA

THOMAS TRAHERNE

No more shall walls, no more shall walls confine
That glorious soul which in my flesh doth shine:
    No more shall walls of clay or mud
      Nor ceilings made of wood,
    Nor crystal windows, bound my sight,

But rather shall admit delight.
The skies that seem to bound
My joys and treasures,
Of more endearing pleasures
Themselves become a ground:
While from the center to the utmost sphere
My goods are multiplièd everywhere.

The Deity, the Deity to me
Doth all things give, and make me clearly see
The moon and stars, the air and sun
Into my chamber come;
The seas and rivers hither flow,
Yea, here the trees of Eden grow,
The fowls and fishes stand,
Kings and their thrones,
As 'twere, at my command;
God's wealth, his holy ones,
The ages too, and angels all conspire:
While I, that I the center am, admire.

No more, no more shall clouds eclipse my treasures,
Nor viler shades obscure my highest pleasures;
No more shall earthen husks confine
My blessings which do shine
Within the skies, or else above:
Both worlds one Heaven made by love,
In common happy I
With angels walk
And there my joys espy;
With God himself I talk;
Wondering with ravishment all things to see
Such real joys, so truly mine, to be.

No more shall trunks and dishes be my store,
Nor ropes of pearl, nor chains of golden ore;
As if such beings yet were not,
They all shall be forgot.
No such in Eden did appear,
No such in Heaven: Heaven here
Would be, were those removed;
The sons of men
Live in Jerusalem,
Had they not baubles loved.

These clouds dispersed, the heavens clear I see.
Wealth new-invented, mine shall never be.

Transcendent objects doth my God provide,
In such convenient order all contrived,
    That all things in their proper place
      My soul doth best embrace,
    Extends its arms beyond the seas,
    Above the heavens its self can please,
      With God enthroned may reign;
        Like sprightly streams
      My thoughts on things remain,
      Even as some vital beams
They reach to, shine on, quicken things, and make
Them truly useful; while I *All* partake.

For me the world created was by love;
For me the skies, the seas, the sun do move;
    The Earth for me doth stable stand;
      For me each fruitful land
For me the very angels God made His
And my companions in bliss:
      His laws command all men
        That they love me,
      Under a penalty
      Severe, in case they miss:
His laws require his creatures all to praise
His Name, and when they do't be most my joys.

JOHN 12:14–15 **And Jesus, when he had found a young ass, sat thereon; as it is written, Fear not, daughter of Sion: behold, thy King cometh, sitting on an ass's colt.**

Upon the Ass that bore our Savior

Richard Crashaw

Hath only anger an omnipotence
    In eloquence?
Within the lips of love and joy doth dwell
    No miracle?

Why else had Balaam's ass a tongue to chide
                    His masters pride?
And thou (Heaven-burdened beast) hast ne'er a word
                    To praise thy Lord?
That he should find a tongue and vocal thunder,
                    Was a great wonder.
But o methinks 'tis a far greater one
                    That thou find'st none.

LUKE 19:39–40   And some of the Pharisees from among the multitude said unto him, Master, rebuke thy disciples. And he answered and said unto them, I tell you that, if these should hold their peace, the stones would immediately cry out.

A CHRISTMAS HYMN

RICHARD WILBUR

A stable-lamp is lighted
Whose glow shall wake the sky;
The stars shall bend their voices,
And every stone shall cry.
And every stone shall cry,
And straw like gold shall shine;
A barn shall harbor heaven,
A stall become a shrine.

This child through David's city
Shall ride in triumph by;
The palm shall strew its branches,
And every stone shall cry.
And every stone shall cry,
Though heavy, dull, and dumb,
And lie within the roadway
To pave his kingdom come.

Yet he shall be forsaken,
And yielded up to die;
The sky shall groan and darken,
And every stone shall cry.

And every stone shall cry
For stony hearts of men:
God's blood upon the spearhead,
God's love refused again.

But now, as at the ending,
The low is lifted high;
The stars shall bend their voices,
And every stone shall cry.
And every stone shall cry
In praises of the child
By whose descent among us
The worlds are reconciled.

MATTHEW 21:13   And said unto them, It is written, My house shall be called the house of prayer; but ye have made it a den of thieves.

THE HOUSE OF PRAYER

WILLIAM COWPER

Thy mansion is the christian's heart,
O Lord, thy dwelling-place secure!
Bid the unruly throng depart,
And leave the consecrated door.

Devoted as it is to thee,
A thievish swarm frequents the place;
They steal away my joys from me,
And rob my Savior of his praise.

There too a sharp designing trade
Sin, Satan, and the world maintain;
Nor cease to press me, and persuade,
To part with ease and purchase pain.

I know them, and I hate their din,
Am weary of the bustling crowd;
But while their voice is heard within,
I cannot serve thee as I would.

Oh! for the joy thy presence gives,
What peace shall reign when thou art here!
Thy presence makes this den of thieves,
A calm delightful house of prayer.

And if thou make thy temple shine,
Yet, self-abased, will I adore;
The gold and silver are not mine,
I give thee what was thine before.

MARK 11:19–21 **And when even was come, he went out of the city. And in the morning, as they passed by, they saw the fig tree dried up from the roots. And Peter calling to remembrance saith unto him, Master, behold, the fig tree which thou cursedst is withered away.**

A SMALL FIG TREE

DONALD HALL

I am dead, to be sure,
for thwarting Christ's pleasure,
Jesus Christ called Saviour.

I was a small fig tree.
Unjust it seems to me
that I should withered be.

If justice sits with God,
Christ is cruel Herod
and I by magic dead.

If there is no justice
where great Jehovah is,
I will the devil kiss.

MARK 12:29–31 **And Jesus answered him, The first of all the commandments is, Hear, O Israel; The Lord our God is one Lord: And thou shalt love the Lord thy God with all thy heart, and with all thy soul, and with all thy mind, and with all thy strength: this is the first commandment.**

And the second is like, namely this, Thou shalt love thy neighbour as thyself. There is none other commandment greater than these.

LOVE THY NEIGHBOUR

D. H. LAWRENCE

I love my neighbour
but
are these things my neighbours?
these two-legged things that walk and talk
and eat and cachinnate, and even seem to smile
seem to smile, ye gods!

Am I told that these things are my neighbours?

All I can say then is Nay! nay! nay! nay! nay!

MATTHEW 22:41–46   While the Pharisees were gathered together, Jesus asked them, Saying, What think ye of Christ? whose son is he? They say unto him, The son of David. He saith unto them, How then doth David in spirit call him Lord, saying, The LORD said unto my Lord, Sit thou on my right hand, till I make thine enemies thy footstool? If David then call him Lord, how is he his son? And no man was able to answer him a word, neither durst any man from that day forth ask him any more questions.

NEITHER DURST ANY MAN FROM THAT DAY
ASK HIM ANY MORE QUESTIONS

RICHARD CRASHAW

Midst all the dark and knotty snares,
Black wit or malice can or dares,
Thy glorious wisdom breaks the nets,
And treads with uncontrolled steps.
Thy quelled foes are not only now
Thy triumphs, but thy trophies too:
They, both at once thy conquests be,
And thy conquests' memory.
Stony amazement makes them stand
Waiting on thy victorious hand,
Like statues fixed to the fame

Of thy renown, and their own shame.
As if they only meant to breath,
To be the Life of their own Death.
'Twas time to hold their peace when they,
Had ne'er another word to say:
Yet is their silence unto thee,
The full sound of thy victory.
Their silence speaks aloud, and is
Thy well pronounced *Panegyris.*
While they speak nothing, they speak all
Their share, in thy memorial.
While thy speak nothing, they proclaim
Thee, with the shrillest trump of fame.
    To hold their peace is all the ways,
    These wretches have to speak thy praise.

MATTHEW 23:1–14   Then spake Jesus to the multitude, and to his disciples, Saying The scribes and the Pharisees sit in Moses' seat: All therefore whatsoever they bid you observe, that observe and do; but do not ye after their works: for they say, and do not.

On Worldly Prelates

Charles Wesley

Alas, for us, who need beware
Of men, that sit in Moses' chair,
    And should to heaven the people guide!
Men with the pomp of office clad,
In robes pontifical arrayed,
    But stained with avarice and pride:
They love to be preferred, adored
Affect the state and style of lord,
    And shine magnificently great:
They for precedency contend,
And on ambition's scale ascend
    Hard-laboring for the highest seat.

The church they call their proper care,
The temple of the Lord they are,
    Abusers of their legal power;

Greedy the church's goods to seize,
Their wealth they without end increase,
  And the poor widow's house devour.
O what a change they soon shall know,
When torn away by death, they go
  Reluctant from their splendid feasts,
Condemned in hottest flames to dwell,
And find the spacious courts of hell
  Paved with the skulls of Christian Priests!

MATTHEW 23:27–33 Woe unto you, scribes and Pharisees, hypocrites! for ye are like unto whited sepulchres, which indeed appear beautiful outward, but are within full of dead men's bones, and of all uncleanness. Even so ye also outwardly appear righteous unto men, but within ye are full of hypocrisy and iniquity. Woe unto you, scribes and Pharisees, hypocrites! because ye build the tombs of the prophets, and garnish the sepulchres of the righteous, And say, If we had been in the days of our fathers, we would not have been partakers with them in the blood of the prophets. Wherefore ye be witnesses unto yourselves, that ye are the children of them which killed the prophets. Fill ye up then the measure of your fathers. Ye serpents, ye generation of vipers, how can ye escape the damnation of hell?

THE PLACE OF THE DAMNED

BY J.S.D.D.D.S.P.D.

JONATHAN SWIFT

All folks who pretend to religion and grace,
Allow there's a Hell, but dispute of the place;
But if Hell may by logical rules be defined,
The place of the Damned,—I will tell you my mind.
  Wherever the Damned do chiefly abound,
Most certainly there is Hell to be found,
Damned Poets, Damned Critics, Damned Block-Heads, Damned
  Knaves,
Damned Senators bribed, Damned prostitute Slaves;
Damned Lawyers and Judges, Damned Lords and Damned Squires,
Damned Spies and Informers, Damned Friends and Damned Liars;
Damned Villains, corrupted in every station,
Damned Time-Serving Priests all over the nation;

And into the bargain, I'll readily give you,
Damned Ignorant Prelates, and Councillors Privy.
Then let us no longer by parsons be flammed,
For we know by these marks, the place of the Damned;
And Hell to be sure is at Paris or Rome,
How happy for us, that it is not at home.

**JOHN 12:35–36   Then Jesus said unto them, Yet a little while is the light
with you. Walk while ye have the light, lest darkness come upon you: for
he that walketh in darkness knoweth not whither he goeth. While ye have
light, believe in the light, that ye may be the children of light. These
things spake Jesus, and departed, and did hide himself from them.**

YET A LITTLE WHILE IS THE LIGHT WITH YOU

FRANCIS QUARLES

The day grows old, the low-pitched lamp hath made
        No less than treble shade,
And the descending damp doth now prepare
        T' uncurl bright Titan's hair;
Whose western wardrobe now begins t' unfold
        Her purples, fringed with gold;
To clothe his evening glory, when th' alarms
Of rest shall call to rest in restless Thetis' arms.

Nature now calls to supper, to refresh
        The spirits of all flesh;
The toiling plowman drives his thirsty teams,
        To taste the slippery streams:
The droiling swineherd knocks away, and feasts
        His hungry whining guests:
The boxbill ouzel, and the dappled thrush
Like hungry rivals meet at their beloved bush.

And now the cold autumnal dews are seen
        To cobweb every green;
And by the low-shorn rowans doth appear
        The fast-declining year:

The sapless branches doff their summer suits
    And wane their winter fruits;
And stormy blasts have forced the quaking trees
To wrap their trembling limbs in suits of mossy freeze.

Our wasted taper now hath brought her light
    To the next door to night;
Her spriteless flame grown great with snuff, doth turn
    Sad as her neighboring urn:
Her slender inch, that yet unspent remains,
    Lights but to further pains,
And in a silent language bids her guest
Prepare his weary limbs to take eternal rest.

Now carkful age hath pitched her painful plough
    Upon the furrowed brow;
And snowy blasts of discontented care
    Have blanched the falling hair:
Suspicious envy mixed with jealous spite
    Disturbs his weary night:
He threatens youth with age; and now alas,
He owns not what he is, but vaunts the man he was.

Gray-hairs, peruse thy days, and let thy past
    Read lectures to thy last:
Those hasty wings that hurried them away
    Will give these days no day:
The constant wheels of Nature scorn to tire
    Until her works expire:
That blast that nipped thy youth, will ruin thee;
The hand that shook the branch will quickly strike the tree.

MARK 13:1–2 And as he went out of the temple, one of his disciples saith unto him, Master, see what manner of stones and what buildings are here! And Jesus answering said unto him, Seest thou these great buildings? there shall not be left one stone upon another, that shall not be thrown down.

from THE DESTRUCTION OF JERUSALEM

THOMAS DELONEY

Christ's Prophecy of the destruction of this City
and how it came to pass accordingly within Forty years after.

Our Savior Christ tracing the bordering hills,
When he on this fair city cast his eye
The tears along his royal cheeks distills:
Mourning for their destruction drawing nigh.
     O *Jerusalem Jerusalem* (quoth hee)
     My heart bewails thy great calamity.

The time shall come and near it is at hand,
When furious foes shall trench thee round about,
And batter down thy towers that stately stand,
All thy strong holds within thee and without:
     Thy golden buildings shall they quite confound,
     And make thee equal with the lowly ground.

O woe to them that then gives suck (he says)
And lulls their infants on their tender knees,
More woe to them that be with child those days,
Wherein shall be such extreme miseries:
     Thou mightst have shunned these plagues, hadst thou been wise,
     Which now for sin is hidden from thy eyes.

This dreadful prophecy spoken by our Lord,
The stubborn people naught at all regarded,
Whose adamantine hearts did still accord,
To follow sin, which was with shame rewarded:
     They flouted him for telling of this story,
     And crucified in spite the Lord of glory.

Reproachfully they fleered in his face,
That wept for them in tender true compassion,
They wrought his death and did him all disgrace,
That sought their life, and wailed their desolation:
     Their hardened hearts believed not what was said,
     Until they saw the siege about them laid.

Full forty years after Christ's passion,
Did these proud people live in peace and rest,

Whose wanton eyes seeing no alteration,
Christ's words of truth, they turned to a jest:
    But when they thought themselves the surest of all,
    Lo then began their never raised fall.

Their mounting minds that towered past their strength
Scorning subjection to the Roman state,
In boiling hatred loathed their lords at length,
Despised the Emperor with a deadly hate:
    Rejecting his authority each hour,
    Sought to expel the pride of foreign power.

Which foul contempt the Emperor's wrath inflamed,
Mighty Vespasian hot revenge did threat,
But all in vain they would not be reclaimed;
Relying on their strength and courage great:
    And hereupon began the deadly jar,
    And after followed bloody woeful war.

MARK 13:33   **Take ye heed, watch and pray: for ye know not when the time is.**

TAKE YE HEED, WATCH AND PRAY

JONES VERY

Come suddenly, O Lord, or slowly come,
    I wait Thy will, Thy servant ready is;
Thou hast prepared Thy follower a home,
    The heaven in which Thou dwellest, too, is his.

Come in the morn, at noon, or midnight deep,
    Come, for Thy servant still doth watch and pray
E'en when the world around is sunk in sleep,
    I wake, and long to see Thy glorious day.

I would not fix the time, the day, nor hour,
    When Thou with all Thine angels shalt appear;
When in Thy kingdom Thou shalt come with power,
    E'en now, perhaps, the promised day is near!

For though, in slumber deep, the world may lie,
　　And e'en Thy church forget Thy great command;
Still year by year Thy coming draweth nigh,
　　And in its power Thy kingdom is at hand.

Not in some future world alone 't will be,
　　Beyond the grave, beyond the bounds of Time;
But on the earth Thy glory we shall see,
　　And share Thy triumph, peaceful, pure, sublime.

Lord! help me that I faint not, weary grow,
　　Nor at Thy coming slumber too, and sleep;
For Thou hast promised, and full well I know,
　　Thou wilt to us Thy word of promise keep.

MARK 13:34–37 **For the Son of Man is as a man taking a far journey, who left his house, and gave authority to his servants, and to every man his work, and commanded the porter to watch. Watch ye therefore: for ye know not when the master of the house cometh, at even, or at midnight, or at the cockcrowing, or in the morning: Lest coming suddenly he find you sleeping. And what I say unto you I say unto all, Watch.**

THE LAMP

HENRY VAUGHAN

'Tis dead night round about: Horror doth creep
And move on with the shades; stars nod, and sleep,
And through the dark air spin a fiery thread
Such as doth gild the lazy glow-worm's bed.
　　Yet, burnst thou here, a full day; while I spend
My rest in cares, and to the dark world lend
These flames, as thou dost thine to me, I watch
That hour, which must thy life, and mine dispatch;
But still thou dost out-go me, I can see
Met in thy flames, all acts of piety;
Thy light, is charity; thy heat, is zeal;
And thy aspiring, active fires reveal
Devotion still on wing; Then, thou dost weep
Still as thou burnst, and the warm droppings creep
To measure out thy length, as if thou'dst know

What stock, and how much time were left thee now;
Nor dost thou spend one tear in vain, for still
As thou dissolvst to them, and they distill,
They're stored up in the socket, where they lie,
When all is spent, thy last, and sure supply,
And such is true repentance, every breath
We spend in sighs, is treasure after death;
Only, one point escapes thee; That thy oil
Is still out with thy flame, and so both fail;
But whensoe'er I'm out, both shall be in,
And where thou mad'st an end, there I'll begin.

MATTHEW 24:37–25:12 But as the days of Noe were, so shall also the coming of the Son of man be. . . . Then shall the kingdom of heaven be likened unto ten virgins, which took their lamps, and went forth to meet the bridegroom. And five of them were wise, and five were foolish. They that were foolish took their lamps, and took no oil with them: But the wise took oil in their vessels with their lamps. While the bridegroom tarried, they all slumbered and slept. And at midnight there was a cry made, Behold, the bridegroom cometh; go ye out to meet him. Then all those virgins arose, and trimmed their lamps. And the foolish said unto the wise, Give us of your oil; for our lamps are gone out. But the wise answered, saying, Not so; lest there be not enough for us and you: but go ye rather to them that sell, and buy for yourselves. And while they went to buy, the bridegroom came; and they that were ready went in with him to the marriage: and the door was shut. Afterward came also the other virgins, saying, Lord, Lord, open to us. But he answered and said, Verily I say unto you, I know you not.

SONNET: LADY, THAT IN THE PRIME

JOHN MILTON

Lady that in the prime of earliest youth,
  Wisely hast shunned the broad way and the green,
  And with those few art eminently seen
  That labor up the hill of heavenly truth,
The better part with Mary and with Ruth
  Chosen thou hast; and they that overween,
  And at thy growing virtues fret their spleen,
  No anger find in thee, but pity and ruth.

Thy care is fixed and zealously attends
  To fill thy odorous lamp with deeds of light,
  And hope that reaps not shame. Therefore be sure
Thou, when the Bridegroom with his feastful friends
  Passes to bliss at the mid-hour of night,
  Hast gained thy entrance, virgin wise and pure.

MATTHEW 25:13–26 Watch therefore, for ye know neither the day nor the hour wherein the Son of man cometh. For the kingdom of heaven is as a man travelling into a far country, who called his own servants, and delivered unto them his goods. And unto one he gave five talents, to another two, and to another one; to every man according to his several ability; and straightway took his journey. Then he that had received the five talents went and traded with the same, and made them other five talents. And likewise he that had received two, he also gained other two. But he that had received one went and digged in the earth, and hid his lord's money. After a long time the lord of those servants cometh, and reckoneth with them. And so he that had received five talents came and brought other five talents, saying, Lord, thou deliveredst unto me five talents: behold, I have gained beside them five talents more. His lord said unto him, Well done, thou good and faithful servant: thou hast been faithful over a few things, I will make thee ruler over many things: enter thou into the joy of thy lord. He also that had received two talents came and said, Lord, thou deliveredst unto me two talents: behold, I have gained two other talents beside them. His lord said unto him, Well done, good and faithful servant; thou hast been faithful over a few things, I will make thee ruler over many things: enter thou into the joy of thy lord. Then he which had received the one talent came and said, Lord, I knew thee that thou art an hard man, reaping where thou hast not sown, and gathering where thou hast not strawed: And I was afraid, and went and hid thy talent in the earth: lo, there thou hast that is thine. His lord answered and said unto him, Thou wicked and slothful servant, thou knewest that I reap where I sowed not, and gather where I have not strawed:

SONNET: WHEN I CONSIDER

JOHN MILTON

When I consider how my light is spent,
  Ere half my days, in this dark world and wide,
  And that one talent which is death to hide,
  Lodged with me useless, though my soul more bent

To serve therewith my maker, and present
    My true account, lest he returning chide,
    "Doth God exact day-labor, light denied,"
    I fondly ask; But patience to prevent
That murmur, soon replies, "God doth not need
    Either man's work or his own gifts; who best
    Bear his mild yoke, they serve him best; his state
Is kingly. Thousands at his bidding speed
    And post o'er land and ocean without rest:
    They also serve who only stand and wait."

MATTHEW 25:27–29   **Thou oughtest therefore to have put my money to the exchangers, and then at my coming I should have received mine own with usury. Take therefore the talent from him, and give it unto him which hath ten talents. For unto every one that hath shall be given, and he shall have abundance: but from him that hath not shall be taken away even that which he hath.**

On the Death of Dr. Robert Levet

Samuel Johnson

Condemned to hope's delusive mine,
    As on we toil from day to day,
By sudden blasts, or slow decline,
    Our social comforts drop away.

Well tried through many a varying year,
    See Levet to the grave descend;
Officious, innocent, sincere,
    Of every friendless name the friend.

Yet still he fills affection's eye,
    Obscurely wise, and coarsely kind;
Nor, lettered arrogance, deny
    Thy praise to merit unrefined.

When fainting nature called for aid,
    And hovering death prepared the blow
His vigorous remedy displayed
    The power of art without the show.

In misery's darkest caverns known,
    His useful care was ever nigh,
Where hopeless anguish poured his groan,
    And lonely want retired to die.

No summons mocked by chill delay,
    No petty gain disdained by pride,
The modest wants of every day
    The toil of every day supplied.

His virtues walked their narrow round,
    Nor made a pause, nor left a void;
And sure th' Eternal Master found
    The single talent well employed.

The busy day, the peaceful night,
    Unfelt, uncounted, glided by;
His frame was firm, his powers were bright,
    Though now his eightieth year was nigh.

Then with no throbbing fiery pain,
    No cold gradations of decay,
Death broke at once the vital chain,
    And forced his soul the nearest way.

MATTHEW 25:30–33 And cast ye the unprofitable servant into outer darkness: there shall be weeping and gnashing of teeth. When the Son of man shall come in his glory, and all the holy angels with him, then shall he sit upon the throne of his glory: And before him shall be gathered all nations: and he shall separate them one from another, as a shepherd divideth his sheep from the goats: And he shall set the sheep on his right hand, but the goats on the left.

THE TRIBUNAL

CHRIS WALLACE-CRABBE

After death, suppose we were judged by animals:
the harmless pigs and sheep,
each throat still bearing its long scar,
their eyes not meeting ours,
stand firm behind the bar of judgement

where scales flaunt their brightness
weighing us up.
'The sheep from the goats,' they would say
and laugh to themselves at the joke.

'The goats from the sheep, indeed,
that's a good one.'
Our critics chuckle away at their beastly job
separating friend from friend
and nice girl from her bloke,
sifting us finally, neatly out
with a good horse-laugh at our pride
which came to this in the end.

MATTHEW 26:26 And as they were eating, Jesus took bread, and blessed it, and brake it, and gave it to the disciples, and said, Take, eat; this is my body.

THIS BREAD I BREAK

DYLAN THOMAS

This bread I break was once the oat,
This wine upon a foreign tree
Plunged in its fruit;
Man in the day or wind at night
Laid the crops low, broke the grape's joy.

Once in this wine the summer blood
Knocked in the flesh that decked the vine,
Once in this bread
The oat was merry in the wind;
Man broke the sun, pulled the wind down.

This flesh you break, this blood you let
Make desolation in the vein,
Were oat and grape
Born of the sensual root and sap;
My wine you drink, my bread you snap.

JOHN 13:1–9 Now before the feast of the passover, when Jesus knew that his hour was come that he should depart out of this world unto the Father, having loved his own which were in the world, he loved them unto the end. And supper being ended, the devil having now put into the heart of Judas Iscariot, Simon's son, to betray him; Jesus knowing that the Father had given all things into his hands, and that he was come from God, and went to God; He riseth from supper, and laid aside his garments; and took a towel, and girded himself. After that he poureth water into a bason, and began to wash the disciples' feet, and to wipe them with the towel wherewith he was girded. Then cometh he to Simon Peter: and Peter saith unto him, Lord, dost thou wash my feet? Jesus answered and said unto him, What I do thou knowest not now; but thou shalt know hereafter. Peter saith unto him, Thou shalt never wash my feet. Jesus answered him, If I wash thee not, thou hast no part with me. Simon Peter saith unto him, Lord, not my feet only, but also my hands and my head.

St. Peter

Christina Georgina Rossetti

St Peter once: 'Lord, dost thou wash my feet?'—
    Much more I say: Lord, dost thou stand and I
    At my closed heart more rugged than a rock,
Bolted and barred, for thy soft touch unmeet,
Nor garnished nor in any wise made sweet?
    Owls roost within and dancing satyrs mock.
    Lord, I have heard the crowing of the cock
And have not wept: ah, Lord, thou knowest it.
Yet still I hear thee knocking, still I hear:
    'Open to me, look on me eye to eye,
That I may wring thy heart and make it whole;
And teach thee love because I hold thee dear
    And sup with thee in gladness soul with soul,
And sup with thee in glory by and by.'

JOHN 13:10–14 Jesus saith to him, He that is washed needeth not save to wash his feet, but is clean every whit: and ye are clean, but not all. For he knew who should betray him; therefore said he, Ye are not all clean. So after he had washed their feet, and had taken his garments, and was set down again, he said unto them, Know ye what I have done to you? Ye call me Master and Lord: and ye say well; for so I am. If I then, your Lord and Master, have washed your feet; ye also ought to wash one another's feet.

The Foot-Washing

A. R. Ammons

Now you have come,
the roads
humbling your feet with dust:

I will wash your feet
with springwater
and silver care:

the odor of your feet
is newly earthen,
honeysuckled

bloodwork in blue
raisures over the white
skinny anklebone:

if I have wronged you
cleanse me with the falling
water of forgiveness.

And woman, your flat feet
yellow, gray with dust,
your orphaned udders flat,

lift your dress
up to your knees
and I will wash your feet:

feel the serenity
cool as cool springwater
and hard to find:

if I have failed to know
the grief in your gone time,
forgive me wakened now.

JOHN 13:22–29   Then the disciples looked one on another, doubting of
whom he spake. Now there was leaning on Jesus' bosom one of his disciples, whom Jesus loved. Simon Peter therefore beckoned to him, that he

should ask who it should be of whom he spake. He then lying on Jesus'
breast saith unto him, Lord, who is it? Jesus answered, He it is, to whom
I shall give a sop, when I have dipped it. And when he had dipped the sop,
he gave it to Judas Iscariot, the son of Simon. And after the sop Satan
entered into him. Then said Jesus unto him, That thou doest, do quickly.
Now no man at the table knew for what intent he spake this unto him. For
some of them thought, because Judas had the bag, that Jesus had said
unto him, Buy those things that we have need of against the feast; or, that
he should give something to the poor.

THE BOTTLE

RALPH KNEVET

Thou bearst the bottle, I the bag (oh Lord)
Which daily I do carry at my back,
So stuffed with sin, that ready 'tis to crack:
I have no unfeigned nectar for thy gourd,
Mine eyes will no such precious drink afford:
Yet both my heart, and eyes, are deserts dry,
Even Lybian sands, where serpents crawl and fly.

Yea the two extreme zones took up my heart,
For unto good, as cold as ice, I am;
But unto evil, like an Ætna flame:
I paralytical seem in each part,
One utterly deprived of strength, and art,
When I should execute my master's will,
But active am as fire, t'accomplish ill.

I bear the bag like Judas: (Lord) do Thou,
From this unwieldy burden me dismiss,
And this bag empty, which so heavy is:
Then shall my tears into thy bottle flow;
Not only tears, which do from sorrow grow,
But cooler drops, which do from joy distill,
And to the brim, these shall thy bottle fill.

MATTHEW 26:35 Verily I say unto thee, That this night, before the
cock crow, thou shalt deny me thrice. Peter said unto him, Though I
should die with thee, yet will I not deny thee. Likewise also said all the
disciples.

DREAM SONG 55

JOHN BERRYMAN

Peter's not friendly. He gives me sideways looks.
The architecture is far from reassuring.
I feel uneasy.
A pity,—the interview began so well:
I mentioned fiendish things, he waved them away
and sloshed out a martini

strangely needed. We spoke of indifferent matters—
God's health, the vague hell of the Congo,
John's energy,
anti-matter matter. I felt fine.
Then a change came backward. A chill fell.
Talk slackened,

died, and he began to give me sideways looks.
'Christ,' I thought 'what now?' and would have askt for another
but didn't dare.
I feel my application failing. It's growing dark,
some other sound is overcoming. His last words are:
'We betrayed me.'

**JOHN 15:12–13 This is my commandment, That ye love one another, as
I have loved you. Greater love hath no man than this, that a man lay
down his life for his friends.**

AT A CALVARY NEAR THE ANCRE

WILFRED OWEN

One ever hangs where shelled roads part.
    In this war He too lost a limb,
But His disciples hide apart;
    And now the Soldiers bear with Him.

Near Golgotha strolls many a priest,
    And in their faces there is pride
That they were flesh-marked by the Beast
    By whom the gentle Christ's denied.

The scribes on all the people shove
And bawl allegiance to the state,
But they who love the greater love
Lay down their life; they do not hate.

JOHN 15:24 **If I had not done among them the works which none other man did, they had not had sin: but now have they both seen and hated both me and my Father.**

MEDITATION FIFTY-SIX

Second Series

EDWARD TAYLOR

Should I with silver tools delve through the hill
Of Cordilera for rich thoughts, that I
My Lord, might weave with an angelic skill
A damask web of velvet verse, thereby
To deck thy works up, all my web would run
To rags and jags: so snick-snarled to the thrum.

Thine are so rich: within, without refined:
No work like thine. No fruits so sweet that grow
On th' trees of righteousness of angel kind,
And saints, whose limbs reeved with them bow down low.
Should I search o'er the nutmeg gardens shine,
Its fruits in flourish are but skegs to thine.

The clove, when in its white-greened blossoms shoots,
Some call the pleasantest scent the world doth show,
None eye e'er saw, nor nose e'er smelt such fruits,
My Lord, as thine, thou Tree of Life in'ts blow.
Thou Rose of Sharon, valley's lily true,
Thy fruits most sweet and glorious ever grew.

Thou art a tree of perfect nature trim,
Whose golden lining is of perfect grace,
Perfumed with Deity unto the brim,
Whose fruits, of the perfection, grow, of grace.
Thy buds, thy blossoms, and thy fruits adorn
Thyself and works, more shining than the morn.

Art, nature's ape, hath many brave things done:
    As th' Pyramids, the Lake of Moeris vast,
The pensile orchards built in Babylon,
      Psammitich's labyrinth, (arts cramping task)
      Archimedes his engines made for war,
      Rome's golden house, Titus his theater.

The clock of Strasburgh, Dresden's table-sight,
    Regsamont's fly of steel about that flew,
Turrian's wooden sparrows in a flight,
      And th' artificial man Aquinas slew,
      Mark Scaliota's lock and key and chain
      Drawn by a flea, in our Queen Betty's reign.

Might but my pen in nature's inventory
    Its progress make, 't might make such things to jump,
All which are but invention's vents or glory:
      Wit's wantonings, and fancies' frolics plump:
      Within whose maws lies buried times, and treasures,
      Embalmed up in thick daubed sinful pleasures.

Nature doth better work than art, yet thine
    Out vie both works of nature and of art.
Nature's perfection and the perfect shine
      Of grace attend thy deed in every part.
      A thought, a word, and work of thine, will kill
      Sin, Satan, and the Curse: and Law fulfill.

Thou art the Tree of Life in Paradise,
    Whose lively branches are with clusters hung
Of lovely fruits, and flowers more sweet than spice.
      Bend down to us, and do outshine the sun.
      Delightful unto God, do man rejoice
      The pleasantest fruits in all God's Paradise.

Lord, feed mine eyes then with thy doings rare,
    And fat my heart with these ripe fruits thou bearst;
Adorn my life well with thy works; make fair
      My person with apparel thou prepar'st.
      My boughs shall loaded be with fruits that spring
      Up from thy works, while to thy praise I sing.

JOHN 17:13–26   And now come I to thee; and these things I speak in the world, that they might have my joy fulfilled in themselves. I have given them thy word; and the world hath hated them, because they are not of the world, even as I am not of the world. I pray not that thou shouldest take them out of the world, but that thou shouldest keep them from the evil. They are not of the world, even as I am not of the world. Sanctify them through thy truth: thy word is truth. As thou hast sent me into the world, even so have I also sent them into the world. And for their sakes I sanctify myself, that they also might be sanctified through the truth. Neither pray I for these alone, but for them also which shall believe on me through their word; That they all may be one; as thou, Father, art in me, and I in thee, that they also may be one in us: that the world may believe that thou hast sent me. And the glory which thou gavest me I have given them; that they may be one, even as we are one: I in them, and thou in me, that they may be made perfect in one; and that the world may know that thou hast sent me, and hast loved them, as thou hast loved me. Father, I will that they also, whom thou hast given me, be with me where I am; that they may behold my glory, which thou hast given me: for thou lovedst me before the foundation of the world. O righteous Father, the world hath not known thee: but I have known thee, and these have known that thou hast sent me. And I have declared unto them thy name, and will declare it: that the love wherewith thou hast loved me may be in them, and I in them.

I HEARD CHRIST SING

HUGH MACDIARMID

I heard Christ sing quhile roond him dar
The twal' disciples in a ring,
And here's the dance I saw them dance,
And the sang I heard him sing.

Ane, twa, three, and their right feet heich,
Fower, five, six, and doon wi' them,
Seevin, aucht, nine, and up wi' the left,
Ten, eleevin, twal', and doon they came.

And Christ he stude i' the middle there,
And was the thirteenth man,
And sang the bonniest sang that e'er
Was sung sin' Time began.

And Christ he was the centrepiece,
Wi' three on ilka side.

My hert stude still, and the sun stude still
But still the dancers plied.

O I wot it was a maypole,
As a man micht seek to see,
Wi' the twal' disciples dancin' roon',
While Christ sang like a lintie.

The twal' points o' the compass
Made jubilee roon' and roon',
And but for the click-click-clack o' the feet,
Christ's sang was the only soon'.

And there was nae time that could be tauld
Frae a clock wha's haun's stude still,
Quhile the figures a' gaed bizzin roon'
—I wot it was God's will.

    Wersh is the vinegar,
    And the sword is sharp.
    Wi' the tremblin' sunbeams
    Again for my harp,
    I sing to Thee.

    The spirit of man
    Is a bird in a cage,
    That beats on the bars
    Wi' a goodly rage,
    And fain 'ud be free.

    Twice-caged it is,
    In life and in death,
    Yet it claps its wings
    Wi' a restless faith,
    And sings as it may.

    Then fill my mouth
    Wi' the needfu' words,
    That sall turn its wings,
    Into whirlin swords,
    When it hears what I say.

    Hearken my cry,
    And let me speak,
    That when it hears

It sall lift its beak,
And sing as it should.

Sweet is the song
That is lost its throat,
And fain 'ud I hear
Its openin' note
As I hang on the rood.

And when I rise
Again from the dead,
Let me, I pray,
Be accompanied
By the spirit of man.

Yea, as I rise
From earth to Heaven
Fain 'ud I know
That Thou hast given
Consent to my plan—

Even as the stars
Sang here at my birth,
Let Heaven hear
The song of the earth
Then, for my sake.

The thorns are black
And callous the nails.
As a bird its bars
My hand assails
Harpstrings . . . that break!

O I wot they'll lead the warl' a dance
And I wot the sang sall be,
As a white sword loupin' at the hert
O' a' eternity.

Judas and Christ stude face to face,
And mair I couldna' see,
But I wot he did God's will wha made
Siccar o' Calvary.

LUKE 22:39   And he came out, and went, as he was wont, to the mount of Olives; and his disciples also followed him.

A BALLAD OF TREES AND THE MASTER

SIDNEY LANIER

Into the woods my Master went,
Clean forspent, forspent.
Into the woods my Master came,
Forspent with love and shame.
But the olives they were not blind to Him,
The little gray leaves were kind to Him:
The thorn-tree had a mind to Him
When into the woods He came.

Out of the woods my Master went,
And he was well content.
Out of the woods my Master came,
Content with death and shame.
When Death and Shame would woo Him last,
From under the trees they drew Him last:
'Twas on a tree they slew Him—last
When out of the woods He came.

MATTHEW 26:56   But all this was done, that the scriptures of the prophets might be fulfilled. Then all the disciples forsook him, and fled.

THE TWELVE

ALLEN TATE

There by some wrinkled stones round a leafless tree
With beards askew, their eyes dull and wild
Twelve ragged men, the council of charity
Wandering the face of the earth a fatherless child,
Kneel, at their infidelity aghast,
For where was it, somewhere in Syria
Or Palestine when the streams went red,
The victor of Rome, his arms outspread,

His eyes cold with his inhuman ecstasy,
Cried the last word, the accursed last
Of the forsaken that seared the western heart
With the fire of the wind, the thick and the fast
Whirl of the damned in the heavenly storm:
Now the wind's empty and the twelve living dead
Look round them for that promontory Form
Whose mercy flashed from the sheet lightning's head;
But the twelve lie in the sand by the dry rock
Seeing nothing—the sand, the tree, rocks
Without number—and turn away the face
To the mind's briefer and more desert place.

MATTHEW 26:73–74 And after a while came unto him they that stood by, and said to Peter, Surely thou also art one of them; for thy speech bewrayeth thee. Then began he to curse and to swear, saying, I know not the man. And immediately the cock crew.

ROOSTERS

ELIZABETH BISHOP

At four o'clock
in the gun-metal blue dark
we hear the first crow of the first cock

just below
the gun-metal blue window
and immediately there is an echo

off in the distance,
then one from the backyard fence,
then one, with horrible insistence,

grates like a wet match
from the broccoli patch,
flares, and all over town begins to catch.

Cries galore
come from the water-closet door,
the dropping-plastered henhouse floor,

where in the blue blur
their rustling wives admire,
the roosters brace their cruel feet and glare

with stupid eyes
while from their beaks there rise
the uncontrolled, traditional cries.

Deep from protruding chests
in green-gold medals dressed,
planned to command and terrorize the rest,

the many wives
who lead hens' lives
of being courted and despised;

deep from raw throats
a senseless order floats
all over town. A rooster gloats

over our beds
from rusty iron sheds
and fences made from old bedsteads,

over our churches
where the tin rooster perches,
over our little wooden northern houses,

making sallies
from all the muddy alleys,
marking out maps like Rand McNally's:

glass-headed pins,
oil-golds and copper greens,
anthracite blues, alizarins,

each one an active
displacement in perspective;
each screaming, "This is where I live!"

Each screaming
"Get up! Stop dreaming!"
Roosters, what are you projecting?

You, whom the Greeks elected
to shoot at on a post, who struggled
when sacrificed, you whom they labeled

"Very combative . . ."
what right have you to give
commands and tell us how to live,

cry "Here!" and "Here!"
and wake us here where are
unwanted love, conceit and war?

The crown of red
set on your little head
is charged with all your fighting blood.

Yes, that excrescence
makes a most virile presence,
plus all that vulgar beauty of iridescence.

Now in mid-air
by twos they fight each other.
Down comes a first flame-feather,

and one is flying,
with raging heroism defying
even the sensation of dying.

And one has fallen,
but still above the town
his torn-out, bloodied feathers drift down;

and what he sung
no matter. He is flung
on the gray ash-heap, lies in dung

with his dead wives
with open, bloody eyes,
while those metallic feathers oxidize.

St. Peter's sin
was worse than that of Magdalen
whose sin was of the flesh alone;

of spirit, Peter's,
falling, beneath the flares,
among the "servants and officers."

Old holy sculpture
could set it all together
in one small scene, past and future:

Christ stands amazed,
Peter, two fingers raised
to surprised lips, both as if dazed.

But in between
a little cock is seen
carved on a dim column in the travertine,

explained by *gallus canit;*
flet Petrus underneath it.
There is inescapable hope,

yes, and there Peter's tears
run down our chanticleer's
sides and gem his spurs.

Tear-encrusted thick
as a medieval relic
he waits. Poor Peter, heart-sick,

still cannot guess
those cock-a-doodles yet might bless,
his dreadful rooster come to mean forgiveness,

a new weathervane
on basilica and barn,
and that outside the Lateran

there would always be
a bronze cock on a porphyry
pillar so the people and the Pope might see

that even the Prince
of the Apostles long since
had been forgiven, and to convince

all the assembly
that "Deny deny deny"
is not all the roosters cry.

In the morning
a low light is floating
in the backyard, and gilding

from underneath
the broccoli, leaf by leaf;
how could the night have come to grief?

gilding the tiny
floating swallow's belly
and lines of pink cloud in the sky,

the day's preamble
like wandering lines in marble.
The cocks are now almost inaudible

The sun climbs in,
following "to see the end,"
faithful as enemy, or friend.

MATTHEW 27:3–4   Then Judas, which had betrayed him, when he saw
that he was condemned, repented himself, and brought again the thirty
pieces of silver to the chief priests and elders, Saying, I have sinned in
that I have betrayed the innocent blood. And they said, What is that to
us? see thou to that.

THE HOUND OF HEAVEN

FRANCIS THOMPSON

I fled Him, down the nights and down the days;
    I fled Him, down the arches of the years;
I fled Him, down the labyrinthine ways
        Of my own mind; and in the midst of tears
I hid from Him, and under running laughter.
            Up vistaed hopes I sped;
            And shot, precipitated,

Adown titanic glooms of chasméd fears,
From those strong feet that followed, followed after.
But with unhurrying chase,
And unperturbéd pace,
Deliberate speed, majestic instancy,
They beat—and a voice beat
More instant than the feet—
"All things betray thee, who betrayest Me."

I pleaded, outlaw-wise,
By many a hearted casement, curtained red,
Trellised with intertwining charities
(For, though I knew His love Who followéd,
Yet was I sore adread
Lest, having Him, I must have naught beside);
But, if one little casement parted wide,
The gust of His approach would clash it to.
Fear wist not to evade, as Love wist to pursue.
Across the margent of the world I fled,
And troubled the gold gateways of the stars,
Smiting for shelter on their clangéd bars;
Fretted to dulcet jars
And silvern chatter the pale ports o' the moon.
I said to dawn, Be sudden; to eve, Be soon;
With thy young skiey blossoms heap me over
From this tremendous lover!
Float thy vague veil about me, lest He see!
I tempted all His servitors, but to find
My own betrayal in their constancy,
In faith to Him their fickleness to me,
Their traitorous trueness, and their loyal deceit.
To all swift things for swiftness did I sue;
Clung to the whistling mane of every wind,
But whether they swept, smoothly fleet,
The long savannahs of the blue;
Or whether thunder-driven
They clanged his chariot 'thwart a heaven
Plashy with flying lightnings round the spurn o' their feet:—
Fear wist not to evade as Love wist to pursue—
Still with unhurrying chase,
And unperturbéd pace,
Deliberate speed, majestic instancy,
Came on the following feet,
And a voice above their beat—
"Naught shelters thee, who wilt not shelter Me."

I sought no more that after which I strayed
       In face of man or maid;
But still within the little children's eyes
       Seems something, something that replies;
They at least are for me, surely for me!
I turned me to them very wistfully;
But, just as their young eyes grew sudden fair
       With dawning answers there,
Their angel plucked them from me by the hair.
"Come then, ye other children, Nature's—share
With me" (said I) "your delicate fellowship;
       Let me greet you lip to lip,
       Let me twine with you caresses,
          Wantoning
       With our Lady-Mother's vagrant tresses,
          Banqueting
       With her in her wind-walled palace,
       Underneath her azured daïs,
       Quaffing as your taintless way is,
          From a chalice
Lucent-weeping out of the dayspring.
          So it was done:
I in their delicate fellowship was one—
Drew the bolts of Nature's secrecies.
I knew all the swift importings
       On the willful face of skies;
       I knew how the clouds arise
       Spuméd of the wild sea-snortings;
          All that's born or dies
       Rose and drooped with—made them shapers
Of mine own moods, or wailful or divine—
       With them joyed and was bereaven.
       I was heavy with the even,
       When she lit her glimmering tapers
       Round the day's dead sanctities.
       I laughed in the morning's eyes.
I triumphed and I saddened with all weather,
       Heaven and I wept together,
And its sweet tears were salt with mortal mine;
Against the red throb of its sunset-heart
       I laid my own to beat,
       And share commingling heat;
But not by that, by that, was eased my human smart.
In vain my tears were wet on Heaven's grey cheek.

For ah! we know not what each other says,
>   These things and I; in sound *I* speak—
Their sound is but their stir, they speak by silences.
Nature, poor stepdame, cannot slake my drouth;
>   Let her, if she would owe me,
Drop yon blue bosom-veil of sky, and show me
>   The breasts o' her tenderness:
Never did any milk of hers once bless
>   My thirsting mouth.
>   Nigh and nigh draws the chase,
>   With unperturbéd pace,
>   Deliberate speed, majestic instancy;
>   And past those noiséd feet
>   A voice comes yet more fleet—
"Lo! naught contents thee, who content'st not Me."

Naked I wait Thy love's uplifted stroke!
My harness piece by piece Thou hast hewn from me,
>   And smitten me to my knee;
>   I am defenceless utterly.
>   I slept, methinks, and woke,
And, slowly gazing, find me stripped in sleep.
In the rash lustihead of my young powers,
>   I shook the pillaring hours
And pulled my life upon me; grimed with smears,
I stand amid the dust o' the mounded years—
My mangled youth lies dead beneath the heap.
My days have crackled and gone up in smoke,
Have puffed and burst as sun-starts on a stream.
>   Yea, faileth now even dream
The dreamer, and the lute the lutanist;
Even the linkéd fantasies, in whose blossomy twist
I swung the earth a trinket at my wrist,
Are yielding; cords of all too weak account
For earth with heavy griefs so overplussed.
>   Ah! is Thy love indeed
A weed, albeit an amaranthine weed,
Suffering no flowers except its own to mount?
>   Ah! must—
>   Designer infinite!—
Ah! must Thou char the wood ere Thou canst limn
My freshness spent its wavering shower i' the dust;
And now my heart is as a broken fount,

Wherein tear-droppings stagnate, spilt down ever
          From the dank thoughts that shiver
Upon the sighful branches of my mind.
          Such is; what is to be?
The pulp so bitter, how shall taste the rind?
I dimly guess what Time in mists confounds;
Yet ever and anon a trumpet sounds
From the hid battlements of Eternity;
Those shaken mists a space unsettle, then
Round the half-glimpséd turrets slowly wash again.
          But not ere him who summoneth
          I first have seen, enwound
With glooming robes purpureal, cypress-crowned;
His name I know, and what his trumpet saith.
Whether man's heart or life it be which yields
          Thee harvest, must Thy harvest fields
          Be dunged with rotten death?

          Now of that long pursuit
          Comes on at hand the bruit;
          That voice is round me like a bursting sea:
          "And is thy earth so marred,
          Shattered in shard on shard?
          Lo, all things fly thee, for thou fliest Me!
          Strange, piteous, futile thing!
Wherefore should any set thee love apart?
Seeing none but I makes much of naught"
          (He said)
"And human love needs human meriting:
          How hast thou merited—
Of all man's clotted clay the dingiest clot?
          Alack, thou knowest not
How little worthy of any love thou art!
Whom wilt thou find to love ignoble thee
          Save Me, save only Me?
All which I took from thee I did but take,
          Not for thy harms,
But just that thou might'st seek it in My arms.
          All which thy child's mistake
Fancies as lost, I have stored for thee at home;
          Rise, clasp My hand, and come!"
          Halts by me that footfall:
          Is my gloom, after all,

> Shade of His hand, outstretched caressingly?
> "Ah, fondest, blindest, weakest,
> I am He whom thou seekest!
> Thou dravest love from thee, who dravest Me."

MATTHEW 27:5   And he cast down the pieces of silver in the temple, and departed, and went and hanged himself.

JUDAS

VASSAR MILLER

Always I lay upon the brink of love,
Impotent, waiting till the waters stirred,
And no one healed my weakness with a word;
For no one healed me who lacked words to prove
My heart, which, when the kiss of Mary wove
His shroud, my tongueless anguish spurred
To cool dissent, and which, each time I heard
John whisper to Him, moaned, but could not move.

While Peter deeply drowsed within love's deep
I cramped upon its margin, glad to share
The sop Christ gave me, yet its bitter bite
Dried up my ducts. Praise Peter, who could weep
His sin away, but never see me where
I hang, huge teardrop on the cheek of night.

MARK 15:2–3   And Pilate asked him, Art thou the King of the Jews? And he answering said unto them, Thou sayest it. And the chief priests accused him of many things: but he answered nothing.

AND HE ANSWERED THEM NOTHING

RICHARD CRASHAW

O Mighty *Nothing!* unto thee,
Nothing, we owe all things that be.

God spake once when he all things made,
He saved all when he *Nothing* said.
The world was made of *Nothing* then;
'Tis made by *Nothing* now again.

JOHN 19:1–5   Then Pilate therefore took Jesus, and scourged him. And the soldiers platted a crown of thorns, and put it on his head, and they put on him a purple robe, And said, Hail, King of the Jews! and they smote him with their hands. Pilate therefore went forth again, and saith unto them, Behold, I bring him forth to you, that ye may know that I find no fault in him. Then came Jesus forth, wearing the crown of thorns, and the purple robe. And Pilate saith unto them, Behold the man!

ECCE HOMO

DAVID GASCOYNE

Whose is this horrifying face,
This putrid flesh, discoloured, flayed,
Fed on by flies, scorched by the sun?
Whose are these hollow red-filmed eyes
And thorn-spiked head and spear-struck side?
Behold the Man: He is Man's Son.

Forget the legend, tear the decent veil
That cowardice or interest devised
To make their mortal enemy a friend,
To hide the bitter truth all His wounds tell,
Lest the great scandal be no more disguised:
He is in agony till the world's end,

And we must never sleep during that time!
He is suspended on the cross-tree now
And we are onlookers at the crime,
Callous contemporaries of the slow
Torture of God. Here is the hill
Made ghastly by His spattered blood

Whereon He hangs and suffers still:
See, the centurions wear riding-boots,
Black shirts and badges and peaked caps,

Greet one another with raised-arm salutes;
They have cold eyes, unsmiling lips;
Yet these His brothers know not what they do.

And on his either side hang dead
A labourer and a factory hand,
Or one is maybe a lynched Jew
And one a Negro or a Red,
Coolie or Ethiopian, Irishman,
Spaniard or German democrat.

Behind His rolling head the sky
Glares like a fiery cataract
Red with the murders of two thousand years
Committed in His name and by
Crusaders, Christian warriors
Defending faith and property.

Amid the plain beneath His transfixed hands,
Exuding darkness as indelible
As guilty stains, fanned by funereal
And lurid airs, besieged by drifting sands
And clefted landslides our about-to-be
Bombed and abandoned cities stand.

He who wept for Jerusalem
Now sees His prophecy extend
Across the greatest cities of the world,
A guilty panic reason cannot stem
Rising to raze them all as He foretold;
And He must watch this drama to the end.

Though often named, He is unknown
To the dark kingdoms at His feet
Where everything disparages His words,
And each man bears the common guilt alone
And goes blindfolded to his fate,
And fear and greed are sovereign lords.

The turning point of history
Must come. Yet the complacent and the proud
And who exploit and kill, may be denied—
Christ of Revolution and of Poetry—
The resurrection and the life
Wrought by your spirit's blood.

Involved in their own sophistry
The black priest and the upright man
Faced by subversive truth shall be struck dumb,
Christ of Revolution and of Poetry,
While the rejected and condemned become
Agents of the divine.

Not from a monstrance silver-wrought
But from the tree of human pain
Redeem our sterile misery,
Christ of Revolution and of Poetry,
That man's long journey through the night
May not have been in vain.

MATTHEW 27:29 And when they had platted a crown of thorns, they put it upon his head, and a reed in his right hand: and they bowed the knee before him, and mocked him, saying, Hail, King of the Jews!

ONE CROWN THAT NO ONE SEEKS

EMILY DICKINSON

One crown that no one seeks
And yet the highest head
Its isolation coveted
Its stigma deified

While Pontius Pilate lives
In whatsoever hell
That coronation pierces him
He recollects it well.

MATTHEW 27:32 And as they came out, they found a man of Cyrene, Simon by name: him they compelled to bear his cross.

SIMON THE CYRENIAN SPEAKS

COUNTEE CULLEN

He never spoke a word to me,
    And yet He called my name;

He never gave a sign to me,
    And yet I knew he came.

At first I said, "I will not bear
    His cross upon my back;
He only seeks to place it there
    Because my skin is black."

But He was dying for a dream,
    And He was very meek.
And in His eyes there shone a gleam
    Men journey far to seek.

It was Himself my pity bought,
    I did for Christ alone
What all of Rome could not have wrought
    With bruise of lash or stone.

LUKE 23:27 **And there followed him a great company of people, and of women, which also bewailed and lamented him.**

HIS SAVIOR'S WORDS, GOING TO THE CROSS

ROBERT HERRICK

Have, have ye no regard, all ye
Who pass this way, to pity me,
Who am a man of misery!

A man both bruised, and broke, and one
Who suffers not here for mine own,
But for my friends transgression!

Ah! Sion's Daughters, do not fear
The Cross, the Cords, the Nails, the Spear,
The Myrrh, the Gall, the Vinegar:

For Christ, your loving Savior, hath
Drunk up the wine of God's fierce wrath;
Only, there's left a little froth,

Less for to taste, than for to show,
What bitter cups had been your due,
Had He not drank them up for you.

MATTHEW 27:33   And when they were come unto a place called Golgotha, that is to say, a place of a skull,

GOLGOTHA

ANDREW LANSDOWN

Finally, one arrives at the place
Of the skull because there is nowhere
Else to go. And there before the face
Of bone one pauses to despair.

The culmination of all evil
Is displayed before one's eyes:
Man's heart conspired with the devil
And cared little for disguise.

MATTHEW 27:34   They gave him vinegar to drink mingled with gall: and when he had tasted thereof, he would not drink.

EARLY LYNCHING

CARL SANDBURG

Two Christs were at Golgotha.
One took the vinegar, another looked on.
One was on the cross, another in the mob.
One had the nails in his hands, another the stiff fingers holding a
        hammer driving nails.
There were many more Christs at Golgotha, many more thief pals,
        many many more in the mob howling the Judean equivalent of "Kill
        Him! Kill Him!"
The Christ they killed, the Christ they didn't kill, those were the two at
        Golgotha.

Pity, pity, the bones of these broken ankles.
Pity, pity, the slimp of these broken wrists.
The mother's arms are strong to the last.
She holds him and counts the heart drips.

The smell of the slums was on him,
Wrongs of the slums lit his eyes.
Songs of the slums wove in his voice,
The haters of the slums hated his slum heart.

The leaves of a mountain tree,
Leaves with a spinning star shook in them,
Rocks with a song of water, water, over them,
Hawks with an eye for death any time, any time,
The smell and the sway of these were on his sleeves, were in his nostrils,
     his words.

The slum man they killed, the mountain man lives on.

CANTICLE FOR GOOD FRIDAY

GEOFFREY HILL

The cross staggered him. At the cliff-top
Thomas, beneath its burden, stood
While the dulled wood
Spat on the stones each drop
Of deliberate blood.

A clamping, cold-figured day
Thomas (not transfigured) stamped, crouched.
Watched
Smelt vinegar and blood. He,
As yet unsearched, unscratched,

And suffered to remain
At such near distance
(A slight miracle might cleanse
His brain
Of all attachments, claw-roots of sense)

In unaccountable darkness moved away,
The strange flesh untouched, carrion-sustenance
Of staunchest love, choicest defiance,
Creation's issue congealing (and one woman's).

MARK 15:25   And it was the third hour, and they crucified him.

CRUCIFYING

JOHN DONNE

By miracles exceeding power of man,
He faith in some, envy in some begat,
For, what weak spirits admire, ambitious, hate;
In both affections many to him ran,
But Oh! the worst are most, they will and can,
Alas, and do, unto the immaculate,
Whose creature fate is, now prescribe a fate,
Measuring self-life's infinity to a span,
Nay to an inch. Lo, where condemned he
Bears his own cross, with pain, yet by and by
When it bears him, he must bear more and die.
Now thou art lifted up, draw me to thee,
And at thy death giving such liberal dole,
Moist, with one drop of thy blood, my dry soul.

JOHN 19:19–22   And Pilate wrote a title, and put it on the cross. And the writing was JESUS OF NAZARETH THE KING OF THE JEWS. This title then read many of the Jews: for the place where Jesus was crucified was nigh to the city: and it was written in Hebrew, and Greek, and Latin. Then said the chief priests of the Jews to Pilate, Write not, The King of the Jews; but that he said, I am King of the Jews. Pilate answered, What I have written I have written.

On the Inscription over the head of Christ on the Cross

Henry Colman

Anacrostica. Joh: 19. Cap: v: 19.

I am that Savior that vouchsafed to die
                For sin-sick souls, behold me it is I
Even unto my self that was content to be
                Scourged, buffeted, despised, bethorned for yE
Suffered the death o'th'Cross, suffered no less
                Than all my Father's wrath that happineS
Unto the world might come, and peace ensue
                To those that would repent, to heaven be trU
Suffer I did such wounds, such killing groans
                As would have moved to ruth the senseless stoneS

O let it pity then move in you so
                As may constrain you to repentance gO
Ferret remorse, and that enjoin you doff
                Sin's damned garment, and all vice put ofF

No more let sin abound, but may contrition
                For me, and for your sins make good remissioN
All else in vain I suffer, and Abba
                In vain you cry not having learned your A
Zeal is but cold in you, howe'er the blaze
                May make such as your self with wonder gaZ
All your devotion is not worth a flea
                Unless it have more than an outward pleA
Repent then quickly that my sepulcher
                May bury all your sins, and may you eveR
Ever remember him that did deny
                No pains, no torments, that might remediE
The misery of you; for my sake set
                Light by all pleasure, and let no man freT
Himself with the world's business, I am nigh
                To all that love me, will assist from higH

Trust not in worldly wealth for cankered rust
                    Will soon consume it, but among the jusT
Heap up your treasure, for in heaven nor moth,
                    Nor thief, nor can consume, nor pilfer dotH
Earth, and its choicest pleasures are but dross
                    And rob the soul of bliss, then fly such lossE

Knit, and ingrafted into me, the rack
                    Ye need not fear, though whips furrow your bacK
I will be with you still, pity your cry
                    Wipe off your tears, make your tormentors dI
Not death it self shall hurt you, I upon
                    Your heads (in spite of death) will set the CrowN
Glory shall be your reward, every dreg
                    Of frail mortality, and pollution's raG

Off you shall purged be, and you shall know
                    Eternal pleasures, 'stead of these belO
Fear not then quickly for my sake to doff
                    Sin's damned garment, and all vice put ofF

Then shall you welcome be, for I was sent
                    Only to save such as are penitenT
Heal such as seek for ease, bestow new birth
                    On the repentant and obedient eartH
Even for such, and none but such I give
                    Freely my life that they may ever livE

I will revenge my blood on those that fly
                    Far from my love, for ever let them frI
Even in the flames of hell, and may a curse
                    Fall on them greater if there may be worsE
Well I am come to heal, and as I bow
                    For sinners, so I would have them to voW
Eternally themselves to me, and keep
                    Those vows most constant, then though now I weepE
Sorrow shall be exiled, and I no less
                    Happy in death, than you in happineS

JOHN 19:23–24   **Then the soldiers, when they had crucified Jesus, took his garments, and made four parts, to every soldier a part; and also his coat: now the coat was without seam, woven from the top throughout. They said therefore among themselves, Let us not rend it, but cast lots for it, whose it shall be: that the scripture might be fulfilled, which saith, They parted my raiment among them, and for my vesture they did cast lots. These things therefore the soldiers did.**

On the Cards, and Dice

Sir Walter Raleigh

Before the sixth day of the next new year,
Strange wonders in this kingdom shall appear.
Four kings shall be assembled in this Isle,
Where they shall keep great tumult for a while.
Many men then shall have an end of crosses,
And many likewise shall sustain great losses.
Many that now full joyful are and glad,
Shall at that time be sorrowful and sad.
Full many a Christian's heart shall quake for fear,
The dreadful sound of trump when he shall hear.
Dead bones shall then be tumbled up and down,
In every city, and in every town.
By day or night this tumult shall not cease,
Until an herald shall proclaim a peace,
An herald strange, the like was never born
Whose very beard is flesh, and mouth is horn.[*]

JOHN 19:24   These things therefore the soldiers did.   LUKE 23:35   And the people stood beholding.

[*] Raleigh's poem paraphrases DANIEL 7:17–23.

THIS CROSS-TREE HERE

ROBERT HERRICK

This   Cross-Tree   here
Doth   Jesus   bear,
Who   sweetened   first,
The   Death accursed.

Here all things ready are, make haste, make haste away;
For, long this work will be, and very short this day.
Why then, go on to act: Here's wonders to be done,
Before the last least sand of thy ninth hour be run;
Or ere dark clouds do dull, or dead the mid-day's sun.

Act when thou wilt,
Blood will be spilt;
Pure balm, that shall
Bring health to all.
Why then, begin
To pour first in
Some drops of wine,
In stead of brine,
To search the wound,
So long unsound:
And, when that's done,
Let oil, next, run,
To cure the sore
Sin made before.
And O! Dear Christ,
E'en as thou di'st,
Look down, and see
Us weep for Thee.
And tho' (Love knows)
Thy dreadful woes
We cannot ease;
Yet do thou please,
Who mercy art,
T' accept each heart,
That gladly would
Help, if it could.
Mean while, let me,
Beneath this Tree,
This honor have,
To make my grave.

MATTHEW 27:39–40 **And they that passed by reviled him, wagging their heads, And saying, Thou that destroyest the temple, and buildest it in three days, save thyself. If thou be the Son of God, come down from the cross.**

THE CARPENTER'S SON

A. E. HOUSMAN

'Here the hangman stops his cart:
Now the best of friends must part.
Fare you well, for ill fare I:
Live, lads, and I will die.

'Oh, at home had I but stayed
'Prenticed to my father's trade,
Had I stuck to plane and adze,
I had not been lost, my lads.

'Then I might have built perhaps
Gallows-trees for other chaps,
Never dangled on my own,
Had I but left ill alone.

'Now, you see, they hang me high,
And the people passing by
Stop to shake their fists and curse;
So 'tis come from ill to worse.

'Here hang I, and right and left
Two poor fellows hang for theft:
All the same's the luck we prove,
Though the midmost hangs for love.

'Comrades all, that stand and gaze,
Walk henceforth in other ways;
See my neck and save your own:
Comrades all, leave ill alone.

'Make some day a decent end,
Shrewder fellows than your friend.
Fare you well, for ill fare I:
Live, lads, and I will die.'

LUKE 23:39–43   And one of the malefactors which were hanged railed on
him, saying, If thou be Christ, save thyself and us. But the other answering rebuked him, saying, Dost not thou fear God, seeing thou art in the
same condemnation? And we indeed justly; for we receive the due reward
of our deeds: but this man hath done nothing amiss. And he said unto
Jesus, Lord, remember me when thou comest into thy kingdom. And
Jesus said unto him, Verily I say unto thee, To day shalt thou be with me
in paradise.

"REMEMBER ME" IMPLORED THE THIEF!

EMILY DICKINSON

"Remember me" implored the Thief!
Oh Hospitality!
My Guest "Today in Paradise"
I give thee guaranty.

That Courtesy will fair remain
When the Delight is Dust
With which we cite this mightiest case
Of compensated Trust.

Of all we are allowed to hope
But Affidavit stands
That this was due where most we fear
Be unexpected Friends.

MATTHEW 27:48–49   And straightway one of them ran, and took a
spunge, and filled it with vinegar, and put it on a reed, and gave him to
drink. The rest said, Let be, let us see whether Elias will come to save
him.

CHRIST'S PASSION

ABRAHAM COWLEY

Enough, my Muse, of earthly things,
And inspirations but of wind,
Take up thy lute, and to it bind
Loud and everlasting strings;

And on 'em play and to 'em sing,
The happy mournful stories,
The lamentable glories,
Of the great Crucified King.
Mountainous heap of wonders! which dost rise
Till earth thou joinest with the skies!
Too large at bottom, and at top too high,
To be half seen by mortal eye.
How shall I grasp this boundless thing?
What shall I play? what shall I sing?
I'll sing the mighty riddle of mysterious love,
Which neither wretched men below, nor blessed spirits above
With all their comments can explain;
How all the Whole World's Life to die did not disdain.

I'll sing the searchless depths of the compassion divine,
The depths unfathomed yet
By reasons plummet, and the line of wit,
Too light the plummet, and too short the line,
How the Eternal Father did bestow
His own Eternal Son as ransom for his Foe,
I'll sing aloud, that all the world may hear,
The triumph of the buried conquerer.
How hell was by its prisoner captive led,
And the great slayer Death slain by the dead.

Me thinks I hear of murdered men the voice,
Mixed with the murderers' confused noise,
Sound from the top of Calvary;
My greedy eyes fly up the hill, and see
Who 'tis hangs there midmost of the three;
Oh how unlike the others he!
Look how he bends head with blessings from the Tree!
His gracious hands ne'er stretched but to do good,
Are nailed to the infamous wood:
And sinful Man does fondly bind
The arms, which he extends t'embrace all human kind.

Unhappy, canst thou stand by, and see
        All this as patient, as he?
        Since he thy sins does bear,
        Make thou his sufferings thine own,
        And weep, and sigh, and groan,
        And beat thy breast, and tear,
        Thy garments, and thy hair,
        And let thy grief, and let thy love
        Through all thy bleeding bowels move.
Dost thou not see thy Prince in purple clad all o'er,
     Not purple brought from the Sidonian shore,
        But made at home with richer gore?
Dost thou not see the roses, which adorn
        The thorny garland, by him worn?
        Dost thou not see the livid traces
        Of the sharp scourges rude embraces?
        If yet thou feelest not the smart
        Of thorns and scourges in thy heart,
        If that be yet not crucified,
Look on his hands, look on his feet, look on his side.

Open, Oh! open wide the fountains of thine eyes,
        And let 'em call
    Their stock of moisture forth, where e'er it lies,
        For this will ask it all.
        'Twould all (alas) too little be,
        Though thy salt tears came from a sea:
        Canst thou deny him this, when he
Has opened all his vital springs for thee?
Take heed; for by his sides mysterious flood
        May well be understood,
That he will still require some waters to his blood.

LUKE 23:46 And when Jesus had cried with a loud voice, he said, Father, into thy hands I commend my spirit: and having said thus, he gave up the ghost.

HYMN

ALEXANDER POPE

Thou art my God, sole object of my love;
Not for hope of endless joys above;

Not for the fear of endless pains below,
Which they who love thee must not undergo.
For me, and such as me, thou deignst to bear
An ignominious cross, the nails, the spear:
A thorny crown transpierced thy sacred brow,
While bloody sweats from every member flow.
For me in tortures thou resignst thy breath,
Embraced me on the cross, and saved me by death.
And can these sufferings fail my heart to move?
Such as then was, and is, thy love to me,
Such is, and shall be still, my love to thee—
To thee, Redeemer! mercy's sacred spring!
My God, my Father, Maker, and my King!

MATTHEW 27:51–53 And, behold, the veil of the temple was rent in twain from the top to the bottom; and the earth did quake, and the rocks rent; And the graves were opened; and many bodies of the saints which slept arose, And came out of the graves after his resurrection, and went into the holy city, and appeared unto many.

On the strange apparitions at Christ's death

Henry Colman

What strange unusual prodigy is here,
The height of day and yet no sun appear,
Nothing but darkness to be seen? what fright
Hath caused the day thus to be turned to night?
Sure th'old Chaos, or the Day of Doom,
Heaven, and earth's fabric to dissolve is come,
For so graves open, and in every street
The dead are seen to stand upon their feet,
Nor is the Temple safe, its vale in sunder
Is rent, by a prodigious clap of thunder,
And all disordered is: God's Son is dead.
No marvel then, the Sun doth hide its head.
Black death hath seized upon the God of light,
'Tis equal then day mourn in sable night.
Nor is it fit the graves should peopled be
With dead, when earth receives eternity.
The Temple's vale must rent in pieces be

Lest there should want a winding-sheet for thee.
Nor is 't a wonder that all things do lie
Disordered, and are sick when God can die.

LUKE 23:48   **And all the people that came together to that sight, beholding the things which were done, smote their breasts, and returned.**

THE CRUCIFIXION OF OUR BLESSED LORD

CHRISTOPHER SMART

The world is but a sorry scene,
Untrue, unhallowed, and unclean,
    And hardly worth a man;
The fiend upon the land prevails,
And o'er the floods in triumph sails,
    Do goodness all she can.

How many works for such a day?
How glorious? that ye scourge and slay
    Ye blind, by blinder led;
All hearts at once devising bad,
Hands, mouths against their Maker mad,
    With Satan at the head—

Are these the race of saints professed,
That for authorities contest,
    And question and debate?
Yet in so foul a deed rebel,
Beyond example, even from hell,
    To match its barbarous hate.

Behold the man! the tyrant said,
As in the robes of scoff arrayed,
    And crowned with thorns he stood;
And feigning will to let him go
He chose Barabbas, open foe
    Of human kind and good.

And was it He, whose voice divine,
Could change the water into wine,
    And first his power averred;

Which fed in Galilea's groves
The fainting thousands with the loaves
    And fishes of his word!

And was it He, whose mandate freed
The palsied suppliant, and in deed
    The sabbath-day revered;
Which bade the thankful dumb proclaim
The Lord omnipotent by name,
    Till loosened deafness heard!

And was it He, whose hand was such,
As lightened blindness at a touch,
    And made the lepers whole;
Could to the dropsy health afford,
And to the lunatic restored
    Serenity of soul!

The daughter that so long a term
By Satan's bonds had been infirm,
    Was rescued and received;
Yea, with the foes of faith and hope
His matchless charity could cope,
    When Malchus was relieved.

The woman in his garment's hem
Conceived a prevalence to stem
    The sources of her pain;
He calls—the dead from death arise,
And as their legions he defies
    The devils descend again.

His irresistable command
Conveyed the vessel to the land,
    As instant as his thought;
He caused the tempest to forget
Its rage, and into Peter's net,
    The wondrous capture brought.

The roarings of the billows cease
To hear the gospel of his peace
    Upon the still profound—
He walked the waves—and at his will,
The fish to pay th' exactor's bill
    To Judah's coast was bound.

The withered hand he saw and cured,
And health from general ail secured
      Where'er disease was rife;
And was omniscient to tell
The woman at the patriarch's well
      The story of her life.

But never since the world was known,
One so stupendous as his own,
      And rich of vast event;
From love adored, as soon as seen,
Had not his hated message been
      To bid the world repent.

Ah, still desirous of a king,
To give voluptuous vice its swing
      With passions like a brute;
By Jesus Christ came truth and grace,
But none indulgence, pension, place,
      The slaves of self to suit.

The Lord on Gabbatha they doom,
Before the delegate of Rome,
      Deserted and exposed—
They might have thought on Israel's God,
Which on the sapphire pavement trod,
      To seventy seers disclosed.

They might have thought upon the loss
Of Eden, and the dreadful cross
      That happened by a tree;
Ere yet with cursed throats they shout
To bring the dire event about,
      Though prophesied to be.

O God, the bonds of sin enlarge,
Lay not this horror to our charge,
      But as we fast and weep,
Pour out the streams of love profuse,
Let all the powers of mercy loose,
      While wrath and vengeance sleep.

MARK 15:40   **There were also women looking on afar off: among whom was Mary Magdalene, and Mary the mother of James the less and of Joses, and Salome;**

GOOD FRIDAY, 1613. RIDING WESTWARD

JOHN DONNE

Let man's soul be a sphere, and then, in this,
The intelligence that moves, devotion is,
And as the other spheres, by being grown
Subject to foreign motions, lose their own,
And being by others hurried every day,
Scarce in a year their natural form obey;
Pleasure or business, so, our souls admit
For their first mover, and are whirled by it.
Hence is't, that I am carried towards the West
This day, when my soul's form bends towards the East.
There I should see a sun, by rising, set,
And by that setting endless day beget:
But that Christ on this Cross did rise and fall,
Sin had eternally benighted all.
Yet dare I almost be glad I do not see
That spectacle, of too much weight for me.
Who sees God's face, that is self life, must die;
What a death were it then to see God die?
It made his own lieutenant nature, shrink;
It made his footstool crack, and the sun wink.
Could I behold those hands which span the poles,
And tune all spheres at once, pierced with those holes?
Could I behold that endless height which is
Zenith to us, and our Antipodes,
Humbled below us? Or that blood which is
The seat of all our souls, if not of His,
Make dirt of dust, or that flesh which was worn
By God, for his apparel, ragged and torn?
If on these things I durst not look, durst I
Upon his miserable mother cast mine eye,
Who was God's partner here, and furnished thus
Half of that sacrifice which ransomed us?
Though these things, as I ride, be from mine eye,
They are present yet unto my memory,
For that looks towards them; and thou lookst towards me,
O Savior, as thou hangst upon the tree.

I turn my back to Thee but to receive
Corrections, till thy mercies bid thee leave.
O think me worth thine anger; punish me;
Burn off my rusts, and my deformity,
Restore thine Image so much, by thy grace
That thou mayst know me, and I'll turn my face.

GOOD FRIDAY

CHRISTINA GEORGINA ROSSETTI

Am I a stone and not a sheep
    That I can stand, O Christ, beneath thy Cross,
    To number drop by drop thy blood's slow loss,
And yet not weep?

Not so those women loved
    Who with exceeding grief lamented thee;
    Not so fallen Peter weeping bitterly;
Not so the thief was moved;

Not so the sun and moon
    Which hid their faces in a starless sky,
    A horror of great darkness at broad noon—
I, only I.

Yet give not o'er,
    But seek thy sheep, true Shepherd of the flock;
    Greater than Moses, turn and look once more
And smite a rock.

JOHN 19:31–34 **The Jews therefore, because it was the preparation, that the bodies should not remain upon the cross on the sabbath day, (for that sabbath day was an high day,) besought Pilate that their legs might be broken, and that they might be taken away. Then came the soldiers, and brake the legs of the first, and of the other which was crucified with him. But when they came to Jesus, and saw that he was dead already, they brake not his legs: But one of the soldiers with a spear pierced his side, and forthwith came there out blood and water.**

'O, MY HEART IS WOE'

ANONYMOUS

'O, my heart is woe!' Mary she said so,
'For to see my dear son die, and sons I have no mo.'

'When that my sweet son was thirty winter old,
Then the traitor Judas waxed very bold:
For thirty plates of money his master he had sold.
But when I it wist, Lord, my heart was cold!

'Upon Shere Thursday then truly it was
On my son's death that Judas did compass.
Many were the false Jews that followed him by trace;
And there before them all he kissed my son's face.

'My son before Pilate brought was he,
And Peter said three times he knew him not, pardee.
Pilate said unto the Jews: 'What say ye?'
Then they cried with one voice: 'Crucify!'

'On Good Friday, at the mount of Calvary,
My son was done on the cross, nailed with nails three.
Of all the friends that he had, never one could he see
But gentle John the Evangelist, that still stood him by.

'Though I were sorrowful, no man have at it wonder;
For huge was the earthquake, horrible was the thunder.
I looked on my sweet son on the cross that I stood under;
Then came Longeus with a spear and cleft his heart in sunder.'

JOHN 19:35–37 And he that saw it bare record, and his record is true:
and he knoweth that he saith true, that ye might believe. For these things
were done, that the scripture should be fulfilled, A bone of him shall not
be broken. And again another scripture saith, They shall look on him
whom they pierced.

ODE ON THE PASSION

THOMAS WARTON THE ELDER

In sable clad, Urania come,
    Dictate a pity-moving lay,
Such as may paint a dying God,
    And all his wounds and pangs display:
What time the blissful saints above,
Struck with his sufferings and his love,
    Began to heave unusual sighs;
Each seraph tore his palmy-crown,
Each threw his harp or trumpet down,
    And grief a while usurped the skies.

But hark! I hear triumphant shouts,
    Of Jews that dare insult their Lord;
At whose approach pale sickness fled,
    Madness and storms obeyed his Word:
This gracious benefactor see,
Stretched out in anguish on the tree!
    How deep the traces of the scourge!
        His bending head how pale!
    The spear has gored his snowy side,
        His tender feet the nail!

Sudden the graves their dreary depths disclose,
    Low, dreadful sounds run murmuring through the air;
The shrouded bodies from the charnels rose,
    And gliding by, their trembling kindred fear;
The twisting rocks their sulphurous beds displayed,
    Earth's deep foundations to the center shook;
The sun was covered with a ten-fold shade,
    Unable on Messiah's pains to look:
Remotest lands the dreadful portents felt,
And, for a time, in wonder, fear, and darkness dwelt.

Beneath, lo! Mary weeping stands,
    In tears most pitifully fair,

And beats the breast, where Christ had hung,
    And tears her long dishevelled hair—
    "Where can I lay my mournful head?
    "My son, my king, my God is dead!
        "To gloomy deserts let me go,
    "Among the horrid rocks and woods,
    "The caves, and pensive-falling floods,
        "Indulging solitude and woe!"—

And shall not vile, ungrateful man,
    Bear in these griefs a wretched part,
Roll in the dust, and beat his face,
    Bleed in his bowels, and his heart?
While stern repentance near him stands,
Pointing to Heaven with meager hands!
    O let us weep and humbly pray,
        That faith no longer mourn,
    That peace may raise her olived head,
        And righteousness return.

Then pride no more shall swell her purple crest,
    Or mad ambition kindle lawless strife;
Pale envy then shall leave the tortured breast,
    And frowning murder break his reeking knife;
Old avarice his heaps of gold forego,
    Sly theft no more the traveller beguile,
Lust shall grow whiter than the new-fallen snow,
    And rage be calmed, and malice learn to smile:
Even Satan's self shall feel a heavier chain
And gnash his teeth, and shake his burning spear in vain.

Alas! far other scenes appear,
    Man still enslaved to tenfold guilt,
Tossed on from vanity to vice,
    Forgets his Savior's blood was spilt:
Forgets he left the realms of day,
Changing his glorious robes for clay:
    With inexpressive mercy filled,
His angels left, and emerald throne,
Deigning as mortal to come down,
    To be despised, forsaken, killed.

Yet there remains a dreadful day,
    When, after years in follies spent,
This vain, fantastic world shall fall,
    With every melting element.
Methinks I hear the Angel— "Come—
    "This Trumpet calls ye to your doom."—
        The simple Indian starts amazed,
            The Jew now dreads the rod,
        Cursed is the *Koran* by the Turk,
            The atheist owns a God.

Down rides Messiah on the wings of wind,
    His fiery sword of justice blazing round;
To vengeance comes He, yet with mercy kind,
    Satan and Death behind his chariot bound.
O turn we from the burning sinner's pains,
    His agonizing struggles, piercing plaints;
And let us listen to the rapturous strains,
    Sung by the just, the seraphs, and the saints:
How for mankind the filial godhead bled,
And proud captivity an humbled captive led!

MARK 15:46 And he bought fine linen, and took him down, and wrapped him in the linen, and laid him in a sepulchre which was hewn out of a rock, and rolled a stone unto the door of the sepulchre.

UPON OUR SAVIOR'S TOMB WHEREIN NEVER MAN WAS LAID

RICHARD CRASHAW

How Life and Death in thee
        Agree!
Thou hadst a virgin Womb
        And Tomb.
A Joseph did betroth
        Them both.

LUKE 23:54 And that day was the preparation, and the sabbath drew on.

EASTER NIGHT

ALICE MEYNELL

All night had shout of men and cry
    Of woeful women filled his way;
Until that noon of sombre sky
    On Friday, clamour and display
Smote him; no solitude had he,
No silence, since Gethsemane.

Public was death; but power, but might,
    But life again, but victory,
Were hushed within the dead of night,
    The shuttered dark, the secrecy.
And all alone, alone, alone
He rose again behind the stone.

LUKE 23:55–56 **And the women also, which came with him from Galilee, followed after, and beheld the sepulchre, and how his body was laid. And they returned, and prepared spices and ointments; and rested the sabbath day according to the commandment.**

OBSERVATION

ROBERT HERRICK

The Virgin-Mother stood at distance (there)
From her son's cross, not shedding once a tear:
Because the Law forbad to sit and cry
For those, who did as malefactors die.
So she, to keep her mighty woes in awe,
Tortured her love, not to transgress the Law.
Observe we may, how Mary Joses then,
And th'other Mary (Mary Magdalen)
Sat by the grave; and sadly sitting there,
Shed for their master many a bitter tear:
But 'twas not till their dearest Lord was dead;
And then to weep they both were licensed.

MATTHEW 27:62–64 Now the next day, that followed the day of the preparation, the chief priests and Pharisees came together unto Pilate, Saying, Sir, we remember that that deceiver said, while he was yet alive, After three days I will rise again. Command therefore that the sepulchre be made sure until the third day, lest his disciples come by night, and steal him away, and say unto the people, He is risen from the dead: so the last error shall be worse than the first.

EPILOGUE

ROBERT BROWNING

First speaker

On the first of the Feast of Feasts,
    The dedication day,
When the Levites joined the priests
    At the altar in robed array,
Gave signal to sound and say,—

When the thousands, rear and van,
    Swarming with one accord,
Became as a single man,
(Look, gesture, thought and word)
    In praising and thanking the Lord,—

When the singers lift up their voice,
    And the trumpets made endeavour,
Sounding, "In God rejoice!"
    Saying, "In Him rejoice
Whose mercy endureth for ever!"—

Then the Temple filled with a cloud,
    Even the House of the Lord;
Porch bent and pillar bowed:
    For the presence of the Lord,
In the glory of His cloud,
    Had filled the House of the Lord.

Second Speaker.

Gone now! All gone across the dark so far,
      Sharpening fast, shuddering ever, shutting still,
Dwindling into the distance, dies that star
      Which came, stood, opened once! We gazed our fill
With upturned faces on as real a face
      That, stooping from grave music and mild fire,
Took in our homage, made a visible place
      Through many a depth of glory, gyre on gyre,
For the dim human tribute. Was this true?
      Could man indeed avail, mere praise of his,
To help by rapture God's own rapture too,
      Thrill with a heart's red tinge that pure pale bliss?
Why did it end? Who failed to beat the breast,
      And shriek, and throw the arms protesting wide,
When a first shadow showed the star addressed
      Itself to motion, and on either side
The rims contracted as the rays retired;
      The music, like a fountain's sickening pulse,
Subsided on itself; awhile transpired
      Some vestige of a face no pangs convulse,
No prayers retard; then even this was gone,
      Lost in the night at last. We, lone and left
Silent through centuries, ever and anon
      Venture to probe again the vault bereft
Of all now save the lesser lights, a mist
      Of multitudinous points, yet suns, men say—
And this leaps ruby, this lurks amethyst,
      But where may hide what came and loved our clay?
How shall the sage detect in yon expanse
      The star which chose to stoop and stay for us?
Unroll the records! Hailed ye such advance
      Indeed, and did your hope evanish thus?
Watchers of twilight, is the worst averred?
      We shall not look up, know ourselves are seen,
Speak, and be sure that we again are heard,
      Acting or suffering, have the disk's serene
Reflect our life, absorb an earthly flame,
      Nor doubt that, were mankind inert and numb,
Its core had never crimsoned all the same,
      Nor, missing ours, its music fallen dumb?
Oh, dread succession to a dizzy post,
      Sad sway of sceptre whose mere touch appals,

Ghastly dethronement, cursed by those the most
    On whose repugnant brow the crown next falls!

Third Speaker.

Witless alike of will and way divine,
How Heaven's high with earth's low should intertwine!
Friends, I have seen through your eyes: now use mine.

Take the least man of all mankind, as I;
Look at his head and heart, find how and why
He differs from his fellows utterly:

Then, like me, watch when nature by degrees
Grows alive round him, as in Arctic seas
(They said of old) the instinctive water flees

Toward some elected point of central rock,
As though, for its sake only, roamed the flock
Of waves about the waste: awhile they mock

With radiance caught for the occasion,—hues
Of blackest hell now, now such reds and blues
As only heaven could fitly interfuse,—

The mimic monarch of the whirlpool, king
O' the current for a minute: then they wring
Up by the roots and oversweep the thing,

And hasten off, to play again elsewhere
The same part, choose another peak as bare,
They find and flatter, feast and finish there.

When you see what I tell you,—nature dance
About each man of us, retire, advance,
As though the pageant's end were to enhance

His worth, and—once the life, his product, gained—
Roll away elsewhere, keep the strife sustained,
And show thus real, a thing the North but feigned,—

When you acknowledge that one world could do
All the diverse work, old yet ever new.
Divide us, each from other, me from you,—

Why, where's the need of Temple, when the walls
O' the world are that? What use of swells and falls
From Levites' choir, priests' cries, and trumpet-calls?

That one Face, far from vanish, rather grows,
Or decomposes but to recompose,
Become my universe that feels and knows!

MATTHEW 27:65–66 Pilate said unto them, Ye have a watch: go your way, make it as sure as ye can. So they went, and made the sepulchre sure, sealing the stone, and setting a watch.

EASTER HYMN

A. D. HOPE

Make no mistake; there will be no forgiveness;
No voice can harm you and no hand will save;
Fenced by the magic of deliberate darkness
You walk on the sharp edges of the wave;

Trouble with soul again the putrefaction
Where Lazarus three days rotten lies content.
Your human tears will be the seed of faction,
Murder the sequel to your sacrament.

The City of God is built like other cities:
Judas negotiates the loans you float;
You will meet Caiaphas upon committees;
You will be glad of Pilate's casting vote.

Your truest lovers still the foolish virgins,
Your heart will sicken at the marriage feasts
Knowing they watch you from the darkened gardens
Being polite to your official guests.

MATTHEW 28:1 **In the end of the sabbath, as it began to dawn toward the first day of the week, came Mary Magdalene and the other Mary to see the sepulchre.**

RESURRECTION, IMPERFECT

JOHN DONNE

Sleep sleep old sun, thou canst not have repast
As yet, the wound thou tookst on Friday last;
Sleep then, and rest; The world may bear thy stay,
A better sun rose before thee to day,
Who, not content to enlighten all that dwell
On the earth's face, as thou, enlightened hell,
And made the dark fires languish in that vale,
As, at thy presence here, our fires grow pale.
Whose body having walked on earth, and now
Hasting to Heaven, would, that he might allow
Himself unto all stations, and fill all,
For these three days become a mineral;
He was all gold when he lay down, but rose
All tincture, and doth not alone dispose
Leaden and iron wills to good, but is
Of power to make even sinful flesh like his.
Had one of those, whose credulous piety
Thought, that a soul one might discern and see
Go from a body, at this sepulcher been,
And, issuing from the sheet, this body seen,
He would have justly thought this body a soul,
If not of any man, yet of the whole.

MARY'S SONG

SYLVIA PLATH

The Sunday lamb cracks in its fat.
The fat
Sacrifices its opacity. . . .

A window, holy gold.
The fire makes it precious,
The same fire

Melting the tallow heretics,
Ousting the Jews.
Their thick palls float

Over the cicatrix of Poland, burnt-out
Germany.
They do not die.

Grey birds obsess my heart,
Mouth-ash, ash of eye.
They settle. On the high

Precipice
That emptied one man into space
The ovens glowed like heavens, incandescent.

It is a heart,
This holocaust I walk in,
O golden child the world will kill and eat.

LUKE 24:1   Now upon the first day of the week, very early in the morning, they came unto the sepulchre, bringing the spices which they had prepared, and certain others with them.

HIS OFFERING, WITH THE REST, AT THE SEPULCHER

ROBERT HERRICK

To join with them, who here confer
Gifts to my Savior's sepulcher;
Devotion bids me hither bring
Somewhat for my thank-offering.
Lo! Thus I give a virgin-flower,
To dress my maiden-Savior.

**MARK 16:3–4   And they said among themselves, Who shall roll us away
the stone from the door of the sepulchre? And when they looked, they saw
that the stone was rolled away: for it was very great.**

TO JESUS ON HIS BIRTHDAY

EDNA ST. VINCENT MILLAY

For this your mother sweated in the cold,
For this you bled upon the bitter tree:
A yard of tinsel ribbon bought and sold;
A paper wreath; a day at home for me.
The merry bells ring out, the people kneel;
Up goes the man of God before the crowd;
With voice of honey and with eyes of steel
He drones your humble gospel to the proud.
Nobody listens. Less than the wind that blows
Are all your words to us you died to save.
O Prince of Peace ! O Sharon's dewy Rose !
How mute you lie within your vaulted grave.
        The stone the angel rolled away with tears
        Is back upon your mouth these thousand years.

EASTER MORNING

AMY CLAMPITT

a stone at dawn
cold water in the basin

these walls' rough plaster
imageless
after the hammering
of so much insistence
on the need for naming
after the travesties
that passed as faces,
grace: the unction
of sheer nonexistence
upwelling in this
hyacinthine freshet
of the unnamed
the faceless

MATTHEW 28:5–6 And the angel answered and said unto the women, Fear not ye: for I know that ye seek Jesus, which was crucified. He is not here: for he is risen, as he said. Come, see the place where the Lord lay.

COME SEE THE PLACE WHERE THE LORD LAY

RICHARD CRASHAW

Show me himself, himself (bright Sir) O show
    Which way my poor tears to himself may go,
Were it enough to show the place, and say,
    Look, *Mary,* here see, where thy Lord once lay,
Then could I show these arms of mine, and say
    Look, *Mary,* here see, where thy Lord once lay.

LUKE 24:6–8 He is not here, but is risen: remember how he spake unto you when he was yet in Galilee, Saying, The Son of man must be delivered into the hands of sinful men, and be crucified, and the third day rise again. And they remembered his words,

RESURRECTION

JOHN DONNE

Moist with one drop of thy blood, my dry soul
Shall (though she now be in extreme degree

Too stony hard, and yet too fleshly,) be
Freed by that drop, from being starved, hard, or foul,
And life, by this death abled, shall control
Death, whom thy death slew; nor shall to me
Fear of first or last death, bring misery,
If in thy little book my name thou enrol,
Flesh in that long sleep is not putrified,
But made that there, of which, and for which 'twas;
Nor can by other means be glorified.
May then sins sleep, and deaths soon from me pass,
That waked from both, I again risen may
Salute the last, and everlasting day.

JOHN 20:1–2 Mary Magdalene runneth, and cometh to Simon Peter, and to the other disciple, whom Jesus loved, and saith unto them, They have taken away the Lord out of the sepulchre, and we know not where they have laid him.

APRIL FOOL'S DAY, OR, ST MARY OF EGYPT

JOHN BERRYMAN

—Thass a funny title, Mr Bones.
—When down she saw her feet, sweet fish, on the threshold,
she considered her fair shoulders
and all them hundreds who have held them, all
the more who to her mime thickened & maled
from the supple stage,

and seeing her feet, in a visit, side by side
paused on the sill of The Tomb, she shrank: 'No.
They are not worthy,
fondled by many' and rushed from The Crucified
back through her followers out of the city ho
across the suburbs, plucky

to dare my desert in her late daylight
of animals and sands. She fall prone.
Only wind whistled.
And forty-seven years went by like Einstein.
We celebrate her feast with our caps on,
whom God has not visited.

JOHN 20:3–5   Peter therefore went forth, and that other disciple, and came to the sepulchre. So they ran both together: and the other disciple did outrun Peter, and came first to the sepulchre. And he stooping down, and looking in, saw the linen clothes lying; yet went he not in.

COMPOSED IN ONE OF THE VALLEYS OF WESTMORELAND, ON EASTER SUNDAY

WILLIAM WORDSWORTH

With each recurrence of this glorious morn
That saw the Saviour in his human frame
Rise from the dead, erewhile the cottage-dame
Put on fresh raiment—till that hour unworn:
Domestic hand the home-bred wool had shorn,
And she who span it culled the daintiest fleece,
In thoughtful reverence to the Prince of Peace,
Whose temples bled beneath the platted thorn.
A blessed estate when piety sublime
These humble props disdained not! O green dales!
Sad may *I* be who heard your sabbath chime
When art's abused inventions were unknown;
Kind nature's various wealth was all your own;
And benefits were weighed in reason's scales!

JOHN 20:6–10   Then cometh Simon Peter following him, and went into the sepulchre, and seeth the linen clothes lie, And the napkin, that was about his head, not lying with the linen clothes, but wrapped together in a place by itself. Then went in also that other disciple, which came first to the sepulchre, and he saw, and believed. For as yet they knew not the scripture, that he must rise again from the dead. Then the disciples went away again unto their own home.

EASTER 1984

LES MURRAY

When we saw human dignity
healing humans in the middle of the day

we moved in on him slowly
under the incalculable gravity

of old freedom, of our own freedom,
under atmospheres of consequence, of justice

under which no one needs to thank anyone.
If this was God, we would get even.

And in the end we nailed him,
lashed, spittled, stretched him limb from limb.

We would settle with dignity
for the anguish it had caused us,

we'd send it to be abstract again, we would set it free.

•

But we had raised up evolution.
It would not stop being human.

Ever afterwards, the accumulation
of freedom would end in this man

whipped, bloodied, getting the treatment.
It would look like man himself getting it.

He was freeing us, painfully, from freedom,
justice, dignity—he was discharging them

of their deadly ambiguous deposit,
remaking out of them the primal day

in which he was free not to have borne it
and we were free not to have done it,

free never to torture man again,
free to believe him risen.

•

Remember the day when life increased,
explainably or outright, was haloed in poignancy,

straight life, given not attained, unlurching ecstasy,
arrest of the guards for once, and ourself released,

splendour taking detail, beyond the laughter-and-tears
as if these were gateway to it, a still or moving utterness

in and all around us? Some have been this human
night and day, steadily. Flashes of it have drawn others on.

A laser of this would stand the litter-bound or Lazarus
upright, stammering, or unshroud absent Jesus

whose anguish was to be for a whole day lost to this,
making of himself the companionway of our species

up from where such love is an unreal, half-forgotten
peak, and not yet the baseline of the human.

APPEARANCES

LUKE 24:33–43 And they rose up the same hour, and returned to Jerusalem, and found the eleven gathered together, and them that were with them, Saying, The Lord is risen indeed, and hath appeared to Simon. And they told what things were done in the way, and how he was known of them in breaking of bread. And as they thus spake, Jesus himself stood in the midst of them, and saith unto them, Peace be unto you. But they were terrified and affrighted, and supposed that they had seen a spirit. And he said unto them, Why are ye troubled? and why do thoughts arise in your hearts? Behold my hands and my feet, that it is I myself: handle me, and see; for a spirit hath not flesh and bones, as ye see me have. And when he had thus spoken, he shewed them his hands and his feet. And while they yet believed not for joy, and wondered, he said unto them, Have ye here any meat? And they gave him a piece of a broiled fish, and of an honeycomb. And he took it, and did eat before them.

BALLAD OF THE GOODLY FERE

EZRA POUND

Simon Zelotes speaking after the Crucifixion. Fere=Mate, Companion

Ha' we lost the goodliest fere o' all
For the priests and the gallows tree?
Aye lover was he of brawny men,
O' ships and the open sea.

When they came wi' a host to take Our Man
His smile was good to see,
"First let these go!" quo' our Goodly Fere,
"Or I'll see ye damned," says he.

Aye he sent us out through the crossed high spears
And the scorn of his laugh rang free,
"Why took ye not me when I walked about
Alone in the town?" says he.

Oh we drank his "Hale" in the good red wine
When we last made company,
No capon priest was the Goodly Fere
But a man o' men was he.

I ha' seen him drive a hundred men
Wi' a bundle o' cords swung free,
That they took the high and holy house
For their pawn and treasury.

They'll no' get him a' in a book I think
Though they write it cunningly;
No mouse of the scrolls was the Goodly Fere
But aye loved the open sea.

If they think they ha' snared our Goodly Fere
They are fools to the last degree.
"I'll go to the feast," quo' our Goodly Fere,
"Though I go to the gallows tree."

"Ye ha' seen me heal the lame and blind,
And wake the dead," says he,
"Ye shall see one thing to master all:
'Tis how a brave man dies on the tree."

A son of God was the Goodly Fere
That bade us his brothers be.
I ha' seen him cow a thousand men.
I have seen him upon the tree.

He cried no cry when they drave the nails
And the blood gushed hot and free.
The hounds of the crimson sky gave tongue
But never a cry cried he.

I ha' seen him cow a thousand men
On the hills o' Galilee,
They whined as he walked out calm between,
Wi' his eyes like the grey o' the sea,

Like the sea that brooks no voyaging
With the winds unleashed and free,
Like the sea that he cowed at Genseret
Wi' twey words spoke' suddenly.

A master of men was the Goodly Fere,
A mate of the wind and sea,
If they think they ha' slain our Goodly Fere
They are fools eternally.

I ha' seen him eat o' the honey-comb
Sin' they nailed him to the tree.

LUKE 24:44–51 And he said unto them, These are the words which I spake unto you, while I was yet with you, that all things must be fulfilled, which were written in the law of Moses, and in the prophets, and in the psalms, concerning me. Then opened he their understanding, that they might understand the scriptures, And said unto them, Thus it is written, and thus it behoved Christ to suffer, and to rise from the dead the third day: And that repentance and remission of sins should be preached in his name among all nations, beginning at Jerusalem. And ye are witnesses of these things. And, behold, I send the promise of my Father upon you: but tarry ye in the city of Jerusalem, until ye be endued with power from on high. And he led them out as far as to Bethany, and he lifted up his hands, and blessed them. And it came to pass, while he blessed them, he was parted from them, and carried up into heaven.

ASCENTION

JOHN DONNE

Salute the last and everlasting day,
Joy at the uprising of this Sun, and Son,
Ye whose just tears, or tribulation
Have purely washed, or burnt your drossy clay;
Behold the Highest, parting hence away,
Lightens the dark clouds, which he treads upon,

Nor doth he by ascending, show alone,
But first he, and he first enters the way.
O strong Ram, which hast battered heaven for me,
Mild Lamb, which with thy blood, hast marked the path;
Bright Torch, which shin'st, that I the way may see,
Oh, with thy own blood quench thy own just wrath,
And if thy holy Spirit, my Muse did raise,
Deign at my hands this crown of prayer and praise.

ASCENSION

DENIS DEVLIN

It happens through the blond window, the trees
With diverse leaves divide the light, light birds;
Aengus, the god of Love, my shoulders brushed
With birds, you could say lark or thrush or thieves

And not be right yet—or ever right—
For it was God's Son foreign to our moor:
When I looked out the window, all was white,
And what's beloved in the heart was sure,

With such a certainty ascended He,
The Son of Man who deigned Himself to be:
That when we lifted out of sleep, there was
Life with its dark, and love above the laws.

MARK 16:9–10   Now when Jesus was risen early the first day of the week, he appeared first to Mary Magdalene, out of whom he had cast seven devils. And she went and told them that had been with him, as they mourned and wept.

from MADELEINE IN CHURCH

CHARLOTTE MEW

'Find rest in Him!' One knows the parsons' tags –
Back to the fold, across the evening fields, like any flock of baa-ing
sheep:

Yes, it may be, when He was shorn, led us to slaughter, torn the bleating
     soul in us to rags,
          For so He giveth His beloved sleep.
     Oh! He will take us stripped and done,
     Driven into His heart. So we are won:
Then safe, safe are we? in the shelter of His everlasting wings –
I do not envy Him his victories. His arms are full of broken things.

     But I shall not be in them. Let Him take
          The finer ones, the easier to break.
And they are not gone, yet, for me, the lights, the colours, the perfumes,
     Though now they speak rather in sumptuous rooms,
          In silks and in gem-like wines;
Here, even, in this corner where my little candle shines
          And overhead the lancet-window glows
     With golds and crimsons you could almost drink
To know how jewels taste, just as I used to think
There was a scent in every red and yellow rose
     Of all the sunsets. But this place is grey,
          And much too quiet. No one here,
          Why, this is awful, this is fear!
               Nothing to see, no face,
     Nothing to hear except your heart beating in space
          As if the world was ended! Dead at last!
          Dead soul, dead body, tied together fast.
     These to go on with and alone, to the slow end:
No one to sit with, really, or speak to, friend to friend:
     Out of the long procession, black or white or red,
Not one left now to say 'Still I am here, then see you, dear, lay here your
     head.'
     Only the doll's house looking on the Park
  To-night, all nights, I know, when the man puts the lights out, very
     dark.
With upstairs, in the blue and gold box of a room, just the maids'
     footsteps overhead
Then utter silence and the empty world – the room – the bed –
     The corpse! No, not quite dead, while this cries out in me,
          But nearly: very soon to be
     A handful of forgotten dust –
     There must be someone. Christ! there must,
          Tell me there will be someone. Who?
     If there were no one else, could it be You?

How old was Mary out of whom You cast
So many devils? Was she young or perhaps for years
She had sat staring, with dry eyes, at this and that man going past
Till suddenly she saw You on the steps of Simon's house
And stood and looked at You through tears.
I think she must have known by those
The thing, for what it was that had come to her.
For some of us there is a passion, I suppose,
So far from earthly cares and earthly fears
That in its stillness you can hardly stir
Or in its nearness, lift your hand,
So great that you have simply got to stand
Looking at it through tears, through tears.
Then straight from these there broke the kiss,
I think You must have known by this
The thing for what it was, that had come to You:
She did not love You like the rest,
It was in her own way, but at the worst, the best,
She gave You something altogether new.
And through it all, from her, no word.
She scarcely saw You, scarcely heard:
Surely You knew when she so touched You with her hair
Or by the wet cheek lying there
And while her perfume clung to You from head to feet all through the
day
That you can change the things for which we care,
But even You, unless You kill us, not the way.
This, then was peace for her, but passion too.
I wonder was it like a kiss that once I knew,
The only one that I would care to take
Into the grave with me, to which, if there afterwards, to wake.
Almost as happy as the carven Dead
In some dim chancel lying head by head
We slept with it, but face to face, the whole night through –
One breath, one throbbing quietness, as if the thing behind our lips was
endless life,
Lost, as I woke, to hear in the strange earthly dawn, his 'Are you
there?'
And lie still, listening to the wind outside, among the firs.

So Mary chose the dream of Him for what was left to her of night
and day,

It is the only truth: it is the dream in us that neither life nor death nor
    any other thing can take away:
        But if she had not touched Him in the doorway of the dream could
            she have cared so much?
        She was a sinner, we are what we are: the spirit afterwards, but first,
            the touch.

And He has never shared with me my haunted house beneath the trees.
Of Eden and Calvary, with its ghosts that have not any eyes for tears,
And the happier guests who would not see, or if they did, remember
    these,
                Though they lived there a thousand years.
             Outside, too gravely looking at me, He seems to stand,
             And looking at Him, if my forgotten spirit came
                Unwillingly back, what could it claim
                Of those calm eyes, that quiet speech,
             Breaking like a slow tide upon the beach,
                The scarred, not quite human hand?

        Unwillingly back to the burden of old imaginings
           When it has learned so long not to think, not to be;
Again, again it would speak as it has been spoken to me of things
                That I shall not see!

I cannot bear to look at this divinely bent and gracious head:
        When I was small I never quite believed that He was dead:
             And at the Convent School I used to lie awake in bed
        Thinking about His hands. It did not matter what they said,
He was alive to me, so hurt, so hurt! And most of all in Holy Week
             When there was no one else to see
           I used to think it would not hurt me too, so terribly,
               If He had ever seemed to notice me
               Or if, for once, He would only speak.

MARK 16:11   **And they, when they had heard that he was alive, and had been seen of her, believed not.**

To St Mary Magdalen

Henry Constable

For few night's solace in delicious bed,
    where heat of lust, did kindle flames of hell:
    thou nak'd on naked rock in desert cell
    lay thirty years, and tears of grief did shed.
But for that time, thy heart there sorrowed,
    thou now in heaven eternally dost dwell,
    and for each tear, which from thine eyes then fell,
    a sea of pleasure now is rendered.
If short delights entice my hart to stray,
    let me by thy long penance learn to know
    how dear I should for trifling pleasures pay:
And if I virtue's rough beginning shun,
    Let thy eternal joys unto me show
    what high reward, by little pain is won.

MARK 16:12–20 After that he appeared in another form unto two of them, as they walked, and went into the country. And they went and told it unto the residue: neither believed they them.

Afterward he appeared unto the eleven as they sat at meat, and upbraided them with their unbelief and hardness of heart, because they believed not them which had seen him after he was risen. And he said unto them, Go ye into all the world, and preach the gospel to every creature. He that believeth and is baptized shall be saved; but he that believeth not shall be damned. And these signs shall follow them that believe; In my name shall they cast out devils; they shall speak with new tongues; They shall take up serpents; and if they drink any deadly thing, it shall not hurt them; they shall lay hands on the sick, and they shall recover.

So then after the Lord had spoken unto them, he was received up into heaven, and sat on the right hand of God. And they went forth, and preached every where, the Lord working with them, and confirming the word with signs following. Amen.

The Airy Christ

Stevie Smith

(After reading Dr. Rieu's translation of St. Mark's Gospel)

Who is this that comes in splendour, coming from the blazing East?
This is he we had not thought of, this is he the airy Christ.

Airy, in an airy manner in an airy parkland walking,
Others take him by the hand, lead him, do the talking.

But the Form, the airy One, frowns an airy frown,
What they say he knows must be, but he looks aloofly down,

Looks aloofly at his feet, looks aloofly at his hands,
Knows they must, as prophets say, nailèd be to wooden bands.

As he knows the words he sings, that he sings so happily
Must be changed to working laws, yet sings he ceaselessly.

Those who truly hear the voice, the words, the happy song,
Never shall need working laws to keep from doing wrong.

Deaf men will pretend sometimes they hear the song, the words,
And make excuse to sin extremely; this will be absurd.

Heed it not. Whatever foolish men may do the song is cried
For those who hear, and the sweet singer does not care that he was
     crucified.

For he does not wish that men should love him more than anything
Because he died; he only wishes they would hear him sing.

**JOHN 20:11–15   But Mary stood without at the sepulchre weeping: and
as she wept, she stooped down, and looked into the sepulchre, And seeth
two angels in white sitting, the one at the head, and the other at the feet,
where the body of Jesus had lain. And they say unto her, Woman, why
weepest thou? She saith unto them, Because they have taken away my
Lord, and I know not where they have laid him. And when she had thus
said, she turned herself back, and saw Jesus standing, and knew not that
it was Jesus. Jesus saith unto her, Woman, why weepest thou? whom
seekest thou? She, supposing him to be the gardener, saith unto him, Sir,
if thou have borne him hence, tell me where thou hast laid him, and I will
take him away.**

Mary Magdalen's Complaint at Christ's Death

Robert Southwell

Sith my life from life is parted,
     Death come take thy portion;

Who survives when life is murdered,
      Lives by mere extortion;
All that live, and not in God,
Couch their life in death's abode.

Seely stars must needs leave shining
      When the sun is shadowèd,
Borrowed streams refrain their running
      When head-springs are hindered:
One that lives by other's breath,
      Dieth also by his death.

O true life! Since Thou hast left me,
      Mortal life is tedious;
Death it is to live without Thee,
      Death of all most odious:
Turn again or take me to Thee,
Let me die or live Thou in me!

Where the truth once was and is not,
      Shadows are but vanity,
Showing wan, that help they cannot,
      Signs, not salves, of misery;
Painted meat no hunger feeds,
Dying life each death exceeds.

With my love my life was nestled
      In the sum of happiness:
From my love my life is wrested
      To a world of heaviness:
O let love my life remove,
Sith I live not where I love!

O my soul! what did unloose thee
      From thy sweet captivity,
God, not I, did still possess thee,
      His, not mine, thy liberty:
O too happy thrall thou wert,
When thy prison was His heart.

Spiteful spear that breakst this prison,
      Seat of all felicity,
Working thus with double treason
      Love's and life's delivery:

Though my life thou drav'st away,
Maugré thee my love shall stay.

JOHN 20:24–25   But Thomas, one of the twelve, called Didymus, was not with them when Jesus came. The other disciples therefore said unto him, We have seen the Lord. But he said unto them, Except I shall see in his hands the print of the nails, and put my finger into the print of the nails, and thrust my hand into his side, I will not believe.

St. Thomas

Christopher Smart

Ah! Thomas, wherefore wouldst thou doubt,
    And put the Lord in pain,
And mad'st his wounds to spout
    Anew from every vein?

Lo! those of God are blessed most,
    Which, simple and serene,
Believe the Holy Ghost,
    That operates unseen.

This is that great and prior proof
    Of God and of his Son,
Beneath whose sacred roof
    To-day the duty's done.

Though seventeen hundred years remote,
    We can perform our part,
And to the Lord devote
    The tribute of our heart.

O Lord, the slaves of sin release,
    Their ways in Christ amend,
Our faith and hope increase,
    Our charities extend.

Make thou our altered lives of use
    To all the skirts around.
And purge from each abuse
    Thy church, so much renowned.

Enlarge from Mammon's spells her priests,
    And from all carnal cares,
And bid to ghostly feasts,
    To pure cherubic airs.

Thy people in that choir employ
    Whose business is above,
In gratitude and joy,
    In wonder, praise, and love.

JOHN 20:26–29 And after eight days again his disciples were within, and Thomas with them: then came Jesus, the doors being shut, and stood in the midst, and said, Peace be unto you. Then saith he to Thomas, Reach hither thy finger, and behold my hands; and reach hither thy hand, and thrust it into my side: and be not faithless, but believing. And Thomas answered and said unto him, My Lord and my God. Jesus saith unto him, Thomas, because thou hast seen me, thou hast believed: blessed are they that have not seen, and yet have believed.

SPLIT THE LARK – AND YOU'LL FIND THE MUSIC –

EMILY DICKINSON

Split the Lark – and you'll find the Music –
Bulb after Bulb, in Silver rolled –
Scantily dealt to the Summer Morning
Saved for your Ear when Lutes be old.

Loose the Flood – you shall find it patent –
Gush after Gush, reserved for you –
Scarlet Experiment! Sceptic Thomas!
Now, do you doubt that your Bird was true?

JOHN 21:15–16 So when they had dined, Jesus saith to Simon Peter, Simon, son of Jonas, lovest thou me more than these? He saith unto him, Yea, Lord; thou knowest that I love thee. He saith unto him, Feed my lambs. He saith to him again the second time, Simon, son of Jonas, lovest thou me? He saith unto him, Yea, Lord; thou knowest that I love thee. He saith unto him, Feed my sheep.

LOVEST THOU ME?

WILLIAM COWPER

Hark, my soul! it is the Lord;
'Tis thy Savior, hear his word;
Jesus speaks, and speaks to thee;
'Say, poor sinner, lovst thou me?

I delivered thee when bound,
And, when wounded, healed thy wound;
Sought thee wandering, set thee right,
Turned thy darkness into light.

Can a woman's tender care
Cease, towards the child she bare?
Yes, she may forgetful be,
Yet will I remember thee.

Mine is an unchanging love,
Higher than the heights above;
Deeper than the depths beneath,
Free and faithful, strong as death.

Thou shalt see my glory soon,
When the work of grace is done;
Partner of my throne shalt be,
Say, poor sinner, lovst thou me?'

Lord, it is my chief complaint,
That my love is weak and faint;
Yet I love thee and adore,
Oh for grace to love thee more!

JOHN 21:18–19 Verily, verily, I say unto thee, When thou wast young, thou girdedst thyself, and walkedst whither thou wouldest: but when thou shalt be old, thou shalt stretch forth thy hands, and another shall gird thee, and carry thee whither thou wouldest not. This spake he, signifying by what death he should glorify God. And when he had spoken this, he saith unto him, Follow me.

THE CROWN

JOHN DONNE

Deign at my hands this crown of prayer and praise,
Weaved in my low devout melancholy,
Thou which of good, hast, yea art treasury,
All changing unchanged Ancient of days;
But do not, with a vile crown of frail bays,
Reward my muses white sincerity,
But what thy thorny crown gained, that give me,
A crown of glory, which doth flower always;
The ends crown our works, but thou crownst our ends,
For, at our end begins our endless rest;
The first last end, now zealously possessed,
With a strong sober thirst, my soul attends.
'Tis time that heart and voice be lifted high,
Salvation to all that will is nigh.

THE ACTS *of the Apostles* *and* THE EPISTLES

ACTS 1:15–22   And in those days Peter stood up in the midst of the disciples, and said, (the number of names together were about an hundred and twenty,) Men and brethren, this scripture must needs have been fulfilled, which the Holy Ghost by the mouth of David spake before concerning Judas, which was guide to them that took Jesus. . . . Wherefore of these men which have companied with us all the time that the Lord Jesus went in and out among us, Beginning from the baptism of John, unto that same day that he was taken up from us, must one be ordained to be a witness with us of his resurrection.

THE BALLAD OF JOKING JESUS

JAMES JOYCE

—I'm the queerest young fellow that you ever heard.
  My mother's a jew, my father's a bird.

With Joseph the joiner I cannot agree,
So here's to disciples and Calvary.

—If anyone thinks that I amn't divine
He'll get no free drinks when I'm making the wine
But have to drink water and wish it were plain
That I make when the wine becomes water again.

—Goodbye, now, goodbye. Write down all I said
And tell Tom, Dick and Harry I rose from the dead.
What's bred in the bone cannot fail me to fly
And Olivet's breezy . . . Goodbye, now, goodbye.

BALLAD OF THE SCARECROW CHRIST

ELDER OLSON

"My son, come pierce my soul with a sword,
Scrape death from these bones,
Build them into a gay cathedral,
It will sing in all its stones.

"All the carved angels and holy images
Will sing, to cymbal and psaltery,
Till the long winter of Eden ends,
And Christ lies easy on his Cross,
And the Cross turns into a Tree."

O Christ hangs high upon the Cross,
The cathedral glitters as if afire,
But demons glare from coign and finial,
Couple with the gargoyles, howl in the choir.

Farewell, cries the son, to the crow-roost scarecrow,
Farewell to a country curst with foul crows,
Take ship and sail from this haunted land,
No Garden is hidden beneath these snows.

O see the angry wanderer:
It is his breath in the sail
Drives him alone through a world of waters
In a ship of his own will.

Look, look! amid what pomp of waters
He lordly rides like the light of day;
All the sea-robed waves throng round,
Sea-foam garlands all his way,

O see the sleek sea-people raining with jewels,
The salt-blue flashing with fin, with wing!
Continents rear from the sea at his coming,
Foaming into instant spring,

Amorous, the hills bend toward him,
Hanging gardens kiss his hand,
Ocean murmurs in lamentation
As his foot summers all the land.

O all the air is sharp with spires
O all the air bubbles with domes
O all the air is afloat with palaces
Towering terraces
Fountains and peacocks on all the terraces
And brilliant millions on all the terraces
And the dead burst singing from their tombs
Singing singing the living and the dead
Spires domes palaces terraces
And stairs stairs the tallest tower
Candles flowers a feast is laid.
Now. Now. A feast laid.

O what is this festival, what the feast,
What is this host, what this homage?
Millions millions smiling millions:
And every one of them his image.

All faces are his mirrored face
Whether the living or the dead;
And for that long banquet laid
Cups blaze with his blood, his body is the bread.

Candles quiver and smoke,
O the sky runs wild, the air turns brown,
Every building rocks and walks
And cracks to cascades roaring down,
Air mutters and glares and then goes black;
Pursued by a million cannibal images

Down, down the great stair of the terraces
He is running running like a man afire
With a lightning-bolt at his back.

Noah alone on the bulging flood
He sails to drown a million selves
But the Ark heaves him into a hissing and hackled
Green-black ocean that boils and halves
And spews him Jonah to a far dim shore
And the land turns horseback to hurl him off;
Forests wither, stones singe and shriek;
Fire, water, flee him like the wind;
Towers and houses shrink aside;
Look, look; Judas, without kin or kind.

Every puddle pukes to see him,
Every rivulet coils and strikes;
Crawling over quaking mountains and valleys
(Husks, husks) like an old volcano
He rages to retch soul-fires: fails.
He oozes in sewers, dogs drop him in alleys.

Now all the aureoled saints and martyrs
Had breathed but one breath of eternal bliss
And the damned who dance the dance of the burning
Had screamed for twelve eternities

And so much earthly time had passed
As turns green forests into coal
And that coal into diamond
And that diamond into dust:

Now in a stark field without stalk
In a country of cold slag
Too poor for hour or season
Too starved for crow or hawk

O what is that on its knees
And what is that in darkling air?
A hanged man there?
No, no:

Anybody could,
Anyone can

With a rag or two and a cross of wood
Make an image of man:
It is a scarecrow.

"If for insulted suffering
Other suffering may atone,
Lie easy on your cross of wood,
I perish on my cross of bone.

"And what if all suffering be in vain?
I honor still that agony:
Christ or Judas, each in pain,
Perished upon a bitter tree."

O see, see: he stands
In a vast hollow like the inside of a mountain
Arch on arch
A Church
(Is it a bell that rings? Who brings
All these flames? Who sings?
Can it be that stone sings?)

—All the carved angels and holy images
Sing, to cymbal and psaltery,
And the long winter of Eden ends,
And Christ lies easy on his Cross,
And the Cross turns into a Tree.

ACTS 3:2–8   And a certain man lame from his mother's womb was carried, whom they laid daily at the gate of the temple which is called Beautiful, to ask alms of them that entered into the temple; Who seeing Peter and John about to go into the temple asked an alms. And Peter, fastening his eyes upon him with John, said, Look on us. And he gave heed unto them, expecting to receive something of them. Then Peter said, Silver and gold have I none; but such as I have give I thee: In the name of Jesus Christ of Nazareth rise up and walk. And he took him by the right hand, and lifted him up: and immediately his feet and ancle bones received strength. And he leaping up stood, and walked, and entered with them into the temple, walking, and leaping, and praising God. And all the people saw him walking and praising God:

Faith Healing

Philip Larkin

Slowly the women file to where he stands
Upright in rimless glasses, silver hair,
Dark suit, white collar. Stewards tirelessly
Persuade them onwards to his voice and hands,
Within whose warm spring rain of loving care
Each dwells some twenty seconds. Now, dear child,
What's wrong, the deep American voice demands,
And, scarcely pausing, goes into a prayer
Directing God about this eye, that knee.
Their heads are clasped abruptly; then, exiled

Like losing thoughts, they go in silence; some
Sheepishly stray, not back into their lives
Just yet; but some stay stiff, twitching and loud
With deep hoarse tears, as if a kind of dumb
And idiot child within them still survives
To re-awake at kindness, thinking a voice
At last calls them alone, that hands have come
To lift and lighten; and such joy arrives
Their thick tongues blort, their eyes squeeze grief, a crowd
Of huge unheard answers jam and rejoice –

What's wrong! Moustached in flowered frocks they shake:
By now, all's wrong. In everyone there sleeps
A sense of life lived according to love.
To some it means the difference they could make
By loving others, but across most it sweeps
As all they might have done had they been loved.
That nothing cures. An immense slackening ache,
As when, thawing, the rigid landscape weeps,
Spreads slowly through them – that, and the voice above
Saying *Dear child,* and all time has disproved.

ACTS 5:29–32   **Then Peter and the other apostles answered and said, We ought to obey God rather than men. The God of our fathers raised up Jesus, whom ye slew and hanged on a tree. Him hath God exalted with his right hand to be a Prince and a Saviour, for to give repentance to Israel,** and forgiveness of sins. And we are his witnesses of these things; and so is also the Holy Ghost, whom God hath given to them that obey him.

THERE WAS A SAVIOUR

DYLAN THOMAS

There was a saviour
Rarer than radium,
Commoner than water, crueller than truth;
Children kept from the sun
Assembled at his tongue
To hear the golden note turn in a groove,
Prisoners of wishes locked their eyes
In the jails and studies of his keyless smiles.

The voice of children says
From a lost wilderness
There was calm to be done in his safe unrest,
When hindering man hurt
Man, animal, or bird
We hid our fears in that murdering breath,
Silence, silence to do, when earth grew loud,
In lairs and asylums of the tremendous shout.

There was glory to hear
In the churches of his tears,
Under his downy arm you sighed as he struck,
O you who could not cry
On to the ground when a man died
Put a tear for joy in the unearthly flood
And laid your cheek against a cloud-formed shell:
Now in the dark there is only yourself and myself.

Two proud, blacked brothers cry,
Winter-locked side by side,
To this inhospitable hollow year,
O we who could not stir
One lean sigh when we heard
Greed on man beating near and fire neighbour
But wailed and nested in the sky-blue wall
Now break a giant tear for the little known fall,

For the drooping of homes
That did not nurse our bones,
Brave deaths of only ones but never found,
Now see, alone in us,
Our own true strangers' dust
Ride through the doors of our unentered house.
Exiled in us we arouse the soft,
Unclenched, armless, silk and rough love that breaks all rocks.

ACTS 7:59–60   And they stoned Stephen, calling upon God, and saying, Lord Jesus, receive my spirit. And he kneeled down, and cried with a loud voice, Lord, lay not this sin to their charge. And when he had said this, he fell asleep.

UPON STEPHEN STONED

SIR JOHN SUCKLING

Under this heap of stones interred lies
No holocaust, but stoned sacrifice
Burnt not by altar-coals, but by the fire
Of Jewish ire,
Whose softest words in their hard hearts alone
Congealed to stone,
Not piercing them recoiled in him again,
Who being slain
As not forgetful, whence they once did come,
Now being stones he found them in a tomb.

STEPHEN TO LAZARUS

C. S. LEWIS

But was I the first martyr, who
Gave up no more than life, while you,
Already free among the dead,
Your rags stripped off, your fetters shed,
Surrendered what all other men
Irrevocably keep, and when

Your battered ship at anchor lay
Seemingly safe in the dark bay
No ripple stirs, obediently
Put out a second time to sea
Well knowing that your death (in vain
Died once) must all be died again?

ACTS 8:26–31 And the angel of the Lord spake unto Philip, saying, Arise, and go toward the south unto the way that goeth down from Jerusalem unto Gaza, which is desert. And he arose and went: and, behold, a man of Ethiopia, an eunuch of great authority under Candace queen of the Ethiopians, who had the charge of all her treasure, and had come to Jerusalem for to worship, Was returning, and sitting in his chariot read Esaias the prophet. Then the Spirit said unto Philip, Go near, and join thyself to this chariot. And Philip ran thither to him, and heard him read the prophet Esaias, and said, Understandest thou what thou readest? And he said, How can I, except some man should guide me?

ON THE BAPTIZED ETHIOPIAN

RICHARD CRASHAW

Let it no longer be a forlorn hope
             To wash an Ethiope:
He's washed, his gloomy skin a peaceful shade
             For his white soul is made:
And now, I doubt not, the Eternal Dove,
             A black-faced house will love.

ACTS 9:1–9 And Saul, yet breathing out threatenings and slaughter against the disciples of the Lord, went unto the high priest, And desired of him letters to Damascus to the synagogues, that if he found any of this way, whether they were men or women, he might bring them bound unto Jerusalem. And as he journeyed, he came near Damascus: and suddenly there shined round about him a light from heaven: And he fell to the earth, and heard a voice saying unto him, Saul, Saul, why persecutest thou me? And he said, Who art thou, Lord? And the Lord said, I am Jesus whom thou persecutest: it is hard for thee to kick against the pricks. And he trembling and astonished said, Lord, what wilt thou have me to do? And the Lord said unto him, Arise, and go into the city, and it shall be

told thee what thou must do. And the men which journeyed with him
stood speechless, hearing a voice, but seeing no man.

    And Saul arose from the earth; and when his eyes were opened, he
saw no man: but they led him by the hand, and brought him into Damascus. And he was three days without sight, and neither did eat nor drink.

Near Damascus

W. S. Di Piero

The antlered scarab rolled a dungball
for its brood; a red ant, tipsy,
bulldozed a flinty wedge of chaff.
Mud slots from the recent rain,
now crusted over by the heat—
moon mountains seen close up; my mouth
plugged with road grit and surprise
just when I tried to shout *no*
to the blunt lightning spike that stopped me . . .

In the mountains of the moon I saw
a wasp dragging a grasshopper
to a frothing nest, grubs lingering
through their episode, and larvae
I'd have chewed like honeycomb
if it would have saved my sight.
Antaeus inhaled force from dirt;
he was luckier, never much
for visions, and too far gone.

In my head, I see this body
dumped flat. Painted in above,
the horse twists and straddles me,
his eyes flare, ecstatic, new,
contemptuous of the thing that fell,
while the light-shaft curries his flank
and nails me down, the unloved me,
rousted, found out, blasted, saved
down in the road's pearly filth.

ACTS 9:17–18   And Ananias went his way, and entered into the house; and putting his hands on him said, Brother Saul, the Lord, even Jesus, that appeared unto thee in the way as thou camest, hath sent me, that thou mightest receive thy sight, and be filled with the Holy Ghost. And immediately there fell from his eyes as it had been scales: and he received sight forthwith, and arose, and was baptized.

THE CONVERSION OF S. PAUL

GEORGE WITHER

A blessed conversion, and a strange
Was that, when Saul a Paul became:
And, Lord, for making such a change,
We praise and glorify thy name.
　　　For whilst he went from place to place,
To persecute thy truth and thee;
(And running to perdition was)
By powerful grace called back was he.

When from thy truth we go astray,
(Or wrong it through our blinded zeal)
Oh come, and stop us in the way,
And then thy will to us reveal;
　　　That brightness show us from above
Which proves the sensual eyesight blind:
And from our eyes those scales remove,
That hinder us the way to find.

And as thy blessed servant Paul,
When he a convert once became,
Exceeded thy Apostles all,
In painful preaching of thy name:
　　　So grant that those who have in sin
Exceeded others heretofore,
The start of them in faith may win,
Love, serve, and honor thee the more.

ST. PAUL

THOMAS MERTON

When I was Saul, and sat among the cloaks,
My eyes were stones, I saw no sight of heaven,

Open to take the spirit of the twisting Stephen.
When I was Saul, and sat among the rocks,
I locked my eyes, and made my brain my tomb,
Sealed with what boulders rolled across my reason!

When I was Saul and walked upon the blazing desert
My road was quiet as a trap.
I feared what word would split high noon with light
And lock my life, and try to drive me mad:
And thus I saw the Voice that struck me dead.

Tie up my breath, and wind me in white sheets of anguish,
And lay me in my three days' sepulchre
Until I find my Easter in a vision.

Oh Christ! Give back my life, go, cross Damascus,
Find out my Ananias in that other room:
Command him, as you do, in this my dream;
He knows my locks, and owns my ransom,
Waits for Your word to take his keys and come.

ACTS 9:36–42 Now there was at Joppa a certain disciple named Tabitha, which by interpretation is called Dorcas: this woman was full of good works and almsdeeds which she did. And it came to pass in those days, that she was sick, and died: whom when they had washed, they laid her in an upper chamber. And forasmuch as Lydda was nigh to Joppa, and the disciples had heard that Peter was there, they sent unto him two men, desiring him that he would not delay to come to them. Then Peter arose and went with them. When he was come, they brought him into the upper chamber: and all the widows stood by him weeping, and shewing the coats and garments which Dorcas made, while she was with them. But Peter put them all forth, and kneeled down, and prayed; and turning him to the body said, Tabitha, arise. And she opened her eyes: and when she saw Peter, she sat up. And he gave her his hand, and lifted her up, and when he had called the saints and widows, presented her alive. And it was known throughout all Joppa; and many believed in the Lord.

THE WIDOWS' TEARS: OR, DIRGE OF DORCAS

ROBERT HERRICK

Come pity us, all ye, who see
Our harps hung on the willow-tree:
Come pity us, ye passers by,

Who see, or hear poor widows cry:
Come pity us; and bring your ears,
And eyes, to pity widows' tears.
    Chor. And when you are come hither;
          Then we will keep
          A fast, and weep
        Our eyes out all together.

For Tabitha, who dead lies here,
Clean washed, and laid out for the bier;
O modest matrons, weep and wail!
For now the corn and wine must fail:
The basket and the bin of bread,
Wherewith so many souls were fed
    Chor. Stand empty here for ever:
          And ah! the poor,
          At thy worn door,
        Shall be relieved never.

Woe worth the time, woe worth the day,
That reaved us of thee Tabitha!
For we have lost, with thee, the meal,
The bits, the morsels, and the deal
Of gentle paste, and yielding dough,
That thou on widows didst bestow.
    Chor. All's gone, and death hath taken
          Away from us
          Our maundy; thus,
        Thy widows stand forsaken.

Ah Dorcas, Dorcas! now adieu
We bid the cruse and pannier too:
I and the flesh, for and the fish,
Doled to us in that lordly dish.
We take our leaves now of the loom,
From whence the house-wives cloth did come.
    Chor. The web affords now nothing;
          Thou being dead,
          The worsted thread
        Is cut, that made us clothing.

Farewell the flax and reaming wool,
With which thy house was plentiful.
Farewell the coats, the garments, and

The sheets, the rugs, made by thy hand.
Farewell thy fire and thy light,
That ne'er went out by day or night:
    Chor. No, or thy zeal so speedy,
          That found a way
          By peep of day,
        To feed and cloth the needy.

But, ah, alas! the almond bough,
And olive branch is withered now.
The wine press now is ta'en from us,
The saffron and the calamus.
The spice and spikenard hence is gone,
The storax and the cinnamon,
    Chor. The carol of our gladness
          Has taken wing,
          And our late spring
        Of mirth is turned to sadness.

How wise wast thou in all thy ways!
How worthy of respect and praise!
How matron-like didst thou go dressed!
How soberly above the rest
Of those that prank it with their plumes;
And jet it with their choice perfumes.
    Chor. Thy vestures were not flowing:
          Nor did the street
          Accuse thy feet
        Of mincing in their going.

And though thou here li'st dead, we see
A deal of beauty yet in thee.
How sweetly shows thy smiling face,
Thy lips with all diffused grace!
Thy hands (though cold) yet spotless, white,
And comely as the chrysolite.
    Chor. Thy belly like a hill is,
          Or as a neat
          Clean heap of wheat,
        All set about with lilies.

Sleep with thy beauties here, while we
Will show these garments made by thee;
These were the coats, in these are read

The monuments of Dorcas dead.
These were thy acts, and thou shalt have
These hung, as honors o'er thy grave,
  Chor. And after us (distressed)
     Should fame be dumb;
     Thy very tomb
    Would cry out, *Thou art blessed.*

ACTS 16:22–24 And the multitude rose up together against them: and the magistrates rent off their clothes, and commanded to beat them. And when they had laid many stripes upon them, they cast them into prison, charging the jailor to keep them safely: Who, having received such a charge, thrust them into the inner prison, and made their feet fast in the stocks.

OF PAUL AND SILAS IT IS SAID

EMILY DICKINSON

Of Paul and Silas it is said
They were in Prison laid
But when they went to take them out
They were not there instead.

Security the same insures
To our assaulted Minds–
The staple must be optional
That an Immortal binds.

ACTS 17:22–28 Then Paul stood in the midst of Mars' hill, and said, Ye men of Athens, I perceive that in all things ye are too superstitious. For as I passed by, and beheld your devotions, I found an altar with this inscription, TO THE UNKNOWN GOD. Whom therefore ye ignorantly worship, him declare I unto you. God that made the world and all things therein, seeing that he is Lord of heaven and earth, dwelleth not in temples made with hands; Neither is worshipped with men's hands, as though he needed any thing, seeing he giveth to all life, and breath, and all things; And hath made of one blood all nations of men for to dwell on all the face of the earth, and hath determined the times before appointed, and the bounds of their habitation; That they should seek the Lord, if

haply they might feel after him, and find him, though he be not far from
every one of us: For in him we live, and move, and have our being; as
certain also of your own poets have said, For we are also his offspring.

THE SEARCH

HENRY VAUGHAN

'Tis now clear day: I see a rose
Bud in the bright East, and disclose
The pilgrim-sun; all night have I
Spent in a roving ecstasy
To find my Savior; I have been
As far as Beth'lem, and have seen
His inn, and cradle; Being there
I met the Wise-men, asked them where
He might be found, or what star can
Now point him out, grown up a man?
To Egypt hence I fled, ran o'er
All her parched bosom to Nile's shore
Her yearly nurse; came back, enquired
Amongst the Doctors, and desired
To see the Temple, but was shown
A little dust, and for the town
A heap of ashes, where some said
A small bright sparkle was a bed,
Which would one day (beneath the pole,)
Awake, and then refine the whole.
      Tired here, I come to Sychar; thence
To Jacob's well, bequeathed since
Unto his sons, (where often they
In those calm, golden evenings lay
Watering their flocks, and having spent
Those white days, drove home to the tent
Their well-fleeced train;) And here (O fate!)
I sit, where once my Savior sat;
The angry spring in bubbles swelled
Which broke in sighs still, as they filled,
And whispered, *Jesus had been there*
But *Jacob's children would not hear.*
Loth hence to part, at last I rise
But with the fountain in my eyes,
And here a fresh search is decreed

He must be found, where he did bleed;
I walk the garden, and there see
Ideas of his agony,
And moving anguishments that set
His blest face in a bloody sweat;
I climbed the hill, perused the Cross
Hung with my gain, and his great loss,
Never did tree bear fruit like this,
Balsam of Soul, the body's bliss;
But, O his grave! where I saw lent
(For he had none,) a monument,
An undefiled, and new-hewed one,
But there was not the corner-stone;
Sure (then said I,) my quest is vain,
He'll not be found, where he was slain,
So mild a Lamb can never be
'Midst so much blood, and cruelty;
I'll to the Wilderness, and can
Find beasts more merciful than man,
He lived there safe, 'twas his retreat
From the fierce Jew, and Herod's heat,
And forty days withstood the fell,
And high temptations of hell;
With seraphims there talked he
His father's flaming ministry,
He heavened their walks, and with his eyes
Made those wild shades a Paradise,
Thus was the desert sanctified
To be the refuge of his bride;
I'll thither then; See, it is day,
The sun's broke through to guide my way.
      But as I urged thus, and writ down
What pleasures should my journey crown,
What silent paths, what shades, and cells,
Fair, virgin-flowers, and hallowed wells
I should rove in, and rest my head
Where my dear Lord did often tread,
Sugaring all dangers with success,
Me thought I heard one singing thus:

          Leave, leave, thy gadding thoughts;
                Who pores
                and spies

Still out of doors
descries
Within them nought.

The skin, and shell of things
Though fair,
are not
Thy wish, nor prayer
but got
My mere despair
of wings.

To rack old elements,
or dust
and say
Sure here he must
needs stay
Is not the way,
nor just.

Search well another world; who studies this,
Travels in clouds, seeks manna, where none is.

ACTS 18:12–17 **And when Gallio was the deputy of Achaia, the Jews made insurrection with one accord against Paul, and brought him to the judgment seat, Saying, This fellow persuadeth men to worship God contrary to the law. And when Paul was now about to open his mouth, Gallio said unto the Jews, If it were a matter of wrong or wicked lewdness, O ye Jews, reason would that I should bear with you: But if it be a question of words and names, and of your law, look ye to it; for I will be no judge of such matters. And he drave them from the judgment seat. Then all the Greeks took Sosthenes, the chief ruler of the synagogue, and beat him before the judgment seat. And Gallio cared for none of those things.**

GALLIO'S SONG

RUDYARD KIPLING

All day long to the judgment-seat
The crazed Provincials drew—

All day long at their ruler's feet
Howled for the blood of the Jew.
Insurrection with one accord
Banded itself and woke,
And Paul was about to open his mouth
When Achaia's Deputy spoke—

"Whether the God descend from above
Or the Man ascend upon high,
Whether this maker of tents be Jove
Or a younger deity—
I will be no judge between your gods
And your godless bickerings.
Lictor, drive them hence with rods—
I care for none of these things!

Were it a question of lawful due
Or Cæsar's rule denied,
Reason would I should bear with you
And order it well to be tried;
But this is a question of words and names.
I know the strife it brings.
I will not pass upon any your claims.
I care for none of these things.

One thing only I see most clear,
As I pray you also see.
Claudius Cæsar hath set me here
Rome's Deputy to be.
It is Her peace that ye go to break—
Not mine, nor any king's.
But, touching your clamour of 'Conscience sake,'
I care for none of these things.

Whether ye rise for the sake of a creed,
Or riot in hope of spoil,
Equally will I punish the deed,
Equally check the broil;
Nowise permitting injustice at all
From whatever doctrine it springs—
But—whether ye follow Priapus or Paul,
I care for none of these things!"

ACTS 20:9–12   And there sat in a window a certain young man named Eutychus, being fallen into a deep sleep: and as Paul was long preaching, he sunk down with sleep, and fell down from the third loft, and was taken up dead. And Paul went down, and fell on him, and embracing him said, Trouble not yourselves; for his life is in him. When he therefore was come up again, and had broken bread, and eaten, and talked a long while, even till break of day, so he departed. And they brought the young man alive, and were not a little comforted.

EUTYCHUS

ROSEMARY DOBSON

The first day of the week he spoke to them
In Troas when they met to break their bread,
And preached till midnight. Eutychus afterwards
Could not remember anything he said.

This was an irony not easily faced:
Indeed, he kept it largely unconfessed
That after travelling many days and nights
In dangers often, and by hardships pressed,

To hear the words of Paulus and receive
Some healing comfort for his troubled mind
He could not fix his thoughts, was sorely vexed
By others pushing in the crowd behind,

Till, smarting with discomfiture and grief,
He reached a window not above his height
And climbing on the sill and looking out
Breathed in the soporific airs of night.

To saints who have received the word of God
One lifetime is too short for telling all
The joyful news. And certainly an hour
Did not suffice in Troas for Saint Paul.

His discourse lengthened. Eutychus's head
Sank on his chest (and for his sake we weep),
The saint in words that none who heard forgot
Spoke of Damascus. Eutychus was asleep.

Now they were gathered in an upper room
That rose three lofts above, as it is said,

And from his window Eutychus fell down
And those that took him up pronounced him dead.

Saint Paul went straightway to the youth and held
His body in his arms, and cried to those
Who stood about, 'Be troubled not. For see
His life is in him.' And the young man rose,

His troubled mind at peace, his body healed.
And others there were saved that else were lost.
And in the morning Paul went on afoot
To reach Jerusalem by Pentecost.

I like this story of young Eutychus
For I, like him, am troubled too, and weak,
And may, like him, be too preoccupied
To listen if a saint should come to speak.

And yet, I think, if some event befall
To bring me face to face with holiness,
I should not fail to recognize the truth
And spring to life again, like Eutychus.

ACTS 28:3–6 And when Paul had gathered a bundle of sticks, and laid them on the fire, there came a viper out of the heat, and fastened on his hand. And when the barbarians saw the venomous beast hang on his hand, they said among themselves, No doubt this man is a murderer, whom, though he hath escaped the sea, yet vengeance suffereth not to live. And he shook off the beast into the fire, and felt no harm. Howbeit they looked when he should have swollen, or fallen down dead suddenly: but after they had looked a great while, and saw no harm come to him, they changed their minds, and said that he was a god.

HE SHOOK OFF THE BEAST

CHARLES WESLEY

Our Christian savages expect
    That by the hellish viper stung
We soon shall feel the dire effect,
    The poison of a slanderous tongue,
And gasp our last infected breath,
And die the everlasting death.

But lo, the tooth of calumny
 Calm and unmoved we still abide,
From nature's fretful passion free,
 Hasty revenge and swelling pride;
Men cannot their own spirit impart,
Or taint a pure, believing heart.

Ourselves with Jesus' mind we arm,
 And our envenomed foes confound,
Defy their sharpest words to harm,
 Or once inflict the slightest wound
While all the power of faith we prove
In meek invulnerable love.

Let Satan still their tongues employ,
 The vipers fastened on our fame,
The deadly things can not annoy,
 Shook off at last into the flame:
But O, they never can expire,
The worms in that infernal fire!

ROMANS 2:1–3 Therefore thou art inexcusable, O man, whosoever thou art that judgest: for wherein thou judgest another, thou condemnest thyself; for thou that judgest doest the same things. But we are sure that the judgment of God is according to truth against them which commit such things. And thinkest thou this, O man, that judgest them which do such things, and doest the same, that thou shalt escape the judgment of God?

DIES IRÆ

THOMAS BABINGTON MACAULAY

On that great, that awful day,
This vain world shall pass away.
Thus the sibyl sang of old,
Thus hath holy David told.
There shall be a deadly fear
When the Avenger shall appear,
And unveiled before his eye
All the works of man shall lie.

Hark I to the great trumpet's tones
Pealing o'er the place of bones:
Hark! it waketh from their bed
All the nations of the dead,—
In a countless throng to meet,
At the eternal judgment seat.
Nature sickens with dismay,
Death may not retain its prey;
And before the Maker stand
All the creatures of his hand.
The great book shall be unfurled,
Whereby God shall judge the world:
What was distant shall be near,
What was hidden shall be clear.
To what shelter shall I fly?
To what guardian shall I cry?
Oh, in that destroying hour,
Source of goodness, Source of power,
Show thou, of thine own free grace,
Help unto a helpless race.
Though I plead not at thy throne
Aught that I for thee have done,
Do not thou unmindful be,
Of what thou hast borne for me:
Of the wandering, of the scorn,
Of the scourge, and of the thorn.
Jesus, hast thou borne the pain,
And hath all been borne in vain?
Shall thy vengeance smite the head
For whose ransom thou hast bled?
Thou, whose dying blessing gave
Glory to a guilty slave:
Thou, who from the crew unclean
Didst release the Magdalene:
Shall not mercy vast and free,
Evermore be found in thee?
Father, turn on me thine eyes,
See my blushes, hear my cries;
Faint though be the cries I make,
Save me for thy mercy's sake,
From the worm, and from the fire,
From the torments of thine ire.
Fold me with the sheep that stand
Pure and safe at thy right hand.

Hear thy guilty child implore thee,
Rolling in the dust before thee.
Oh the horrors of that day!
When this frame of sinful clay,
Starting from its burial place,
Must behold thee face to face.
Hear and pity, hear and aid,
Spare the creatures thou hast made.
Mercy, mercy, save, forgive,
Oh, who shall look on thee and live?

ROMANS 5:6–14   For when we were yet without strength, in due time Christ died for the ungodly. For scarcely for a righteous man will one die: yet peradventure for a good man some would even dare to die. But God commendeth his love toward us, in that, while we were yet sinners, Christ died for us. Much more then, being now justified by his blood, we shall be saved from wrath through him. For if, when we were enemies, we were reconciled to God by the death of his Son, much more, being reconciled, we shall be saved by his life. And not only so, but we also joy in God through our Lord Jesus Christ, by whom we have now received the atonement. Wherefore, as by one man sin entered into the world, and death by sin; and so death passed upon all men, for that all have sinned: (For until the law sin was in the world: but sin is not imputed when there is no law. Nevertheless death reigned from Adam to Moses, even over them that had not sinned after the similitude of Adam's transgression, who is the figure of him that was to come. . .)

MEDITATION THREE

Second Series

EDWARD TAYLOR

Like to the marigold, I blushing close
        My golden blossoms when thy sun goes down:
Moistening my leaves with dewy sighs, half froze
        By the nocturnal cold, that hoars my crown.
        Mine apples ashes are in apple shells
        And dirty too: strange and bewitching spells!

When Lord, mine eye doth spy thy grace to beam
        Thy mediatorial glory in the shine

Out spouted so from Adam's typic stream
  And emblemized in Noah's polished shrine
  Thine theirs outshines so far it makes their glory
  In brightest colors, seem a smoky story.

But when mine eye full of these beams, doth cast
  Its rays upon my dusty essence thin
Impregnate with a spark divine, defaced,
  All candied o'er with leprosy of sin,
  Such influences on my spirits light,
  Which them as bitter gall, or cold ice smite.

My bristled sins hence do so horrid 'pear,
  None but thyself, (and thou decked up must be
In thy transcendent glory sparkling clear)
  A mediator unto God for me.
  So high they rise, faith scarce can toss a sight
  Over their head upon thyself to light.

Is't possible such glory, Lord, e'er should
  Center its love on me sin's dunghill else?
My case up take? make it its own? Who would
  Wash with his blood my blots out? Crown his shelf
  Or dress his golden cupboard with such ware?
  This makes my pale faced hope almost despair.

Yet let my Titimouse's quill suck in
  Thy grace's milk pails some small drop: or cart
A bit, or splinter of some ray, the wing
  Of grace's sun sprindged out, into my heart:
  To build there wonders chapel where thy praise
  Shall be the Psalms sung forth in gracious lays.

ROMANS 5:18–21 **Therefore as by the offence of one judgment came upon all men to condemnation; even so by the righteousness of one the free gift came upon all men unto justification of life. For as by one man's disobedience many were made sinners, so by the obedience of one shall many be made righteous. Moreover the law entered, that the offence might abound. But where sin abounded, grace did much more abound: That as sin hath reigned unto death, even so might grace reign through righteousness unto eternal life by Jesus Christ our Lord.**

EASTER HYMN

HENRY VAUGHAN

Death and darkness get you packing,
Nothing now to man is lacking;
All your triumphs now are ended,
And what Adam marred is mended;
Graves are beds now for the weary,
Death a nap, to wake more merry;
Youth now, full of pious duty,
Seeks in thee for perfect beauty;
The weak and aged, tired with length
Of days, from thee look for new strength;
And infants with thy pangs contest
As pleasant, as if with the breast.
  Then, unto Him, who thus hath thrown
Even to contempt thy kingdom down,
And by His blood did us advance
Unto His own inheritance,
To Him be glory, power, praise,
From this, unto the last of days!

ROMANS 6:8–9   Now if we be dead with Christ, we believe that we shall also live with him: Knowing that Christ being raised from the dead dieth no more; death hath no more dominion over him.

AND DEATH SHALL HAVE NO DOMINION

DYLAN THOMAS

And death shall have no dominion.
Dead men naked they shall be one
With the man in the wind and the west moon;
When their bones are picked clean and the clean bones gone,
They shall have stars at elbow and foot;
Though they go mad they shall be sane,
Though they sink through the sea they shall rise again;
Though lovers be lost love shall not;
And death shall have no dominion.

And death shall have no dominion.
Under the windings of the sea
They lying long shall not die windily;
Twisting on racks when sinews give way,
Strapped to a wheel, yet they shall not break;
Faith in their hands shall snap in two,
And the unicorn evils run them through;
Split all ends up they shan't crack;
And death shall have no dominion.

And death shall have no dominion.
No more may gulls cry at their ears
Or waves break loud on the seashores;
Where blew a flower may a flower no more
Lift its head to the blows of the rain;
Though they be mad and dead as nails,
Heads of the characters hammer through daisies;
Break in the sun till the sun breaks down,
And death shall have no dominion.

**ROMANS 6:21–23   What fruit had ye then in those things whereof ye are
now ashamed? for the end of those things is death. But now being made
free from sin, and become servants to God, ye have your fruit unto holiness, and the end everlasting life. For the wages of sin is death; but the
gift of God is eternal life through Jesus Christ our Lord.**

AIDS, AMONG OTHER THINGS

PETER KOCAN

The wages of sin is death. These words run
With a quiet persistence in my brain,
As though that biblical archaic phrase
Had been precisely meant to diagnose
What's bothering an unreligious man

Like me today. The blasphemy was met
By sins of silence, cowardice and doubt,
And so we muddied what clear light might thresh
The good from the bad or merely foolish
When the consequences begin to hit.

I fear that we have too glibly mocked
For too long in the word and in the act
To hope we've any second chances owed
Or plead extenuation when we're paid
The wages we knew always to expect.

We acquiesce to birth-in-bottles now,
Dissimulate on every law we knew
Was solemn in the covenants we had
With whatever we call Nature or God,
Yet we never think to reap what we sow.

The ills multiply as we unlearn
That ancient wise humility of men
Who saw, beyond the wreckage of taboos,
Despair and madness, hatred and disease
The promised payment in the promised coin.

ROMANS 7:14–21 **For we know that the law is spiritual: but I am carnal, sold under sin. For that which I do I allow not: for what I would, that do I not; but what I hate, that do I. If then I do that which I would not, I consent unto the law that it is good. Now then it is no more I that do it, but sin that dwelleth in me. For I know that in me (that is, in my flesh,) dwelleth no good thing: for to will is present with me; but how to perform that which is good I find not. For the good that I would I do not: but the evil which I would not, that I do. Now if I do that I would not, it is no more I that do it, but sin that dwelleth in me. I find then a law, that, when I would do good, evil is present with me.**

HOLY SONNET XIX

JOHN DONNE

Oh, to vex me, two contraries meet in one:
Inconstancy unnaturally hath begot
A constant habit, that when I would not
I change in vows, and in devotion.
As humorous is my contrition
As my profane love, and as soon forgot:
As ridingly distempered, cold and hot,
As praying, as mute; as infinite, as none.
I durst not view heaven yesterday; and today

In prayers, and flattering speeches, I court God:
Tomorrow I quake with true fear of his rod.
So my devout fits come and go away
Like a fantastic ague: save that here
Those are my best days, when I shake with fear.

**ROMANS 7:22–24   For I delight in the law of God after the inward man:
But I see another law in my members, warring against the law of my
mind, and bringing me into captivity to the law of sin which is in my
members. O wretched man that I am! who shall deliver me from the
body of this death?**

TO HEAVEN

BEN JONSON

Good, and great God, can I not think of thee,
    But it must, straight, my melancholy be?
Is it interpreted in me disease,
    That, laden with my sins, I seek for ease?
O, be thou witness, that the reins dost know,
    And hearts of all, if I be sad for show,
And judge me after: if I dare pretend
    To ought but grace, or aim at other end.
As thou art all, so be thou all to me,
    First, midst, and last, converted one, and three;
My faith, my hope, my love: and in this state,
    My judge, my witness, and my advocate.
Where have I been this while exiled from thee?
    And whither raped, now thou but stoopst to me?
Dwell, dwell here still O, being every-where,
    How can I doubt to find thee ever, here?
I know my state, both full of shame, and scorn,
    Conceived in sin, and unto labor born,
Standing with fear, and must with horror fall,
    And destined unto judgement, after all.
I feel my griefs too, and there scarce is ground,
    Upon my flesh t'inflict another wound.
Yet dare I not complain, or wish for death
    With holy Paul, lest it be thought the breath
Of discontent; or that these prayers be
    For weariness of life, not love of thee.

ROMANS 8:1–2   There is therefore now no condemnation to them which are in Christ Jesus, who walk not after the flesh, but after the Spirit. For the law of the Spirit of life in Christ Jesus hath made me free from the law of sin and death.

THE FLESH AND THE SPIRIT

ANNE BRADSTREET

In secret place where once I stood
Close by the banks of *Lacrim* flood
I heard two sisters reason on
Things that are past, and things to come;
One Flesh was called, who had her eye
On worldly wealth and vanity;
The other Spirit, who did rear
Her thoughts unto a higher sphere:
Sister, quoth Flesh, what livst thou on
Nothing but meditation?
Doth contemplation feed thee so
Regardlessly to let earth go?
Can speculation satisfy
Notion without reality?
Dost dream of things beyond the moon
And dost thou hope to dwell there soon?
Hast treasures there laid up in store
That all in th' world thou countst but poor?
Art fancy sick, or turned a sot
To catch at shadows which are not?
Come, come, I'll show unto thy sense,
Industry hath its recompense.
What canst desire, but thou mayst see
True substance in variety?
Doth honor like? acquire the same,
As some to their immortal fame:
And trophies to thy name erect
Which wearing time shall ne'er deject.
For riches dost thou long full sore?
Behold enough of precious store.
Earth hath more silver, pearls and gold,
Than eyes can see, or hands can hold.
Affectest thou pleasure? take thy fill,
Earth hath enough of what you will.
Then let not go, what thou mayst find,

For things unknown, only in mind.
Spir.   Be still thou unregenerate part;
Disturb no more my settled heart,
For I have vowed (and so will do)
Thee as a foe, still to pursue
And combat with thee will and must,
Until I see thee laid in th' dust.
Sisters we are, yea twins we be,
Yet deadly feud 'twixt thee and me;
For from one father are we not,
Thou by old Adam wast begot,
But my arise is from above,
Whence my dear father I do love.
Thou speakst me fair, but hat'st me sore,
Thy flattering shows I'll trust no more.
How oft thy slave, hast thou me made,
When I believed, what thou hast said,
And never had more cause of woe
Then when I did what thou bad'st do.
I'll stop mine ears at these thy charms,
And count them for my deadly harms.
Thy sinful pleasures I do hate,
Thy riches are to me no bait,
Thine honours do, nor will I love;
For my ambition lies above.
My greatest honor it shall be
When I am victor over thee,
And triumph shall, with laurel head,
When thou my captive shalt be led,
How I do live, thou needst not scoff,
For I have meat thou knowst not of;
The hidden manna I do eat,
The word of life it is my meat.
My thoughts do yield me more content
Than can thy hours in pleasure spent.
Nor are they shadows which I catch,
Nor fancies vain at which I snatch
But reach at things that are so high,
Beyond thy dull capacity;
Eternal substance I do see,
With which enriched I would be:

Mine eye doth pierce the heavens, and see
What is invisible to thee.
My garments are not silk nor gold,
Nor such like trash which Earth doth hold,
But royal robes I shall have on,
More glorious then the glistering sun;
My crown not diamonds, pearls, and gold,
But such as Angels' heads enfold.
The city where I hope to dwell,
There's none on Earth can parallel;
The stately walls both high and strong,
Are made of precious jasper stone;
The gates of pearl, both rich and clear,
And Angels are for porters there;
The streets thereof transparent gold,
Such as no eye did e'er behold,
A crystal river there doth run,
Which doth proceed from the Lamb's Throne:
Of life, there are the waters sure,
Which shall remain for ever pure,
Nor sun, nor moon, they have no need,
For glory doth from God proceed:
No candle there, nor yet torch light,
For there shall be no darksome night.
From sickness and infirmity,
For evermore they shall be free,
Nor withering age shall e'er come there,
But beauty shall be bright and clear;
This city pure is not for thee,
For things unclean there shall not be:
If I of Heaven may have my fill,
Take thou the world, and all that will.

ROMANS 11:33–36 O the depth of the riches both of the wisdom and knowledge of God! how unsearchable are his judgments, and his ways past finding out! For who hath known the mind of the Lord? or who hath been his counsellor? Or who hath first given to him, and it shall be recompensed unto him again? For of him, and through him, and to him, are all things: to whom be glory for ever. Amen.

THE OVER-HEART

JOHN GREENLEAF WHITTIER

Above, below, in sky and sod,
　　In leaf and spar, in star and man,
　　Well might the wise Athenian scan
The geometric signs of God,
　　The measured order of His plan.

And India's mystics sang aright,
　　Of the one life pervading all,—
　　One being's tidal rise and fall
In soul and form, in sound and sight,—
　　Eternal outflow and recall.

God is: and man in guilt and fear
　　The central fact of nature owns;
　　Kneels, trembling by his altar stones,
And darkly dreams the ghastly smear
　　Of blood appeases and atones.

Guilt shapes the terror: deep within
　　The human heart the secret lies
　　Of all the hideous deities;
And, painted on a ground of sin,
　　The fabled gods of torment rise!

And what is He? The ripe grain nods,
　　The sweet dews fall, the sweet flowers blow;
　　But darker signs His presence show:
The earthquake and the storm are God's,
　　And good and evil interflow.

O hearts of love! O souls that turn
　　Like sunflowers to the pure and best!
　　To you the truth is manifest:
For they the mind of Christ discern
　　Who lean like John upon His breast!

In him of whom the sybil told,
　　For whom the prophet's harp was toned,
　　Whose need the sage and magian owned,

The loving heart of God behold,
    The hope for which the ages groaned!

Fade, pomp of dreadful imagery
    Wherewith mankind have deified
    Their hate, and selfishness, and pride!
Let the scared dreamer wake to see
    The Christ of Nazareth at his side!

What doth that holy Guide require?
    No rite of pain, nor gift of blood,
    But man a kindly brotherhood,
Looking, where duty is desire,
    To Him, the beautiful and good.

Gone be the faithlessness of fear,
    And let the pitying heaven's sweet rain
    Wash out the altar's bloody stain;
The law of hatred disappear,
    The law of love alone remain.

How fall the idols false and grim!
    And lo! their hideous wreck above
    The emblems of the Lamb and Dove!
Man turns from God, not God from him;
    And guilt, in suffering, whispers Love!

The world sits at the feet of Christ,
    Unknowing, blind, and unconsoled;
    It yet shall touch his garment's fold,
And feel the heavenly alchemist
    Transform its very dust to gold.

The theme befitting angel tongues
    Beyond a mortal's scope has grown.
    O heart of mine! with reverence own
The fulness which to it belongs,
And trust the unknown for the known.

**FIRST CORINTHIANS 1:17–19 For Christ sent me not to baptize, but
to preach the gospel: not with wisdom of words, lest the cross of Christ
should be made of none effect. For the preaching of the cross is to them**

that perish foolishness; but unto us which are saved it is the power of God. For it is written, I will destroy the wisdom of the wise, and will bring to nothing the understanding of the prudent.

Perdam Sapientiam Sapientum

WILLIAM HABINGTON

To the Right Honorable the Lord Windsor.
    My Lord,
Forgive my envy to the World; while I
Commend those sober thoughts persuade you fly
The glorious troubles of the court. For though
The vale lies open to each overflow,
And in the humble shade we gather ill
And aguish airs: yet lightnings oftener kill
O'th' naked heights of mountains, whereon we
May have more prospect, not security.
For when with loss of breath, we have o'ercome
Some steep ascent of power, and forced a room
On the so envied hill; how do our hearts
Pant with the labor, and how many arts
More subtle must we practise, to defend
Our pride from sliding, then we did t'ascend?
How doth success delude the mysteries
And all th' involved designments of the wise?
How doth that power, our politics call chance
Rack them till they confess the ignorance
Of human wit? Which, when 'tis fortified
So strong with reason that it doth deride
All adverse force o'th' sudden finds its head
Intangled in a spider's slender thread.
Celestial Providence! How thou dost mock
The boast of earthly wisdom? On some rock
When man hath raised a structure, with such art,
It doth disdain to tremble at the dart
Of thunder, or to shrink opposed by all
The angry winds, it of itself doth fall,
Even in a calm so gentle that no air
Breathes loud enough to stir a virgin's hair!
But misery of judgement! Though past times
Instruct us by th' ill fortune of their crimes,
And show us how we may secure our state
From pitied ruin, by another's fate;

Yet we contemning all such sad advice,
Pursue to build though on a precipice.
    But you (my Lord) prevented by foresight
To engage your self to such an unsafe height,
And in your self both great and rich enough
Refused t' expose your vessel to the rough
Uncertain sea of business: whence even they
Who make the best return, are forced to say:
The wealth we by our worldly traffic gain,
Weighs light if balanced with the fear or pain.

FIRST CORINTHIANS 5:6–8   Your glorying is not good. Know ye not that a little leaven leaveneth the whole lump? Purge out therefore the old leaven, that ye may be a new lump, as ye are unleavened. For even Christ our passover is sacrificed for us: Therefore let us keep the feast, not with old leaven, neither with the leaven of malice and wickedness; but with the unleavened bread of sincerity and truth.

ON A FEAST

FRANCIS QUARLES

The Lord of Heaven and Earth has made a feast,
And every soul is an invited guest:
The Word's the food; the Levites are the cooks;
The Fathers' Writings are their diet-books;
But seldom used; for 'tis a fashion grown,
To recommend made dishes of their own:
What they should boil, they bake; what roast, they broil,
Their luscious salads are too sweet with oil:
In brief, 'tis nowadays too great a fault,
T'have too much pepper, and too little salt.

FIRST CORINTHIANS 9:19–23   For though I be free from all men, yet have I made myself servant unto all, that I might gain the more. And unto the Jews I became as a Jew, that I might gain the Jews; to them that are under the law, as under the law, that I might gain them that are under the law; To them that are without law, as without law, (being not without law to God, but under the law to Christ,) that I might gain them that are without law. To the weak became I as weak, that I might gain the

weak: I am made all things to all men, that I might by all means save some. And this I do for the gospel's sake, that I might be partaker thereof with you.

At his Execution

RUDYARD KIPLING

"The manner of men"

I am made all things to all men—
    Hebrew, Roman, and Greek—
    In each one's tongue I speak,
Suiting to each my word,
That some may be drawn to the Lord!

I am made all things to all men—
    In city or wilderness
    Praising the crafts they profess
That some may be drawn to the Lord—
By any means to my Lord!

Since I was overcome
    By that great Light and Word,
I have forgot or forgone
The self men call their own
(Being made all things to all men)
    So that I might save some
    At such small price, to the Lord,
As being all things to all men.

I was made all things to all men,
But now my course is done—
And now is my reward . . .
Ah, Christ, when I stand at Thy Throne
With those I have drawn to the Lord,
Restore me my self again!

FIRST CORINTHIANS 10:1–5 Moreover, brethren, I would not that ye should be ignorant, how that all our fathers were under the cloud, and all

**passed through the sea; And were all baptized unto Moses in the cloud
and in the sea; And did all eat the same spiritual meat; And did all drink
the same spiritual drink: for they drank of that spiritual Rock that followed them: and that Rock was Christ. But with many of them God was
not well pleased: for they were overthrown in the wilderness.**

MEDITATION SIXTY

Second Series

EDWARD TAYLOR

Ye Angels bright, pluck from your wings a quill.
    Make men a pen thereof that best will write.
Lend me your fancy, and angelic skill
        To treat this theme, more rich than rubies bright.
        My muddy ink, and cloudy fancy dark,
        Will dull its glory, lacking highest art.

An eye at center righter may describe
        The world's circumferential glory vast
As in its nutshell bed it snugs fast tide,
        Than any angel's pen can glory cast
        Upon this drink drawn from the rock, tapped by
        The rod of God, in Horeb, typicly.

Sea water strained through minerals, rocks, and sands
        Well clarified by sunbeams, dulcified,
Insipid, sordid, swill, dishwater stands.
        But here's a rock of *aqua vitae* tried.
        When once God broached it, out a river came
        To bath and bibble in, for Israel's train.

Some rocks have sweat. Some pillars bled out tears.
        But here's a river in a rock up tunned
Not of sea water nor of swill. It's beer.
        No nectar like it. Yet it once unbunged
        A river down it runs through ages all.
A fountain oped, to wash off sin and fall.

Christ is this Horeb's rock, the streams that slide
        A river is of *aqua vitae* dear

Yet costs us nothing, gushing from his side,
　　Celestial wine our sinsunk souls to cheer.
　　This rock and water, sacramental cup
　　Are made, Lord's Supper wine for us to sup.

This rock's the grape that Zion's vineyard bore
　　Which Moses rod did smiting pound, and press
Until its blood, the brook of life, run o'er.
　　All glorious grace, and gracious righteousness.
　　We in this brook must bath: and with faith's quill
　　Suck grace, and life out of this rock our fill.

Lord, oint me with this petro oil. I'm sick.
　　Make me drink water of the rock. I'm dry.
Me in this fountain wash. My filth is thick.
　　I'm faint, give *aqua vitae* or I die.
　　If in this stream thou cleanse and cherish me
　　My heart thy Hallelujah's Pipe shall be.

FIRST CORINTHIANS 13:6–7　Rejoiceth not in iniquity, but rejoiceth in the truth; Beareth all things, believeth all things, hopeth all things, endureth all things.

FORBEARANCE

SAMUEL TAYLOR COLERIDGE

Gently I took that which ungently came,
And without scorn forgave:—Do thou the same.
A wrong done to thee think a cat's eye spark
Thou wouldst not see, were not thine own heart dark.
Thine own keen sense of wrong that thirsts for sin,
Fear that—the spark self-kindled from within,
Which blown upon will blind thee with its glare,
Or smothered stifle thee with noisome air.
Clap on the extinguisher, pull up the blinds,
And soon the ventilated spirit finds
Its natural daylight. If a foe have kenned,
Or worse than foe, an alienated friend,
A rib of dry rot in thy ship's stout side,
Think it God's message, and in humble pride

With heart of oak replace it;—thine the gains—
Give him the rotten timber for his pains!

FIRST CORINTHIANS 13:11–12   When I was a child, I spake as a child,
I understood as a child, I thought as a child: but when I became a man, I
put away childish things. For now we see through a glass, darkly; but
then face to face: now I know in part; but then shall I know even as also I
am known.

ECCE PUER

JAMES JOYCE

Of the dark past
A child is born
With joy and grief
My heart is torn

Calm in his cradle
The living lies.
May love and mercy
Unclose his eyes!

Young life is breathed
On the glass;
The world that was not
Comes to pass.

A child is sleeping:
An old man gone.
O, father forsaken,
Forgive your son!

FIRST CORINTHIANS 13:13   And now abideth faith, hope, charity,
these three; but the greatest of these is charity.

FAITH, HOPE, AND CHARITY

Are the Prospects of Manhood

LEIGH HUNT

'Tis said that faith declines; believe it not;
Faith grows and spreads. Faith in the happier lot
Of human kind; therefore, sweet hope, in thee;
And faith in God's own climax, charity.
'Tis strange that Christians should be proud, who hold
Prospects in scorn, by Christ himself foretold.
What was the song sung on this blessed night,
When round the shepherds fell the golden light
That held the angel, and he said 'Fear not'?
What but the promise of that happier lot
Fit to bring angels down, as it did then,
Of 'peace on earth and good-will towards men'?

FIRST CORINTHIANS 14:5–10 I would that ye all spake with tongues but rather that ye prophesied: for greater is he that prophesieth than he that speaketh with tongues, except he interpret, that the church may receive edifying. Now, brethren, if I come unto you speaking with tongues, what shall I profit you, except I shall speak to you either by revelation, or by knowledge, or by prophesying, or by doctrine? And even things without life giving sound, whether pipe or harp, except they give a distinction in the sounds, how shall it be known what is piped or harped? For if the trumpet give an uncertain sound, who shall prepare himself to the battle? So likewise ye, except ye utter by the tongue words easy to be understood, how shall it be known what is spoken? for ye shall speak into the air. There are, it may be, so many kinds of voices in the world, and none of them is without signification.

REVELATION

ROBERT FROST

We make ourselves a place apart
        Behind light words that tease and flout,
But oh, the agitated heart
        Till someone really find us out.

'Tis pity if the case require
    (Or so we say) that in the end
We speak the literal to inspire
    The understanding of a friend.

But so with all, from babes that play
    At hide-and-seek to God afar,
So all who hide too well away
    Must speak and tell us where they are.

FIRST CORINTHIANS 15:24–31 Then cometh the end, when he shall have delivered up the kingdom to God, even the Father; when he shall have put down all rule and all authority and power. For he must reign, till he hath put all enemies under his feet. The last enemy that shall be destroyed is death. For he hath put all things under his feet. But when he saith all things are put under him, it is manifest that he is excepted, which did put all things under him. And when all things shall be subdued unto him, then shall the Son also himself be subject unto him that put all things under him, that God may be all in all. Else what shall they do which are baptized for the dead, if the dead rise not at all? why are they then baptized for the dead? And why stand we in jeopardy every hour? I protest by your rejoicing which I have in Christ Jesus our Lord, I die daily.

OF THE RESURRECTION

MILES COVERDALE

Christ is now risen again
From his death and all his pain:
Therefore will we merry be,
And rejoice with him gladly.

                  Kyrieleison.

Had he not risen again,
We had been lost, this is plain:
But since he is risen in deed,
Let us love him all with speed.

                  Kyrieleison.

Now is time of gladness,
To sing of the Lord's goodness:
Therefore glad now will we be,
And rejoice in him only.

                  Kyrieleison.

FIRST CORINTHIANS 15:32   **If after the manner of men I have fought with beasts at Ephesus, what advantageth it me, if the dead rise not? let us eat and drink; for to morrow we die.**

THE CHOICE

DANTE GABRIEL ROSSETTI

Eat thou and drink; tomorrow thou shalt die.
 Surely the earth, that's wise being very old,
 Needs not our help. Then loose me, love, and hold
Thy sultry hair up from my face; that I
May pour for thee this golden wine, brim-high,
 Till round the glass thy fingers glow like gold.
 We'll drown all hours: thy song, while hours are tolled,
Shall leap, as fountains veil the changing sky.

Now kiss, and think that there are really those,
 My own high-bosomed beauty, who increase
  Vain gold, vain lore, and yet might choose our way!
  Through many years they toil; then on a day
 They die not,—for their life was death,—but cease;
And round their narrow lips the mould falls close.

Watch thou and fear; to-morrow thou shalt die.
 Or art thou sure thou shalt have time for death?
 Is not the day which God's word promiseth
To come man knows not when? In yonder sky
Now while we speak, the sun speeds forth: can I
 Or thou assure him of his goal? God's breath
 Even at this moment haply quickeneth
The air to a flame; till spirits, always nigh
Though screened and hid, shall walk the daylight here.
 And dost thou prate of all that men shall do?
  Canst thou, who hast but plagues, presume to be
  Glad in his gladness that comes after thee?
 Will *his* strength slay *thy* worm in Hell? Go to:
Cover thy countenance, and watch, and fear.

Think thou and act; to-morrow thou shalt die.
>   Outstretched in the sun's warmth upon the shore,
>   Thou sayst: "Man's measured path is all gone o'er:
Up all his years, steeply, with strain and sigh,
Man clomb until he touched the truth; and I,
>   Even I, am he whom it was destined for."
>   How should this be? Art thou then so much more
Than they who sowed, that thou shouldst reap thereby?

Nay, come up hither. From this wave-washed mound
>   Unto the furthest flood-brim look with me;
Then reach on with thy thought till it be drowned.
>   Miles and miles distant though the last line be,
And though thy soul sail leagues and leagues beyond,—
>   Still, leagues beyond those leagues, there is more sea.

FIRST CORINTHIANS 15:41–43 There is one glory of the sun, and another glory of the moon, and another glory of the stars: for one star differeth from another star in glory. So also is the resurrection of the dead. It is sown in corruption; it is raised in incorruption: It is sown in dishonour; it is raised in glory: it is sown in weakness; it is raised in power:

"SOWN IN DISHONOR"!

EMILY DICKINSON

"Sown in dishonor"!
Ah! Indeed!
May *this* "dishonor" be?
If I were half so fine myself
I'd notice nobody!

"Sown in corruption"!
Not so fast!
Apostle is askew!
Corinthians I. 15. narrates
A Circumstance or two!

FIRST CORINTHIANS 15:46–55 Howbeit that was not first which is spiritual, but that which is natural; and afterward that which is spiritual. The first man is of the earth, earthy; the second man is the Lord from heaven. As is the earthy, such are they also that are earthy: and as is the heavenly, such are they also that are heavenly. And as we have borne the image of the earthy, we shall also bear the image of the heavenly. Now this I say, brethren, that flesh and blood cannot inherit the kingdom of God; neither doth corruption inherit incorruption. Behold, I shew you a mystery; We shall not all sleep, but we shall all be changed, In a moment, in the twinkling of an eye, at the last trump: for the trumpet shall sound, and the dead shall be raised incorruptible, and we shall be changed. For this corruptible must put on incorruption, and this mortal must put on immortality. So when this corruptible shall have put on incorruption, and this mortal shall have put on immortality, then shall be brought to pass the saying that is written, Death is swallowed up in victory. O death, where is thy sting? O grave, where is thy victory?

ODE: THE DYING CHRISTIAN TO HIS SOUL

ALEXANDER POPE

Vital spark of heavenly flame!
Quit, oh quit this mortal frame:
    Trembling, hoping, lingering, flying,
    Oh the pain, the bliss of dying!
Cease, fond nature, cease thy strife,
And let me languish into life.

Hark! they whisper; Angels say,
Sister Spirit, come away.
    What is this absorbs me quite?
    Steals my senses, shuts my sight,
Drowns my spirits, draws my breath?
Tell me, my soul, can this be death?

The world recedes; it disappears!
Heaven opens on my eyes! my ears
    With sounds seraphic ring:
Lend, lend your wings! I mount! I fly!
O grave! where is thy victory?
    O death! where is thy sting?

To a Child in Death

Charlotte Mew

You would have scoffed if we had told you yesterday
Love made us feel—or so it was with me—like some great bird
    Trying to hold and shelter you in its strong wing;—
A gay little shadowy smile would have tossed us back such a solemn
  word,
    And it was not for that you were listening
    When so quietly you slipped away
With half the music of the world unheard.
What shall we do with this strange Summer, meant for you,—
    Dear, if we see the Winter through
    What shall be done with Spring—?
This, this is the victory of the grave; here is death's sting.
That it is not strong enough, our strongest wing.

But what of His who like a Father pitieth—?
His Son was also, once, a little thing,
The wistfulest child that ever drew breath,
Chased by a sword from Bethlehem and in the busy house at Nazareth
Playing with little rows of nails, watching the carpenter's hammer swing,
Long years before His hands and feet were tied
And by a hammer and the three great nails He died,
    Of youth, of Spring,
Of sorrow, of loneliness, of victory the king,
    Under the shadow of that wing.

FIRST CORINTHIANS 15:56–16:13 The sting of death is sin; and the
strength of sin is the law. But thanks be to God, which giveth us the victory through our Lord Jesus Christ. Therefore, my beloved brethren, be ye
stedfast, unmoveable, always abounding in the work of the Lord, forasmuch as ye know that your labour is not in vain in the Lord. . . .
    Watch ye, stand fast in the faith, quit you like men, be strong.

FORTITUDE

CHRISTOPHER SMART

Stand fast, my child, and after all
Yet still stand fast, says holy Paul;
Thy resolution be renewed,
For this is Christian fortitude.

Repeat the Lord's own prayer for grace,
At every hour, in every place;
Spring up from human to divine,
For strength invincible is thine.

Then, as the great Apostle saith,
'Bove all things take the shield of faith,
Salvation's helm, and for thy sword,
E'en God's good spirit and his Word.

And now in dangerous giddy youth,
Your loins begirt about with truth;
Your feet with Gospel-peace be shod,
Your breast-plate righteousness from God.

When to the ghostly fight alarmed,
Know, soldier, thou'rt completely armed,
And free from terror or dismay,
March on, engage, and win the day.

SECOND CORINTHIANS 2:14–16 Now thanks be unto God, which always causeth us to triumph in Christ, and maketh manifest the savour of his knowledge by us in every place. For we are unto God a sweet savour of Christ, in them that are saved, and in them that perish: To the one we are the savour of death unto death; and to the other the savour of life unto life. And who is sufficient for these things?

THE ODOUR. 2. COR. 2

GEORGE HERBERT

How sweetly doth *My Master* sound! *My Master!*
　　As ambergris leaves a rich scent
　　　　Unto the taster:
　　So do these words a sweet content,
An oriental fragrancy, *My Master.*

With these all day I do perfume my mind,
　　My mind even thrust into them both:
　　　　That I might find
　　What cordials make this curious broth,
This broth of smells, that feeds and fats my mind.

My Master, shall I speak? O that to thee
　　My servant were a little so,
　　　　As flesh may be;
　　That these two words might creep and grow
To some degree of spiciness to thee!

Then should the pomander, which was before
　　A speaking sweet, mend by reflection,
　　　　And tell me more:
　　For pardon of my imperfection
Would warm and work it sweeter then before.

For when *My Master,* which alone is sweet,
　　And even in my unworthiness pleasing,
　　　　Shall call and meet,
　　My servant, as thee not displeasing,
That call is but the breathing of the sweet.

This breathing would with gains by sweetening me
　　(As sweet things traffic when they meet)
　　　　Return to thee.
　　And so this new commerce and sweet
Should all my life employ, and busy me.

SECOND CORINTHIANS 5:10 **For we must all appear before the judg-ment seat of Christ; that every one may receive the things done in his body, according to that he hath done, whether it be good or bad.**

SONNET

On the Religious Memory of Mrs. Catharine Thomason, My Christian Friend, Deceased 16 December, 1646

JOHN MILTON

When faith and love which parted from thee never,
    Had ripened thy just soul to dwell with God,
    Meekly thou didst resign this earthy load
Of death, called life; which us from life doth sever.
Thy works and alms and all thy good endeavor
    Stayed not behind, nor in the grave were trod;
    But, as faith pointed with her golden rod,
Followed thee up to joy and bliss for ever.
Love led them on, and faith who knew them best
    Thy handmaids, clad them o'er with purple beams
    And azure wings, that up they flew so dressed,
And spake the truth of thee in glorious themes
    Before the Judge, who thenceforth bid thee rest
    And drink thy fill of pure immortal streams.

GALATIANS 6:14   But God forbid that I should glory, save in the cross of our Lord Jesus Christ, by whom the world is crucified unto me, and I unto the world.

GALATIANS 6. 14

FRANCIS QUARLES

Can nothing settle my uncertain breast
    And fix my rambling love?
Can my affections find out nothing blessed?
    But still and still remove?
Has earth no mercy? will no ark of rest
    Receive my restless dove?
Is there no good, than which there's nothing higher,
    To bless my full desire
With joys that never change; with joys that never expire?

I wanted wealth; and at my dear request,
    Earth lent a quick supply;
I wanted mirth to charm my sullen breast;
    And who more brisk than I?
I wanted fame to glorify the rest;
    My fame flew eagle-high:
My joy not fully ripe, but all decayed;
    Wealth vanished like a shade,
My mirth began to flag, my fame began to fade.

The world's an ocean, hurried to and fro
    With every blast of passion:
Her lustful streams, when either ebb or flow,
    Are tides of man's vexation:
They alter daily, and they daily grow
    The worse by alteration:
The earth's a cask full-tunned, yet wanting measure;
    Her precious wind, is pleasure;
Her yeast is honor's puff; her lees are worldly treasure.

My trust is in the Cross: let beauty flag
    Her loose, her wanton sail;
Let countenance-gilding honor cease to brag
    In courtly terms, and veil;
Let ditch-bred wealth henceforth forget to wag
    Her base though golden tail;
False beauty's conquest is but real loss,
    And wealth but golden dross;
Best honor's but a blast: my trust is in the Cross.

My trust is in the Cross: There lies my rest;
    My fast, my sole delight:
Let cold-mouthed Boreas, or hot-mouthed East
    Blow till they burst with spite:
Let earth and hell conspire their worst, their best,
    And join their twisted might:
Let showers of thunderbolts dart down and wound me,
    And troops of fiends surround me,
All this may well confront; all this shall never confound me.

EPHESIANS 4:4–10   There is one body, and one Spirit, even as ye are called in one hope of your calling; One Lord, one faith, one baptism, One God and Father of all, who is above all, and through all, and in you all. But unto every one of us is given grace according to the measure of the gift of Christ. Wherefore he saith, When he ascended up on high, he led captivity captive, and gave gifts unto men. (Now that he ascended, what is it but that he also descended first into the lower parts of the earth? He that descended is the same also that ascended up far above all heavens, that he might fill all things.)

ADAM LAY I-BOUNDEN

ANONYMOUS

Adam lay i-bounden, bounden in a bond;
Four thousand winter thought he not too long.
And all was for an apple, an apple that he took,
As clerks finden written in their book.

Ne had the apple taken been, the apple taken been,
Ne had never our Lady aye been Heaven's queen.
Blessed be the time that apple taken was,
Therefore may we singen, *"Deo gracias!"*

ON THE RESURRECTION OF CHRIST

WILLIAM DUNBAR

Done is a battle on the dragon black,
Our champion Christ confounded has his force;
The gates of hell are broken with a crack
The sign triumphal raised is of the cross,
The devil trembles with hideous voice,
The souls are harrowed and to the bliss can go,
Christ with his blood our ransoms does endorse:
Surrexit Dominus de sepulchro.

Dungeoned is the deadly dragon Lucifer,
The cruel serpent with the mortal sting;
The old keen tiger with his teeth on char,
Which in a wait has lain for us so long,
Thinking to grip us in his claws strong;
The merciful Lord would not that it were so,

He made him for to fail of that fang:
Surrexit Dominus de sepulchro.

He for our sake that suffered to be slain,
And like a lamb in sacrifice was dight,
Is like a lion risen up again,
And as a giant raised him on high;
Sprung is Aurora radiant and bright,
Aloft is gone the glorious Apollo,
The blissful day departed from the night:
Surrexit Dominus de sepulchro.

The great victor again is risen on high,
That for our quarrel to the death was wounded;
The sun that waxed all pale now shines bright,
And darkness cleared, our faith is now refounded;
The knell of mercy from the heaven is sounded,
The Christian are delivered of their woe,
The Jews and their error are confounded:
Surrexit Dominus de sepulchro.

The foe is chased, the battle is done cease,
The prison broken, the jailers fled and flamed;
The war is gone, confirmed is the peace,
The fetters loosened and the dungeon tamed,
The ransom made, the prisoners redeemed;
The field is won, o'ercome is the foe,
Dispoiled of the treasure that he claimed:
Surrexit Dominus de sepulchro.

AMORETTI. SONNET LXVIII

EDMUND SPENSER

Most glorious Lord of life, that on this day
 Didst make thy triumph over death and sin,
 And having harrowed hell, didst bring away
 Captivity thence captive, us to win:
This joyous day, dear Lord, with joy begin,
 And grant that we, for whom thou diddest die,
 Being with thy dear blood clean washed from sin,
 May live for ever in felicity:

And that thy love we weighing worthily,
> May likewise love thee for the same again;
> And for thy sake, that all like dear didst buy,
> May love with one another entertain.
So let us love, dear love, like as we ought:
Love is the lesson which the Lord us taught.

EPHESIANS 5:25–27 Husbands, love your wives, even as Christ also loved the church, and gave himself for it; That he might sanctify and cleanse it with the washing of water by the word, That he might present it to himself a glorious church, not having spot, or wrinkle, or any such thing; but that it should be holy and without blemish.

MEDITATION TWENTY-FIVE

EDWARD TAYLOR

Why should my bells, which chime thy praise, when thou
> My shew-bread, on thy table wast, my King,
Their clappers, or their bell-ropes want even now?
> Or those that can thy changes sweetly ring?
> What! is a scar-fire broken out? No, no.
> The bells would backward ring if it was so.

Its true: and I do all things backward run;
> Poor pillard, I have a sad tale to tell:
My soul stark naked, rolled all in mire, undone,
> Thy bell may toll my passing peal to Hell.
> None in their winding sheet more naked stay
> Nor dead than I. Hence oh! the Judgment Day.

When I behold some curious piece of art,
> Or pretty bird, flower, star, or shining sun,
Pour out o'erflowing glory: oh! my heart
> Aches seing how my thoughts in snick-snarls run.
But all this glory to my Lord's a spot,
While I instead of any, am all blot.

But, my sweet Lord, what glorious robes are those
> That thou hast brought out of thy grave for thine?

They do outshine the sunshine, grace the rose:
    I leap for joy to think, shall these be mine?
Such are, as wait upon thee in thy wars,
    Clothed with the sun, and crowned with twelve stars.

Dost thou adorn some thus, and why not me?
    I'll not believe it. Lord, thou art my chief.
Thou me commandest to believe in thee:
    I'll not affront thee thus with unbelief.
    Lord, make my soul obedient: and whenso
    Thou sayst Believe, make it reply, I do.

I fain the choicest love my soul can get,
    Would to thy gracious self a gift present.
But cannot now unscrew love's cabinet.
    Say not this is a niggard's compliment:
    For seeing it is thus, I choose now rather
    To send thee th' cabinet and pearl together.

PHILIPPIANS 1:21–23 For to me to live is Christ, and to die is gain. But if I live in the flesh, this is the fruit of my labour: yet what I shall choose I wot not. For I am in a strait betwixt two, having a desire to depart, and to be with Christ; which is far better:

PHILIPPIANS 1. 23

FRANCIS QUARLES

What meant our careful parents so to wear,
    And lavish out their ill-expended hours,
To purchase for us large possessions here,
    Which (though unpurchased) are too truly ours?
    What meant they, ah, what meant they to endure
    Such loads of needless labor, to procure
And make that thing our own, which was our own too sure!

What mean these liveries and possessive keys?
    What mean these bargains, and these needless sales?

What need these jealous, these suspicious ways
    Of law-devised, and law-dissolved entails?
        No need to sweat for gold, wherewith to buy
        Estates of high-prized land; no need to tie
Earth to their heirs, were they but clogged with earth as I.

O were their souls but clogged with earth as I,
    They would not purchase with so salt an itch;
They would not take of alms, what now they buy;
    Nor call him happy, whom the world counts rich:
        They would not take such pains, project and prog,
        To charge their shoulders with so great a log:
Who hath the greater lands, hath but the greater clog.

I cannot do an act which earth disdains not;
    I cannot think a thought which earth corrupts not;
I cannot speak a word which earth profanes not;
    I cannot make a vow earth interrupts not:
        If I but offer up an early groan,
        Or spread my wings to Heaven's long longed-for throne,
She darkens my complaints, and drags my offering down.

Even like the hawk, (whose keeper's wary hands
    Have made a prisoner to her wethering stock)
Forgetting quite the power of her fast bands,
    Makes a rank bate from her forsaken block;
        But her too faithful leash doth soon restrain
        Her broken flight, attempted oft in vain;
It gives her loins a twitch, and tugs her back again.

So, when my soul directs her better eye
    To Heaven's bright palace (where my treasure lies)
I spread my willing wings, but cannot fly;
    Earth hales me down, I cannot, cannot rise:
        When I but strive to mount the least degree,
        Earth gives a jerk, and foils me on my knee;
Lord, how my soul is racked betwixt the world and thee!

Great God, I spread my feeble wings in vain;
    In vain I offer my extended hands:
I cannot mount till thou unlink my chain;

I cannot come till thou release my bands:
    Which if thou please to break, and then supply
    My wings with spirit, th' Eagle shall not fly
A pitch that's half so fair, nor half so swift as I.

PHILIPPIANS 1:24   **Nevertheless to abide in the flesh is more needful for you.**

Cupio dissolvi

WILLIAM HABINGTON

The soul which doth with God unite,
Those gaieties how doth she slight
    Which o'er opinion sway?
Like sacred virgin wax, which shines
On altars or on martyrs' shrines
    How doth she burn away?

How violent are her throes till she
From envious earth delivered be,
    Which doth her flight restrain?
How doth she dote on whips and racks,
On fires and the so dreaded axe,
    And every murdering pain?

How soon she leaves the pride of wealth,
The flatteries of youth and health
    And fame's more precious breath.
And every gaudy circumstance
That doth the pomp of life advance
    At the approach of death?

The cunning of astrologers
Observes each motion of the stars
    Placing all knowledge there:
And lovers in their mistress' eyes
Contract those wonders of the skies,
    And seek no higher sphere.

The wandering pilot sweats to find
The causes that produce the wind
    Still gazing on the Pole.
The politician scorns all art
But what doth pride and power impart,
    And swells the ambitious soul.

But he whom heavenly fire doth warm,
And 'gainst these powerful follies arm,
    Doth soberly disdain
All these fond human mysteries
As the deceitful and unwise
    Distempers of our brain.

He as a burden bears his clay,
Yet vainly throws it not away
    On every idle cause:
But with the same untroubled eye
Can or resolve to live or die,
    Regardless of th' applause.

My God! If 'tis thy great decree
That this must the last moment be
    Wherein I breath this air;
My heart obeys joyed to retreat
From the false favors of the great
    And treachery of the fair.

When thou shalt please this soul t' enthrone,
Above impure corruption;
    What should I grieve or fear,
To think this breathless body must
Become a loathsome heap of dust
    And ne'er again appear.

For in the fire when ore is tried;
And by that torment purified:
    Do we deplore the loss?
And when thou shalt my soul refine,
That it thereby may purer shine
    Shall I grieve for the dross?

PHILIPPIANS 3:8–11   Yea doubtless, and I count all things but loss for the excellency of the knowledge of Christ Jesus my Lord: for whom I have suffered the loss of all things, and do count them but dung, that I may win Christ, And be found in him, not having mine own righteousness, which is of the law, but that which is through the faith of Christ, the righteousness which is of God by faith: That I may know him, and the power of his resurrection, and the fellowship of his sufferings, being made conformable unto his death; If by any means I might attain unto the resurrection of the dead.

THE LITANY OF THE DARK PEOPLE

COUNTEE CULLEN

Our flesh that was a battle-ground
Shows now the morning-break;
The ancient deities are drowned
For thy eternal sake.
Now that the past is left behind,
Fling wide thy garment's hem
To keep us one with Thee in mind,
Thou Christ of Bethlehem.

The thorny wreath may ridge our brow,
The spear may mar our side,
And on white wood from a scented bough
We may be crucified;
Yet no assaults the old gods make
Upon our agony
Shall swerve our footsteps from the wake
Of Thine toward Calvary.

And if we hunger now and thirst,
Grant our withholders may,
When heaven's constellations burst
Upon Thy crowning day,
Be fed by us, and given to see
Thy mercy in our eyes,
When Bethlehem and Calvary
Are merged in Paradise.

PHILIPPIANS 4:9–12   Those things, which ye have both learned, and received, and heard, and seen in me, do: and the God of peace shall be with you. But I rejoiced in the Lord greatly, that now at the last your care

of me hath flourished again; wherein ye were also careful, but ye lacked opportunity. Not that I speak in respect of want: for I have learned, in whatsoever state I am, therewith to be content. I know both how to be abased, and I know how to abound: every where and in all things I am instructed both to be full and to be hungry, both to abound and to suffer need.

CONTENTMENT

WILLIAM COWPER

Fierce passions discompose the mind,
    As tempests vex the sea:
But calm content and peace we find,
    When, Lord, we turn to thee.

In vain by reason and by rule
    We try to bend the will;
For none but in the Savior's school
    Can learn the heavenly skill.

Since at his feet my soul has sat,
    His gracious words to hear,
Contented with my present state,
    I cast on him my care.

"Art thou a sinner, soul?" he said,
    "Then how canst thou complain?
How light thy troubles here, if weighed
    With everlasting pain!

"If thou of murmuring wouldst be cured,
    Compare thy griefs with mine;
Think what my love for thee endured,
    And thou wilt not repine.

" 'Tis I appoint thy daily lot,
    And I do all things well;
Thou soon shalt leave this wretched spot,
    And rise with me to dwell.

"In life my grace shall strength supply,
    Proportioned to thy day;
At death thou still shalt find me nigh,
    To wipe thy tears away."

Thus I, who once my wretched day
In vain repinings spent,
Taught in my Savior's school of grace,
Have learnt to be content.

**COLOSSIANS 3:1–4 If ye then be risen with Christ, seek those things
which are above, where Christ sitteth on the right hand of God. Set your
affection on things above, not on things on the earth. For ye are dead,
and your life is hid with Christ in God. When Christ, who is our life, shall
appear, then shall ye also appear with him in glory.**

COLOSS. 3.3

GEORGE HERBERT

My words and thoughts do both express this notion,
That *Life* hath with the sun a double motion.
The first   *Is* straight, and our diurnal friend,
The other   *Hid* and doth obliquely bend.
One life is wrapped   *In* flesh, and tends to earth.
The other winds towards *Him,* whose happy birth
Taught me to live here so,   *That* still one eye
Should aim and shoot at that which *Is* on high:
Quitting   with   daily   labor   all   *My* pleasure,
To   gain at harvest   an   eternal   *Treasure.*

**COLOSSIANS 3:8–16 But now ye also put off all these; anger, wrath,
malice, blasphemy, filthy communication out of your mouth. Lie not one
to another, seeing that ye have put off the old man with his deeds; And
have put on the new man, which is renewed in knowledge after the image
of him that created him: Where there is neither Greek nor Jew, circumcision nor uncircumcision, Barbarian, Scythian, bond nor free: but Christ
is all, and in all. Put on therefore, as the elect of God, holy and beloved,
bowels of mercies, kindness, humbleness of mind, meekness, longsuffering; Forbearing one another, and forgiving one another, if any man have
a quarrel against any: even as Christ forgave you, so also do ye. And
above all these things put on charity, which is the bond of perfectness.
And let the peace of God rule in your hearts, to the which also ye are
called in one body; and be ye thankful. Let the word of Christ dwell in you
richly in all wisdom; teaching and admonishing one another in psalms
and hymns and spiritual songs, singing with grace in your hearts to the
Lord.**

CONTENT AND RICH

ROBERT SOUTHWELL

I dwell in grace's court,
    Enriched with virtue's rights;
Faith guides my wit; love leads my will,
    Hope all my mind delights.

In lowly vales I mount
    To pleasure's highest pitch;
My seely shroud true honors brings,
    My poor estate is rich.

My conscience is my crown,
    Contented thoughts my rest;
My heart is happy in it self,
    My bliss is in my breast.

Enough, I reckon wealth;
    A mean the surest lot,
That lies too high for base contempt,
    Too low for envy's shot.

My wishes are but few,
    All easy to fulfill,
I make the limits of my power
    The bounds unto my will.

I have no hopes but one,
    Which is of heavenly reign;
Effects attained, or not desired,
    All lower hopes refrain.

I feel no care of coin,
    Well-doing is my wealth;
My mind to me an empire is,
    While grace affordeth health.

I clip high-climbing thoughts;
    The wings of swelling pride;
Their fall is worst, that from the height
    Of greatest honors slide.

Sith sails of largest size
　　The storm doth soonest tear,
I bear so low and small a sail
　　As freeth me from fear.

I wrestle not with rage,
　　While fury's flame doth burn;
It is in vain to stop the stream
　　Until the tide do turn.

But when the flame is out,
　　And ebbing wrath doth end,
I turn a late enragèd foe
　　Into a quiet friend.

And taught with often proof,
　　A tempered calm I find
To be most solace to it self,
　　Best cure for angry mind.

Spare diet is my fare,
　　My clothes more fit than fine;
I know I feed and clothe a foe
　　That pampered would repine.

I envy not their hap,
　　Whom favor doth advance;
I take no pleasure in their pain,
　　That have less happy chance.

To rise by other's fall
　　I deem a loosing gain;
All states with others' ruins built,
　　To ruin run amain.

No change of fortune's calms
　　Can cast my comforts down;
　　When fortune smiles, I smile to think
How quickly she will frown.

And when in froward mood
　　She proves an angry foe,
Small gain I found to let her come,
　　Less loss to let her go.

FIRST THESSALONIANS 5:1–3 But of the times and the seasons, brethren, ye have no need that I write unto you. For yourselves know perfectly that the day of the Lord so cometh as a thief in the night. For when they shall say, Peace and safety; then sudden destruction cometh upon them, as travail upon a woman with child; and they shall not escape.

THE JUDGMENT DAY

JAMES WELDON JOHNSON

In that great day,
People, in that great day
God's a-going to rain down fire.
God's a-going to sit in the middle of the air
To judge the quick and the dead.

Early one of these mornings,
God's a-going to call for Gabriel,
That tall, bright angel, Gabriel;
And God's a-going to say to him: Gabriel,
Blow your silver trumpet,
And wake the living nations.

And Gabriel's going to ask him: Lord,
How loud must I blow it?

And God's a-going to tell him: Gabriel,
Blow it calm and easy.
Then putting one foot on the mountain top,
And the other in the middle of the sea,
Gabriel's going to stand and blow his horn,
To wake the living nations.

Then God's a-going to say to him: Gabriel,
Once more blow your silver trumpet,
And wake the nations underground.

And Gabriel's going to ask him: Lord
How loud must I blow it?
And God's a-going to tell him: Gabriel,
Like seven peals of thunder.
Then the tall, bright angel, Gabriel,
Will put one foot on the battlements of heaven
And the other on the steps of hell,

And blow that silver trumpet
Till he shakes old hell's foundations.

And I feel Old Earth a-shuddering—
And I see the graves a-bursting—
And I hear a sound,
A blood-chilling sound.
What sound is that I hear?
It's the clicking together of the dry bones,
Bone to bone—the dry bones.
And I see coming out of the bursting graves,
And marching up from the valley of death,
The army of the dead.
And the living and the dead in the twinkling of an eye
Are caught up in the middle of the air,
Before God's judgment bar.

Oh-o-oh, sinner,
Where will you stand,
In that great day when God's a-going to rain down fire?
Oh, you gambling man—where will you stand?
You whore-mongering man—where will you stand?
Liars and backsliders—where will you stand,
In that great day when God's a-going to rain down fire?

And God will divide the sheep from the goats,
The one on the right, the other on the left.
And to them on the right God's a-going to say:
Enter into my kingdom.
And those who've come through great tribulations,
And washed their robes in the blood of the Lamb,
They will enter in—
Clothed in spotless white,
With starry crowns upon their heads,
And silver slippers on their feet,
And harps within their hands;—

And two by two they'll walk
Up and down the golden street,
Feasting on the milk and honey
Singing new songs of Zion,
Chattering with the angels
All around the Great White Throne.

And to them on the left God's a-going to say:
Depart from me into everlasting darkness,
Down into the bottomless pit.
And the wicked like lumps of lead will start to fall,
Headlong for seven days and nights they'll fall,
Plumb into the big, black, red-hot mouth of hell,
Belching out fire and brimstone.
And their cries like howling, yelping dogs,
Will go up with the fire and smoke from hell,
But God will stop his ears.

Too late, sinner! Too late!
Good-bye, sinner! Good-bye!
In hell, sinner! In hell!
Beyond the reach of the love of God.

And I hear a voice, crying, crying:
Time shall be no more!
Time shall be no more!
Time shall be no more!
And the sun will go out like a candle in the wind,
The moon will turn to dripping blood,
The stars will fall like cinders,
And the sea will burn like tar;
And the earth shall melt away and be dissolved,
And the sky will roll up like a scroll.
With a wave of his hand God will blot out time,
And start the wheel of eternity.

Sinner, oh, sinner,
Where will you stand
In that great day when God's a-going to rain down fire?

FIRST TIMOTHY 6:3–10 If any man teach otherwise, and consent not to wholesome words, even the words of our Lord Jesus Christ, and to the doctrine which is according to godliness; He is proud, knowing nothing, but doting about questions and strifes of words, whereof cometh envy, strife, railings, evil surmisings, Perverse disputings of men of corrupt minds, and destitute of the truth, supposing that gain is godliness: from such withdraw thyself. But godliness with contentment is great gain. For we brought nothing into this world, and it is certain we can carry nothing out. And having food and raiment let us be therewith content. But they that will be rich fall into temptation and a snare, and into many foolish and hurtful lusts, which drown men in destruction and perdition. For the love of money is the root of all evil: which while some coveted after, they have erred from the faith, and pierced themselves through with many sorrows.

The Root of our Evil

D. H. Lawrence

The root of our present evil is that we buy and sell.
Ultimately, we are all busy buying and selling one another.

It began with Judas, and goes on in the wage-system.
Men sell themselves for a wage, and employers look out for a bargain.
And employers are bought by financiers, and financiers are sold to the
    devil.

—Get thou behind me, Satan!—
That was just what Satan wanted to do,
for then nobody would have their eye on him.

And Jesus never looked round.
That is the great reproach we have against him.
He was frightened to look round
and see Satan bargaining the world away
and men, and the bread of men
behind his back
with satanically inspired financiers.

If Jesus had kept a sharp eye on Satan,
and refused to let so many things happen behind his back
we shouldn't be where we are now.

Come, Satan, don't go dodging behind my back any longer.
If you've got the goods, come forward, boy, and let's see 'em.
I'm perfectly willing to strike a decent bargain.
But I'm not having any dodging going on behind my back.

What we want is some sort of communism
not based on wages, nor profits, nor any sort of buying and selling
but on a religion of life.

FIRST TIMOTHY 6:11–16 But thou, O man of God, flee these things; and follow after righteousness, godliness, faith, love, patience, meekness. Fight the good fight of faith, lay hold on eternal life, whereunto thou art also called, and hast professed a good profession before many witnesses. I give thee charge in the sight of God, who quickeneth all things, and before Christ Jesus, who before Pontius Pilate witnessed a good confession; That thou keep this commandment without spot, unrebukeable, until the appearing of our Lord Jesus Christ: Which in his times he shall show, who is the blessed and only Potentate, the King of kings, and Lord of lords; Who only hath immortality, dwelling in the light which no man can approach unto; whom no man hath seen, nor can see: to whom be honour and power everlasting. Amen.

PILATE REMEMBERS

WILLIAM E. BROOKS

I wonder why that scene comes back tonight,
That long-forgotten scene of years ago.
Perhaps this touch of spring, that full white moon,
For it was spring, and spring's white moon hung low
Above my garden on the night He died.
I still remember how I felt disturbed
That I must send Him to a felon's cross
On such a day when spring was in the air,
And in His life, for He was young to die.
How tall and strong He stood, how calm His eyes,
Fronting me straight and while I questioned Him;
His fearless heart spoke to me through His eyes.
Could I have won Him as my follower,
And a hundred more beside, my way had led
To Cæsar's palace and I'd wear today
The imperial purple. But He would not move
One little bit from His wild madcap dream
Of seeking truth. What wants a man with "truth"
When He is young and spring is at the door?
He would not listen, so He had to go.
One mad Jew less meant little to the state,
And pleasing Annas made my task the less.
And yet for me He spoiled that silver night,—
Remembering it was spring and he was young.

SECOND TIMOTHY 2:10–13 Therefore I endure all things for the elect's sakes, that they may also obtain the salvation which is in Christ

**Jesus with eternal glory. It is a faithful saying: For if we be dead with
him, we shall also live with him: If we suffer, we shall also reign with
him: if we deny him, he also will deny us: If we believe not, yet he abideth
faithful: he cannot deny himself.**

The Life is Long

Sir John Harington

The life is long that loathesomely doth last
the doleful days draw slowly to their date
the present pangs and painful plague scarce past
yields grief aye green to stablish thy estate
so that I find in this great storm and strife
that death is sweet that shorteth such a life

Yet by the stroke of this strange overthrow
at which conflict in thralldom I was thrust
my God I thank I am well taught to know
from whence man came and eke whereto he must
and by the way upon how feeble force
his term doth stand till death shall end his course

The pleasant years that seem so swiftly run
the merry days to end so fast that fleet
the joyful nights of which day dawnth so soon
the happy hours which more do miss than meet
do all consume as snow against the sun
and death makes end of all that life begun

Since death shall dure till all the world lie waste
what meaneth man to shun death then so sore
as man might make that life should always last
without regard the Lord hath lead before
the dance of death which all must run on row
though how or when himself doth only know

If man would mind what burdens life doth bring
what grievous crimes to god he doth commit
what griefs do grow what dangers daily spring
with no safe hour in all his days to sit
he would sure think as with great cause I do
the day of death were better of the two

Death is a port whereby we pass to joy
Life is a lake that drowneth all in pain
Death is so dear it ceaseth all annoy
Life is so lewd that all it yields is vain
For as by life to bondage man was brought
Even so by death was freedom likewise wrought

Wherefore with Paul let all flesh wish and pray
to be dissolved from this foul fleshy mass
or at the least be armed against the day
that they be found good soldiers pressed to pass
From life to death from death to life again
to such a life as ever shall remain

**SECOND TIMOTHY 4:6–8   For I am now ready to be offered, and the
time of my departure is at hand. I have fought a good fight, I have finished
my course, I have kept the faith: Henceforth there is laid up for me a crown
of righteousness, which the Lord, the righteous judge, shall give me at that
day: and not to me only, but unto all them also that love his appearing.**

CROSSING THE BAR

ALFRED, LORD TENNYSON

Sunset and evening star,
    And one clear call for me!
And may there be no moaning of the bar,
    When I put out to sea,

But such a tide as moving seems asleep,
    Too full for sound and foam,
When that which drew from out the boundless deep
    Turns again home.

Twilight and evening bell,
    And after that the dark!
And may there be no sadness of farewell,
    When I embark;

For though from out our bourn of Time and Place
    The flood may bear me far,
I hope to see my Pilot face to face
    When I have crossed the bar.

TITUS 1:10–12   For there are many unruly and vain talkers and deceivers, specially they of the circumcision: Whose mouths must be stopped, who subvert whole houses, teaching things which they ought not, for filthy lucre's sake. One of themselves, even a prophet of their own, said, The Cretians are alway liars, evil beasts, slow bellies.

FOR A POET

GEORGE WITHER

Poets are prophets, not only in the vulgar acception, among human authors, but so called by St. Paul, Tit. i. 12. By this hymn, therefore, such poets as are not past grace may be remembered to exercise their faculty to that end for which it was given unto them by God.

By art a poet is not made;
For though by art some bettered be,
Immediately his gift he had
From thee, O God, from none but thee.
 And fitted in the womb he was
To be, by what thou didst inspire,
In extraordinary place,
A chaplain of this lower choir.
 Most poets future things declare,
 And prophets, true or false, they are.
They who with meekness entertain,
And with a humble soul admit
Those raptures which thy grace doth deign,
Become for thy true service fit.
 And though the scapes which we condemn
In these may otherwhile be found,
Thy secrets thou revealest by them,
And mak'st their tongues thy praise to sound.
 Such Moses was, such David proved,
 Men famous, holy, and beloved.
And such, though lower in degree,
Are some who live among us yet;
And they with truth inspirëd be,
By musing on thy holy writ.
 In ordinary, some of those
Upon thy service do attend;
Divulging forth in holy prose
The messages which thou dost send;
 And some of these thy truths display,
 Not in an ordinary way.

But where this gift puffs up with pride,
The devil enters in thereby,
And through the same doth means provide
To raise his own inventions high;
    Blasphemous fancies are infused,
All holy new things are expelled.
He that hath most profanely mused
Is famed as having most excelled;
    And those are priests and prophets made
    To him from whom their strains they had.
Such were those poets who of old
To heathen gods their hymns did frame;
Or have blasphemous fables told,
To truth's abuse and virtue's blame.
    Such are these poets in these days
Who vent the fumes of lust and wine,
Then crown each others' heads with bays,
As if their poems were divine.
    And such, though they some truths foresee,
    False-hearted and false prophets be.
Therefore, since I reputed am
Among these few on whom the times
Imposèd have a poet's name,
Lord, give me grace to shun their crimes;
    My precious gift let me employ
Not, as imprudent poets use,
That grace and virtue to destroy
Which I should strengthen by my muse;
    But help to free them of the wrongs
    Sustained by drunkards' rhymes and songs.
Yea, whilst thou shalt prolong my days,
Lord, all the musings of my heart,
To be advancements of thy praise,
And to the public weal convert;
    That when to dust I must return,
It may not justly be my thought
That to a blessing I was born,
Which, by abuse, a curse hath brought.
    But let my conscience truly say,
    My soul in peace departs away.

HEBREWS 3:15–4:2   **While it is said, To day if ye will hear his voice, harden not your hearts, as in the provocation. For some, when they had heard, did provoke: howbeit not all that came out of Egypt by Moses. But with whom was he grieved forty years? was it not with them that had sinned, whose carcases fell in the wilderness? And to whom sware he that they should not enter into his rest, but to them that believed not? So we see that they could not enter in because of unbelief.**

Let us therefore fear, lest, a promise being left us of entering into his rest, any of you should seem to come short of it. For unto us was the gospel preached, as well as unto them: but the word preached did not profit them, not being mixed with faith in them that heard it.

OLD TESTAMENT GOSPEL

WILLIAM COWPER

Israel, in ancient days
  Not only had a view
Of Sinai in a blaze,
  But learned the Gospel too;
The types and figures were a glass
In which they saw a Savior's face.

The paschal sacrifice
  And blood-besprinkled door,
Seen with enlightened eyes,
  And once applied with power,
Would teach the need of other blood,
To reconcile an angry God.

The Lamb, the Dove, set forth
  His perfect innocence,
Whose blood of matchless worth
  Should be the soul's defence;
For he who can for sin atone,
Must have no failings of his own.

The scape-goat on his head
  The people's trespass bore,
And, to the desert led,
  Was to be seen no more:
In him our surety seemed to say,
"Behold, I bear your sins away."

Dipped in his fellow's blood,
            The living bird went free;
The type, well understood,
            Expressed the sinner's plea;
Described a guilty soul enlarged,
And by a Savior's death discharged.

Jesus, I love to trace,
            Throughout the sacred page,
The footsteps of thy grace,
            The same in every age!
O grant that I may faithful be
To clearer light vouchsafed to me!

HEBREWS 6:16–19 For men verily swear by the greater: and an oath for confirmation is to them an end of all strife. Wherein God, willing more abundantly to shew unto the heirs of promise the immutability of his counsel, confirmed it by an oath: That by two immutable things, in which it was impossible for God to lie, we might have a strong consolation, who have fled for refuge to lay hold upon the hope set before us: Which hope we have as an anchor of the soul, both sure and steadfast, and which entereth into that within the veil;

HOPE

GEORGE HERBERT

I gave to Hope a watch of mine: but he
            An anchor gave to me.
Then an old prayer-book I did present:
            And he an optic sent.
With that I gave a vial full of tears:
            But he a few green ears:
Ah Loiterer! I'll no more, no more I'll bring:
            I did expect a ring.

HEBREWS 10:28–31 He that despised Moses' law died without mercy under two or three witnesses: Of how much sorer punishment, suppose ye, shall he be thought worthy, who hath trodden under foot the Son of God, and hath counted the blood of the covenant, wherewith he was

sanctified, an unholy thing, and hath done despite unto the Spirit of grace? For we know him that hath said, Vengeance belongeth unto me, I will recompense, saith the Lord. And again, The Lord shall judge his people. It is a fearful thing to fall into the hands of the living God.

THE HANDS OF GOD

D. H. LAWRENCE

It is a fearful thing to fall into the hands of the living God.
But it is a much more fearful thing to fall out of them.

Did Lucifer fall through knowledge?
oh then, pity him, pity him that plunge!

Save me, O God, from falling into the ungodly knowledge
of myself as I am without God.
Let me never know, O God
let me never know what I am or should be
when I have fallen out of your hands, the hands of the living God.

That awful and sickening endless sinking, sinking
through the slow, corruptive levels of disintegrative knowledge
when the self has fallen from the hands of God,
and sinks, seething and sinking, corrupt
and sinking still, in depth after depth of disintegrative consciousness
sinking in the endless undoing, the awful katabolism into the abyss!
Even of the soul, fallen from the hands of God!

Save me from that, O God!
Let me never know myself apart from the living God!

HEBREWS 11:13–16　These all died in faith, not having received the promises, but having seen them afar off, and were persuaded of them, and embraced them, and confessed that they were strangers and pilgrims on the earth. For they that say such things declare plainly that they seek a country. And truly, if they had been mindful of that country from whence they came out, they might have had opportunity to have returned. But now they desire a better country, that is, an heavenly: wherefore God is not ashamed to be called their God: for he hath prepared for them a city.

THE PILGRIMAGE

HENRY VAUGHAN

As travellers when the twilight's come,
And in the sky the stars appear,
The past days accidents do sum
With, *Thus we saw there, and thus here.*

Then Jacob-like lodge in a place
(A place, and no more, is set down,)
Where till the day restore the race
They rest and dream homes of their own.

So for this night I linger here,
And full of tossings too and fro,
Expect still when thou wilt appear
That I may get me up, and go.

I long, and groan, and grieve for thee,
For thee my words, my tears do gush,
O that I were but where I see!
Is all the note within my bush.

As birds robbed of their native wood,
Although their diet may be fine,
Yet neither sing, nor like their food,
But with the thought of home do pine;

So do I mourn, and hang my head,
And though thou dost me fullness give,
Yet look I for far better bread
Because by this man cannot live.

O feed me then! and since I may
Have yet more days, more nights to count,
So strengthen me, Lord, all the way,
That I may travel to thy Mount.

HEBREWS 11:28–40   **Through faith he kept the passover, and the sprin-
kling of blood, lest he that destroyed the firstborn should touch them. By
faith they passed through the Red sea as by dry land: which the Egyptians**

assaying to do were drowned. By faith the walls of Jericho fell down, after they were compassed about seven days. By faith the harlot Rahab perished not with them that believed not, when she had received the spies with peace. And what shall I more say? for the time would fail me to tell of Gideon, and of Barak, and of Samson, and of Jephthah; of David also, and Samuel, and of the prophets: Who through faith subdued kingdoms, wrought righteousness, obtained promises, stopped the mouths of lions. Quenched the violence of fire, escaped the edge of the sword, out of weakness were made strong, waxed valiant in fight, turned to flight the armies of the aliens. Women received their dead raised to life again: and others were tortured, not accepting deliverance; that they might obtain a better resurrection: And others had trial of cruel mockings and scourgings, yea, moreover of bonds and imprisonment: They were stoned, they were sawn asunder, were tempted, were slain with the sword: they wandered about in sheepskins and goatskins; being destitute, afflicted, tormented; (Of whom the world was not worthy:) they wandered in deserts, and in mountains, and in dens and caves of the earth. And these all, having obtained a good report through faith, received not the promise: God having provided some better thing for us, that they without us should not be made perfect.

THE PRAISE OF FAITH

JOHN HALL

If I shall enterprise to make
A due praise unto faith:
I can in no wise better that,
Which written is of Paul
In his Epistle to the Jews:
Mark therefore what he sayeth,
Though not each word, yet will I here
Recite the sum of all.

Faith is a perfect confidence,
Of things that hoped are,
And a most constant certainty,
Of things which are not seen.
For thereby did the fathers old,
(As scripture doth declare,)
Obtain a just and good report,
That long time since hath been.

And we through faith do understand,
God did the world ordain,

By Christ his son the blessed word,
That no beginning had.
By it also how things were wrought,
We do knowledge obtain:
Things that are seen by things not seen,
Were ordained and made.

By faith also (as we do read,)
The righteous man Abel
Did offer up a sacrifice,
More plentiful than Cain:
And thereby had a witness true,
(As holy writ doth tell,)
That he was just: Though he be dead,
His fame doth still remain.

By faith Enoch translated was,
That death he should not see,
And was not found: for god therefore
Had taken him away.
Before which time he won the name,
A righteous man to be,
Because he did the will of God,
And pleased him night and day.

But sure without a lively faith
It can be in no wise,
That any man by any mean
The living god should please:
For all that come to God believe,
(And their faith exercise,)
That he rewardeth them that seek
Him, with eternal ease.

By faith Noah (being warned of God,)
Unseen things did eschew,
Prepared an ark, and saved his folk,
As holy scripture sayth.
Whereby he did condemn the world,
That sin did still ensue:
And became heir of righteousness,
According unto faith.

By faith our father Abraham,
When he first called was,

To go into a place most strange,
Did by and by obey.
Which place though he inherit should,
As after came to pass:
When he went forth he knew it not,
Nor no part of the way.

By faith into the promised land,
I say he did remove,
A strange country where he did long
In tabernacles dwell:
And so did Isaac and Jacob,
Heirs with him from above.
All these did for a city look,
Which God had builded well.

Through faith Sara received strength,
When she was now past age,
To conceive and bring forth a son
That perfect was and pure:
Because she judged the promiser
Both faithful, true, and sage.
Lo thus by faith there sprang great health,
Where thought was no recure.

And therefore sprang there forth of one,
That dead was to esteem,
As many folk in multitude
As are stars in the sky:
And as the sand on the sea shore
Her offspring then did seem,
The which without number to be,
No creature can deny.

These died in faith, yet the promise
None of them did receive:
But seeing it as afar off,
They did right well believe,
That as many as so it saw
And to the same did cleave,
Saluting it by lively faith,
None evil should them grieve.

These faithful men the fathers old,
As truth was did confess,

That they strangers and pilgrims were
Upon this earthly vale.
For they that see such things before
Of truth declare no less,
But that they do a country seek
Right high above this dale.

Also if they had minded once,
The country whence they came,
They had leisure to turn again
To that which they did love:
But now it shows they did desire
A thing of better fame,
That is to say a heavenly soil,
With God the lord above.

Wherefore the living God himself
Esteemeth it no shame
To be called the God of these,
And suchlike godly men:
For he a city excellent
Hath builded for the same,
And thinketh nothing ill bestowed
That may well pleasure them.

Who so the text will farther read,
To follow there shall find
That Isaac, Jacob, and Joseph,
And Moses did the like:
By faith how the Red Sea went back,
Contrary to his kind:
As on dry land how Israel
Did pass through that dry dyke.

The Egyptians when they the like
Would seem to enterprise,
They lacking faith were drowned all,
As for their just reward.
By faith the walls of Jericho
Did fall down in like wise,
No force or engine of the wars
Against it once prepared.

The harlot Rahab in like wise,
How she did save her life,

And perished not with them that did
Resist the will of God:
When she the spies received well
In peace without all strife:
For she believed, that god would plague
That country with his rod.

What should be said of Gideon,
Of Barak, and Samson:
Jephthah, David, and Samuel,
And eke the prophets all,
Who did by faith great realms subdue
And mighty kingdoms won:
They turned their enemies to flight,
And gave their foes a fall.

By faith some stopped the lions' mouths,
Some quenched the rage of fire:
By faith some wrought out righteousness,
Some promise did obtain.
Some 'scaped the sword, some were made strong
Whom weakness erst did tire:
And women did their dead receive
To perfect life again.

Some racked were, and would not void
The danger of that woe,
Knowing that they should rise again,
Possessing better joy.
With mocks and scorns and prisonment,
Lo some were tried so:
Some were stoned, some were tempted,
Thus did the world them 'noy.

Some hewed were asunder quite,
Some with the sword were slain:
Some in the skins of sheep and goats
Disdained not to go,
In trouble and necessity,
They were content to reign
In mountains, deserts, and in dens,
By faith this could they do.

These, was the world not worthy of,
Yet did it them despise.

Though they did all (through lively faith)
Obtain a good report:
Yet did they not that time receive,
That God did them promise:
That we with them, and they with us,
Might jointly have comfort.

For Christ that holy promise was,
The fruit of all our faith:
Without whom none can saved be,
No neither we nor they,
For in him all fulfilled is,
That holy scripture sayth:
Ye Christ is he in whom both we
And they our faith do stay.

For which all honor laud and praise
To God ascribed be,
To the father, and to the son,
And to the holy spirit:
In unity, and trinity,
One God and persons three,
As hath been, is and shall be still,
For ever so be it.

HEBREWS 13:8–10   Jesus Christ the same yesterday, and to day, and for ever. Be not carried about with divers and strange doctrines. For it is a good thing that the heart be established with grace; not with meats, which have not profited them that have been occupied therein. We have an altar, whereof they have no right to eat which serve the tabernacle.

MEDITATION EIGHTEEN

Second Series

EDWARD TAYLOR

A bran, a chaff, a very barley awn,
     An husk, a shell, a nothing, nay yet worse,

A thistle, briar prickle, pricking thorn
    A lump of lewdness, pouch of sin, a purse
    Of naughtiness, I am, yea what not Lord?
    And wilt thou be mine altar? and my board?

Mine heart's a park or chase of sins: mine head
    'S a bowling alley. Sins play ninehole here.
Fant'sy's a green: sin barley breaks in't led.
    Judgment's a pingle. Blindman's Buff's played there.
    Sin plays at Course-a-park within my mind.
    My wills a walk in which it airs what's blind.

Sure then I lack atonement. Lord me help.
    Thy shittim wood o'er laid with wealthy brass
Was an atoning altar, and sweet smelt:
    But if o'er laid with pure pure gold it was
    It was an incense altar, all perfumed
    With odors, wherein Lord thou thus was bloomed.

Did this e'er-during wood when thus o'erspread
    With these e'erlasting metals altarwise
Type thy eternal plank of godhead, wed
    Unto our mortal chip, its sacrifice?
    Thy Deity mine altar. Manhood thine.
    Mine off'ring on't for all men's sins, and mine?

This golden altar puts such weight into
    The sacrifices offered on't that it
O'er weighs the weight of all the sins that flow
    In thine elect. This wedge, and beetle split
    The knotty logs of vengeance too to shivers:
    And from their guilt and shame them clear delivers.

This holy altar by its heavenly fire
    Refines our offerings: casts out their dross
And sanctifies their gold by its rich 'tire
    And all their steams with holy odors boss.
    Pillars of frankincense and rich perfume
    They 'tone Gods nostrils with, off from this loom.

Good news, good sirs, more good than comes within
    The canopy of angels. Heavens hall

Allows no better: this atones for sin,
>My glorious God, whose grace here thickest falls.
>May I my barley awn, bran, briar claw,
>Lay on't a sacrifice? or chaff or straw?

Shall I my sin pouch lay, on thy gold bench
>My offering, Lord, to thee? I've such alone
But have no better. For my sins do drench
>My very best unto their very bone.
>And shall mine offering by thine altars fire
>Refined, and sanctified to God aspire?

Amen, even so be it. I now will climb
>The stairs up to thine altar, and on't lay
Myself, and services, even for its shrine.
>My sacrifice brought thee accept I pray.
>My morn, and evening offerings I'll bring
>And on this golden altar incense fling.

Lord let thy deity mine altar be
>And make thy manhood, on't my sacrifice.
For mine atonement: make them both for me
>My altar t'sanctify my gifts likewise
>That so myself and service on't may bring
>Its worth along with them to thee my king.

The thoughts whereof, do make my tunes as fume,
>From off this altar rise to thee most high
And all their steams stuffed with thy altar's blooms,
>My sacrifice of praise in melody.
>Let thy bright angels catch my tune, and sing it.
>That equals David's Michtam which is in it.

JAMES 1:4–11 But let patience have her perfect work, that ye may be perfect and entire, wanting nothing. If any of you lack wisdom, let him ask of God, that giveth to all men liberally, and upbraideth not; and it shall be given him. But let him ask in faith, nothing wavering. For he that wavereth is like a wave of the sea driven with the wind and tossed. For let not that man think that he shall receive any thing of the Lord. A double minded man is unstable in all his ways. Let the brother of low degree rejoice in that he is exalted: But the rich, in that he is made low: because as the flower of the grass he shall pass away. For the sun is no sooner risen with a burning heat, but it withereth the grass, and the flower thereof falleth, and the grace of the fashion of it perisheth: so also shall the rich man fade away in his ways.

from *JUBILATE AGNO*

CHRISTOPHER SMART

For the doubling of flowers is the improvement of the gardener's talent.
For the flowers are great blessings.
For the Lord made a nosegay in the meadow with his disciples and
    preached upon the lily.
For the angels of God took it out of his hand and carried it to the
    Height.
For a man cannot have public spirit, who is void of private benevolence.
For there is no Height in which there are not flowers.
For flowers have great virtues for all the senses.
For the flower glorifies God and the root parries the adversary.
For the flowers have their angels even the words of God's Creation.
For the warp and woof of flowers are worked by perpetual moving
    spirits.
For flowers are good both for the living and the dead.
For there is a language of flowers.
For there is a sound reasoning upon all flowers.
For elegant phrases are nothing but flowers.
For flowers are peculiarly the poetry of Christ.
For flowers are medicinal.
For flowers are musical in ocular harmony.
For the right names of flowers are yet in heaven. God make gardeners
    better nomenclators.
For the poor man's nosegay is an introduction to a Prince.

JAMES 1:26–27 If any man among you seem to be religious, and bridleth not his tongue, but deceiveth his own heart, this man's religion is vain. Pure religion and undefiled before God and the Father is this, To visit the fatherless and widows in their affliction, and to keep himself unspotted from the world.

WORSHIP

JOHN GREENLEAF WHITTIER

The Pagan's myths through marble lips are spoken,
  And ghosts of old Beliefs still flit and moan
Round fane and altar overthrown and broken,
  O'er tree-grown barrow and gray ring of stone.

Blind faith had martyrs in those old high places,
  The Syrian hill grove and the Druid's wood,
With mothers offering, to the Fiend's embraces,
  Bone of their bone, and blood of their own blood.

Red altars, kindling through that night of error,
  Smoked with warm blood beneath the cruel eye
Of lawless power and sanguinary terror,
  Throned on the circle of a pitiless sky;

Beneath whose baleful shadow, over-casting
  All heaven above, and blighting earth below,
The scourge grew red, the lip grew pale with fasting,
  And man's oblation was his fear and woe!

Then through great temples swelled the dismal moaning
  Of dirge-like music and sepulchral prayer;
Pale wizard priests, o'er occult symbols droning,
  Swung their white censers in the burdened air:

As if the pomp of rituals, and the savor
  Of gums and spices could the Unseen One please;
As if His ear could bend, with childish favor,
  To the poor flattery of the organ keys!

Feet red from war-fields trod the church aisles holy,
  With trembling reverence: and the oppressor there,
Kneeling before his priest, abased and lowly,
  Crushed human hearts beneath his knee of prayer.

Not such the service the benignant Father
  Requireth at His earthly children's hands:
Not the poor offering of vain rites, but rather
  The simple duty man from man demands.

For Earth he asks it: the full joy of heaven
    Knoweth no change of waning or increase;
The great heart of the Infinite beats even,
    Untroubled flows the river of His peace.

He asks no taper lights, on high surrounding
    The priestly altar and the saintly grave,
No dolorous chant nor organ music sounding,
    Nor incense clouding up the twilight nave.

For he whom Jesus loved hath truly spoken:
    The holier worship which he deigns to bless
Restores the lost, and binds the spirit broken,
    And feeds the widow and the fatherless!

Types of our human weakness and our sorrow!
    Who lives unhaunted by his loved ones dead?
Who, with vain longing, seeketh not to borrow
    From stranger eyes the home lights which have fled?

O brother man! fold to thy heart thy brother;
    Where pity dwells, the peace of God is there;
To worship rightly is to love each other,
    Each smile a hymn, each kindly deed a prayer.

Follow with reverent steps the great example
    Of Him whose holy work was 'doing good';
So shall the wide earth seem our Father's temple,
    Each loving life a psalm of gratitude.

Then shall all shackles fall; the stormy clangor
    Of wild war music o'er the earth shall cease;
Love shall tread out the baleful fire of anger,
    And in its ashes plant the tree of peace!

FIRST PETER 3:17–20 **For it is better, if the will of God be so, that ye suffer for well doing, than for evil doing. For Christ also hath once suffered for sins, the just for the unjust, that he might bring us to God, being put to death in the flesh, but quickened by the Spirit: By which also he went and preached unto the spirits in prison; Which sometime were disobedient, when once the longsuffering of God waited in the days of Noah, while the ark was a preparing, wherein few, that is, eight souls were saved by water.**

MEDITATION TWENTY-NINE

Second Series

EDWARD TAYLOR

What shall I say, my Lord? with what begin?
    Immense profaneness wormholes every part.
The world is saddlebacked with loads of sin.
        Sin cracks the axle tree of this great cart.
        Floodgates of fiery vengeance open fly
        And smoky clouds of wrath darken the sky.

The fountains of the deep up broken are.
        The cataracts of heaven do boil o'er
With wallowing seas. Thunder, and lightnings tear
        Spouts out of Heaven, floods out from hell do roar
        To overflow, and drown the world all drowned
        And overflown with sin, that doth abound.

Oh! for an ark: an ark of gopher wood.
        This flood's too stately to be rode upon
By other boats, which are base swilling tubs.
        It gulps them up as gudgeons. And they're gone.
        But thou, my Lord, dost antitype this ark,
        And rod'st upon these waves that toss and bark.

Thy human nature, (oh choice timber rich)
        Bituminated ore within, and out
With dressing of the Holy Spirits pitch
        Propitiatory grace parged round about.
        This ark will ride upon the Flood, and live
        Nor passage to a drop through chink holes give.

This ark will swim upon the fiery flood:
        All showers of fire the heavens rain on't will
Slide off: though hells and heavens spouts out stood
        And meet upon't to crush't to shivers, still
        It neither sinks, breaks, fires, nor leaky proves,
        But lives upon them all and upward moves.

All that would not be drownded must be in't,
        Be arked in Christ, or else the cursed rout

Of crimson sins their cargo will them sink
>And suffocate in Hell, because without.
>Then ark me, Lord, thus in thyself that I
>May dance upon these drownding waves with joy.

Sweet ark, with concord sweetened, in thee feed
>The calf, and bear, lamb, lion at one crib.
Here rattlesnake and squirrel jar not, breed.
>The hawk and dove, the leopard, and the kid
>Do live in peace, the child, and cockatrice.
>As if red sin tantarrowed in no vice.

Take me, my Lord, into thy golden ark.
>Then when thy flood of fire shall come, I shall
Though Hell spews streams of flames, and th' heavens spark
>Out storms of burning coals, swim safe o'er all.
>I'll make thy curled flames my cittern's wire
>To toss my songs of praise rung on them, higher.

FIRST PETER 4:7–8   But the end of all things is at hand: be ye therefore sober, and watch unto prayer. And above all things have fervent charity among yourselves: for charity shall cover the multitude of sins.

DAY OF JUDGEMENT

HENRY VAUGHAN

When through the North a fire shall rush
>And roll into the East,
And like a fiery torrent brush
>And sweep up South, and West,

When all shall stream, and lighten round
>And with surprising flames
Both stars, and elements confound
>And quite blot out their names,

When thou shalt spend thy sacred store
>Of thunders in that heat
And low as e'er they lay before
>Thy six-days-buildings beat,

When like a scroll the heavens shall pass
      And vanish clean away,
And nought must stand of that vast space
      Which held up night, and day,

When one loud blast shall rend the deep,
      And from the womb of earth
Summon up all that are asleep
      Unto a second birth,

When thou shalt make the clouds thy seat,
      And in the open air
The quick, and dead, both small and great
      Must to thy bar repair;

O then it will be all too late
      To say, *What shall I do?*
Repentance there is out of date
      And so is mercy too;

Prepare, prepare me then, O God!
      And let me now begin
To feel my loving father's rod
      Killing the man of sin!

Give me, O give me crosses here,
      Still more afflictions lend,
That pill, though bitter, is most dear
      That brings health in the end;

Lord, God! I beg nor friends, nor wealth
      But pray against them both;
Three things I'd have, my souls chief health!
      And one of these seem loth,

A living *FAITH*, a *HEART* of flesh,
      The *WORLD* an enemy,
This last will keep the first two fresh,
      And bring me, where I'd be.

SECOND PETER 3:8   But, beloved, be not ignorant of this one thing, that one day is with the Lord as a thousand years, and a thousand years as one day.

ON THE LIFE OF MAN

FRANCIS QUARLES

A thousand years, with God (the Scriptures say)
    Are reckoned but a day;
By which account, this measured life of ours
    Exceeds not much an hour;
The half whereof nature does claim and keep
    As her own debt for sleep:
A full sixth part of what remains, we riot
    In more than needful diet:
Our infancy, our childhood, and the most
    Of our green youth is lost:
The little that is left, we thus divide;
    One part to clothe our pride,
An other share we lavishly deboise
    To vain, or sinful joys;
If then, at most, the measured life of man
    Be counted but a span,
Being halved and quartered, and disquartered thus,
    What, what remains for us?
Lord, if the total of our days do come
    To so-so poor a sum;
And if our shares so small, so nothing be,
Out of that nothing, what remains to Thee?

SECOND PETER 3:9–12   The Lord is not slack concerning his promise, as some men count slackness; but is longsuffering to us-ward, not willing that any should perish, but that all should come to repentance. But the day of the Lord will come as a thief in the night; in the which the heavens shall pass away with a great noise, and the elements shall melt with fervent heat, the earth also and the works that are therein shall be burned up. Seeing then that all these things shall be dissolved, what manner of persons ought ye to be in all holy conversation and godliness, Looking for and hasting unto the coming of the day of God, wherein the heavens being on fire shall be dissolved, and the elements shall melt with fervent heat?

A Dream

Sir John Suckling

Scarce had I slept my wonted round
But that methoughts I heard the last Trump sound:
And in a moment Earth's fair frame did pass,
The heavens did melt, and all confusion was.
My thoughts straight gave me, Earth's great day was come,
And that I was now to receive my doom.
'Twixt hope and fear, whilst I thus trembling stood
Fearing the bad, and yet expecting good:
Summoned I was, to show how I had spent,
That span-long time which God on earth me lent.
Cold fears possessed me; for I knew no lies
(Though gilded o'er) could blind th' Eternal's eyes.
Besides my bosom friend my conscience me accused,
That I too much this little time abused.
And now no sums of gold, no bribes (alas)
Could me reprieve, sentence must straightway pass.
Great friends could nothing do, no lustful peer,
No smooth-faced Buckingham, was favorite here.
These helps were vain; what could I then say more?
I had done ill, and death lay at the door.
But yet methoughts it was too much to die,
To die a while, much less eternally:
And therefore straight I did my sins unmask
And in Christ's name, a pardon there did ask
Which God then granted; and God grant he may
Make this my dream prove true i'th' latter day.

FIRST JOHN 2:15–17 **Love not the world, neither the things that are in the world. If any man love the world, the love of the Father is not in him. For all that is in the world, the lust of the flesh, and the lust of the eyes, and the pride of life, is not of the Father, but is of the world. And the world passeth away, and the lust thereof: but he that doeth the will of God abideth for ever.**

THE WORLD

HENRY VAUGHAN

I saw Eternity the other night
Like a great ring of pure and endless light,
   All calm, as it was bright,
And round beneath it, time in hours, days, years
     Driven by the spheres
Like a vast shadow moved, in which the world
   And all her train were hurled;
The doting lover in his quaintest strain
     Did there complain,
Near him, his lute, his fancy, and his flights,
     Wit's sour delights,
With gloves, and knots the silly snares of pleasure
     Yet his dear treasure
All scattered lay, while he his eyes did pour
     Upon a flower.

The darksome statesman hung with weights and woe
Like a thick midnight-fog moved there so slow
   He did nor stay, nor go;
Condemning thoughts (like sad eclipses) scowl
     Upon his soul,
And clouds of crying witnesses without
     Pursued him with one shout.
Yet digged the mole, and lest his ways be found
     Worked under ground,
Where he did clutch his prey, but one did see
     That policy,
Churches and altars fed him, perjuries
     Were gnats and flies,
It rained about him blood and tears, but he
     Drank them as free.

The fearful miser on a heap of rust
Sat pining all his life there, did scarce trust
     His own hands with the dust,
Yet would not place one piece above, but lives
     In fear of thieves.

Thousands there were as frantic as himself
      And hugged each one his pelf,
The down-right epicure placed heaven in sense
      And scorned pretence
While others slipped into a wide excess
      Said little less;
The weaker sort slight, trivial wares enslave
      Who think them brave,
And poor, despised truth sat counting by
      Their victory.

Yet some, who all this while did weep and sing,
And sing, and weep, soared up into the ring,
      But most would use no wing.
O fools (said I,) thus to prefer dark night
      Before true light,
To live in grots, and caves, and hate the day
      Because it shows the way,
The way which from this dead and dark abode
      Leads up to God,
A way where you might tread the sun, and be
      More bright than he.
But as I did their madness so discuss
      One whispered thus,
This ring the Bride-groom did for none provide
      But for his bride.

FIRST JOHN 3:1–2 Behold, what manner of love the Father hath bestowed upon us, that we should be called the sons of God: therefore the world knoweth us not, because it knew him not. Beloved, now are we the sons of God, and it doth not yet appear what we shall be: but we know that, when he shall appear, we shall be like him; for we shall see him as he is.

WHAT WE, WHEN FACE TO FACE

ARTHUR HUGH CLOUGH

What we, when face to face we see
The Father of our souls, shall be,
John tells us, doth not yet appear;
Ah! did he tell what we are here!

A mind for thoughts to pass into,
A heart for loves to travel through,
Five senses to detect things near,
Is this the whole that we are here?

Rules baffle instincts—instincts rules,
Wise men are bad—and good are fools,
Facts evil—wishes vain appear,
We cannot go, why are we here?

O may we for assurance' sake,
Some arbitrary judgement take,
And wilfully pronounce it clear,
For this or that 'tis we are here?

Or is it right, and will it do,
To pace the sad confusion through,
And say:—It doth not yet appear,
What we shall be, what we are here?

Ah yet, when all is thought and said,
The heart still overrules the head;
Still what we hope we must believe,
And what is given us receive;

Must still believe, for still we hope
That in a world of larger scope,
What here is faithfully begun
Will be completed, not undone.

My child, we still must think, when we
That ampler life together see,
Some true result will yet appear
Of what we are, together, here.

FIRST JOHN 4:4–21 Ye are of God, little children, and have overcome them: because greater is he that is in you, than he that is in the world. They are of the world: therefore speak they of the world, and the world heareth them. We are of God: he that knoweth God heareth us; he that is not of God heareth not us. Hereby know we the spirit of truth, and the spirit of error. Beloved, let us love one another: for love is of God; and every one that loveth is born of God, and knoweth God. . . . There is no

fear in love; but perfect love casteth out fear: because fear hath torment.
He that feareth is not made perfect in love. We love him, because he first
loved us. If a man say, I love God, and hateth his brother, he is a liar: for
he that loveth not his brother whom he hath seen, how can he love God
whom he hath not seen? And this commandment have we from him, That
he who loveth God love his brother also.

THE PRAISE OF GODLY LOVE

Out of 1 John. 4

JOHN HALL

Saint John divinely counsels us
One another to love,
For every one that loves sayeth he,
Of God is truly born.
For love doth ever surely come
From God the lord above:
Such as love not, do not know God,
But rather do him scorn.

In this the love of God to us
Doth perfectly appear.
He (but not we) did truly love
And pain for us did take:
For he into this world did send
His only son so dear,
That for our sins he might thereby
A full agreement make.

Wherefore (my loving brethren dear)
If God so loved us,
That we should one another love,
We certainly are bound:
If we love one another then,
Our love doth plain discuss,
That god in us doth dwell and reign,
And hath a perfect ground.

For God is love, and who so doth
In love abide or dwell,
Dwelleth in God and God in him,
Thus love in us is sure:

That in the day of judgement just
We should in hope excel.
For in this world we are like him,
By love perfect and pure.

By this we know the godly love,
That there in is no fear:
It casteth out all fear and doubt
Wherein is painfulness.
Where timor is, the perfect love
In no wise can be there,
For love doth always fix her self
On peace and gentleness.

If we love God, he loved us first,
Then whereof can we boast?
But whoso sayeth he loveth God
And doth his brother hate:
He is a liar verily,
And none of Christës host:
And thereby doth provoke the plague
To light upon his pate.

For how can he that loveth not
His brother in this life,
Whom he may with his eyes behold,
At all times when he will:
How can he with the living God
Be other then at strife?
Or love him which he can not see
By nature or by skill?

Therefore hath Christ commanded us,
That he which loveth God,
By perfect love as he forbears
All that God doth abhor:
That he also his brother love,
All hate is him forbad.
All honor praise and laud to God
For this now ever more.
      Amen.

JUDE 1:5–6 I will therefore put you in remembrance, though ye once knew this, how that the Lord, having saved the people out of the land of Egypt, afterward destroyed them that believed not. And the angels which kept not their first estate, but left their own habitation, he hath reserved in everlasting chains under darkness unto the judgment of the great day.

THE DAY OF JUDGMENT

ISAAC WATTS

When the fierce north wind with his airy forces
Rears up the Baltic to a foaming fury,
And the red lightning with a storm of hail comes
                  Rushing amain down,

How the poor sailors stand amazed and tremble,
While the hoarse thunder, like a bloody trumpet,
Roars a loud onset to the gaping waters,
                  Quick to devour them!

Such shall the noise be and the wild disorder,
(If things eternal may be like these earthly)
Such the dire terror, when the great Archangel
                  Shakes the creation,

Tears the strong pillars of the vault of heaven,
Breaks up old marble, the repose of princes;
See the graves open, and the bones arising,
                  Flames all around 'em!

Hark, the shrill outcries of the guilty wretches!
Lively bright horror and amazing anguish
Stare through their eyelids, while the living worm lies
                  Gnawing within them.

Thoughts like old vultures prey upon their heart-strings,
And the smart twinges, when the eye beholds the
Lofty Judge frowning, and a flood of vengeance
                  Rolling afore him.

Hopeless immortals! how they scream and shiver,
While devils push them to the pit wide-yawning
Hideous and gloomy, to receive them headlong
                  Down to the center.

Stop here, my fancy: (all away ye horrid
Doleful ideas); come, arise to Jesus;
How He sits God-like! and the saints around him
                    Throned, yet adoring!

Oh may I sit there when he comes triumphant
Dooming the nations! then ascend to glory
While our hosannas all along the passage
                    Shout the Redeemer.

THE REVELATION

of St. John the Divine

1:1–19 . . . **I John, who also am your brother, and companion in tribulation, and in the kingdom and patience of Jesus Christ, was in the isle that is called Patmos, for the word of God, and for the testimony of Jesus Christ. I was in the Spirit on the Lord's day, and heard behind me a great voice, as of a trumpet, Saying, I am Alpha and Omega, the first and the last: and, What thou seest, write in a book, and send it unto the seven churches which are in Asia; unto Ephesus, and unto Smyrna, and unto Pergamos, and unto Thyatira, and unto Sardis, and unto Philadelphia, and unto Laodicea. And I turned to see the voice that spake with me. . . . And when I saw him, I fell at his feet as dead. And he laid his right hand upon me, saying unto me, Fear not; I am the first and the last: I am he that liveth, and was dead; and, behold, I am alive for evermore, Amen; and have the keys of hell and of death. Write the things which thou hast seen, and the things which are, and the things which shall be hereafter;**

TO GOD

ROBERT HERRICK

Do with me, God! as Thou didst deal with John,
(Who writ that heavenly *Revelation*)
Let me (like him) first cracks of thunder hear;
Then let the harp's enchantments strike mine ear;
Here give me thorns; there, in thy Kingdom, set

Upon my head the golden coronet;
There give me day; but here my dreadful night:
My sackcloth here; but there my stole of white.

BREAD-WORD GIVER

JOHN WHEELWRIGHT

For John, Unborn

John, founder of towns,—dweller in none;
Wheelwright, schismatic,—schismatic from schismatics;
friend of great men whom these great feared greatly;
Saint, whose name and business I bear with me;
rebel New England's rebel against dominion;
who made bread-giving words for bread makers;
whose blood floods me with purgatorial fire;
I, and my unliving son, adjure you:
keep us alive with your ghostly disputation
make our renunciation of dominion
mark not the escape, but the permanent of rebellion.

Speak! immigrant ancestor in blood; brain
ancestor of all immigrants I like. Speak,
who unsealed sealed wells with a flame and sword:
    'The springs that we dug clean must be kept flowing.
    If Philistines choke wells with dirt,—open
    'em up clear. And we have a flaming flare
    whose light is the flare that flames up in the people.

    'The way we take (who will not fire and water
    taken away) is this: prepare to fight. If we
    fight not for fear in the night, we shall be surprised.
    Wherever we live, who want present abundance
    take care to show ourselves brave. If *we* do not try
    they prevail. Come out,—get ready for war;
    stalwart men, out and fight. Cursed
    are all who'll come not against strong wrong.
    First steel your swordarm and first sword.
    But the second way to go? and deed to do?

'That is this: Take hold upon our foes and kill.
We are they whose power underneath a nation
breaks it in bits as shivered by iron bars.
What iron bars are these but working wills?
Toothed as spiked threshing flails we beat
hills into chaff. Wherefore, handle our second
swords with awe. They are two-edged. They cut their wielders'
    hearts.'

3:1–6 And unto the angel of the church in Sardis write; These things saith he that hath the seven Spirits of God, and the seven stars; I know thy works, that thou hast a name that thou livest, and art dead. Be watchful, and strengthen the things which remain, that are ready to die: for I have not found thy works perfect before God. Remember therefore how thou hast received and heard, and hold fast, and repent. If therefore thou shalt not watch, I will come on thee as a thief, and thou shalt not know what hour I will come upon thee. Thou hast a few names even in Sardis which have not defiled their garments; and they shall walk with me in white: for they are worthy. He that overcometh, the same shall be clothed in white raiment; and I will not blot out his name out of the book of life, but I will confess his name before my Father, and before his angels. He that hath an ear, let him hear what the Spirit saith unto the churches.

SARDIS

WILLIAM COWPER

"Write to Sardis," saith the Lord,
    And write what he declares,
He whose Spirit and whose word,
    Upholds the seven stars:
"All thy works and ways I search,
    Find thy zeal and love decayed:
Thou art called a living church,
    But thou art cold and dead.

"Watch, remember, seek, and strive,
    Exert thy former pains;
Let thy timely care revive,
    And strengthen what remains:
Cleanse thine heart, thy works amend,
    Former times to mind recall,

Lest my sudden stroke descend,
    And smite thee once for all.

"Yet I number now in thee
    A few that are upright:
These my Father's face shall see,
    And walk with me in white,
When in judgment I appear,
    They for mine shall be confessed;
Let my faithful servants hear,
    And woe be to the rest!"

7:1–3 And after these things I saw four angels standing on the four corners of the earth, holding the four winds of the earth, that the wind should not blow on the earth, nor on the sea, nor on any tree. And I saw another angel ascending from the east, having the seal of the living God: and he cried with a loud voice to the four angels, to whom it was given to hurt the earth and the sea, Saying, Hurt not the earth, neither the sea, nor the trees, till we have sealed the servants of our God in their foreheads.

THE TREES ARE DOWN

CHARLOTTE MEW

They are cutting down the great plane-trees at the end of the gardens.
For days there has been the grate of the saw, the swish of the branches
    as they fall,
The crash of trunks, the rustle of trodden leaves,
With the "Whoops" and the "Whoas," the loud common talk, the loud
    common laughs of the men, above it all.

I remember one evening of a long past Spring
Turning in at a gate, getting out of a cart, and finding a large dead rat in
    the mud of the drive.
I remember thinking: alive or dead, a rat was a god-forsaken thing,
But at least, in May, that even a rat should be alive.

The week's work here is as good as done. There is just one bough
    On the roped bole, in the fine gray rain,
        Green and high
        And lonely against the sky.
           (Down now!)
        And but for that,
        If an old dead rat

Did once, for a moment, unmake the Spring, I might never have
        thought of him again.

It is not for a moment the Spring is unmade today;
These were great trees, it was in them from root to stem:
When the men with the "Whoops" and the "Whoas" have carted the
        whole of the whispering loveliness away,
Half the Spring, for me, will have gone with them.

It is going now, and my heart has been struck with the hearts of the
        planes;
Half my life it has beat with these, in the sun, in the rains,
        In the March wind, the May breeze,
In the great gales that came over to them across the roofs from the great
        seas.
        There was only a quiet rain when they were dying;
        They must have heard the sparrows flying,
And the small creeping creatures in the earth where they were lying—
        But I, all day, I heard an angel crying:
        "Hurt not the trees."

7:13–17   And one of the elders answered, saying unto me, What are these which are arrayed in white robes? and whence came they? And I said unto him, Sir, thou knowest. And he said to me, These are they which came out of great tribulation, and have washed their robes, and made them white in the blood of the Lamb. Therefore are they before the throne of God, and serve him day and night in his temple: and he that sitteth on the throne shall dwell among them. They shall hunger no more, neither thirst any more; neither shall the sun light on them, nor any heat. For the Lamb which is in the midst of the throne shall feed them, and shall lead them unto living fountains of waters: and God shall wipe away all tears from their eyes.

GENERAL WILLIAM BOOTH[*] ENTERS INTO HEAVEN

VACHEL LINDSAY

*(To be sung to the tune of 'The Blood of the Lamb'
with indicated instrument)*

(Bass drum beaten loudly.)
Booth led boldly with his big bass drum—
(Are you washed in the blood of the Lamb?)

---

[*]Englishman (1829–1912), founder and commander-in-chief of the Salvation Army.

The Saints smiled gravely and they said: 'He's come.'
(Are you washed in the blood of the Lamb?)
Walking lepers followed, rank on rank,
Lurching bravos from the ditches dank
Drabs from the alleyways and drug fiends pale—
Minds still passion-ridden, soul-powers frail:—
Vermin-eaten saints with moldy breath,
Unwashed legions with the ways of Death—
(Are you washed in the blood of the Lamb?)

    (Banjos.)
Every slum had sent its half-a-score
The round world over. (Booth had groaned for more.)
Every banner that the wide world flies
Bloomed with glory and transcendent dyes.
Big-voiced lasses made their banjos bang,
Tranced, fanatical they shrieked and sang:—
'Are you washed in the blood of the Lamb?'
Hallelujah! It was queer to see
Bull-necked convicts with that land make free.
Loons with trumpets blowed a blare, blare, blare
On, on upward through the golden air!
(Are you washed in the blood of the Lamb?)

    (Bass drum slower and softer.)
Booth died blind and still by faith he trod,
Eyes still dazzled by the ways of God.
Booth led boldly, and he looked the chief
Eagle countenance in sharp relief,
Beard a-flying, air of high command
Unabated in that holy land.

    (Sweet flute music.)
Jesus came from out the court-house door
Stretched his hands above the passing poor.
Booth saw not, but led his queer ones there
Round and round the mighty court-house square.
Then, in an instant all that blear review
Marched on spotless, clad in raiment new.
The lame were straightened, withered limbs uncurled
And blind eyes opened on a new, sweet world.

(Bass drum louder.)
Drabs and vixens in a flash made whole!
Gone was the weaselhead, the snout, the jowl!
Sages and sibyls now, and athletes clean,
Rulers of empires, and of forests green!

(Grand chorus of all instruments. Tambourines to the foreground.)
The hosts were sandalled, and their wings were fire!
(Are you washed in the blood of the Lamb?)
But their noise played havoc with the angel-choir.
(Are you washed in the blood of the Lamb?)
Oh, shout Salvation! It was good to see
Kings and Princes by the Lamb set free.
The banjos rattled and the tambourines
Jing-jing-jingled in the hands of Queens.

(Reverently sung, no instruments.)
And when Booth halted by the curb for prayer
He saw his Master through the flag-filled air.
Christ came gently with a robe and crown
For Booth the soldier, while the throng knelt down.
He saw King Jesus. They were face to face,
And he knelt a-weeping in that holy place.
Are you washed in the blood of the Lamb?

8:1–7 And when he had opened the seventh seal, there was silence in heaven about the space of half an hour. And I saw the seven angels which stood before God; and to them were given seven trumpets. And another angel came and stood at the altar, having a golden censer; and there was given unto him much incense, that he should offer it with the prayers of all saints upon the golden altar which was before the throne. And the smoke of the incense, which came with the prayers of the saints, ascended up before God out of the angel's hand. And the angel took the censer, and filled it with fire of the altar, and cast it into the earth: and there were voices, and thunderings, and lightnings, and an earthquake. And the seven angels which had the seven trumpets prepared themselves to sound.

HOLY SONNET VII

JOHN DONNE

At the round Earth's imagined corners, blow
Your trumpets, Angels, and arise, arise

From death, you numberless infinities
Of souls, and to your scattered bodies go,
All whom the flood did, and fire shall o'erthrow,
All whom war, dearth, age, agues, tyrannies,
Despair, law, chance, hath slain, and you whose eyes,
Shall behold God, and never taste death's woe.
But let them sleep, Lord, and me mourn a space,
For, if above all these, my sins abound,
'Tis late to ask abundance of thy grace,
When we are there; here on this lowly ground,
Teach me how to repent; for that's as good
As if thou hadst sealed my pardon, with thy blood.

9:1–2 And the fifth angel sounded, and I saw a star fall from heaven unto the earth: and to him was given the key of the bottomless pit. And he opened the bottomless pit; and there arose a smoke out of the pit, as the smoke of a great furnace; and the sun and the air were darkened by reason of the smoke of the pit.

THE CROSS

ALLEN TATE

There is a place that some men know,
I cannot see the whole of it
Nor how I came there. Long ago
Flame burst out of a secret pit
Crushing the world with such a light
The day-sky fell to moonless black,
The kingly sun to hateful night
For those, once seeing, turning back:
For love so hates mortality
Which is the providence of life
She will not let it blessèd be
But curses it with mortal strife,
Until beside the blinding rood
Within that world-destroying pit
—Like young wolves that have tasted blood—
Of death, men taste no more of it.
So blind, in so severe a place
(All life before in the black grave)

The last alternatives they face
Of life, without the life to save,
Being from all salvation weaned—
A stag charged both at heel and head:
Who would come back is turned a fiend
Instructed by the fiery dead.

12:1–6   And there appeared a great wonder in heaven; a woman clothed with the sun, and the moon under her feet, and upon her head a crown of twelve stars: And she being with child cried, travailing in birth, and pained to be delivered. And there appeared another wonder in heaven; and behold a great red dragon, having seven heads and ten horns, and seven crowns upon his heads. And his tail drew the third part of the stars of heaven, and did cast them to the earth: and the dragon stood before the woman which was ready to be delivered, for to devour her child as soon as it was born. And she brought forth a man child, who was to rule all nations with a rod of iron: and her child was caught up unto God, and to his throne. And the woman fled into the wilderness, where she hath a place prepared of God, that they should feed her there a thousand two hundred and threescore days.

THE MENTAL TRAVELLER

WILLIAM BLAKE

I travelled through a Land of Men,
A Land of Men and Women too,
And heard and saw such dreadful things
As cold Earth wanderers never knew.

For there the Babe is born in joy
That was begotten in dire woe;
Just as we Reap in joy the fruit
Which we in bitter tears did sow.

And if the Babe is born a Boy
He's given to a Woman Old,
Who nails him down upon a rock,
Catches his shrieks in cups of gold.

She binds iron thorns around his head,
She pierces both his hands and feet,

She cuts his heart out at his side
To make it feel both cold and heat.

Her fingers number every Nerve,
Just as a Miser counts his gold;
She lives upon his shrieks and cries,
And she grows young as he grows old.

Till he becomes a bleeding youth,
And she becomes a Virgin bright;
Then he rends up his Manacles
And binds her down for his delight.

He plants himself in all her Nerves,
Just as a Husbandman his mould;
And she becomes his dwelling place
And Garden fruitful seventy fold.

An aged Shadow, soon he fades,
Wand'ring round an Earthly Cot,
Full filled all with gems and gold
Which he by industry had got.

And these are the gems of the Human Soul,
The rubies and pearls of a lovesick eye,
The countless gold of the aching heart,
The martyr's groan and the lover's sigh.

They are his meat, they are his drink;
He feeds the Beggar and the Poor
And the wayfaring Traveller:
For ever open is his door.

His grief is their eternal joy;
They make the roofs and walls to ring;
Till from the fire on the hearth
A little Female Babe does spring.

And she is all of solid fire
And gems and gold, that none his hand
Dares stretch to touch her Baby form
Or wrap her in his swaddling-band.

But She comes to the Man she loves,
If young or old, or rich or poor;

They soon drive out the aged Host,
A Beggar at another's door.

He wanders weeping far away,
Until some other take him in;
Oft blind and age-bent, sore distrest,
Until he can a Maiden win.

And to allay his freezing Age
The Poor Man takes her in his arms;
The Cottage fades before his sight,
The Garden and its lovely Charms.

The Guests are scattered through the land,
For the Eye altering alters all;
The Senses roll themselves in fear,
And the flat Earth becomes a Ball;

The stars, sun, Moon, all shrink away,
A desart vast without a bound,
And nothing left to eat or drink,
And a dark desart all around.

The honey of her Infant lips,
The bread and wine of her sweet smile,
The wild game of her roving Eye,
Does him to Infancy beguile;

For as he eats and drinks he grows
Younger and younger every day;
And on the desart wild they both
Wander in terror and dismay.

Like the wild Stag she flees away,
Her fear plants many a thicket wild;
While he pursues her night and day,
By various arts of Love beguiled,

By various arts of Love and Hate,
Till the wide desart planted o'er
With Labyrinths of wayward Love,
Where roam the Lion, Wolf and Boar,

Till he becomes a wayward Babe,
And she a weeping Woman Old.

Then many a Lover wanders here;
The Sun and Stars are nearer rolled.

The trees bring forth sweet Extacy
To all who in the desert roam;
Till many a City there is Built,
And many a pleasant Shepherd's home.

But when they find the frowning Babe,
Terror strikes through the region wide:
They cry "The Babe! the Babe is Born!"
And flee away on Every side.

For who dare touch the frowning form,
His arm is withered to its root;
Lions, Boars, Wolves, all howling flee,
And every Tree does shed its fruit.

And none can touch that frowning form,
Except it be a Woman Old;
She nails him down upon the Rock,
And all is done as I have told.

12:7–9 And there was war in heaven: Michael and his angels fought against the dragon; and the dragon fought and his angels, And prevailed not; neither was their place found any more in heaven. And the great dragon was cast out, that old serpent, called the Devil, and Satan, which deceiveth the whole world: he was cast out into the earth, and his angels were cast out with him.

TO ST MICHAEL THE ARCHANGEL

HENRY CONSTABLE

When as the prince of Angels puffed with pride
        stirred his seditious spirits to rebel:
        God choose for chief, his champion Michael:
        and gave him charge the host of heaven to guide.
And when the Angels of the rebel's side
        vanquished in battle from their glory fell,
        the pride of heaven became the Drake of hell,
        and in the dungeon of despair was tied.

> This Dragon since let loose, God's Church assailed,
>   and she by help of Michael's sword prevailed.
>   Who ever tried adventures like this knight?
> Which general of heaven, hell overthrew;
>   for such a Lady as God's spouse did fight:
>   and such a monster as the Devil subdue.

13:1–3 And I stood upon the sand of the sea, and saw a beast rise up out of the sea, having seven heads and ten horns, and upon his horns ten crowns, and upon his heads the name of blasphemy. And the beast which I saw was like unto a leopard, and his feet were as the feet of a bear, and his mouth as the mouth of a lion: and the dragon gave him his power, and his seat, and great authority. And I saw one of his heads as it were wounded to death; and his deadly wound was healed: and all the world wondered after the beast.

Sonnet XII

Edmund Spenser

I saw an ugly beast come from the sea,
   That seven heads, ten crowns, ten horns did bear,
   Having thereon the vile blaspheming name.
The cruel leopard she resembled much:
   Feet of a bear, a lion's throat she had.
   The mighty dragon gave to her his power.
One of her heads yet there I did espy,
   Still freshly bleeding of a grievous wound.
   One cried aloud. What one is like (quoth he)
This honored dragon, or may him withstand?
   And then came from the sea a savage beast,
   With dragon's speech, and showed his force by fire,
With wondrous signs to make all wights adore
   The beast, in setting of her image up.

16:1–18 And I heard a great voice out of the temple saying to the seven angels, Go your ways, and pour out the vials of the wrath of God upon the earth. And the first went, and poured out his vial upon the earth; and there fell a noisome and grievous sore upon the men which had the mark of the beast, and upon them which worshipped his image. And the second

angel poured out his vial upon the sea; and it became as the blood of a
dead man: and every living soul died in the sea. And the third angel
poured out his vial upon the rivers and fountains of waters; and they
became blood. And I heard the angel of the waters say, Thou art
righteous, O Lord, which art, and wast, and shalt be, because thou
hast judged thus. For they have shed the blood of saints and prophets,
and thou hast given them blood to drink; for they are worthy. And I
heard another out of the altar say, Even so, Lord God Almighty, true
and righteous are thy judgments. And the fourth angel poured out his
vial upon the sun; and power was given unto him to scorch men with fire.
And men were scorched with great heat, and blasphemed the name of
God, which hath power over these plagues: and they repented not to give
him glory. And the fifth angel poured out his vial upon the seat of the
beast; and his kingdom was full of darkness; and they gnawed their
tongues for pain, And blasphemed the God of heaven because of their
pains and their sores, and repented not of their deeds. And the sixth
angel poured out his vial upon the great river Euphrates; and the water
thereof was dried up, that the way of the kings of the east might be prepared.

And I saw three unclean spirits like frogs come out of the mouth of
the dragon, and out of the mouth of the beast, and out of the mouth of the
false prophet. For they are the spirits of devils, working miracles, which
go forth unto the kings of the earth and of the whole world, to gather
them to the battle of that great day of God Almighty. Behold, I come as a
thief. Blessed is he that watcheth, and keepeth his garments, lest he walk
naked, and they see his shame. And he gathered them together into a
place called in the Hebrew tongue Armageddon. And the seventh angel
poured out his vial into the air; and there came a great voice out of the
temple of heaven, from the throne, saying, It is done. And there were
voices, and thunders, and lightnings; and there was a great earthquake,
such as was not since men were upon the earth, so mighty an earthquake,
and so great.

ARMAGEDDON

JOHN CROWE RANSOM

Antichrist, playing his lissome flute and merry
As was his wont, debouched upon the plain;
Then came a swirl of dust, and Christ drew rein,
Brooding upon his frugal breviary.

Now which shall die, the roundel, rose, and hall,
Or else the tonsured beadsman's monkery?
For Christ and Antichrist arm cap-a-pie,
The prospect charms the soul of the lean jackal.

But Antichrist got down from the Barbary beast
And doffed his plume in courteous prostration;
Christ left his jennet's back in deprecation
And raised him, his own hand about the waist.

Then next they fingered chivalry's quaint page,
Of precedence discoursing by the letter.
The oratory of Antichrist was better,
He invested Christ with the elder lineage.

He set Christ on his own Mahomet's back
Where Christ sat fortressed up like Diomede;
The cynical hairy jennet was his steed.
Obtuse, and most indifferent to attack.

The lordings measured lances and stood still,
And each was loath to let the other's blood;
Originally they were one brotherhood;
There stood the white pavilion on the hill.

To the pavilion went then the hierarchs,
If they might truce their honorable dispute;
Firm was the Christian's chin and he was mute,
And Antichrist ejected scant remarks.

Antichrist tendered a spray of rosemary
To serve his brother for a buttonhole;
Then Christ about his adversary's poll
Wrapped a dry palm that grew on Calvary.

Christ wore a dusty cassock, and the knight
Did him the honors of his tiring-hall,
Whence Christ did not come forth too finical,
But his egregious beauty richly dight.

With feasting they concluded every day,
And when the other shaped his phrases thicker
Christ, introducing water in the liquor,
Made wine of more ethereal bouquet.

At wassail Antichrist would pitch the strain
For unison of all the retinue;
Christ beat the time, and hummed a stave or two,
But did not say the words, which were profane.

Perruquiers were privily presented,
Till, knowing his need extreme and his heart pure,
Christ let them dress him his thick chevelure,
And soon his beard was glozed and sweetly scented.

And so the Wolf said Brother to the Lamb,
The True Heir keeping with the poor Impostor,
The rubric and the holy paternoster
Were jangled strangely with the dithyramb.

It could not be. There was a patriarch,
A godly liege of old malignant brood,
Who could not fathom the new brotherhood
Between the children of the light and dark.

He sought the ear of Christ on these strange things,
But in the white pavilion when he stood,
And saw them favored and dressed like twins at food,
Profound and mad became his misgivings.

The voices, and their burdens, he must hear,
But equal between the pleasant Princes flew
Theology, the arts, the old customs and the new;
Hoarsely he ran and hissed in the wrong ear.

He was discomfited, but Christ much more.
Christ sheds unmannerly his devil's pelf,
Takes ashes from the hearth and smears himself,
Calls for his smock and jennet as before.

His trump recalls his own to right opinions,
With scourge they mortify their carnal selves,
With stone they whet the ax-heads on the helves
And seek the Prince Beelzebub and minions.

Christ and his myrmidons, Christ at the head,
Chanted of death and glory and no complaisance;
Antichrist and the armies of malfeasance
Made songs of innocence and no bloodshed.

The immortal Adversary shook his head:
If now they fought too long, then he would famish;
And if much blood was shed, why, he was squeamish:
"These Armageddons weary me much," he said.

17:1–5 And there came one of the seven angels which had the seven vials, and talked with me, saying unto me, Come hither; I will shew unto thee the judgment of the great whore that sitteth upon many waters: With whom the kings of the earth have committed fornication, and the inhabitants of the earth have been made drunk with the wine of her fornication. So he carried me away in the spirit into the wilderness: and I saw a woman sit upon a scarlet coloured beast, full of names of blasphemy, having seven heads and ten horns. And the woman was arrayed in purple and scarlet colour, and decked with gold and precious stones and pearls, having a golden cup in her hand full of abominations and filthiness of her fornication: And upon her forehead was a name written, MYSTERY, BABYLON THE GREAT, THE MOTHER OF HARLOTS AND ABOMINATIONS OF THE EARTH.

SONNET XIII

EDMUND SPENSER

I saw a woman sitting on a beast
Before mine eyes, of orange color hue:
Horror and dreadful name of blasphemy
Filled her with pride. And seven heads I saw,
Ten horns also the stately beast did bear.
She seemed with glory of the scarlet fair,
And with fine pearl and gold puffed up in heart.
The wine of whoredom in a cup she bare.
The name of Mystery writ in her face.
The blood of martyrs dear were her delight.
Most fierce and fell this woman seemed to me.
An angel then descending down from Heaven,
With thundering voice cried out aloud, and said,
Now for a truth great Babylon is fallen.

18:1–2 And after these things I saw another angel come down from heaven, having great power; and the earth was lightened with his glory. And he cried mightily with a strong voice, saying, Babylon the great is fallen, is fallen, and is become the habitation of devils, and the hold of every foul spirit, and a cage of every unclean and hateful bird.

LET GO THE WHORE OF BABYLON

MILES COVERDALE

Let go the whore of Babylon,
    Her kingdom falleth sore
Her merchants begin to make their moan
    The Lord be praised therefore.
Their ware is naught / it will not be bought
Great falsehood is found therein.
Let go the whore of Babylon
    The mother of all sin.

No man will drink her wine any more
    The poison is come to light,
That maketh her merchants to weep so sore
    The blind have gotten their sight
For now we see / gods grace seely
Is Christ offered us so fair
Let go the whore of Babylon
    And buy no more her ware.

Of Christian blood so much she shed
    That she was drunken withal
But now Gods word hath broken her head
    And she hath gotten a fall
God hath raised / some men in deed
To utter her great wickedness
Let go the whore of Babylon
    And her ungodliness.

Ye hypocrites what can ye say?
    Woe be unto you all
Ye have beguiled us many a day
    Heretics ye did us call
For loving the word / of Christ the Lord
Whom ye do always resist
Let go the whore of Babylon
    That rideth upon the beast.

Ye proud and cruel Egyptians
    That did us so great wrong
The lord hath sent us deliverance
    Though ye have troubled us long

Your Pharaoh / with other mo
He drowned in the Reed Sea
Let go the whore of Babylon
  With her captivity.

Ye Canaanites ye enemies all
  Though ye were many in deed
Yet hath the lord given you a fall
  And us delivered
Even in your land / do we now stand
Our lord god hath brought us in
Let go the whore of Babylon
  And flee from all her sin.

Dagon Dagon that false idol
  The Philistine's god
Which hath deceived many a soul
  In such honor he stood
But now the lord / with his sweet word
  Hath broken him down before the ark
Let go the whore of Babylon
  And forsake the beastës mark.

Balaam Balaam thou false prophet
  Thou hast cursed us right sore
Yet into a blessing hath god turned it
  No thank to thee therefore
For thy belly / thou wouldest lie
  Though God make thee to say the sooth
Let go the whore of Babylon
  And turn you to the truth.

Thy God be praised o Daniel
  For his goodness so great
The greedy priests of the Idol Bel
  Were wont too much to eat
And that privily / no man did see
But now the king hath spied their cast
Let go the whore of Babylon
  For Bel is destroyed at the last.

O glorious God full of mercy
  We thank thee evermore
Thou hast showed us thy verity
  Thy name be praised therefore

For thy sweet word / O gracious Lord
Let us be ever thankful to thee
And send the whore of Babylon
    Into captivity.

Rejoice with me thou heaven above
    And ye Apostles all
Be glad ye people for Christ's love
    That the whore hath gotten a fall
Be thankful now / I require you
Amend your lives while ye have space
Let go the whore of Babylon
    And thank god of his grace.

19:11–13 And I saw heaven opened, and behold a white horse; and he that sat upon him was called Faithful and True, and in righteousness he doth judge and make war. His eyes were as a flame of fire, and on his head were many crowns; and he had a name written, that no man knew, but he himself. And he was clothed with a vesture dipped in blood: and his name is called The Word of God.

SONNET XIV

EDMUND SPENSER

Then might I see upon a white horse set
The faithful man with flaming countenance,
His head did shine with crowns set thereupon.
The word of God made him a noble name.
His precious robe I saw embrewed with blood.
Then saw I from the heaven on horses white,
A puissant army come the self-same way.
Then cried a shining angel as me thought,
That birds from air descending down on earth
Should war upon the kings, and eat their flesh.
Then did I see the beast and kings also
Joining their force to slay the faithful man.
But this fierce hateful beast and all her train,
Is pitiless thrown down in pit of fire.

20:1–4 And I saw an angel come down from heaven, having the key of
the bottomless pit and a great chain in his hand. And he laid hold on the
dragon, that old serpent, which is the Devil, and Satan, and bound him a
thousand years, And cast him into the bottomless pit, and shut him up,
and set a seal upon him, that he should deceive the nations no more, till
the thousand years should be fulfilled: and after that he must be loosed a
little season. And I saw thrones, and they sat upon them, and judgment
was given unto them: and I saw the souls of them that were beheaded for
the witness of Jesus, and for the word of God, and which had not worshipped the beast, neither his image, neither had received his mark upon
their foreheads, or in their hands; and they lived and reigned with Christ
a thousand years.

from THE CRY OF A STONE

ANNA TRAPNELL

Therefore *John* read how that thou wouldst
  the earth again restore.
None shall hinder them from those thrones
  which *John* there did declare:
Oh a sea of glass there crystal was
  which none could it compare:
But oh your standing on the earth,
  on glass that brittle is,
Which shall crumble under your feet
  when that there comes forth this,
This sea of glass which is indeed,
  that where thine thee behold:
Oh they may look up unto thee,
  and thorough it extol
Thy love that did a book write sweet,
  and many things there in store
Of royalties which should come out,
  and be given more and more,
Unto those that deny thy foes,
  and Antichrist also,
They that go forth to strike at him,
  thou wilt upon them blow,
Thy spirit upon them shall come forth
  and Antichrist shall fall

Both in person, and also too,
    in his coming principal.
Oh it is Lord, then sweet surely,
    to read of such things here,
And *John* he mourned abundantly,
    that th' mystery might draw near,
That new Jerusalem above,
    might come down here below,
And that they might see their High,
    when that forth he doth go.

20:5–6 **But the rest of the dead lived not again until the thousand years were finished. This is the first resurrection. Blessed and holy is he that hath part in the first resurrection: on such the second death hath no power, but they shall be priests of God and of Christ, and shall reign with him a thousand years.**

'WOEFULLY ARRAYED'

JOHN SKELTON?

Woefully arrayed,
My blood, man,
For thee ran,
It may not be nayed:
My body blue and wan,
Woefully arrayed.

Behold me, I pray thee, with all thine whole reason,
And be not hard-hearted for this encheason,
That I for thy soul's sake was slain in good season,
Beguiled and betrayed by Judas' false treason,
    Unkindly entreated,
    With sharp cords sore fretted,
    The Jewës me threated,
They mowed, they spitted and despised me
Condemned to death, as thou mayst see.

Thus naked am I nailed, O man, for thy sake.
I love thee, then love me. Why sleepest thou? Awake!
Remember my tender heart-root for thee brake,

With pains my veins constrained to crack.
>   Thus was I defaced,
>   Thus was my flesh rased,
>   And I to death chased,
>   Like a lamb led unto sacrifice,
>   Slain I was in most cruel wise.

Of sharp thorn I have worn a crown on my head
So rubbed, so bobbed, so rueful, so red;
Sore pained, sore strained, and for thy love dead,
Unfeigned, not deemed, my blood for thee shed;
>   My feet and hands sore
>   With sturdy nails bore.
>   What might I suffer more
>   Than I have suffered, man, for thee.
>   Come when thou wilt and welcome to me!

Dear brother, none other thing I desire
But give me thy heart free, to reward mine hire.
I am he that made the earth, water and fire.
Sathanas, that sloven, and right loathly sire,
>   Him have I overcast
>   In hell-prison bound fast,
>   Where aye his woe shall last.
I have purveyed a place full clear
For mankind, whom I have bought dear.

20:12–13 And I saw the dead, small and great, stand before God; and the books were opened: and another book was opened, which is the book of life: and the dead were judged out of those things which were written in the books, according to their works. And the sea gave up the dead which were in it; and death and hell delivered up the dead which were in them: and they were judged every man according to their works.

THE RESURRECTION

ABRAHAM COWLEY

Not winds to voyagers at sea,
Not showers to earth more necessary be,

(Heavens vital seed cast on the womb of earth
　　　To give the fruitful year a birth)
　　　Than verse to virtue, which can do
The midwife's office, and the nurse's too;
It feeds it strongly, and it clothes it gay,
　　　And when it dies, with comely pride
Embalms it, and erects a pyramid
　　　That never will decay
　　Till Heaven itself shall melt away,
And nought behind it stay.

Begin the song, and strike the living lyre;
Lo how the years to come, a numerous and well-fitted choir,
All hand in hand do decently advance,
And to my song with smooth and equal measures dance.
Whilst the dance lasts, how long so e'er it be,
My music's voice shall bear it company.
　　　Till all gentle notes be drowned
　　　In the last Trumpet's dreadful sound.
That to the spheres themselves shall silence bring,
　　　Untune the universal string.
　　　Then all the wide extended sky,
　　　And all th'harmonious worlds on high,
　　　And Virgil's sacred work shall die.
And he himself shall see in one fire shine
Rich nature's ancient Troy, though built by hands divine.

　　　Whom thunders dismal noise,
And all that Prophets and Apostles louder spake,
And all the creatures plain conspiring voice,
　　　Could not whilst they lived, awake,
　　　This mightier sound shall make
　　　When dead t'arise,
　　　And open tombs, and open eyes
To the long sluggards of five thousand years.
This mightier sound shall make its hearers ears.

Then shall the scattered atoms crowding come
        Back to their ancient home,
        Some from birds, from fishes some,
        Some from earth, and some from seas,
        Some from beasts, and some from trees.
        Some descend from clouds on high,
        Some from metals upwards fly,
And where th'attending soul naked, and shivering stands,
        Meet, salute, and join their hands.
As dispersed soldiers at the trumpet's call,
        Haste to their colors all.
      Unhappy most, like tortured men,
Their joints new set, to be new racked again.
      To mountains they for shelter pray,
The mountains shake, and run about no less confused than they.

Stop, stop, my Muse, allay thy vigorous heat,
        Kindled at a hint so great.
Hold thy Pindaric Pegasus closely in,
        Which does to rage begin,
And this steep hill would gallop up with violent course,
'Tis an unruly, and a hard-mouthed horse,
        Fierce, and unbroken yet,
        Impatient of the spur or bit.
Now prances stately, and anon flies o'er the place,
Disdains the servile law of any settled pace,
Conscious and proud of his own natural force.
        'Twill no unskillful touch endure,
But flings writer, and reader too, that sits not sure.

21:1–3 **And I saw a new heaven and a new earth: for the first heaven and the first earth were passed away; and there was no more sea. And I John saw the holy city, new Jerusalem, coming down from God out of heaven, prepared as a bride adorned for her husband. And I heard a great voice out of heaven saying, Behold, the tabernacle of God is with men, and he will dwell with them, and they shall be his people, and God himself shall be with them, and be their God.**

A Vision of Sunday in Heaven

Victor Daley

At a meeting of the Presbyterian General Assembly, the Rev. Mr. Meiklejohn made a statement to the effect that 'It was a matter upon which every right-minded man should congratulate himself that recent attempts to throw open the Museum and Libraries on Sunday had not been successful.'

Methought, one night, I saw, in trance sublime,
    With wonder, and with terror, and with awe,
Builded beyond the bounds of Space and Time,
    The glorious city John in Patmos saw.

Mighty and high it shone, a living glow,
    A splendid sun of suns in azure pendent:
Not all the wealth of all this world below
    Would make a string-course for its walls resplendent.

For every brick therein was solid gold
    (Of diamond were the turrets and pilasters)
For one of them you might have bought, behold,
    The Presbyterian Church with all its pastors!

Even in my trance, though a good Catholic,
    I could not at this sight my envy smother:
I could pay all my debts with half-a-brick
    I saw one little saint throw at another.

Too much, mayhap, of democratic leaven
    Remains in me; but, on its bright outside, as
I gazed, this city looked to me like Heaven
    According to the gospel of St. Midas.

So dazzling-new it seemed hung in the skies!
    It would have pleased me more had it been duller
In tone; its dreadful splendour scorched mine eyes
    Accustomed to the cult of quiet colour.

Ah, purblind eyes! It was God's Golden Rose
    To music grand unfolding every petal,
Flooding all space with solemn overflows—
    The Choir Invisible was on its mettle.

But suddenly there came before my view
    A Shape lugubrious: 'twas another mortal,

Attired in garments of funereal hue,
    A-knocking sadly at the Heavenly Portal.

His face was sour to see, with lips down-drawn,
    And bilious eyes. A foe to all jocoseness
He seemed; a victim to a woe-begone,
    Incurable, inherited moroseness.

The Portal opened with melodious clang,
    And forth came Peter, in a style theatric,
And down the gulfs of space his laughter rang—
    'Twas at a joke, he said, made by St. Patrick.

The Shape frowned gloomily, and said, 'I am
    The Reverend Meiklejohn.' Then, very slyly,
Winking at one inside the Gate, 'Salaam!
    I've often heard of you,' quoth Peter, dryly.

'We've no free passes here, but if you stand
    Beside me, you may look.' At this grown bolder
I also ranged up on his other hand—
    I think the good saint saw me o'er his shoulder.

Then soared into the crystal air above
    A song seraphic, pulsing, glowing, thrilling
With heavenly heart-notes of immortal love,
    The infinite blue dome with rapture filling.

Ah, hymn divine, I ne'er may hear again!
    Song of the full-voiced soul, freed from the yearning
Known here on earth! I listened to the strain,
    And mine own soul I felt within me burning.

St. Peter spake; with pride his visage shone:
    'What think you, reverend sir, of our intoning?'
He shook his head, the Reverend Meiklejohn—
    He missed the good old Presbyterian droning.

But now the inner glory of the place
    Was visible, and, desperately folding
His hands, the trembling pastor hid his face.
    His grief was terrible, such sights beholding

Upon a Sabbath-day. For, lo, he saw
    Angels and saints—confessor, martyr, virgin—

Holding high sport, and—spectacle of awe!—
    Leading the revels the late Reverend Spurgeon!

'Have sense! You're now too good for us by half,'
    Said Peter. 'Take a hint from yonder trio!
The red-faced saint is Luther—hear him laugh!—
    Huss has some jest told to the Tenth Pope Leo. '

The pastor lost what sense he had to lose,
    When, down a jasper-kerbed celestial strada,
Came, chatting pleasantly with Moors and Jews,
    His Eminence the General, Torquemada.

And then passed by, linked arm in arm, a pair:
    ' 'Tis Cyril and Hypatia, talking sweet as
Two seraphs. In the alley over there
    Is Calvin, playing skittles with Servetus.'

Thus Peter. Beatrice and Dante then
    We saw; the Poet's brow no more was wrinkled.
He looked the mirthfullest of sainted men—
    The very laurels on his forehead twinkled.

And, on a slope abloom with asphodel,
    Grandly aloof from all amusements petty,
We saw Rossetti's Blessed Damozel,
    And, at her feet, reciting verse, Rossetti.

A ring of dancing angels next we spied—
    To tell the truth I liked their style extremely—
But Reverend Meiklejohn was shocked, and cried,
    'Oh, Peter, Peter, mon—it's maist onseemly.'

St. Peter smiled—'Judge not of anything
    In haste; all things are pure unto the pure,' he
Remarked: 'Observe John Knox outside the ring
    Clapping his hands with corybantic fury!'

There was a spice of malice, nowise lost,
    In that last sentence by St. Peter spoken;
He would have stood a jest at his own cost,
    But Reverend Meiklejohn was too heart-broken.

'And whaur's the Scarlet Woman—she of Rome?'
    The pastor cried, his temper tried severely.

St. Peter frowned: 'Sir, this is not a Home
    For Presbyterian myths,' he said, austerely.

Just as the pastor's hand was raised on high
    In act to pass on all he saw stern stricture,
He caught Fra Lippo Lippi's merry eye,
    And saw him slyly sketching out his picture.

Then Peter kindly said, 'Laugh more; groan less;
    That Heaven is dull is simply Satan's rumour;
The ways of God are ways of pleasantness,
    And well He loves a saint with wit and humour.'

'I've neither,' sighed the Reverend Meiklejohn.
    And with these words the conversation ended—
'I doot that God's nae a richt-thinkin' mon!'
    He said, and sadly to the earth descended.

21:9–11 **And there came unto me one of the seven angels which had the seven vials full of the seven last plagues, and talked with me, saying, Come hither, I will shew thee the bride, the Lamb's wife. And he carried me away in the spirit to a great and high mountain, and shewed me that great city, the holy Jerusalem, descending out of heaven from God, Having the glory of God: and her light was like unto a stone most precious, even like a jasper stone, clear as crystal;**

NOT FOR THAT CITY

CHARLOTTE MEW

Not for that city of the level sun,
    Its golden streets and glittering gates ablaze –
    The shadeless, sleepless city of white days,
White nights, or nights and days that are as one –
We weary, when all is said, all thought, all done.
    We strain our eyes beyond this dusk to see
    What, from the threshold of eternity,
We shall step into. No, I think we shun
The splendour of that everlasting glare,
    The clamour of that never-ending song.
    And if for anything we greatly long,

It is for some remote and quiet stair
    Which winds to silence and a space of sleep
    Too sound for waking and for dreams too deep.

21:21 And the twelve gates were twelve pearls: every several gate was of one pearl: and the street of the city was pure gold, as it were transparent glass.

SONNET XV

EDMUND SPENSER

I saw new Earth, new Heaven, said Saint John.
And lo, the sea (quoth he) is now no more.
The holy City of the Lord, from high
Descendeth garnished as a loved spouse.
A voice then said, behold the bright abode
Of God and men. For he shall be their God.
And all their tears he shall wipe clean away.
Her brightness greater was than can be found.
Square was this city, and twelve gates it had.
Each gate was of an orient perfect pearl,
The houses gold, the pavement precious stone.
A lively stream, more clear than crystal is,
Ran through the mid, sprung from triumphant seat.
There grows life's fruit unto the Churches good.

22:10–11 And he saith unto me, Seal not the sayings of the prophecy of this book: for the time is at hand. He that is unjust, let him be unjust still: and he which is filthy, let him be filthy still: and he that is righteous, let him be righteous still: and he that is holy, let him be holy still.

A COMMINATION

A. D. HOPE

Like John on Patmos, brooding on the Four
Last Things, I meditate the ruin of friends

Whose loss, Lord, brings this grand new Curse to mind.
Now send me foes worth cursing, or send more
—Since means should be proportionate to ends—
For mine are few and of the piddling kind:

Drivellers, snivellers, writers of bad verse,
Backbiting bitches, snipers from a pew,
Small turds from the great arse of self-esteem;
On such as these I would not waste my curse.
God send me soon the enemy or two
Fit for the wrath of God, of whom I dream:

Some Caliban of Culture, some absurd
Messiah of the Paranoiac State,
Some Educator wallowing in his slime,
Some Prophet of the Uncreating Word
Monsters and man might reasonably hate,
Masters of Progress, Leaders of our Time;

But chiefly the Suborners: Common Tout
And Punk, the Advertiser, him I mean
And his smooth hatchet-man, the Technocrat,
Them let my malediction single out,
These modern Dives with their talking screen
Who lick the sores of Lazarus and grow fat,

Licensed to pimp, solicit and procure
Here in my house, to foul my feast, to bawl
Their wares while I am talking with my friend,
To pour into my ears a public sewer
Of all the Strumpet Muses sell and all
That prostituted science has to vend.

In this great Sodom of a world, which turns
The Treasure of the Intellect to dust
And every gift to some perverted use,
What wonder if the human spirit learns
Recourses of despair or of disgust,
Abortion, suicide and self-abuse.

But let me laugh, Lord; let me crack and strain
The belly of this derision till it burst;
For I have seen too much, have lived too long
A citizen of Sodom to refrain,

And in the stye of Science, from the first,
Have watched the pearls of Circe drop on dung.

Let me not curse my children, nor in rage
Mock at the just, the helpless and the poor,
Foot-fast in Sodom's rat-trap; make me bold
To turn on the Despoilers all their age
Invents: damnations never felt before
And hells more horrible than hot and cold.

And, since in Heaven creatures purified,
Rational, free, perfected in their kinds
Contemplate God and see Him face to face,
In Hell, for sure, spirits transmogrified,
Paralysed wills and parasitic minds
Mirror their own corruption and disgrace.

Now let this curse fall on my enemies,
My enemies, Lord, but all mankind's as well,
Prophets and panders of their golden calf;
Let Justice fit them all in their degrees;
Let them, still living, know that state of hell,
And let me see them perish, Lord, and laugh.

Let them be glued to television screens
Till their minds fester and the trash they see
Worm their dry hearts away to crackling shells;
Let ends be so revenged upon their means
That all that once was human grows to be
A flaccid mass of phototropic cells;

Let the dog love his vomit still, the swine
Squelch in the slough; and let their only speech
Be Babel; let the specious lies they bred
Taste on their tongues like intellectual wine;
Let sung commercials surfeit them, till each
Goggles with nausea in his nauseous bed.

And, lest with them I learn to gibber and gloat,
Lead me, for Sodom is my city still,
To seek those hills in which the heart finds ease;
Give Lot his leave; let Noah build his boat,
And me and mine, when each has laughed his fill,
View thy damnation and depart in peace.

22:12–16 And, behold, I come quickly; and my reward is with me, to give every man according as his work shall be.

I am Alpha and Omega, the beginning and the end, the first and the last. Blessed are they that do his commandments, that they may have right to the tree of life, and may enter in through the gates into the city. For without are dogs, and sorcerers, and whoremongers, and murderers, and idolaters, and whosoever loveth and maketh a lie. I Jesus have sent mine angel to testify unto you these things in the churches. I am the root and the offspring of David, and the bright and morning star.

from CHRIST'S TRIUMPH AFTER DEATH

GILES FLETCHER

stanzas 30–44

Here let my Lord hang up his conquering lance,
And bloody armor with late slaughter warm,
And looking down on his weak militants,
Behold his saints, midst of their hot alarm,
Hang all their golden hopes upon his arm.
    And in this lower field dispacing wide,
      Through windy thoughts, that would their sails misguide,
Anchor their fleshly ships fast in his wounded side.

Here may the band, that now in triumph shines,
And that (before they were invested thus)
In earthly bodies carried heavenly minds,
Pitched round about in order glorious,
Their sunny tents, and houses luminous,
    All their eternal day in songs employing,
      Joying their end, without end of their joying,
While their almighty Prince destruction is destroying.

Full, yet without satiety, of that
Which whets, and quiets greedy appetite,
Where never sun did rise, nor ever sat,
But one eternal day, and endless light

Gives time to those, whose time is infinite,
    Speaking with thought, obtaining without fee,
    Beholding him, whom never eye could see,
And magnifying him, that cannot greater be.

How can such joy as this want words to speak?
And yet what words can speak such joy as this ?
Far from the world, that might their quiet break,
Here the glad souls the face of beauty kiss,
Poured out in pleasure, on their beds of bliss.
    And drunk with nectar torrents, ever hold
    Their eyes on him, whose graces manifold,
The more they do behold, the more they would behold.

Their sight drinks lovely fires in at their eyes,
Their brain sweet incense with fine breath accloys,
That on God's sweating altar burning lies,
Their hungry cares feed on their heavenly noise,
That angels sing, to tell their untold joys;
    Their understanding naked truth, their wills
    The all, and self-sufficient goodness fills,
That nothing here is wanting, but the want of ills.

No sorrow now hangs clouding on their brow,
No bloodless malady empales their face,
No age drops on their hairs his silver snow,
No nakedness their bodies doth embase,
No poverty themselves, and theirs disgrace,
    No fear of death the joy of life devours.
    No unchaste sleep their precious time deflowers,
No loss, no grief, no change wait on their winged hours.

But now their naked bodies scorn the cold,
And from their eyes joy looks, and laughs at pain,
The infant wonders how he came so old,
And old man how he came so young again;
    Still resting, though from sleep they still refrain,
    Where all are rich, and yet no gold they owe,
And all are kings, and yet no subjects know,

For things that pass are past, and in this field,
The indeficient spring no winter fears,
The trees together fruit, and blossom yield,
Th' unfading lily leaves of silver bears,
And crimson rose a scarlet garment wears:
    And all of these on the saints' bodies grow,
    Not, as they wont, on baser earth below;
Three rivers here of milk, and wine, and honey flow.

About the holy city rolls a flood
Of molten crystal, like a sea of glass,
On which weak stream a strong foundation stood,
Of living diamonds the building was,
That all things else, besides it self, did pass.
    Her streets, instead of stones, the stars did pave,
    And little pearls, for dust, it seemed to have,
On which soft-streaming manna, like pure snow, did wave.

In midst of this city celestial,
Where the eternal temple should have rose,
Lightened th' Idea Beatifical:
End, and beginning of each thing that grows,
Whose self no end, nor yet beginning knows,
    That hath no eyes to see nor ears to hear,
    Yet sees, and hears, and is all-eye, all-ear,
That no where is contained, and yet is every where.

Changer of all things, yet immutable,
Before, and after all, the first, and last,
That moving all, is yet immoveable,
Great without quantity, in whose forecast,
Things past are present, things to come are past,
    Swift without motion, to whose open eye
    The hearts of wicked men unbreasted lie,
At once absent, and present to them, far, and nigh.

It is no flaming luster, made of light,
No sweet concent, or well-timed harmony,

Ambrosia, for to feast the appetite,
Or flowery odor, mixed with spicery.
No soft embrace, or pleasure bodily,
    And yet it is a kind of inward feast,
    A harmony, that sounds within the breast,
An odor, light, embrace, in which the soul doth rest.

A heavenly feast, no hunger can consume,
A light unseen, yet shines in every place,
A sound, no time can steal, a sweet perfume,
No winds can scatter, an entire embrace,
That no satiety can e'er unlace,
    Ingraced into so high a favor, there
    The saints, with their beau-peres, whole worlds outwear,
And things unseen do see, and things unheard do hear.

Ye blessed souls, grown richer by your spoil,
Whose loss, though great, is cause of greater gains,
Here may your weary spirits rest from toil,
Spending your endless evening, that remains,
Among those white flocks, and celestial trains,
    That feed upon their shepherd's eyes, and frame
    That heavenly music of so wondrous fame,
Psalming aloud the holy honors of his name.

Had I a voice of steel to tune my song,
Were every verse as smoothly filed as glass,
And every member turned to a tongue,
And every tongue were made of sounding brass,
Yet all that skill, and all this strength, alas,
    Should it presume to gild, wear misadvised,
    The place, where David hath new songs devised,
As in his burning throne he sits emparadised.

22:17 And the Spirit and the bride say, Come. And let him that heareth say, Come. And let him that is athirst come. And whosoever will, let him take the water of life freely.

PARADISE RE-ENTERED

D. H. LAWRENCE

Through the strait gate of passion,
Between the bickering fire
Where flames of fierce love tremble
On the body of fierce desire:

To the intoxication,
The mind, fused down like a bead,
Flees in its agitation
The flames' stiff speed:

At last to calm incandescence,
Burned clean by remorseless hate,
Now, at the day's renascence
We approach the gate.

Now, from the darkened spaces
Of fear, and of frightened faces,
Death, in our awed embraces
Approached and passed by;

We near the flame-burnt porches
Where the brands of the angels, like torches,
Whirl,—in these perilous marches
Pausing to sigh;

We look back on the withering roses,
The stars, in their sun-dimmed closes,
Where 'twas given us to repose us
Sure on our sanctity;

Beautiful, candid lovers,
Burnt out of our earthly covers,
We might have nestled like plovers
In the fields of eternity.

There, sure in sinless being,
All-seen, and then all-seeing,
In us life unto death agreeing,
We might have lain.

But we storm the angel-guarded
Gates of the long discarded
Garden, which God has hoarded
Against our pain.

The Lord of Hosts and the Devil
Are left on Eternity's level
Field, and as victors we travel
To Eden home.

Back beyond good and evil
Return we. Eve dishevel
Your hair for the bliss-drenched revel
On our primal loam.

22:18–20 For I testify unto every man that heareth the words of the
prophecy of this book, If any man shall add unto these things, God shall
add unto him the plagues that are written in this book: And if any man
shall take away from the words of the book of this prophecy, God shall
take away his part out of the book of life, and out of the holy city, and
from the things which are written in this book.

He which testifieth these things saith, Surely I come quickly. Amen.

THE SECOND COMING

WILLIAM BUTLER YEATS

Turning and turning in the widening gyre
The falcon cannot hear the falconer;
Things fall apart; the centre cannot hold;
Mere anarchy is loosed upon the world,
The blood-dimmed tide is loosed, and everywhere
The ceremony of innocence is drowned;
The best lack all conviction, while the worst
Are full of passionate intensity.

Surely some revelation is at hand;
Surely the Second Coming is at hand.
The Second Coming! Hardly are those words out
When a vast image out of *Spiritus Mundi*
Troubles my sight: somewhere in sands of the desert
A shape with lion body and the head of a man,

A gaze blank and pitiless as the sun,
Is moving its slow thighs, while all about it
Reel shadows of the indignant desert birds.
The darkness drops again; but now I know
That twenty centuries of stony sleep
Were vexed to nightmare by a rocking cradle,
And what rough beast, its hour come round at last,
Slouches towards Bethlehem to be born?

INDEX OF TITLES

INDEX OF FIRST LINES

INDEX OF POETS